Fit your coursework into your hectic life.

Make the most of your time by learning your way. Access the resources you need to succeed wherever, whenever.

 Study with digital flashcards, listen to audio textbooks and take quizzes.

 Review your current course grade and compare your progress with your peers.

 Get the free Cengage Mobile App and learn wherever you are.

Break Limitations. Create your own potential, and be unstoppable with *MindTap*.

MindTap. Powered by You.

cengage.com/mindtap

WESTERN CIVILIZATION

VOLUME I: TO 1715

Eleventh
Edition

WESTERN CIVILIZATION

VOLUME I: TO 1715

Jackson J. Spielvogel

The Pennsylvania State University

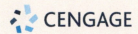

Australia • Brazil • Mexico • Singapore • United Kingdom • United States

Western Civilization, Eleventh Edition
Volume I: To 1715
Jackson J. Spielvogel

Senior Product Manager: Joseph D. Potvin

Product Assistant: Haley Gaudreau

Senior Marketing Manager: Valerie A. Hartman

Senior Content Manager: Philip Lanza

IP Analyst: Deanna Ettinger

IP Project Manager: Carly B. Belcher

Production Service/Compositor: MPS Limited

Art Director: Sarah Cole

Text Designer: Dutton & Sherman Design

Cover Designer: Sarah Cole

Cover Image: Anonymous, 15th century fresco, The Month of January (Snowball Fight). Scala/Art Resource, NY.

© 2021, 2018, 2015 Cengage Learning, Inc.

Unless otherwise noted, all content is © Cengage.

ALL RIGHTS RESERVED. No part of this work covered by the copyright herein may be reproduced or distributed in any form or by any means, except as permitted by U.S. copyright law, without the prior written permission of the copyright owner.

For product information and technology assistance, contact us at **Cengage Customer & Sales Support, 1-800-354-9706 or support.cengage.com.**

For permission to use material from this text or product, submit all requests online at **www.cengage.com/permissions.**

Library of Congress Control Number: 2019920584

Student Edition:
ISBN: 978-0-357-36298-3

Loose-leaf Edition:
ISBN: 978-0-357-36313-3

Cengage
200 Pier 4 Boulevard
Boston, MA 02210
USA

Cengage is a leading provider of customized learning solutions with employees residing in nearly 40 different countries and sales in more than 125 countries around the world. Find your local representative at **www.cengage.com**.

Cengage products are represented in Canada by Nelson Education, Ltd.

To learn more about Cengage platforms and services, register or access your online learning solution, or purchase materials for your course, visit **www.cengage.com.**

Printed at CLDPC, USA, 06-20

ABOUT THE AUTHOR

JACKSON J. SPIELVOGEL is associate professor emeritus of history at The Pennsylvania State University. He received his Ph.D. from The Ohio State University, where he specialized in Reformation history under Harold J. Grimm. His articles and reviews have appeared in such journals as *Moreana, Journal of General Education, Catholic Historical Review, Archiv für Reformationsgeschichte,* and *American Historical Review.* He has also contributed chapters or articles to *The Social History of the Reformation, The Holy Roman Empire: A Dictionary Handbook,* the *Simon Wiesenthal Center Annual of Holocaust Studies,* and *Utopian Studies.* His work has been supported by fellowships from the Fulbright Foundation and the Foundation for Reformation Research. At Penn State, he helped inaugurate the Western civilization courses as well as a popular course on Nazi Germany. His book *Hitler and Nazi Germany* was published in 1987 (seventh edition, 2014). He is the coauthor (with William Duiker) of *World History,* first published in 1998 (ninth edition, 2019), and *The Essential World History* (ninth edition, 2020). Professor Spielvogel has won five major university-wide teaching awards. In 1988–1989, he held the Penn State Teaching Fellowship, the university's most prestigious teaching award. He won the Dean Arthur Ray Warnock Award for Outstanding Faculty Member in 1996 and the Schreyer Honors College Excellence in Teaching Award in 2000.

TO DIANE,
WHOSE LOVE AND SUPPORT MADE IT ALL POSSIBLE
J.J.S.

BRIEF CONTENTS

CONTENTS

Contents ■ XI

16   Toward a New Heaven and a New Earth: The Scientific Revolution and the Emergence of Modern Science   486

DOCUMENTS

MAPS

FEATURES

PREFACE

DURING A VISIT TO GREAT BRITAIN, where he studied as a young man, Mohandas Gandhi, the leader of the effort to liberate India from British colonial rule, was asked what he thought of Western civilization. "I think it would be a good idea," he replied. Gandhi's response was as correct as it was clever. Western civilization has led to great problems as well as great accomplishments, but it remains a good idea. And any complete understanding of today's world must take into account the meaning of Western civilization and the role Western civilization has played in history. Despite modern progress, we still greatly reflect our religious traditions, our political systems and theories, our economic and social structures, and our cultural heritage. I have written this history of Western civilization to assist a new generation of students in learning more about the past that has helped create them and the world in which they live.

At the same time, for the eleventh edition, as in the tenth, I have added new material on world history to show the impact other parts of the world have made on the West. Certainly, the ongoing struggle with terrorists since 2001 has made clear the intricate relationship between the West and the rest of the world. It is important then to show not only how Western civilization has affected the rest of the world but also how it has been influenced and even defined since its beginnings by contacts with other peoples around the world.

Another of my goals was to write a well-balanced work in which the political, economic, social, religious, intellectual, cultural, and military aspects of Western civilization have been integrated into a chronologically ordered synthesis. I have been especially aware of the need to integrate the latest research on social history and women's history into each chapter of the book rather than isolating it either in lengthy topical chapters, which confuse the student by interrupting the chronological narrative, or in separate sections that appear at periodic intervals between chapters.

Another purpose in writing this history of Western civilization has been to put the *story* back in history. That story is an exciting one, yet many textbooks fail to capture the imagination of their readers. Narrative history effectively transmits the knowledge of the past and is the form that best aids remembrance. At the same time, I have not overlooked the need for the kind of historical analysis that makes students aware that historians often disagree on their interpretations of the past.

Features of the Text

To enliven the past and to let readers see for themselves the materials that historians use to create their pictures of the past, I have included in each chapter **primary sources** (**Historical Voices**) that are keyed to the discussion in the text. The documents include examples of the religious, artistic, intellectual, social, economic, and political aspects of Western life. Such varied sources as a Renaissance banquet menu, a debate in the Reformation era, the Declaration of the Rights of Woman and the Female Citizen in the French Revolution, and letters exchanged between a woman and her fiancé on the battle front in World War I all reveal in vivid fashion what Western civilization meant to the individual men and women who shaped it by their activities. I have included a focus question at the beginning of each Historical Voices presentation to help students in analyzing the documents.

To help students examine how and why historians differ in their interpretation of specific topics, new historiographical sections were introduced in the ninth edition. Examples include "Was There a United Kingdom of Israel?"; "Was There a Renaissance for Women?"; "Was There an Agricultural Revolution?"; "The Retreat from Democracy: Did Europe Have Totalitarian States?"; and "Why Did the Soviet Union Collapse?" Each of these sections is now preceded by the heading **Historians Debate** to make students more aware of the interpretive nature of history.

An additional feature that began in the seventh edition is **Images of Everyday Life**, which combines two or more illustrations with a lengthy caption to provide insight into various aspects of social life and includes such topics as "Children in the Roman World," "Family and Marriage in Renaissance Italy," "Women and the Enlightenment Salon," and "Political Cartoons: Attacks on the King." **Movies & History**, which appears in a brief format, can be found in eighteen chapters; the features reference twenty-two films.

Each chapter has an introduction and illustrated chapter summary to help maintain the continuity of the narrative and to provide a synthesis of important themes. Anecdotes in the chapter introductions dramatically convey the major theme or themes of each chapter. Detailed chronologies reinforce the events discussed in the text, and a **Chapter Timeline** at the end of each chapter enables students to review at a glance the chief developments of an era. Some of the timelines also show parallel developments in different cultures or nations. Beginning with the eighth edition, a new format was added at the end of each chapter. The **Chapter Summary** is illustrated with thumbnail images of chapter illustrations and combined with the **Chapter Timeline**. A **Chapter Review** assists students in studying the chapter. This review includes **Upon Reflection** essay questions and a list of **Key Terms** from the chapter. The **Suggestions for Further Reading** at the end of each chapter has been thoroughly updated for this new edition and is organized under subheadings to make it more useful.

Updated maps and extensive illustrations serve to deepen the reader's understanding of the text. Detailed map captions are designed to enrich students' awareness of the importance of geography to history, and numerous spot maps enable readers to see at a glance the region or subject being discussed in the text. Map captions also include a map question to guide students' reading of the map. To facilitate understanding of cultural movements, images of artistic works discussed in the text are placed near the discussions. Throughout the text, image captions have been revised and expanded to further students' understanding of the past. New to this edition, many images now include critical thinking questions to guide students in analyzing their significance. Chapter outlines and focus questions at the beginning of each chapter give students a useful overview and guide them to the main subjects of each chapter. The section **Connections to Today** at the beginning of each chapter is intended to help students appreciate the relevance of history by asking them to draw connections between the past and present.

The focus questions are then repeated at the beginning of each major section in the chapter. A glossary of important terms (boldfaced in the text when they are introduced and defined) is provided at the back of the book to maximize reader comprehension. A guide to pronunciation is provided in the text in parentheses following the first mention of a complex name or term, and **Chapter Notes** appear at the end of each chapter.

New to This Edition

While preparing the revision of *Western Civilization*, I reexamined the entire book and analyzed the comments and reviews of many colleagues who have found the book to be a useful instrument for introducing their students to the history of Western civilization. In preparing the eleventh edition, I sought to build on the strengths of the first ten editions and, above all, to maintain the balance, synthesis, and narrative qualities that characterized those editions. In addition to revising Connections to Today questions and adding new focus questions, to keep up with the ever-growing body of historical scholarship, new or revised material has been added throughout the book on the following topics:

Chapter 1 Australopithecines; Neanderthals; domestication of animals; Hatshepsut; new document, "The Instructions of Shuruppag"; new Map 1.2 The Emergence of Civilizations Around the World.

Chapter 2 the Hebrew Psalms; the Phoenicians.

Chapter 3 Minoan Crete; Greece in a Dark Age; "hoplite revolution"; the reforms of Solon, Cleisthenes, and Pericles; the pre-Socratics; the Greek Olympics; Greek slavery.

Chapter 4 Philip II's military reforms; Alexander's early life; new document, "The Wrath of Alexander."

Chapter 5 the Twelve Tables; Roman warfare; Roman religion; slavery in the Roman world; Roman women; Tiberius Gracchus.

Chapter 6 Augustus; the Augustan social order; new document, "The Resistance to Rome: The Exhortations of Galgacus"; Trier, in Rome in Germany photo caption;

Romanization and cities; changes in population issues in late second century c.e.; the crises in the third century.

Chapter 7 Christology; the emperor Constantine; Augustine of Hippo; the Byzantine Empire; the rise of Islam.

Chapter 8 the government of Charlemagne; new document, "Charlemagne's Goal of Learning"; the Carolingian Renaissance; Louis the Pious; Vikings as traders; the Byzantine Empire; the expansion of Islam.

Chapter 9 the new agriculture; Gothic cathedrals.

Chapter 10 women in the High Middle Ages; Bernard and the humanization of Christ; the pilgrimage.

Chapter 11 the Black Death in North Africa; replaced use of terms feminism and anti-Semitism; shortened discussion of the Hundred Year' War; Venice's trade with the Muslim world.

Chapter 12 new document, "The Problems of Renaissance City Governments"; male homosexuality in the Renaissance; female humanists; Northern High Renaissance art.

Chapter 13 Erasmus; the break between Luther and Erasmus; new section, "Response to the Wars of Religion: Michel de Montaigne."

Chapter 14 Peru and the Incan conquest; the *mita* labor system; sugar production and its impact as a global driver; slavery; the British East India Company; Christian missionaries in Japan.

Chapter 15 Louis XIV; Peter the Great; Oliver Cromwell.

Chapter 16 Newton and religion; Galileo; medicine; Boyle and air; scientific societies.

Chapter 17 Voltaire; women in the Enlightenment; innovations in art and architecture; "Grub Street" writers.

Chapter 18 King Frederick William I of Prussia; King Frederick II of Prussia; the Seven Years' War.

Chapter 19 the impact of the American Revolution on Europeans; the Tennis Court Oath; the role of women in the French Revolution; new document, "Disaster in Russia."

Chapter 20 revolt of silk workers of Lyon; the Sadler report.

Chapter 21 Metternich; new document: "The Voice of Utopian Socialism"; Owen's New Lanark model industrial community; the 1848 revolution in the Austrian Empire; Romanticism, the work of Turner.

Chapter 22 the Crimean War; Bismarck; the Victorian Age.

Chapter 23 re-organized section 23-2 to become new sections 23-2 "Urbanization and Population Movements" and 23-3 "The Emergence of a Mass Society"; German industrial leadership; the Second Industrial Revolution and communications; population growth in the nineteenth century; emigration; urbanization; mass consumption; Germany; Russia.

Chapter 24 imperialism; J. A. Hobson's *Imperialism*; King Leopold's reign of terror in Central Africa; ant-Western thought in the colonies after World War I; the Bismarckian system of alliances.

Chapter 25 the Russian revolution; the role of Lenin; women working in factories; women's opposition to the war; Britain's decision to go to war; divided subsection entitled "The Social Impact of the War" into two subsections entitled "The Social Impact of the War" and "New Roles for Women," with new material.

Chapter 26 the depression in the United States; new document, "Daily Life in the Collective Farms"; revised Map 26.2 Territory Gained by Italy; fear of communism in Europe and specifically Germany; Carl Jung.

Chapter 27 Asian war before Pearl Harbor, especially China and Japan; the role of Spain; context of the American decision to drop atomic bombs on Japan.

Chapter 28 the Marshall Plan; the Algerian War; the Vietnam War; Americanization and the Cold War; new document, "The Berlin Air Lift."

Chapter 29 Margaret Thatcher; West German politics; changes in Italy; the Second Vietnam War; new document, "The Current Malaise."

Chapter 30 new document, "Emmanuel Macron and European Sovereignty"; Russia; Poland; Germany; Great Britain; France; Italy; the United States; Canada; new section on the United States; terrorism; new section, "The Great Recession"; Greece; the women's movement; the European Union.

The enthusiastic response to the primary sources (Historical Voices) led me to evaluate the content of each document carefully and add new documents throughout the text. The feature **Opposing Viewpoints**, which was introduced in the seventh edition, presents a comparison of two or three primary sources in order to facilitate student analysis of historical documents. This feature now appears in almost every chapter and includes such topics as "The Great Flood: Two Versions," "The Black Death: Contemporary Views," "A New Heaven: Faith Versus Reason," "The Response to Revolution," and "Czechoslovakia, 1968: Two Faces of Communism." Focus questions are included to help students evaluate the documents.

Introduced in the tenth edition was a feature entitled **Global Perspectives**, which reinforces the relationship between the West and other parts of the world. This new feature, which is found in twenty chapters, includes such topics as "The Stele in the Ancient World," "Women in the Roman and Han Empires," "Medieval Monastic Life in West and East," "Revolution and Revolt in France and China," "West and East: Textile Factory Work," and "The New Global Economy: Fast Fashion."

Because courses in Western civilization at American and Canadian colleges and universities follow different chronological divisions, the text is available in both one-volume and two-volume versions to fit the needs of instructors. Teaching and learning ancillaries include the following.

Resources

CENGAGE | MINDTAP **MindTap** for *Western Civilization*, eleventh edition, is a flexible online learning platform that provides students with resources to help them succeed in their history course and beyond. The platform provides students with a relevant and engaging learning experience that supports them as they develop historical understanding, improve reading and writing skills, and build critical thinking and analysis skills.

MindTap gives students the tools to help them master all-important course concepts from the moment they log in. History Skills Tutorials helps them understand how to analyze maps and images, research and write a history paper, work with primary and secondary sources, and much more. Tutorials such as these inspire confidence as students begin to interact with the material.

Everything in MindTap is built around its interactive ebook. As students work through the readings in each chapter, Check Your Understanding quizzes test reading comprehension and help reinforce key concepts. In addition to encountering maps, images, and other figures, students will find short video clips and Google Arts & Culture links at various points throughout the readings that allow them to explore relevant content and resources beyond the text.

A hallmark feature of MindTap is the wealth of opportunities for primary source analysis. Each chapter begins with an auto-graded Image Analysis Primary Source Activity. Then, end-of-chapter Primary Source Writing Activities have students writing comparatively about multiple primary sources and putting critical thinking skills to work. Beyond the chapter-level content, other thematically organized auto-graded primary source activities cover such topics as Religion in Ancient Egypt; Money, Power, and Diversion in Imperial Rome; Court Life at Versailles; Enlightenment Thinkers; the Rise of Nationalism in Europe; and Poets of World War I. Course-level thematic writing activities ask students to formulate a thesis and defend it with analysis of primary source material.

MindTap also allows instructors to customize their content, providing tools that integrate YouTube clips (without ads), outside websites, and their own content directly into the learning path with the click of a button. Instructors can also add thousands of additional primary and secondary sources to their course with MindTap's Activity Builder. To learn more, ask your Cengage sales representative to demo it for you—or go to **www.cengage.com/mindtap**.

Instructor's Companion Website The Instructor's Companion Website, accessed through the Instructor Resource Center (**login.cengage.com**), houses all of the supplemental materials you can use for your course. This includes a Test Bank, Instructor's Manual, and PowerPoint Lecture Presentations.

- **Test Bank** The Test Bank contains multiple-choice questions for each chapter and is available in **Cognero®** and within MindTap. The Cognero® version of the Test Bank also includes essay and short answer historical identification questions. Cognero® is a flexible, online system that allows you to author, edit, and manage test bank content for *Western Civilization*, eleventh edition. With Cognero®, you can create multiple test versions instantly and deliver them through your LMS from your classroom or wherever you may be, with no special software installs or downloads required. The following format types are available for download from the Instructor Companion Site: Blackboard, Angel, Moodle, Canvas, and Desire2Learn. You can import these files directly into your LMS to edit, manage questions, and create tests.

- **PowerPoint Lectures** These are ADA-compliant slide decks that collate the key takeaways from the chapter in concise visual formats perfect for in-class presentations or for student review. Each slide deck also includes the chapter's full set of images and maps. New to this edition, the PowerPoints now include six different types of Activity slides to enhance student engagement. The activities include "Think, Pair, Share"; "Quick Check"; "Written Reflection"; "Discussion"; "Diary"; and "Self-Assessment."

- **Instructor's Resource Manual** The Instructor's Resource Manual closely complements the PowerPoint Lecture slides and is focused on supporting instructors who are new to teaching or new to using *Western Civilization*. It includes instructional objectives, chapter summaries, chapter outlines, brief descriptions of specific chapter features (Historical Voices, Opposing Viewpoints, Global Perspectives, Images of Everyday Life, Movies & History), and notes for using the Activity slides featured in the PowerPoint deck for each chapter. Each chapter concludes with a Learning Plan table that correlates chapter sections with associated PowerPoint slides and Learning Objectives.

Cengage.com/student Save your students time and money. Direct them to **cengage.com/student** for a choice in formats and savings and a better chance to succeed in your class. Cengage.com/student, Cengage's online store, is a single destination for more than 10,000 new textbooks, ebooks, study tools, and audio supplements. Students have the freedom to purchase à la carte exactly what they need and when they need it. Students can save up to 70 percent on the ebook electronic version of their textbook.

CENGAGE *UNLIMITED* **Cengage Unlimited** is the first-of-its-kind digital subscription that empowers students to learn more for less. One student subscription includes total access to every Cengage online textbook, platform, career and college success centers, and more—in one place. Learn across courses and disciplines with confidence that you won't pay more to access more. Available now in bookstores and online. Available only in select markets. For more information, please contact your local Learning Consultant or visit **cengage.com/unlimited**.

Doing History: Research and Writing in the Digital Age, **2e** (ISBN: 9781133587880) Prepared by Michael J. Galgano, J. Chris Arndt, and Raymond M. Hyser of James Madison University. Whether you're starting down the path as a history major or simply looking for a straightforward, systematic guide to writing a successful paper, this text's "soup to nuts" approach to researching and writing about history addresses every step of the process: locating your sources, gathering information, writing and citing according to various style guides, and avoiding plagiarism.

Reader Program Cengage Learning publishes a number of readers. Some contain exclusively primary sources, others are devoted to essays and secondary sources, and still others provide a combination of primary and secondary sources. All of these readers are designed to guide students through the process of historical inquiry. Visit **cengage.com/history** for a complete list of readers.

Custom Options Nobody knows your students like you, so why not give them a text that tailor-fits their needs? Cengage Learning offers custom solutions for your course—whether it's making a small modification to *Western Civilization*, 11e, to match your syllabus or combining multiple sources to create something truly unique. Contact your Cengage Learning representative to explore custom solutions for your course.

ACKNOWLEDGMENTS

I BEGAN TO TEACH at age five in my family's grape arbor. By the age of ten, I wanted to know and understand everything in the world, so I set out to memorize our entire set of encyclopedia volumes. At seventeen, as editor of the high school yearbook, I chose "patterns" as its theme. With that as my early history, followed by many rich years of teaching, writing, and family nurturing, it seemed quite natural to accept the challenge of writing a history of Western civilization as I approached that period in life often described as the age of wisdom. Although I see this writing adventure as part of the natural unfolding of my life, I gratefully acknowledge that without the generosity of many others, it would not have been possible.

David Redles gave generously of his time and ideas, especially for Chapters 28, 29, and 30. Chris Colin provided research on the history of music, while Laurie Batitto, Alex Spencer, Stephen Maloney, Shaun Mason, Peter Angelos, and Fred Schooley offered valuable editorial assistance. I deeply appreciate the valuable technical assistance provided by Dayton Coles. I am deeply grateful to John Soares for his assistance in preparing the map captions and to Charmarie Blaisdell of Northeastern University for her detailed suggestions on women's history. Daniel Haxall of Kutztown University provided valuable assistance with materials on postwar art, popular culture, postmodern art and thought, and the Digital Age. I am especially grateful to Kathryn Spielvogel for her work as editorial associate for Chapters 15–30. I am also thankful to the thousands of students whose questions and responses caused me to see many aspects of Western civilization in new ways.

My ability to undertake a project of this magnitude was in part due to the outstanding European history teachers that I had as both an undergraduate and graduate student. These included Kent Forster (modern Europe) and Robert W. Green (early modern Europe) at The Pennsylvania State University and Franklin Pegues (medieval), Andreas Dorpalen (modern Germany), William MacDonald (ancient), and Harold J. Grimm (Renaissance and Reformation) at The Ohio State University. These teachers provided me with profound insights into Western civilization and also taught me by their examples that learning only becomes true understanding when it is accompanied by compassion, humility, and open-mindedness.

I would like to thank the many teachers and students who have used the first ten editions. Their enthusiastic response to a textbook that was intended to put the story back in history and capture the imagination of the reader has been very gratifying. I especially thank the many teachers and students who made the effort to contact me personally to share their enthusiasm. Thanks to Cengage's comprehensive review process, many historians were asked to evaluate my manuscript and review each edition. I am grateful to the following people for their innumerable suggestions over the course of the first ten editions, which have greatly improved my work:

Anne J. Aby
Minnesota West Community and Technical College, Worthington Campus

Paul Allen
University of Utah

Randall Allen
Bay de Noc Community College

Betsy Anderson
East Central Community College

Gerald Anderson
North Dakota State University

Susan L. H. Anderson
Campbell University

Letizia Argenteri
University of San Diego

Roy A. Austensen
Illinois State University

James A. Baer
Northern Virginia Community College— Alexandria

James T. Baker
Western Kentucky University

Patrick Bass
Morningside College

John F. Battick
University of Maine

Frederic J. Baumgartner
Virginia Polytechnic Institute

Phillip N. Bebb
Ohio University

Anthony Bedford
Modesto Junior College

F. E. Beemon
Middle Tennessee State University

Leonard R. Berlanstein
University of Virginia

Cyriaque Beurtheret
Salt Lake Community College

Douglas T. Bisson
Belmont University

Charmarie Blaisdell
Northeastern University

Benay Blend
Central New Mexico Community College

Stephen H. Blumm
Montgomery County Community College

John Bohstedt
University of Tennessee—Knoxville

Hugh S. Bonar
California State University

Werner Braatz
University of Wisconsin—Oshkosh

Alfred S. Bradford
University of Missouri

Owen Bradley
Columbia College at Coast Guard Island

Janet Brantley
Texarkana College

Patrick Brennan
Gulf Coast State College

Matt Brent
Rappahannock Community College

Maryann E. Brink
College of William & Mary

Jerry Brookshire
Middle Tennessee State University

Daniel Patrick Brown
Moorpark College

Gregory S. Brown
University of Nevada—Las Vegas

Robert Brown
SUNY—Finger Lakes Community College

Blaine T. Browne
Broward Community College

Daniel Bubb
Gonzaga University

Claire Cage
University of South Alabama

Kevin W. Caldwell
Blue Ridge Community College

J. Holden Camp Jr.
Hillyer College, University of Hartford

Jack Cargill
Rutgers University

Martha Carlin
*University of Wisconsin—
Milwaukee*

Elizabeth Carney
Clemson University

Susan Carrafiello
Wright State University

Jane Laurel Carrington
St. Olaf College

Joseph J. Casino
St. Joseph's University

Eric H. Cline
Xavier University

Robert G. Clouse
Indiana State University

Robert Cole
Utah State University

Elizabeth Collins
Triton College

William J. Connell
Rutgers University

Nancy Conradt
College of DuPage

Marc Cooper
Southwest Missouri State

Richard A. Cosgrove
University of Arizona

David A. Crain
South Dakota State University

Michael A. Crane Jr. (student)
Everett Community College

Luanne Dagley
*Pellissippi State Technical Community
College*

John Davies
University of Delaware

Michael Dolski
Ball State University

Michael F. Doyle
Ocean County College

Hugh Dubrulle
Saint Anselm College

Joseph J. Eble
Burlington County College

James W. Ermatinger
University of Nebraska—Kearney

Christine Eubank
Bergen Community College

Porter Ewing
Los Angeles City College

Carla Falkner
Northeast Mississippi Community College

Steven Fanning
University of Illinois—Chicago

Ellsworth Faris
California State University—Chico

Gary B. Ferngren
Oregon State University

Mary Helen Finnerty
Westchester Community College

Jennifer Foray
Purdue University

Amy Forbes
Millsaps College

Jennifer E. Forster
Lakeland Community College

Eric Fournier
West Chester University of Pennsylvania

Patricia Frank
St. Clair County Community College

A. Z. Freeman
Robinson College

Marsha Frey
Kansas State University

Frank J. Frost
University of California—Santa Barbara

Frank Garosi
California State University—Sacramento

Laura Gellott
University of Wisconsin—Parkside

Richard M. Golden
University of North Texas

Stella Gomezdelcampo
Roane State Community College

Manuel G. Gonzales
Diablo Valley College

Amy G. Gordon
Denison University

Richard J. Grace
Providence College

Charlotte M. Gradie
Sacred Heart University

Candace Gregory
California State University—Sacramento

Katherine Gribble
Highline Community College

Hanns Gross
Loyola University

John F. Guilmartin
Ohio State University

Paul Hagenloh
The University of Alabama

Awad Halabi
Wright State University

Jeffrey S. Hamilton
Gustavus Adolphus College

J. Drew Harrington
Western Kentucky University

James Harrison
Siena College

Doina Pasca Harsanyi
Central Michigan University

Jay Hatheway
Edgewood College

A. J. Heisserer
University of Oklahoma

Carol Herringer
Wright State University

Betsey Hertzler
Mesa Community College

Robert Herzstein
University of South Carolina

Michael C. Hickey
Bloomsburg University

Shirley Hickson
North Greenville College

Martha L. Hildreth
University of Nevada

Boyd H. Hill Jr.
University of Colorado—Boulder

Michael Hofstetter
Bethany College

Donald C. Holsinger
Seattle Pacific University

Frank L. Holt
University of Houston

W. Robert Houston
University of South Alabama

Michael W. Howell
College of the Ozarks

Anne Huebel
Franklin Pierce University

David Hudson
California State University— Fresno

Paul J. L. Hughes
Sussex County Community College

Richard A. Jackson
University of Houston

Fred Jewell
Harding University

Nicole Jobin
University of Colorado

Jenny M. Jochens
Towson State University

William M. Johnston
University of Massachusetts

Sarah Jurenka
Bishop State

George Kaloudis
Rivier College

Jeffrey A. Kaufmann
Muscatine Community College

David O. Kieft
University of Minnesota

Patricia Killen
Pacific Lutheran University

Jay Kilroy
Mesa Community College

William E. Kinsella Jr.
Northern Virginia Community College—Annandale

James M. Kittelson
Ohio State University

Doug Klepper
Santa Fe Community College

Cynthia Kosso
Northern Arizona University

Ed Krzemienski
The Citadel

Paul E. Lambert
Nichols College

Clayton Miles Lehmann
University of South Dakota

Diana Chen Lin
Indiana University, Northwest

Paul Douglas Lockhart
Wright State University

Ursula W. MacAffer
Hudson Valley Community College

Harold Marcuse
University of California—Santa Barbara

Mike Markowski
Westminster College

Michael Martin
Fort Lewis College

Mavis Mate
University of Oregon

Derek Maxfield
Genesee Community College

Priscilla McArthur
Troy State University—Dothan

T. Ronald Melton
Brewton Parker College

Martin Menke
Rivier College

Jack Allen Meyer
University of South Carolina

Eugene W. Miller Jr.
The Pennsylvania State University—Hazleton

David B. Mock
Tallahassee Community College

Thomas Mockaitis
DePaul University

John Patrick Montano
University of Delaware

Rex Morrow
Trident Technical College

Wyatt S. Moulds
Jones County Junior College

Kenneth Mouré
University of California—Santa Barbara

Thomas M. Mulhern
University of North Dakota

Pierce Mullen
Montana State University

Cliona Murphy
California State University—Bakersfield

Frederick I. Murphy
Western Kentucky University

William M. Murray
University of South Florida

Otto M. Nelson
Texas Tech University

Sam Nelson
Willmar Community College

John A. Nichols
Slippery Rock University

Lisa Nofzinger
Albuquerque Technical Vocational Institute

Chris Oldstone-Moore
Augustana College

Donald Ostrowski
Harvard University

James O. Overfield
University of Vermont

Matthew L. Panczyk
Bergen Community College

Kathleen A. Parrow
Black Hills State University

Kathleen Paul
University of South Florida

Jody Peterson
Centralia College

Ted Petro
New England College

Carla Rahn Phillips
University of Minnesota

Keith Pickus
Wichita State University

Linda J. Piper
University of Georgia

Jeff Plaks
University of Central Oklahoma

Marjorie Plummer
Western Kentucky University

Janet Polasky
University of New Hampshire

Ann Pond
Bishop State Community College

Thomas W. Porter
Randolph-Macon College

Charles A. Povlovich
California State University—Fullerton

Penne L. Prigge
Rockingham Community College

Timothy Pytell
California State University— San Bernardino

Nancy Rachels
Hillsborough Community College

Norman G. Raiford
Greenville Technical College

Charles Rearick
University of Massachusetts—Amherst

Jerome V. Reel Jr.
Clemson University

Roger Reese
Texas A&M University

William Roba
Scott Community College

Kevin Robbins
Indiana University Purdue University—Indianapolis

Eric C. Roberson
Wake Technical Community College

Joseph Robertson
Gadsden State Community College

Jonathan Roth
San Jose State University

Constance M. Rousseau
Providence College

Beverly J. Rowe
Texarkana College

Matthew Ruane
Florida Institute of Technology

Julius R. Ruff
Marquette University

Mark Edward Ruff
Saint Louis University

David L. Ruffley
Pikes Peak Community College

Geraldine Ryder
Ocean County College

Richard Saller
University of Chicago

Magdalena Sanchez
Texas Christian University

Thomas J. Schaeper
St. Bonaventure University

Jack Schanfield
Suffolk County Community College

Roger Schlesinger
Washington State University

Joanne Schneider
Rhode Island College

Thomas C. Schunk
University of Wisconsin—Oshkosh

Kyle C. Sessions
Illinois State University

Linda Simmons
Northern Virginia Community College—Manassas

Donald V. Sippel
Rhode Island College

Stuart Smyth
University at SUNY—Albany

Glen Spann
Asbury College

Heath A. Spencer
Seattle University

John W. Steinberg
Georgia Southern University

Barbara Stengel
Yuba College

Robert P. Stephens
Virginia Tech

Paul W. Strait
Florida State University

James E. Straukamp
California State University—Sacramento

Brian E. Strayer
Andrews University

Fred Suppe
Ball State University

Roger Tate
Somerset Community College

Tom Taylor
Seattle University

Emily Teipe
Fullerton College

David Tengewall
Anne Arundel Community College

Jack W. Thacker
Western Kentucky University

Thomas Turley
Santa Clara University

John G. Tuthill
University of Guam

Maarten Ultee
University of Alabama

Donna L. Van Raaphorst
Cuyahoga Community College

J. Barry Vaughn
University of Alabama

Allen M. Ward
University of Connecticut

Richard D. Weigel
Western Kentucky University

Michael Weiss
Linn-Benton Community College

Alison Williams
Saint Joseph's University

Steven J. Williams
New Mexico Highlands University

Arthur H. Williamson
California State University—Sacramento

Julianna Wilson
Pima Community College

Daniel Woods
Ferrum College

Katherine Workman
Wright State University

Judith T. Wozniak
Cleveland State University

Walter J. Wussow
University of Wisconsin—Eau Claire

Edwin M. Yamauchi
Miami University

Robert W. Young
Carroll Community College

Sergei Zhuk
Ball State University

The following individuals contributed suggestions for the eleventh edition:

Onek Adyanga
Millersville University

Matthew Avitabile
SUNY Oneonta

Lyn Blanchfield
SUNY Oswego

Cullen Chandler
Lycoming College

Dane Daniel
Wright State University, Lake Campus

Dr. Benjamin Esswein
Liberty University

Robert M. Leo
SUNY Onondaga Community College

Dale Moler
Central Michigan University

John Mulloy
Delta College

Michal Yadlin
Treasure Valley Community College

The editors at Cengage have been both helpful and congenial at all times. I especially wish to thank Clark Baxter, who originally asked me to do this project, and whose clever wit, wisdom, gentle prodding, and good friendship added great depth to our working relationship. As Senior Product Manager, Joseph Potvin provided a smoothly organized supervision of this project. As Senior Content Manager, Philip Lanza thoughtfully, wisely, efficiently, and pleasantly guided the overall development of the eleventh edition. I thank Matt Kennedy for his valuable content suggestions and also want to express my gratitude to Kate MacLean and Haley Gaudreau, two other members of Cengage's history team who made valuable recommendations. Above all, I thank my family for their support. The gifts of love, laughter, and patience from my daughters, Jennifer and Kathryn; my sons, Eric and Christian; my daughters-in-law, Liz and Laurie; and my sons-in-law, Daniel and Eddie, were enormously appreciated. I also wish to acknowledge my grandchildren, Devyn, Bryn, Drew, Elena, Sean, Emma, Jackson, and Henry who bring great joy to my life. My wife and best friend, Diane, contributed editorial assistance, wise counsel, good humor, and the loving support that made it possible for me to accomplish a project of this magnitude. I could not have written the book without her.

INTRODUCTION TO STUDENTS OF WESTERN CIVILIZATION

CIVILIZATION, AS HISTORIANS DEFINE IT, first emerged between five and six thousand years ago when people in different parts of the world began to live in organized communities with distinct political, military, economic, and social structures. Religious, intellectual, and artistic activities assumed important roles in these early societies. The focus of this book is on Western civilization, a civilization that many people identify with the continent of Europe.

Defining Western Civilization

Western civilization itself has evolved considerably over the centuries. Although the concept of the West did not yet exist at the time of the Mesopotamians and Egyptians, their development of writing, law codes, and different roles based on gender all eventually influenced what became Western civilization. Although the Greeks did not conceive of Western civilization as a cultural entity, their artistic, intellectual, and political contributions were crucial to the foundations of Western civilization. The Romans produced a remarkable series of accomplishments that were fundamental to the development of Western civilization, a civilization that came to consist largely of lands in Europe conquered by the Romans, in which Roman cultural and political ideals were gradually spread. Nevertheless, people in these early civilizations viewed themselves as subjects of states or empires, not as members of Western civilization.

With the rise of Christianity during the Late Roman Empire, however, peoples in Europe began to identify themselves as part of a civilization different from others, such as that of Islam, leading to a concept of a Western civilization different from other civilizations. In the fifteenth century, Renaissance intellectuals began to identify this civilization not only with Christianity but also with the intellectual and political achievements of the ancient Greeks and Romans.

Important to the development of the idea of a distinct Western civilization were encounters with other peoples. Between 700 and 1500, encounters with the world of Islam helped define the West. After 1500, however, as European ships began to move into other parts of the world, encounters with peoples in Asia, Africa, and the Americas not only had an impact on the civilizations found there but also affected how people in the West defined themselves. At the same time, as they set up colonies, Europeans began to transplant a sense of Western identity to other areas of the world, especially North America and parts of Latin America, that have come to be considered part of Western civilization.

As the concept of Western civilization has evolved over the centuries, so have the values and unique features associated with that civilization. Science played a crucial role in the development of modern Western civilization. The societies of the Greeks, Romans, and medieval Europeans were based largely on a belief in the existence of a spiritual order; a dramatic departure to a natural or material view of the universe occurred in the seventeenth-century Scientific Revolution. Science and technology have been important in the growth of today's modern and largely secular Western civilization, although antecedents to scientific development also existed in Greek and medieval thought and practice, and religion remains an important component of the Western world today.

Many historians have viewed the concept of political liberty, belief in the fundamental value of every individual, and a rational outlook based on a system of logical, analytical thought as unique aspects of Western civilization. Of course, the West has also witnessed horrendous negations of liberty, individualism, and reason. Racism, slavery, violence, world wars, totalitarian regimes—these too form part of the complex story of what constitutes Western civilization.

The Dating of Time

In our examination of Western civilization, we also need to be aware of the dating of time. In recording the past, historians try to determine the exact time when events occurred. World War II in Europe, for example, began on September 1, 1939, when Hitler sent German troops into Poland, and ended on May 7, 1945, when Germany surrendered. By using dates, historians can place events in order and try to determine the development of patterns over periods of time.

If someone asked you when you were born, you would reply with a number, such as 2002. In the United States, we would all accept that number without question because it is part of the dating system followed in the Western world (Europe and the Western Hemisphere). In this system, events are dated by counting backward or forward from the year 1. When the system was first devised, the year 1 was assumed to be the year of the birth of Jesus, and the abbreviations B.C. (before Christ) and A.D. (for the Latin *anno Domini*, meaning "in the year of the Lord") were used to refer to the periods before and after the birth of Jesus, respectively. Historians now generally prefer to refer to the year 1 in nonreligious terms as the beginning of the "common era." The abbreviations B.C.E. (before the common era) and C.E. (common era) are used instead of B.C. and A.D., although the years are the same. Thus, an event that took place four hundred years before the year 1 would be dated 400 B.C.E. (before the common era)—or the date could be expressed as 400 B.C. Dates after the year 1 are labeled C.E. Thus, an event that took place two hundred years after the year 1 would be dated 200 C.E. (common era), or the date could be written as

A.D. 200. It can also be written simply as 200, just as you would not give your birth year as 2002 C.E., but simply as 2002. In keeping with the current usage by most historians, this book will use the abbreviations B.C.E. and C.E.

Historians also make use of other terms to refer to time. A *decade* is ten years, a *century* is one hundred years, and a *millennium* is one thousand years. Thus, "the fourth century B.C.E." refers to the fourth period of one hundred years counting backward from the year 1, the beginning of the common era. Since the first century B.C.E. would be the years 100 B.C.E. to 1 C.E., the fourth century B.C.E. would be the years 400 B.C.E. to 301 B.C.E. We could say, then, that an event in 350 B.C.E. took place in the fourth century B.C.E.

Similarly, "the fourth century C.E." refers to the fourth period of one hundred years after the beginning of the common era. Since the first period of one hundred years would be the years 1 to 100, the fourth period or fourth century would be the years 301 to 400. We could say, then, that an event in 350 took place in the fourth century. Likewise, the first millennium B.C.E. refers to the years 1000 B.C.E. to 1 C.E.; the second millennium C.E. refers to the years 1001 to 2000.

The dating of events can also vary from people to people. Most people in the Western world use the Western calendar, also known as the Gregorian calendar after Pope Gregory XIII, who refined it in 1582. The Hebrew calendar uses a different system in which the year 1 is the equivalent of the Western year 3760 B.C.E., considered to be the date of the creation of the world according to the Bible. Thus, the Western year 2020 is the year 5780 on the Hebrew calendar. The Islamic calendar begins year 1 on the day Muhammad fled Mecca, which is the year 622 on the Western calendar.

STUDYING FROM PRIMARY SOURCE MATERIALS

Astronomers investigate the universe through telescopes. Biologists study the natural world by collecting plants and animals in the field and then examining them with microscopes. Sociologists and psychologists study human behavior through observation and controlled laboratory experiments.

Historians study the past by examining historical "evidence" or "source" materials—church or town records, letters, treaties, advertisements, paintings, menus, literature, buildings, clothing—anything and everything written or created by our ancestors that give clues about their lives and the times in which they lived.

Historians refer to written material as "documents." Excerpts of more than 150 documents—many in feature boxes and others in the text narrative itself—appear in every chapter of this textbook. Each chapter also includes several photographs of buildings, paintings, and other kinds of historical evidence.

As you read each chapter, the more you examine all this "evidence," the more you will understand the main ideas of the course. This introduction to studying historical evidence, along with the visual summaries at the end of each chapter, will help you learn how to look at evidence the way historians do.

Source Material Comes in Two Main Types: Primary and Secondary

Primary evidence is material that comes to us exactly as it left the pen of the person who wrote it. Letters between King Louis XIV of France and the king of Tonkin (now Vietnam) are primary evidence (p. 430). So is the court transcript of a witchcraft trial in France (p. 447), or a diagram of the solar system drawn by Copernicus (p. 491).

Secondary evidence is an account by someone about the life or activity of someone else. A story about Abraham Lincoln written by his secretary of war would give us primary source information about Lincoln by someone who knew him. Reflections about Lincoln's presidency written by a historian might give us insights into how, for example, Lincoln governed during wartime. But because the historian did not know Lincoln in person, we would consider this a secondary source of information about Lincoln. Secondary sources such as historical essays (and textbooks such as this one) can therefore by very helpful in understanding the past. But it is important to remember that a secondary source can reveal as much about its author as it does about its subject.

Reading Documents

We will turn to a specific document in a moment and analyze it in some detail. For now, however, the following are a few basic things to be aware of—and to ask yourself—as you read any written document.

1. Who wrote it? The author of the textbook answers this question for you at the beginning of each document in the book. But your instructors may give you other documents to read, and the authorship of each document is the first question you need to answer.
2. What do we know about the author of the document? The more you know about the author, the more meaningful and reliable the information you can extract from the document.
3. Is it a primary or secondary source document?
4. When was the document written?
5. What is the purpose of the document? Closely tied to the question of document type is the document's purpose. A work of fiction might have been written to entertain, whereas an official document would have been written to convey a particular law or decree to subjects, citizens, or believers.
6. Who was the intended audience? A play is meant to be performed by actors on a stage before a group of onlookers, whereas Martin Luther's Ninety-Five Theses were posted publicly and intended to be seen by all ordinary citizens.
7. Can you detect a bias in this document? As the two documents on the siege of Jerusalem (p. 302) suggest, first-hand accounts of the Crusades written by Christians and Muslims tend to differ. Each may be "accurate" as far as the writer is concerned, but your job as a historian is to decide whether this written evidence gives a reliable account of

Snark/Art Resource, NY

Medieval Town

what happened. You cannot always believe everything you read, but the more you read, the more you can decide what is, in fact, accurate.

"Reading" and Studying Photographs and Artwork

This book pays close attention to primary source and written documents, but contemporary illustrations can also be analyzed to provide an understanding of a historical period.

A historian might ask questions about a painting like the one above to learn more about life in a medieval town. The more you study and learn about medieval social history, the more information this painting will reveal. To help you look at and interpret art like a historian, ask yourself the following questions:

1. By looking closely at just the buildings, what do you learn about the nature of the medieval town dwellings and the allotment of space within the town? Why were medieval towns arranged in this fashion? Why would this differ from modern urban planning?
2. Based on the various activities shown, what kinds of groups would you expect to find in a medieval town? What do you learn about medieval methods of production? How do they differ from modern methods of production? What difference would this make in the nature of community organization and life?
3. Based on what the people in the street are wearing, what do you think their economic status was? Would that be typical of a medieval town? Why or why not?
4. What do you think the artist who created this piece was trying to communicate about life in a medieval town? Based on your knowledge of medieval towns, would you agree with the artist's assessment? Why or why not?
5. What do you think was the social class of the artist? Why?

Reading and Studying Maps

Historical events do not just "happen"; they happen in a specific place. It is important to learn all you can about that place, and a good map can help you do this.

Your textbook includes several kinds of maps. The map of Europe on pages xxxvi-xxxvii before Chapter 1 is a good place to start. Map basics include taking care to read and understand every label on whatever map you study. The map of Europe has labels for six kinds of information. Each of the following is important:

1. Names of countries.
2. Names of major cities.
3. Names of oceans and large bodies of water.
4. Names of rivers.
5. Longitude and latitude. Lines of longitude extend from the North Pole to the South Pole; one such line intersects Iceland in the top left (or northwest) corner of the map. Lines of latitude circle the globe east to west and intersect lines of longitude. These imaginary lines place countries and oceans in their approximate setting on the face of the earth. Not every map includes latitude and longitude.
6. Mileage scale. A mileage scale shows how far apart, in miles and kilometers, each location is from other locations.

Most Maps Include Three Basic Types of Information

1. The boundaries of countries, cities, empires, and other kinds of "political" information. A good map shows each political division in a different color to make them all easy to find. The color of each region or country is the decision of the mapmaker (also known as a cartographer).
2. Mountains, oceans, rivers, and other "physical" or "topographic" information. The mountains on this kind of map have been rendered by the cartographer: Switzerland and Norway are mountainous; Germany and Belarus are relatively flat.
3. Latitude, longitude, a mileage scale, and other information. These elements help the reader place the information in some kind of context. Some maps include an "N" with an arrow that points north. Most maps show northern areas (Alaska, Norway, etc.) at the top. A map that does not do this is not misleading or wrong. But if an "N" arrow does not appear on the map, be sure you know where north is.

"Political" information tends to change a great deal: maps may change after a major war if the winners take more territory, for example. "Physical" information changes slowly: latitude, rivers, distances, and the like do not change or generally change very slowly.

In addition, many maps include information about the spread of disease, the location of cathedrals and universities, trade routes, and any number of other things. There is no real limit to the kinds of information a map can show, and the more information a map can display clearly, the more useful it is. Any good map will include a "legend" stating the information that makes the map useful. The more detailed the map, the more information the mapmaker should provide in the legend.

Again, note that only the oceans, large bodies of water, and rivers—the "physical" features in a map—really exist in nature. They are relatively changeless. All other features on a map are made up and change fairly often. The maps you see on this page all show the same familiar "boot" we call Italy. But all or part of this landmass has also been called Latium, Campania, the duchy of Benevento, the Papal States, the kingdom of the Two Sicilies, Tuscany, Lombardy, Piedmont, and Savoy. Populations and place names change; mountains and oceans do not, at least not much. Whenever you have trouble finding a region or a place on a map, look for a permanent feature to get your bearings.

In addition to kingdoms, cities, and mountains, maps can show the physical proximity of any two or more ideas, movements, or developments. Map 10.9 (p. 301) shows the routes of several crusades of the eleventh and twelfth centuries. Note that the legend associates the color of a crusade's route (shown as a line) with its duration in years. This map makes it possible to see a number of useful things at a glance that could take several maps to describe, including the following:

1. Where each crusade began. (Note the places that send the most crusades and those that send none.)
2. How far each crusade traveled. (Note the mileage key.)
3. Which route each crusade took. (Why did no Crusaders make the trip only on land?)
4. How much time passed between the end of one crusade and the beginning of another. (Did the rate of Crusades accelerate or slow down over time? What does this suggest?)
5. Which Crusaders actually made it to the eastern Mediterranean and which did not. (Consider any correlation between route and timing.)
6. The names of the crusader states themselves.

Another kind of invasion appears in Map 11.1 (p. 310). This map shows the steady progress of the Black Death from the Black Sea and the Mediterranean north and west through Europe. Using the legend, find the shade of color that corresponds to the first outbreak of plague, in December 1347, and follow the spread of disease, shown here in six-month intervals, as you follow the colors northward.

The documents on p. 309 give a sense of how contemporaries tried to explain the plague, and the image on p. 312 vividly illustrates how some people responded to the horrors of the

The Carolingian Empire

Ancient Italy

The Unification of Italy

plague. Map 11.1 brings to mind another aspect of this horror by tracking the plague's ruthless and irresistible advance, month by month, year by year. The more information you can gather from the map, the more the document and illustrations can tell you about the horrors of the plague.

A happier kind of movement, the advance of learning, appears in Map 9.3 (p. 263). For this map, it is important to identify the symbols for universities and schools and to see where they appear on the map. Because education does not tend to move as a wave, as the plague did, each symbol represents a place where learning flourished more than it did in places without a symbol of some kind.

Map 11.1 makes it clear that the plague began in one part of Europe and touched nearly every region as it passed through it. Map 9.3 shows that education works differently; some people have better access to it than others. Your job as a historian is to recognize this and then to figure out why.

Putting It Together: Reading and Studying Documents, Supported by Images

Learning to read a document is no different from learning to read a restaurant menu. The more you practice, the quicker your eyes will find the lobster and pastries.

Let Us Explore a Pair of Primary Sources

As the introduction to the reading on the next page makes clear, King Louis XIV of France is writing the king of Tonkin to ask permission to send Christian missionaries to Southeast Asia. But this exchange of letters tells a great deal more than that.

Before you read this document, take a careful look at this portrait of Louis XIV. As this image makes clear, Louis lived during an age of flourishes and excess. Among many other questions, including some that appear later, you may ask yourself how Louis's manner of speaking reflects the public presentation you see in his portrait.

Your textbook does not show a corresponding portrait of the king of Tonkin, but you might try to create a picture of him in your mind as you read this response to the letter he receives from his fellow ruler.

The following questions about this document are the kinds of questions your instructor would ask about the document.

1. Why does Louis refer to the king of Tonkin, whom he never met, as his "very dear and good friend" (line 2)? Do you think that this French king would begin a conversation with, say, a French shopkeeper in quite the same way? If not, why does he identify more with a fellow king than with a fellow Frenchman?

2. How often do you imagine that the king of France had to persuade people to do what he wanted rather than order them to do so? Who might the people that he had to persuade have been?

3. Note that Louis uses what is referred to as the "royal we," referring to himself in the plural. When does the king of Tonkin refer to himself in the singular ("he," "my"), and when does he refer to himself in the plural ("we")?

RMN-Grand Palais/Art Resource, NY

King Louis XIV

4. Why does Louis say that he is writing at that particular time rather than earlier (lines 15–21)?

5. Why does Louis say that Christian missionaries will be good for Tonkin and its people (lines 32–38)? What reason in Louis's own letter makes you wonder if converting the people of Tonkin to Christianity is "the one thing in the world which we desire most"?

6. Does the king of Tonkin seem pleased to hear from Louis and to receive his request (lines 49–60)? How does he refer to the gift Louis offers him?

7. Louis mentions his gratitude for the good treatment of some French subjects when they were "in your realm." What do you think these Frenchmen were doing there? Do you think they were invited, or did they arrive on their own? How does the king of Tonkin respond when Louis mentions his appreciation for the "protection" they were accorded (lines 61–65)? Protection from what, do you suppose?

8. What reason does the king of Tonkin give for refusing Louis's offer of Christian missionaries (lines 67–73)? He takes care to explain to Louis that "without fidelity [to edicts] nothing is stable." What does this suggest about the king of Tonkin's attitude toward Louis and the "incomparable blessing" of faith in the Christian god? How many French people (or Europeans, for that matter) is the king of Tonkin likely to have met? What French person or persons might have already expressed to the king the ideas that Louis offers?

9. Compare the final lines of each letter. What significance do you draw from the fact that Louis names the day, month, year, and location in which he writes? Apart from later historians, to whom in particular would this information be of greatest interest? What is the significance of the king of Tonkin's closing line?

If you can propose thoughtful answers to these questions, you will have come to know the material very well and should be ready for whatever examinations and papers await you in your course.

A Letter to the King of Tonkin from Louis XIV

1. Most high, most excellent, most mighty and most
2. magnanimous Prince, our very dear and good friend, may it
3. please God to increase your greatness with a happy end!
4.   We hear from our subjects who were in your Realm
5. what protection you accorded them. We appreciate this
6. all the more since we have for you all the esteem that one
7. can have for a prince as illustrious through his military
8. valor as he is commendable for the justice which he
9. exercises in his Realm. We have even been informed
10. that you have not been satisfied to extend this general
11. protection to our subjects but, in particular, that you gave
12. effective proofs of it to Messrs. Deydier and de Bourges.
13. We would have wished that they might have been able
14. to recognize all the favors they received from you by
15. having presents worthy of you offered you; but since the
16. war which we have had for several years, in which all of
17. Europe had banded together against us, prevented our
18. vessels from going to the Indies, at the present time,
19. when we are at peace after having gained many victories
20. and expanded our Realm through the conquest of several
21. important places, we have immediately given orders to
22. the Royal Company to establish itself in your kingdom as
23. soon as possible, and have commanded Messrs. Deydier
24. and de Bourges to remain with you in order to maintain
25. a good relationship between our subjects and yours, also
26. to warn us on occasions that might present themselves
27. when we might be able to give you proofs of our esteem
28. and of our wish to concur with your satisfaction as well as
29. with your best interests.
30.   By way of initial proof, we have given orders to have
31. brought to you some presents which we believe might be
32. agreeable to you. But the one thing in the world which we
33. desire most, both for you and for your Realm, would be to
34. obtain for your subjects who have already embraced the
35. law of the only true God of heaven and earth, the freedom
36. to profess it, since this law is the highest, the noblest,
37. the most sacred and especially the most suitable to have
38. kings reign absolutely over the people.
39.   We are even quite convinced that, if you knew the
40. truths and the maxims which it teaches, you would
41. give first of all to your subjects the glorious example of
42. embracing it. We wish you this incomparable blessing
43. together with a long and happy reign, and we pray God
44. that it may please Him to augment your greatness with the
45. happiest of endings.
46. Written at Saint-Germain-en-Laye, the 10th day of January, 1681,
47.   Your very dear and good friend,
48.   Louis

Answer from the King of Tonkin to Louis XIV

49. The King of Tonkin sends to the King of France a letter to
50. express to him his best sentiments, saying that he was happy
51. to learn that fidelity is a durable good of man and that justice
52. is the most important of things. Consequently practicing of
53. fidelity and justice cannot but yield good results. Indeed,
54. though France and our Kingdom differ as to mountains,
55. rivers, and boundaries, if fidelity and justice reign among
56. our villages, our conduct will express all of our good feelings
57. and contain precious gifts. Your communication, which
58. comes from a country which is a thousand leagues away,
59. and which proceeds from the heart as a testimony of your
60. sincerity, merits repeated consideration and infinite praise.
61. Politeness toward strangers is nothing unusual in our country.
62. There is not a stranger who is not well received by us. How
63. then could we refuse a man from France, which is the most
64. celebrated among the kingdoms of the world and which for
65. love of us wishes to frequent us and bring us merchandise?
66. These feelings of fidelity and justice are truly worthy to be
67. applauded. As regards your wish that we should cooperate
68. in propagating your religion, we do not dare to permit it,
69. for there is an ancient custom, introduced by edicts, which
70. formally forbids it. Now, edicts are promulgated only to be
71. carried out faithfully; without fidelity nothing is stable. How
72. could we disdain a well-established custom to satisfy a
73. private friendship?...
74.   We beg you to understand well that this is our
75. communication concerning our mutual acquaintance. This
76. then is my letter. We send you herewith a modest gift, which
77. we offer you with a glad heart.
78.   This letter was written at the beginning of winter and on
79. a beautiful day.

Elevation

Meters	Feet
4,000	13,120
2,000	6,560
500	1,640
200	656
Sea level	Sea level
Below sea level	Below sea level

⊛ National capital
• Other city

30°W 20°W 10°W 0° 10°E 20°E

Reykjavik

ICELAND

Arctic Circle

Faroe Islands
(Den.)

Shetland
Islands
(U.K.)

SWEDEN

NORWAY

Oslo

*North
Sea*

Stockholm

**NORTHERN
IRELAND**

Edinburgh

Belfast

IRELAND

Dublin

**UNITED
KINGDOM**

Cardiff

London

DENMARK

Copenhagen

Baltic Sea

Kaliningrad

Rig

LITH

(RUSSIA)

Hamburg

Gdansk

Elbe R.

NETHERLANDS

Amsterdam

Berlin

POLAND

War

Vistula R.

*ATLANTIC
OCEAN*

Brussels

Bonn

Leipzig

GERMANY

BELGIUM

Paris

Seine R.

LUX.

Luxembourg

Frankfurt

Prague

**CZECH
REPUBLIC**

Loire R.

Stuttgart

SLOVAKIA

Munich

LIECH.

Vienna

Bratislava

FRANCE

Zurich

Bern

Geneva

SWITZ.

Vaduz

AUSTRIA

Budapest

HUNGARY

Rhine R.

Lyons

Turin

Milan

Ljubljana

Po R.

SLOVENIA

Zagreb

Porto

ANDORRA

Monaco

San
Marino

CROATIA

Belgra

PORTUGAL

SPAIN

Andorra
la Vella

MONACO

**SAN
MARINO**

**BOSNIA &
HERZEGOVINA**

SERBIA

Lisbon

Madrid

Barcelona

*Corsica
(Fr.)*

Rome

Sarajevo

KOSOVO

Tagus R.

MONT.

Podgorica

*Balearic Islands
(Sp.)*

**VATICAN
CITY**

ITALY

Naples

ALBANIA

Tiranë

Sk

MACE

*Sardinia
(It.)*

Gibraltar
(U.K.)

Mediterranean

Algiers

GREEC

Rabat

MOROCCO

Tunis

*Sicily
(It.)*

Valletta

MALTA

ALGERIA

0   200   400 Km.

0   200   400 Mi.

TUNISIA

Sea

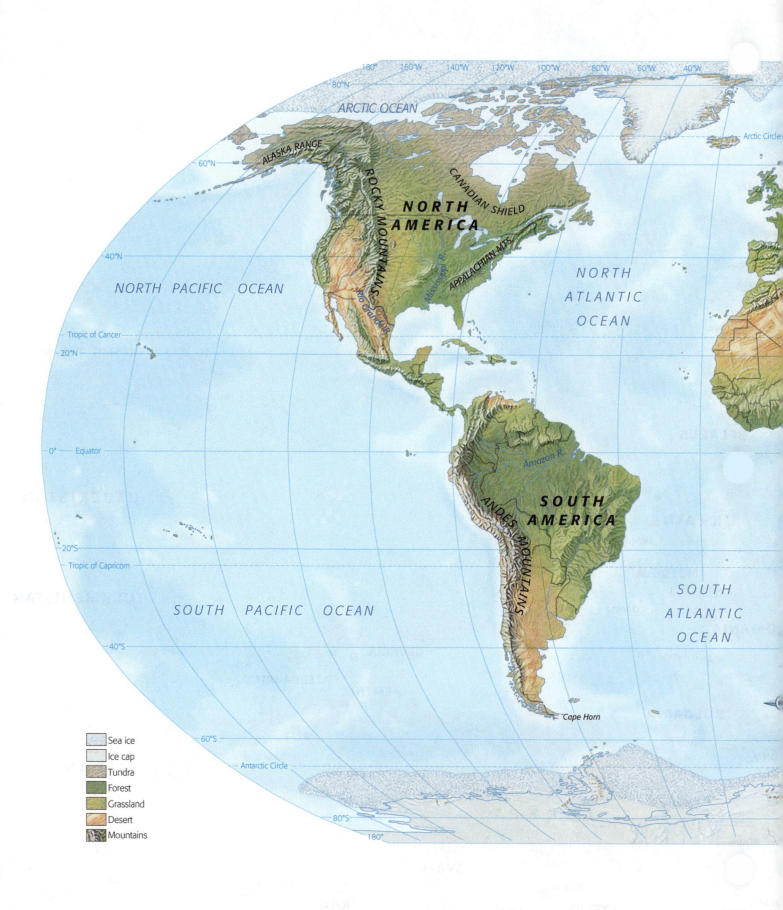

ARCTIC OCEAN

80°N

Arctic Circle

60°N

ALASKA RANGE

CANADIAN SHIELD

ROCKY MOUNTAINS

NORTH AMERICA

40°N

NORTH PACIFIC OCEAN

Mississippi R.

APPALACHIAN MTS.

Rio Grande R.

NORTH ATLANTIC OCEAN

Tropic of Cancer

20°N

0°   Equator

Amazon R.

SOUTH AMERICA

ANDES MOUNTAINS

20°S

Tropic of Capricorn

SOUTH PACIFIC OCEAN

SOUTH ATLANTIC OCEAN

40°S

Cape Horn

60°S

Antarctic Circle

80°S

180°

	Sea ice
	Ice cap
	Tundra
	Forest
	Grassland
	Desert
	Mountains

ARCTIC OCEAN

80°N

60°N

40°N

EUROPE

ALPS

ASIA

URAL MTS.

Volga R.

Ob R.

GOBI

HINDU KUSH

HIMALAYA MTS.

Indus R.

Ganges R.

SAHARA

SYRIAN DESERT

AFRICA

Nile R.

DECCAN PLATEAU

Tropic of Cancer

20°N

PACIFIC OCEAN

0°

INDIAN OCEAN

NAMIB DESERT

KALAHARI DESERT

GREAT SANDY DESERT

20°S

Tropic of Capricorn

AUSTRALIA

Cape of Good Hope

60°S

Antarctic Circle

0   1,000   2,000 Km.

0   1,000   2,000 Mi.

ANTARCTICA

80°S

180°

40°E   60°E   80°E   100°E   120°E   140°E   160°E   180°

WESTERN CIVILIZATION

VOLUME I: TO 1715

CHAPTER 1

The Ancient Near East: The First Civilizations

IMAGE 1.1 **Excavation of Warka Showing the Ruins of Uruk**

ESSAM AL-SUDANI/AFP/Getty Images

CHAPTER OUTLINE AND FOCUS QUESTIONS

1-1 The First Humans

Q How did the Paleolithic and Neolithic Ages differ? How did the Neolithic Revolution affect the lives of men and women?

1-2 The Emergence of Civilization

Q What characteristics do some scholars use when speaking about the idea of civilization? What are some explanations for why early civilizations emerged?

1-3 Civilization in Mesopotamia

Q How are the chief characteristics of civilization evident in ancient Mesopotamia?

1-4 Egyptian Civilization: "The Gift of the Nile"

Q What are the basic features of the three major periods of Egyptian history? What elements of continuity are there in these periods? What are their major differences?

1-5 On the Fringes of Civilization

Q What is the significance of the Indo-European-speaking peoples?

CONNECTIONS TO TODAY

What lessons can you learn from the decline and fall of early civilizations, and can you apply those lessons to today's civilizations? Why or why not?

IN 1849, A DARING YOUNG ENGLISHMAN made a hazardous journey into the deserts and swamps of southern Iraq. Moving south down the banks of the Euphrates (yoo-FRAY-teez) River while braving high winds and temperatures that reached 120°F, William Loftus led a small expedition in search of the roots of civilization. As he said, "From our childhood we have been led to regard this place as the cradle of the human race."

Guided by native Arabs into the southernmost reaches of Iraq, Loftus and his small group of explorers were soon overwhelmed by what they saw. He wrote, "I know of nothing more exciting or impressive than the first sight of one of these great piles, looming in solitary grandeur from the surrounding plains and marshes." One of these piles, known to the natives as the mound of Warka, contained the ruins of Uruk, one of the first cities in the world and part of one of the world's first civilizations.

Southern Iraq in Southwest Asia was one area in the world where civilization began. In fact, people in both Southwest Asia and Egypt developed organized societies, invented writing, and created the ideas and institutions that we associate with civilization. The Greeks and Romans, who later played such a crucial role in the foundation of what became Western civilization, were themselves nourished and influenced by these older societies. It is appropriate, therefore, to begin our story of Western civilization with the early civilizations of Southwest Asia and Egypt. Before considering these civilizations, however, we must briefly examine humankind's prehistory and observe how human beings made the shift from hunting and gathering to agricultural communities and ultimately to cities and civilization.

1-1 The First Humans

 FOCUS QUESTIONS: How did the Paleolithic and Neolithic Ages differ? How did the Neolithic Revolution affect the lives of men and women?

Historians rely primarily on documents to create their pictures of the past, but no written records exist for the prehistory of humankind. In their absence, the story of early humanity depends on archaeological and, more recently, biological information, which anthropologists and archaeologists use to formulate theories about our early past. Although modern science has given us more precise methods for examining prehistory, much of our understanding of early humans still relies on conjecture.

The earliest humanlike creatures—known as **hominids**—existed in Africa as long as 3 to 4 million years ago. Known as Australopithecines (aw-stray-loh-PITH-uh-synz), they flourished in East and South Africa and were the first hominids to make simple stone tools. They were bipedal with a brain size similar to that of modern apes. New hominids continue to be found, although considerable controversy can surround them. For example, the contention that a 2003 discovery in Indonesia of a hominid species known as the hobbit because of its small body is a distinct hominid species has been challenged by other scientists.

Another stage in early human development occurred around 1.5 million years ago when *Homo erectus* ("upright human being") emerged. *Homo erectus* made use of larger and more varied tools and was the first hominid to leave Africa and move into both Europe and Asia.

1-1a The Emergence of *Homo sapiens*

Around 250,000 years ago, a crucial stage in human development began with the emergence of *Homo sapiens* (HOH-moh SAY-pee-unz) ("wise human being"). The first anatomically modern humans, known as *Homo sapiens sapiens* ("wise, wise human being"), appeared in Africa between 200,000 and 150,000 years ago. Recent evidence indicates that they began to spread outside Africa around 70,000 years ago. Map 1.1 shows probable dates for different movements, although many of these dates are still controversial.

These modern humans, who were our direct ancestors, soon encountered other hominids, such as the Neanderthals, whose remains were first found in 1856 in the Neander valley in Germany. Neanderthal remains have since been found in both Europe and Asia and have been dated to between 200,000 and 30,000 B.C.E.

New genetic evidence since 2010 has indicated that European humans interbred with Neanderthals, and East Asian humans even more so. Neanderthals relied on a variety of stone tools and were the first early people to bury their dead. By 30,000 B.C.E., *Homo sapiens sapiens* had replaced the Neanderthals, who had largely become extinct.

HISTORIANS DEBATE **The Spread of Humans: Out of Africa or MultiRegional?** The movements of the first modern humans were rarely sudden or rapid. Groups of people advanced beyond their old hunting grounds at a rate

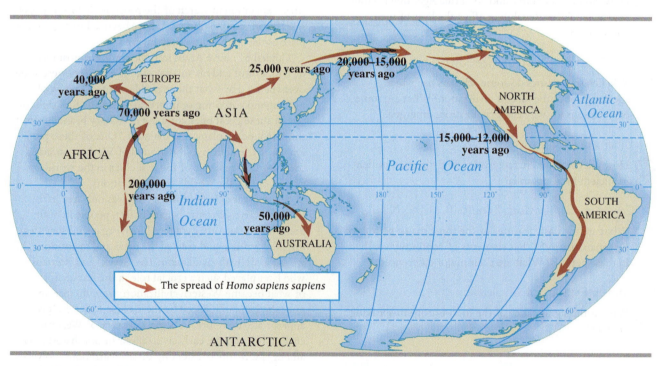

MAP 1.1 The Spread of *Homo sapiens sapiens*. *Homo sapiens sapiens* spread from Africa beginning about 70,000 years ago. Living and traveling in small groups, these anatomically modern humans were hunter-gatherers.

 Given that some diffusion of humans occurred during ice ages, how would such climate change affect humans and their movements, especially from Asia to Australia and Asia to North America?

CHRONOLOGY	The First Humans
Australopithecines	Flourished ca. 2–4 million years ago
Homo erectus	Flourished ca. 100,000–1.5 million years ago
Neanderthals	Flourished ca. 200,000–30,000 B.C.E.
Homo sapiens sapiens	Emerged ca. 200,000 B.C.E.

of only two or three miles per generation, but this was enough to populate the world in some tens of thousands of years. Some scholars who advocate a multiregional theory have suggested that advanced human creatures may have emerged independently in different parts of the world rather than in Africa alone. But the latest genetic, archaeological, and climatic evidence strongly supports the out-of-Africa theory as the most likely explanation of human origin. In any case, by 10,000 B.C.E., *Homo sapiens sapiens* could be found throughout the world. By that time, it was the only human species left. All humans today, whether Europeans, Australian Aborigines, or Africans, belong to the same subspecies of human being.

1-1b The Hunter-Gatherers of the Old Stone Age

One of the basic distinguishing features of the human species is the ability to make tools. The earliest tools were made of stone, and so scholars refer to this early period of human history (ca. 2,500,000–10,000 B.C.E.) as the **Paleolithic Age** (*paleolithic* is Greek for "old stone").

For hundreds of thousands of years, humans relied on gathering and hunting for their daily food. Paleolithic peoples had a close relationship with the world around them and over time came to know which plants to eat and which animals to hunt. They did not know how to grow crops or raise animals, however. They gathered wild nuts, berries, fruits, and a variety of wild grains and green plants. Around the world, they hunted and consumed various animals, including buffalo, horses, bison, wild goats, and reindeer. In coastal areas, fish were a rich source of nourishment.

The gathering of wild plants and the hunting of animals no doubt led to certain patterns of living. Archaeologists and anthropologists have speculated that Paleolithic people lived in small bands of twenty or thirty people. They were nomadic, moving from place to place to follow animal migrations and vegetation cycles. Hunting depended on careful observation of animal behavior patterns and required a group effort for success. Over the years, tools became more refined and useful. The invention of the spear, and later the bow and arrow, made hunting considerably easier. Harpoons and fishhooks made of bone increased the catch of fish.

Both men and women were responsible for finding food—the chief work of Paleolithic people. Since women bore and raised the children, they generally stayed close to the camps, but they played an important role in acquiring food by gathering berries, nuts, and grains. Men hunted wild animals, an activity that often took them far from camp. Because both men and women played important roles in providing for the band's survival, many scientists believe that a rough equality existed between men and women. Indeed, some speculate that both men and women made the decisions that affected the activities of the Paleolithic band.

Some groups of Paleolithic peoples found shelter in caves, but over time, they also created new types of shelter. Perhaps the most common was a simple structure of wooden poles or sticks covered with animal hides. Where wood was scarce, Paleolithic hunter-gatherers might use the bones of mammoths to build frames that were then covered with animal hides. The systematic use of fire, which archaeologists believe began around 500,000 years ago, made it possible for the caves and human-made structures to have a source of light and heat. Fire also enabled early humans to cook their food, making it taste better, last longer, and, in the case of some plants, such as wild grain, easier to chew and digest.

The making of tools and the use of fire—two important technological innovations of Paleolithic peoples—remind us how crucial the ability to adapt was to human survival. But Paleolithic peoples did more than just survive. The cave paintings of large animals found in southwestern France and northern Spain bear witness to the cultural activity of Paleolithic peoples. A cave discovered in southern France in 1994—known as the Chauvet (shoh-VAY) cave after the leader of the expedition that found it—contains more than three hundred paintings of lions, oxen, owls, bears, and other animals (see Image 1.2). Most of these are animals that Paleolithic peoples did not hunt, which suggests to some scholars that the paintings were made for religious or even decorative purposes. The discoverers were overwhelmed by what they saw: "There was a moment of ecstasy. . . . They overflowed with joy and emotion in their turn. . . . These were moments of indescribable madness."[1]

1-1c The Neolithic Revolution (ca. 10,000–4000 B.C.E.)

The end of the last ice age around 10,000 B.C.E. was followed by what scholars call the **Neolithic Revolution**, a significant change in living patterns that occurred in the New Stone Age (*neolithic* is Greek for "new stone"). The name is misleading, however. Although Neolithic peoples made a new type of polished stone ax, this was not the major change that occurred after 10,000 B.C.E.

An Agricultural Revolution The biggest change in living patterns was the shift from gathering plants and hunting animals for sustenance (food gathering) to producing food by systematic agriculture (food production). The planting of grains and vegetables provided a regular supply of food. Dogs and sheep were among the first animals to be domesticated, and the domestication of animals such as goats, cattle, pigs, and sheep provided a steady source of meat, milk, and fibers such as wool for clothing. Larger animals could also be used for work as beasts of burden. The growing of crops and the taming of food-producing animals created a new relationship between humans and nature. Historians

IMAGE 1.2 **Paleolithic Cave Painting: The Lascaux Cave.** Cave paintings of large animals reveal the cultural creativity of Paleolithic peoples. This scene is part of a large underground chamber found accidentally in 1940 at Lascaux, France, by some boys looking for their dog. This work is dated around 15,000 B.C.E. To make their paintings, Paleolithic artists used stone lamps that burned animal fat to illuminate the cave walls and mixed powdered mineral ores with animal fat to create red, yellow, and black pigments. Some artists even made brushes out of animal hairs with which to apply the paints.

 What does this painting reveal about Paleolithic peoples?

speak of this as the agricultural revolution. Revolutionary change is dramatic and requires great effort, but the ability to acquire food on a regular basis gave humans greater control over their environment. It also allowed them to give up their nomadic way of life and begin to live in settled communities.

Systematic agriculture probably developed independently between 8000 and 7000 B.C.E. in four different areas of the world. Different plants were cultivated in each area: wheat, barley, and lentils in the Near East; rice and millet in South Asia; millet and yams in West Africa; and beans, potatoes, and corn (maize) in the Americas. The Neolithic Revolution needed a favorable environment. In the Near East, the upland areas above the Fertile Crescent (present-day northern Iraq and southern Turkey) were initially more conducive to systematic farming than the river valleys. This region received the necessary rainfall and was the home of two wild plant (barley and wheat) and four wild animal (pigs, cows, goats, and sheep) species that humans eventually domesticated.

Neolithic Farming Villages The growing of crops on a regular basis gave rise to more permanent settlements that historians refer to as Neolithic farming villages or towns. One of the oldest and most extensive agricultural villages was Çatal Hüyük (chaht-ul hoo-YOOK), which is located in modern-day Turkey. Its walls enclosed thirty-two acres, and its population probably reached six thousand during its high point from 6700 to 5700 B.C.E. People lived in simple mudbrick houses that were built so close to one another that there were few streets. To get to their homes, people had to walk along the rooftops and then enter the house through a hole in the roof.

Archaeologists have discovered twelve cultivated products at Çatal Hüyük, including fruits, nuts, and three kinds of wheat. Artisans made weapons and jewelry that were traded with neighboring peoples. Religious shrines housing figures of gods and goddesses have been found at Çatal Hüyük, as have a number of female statuettes. Molded with noticeably large breasts and buttocks, these "earth mothers" perhaps symbolically represented the fertility of both mother earth and human mothers. The shrines and statues point to the important role of religious practices in the lives of these Neolithic people (see Image 1.3).

Consequences of the Neolithic Revolution The Neolithic Revolution had far-reaching consequences. Once people settled in villages or towns, they built houses for protection and other structures for storing goods. As organized communities stored food and accumulated material goods, they began to engage in trade. People also began to specialize in certain crafts, and a division of labor consequently developed. Pottery was made from clay and baked in fire to make it hard. The pots were used for cooking and for storing grains. Woven baskets were also used for storage. Stone tools became refined as flint blades were developed to make sickles and hoes for use in the fields. Obsidian—a volcanic glass that was easily flaked—was also used to create very sharp tools. In the course of the Neolithic Age, many of the food plants still in use today began to be cultivated. Moreover, vegetable fibers from such plants as flax were used to make thread that was woven into cloth.

The change to systematic agriculture in the Neolithic Age also had consequences for the relationship between men and women. Men assumed the primary responsibility for working in the fields and herding animals—jobs that kept them away from home. Although women also worked in the fields, many remained close to home, caring for the children, weaving cloth, and performing other household tasks. In time, as work outside the home was increasingly perceived as more important than work done at home, men came to play the more dominant role in human society, which gave rise to the practice of **patriarchy** (PAY-tree-ark-ee), or a society dominated by men, a basic pattern that has persisted until our own times.

of metals marked a new level of human control over the environment and its resources. Already before 4000 B.C.E., craftspeople had discovered that certain rocks could be heated to liquefy metals embedded within them. The metals could then be cast in molds to produce tools and weapons that were more refined than stone instruments. Although copper was the first metal to be used in producing tools, after 4000 B.C.E. craftspeople in West Asia discovered that combining copper and tin produced bronze, a much harder and more durable metal than copper. Its widespread use led historians to call the period from around 3000 to 1200 B.C.E. the Bronze Age; thereafter, bronze was increasingly replaced by iron.

At first, Neolithic settlements were mere villages. But as their inhabitants mastered the art of farming, more complex human societies emerged. As wealth increased, these societies began to develop armies and to build walled cities. By the beginning of the Bronze Age, the concentration of larger numbers of people in the river valleys of Southwest Asia and Egypt was leading to an entirely new pattern for human life.

1-2 The Emergence of Civilization

 FOCUS QUESTIONS: What characteristics do some scholars use when speaking about the idea of civilization? What are some explanations for why early civilizations emerged?

As we have seen, early human beings formed small groups that developed a simple culture that enabled them to survive. As human societies grew and developed greater complexity, a new form of human existence—called civilization—came into being. A **civilization** is a complex culture in which large numbers of human beings share a variety of common elements. Historians have identified a number of basic characteristics of civilization. These include (1) an urban focus: cities became the centers of political, economic, social, cultural, and religious development; (2) a distinct religious structure: the gods were deemed crucial to the community's success, and professional priestly classes, as stewards of the gods' property, regulated relations with the gods; (3) new political and military structures: an organized government bureaucracy arose to meet the administrative demands of the growing population, and armies were organized to gain land and power and for defense; (4) a new social structure based on economic power: while kings and an upper class of priests, political leaders, and warriors dominated, there also existed a large group of free people (farmers, artisans, craftspeople) and at the very bottom, socially, a class of slaves; (5) the development of writing: kings, priests, merchants, and artisans used writing to keep records; and (6) new forms of significant artistic and intellectual activity: for example, monumental architectural structures, usually religious, occupied a prominent place in urban environments.

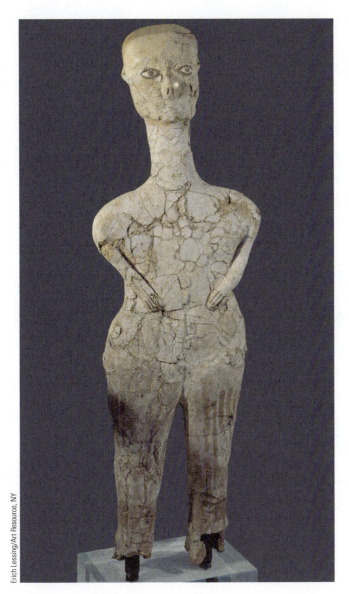

IMAGE 1.3 **Statue from Ain Ghazal.** This life-size statue made of plaster, sand, and crushed chalk was discovered in 1984 in Ain Ghazal, an archaeological site near Amman, Jordan. Dating from 6500 B.C.E., it is among the oldest known statues of the human figure. Although it appears lifelike, its features are considered generic rather than a portrait of an individual face. The purpose and meaning of this sculpture may never be known.

Erich Lessing/Art Resource, NY

Other patterns set in the Neolithic Age also proved to be enduring elements of human history. Fixed dwellings, domesticated animals, regular farming, a division of labor, men holding power—all of these are a part of the human story. Despite all our modern scientific and technological progress, human survival still depends on the growing and storing of food, an accomplishment of peoples in the Neolithic Age. The Neolithic Revolution was truly a turning point in human history.

Between 4000 and 3000 B.C.E., significant technical developments began to transform Neolithic towns. The invention of writing enabled records to be kept, and the use

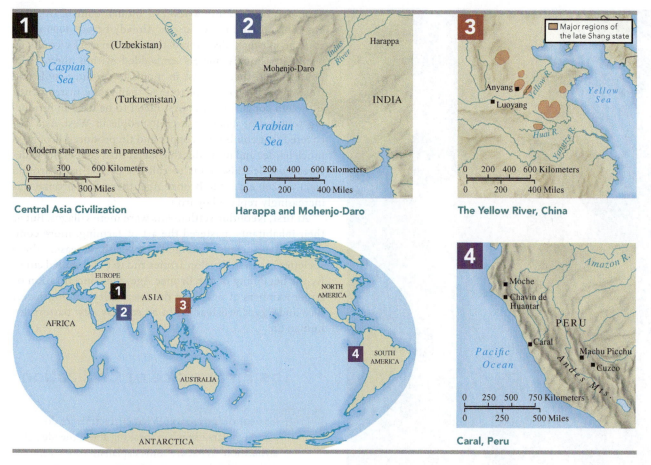

MAP 1.2 **Emergence of Civilizations Around the World.** Many historians maintain that civilizations developed independently in different parts of the world. As seen on this map, in addition to those in Southwest Asia and Egypt that will be examined in this chapter, civilizations emerged in India, China, Central Asia, and South America.

Q *What common features might explain the emergence of civilization in these areas?*

The civilizations that developed in Southwest Asia and Egypt will be examined in detail in this chapter. But civilization also developed independently in other parts of the world (see Map 1.2). Between 3000 and 1500 B.C.E., the valleys of the Indus River in India supported a flourishing civilization that extended hundreds of miles from the Himalayas to the coast of the Arabian Sea. Two major cities—Harappa (huh-RAP-uh) and Mohenjo-Daro (moh-HEN-joh-DAH-roh)—were at the heart of this South Asian civilization. Many written records of the Indus valley civilization exist, but their language has not yet been deciphered. This Indus valley civilization carried on extensive trade with city-states in Southwest Asia.

Another river valley civilization emerged along the Yellow River in northern China about 4,000 years ago. Under the Shang (SHAHNG) dynasty of kings, which ruled from 1570 to 1045 B.C.E., this civilization contained impressive cities with huge outer walls, royal palaces, and large royal tombs. A system of irrigation enabled early Chinese civilization to maintain a prosperous farming society ruled by an aristocratic class whose major concern was war.

Scholars long believed that civilization emerged in only four areas: the fertile river valleys of the Tigris and Euphrates, the Nile, the Indus, and the Yellow River—that is, in Southwest Asia, Egypt, India, and China. Recently, however, archaeologists have discovered two other early civilizations. One of these flourished in Central Asia (in what are now the republics of Turkmenistan and Uzbekistan) around 4,000 years ago. People in this civilization built mudbrick buildings, raised sheep and goats, had bronze tools, used a system of irrigation to grow wheat and barley, and had a writing system.

Another early civilization emerged in the Supe River valley of Peru. At the center of this civilization was the city of Caral, which flourished around 2600 B.C.E. It contained buildings for officials, apartment houses, and grand residences—all built of stone. The inhabitants of Caral also developed a system of irrigation by diverting a river more than a mile upstream into their fields.

CHRONOLOGY	The Birth of Early Civilizations
Egypt	ca. 3100 B.C.E.
Mesopotamia	ca. 3000 B.C.E.
India	ca. 3000 B.C.E.
Peru	ca. 2600 B.C.E.
China	ca. 2000 B.C.E.
Central Asia	ca. 2000 B.C.E.

HISTORIANS DEBATE 1-2a **Why Did Early Civilizations Develop?**

Since civilizations developed independently in different parts of the world, can general causes be identified that would explain why all of these civilizations emerged? A number of possible explanations of the beginning of civilization have been suggested. One theory maintains that challenges forced human beings to make efforts that resulted in the rise of civilization. Some scholars have adhered to a material explanation and have argued that material forces, such as the growth of food surpluses, made possible the specialization of labor and development of large communities with bureaucratic organization. But the area of the Fertile Crescent, in which civilization emerged in Southwest Asia (see Map 1.2), was not naturally conducive to agriculture. Abundant food could be produced only with massive human effort to manage the water, an undertaking that required organization and led to civilized cities. Other historians have argued that nonmaterial forces, primarily religious, provided the sense of unity and purpose that made such organized activities possible. Finally, some scholars doubt that we will ever discover the actual causes of early civilization.

1-3 Civilization in Mesopotamia

FOCUS QUESTION: How are the chief characteristics of civilization evident in ancient Mesopotamia?

The Greeks spoke of the valley between the Tigris and Euphrates Rivers in Southwest Asia as **Mesopotamia** (mess-uh-puh-TAY-mee-uh), the "land between the rivers." The region receives little rain, but the soil of the plain of southern Mesopotamia was enlarged and enriched over the years by layers of silt deposited by the two rivers. In late spring, the Tigris and Euphrates overflow and deposit their fertile silt, but since this flooding depends on the melting of snows in the upland mountains where the rivers begin, it is unpredictable and sometimes catastrophic. In such circumstances, people could raise crops only by building a complex system of irrigation and drainage ditches to control the flow of the rivers. Large-scale irrigation made possible the

expansion of agriculture in this region, and the abundant food provided the material base for the emergence of civilization in Mesopotamia.

1-3a The City-States of Ancient Mesopotamia

The creators of Mesopotamian civilization were the Sumerians (soo-MER-ee-unz *or* soo-MEER-ee-unz), a people whose origins remain unclear. By 3000 B.C.E., the Sumerians had established a number of independent cities in southern Mesopotamia, including Eridu, Ur, Uruk, Umma, and Lagash (see Map 1.3). There is evidence that they were not the first people in the region, however. A number of Sumerian agricultural and craft terms are not Sumerian in origin, indicating that the Sumerians adopted some aspects of preexisting settlements. As the Sumerian cities grew larger, they came to exercise political and economic control over the surrounding countryside, forming city-states. These city-states were the basic units of Sumerian civilization.

Sumerian Cities Sumerian cities were surrounded by walls. Uruk, for example, occupied an area of approximately 1,000 acres encircled by a wall 6 miles long with defense towers located every 30 to 35 feet along the wall. City dwellings, built of sun-dried bricks, included both the small flats of peasants and the larger dwellings of the civic and priestly officials. Although Mesopotamia had little stone or wood for building purposes, it did have plenty of mud. Mudbricks, easily shaped by hand, were left to bake in the hot sun until they were hard enough to use for building. People in Mesopotamia were remarkably inventive with mudbricks, inventing the arch and constructing some of the largest brick buildings in the world.

The most prominent building in a Sumerian city was the temple, which was dedicated to the chief god or goddess of the city and often built atop a massive stepped tower called a **ziggurat** (ZIG-uh-rat). The Sumerians believed that gods and goddesses owned the cities, and much wealth was used to build temples as well as elaborate houses for the priests and priestesses who served the gods and supervised the temples and their property. The priests and priestesses had great power. In fact, historians believe that in the early stages of a few city-states, priests and priestesses may have played an important role in ruling. The Sumerians believed that the gods ruled the cities, making the state a **theocracy** (government by a divine authority). Actual ruling power, however, was primarily in the hands of worldly figures known as kings.

Kingship Sumerians viewed kingship as divine in origin—kings, they believed, derived their power from the gods and were the agents of the gods. As one person said in a petition to his king: "You in your judgment, you are the son of Anu [god of the sky]; your commands, like the word of a god, cannot be reversed; your words, like rain pouring down from heaven, are without number."[2] Regardless of their origins, kings had power—they led armies, issued laws, supervised the building

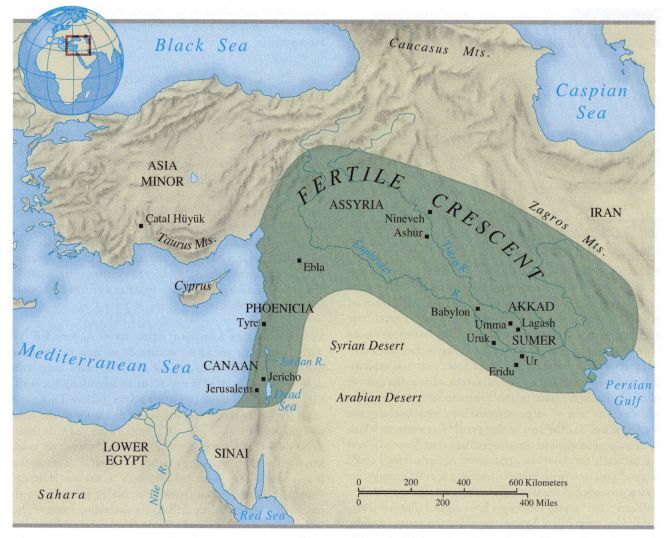

MAP 1.3 **The Ancient Near East.** The Fertile Crescent encompassed land with access to water. Employing flood management and irrigation systems, the peoples of the region established civilizations based on agriculture. These civilizations developed writing, law codes, and economic specialization.

Q *What geographic aspects of the Mesopotamian city-states made conflict between them likely?*

of public works, provided courts, and organized workers for the irrigation projects on which Mesopotamian agriculture depended. The army, government bureaucracy, and priests and priestesses all aided the kings in their rule (see Image 1.4). Befitting their power, Sumerian kings lived in large palaces with their wives and children.

Economy and Society The economy of the Sumerian city-states was primarily agricultural, but commerce and industry became important as well. The people of Mesopotamia produced woolen textiles, pottery, and metalwork. Foreign trade, which was primarily a royal monopoly, could be extensive. Royal officials imported luxury items, such as copper and tin, aromatic woods, and fruit trees, in exchange for dried fish, wool, barley, wheat, and the goods produced by Mesopotamian metalworkers. Traders traveled by land to the eastern Mediterranean in the

west and by sea to India in the east. The invention of the wheel around 3000 B.C.E. led to the development of carts with wheels that made the transport of goods easier.

Sumerian city-states probably contained four major social groups: elites, dependent commoners, free commoners, and slaves. Elites included royal and priestly officials and their families. Dependent commoners included the elites' clients who worked for the palace and temple estates. Free commoners worked as farmers, merchants, fishers, scribes, and craftspeople. Probably 90 percent or more of the population were farmers. They could exchange their crops for the goods of the artisans in free town markets. Slaves belonged to palace officials, who used them mostly in building projects; temple officials, who used mostly female slaves to weave cloth and grind grain; and rich landowners, who used them for farming and domestic work.

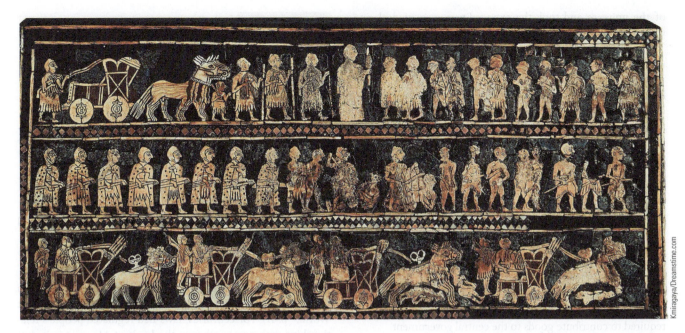

IMAGE 1.4 **The Royal Standard of Ur.** This detail is from the Royal Standard of Ur, a box dating from around 2700 b.c.e. that was discovered in a stone tomb from the royal cemetery of the Sumerian city-state of Ur. The scenes on one side of the box depict the activities of the king and his military forces. Shown in the bottom panel are four Sumerian battle chariots. Each chariot held two men, one who held the reins and the other armed with a spear for combat. A special compartment in the chariot held a number of spears. The charging chariots are seen defeating the enemy. In the middle band, the Sumerian soldiers round up the captured enemies. In the top band, the captives are presented to the king, who has alighted from his chariot and is shown standing above all the others in the center of the panel.

 What do these scenes reveal about the importance of war in Sumerian society? Why was war so important?

1-3b Empires in Ancient Mesopotamia

As the number of Sumerian city-states grew and the states expanded, new conflicts arose as city-state fought city-state for control of land and water. During the Early Dynastic Age (3000–2340 b.c.e.), the fortunes of various cities rose and fell over the centuries. The constant wars, with their burning and sacking of cities, left many Sumerians in deep despair, as is evident in the following lines from the Sumerian poem "Lament from Ur": "Ur is destroyed, bitter is its lament. The country's blood now fills its holes like hot bronze in a mold. Bodies dissolve like fat in the sun. Our temple is destroyed, the gods have abandoned us, like migrating birds. Smoke lies on our city like a shroud."[3]

The Akkadian Empire Located on the flat, open land of Mesopotamia, the Sumerian city-states were also vulnerable to invasion. To the north of the Sumerian city-states were the Akkadians (uh-KAY-dee-unz). We call them a Semitic people because of the language they spoke (see Table 1.1). Around 2340 b.c.e., Sargon, leader of the Akkadians, overran the Sumerian city-states and established a dynastic empire. Sargon used the former rulers of the conquered city-states as his governors. His power was based on the military—namely, his army of 5,400 men. Sargon's empire, including all of Mesopotamia as well as lands westward to the Mediterranean, inspired generations of Near Eastern leaders to emulate his accomplishment. Even in the first millennium b.c.e., Sargon was still remembered in chronicles as a king of

TABLE 1.1	Some Semitic Languages	
Akkadian	Assyrian	Hebrew
Arabic	Babylonian	Phoenician
Aramaic	Canaanitic	Syriac

Note: Languages in *italic* type are no longer spoken.

Akkad who "had no rival or equal, spread his splendor over all the lands, and crossed the sea in the east. In his eleventh year, he conquered the western land to its furthest point, and brought it under his sole authority."[4]

Sargon also used religion as a unifying force in his empire. He made his daughter high priestess of the moon god Nanna at Ur in Sumer. She was given the Sumerian name of Enheduanna, "chief priestess, ornament of heaven." Sargon trusted her to unify the Sumerian and Akkadian gods in order to bring stability to his empire. This Akkadian princess also composed a number of religious hymns for the temples in Sumer, making her one of the first authors in history known by name.

One of Sargon's successors, his grandson Naram-Sin (ca. 2260–2223 b.c.e.), continued the greatness of the Akkadian empire. Like his grandfather, Naram-Sin waged numerous military campaigns that led him to an extreme level of self-glorification. He called himself the king of the four corners of the universe and took the extraordinary step of declaring himself a god. An inscription found in northern Iraq reads: "Naram-Sin, the strong one, king of Akkad, when the four corners [of the universe] together were hostile to him, he remained victorious in nine battles in a single year. . . . Because he had been able to preserve his city in the time of crisis, [the inhabitants of] his city asked . . . that he be the god of their city Akkad, and built a temple for him in the midst of Akkad."[5] By the end of his reign, however, Naram-Sin was battling hill peoples, who finally caused the fall of the Akkadian empire by 2150 B.C.E.

The Third Dynasty of Ur The end of the Akkadian empire brought a return to independent city-states in Mesopotamia. Much confusion ensued, as is evident in the recorded Sumerian king list, which stated bluntly, "Who was king? Who was not king?" The confusion ended when Ur-Nammu established a new dynasty that reunified much of Mesopotamia with its capital at Ur. This Third Dynasty of Ur (ca. 2112–2000 B.C.E.) witnessed a final flowering of Sumerian culture. The economy flourished, and new temples and canals were built. Each province was required to contribute goods to the central government.

Around 2000 B.C.E., however, invaders from Iran destroyed Ur and brought an end to the Third Dynasty. Even earlier, the Amorites, a large group of Semitic-speaking semi-nomads, described by Sumerian scribes as dressed in sheepskins, living in tents, and eating raw meat, had entered the region and battled the kings of the Third Dynasty. The Amorites, or Old Babylonians, gradually settled down and over the next two hundred years established their influence throughout much of Mesopotamia. One of their kings, Hammurabi (ham-uh-RAH-bee), managed to establish power and create a new empire.

Hammurabi's Empire Hammurabi (1792–1750 B.C.E.) had a well-disciplined army of foot soldiers who carried axes, spears, and copper or bronze daggers. He learned to divide his opponents and subdue them one by one. Using such methods, he gained control of Sumer and Akkad and reunified Mesopotamia almost to the old borders established by Sargon (see Map 1.4). After his conquests, Hammurabi called himself "the sun of Babylon, the king who made the four quarters of the world obedient," and established his capital at Babylon.

Hammurabi, the man of war, was also a man of peace. He followed in the footsteps of previous conquerors by assimilating Mesopotamian culture; as a result, Sumerian ways continued to exist despite the end of the Sumerians as a political entity. A collection of his letters, found by archaeologists, reveals that the king took a strong interest in state affairs. He built temples, defensive walls, and irrigation canals; encouraged trade; and brought about an economic revival. Indeed, Hammurabi saw himself as a shepherd to his people: "I am indeed the shepherd who brings peace, whose scepter is just. My benevolent shade was spread over my city. I held the people of the lands of Sumer and Akkad safely on my lap."[6]

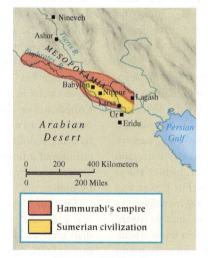

MAP 1.4 Hammurabi's Empire

CHRONOLOGY	Chief Events in Mesopotamian History
Sumerian city-states: Early Dynastic Age	ca. 3000–2340 B.C.E.
Sargon	ca. 2340–2279 B.C.E.
Naram-Sin	ca. 2260–2223 B.C.E.
Third Dynasty of Ur	ca. 2112–2000 B.C.E.
Hammurabi's reign	1792–1750 B.C.E.
Invasion by Kassites	ca. 1550 B.C.E.

Hammurabi left his dynasty strong enough that it survived until the 1550s B.C.E., when the Kassites from the northeast took over.

1-3c The Code of Hammurabi

Hammurabi is best remembered for his law code, a collection of 282 laws (see Global Perspectives, "The Stele in the Ancient World," p. 11). For centuries, laws had regulated people's relationships with one another in the lands of Mesopotamia, but only fragments of these earlier codes survive. Although many scholars today view Hammurabi's collection less as a code of laws and more as an attempt by Hammurabi to portray himself as the source of justice to his people, the code still gives us a glimpse of the Babylonian society of his time (see Historical Voices, "The Code of Hammurabi," p. 12).

The Code of Hammurabi reveals a society with a system of strict justice. Penalties for criminal offenses were severe and varied according to the social class of the victim. A crime against a member of the upper class (a noble) was punished more severely than the same offense against a member of the lower class. Moreover, the principle of an eye for an eye, tooth for a tooth was fundamental to this system of justice. This meant that punishments should fit the crime: "If a freeman has destroyed the eye of a member of the aristocracy, they shall destroy his eye." Hammurabi's code had an impact on legal ideas in Southwest Asia for hundreds of years, as the following verse from the Hebrew Bible (Leviticus 24:19–20) demonstrates: "If anyone injures his neighbor, whatever he has done must be done to him: fracture for fracture, eye for eye, tooth for tooth. As he has injured the other, so is he to be injured."

Hammurabi's code took the responsibilities of public officials very seriously. The governor of an area and city officials were expected to catch burglars. If they failed to do so, the officials in the district where the crime was committed had to replace the lost property. If the officials did not apprehend a murderer, they had to pay a fine to the relatives of the murdered person.

The code also furthered the proper performance of work with what amounted to consumer protection laws. Builders were held responsible for the buildings they constructed. If a house collapsed, killing the

The Stele in the Ancient World

 Why was the stele so widely used in ancient civilizations? Why was the stele of Hammurabi especially important in Mesopotamia?

A STELE IS AN UPRIGHT STONE SLAB OR PILLAR that usually contains an inscription and sculpture. Stelae were often used to commemorate the achievements of a ruler. One prominent stele from antiquity, shown in Image 1.5a, was the stele of Hammurabi. Although the Sumerians had compiled earlier law codes, Hammurabi's code was the most famous in early Mesopotamian history. The upper part of the stele depicts Hammurabi standing in front of the seated sun god Shamash. The king raises his hand in deference to the god, who gives Hammurabi the power to rule and orders the king to record the law. The lower portion of the stele contains the actual code.

Shown in Image 1.5b is the tallest of the Axum stelae still standing in present-day Ethiopia. Axum was a prosperous trading state in Africa by the third century C.E., and in the fourth century rulers of Axum erected stelae to mark the site of royal tombs with inscriptions commemorating the achievements of the kings.

Image 1.5c shows a polished sandstone column, 32 feet high, erected in the third century B.C.E. during the reign of Ashoka (269–232 B.C.E.), who is considered one of India's greatest rulers. This and other pillars were used to commemorate events in the life of the Buddha and were inscribed with Buddhist sayings to guide people in the proper way. Stelae were also used in ancient China, Greece, and Mexico.

RMN-Grand Palais/Art Resource, NY

IMAGE 1.5a

Werner Forman/Art Resource, NY

IMAGE 1.5b

Borromeo/Art Resource, NY

IMAGE 1.5c

owner, the builder was put to death. If the collapse caused the death of the son of the owner, the son of the builder was put to death. If the collapse destroyed goods, they had to be replaced and the house itself reconstructed at the builder's expense.

The number of laws in Hammurabi's code dedicated to land tenure and commerce reveals the importance of agriculture and trade in the Mesopotamian economy. Laws concerning land use and irrigation were especially strict, an indication of the danger

The Code of Hammurabi

 What do the laws from the Code of Hammurabi reveal about Mesopotamian society?

HAMMURABI'S CODE is the most complete Mesopotamian law code, although not the earliest. It was inscribed on a stone stele (STEE-lee), or pillar, topped by a bas-relief picturing Hammurabi receiving the inspiration for the law code from the sun god Shamash, who was also the god of justice. As the following examples illustrate, the law code emphasized the principle of "an eye for an eye" and punishments that varied according to the victim's social status.

The Code of Hammurabi

25. If a fire break out in a man's house and a man who goes to extinguish it cast his eye on the furniture of the owner of the house, and take the furniture of the owner of the house, that man shall be thrown into that fire.

129. If the wife of a man be taken in lying with another man, they shall bind them and throw them into the water. If the husband of the woman would save his wife, or if the king would save his male servant (he may).

131. If a man accuse his wife and she has not been taken in lying with another man, she shall take an oath in the name of god and she shall return to her house.

196. If a man destroy the eye of another man, they shall destroy his eye.

198. If one destroy the eye of a freeman or break the bone of a freeman, he shall pay one mina of silver.

199. If one destroy the eye of a man's slave or break a bone of a man's slave he shall pay one-half his price.

209. If a man strike a man's daughter and bring about a miscarriage, he shall pay ten shekels of silver for her miscarriage.

210. If that woman die, they shall put his daughter to death.

211. If, through a stroke, he bring about a miscarriage to the daughter of a freeman, he shall pay five shekels of silver.

212. If that woman die, he shall pay one-half mana of silver.

213. If he strike the female slave of a man and bring about a miscarriage, he shall pay two shekels of silver.

214. If that female slave die, he shall pay one-third mana of silver.

Source: Hammurabi, *The Code of Hammurabi, King of Babylon*, ed. R. F. Harper, 2nd edition (Chicago: The University of Chicago Press, 1904).

of declining crop yields if the land was used incompetently. If landowners and tenants failed to keep dikes in good repair or to control water flow properly, thereby causing damage to others' crops, they were required to pay for the grain that was destroyed.

Commercial activity was carefully regulated. Rates of interest on loans were watched closely. If the lender raised the interest rate after a loan was made, he lost the entire amount of the loan. The Code of Hammurabi even specified the precise wages of laborers and artisans, such as brickmakers and jewelers.

Most laws in the code focused on marriage and the family. Parents arranged marriages for their children. After marriage, the parties involved signed a marriage contract; without it, no one was considered legally married. The husband provided a bridal payment, and the woman's parents were responsible for a dowry to the new husband.

As in many patriarchal societies, women had far fewer privileges and rights in the married relationship than men. A woman's place was in the home, and failure to fulfill her expected duties was grounds for divorce. If she was not able to bear children, her husband could divorce her, but he had to return the dowry to her family. If a wife tried to leave home to engage in business, thus neglecting her house, her husband could divorce her and did not have to repay the dowry. Furthermore, a wife who was a "gad-about . . . neglecting her house [and] humiliating her husband" could be drowned. We do know that in practice not all women remained at home. Some worked in the fields and others in business, where they were especially prominent in running taverns.

Women did have some rights, however. A husband who divorced his wife without good reason had to return her dowry. A woman could seek a divorce and get her dowry back if her husband was unable to show that she had done anything wrong. In theory, a wife was guaranteed the use of her husband's legal property in the event of his death. A mother could also decide which of her sons would receive an inheritance.

Sexual relations were strictly regulated as well. Husbands, but not wives, were permitted sexual activity outside marriage. A wife and her lover caught committing adultery were pitched into the river, although if the husband pardoned his wife, the king could pardon the guilty man. Incest was strictly forbidden. If a father had incestuous relations with his daughter, he would be banished. Incest between a son and his mother resulted in both being burned.

Fathers ruled their children as well as their wives. Obedience was duly expected: "If a son has struck his father, they shall cut off his hand." If a son committed a serious offense, his father could disinherit him.

1-3d The Culture of Mesopotamia

A spiritual worldview was of fundamental importance to Mesopotamian culture. To the peoples of Mesopotamia, the gods were living realities who affected all aspects of life. It was crucial, therefore, that the correct hierarchies be observed. Leaders could prepare armies for war, but success really depended on a favorable relationship with the gods. This helps explain the importance of the priestly class and is the reason why even the kings took great care to dedicate offerings and monuments to the gods.

The Importance of Religion One of the most famous accounts of the creation of the universe from the ancient Near East is the Babylonian creation epic known as the *Enûma Eliš*. The name comes from the first three words of the first two lines of the poem:

> *When on high the heavens were not yet named,*
> *And below, the earth was not called by a name*

The *Enûma Eliš* tells how the god Marduk was endowed with absolute power by the other gods to do battle with Tiamat, a primordial goddess who personified the forces of watery chaos. Marduk defeats Tiamat in battle and proceeds to create the universe by dividing Tiamat in two, one part becoming the heavens and the other the earth (with her breasts as mountains). From her eyes came the Tigris and Euphrates Rivers. The *Enûma Eliš* was recited during the New Year Festival celebrated in honor of Marduk in the city of Babylon, which the all-powerful god founded as an earthly residence for the gods after he created the universe.

The Mesopotamians viewed their city-states as earthly copies of a divine model and order. Each city-state was sacred because it was linked to a god or goddess. Hence, Nippur, the earliest center of Sumerian religion, was dedicated to Enlil (EN-lil), the god of wind. Moreover, located at the heart of each major city-state was a temple complex. Occupying several acres, this sacred area consisted of a ziggurat with a temple at the top dedicated to the god or goddess who owned the city. The temple complex was the true center of the community. The main god or goddess dwelt there symbolically in the form of a statue, and the ceremony of dedication included a ritual that linked the statue to the god or goddess and thus supposedly harnessed the power of the deity for the city's benefit. Considerable wealth was poured into the construction of temples and other buildings used for the residences of priests and priestesses who served the gods. Although the gods literally owned the city, the temple complex used only part of the land and rented out the remainder. The temples dominated individual and commercial life, an indication of the close relationship between Mesopotamian religion and culture.

The physical environment had an obvious impact on the Mesopotamian view of the universe. Ferocious floods, heavy downpours, scorching winds, and oppressive humidity were all part of the Mesopotamian climate. These conditions and the resulting famines easily convinced Mesopotamians that this world was controlled by supernatural forces and that the days of human beings "are numbered; whatever he may do, he is but wind," as *The Epic of Gilgamesh* laments (see "Mesopotamian Literature," later in this section). In the presence of nature, Mesopotamians could easily feel helpless, as this poem relates:

> *The rampant flood which no man can oppose,*
> *Which shakes the heavens and causes earth to tremble,*
> *In an appalling blanket folds mother and child,*
> *Beats down the canebrake's full luxuriant greenery,*
> *And drowns the harvest in its time of ripeness.*[7]

The Mesopotamians discerned cosmic rhythms in the universe and accepted its order but perceived that it was not completely safe because of the presence of willful and powerful cosmic forces that they identified with gods and goddesses.

With its numerous gods and goddesses animating all aspects of the universe, Mesopotamian religion was **polytheistic**. The four most important deities were An, Enlil, Enki (EN-kee), and Ninhursaga (nin-HUR-sah-guh). An was the god of the sky and hence the most important force in the universe. Since his basic essence was authority, he was also viewed as the source or active principle of all authority, including the earthly power of rulers and fathers alike. In one myth, the gods address him thus:

> *What you have ordered comes true!*
> *The utterance of prince and lord is but what you have*
> *ordered, do agree with.*
> *O An! your great command takes precedence, who*
> *could gainsay it?*
> *O father of the gods, your command, the very*
> *foundations of heaven and earth, what god*
> *could spurn it?*[8]

Enlil, god of wind, was considered the second greatest power of the visible universe. In charge of the wind and thus an expression of the legitimate use of force, Enlil became the symbol of the proper use of force on earth as well. Enki was the god of the earth. Since the earth was the source of life-giving waters, Enki was also the god of rivers, wells, and canals. More generally, he represented the waters of creativity and was responsible for inventions and crafts. Ninhursaga began as a goddess associated with soil, mountains, and vegetation. Eventually, however, she was worshiped as a mother goddess, a "mother of all children," who manifested her power by giving birth to kings and conferring the royal insignia on them.

Human beings' relationship with their gods was based on subservience because, according to Sumerian myth, human beings were created to do the manual labor the gods were unwilling to do for themselves. Moreover, humans were insecure because they could never be sure what the gods would do. But humans did make attempts to circumvent or relieve their anxiety by discovering the intentions of the gods and by trying to influence them as well; these efforts gave rise to the development of the arts of **divination**.

Divination took a variety of forms. A common form, at least for kings and priests who could afford it, involved killing animals such as sheep or goats and examining their livers or other organs. Supposedly, features seen in the organs of the sacrificed animals foretold events to come. Thus, one handbook states that if the animal organ has shape x, the outcome of the military campaign will be y. Private individuals relied on cheaper divinatory techniques. These included interpreting shapes in the smoke from burning incense or the pattern formed when oil was poured into water. The Mesopotamian arts of divination arose out of the desire to discover the purposes of the gods and goddesses. If people could decipher the signs that foretold events, the events would be predictable and humans could act wisely.

IMAGE 1.6 **The Development of Cuneiform.** Pictured here is the cone of Uruinimgina, an example of cuneiform script from an early Sumerian dynasty. The inscription announces reductions in taxes.

Rmn-Grand Palais/Art Resource, NY

hundred thousand that have been found so far have provided a valuable source of information for modern scholars. Sumerian writing evolved from pictures of concrete objects to simplified and stylized signs, leading eventually to a phonetic system that made possible the written expression of abstract ideas (see Table 1.2). Sumerian was the chief spoken and written language of Mesopotamia in the third millennium B.C.E., but it was replaced in the second millennium by Akkadian.

Mesopotamian peoples used writing primarily for record keeping. The most common cuneiform tablets record transactions of daily life: tallies of cattle kept by cowherds for their owners, production figures, lists of taxes and wage payments, accounts, contracts, and court decisions dealing with business matters. There are also monumental texts, documents that were intended to last forever, such as inscriptions etched in stone on statues and royal buildings.

Still another category of cuneiform inscriptions includes a large body of basic texts produced for teaching purposes. Schools for scribes were in operation by 2500 B.C.E. They were necessary because considerable time was needed to master the cuneiform system of writing. The primary goal of scribal education was to produce professionally trained scribes for careers in the temples and palaces, the military, and government service. Pupils were male and primarily from wealthy families.

Writing The realization of writing's great potential was another aspect of Mesopotamian culture. The oldest Mesopotamian texts date to around 3000 B.C.E. and were written by the Sumerians, who used a **cuneiform** (kyoo-NEE-uh-form) ("wedge-shaped") system of writing (see Image 1.6). Using a reed stylus, they made wedge-shaped impressions on clay tablets, which were then baked or dried in the sun. Once dried, these tablets were virtually indestructible, and the several

Mesopotamian Literature Writing was important because it enabled a society to keep records and maintain knowledge of previous practices and events. Writing also made it possible for people to communicate ideas in new ways, which is especially evident in Mesopotamian literary works (see Historical Voices, "The Advice of Shuruppag," p. 15). The most famous piece of Mesopotamian literature was *The Epic of Gilgamesh*, an elaborate poem that records the exploits of a legendary king of

TABLE 1.2	Evolution of Writing from Pictographic Signs to Cuneiform Script								
Pictographic sign, ca. 3100 B.C.E.									
Interpretation	star	?sun over horizon	?stream	ear of barley	bull's head	bowl	head + bowl	lower leg	?shrouded body
Cuneiform sign, ca. 2400 B.C.E.									
Cuneiform sign ca. 700 B.C.E. (turned through 90°)									
Phonetic value*	dingir, an	u_4, ud	a	še	gu_4	nig_2, ninda	ku_2	du, gin, gub	lu_2
Meaning	god, sky	day, sun	water, seed, son	barley	ox	food, bread	to eat	to walk, to stand	man

*Some signs have more than one phonetic value, and some sounds are represented by more than one sign; for example, u_4 means the fourth sign with the phonetic value u.

From the *Cultural Atlas of Mesopotamia & the Ancient Near East* by Michael Roaf/Courtesy of Andromeda Oxford Limited, Oxford, England.

The Advice of Shuruppag

 What does this document tell you about the position of men and women in Sumerian society? How would you compare ancient Sumerian values with those of Hammurabi and those of today?

IN THE LATE THIRD MILLENNIUM B.C.E. a Sumerian king named Shuruppag gave instructions to his son Ziusudra. The instructions included bits of wisdom on a variety of practical subjects.

The Instructions of Shuruppag

My son, let me give you instructions: you should pay attention! Ziusudra, let me speak a word to you: you should pay attention! Do not neglect my instructions! Do not transgress the words I speak! The instructions of an old man are precious: you should comply with them.

You should not steal anything. . . . You should not break into a house. . . . My son, you should not commit robbery. . . .

You should not play around with a married young woman: the slander could be serious. My son, you should not sit alone in a chamber with a married woman. . . .

You should not speak improperly, later it will lay a trap for you. . . .

You should not curse strongly: it rebounds on you. . . .

My son, you should not use violence. . . . You should not commit rape on someone's daughter; the courtyard will learn of it. . . .

You should not boast in beer halls like a deceitful man: then your words will be trusted. . . .

You should not pass judgment when you drink beer. . . .

At harvest time, at the most priceless time, collect like a slave girl, eat like a queen; my son, to collect like a slave girl, to eat like a queen, this is how it should be. . . .

The elder brother is indeed like a father; the elder sister is indeed like a mother. Listen therefore to your elder brother, and you should be obedient to your elder sister as if she were your mother. . . .

The negligent one ruins his family. . . .

When you bring a slave girl from the hills, she brings both good and evil with her. The good is in the hands; the evil is in the heart. The heart does not let go of the good, but the heart cannot let go of the evil either. . . .

A loving heart maintains a family; a hateful heart destroys a family.

To have authority, to have possessions and to be steadfast are princely divine powers. You should submit to the respected; you should be humble before the powerful. My son, you will then survive against the wicked. . . .

You should not speak arrogantly to your mother; that causes hatred for you. You should not question the words of your mother and your personal god. The mother gives birth to the man; the father, like a god, makes him bright. The father is like a god: his words are reliable. The instructions of the father should be complied with.

Source: The Electronic Text Corpus of Sumerian Literature, Oxford 1998–2006.

Uruk. Gilgamesh (GILL-guh-mesh), wise, strong, and perfect in body, part man, part god, abused the citizens of Uruk:

> "Gilgamesh sounds the tocsin for his amusement," the people complained, "his arrogance has no bounds by day or night. No son is left with his father, for Gilgamesh takes them all, even the children. . . . His lust leaves no virgin to her lover, neither the warrior's daughter nor the wife of the noble."[9]

The citizens ask the gods to send a competitor to oppose Gilgamesh and keep him busy. The gods comply and send a hairy, barbaric beast named Enkidu who Gilgamesh tries to weaken by sending a prostitute to seduce him. When Enkidu finally comes to Uruk, he and Gilgamesh engage in a fierce struggle that neither can win. The two become fast friends and set off in pursuit of heroic deeds. Ishtar (Sumerian Inanna), the goddess of love, attempts to seduce Gilgamesh, but he refuses her advances. In anger, she convinces her father Anu (Sumerian An) to send the Bull of Heaven to kill Gilgamesh and Enkidu. They manage to kill the bull instead, but the gods decide that in return one of them must die. When Enkidu dies, Gilgamesh experiences the pain of mortality and begins a search for the secret of immortality. He finds Utnapishtim, a man who had been granted everlasting life by the gods. Utnapishtim tells how he survived the Great Flood sent by the gods to destroy humankind (see Opposing Viewpoints, "The Great Flood: Two Versions," p. 16). Regretting what they had done, the gods bestowed immortality on Utnapishtim, who then instructed Gilgamesh to dive to the bottom of a river and find a certain plant that gives the power to grow younger. Although Gilgamesh finds the plant, a snake snatches it away before he can eat it. Gilgamesh remains mortal. The desire for immortality, one of humankind's great searches, ends in frustration. Everlasting life, as this Mesopotamian epic makes clear, is only for the gods.

Mathematics and Astronomy People in Mesopotamia made outstanding developments in mathematics and astronomy. In math, the Sumerians devised a number system based on 60, using combinations of 6 and 10 for practical solutions. They used the processes of multiplication and division and compiled tables for the computation of interest. Geometry was used for practical purposes, such as measuring fields and building projects. In

The Great Flood: Two Versions

 What does this selection from the Epic of Gilgamesh tell you about the relationship between the Mesopotamians and their gods? How might you explain the similarities and differences between the Mesopotamian account and the flood story in Genesis?

BOTH THE MESOPOTAMIAN *EPIC OF GILGAMESH* and the Hebrew Bible (Old Testament) include accounts of a great flood. In the first selection, taken from *The Epic of Gilgamesh*, Utnapishtim tells Gilgamesh the story of how he survived the flood unleashed by the gods to destroy humankind. Utnapishtim recounts how the god Ea advised him to build a boat and how he came to land the boat at the end of the flood. The second selection is the account of the great flood that appears in the book of Genesis in the Hebrew Bible. The biblical Noah appears to be a later version of the Mesopotamian Utnapishtim.

The *Epic of Gilgamesh*

"In those days the world teemed, the people multiplied, the world bellowed like a wild bull, and the great god was aroused by the clamor. Enlil heard the clamor and he said to the gods in council, 'The uproar of mankind is intolerable and sleep is no longer possible by reason of the babel.' So the gods agreed to exterminate mankind. Enlil did this, but Ea [Sumerian Enki, god of the waters] because of his oath warned me in a dream . . . 'tear down your house and build a boat, abandon possessions and look for life, despise worldly goods and save your soul alive. Tear down your house, I say, and build a boat. . . . Then take up into the boat the seed of all living creatures.' [Utnapishtim did as he was told, and then the destruction came.]

"For six days and six nights the winds blew, torrent and tempest and flood overwhelmed the world, tempest and flood raged together like warring hosts. When the seventh day dawned, the storm from the south subsided, the sea grew calm, the flood was stifled; I looked at the face of the world and there was silence, all mankind was turned to clay. The surface of the sea stretched as flat as a rooftop; I opened a hatch and the light fell on my face. Then I bowed low, I sat down and I wept, the tears streamed down my face, for on every side was the waste of water. I looked for land in vain, but fourteen leagues distant there appeared a mountain, and there the boat grounded; on the mountain of Nisir the boat held fast, she held fast and did not budge. . . .

"When the seventh day dawned, I loosed a dove and let her go. She flew away, but finding no resting-place she returned. Then I loosed a swallow, and she flew away but finding no resting-place she returned. I loosed a raven, she saw that the waters had retreated, she ate, she flew around, she cawed, and she did not come back. Then I threw everything open to the four winds, I made a sacrifice and poured out a libation on the mountain top."

Genesis 6:11–15, 17–19; 7:24; 8:3, 13–21

Now the earth was corrupted in God's sight and was full of violence. God saw how corrupt the earth had become, for all the people on earth had corrupted their ways. So God said to Noah, "I am going to put an end to all people, for the earth is filled with violence because of them. I am surely going to destroy both them and the earth. So make yourself an ark of cypress wood: make rooms in it and coat it with pitch inside and out. . . . I am going to bring flood waters on the earth to destroy all life under the heavens, every creature that has the breath of life in it. Everything on earth will perish. But I will establish my covenant with you, and you will enter the ark— you and your sons and your wife and your sons' wives with you. You are to bring into the ark two of all living creatures, male and female, to keep them alive with you. . . ."

The waters flooded the earth for a hundred and fifty days. . . . By the first day of the first month of Noah's six hundred and first year, the water had dried up from the earth. Noah then removed the covering from the ark and saw that the surface of the ground was dry. . . . Then God said to Noah, "Come out of the ark, you and your wife and your sons and their wives. Bring out every kind of living creature that is with you—the birds, the animals, and all the creatures that move along the ground—so they can multiply on the earth and be fruitful and increase in number upon it." So Noah came out, together with his sons and his wife and his son's wives . . . [and all the animals]. Then Noah built an altar to the Lord and, taking some of all the clean animals and clean birds, he sacrificed burnt offerings on it. The Lord smelled the pleasing aroma and said in his heart. "Never again will I curse the ground because of man, even though every inclination of his heart is evil from childhood. And never again will I destroy all living creatures, as I have done."

Sources: *The Epic of Gilgamesh*, trans. with an introduction by N. K. Sandars (London: Penguin Classics, 1960), and the Holy Bible, New International Version (Colorado Springs, CO: Biblica, 1973).

Significance of the Nile River and the Pharaoh

 How do the two hymns presented here underscore the importance of the Nile River and the institution of the pharaoh to Egyptian civilization?

TWO OF THE MOST IMPORTANT SOURCES of life for the ancient Egyptians were the Nile River and the pharaoh. Egyptians perceived that the Nile River made possible the abundant food that was a major source of their well-being. The first selection, *Hymn to the Nile*, probably from the nineteenth and twentieth dynasties in the New Kingdom, expresses the gratitude Egyptians felt for the Nile. The Egyptian king, or pharaoh, was viewed as a god and the absolute ruler of Egypt. His significance and the gratitude of the Egyptian people for his existence are evident in the second selection, a hymn from the reign of Sesotris III (ca. 1880–1840 B.C.E.).

"Hymn to the Nile"

*Hail to you, O Nile, that issues from the earth and
   comes to keep Egypt alive! . . .
He that waters the meadows which Re [Ra] created, in
   order to keep every kid alive.
He that makes to drink the desert and the place
   distant from water: that is his dew coming down
   from heaven. . . .
The lord of fishes, he who makes the marsh-birds to
   go upstream. . . .
He who makes barley and brings emmer [wheat] into
   being, that he may make the temples festive.*

*If he is sluggish, then nostrils are stopped up, and
   everybody is poor. . . .
When he rises, then the land is in jubilation, then
   every belly is in joy, every backbone takes on
   laughter, and every tooth is exposed.
The bringer of food, rich in provisions, creator of all
   good, lord of majesty, sweet of fragrance. . . .
He who makes every beloved tree to grow, without
   lack of them.*

"Hymn to the Pharaoh"

*He has come to us, he has taken the land of the well,
   the double crown [crown of Upper and Lower Egypt]
   is placed on his head.
He has come, he has united the two lands,
   he has joined the kingdom of the upper land with
   the lower.
He has come, he has ruled Egypt,
   he has placed the desert in his power.
He has come, he has protected the two lands,
   he has given peace in the two regions.
He has come, he has made Egypt to live,
   he has destroyed its afflictions.
He has come, he has made the aged to live,
   he has opened the breath of the people.
He has come, he has trampled on the nations,
   he has smitten the [enemies], who knew not his terror.
He has come, he has protected his frontier,
   he has rescued the robbed.*

Source: "Hymn to the Nile" from J. Pritchard, ed., *Ancient Near Eastern Texts Related to the Old Testament*, 3rd revised edition with supplement (Princeton, N.J.: Princeton University Press, 1969). Reprinted by permission of Princeton University Press. "Hymn to the Pharaoh" from W. M. Flinders Petrie, *A History of Egypt* (Cambridge, U.K.: Cambridge University Press, 1903), vol. 1, p. 183.

---

astronomy, the Sumerians made use of units of 60 and charted the chief heavenly constellations. Their calendar was based on twelve lunar months and was brought into harmony with the solar year by adding an extra month from time to time.

1-4 Egyptian Civilization: "The Gift of the Nile"

 FOCUS QUESTION: What are the basic features, elements of continuity, and differences in the three major periods of Egyptian history?

Although contemporaneous with Mesopotamia, civilization in Egypt evolved along somewhat different lines. Of central importance to the development of Egyptian civilization was the Nile River. That the Egyptian people recognized its significance is apparent in the *Hymn to the Nile* (see Historical Voices, "Significance of the Nile River and the Pharaoh," above): "The bringer of food, rich in provisions, creator of all good, lord of majesty, sweet of fragrance. . . . He who . . . fills the magazines, makes the granaries wide, and gives things to the poor. He who makes every beloved tree to grow."[10] Egypt, like Mesopotamia, was a river valley civilization.

1-4a The Impact of Geography

The Nile is a unique river, beginning in the heart of Africa and coursing northward for thousands of miles. It is the longest river in the world. Thanks to the Nile, an area several miles wide on both banks of the river was capable of producing abundant harvests. The miracle of the Nile was its annual flooding. The river rose in the summer from rains in Central Africa and

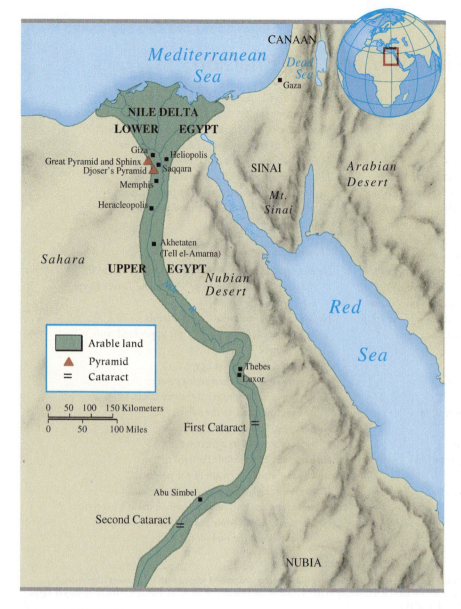

MAP 1.5 **Ancient Egypt.** Egyptian civilization centered on the life-giving water and flood silts of the Nile River, with most of the population living in Lower Egypt, where the river splits to form the Nile delta. Most of the pyramids, built during the Old Kingdom, are clustered at the entrance to the delta.

Q *How did the lands to the east and west of the river help to protect Egypt from invasion?*

consequently tended to remain more rural, with many small population centers congregated along a narrow band on both sides of the Nile. About 100 miles before it empties into the Mediterranean, the river splits into two major branches, forming the delta, a triangular-shaped territory called Lower Egypt to distinguish it from Upper Egypt, the land upstream to the south (see Map 1.5). Egypt's important cities developed at the tip of the delta. Even today, most of Egypt's people are crowded along the banks of the Nile River.

The surpluses of food that Egyptian farmers grew in the fertile Nile valley made Egypt prosperous. But the Nile also served as a unifying factor in Egyptian history. In ancient times, the Nile was the fastest way to travel, making both transportation and communication easier. Winds from the north pushed sailboats south, and the current of the Nile carried them north. Often when they headed downstream (north), people used long poles or paddles to propel their boats forward.

Unlike Mesopotamia, which was subject to constant invasion, Egypt was blessed by natural barriers that protected it from invasion and gave it a sense of security. These barriers included the deserts to the west and east; the cataracts (rapids) on the southern part of the Nile, which made defense relatively easy; and the Mediterranean Sea to the north. These barriers, however, were effective only when they were combined with Egyptian fortifications at strategic locations, and they did not prevent the development of trade. Indeed, there is evidence of very early trade between Egypt and Mesopotamia.

In essence, Egyptian geography and topography played important roles in the early history of the country. The regularity of the Nile floods and the relative isolation of the Egyptians created a sense of security that was accompanied by a feeling of changelessness. As the ancient Egyptians said, when the Nile floods each year "the fields laugh and people's faces light up." Unlike people in Mesopotamia, Egyptians faced life with a spirit of confidence in the stability of things. Egyptian civilization was characterized by a remarkable degree of continuity over thousands of years.

1-4b The Old and Middle Kingdoms

Manetho (MAN-uh-thoh), an Egyptian priest and historian who lived in the early third century B.C.E., provided the basic framework for the study of Egyptian history. He divided Egyptian

the Ethiopian highlands, crested in Egypt in September and October, and left a deposit of silt that enriched the soil. The Egyptians called this fertile land, dark from the silt and the lush crops that grew on it, the Black Land. Beyond these narrow strips of fertile fields lay the deserts (the Red Land).

Unlike the floods of Mesopotamia's rivers, the flooding of the Nile was gradual and usually predictable, and the river itself was seen as life-enhancing, not life-threatening. Although a system of organized irrigation was still necessary, the small villages along the Nile could make the effort without the massive state intervention that was required in Mesopotamia. Egyptian civilization

history into thirty-one dynasties of kings. Using Manetho's and other lists of kings, modern historians have divided Egyptian history into three major periods: the Old Kingdom, the Middle Kingdom, and the New Kingdom. These were periods of long-term stability characterized by strong monarchical authority, competent bureaucracy, freedom from invasion, much construction of temples and pyramids, and considerable intellectual and cultural activity. But between the periods of stability were intervals known as the Intermediate Periods, which were characterized by weak political structures and rivalry for leadership, invasions, a decline in building activity, and a restructuring of society.

The Old Kingdom According to the Egyptians' own tradition, their land consisted initially of numerous populated areas ruled by tribal chieftains. Around 3100 B.C.E., during the Early Dynastic Period, the first Egyptian royal dynasty, under a king called Menes (MEE-neez), united both Upper and Lower Egypt into a single kingdom. Henceforth, the king would be called King of Upper and Lower Egypt, and one of the royal crowns would be the Double Crown, combining the White Crown of Upper Egypt and the Red Crown of Lower Egypt. Just as the Nile united Upper and Lower Egypt physically, kingship united the two areas politically.

The Old Kingdom encompassed the fourth through eighth dynasties of Egyptian kings and lasted from around 2575 to 2125 B.C.E. It was an age of prosperity and splendor, made visible in the construction of the greatest and largest pyramids in Egyptian history. The capital of the Old Kingdom was located at Memphis, south of the delta.

Kingship was a divine institution in ancient Egypt and formed part of a universal cosmic scheme (see Historical Voices, "Significance of the Nile River and the Pharaoh," p. 17): "What is the king of Upper and Lower Egypt? He is a god by whose dealings one lives, the father and mother of all men, alone by himself, without an equal."[11] In obeying their king, subjects helped maintain the cosmic order. A breakdown in royal power could only mean that citizens were offending divinity and weakening the universal structure. Among the various titles of Egyptian kings, that of pharaoh (originally meaning "great house" or "palace") eventually came to be the most common.

Although they possessed absolute power, Egyptian kings were supposed to rule not arbitrarily but according to set principles. The chief principle was called *Ma'at* (muh-AHT), a spiritual precept that conveyed the idea of truth and justice, especially right order and harmony. To ancient Egyptians, this fundamental order and harmony had existed throughout the universe since the beginning of time. Pharaohs were the divine instruments who maintained it and were themselves subject to it.

Although theoretically absolute in their power, in practice Egyptian kings did not rule alone. Initially, members of the king's family performed administrative tasks, but by the fourth dynasty a bureaucracy with regular procedures had developed. Especially important was the office of vizier, "steward of the whole land." Directly responsible to the king, the vizier was in charge of the bureaucracy, with its numerous departments, including police, justice, river transport, and public works. Agriculture and the treasury were the most important departments.

Agriculture was, of course, the backbone of Egyptian prosperity, and the treasury collected the taxes, which were paid in kind. A careful assessment of land and tenants was undertaken to establish the tax base.

For administrative purposes, Egypt was divided into twenty-two provinces (or nomes as they were later called by the Greeks) in Upper Egypt and twenty in Lower Egypt. A governor, called by the Greeks a nomarch, was head of each nome and was responsible to the king and vizier. Nomarchs, however, tended to build up large holdings of land and power within their nomes, creating a potential rivalry with the pharaohs.

The Middle Kingdom A decline in centralized authority, a drought caused by low levels of the Nile and a decline in rainfall, and economic troubles brought about the collapse of the Old Kingdom, ushering in the First Intermediate Period (ca. 2125–2010 B.C.E.). A so-called prophet named Nefer-Rohu (Neferti) described the scene:

> This land is so damaged that there is no one who is concerned with it, no one who speaks, no one who weeps. . . . The sun disk is covered over. It will not shine so that people may see. . . . The rivers of Egypt are empty, so that the water is crossed on foot. Men seek for water for the ships to sail on it. . . . This land is helter-skelter, and no one knows the result that will come about, which is hidden from speech, sight, or hearing.[12]

Eventually, a new royal dynasty managed to pacify all Egypt and inaugurated the Middle Kingdom, a new period of stability lasting from around 2010 to 1630 B.C.E.

Much of the Middle Kingdom's history centered around the twelfth dynasty founded by Amenemhet I, a vizier who established himself and his successors as pharaohs. Egyptians later portrayed the Middle Kingdom as a golden age, a clear indication of its stability. Several factors contributed to its vitality. The nome structure was reorganized. The boundaries of each nome were now settled precisely, and the obligations of the nomes to the state were clearly delineated. Nomarchs were confirmed as hereditary officeholders but with the understanding that their duties must be performed faithfully. These included the collection of taxes for the state and the recruitment of labor forces for royal projects, such as stone quarrying.

The Middle Kingdom was characterized by a new concern on the part of the pharaohs for the people. In the Old Kingdom, the pharaoh had been viewed as an inaccessible god-king. Now he was portrayed as the shepherd of his people with the responsibility to build public works and provide for the public welfare. As one pharaoh expressed it: "He [a particular god] created me as one who should do that which he had done, and to carry out that which he commanded should be done. He appointed me herdsman of this land, for he knew who would keep it in order for him."[13]

As confirmation of its newfound strength, Egypt embarked on a period of expansion. Lower Nubia was conquered, and fortresses were built to protect the new southern frontier. The government also sent military expeditions into Canaan and Syria. Although they did not remain there, this campaign marks the beginning of Egyptian imperialism in those areas.

1-4c Society and Economy in Ancient Egypt

Egyptian society had a simple structure in the Old and Middle Kingdoms; basically, it was organized along hierarchical lines with the god-king at the top. The king was surrounded by an upper class of nobles and priests who participated in the elaborate rituals of life that surrounded the pharaoh. The members of this ruling class ran the government and managed their own landed estates, which provided much of their wealth.

Below the upper classes were merchants and artisans. Merchants engaged in active trade up and down the Nile as well as in town and village markets. Some merchants also engaged in international trade; they were sent by the king to Crete and Syria, where they obtained wood and other products. Expeditions traveled into Nubia for ivory and down the Red Sea to Punt for incense and spices. Egyptian artisans displayed unusually high standards of craftsmanship and physical beauty (see Image 1.7) and produced an incredible variety of goods: stone dishes; beautifully painted boxes made of clay; wooden furniture, especially of Lebanon cedar; gold, silver, and copper tools and containers; jewelry; paper and rope made of papyrus; and linen clothes.

Most people in Egypt simply worked the land. In theory, the king owned all the land but granted portions of it to his subjects. Large sections were in the possession of nobles and the temple complexes. Most of the lower classes were serfs, common people who were bound to the land and cultivated the estates. They paid taxes in the form of crops to the king, nobles, and priests; lived in small villages or towns; and provided military service and labor for building projects.

The Trustees of the British Museum /Art Resource, NY

IMAGE 1.7 The Making of Jewelry. In ancient Egypt, people used jewelry for self-adornment as well as a mark of social status. This photo of a wall fragment from a tomb in Thebes around 1400 B.C.E. shows jewelers and metal craftsmen at work. At the top jewelers are seen drilling holes in hard-stone beads with three or four bow-drills. The beads were then polished and strung in collars, as seen in the lower panel.

1-4d The Culture of Egypt

Egypt produced a culture that dazzled and awed its later conquerors. The Egyptians' technical achievements alone, especially visible in the construction of the pyramids, demonstrated a measure of skill unique to the world at that time. To the Egyptians, all of these achievements were part of a cosmic order suffused with the presence of the divine.

Spiritual Life in Egyptian Society The Egyptians had no word for religion because it was an inseparable element of the world order to which Egyptian society belonged. Egypt was part of the universal cosmic scheme, and the pharaoh was the divine being whose duty was to preserve Egypt's place within that divinely ordained cosmic order.

This perspective helps explain the importance of ritual in ancient Egypt. Through their rituals, Egyptians worked to maintain the cosmic order by appeasing the gods and goddesses who controlled the universe. An Egyptian ritual ceremony focused on an image of a deity and provided it with food and sustenance, thereby performing an act of ritual worship to appease the god.

The pharaoh was at the heart of Egypt's ritual life. He supervised the sacred ceremonies that were performed in the temples, although in practice the pharaoh's religious deputies—the priests—carried out the daily ceremonies.

The Egyptians had a remarkable number of gods associated with heavenly bodies and natural forces, hardly unusual in view of how important the sun, river, and fertile land were to Egypt's well-being. The sun was the source of life and hence worthy of worship. A sun cult developed, and the sun god took on different forms and names depending on his specific function. He was worshiped as Atum in human form and as Re (or Ra), who had a human body but the head of a falcon. The pharaoh took the title Son of Re because he was regarded as the earthly embodiment of Re.

River and land deities included Osiris (oh-SY-russ) and Isis (Y-sis) with their child Horus, who was related to both the Nile and the sun. Osiris became especially important as a symbol of resurrection. A famous Egyptian myth told of the struggle between Osiris, who brought civilization to Egypt, and his evil brother Seth, who killed him, cut his body into fourteen parts, and tossed them into the Nile. Isis, the faithful wife of Osiris, found the pieces and, with help from other gods, restored Osiris to life. As a symbol of resurrection and as judge of the dead, Osiris took on an important role for the Egyptians (see Image 1.8). By identifying with Osiris, one could hope to gain new life, just as Osiris had done. The dead, embalmed and mummified, were placed in tombs (in pyramidal tombs in the case of kings), given the name of Osiris, and by a process of magical identification became Osiris. Like Osiris, they would then be reborn. The flood of the Nile and the new life it brought to Egypt were symbolized by Isis gathering all of the parts of Osiris together and were celebrated each spring in the festival of the new land.

Later Egyptian spiritual practice began to emphasize morality by stressing the role of Osiris as judge of the dead. The dead were asked to give an account of their earthly deeds to show whether they deserved a reward. Other means were also employed to gain immortality. As seen in the *Book of the Dead* from the period of

© The Trustees of the British Museum/Art Resource, NY

IMAGE 1.8 **Osiris as Judge of the Dead.** According to the *Book of the Dead*, after making a denial of offenses (the "negative confession"), the deceased experienced the "weighing of the heart." Shown here is a judgment scene from the *Book of the Dead* of Hunefer, a royal scribe who died around 1285 B.C.E. Hunefer's heart is placed on one side of a balance scale; on the other side is the feather of Ma'at, the goddess of truth. For Hunefer, heart and feather are of equal weight, so the god Anubis ushers him into the presence of Osiris, seated on his throne at the right. A "Swallowing Monster," a hybrid creature combining crocodile, lion, and hippopotamus, stood ready at the scale to devour the deceased if he failed the test.

 What is the significance of the ritual that is described here?

the New Kingdom, magical incantations were used to ensure a favorable journey to a happy afterlife. Specific instructions explained what to do when confronted by the judge of the dead. These instructions had two aspects. In the negative confession, the deceased gave a detailed list of what he had not done:

> *I have not committed evil against men.*
> *I have not mistreated cattle. . . .*
> *I have not blasphemed a god. . . .*
> *I have not done violence to a poor man. . . .*
> *I have not made anyone sick. . . .*
> *I have not killed. . . .*
> *I have not caused anyone suffering. . . .*
> *I have not had sexual relations with a boy.*
> *I have not defiled myself. . . .*
> *I have not driven cattle away from their pasturage.*[14]

Later the supplicant made a speech listing his good actions: "I have done that which men said and that with which gods are content. . . . I have given bread to the hungry, water to the thirsty, clothing to the naked, and a ferry-boat to him who was marooned. I have provided divine offerings for the gods and mortuary offerings for the dead."[15]

At first the Osiris cult was reserved for the very wealthy, who could afford to take expensive measures to preserve the body after death. During the Middle Kingdom, however, the cult became "democratized" and was extended to all Egyptians who aspired to an afterlife.

The Pyramids One of the great achievements of Egyptian civilization, the building of pyramids, occurred during the Old Kingdom. Pyramids were not built in isolation but as part of a larger complex dedicated to the dead—in effect, a city of the dead. The area included a large pyramid for the king's burial, smaller pyramids for his family, and mastabas (MAS-tuh-buhs), rectangular structures with flat roofs, as tombs for the pharaoh's noble officials. The tombs were well prepared for their residents. The rooms were furnished and stocked with numerous supplies, including chairs, boats, chests, weapons, games, dishes, and a variety of foods. The Egyptians believed that human beings had two bodies, a physical one and a spiritual one, which they called the ka. If the physical body was properly preserved (i.e., mummified) and the tomb furnished with all the various objects of regular life, the *ka* could return and continue its life despite the death of the physical body.

To preserve the physical body after death, the Egyptians practiced mummification, a process of slowly drying a dead body to prevent it from rotting. Special workshops, run by priests, performed this procedure, primarily for the wealthy families who could afford it. According to Herodotus, an ancient Greek historian (see Chapter 3) who visited Egypt around 450 B.C.E., "The most refined method is as follows: first of all they draw out the brain through the nostrils with an iron hook. . . . Then they make an incision in the flank with a sharp Ethiopian stone through which they extract all the internal organs."[16] The liver, lungs, stomach, and intestines were then placed in four special jars that were put in the tomb with the mummy. The priests then covered the corpse with a natural salt that absorbed the body's water. Later, they filled the body with spices and wrapped it with layers of linen soaked in resin. At the end of the process, which took about seventy days, a lifelike mask was placed over the head and shoulders of the mummy, which was then sealed in a case and placed in its tomb.

Pyramids were tombs for the mummified bodies of pharaohs. The first pyramid was a step pyramid built at Saqqara in the third dynasty during the reign of King Djoser (ZHOH-sur). The first real pyramid, with each side filled in to make an even surface, was constructed around 2600 B.C.E. by King Snefru, who built three pyramids. But the largest and most magnificent of all was built under Snefru's son Khufu. Constructed at Giza around 2540 B.C.E., the famous Great Pyramid covers 13 acres, measures 756 feet at each side of its base, and stands 481 feet high. Its four sides are almost precisely oriented to the four points of the compass (see Image 1.9).

The building of the Great Pyramid was an enormous construction project that used limestone blocks as well as granite from Upper Egypt. Herodotus reported that it took 100,000 Egyptians twenty years to build the Great Pyramid. But Herodotus wrote two thousand years after the event, and considerable controversy and speculation still surround the construction of the Great Pyramid, especially in view of the precision with which it was built. The stone slabs on the outside of the pyramid, for example, fit so closely side by side that a hair cannot be pushed into the joints between them. The Great Pyramid still stands as a symbol of the power of Egyptian kings of the Old Kingdom. No later pyramid ever matched its size or splendor. But an Egyptian pyramid was not just the king's tomb; it was also an important symbol of royal power. It could be seen for miles away as a visible reminder of the glory and might of the ruler, a living god on earth.

Art and Writing Commissioned by kings or nobles for use in temples and tombs, Egyptian art was largely functional. Wall paintings and statues of gods and kings in temples served a strictly spiritual purpose. They were an integral part of the performance of ritual, which was thought necessary to preserve the cosmic order and hence the well-being of Egypt. Likewise, the mural scenes and sculptured figures found in the tombs had a specific function. They were supposed to aid the journey of the deceased into the afterworld.

Egyptian art was also formulaic. Artists and sculptors were expected to observe a strict canon of proportions that determined both form and presentation. This canon gave Egyptian art a distinctive appearance for thousands of years. Especially characteristic was the convention of combining the profile, semi-profile, and frontal views of the human body in relief work and painting in order to represent each part of the body accurately. This fashion created an art that was highly stylized yet still allowed distinctive features to be portrayed.

Writing emerged in Egypt during the first two dynasties. It was the Greeks who later labeled Egyptian writing **hieroglyphics**, meaning "priest carvings" or "sacred writings." Hieroglyphs (HY-uh-roh-glifs) were signs that depicted objects and had a sacred value at the same time. Although hieroglyphs were later simplified for writing purposes into two scripts, they never developed into an alphabet. Egyptian hieroglyphs were initially carved in stone, but later the two simplified scripts were written on papyrus, a paper made from the papyrus reed that grew along the Nile. Most of the ancient Egyptian literature that has come down to us was written on papyrus rolls and wooden tablets.

1-4e Disorder and a New Order: The New Kingdom

The Middle Kingdom came to an end in the midst of another period of instability. An incursion into the delta region by a people known as the Hyksos (HIK-sos) initiated this second age of disorder. The Hyksos, a Semitic-speaking people, infiltrated Egypt in the seventeenth century B.C.E. and came to dominate much of Egypt. The presence of the Hyksos was not entirely negative for Egypt, however. They taught the Egyptians how to use bronze to make agricultural tools and weapons. The Hyksos also introduced new aspects of warfare, including the horse-drawn war chariot, a heavier sword, and the compound bow. Eventually, the Egyptians made use of their new weapons to throw off Hyksos domination.

The Egyptian Empire It was the pharaoh Ahmose I who managed to defeat and expel the Hyksos from Egypt. He reunited Egypt, founded the eighteenth dynasty, established the New Kingdom (ca. 1539–1069 B.C.E.), and launched the Egyptians along a new militaristic and imperialistic path characterized by the development of a more professional

IMAGE 1.9 **The Pyramids at Giza.** The three pyramids at Giza, across the Nile River from Cairo, are the most famous in Egypt. At the rear is the largest of the three pyramids—the Great Pyramid of Khufu. Next to it is the pyramid of Khafre. In the foreground is the smaller pyramid of Menkaure standing behind the even smaller pyramids for the pharaohs' wives. Covering almost 13 acres, the Great Pyramid of Khufu is immense. It is estimated that the Great Pyramid contains 2.3 million stone blocks, each weighing about 2.5 tons.

Pius Lee/Shutterstock.com

Q *What is the significance of the pyramids in the spiritual life of Egypt?*

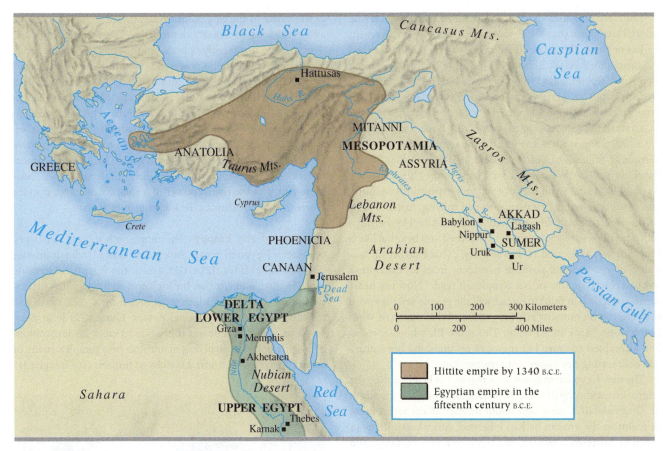

MAP 1.6 **The Egyptian and Hittite Empires.** The Hittite empire was the dominant power north of Egypt for roughly two centuries. The Hittites assimilated important linguistic, political, and religious aspects of the peoples they conquered and thus helped transmit Mesopotamian culture to the eastern Mediterranean.

Q *What made both the Hittite and Egyptian empires vulnerable to invasion?*

army. No longer content to remain in isolation, Egypt now pursued an active political and diplomatic policy.

During the period of the New Kingdom, Egypt became the most powerful state in the ancient Near East (see Map 1.6). Thutmose (thoot-MOH-suh) I (ca. 1493–1481 B.C.E.) expanded Egypt's border to the south by conquering the African kingdom of Nubia. The warrior Thutmose III (ca. 1479–1425 B.C.E.)

led seventeen military campaigns into Canaan and Phoenicia. The Egyptians occupied these lands but permitted local native princes to rule. Amenhotep (ah-mun-HOH-tep) II (ca. 1426–1400 B.C.E.), the successor of Thutmose III, also campaigned in the Near East and not only solidified the Egyptian empire but also increased Egypt's prosperity by bringing back enormous quantities of booty (see Image 1.10).

IMAGE 1.10 **Nubians in Egypt.** During the New Kingdom, Egypt expanded to the north, into Canaan and Syria, and to the south, into the African kingdom of Nubia. Nubia had first emerged as an African kingdom around 2300 B.C.E. Shown here in a fourteenth-century B.C.E. painting from an Egyptian official's tomb in Nubia are Nubians arriving in Egypt with bags and rings of gold. Nubia was a rich source of gold for the Egyptians.

Erich Lessing/Art Resource, NY

The New Kingdom also witnessed one of Egypt's six female rulers: Hatshepsut (hat-SHEP-soot). She initially served as regent for her nephew Thutmose III when he was a child but assumed the throne for herself. Although Thutmose III was considered a co-ruler, she remained in power until her death. In order to remain in power, Hatshepsut had to create many new positions for the elites who supported her. Her reign (ca. 1473–1458 B.C.E.) was a prosperous one, as is especially evident in her building activity. She is most famous for the temple, known as the Temple of Millions of Years, she dedicated to herself at Deir el Bahri (dayr ahl BAH-ree) on the west bank of the Nile at Thebes. As pharaoh, Hatshepsut sent out military expeditions, securing and expanding boundaries, encouraged mining, fostered agriculture, and sent a trading expedition up the Nile. Hatshepsut's official statues sometimes show her clothed and bearded like a king. She was addressed as "His Majesty." That Hatshepsut was aware of her unusual position is evident from an inscription she had placed on one of her temples. It read: "Now my heart turns to and fro, in thinking what will the people say, they who shall see my monument in after years, and shall speak of what I have done." Late in his reign, Thutmose III, who succeeded her, attempted to erase her memory by smashing her statues and obliterating her image from monuments.

The new Egyptian imperial state reached its height during the reign of Amenhotep III (ca. 1390–1353 B.C.E.), the great-grandson of Thutmose III. Caring little about military affairs and content to maintain the empire he had inherited, Amenhotep III spent much of his reign constructing magnificent new buildings and temples. Especially famous were the temple centers at Karnak and Luxor and the immense statues of Amenhotep III in front of the mortuary temples along the Nile.

By the end of his reign, Amenhotep III faced a growing military challenge from a people known as the Hittites (see "1-5b The Hittite Empire," later in this chapter). His son, Amenhotep IV (ca. 1353–1336 B.C.E.), proved even less able to deal with this threat, a failure that was due in large part to a religious upheaval that he had initiated in Egypt.

Akhenaten and Religious Change Amenhotep IV introduced the worship of Aten, god of the sun disk, as the supreme god and later in his reign as the only god (see Historical Voices, "Akhenaten's 'Hymn to Aten'," p. 25). In the pharaoh's eyes, he and Aten had become co-rulers of Egypt. Changing his own name to Akhenaten (ah-kuh-NAH-tun) ("Servant of Aten"), the pharaoh closed the temples of other gods and especially endeavored to lessen the power of the priesthood dedicated to the god Amon-Re at Thebes. Akhenaten strove to reduce the priests' influence by replacing Thebes as the capital of Egypt with Akhetaten ("Horizon of Aten"), a new city located at modern Tell el-Amarna, 200 miles north of Thebes. The pharaoh decreed that Akhetaten, not Thebes, would be his final resting place: "If I die in any town of the north, the south, the west, or the east in these millions of years, let me be brought back so that I may be buried in Akhetaten."[17]

Akhenaten's attempt at religious change failed. It was too much to ask Egyptians to ignore their traditional ways and beliefs, especially since they saw the destruction of the old gods

as subversive of the very cosmic order on which Egypt's survival and continuing prosperity depended. Moreover, the priests at Thebes were unalterably opposed to the changes, which diminished their influence and power. At the same time, Akhenaten's preoccupation with religion caused him to ignore foreign affairs and led to the loss of both Syria and Canaan. Akhenaten's changes were soon undone after his death by those who influenced his successor, the boy-pharaoh Tutankhamun (toot-ahng-KAH-muhn) (ca. 1332–1322 B.C.E.). Tutankhamun returned the government to Thebes and restored the old gods. The Aten experiment had failed to take hold, and the eighteenth dynasty itself came to an end with the rise to power of a military officer and vizier, Horemhab, who assumed the kingship in 1319 B.C.E.

The End of the Empire The nineteenth dynasty managed to restore Egyptian power one more time. Under Ramesses (RAM-uh-seez) II (ca. 1279–1213 B.C.E.), the Egyptians went on the offensive, and after an inconclusive struggle with the Hittites at the Battle of Kadesh, regained control of Canaan and restored Egypt as an imperial power. During his long sixty-seven-year reign, Ramesses II provided visible demonstrations of his power by constructing mammoth new temples, many of them adorned with colossal statues of himself (see Image 1.11).

IMAGE 1.11 **Statues of Ramesses II at Abu Simbel.** After being driven out of Canaan and Syria by the Hittites, Egypt grew to power one final time under Ramesses II. He succeeded in reconquering Canaan but was unable to restore the boundaries of the previous empire. The massive Temple of Ramesses II, located at Abu Simbel, was carved out of a cliff of Nubian sandstone. The giant statues represent Ramesses II.

Q *What message do these statues convey?*

Akhenaten's *"Hymn to Aten"*

 Q *What does Akhenaten's Hymn to Aten tell you about the religion of the Egyptians and Akhenaten's attempt to change it? Why did so many Egyptians oppose the basic premise of the hymn?*

AMENHOTEP IV, MORE COMMONLY KNOWN AS AKHENATEN, created a religious upheaval in Egypt by introducing the worship of Aten, god of the sun disk, as the chief god. Akhenaten's reverence for Aten is evident in this hymn. Some authorities have noted a similarity in spirit and wording to the 104th Psalm of the Old Testament.

"Hymn to Aten"

Your rays suckle every meadow.
When you rise, they live, they grow for you.
You make the seasons in order to rear all that you
*   have made,*
The winter to cool them,
And the heat that they may taste you.
You have made the distant sky in order to rise
*   therein,*
In order to see all that you do make.

While you were alone,
Rising in your form as the living Aten,
Appearing, shining, withdrawing or approaching,
You made millions of forms of yourself alone.

Cities, towns, fields, road, and river—
Every eye beholds you over against them,
For you are the Aten of the day over the earth. . . .
The world came into being by your hand,
According as you have made them.
When you have risen they live,
When you set they die.
You are lifetime your own self,
For one lives only through you.
Eyes are fixed on beauty until you set.
All work is laid aside when you set in the west. . . .
But when you rise again,
Everything is made to flourish for the king.
Since you did found the earth
And raise them up for your son,
Who came forth from your body: the King of Upper
*   and Lower Egypt . . . Akh-en-Aten . . . and the*
Chief Wife of the King . . . Nefert-iti, living and
*   youthful forever and ever.*

Source: "Hymn to Aten" from J. Pritchard, ed., *Ancient Near Eastern Texts Related to the Old Testament*, 3rd revised edition with supplement (Princeton, N.J.: Princeton University Press, 1969). Reprinted by permission of Princeton University Press.

After the death of Ramesses II, struggles for the throne weakened the government, and new invasions in the twelfth century by the Sea Peoples, as the Egyptians called them, destroyed Egyptian power in Canaan and drove the Egyptians back within their old frontiers. The days of the Egyptian empire were ended, and the New Kingdom itself expired with the twentieth dynasty in 1069 B.C.E. For the next thousand years, despite periodic revivals of strength, Egypt was dominated by Libyans, Nubians, Assyrians, Persians, and finally Macedonians after the conquest of Alexander the Great (see Chapter 4). In the first century B.C.E., Egypt became a province in Rome's mighty empire.

1-4f Daily Life in Ancient Egypt

Ancient Egyptians had a very positive attitude toward daily life on earth and followed the advice of the wisdom literature, which suggested that people marry young and establish a home and family. Monogamy was the general rule, although a husband was allowed to keep additional wives if his first wife was childless. Pharaohs were entitled to harems, although the queen was acknowledged as the Great Wife, with a status higher than that of the other wives. As in all patriarchal societies, the husband was master in the house, but wives were very

CHRONOLOGY	The Egyptians
Early Dynastic Period (dynasties 1–3)	ca. 3100–2575 B.C.E.
Old Kingdom (dynasties 4–8)	ca. 2575–2125 B.C.E.
First Intermediate Period (dynasties 9–11)	ca. 2125–2010 B.C.E.
Middle Kingdom (dynasties 12–13)	ca. 2010–1630 B.C.E.
Second Intermediate Period (dynasties 14–17)	ca. 1630–1539 B.C.E.
New Kingdom (dynasties 18–20)	ca. 1539–1069 B.C.E.
Postempire Egypt (dynasties 21–31)	1069–30 B.C.E.

much respected and in charge of the household and education of the children (see Historical Voices, "Respect for Women," p. 26). From a book of wise sayings (which the Egyptians referred to as instructions) came this advice:

If you are a man of standing, you should found your household and love your wife at home as is fitting. Fill her belly; clothe her

Respect for Women

 What does this advice to a young man reveal about the circumstances of upper-class Egyptian women? How does this advice compare to that of the Sumerians as seen in the document, The Instructions of Shuruppag?

BECAUSE OF THE HIGH infant and child mortality rate, women were considered important for their role as childbearers and hence due respect. Any, a scribe at the court of Nefertari, one of the wives of Ramesses II, provided this advice concerning women to a young man around 1270 B.C.E.

Any, *Advice to a Young Man Concerning Women*

Beware of the woman who is a stranger, who is not known in her town. Do not stare at her as she passes by and do not have intercourse with her. A woman who is away from her husband is a deep water whose course is unknown.

Take a wife while you're young,
That she make a son for you;
She should bear for you while you're youthful.
It is proper to make people.
Happy the man whose people are many.
He is saluted on account of his progeny.

Do not control your wife in her house,
When you know she is efficient;
Don't say to her: "Where is it?" "Get it!"
When she has put it in the right place.
Let your eye observe her in silence,
Then you will recognize her skill;
It is a joy when your hand is with her,
There are many who don't know this.

Source: J. E. Lewis, ed., The *Mammoth Book of Eyewitness: Ancient Egypt* (New York: Caroll & Graf Publishers, 2003), p. 184.

---

back. Ointment is the prescription for her body. Make her heart glad as long as you live. She is a profitable field for her lord. You should not contend with her at law, and keep her far from gaining control. . . . Let her heart be soothed through what may accrue to you; it means keeping her long in your house.[18]

Women's property and inheritances remained in their hands, even after marriage. Although most careers and public offices were closed to women, some did operate businesses. Peasant women worked long hours in the fields and at numerous domestic tasks, especially weaving cloth. Upper-class women could function as priestesses, and a few queens even became pharaohs in their own right. Most famous, as we have seen, was Hatshepsut in the New Kingdom.

Marriages were arranged by parents. The primary concerns were family and property, and the chief purpose of marriage was to produce children, especially sons (see Historical Voices, "A Father's Advice," p. 27). Daughters were not slighted, however. Numerous tomb paintings show the close and affectionate relationship parents had with both sons and daughters. Marriages could and did end in divorce, which was allowed, apparently with compensation for the wife. Adultery, however, was strictly prohibited, and punishments were severe, especially for women, who could have their noses cut off or be burned at the stake.

Under normal circumstances, Egypt was blessed by a material abundance that not only kept its entire population fed but also enabled its upper classes to lead a life of gracious leisure.

These wealthy families had attractive homes located on walled estates. Much energy was devoted to the garden, which contained fruit trees and vegetables as well as tree-lined paths and pools for the family's leisure time.

Tomb paintings indicate that the upper classes participated in numerous banquets where guests were lavishly fed and entertained (see Images of Everyday Life, "The Egyptian Diet," p. 28). Although some people obviously got drunk, a collection of "instructions" advises more circumspect behavior:

If you are one of those sitting at the table of one greater than yourself, take what he may give, when it is set before your nose. You should gaze at what is before you. . . . Let your face be cast down until he addresses you, and you should speak only when he addresses you. Laugh after he laughs, and it will be very pleasing to his heart and what you may do will be pleasing to the heart.[19]

The same collection of instructions warns that when one has been invited to a party, "beware of approaching the women. It does not go well with the place where that is done."[20]

Entertainment, especially music, was a regular feature of parties. The Egyptians used an astonishing variety of instruments: drums, tambourines, flutes, trumpets, and stringed instruments that were plucked rather than played with a bow. Singers, accompanying themselves on the lute or harp, presented songs in praise of the host's generosity and of enjoying life.

A Father's Advice

 According to this document, what social and political skills were prized by members of the Egyptian governing elite? What does the passage reveal about Egyptian bureaucrats?

UPPER-CLASS EGYPTIANS enjoyed compiling collections of wise sayings to provide guidance for leading an upright and successful life. This excerpt is taken from "The Instruction of Ptah-hotep" and dates from around 2450 B.C.E. The vizier was the pharaoh's chief official. In this selection, Ptah-hotep advises his son on how to be a successful official.

"The Instruction of Ptah-hotep"

Then he said to his son:

Let not your heart be puffed-up because of your knowledge; be not confident because you are a wise man. Take counsel with the ignorant as well as the wise. The full limits of skill cannot be attained, and there is no skilled man equipped to his full advantage. Good speech is more hidden than the emerald, but it may be found with maidservants at the grindstones. . . .

If you are a leader commanding the affairs of the multitude, seek out for yourself every beneficial deed, until it may be that your own affairs are without wrong. Justice is great, and its appropriateness is lasting; it has been disturbed since the time of him who made it, whereas there is punishment for him who passes over its laws. It is the right path before him who knows nothing. Wrongdoing has never brought its undertaking into port. It may be that it is fraud that gains riches, but the strength of justice is that it lasts. . . .

If you are a man of intimacy, whom one great man sends to another, be thoroughly reliable when he sends you. Carry out the errand for him as he has spoken. Do not be reserved about what is said to you, and beware of any act of forgetfulness. Grasp hold of truth, and do not exceed it. Mere gratification is by no means to be repeated. Struggle against making words worse, thus making one great man hostile to another through vulgar speech. . . .

If you are a man of standing and found a household and produce a son who is pleasing to god, if he is correct and inclines toward your ways and listens to your instruction, while his manners in your house are fitting, and if he takes care of your property as it should be, seek out for him every useful action. He is your son . . . you should not cut your heart off from him.

But a man's seed often creates enmity. If he goes astray and transgresses your plans and does not carry out your instruction, so that his manners in your household are wretched, and he rebels against all that you say, while his mouth runs on in the most wretched talk, quite apart from his experience, while he possesses nothing, you should cast him off: he is not your son at all. He was not really born to you. Thus, you enslave him entirely according to his own speech. He is one whom god has condemned in the very womb.

Source: "The Instruction of Ptah-hotep" from J. Pritchard, ed., *Ancient Near Eastern Texts Related to the Old Testament*, 3rd revised edition with supplement (Princeton, N.J.: Princeton University Press, 1969). Reprinted by permission of Princeton University Press.

Judging from the paintings in their tombs, the upper classes found myriad ways to entertain themselves as well. Fowling in the stands of papyrus reeds that grew along the riverbanks was a favorite pastime. So was hunting animals, but only for the men. Armed with bows and arrows, the hunters rode in chariots and used dogs to pursue antelope, gazelles, and other creatures. Indoor activities included board games. The earliest known board games in the world have been found in Egyptian tombs. Many are made of wood decorated with ivory or ebony. The games played on them involved moving pieces on the boards according to the roll of the dice.

The gulf between the upper and lower classes of Egyptian society was especially evident in health care. While the elite had a healthy diet and could call on doctors and dentists for medical help, the peasants suffered from numerous debilitating diseases. The ailments of women, especially those related to fertility, pregnancy, and childbirth, attracted special attention from the medical world.

Regardless of class, most Egyptians believed that disease came from bad spirits or incorrect behavior. To protect themselves, people used magic spells and amulets that carried images of protective deities. Nevertheless, Egyptian records include lists of prescriptions for broken bones, wounds, stomach problems, rashes, and numerous other ailments.

1-5 On the Fringes of Civilization

 FOCUS QUESTION: What is the significance of the Indo-European-speaking peoples?

Mesopotamia and Egypt have dominated our story of the beginnings of Western civilization, but significant developments were also taking place on the fringes of these civilizations. Farming had spread into the Balkan peninsula of Europe by 6500 B.C.E., and by 4000 B.C.E. it was well established in southern

The Egyptian Diet

 What were the differences in the diets of the upper and lower classes? Why were they so different?

THE DIETS OF THE UPPER AND LOWER CLASSES in ancient Egypt differed considerably. Various types of meat and fowl, including beef, goat, pork, goose, and pigeon, were on the tables of the rich. Fish was also an important part of the upper-class Egyptian diet. Although done for sport as well as food, hunting waterfowl in the stands of papyrus reeds that grew along the river's banks was a favorite pastime of the Egyptian upper classes. Image 1.12a shows a hunting scene from the eighteenth-dynasty tomb of Nebamun in Thebes. Nebamun, a nobleman, is seen standing in his boat using his throwstick to hunt birds. He holds three birds in his right hand while a cat retrieves two in its claws and holds the wings of another in its teeth.

The basic diet of the poor consisted chiefly of bread, beer made from barley, and onions. The baking of bread was an important task in all households. The tomb painting in Image 1.12b from the eighteenth-dynasty tomb of Mennah shows two men carrying grain while slave girls fight over leftovers in the background.

Vegetables and fruits were also part of the Egyptian diet. Among the vegetables were lettuce, radishes, squash, and cucumbers. Fruits included figs, dates, and grapes,

which were mainly used by the upper classes for making wine. Image 1.12c shows peasants harvesting grapes from grapevines that have been attached to a trellis. Both sweet and dry wines were produced from a variety of dark and pale grapes.

IMAGE 1.12a

Werner Forman/Art Resource, NY

IMAGE 1.12b

Erich Lessing/Art Resource, NY

IMAGE 1.12c

Erich Lessing/Art Resource, NY

France, central Europe, and the coastal regions of the Mediterranean. Although migrating farmers from the Near East may have brought some farming techniques into Europe, historians now believe that the Neolithic peoples of Europe domesticated animals and began to farm largely on their own.

One outstanding feature of late Neolithic Europe was the building of megalithic structures. *Megalith* is Greek for "large stone." Radiocarbon dating, a technique that allows scientists to determine the age of objects, shows that the first megalithic structures were built around 4000 B.C.E., more than a thousand years before the great pyramids were built in Egypt. Between 3200 and 1500 B.C.E., standing stones placed in circles or lined up in rows were erected throughout the British Isles and northwestern France. Other megalithic constructions have been found as far north as Scandinavia and as far south as the islands of Corsica, Sardinia, and Malta (see Map 1.7). Some archaeologists have demonstrated that the stone circles were used as observatories to detect not only such simple

MAP 1.7 **Stonehenge and Other Megalithic Sites in Europe**

astronomical phenomena as the midwinter and midsummer sunrises but also such sophisticated observations as the major and minor standstills of the moon.

By far the most famous of these megalithic constructions is Stonehenge in England (see Image 1.13). Stonehenge consists of a series of concentric rings of standing stones. Its construction sometime between 2100 and 1900 B.C.E. was no small accomplishment. The eighty bluestones used at Stonehenge weigh 4 tons each and were transported to the site from their original source 135 miles away. Like other megalithic structures, Stonehenge indicates a remarkable awareness of astronomy on the part of its builders, as well as an impressive coordination of workers.

1-5a The Impact of the Indo-Europeans

For many historians, both the details of construction and the purpose of the megalithic structures of Europe remain a mystery. Also puzzling is the role of the Indo-European people. The term *Indo-European* refers to people who used a language derived from a single parent tongue. Indo-European languages include Greek, Latin, Persian, Sanskrit, and the Germanic languages (see Table 1.3). It has been suggested that the original Indo-European-speaking peoples were based somewhere in the steppe region north of the Black Sea or in southwestern Asia, in modern Iran or Afghanistan. Although there had been earlier migrations, around 2000 B.C.E. they began major nomadic movements into Europe (including present-day Italy and Greece), India, and the Near East. The Indo-Europeans who moved into Asia Minor and Anatolia (modern Turkey) coalesced with the native peoples to form the first Hittite kingdom, known as the Old Kingdom (ca. 1700–1400 B.C.E.), with its capital at Hattusas (Boğazköy in modern-day Turkey).

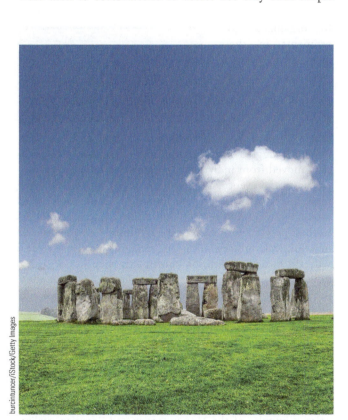

IMAGE 1.13 **Stonehenge.** The Bronze Age in northwestern Europe is known for its megaliths, large standing stones that were placed in circles or lined up in rows. By far the most famous of these megalithic constructions is Stonehenge in England.

TABLE 1.3	Some Indo-European Languages
SUBFAMILY	**LANGUAGES**
Indo-Iranian	*Sanskrit*, Persian
Balto-Slavic	Russian, Serbo-Croatian, Czech, Polish, Lithuanian
Hellenic	Greek
Italic	*Latin*, Romance languages (French, Italian, Spanish, Portuguese, Romanian)
Celtic	Irish, Gaelic
Germanic	Swedish, Danish, Norwegian, German, Dutch, English

Note: Languages in *italic* type are no longer spoken.

1-5b The Hittite Empire

The Hittites began to spread outward around 1600 B.C.E., but it was not until around two hundred years later that a new line of kings created the Hittite New Kingdom or Hittite Empire. Especially notable was Suppiluliumas (suh-PIL-oo-LEE-uh-muss) I (ca. 1370–1330 B.C.E.), one of the strongest rulers of the era, who established Hittite control from western Turkey to northern Syria. Suppiluliumas formed an alliance with the Egyptians and then conquered Syria. The Hittites were the first of the Indo-European peoples to make use of iron, enabling them to construct weapons that were stronger and cheaper to make because of the widespread availability of iron ore.

For the next hundred years, the Hittites were in conflict with Egypt until the Egyptian pharaoh Ramesses II crafted a remarkable nonaggression treaty that stabilized relations between Egypt and the Hittites. The end of Hittite power came in part from internal problems but also as a result of attacks by the Sea Peoples from the west around 1200 B.C.E. and by a group of aggressive tribespeople who raided Hittite cities. By 1190 B.C.E., Hittite power had come to an end.

During its heyday, however, the Hittite Empire was one of the great powers in West Asia. The Hittite ruler, known as the Great King, controlled the core areas of the kingdom, but in western and southern Anatolia and Syria he allowed local rulers to swear allegiance to him as his vassals. Constant squabbling over succession to the throne, however, tended to weaken the royal authority at times.

During its height, the Hittite Empire also demonstrated an interesting ability to assimilate other cultures into its own. In language, literature, art, law, and religion, the Hittites borrowed much from Mesopotamia as well as from the native peoples they had subdued. Recent scholarship has stressed the important role of the Hittites in transmitting Mesopotamian culture, as they transformed it, to later civilizations in the Mediterranean area, especially to the Mycenaean Greeks (see Chapter 3).

CHAPTER SUMMARY

Humanlike creatures first emerged in Africa more than 3 to 4 million years ago. Over a long period of time, Paleolithic people learned how to create more sophisticated tools, to use fire, and to adapt to and even change their physical environment. Paleolithic people were primarily nomads who hunted animals and gathered wild plants for survival. Nevertheless, they created a culture that included sophisticated cave paintings.

The agricultural revolution of the Neolithic Age, which began around 10,000 B.C.E., dramatically changed human patterns of living. The growing of food on a regular basis and the taming of animals made it possible for humans to stop their nomadic ways and settle in more permanent settlements.

These organized communities gradually gave rise to more complex human societies.

These more complex human societies, which we call the first civilizations, emerged around 3000 B.C.E. in the river valleys of Mesopotamia, Egypt, India, and China. An increase in food production in these regions led to a significant growth in human population and the rise of cities. Efforts to control the flow of water for farming also led to organized governments in these new urban civilizations. The peoples of Southwest Asia and Egypt laid the foundations of what

would become Western civilization. They developed cities and struggled with the problems of organized states as they moved from individual communities to larger territorial units and eventually to empires. They invented writing to keep records and created literature. They constructed monumental buildings to please their gods, give witness to their power, and preserve their culture. They developed new political, military, social, and religious structures to deal with the basic problems of human existence and organization. These first civilizations left detailed records that allow us to view how they grappled with three of the fundamental problems that humans have pondered: the nature of human relationships, the nature of the universe, and the role of divine forces in the cosmos. Although later people would provide different answers from those of the Mesopotamians and Egyptians, it was they who first posed the questions, gave answers, and wrote them down.

By the middle of the second millennium B.C.E., much of the creative impulse of the Mesopotamian and Egyptian civilizations was beginning to wane. As we shall see in Chapter 2, by 1200 B.C.E. a whole new pattern of petty states and new kingdoms would lead to the largest empires the ancient Near East had seen.

CHAPTER TIMELINE

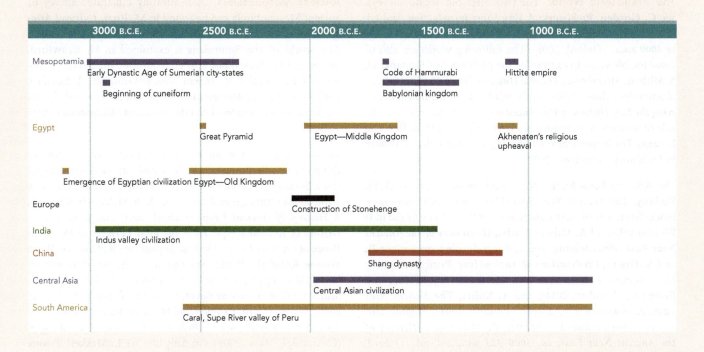

	3000 B.C.E.	2500 B.C.E.	2000 B.C.E.	1500 B.C.E.	1000 B.C.E.

Mesopotamia
Early Dynastic Age of Sumerian city-states
Beginning of cuneiform
Code of Hammurabi
Babylonian kingdom
Hittite empire

Egypt
Great Pyramid
Egypt—Middle Kingdom
Akhenaten's religious upheaval
Emergence of Egyptian civilization   Egypt—Old Kingdom

Europe
Construction of Stonehenge

India
Indus valley civilization

China
Shang dynasty

Central Asia
Central Asian civilization

South America
Caral, Supe River valley of Peru

CHAPTER REVIEW

Upon Reflection

Q What achievements did early humans make during the Paleolithic and Neolithic Ages, and how did those achievements eventually make possible the emergence of civilization?

Q Explain the ways in which the civilizations of Mesopotamia and Egypt were alike and how they were different. How significant are the differences?

Q What roles did geography, environmental conditions, religion, politics, economics, and women and families play in the civilizations of Southwest Asia and Egypt?

Q What do you think Western civilization has derived from the civilizations of the ancient Near East?

Key Terms

hominids (p. 2)
Paleolithic Age (p. 3)
Neolithic Revolution (p. 3)
patriarchy (p. 4)
civilization (p. 5)
Mesopotamia (p. 7)

ziggurat (p. 7)
theocracy (p. 7)
polytheistic (p. 13)
divination (p. 13)
cuneiform (p. 14)
hieroglyphics (p. 22)

Full definitions also appear in the Glossary at the end of the book.

Suggestions for Further Reading

The Prehistoric World   For two brief but sound surveys, see **C. Gosden**, *Prehistory: A Very Short Introduction*, 2nd ed. (New York, 2018), and **I. Tattersall**, *The World from Beginnings to 4000 B.C.E.* (Oxford, 2008). The following works are also of considerable value in examining the prehistory of humankind: **S. Mithen**, *After the Ice: A Global Human History, 20,000–5000 B.C.* (Cambridge, Mass., 2006), and **N. Wade**, *Before the Dawn: Recovering the Lost History of Our Ancestors* (New York, 2006). On the role of women in prehistory, see **J. M. Adovasio, O. Soffer**, and **J. Page**, *The Invisible Sex: Uncovering the True Roles of Women in Prehistory* (New York, 2007).

The Ancient Near East   For a brief introduction, see **A. H. Podany**, *The Ancient Near East* (New York, 2014). An excellent reference tool on the ancient Near East can be found in **P. Bienkowski** and **A. Milward, eds.**, *Dictionary of the Ancient Near East* (Philadelphia, 2000). For a detailed survey, see **B. and K. Foster**, *Civilizations of Ancient Iraq* (Princeton, 2009); **M. Liverani**, **The Ancient Near East: History, Society and Economy** (London, 2014); and **A. Kuhrt**, **The Ancient Near East, c. 3000–330 B.C.**, 2 vols. (London, 1995). A good survey can also be found in **M. van de Mieroop,** *A History of the Ancient Near East, ca. 3000–323 B.C.,* 2nd ed. (Oxford, 2006). **G. Leick**, *The Babylonians* (London, 2003), provides an overview of the peoples of ancient Mesopotamia. On the economic and social history of the ancient Near East, see **D. C. Snell**, *Life in the Ancient Near East* (New Haven, Conn., 1997).

Ancient Mesopotamia   A beautifully illustrated survey of ancient Mesopotamia can be found in **M. Roaf, *Cultural Atlas of Mesopotamia and the Ancient Near East*** (New York, 1996). The world of the Sumerians is examined in **H. Crawford, *Sumer and the Sumerians,*** 2nd ed. (Cambridge, 2004). On the spiritual perspective of ancient Mesopotamia, see **J. Bottéro,** *Religion in Ancient Mesopotamia* (Chicago, 2001). On daily life, see **S. Bertman,** *Handbook to Life in Ancient Mesopotamia* (New York, 2003).

Ancient Egypt   For an excellent introduction to ancient Egypt, see **T. Wilkinson, *The Rise and Fall of Ancient Egypt*** (New York, 2010). A brief survey is **I. Shaw,** *Ancient Egypt* (New York, 2004). Other general surveys include **M. Van de Mieroop,** *A History of Ancient Egypt* (Oxford, 2011) and **J. Romer,** *A History of Ancient Egypt: From the First Farmers to the Great Pyramid* on early Egypt. On Hatshepsut, see **K. Cooney, *When Women Ruled the World: Six Queens of Egypt*** (Washington, D.C., 2018). Egyptian religion is covered in **J. Assmann,** *The Search for God in Ancient Egypt,* trans. D. Lorton (Ithaca, N.Y., 2001), and **R. David,** *Religion and Magic in Ancient Egypt* (New York, 2002). On art, see **G. Robins,** *The Art of Ancient Egypt* (Cambridge, Mass., 2008). On daily life, see **L. Meskell,** *Private Life in New Kingdom Egypt* (Princeton, N.J., 2004).

Hittites   On the Hittites, see **T. Bryce, *The Kingdom of the Hittites,*** 2nd ed. (Oxford, 2006) and *Life and Society in the Hittite World* (Oxford, 2002).

Notes

1. J.-M. Chauvet et al., *Dawn of Art: The Chauvet Cave* (New York, 1996), pp. 49–50.
2. Quoted in A. Kuhrt, *The Ancient Near East, c. 3000–330 B.C.*, vol. 1 (London, 1995), p. 68.
3. Quoted in M. Wood, *Legacy: The Search for Ancient Cultures* (New York, 1995), p. 34.
4. Quoted in M. van de Mieroop, *A History of the Ancient Near East, ca. 3000–323 B.C.* (Oxford, 2004), p. 69.
5. Ibid., p. 64.
6. Ibid., p. 106.
7. Quoted in T. Jacobsen, "Mesopotamia," in H. Frankfort et al., *Before Philosophy* (Baltimore, 1949), p. 139.
8. Quoted in T. Jacobsen, *The Treasures of Darkness: A History of Mesopotamian Religion* (New Haven, Conn., 1976), p. 97.
9. *The Epic of Gilgamesh*, trans. N. K. Sandars (London, 1972), p. 62.
10. J. B. Pritchard, *Ancient Near Eastern Texts*, 3rd edition (Princeton, N.J., 1969), p. 372.
11. Quoted in A. P. Thomas, *Egyptian Gods and Myths* (London, 1986), p. 25.
12. Pritchard, *Ancient Near Eastern Texts*, p. 445.
13. Quoted in B. G. Trigger, B. J. Kemp, D. O'Connor, and A. B. Lloyd, *Ancient Egypt: A Social History* (Cambridge, 1983), p. 74.
14. Pritchard, *Ancient Near Eastern Texts*, p. 34.
15. Ibid., p. 36.
16. Quoted in R.-M. Hagen and R. Hagen, *Egypt: People, Gods, Pharaohs* (Cologne, 2002), p. 148.
17. Quoted in T. Wilkerson, *The Rise and Fall of Ancient Egypt* (New York, 2010), p. 262.
18. Pritchard, *Ancient Near Eastern Texts*, p. 413.
19. Ibid., p. 412.
20. Ibid., p. 413.

 **MindTap** *Tips*   What's a primary source? What's visual literacy? Get acquainted with all-important course concepts with the History Skills Tutorials in MindTap. These tutorials and associated online activities will help you succeed in the course!

CHAPTER 2

The Ancient Near East: Peoples and Empires

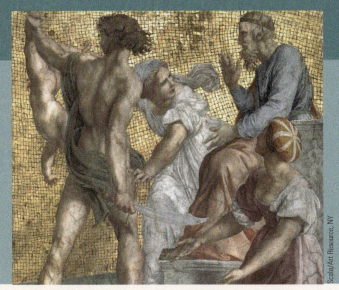

IMAGE 2.1 **The Judgment of Solomon as Painted by Raphael in the Sixteenth Century**

Scala/Art Resource, NY

CHAPTER OUTLINE AND FOCUS QUESTIONS

2-1 The Hebrews: "The Children of Israel"

Q How did the Israelites establish a united state, and what became of it? In what ways was the Jewish faith unique in the ancient Near East? How did it evolve over time?

2-2 The Neighbors of the Israelites

Q Who were the neighbors of the Israelites, and what was their significance?

2-3 The Assyrian Empire

Q What methods and institutions did the Assyrians use to amass and maintain their empire?

2-4 The Neo-Babylonian Empire

Q What was the significance of the Neo-Babylonian Empire?

2-5 The Persian Empire

Q What methods and institutions did the Persians use to amass and maintain their empire? How did these methods and institutions differ from those of the Assyrians?

CONNECTIONS TO TODAY

What effect. if any, does the history of ancient Israel have on the contemporary state of Israel?

AROUND 970 B.C.E., SOLOMON came to the throne of Israel, a small state in Western Asia. According to the biblical account, he was lacking in military prowess but excelled in many other ways. Through trade and a series of foreign alliances, he created a strong, flourishing state. But he was especially famed for another of his qualities. When confronted with two women who each claimed that the child before them was her natural child, Solomon ordered his servant to cut the child in half and give half to each woman. The first woman cried out, "Please, my lord, give her the living baby! Don't kill him!" The second woman replied, "Neither I nor you shall have him. Cut him in two!" Then Solomon rendered his judgment: "Give the living baby to the first woman. Do not kill him; she is his mother." According to the biblical account, "when all Israel heard the verdict the king had given, they held the king in awe, because they saw that he had wisdom from God to administer justice." After Solomon's death, Israel began to disintegrate. But how had such a small nation been able to survive for as long as it did in a Near East dominated by mighty empires?

The destruction of the Hittite kingdom and the weakening of Egypt around 1200 B.C.E. temporarily left a power vacuum in the Near East, allowing a patchwork of petty kingdoms and city-states to emerge, especially in Syria and Canaan. One of these small states, the nation of Israel, has played a role in Western civilization completely disproportionate to its size. The Israelites were a minor factor in the politics of the ancient Near East, but their spiritual heritage—the Judeo-Christian values—is one of the basic pillars of Western civilization.

The small states did not last, however. Ever since the first city-states had arisen in the Near East around

3000 B.C.E., there had been a movement toward the creation of larger territorial states with more sophisticated systems of control. This process reached a high point in the first millennium B.C.E. with the appearance of empires that embraced the entire Near East. Between 1000 and 500 B.C.E., the Assyrians, Chaldeans, and Persians all created empires that encompassed most or all of the ancient Near East. Each had impressive and grandiose capital cities that emphasized the power and wealth of its rulers. Each brought peace and order for a period of time by employing new administrative techniques. Each eventually fell to other conquerors. In the long run, these large empires had less impact on Western civilization than the Hebrew people of Israel did. In human history, the power of ideas is often more significant than the power of empires.

2-1 The Hebrews: "The Children of Israel"

 FOCUS QUESTIONS: How did the Israelites establish a united state, and what became of it? In what ways was the Jewish faith unique in the ancient Near East? How did it evolve over time?

The Hebrews were a Semitic-speaking people who had a tradition concerning their origins and history that was eventually written down as part of the Hebrew Bible, known to Christians as the Old Testament. Describing themselves originally as nomads organized into clans, the Hebrews' tradition states that they were descendants of the patriarch Abraham, who had migrated from Mesopotamia to the land of Canaan, where they became identified as the "Children of Israel." Again according to tradition, a drought in Canaan caused many Hebrews to migrate to Egypt, where they lived peacefully until they were enslaved by pharaohs who used them as laborers on building projects. These Hebrews remained in bondage until Moses supposedly led them eastward out of Egypt in the Exodus in the first half of the thirteenth century B.C.E. According to the biblical account, the Hebrews then wandered for many years in the desert until they entered Canaan. Organized into twelve tribes, they became embroiled in conflict with the Philistines, a people who had settled in the coastal area of Canaan but were beginning to move inland.

Many scholars today doubt that the early books of the Hebrew Bible reflect the true history of the early Israelites. The Hebrew Bible is a collection of twenty-four books written over hundreds of years. Dating of the biblical books is problematic, although scholars have advanced a documentary hypothesis that maintains that a series of authors wrote different books of the Bible over a period of hundreds of years until the books were finally consolidated around 250 B.C.E. They argue that the early books of the Bible, written centuries after the events described, preserve only the cultural memory of what the Israelites came to believe about themselves and that recent archaeological evidence often contradicts the details of the biblical account. There is, for example, no archaeological or other evidence for the Exodus from Egypt. These scholars also argue that the Israelites were not nomadic invaders but indigenous peoples in the Canaanite hill country. What is generally agreed upon, however, is that between 1200 and 1000 B.C.E. the Israelites emerged as a distinct group of people who were possibly organized into tribes or a league of tribes.

HISTORIANS DEBATE — 2-1a Was There a United Kingdom of Israel?

According to the Hebrew Bible, the Israelites established a united kingdom of Israel beginning with Saul (ca. 1020–1000 B.C.E.), who supposedly achieved some success in the ongoing struggle with the Philistines. After his death, however, a brief period of anarchy ensued until one of Saul's lieutenants, David (ca. 1000–970 B.C.E.), reunited the Israelites, defeated the Philistines, and established control over all of Canaan. According to the biblical account, some of his conquests led to harsh treatment for the conquered people: "David also defeated the Moabites. He made them lie down on the ground and measured them off with a length of cord. Every two lengths of them were put to death, and the third length was allowed to live. So the Moabites became subject to David and brought tribute."[1] Among David's conquests was the city of Jerusalem, which he supposedly made into the capital of a united kingdom.

According to the biblical account, David's son Solomon (ca. 970–930 B.C.E.) did even more to strengthen royal power. He expanded the political and military establishments and extended the trading activities of the Israelites. Solomon is portrayed as a great builder who was responsible for the temple in the city of Jerusalem. The Israelites viewed the temple as the symbolic center of their religion and hence of the kingdom of Israel itself. Under Solomon, ancient Israel was supposedly at the height of its power (see Map 2.1).

The accuracy of this biblical account of the united kingdom of Israel under Saul, David, and Solomon has been recently challenged by a new generation of archaeologists and historians. Although they mostly accept Saul, David, and Solomon as historical figures, they portray them more as chief warlords than as kings. If a kingdom of Israel did exist during these years, it was not as powerful or as well organized as the Hebrew Bible says. Furthermore, they argue, there is no definitive archaeological evidence that Solomon built the temple in Jerusalem.

2-1b The Kingdoms of Israel and Judah

There may or not have been a united kingdom of Israel, but after Solomon's death tensions between northern and southern tribes in Israel led to the establishment of two separate kingdoms—the kingdom of Israel, composed of the ten northern tribes, with its capital eventually at Samaria, and the southern kingdom of Judah, consisting of two tribes, with its capital at Jerusalem. The northern kingdom of Israel joined with some

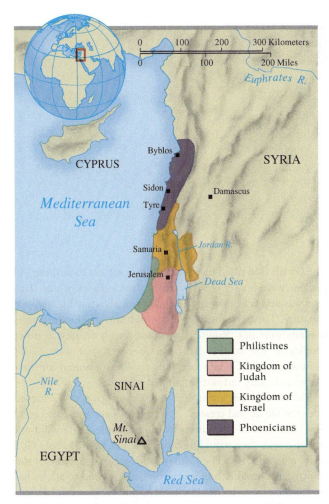

MAP 2.1 **The Israelites and Their Neighbors in the First Millennium B.C.E.** United under Saul, David, and Solomon according to the biblical account, greater Israel split into two states—Israel and Judah—after the death of Solomon. With power divided, the Israelites could not resist invasions that dispersed many of them from Canaan. Some, such as the "ten lost tribes," never returned. Others were sent to Babylon but were later allowed to return under the rule of the Persians.

Q *Why was Israel more vulnerable to the Assyrian Empire than Judah was?*

small Syrian states to temporarily stop the onslaught of the Assyrians (uh-SEER-ee-unz), who had consolidated their kingdom to the northeast (see "2-3 The Assyrian Empire," later in this chapter). But the power of the kingdom of Israel declined, and by the end of the ninth century, Israel was forced to pay tribute to Assyria (see Image 2.2). In the next century, Israel itself was destroyed. The Assyrians overran the kingdom, destroyed the capital of Samaria in 722 or 721 B.C.E., and deported many Israelites to other parts of the Assyrian Empire. These dispersed Israelites (the ten lost tribes) merged with neighboring peoples and gradually lost their identity.

The southern kingdom of Judah was also forced to pay tribute to Assyria but managed to survive as an independent state as Assyrian power declined (see Image 2.3). A new enemy, however, appeared on the horizon. The Chaldeans (kal-DEE-unz) first demolished Assyria and then, under King Nebuchadnezzar (neb-uh-kud-NEZZ-ur) II, conquered Judah and completely destroyed Jerusalem in 586 B.C.E. Many upper-class people from Judah were deported to Babylonia. The memory of their exile is still evoked in the stirring words of Psalm 137 (the Israelites mistakenly believed that these sacred songs—part of the Hebrew Bible—had been composed by King David):

> By the rivers of Babylon, we sat and wept when we
>   remembered Zion. . . .
> How can we sing the songs of the Lord while in a
>   foreign land?
> If I forget you, O Jerusalem, may my right hand forget
>   its skill.
> May my tongue cling to the roof of my mouth if I do
>   not remember you, if I do not consider Jerusalem
>   my highest joy.[2]

But the Babylonian captivity of the people of Judah did not last. A new set of conquerors, the Persians, destroyed the Chaldean kingdom but allowed the people of Judah to return to Jerusalem and rebuild their city and temple. The revived kingdom of Judah remained under Persian control until the conquests of Alexander the Great in the fourth century B.C.E. The people of Judah survived, eventually becoming known as the

IMAGE 2.2 **The King of Israel Pays Tribute to the King of Assyria.** By the end of the ninth century B.C.E., the kingdom of Israel had been forced to pay tribute to the Assyrian Empire. The Assyrians overran the kingdom in 722 or 721 B.C.E. and destroyed the capital city of Samaria. In this scene from a black obelisk, Jehu, the king of Israel, is shown paying tribute to Shalmaneser III, the king of Assyria.

Erich Lessing/Art Resource, NY

IMAGE 2.3 Prisoners from Judah. The Assyrians overran the kingdom of Israel in 722 or 721 B.C.E., destroyed the capital city of Samaria, and then began an assault on the kingdom of Judah. In this eighth-century B.C.E. relief from the palace of Sennacherib at Nineveh, Assyrian soldiers are seen impaling Jewish prisoners after their conquest of the fortified town of Lachish in Judah in 701 B.C.E.

Q *What does this image tell you about the reputation of Assyrian soldiers?*

Jews and giving their name to Judaism, the religion of Yahweh (YAH-way), God of Israel.

2-1c The Spiritual Dimensions of Israel

The spiritual perspective of the Israelites evolved over time. Early Israelites probably worshiped many gods, including nature spirits dwelling in trees and rocks. For some Israelites, Yahweh was the chief god of Israel, but many, including kings of Israel and Judah, worshiped other gods as well. It was among the Babylonian exiles in the sixth century B.C.E. that Yahweh—God of Israel—came to be seen as the *only* God. After these exiles returned to Judah, their point of view eventually became dominant, and pure **monotheism**, or the belief that there is only one God for all peoples, came to be the major tenet of Judaism.

"I Am the Lord Your God": Ruler of the World According to the Jewish conception, there is but one God, whom the Jews called Yahweh. God is the creator of the world and everything in it. To the Jews, the gods of all other peoples were mere idols.

CHRONOLOGY	The Israelites
Saul	ca. 1020–1000 B.C.E.
David	ca. 1000–970 B.C.E.
Solomon	ca. 970–930 B.C.E.
Northern kingdom of Israel destroyed by Assyria	722 or 721 B.C.E.
Southern kingdom of Judah falls to Chaldeans; destruction of Jerusalem	586 B.C.E.
Return of exiles to Jerusalem	538 B.C.E.

The Jewish God ruled the world; he was subject to nothing. All peoples were his servants, whether they knew it or not. This God was also transcendent. He had created nature but was not in nature. The stars, moon, rivers, wind, and other natural phenomena were not divinities or suffused with divinity, as other peoples of the ancient Near East believed, but were God's handiwork. All of God's creations could be admired for their awesome beauty but not worshiped as gods.

This omnipotent creator of the universe was not removed from the life he had created, however, but was a just and good God who expected goodness from his people. If they did not obey his will, they would be punished. But he was also a God of mercy and love: "The Lord is gracious and compassionate, slow to anger and rich in love. The Lord is good to all; he has compassion on all he has made."[3] Despite the powerful dimensions of God as creator and sustainer of the universe, the Jewish message also emphasized that each person could have a personal relationship with this omnipotent being. As the psalmist sang: "My help comes from the Lord, the Maker of heaven and earth. He will not let your foot slip—he who watches over you will not slumber."[4]

The chief source of information about Israel's spiritual conceptions is the Hebrew Bible. Its purpose was to teach the essential beliefs about the God of Israel after the Babylonian captivity of the Jews and their dispersal. During and after the Babylonian exile, the Jews recorded many of their traditions in order to create and preserve their identity. These writings became the core of the Hebrew Bible. The first five books, known as the **Pentateuch** (PEN-tuh-took), which cover the time from the beginning of the world until the Israelites' arrival in Canaan, constitute the **Torah** (TOR-uh), or law code, governing the lives of worshipers and their relations to one another and to the non-Jewish population. The Hebrew Bible focuses on one basic theme: the necessity for the Jews to obey their God.

"You Only Have I Chosen": Covenant and Law The covenant, the law, the prophets, and the rabbis are additional aspects of the Jewish religious tradition. The Israelites believed that during the Exodus from Egypt, when Moses supposedly led his people out of bondage into a land of plenty promised to them by Yahweh, a special event occurred that determined the Jewish experience for all time. According to tradition, God

The Covenant and the Law: The Book of Exodus

 What was the nature of the covenant between Yahweh and the Israelites? What was its moral significance for the Israelites? How does it differ from Hammurabi's code, and how might you explain those differences?

ACCORDING TO THE BIBLICAL ACCOUNT, it was during the Exodus from Egypt that the Israelites supposedly made their covenant with Yahweh. They agreed to obey their God and follow his law. In return, Yahweh promised to take special care of his chosen people. These selections from the book of Exodus describe the making of the covenant and God's commandments to the Israelites.

Exodus 19:1–8

In the third month after the Israelites left Egypt—on the very day—they came to the Desert of Sinai. After they set out from Rephidim, they entered the Desert of Sinai, and Israel camped there in the desert in front of the mountain. Then Moses went up to God, and the Lord called to him from the mountain, and said, "This is what you are to say to the house of Jacob and what you are to tell the people of Israel: 'You yourselves have seen what I did to Egypt, and how I carried you on eagles' wings and brought you to myself. Now if you obey me fully and keep my covenant, then out of all nations you will be my treasured possession. Although the whole earth is mine, you will be for me a kingdom of priests and a holy nation.' These are the words you are to speak to the Israelites." So Moses went back and summoned the elders of the people and set before them all the words the Lord had commanded him to speak. The people all responded together, "We will do everything the Lord has said." So Moses brought their answer back to the Lord.

Exodus 20:1–17

And God spoke all these words, "I am the Lord your God, who brought you out of Egypt, out of the land of slavery. You shall have no other gods before me. You shall not make for yourself an idol in the form of anything in heaven above or on the earth beneath or in the waters below. You shall not bow down to them or worship them; for I, the Lord your God, am a jealous God, punishing the children for the sin of the fathers to the third and fourth generation of those who hate me, but showing love to a thousand generations of those who love me and keep my commandments. You shall not misuse the name of the Lord your God, for the Lord will not hold any-one guiltless who misuses his name. Remember the Sabbath day by keeping it holy. Six days you shall labor and do all your work, but the seventh day is a Sabbath to the Lord your God. On it you shall not do any work, neither you, nor your son or daughter, nor your manservant or maidservant, nor your animals, nor the alien within your gates. For in six days the Lord made the heavens and the earth, the sea, and all that is in them, but he rested on the seventh day. Therefore the Lord blessed the Sabbath day and made it holy. Honor your father and your mother, so that you may live long in the land the Lord your God is giving you. You shall not murder. You shall not commit adultery. You shall not steal. You shall not give false testimony against your neighbor. You shall not covet your neighbor's house. You shall not covet your neighbor's wife, or his manservant or maidservant, his ox or donkey, or anything that belongs to your neighbor."

Source: The Holy Bible, New International Version (Colorado Springs, Colo.: Biblica, 1973).

---

entered into a covenant, or contract, with the tribes of Israel, who believed that Yahweh had spoken to them through Moses (see Historical Voices, "The Covenant and the Law," above). The Israelites promised to obey Yahweh and follow his law. In return, Yahweh promised to take special care of his people, "a peculiar treasure unto me above all people."

This covenant between Yahweh and his chosen people could be fulfilled, however, only by obedience to the law of God. Law became a crucial element of the Jewish world and had a number of different dimensions. In some instances, it set forth specific requirements, such as payments for offenses. Most important, since the major characteristic of God was his goodness, ethical concerns stood at the center of the law. Sometimes these took the form of specific standards of moral behavior: "You shall not murder. You shall not commit adultery. You shall not steal."[5] But these concerns were also expressed in decrees that regulated the economic, social, religious, and political life of the community, for God's laws of morality applied to all areas of life (see Image 2.4). These laws made no class distinctions and emphasized the protection of the poor, widows, orphans, and slaves.

The Prophets and Rabbis The Israelites believed that certain religious leaders or holy men, called prophets, were sent by God to serve as his voice to his people. In the ninth century B.C.E., the prophets were particularly vociferous about the tendency of the Israelites to accept other gods, chiefly the fertility and earth gods of other peoples in Canaan. They warned of the terrible retribution that Yahweh would exact from the Israelites if they did not keep the covenant to remain faithful to him alone and just in their dealings with one another.

IMAGE 2.4 Moses and the Ten Commandments. As we have seen, according to the Hebrew Bible, God gave to Moses a set of commandments for the Israelites to obey. Although these commandments are interpreted and numbered differently by religious groups, the early Christian church came to consider the Ten Commandments given to Moses by God as a summary of God's law and a standard for ethical behavior. This is evident in this sixth-century detail of Moses and the Ten Commandments in the Eastern Roman (later known as Byzantine) church of San Vitale in Italy. The Israelites shown in the photo are, of course, garbed in the styles of the sixth century.

The golden age of prophecy began in the mid-eighth century and continued during the time when the people of Israel and Judah were threatened by Assyrian and Chaldean conquerors. These "men of God" went through the land warning the Israelites that they had failed to keep God's commandments and would be punished for breaking the covenant: "I will punish you for all your iniquities." Amos prophesied the fall of the northern kingdom of Israel to Assyria; twenty years later, Isaiah said the kingdom of Judah too would fall (see Historical Voices, "The Hebrew Prophets," p. 39).

Out of the words of the prophets came new concepts that enriched the Jewish tradition and ultimately Western civilization, including a notion of universalism and a yearning for social justice. Although the Jews' religious practices gave them a sense of separateness from other peoples, the prophets transcended this by embracing a concern for all humanity. All nations would someday come to the God of Israel: "All

the earth shall worship you." A universal community of all people under God would someday be established by Israel's effort. This vision encompassed the elimination of war and the establishment of peace for all the nations of the world. In the words of the prophet Isaiah: "He will judge between the nations and will settle disputes for many people. They will beat their swords into plowshares and their spears into pruning hooks. Nation will not take up sword against nation, nor will they train for war anymore."[6]

The prophets also cried out against social injustice. They condemned the rich for causing the poor to suffer, denounced luxuries as worthless, and threatened Israel with prophecies of dire punishments for these sins. God's command was to live justly, share with one's neighbors, care for the poor and the unfortunate, and act with compassion. When God's command was not followed, the social fabric of the community was threatened. These proclamations by Israel's prophets became a source for Western ideals of social justice, even if they have never been perfectly realized.

Although the prophets ultimately developed a sense of universalism, the demands of the Jewish religion—the need to obey their God—encouraged a separation between the Jews and their non-Jewish neighbors. Unlike most other peoples of the Near East, Jews could not simply be amalgamated into a community by accepting the gods of their conquerors and their neighbors. To remain faithful to the demands of their God, they might even have to refuse loyalty to political leaders.

The Babylonian captivity of the Jews also led to an important figure in Judaism—the rabbi. Devoid of the usual community worship of their homeland, Jews faced new challenges and new questions about their faith and began to turn to the rabbi for answers. Although not new figures in Judaism, rabbis now emerged as teachers of Jewish law and became the leaders of the Jews in exile. They not only taught the Torah but also began to interpret it, leading to a body of rabbinical law that greatly affected Jewish life.

2-1d The Social Structure of the Hebrews

Originally, the Israelites were organized along tribal lines, but by the time of the monarchy a new social structure had evolved as the Israelites settled in towns and villages, leaving them with conspicuous "divisions of the population."

Social Patterns The men of rank and influence formed a special group of considerable importance in Hebrew society. This group included officials of the king, military officers, civil officials, and governors. Although simply servants to the kings, they held a privileged position in the society at large. The common people, sometimes called "people of the land," remained a body of free people having basic civil rights. Their livelihood came mostly from the land and from various crafts. These peasants and artisans sold their own produce and products directly to buyers in markets in their local town or village squares, thus avoiding the need for intermediaries or traders. There was no real merchant class in ancient Israel. Commerce was carried on by foreigners, such as the Phoenicians. Not until the **Diaspora** (dy-ASS-pur-uh), when Jews became scattered throughout the ancient world after their exile to Babylon, did they become merchants.

Alfredo Dagli Orti/Art Resource, NY

The Hebrew Prophets: Micah, Isaiah, and Amos

 What did the Hebrew prophets see as the chief transgressions of the Hebrew people? What do these selections tell you about the nature of the Hebrews as a "chosen" people?

THE HEBREW PROPHETS warned the Israelites that they must obey God's commandments or face punishment for breaking their covenant with God. These selections from the prophets Micah, Isaiah, and Amos make clear the dreadful punishments that God would inflict on the Israelites for their sins. Even the Assyrians, as Isaiah indicated, would be used as God's instrument to punish them.

Micah 6:9–16

Listen! The Lord is calling to the city—and to fear your name is wisdom—"Heed the rod and the One who appointed it. Am I still to forget, O wicked house, your ill-gotten treasures? Shall I acquit a man with dishonest scales, with a bag of false weights? Her rich men are violent; her people are liars and their tongues speak deceitfully. Therefore, I have begun to destroy you, to ruin you because of your sins. You will eat but not be satisfied; your stomach will still be empty. You will store up but save nothing, because what you save I will give to the sword. You will plant but not harvest; you will press olives but not use the oil on yourselves, you will crush grapes but not drink the wine. . . . Therefore I will give you over to ruin and your people to derision; you will bear the scorn of the nations."

Isaiah 10:1–6

Woe to those who make unjust laws, to those who issue oppressive decrees, to deprive the poor of their rights and withhold justice from the oppressed of my people, making widows their prey and robbing the fatherless. What will you do on the day of reckoning, when disaster comes from afar? To whom will you run for help? Where will you leave your riches? Nothing will remain but to cringe among the captives or fall among the slain. Yet for all this, his anger is not turned away, his hand is still upraised. "Woe to the Assyrian, the rod of my anger, in whose hand is the club of my wrath! I send him against a godless nation, I dispatch him against a people who anger me, to seize loot and snatch plunder, and to trample them down like mud in the streets."

Amos 3:1–2

Hear this word the Lord has spoken against you, O people of Israel—against the whole family I brought up out of Egypt: "You only have I chosen of all the families of the earth; therefore, I will punish you for all your sins."

Source: The Holy Bible, New International Version (Colorado Springs, Colo.: Biblica, 1973).

Family The family was the central social institution in Hebrew life and consisted of individuals connected by common blood and a common living place. A family living in one house could comprise husband and wife, married sons and their wives, and their children. The Hebrew family was **patriarchal** (pay-tree-AR-kul). The husband-father was master of his wife and possessed absolute authority over his children, including the power of life and death.

Marriage and Women Marriage was an important aspect of Hebrew family life. In ancient Israel, polygamy was an accepted form of marriage, especially for kings and wealthier citizens. Hebrew law limited kings to eighteen wives and citizens to four. In practice, only kings could afford a large harem. When others had more than one wife, it was usually because they desired more children; the first wife, for example, might have been unable to have children or produced only daughters.

Many Hebrews, however, believed that monogamy was the preferred form of marriage. Wives were honored for their faithfulness and dedication to their husbands. The book of Proverbs in the Hebrew Bible provides a picture of what Hebrews considered a perfect wife:

> A wife of noble character who can find? She is worth
>   far more than rubies.
> Her husband has full confidence in her and lacks
>   nothing of value.
> She brings him good, not harm, all the days of her life.
> She selects wool and flax and works with eager hands.
> She is like the merchant ships, bringing her food from
>   a far.
> She gets up while it is still dark; she provides food for
>   her family and portions for her servant girls.
> She considers a field and buys it; out of her earnings
>   she plants a vineyard.
> She sets about her work vigorously; her arms are
>   strong for her tasks. . . .
> She speaks with wisdom, and faithful instruction is
>   on her tongue.
> She watches over the affairs of her household, and
>   does not eat the bread of idleness.
> Her children arise and call her blessed; her husband
>   also, and he praises her.[7]

Women were greatly valued, but their work was obviously never done.

Although the Hebrew Bible, a male-edited work, reveals a society dominated by men, it also includes stories of women who played heroic roles in the early history of Israel. Deborah, for example, played a prominent role in the defeat of the Canaanites at Mount Tabor. After the same battle, Jael killed Sisera, the leader of the Canaanites. According to the Song of Deborah, "Most blessed of women be Jael, . . . most blessed of tent-dwelling women. . . . Her hand reached for the tent peg, her right hand for the workman's hammer. She struck Sisera, she crushed his head, she shattered and pierced his temple. At her feet he sank, he fell; there he lay."[8]

But these accounts are not the norm. In the Hebrew Bible, women are mostly dependent on men. It should not surprise us, then, to learn that a married woman was subject to her husband's authority. A married woman left her parents' home, lived with her husband's family, and became a member of their clan. Her children also belonged to the husband's clan. Since boys and girls were married at a relatively young age, parents took the responsibility for matchmaking. Wives were expected to remain faithful to their husbands, an ideal that would later have an impact on Christian attitudes toward women.

The primary goal of marriage was to produce children. They were the "crown of man," and sons, in particular, were desired. Daughters would eventually leave the family house, but sons carried on the family line. Mothers were in charge of the early education of children, especially in regard to basic moral principles. As boys matured, their fathers took over responsibility for their education, which remained largely informal. This included religious instruction as well as general education for life. The rod was not spared as a matter of principle. Since trades were usually hereditary, fathers also provided their sons' occupational education. As one rabbi warned, "He who does not teach his son a useful trade is bringing him up to be a thief."[9] Additional education for boys came from priests, whose sacred mission was to instruct people in the Torah. The only education girls received was from their mothers, who taught them the basic fundamentals of how to be good wives, mothers, and housekeepers.

2-2 The Neighbors of the Israelites

 FOCUS QUESTION: Who were the neighbors of the Israelites, and what was their significance?

The Israelites were not the only people living in Canaan. The Philistines, who invaded from the sea, established five towns on the coastal plain of the region. They settled down as farmers and eventually came into conflict with the Israelites. The Phoenicians (fuh-NEE-shunz) had resided in Canaan for some time but now found themselves with a new independence. A Semitic-speaking people, the Phoenicians resided along the Mediterranean coast on a narrow band of land 120 miles long (see Map 2.2). They had rebuilt their major cities, Byblos (BIB-uhs), Tyre, and Sidon (SYD-un), after destruction by the Sea Peoples. Their newfound political independence helped the

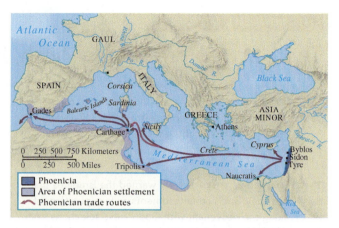

MAP 2.2 **Phoenician Colonies and Trade Routes, ca. 600** B.C.E.

Phoenicians expand the trade that was already the foundation of their prosperity. In fact, Byblos had been the principal distribution center for Egyptian papyrus outside Egypt (the Greek word for book, *biblos*, is derived from the name Byblos).

All three chief cities of Phoenicia were seaports, but they also served as distribution centers for the lands to the east in Mesopotamia. The Phoenicians themselves produced a number of goods for foreign markets, including purple dye, glass, wine, and lumber from the famous cedars of Lebanon. In addition, the Phoenicians improved their ships and became great international sea traders (see Image 2.5). They charted

Relief portraying Phoenician merchant ship, fourth century BC/ DE AGOSTINI EDITORE/Bridgeman Images

IMAGE 2.5 **A Phoenician Merchant Ship.** The Phoenicians, a Semitic-speaking people dwelling in ancient Canaan, became the predominant sea traders of the ancient Near East. The Phoenicians built both warships and trading ships. In their trading ships, they sailed westward from the eastern coast of the Mediterranean Sea and traded with native peoples and set up colonies as far west as the Atlantic coasts of Spain and Morocco, past the Straits of Gibraltar, establishing a reputation as the greatest mariners in the ancient world. Shown here is a fourth-century B.C.E. relief portraying a Phoenician merchant ship with its traditional high prow with a horse head.

 How did the location of the Phoenicians determine their trading patterns?

PHOENICIAN			HEBREW	GREEK				LATIN	
Phoenician	Phoenician Name	Modern Symbol	Hebrew	Early Greek	Classical Greek	Greek Name		Early Latin	Classical Latin
⟨	ʾp	ʾ	𐤀	Λ	A	alpha		A	A
⊴	bēt	b	⊐	ꓭ	B	beta			B
↑	gīml	g	𐤂	⅂	Γ	gamma			C
◁	dālet	d	⊤	△	Δ	delta		◁	D
⸲	hē	h	⊓	ꓯ	E	epsilon		ꓱ	E
Y	wāw	w	⎮	𝈄		digamma		ꓵ	F

Source: Andrew Robinson, *The Story of Writing* (London: Thames & Hudson, 1995), p. 170. Reprinted by permission of Thames & Hudson.

new routes not only in the Mediterranean but also in the Atlantic Ocean, where they sailed south along the west coast of Africa. The Phoenicians established a number of colonies in the western Mediterranean, including settlements in southern Spain, Sicily, and Sardinia. Most of the Phoenician colonies were trading stations, not permanent settlements. A major exception was Carthage, the Phoenicians' most famous colony, located on the North African coast.

Culturally, the Phoenicians are best known as transmitters. Instead of using pictographs or signs to represent whole words and syllables as the Mesopotamians and Egyptians did, the Phoenicians simplified their writing by using twenty-two different signs to represent the sounds of their speech. These twenty-two characters or letters could be used to spell out all the words in the Phoenician language. Although the Phoenicians were not the only people to invent an alphabet, theirs would have special significance because it was eventually passed on to the Greeks. From the Greek alphabet was derived the Roman alphabet that we still use today (see Table 2.1). The Phoenicians achieved much while independent, but they ultimately fell subject to the Assyrians, Chaldeans, and Persians.

2-3 The Assyrian Empire

 FOCUS QUESTION: What methods and institutions did the Assyrians use to amass and maintain their empire?

Independent states in Canaan flourished in the power void that followed the destruction of the Hittite kingdom and the weakening of the Egyptian empire. But this state of affairs did not last; new empires soon came to dominate vast stretches of the ancient Near East. The first of these empires

emerged in Assyria, an area whose location on the upper Tigris River brought it into both cultural and political contact with southern Mesopotamia.

Although part of Mesopotamia, Assyria, with its hills and adequate, if not ample, rainfall, had a different terrain and climate. The Assyrians were a Semitic-speaking people; for much of their early history, they were vassals of foreign rulers, including Sargon of Akkad, the Third Dynasty of Ur, and the Babylonian King Hammurabi (see Chapter 1). From about 1650 to 1360 B.C.E., the Hurrian kingdom of Mitanni in northern Mesopotamia dominated Assyria. The Assyrians finally became independent when the Hittites destroyed Mitanni; we read in Hittite documents from about 1360 B.C.E. of the emergence of the "king of the land of Assyria." For the next 250 years, the Assyrians experienced alternating expansion and decline until the reassertion of Assyrian power under Tiglath-Pileser (TIG-lath-py-LEE-zur) I (1114–1076 B.C.E.), a brutal conqueror whose policy of deliberate terror set a pattern for later Assyrian rulers.

The Assyrian Empire created by Tiglath-Pileser was unable to maintain its strength after his death. A new phase of expansion did not begin until the ninth century with the conquests of Shalmaneser (shal-muh-NEE-zur) III (858–824 B.C.E.), who marched westward into Canaan and southward into Babylonia. Yet Assyrian power did not go unchallenged. The almost continuous warfare on these new frontiers did not end until the reigns of Tiglath-Pileser III (744–727 B.C.E.) and Sargon II (721–705 B.C.E.), who waged military campaigns almost every year, reestablishing control over Mesopotamia and completely subduing Canaan. The conquered territories were then incorporated into the empire as provinces. These two kings were also responsible for centralizing the system of government in order to increase the power of the king. By 700 B.C.E., the Assyrian Empire had reached the height of its power and included Mesopotamia, sections of Asia Minor, Syria, Canaan, and Egypt up to Thebes (see Map 2.3).

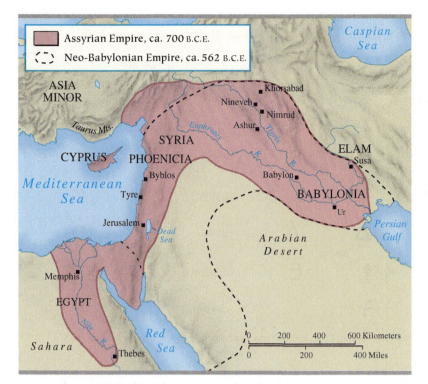

Assyrian Empire, ca. 700 B.C.E.

Neo-Babylonian Empire, ca. 562 B.C.E.

MAP 2.3 **The Assyrian and Neo-Babylonian Empires.** The Assyrian Empire expanded in large part because of its brutal military methods. It maintained its rule by using a common language and religion and by violently suppressing internal revolts. It was overthrown by the Chaldeans in Babylonia, leading to the Neo-Babylonian Empire epitomized by Nebuchadnezzar.

 Why was control of Babylonia crucial to both empires?

Ashurbanipal (ah-shur-BAH-nuh-pahl) (669–627 B.C.E.) was one of the strongest Assyrian rulers, but it was already becoming apparent during his reign that the Assyrian Empire was greatly overextended. Internal strife intensified as powerful Assyrian nobles gained control of vast territories and waged their own private military campaigns. Moreover, subject peoples greatly resented Assyrian rule. The hatred that the Babylonians felt after the brutal Assyrian sack of the city of Babylon in 689 B.C.E., for example, led them to rebel during the reign of Ashurbanipal. Soon after Ashurbanipal's death, the Assyrian Empire began to disintegrate. The capital city of Nineveh fell to a coalition of Chaldeans and Medes (see "2-4 The Neo-Babylonian Empire," later in this chapter) in 612 B.C.E., and in 605 B.C.E. the Neo-Babylonian Empire took over the rest of the empire.

2-3a Organization of the Empire

At its height, kings whose power was considered absolute ruled the Assyrian Empire. Under their leadership, the empire became well organized. By eliminating governorships held by nobles on a hereditary basis and instituting a new hierarchy of local officials directly responsible to the king, the Assyrian kings gained greater control over the resources of the empire. Personal loyalty determined the relationship between the king and his officials. Loyalty to the king was also expected of all people in Assyria. According to King Ashurbanipal, when his father King Esarhaddon appointed him as his successor, he "convened the people of Assyria, great and small, from coast to coast, made them swear a loyalty oath by the gods and established a binding agreement to protect my future kingship over Assyria."[10]

The Assyrians also developed an efficient system of communication to administer their empire more effectively. They established a network of posting stages that used relays of horses (mules or donkeys in mountainous terrain) to carry messages throughout the empire. The system was so effective that a provincial governor anywhere in the empire (except Egypt) could send a question to the king in his palace and receive an answer within a week.

2-3b The Assyrian Military Machine

The ability of the Assyrians to conquer and maintain an empire derived from a combination of factors. Through years of practice, the Assyrians developed effective military leaders and fighters. They were able to enlist and deploy troops numbering in the hundreds of thousands, although most campaigns were not on such a large scale. In 845 B.C.E., Shalmaneser III led an army of 120,000 men across the Euphrates on a campaign. Size alone was not decisive, however. The Assyrian army was extremely well organized and disciplined. It included a standing army of infantry as its core, accompanied by cavalry and horse-drawn war chariots that were used as mobile platforms for shooting arrows. Moreover, the Assyrians had the advantage of having the first large armies equipped with iron weapons. The Hittites (see Chapter 1) had been the first to develop iron metallurgy, but iron came to be used extensively only after new methods for hardening it came into common use after 1000 B.C.E.

Another factor in the Assyrian army's success was its ability to use different kinds of military tactics. The army was capable of waging guerrilla warfare in the mountains and set battles on open ground as well as laying siege to cities. The Assyrians were especially renowned for their siege warfare. They would hammer a city's walls with heavy, wheeled siege towers and armored battering rams while sappers dug tunnels to undermine the walls' foundations and cause them to collapse. The besieging Assyrian armies learned to cut off

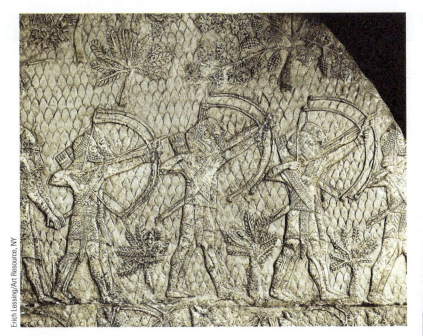

Erich Lessing/Art Resource, NY

IMAGE 2.6a

Alfredo Dagli Orti/The Art Archive at Art Resource, NY

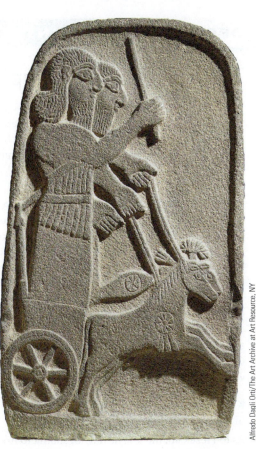

IMAGE 2.6b

IMAGE 2.6 **Assyrian Warriors.** The Assyrians had a highly efficient and well-organized military machine, capable of fighting under a variety of conditions. In Image 2.6a, a stone relief from the palace of Ashurbanipal in Nineveh depicts Assyrian archers at work during the siege of Lachish in Judah. Image 2.6b shows Assyrian warriors in a chariot from an eighth-century B.C.E. stele.

supplies so effectively that if a city did not fall to them, the inhabitants could be starved into submission.

A final factor in the effectiveness of the Assyrian military machine was its ability to create a climate of terror as an instrument of warfare, a policy that one historian has called "calculated frightfulness." The aim of the Assyrians was to encourage their enemies to surrender quickly rather than face a series of atrocities. The Assyrians became famous for their terror tactics, although some historians believe they were no worse than other Near Eastern conquerors. As a matter of regular policy, the Assyrians laid waste to the land in which they were fighting, smashing dams, looting and destroying towns, setting crops on fire, and cutting down trees, particularly fruit trees. The Assyrians were especially known for their brutality toward their captives. King Ashurnasirpal (ah-shur-NAH-zur-pahl) II recorded this account of his treatment of prisoners:

> 3,000 of their combat troops I felled with weapons. . . . Many of the captives taken from them I burned in a fire. Many I took alive; from some of these I cut off their hands to the wrist, from others I cut off their noses, ears, and fingers; I put out the eyes of many of the soldiers. . . . I burned their young men and women to death.

After conquering another city, the same king wrote: "I fixed up a pile of corpses in front of the city's gate. I flayed the nobles, as many as had rebelled, and spread their skins out on the piles. . . . I flayed many within my land and spread their skins out on the walls."[11] Note that this policy of extreme cruelty to prisoners was not used against all enemies but was reserved primarily for those who were already part of the empire and then rebelled against Assyrian rule (see Opposing Viewpoints, "The Governing of Empires: Two Approaches," p. 44).

2-3c Assyrian Society

Unlike the Hebrews, the Assyrians were not fearful of mixing with other peoples. In fact, the Assyrian policy of deporting many prisoners of newly conquered territories to Assyria created a polyglot society in which ethnic differences were not very important. It has been estimated that over a period of three centuries, between 4 and 5 million people were deported to Assyria, resulting in a population that was racially and linguistically mixed. What gave identity to the Assyrians themselves was their language, although even that was akin to that of their southern neighbors in Babylonia. Religion was also a cohesive force. Assyria was literally "the land of Ashur," a reference to its chief god. The king, as the human representative of the god Ashur, brought order to his people and served as a final unifying focus.

Assyrian society was hierarchical. There was a noticeable gap between kings, royal officials, and warriors at the top and the merchants, peasants, and slaves below them. As in other ancient Near East societies, the Assyrian family was patriarchal. The father held authority over his wife and children; women

The Governing of Empires: Two Approaches

 Both Ashurbanipal and Cyrus entered Babylon as conquerors. How did their treatment of the conquered city differ? How do you explain the differences? Which method do you think was more effective? Why?

BOTH THE ASSYRIANS AND THE PERSIANS created large empires that encompassed large areas of the ancient Near East. Although both Assyrian and Persian rulers used military force and violence to attain their empires, their approaches to conquest and ruling sometimes differed. Assyrian rulers were known for their terror tactics and atrocities, as described in the first two selections that follow. Although the kings of Persia used terror when needed, they also had a reputation for less cruelty and more tolerance. Especially noteworthy was Cyrus, as is evident in the third selection from a decree (known as the Cyrus Cylinder) that he issued in 538 B.C.E. The propagandistic value of his words is also apparent, however.

King Sennacherib (704–681 B.C.E.) Describes His Siege of Jerusalem (701 B.C.E.)

As to Hezekiah, the Jew, he did not submit to my yoke, I laid siege to 46 of his strong cities, walled forts and to the countless small villages in their vicinity, and conquered them by means of well-stamped earth-ramps, and battering-rams brought thus near to the walls combined with the attack by foot soldiers, using mines, breaches as well as sapper work. I drove out of them 200,150 people, young and old, male and female, horses, mules, donkeys, camels, big and small cattle beyond counting, and considered them booty. Himself I made a prisoner in Jerusalem, his royal residence, like a bird in a cage. I surrounded him with earthwork in order to molest those who were leaving his city's gate.

King Ashurbanipal (669–627 B.C.E.) Describes His Treatment of Conquered Babylon

I tore out the tongues of those whose slanderous mouths had uttered blasphemies against my god Ashur and had

plotted against me, his god-fearing prince; I defeated them completely. The others, I smashed alive with the very same statues of protective deities with which they had smashed my own grandfather Sennacherib—now finally as a belated burial sacrifice for his soul. I fed their corpses, cut into small pieces, to dogs, pigs, . . . vultures, the birds of the sky and also to the fish of the ocean. After I . . . thus made quiet again the hearts of the great gods, my lords, I removed the corpses of those whom the pestilence had felled, whose leftovers after the dogs and pigs had fed on them were obstructing the streets, filling the places of Babylon, and of those who had lost their lives through the terrible famine.

The Cyrus Cylinder

I am Cyrus, king of the world, great king, legitimate king, king of Babylon, king of Sumer and Akkad, king of the four corners of the earth. . . .

When I entered Babylon as a friend and when I established the seat of the government in the palace of the ruler under jubilation and rejoicing, Marduk, the great lord [the chief Babylonian god], caused the magnanimous inhabitants of Babylon to love me, and I was daily endeavoring to worship him. My numerous troops walked around in Babylon in peace. I did not allow anybody to terrorize any place of the country of Sumer and Akkad. I strove for peace in Babylon and in all his other sacred cities. As to the inhabitants of Babylon . . . I brought relief to their dilapidated housing, putting thus an end to their main complaints. . . .

As to the region from as far as Ashur and Susa . . . I returned to these sacred cities on the other side of the Tigris, the sanctuaries of which have been ruins for a long time, the images which used to live therein and established for them permanent sanctuaries. I also gathered all their former inhabitants and returned to them their dwellings.

Source: All selections from J. Pritchard, ed., *Ancient Near Eastern Texts Related to the Old Testament*, 3rd revised edition with supplement (Princeton, N.J.: Princeton University Press, 1969). Reprinted by permission of Princeton University Press.

were expected to take care of the household and bear children. Although women were not equal to men, legal documents indicate that some Assyrian women could purchase and sell property, take part in business for themselves, and assist their husbands in legal matters. There were also enormous differences between high- and low-class women. The former included the wives and daughters of rulers and royal officials;

the latter included lower-class wives and slaves who worked in households and temples Their lives were regulated by harsh laws (see Historical Voices, "The Code of the Assura," p. 45).

Agriculture formed the principal basis of Assyrian life. Assyria was a land of farming villages with relatively few significant cities, especially in comparison with southern Mesopotamia. Unlike the river valleys, where farming required

The Code of the Assura

 Compare these excerpts from the Code of the Assura with the Code of Hammurabi and The Advice of Shuruppag in Chapter 1. How are they similar? How are they different? What do the differences reveal about Assyrian society?

ASSYRIAN LAW was similar to Sumerian and Babylonian law, but it could be considerably harsher, especially in regard to women. The excerpts that follow are taken from one compilation of Assyrian laws known as the Code of the Assura, which is dated around 1075 B.C.E.

The Code of the Assura

1.7. If a woman bring her hand against a man, they shall prosecute her; 30 manas of lead shall she pay, 20 blows shall they inflict on her.

1.8. If a woman in a quarrel injure the testicle of a man, one of her fingers they shall cut off. And if a physician bind it up and the other testicle which is beside it be infected thereby, or take harm; or in a quarrel she injure the other testicle, they shall destroy both of her eyes.

1.9. If a man bring his hand against the wife of a man, treating her like a little child, and they prove it against him, and convict him, one of his fingers they shall cut off. If he kiss her, his lower lip with the blade of an axe they shall draw down and they shall cut off.

1.13. If the wife of a man go out from her house and visit a man where he lives, and he have intercourse with her, knowing that she is a man's wife, the man and also the woman they shall put to death.

1.15. If a man catch a man with his wife, both of them shall they put to death. If the husband of the woman put his wife to death, he shall also put the man to death. If he cut off the nose of his wife, he shall turn the man into a eunuch, and they shall disfigure the whole of his face.

1.16. If a man have relations with the wife of a man at her wish, there is no penalty for that man. The man shall lay upon the woman, his wife, the penalty he wishes.

1.40. If the wives of a man, or the daughters of a man go out into the street, their heads are to be veiled. The prostitute is not to be veiled. Maidservants are not to veil themselves. Veiled harlots and maidservants shall have their garments seized and 50 blows inflicted on them and bitumen poured on their heads.

1.50. If a man strike the wife of a man, in her first stage of pregnancy, and cause her to drop that which is in her, it is a crime; two talents of lead he shall pay.

1.52. If a woman of her own accord drop that which is in her, they shall prosecute her, they shall convict her, they shall crucify her, they shall not bury her. . . .

1.57. In the case of every crime for which there is the penalty of the cutting-off of ear or nose or ruining or reputation or condition, as it is written it shall be carried out.

1.58. Unless it is forbidden in the tablets, a man may strike his wife, pull her hair, her ear he may bruise or pierce. He commits no misdeed thereby.

Source: Internet Ancient History Sourcebook.

---

the minute organization of large numbers of people to control irrigation, Assyrian farms received sufficient moisture from regular rainfall.

Trade was second to agriculture in economic importance. For internal trade, metals such as gold, silver, copper, and bronze were used as a medium of exchange. Various agricultural products also served as a form of payment or exchange. Because of their geographic location, the Assyrians served as intermediaries and participated in international trade, importing timber, wine, and precious metals and stones while exporting textiles produced in palaces, temples, and private villas.

2-3d Assyrian Culture

The culture of the Assyrian Empire was a hybrid. The Assyrians assimilated much of Mesopotamian civilization and saw themselves as guardians of Sumerian and Babylonian culture. Ashurbanipal, for example, amassed a large library at Nineveh that included the available works of Mesopotamian history. Assyrian religion also reflected this assimilation of other cultures. Although the Assyrians considered their own national god, Ashur, their chief deity, they recognized virtually all of the Mesopotamian gods and goddesses as well.

Among the best-known objects of Assyrian art are the relief sculptures found in the royal palaces in three of the Assyrian capital cities: Nimrud, Nineveh, and Khorsabad. These reliefs, which were begun in the ninth century and reached their apex in the reign of Ashurbanipal in the seventh century, depicted two different kinds of subject matter: ritual or ceremonial scenes revolving around the person of the king and scenes of hunting and war (see Image 2.7). The latter show realistic action scenes of the king and his warriors engaged in battle or hunting animals, especially lions. These reliefs depict a strongly masculine world in which discipline, brute force, and toughness are the enduring values—indeed the very values—of the Assyrian military monarchy.

IMAGE 2.7 **An Assyrian Lion Hunt.** This stone panel was on a wall of the palace of King Ashurbanipal in Nineveh. It was part of a much larger work connected to the royal sport of hunting. Lion hunts were not conducted in the wild but were held under controlled circumstances. The king and his retainers faced lions released from cages in an arena. The purpose of the scene was to glorify the king as a conqueror of the king of beasts. Shown here are the hunt attendants with large dogs whose purpose was to guard the edge of the arena in which the king killed the lions.

Scene of Ashurbanipal hunting. Relief from Royal Palaces of Nineveh, circa 645 B.C./DE AGOSTINI EDITORE/Bridgeman Images

2-4 The Neo-Babylonian Empire

Q **FOCUS QUESTION:** What was the significance of the Neo-Babylonian Empire?

The Chaldeans, a Semitic-speaking people, had gained ascendancy in Babylonia by the seventh century, came to form the chief resistance to Assyrian control of Mesopotamia, and established a new Babylonian monarchy. King Nebuchadnezzar II (605–562 B.C.E.) achieved the final defeat of the Assyrian Empire. Under his rule, the Chaldeans defeated Egypt to gain control of Syria and Canaan, destroyed Jerusalem, carried the people of Judah into exile in Babylon, and in the process regained for Babylonia a position as the leading power in the ancient Near East (see Map 2.3).

During Nebuchadnezzar's reign, Babylonia was renowned for a prosperity based on lush agricultural lands, lucrative trade routes, and industries, especially textiles and metals. Nebuchadnezzar rebuilt Babylon as the center of his empire, giving it a reputation as one of the great cities of the ancient world. Babylon was surrounded by towering walls, 8 miles in length, encircled by a moat filled by the Euphrates River. The Ishtar Gate (see Image 2.8) opened onto the Triumphal Way, which led to the sacred precincts of Marduk, the chief Babylonian god. Babylon was adorned with temples and palaces; most famous of all were the Hanging Gardens, renowned as one of the Seven Wonders of the Ancient World. The gardens were supposedly built to satisfy Nebuchadnezzar's wife, a princess from the land of Media, who missed the mountains of her homeland. A series of terraces led to a plateau, an artificial mountain, at the top of which grew the lush gardens irrigated by water piped to the top. According to the account of

IMAGE 2.8 **Ishtar Gate of Babylon.** Nebuchadnezzar rebuilt Babylon as the center of his empire and adorned it with such architectural wonders as the Ishtar Gate, which was built of blue glazed bricks and opened onto the Triumphal Way. The bricks were made separately and then assembled on the gate walls. Figures of the dragon of Marduk (patron god of the city of Babylon, whose sacred animal was the dragon) and the bull of Adad (god of storms, whose sacred animal was the bull) alternate on the surfaces of the gate. Ishtar was the Babylonian goddess of war and sexual love. This picture shows the Ishtar Gate as it was rebuilt in the Pergamum Museum in Berlin.

bpk, Berlin/(name of museum) /(name of photographer)/Art Resource, NY

The Customs of the Persians

 According to Herodotus, what were the most important customs of the Persians? To what extent do you think this is a realistic account? What bias might Herodotus have had?

IN HIS HISTORY OF THE PERSIAN WARS, written in the fifth century B.C.E., the ancient Greek historian Herodotus, who is often regarded as the father of history (see Chapter 3), gave a detailed account of the customs of the Persians. Herodotus traveled widely in search of his information and obtained it from a variety of sources, especially the stories of local inhabitants. Although the Greek-speaking world was the center of his perceptions, he could be remarkably open-minded about other cultures.

Herodotus, *The Persian Wars*

The customs which I know the Persians to observe are the following. . . . Of all the days in the year, the one which they celebrate most is their birthday. It is customary to have the table furnished on that day with an ampler supply than common. The richer Persians cause an ox, a horse, a camel, and an ass to be baked whole and so served up to them; the poorer classes use the smaller kinds of cattle. They eat little solid food but abundance of dessert, which is set on table a few dishes at a time. It is this custom which makes them say that "the Greeks, when they eat, leave off hungry, having nothing worth mention served up to them after the meats; whereas, if they had more put before them, they would not stop eating."

The Persians are very fond of wine. It is their practice to deliberate upon affairs of weight when they are drunk. . . .

When they meet each other in the streets, you may know that the persons meeting are of equal rank . . . if, instead of speaking, they kiss each other on the lips. In the case where one is a little inferior to the other, the kiss is given on the cheek. Where the difference of rank is great, the inferior prostrates himself upon the ground. . . .

There is no nation which so readily adopts foreign customs as the Persians. Thus, they have taken the dress of the Medes, considering it superior to their own; and in war they wear the Egyptian breastplate. As soon as they hear of any luxury, they instantly make it their own. . . .

Next to bravery in battle, it is regarded as the greatest proof of manly excellence, to be the father of many sons. Every year the king sends rich gifts to the man who can show the largest number; for they hold that number is strength. Their sons are carefully instructed from the fifth to their twentieth year, in three things alone: to ride, to draw the bow, and to speak the truth. Until their fifth year they are not allowed to come into the sight of their father, but pass their lives with the women. This is done that, if the child dies young, the father may not be afflicted by its loss.

Source: Hutton Webster, editor, *Readings in Ancient History* (New York: D.C. Heath & Co., 1913), pp. 9–11.

---

a first-century C.E. author, from a distance the gardens made a remarkable impression:

> On the top of the citadel are the hanging gardens, a wonder celebrated in the tales of the Greeks. . . . Columns of stone were set up to sustain the whole work, and on these was laid a floor of squared blocks, strong enough to hold the earth which is thrown upon it to a great depth, as well as the water with which they irrigate the soil; and the structure supports trees of such great size that the thickness of their trunks equals a measure of eight cubits [about 12 feet]. They tower to a height of fifty feet, and they yield as much fruit as if they were growing in their native soil. . . . To those who look upon the trees from a distance, real woods seem to be overhanging their native mountains.[12]

The splendor of the Neo-Babylonian Empire proved to be short-lived. Nabonidus (nab-uh-NY-duss) (555–539 B.C.E.) was the last king of the Chaldean dynasty. He had a great interest in history and encouraged scholars to collect Sumerian texts and study the Sumerian language. But his policies aroused considerable internal dissent, and when Babylon fell to the Persian conqueror Cyrus in 539 B.C.E., the Babylonians welcomed him as a liberator.

2-5 The Persian Empire

 FOCUS QUESTIONS: What methods and institutions did the Persians use to amass and maintain their empire? How did these methods and institutions differ from those of the Assyrians?

The Persians were an Indo-European-speaking people related to the Medes. Both peoples probably formed part of the great waves of Indo-European migrations into the Mediterranean, the Near East, and India. The Persians lived to the southeast of the Medes, who occupied the western Iranian plateau south of the Caspian Sea. Primarily nomadic, both Medes and Persians were organized in clans. Both peoples were led by petty kings assisted by a group of warriors who formed a class of nobles. Their populations also included both free and unfree people who worked the land, craftspeople, and slaves (see Historical Voices, "The Customs of the Persians," above).

By 735 B.C.E., the Medes had begun to form a confederation of the various tribes, and around the beginning of the

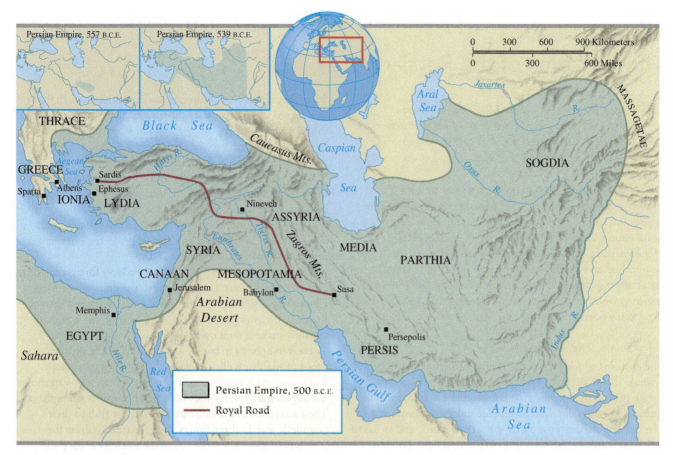

Persian Empire, 500 B.C.E.
—— Royal Road

MAP 2.4 **The Persian Empire at the Time of Darius.** Cyrus the Great united the Persians and led them in the successful conquest of much of the Near East. By the time of Darius, the Persian Empire was the largest the world had yet seen. The Persians allowed a high degree of religious toleration and gave some government positions to natives of conquered territories.

 How did Persian policies attempt to overcome the difficulties of governing far-flung provinces?

seventh century they became unified under a monarchy. The Persians did likewise under the Achaemenid (ah-KEE-muh-nud) dynasty established in Persis in southern Iran. About fifty years later, the Persians were made subject to the Medes. The Medes now constituted a powerful state and joined the Babylonians in attacking the Assyrians. After the capture of Nineveh in 612 B.C.E., King Cyaxares (si-AK-suh-reez) established a Median empire, the first Iranian empire known to the ancient Near East.

2-5a Cyrus the Great

In 559 B.C.E., Cyrus became the leader of the Persians, united them under his rule, and went on the offensive against the Medes. By 550 B.C.E., he had established Persian control over Media, making it the first Persian **satrapy** (SAY-truh-pee), or province. Three years later, Cyrus defeated the prosperous Lydian kingdom in western Asia Minor, and Lydia became another Persian satrapy (see Map 2.4). Cyrus's forces then went on to conquer the Greek city-states that had been established on the Ionian coast of western Asia Minor. Cyrus then turned eastward, subduing the eastern part of the Iranian plateau,

Sogdia, and even western India. His eastern frontiers secured, Cyrus entered Mesopotamia in 539 and captured Babylon (see Historical Voices, "The Fall of Babylon," p. 49). His treatment of Babylonia showed remarkable restraint and wisdom. Babylonia was made into a Persian province under a Persian **satrap** (SAY-trap), or governor, but many government officials were kept in their positions. Cyrus took the title "King of All, Great King, Mighty King, King of Babylon, King of the Land of Sumer and Akkad, King of the Four Rims (of the Earth), the Son of Cambyses the Great King, King of An-shan"[13] and insisted that he stood in the ancient, unbroken line of Babylonian kings. By appealing to the vanity of the Babylonians, he won their loyalty. Cyrus also issued an edict permitting the Jews, who had been brought to Babylon in the sixth century B.C.E., to return to Jerusalem with their sacred temple objects and to rebuild the temple there as well.

From 538 to 530 B.C.E., Cyrus consolidated his empire. Among other things, he constructed forts, especially in the northeast, to protect against nomadic incursions. It was there that he undertook his last campaign. In 530 B.C.E., he marched from Sogdia into the territory of the Massagetae, where he was killed in battle.

The Fall of Babylon

 Do you think this is a realistic account of the fall of Babylon? What image do you have of Cyrus from this account?

Herodotus, *The Persian Wars*

Cyrus, at the beginning of the following spring, resumed his march to Babylon. The Babylonians had taken the field and were awaiting his approach. When he arrived near the city they attacked him, but were defeated and forced to retire inside their defenses; they already knew of Cyrus' restless ambition and had watched his successive acts of aggression against one nation after another, and as they had taken the precaution of accumulating in Babylon a stock of provisions sufficient to last many years, they were able to regard the prospect of a siege with indifference. The siege dragged on, no progress was made, and Cyrus was beginning to despair of success. Then somebody suggested or he himself thought up the following plan: he stationed part of his force at the point where the Euphrates flows into the city and another contingent at the opposite end where it flows out, with orders to both to force an entrance along the riverbed as

soon as they saw that the water was shallow enough. Then, taking with him all his non-combatant troops, he withdrew to the spot where Nitocris had excavated the lake, and proceeded to repeat the operation which the queen had previously performed; by means of a cutting he diverted the river into the lake (which was then a marsh) and in this way so greatly reduced the depth of water in the actual bed of the river that it became fordable, and the Persian army, which had been left at Babylon for the purpose, entered the river, now only deep enough to reach about the middle of a man's thigh, and, making their way along it, got into the town. If the Babylonians had learned what Cyrus was doing or had seen it for themselves in time, they could have let the Persians enter and then, by shutting all the gates which led to the waterside and manning the walls on either side of the river, they could have caught them in a trap and wiped them out. But as it was they were taken by surprise. The Babylonians themselves say that owing to the great size of the city the outskirts were captured without the people in the center knowing anything about it; there was a festival going on, and they continued to dance and enjoy themselves, until they learned the news the hard way. That, then, is the story of the first capture of Babylon.

Source: Herodotus, *The Histories*, trans. Aubrey de Sélincourt (New York: Penguin Books, 2003, pp. 83–84).

To his contemporaries, Cyrus the Great was deserving of his epithet. The Greek historian Herodotus recounted that the Persians viewed him as a "father," a ruler who was "gentle, and procured them all manner of goods."[14] Cyrus must have been an unusual ruler for his time, a man who demonstrated considerable wisdom and compassion in the conquest and organization of his empire (see Opposing Viewpoints, "The Governing of Empires," p. 44). Cyrus obtained the favor of the priesthoods in his conquered lands by restoring temples and permitting religious toleration. He won approval by using not only Persians but also native peoples as government officials in their own states. He allowed Medes to be military commanders. Unlike the Assyrian rulers of an earlier empire, he had a reputation for mercy. Medes, Babylonians, and Jews all accepted him as their legitimate ruler. Some peoples portrayed him as a great leader and peacemaker. Indeed, a Hebrew prophet regarded him as the anointed one of God: "I am the Lord who says of Cyrus, 'He is my shepherd and will accomplish all that I please'; he will say of Jerusalem, 'Let it be rebuilt'; and of the temple, 'Let its foundations be laid.' This is what the Lord says to his anointed, to Cyrus, whose right hand I take hold of to subdue nations before him."[15] Cyrus had a genuine respect for ancient civilizations—in building his palaces, he made use of Assyrian, Babylonian, Egyptian, and

Lydian practices. Indeed, Cyrus believed that he was creating a world empire that included peoples who had ancient and venerable traditions and institutions.

2-5b Expanding the Empire

Upon Cyrus's death in 530 B.C.E., his son Cambyses (kam-BY-seez) II assumed power as the Great King. Four years later, Cambyses undertook the invasion of Egypt, the only kingdom in the Near East not yet brought under Persian control. Aided by the Phoenician fleet, he defeated and captured the pharaoh and the Egyptian forces. Egypt was made into a satrapy with Memphis as its capital. In the summer of 525 B.C.E., Cambyses took the title of pharaoh.

After the death of Cambyses in 522, Darius (duh-RY-uss) emerged as Great King after a year of intense civil war. Once in charge, Darius (521–486 B.C.E.) turned to the task of strengthening the empire (see Image 2.9). He codified Egyptian law and built a canal to link the Red Sea and the Mediterranean. A campaign into western India led to the creation of a new Persian province that extended to the Indus River. Darius also moved into Europe proper, conquering Thrace and making the Macedonian king a vassal. In 499 B.C.E., the Ionian Greek cities in western Asia Minor rose in revolt and temporarily obtained

DEA/W. BUSS/De Agostini/Getty Images

IMAGE 2.9 **Darius, the Great King.** Darius ruled the Persian Empire from 521 to 486 B.C.E. He is shown here on his throne in Persepolis, a new capital city that he built. In his right hand, Darius holds the royal staff. In his left hand, he grasps a lotus blossom with two buds, a symbol of royalty.

Q *What are the similarities and differences between this image of Darius and the image of an Egyptian pharaoh in Chapter 1?*

their freedom. With aid from the Greek mainland, most notably from Athens, the Ionians then invaded Lydia and burned Sardis, center of the Lydian satrapy. This event led to Darius's involvement with the mainland Greeks. After reestablishing control of the Ionian Greek cities, Darius undertook an invasion of the Greek mainland, which culminated in the Athenian victory in the Battle of Marathon in 490 B.C.E. (see Chapter 3).

2-5c Governing the Empire

With the reign of Darius the Persians had created the largest empire the world had yet seen. It not only included all the old centers of power in the Near East, Egypt, Mesopotamia, and Assyria but also extended into Thrace and Asia Minor in the west and into India in the east.

For administrative purposes, the empire had been divided into approximately twenty satrapies. Each satrapy was ruled by a provincial governor or satrap, literally a "protector of the

kingdom." Although Darius had not introduced the system of satrapies, he did see that it was organized more rationally. He created a sensible system for calculating the tribute that each satrapy owed to the central government and gave the satraps specific civil and military duties. They collected tributes, were responsible for justice and security, raised military levies, and normally commanded the military forces within their satrapies. In terms of real power, the satraps were miniature kings who established courts that imitated the Great King's.

From the time of Darius on, satraps were men of Persian descent. The major satrapies were given to princes of the king's family, and their positions became essentially hereditary. The minor satrapies were placed in the hands of Persian nobles. Their offices also tended to pass from father to son. The hereditary nature of the governors' offices made it necessary to provide some checks on their power. Consequently, some historians think that there were officials at the satrapal courts, such as secretaries and generals in charge of the garrison, who reported directly to the Great King, keeping him informed of what was going on within the various satrapal governments. It is also possible that an official known as the "king's eye" or "king's messenger" annually inspected each satrapy.

An efficient system of communication was crucial to sustaining the Persian Empire. Well-maintained roads facilitated the rapid transit of military and government personnel. One in particular, known as the Royal Road, stretched from Sardis, the center of Lydia in Asia Minor, to Susa, the chief capital of the Persian Empire (see Map 2.4). Like the Assyrians, the Persians established staging posts equipped with fresh horses for the king's messengers.

CHRONOLOGY	The Empires	
The Assyrians		
Tiglath-Pileser I		1114–1076 B.C.E.
Shalmaneser III		858–824 B.C.E.
Tiglath-Pileser III		744–727 B.C.E.
Sargon II		721–705 B.C.E.
Ashurbanipal		669–627 B.C.E.
Fall of Nineveh		612 B.C.E.
Assyrian Empire destroyed		605 B.C.E.
The Chaldeans		
Ascendancy in Babylonia		600s B.C.E.
Height of empire under King Nebuchadnezzar II		605–562 B.C.E.
Fall of Babylon		539 B.C.E.
The Persians		
Unification of Persians		600s B.C.E.
Conquests of Cyrus the Great		559–530 B.C.E.
Cambyses II and conquest of Egypt		530–522 B.C.E.
Reign of Darius		521–486 B.C.E.

2-5d The Great King

In this vast administrative system, the Persian king occupied an exalted position. Although not considered a god like the Egyptian pharaoh, he was nevertheless the elected one or regent of the Persian god Ahuramazda (see "2-5e Persian Religion," below). All subjects were the king's servants, and he was the source of all justice, possessing the power of life and death over everyone. Persian kings resided largely in seclusion in a series of splendid palaces and were not easily accessible. Darius in particular was a palace builder on a grand scale. In the construction of a palace in the chief Persian capital of Susa, he used workers and materials from throughout the Persian Empire. But Darius was unhappy with Susa. He did not really consider it his homeland, and it was oppressively hot in the summer months. He built another residence at Persepolis, a new capital located to the east of the old one and at a higher elevation.

The policies of Darius also tended to widen the gap between the king and his subjects. As the Great King himself said of all his subjects, "What was said to them by me, night and day it was done."[16] Over a period of time, the Great Kings in their greed came to hoard immense quantities of gold and silver in the various treasuries located in the capital cities. Both their hoarding of wealth and their later overtaxation of their subjects are seen as crucial factors in the ultimate weakening of the Persian Empire.

In its heyday, however, the empire stood supreme, and much of its power depended on the military. By the time of Darius, the Persian monarchs had created a standing army of professional soldiers. This army was truly international, composed of contingents from the various peoples who made up the empire. At its core was a cavalry force of 10,000 and an elite infantry force of 10,000 Medes and Persians known as the Immortals, so called because their number was never allowed to drop below 10,000; anyone killed would be replaced immediately (see Image 2.10). The Persians made effective use of their cavalry, especially for operating behind enemy lines and breaking up lines of communication. The Persian navy consisted of ships from subject states, including the Phoenicians, Egyptians, Anatolians, and Ionian Greeks.

2-5e Persian Religion

Of all the Persians' cultural contributions, the most original was their religion, **Zoroastrianism**. Zoroaster (ZOR-oh-ass-tur), or Zarathustra, was a semilegendary figure who, according to Persian tradition, was born in 660 B.C.E. After a period of wandering and solitude, he experienced revelations that caused him to be revered as a prophet of the "true religion." It is difficult to know what Zoroaster's original teachings were because the sacred book of Zoroastrianism, the Zend Avesta, was not written down until the third century C.E. Scholars believe, however, that the earliest section of the Zend Avesta, known as the Yasna, consisting of seventeen hymns (gathas), contains the actual writings of Zoroaster. This enables us to piece together his message.

Like the Hebrews, Zoroaster taught a spiritual message of monotheism. To Zoroaster, the religion he preached was the

IMAGE 2.10 **Archers of the Persian Guard.** One of the main pillars supporting the Persian Empire was the military. This frieze, composed of enameled brick, depicts members of the famous infantry force known as the Immortals, They carry the standard lance and bow and arrow of the infantry.

only perfect one, and Ahuramazda (uh-HOOR-uh-MAHZ-duh) was the only God. Ahuramazda (the "Wise Lord") was the supreme deity who brought all things into being:

This I ask [You], O Ahura! tell me aright: Who by generation was the first father of the Righteous Order (within the world)? Who gave the (recurring) sun and stars their (undeviating) way? Who established that whereby the moon waxes, and whereby she wanes, save [You]? . . .

This I ask [You], O Ahura! tell me aright, who from beneath ha[s] sustained the earth and the clouds above that they do not fall? Who made the waters and the plants? Who to the wind has yoked on the storm-clouds, the swift and fleetest two? . . .

This I ask [You], O Ahura! tell me aright; who fashioned Âramaiti (our piety) the beloved, together with [Your] Sovereign Power? Who, through his guiding wisdom, has made the son revering the father? (Who made him beloved?) With (questions such as) these, so abundant, O Mazda! I press [You], O bountiful Spirit, [You] maker of all![17]

According to Zoroaster, Ahuramazda also possessed abstract qualities or states that all humans should aspire to, such as good thought, right, and piety. Although Ahuramazda was supreme,

Rmn-Grand Palais/Art Resource, NY

he was not unopposed. Right is opposed by the lie, truth by falsehood, life by death. At the beginning of the world, the good spirit of Ahuramazda was opposed by the evil spirit (in later Zoroastrianism identified with Ahriman).

Humans also played a role in this cosmic struggle between good and evil. Ahuramazda, the creator, gave all humans free will and the power to choose between right and wrong. The good person chooses the right way of Ahuramazda. Zoroaster taught that there would be an end to the struggle between good and evil. Ahuramazda would eventually triumph, and at the last judgment at the end of the world, the final separation of good and evil would occur. Individuals, too, would be judged. Each soul faced a final evaluation of its actions. The soul of a person who had performed good deeds would achieve paradise; but if the deeds had been evil, the person would be thrown into an abyss of torment. Some historians believe that Zoroastrianism, with its emphasis on good and evil, heaven and hell, and a last judgment, had an impact on Christianity, a religion that eventually surpassed it in significance.

The spread of Zoroastrianism was due to its acceptance by the Great Kings of Persia. The inscriptions of Darius make clear that he believed Ahuramazda was the only God. Although Darius himself may have been a monotheist, dramatic changes in Zoroastrianism occurred over time. Before Zoroaster, Persian religion had focused on the worship of forces of nature, such as the sun, moon, fire, and wind, with the aid of priests known as Magi. As the kings and Magi propagated Zoroaster's teachings on Ahuramazda, Zoroastrianism lost its monotheistic emphasis, and the old nature worship resurfaced. Soon Persian religion had returned to polytheism, with Ahuramazda the chief of a number of gods of light. Mithra, the sun god, became a helper of Ahuramazda and later, in Roman times, the source of another religion. Persian kings were also very tolerant of other religions, and gods and goddesses of those religions tended to make their way into the Persian pantheon. Moreover, as frequently happens to the ideas of founders of religions, Zoroaster's teachings acquired concrete forms that he had never originally intended. The struggle between good and evil was taken beyond the abstractions of Zoroaster into a strong ethical dualism. The spirit of evil became an actual being who had to be warded off by the use of spells and incantations.

CHAPTER SUMMARY

By 1500 B.C.E., much of the creative impulse of the Mesopotamian and Egyptian civilizations was beginning to wane. And by 1200 B.C.E., the decline of the Hittites and Egyptians had created a power vacuum that allowed a patchwork of petty kingdoms and city-states to emerge, especially in the area of Syria and Canaan. One was that of the Phoenicians, who created a trading empire in the Mediterranean as well as an alphabet that was later adapted by the Greeks and Romans.

Of these small states, however, perhaps the most important was that of the Israelites, who created a kingdom under Saul, David, and Solomon. By the tenth century B.C.E., the inhabitants of Israel had divided into a northern kingdom of Israel and a southern kingdom of Judah, but the rise of larger states in the region eventually led to their demise. Israel fell to the Assyrians at the end of the eighth century B.C.E. and Judah to the Chaldeans in the sixth century. Nevertheless, although the Israelites did not create an empire and were dominated by

the Assyrians, Chaldeans, and eventually the Persians, they left a spiritual legacy that influenced much of the later development of Western civilization. The evolution of Hebrew monotheism created in Judaism one of the world's great religions; it influenced the development of both Christianity and Islam. When we speak of the Judeo-Christian heritage of Western civilization, we refer not only to the concept of monotheism but also to ideas of law, morality, and social justice that have become important parts of Western culture.

All of these small states were eventually overshadowed by the rise of the great empires of the Assyrians, Chaldeans, and Persians. The Assyrian Empire, built upon the effective use of military force, was the first to unite almost all of the ancient Near East. Nevertheless, after reaching the height of its power by 700 B.C.E., it gradually succumbed to internal dissension and was overrun by the armies of the Medes and Chaldeans near the end of the seventh century B.C.E. The latter created a Neo-Babylonian Empire, which in turn was short-lived and soon conquered by the Persians. Although the Persian Empire owed much to the administrative organization developed by the Assyrians, the Persian Empire had its own peculiar strengths. Persian rule was tolerant

as well as efficient. Conquered peoples were allowed to keep their own religions, customs, and methods of doing business. The two centuries of relative peace that the Persian Empire brought to the Near East facilitated trade and the general well-being of its peoples. Many Near Eastern peoples, including the Israelites, expressed gratitude for being subjects of the Great Kings of Persia.

CHAPTER TIMELINE

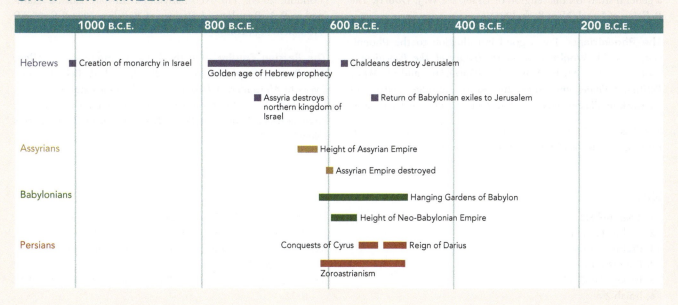

	1000 B.C.E.	800 B.C.E.	600 B.C.E.	400 B.C.E.	200 B.C.E.

Hebrews
- Creation of monarchy in Israel
- Golden age of Hebrew prophecy
- Assyria destroys northern kingdom of Israel
- Chaldeans destroy Jerusalem
- Return of Babylonian exiles to Jerusalem

Assyrians
- Height of Assyrian Empire
- Assyrian Empire destroyed

Babylonians
- Hanging Gardens of Babylon
- Height of Neo-Babylonian Empire

Persians
- Conquests of Cyrus
- Reign of Darius
- Zoroastrianism

CHAPTER REVIEW

Upon Reflection

Q What is the relationship between the political history of the Israelites and the evolution of their religious beliefs?

Q How did the Israelites establish a united state, and what became of it?

Q Compare and contrast the administrative and military structure and attitudes toward subject peoples of the Assyrian and Persian Empires.

Q If the large empires of the Assyrians, Chaldeans, and Persians dominated the entire Near East for centuries, why did the small state of the Israelites have a greater impact on Western civilization?

Key Terms

monotheism (p. 36)
Pentateuch (p. 36)
Torah (p. 36)
Diaspora (p. 38)

patriarchal (p. 39)
satrapy (p. 48)
satrap (p. 48)
Zoroastrianism (p. 51)

Full definitions also appear in the Glossary at the end of the book.

Suggestions for Further Reading

General Surveys For excellent general surveys of the material covered in this chapter, see **A. Kuhrt,** *The Ancient Near East, c. 3000–330 B.C.*, vol. 2 (London, 1995), and **M. van de Mieroop,** *A History of the Ancient Near East, ca. 3000–323 B.C.*, 3rd ed. (Oxford, 2016).

Ancient Israel There is an abundance of literature on ancient Israel. For important revisionist views on the archaeological aspects, see **I. Finkelstein** and **N. Silberman,** *The Bible Unearthed: Archaeology's New Vision of Ancient Israel* (New York, 2002), and **M. Liverani,** *Israel's History and the History of Israel* (London, 2007). For a historical narrative, see **H. Shanks,**

Ancient Israel: A Short History from Abraham to the Roman Destruction of the Temple, 3rd ed. (Englewood Cliffs, N.J., 2010). On the origins of the Israelites, see **W. G. Dever,** *Who Were the Early Israelites and Where Did They Come From?* (Grand Rapids, Mich., 2003). On early Israelite kings, see **I. Finkelstein** and **N. Silberman,** *David and Solomon: In Search of the Bible's Sacred Kings and the Roots of the Western Tradition* (New York, 2006). On the controversies surrounding the history of the Israelites, see **J. M. Golden,** *Ancient Canaan and Israel* (Oxford, 2004). **P. J. King** and **L. E. Stager,** *Life in Biblical Israel* (New York, 2002), is useful in regard to the social institutions of ancient Israel. On women in ancient Israel, see **C. Meyers,** *Discovering*

Eve: Ancient Israelite Women in Context (New York, 1988). For a general study on the religion of Israel, see **W. J. Doorly, *The Religion of Israel*** (New York, 1997).

The Phoenicians   For a good introduction to the Phoenicians, see M. Woolmer, *A Short History of the Phoenicians* (London, 2017); **M. E. Aubet, *The Phoenicians and the West: Politics, Colonies and Trade***, 2nd ed. (Cambridge, 2001); and **G. Markoe, *Phoenicians*** (London, 2000), on Phoenician society.

The Assyrian Empire   For a brief introduction to the Assyrian Empire, see **K. Radner, *Ancient Assyria*** (Oxford, 2015). On

Assyrian culture, see **P. Collins, *Assyrian Palace Sculpture*** (London, 2008). The Neo-Babylonian Empire can be examined in **P-A. Beaulieu, *A History of Babylon, 2000 B.C.-75 AD*** (Hoboken, N.J., 2018).

The Persian Empire   On the Persian Empire see **L. Allen, *The Persian Empire*** (Chicago, 2005), and **P. Briant, *From Cyrus to Alexander: A History of the Persian Empire*** (Winona Lake, Ind., 2006). On the history of Zoroastrianism, see **S. A. Nigosian, *The Zoroastrian Faith: Tradition and Modern Research*** (New York, 1993).

Notes

1. 2 Samuel 8:2.
2. Psalms 137:1, 4–6.
3. Psalms 145:8–9.
4. Psalms 121:2–3.
5. Exodus 20:13–15.
6. Isaiah 2:4.
7. Proverbs 31:10–20, 24–28.
8. Judges 5:24–27.
9. Quoted in R. de Vaux, *Ancient Israel: Its Life and Institutions* (New York, 1961), p. 49.
10. Quoted in M. van de Mieroop, *A History of the Ancient Near East* (Oxford, 2004), p. 242.
11. Quoted in H. W. F. Saggs, *The Might That Was Assyria* (London, 1984), pp. 261–262.
12. John C. Rolfe, trans., *Quintus Curtius I* (Cambridge, Mass., 1971), pp. 337–339.
13. Quoted in J. M. Cook, *The Persian Empire* (New York, 1983), p. 32.
14. Herodotus, *The Persian Wars*, trans. George Rawlinson (New York, 1942), p. 257.
15. Isaiah 44:28, 45:1.
16. Quoted in Cook, *The Persian Empire*, p. 76.
17. Yasna 44:3–4, 7, from The Zend Avesta, Part III, trans. L. H. Mills, *Sacred Books of the East*, vol. 31 (Oxford University Press, 1887), pp. 113–115.

MindTap *Tips*   Every chapter in MindTap begins with an Image Analysis Primary Source Activity. They're an easy way to learn more about a primary source image from the chapter, to practice visual literacy, and build primary source analysis skills that you can apply in bigger writing assignments.

CHAPTER 3

The Civilization of the Greeks

IMAGE 3.1 **A Bust of Pericles**

CHAPTER OUTLINE AND FOCUS QUESTIONS

3-1 Early Greece

Q How did geography affect Greek political, military, and economic developments?

3-2 The Greeks in a Dark Age (ca. 1100–750 B.C.E.)

Q Why do some scholars refer to the period from 1100 to 750 B.C.E. as the Greek Dark Age? Who was Homer, and why was his work used as the basis for Greek education?

3-3 The World of the Greek City-States (ca. 750–500 B.C.E.)

Q What were the chief features of the polis, or city-state, and how did the major city-states of Athens and Sparta differ? What were the effects of expansion and the role of tyranny in the Greek polis?

3-4 The High Point of Greek Civilization: Classical Greece

Q What did the Greeks mean by democracy, and in what ways was the Athenian political system a democracy? What effect did the Persian Wars have on Greek military and political developments? What effect did the Great Peloponnesian War have on Greek economic, military, and political developments?

3-5 Culture and Society of Classical Greece

Q Upon what ideals were Classical Greek art, drama, and religion based, and how were these ideals expressed? What questions did the Greek philosophers pose, and what answers did they suggest? What are the chief features of daily life in Classical Athens?

Scala/Art Resource, NY

CONNECTIONS TO TODAY

What are the similarities and differences between ancient Athenian democracy and modern U.S. democracy?

IN 431 B.C.E., WAR ERUPTED IN GREECE as two dramatically different Greek city-states—Athens and Sparta—fought for domination of the Greek world. The people of Athens felt secure behind their walls and in the first winter of the war held a public funeral to honor those who had died in battle. On the day of the ceremony, the citizens of Athens joined in a procession, with the relatives of the dead wailing for their loved ones. As was the custom in Athens, one leading citizen was asked to address the crowd, and on this day it was Pericles who spoke to the people. He talked about the greatness of Athens and reminded the Athenians of the strength of their political system. "Our constitution," he said, "is called a democracy because power is in the hands not of a minority but of the whole people. When it is a question of settling private disputes, everyone is equal before the law. Just as our political life is free and open, so is our day-to-day life in our relations with each other. . . . Here each individual is interested not only in his own affairs but in the affairs of the state as well."

In this famous funeral oration, Pericles gave voice to the ideal of democracy and the importance of the individual. It was the Greeks who created the intellectual foundations of our Western heritage. They asked some basic questions about human life that still dominate our own intellectual pursuits: What is the nature of the universe? What is the purpose of human existence? What is our relationship to divine forces? What constitutes a community? What constitutes a state? What is true education? What are the true sources of law? What is truth itself, and how do we realize it? The Greeks not only provided answers to these questions but also created a system of logical, analytical thought to examine them. This rational outlook has remained an important feature of Western civilization.

The story of ancient Greek civilization is a remarkable one that begins with the first arrival of the Greeks around 2000 B.C.E. By the eighth century B.C.E., the characteristic institution of ancient Greek life, the **polis** (POH-liss), or city-state, had emerged. Greek civilization flourished and reached its height in the classical era of the fifth century B.C.E., which has come to be closely identified with the achievements of Athenian democracy.

3-1 Early Greece

 FOCUS QUESTION: How did geography affect Greek political, military, and economic developments?

Geography played an important role in the evolution of Greek history. Unlike the landmasses of Mesopotamia and Egypt, Greece occupied a small area, a mountainous peninsula that encompassed only 45,000 square miles of territory, about the size of the state of Louisiana. The mountains and the sea played especially significant roles in the development of Greek history. Much of Greece consists of small plains and river valleys surrounded by mountain ranges 8,000 to 10,000 feet high. The mountainous terrain had the effect of isolating Greeks from one another. Consequently, Greek communities tended to follow their own separate paths and develop their own way of life. Over a period of time, these communities became attached to their independence and were only too willing to fight one another to gain advantage. No doubt the small size of these independent Greek communities fostered participation in political affairs and unique cultural expressions, but the rivalry among these communities also led to the bitter warfare that ultimately devastated Greek society.

The sea also influenced the evolution of Greek society. Greece had a long seacoast dotted by bays and inlets that provided numerous harbors. The Greeks also inhabited a number of islands to the west, the south, and particularly the east of the Greek mainland. It is no accident that the Greeks became seafarers who sailed out into the Aegean and Mediterranean Seas, first to make contact with the outside world and later to establish colonies that would spread Greek civilization throughout the Mediterranean region.

Topography helped to determine the major territories into which Greece was ultimately divided. South of the Gulf of Corinth was the Peloponnesus (pel-uh-puh-NEE-suss), which was virtually an island (see Map 3.1). Consisting

mostly of hills, mountains, and small valleys, the Peloponnesus was the location of Sparta as well as the site of Olympia, where athletic games were held. Northeast of the Peloponnesus was the Attic peninsula (or Attica), the home of Athens, hemmed in by mountains to the north and west and surrounded by the sea to the south and east. Northwest of Attica was Boeotia (bee-OH-shuh) in central Greece, with its chief city of Thebes (THEEBZ). To the north of Boeotia was Thessaly, which contained the largest plains and became a great producer of grain and horses. To the north of Thessaly lay Macedonia, which was not of much importance in Greek history until 338 B.C.E., when a Macedonian king, Philip II, conquered the Greeks.

3-1a Minoan Crete

The earliest civilization in the Aegean region emerged on the large island of Crete, southeast of the Greek mainland. A Bronze Age civilization that used metals, especially bronze, in making weapons had been established there by 2700 B.C.E. This forgotten civilization was rediscovered at the turn of the twentieth century by the English archaeologist Arthur Evans, who named it Minoan (mih-NOH-uhn) after Minos (MY-nuss), a legendary king of Crete. In language and religion, the Minoans were not Greek, although they did have some influence on the peoples of the Greek mainland. The Minoans created a relatively advanced society as evidenced by use of a writing system in their records known as Linear A, which has not yet been deciphered.

Evans's excavations on Crete led to the discovery of what he labeled an enormous palace complex at Knossus (NOSS-suss), near modern Heraklion, that was most likely the center of a far-ranging "sea empire," probably largely commercial. We know from archaeological remains that the people of Minoan Crete witnessed a major development in the use of sailing ships that could cover longer distances and carry more cargo. The Minoans used clay containers to store and transport Cretan olive oil and wine. They made contact with the more advanced civilization of Egypt. Egyptian products have been found in Crete and Cretan products in Egypt. Minoan Cretans also made contact with and exerted influence on the Greek-speaking inhabitants of the Greek mainland.

The Minoan civilization reached its height between 2000 and 1450 B.C.E. The palace at Knossus demonstrates the prosperity and power of this civilization. It was an elaborate structure built around a central courtyard and included numerous private living rooms and workshops for making decorated vases, small sculptures, and jewelry. The complex even included bathrooms with elaborate drains. The rooms were decorated with frescoes in bright colors that depicted sporting events and naturalistic scenes that have led some observers to conclude that the Cretans had a great love of nature. Moreover, some historians have speculated that the presence of both men and women in these frescoes point to a rough equality between men and women, a position that would be unique in the ancient world (see Image 3.2). Storerooms in the

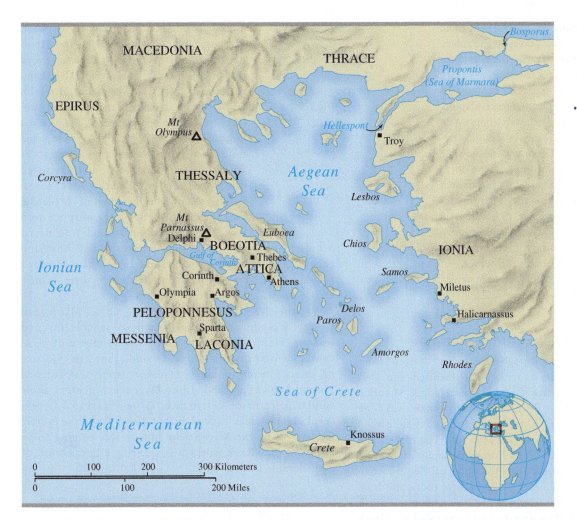

MAP 3.1 **Ancient Greece (ca. 750–338 B.C.E.).** Between 750 and 500 B.C.E., Greek civilization witnessed the emergence of the city-state as the central institution in Greek life and the Greeks' colonization of the Mediterranean and Black Seas. Classical Greece lasted from about 500 to 338 B.C.E. and encompassed the high points of Greek civilization in art, science, philosophy, and politics, as well as the Persian Wars and the Peloponnesian War.

Q *How does the geography of Greece help to explain the rise and development of the Greek city-state?*

Erich Lessing/Art Resource, NY

IMAGE 3.2 **The Minoan Sport of Bull Leaping.** Minoan bull games were held in the great palaces on the island of Crete. As seen in this fresco from the east wing of the palace at Knossus, both women and men (the man in red) acrobatically somersaulted over the back of the bull. Another person waited behind the bull to catch the leapers.

Q *What might the emphasis on bull games tell you about the Cretan economy?*

palace held enormous jars of oil, wine, and grain, presumably paid as taxes to the rulers. Some of the large courtyards were used for great communal feasts for the elite.

Eventually, however, the centers of Minoan civilization on Crete collapsed. Some historians once believed that a tsunami triggered by a powerful volcanic eruption on the island of Thera was responsible for destroying towns and ships on the north coast of Crete, but the latest dating of that eruption places it in the seventeenth century B.C.E. There is evidence that mainland Greeks known as the Mycenaeans invaded and pillaged many centers, including Knossus, which was destroyed around 1400 B.C.E. However, Knossus was soon rebuilt and made the chief administrative center on Crete for the Mycenaeans.

3-1b The First Greek State: Mycenae

The term *Mycenaean* (my-suh-NEE-un) is derived from Mycenae (my-SEE-nee), a remarkable fortified site first excavated by the amateur German archaeologist Heinrich Schliemann (HYN-rikh SHLEE-mahn). Mycenae was one center in a Mycenaean Greek civilization that flourished between 1600 and 1100 B.C.E. (see Map 3.2). The Mycenaean Greeks were part of the Indo-European family of peoples (see Chapter 1) who spread from their original Central Asian location into southern and western Europe, India, and Iran. One group entered the territory of Greece from the north around 1900 B.C.E. and managed to gain control of the Greek mainland and develop a civilization.

Mycenaean civilization, which reached its high point between 1400 and 1200 B.C.E., consisted of a number of powerful monarchies centered in fortified palace complexes. Like Mycenae itself, the palaces were built on hills and surrounded by gigantic stone walls. The royal families lived within the walls of these complexes, while the civilian populations lived in scattered locations outside the walls.

These various centers of power probably formed a loose confederacy of independent states, with Mycenae being the strongest. According to tablets written in an early form of Greek script called Linear B, a Mycenaean king used the title of *wanax*. Next in importance to the king were commanders of the army, priests, and bureaucrats who kept careful records. The free citizenry included peasants, soldiers, and artisans, with the lowest rung of the social ladder consisting of serfs and slaves.

The Mycenaeans were above all a warrior people who prided themselves on their heroic deeds in battle (see Image 3.3). Archaeological evidence also indicates that the Mycenaean monarchies developed an extensive commercial network. Mycenaean pottery has been found throughout the Mediterranean basin, in Syria and Egypt to the east

MAP 3.2 **Minoan Crete and Mycenaean Greece**

and Sicily and southern Italy to the west. But some scholars believe that the Mycenaeans, led by Mycenae itself, also spread outward militarily, conquering Crete and making it part of the Mycenaean world. Some of the Aegean islands also fell subject to Mycenaean control. The most famous of all the Mycenaeans' supposed military adventures has come down to us from the epic poetry of Homer (discussed in the next section). Did the Mycenaeans, led by Agamemnon, king of Mycenae, sack the city of Troy on the northwestern coast of Asia Minor around 1250 B.C.E.? Scholars have debated this question ever since Schliemann began his excavations in 1870. Some believe that Homer's account does have a basis in fact, although there is little archaeological evidence to support it.

By the late thirteenth century B.C.E., Mycenaean Greece was showing signs of serious trouble for two reasons. First, earthquakes and possibly severe drought caused widespread damage. Second, there is evidence of attacks from without. Mycenae itself was torched around 1190 B.C.E., and other Mycenaean centers show similar patterns of destruction as new waves of Greek-speaking invaders moved into Greece from the north. By 1100 B.C.E., the Mycenaean culture was coming to an end, and the Greek world was entering a new period of considerable insecurity.

IMAGE 3.3 **Pair of Lions at the Lion Gate, Mycenae.** The Lion Gate was the chief entryway into the citadel at Mycenae and was a rare piece of monumental sculpture in Mycenaean Greece. It was formed by two standing monoliths that supported a huge lintel topped by two lion sculptures facing a column, as shown here in this photo.

Q *What do you think is the significance of the two lions?*

3-2 The Greeks in a Dark Age (ca. 1100–750 B.C.E.)

 FOCUS QUESTIONS: Why do some scholars refer to the period from 1100 to 750 B.C.E as the Greek Dark Age? Who was Homer, and why was his work used as the basis for Greek education?

After the collapse of the Mycenaean civilization, Greece entered a difficult period in which population declined and food production dropped. Because of the difficult conditions and our lack of knowledge about the period, historians refer to it as the Dark Age, but many historians now view it more as a period of transition from the Bronze Age to the Iron Age in Greece. Iron replaced bronze in the construction of weapons, making them affordable for more people. And farming tools made of iron helped reverse the decline in food production and led to a revival of farming by 850 B.C.E. At the same time, other new developments were forming the basis for a revived Greece.

During this transitional period, large numbers of Greeks left the mainland and migrated across the Aegean Sea to various islands and especially to the southwestern shore of Asia Minor, a strip of territory that came to be called Ionia (y-OH-nee-uh). Based on their dialect, the Greeks who resided there were called Ionians. Two other major groups of Greeks settled in established parts of Greece. The Aeolian (ee-OH-lee-un) Greeks, located in northern and central Greece, colonized the large island of Lesbos and the adjacent territory on the northwestern coast of Asia Minor. The Dorians (DOR-ee-unz) established themselves in southwestern Greece, especially in the Peloponnesus, as well as on some of the southern Aegean islands, including Crete and Rhodes.

Other important activities occurred in this period as well. Beginning around 1050 B.C.E., a new way of decorating pottery known as Geometric provides some indication of more settled conditions in parts of Greece. Greece also saw a revival of some trade and economic activity in addition to agriculture. At some point in the eighth century B.C.E., the Greeks adopted the Phoenician alphabet to give themselves a new system of writing. By reducing all words to a combination of twenty-four letters, the Greeks made learning to read and write simpler. Finally, near the end of this Dark Age appeared the work of Homer, who has come to be viewed as one of the great poets of all time.

3-2a Homer and Homeric Greece

The *Iliad* and the *Odyssey*, the first great epic poems of early Greece, were based on stories that had been passed on from generation to generation. It is generally assumed that early in the eighth century B.C.E., Homer made use of these oral traditions to compose the *Iliad*, his epic of the Trojan War. The war was sparked by Paris, a prince of Troy. By kidnapping Helen, wife of the king of the Greek state of Sparta, he outraged all the Greeks. Under the leadership of the Spartan king's brother, Agamemnon of Mycenae, the Greeks attacked Troy. Ten years later, the Greeks finally won and sacked the city (see Image 3.4).

But the *Iliad* is not so much the story of the war itself as it is the tale of the Greek hero Achilles (uh-KIL-eez) and how the "wrath of Achilles" led to disaster. As is true of all great literature, the *Iliad* abounds in universal lessons. Underlying them all is the clear message, as one commentator has observed, that "men will still come and go like the generations of leaves in the forest; that [man] will still be weak, and the gods strong and incalculable; that the quality of a man matters more than his achievement; that violence and recklessness will still lead to disaster, and that this will fall on the innocent as well as on the guilty."[1]

© The Trustees of the British Museum/Art Resource, NY

IMAGE 3.4 **The Slaying of Hector.** This scene from a late-fifth-century B.C.E. Athenian vase depicts the final battle between Achilles and the Trojan hero Hector. Achilles is shown lunging forward with his spear to deliver the fatal blow to the Trojan prince, a scene taken from Homer's *Iliad*. The *Iliad* is one of Homer's masterpieces and was important to later Greeks as a means of teaching the aristocratic values of courage and honor.

Homer's Ideal of Excellence

 Q *What important ideals for Greek men and women are revealed in this passage from the Iliad?*

THE *ILIAD* AND THE *ODYSSEY*, epics that the Greeks believed were written by Homer, were used as basic texts for educating Greeks for hundreds of years in antiquity. This passage from the *Iliad*, describing a conversation between Hector, prince of Troy, and his wife, Andromache (an-DRAHM-uh-kee), illustrates the Greek ideal of gaining honor through combat. At the end of the passage, Homer also reveals what became the Greek attitude toward women: women are supposed to spin and weave and take care of their households and their children.

Homer, *Iliad*

Hector looked at his son and smiled, but said nothing. Andromache, bursting into tears, went up to him and put her hand in his. "Hector," she said, "you are possessed. This bravery of yours will be your end. You do not think of your little boy or your unhappy wife, whom you will make a widow soon. Some day the Achaeans [Greeks] are bound to kill you in a massed attack. And when I lose you I might as well be dead. . . . I have no father, no mother, now. . . . I had seven brothers too at home. In one day all of them went down to Hades' House. The great Achilles of the swift feet killed them all. . . .

"So you, Hector, are father and mother and brother to me, as well as my beloved husband. Have pity on me now; stay here on the tower; and do not make your boy an orphan and your wife a widow. . . ."

"All that, my dear," said the great Hector of the glittering helmet, "is surely my concern. But if I hid myself like a coward and refused to fight, I could never face the Trojans and the Trojan ladies in their trailing gowns. Besides, it would go against the grain, for I have trained myself always, like a good soldier, to take my place in the front line and win glory for my father and myself. . . ."

As he finished, glorious Hector held out his arms to take his boy. But the child shrank back with a cry to the bosom of his girdled nurse, alarmed by his father's appearance. He was frightened by the bronze of the helmet and the horsehair plume that he saw nodding grimly down at him. His father and his lady mother had to laugh. But noble Hector quickly took his helmet off and put the dazzling thing on the ground. Then he kissed his son, dandled him in his arms, and prayed to Zeus and the other gods: "Zeus, and you other gods, grant that this boy of mine may be, like me, preeminent in Troy; as strong and brave as I; a mighty king of Ilium. May people say, when he comes back from battle, 'Here is a better man than his father.' Let him bring home the bloodstained armor of the enemy he has killed, and make his mother happy."

Hector handed the boy to his wife, who took him to her fragrant breast. She was smiling through her tears, and when her husband saw this he was moved. He stroked her with his hand and said: "My dear, I beg you not to be too much distressed. No one is going to send me down to Hades before my proper time. But Fate is a thing that no man born of woman, coward or hero, can escape. Go home now, and attend to your own work, the loom and the spindle, and see that the maidservants get on with theirs. War is men's business; and this war is the business of every man in Ilium, myself above all."

Source: Homer, the *Iliad*, trans. E. V. Rieu (London: Penguin Classics, 1950; revised translation 2003).

The *Odyssey*, Homer's other masterpiece, is an epic romance that recounts the journeys of one of the Greek heroes, Odysseus (oh-DISS-ee-uss), after the fall of Troy and his ultimate return to his wife. But there is a larger vision here as well: the testing of the heroic stature of Odysseus until, by both cunning and patience, he prevails. In the course of this testing, the underlying moral message is "that virtue is a better policy than vice."[2]

Although the *Iliad* and the *Odyssey* supposedly deal with the heroes of the Mycenaean age of the thirteenth century B.C.E., many scholars believe that they really describe the social conditions of the transitional period from the Bronze to the Iron Age. According to the Homeric view, Greece was a society based on agriculture in which a landed warrior-aristocracy controlled much wealth and exercised considerable power. Homer's world reflects the values of aristocratic heroes.

3-2b Homer's Enduring Importance

This, of course, explains the importance of Homer to later generations of Greeks. Homer did not record history; he made it. The Greeks regarded the *Iliad* and the *Odyssey* as authentic history as recorded by one poet, Homer. These masterpieces gave the Greeks an ideal past with a cast of heroes and came to be used as standard texts for the education of generations of Greek males. As one Athenian stated, "My father was anxious to see me develop into a good man . . . and as a means to this end he compelled me to memorize all of Homer."[3] The values Homer taught were essentially the aristocratic values of courage and honor (see Historical Voices, "Homer's Ideal of Excellence," above). A hero strives for excellence, which the Greeks called *arete* (ahr-ih-TAY). In the warrior-aristocratic world of Homer, arete is won in a struggle or contest. Through his willingness to fight, the hero protects his family and friends, preserves his own honor and that of his family, and earns his reputation.

In the Homeric world, aristocratic women were also expected to pursue excellence. Penelope, for example, the wife of Odysseus, the hero of the *Odyssey*, remains faithful to her husband and displays great courage and intelligence in preserving their household during her husband's long absence. Upon his return, Odysseus praises her for her excellence: "Madame, there is not a man in the wide world who could find fault with you. For your fame has reached heaven itself, like that of some perfect king, ruling a populous and mighty state with the fear of god in his heart, and upholding the right."[4] Homer gave the Greeks a model of heroism, honor, and nobility. But in time, as a new world of city-states emerged and Greece became the first urban culture to emerge on the continent of Europe, new values of cooperation and community also transformed what the Greeks learned from Homer.

3-3 The World of the Greek City-States (ca. 750–500 B.C.E.)

 FOCUS QUESTIONS: What were the chief features of the polis, or city-state, and how did the major city-states of Athens and Sparta differ? What were the effects of expansion and the role of tyranny in the Greek polis?

In the eighth century B.C.E., Greek civilization burst forth with new energies, beginning the period that historians have called the Archaic Age of Greece. Two major developments stand out in this era: the evolution of the polis, or city-state, as the central institution in Greek life and the movement of people from the Greek states into lands bordering the Mediterranean and Black Seas.

3-3a The Polis

The Greek polis (plural, *poleis*) developed slowly but by the eighth century B.C.E. had emerged as a unique and fundamental institution in Greek society. In a physical sense, the polis encompassed a town or city or even a village and its surrounding countryside. But each had a central place where the citizens of the polis could assemble for political, social, and religious activities. In some poleis, this central meeting point was a hill that could serve as a place of refuge during an attack and later in some locales came to be the religious center where temples and public monuments were erected. Below this *acropolis* (uh-KROP-uh-liss) would be an *agora* (AG-er-uh), an open space that served both as a place where citizens could assemble and as a marketplace.

Poleis varied greatly in size, from a few square miles to a few hundred square miles. The larger ones were the product of consolidation. The territory of Attica, for example, had once had twelve poleis but eventually became a single polis (Athens) through a process of amalgamation. The population of Athens grew to about 250,000 by the fifth century B.C.E. Most poleis were much smaller, consisting of only a few hundred to several thousand people.

Although our word *politics* is derived from the Greek term polis, the polis itself was much more than just a political institution. It was, above all, a community of citizens in which all political, economic, social, cultural, and religious activities were focused. As a community, the polis consisted of citizens with political rights (adult males), citizens with no political rights (women and children), and noncitizens (slaves and resident aliens). All citizens of a polis possessed rights, but these rights were coupled with responsibilities. The Greek philosopher Aristotle argued that the citizen did not belong just to himself: "We must rather regard every citizen as belonging to the state." The unity of citizens was important and often meant that states would take an active role in directing the patterns of life. This idea of citizenship created a Greek society that was quite different from the societies of the despotic states we have examined and was an important element in the Greeks' contribution to Western civilization.

Nevertheless, the loyalty that citizens had to their poleis also had a negative side. Poleis distrusted one another, and the division of Greece into fiercely patriotic sovereign units helped bring about its ruin. Greece was not a united country but a geographic location. The cultural unity of the Greeks did not mean much politically. And, as we shall see, it took until the sixth century B.C.E. for the Greeks to even begin establishing a common Greek identity.

A New Military System: The Greek Way of War As the polis developed, so did a new military system. In earlier times, wars in Greece had been fought by aristocratic cavalry—nobles on horseback. These aristocrats, who were large landowners, also dominated the political life of their poleis. But by the end of the eighth century, a new military order came into being that was based on **hoplites** (HAHP-lyts), heavily armed infantrymen who wore bronze or leather helmets, breastplates, and greaves (shin guards). Each carried a round shield, a short sword, and a thrusting spear about 9 feet long. Hoplites advanced into battle as a unit, shoulder to shoulder, forming a **phalanx** (a rectangular formation) in tight order, usually eight ranks deep (see Image 3.5). As long as the hoplites kept their order, were not outflanked, and did not break, they either secured victory or, at the very least, suffered no harm. The phalanx was easily routed, however, if it broke its order. The safety of the phalanx thus depended on the solidarity and discipline of its members. As one seventh-century B.C.E. poet observed, a good hoplite was "a short man firmly placed upon his legs, with a courageous heart, not to be uprooted from the spot where he plants his legs."[5]

The hoplite force, which apparently developed first in the Peloponnesus, had political as well as military repercussions. The aristocratic cavalry was now outdated. Since each hoplite provided his own armor, men of property, both aristocrats and small farmers, made up the new phalanx. Those who could become hoplites and fight for the state could also challenge aristocratic control. Thus, the development of the hoplite and

Scala/Art Resource, NY

IMAGE 3.5 **The Hoplite Forces.** The Greek hoplites were infantrymen equipped with large round shields and long thrusting spears. In battle, they advanced in tight phalanx formation and were dangerous opponents as long as this formation remained unbroken. This vase painting from the seventh century B.C.E. shows two groups of hoplite warriors engaged in battle. The piper on the left is leading another line of soldiers preparing to enter the fray.

 Do you think the role of the piper was important? Why or why not?

phalanx became an important factor in the rise of democracy in Greece.

Some historians have questioned this idea of a hoplite revolution. They argue that early hoplites continued to be aristocrats because only they could afford the required equipment and only gradually did they recruit nonaristocrats to join their ranks. Others have argued that the phalanx developed gradually over the centuries and that the phalanx did not hold together nor crash into one another, arguing that there was no military revolution that led to a political revolution.

In the new world of the Greek city-states, war became an integral part of the Greek way of life. The Greek philosopher Plato described war as "always existing by nature between every Greek city-state."[6] The Greeks created a tradition of warfare that became a prominent element of Western civilization. For example, the Greeks devised excellent weapons and body armor, making effective use of technological improvements. Greek armies included a wide number of citizen-soldiers, who gladly accepted the need for training and discipline, giving them an edge over their opponents' often far-larger armies of mercenaries. Moreover, the Greeks displayed a willingness to engage the enemy head-on, thus deciding a battle quickly and with as few casualties as possible. Finally, the Greeks demonstrated the effectiveness of heavy infantry in determining the outcome of

a battle. All of these features of Greek warfare remained part of Western warfare for centuries.

3-3b Greek Expansion and the Growth of Trade

Greek expansion overseas was another major development of the Archaic Age. Between 750 and 550 B.C.E., large numbers of Greeks from different city-states left their homeland to settle in distant lands. Poverty and land hunger created by the growing gulf between rich and poor and the development of trade were all factors that led to the establishment of colonies. Some Greek settlements were simply trading posts or centers for the transshipment of goods to Greece. Most were larger settlements that included fertile agricultural land taken from the native populations in those areas. Each colony was founded as a *polis* and was usually independent of the *metropolis* ("mother polis") that had established it.

In the western Mediterranean, new Greek settlements were established along the coastline of southern Italy, including the cities of Tarentum (Taranto) and Neapolis (Naples) (see Map 3.3). So many Greek communities were established in southern Italy that the Romans later called it *Magna Graecia* (MAG-nuh GREE-shuh) ("Great Greece"). An important city was founded at Syracuse in eastern Sicily in 734 B.C.E. by the

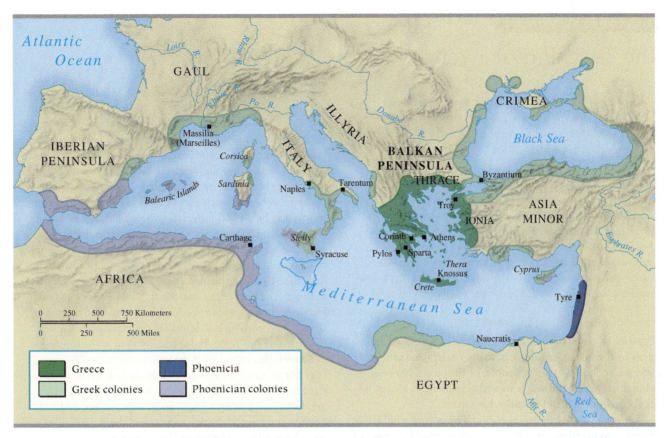

MAP 3.3 Greece and Its Colonies in the Archaic Age. Impelled by a variety of factors, Greeks spread out from their homelands during the Archaic Age, establishing colonies in many parts of the Mediterranean. The colonies were independent city-states that traded with the older Greek city-states.

 What aspects of the colonies' locations facilitated trade between them and city-states in Greece?

city-state of Corinth, one of the most active Greek states in establishing colonies. Greek settlements were also established in southern France at Massilia—modern Marseilles (mar-SAY)—in eastern Spain, and in northern Africa west of Egypt.

To the north, some Greek states set up colonies in Thrace, where they sought good agricultural lands to grow grains. Others also settled along the shores of the Black Sea and secured the approaches to it with cities on the Hellespont and Bosporus, most notably Byzantium, site of the later Constantinople (Istanbul). A trading post was established in Egypt, giving some Greeks access to both the products and the advanced culture of the East.

The Effects of Expansion The establishment of these settlements over such a wide area had important effects. For one thing, they contributed to the diffusion of aspects of Greek culture throughout the Mediterranean basin. The later Romans had their first contacts with the Greeks through the settlements in southern Italy. Furthermore, expansion helped the Greeks foster a greater sense of Greek identity. Before the eighth century, Greek communities were mostly isolated from one another, leaving many neighboring states on unfriendly terms. Once Greeks from different communities went abroad and encountered peoples with different languages

and customs, they became more aware of their own linguistic and cultural similarities, thus aiding in the development of a common Greek identity.

Expansion abroad also led to increased trade and industry. The Greeks sent their pottery, wine, and olive oil to these areas; in return, they received grains and metals from the west and fish, timber, wheat, metals, and slaves from the Black Sea region. In many poleis, the expansion of trade and industry created a new group of rich men who perceived that the decisions of the polis could affect their businesses. They now desired new political privileges but found them impossible to gain because of the power of the ruling aristocrats. This desire for change soon led to political crisis in many Greek states.

3-3c Tyranny in the Greek Polis

When the polis emerged as an important institution in Greece in the eighth century B.C.E., monarchical power waned, and kings virtually disappeared in most Greek states or survived only as ceremonial figures with little or no real power. Instead, political power passed into the hands of local aristocracies. But increasing divisions between rich and poor and the aspirations of newly rising industrial and commercial groups in Greek poleis opened the door to the rise of the **tyrant** in

The Teaching of Tyranny

 What advice does Thrasybulus give to Periander? Why did the advice ultimately lead to the end of tyranny in Corinth? What do we learn about tyranny in Greece from this excerpt?

TYRANNY, AS THE GREEKS PRACTICED IT, was a relatively short experience for most Greek states. But it did lead to some extreme practices that helped lead to its own downfall. In this excerpt, the Greek historian Herodotus (see "3-5a The Writing of History," later in the chapter) discusses how one tyrant—Thrasybulus of Miletus—taught another tyrant—Periander of Corinth—the ways of tyranny. The lesson ultimately led to disaster for Periander's family.

Herodotus, *The Persian Wars*

[Cypselus] showed himself a harsh ruler. Many of the Corinthians he drove into banishment, many he deprived of their fortunes, and a still greater number, of their lives. His reign lasted thirty years, and was prosperous to its close; so that he left the government to Periander, his son.

This ruler, at the beginning of his reign, was of a milder temper than his father; but after he corresponded by means of messengers with Thrasybulus, tyrant of Miletus, he became ever more bloodthirsty. On one occasion he sent a herald to ask Thrasybulus what mode of government it was safest to set up in order to rule with honor. Thrasybulus led the messenger without the city, and took him into a field of corn, through which he began to walk. While Thrasybulus asked him again and again concerning his coming from Corinth, he broke off and threw away such ears of corn as overtopped the rest. In this way he went through the whole field, and destroyed all the best and richest parts of the crop. Then, without a word, he sent the messenger back. On the return of the man to Corinth, Periander was eager to know what Thrasybulus had counseled, but the messenger reported that he had said nothing. The messenger wondered that Periander had sent him to so strange a man, who seemed to have lost his senses, since he did nothing but destroy his own property. Upon this he told how Thrasybulus had behaved at the interview. Periander, perceiving what the action meant, and knowing that Thrasybulus advised the destruction of all the leading citizens, treated his subjects from this time forward with the greatest cruelty. Where Cypselus had spared any, and had neither put them to death nor banished them, Periander completed what his father had left unfinished.

Source: Hutton Webster, *Readings in Ancient History* (Boston: D.C. Heath & Co., 1913), pp. 53–54.

the seventh and sixth centuries B.C.E. They were not necessarily oppressive or wicked, as our word *tyrant* connotes. Greek tyrants were rulers who seized power by force and who were not subject to the law. Support for the tyrants came from the new rich, who made their money in trade and industry, as well as from poor peasants, who were in debt to landholding aristocrats. Both groups opposed the domination of political power by the aristocrats.

Tyrants usually achieved power by a local coup d'état and maintained it by using mercenary soldiers. Once in power, they built new marketplaces, temples, and walls that created jobs, glorified the city, and enhanced their own popularity. Tyrants also favored the interests of merchants and traders by encouraging the founding of new colonies, developing new coinage, and establishing new systems of weights and measures. In many instances, they added to the prosperity of their cities. By their patronage of the arts, they encouraged cultural development.

The Example of Corinth One of the most famous examples of tyranny can be found in Corinth (KOR-inth). During the eighth and early seventh centuries B.C.E., Corinth had become one of the most prosperous states in Greece under the rule of an **oligarchy** led by members of the Bacchiad family. Their violent activities, however, made them unpopular and led Cypselus (SIP-suh-luss), a member of the family, to overthrow the oligarchy and assume sole control of Corinth.

Cypselus was so well liked that he could rule without a bodyguard. During his tyranny, Corinth prospered by exporting vast quantities of pottery and founding new colonies to expand its trade empire. Cypselus's son, Periander, took control of Corinth after his father's death (see Historical Voices, "The Teaching of Tyranny," above). But he ruled with such cruelty that shortly after he died in 585 B.C.E., his son, who succeeded him, was killed, and a new oligarchy soon ruled Corinth.

As in Corinth, tyranny elsewhere in Greece was largely extinguished by the end of the sixth century B.C.E. The children and grandchildren of tyrants, who tended to be corrupted by their inherited power and wealth, often became cruel and unjust rulers, making tyranny no longer seem such a desirable institution. Its very nature as a system outside the law seemed contradictory to the ideal of law in a Greek community. Tyranny did not last, but it played a significant role in the evolution of Greek history. The rule of narrow aristocratic oligarchies was destroyed. Once the tyrants were eliminated, the door was opened to the participation of more people in the affairs of the community. Although this trend culminated in the development of democracy in some communities, in other states expanded oligarchies of one kind or another managed to remain in power. Greek states exhibited considerable variety in their governmental structures; this can perhaps best be seen by examining the two most famous and most powerful Greek city-states, Sparta and Athens.

3-3d Sparta

The Greeks of Sparta and Athens spoke different dialects and developed different political systems. The Spartans sought stability and conformity and emphasized order. The Athenians allowed for individual differences and stressed freedom. Although the two states shared a common heritage, their differences grew so large in their own minds that they were ultimately willing to engage in a life-and-death struggle to support their separate realities. When they did so, the entire Greek world was the real loser.

Located in the southeastern Peloponnesus, in an area known as Laconia (luh-KOH-nee-uh), the Spartans had originally occupied four small villages that eventually became unified into a single polis (a fifth soon joined the others). This unification made Sparta a strong community in Laconia and enabled the Spartans to conquer the neighboring Laconians. Many Laconians became *perioikoi* (per-ee-EE-koh-ee), free inhabitants (but not citizens) who were required to pay taxes and perform military service for Sparta. Other Laconians became known as **helots** (HEL-uts) (derived from the Greek word for "capture"). They were bound to the land and forced to work on farms and as household servants for the Spartans.

When the land in Laconia proved incapable of maintaining the growing number of Spartan citizens, the Spartans looked for land nearby and, beginning around 730 B.C.E., undertook the conquest of neighboring Messenia despite its larger size and population. Messenia possessed a spacious, fertile plain ideal for growing grain. After its conquest, which was not completed until the seventh century B.C.E., the Messenians were made helots and forced to work for the Spartans. But the helots drastically outnumbered the Spartan citizens (some estimates are ten to one) and constantly threatened to revolt. To ensure control over them, the Spartans made a conscious decision to create a military state.

Sometime between 800 and 600 B.C.E., the Spartans instituted a series of reforms that are associated with the name of the lawgiver Lycurgus (ly-KUR-guss) (see Historical Voices, "The Lycurgan Reforms," p. 66). Although historians are not sure that Lycurgus ever existed, there is no doubt about the result of the reforms that were made: Sparta was transformed into a perpetual military camp.

The New Sparta The lives of Spartans were now rigidly organized. At birth, all children were examined by state officials who decided whether they were fit to live. Those judged unfit were exposed to the elements and left to die. Boys were taken from their mothers at the age of seven and put under control of the state. They lived in barracks, where they were subjected to harsh discipline to make them tough and given an education that stressed military training and obedience to authority. At twenty, Spartan males were enrolled in the army for regular military service. Although allowed to marry, they continued to live in the barracks and ate their meals in public dining halls with their fellow soldiers. Meals were simple; the famous Spartan black broth consisted of a piece of pork boiled in animal blood, salt, and vinegar, causing a visitor who ate in a public mess to remark that he now understood why Spartans were not afraid to die. At thirty, Spartan males were recognized as mature and allowed to vote in the assembly and live at home, but they remained in the army until the age of sixty.

While their husbands remained in military barracks until age thirty, Spartan women lived at home. Because of this separation, Spartan women had greater freedom of movement. Permitted to own and inherit land, Spartan women had more power in the household than was common for women elsewhere in Greece and could even supervise large estates. They were encouraged to exercise and remain fit to bear and raise healthy children. Like the men, Spartan women engaged in athletic exercises in the nude. At solemn feasts, the young women would march naked in processions, and in the presence of the young men, they would sing songs about those who had shown special gallantry or cowardice on the battlefield. Many Spartan women upheld the strict Spartan values, expecting their husbands and sons to be brave in war. The story is told that as a Spartan mother was burying her son, an old woman came up to her and said, "You poor woman, what a misfortune." "No," replied the other, "because I bore him so that he might die for Sparta and that is what has happened, as I wished."[7] Another Spartan woman saw her son off to war by telling him to come back carrying his shield or carried on it.

The Spartan social structure was rigidly organized. At the summit were the *Spartiates* (spar-tee-AH-teez)—full Spartan citizens. Each Spartan citizen owned a piece of land, worked by the helots, to provide economic sustenance. With their material needs provided for them, Spartan citizens could dedicate themselves to their duties as a ruling class. Below the Spartiates were the *perioikoi*. Though free, they did not possess the privileges of citizenship and served as small merchants and artisans. They were subject to military duty, however. At the bottom of the social scale were the *helots*, perpetually bound to the land. They were assigned to the lands of the Spartan citizens. The helots farmed the land and gave their masters half of the produce. According to one seventh-century Spartan poet, helots worked "like donkeys exhausted under heavy loads." A secret police force lived among them and was permitted to kill any helot considered dangerous. To legalize this murder, the state officially declared war on the helots at the beginning of each year.

The Spartan State The so-called Lycurgan reforms also reorganized the Spartan government, creating an oligarchy. Two kings from different families were primarily responsible for military affairs and served as the leaders of the Spartan army on its campaigns. Five men, known as *ephors* (EFF-urz), were elected each year and were responsible for the education of youth and conduct of all citizens. A council of elders, composed of the two kings and twenty-eight citizens over the age of sixty, decided what issues would be presented to an assembly of all male citizens. This assembly did not debate but only voted on the proposals put before it by the council of elders. The assembly also elected the council of elders and the ephors.

The Lycurgan Reforms

 What does this passage from Plutarch's account of Lycurgus tell you about the nature of the Spartan state? Why would the entire program have been distasteful to the Athenians?

TO MAINTAIN THEIR CONTROL over the helots, the Spartans instituted the reforms that created their military state. In this account of the lawgiver Lycurgus, the Greek historian Plutarch discusses the effect of these reforms on the treatment and education of boys.

Plutarch, *Lycurgus*

Lycurgus was of another mind; he would not have masters bought out of the market for his young Spartans . . . nor was it lawful, indeed, for the father himself to breed up the children after his own fancy; but as soon as they were seven years old they were to be enrolled in certain companies and classes, where they all lived under the same order and discipline, doing their exercises and taking their play together. Of these, he who showed the most conduct and courage was made captain; they had their eyes always upon him, obeyed his orders, and underwent patiently whatsoever punishment he inflicted; so that the whole course of their education was one continued exercise of a ready and perfect obedience. The old men, too, were spectators of their performances, and often raised quarrels and disputes among them, to have a good opportunity of finding out their different characters, and of seeing which would be valiant, which a coward, when they should come to more dangerous encounters. Reading and writing they gave them just enough to serve their turn; their chief care was to make them good subjects, and to teach them to endure pain and conquer in battle. To this end, as they grew in years, their discipline was proportionately increased; their heads were close-clipped, they were accustomed to go barefoot, and for the most part to play naked.

After they were twelve years old, they were no longer allowed to wear any undergarments, they had one coat to serve them a year; their bodies were hard and dry, with but little acquaintance of baths and unguents; these human indulgences they were allowed only on some few particular days in the year. They lodged together in little bands upon beds made of the rushes which grew by the banks of the river Eurotas, which they were to break off with their hands with a knife; if it were winter, they mingled some thistledown with their rushes, which it was thought had the property of giving warmth. By the time they were come to this age there was not any of the more hopeful boys who had not a lover to bear him company. The old men, too, had an eye upon them, coming often to the grounds to hear and see them contend either in wit or strength with one another, and this as seriously . . . as if they were their fathers, their tutors, or their magistrates; so that there scarcely was any time or place without someone present to put them in mind of their duty, and punish them if they had neglected it.

[Spartan boys were also encouraged to steal their food.] They stole, too, all other meat they could lay their hands on, looking out and watching all opportunities, when people were asleep or more careless than usual. If they were caught, they were not only punished with whipping, but hunger, too, being reduced to their ordinary allowance, which was but very slender, and so contrived on purpose, that they might set about to help themselves, and be forced to exercise their energy and address. This was the principal design of their hard fare.

Source: Plutarch, *The Lives of the Noble Grecians and Romans,* edited by A. H. Clough and translated by J. Dryden (New York: Modern Library, 1992).

To make their new military state secure, the Spartans deliberately turned their backs on the outside world. Foreigners, who might bring in new ideas, were discouraged from visiting Sparta. Nor were Spartans, except for military reasons, encouraged to travel abroad where they might pick up new ideas. Trade and commerce were likewise minimized. Spartan citizens were discouraged from pursuing philosophy, literature, the arts, or any other subject that might foster novel thoughts dangerous to the stability of the state. The art of war and ruling was the Spartan ideal. All other arts were frowned upon.

In the sixth century, Sparta used its military might and the fear it inspired to gain greater control of the Peloponnesus by organizing an alliance of almost all the Peloponnesian states. Sparta's strength enabled it to dominate this Peloponnesian League and determine its policies. By 500 B.C.E., the Spartans had organized a powerful military state that maintained order and stability in the Peloponnesus. Raised from early childhood to believe that total loyalty to the Spartan state was the basic reason for existence, the Spartans viewed their strength as justification for their militaristic ideals and regimented society.

3-3e Athens

By 700 B.C.E., Athens had established a unified polis on the peninsula of Attica. Although early Athens had been ruled by a monarchy, by the seventh century B.C.E. it had fallen under the control of its aristocrats. The aristocrats possessed the best land and controlled political and religious life by means of a council of nobles called the Areopagus (ar-ee-OP-uh-guss), assisted by a board of nine archons. Although there was an Assembly of full citizens, it possessed few powers.

Near the end of the seventh century B.C.E., Athens faced political turmoil because of serious economic problems. Many Athenian farmers found themselves sold into slavery when they were unable to repay the loans they had borrowed from their aristocratic neighbors, pledging themselves as collateral. Over and over, there were cries to cancel the debts and give land to the poor. Athens seemed on the verge of civil war.

The Reforms of Solon Hoping to avoid tyranny, the ruling Athenian aristocrats responded to this crisis by choosing Solon (SOH-lun), a reform-minded aristocrat, as sole archon in 594 B.C.E. and giving him full power to make reforms. Solon's reforms dealt with both the economic and political problems. Solon canceled all current land debts, outlawed new loans based on humans as collateral, and freed people who had fallen into slavery for debt. He refused, however, to carry out the redistribution of the land and hence failed to deal with the basic cause of the economic crisis.

Like his economic reforms, Solon's political measures were also a compromise. Though by no means eliminating the power of the aristocracy, they opened the door to the participation of new people, especially the nonaristocratic wealthy, in the government. Wealth instead of birth now qualified people for holding political office, thus creating upward political mobility. Solon divided all Athenian citizens into four classes on the basis of wealth. Only men in the first two classes (the wealthiest classes) could hold the archonship and be members of the Areopagus. Men in the third class could be elected to a new council of 400, whose function it was to prepare the agenda for the Assembly. The fourth (and poorest) class, though not allowed to hold any political offices, could now vote in the Assembly.

The Move to Tyranny But Solon's reforms, though popular, did not solve Athens's problems. Aristocratic factions continued to vie for power, and the poorer peasants resented Solon's failure to institute land redistribution. Internal strife finally led to the very institution Solon had hoped to avoid—tyranny. Pisistratus (puh-SIS-truh-tuss), an aristocrat and distant relative of Solon's, seized power in 560 B.C.E. and made himself a tyrant.

Pisistratus did not tamper very much with the constitution. The Assembly, councils, and courts continued to function while he made sure that his supporters were elected as magistrates and council members. Pisistratus curried favor with the small farmers by offering land and loans to the needy. His ambitious building program, aimed at beautifying the city, also created jobs. Pursuing a foreign policy that aided Athenian trade, Pisistratus also maintained the support of the mercantile and industrial classes. Pisistratus's mild tyranny was popular with many Athenians, but they rebelled against his son and ended the tyranny in 510 B.C.E. Although the aristocrats attempted to reestablish an aristocratic oligarchy, Cleisthenes (KLYSS-thuh-neez), an aristocratic reformer, opposed this plan and, with the backing of the Athenian people, gained the upper hand in 508 B.C.E. The reforms of Cleisthenes now established the basis for Athenian democracy.

The Reforms of Cleisthenes A major aim of Cleisthenes's reforms was to weaken the power of traditional localities and

CHRONOLOGY	Archaic Greece: Sparta and Athens	
Sparta		
Conquest of Messenia	ca. 730–710 B.C.E.	
Beginning of Peloponnesian League	ca. 560–550 B.C.E.	
Athens		
Solon's reforms	594–593 B.C.E.	
Tyranny of Pisistratus	ca. 560–556 and 546–527 B.C.E.	
End of tyranny	510 B.C.E.	
Cleisthenes's reforms	ca. 508–501 B.C.E.	

regions, which had provided the foundation for aristocratic strength. He made the *demes*, the 139 villages and townships of Attica, the basic units of political life. Cleisthenes enrolled all the citizens of the demes in ten new tribes, each of which contained inhabitants located in the country districts of Attica, the coastal areas, and Athens itself. The ten tribes thus contained a cross-section of the population and reflected all of Attica, a move that gave local areas a basic role in the political structure. Cleisthenes' ten new tribes were then linked to a new council of 500 that replaced Solon's council of 400. Each of the ten tribes chose fifty members by lot each year for the new council. No one was allowed to serve more than two years (and then not in succession) on the council. It met on a regular basis and was responsible for the administration of both foreign and financial affairs and prepared the business that would be handled by the Assembly. This Assembly of all male citizens had final authority in the passing of laws after free and open debate; thus, Cleisthenes's reforms strengthened the central role of the Assembly of citizens in the Athenian political system. Cleisthenes also established new courts with juries for both private and public cases. Jurors were chosen by lot from the ten tribes and swore an oath to uphold the laws.

The reforms of Cleisthenes laid the foundations for Athenian democracy. More changes would come in the fifth century when the Athenians themselves would begin to use the word *democracy* (from the Greek words *demos*, "people," and *kratia*, "power"; thus, "power to the people") to describe their system. By 500 B.C.E., Athens was more united than it had been and was about to assume a more important role in Greek affairs.

3-3f Greek Culture in the Archaic Age

The Archaic Age witnessed a revitalization of Greek life that is also evident in Greek art and literature. Some aspects of Archaic Greek culture, such as sculpture and pottery, were especially influenced by the East (see Global Perspectives, "The Influence of the East on the Greeks," p. 68). Greek sculpture demonstrates the impact of the considerably older Egyptian civilization in the life-size stone statues of young male nudes known as *kouros* (KOO-rohss) figures. The kouros bears considerable resemblance to Egyptian statues of the New Kingdom. The figures are not realistic but stiff, with a slight smile; one leg is advanced ahead of the other, and the arms are held rigidly at the sides of the body.

The Influence of the East on the Greeks

Q *What was the influence of the Near East on Greek sculpture and pottery? Why were Greek and Egyptian statues different? How do you explain the significance of the Near East on Greece?*

AS THE GREEKS MOVED OUT into the eastern Mediterranean, they came into increased contact with the older civilizations of the Near East and Egypt, which had a strong impact on early Greek culture. Greek sculpture, especially that of the Ionian Greek settlements in southwestern Asia Minor, demonstrates the impact of the considerably older Egyptian civilization. There we first see the life-size statues of young male nudes known as *kouros*. As seen in the photos, Image 3.6a shows a statue of a young male nude around 600 B.C.E., making it an early example of Greek kouros sculpture. Such statues, which were placed in temples along with companion figures of clothed young women, known as *korai*, were meant to be representations for the faithful dedicated to the gods. Image 3.6b shows an early-seventh-century B.C.E. statue of an Egyptian nobleman. Clearly, Egyptian sculpture had a strong influence on Greek art. Unlike the Egyptians, however, Greek sculptors preferred depicting male figures in the nude.

In addition, Greek pottery in the eighth and seventh centuries B.C.E. began to use new motifs—such as floral and animal designs— borrowed from the Near East. Seen here are two examples of Greek vases. Image 3.6c shows a ninth-century vase in the Greek geometric style featuring mostly abstract motifs. Image 3.6d shows a Greek vase from the seventh century in which a Greek artist demonstrated his fascination with the East by combining a floral motif with exotic Eastern animals such as griffons, sphinxes, and wild goats.

The Phoenicians especially played an important role as middlemen in transmitting Near Eastern culture to the Greeks. We have already seen that the Greeks borrowed from the Phoenicians to create a truly phonetic alphabet, making it easier to write the poetry, philosophical treatises, and other literary works that distinguish Greek culture.

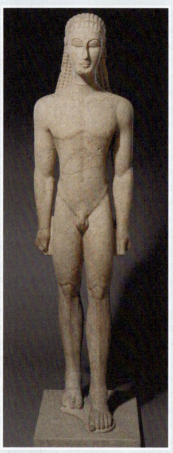

IMAGE 3.6a

IMAGE 3.6b

IMAGE 3.6c

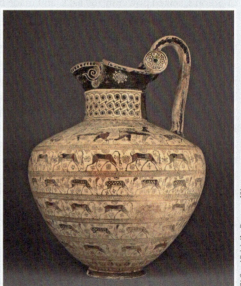

IMAGE 3.6d

Greek literature of the seventh century is perhaps best known for its lyric poetry. The lyric is considerably shorter than epic poetry (such as Homer's) and focuses on personal emotions, usually the power of love and its impact on human lives. Later Greeks acknowledged Sappho as their greatest female lyric poet. Born in the seventh century, Sappho lived on the island of Lesbos in the Aegean Sea, where she taught music and poetry to her young charges. Many of her poems are love songs to her female students, as seen in these words from one of her poems:

> But remember me, for surely you
> know how I worshiped you. If not,
> then I want you to remember all
> the exquisite days we too shared;
> how when near me you would adorn
> your hanging locks with violets and
> tiny roses and your sapling throat
> with necklets of a hundred blossoms;
> how your young flesh was rich with kingly
> myrrh as you leaned near my breasts on
> the soft couch where delicate girls
> served us all an Ionian could desire. . .[8]

Our word *lesbian* is derived from Sappho's island of Lesbos. Sappho, like many upper-class Greeks, accepted that homosexual and heterosexual feelings could exist in the same individual. Sappho was a wife and a mother who also wrote poems about love between men and between women.

Archaic Greece is also known for poets who reflected the lifestyles of both aristocrats and peasants. A wide gulf, however, separated the wealthy aristocrat with his large landed estates from the poor peasants and small farmers who eked out their existence as best they could. Hesiod (HEE-see-uhd), a poet from Boeotia in central Greece who lived around 700 B.C.E., wrote a lengthy epic poem titled *Works and Days*. Himself a farmer, Hesiod distrusted aristocrats and looked down on what he considered the aristocratic emphasis on pride and war. One of his aims was to show that the gods punished injustice and that the way to success was to work: "Famine and blight do not beset the just, who till their well-worked fields and feast. The earth supports them lavishly." Therefore,

> . . . you must learn to organize your work
> So you may have full barns at harvest time.
> From working, men grow rich in flocks and gold
> And dearer to the deathless gods. In work
> There is no shame; shame is in idleness.[9]

Works and Days is the first known paean to work in Western literature.

Theognis of Megara (THEE-og-niss of MEG-er-uh) described a way of life considerably different from Hesiod's. Theognis was an aristocrat who lived and wrote primarily in the sixth century B.C.E. As a result of revolutionary upheaval, he, like other aristocrats in sixth-century poleis, lost his position and probably his wealth. Sent into exile, he became a bitter man. In his poetry, he portrayed aristocrats as the only good people, who are distinguished from others by their natural intelligence, virtue, honor, and moderation. The lower classes or common people were by nature bad and debased. Aristocrats, then, should associate only with other aristocrats: "Avoid low company, mix only with the better sort of men. . . . From them you will learn goodness. Men of little worth will spoil the natural beauty of your birth." The poems of Theognis reveal the political views and biases of a typical sixth-century aristocrat.

3-4 The High Point of Greek Civilization: Classical Greece

 FOCUS QUESTIONS: What did the Greeks mean by democracy, and in what ways was the Athenian political system a democracy? What effect did the Persian Wars have on Greek military and political developments? What effect did the Great Peloponnesian War have on Greek economic, military, and political developments?

Classical Greece is the name given to the period of Greek history from around 500 B.C.E. to the conquest of Greece by the Macedonian king Philip II in 338 B.C.E. It was a period of brilliant achievement, much of it associated with the flowering of democracy in Athens under the leadership of Pericles. Many of the lasting contributions of the Greeks occurred during this period. The age began with a mighty confrontation between the Greek states and the mammoth Persian Empire.

3-4a The Challenge of Persia

As Greek civilization expanded throughout the Mediterranean region, it was inevitable that it would come into contact with the Persian Empire to the east. In his play *The Persians*, the Greek playwright Aeschylus (ESS-kuh-luss) expressed what some Greeks perceived to be the essential difference between themselves and the Persians. The Persian queen, curious to find out more about the Athenians, asks: "Who commands them? Who is shepherd of their host?" The chorus responds: "They are slaves to none, nor are they subject."[10] Thus, at least some Greeks saw the struggle with the Persians as a contest between freedom and slavery. To the Greeks, a person was a citizen of the state, not a subject. And for the Greeks, who were still divided into independent city-states, the growing Persian threat would serve to deepen a growing sense of Greek cultural identity.

The Ionian Greek cities in southwestern Asia Minor had already fallen subject to the Persian Empire by the mid-sixth century B.C.E. (see Chapter 2). An unsuccessful revolt by the Ionian cities in 499, assisted by the Athenian navy, led the Persian ruler Darius to seek revenge by attacking the mainland Greeks in 490. Darius may also have wished to expand his empire westward.

The First Persian Attack The Persians sailed across the Aegean, captured Eretria (which had also aided the Ionian rebels) on the island of Euboea across from Attica, and then transferred their army to the plain of Marathon, only 26 miles from Athens (see Map 3.4). The Athenians, aided by the Plataeans (from a neighboring town in Boeotia), confronted

MAP 3.4 The Persian Wars. The Athenians defeated Persia in 490 B.C.E. at Marathon. Athens later led a coalition of Greek city-states that decisively defeated Xerxes's navy at the Battle of Salamis in 480 B.C.E., causing Xerxes to withdraw most of his troops back to Asia.

 How far did the Persian army have to walk to get to Athens, and through what types of terrain?

the Persians without additional assistance. The two armies were quite different. The Persians, with their light-armed troops, were more mobile and flexible and relied heavily on missiles; the Greek hoplites were armed with heavy shields and relied on spear thrusts at close range. The Athenians and Plataeans were clearly outnumbered, but led by Miltiades (mil-TY-uh-deez), one of the Athenian leaders who insisted on attacking, the Greek hoplites charged across the plain of Marathon and crushed the Persian forces (see Historical Voices, "The Battle of Marathon," p. 71). The Persians did not mount another attack against mainland Greece for ten years.

In the meantime, Athens had acquired a new leader, Themistocles (thuh-MISS-tuh-kleez), a man lacking in aristocratic connections but strongly favored by Athenian merchants and highly skilled in speaking in the democratic assembly. Themistocles persuaded his fellow citizens to pursue a new military policy, namely, the development of a navy. The Athenians used a newly discovered vein of silver from Laurium to finance the construction of ships and new port facilities. By 480 B.C.E.,

Athens had produced a navy of about two hundred vessels, primarily triremes (TRY-reemz) (ships with three banks of oars).

A revolt in Egypt, compounded by the death of Darius in 486 B.C.E., kept the Persians from mounting another attack on Greece. Xerxes (ZURK-seez), the new Persian monarch, was bent on revenge and expansion, however. Some of the Greeks prepared by forming a defensive league under Spartan leadership, although many Greek states remained neutral; some even fought on the Persian side.

The Invasion of Xerxes The Persians under Xerxes mounted their invasion in 480 B.C.E. Their military forces were massive: close to 150,000 troops, almost seven hundred naval ships, and hundreds of supply ships to feed their large army. The Persians crossed the Hellespont by forming a bridge of ships and then moved through Thrace and Macedonia on their way into Greece. The Greek plan, as it evolved, was to fight a holding action at the pass of Thermopylae (thur-MAHP-uh-lee) along the main road from Thessaly into Boeotia, probably to give the Greek fleet

The Battle of Marathon

 How does this passage reflect Herodotus's pride in the Greeks?

THE BATTLE OF MARATHON (490 B.C.E.) was an important event in the struggle between the Greeks and the Persians. The defeat of the mighty Persians gave Athenian confidence a tremendous boost. In *The Persian Wars,* the Greek historian Herodotus gave an account of this momentous battle.

Herodotus, *The Persian Wars*

So when the battle was set in array, and the victims showed themselves favorable, instantly the Athenians, so soon as they were let go, charged the barbarians at a run. Now the distance between the two armies was little short of a mile. The Persians, therefore, when they saw the Greeks coming on at speed, made ready to receive them, although it seemed to them that the Athenians were bereft of their senses, and bent upon their own destruction; for they saw a mere handful of men coming on at a run without either horsemen or archers. Such was the opinion of the barbarians; but the Athenians in close array fell upon them, and fought in a manner worthy of being recorded. They were the first of the Greeks, so far as I know, who introduced the custom of charging the enemy at a run, and they were likewise the first who dared to look upon the Median garb, and to face men clad in that fashion. Until this time the very name of the Medes had been a terror to the Greeks to hear.

The two armies fought together on the plain of Marathon for a length of time; and in the midbattle, where the Persians themselves and the Sacae had their place, the barbarians were victorious, and broke and pursued the Greeks into the inner country; but on the two wings the Athenians and the Plataeans defeated the enemy. Having so done, they suffered the routed barbarians to fly at their ease, and joining the two wings in one, fell upon those who had broken their own center, and fought and conquered them. These likewise fled, and now the Athenians hung upon the runaways and cut them down, chasing them all the way to the shore, on reaching which they laid hold of the ships and called for fire. . . .

After the full of the moon 2,000 Lacedaemonians [Spartans] came to Athens. So eager had they been to arrive in time, that they took but three days to reach Attica from Sparta. They came, however, too late for the battle; yet, as they had a longing to behold the Medes, they continued their march to Marathon and there viewed the slain. Then, after giving the Athenians all praise for their achievement, they departed and returned home.

Source: Herodotus, *The Persian Wars*, trans. George Rawlinson (New York: Modern Library, 1942).

---

of three hundred ships at Artemisium, off northern Euboea, the chance to fight the Persian fleet. The Greeks knew that the Persian army depended on the fleet for supplies. Under the leadership of the Spartan king Leonidas (lee-AHN-ih-duss) and his contingent of three hundred Spartans, a Greek force numbering close to nine thousand held off the Persian army at Thermopylae for two days. The Spartan troops were especially brave. When told that Persian arrows would darken the sky in battle, one Spartan warrior supposedly responded, "That is good news. We will fight in the shade!" Unfortunately for the Greeks, a traitor told the Persians of a mountain path they could use to outflank the Greek force. King Leonidas and the three hundred Spartans fought to the last man (see Movies & History, *300*).

The Athenians, now threatened by the onslaught of the Persian forces, decided to abandon Athens and evacuate the population of Attica to the offshore island of Salamis (SAH-luh-miss). Meanwhile, the Greek fleet remained in the straits off Salamis while the Persians sacked Athens. The Peloponnesians wanted the Greeks to retreat to the Peloponnesus and the Greek ships to move to the isthmus. Themistocles's refusal and his threat to withdraw the Athenian ships altogether if a fight was not made forced the ships to remain and set up the naval Battle of Salamis. Although the Greeks were outnumbered, they managed to outmaneuver the Persian fleet (mostly Phoenicians and Ionians) and decisively defeated it. The Persians still had their army and much of their fleet intact, but Xerxes, frightened at the prospect of another Ionian revolt, returned to Asia but left a Persian force in Thessaly.

MOVIES & HISTORY
300 (2007)

Watch *300*, an action film adapted from a graphic novel. A fictional portrayal of the Battle of Thermopylae in 480 B.C.E., *300* is a strange mix of history and fantasy. Because the film is adapted from a graphic novel, it has a surreal quality in which special visual effects play a dominant role. Battle scenes rely on stylized violence using slow-motion techniques, but they do capture the bloody nature of ancient warfare.

WARNER BROS. PICTURES/Album/Superstock

 How accurate is this portrayal of the Battle of Thermopylae? How does it reflect Greek warfare? How does the film portray Greek sexual practices? How does the film represent differences between the Greeks and Persians?

Persian control of Greek cities in southwestern Asia Minor	By 540s B.C.E.
Rebellion of Greek cities in Asia Minor	499–494 B.C.E.
Battle of Marathon	490 B.C.E.
Xerxes invades Greece	480–479 B.C.E.
Battles of Thermopylae and Salamis	480 B.C.E.
Battles of Plataea and Mycale	479 B.C.E.

Early in 479 B.C.E., the Greeks formed the largest Greek army seen up to that time. The Athenians forced the Spartans to move north of the Peloponnesus and take on the Persians at Plataea (pluh-TEE-uh), northwest of Athens, where the Greek forces decisively defeated the Persian army. The remnants of the Persian forces retreated to Asia. At the same time, the Greeks destroyed much of the Persian fleet in a naval battle at Mycale (MIH-kuh-lee) in Ionia. The Greeks were overjoyed at their victory but remained cautious. Would the Persians try again?

3-4b The Growth of an Athenian Empire

After the defeat of the Persians, Athens stepped in to provide new leadership against the Persians by forming a confederation called the Delian League. Organized in the winter of 478–477 B.C.E., the Delian League was dominated by the Athenians from the beginning. Its main headquarters was the island of Delos (DEE-lahs), sacred to the Ionian Greeks, but its chief officials, including the treasurers and commanders of the fleet, were Athenians. Athens also provided most of the league's three hundred ships. Under the leadership of the Athenians, the Delian League pursued the attack against the Persian Empire. Virtually all of the Greek states in the Aegean were liberated from Persian control, and the Persian fleet and army were decisively defeated in 469 B.C.E. in southern Asia Minor. Arguing that the Persian threat was now over, some members of the Delian League wished to withdraw. Naxos did so in 470 and Thasos in 465 B.C.E. The Athenians responded vigorously. They attacked both states, destroyed their walls, took over their fleets, eliminated their liberty, and forced them to pay tribute. "No secession" became Athenian policy. The Delian League was rapidly becoming an instrument of Athenian imperialism and the nucleus of an Athenian empire.

The Age of Pericles At home, Athenians favored the new imperial policy, especially in the 450s B.C.E., when an aristocrat named Pericles (PER-i-kleez) began to play an important political role. Under Pericles, Athens embarked on a policy of expanding democracy at home while severing its ties with Sparta and expanding its new empire abroad. This period of Athenian and Greek history, which historians have subsequently labeled the Age of Pericles, witnessed the height of Athenian power and the culmination of its brilliance as a civilization.

In the Age of Pericles, the Athenians became deeply attached to their democratic system. The sovereignty of the people was embodied in the Assembly, which consisted of all male citizens over eighteen years of age. In the 440s, that was probably a group of about 43,000; women, slaves, and foreigners, who made up a majority of Attica's approximately 300,000 residents, were excluded from participation in government. Meetings of the Assembly were held every ten days on the hillside of the Pnyx (NIKS), east of the Acropolis. Not all could attend, and the number present seldom exceeded 6,000, which was its capacity. The Assembly passed all laws and made final decisions on war and foreign policy. Although anyone could speak, usually only respected leaders did so, a feat that required considerable ability in such a large crowd.

The reforms of Cleisthenes had introduced the Council of Five Hundred, elected by lot from the ten tribes. It prepared the agenda for the Assembly and made recommendations for action. Thus, the council served as a control on the Assembly. The council was divided into ten smaller groups of fifty called prytanies. Each prytany held office for one-tenth of the year to supervise the execution of the laws passed by the Assembly.

Routine administration of public affairs was handled by a large body of city magistrates that were usually chosen by lot without regard to class and usually served only one-year terms. This meant that many male citizens held public office at some time during their lives. A board of ten officials known as generals—*strategoi* (strah-tay-GOH-ee)—was elected by public vote to guide the affairs of the state, although their power depended on the respect they had attained. Generals were usually wealthy aristocrats, even though the people were free to select otherwise. The generals could be reelected, enabling individual leaders to play an important political role. Pericles's frequent reelection (fifteen times) as one of the ten generals made him one of the leading politicians between 461 and 429 B.C.E.

All public officials were subject to scrutiny and could be deposed from office if they lost the people's confidence. After 488 B.C.E., the Athenians occasionally made use of a tactic called *ostracism*. Members of the assembly could write on a broken pottery fragment, or *ostrakon* (AHSS-truh-kahn), the name of the person they most disliked or considered most harmful to the polis. Frequently, this was someone whose policy, approved at first by the assembly, had failed. A person who received a majority (if at least six thousand votes were cast) was exiled for ten years, although the practical Athenians often recalled a man from exile if they needed him.

Pericles expanded the Athenians' involvement in democracy, which was by now what Athenians had come to call their form of government (see Historical Voices, "Athenian Democracy," p. 73). Power was in the hands of the people: male citizens voted in the assemblies and served as jurors in the courts. Lower-class citizens were now eligible for public offices formerly closed to them. Pericles also introduced state pay for officeholders, including the widely held jury duty. This meant that even poor citizens could hold public office and afford to participate in public affairs. Nevertheless, although the Athenian system of government was unique in its time in that citizens had equal rights and the people were the government, aristocrats continued to hold the most important offices, and many people, including women, slaves, and foreigners residing in Athens, were not given the same political rights.

Athenian Democracy: The Funeral Oration of Pericles

 In the eyes of Pericles, what are the ideals of Athenian democracy? In what ways does Pericles exaggerate his claims? Why would the Athenian passion for debate described by Pericles have been distasteful to the Spartans?

IN HIS *HISTORY OF THE PELOPONNESIAN WAR*, the Greek historian Thucydides presented his reconstruction of the eulogy given by Pericles in the winter of 431–430 B.C.E. to honor the Athenians killed in the first campaigns of the Great Peloponnesian War. It is a magnificent, idealized description of the Athenian democracy at its height.

Thucydides, *History of the Peloponnesian War*

Our constitution is called a democracy because power is in the hands not of a minority but of the whole people. When it is a question of settling private disputes, everyone is equal before the law; when it is a question of putting one person before another in positions of public responsibility, what counts is not membership of a particular class, but the actual ability which the man possesses. No one, so long as he has it in him to be of service to the state, is kept in political obscurity because of poverty. And, just as our political life is free and open, so is our day-to-day life in our relations with each other. We do not get into a state with our next-door neighbor if he enjoys himself in his own way, nor do we give him the kind of black looks which, though they do no real harm, still do hurt people's feeling. We are free and tolerant in our private lives; but in public affairs we keep to the law. This is because it commands our deep respect.

We give our obedience to those whom we put in positions of authority, and we obey the laws themselves, especially those which are for the protection of the oppressed, and those unwritten laws which it is an acknowledged shame to break. . . . Here each individual is interested not only in his own affairs but in the affairs of the state as well: even those who are mostly occupied with their own business are extremely well-informed on general politics—this is a peculiarity of ours: we do not say that a man who takes no interest in politics is a man who minds his own business; we say that he has no business here at all. We Athenians, in our own persons, take our decisions on policy or submit them to proper discussions: for we do not think that there is an incompatibility between words and deeds; the worst thing is to rush into action before the consequences have been properly debated. . . . Taking everything together then, I declare that our city is an education to Greece, and I declare that in my opinion each single one of our citizens, in all the manifold aspects of life, is able to show himself the rightful lord and owner of his own person and do this, moreover, with exceptional grace and exceptional versatility. And to show that this is no empty boasting for the present occasion, but real tangible fact, you have only to consider the power which our city possesses and which has been won by those very qualities which I have mentioned.

Source: Thucydides, *The History of the Peloponnesian War*, trans. R. Warner (London: Penguin Classics, 1954; revised edition 1972).

Athenian Imperialism The Athenian pursuit of democracy at home was coupled with increasing imperialism abroad as Athens attempted to create both a land empire in Greece and a maritime empire in the Aegean. As we have seen, after 470 B.C.E., Athenian policies had the effect of converting the voluntary allies of the Delian League into the involuntary subjects of an Athenian naval empire. After 462 B.C.E., Athens attempted to expand its empire on the Greek mainland as well. The creation of a land empire, however, overextended the Athenians and involved them in a series of skirmishes with Sparta and its allies known as the First Peloponnesian War (ca. 460–445 B.C.E.). After a series of defeats in 445 B.C.E., the land empire of Athens disintegrated, and Athens agreed to a thirty years' peace with the Spartans in the following year. Athens consented to give up most of its land empire, and in return, Sparta recognized the existence of Athens's maritime empire.

While building its land empire, Athens continued its offensive against Persia and at the same time tightened its control over the Delian League. Citing the threat of the Persian fleet in the Aegean, the Athenians moved the treasury of the league from the island of Delos to Athens itself, possibly in 454 B.C.E.

Members were, in effect, charged a fee (tribute) for the protection that Athens claimed to provide. Pericles also used the treasury money of the league, without the approval of its members, to build new temples in Athens, an arrogant reminder that the Delian League had become the Athenian empire. The pursuit of imperialism, both in Greece and abroad, took its toll, however. Pericles recognized the dangers of Athenian exhaustion and sought a lull. After peace was made with Sparta in 445 B.C.E., the Athenians had a breathing space in which to beautify Athens and enjoy the fruits of empire, but it was not long before all of Greece was plunged into a new and prolonged struggle.

3-4c The Great Peloponnesian War (431–404 B.C.E.)

In his classic *History of the Peloponnesian War*, the great Greek historian Thucydides (thoo-SID-uh-deez) (see "3-5a The Writing of History," later in this chapter) pointed out that the fundamental, long-range cause of the war that began in 431 B.C.E. was the fear that Athens and its empire inspired in Sparta. The Spartans were especially concerned that Athens would use its superior naval power to weaken Sparta's control of the Peloponnesian League. The immediate causes of the war involved conflicts between Corinth and Athens and between Athens and Megara. When these two allies of Sparta threatened to withdraw from the Peloponnesian League if Sparta did not back them, the Spartans sent an ultimatum to Athens: if the Athenians did not back down in their disputes

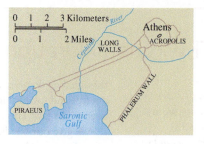

MAP 3.5 **Piraeus and Athens**

with Corinth and Megara, it would mean war. The Athenians refused to compromise when Pericles convinced them that if they accepted Sparta's ultimatum, they would be admitting that Sparta was the dominant power in Greece.

At the beginning of the war in 431 B.C.E., both sides believed they had winning strategies. The Athenian plan was based on the navy. The citizens of Attica would be brought

in behind the protective walls of Athens and the port of Piraeus (py-REE-uss or pih-RAY-uss), while the overseas empire and the navy would keep them supplied (see Map 3.5). Pericles knew perfectly well that the Spartans and their allies could beat the Athenians in pitched battles, which, of course, formed the focus of the Spartan strategy. The Spartans and their allies invaded Attica and ravaged the fields and orchards, hoping that the Athenians would send out their army to fight beyond the walls. But Pericles was convinced that Athens was secure behind its walls and retaliated by sending out naval excursions to ravage the seacoast of the Peloponnesus (see Map 3.6).

In the second year of the war, however, a plague devastated the crowded city of Athens and wiped out up to one-third of the population. Pericles himself died the following year

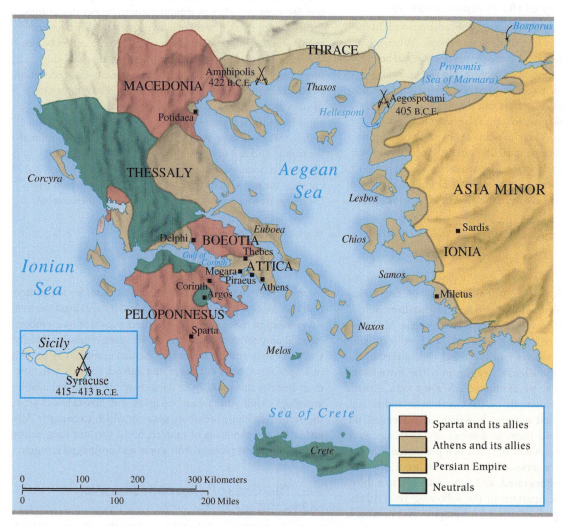

MAP 3.6 **The Great Peloponnesian War (431–404 B.C.E.): Alliances and Battles.** During much of the fifth century B.C.E., Athens sought to dominate Greece and the Aegean Sea. The Peloponnesian War ultimately saw Sparta and the Peloponnesian League defeat Athens and its allies, culminating in the destruction of the Athenian navy and the dismantling of its empire in 404 B.C.E.

Q *How did Athens use its proximity to the sea to forge and maintain its empire and to conduct the war?*

Disaster in Sicily

 What happened to the Athenian soldiers captured in Sicily? In what way was this not typical of the Greek way of war? How would you explain this change?

AT THE BEGINNING of his *History of the Peloponnesian War*, the Greek historian Thucydides wrote, "The Peloponnesian War . . . not only lasted for a long time, but throughout its course brought with it unprecedented suffering for Greece. Never before had so many cities been captured and then devastated . . . never had there been so many exiles; never such loss of life." The greatest defeat for Athens came in Sicily in 413 B.C.E. In his history, Thucydides described what happened to the captured Athenians.

Thucydides, *History of the Peloponnesian War*

The Syracusans and their allies now brought their forces together into one, took up the spoils and as many of the prisoners as they could, and went back to their city. They put the Athenian and allied prisoners whom they had taken into the stone quarries, thinking that this was the safest way of keeping them. . . .

Those who were in the stone quarries were treated badly by the Syracusans at first. There were many of them, and they were crowded together in a narrow pit, where, since there was no roof over their heads, they suffered first from the heat of the sun and the closeness of the air; and then, in contrast, came on the cold autumnal nights, and the change in temperature brought disease among them. Lack of space made it necessary for them to do everything on the same spot; and besides there were the bodies all heaped together on top of one another of those who had died from their wounds or from the change of temperature or other such causes, so that the smell was insupportable. At the same time they suffered from hunger and from thirst. During eight months the daily allowance for each man was half a pint of water and a pint of corn. In fact they suffered everything which one could imagine might be suffered by men imprisoned in such a place. For about ten weeks they lived like this all together; then, with the exception of the Athenians and any Greeks from Italy or Sicily who had joined the expedition, the rest were sold as slaves. It is hard to give the exact figure, but the whole number of prisoners must have been at least 7,000.

This was the greatest Hellenic action that took place during this war, and, in my opinion, the greatest action that we know of in Hellenic history—to the victors the most brilliant of successes, to the vanquished the most calamitous of defeats; for they were utterly and entirely defeated; their sufferings were on an enormous scale; their losses were, as they say, total; army, navy, everything was destroyed, and, out of many, only few returned. So ended the events in Sicily.

Source: Thucydides, *The History of the Peloponnesian War*, trans. R. Warner (London: Penguin Classics, 1954; revised edition 1972).

(429 B.C.E.), a severe loss to Athens. Dominance now passed to Cleon, leader of the war party, who was opposed by Nicias (NISS-ee-uss), head of a conservative faction that favored peace. Despite the losses from the plague, the Athenians fought on in a struggle that witnessed numerous instances of futile destruction. Cleon achieved some successes for the Athenians; Brasidas (BRASS-i-duss) came to be a dynamic general for the Spartans. At the Battle of Amphipolis (am-FIPP-oh-liss) in 422 B.C.E., both generals were killed, and the new Athenian leader, Nicias, negotiated the Peace of Nicias (421 B.C.E.). Although both parties agreed to keep the peace for fifty years, the truce did not solve the problems that had caused the war in the first place.

A second phase of the war began only six years after the fifty-year truce. This phase was initiated by Alcibiades (al-suh-BY-uh-deez), a nephew of Pericles. Elected to the generalship in 420 B.C.E., he proved to be a poor choice because of his recklessness and ambition. In 415 B.C.E., he convinced the Athenians to invade the island of Sicily, arguing that its conquest would give the Athenians a strong source of support to carry on a lengthy war. A large expedition consisting of five thousand Athenian hoplites was sent out in 415 B.C.E.

and reinforced two years later by an even larger army of Athenians and allies. All was in vain. The Athenians failed to take Syracuse and were captured during their retreat. All of the Athenians were killed or sold into slavery (see Historical Voices, "Disaster in Sicily," above). These heavy losses at Syracuse had immediate domestic repercussions. The democracy was weakened, and an aristocratic oligarchy was temporarily established (411–410 B.C.E.).

Despite the disaster, the Athenians refused to give up; they raised new armies and sent out new fleets. The final

CHRONOLOGY	The Great Peloponnesian War
Invasion of Attica	431 B.C.E.
Battle of Amphipolis	422 B.C.E.
Peace of Nicias	421 B.C.E.
Athenian invasion of Sicily	415–413 B.C.E.
Battle of Aegospotami	405 B.C.E.
Surrender of Athens	404 B.C.E.

crushing blow, however, came in 405 B.C.E., when the Athenian fleet was destroyed at Aegospotami (ee-guh-SPAH-tuh-my) on the Hellespont. Athens was besieged and surrendered the next year. Its walls were torn down, the navy was disbanded, and the Athenian empire was dissolved. The great war was finally over.

3-4d The Decline of the Greek States (404–338 B.C.E.)

The next seventy years witnessed continuing warfare among the Greeks, with the leading roles shifting among Sparta, Athens, and a new Greek power, the city-state of Thebes. After the defeat of Athens in 404 B.C.E., the Spartans established their own control over Greece. The Athenian empire was no more. Oligarchies, headed by local ten-man boards in cooperation with Spartan garrisons, were placed in control of the states "liberated" from Athenian imperialism. But oligarchical control proved ineffective, especially in Athens, where the ruling oligarchical faction of thirty, set up by the Spartans, earned the nickname of "Thirty Tyrants" by executing about fifteen hundred of their democratic opponents. This led to a reaction in which the Athenians were able to reestablish their democracy in 403 B.C.E. They also rebuilt their navy and again became an important force in the Greek world.

To maintain its new leadership in Greek affairs, Sparta encouraged a Panhellenic crusade against the Persians as a common enemy. The Persians had taken advantage of the Greeks' internal struggle to reimpose their control over the Greek states in western Asia Minor. But the Persians had learned the lessons of Greek politics. They now offered financial support to Athens, Thebes, and other Greek states to oppose Spartan power within Greece itself, thus beginning a new war, the Corinthian War (395–386 B.C.E.). The war ended when the Greek states, weary of the struggles, accepted the king's peace, dictated by the Great King of Persia.

The city-state of Thebes, in Boeotia north of Athens, now began to exert its influence. Under their leader Epaminondas (ih-PAM-uh-NAHN-duss), the Thebans dramatically defeated the Spartan army at the Battle of Leuctra (LOOK-tra) in 371 B.C.E. Playing an important role in the Theban victory was an elite group known as the Sacred Band of Thebans. This was a force, according to one Greek writer, made up of 150 pairs of men "devoted to each other by mutual obligations of love." After the Spartan defeat, the Thebans liberated Messenia (land of the helots) from Spartan control and established a new polis of Messene. The loss of Messenia meant the end of Sparta as a major Greek power and the ascendancy of the Thebans.

But Theban power was short-lived. After the death of Epaminondas in the Battle of Mantinea (man-tuh-NEE-uh) in 362 B.C.E., the Thebans could no longer dominate Greek politics. And yet the Greek states continued their petty wars, seemingly oblivious to the growing danger to the north, where King Philip II of Macedonia was developing a unified state that would finally end the destructive fratricide of the Greek states by imposing Macedonian authority.

3-5 Culture and Society of Classical Greece

FOCUS QUESTIONS: Upon what ideals were Classical Greek art, drama, and religion based, and how were these ideals expressed? What questions did the Greek philosophers pose, and what answers did they suggest? What are the chief features of daily life in Classical Athens?

Classical Greece saw a period of remarkable intellectual and cultural growth throughout the Greek world. Historians agree, however, that Periclean Athens was the most important center of classical Greek culture.

3-5a The Writing of History

History as we know it, the systematic analysis of past events, was a Greek creation. Herodotus (huh-ROD-uh-tuss) (ca. 484–425 B.C.E.) was the author of *The Persian Wars*, a work commonly regarded as the first real history in Western civilization. The Greek word *historia* (from which we derive our word *history*) means "research" or "investigation," and it is in the opening line of Herodotus's work that we find the first recorded use of the word:

> Here are presented the researches [*historiae*] carried out
> by Herodotus of Halicarnassus. The purpose is to prevent
> the traces of human events from being erased by time,
> and to preserve the fame of the important and remarkable
> achievements produced by both Greeks and non-Greeks;
> among the matters covered is, in particular, the cause of the
> hostilities between Greeks and non-Greeks.[11]

The central theme of Herodotus's work is the conflict between the Greeks and the Persians, which he viewed as a struggle between Greek freedom and Persian despotism. Herodotus traveled widely for his information and was dependent for his sources on what we today would call oral history. Although he was a master storyteller and sometimes included considerable fanciful material, Herodotus was also capable of exhibiting a critical attitude toward the materials he used. Regardless of its weaknesses, Herodotus's history is an important source of information on the Persians and our chief source on the Persian Wars themselves.

Thucydides Thucydides (ca. 460–400 B.C.E.) was a far better historian; in fact, modern historians consider him the greatest of the ancient world. Thucydides was an Athenian and participant in the Peloponnesian War. He had been elected a general, but a defeat in battle led the Athenian assembly to send him into exile. In *History of the Peloponnesian War*, he described his activities:

> I lived through the whole of it, being of an age to understand
> what was happening, and I put my mind to the subject so
> as to get an accurate view of it. It happened, too, that I
> was banished from my country for twenty years after my

command at Amphipolis [422 B.C.E.]; I saw what was being done on both sides, particularly on the Peloponnesian side, because of my exile, and this leisure gave me rather exceptional facilities for looking into things.[12]

Unlike Herodotus, Thucydides was not concerned with underlying divine forces or gods as explanatory causal factors in history. He saw war and politics in purely rational terms, as the activities of human beings. He examined the long-range and immediate causes of the Peloponnesian War in a clear, methodical, objective fashion. Thucydides placed much emphasis on accuracy and the precision of his facts. As he stated:

And with regard to my factual reporting of the events of the war I have made it a principle not to write down the first story that came my way, and not even to be guided by my own general impressions; either I was present myself at the events which I have described or else I heard of them from eyewitnesses whose reports I have checked with as much thoroughness as possible.[13]

Thucydides also provided remarkable insight into the human condition. He believed that human nature was a constant: "It will be enough for me, however, if these words of mine are judged useful by those who want to understand clearly the events which happened in the past and which (human nature being what it is) will, at some time or other and in much the same ways, be repeated in the future."[14] He was not so naive as to believe in an exact repetition of events but felt that political situations recur in similar fashion and that the study of history is of great value in understanding the present.

3-5b Greek Drama

Drama as we know it was created by the Greeks and was clearly intended to do more than entertain. It was used to educate citizens and was supported by the state for that reason. Plays were presented in outdoor theaters as part of religious festivals (see Image 3.7). The form of Greek plays remained rather stable. Three male actors who wore masks acted all the parts. A chorus, also male, spoke the important lines that explained what was going on. Action was very limited because the emphasis was on the story and its meaning.

Aeschylus The first Greek dramas were tragedies, plays based on the suffering of a hero and usually ending in disaster. Aeschylus (525–456 B.C.E.) is the first tragedian whose plays are known to us. Although he wrote ninety tragedies, only seven

IMAGE 3.7a

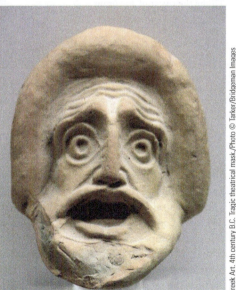

IMAGE 3.7b

IMAGE 3.7 **The Amphitheater at Epidaurus.** Image 3.7a shows the ancient Greek amphitheater at Epidaurus in the eastern Peloponnesus. It held 18,000 onlookers for the theatrical presentations and athletic games that were part of the religious festivals dedicated to Asclepius, the god of healing. Image 3.7b shows an example of a tragic theatrical mask worn by actors. Since Greek dramas used only three male actors who might play several roles, masks were necessary to distinguish the characters.

LatitudeStock - Ron Badkin/Getty Images

Greek Art. 4th century B.C. Tragic theatrical mask./Photo © Tarker/Bridgeman Images

Sophocles: "The Miracle of Man"

 What is Sophocles's view of humans and their achievements? What limitations did he see to human accomplishments?

IN *ANTIGONE*, SOPHOCLES PRESENTS a thoughtful analysis of the painful dilemmas in human existence. In one outstanding passage, the chorus expresses an exalted message on human resourcefulness and the achievements of human beings.

Sophocles, Antigone

Is there anything more wonderful on earth,
Our marvelous planet,
Than the miracle of man!
With what arrogant ease
He rides the dangerous seas,
From the waves' towering summit
To the yawning trough beneath.
The earth mother herself, before time began,
The oldest of the ageless gods,
Learned to endure his driving plough,
Turning the earth and breaking the clods
Till by the sweat of his brow
She yielded up her fruitfulness. . . .

He has mastered the mysteries of language:
And thought, which moves faster than the wind,

He has tamed, and made rational.
Political wisdom too, all the knowledge
Of people and States, all the practical
Arts of government he has studied and refined,
Built cities to shelter his head
Against rain and anger and cold
And ordered all things in his mind.
There is no problem he cannot resolve
By the exercise of his brains or his breath,
And the only disease he cannot salve
Or cure, is death.

In action he is subtle beyond imagination,
Limitless is his skill, and these gifts
Are both enemies and friends,
As he applies them, with equal determination,
To good or evil ends.
All men honor, and the State uplifts
That man to the heights of glory, whose powers
Uphold the constitution, and the gods, and their laws.
His city prospers. But if he shifts
His ground, and takes the wrong path,
Despising morality, and blown up with pride,
Indulges himself and his power, at my hearth
May he never warm himself, or sit at my side.

Source: Sophocles, *Antigone*, trans. D. Taylor (London: Methuen, 2006), pp. 17–18.

---

have survived. As was customary in Greek tragedy, his plots are simple. The entire drama focuses on a single tragic event and its meaning. Greek tragedies were sometimes presented in a trilogy (a set of three plays) built around a common theme. The only complete trilogy we possess, the *Oresteia* (uh-res-TY-uh), was composed by Aeschylus. The theme of this trilogy is derived from Homer. Agamemnon, the king of Mycenae, returns a hero after the defeat of Troy. His wife, Clytemnestra, avenges the sacrificial death of her daughter Iphigenia by murdering Agamemnon, who had been responsible for Iphigenia's death. In the second play of the trilogy, Agamemnon's son Orestes (uh-RES-teez) avenges his father by killing his mother. Orestes is now pursued by the avenging Furies, who torment him for killing his mother. Evil acts breed evil acts, and suffering is one's lot, suggests Aeschylus. But Orestes is put on trial and acquitted by Athena, the patron goddess of Athens. Personal vendetta has been eliminated, and law has prevailed.

Sophocles The most successful writer of Greek tragedies was the Athenian playwright Sophocles (SAHF-uh-kleez) (ca. 496–406 B.C.E.), whose background included holding some

important public offices in Athens. He won many first prizes in festival competitions for best tragedy, although only 7 of his 123 plays have survived. His most famous play is *Oedipus the King*. The oracle of Apollo foretells that a man (Oedipus) will kill his own father and marry his mother. Despite all attempts at prevention, the tragic events occur. Although it appears that Oedipus suffered the fate determined by the gods, Oedipus also accepts that he himself as a free man must bear responsibility for his actions: "It was Apollo, friends, Apollo, that brought this bitter bitterness, my sorrows to completion. But the hand that struck me was none but my own."[15]

In Sophocles's play *Antigone*, Antigone (an-TIG-uh-nee), the daughter of Oedipus, is caught in a terrible dilemma. Her brother Polynices (pol-uh-NY-seez) has died in an attempt to seize the throne of Thebes, and now the king of Thebes, Antigone's uncle Cleon, has forbidden his burial as a traitor to the state. Should Antigone adhere to her principles and fulfill her obligation to the gods by burying her brother or face death by defying the authority of the state? In the confrontation between Cleon and Antigone, Sophocles bears witness to the complexity of human existence (see Historical Voices, "Sophocles: 'The Miracle of Man'," above).

Euripides The third outstanding Athenian tragedian, Euripides (uoo-RIP-i-deez) (ca. 485–406 B.C.E.), moved beyond his predecessors in creating more realistic characters. His plots also became more complex, reflecting a greater interest in real-life situations. Perhaps the greatest of all his plays is *The Bacchae*, which deals with the introduction of the rites associated with Dionysus (dy-uh-NY-suss), god of wine. These rites introduced an element of spiritual ecstasy in Greek religion. Euripides was also critical of the traditional view that war was glorious. He portrayed war as brutal and expressed deep compassion for the women and children who suffered from it.

The Themes of Greek Tragedies Greek tragedies dealt with universal themes that are still relevant in our day. They probed such problems as the nature of good and evil, the conflict between spiritual values and the demands of the state or family, the rights of the individual, the nature of divine forces, and the nature of human beings. Over and over again, the tragic lesson was repeated: humans were free and yet could operate only within limitations imposed by the gods. The real task was to cultivate the balance and moderation that led to awareness of one's true position. But the pride in human accomplishment and independence is real. As the chorus chants in Sophocles's *Antigone:* "Is there anything more wonderful on earth, our marvelous planet, than the miracle of man?"[16]

Greek Comedy Greek comedy developed later than tragedy. The plays of Aristophanes (ar-is-STAH-fuh-neez) (ca. 450–385 B.C.E.), who used both grotesque masks and obscene jokes to entertain the Athenian audience, are examples of Old Comedy, which was used to attack or savagely satirize both politicians and intellectuals. In *The Clouds,* for example, Aristophanes characterizes the philosopher Socrates as the operator of a thought factory where people could learn deceitful ways to handle other people. Later plays give up the element of personal attack and focus on contemporary issues. Of special importance to Aristophanes was his opposition to the Peloponnesian War. *Lysistrata,* performed in 411 B.C.E. at a time when Athens was in serious danger of defeat, has a comic but effective message against the war.

3-5c The Arts: The Classical Ideal

The artistic standards established by the Greeks of the classical period largely dominated the arts of the Western world until the nineteenth and twentieth centuries. Classical Greek art did not aim at experimentation for experiment's sake but was concerned with expressing eternally true ideals. Its subject matter was basically the human being, expressed harmoniously as an object of great beauty. The classical style, based on the ideals of reason, moderation, symmetry, balance, and harmony in all things, was meant to civilize the emotions.

In architecture, the most important form was the temple dedicated to a god or goddess. Since Greek religious ceremonies were held at altars in the open air, temples were not used to enclose the faithful as modern churches are. At the center of Greek temples were walled rooms that housed the statues of deities and treasuries in which gifts to the gods and goddesses were safeguarded. These central rooms were surrounded by a screen of columns that made Greek temples open structures rather than closed ones. The columns were originally made of wood but changed to limestone in the seventh century and to marble in the fifth century B.C.E. The most significant formal element in Greek temples was the shape and size of the columns in combination with the features above and below the column (see Image 3.8).

Some of the finest examples of classical Greek architecture were built in fifth-century B.C.E. Athens. The development of Athenian architecture was aided tremendously by the massive rebuilding program funded from the treasury of the Delian League and instituted almost a half-century after the Persians destroyed Athens in the Persian Wars. Especially important was a series of constructions on the Acropolis begun in 448 B.C.E. that included a monumental entrance gate, a temple to Athena Nike (the Bringer of Victory), and the Erechtheum, a multilevel temple. These temples honored the gods and heroes who protected Athens.

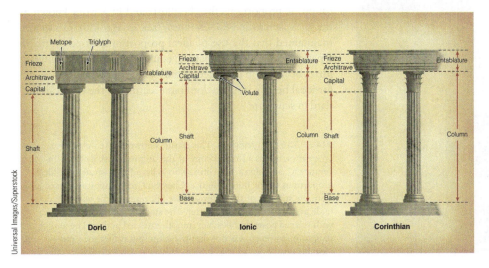

IMAGE 3.8 **Doric, Ionic, and Corinthian Orders.** The size and shape of a column constituted one of the most important aspects of Greek temple architecture. The Doric order, with plain capitals and no base, developed first in the Dorian Peloponnesus and was rather simple in comparison to the slender Ionic column, which had an elaborate base and spiral-shaped capitals, and the Corinthian column, which featured leaf-shaped capitals.

IMAGE 3.9 **The Parthenon.** The arts in classical Greece were designed to express the eternal ideals of reason, moderation, symmetry, balance, and harmony. In architecture, the most important form was the temple, and the classic example of this kind of architecture is the Parthenon, built between 447 and 432 B.C.E. Located on the Acropolis in Athens, the Parthenon was dedicated to Athena, the patron goddess of the city, but it also served as a shining example of the power and wealth of the Athenian empire.

The most famous building, regarded as the greatest example of the classical Greek temple, was the Parthenon, built between 447 and 432 B.C.E. and consecrated to Athena, the patron goddess of Athens (see Image 3.9). The Parthenon typifies the principles of classical architecture: the search for calm, clarity, and freedom from superfluous detail. The individual parts of the temple were constructed in accordance with certain mathematical ratios found in nature. The architects' concern with the laws of proportion is paralleled by the attempt of Greek philosophers to understand the general laws of nature.

Greek sculpture also developed a classical style that differed significantly from the artificial stiffness of the kouros figure of the Archaic Period. Statues of the male nude, the favorite subject of Greek sculptors, now exhibited more relaxed attitudes; their faces were self-assured, their bodies flexible and smooth-muscled. Although the figures possessed natural features that made them lifelike, Greek sculptors sought to achieve not realism but a standard of ideal beauty. Polyclitus (pahl-ee-KLY-tuss), a fifth-century B.C.E. sculptor, wrote a treatise (now lost) on a canon of proportions that he illustrated in a work known as the *Doryphoros* (doh-RIF-uh-rohss) (see Image 3.10). His theory maintained that the use of ideal proportions, based on mathematical ratios found in nature, could produce an ideal human form, beautiful in its perfected and refined features. This search for ideal beauty was the dominant feature of the classical standard in sculpture.

IMAGE 3.10 *Doryphoros.* This statue, known as the *Doryphoros*, or spear carrier, is a Roman copy of the original work by the fifth-century B.C.E. sculptor Polyclitus, who believed it illustrated the ideal proportions of the human figure. Classical Greek sculpture moved away from the stiffness of the kouros figure but retained the young male nude as its favorite subject matter. The statues became more lifelike, with relaxed poses and flexible, smooth-muscled bodies. The aim of sculpture, however, was not simply realism but rather the expression of ideal beauty.

3-5d The Greek Love of Wisdom

Philosophy is a Greek word that literally means "love of wisdom." Early Greek philosophers were concerned with the development of critical or rational thought about the nature of the universe and the place of divine forces and souls within it.

Much of early Greek philosophy focused on the attempt to explain the universe on the basis of unifying principles. Thales of Miletus (THAY-leez of my-LEE-tuss), an Ionian Greek who lived around 600 B.C.E., expressed an interest in explaining the events of nature. He postulated the unity of the universe, arguing that all things were linked by water as the basic substance. Another Ionian Greek, Pythagoras (puh-THAG-uh-russ) (ca. 580–490 B.C.E.), an important figure in the development of mathematics, taught that the essence of the universe could be found in music and numbers. These early Greek philosophers may have eliminated the role of the gods as they were portrayed in Greek myths, but they did not eliminate divinity itself from the world, tending instead to identify it with the underlying, unchanging forces that govern the universe.

Another major preoccupation of the so-called pre-Socratic philosophers (Greek philosophers before Socrates) was the nature of reality. Some philosophers saw change as the only reality, while others took the opposite view that all change is merely an illusion of the senses. Empedocles (ca. 493–433 B.C.E.) arrived at a compromise, believing that there are four basic substances: earth, air, fire, and water. They are unchanging, but their interaction makes up the physical universe and produces the appearance of change.

Many Greeks, however, were simply not interested in speculations on the nature of the universe. The **Sophists** (SAHF-ists) were a group of philosophical teachers in the fifth century who rejected such speculation as foolish; they argued that understanding the universe was beyond the reach of the human mind. It was more important for individuals to improve themselves, so the only worthwhile object of study was human behavior. The Sophists were wandering scholars who sold their services as professional teachers to the young men of Greece, especially those of Athens. The Sophists stressed the importance of **rhetoric** (the art of persuasive speaking) in winning debates and swaying an audience, a skill that was especially valuable in democratic Athens. To the Sophists, there was no absolute right or wrong—what was right for one individual might be wrong for another. True wisdom consisted of being able to perceive one's own good and to pursue its acquisition. Many people, however, viewed the Sophists as a threat to the traditional values of society and especially dangerous to the values of young people.

In classical Greece, Athens became the foremost intellectual and artistic center. Its reputation is perhaps strongest of all in philosophy. After all, Socrates, Plato, and Aristotle raised basic questions that have been debated for more than two thousand years; these are still largely the same philosophical questions we wrestle with today.

Socrates Socrates (SAHK-ruh-teez) (469–399 B.C.E.) left no writings, but we know about him from his pupils, especially his most famous one, Plato. By occupation, Socrates was a stonemason, but his true love was philosophy. He taught a number of pupils, but not for pay, because he believed that the goal of education was only to improve the individual. He made use of a teaching method that is still known by his name. The **Socratic method** employs a question-and-answer technique to lead pupils to see things for themselves using their own reason. Socrates believed that all real knowledge is within each person; only critical examination was needed to call it forth. This was the real task of philosophy, since "the unexamined life is not worth living."

Socrates's questioning of authority and public demonstrations of others' lack of knowledge led him into trouble. Athens had had a tradition of free thought and inquiry, but its defeat in the Peloponnesian War created an environment intolerant of open debate and soul-searching. Socrates was accused and convicted of corrupting the youth of Athens by his teaching, and an Athenian jury sentenced him to death.

Plato One of Socrates's disciples was Plato (PLAY-toh) (ca. 429–347 B.C.E.), considered by many scholars the greatest philosopher of Western civilization. Unlike his master Socrates, who wrote nothing, Plato wrote a great deal. He was fascinated with the question of reality: How do we know what is real?

According to Plato, a higher world of eternal, unchanging Ideas or Forms has always existed. To know these Forms is to know Truth. These ideal Forms constitute reality and can be apprehended only by a trained mind, which, of course, is the goal of philosophy. The objects that we perceive with our senses are simply reflections of the ideal Forms. Hence, they are shadows, while reality is found in the Forms themselves.

Plato's ideas of government were set out in a dialogue titled *The Republic.* Based on his experience in Athens, Plato had come to distrust the workings of democracy. It was obvious to him that individuals could not attain an ethical life unless they lived in a just and rational state. This insight led him to construct an ideal state in which the population was divided into three basic groups. At the top was an upper class, a ruling elite, the famous philosopher-kings: "Unless either philosophers become kings in their countries or those who are now called kings and rulers come to be sufficiently inspired with a genuine desire for wisdom; unless, that is to say, political power and philosophy meet together . . . there can be no rest from troubles . . . for states, nor yet, as I believe, for all mankind."[17] The second group consisted of the courageous; they would be the warriors who protected the society. All the rest made up the masses, essentially people driven not by wisdom or courage but by desire. They would be the producers of society—the artisans, tradesmen, and farmers.

In Plato's ideal state, each group fulfilled its assigned role, creating a society that functioned harmoniously. The needs of the community rather than the happiness of the individual were Plato's concern, and he focused on the need for the guardians or rulers, above all, to be removed from any concerns for wealth or prestige so that they could strive for what was best for the community. To rid the guardians of these desires, Plato urged that they live together, forgoing both private property and family life. Plato believed that women, too, could be rulers; in this he departed radically from the actual practices of the Greek states.

Aristotle Plato established a school at Athens known as the Academy. One of his pupils, who studied there for twenty

The *Politics* of Aristotle

 What do Aristotle's comments suggest about the importance of the polis to the ancient Greeks? How does Aristotle distinguish humans from other animals, and what is the relationship between humanity and the polis?

ARISTOTLE WAS ONE OF THE GREAT PHILOSOPHERS of ancient Athens. His philosophical and political ideas would play an important role in the evolution of Western thought during the Middle Ages. In this selection from his *Politics,* Aristotle examines the nature of political community and of the polis.

Aristotle, *Politics*

From these considerations it is evident that the *polis* belongs to the class of things that exist by nature, and that man is by nature an animal intended to live in a *polis.* He who is without a *polis,* by reason of his own nature and not of some accident, is either a poor sort of being, or a being higher than man: he is the man of whom Homer wrote in denunciation: "Clanless and lawless and heartless is he." The man who is such by

nature [unable to join in the society of a polis] at once plunges into a passion for war; he is in the position of a solitary advanced piece in a game of [checkers].

The reason why man is a being meant for political association, in a higher degree than bees or other gregarious animals can ever associate, is evident. Nature, according to our theory, makes nothing in vain; and man alone of the animals is furnished with the faculty of language. The mere making of sounds serves to indicate pleasure and pain, is thus a faculty that belongs to animals in general: their nature enables them to attain the point at which they have perceptions of pleasure and pain, and can signify those perceptions to one another. But language serves to declare what is advantageous and what is the reverse, and it therefore serves to declare what is just and what is unjust. It is the peculiarity of man, in comparison with the rest of the animal world, that he alone possesses perception of good and evil, of the just and the unjust, and of other similar qualities; and it is association in [a common perception of] these things which makes a family and a *polis.*

We now proceed to add that [though the individual and the family are prior in the order of time] the *polis* is prior in the order of nature to the family and the individual.

Source: Aristotle, *Politics*, trans. E. Barker (Oxford: Clarendon Press, 1946).

years, was Aristotle (AR-iss-tot-ul) (384–322 B.C.E.), who later became a tutor to Alexander the Great. Aristotle did not accept Plato's theory of ideal Forms. He believed that by examining individual objects, we can perceive their form and arrive at universal principles, but they do not exist as a separate higher world of reality beyond material things; rather they are a part of things themselves. Aristotle's interests, then, lay in analyzing and classifying things based on thorough research and investigation. His interests were wide-ranging, and he wrote treatises on an enormous number of subjects: ethics, logic, politics, poetry, astronomy, geology, biology, and physics.

Like Plato, Aristotle wished for an effective form of government that would rationally direct human affairs. Unlike Plato, he did not seek an ideal state based on the embodiment of an ideal form of justice; he tried to find the best form of government by a rational examination of existing governments. For his *Politics* (see Historical Voices, "The *Politics* of Aristotle," above), Aristotle examined the constitutions of 158 states and arrived at general categories for organizing governments. He identified three good forms of government: monarchy, aristocracy, and constitutional government. But based on his examination, he warned that monarchy can easily turn into tyranny, aristocracy into oligarchy, and constitutional government into radical democracy or anarchy. He favored constitutional government as the best form for most people.

Aristotle's philosophical and political ideas played an enormous role in the development of Western thought during the Middle Ages (see Chapter 9). So did his ideas on women. Aristotle believed that marriage was meant to provide mutual comfort between man and woman and contributed to the overall happiness of a community: "The community needs both male and female excellences or it can only be half-blessed." Nevertheless, Aristotle maintained that women were biologically inferior to men: "A woman is, as it were, an infertile male. She is female in fact on account of a kind of inadequacy." Therefore, according to Aristotle, women must be subordinated to men, not only in the community but also in marriage: "The association between husband and wife is clearly an aristocracy. The man rules by virtue of merit, and in the sphere that is his by right; but he hands over to his wife such matters as are suitable for her."[18]

3-5e Greek Religion

Greek religion was intricately connected to every aspect of daily life; it was both social and practical. Public festivals, which originated from religious practices, served specific functions: boys were prepared to be warriors, girls to be mothers. Since religion was related to every aspect of life, citizens had to have a proper attitude toward the gods. Religion was a civic cult necessary for the well-being of the state. Temples dedicated to a god or goddess were the major buildings of Greek society.

Homer gave an account of the gods that provided a definite structure to Greek religion. Over a period of time, most Greeks came to accept a common religion based on twelve chief gods who supposedly lived on Mount Olympus, the highest mountain in Greece. Among the twelve were Zeus (ZOOSS), the chief deity and father of the gods; Athena, goddess of wisdom and crafts; Apollo, god of the sun and poetry; Aphrodite (af-fruh-DY-tee), goddess of love; and Poseidon (puh-SY-duhn), brother of Zeus and god of the seas and earthquakes.

The twelve Olympian gods were common to all Greeks, who thus shared a basic polytheistic religion. Each polis usually singled out one of the twelve Olympians as a guardian deity of its community. Athena was the patron goddess of Athens, for example. Because it was desirable to have the gods look favorably on one's activities, ritual assumed enormous proportions in Greek religion. Prayers were often combined with gifts to the gods based on the principle "I give so that you, the gods, will give in return." Ritual meant sacrifices, whether of animals or agricultural products. Animals were burned on an altar in front of a temple or on a small altar in front of a home.

As another practical side of Greek religion, Greeks wanted to know the will of the gods. The most famous method of divining the will of the gods was the use of the oracle, a sacred shrine dedicated to a god or goddess who revealed the future. The most famous was the oracle of Apollo at Delphi, located on the side of Mount Parnassus, overlooking the Gulf of Corinth. At Delphi, a priestess listened to questions while in a state of ecstasy that was believed to be induced by Apollo. The priests interpreted her responses and gave them in verse form to the person asking the questions. Both representatives of states and individuals traveled to Delphi to consult the oracle of Apollo. States might inquire whether they should undertake a military expedition; individuals might raise such questions as "Heracleidas asks the god whether he will have offspring from the wife he has now." Responses were often enigmatic and could be interpreted in more than one way. Croesus (KREE-suss), the king of Lydia in Asia Minor who was known for his incredible wealth, sent messengers to the oracle at Delphi asking whether he should go to war with the Persians. The oracle replied that if Croesus attacked the Persians, a mighty empire would be destroyed. Overjoyed to hear these words, Croesus made war on the Persians but was crushed by his enemy. A mighty empire was indeed destroyed—Croesus's own.

Festivals also developed as a way to honor the gods and goddesses. Some of these (the Panhellenic celebrations) were important to all Greeks and were held at special locations, such as those dedicated to the worship of Zeus at Olympia, to Poseidon at the Isthmus of Corinth, and to Apollo at Delphi. The great festivals incorporated numerous events in honor of the gods, including athletic competitions to which all Greeks were invited.

According to tradition, such athletic games were first held at the Olympic festival in 776 B.C.E. and then held every four years thereafter to honor Zeus. Initially, the Olympic contests consisted of foot races and wrestling, but later boxing,

javelin throwing, and various other contests were added (see Image 3.11). Competitions were always between individuals, not groups. The Greeks regarded winning athletes as great heroes and often rewarded them with parades, as well as money and free rent for life.

Olympic games were not without danger to the participants, however. Athletes competed in the nude, and rules were rather relaxed. Wrestlers, for example, were allowed to gouge the eyes of their competitors and even pick them up and drop them head first onto a hard surface. Boxers wrapped their hands and forearms with heavy leather thongs to make their blows more damaging. Occasionally, athletes were killed during the games. Given the animosity that often existed between city-states in ancient Greece, the deaths were not always accidental.

The Olympic games, combined with other all-Greek athletic games, served a valuable role. The system of Greek poleis had led to separation and individual goals. But participation in these

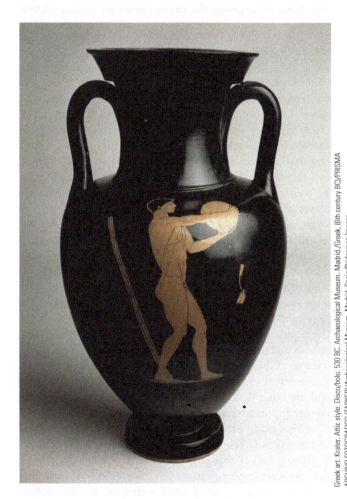

Greek art. Krater. Attic style. Disco/bolo. 530 BC. Archaeological Museum. Madrid./Greek, (6th century BC)/PRISMA ARCHIVO FOTOGRAFICO (TARKER)/Archaeological Museum, Madrid, Spain/Bridgeman Images

IMAGE 3.11 Olympic Athlete. Athletic games were a feature of festivals honoring Greek gods and goddesses. Those at the Olympic festival honoring Zeus were especially prominent. Shown here in a sixth-century Attic krater (a krater was a large vase, usually used for watering down wine) is a Greek athlete preparing to throw a discus. The discus throw was one of the first five events of the Greek Olympics, As seen here, Greek athletes competed in the nude. Originally, the discus was made of stone, but later changed to lead, bronze, or iron.

games also caused Greeks to become more aware of a wider sense of community as Greeks. By the sixth century, this led to an emerging sense of Greekness. And as we have seen, the later threat from the Persians would serve to solidify this growing cultural identity.

3-5f Life in Classical Athens

The Greek city-state was, above all, a male community: only adult male citizens took part in public life. In Athens, this meant the exclusion of women, slaves, and foreign residents, or roughly 85 percent of the total population of Attica. In the fifth century, Athens had the largest population of all the Greek city-states. There were probably 150,000 citizens, of whom about 43,000 were adult males who exercised political power. Resident foreigners, known as **metics**, numbered about 35,000 and received the protection of the laws, but they were also subject to some of the responsibilities of citizens, namely military service and the funding of festivals. The remaining social group, the slaves, numbered around 100,000.

Slavery and the Economy Slavery was a common institution in the ancient world. It was useful to own at least one slave, although the very poor in Athens did not own any. A soldier on campaign usually took along one slave to carry his armor. The really wealthy might own large numbers of slaves, but those who did usually employed them in industry. Most often slaves in Athens performed domestic tasks as cooks and maids or worked in the fields. Few peasants could afford more than one or two. Other slaves worked as unskilled or skilled laborers. Slaves who worked in public construction were paid the same as metics or citizens. Slaves who were used as pearl-divers, rowers in trading ships, and workers in silver mines suffered horrible, and usually short, lives.

The Athenian economy was largely agricultural but highly diversified. Athenian farmers grew grains, vegetables, and fruit for local consumption; cultivated vines and olives for wine and olive oil, which were exportable products; and raised sheep and goats for wool and milk products. Given the size of the population in Attica and the lack of abundant fertile land, Athens had to import between 50 and 80 percent of its grain, a staple in the Athenian diet. Trade was thus very important to the Athenian economy. The building of the port at Piraeus and the Long Walls (a series of defensive walls 41 miles long connecting Athens and Piraeus) created the physical conditions that made Athens the leading trade center in the fifth-century B.C.E. Greek world.

Athens did not have large numbers of artisans, but those it did have were important to the economy. Athens was the chief producer of high-quality painted pottery in the fifth century B.C.E. Other crafts had moved beyond the small workshop into the factory through the use of slave labor.

A Simple Lifestyle The Athenian lifestyle was basically simple. Athenian houses were furnished with necessities bought from artisans, such as beds, couches, tables, chests, pottery, stools, baskets, and cooking utensils. Wives and slaves made clothes and blankets at home (see Images of Everyday Life, "Activities of Athenian Women," p. 85). The Athenian diet was rather plain. Basic foods included barley, wheat, millet, lentils, grapes, figs, olives, almonds, bread made at home, vegetables, eggs, fish, cheese, and chicken. Olive oil was widely used not only for eating but also for lighting lamps and for rubbing on the body after washing and exercise. Owners of country houses kept animals for reasons other than their flesh: oxen for plowing, sheep for wool, and goats for milk and cheese. Meat was consumed only on special occasions, such as festivals, when animals were sacrificed, cooked, and then eaten.

Family and Relationships The family was an important institution in ancient Athens. It was composed of husband, wife, and children (a nuclear family), although other dependent relatives and slaves were regarded as part of the family because of its economic unity. The family's primary social function was to produce new citizens. Strict laws of the fifth century B.C.E. had stipulated that a citizen must be the offspring of a legally acknowledged marriage between two Athenian citizens.

Women were citizens who could participate in most religious cults and festivals but were otherwise excluded from public life. They could not own property beyond personal items and always had a male guardian: if unmarried, a father or male relative; if married, a husband; if widowed, a son or male relative.

The function of the Athenian woman as wife was very clear. Her foremost obligation was to bear children, especially male children who would preserve the family line. The marriage formula that Athenians used put it succinctly: "I give this woman for the procreation of legitimate children." A wife was also expected to take care of her family and her house, either doing the household work herself or supervising the slaves who did the actual work (see Opposing Viewpoints, "Women in Athens and Sparta," p. 86).

Women were kept under strict control. Since they were married at fourteen or fifteen, they were taught about their responsibilities at an early age. Although many managed to learn to read and play musical instruments, they were often cut off from any formal education. And women were expected to remain at home out of sight unless they attended funerals or festivals. If they left the house, they were to be accompanied.

Women in Athens served males in other ways as well. Prostitution was common in classical Athens. Most female prostitutes were slaves in brothels run as a business or trade by an Athenian citizen. Another class of prostitutes in Athenian society occupied a more favorable position; these more refined courtesans were known as **hetairai** (huh-TY-ree), literally "female companions." Usually ex-slaves or foreigners, these women were more sophisticated than ordinary prostitutes and were known for their intellectual and musical achievements as well as their physical ones. Athenian males continued the aristocratic practice of the *symposium*, a sophisticated drinking party at which hetairai were often present. Symposia were held in the men's dining rooms, and wives were not present. Hetairai danced, played musical instruments, and provided entertainment,

Activities of Athenian Women

Q *If women were barred from political activity, why do you think they were allowed to participate in religious festivals?*

IN ATHENS, WOMEN WERE CONSIDERED CITIZENS and could participate in religious cults and festivals, but they were barred from any political activity. Women were thought to belong in the house, caring for the children and the needs of the household. A principal activity of Greek women was the making of clothes. The scene in Image 3.12a from the side of a fifth-century B.C.E. Greek vessel shows one woman

spinning while another holds a small hand loom. Image 3.12b from a mid-sixth-century B.C.E. amphora (a jar or vase) shows another activity of Athenian women—participating in religious rituals. This scene shows a priestess dressed in an elaborate gown holding ceremonial branches and scattering holy water upon an altar while the men behind her are leading a bull to be sacrificed. It has recently been argued that the prominent position of the priestess standing in the center before the goddess Athena shows that the priestess was the chief supervisor of the sacrifice and, thus, an indication that women as priestesses played important public roles in ancient Greece.

IMAGE 3.12a

IMAGE 3.12b

including sex. Some hetairai achieved fortune and considerable renown. Aspasia was the most famous. A friend of Socrates and known for her learning, she was the mistress of Pericles and eventually became his wife.

Male homosexuality was also a prominent feature of classical Athens. It was widely practiced and tolerated. Athenian law disenfranchised a citizen who had prostituted his body to another male, but nothing was done to males who engaged in homosexual love with male prostitutes or other adult males for love or pleasure. The law did not eliminate male prostitution but ensured that male prostitutes would be foreigners, not Athenian citizens.

The Greek homosexual ideal was a relationship between a mature man and a young male. It is most likely that this was primarily an aristocratic ideal. While the relationship was frequently physical, the Greeks also viewed it as educational. The older male (the "lover") won the love of his "beloved" by his value as a teacher and by the devotion he demonstrated in training his charge. In a sense, this love relationship was seen as a way of initiating young males into the male world of political and military dominance. The Greeks did not feel that the coexistence of homosexual and heterosexual predilections created any special problems for individuals or their society.

Women in Athens and Sparta

 In what ways were the lifestyles of Athenian and Spartan women the same? In what ways were they different? How did the Athenian and Spartan views of the world shape their conceptions of gender and gender roles, and why were those conceptions different?

IN CLASSICAL ATHENS, a woman's place was in the home. She had two major responsibilities as a wife—bearing and raising children and managing the household. In the first selection, from a dialogue on estate management, Xenophon (ZEN-uh-fuhn) relates the instructions of an Athenian to his new wife. Although women in Sparta had the same responsibilities as women in Athens, they assumed somewhat different roles as a result of the Spartan lifestyle. The second, third, and fourth selections demonstrate these differences as seen in the accounts of three ancient Greek writers.

Xenophon, *Oeconomicus*

[Ischomachus addresses his new wife:] For it seems to me, dear, that the gods with great discernment have coupled together male and female, as they are called, chiefly in order that they may form a perfect partnership in mutual service. For, in the first place that the various species of living creatures may not fail, they are joined in wedlock for the production of children. Secondly, offspring to support them in old age is provided by this union, to human beings, at any rate. Thirdly, human beings live not in the open air, like beasts, but obviously need shelter. Nevertheless, those who mean to win stores to fill the covered place, have need of someone to work at the open-air occupations; since plowing, sowing, planting and grazing are all such open-air employments; and these supply the needful food. . . . For he made the man's body and mind more capable of enduring cold and heat, and journeys and campaigns; and therefore imposed on him the outdoor tasks. To the woman, since he had made her body less capable of such endurance, I take it that God has assigned the indoor tasks. And knowing that he had created in the woman and had imposed on her the nourishment of the infants, he meted out to her a larger portion of affection for newborn babes than to the man. . . .

Your duty will be to remain indoors and send out those servants whose work is outside, and superintend those who are to work indoors, and to receive the incomings, and distribute so much of them as must be spent, and watch over so much as is to be kept in store, and take care that the sum laid by for a year be not spent in a month. And when wool is brought to you, you must see that cloaks are made for those that want them. You must see too that the dry corn is in good condition for making food. One of the duties that fall to you, however, will perhaps seem rather thankless: you will have to see that any servant who is ill is cared for.

Xenophon, *Constitution of the Spartans*

First, to begin at the beginning, I will take the begetting of children. In other states the girls who are destined to become mothers and are brought up in the approved fashion, live on the very plainest fare, with a most meagre allowance of delicacies. Wine is either withheld altogether, or, if allowed them, is diluted with water. The rest of the Greeks expect their girls to imitate the sedentary life that is typical of handicraftsmen—to keep quiet and do wool-work. How, then, is it to be expected that women so brought up will bear fine children?

But Lycurgus thought the labour of slave women sufficient to supply clothing. He believed motherhood to be the most important function of freeborn woman. Therefore, in the first place, he insisted on physical training for the female no less than for the male sex: moreover, he instituted races and trials of strength for women competitors as for men, believing that if both parents are strong they produce more vigorous offspring.

Aristotle, *Politics*

Now, this license of the [Spartan] women, from the earliest times, was to be expected. For the men were absent from home for long periods of time on military expeditions, fighting the war against the Argives and again against the Arkadians and Messenians. . . . And nearly two-fifths of the whole country is in the hands of women, both because there have been numerous heiresses, and because large dowries are customary. And yet it would have been better to have regulated them, and given none at all or small or even moderate ones. But at present it is possible for a man to give an inheritance to whomever he chooses.

Plutarch, *Lycurgus*

Since Lycurgus regarded education as the most important and finest duty of the legislator, he began at the earliest stage by looking at matters relating to marriages and births. . . . For he exercised the girls' bodies with races and wrestling and discus and javelin throwing, so that the embryos formed in them would have a strong start in strong bodies and develop better, and they would undergo their pregnancies with vigor and would cope well and easily with childbirth. He got rid of daintiness and sheltered upbringing and effeminacy of all kinds, by accustoming the girls no less than the young men to walking naked in processions and dancing and singing at certain festivals, when young men were present and watching. . . . The nudity of the girls had nothing disgraceful in it for modesty was present and immorality absent, but rather it made them accustomed to simplicity and enthusiastic as to physical fitness, and gave the female sex a taste of noble spirit, in as much as they too had a share in valor and ambition.

Sources: Xenophon, *Oeconomicus*, in *Xenophon, Memorabilia and Oeconomicus*, trans. E. C. Marchant and O. J. Todd (Cambridge, Mass.: Harvard University Press, 1930); Xenophon, *Constitution of the Spartans*, in *Xenophon in Seven Volumes*, edited by E. C. Marchant and translated by G. W. Bowersock (Cambridge, Mass.: Harvard University Press, 1925); Aristotle, *Politics*, in *Aristotle, A Treatise on Government*, trans. W. Ellis (London, J. M. Dent & Sons, 1912); Plutarch, *Lycurgus*, in *Ideal Commonwealths: Plutarch's Lycurgus*, ed. H. Morley, 5th edition (London: George Routledge and Sons, 1890).

CHAPTER SUMMARY

The earliest Greek-speaking people migrated into Greece about 2000 B.C.E. and by 1600 B.C.E. had established a Greek civilization, known as the Mycenaean civilization from Mycenae, one of its major cities. After its collapse in the twelfth century B.C.E., Greece entered what some historians have called a Dark Age. With the end of this transitional period around 800 B.C.E., the era of the polis, or city-state, began. The polis was a community of citizens ruled by its male citizens. The two most famous city-states were Sparta, a militaristic polis ruled by an oligarchy, and Athens, which became known for its democratic institutions in spite of the fact that slaves and women had no political rights.

The Greek city-states flourished and reached their height in the classical era of the fifth century B.C.E. The century began with the Persian Wars, which temporarily unified the Greeks, who were victorious against the powerful Persian Empire. But the growth of an Athenian empire led to a mighty conflict between Athens and Sparta—the Great Peloponnesian War—that weakened the Greek city-states and ultimately opened the door to an invasion by Philip II of Macedonia that put an end to their freedom in 338 B.C.E.

The civilization of the ancient Greeks was the fountainhead of Western culture. Socrates, Plato, and Aristotle

established the foundations of Western philosophy. Herodotus and Thucydides created the discipline of history. Our literary forms are largely derived from Greek poetry and drama. Greek notions of harmony, proportion, and beauty remained for centuries the touchstones for subsequent Western art and architecture. A rational method of inquiry, so important to modern science, was conceived in ancient Greece. Many of our political terms are Greek in origin, as are our concepts of the rights and duties of citizenship, especially as they were conceived in Athens, which gave the idea of democracy to the Western world. Especially during the classical period, the Greeks raised and debated fundamental questions about the purpose of human existence, the structure of human society, and the nature of the universe that have concerned Western thinkers ever since. Although the Greeks did not conceive of Western civilization as a cultural entity, their artistic, intellectual, and political contributions were crucial to the foundations of Western civilization.

All of these achievements came from a group of small city-states in ancient Greece. And yet there remains an element of tragedy about Greek civilization. For all of their brilliant accomplishments, the Greeks were unable to rise above the divisions and rivalries that caused them to fight each other and undermine their own civilization. Fortunately, their contributions to Western civilization survived their political struggles.

CHAPTER TIMELINE

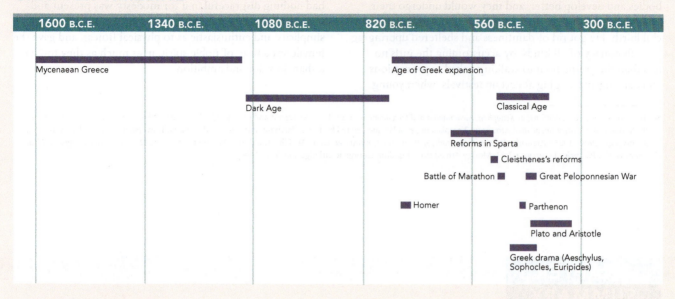

1600 B.C.E.	1340 B.C.E.	1080 B.C.E.	820 B.C.E.	560 B.C.E.	300 B.C.E.

Mycenaean Greece

Dark Age

Age of Greek expansion

Classical Age

Reforms in Sparta

Cleisthenes's reforms

Battle of Marathon

Great Peloponnesian War

Homer

Parthenon

Plato and Aristotle

Greek drama (Aeschylus, Sophocles, Euripides)

CHAPTER REVIEW

Upon Reflection

Q Why are the Greeks considered the cornerstone of the Western intellectual tradition?

Q What was the polis, and why have many historians considered it to be an important development in the political history of Western civilization?

Q Discuss the structure of the Athenian political system. In what ways was it a democracy? In what ways was Athenian democracy limited?

Q The classical age in Greece is known for its literary, artistic, and intellectual achievements. What basic characteristics of Greek culture are reflected in the major achievements of the Greeks in the writing of history, drama, the arts, and philosophy? What universal human concerns did these same achievements reflect?

Key Terms

polis (p. 56)
hoplites (p. 61)
phalanx (p. 61)
tyrant (p. 63)
oligarchy (p. 64)
perioikoi (p. 65)

helots (p. 65)
Sophists (p. 81)
rhetoric (p. 81)
Socratic method (p. 81)
metics (p. 84)
hetairai (p. 86)

Full definitions also appear in the Glossary at the end of the book.

Suggestions for Further Reading

General Works Two good general introductions to Greek history are **W. Donlan et al.,** *Ancient Greece: A Political, Social, and Cultural History,* 4th ed. (New York, 2017), and **V. Parker,** *A History of Greece, 1300 to 30 B.C.* (Hoboken, N.J., 2013). On the Greek way of war, see **V. D. Hanson,** *The Wars of the Ancient Greeks,* revised edition (London, 2006). On the Minoans, see **J. Bennet,** *A Short History of the Minoans* (London, 2014).

Early Greek History Early Greek history is examined in **L. Schofield,** *The Mycenaeans* (Los Angeles, 2007), and **O. Murray,** *Early Greece,* 2nd edition (Cambridge, Mass., 2010).

On the Trojan War, see **B. Strauss,** *The Trojan War: A New History* (New York, 2006).

Archaic Greece A good general work on Archaic Greece is **J. Hall,** *History of the Archaic Greek World, c. 1200–479 B.C.* (London, 2006). On Sparta, see **P. A. Cartledge,** *The Spartans* (New York, 2003). On early Athens, see **R. Osborne,** *Athens and Athenian Democracy* (New York, 2010). The Persian Wars are examined in **T. Holland,** *Persian Fire* (London, 2005). On the polis, see **M. H. Hansen,** *Polis: An Introduction to the Ancient Greek City-State* (Oxford, 2006).

Classical Greece A general history of Classical Greece can be found in **P. J. Rhodes**, *A History of the Greek Classical World, 478–323 B.C.* (London, 2006), and **J. Ober**, *The Rise and Fall of Classical Greece* (Princeton, N.J., 2016) Valuable works on Athens include **D. Kagan**, *Pericles of Athens and the Birth of Democracy* (New York, 1991), and **K. A. Raaflaub et al.**, *Origins of Democracy in Ancient Greece* (Berkeley, Calif., 2007). For an account of the Great Peloponnesian War, see **N. Bagnall**, *The Peloponnesian War: Athens, Sparta, and the Struggle for Greece* (New York, 2006).

Greek Culture For a history of Greek art, see **A. Stewart**, *Classical Greece and the Birth of Western Art* (New York, 2008). On Greek drama, see the general work by **J. De Romilly**, *A Short History of Greek Literature* (Chicago, 1985). On Greek history writing, see **D. Shanske**, *Thucydides and the Philosophical Origin of History* (Cambridge, 2006).

Greek Religion On Greek religion, see **J. N. Bremmer**, *Greek Religion* (Oxford, 1994), and **M. Dillon**, *Girls and Women in Classical Greek Religion* (New York, 2002). On athletic competitions, see **S. G. Miller**, *Ancient Greek Athletics* (New Haven, Conn., 2004).

Family and Gender Issues On the family and women, see **C. B. Patterson**, *The Family in Greek History* (New York, 1998); **S. B. Pomeroy**, *Spartan Women* (Oxford, 2002); and **S. Blundell**, *Women in Ancient Greece* (London, 1995).

Notes

1. H. D. F. Kitto, *The Greeks* (Harmondsworth, England, 1951), p. 64.
2. Homer, *Odyssey*, trans. E. V. Rieu (Harmondsworth, England, 1946), p. 337.
3. Xenophon, *Symposium*, trans. O. J. Todd (Cambridge, Mass., 1968), 3.5.
4. Homer, *Odyssey*, pp. 290–291.
5. Quoted in T. R. Martin, *Ancient Greece* (New Haven, Conn., 1996), p. 62.
6. Quoted in V. D. Hanson, *The Wars of the Ancient Greeks*, revised edition (London, 2006), p. 14.
7. These words from Plutarch are quoted in E. Fantham et al., *Women in the Classical World* (New York, 1994), p. 64.
8. Willis Barnstone, *Ancient Greek Lyrics* (Bloomington, Ind., 1988), p. 63.
9. Hesiod, *Works and Days,* trans. Dorothea Wender (Harmondsworth, England, 1973), pp. 68, 71, 77.
10. Aeschylus, *The Persians*, in *The Complete Greek Tragedies*, vol. 1, eds. D. Grene and R. Lattimore (Chicago, 1959), p. 229.
11. Herodotus, *The Persian Wars*, trans. R. Waterfield (New York, 1998), p. 3.
12. Thucydides, *History of the Peloponnesian War*, trans. R. Warner (Harmondsworth, England, 1954), p. 24.
13. Ibid.
14. Ibid.
15. Sophocles, *Oedipus the King*, trans. David Grene (Chicago, 1959), pp. 68–69.
16. Sophocles, *Antigone*, trans. Don Taylor (London, 1986), p. 146.
17. Plato, *The Republic*, trans. F. M. Cornford (New York, 1945), pp. 178–179.
18. Quoted from S. Blundell, *Women in Ancient Greece* (London, 1995), pp. 106, 186.

MindTap *Tips*

What's the big idea? Check Your Understanding practice quizzes appear after each section reading in MindTap. Use these self-checks to be sure you're keying into the main ideas of your reading.

CHAPTER 4

The Hellenistic World

IMAGE 4.1 **Roman Statuette of Alexander the Great Wearing a Helmet**

© Rmn-Grand Palais/Art Resource, NY

CHAPTER OUTLINE AND FOCUS QUESTIONS

4-1 Macedonia and the Conquests of Alexander

Q How did Philip II prepare the way for the conquests of his son Alexander? How was Alexander able to amass his empire, and what might his rule have been like had he lived longer?

4-2 The World of the Hellenistic Kingdoms

Q What were the main features of the political and military organization of the Hellenistic kingdoms, and how did the new political systems differ from those of the Greek city-states?

4-3 Hellenistic Society

Q What were the main social developments in the Hellenistic world?

4-4 Culture in the Hellenistic World

Q What achievements in literature, art, science, medicine, and philosophy occurred during the Hellenistic period?

4-5 Religion in the Hellenistic World

Q Which religions were prominent during the Hellenistic period, and what does their popularity suggest about Hellenistic society?

CONNECTIONS TO TODAY

What role would a military leader like Alexander play in a military system today?

IN 334 B.C.E., ALEXANDER THE GREAT led an army of Macedonians and Greeks into West Asia to launch his attack on the Persian Empire. Years of campaigning resulted in the complete defeat of the Persians, and in 327 B.C.E., Alexander and his troops pushed eastward into India. But two more years of fighting in an exotic and difficult terrain exhausted his troops, who rebelled and refused to go on. Reluctantly, Alexander turned back, leading his men across the arid lands of southern Persia. Conditions in the desert were appalling; the blazing sun and lack of water led to thousands of deaths. At one point, when a group of his soldiers found a little water, they scooped it up in a helmet and gave it to Alexander. Then, according to Arrian, an ancient Greek historian, Alexander, "with a word of thanks for the gift, took the helmet and, in full view of his troops, poured the water on the ground. So extraordinary was the effect of this action that the water wasted by Alexander was as good as a drink for every man in the army." According to Arrian, Alexander, ever the great military leader, had found yet another way to inspire his troops.

Alexander the Great was the son of King Philip II of Macedonia, who in 338 B.C.E. defeated the Greeks and established his control over the Greek peninsula. After Philip's death, Alexander became king and led the Macedonians and Greeks on a spectacular conquest of the Persian Empire, opening the door to the spread of Greek culture throughout the ancient Near East. Greek settlers poured into these lands as bureaucrats, traders, soldiers, and scholars. Alexander's triumph created a new series of kingdoms that blended the achievements of the eastern world with the cultural outlook and attitudes of the Greeks. We use the term **Hellenistic** to designate this new order. The Hellenistic world was the world of Greeks and non-Greek easterners, and it resulted, in its own way, in a remarkable series of accomplishments that are sometimes underestimated. They form the story of this chapter.

4-1 Macedonia and the Conquests of Alexander

 FOCUS QUESTIONS: How did Philip II prepare the way for the conquests of his son Alexander? How was Alexander able to amass his empire, and what might his rule have been like had he lived longer?

While the Greek city-states were continuing their fratricidal warfare, to their north a new and ultimately powerful kingdom was emerging in its own right. The Macedonians were probably not Greek; scholars are still unsure whether the Macedonian language was an archaic dialect of Greek or an altogether separate language. The Greeks certainly viewed the Macedonians as barbarians but did allow them to participate as "Greeks" in the Olympic games beginning in the fifth century B.C.E.

Unlike the Greeks, the Macedonians were mostly rural folk and were organized in tribes, not city-states. Not until the end of the fifth century B.C.E., during the reign of King Archelaus (ca. 413–399 B.C.E.), did Macedonia emerge as an important kingdom. But his reign was followed by decades of repeated foreign invasions and internal strife until King Philip II (359–336 B.C.E.) took control and turned Macedonia into the chief power of the Greek world.

4-1a Philip and the Conquest of Greece

Philip had spent three years as a hostage in Thebes, where he had gained a great admiration for Greek culture and absorbed the latest Greek military developments. Philip understood the importance of having an efficient army if Macedonia was to be a strong state. He used Macedonian countrymen, sturdy peasants and shepherds, as the core of his phalanx of infantrymen. From the gold mines of Mount Pangaeus, he obtained the wealth to pay these soldiers and establish a standing professional army that could fight year-round.

Philip also instituted military reforms that transformed Macedonia into a major military power. He created a new phalanx of infantrymen who were more lightly armed than Greek hoplites; each carried a smaller shield and shorter sword. Instead, the Macedonian infantryman's chief weapon was a long thrusting spear—18 feet in length, or twice as long as the Greek hoplite's spear. In this way, Macedonian infantrymen could impale an opposing hoplite force before the hoplites could even reach them. The Macedonian phalanx was supported by strong cavalry contingents that helped to break the opposing line of battle and create disorder in the enemy's ranks. Philip also recognized the value of technological improvements in warfare and created a group of engineers to design new catapults to destroy an enemy's fortifications. He began a policy, later used by his son Alexander, of paying poor Macedonian farmers to commit full-time to military service, both in training and campaigning year-round. Moreover, the king established an officer class based on talent that could not only command in battle but also later be used to administer conquered territories. Finally, Philip strengthened the bonds between the army and its leaders. Even the king shared directly in the dangers of battle, as is evident from his many wounds. Philip's new army defeated the Illyrians to the west and the Thracians to the north and east and was then drawn into the Greeks' interstate conflicts.

The Greeks had mixed reactions to Philip's growing strength. Many Athenians, especially the orator Demosthenes (duh-MAHSS-thuh-neez), came to strongly distrust the Macedonian leader's intentions. Demosthenes delivered a series of orations, known as the *Philippics*, in which he portrayed Philip as ruthless, deceitful, treacherous, and barbaric and called on the Athenians to oppose him. Other Athenians, such as Isocrates (eye-SAHK-ruh-teez), a teacher of rhetoric, viewed Philip as a savior who would rescue the Greeks from themselves by uniting them and organizing the entire Greek world in a crusade against the common enemy, the Persians (see Opposing Viewpoints, "Demosthenes and Isocrates Address Philip of Macedonia," p. 92).

Demosthenes's repeated calls for action, combined with Philip's rapid expansion, finally spurred Athens into action. Allied with Thebes and some smaller states, Athens fought the Macedonians at the Battle of Chaeronea (ker-uh-NEE-uh), near Thebes, in 338 B.C.E. The Macedonian army crushed the Greek allies, and Philip was now free to consolidate his control over the Greek peninsula. While Thebes was punished severely, Athens was treated leniently out of respect for its past and expected cooperation in the future. The Greek states were joined together in an alliance that we call the Corinthian League because they met at Corinth. All members took an oath of loyalty: "I swear by Zeus, Earth, Sun, Poseidon, Athena, Ares, and all the gods and goddesses. I will abide by the peace, and I will not break the agreements with Philip the Macedonian, nor will I take up arms with hostile intent against any one of those who abide by the oaths either by land or by sea."[1]

Though based on the principle of self-governing, independent states, the league did have an army and a council. Philip of Macedon was recognized as *hegemon* (HEJ-uh-mun) (leader) of the league and its army. Although Philip allowed the Greek city-states autonomy in domestic affairs, he retained the general direction of their foreign affairs. Many Greeks still objected to being subject to the less civilized master from the north, but Philip insisted that the Greek states end their bitter rivalries and cooperate with him in a war against Persia.

Before Philip could undertake his invasion of Asia, however, he was assassinated by a jilted male lover, leaving the task to his son Alexander. Although Alexander justly deserves credit for the destruction of the Persian Empire, it was Philip who paved the way for the conquest. He had unified Macedonia, created a powerful military machine, and subdued the Greeks.

4-1b Alexander the Great

Alexander was only twenty when he became king of Macedonia. In the next twelve years, he achieved so much that he has ever since been called Alexander the Great (see Image 4.2).

Demosthenes and Isocrates Address Philip of Macedonia

 What are Demosthenes's criticisms of Philip II? What appeal does Isocrates make to Philip? What do these documents tell you about the persistent factionalism and communal tensions within the Greek world? In light of subsequent events, who—Demosthenes or Isocrates—made the stronger argument? Why?

AMONG THE GREEKS, Demosthenes reacted most strongly to the growing strength and expansionary policies of the Macedonian king Philip II. Demosthenes delivered a series of orations to the Athenian assembly in which he portrayed Philip as a ruthless barbarian. The first selection is from Demosthenes's *Third Philippic,* delivered around 341 B.C.E. Isocrates, an Athenian teacher of rhetoric, saw Philip in a different light and appealed to him to lead both Greeks and Macedonians in a war against the Persians. The second selection is from Isocrates's *Address to Philip,* written in 346 B.C.E.

Demosthenes, *The Third Philippic*

I observe, however, that all men, and you first of all, have conceded to him something which has been the occasion of every war that the Greeks have ever waged. And what is that? The power of doing what he likes, of calmly plundering and stripping the Greeks one by one, and of attacking their cities and reducing them to slavery. Yet your hegemony in Greece lasted seventy-three years, that of Sparta twenty-nine, and in these later times Thebes too gained some sort of authority after the battle of Leuctra. But neither to you nor to the Thebans nor to the Spartans did the Greeks ever yet, men of Athens, concede the right of unrestricted action, or anything like it. On the contrary, when you, or rather the Athenians of that day, were thought to be showing a want of consideration in dealing with others, all felt it their duty, even those who had no grievance against them, to go to war in support of those who had been injured. . . . Yet all the faults committed by the Spartans in those thirty years, and by our ancestors in their seventy years of supremacy, are fewer, men of Athens, than the wrongs which Philip has done to the Greeks in the thirteen incomplete years in

which he has been coming to the top—or rather, they are not a fraction of them. . . . Ay, and you know this also, that the wrongs which the Greeks suffered from the Spartans or from us, they suffered at all events at the hands of true-born sons of Greece, and they might have been regarded as the acts of a legitimate son, born to great possessions, who should be guilty of some fault or error in the management of his estate: so far he would deserve blame and reproach, yet it could not be said that it was not one of the blood, not the lawful heir who was acting thus. But if some slave or illegitimate bastard had wasted and squandered what he had no right to, heavens! how much more monstrous and exasperating all would have called it! Yet they have no such qualms about Philip and his present conduct, though he is not only no Greek, nor related to the Greeks, but not even a barbarian from any place that can be named with honor, but a pestilent knave from Macedonia, from where it was never yet possible to buy a decent slave.

Isocrates, *Address to Philip*

I chose to address to you what I have to say. . . . I am going to advise you to champion the cause of concord among the Hellenes and of a campaign against the barbarians; and as persuasion will be helpful in dealing with the Hellenes, so compulsion will be useful in dealing with the barbarians.

I affirm that, without neglecting any of your own interests, you ought to make an effort to reconcile Argos and Sparta and Thebes and Athens; for if you can bring these cities together, you will not find it hard to unite the others as well. . . .

You see how utterly wretched these states have become because of their warfare, and how like they are to men engaged in a personal encounter; for no one can reconcile the parties to a quarrel while their wrath is rising; but after they have punished each other badly, they need no mediator, but separate of their own accord. And that is just what I think these states also will do unless you first take them in hand. . . .

Now regarding myself, and regarding the course which you should take toward the Hellenes, perhaps no more need be said. But as to the expedition against Asia, we shall urge upon the cities which I have called upon you to reconcile that it is their duty to go to war with the barbarians.

Sources: Demosthenes, *The Third Philippic,* trans. J. H. Vince (Cambridge, Mass.: Harvard University Press, 1930); Isocrates, *Address to Philip,* trans. G. Norlin (Cambridge, Mass.: Harvard University Press, 1928).

The illustrious conqueror was in many ways groomed for kingship by his father, who had taken Alexander along on military campaigns and at the important Battle of Chaeronea had given him control of the cavalry. His early upbringing was typical of a Macedonian noble youth: learning to read, ride, fight, and hunt.

His father had also provided him at the age of thirteen with a Greek education by hiring the philosopher Aristotle to be his tutor. Alexander grew to have a love of Greek theater, Greek athletic contests, and Greek philosophers. He was reputed to maintain a copy of Homer under his bed pillow.

© The Trustees of the British Museum/Art Resource, NY

IMAGE 4.2 **Alexander the Great.** This marble head of Alexander the Great was made in the second or first century B.C.E. The long hair and tilt of his head reflect the descriptions of Alexander in the literary sources of the time. This portrait shows a youthful and even godlike appearance. Alexander claimed to be descended from Heracles, a Greek hero worshiped as a god, and as pharaoh of Egypt, he gained recognition as a living deity. It is reported that one statue, now lost, showed Alexander gazing at Zeus. At the base of the statue were the words "I place the earth under my sway; you, O Zeus, keep Olympus."

 How does this marble head reflect the principles of Greek art that were examined in Chapter 3?

After his father's assassination, Alexander moved quickly to assert his authority, securing the Macedonian frontiers and smothering a rebellion in Greece by sacking the city of Thebes, killing most of its male inhabitants, and selling the women and children into slavery. He then turned to his father's dream, the invasion of the Persian Empire.

Alexander's Conquests There is no doubt that Alexander was taking a chance in attacking the Persian Empire. Although weakened in some respects, it was still a strong state. Alexander's fleet was inferior to the Persian navy, which drew its ships from the Phoenicians and other coastal peoples of West Asia, and his finances were shaky at best. His army would have to live off the countryside and win quick victories to gain the resources needed to continue the struggle. In the spring of 334 B.C.E., Alexander entered Asia Minor with an army of some 37,000 men. About half were Macedonians; the rest were Greeks and other allies. The cavalry, which would play an important role as a strike force, numbered about five thousand.

Architects, engineers, historians, and scientists accompanied the army, a clear indication of Alexander's grand vision and positive expectations at the beginning of his campaign.

His first confrontation with the Persians, at the Granicus River in 334 B.C.E. (see Map 4.1), nearly cost him his life but resulted in a major victory. By the following spring, the entire western half of Asia Minor was in Alexander's hands, and the Ionian Greek cities of southwestern Asia Minor had been "liberated" from the Persian oppressor. Not all of them wished to be liberated, however, and many regarded Alexander simply as their new master.

Meanwhile, the Persian king, Darius III, mobilized his forces to stop Alexander's army. Although the Persian troops outnumbered Alexander's, the Battle of Issus (ISS-uss) was fought on a narrow field that canceled the advantage of superior numbers and resulted in another Macedonian success (see Image 4.3). (The Persian cause was not helped when Darius made a spectacular exit from the battlefield before it was even clear who would be victorious.) After his victory at Issus in 333 B.C.E., Alexander laid siege to the port cities of Tyre and Gaza to prevent Persian control of the sea. The siege of Tyre provides an example of Alexander's military and engineering skills. Tyre stood on an island just off the coast. Lacking adequate naval resources to attack the city from the sea, Alexander built a causeway from the coast to the city, a project that took six months but enabled him to use his siege machines against the city. After seven months, Tyre finally fell to Alexander's forces. Six thousand of the inhabitants were killed and 30,000 sold into slavery.

Egypt surrendered without a fight, and by the winter of 332 B.C.E., Syria, Palestine, and Egypt were under Alexander's domination. He took the traditional title of pharaoh of Egypt and was hailed as the "son of Amon," to the Greeks the equivalent of being called the son of Zeus. Alexander also built the first of a series of cities named after him (Alexandria) as the Greek administrative capital of Egypt. It became one of the most important cities in the Mediterranean world.

In the meantime, Darius indicated his willingness to make a peace settlement, offering to cede all land west of the Euphrates River to Alexander. Alexander refused and renewed the offensive. He moved now into the territory of the ancient Mesopotamian kingdoms and fought a decisive battle with the Persians at Gaugamela (gaw-guh-MEE-luh) in the summer of 331 B.C.E. At Gaugamela, Alexander's men were clearly outnumbered by the Persian forces, which had established the battle site on a broad open plain where their war chariots could maneuver to best advantage. Alexander was able to break through the center of the Persian line with his heavy cavalry, followed by the infantry. The battle turned into a rout, although Darius managed to escape. After his victory, Alexander entered Babylon and then proceeded to the Persian capitals at Susa and Persepolis, where he acquired the Persian treasuries and took possession of vast quantities of gold and silver.

By 330 B.C.E., Alexander was again on the march. After Darius was killed by one of his own men, Alexander took the title and office of the Great King of the Persians. But he was not content to rest with the spoils of the Persian Empire. Over the next three

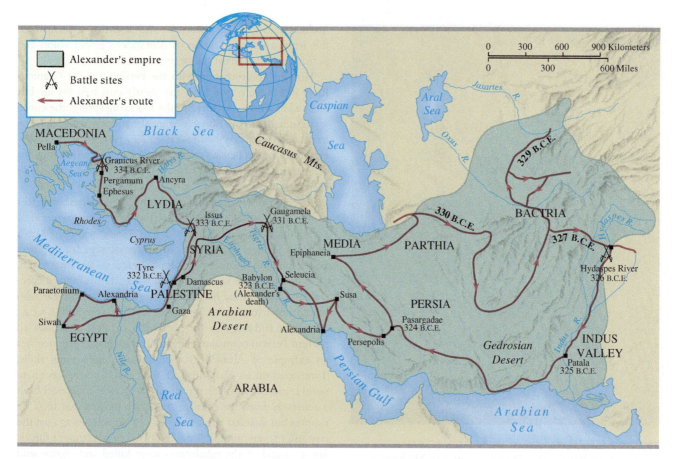

MAP 4.1 **The Conquests of Alexander the Great.** In just twelve years, Alexander the Great conquered vast territories. Dominating lands from west of the Nile to east of the Indus, he brought the Persian Empire, Egypt, and much of the Middle East under his control and laid the foundations for the Hellenistic world.

 Approximately how far did Alexander and his troops travel during those twelve years?

Erich Lessing/Art Resource, NY

IMAGE 4.3 **Alexander and Darius at the Battle of Issus.** This late-second or early-first-century B.C.E. mosaic from the floor of a Roman villa at Pompeii is thought to be a copy of a panel painting made by Philoxenos of Eretria about 310 B.C.E. The mosaic depicts the battle between Alexander and Darius III, king of Persia, at Issus in 333 B.C.E. Alexander is seen at the left on horseback, recklessly leading his troops into battle. Darius is shown in his chariot, already turning around to flee from the battlefield.

 What does this image reveal about Alexander as a military commander?

Alexander Meets an Indian King

 What do we learn from Arrian's account about Alexander's military skills and Indian methods of fighting? What bias do you detect in this account?

IN HIS CAMPAIGNS IN INDIA, Alexander fought a number of difficult battles. At the Battle of the Hydaspes River, he faced a strong opponent in the Indian king Porus. After defeating Porus, Alexander treated him with respect, according to Arrian, Alexander's ancient biographer.

Arrian, *The Campaigns of Alexander*

Throughout the action Porus had proved himself a man indeed, not only as a commander but as a soldier of the truest courage. When he saw his cavalry cut to pieces, most of his infantry dead, and his elephants killed or roaming riderless and bewildered about the field, his behavior was very different from that of the Persian King Darius: unlike Darius, he did not lead the scramble to save his own skin, but so long as a single unit of his men held together, he fought bravely on. It was only when he was himself wounded that he turned the elephant on which he rode and began to withdraw. . . . Alexander, anxious to save the life of this great and gallant soldier, sent . . .

[to him] an Indian named Meroes, a man he had been told had long been Porus's friend. Porus listened to Meroes's message, stopped his elephant, and dismounted; he was much distressed by thirst, so when he had revived himself by drinking, he told Meroes to conduct him with all speed to Alexander.

Alexander, informed of his approach, rode out to meet him. . . . When they met, he reined in his horse and looked at his adversary with admiration: he was a magnificent figure of a man, over seven feet high and of great personal beauty; his bearing had lost none of its pride; his air was of one brave man meeting another, of a king in the presence of a king, with whom he had fought honorably for his kingdom.

Alexander was the first to speak. "What," he said, "do you wish that I should do with you?" "Treat me as a king ought," Porus is said to have replied. "For my part," said Alexander, pleased by his answer, "your request shall be granted. But is there not something you would wish for yourself? Ask it." "Everything," said Porus, "is contained in this one request."

The dignity of these words gave Alexander even more pleasure, and he restored to Porus his sovereignty over his subjects, adding to his realm other territory of even greater extent. Thus, he did indeed use a brave man as a king ought, and from that time forward found him in every way a loyal friend.

Source: Arrian, *The Campaigns of Alexander the Great*, trans. A. de Selincourt (London: Penguin Classics, 1958; revised edition 1971).

---

years, he moved east and northeast, as far as modern Pakistan. By the summer of 327 B.C.E., he had entered India, which at that time was divided into a number of warring states. In 326 B.C.E., Alexander and his armies arrived in the plains of northwestern India. At the Battle of the Hydaspes (hy-DAS-peez) River, Alexander won a brutally fought battle (see Historical Voices, "Alexander Meets an Indian King," above). When Alexander made clear his determination to march east to conquer more of India, his soldiers, weary of campaigning year after year, mutinied and refused to go further. Alexander surrendered to their demands and agreed to return, leading his troops through southern Persia across the Gedrosian Desert, where they suffered heavy losses from appalling desert conditions. Alexander and the remnants of his army went to Susa and then Babylon, where he planned more campaigns. But in June 323 B.C.E., weakened from wounds, fever, and probably excessive alcohol, he died at the young age of thirty-two (see Movies & History, *Alexander*).

Alexander's Military Success Historians, both ancient and modern, generally agree that Alexander was an outstanding military leader. How do they explain his success? For one thing, Alexander demonstrated superb tactical skills. His success in his numerous battles was based to a large extent on his ability to assess the topography of the battlefield and make plans that took advantage of the strengths and weaknesses

of his enemy's forces as well as his own. Within hours after arriving at a potential battlefield, Alexander was able to plan troop formations and tactics appropriate to the landscape on which he was fighting. Then, too, if something went wrong

MOVIES & HISTORY
Alexander (2004)

Picture Lux/The Hollywood Archive/Alamy Stock Photo

Watch **Alexander**, a product of director Oliver Stone's lifelong fascination with Alexander. His epic film cost $150 million, which resulted in an elaborate and stunningly visual spectacle, but as history the film leaves much to be desired. The character of Alexander is never developed in depth.

 Was Alexander an idealistic dreamer, as Stone believes, or was he a brutal military leader who was responsible for mass slaughter in pursuing his dream? What do we learn about the character and sexual practices of Alexander? How accurate are the battle scenes? What objection could be made about the depiction of the Persian forces?

after the battle began, he was quick to adapt to changing circumstances.

Alexander pushed his troops mercilessly, often catching his enemy by surprise as a result of a quick march. But he also maintained a personal interest in his troops and for the most part, until the campaign in India, kept their intense loyalty. His willingness to lead by personal example inspired his troops, although it often led to risks that endangered his own life. He did not hesitate to lead cavalry attacks into the ranks of his enemies. In India, he was injured when he led his troops up a ladder in their assault on the Mallians. He was, in fact, wounded eight times in battle.

Alexander also paid attention to details. All aspects of his campaigns were well organized, from obtaining supplies and reinforcements to doing advanced planning for excursions into little known territories. As the number of Macedonian troops declined from deaths in battle or from being assigned to occupy new conquests, Alexander recruited Persian troops. He also took advantage of his father's technical developments and made good use of siege warfare.

But there is also an uglier side to Alexander's military greatness. Did he become accustomed, as some historians have recently argued, to killing his enemies on a scale that far outstripped what was usual in Greek and Macedonian warfare?

HISTORIANS DEBATE   **The Legacy—Was Alexander Great?** Alexander is one of the most puzzling significant figures in history. Historians relying on the same sources give vastly different pictures of him. For some, his military ability, extensive conquests, and creation of a new empire alone justify calling him Alexander the Great. Other historians also praise Alexander's love of Greek culture and his intellectual brilliance, especially in matters of warfare. In the lands that he conquered, Alexander attempted to fuse the Macedonians, Greeks, and Persians into a new ruling class. Did he do this because he was an idealistic visionary who believed in a concept of universal humanity, as some suggest? Or was he merely trying to bolster his power and create an autocratic monarchy?

CHRONOLOGY	Macedonia and the Conquests of Alexander	
Reign of Philip II	359–336 B.C.E.	
Battle of Chaeronea; Philip II conquers Greece	338 B.C.E.	
Reign of Alexander the Great	336–323 B.C.E.	
Alexander invades Asia; Battle of Granicus River	334 B.C.E.	
Battle of Issus	333 B.C.E.	
Battle of Gaugamela	331 B.C.E.	
Fall of Persepolis, the Persian capital	330 B.C.E.	
Alexander enters India	327 B.C.E.	
Battle of the Hydaspes River	326 B.C.E.	
Death of Alexander	323 B.C.E.	

Those historians who see Alexander as aspiring to autocratic monarchy present a very different portrait of him as a ruthless Machiavellian. One has titled his biography *Alexander the Great Failure*. These critics ask whether a man who slaughtered indigenous peoples, who risked the lives of his soldiers for his own selfish reasons, whose fierce temper led him to kill his friends, and whose neglect of administrative duties weakened his kingdom can really be called great (see Historical Voices, "The Wrath of Alexander," p. 97).

But how did Alexander view himself? We know that he sought to imitate Achilles, the warrior-hero of Homer's *Iliad*. Alexander supposedly kept a copy of the *Iliad*—and a dagger—under his pillow. He also claimed to be descended from Heracles, the Greek hero who came to be worshiped as a god. No doubt Alexander aspired to divine honors; as pharaoh of Egypt, he became a living god according to Egyptian tradition and at one point even sent instructions to the Greek cities to "vote him a god."

Regardless of his ideals, motives, or views about himself, one fact stands out: Alexander created a new age, the Hellenistic era. The word *Hellenistic* is derived from a Greek word meaning "to imitate Greeks." It is an appropriate way to describe an age that saw the extension of the Greek language and ideas to the non-Greek world of the ancient Near East. Alexander's destruction of the Persian monarchy had extended Greco-Macedonian rule over an enormous area. It created opportunities for Greek engineers, intellectuals, merchants, soldiers, and administrators. While the Greeks on the mainland might remain committed to the ideals of their city-states, those who followed Alexander and his successors participated in a new political unity based on the principle of monarchy—the imperial state. Alexander had transformed his army from a Macedonian force into an international one, owing loyalty only to himself. His successors used force to establish military monarchies that dominated the Hellenistic world after his death. Autocratic power, based on military strength and pretensions of divine rule—the new imperial state—became a regular feature of those Hellenistic monarchies and was part of Alexander's political legacy to the Hellenistic world. His vision of empire no doubt inspired the Romans, who were, of course, Alexander's real heirs.

But Alexander also left a cultural legacy. As a result of his conquests, Greek language, art, architecture, and literature spread throughout the Near East. The urban centers of the Hellenistic Age, many founded by Alexander and his successors, became springboards for the diffusion of Greek culture. Alexander had established a number of cities and military colonies named Alexandria to guard strategic points and supervise wide areas. Most of the settlers were Greek mercenaries. It has been estimated that in the course of his campaigns, Alexander summoned some 60,000 to 65,000 additional mercenaries from Greece, at least 36,000 of whom took up residence in the garrisons and new cities. While the Greeks spread their culture in the Near East, they were also inevitably influenced by eastern ways. Thus, Alexander's legacy became one of the hallmarks of the Hellenistic world: the clash and fusion of different cultures.

The Wrath of Alexander

 What is Plutarch's view of Alexander? What is Arrian's view of Alexander? How do you explain the differences? Based on Plutarch, what were Alexander's motives in making his conquests?

ARRIAN, A SECOND-CENTURY C.E. HISTORIAN, wrote a historical account of Alexander's military campaigns in which he praised Alexander as a bold leader who had "perfect self-control." Plutarch, a first-century Greek historian, gave a quite different view as seen in this excerpt from his *Life of Alexander*.

Plutarch, *Life of Alexander*

After the company had drunk a good deal somebody began to sing the verses of a man named Pranichus . . . which had been written to humiliate and make fun of some Macedonian commanders who had recently been defeated by the barbarians. The older members of the party took offense at this and showed their resentment of both the poet and the singer, but Alexander and those sitting near him listened with obvious pleasure and told the man to continue. Thereupon Cleitus, who had already drunk too much and was rough and hot-tempered by nature, became angrier than ever and shouted that it was not right for Macedonians to be insulted in the presence of barbarians and enemies, even if they had met with misfortune, for they were better men than those who were laughing at them. Alexander retorted that if Cleitus was trying to disguise cowardice as misfortune, he must be pleading his own case. At this Cleitus sprang to his feet and shouted back, "Yes, it was my cowardice that saved your life, you who call yourself the son of the gods, . . . And it is the blood of these Macedonians and their wounds which have made you so great . . . ."

These words made Alexander furious. "You scum," he cried out, "do you think that you can keep on speaking of me like this, and stir up trouble among the Macedonians and not pay for it?" Oh, but we Macedonians do pay for it," Cleitus retorted, "Just think of the rewards we get for all our efforts. It's the dead ones who are happy, because they never lived to see Macedonians . . . begging the Persians for an audience with our own king." Cleitus blurted out all this impulsively, whereupon Alexander's friends jumped up and began to abuse him, while the older men tried to calm down both sides. . . . But Cleitus refused to take back anything and he challenged Alexander to speak out whatever he wished to say in front of the company,. . . . At this Alexander could no longer control his rage . . . As Cleitus still refused to give way. . . . Alexander seized a spear from one of his guards, faced Cleitus as he was drawing aside the curtain of the doorway, and ran him through. With a roar of pain and a groan, Cleitus fell, and immediately the king's anger left him. When he came to himself and saw his friends standing around him speechless, he snatched the weapon out of the dead body and would have plunged it into his own throat if the guards had not forestalled him by seizing his hands and carrying him by force to his chamber.

Source: William S. Davis, ed. *Readings in Ancient History*, vol. 1 (Boston: Allyn and Bacon, 1912), pp. 64–66.

4-2 The World of the Hellenistic Kingdoms

 FOCUS QUESTION: What were the main features of the political and military organization of the Hellenistic kingdoms, and how did the new political systems differ from those of the Greek city-states?

The united empire that Alexander created by his conquests disintegrated after his death. All too soon, Macedonian military leaders were engaged in a struggle for power. By 301 B.C.E., any hope of unity was dead.

4-2a Hellenistic Monarchies

Eventually, four major Hellenistic kingdoms emerged as the successors to Alexander: Macedonia under the Antigonid (an-TIG-uh-nid) dynasty, Syria and the east under the Seleucids (suh-LOO-sids), the Attalid (AT-uh-lid) kingdom of Pergamum (PURR-guh-mum), and Egypt under the Ptolemies (TAHL-uh-meez) (see Map 4.2).

Antigonid Kingdom of Macedonia In Macedonia, the struggles for power led to the extermination of Alexander the Great's dynasty. Not until 276 B.C.E. did Antigonus Gonatus (an-TIG-oh-nuss guh-NAH-tuss), the grandson of one of Alexander's generals, succeed in establishing the Antigonid dynasty as rulers of Macedonia. The Antigonids viewed control of Greece as essential to their power but did not see outright conquest as necessary. Macedonia was, of course, also important to the Greeks. As one ancient commentator noted, "It is in the interest of the Greeks that the Macedonian dominion should be humbled for long, but by no means that it should be destroyed. For in that case . . . [the Macedonians] would very soon experience the lawless violence of the Thracians and Gauls, as they had on more than one occasion."[2] But the Greeks, like the Macedonians, eventually fell subject to Roman power.

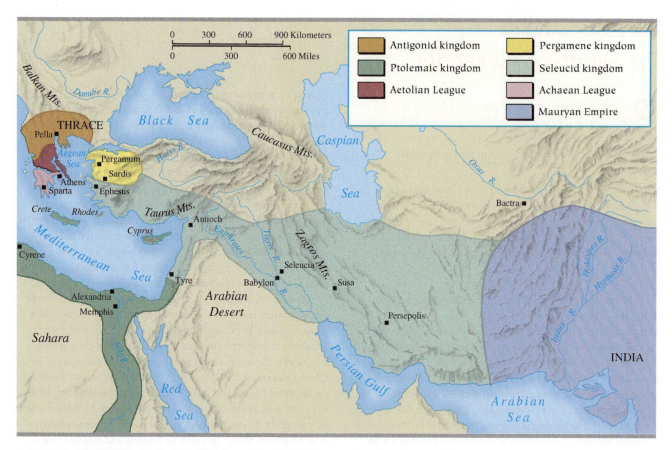

MAP 4.2 **The World of the Hellenistic Kingdoms.** Alexander died unexpectedly at the age of thirty-two and did not designate a successor. Upon his death, his generals struggled for power, eventually establishing monarchies that spread Hellenistic culture and fostered trade and economic development.

Q *Which kingdom encompassed most of the old Persian Empire?*

Seleucid Kingdom Another Hellenistic monarchy was founded by the general Seleucus (suh-LOO-kuss), who established the Seleucid dynasty of Syria. This was the largest of the Hellenistic kingdoms and controlled much of the old Persian Empire from Turkey in the west to India in the east, although the Seleucids found it increasingly difficult to maintain control of the eastern territories. In fact, an Indian ruler named Chandragupta Maurya (chun-druh-GOOP-tuh MOWR-yuh) (324–301 B.C.E.) created a new Indian state, the Mauryan Empire, and drove out the Seleucid forces. His grandson Ashoka (uh-SOH-kuh) (269–232 B.C.E.) extended the empire to include most of India and is considered the greatest ruler in India's history (see Map 4.3). Ashoka, a pious Buddhist, sought to convert the remaining Greek communities in northwestern India to his religion and even sent Buddhist missionaries to Greek rulers.

The Seleucid rulers maintained relations with the Mauryan Empire. Trade was fostered, especially in such luxuries

as spices and jewels. Seleucus also sent Greek and Macedonian ambassadors to the Mauryan court. Best known of these was Megasthenes (muh-GAS-thuh-neez), whose report on the people of India remained one of the West's best sources of information on India until the Middle Ages.

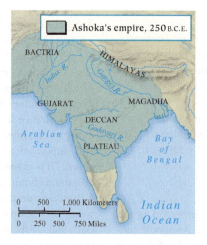

MAP 4.3 **The Mauryan Empire Under Ashoka**

Kingdom of Pergamum A third Hellenistic kingdom came into being by freeing itself from the Seleucids. This was the kingdom of Pergamum in western Asia Minor under the Attalid dynasty. It was Pergamum that brought the Romans into the area by seeking their aid first against the Antigonids and then against the Seleucids. This led to the Roman defeat of Antiochus (an-TY-uh-kuss) III, probably the strongest of the Seleucid monarchs, in 191 B.C.E. The Seleucids declined thereafter until their small remaining territory was made a Roman province in 63 B.C.E. Seventy years before that, the last of the Attalid dynasty had bequeathed his kingdom to Rome in his will.

Ptolemaic Kingdom of Egypt The fourth Hellenistic monarchy was Egypt, which had come under the control of Ptolemy (TAHL-uh-mee), another Macedonian general. Named governor of Egypt after Alexander's death, Ptolemy had established himself as king by 305 B.C.E., creating the Ptolemaic (tahl-uh-MAY-ik) dynasty of pharaohs.

The Ptolemaic kings were especially active in demonstrating their Greek identity. They did so in elaborate festivals that featured statues of the dynasty's founder, Ptolemy I, as well as Alexander. The Ptolemaic rulers also presented themselves as the defenders of Greek liberty.

Hellenistic Egypt lasted longer than all the other Hellenistic monarchies; it was not until the reign of Cleopatra VII, who allied herself with the wrong side in the Roman civil wars (see Chapter 5), that Egypt fell to the Romans in 30 B.C.E.

Other Hellenistic Kingdoms To the east of the four major Hellenistic kingdoms were two smaller kingdoms, the Greco-Bactrian kingdom and the Indo-Greek kingdom. The Greco-Bactrian kingdom was founded around 250 B.C.E. when Diodotus I of Bactria broke away from the Seleucid Empire and established a prosperous kingdom of his own. It encompassed territory around the northern part of present-day Afghanistan. The army was composed of different local peoples, with Greek colonists serving primarily as infantry. Greek influence was evident in the major cities. The Greco-Bactrian kingdom made contact with the Han Chinese Empire, and its ties to the Mauryan kingdom in India led to some conversions to Buddhism. Invasions by nomadic peoples and the Parthians led to the end of the kingdom by 125 B.C.E.

The invasion of India by a Greco-Bactrian army in 175 B.C.E. led to the creation of an Indo-Greek kingdom in northwestern India (present-day India and Pakistan). Indo-Greek kings combined the Greek and Indo-Iranian languages, blended Hinduism and Buddhism with traditional Greek practices in religion, and created a Greco-Buddhist art. King Menander, the greatest of the Indo-Greek kings, who ruled from 165 to 155 B.C.E., even converted to Buddhism. Invasions by neighboring peoples brought an end to the kingdom in 10 C.E.

IMAGE 4.4 **A Gaul and His Wife: Monument to the Victory of a Hellenistic King.** This statue of a Gaulish chieftain and his wife is a Roman copy of a bronze original that was part of a larger monument erected around 230–220 B.C.E. to commemorate the victory of Attalus I of Pergamum over the Gauls, a victory that gave Pergamum control over much of Asia Minor. In this scene, the defeated Gaulish leader plunges a sword into his chest just after he has killed his wife to prevent her from being sold into slavery.

4-2b The Threat from the Celts

The Celts, also known as the Gauls, were a people who had occupied large areas of Europe north of the Alps during the Early Iron Age (ca. 800–500 B.C.E.), especially the region to the south and west of the Rhine River, west of the Alps, and north of the Pyrenees (a region known as Gaul).

At the end of the fifth century B.C.E., possibly as a result of overpopulation, Celtic peoples began to migrate south and east. One group sacked the city of Rome in 390 B.C.E. (see Chapter 5). After the death of Alexander the Great, other groups of Celts began to threaten the Hellenistic world. Celts attacked Macedonia early in the third century B.C.E. As one ancient writer reported: "When the defeated Macedonians had fixed themselves within the walls of their cities, the victorious Brennus ravaged the fields of the whole of Macedonia with no one to oppose him."[3] Brennus also led a group of 30,000 Celts into Greece itself and caused considerable damage before being defeated in 278 B.C.E.

Other groups of Celts later attacked Asia Minor, where Attalus I bested them in 230 B.C.E. After his victory, Attalus gained control of much of Asia Minor and declared himself king of Pergamum (see Image 4.4). As a result of these attacks, the Celts, or Gauls, came to be feared everywhere in the Hellenistic world.

4-2c Political and Military Institutions

The Hellenistic monarchies created a semblance of stability for several centuries, even though Hellenistic kings refused to accept the new status quo and periodically engaged in wars to alter it. At the same time, an underlying strain always existed between the new Greco-Macedonian ruling class and the native populations. Together, these factors created a certain degree of tension that never truly ended until the vibrant Roman state to the west stepped in and imposed a new order.

Araldo De Luca/Corbis Historical/Getty Images

The Hellenistic kingdoms shared a common political system that represented a break with their Greek past. To the Greeks, monarchy was an institution for barbarians, associated in their minds with people like the Persians. Although they retained democratic forms of government in their cities, the Greeks of the Hellenistic world were forced to accept monarchy as a new fact of political life.

Although Alexander the Great had apparently planned to fuse Greeks and easterners, Hellenistic monarchs relied primarily on Greeks and Macedonians to form the new ruling class. In the Seleucid kingdom, for example, historians have estimated that only 2.5 percent of the people in authority were non-Greek or non-Macedonian, and most of them were commanders of local military units. Those who did advance to important administrative posts had learned Greek (all government business was transacted in Greek). This often required alienation from one's own culture. Some were willing to do so, since Greekness meant power, giving incentive to local people to become Hellenized in a cultural sense. The policy of excluding non-Greeks from leadership positions was due not to the incompetence of the natives but to the determination of the Greek ruling class to maintain its privileged position. It was the Greco-Macedonian ruling class that provided the only unity in the Hellenistic world.

Since the Hellenistic monarchs created and maintained their kingdoms by military force, warfare continued to be an integral part of the Hellenistic world. The phalanx—still composed of heavily armed infantry with 18-foot-long spears—and cavalry continued to form the core of the Hellenistic forces. But Hellenistic warfare also saw some innovations. Most noticeable were the elephants, "the tanks of ancient warfare," which were especially prominent in the armies of the Seleucids, who procured theirs from India, and the Ptolemies, who obtained them from North Africa. But even more important, since armies quickly learned tricks that neutralized the elephants, was the development of new siege machinery, especially the catapult and siege towers. In classical times, cities with good walls were virtually impregnable; Alexander and later Hellenistic rulers could capture cities by using their new equipment.

4-2d Hellenistic Cities

Cities played an especially important role in the Hellenistic kingdoms. Throughout his conquests, Alexander had founded a series of new cities and military settlements, and Hellenistic kings did likewise. The new population centers varied considerably in size and importance. Military settlements were meant to maintain order and might consist of only a few hundred men heavily dependent on the king. But there were also new independent cities with thousands of inhabitants. Alexandria in Egypt was the largest city in the Mediterranean region by the first century B.C.E. According to one ancient writer, Seleucus was especially active in founding new cities: "The other kings have exulted in destroying existing cities; he, on the other hand, arranged to build cities which did not yet exist. He established so many . . . that they were enough to carry the names of towns in Macedonia as well as the names of those in his family. . . . One can go to Phoenicia to see his cities; one can go to Syria and see even more."[4]

Hellenistic rulers encouraged this massive spread of Greek colonists to the Near East because of their intrinsic value to the new monarchies. Greeks (and Macedonians) provided not only a recruiting ground for the army but also a pool of civilian administrators and workers who would contribute to economic development. Even architects, engineers, dramatists, and actors were in demand in the new Greek cities. Many Greeks and Macedonians were quick to see the advantages of moving to the new urban centers and gladly sought their fortunes in the Near East. Greeks of all backgrounds joined the exodus until around 250 B.C.E., when the outpouring began to slow significantly.

Within the Hellenistic cities, the culture was primarily Greek. Especially noticeable and important to the maintenance of Greek culture was the gymnasium (see "4-3c The Transformation of Education," later in this chapter). The political institutions of the cities were modeled after those of the Greek polis. Greeks of the classical period would easily have recognized the councils, magistracies, assemblies, and codes of law. The physical layout of the new cities was likewise modeled on those of the Greek homeland. Using the traditional rectilinear grid, cities were laid out with temples, altars, and stone amphitheaters.

Many of the new urban centers were completely dominated by Greeks, whereas the native populations remained cut off from all civic institutions. The Greeks commissioned purely Greek sculpture, read literature of the classical period, and had separate law courts for themselves. Complaints from resentful natives have been recorded (see Historical Voices, "Relations Between Greeks and Non-Greeks," p. 101). As we have seen, not only was it difficult for easterners to enter the ranks of the ruling class, but those who did so had to become thoroughly Hellenized. This often required alienation from one's own culture.

The Greeks' belief in their own cultural superiority provided an easy rationalization for their political dominance of the eastern cities. But Greek control of the new cities was also necessary because the kings frequently used the cities as instruments of government, enabling them to rule considerable territory without an extensive bureaucracy. At the same time, for security reasons, the Greeks needed the support of the kings. After all, the Hellenistic cities were islands of Greek culture in a sea of non-Greeks. The relationship between rulers and cities, therefore, was a symbiotic one that bore serious consequences for the cities.

In their political system, religious practices, and architecture, the Greeks tried to recreate the poleis of their homeland in their new cities. But it was no longer possible to do so. The new cities were not autonomous entities and soon found themselves dependent on the power of the Hellenistic monarchies. Although the kings did not rule the cities directly, they restricted the cities' freedom in other ways. City administrators knew they could not conduct an independent foreign policy and did not try to do so. The kings also demanded tribute, which could be a heavy burden.

The Greek cities of the era were the chief agents for the spread of Hellenistic culture in the Near East, as far, in fact, as modern Afghanistan and India. These Greek cities were also remarkably vibrant despite their subordination to the

Relations Between Greeks and Non-Greeks

 Q *What do these documents reveal about the relationship between the conquerors and the conquered? What problems did each face?*

THE RELATIONSHIP BETWEEN the Greek conquerors and the native peoples of the Near East was often a difficult one. Although a number of the local inhabitants learned Greek in order to advance economically and politically, they were often not treated as equals by the dominant Greek minority. These documents reveal two facets of the problem. In the first selection, a member of the local population complains about his treatment by the Greeks. The second selection reveals the dangers Greeks could experience from local peoples.

Letter to Zenon

To Zenon, greeting. You do well if you are healthy. I too am well. You know that you left me in Syria with Krotos and I did everything that was ordered with respect to the camels and was blameless towards you. When you sent an order to give me pay, he gave nothing of what you ordered. When I asked repeatedly that he give me what you ordered and Krotos gave me nothing, but kept telling me to remove myself. . . . So I wrote to you that you might know that Krotos was the cause of it. When you sent me again to Philadelphia to Jason, although I do everything that is ordered, for nine months now he gives me nothing of what you ordered me to have, neither oil nor grain. . . . And I am toiling away both summer and winter. And he orders me to accept sour wine for my ration. Well, they have treated me with scorn because I am a "barbarian." I beg you therefore, if it seems good to you, to give them orders that I am to obtain what is owing and that in future they pay me in full, in order that I may not perish of hunger because I do not know how to speak Greek.

Letter to Dionysios

To Dionysios from Ptolemaios. . . . Being outrageously wronged and often put in danger of my life by the below-listed cleaners from the sanctuary, I am seeking refuge with you thinking that I shall thus particularly receive justice. For in the 21st year, they came to the sanctuary, in which I have been for the aforesaid years, some of them holding stones in their hands, others sticks, and tried to force their way in, so that with this opportunity they might plunder the temple and kill me because I am a Greek, attacking me in concerted fashion. And when I made it to the door of the temple before them and shut it with a great crash, and ordered them to go away quietly, they did not depart; but they struck Diphilos, one of the servants, who showed his indignation at the way they were behaving in the sanctuary, robbing him outrageously and attacking him violently and beating him, so that their illegal violence was made obvious to everybody.

Source: Roger S. Bagnall and Peter Derow, editors, *The Hellenistic Period* (Oxford: Blackwell Publishing, 2004), pp. 230–231, 232.

Hellenistic monarchies and persisted in being a focal point for the loyalty of their citizens.

4-2e Economic Trends in the Hellenistic World

Agriculture was still of primary importance to both the native populations and the new Greek cities of the Hellenistic world. The Greek cities continued their old agrarian patterns. A well-defined body of citizens owned land and worked it with the assistance of slaves. But their farms were isolated units in a vast area of land ultimately owned by the king or assigned to large estate owners and worked by native peasants dwelling in villages. Overall, then, neither agricultural patterns nor methods of production underwent significant changes.

Few new products or manufacturing methods were introduced in the Hellenistic period, but the centers of manufacturing shifted significantly. Industry spread from Greece to the east—especially to Asia Minor, Rhodes, and Egypt. New textile centers were set up at Pergamum, and glass and silver crafts were developed in Syria. Leading all cities in manufacturing was Alexandria in Egypt, which became the center for the production of parchment, textiles, linens, oil, metalwork, and glass.

Commerce expanded considerably in the Hellenistic era. Indeed, trading contacts linked much of the Hellenistic world. The decline in the number of political barriers encouraged more commercial traffic. Although Hellenistic monarchs still fought wars, the conquests of Alexander and the policies of his successors made possible greater trade between east and west. Two major trade routes connected the east with the Mediterranean. The central route was the major one and led by sea from India to the Persian Gulf, up the Tigris River to Seleucia on the Tigris, which became the center for water-borne traffic from the Persian Gulf and overland caravan routes as well. Overland routes from Seleucia then led to Antioch and Ephesus. A southern route wound its way from India by sea but went around Arabia and up the Red Sea to Petra or later Berenice (ber-uh-NY-see). Caravan routes then led overland to Coptos on the Nile and then to Alexandria and the Mediterranean.

An incredible variety of products were traded: gold and silver from Spain; iron from northern Armenia; salt from Asia Minor; timber from Macedonia; purple dye from Tyre; ebony, gems, ivory, and spices from India; frankincense (used on altars) from Arabia; slaves from Thrace, Syria, and Asia Minor; fine wines from Syria and western Asia Minor; olive oil from Athens; and numerous exquisite foodstuffs, such as the famous prunes of Damascus. The greatest trade, however, was in the basic staple of life—grain. The great exporting areas were Egypt, Sicily, and the Black Sea region, while Rhodes and Delos served as the major depots for the international grain trade.

4-3 Hellenistic Society

 FOCUS QUESTION: What were the main social developments in the Hellenistic world?

One of the noticeable features of social life in the Hellenistic world was the emergence of new opportunities for women—at least for upper-class women. No doubt this was related to the changes in Hellenistic society itself, since the subordination of the cities to the kings altered the way men related to their polis and to each other. Some historians maintain that the visible role of Hellenistic queens may also have contributed to a new model for upper-class women.

4-3a New Opportunities for Women

The creation of the Hellenistic monarchies, which represented a considerable departure from the world of the city-state, gave new scope to the role played by the monarchs' wives, the Hellenistic queens. In Macedonia, a pattern of alliances between mothers and sons provided openings for women to take an active role in politics, especially in political intrigue. In Egypt, opportunities for royal women were even greater after the Ptolemaic rulers adopted the Egyptian custom of kings marrying their own sisters. Of the first eight Ptolemaic rulers, four wed their sisters. Ptolemy II and his sister-wife Arsinoë (ahr-SIN-oh-ee) II were both worshiped as gods in their lifetimes. Arsinoë played an energetic role in government and was involved in the expansion of the Egyptian navy. She was also the first Egyptian queen whose portrait appeared on coins with her husband (see Image 4.5). Hellenistic queens also showed an intense interest in culture. They wrote poems, collected art, and corresponded with intellectuals.

The development of the kingdom as the focus of political life in the Hellenistic era also resulted in fewer restrictions on women. In many cities, for example, women of all classes had a new freedom of movement. The most notable gains, especially for upper-class women, came in the economic area. Documents show increasing numbers of women involved in managing slaves, selling property, and making loans. Even then, legal contracts made by women had to include their official male guardians, although often these men were listed only to satisfy legal requirements and no longer played an important role. In Sparta, women were allowed to own land and manage their own economic affairs. As their husbands were often absent or had died in war, many Spartan women became wealthy; females owned 40 percent of the privately held land in Sparta.

IMAGE 4.5a

IMAGE 4.5b

IMAGE 4.5 Queen Arsinoë II. Image 4.5a shows Arsinoë II, sister and wife of King Ptolemy II, depicted on the reverse side of a gold coin from the kingdom of Egypt in 263 B.C.E. Arsinoë, the first Egyptian queen whose portrait appeared on coins with her husband, played an active role in Egyptian political affairs. Image 4.5b shows a third-century B.C.E. cameo relief made in Alexandria depicting Ptolemy II and Arsinoë as Greek gods.

(a): Historic Images/Alamy Stock Photo

(b): The Gonzaga Cameo, depicting Ptolemy II Philadelphus (285–246 bc) and his wife Arsinoe portrayed as gods of the Greek pantheon, made in Alexandria, 3rd century bc (sardonyx), Egyptian Ptolemaic Period (332–30 bc)/ Hermitage, St. Petersburg, Russia/Bridgeman Images

A New Autonomy for Women?

 What specific complaints are contained in each letter? What do these complaints reveal about some women in the Hellenistic world? Judging by these letters, what freedoms did Hellenistic women enjoy? How autonomous were they? Based on your knowledge of gender and gender roles in shaping earlier cultures, how did Hellenistic civilization differ in its conceptions of what was "proper" for men and women?

THERE WERE NOTICEABLE GAINS for upper-class women in Hellenistic society. But even many ordinary women displayed a new assertiveness despite the continuing domination of society by men. The first selection is taken from the letter of a wife to her husband, complaining about his failure to return home. In the second selection, a father complains that his daughter has abandoned him, contrary to Egyptian law providing that children who have been properly raised should support their parents.

Letter from Isias to Hephaistion, 168 B.C.E.

If you are well and other things are going right, it would accord with the prayer that I make continually to the gods. I myself and the child and all the household are in good health and think of you always. When I received your letter from Horos, in which you announce that you are in detention in the Serapeum at Memphis, for the news that you are well I straightway thanked the gods, but about your not coming home, when all the others who had been secluded there have come, I am ill-pleased, because after having piloted myself and your child through such bad times and been driven to every extremity owing to the price of wheat, I thought that now at least, with you at home, I should enjoy some respite, whereas you have not even thought of coming home nor given any regard to our circumstances, remembering how I was in want of everything while you were still here, not to mention this long lapse of time and these critical days, during which you have sent us nothing. As, moreover, Horos who delivered the letter has brought news of your having been released from detention, I am thoroughly ill-pleased. Notwithstanding, as your mother also is annoyed, for her sake as well as for mine please return to the city, if nothing more pressing holds you back. You will do me a favor by taking care of your bodily health. Farewell.

Letter from Ktesikles to King Ptolemy, 220 B.C.E.

I am wronged by Dionysios and by Nike my daughter. For though I raised her, my own daughter, and educated her and brought her to maturity, when I was stricken with bodily ill-health and was losing my eyesight, she was not minded to furnish me with any of the necessities of life. When I sought to obtain justice from her in Alexandria, she begged my pardon, and in the eighteenth year she swore me a written royal oath to give me each month twenty drachmas, which she was to earn by her own bodily labor. . . . But now corrupted by Dionysios, who is a comic actor, she does not do for me anything of what was in the written oath, despising my weakness and ill-health. I beg you, therefore, O King, not to allow me to be wronged by my daughter and by Dionysios the actor who corrupted her, but to order Diophanes the strategus [provincial administrator] to summon them and hear us out; and if I am speaking the truth, let Diophanes deal with her corrupter as seems good to him and compel my daughter Nike to do justice to me. If this is done I shall no longer be wronged but by fleeing to you, O King, I shall obtain justice.

Source: Roger S. Bagnall and Peter Derow, *The Hellenistic Period: Historical Sources in Translation* (Hoboken, N.J.: Blackwell Publishing, 1981), pp. 281–282, 246.

Spartan women, however, were an exception, especially on the Greek mainland. Women in Athens, for example, still remained highly restricted and supervised. Although a few philosophers welcomed female participation in men's affairs, many philosophers rejected equality between men and women and asserted that the traditional roles of wives and mothers were most satisfying for women. In her treatise "On Chastity," Phintys (FIN-tiss) wrote that "serving as generals, public officials, and statesmen is appropriate for men," but "keeping house, remaining within, and taking care of husbands belongs to women."[5]

But the opinions of philosophers did not prevent upper-class women from making gains in areas other than the economic sphere. New possibilities for females arose when women in some parts of the Hellenistic world were allowed to pursue education in the fields of literature, music, and even athletics. Education, then, provided new opportunities for women: female poets appeared again in the third century B.C.E., and there are instances of women involved in both scholarly and artistic pursuits.

Some wealthy aristocratic women even became politically active and participated in running their cities. In the second century B.C.E., a number of cities passed decrees honoring women for their service to the community. Cyme, in Asia Minor, for example, paid homage to Archippe for her enormous financial contributions. In return, some women were given political rights and in a few instances were allowed to hold office as city magistrates. Some cities even erected statues of women in public squares. But often this generosity had an economic motive. When Phile of Priene was made a magistrate of her city, it was probably with the understanding that she would donate funds for public works. Once in office, she built an aqueduct and a reservoir for the community.

Improvements in the position of females were largely limited to upper-class women (see Historical Voices, "A New Autonomy for Women?", above). Although peasant women faced fewer restrictions, they experienced no real benefit as they were still subject to a lifetime of hard work. A large group of women condemned to the practice of prostitution faced an even harsher reality. Inscriptional evidence indicates that small families were common in the Hellenistic world; boys were preferred, and rarely was more than one daughter raised. Unwanted girl babies were often exposed to the elements and left to die. Some of these infants were gathered up by eager entrepreneurs and raised to be slave prostitutes. Only the most beautiful prostitutes came to be the companions (the *hetairai*) of upper-class men.

4-3b The Role of Slavery

The Hellenistic world witnessed the migration of large numbers of people from one area to another. Greeks and Macedonians went into the Hellenistic kingdoms of the east as administrators, mercenaries, engineers, scholars, artists, teachers, and merchants. Moreover, significantly large numbers of non-Greeks moved around for economic and military purposes. But the largest number of uprooted people were slaves. Slavery was viewed as a normal part of life in the Hellenistic world and in antiquity in general.

Slaves were obtained from four chief sources: the children of slaves; children who were sold by their parents or abandoned to perish; persons kidnapped by pirates; and, perhaps the largest source of all, prisoners of war. Delos, a major trading center, could handle 10,000 slaves a day in its markets. Although slaves came from everywhere, Thracians and Syrians were the most numerous. Slaves varied in price; Macedonians, Thracians, and Italians drew the highest prices.

Slaves were put to work in numerous ways in the Hellenistic world. States employed slaves as servants for government officials and in government-run industries such as weaving. Most slaves were used in domestic service, farming, and mines, but the situation could vary from state to state. Egypt had no slave class in the countryside, nor was there much domestic slavery outside Alexandria. But the Egyptians did use slave labor in state-run textile factories and made especially brutal use of them in mining operations (see Historical Voices, "Treatment of Slaves in the Egyptian Gold Mines," p. 105). Women were also sold as slaves to be concubines for Greek and Macedonian soldiers and civilians.

The effects of slavery could also be important. The employment of large numbers of slaves in the Hellenistic kingdoms contributed to the Hellenizing process. Slaves working in homes, farms, or factories had opportunities to absorb Greek ways. This is especially evident in the case of the slave-wives of Hellenistic soldiers.

4-3c The Transformation of Education

In the Hellenistic world, education underwent a significant transformation. In the classical period of Greek history, education had been left largely to private enterprise. Greek cities now began to supervise education in new ways. The Greek **gymnasium**, which had been primarily an athletic institution, evolved into a secondary school. The curriculum centered on music, physical exercise, and literature, especially the poetry of Homer. Wealthy individuals often provided the money for the schools and also specified how it should be spent. An inscription from the city of Teos in Asia Minor specified that Polythroos "gave 34,000 drachmas . . . for there to be appointed each year . . . three grammar-masters to teach the boys and the girls . . . for two gymnastics-masters to be appointed . . . for a lyre—or harp—player to be appointed . . . [to] teach music and lyre—or harp—playing to the children."[6]

The school in Teos was unusual, however, in that education was ordinarily for upper-class male children. An official known as the *gymnasiarch* served as the head of a gymnasium. This was a civic position of considerable prestige. He was not paid and was expected to provide money for sacrifices, competitions, entertainment, and even school repairs. Many cities passed decrees awarding praise and a gold crown to the gymnasiarch for his generosity to the people. The educational year culminated with various musical, academic, and athletic contests in which students competed for the honor of having their names inscribed on a victory column.

Hellenistic kings also served as patrons of gymnasia, recognizing their importance in training youths who might serve later as administrators of the state. The institution of the gymnasium played a significant role in the diffusion of Greek culture throughout the Hellenistic world. "Those from the gymnasium," as the alumni were called, created associations to sustain the gymnasium and the Greek way of life. Whether an upper-class Greek youth lived on the Greek mainland, in Alexandria, or in another city in the east, he could imbibe Greek culture and maintain that sense of superiority that characterized the Greek overlords of the Hellenistic kingdoms.

4-4 Culture in the Hellenistic World

 FOCUS QUESTION: What achievements in literature, art, science, medicine, and philosophy occurred during the Hellenistic period?

Although the Hellenistic kingdoms encompassed vast areas and many diverse peoples, the Greeks provided a sense of unity as a result of the diffusion of Greek culture throughout the Hellenistic world. The Hellenistic era was a period of considerable cultural accomplishment in many fields—literature, art, science, medicine, and philosophy. Although these achievements occurred throughout the Hellenistic world, certain centers, especially the great Hellenistic cities of Alexandria and Pergamum, stood out. In both cities, the rulers themselves encouraged cultural developments. Rich Hellenistic kings had considerable resources with which to patronize culture.

The Ptolemies in Egypt made Alexandria an especially important cultural center. The library became the largest in ancient times, with more than half a million scrolls. The museum (literally, "temple of the Muses") created a favorable environment for scholarly research. As a result, Alexandria became home to scholars of all kinds—poets, writers, philosophers, and scientists.

Treatment of Slaves in the Egyptian Gold Mines

Q *Compare the treatment of slaves in the Egyptian gold mines with the treatment of slaves in Classical Athens. What does your comparison reveal about the nature of slavery in the Greek world?*

SLAVERY WAS A COMMON PRACTICE throughout antiquity. In both classical Greece and the Hellenistic world, the worst-treated slaves were those who worked in the mines. The Egyptians were especially notorious for their treatment of slaves in the gold mines in Nubia, described in this account by Diodorus of Sicily, who lived in the first century B.C.E. His account was based on the now lost work of the second-century writer Agatharchides.

Diodorus of Sicily, *Library of History*

And those who have been condemned in this way—and they are a great multitude and are all bound in chains—work at their task unceasingly both by day and throughout the entire night, enjoying no respite and being carefully cut off from any means of escape; since guards of foreign soldiers who speak a language different from theirs stand watch over them, so that not a man, either by conversation or by some contact of a friendly nature, is able to corrupt one of his keepers. . . . And the entire operations are in charge of a skilled worker who distinguishes the stone and points it out to the laborers; and of those who are assigned to this unfortunate task the physically strongest break the quartz-rock with iron hammers, applying no skill to the task but only force, and cutting tunnels through the stone, not in a straight line but wherever the seam of gleaming rock may lead. Now these men, working in darkness as they do because of the bending and winding of the passages, carry lamps bound on their foreheads; and since much of the time they change the position of their bodies to follow the particular character of the stone they throw the blocks, as they cut them out, on the ground, and at this task they labor without ceasing beneath the sternness and blows of an overseer.

The boys there who have not yet come to maturity, entering through the tunnels into the galleries formed by the removal of the rock, laboriously gather up the rock as it is cast down piece by piece and carry it out into the open to the place outside the entrance. Then those who are above thirty years of age take this quarried stone from them and with iron pestles pound a specified amount of it in stone mortars, until they have worked it down to a smaller size. Thereupon the women and older men receive from them the rock of this size and cast it into mills of which a number stand there in a row, and taking their places in groups of two or three at the spoke or handle of each mill they grind it until they have worked down the amount given them to the consistency of the finest flour. And since no opportunity is afforded any of them to care for his body and they have no garment to cover their shame, no man can look upon the unfortunate wretches without feeling pity for them because of the exceeding hardships they suffer. For no leniency or respite of any kind is given to any man who is sick, or maimed or aged, or in the case of a woman for her weakness, but all without exception are compelled by blows to persevere in their labors, until through ill-treatment they die in the midst of their tortures. Consequently the poor unfortunates believe, because their punishment is so excessively severe, that the future will always be more terrible than the present and therefore look forward to death as more to be desired than life.

Source: Diodorus of Sicily, *Library of History*, vol. 1, trans. C. H. Oldfather (Cambridge, Mass.: Harvard University Press, 1933).

4-4a New Directions in Literature

The Hellenistic Age produced an enormous quantity of literature, most of which has not survived. Hellenistic monarchs, who held literary talent in high esteem, subsidized writers on a grand scale. The Ptolemaic rulers of Egypt were particularly lavish. The combination of their largess and the famous library drew a host of scholars and authors to Alexandria, including a circle of poets. Theocritus (thee-AHK-ruh-tuss) (ca. 315–250 B.C.E.), originally a native of the island of Sicily, wrote "little poems" or idylls dealing with erotic themes, lovers' complaints, and above all, pastoral themes expressing his love of nature and his appreciation of nature's beauty.

In the Hellenistic era, Athens remained the theatrical center of the Greek world. Though little tragedy was produced, a new kind of comedy developed that completely rejected political themes and sought only to entertain and amuse. The Athenian playwright Menander (muh-NAN-dur) (ca. 342–291 B.C.E.) was perhaps the best representative of New Comedy. Plots were simple: typically, a hero falls in love with a not-really-so-bad prostitute who turns out eventually to be the long-lost daughter of a rich neighbor. The hero marries her, and they live happily ever after.

The Hellenistic period saw a great outpouring of historical and biographical literature. The chief historian of the Hellenistic Age was Polybius (puh-LIB-ee-uss) (ca. 203–120 B.C.E.), a Greek who lived for some years in Rome. Many historians regard him as second only to Thucydides among Greek historians. His major work consisted of forty books narrating the history of the "inhabited Mediterranean world" from 221 to 146 B.C.E. Only the first five books are extant, although long

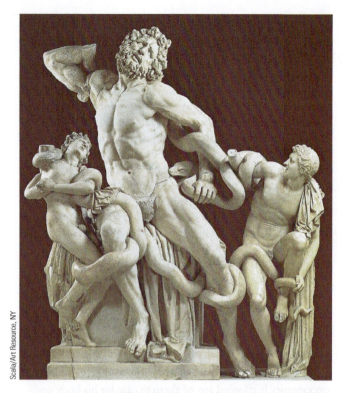

IMAGE 4.6 **Laocoön and His Sons.** Three sculptors from Rhodes created this famous piece. This version is probably a Roman copy of the original. The scene illustrates an episode from the Trojan War when the gods sent serpents into Troy to kill the Trojan priest Laocoön (lay-AHK-oh-wahn) and his sons. The intense struggles of the figures are reflected in the pained expressions on their faces.

extracts from the other books survive. His history focuses on the growth of Rome from a city-state to a vast empire. It is apparent that Polybius understood the significance of the Romans' achievement. He followed Thucydides in seeking rational motives for historical events. He also approached his sources critically and used firsthand accounts.

4-4b Hellenistic Art

In addition to being patrons of literary talent, the Hellenistic monarchs were eager to spend their money to beautify and adorn the cities in their states. The founding of new cities and the rebuilding of old ones provided numerous opportunities for Greek architects and sculptors (see Image 4.6). The structures of the Greek homeland—gymnasia, baths, theaters, and temples—lined the streets of these cities.

Both Hellenistic kings and rich citizens commissioned sculptures. The kings erected thousands of statues, many paid for by their subjects, in towns and cities all over the Hellenistic world. Hellenistic sculptors traveled widely, attracted by the material rewards offered by wealthy patrons. While maintaining the technical skill of the classical period, Hellenistic sculptors moved away from the idealism of fifth-century classicism to a more emotional and realistic art, seen in numerous statues of old women, drunks, and little children at play (see Image 4.7). They also placed a new emphasis on the female nude.

Alexander's incursion into the western part of India also resulted in some Greek cultural influences there, especially during the Hellenistic era in the Greco-Bactrian and Indo-Greek kingdoms. During the first century B.C.E., Indian sculptors began to create statues of the Buddha. The impact of Greek statues is especially evident in the Buddhist statues created in Gandhara, which today is part of Pakistan (see Global Perspectives, "The Influence of the Greeks on India," p. 107).

4-4c A Golden Age of Science and Medicine

The Hellenistic era witnessed a more conscious separation of science from philosophy. In classical Greece, what we would call the physical and life sciences had been divisions of philosophical inquiry. Nevertheless, the Greeks, by the time of Aristotle, had already established an important principle of scientific investigation—empirical research, or systematic observation, as the basis for generalization. In the Hellenistic Age, the sciences tended to be studied in their own right.

One of the traditional areas of Greek science was astronomy, and two Alexandrian scholars continued this exploration.

IMAGE 4.7 **Drunken Old Woman.** Unlike the Greek sculptors of the classical era, Hellenistic sculptors no longer tried to capture ideal beauty in their sculptures but moved toward a more emotional and realistic art. This statue of a drunken old woman is typical of this new trend in art. Old and haggard, mired in poverty, she struggles just to go on living.

The Influence of the Greeks on India

 What impact did Hellenistic art have on India? How do you explain this influence?

ALEXANDER'S INVASION OF INDIA opened the door to the creation of two Hellenistic states—the Greco-Bactrian and Indo-Greek kingdoms. Their location in parts of what are now Afghanistan, Pakistan, and India put them into direct contact with Indian civilization. While the Greeks in the kingdoms became aware of Buddhism, the Indians became aware of Greek art, thus creating a Greco-Buddhist art that combined western and eastern traditions. Greek architects and sculptors were highly valued throughout the Hellenistic world. Image 4.8a shows an example of Hellenistic sculpture—a terra-cotta statuette of a draped young woman made as a tomb offering near Thebes, probably around 300 B.C.E. During the first century B.C.E., Indian sculptors in Gandhara, where the interplay of Greek and Buddhist culture prospered, began to make statues of the Buddha in a style that combined Indian and Hellenistic artistic traditions, evident in the stone sculpture of the Buddha in Image 4.8b. Note the wavy hair topped by a bun tied with a ribbon, which is also a feature of earlier statues of Greek deities. This Buddha is also wearing a Greek-style toga.

IMAGE 4.8a   IMAGE 4.8b

(a): Kanellopoulos Museum, Athens//Gianni Dagli Orti/The Art Archive at Art Resource, NY

(b): National Museum of Pakistan, Karachi//Borromeo/Art Resource, NY

Aristarchus (ar-iss-TAR-kuss) of Samos (ca. 310–230 B.C.E.) developed a *heliocentric* view of the universe, contending that the sun and the fixed stars remain stationary while the earth rotates around the sun in a circular orbit. He also argued that the earth rotates around its own axis. This view was not widely accepted, however, and most scholars clung to the earlier *geocentric* view of the Greeks, which held that the earth was at the center of the universe. Another astronomer, Eratosthenes (er-uh-TAHSS-thuh-neez) (ca. 275–194 B.C.E.), determined that the earth was round and calculated the earth's circumference at 24,675 miles, an estimate that was within 200 miles of the actual figure.

A third Alexandrian scholar was Euclid (YOO-klid), who lived around 300 B.C.E. He established a school in Alexandria but is primarily known for his work *Elements*, which was a systematic organization of the fundamental elements of geometry as they had already been worked out; it became the standard textbook of plane geometry and was used up to modern times.

Archimedes The most famous scientist of the Hellenistic period, Archimedes (ahr-kuh-MEE-deez) (287–212 B.C.E.), came from the western Mediterranean region. Archimedes was especially important for establishing the value of the mathematical constant pi and for creating the science of hydrostatics. Archimedes was also a practical inventor. He may have devised the so-called Archimedean screw used to pump water out of mines and to lift irrigation water, as well as a compound pulley for transporting heavy weights. During the Roman siege of his native city of Syracuse, he constructed a number of devices to thwart attackers. According to Plutarch's account, the Romans became so frightened "that if they did but see a little rope or a piece of wood from the wall, instantly crying out, that there it was again, Archimedes was about to let fly some engine at them, they turned their backs and fled."[7]

Archimedes's accomplishments inspired a wealth of semi-legendary stories. He supposedly discovered specific gravity by observing the water he displaced in his bath and became so excited by his realization that he jumped out of the water and ran home naked, shouting, "Eureka!" ("I have found it!"). He is said to have emphasized the importance of levers by proclaiming to the king of Syracuse: "Give me a lever and a place to stand on, and I will move the earth." The king was so impressed that he encouraged Archimedes to lower his sights and build defensive weapons instead.

Medicine The scientific foundations of medicine also made considerable strides in the Hellenistic period. This represents a continuation from the fifth century when Hippocrates (hih-PAH-kruh-teez), a contemporary of Socrates, is credited with having been the "first to separate medicine from philosophy" by stressing natural explanations and natural cures for disease. Herophilus (huh-ROF-uh-luss) and Erasistratus (er-uh-SIS-truh-tuss), both well-known physicians, were active in Alexandria in the first half of the third century B.C.E. Both were interested in anatomy and used dissection and vivisection (the dissection of living bodies) to expand their knowledge, or so the Roman author Celsus claimed:

> Moreover, as pains, and also various kinds of diseases, arise in the more internal parts, they hold that no one can apply remedies for these who is ignorant about the parts themselves; hence it becomes necessary to lay open the bodies of the dead and to scrutinize their viscera and intestines. They hold that Herophilus and Erasistratus did this in the best way by far, when they laid open men while alive—criminals received out of prison from the kings—and while these were still breathing, observed parts which beforehand nature had concealed, their position, color, shape, size, arrangement, hardness, softness, smoothness, relation, processes and depressions of each, and whether any part is inserted into or is received into another.[8]

Herophilus added significantly to the understanding of the brain, eye, liver, and the reproductive and nervous systems. Erasistratus made discoveries in the process of digestion.

It would be misleading, however, to think of medicine in the Hellenistic world only in terms of scientific advances. Alongside these developments, a wide range of alternative methods of healing continued to exist. These included magical practices, such as the use of amulets to cast off evil spirits, herbal remedies, and the healing powers of deities, especially those of Asclepius (uh-SKLEE-pee-uss), the god of healing.

4-4d Philosophy: New Schools of Thought

While Alexandria and Pergamum became the renowned cultural centers of the Hellenistic world, Athens remained the prime center for philosophy and continued to attract the most illustrious philosophers from the Greek world who established schools there. New schools of philosophical thought—the Epicureans and Stoics—reinforced Athens' reputation as a philosophical center.

Epicureanism Epicurus (ep-i-KYOOR-uss) (341–270 B.C.E.), the founder of **Epicureanism** (ep-i-kyoo-REE-uh-ni-zum), established a school in Athens near the end of the fourth century B.C.E. Epicurus's famous belief in a doctrine of pleasure began with his view of the world. Although he did not deny the existence of the gods, he did not believe they played any active role in the world. The universe ran on its own. This left human beings free to follow self-interest as a basic motivating force. Happiness was the goal of life, and the means to achieve it was the pursuit of pleasure, the only true good. But the pursuit of pleasure was not meant in a physical, hedonistic sense:

> When, therefore, we maintain that pleasure is the end, we do not mean the pleasures of profligates and those that consist in sensuality, as is supposed by some who are either ignorant or disagree with us or do not understand, but freedom from pain in the body and from trouble in the mind. For it is not continuous drinkings and revelings, nor the satisfaction of lusts, nor the enjoyment of fish and other luxuries of the wealthy table, which produce a pleasant life, but sober reasoning, searching out the motives for all choice and avoidance, and banishing mere opinions, to which are due the greatest disturbance of the spirit.

Pleasure was not satisfying one's desire in an active, gluttonous fashion but rather freedom from emotional turmoil and freedom from worry—the freedom that came from a mind at rest. To achieve this passive pleasure, one had to free oneself from public activity: "We must release ourselves from the prison of affairs and politics." They were too strenuous to give peace of mind. But this was not a renunciation of all social life, for to Epicurus, a life could be complete only when it was centered on the basic ideal of friendship: "Of all the things which wisdom acquires to produce the blessedness of the complete life, far the greatest is the possession of friendship."[9] Epicurus's own life in Athens was an embodiment of his teachings. He and his friends created their own private community where they could pursue their ideal of true happiness.

Stoicism Epicureanism was eventually overshadowed by another school of thought known as **Stoicism** (STOH-i-siz-um), which became the most popular philosophy of the Hellenistic world and persisted in the Roman Empire as well. It was the product of a teacher named Zeno (335–263 B.C.E.), who came to Athens and began to teach in a public colonnade known as the Painted Portico (the *Stoa Poikile*—hence the name Stoicism). Like Epicureanism, Stoicism was concerned with how individuals find happiness. But Stoics took a radically different approach. To them, happiness, the supreme good, could be found only in virtue, which meant essentially living in harmony with divine will: "And this very thing constitutes the virtue of the happy man and the smooth current of life, when all actions promote the harmony of the spirit dwelling in the individual man with the will of him who orders the universe."[10] One achieved happiness by choosing to follow divine will through the free exercise of one's own will. To the Stoics, divine will was the same as the will of nature, since nature was simply a manifestation or expression of the gods. "Living according to nature," therefore, meant following divine will or the natural laws that the gods established to run the universe.

Virtuous living, then, was living in accordance with the laws of nature or submitting to divine will (see Historical Voices, "The Stoic Ideal of Harmony with God," p. 109). This led to the acceptance of whatever one received in life because divine will

The Stoic Ideal of Harmony with God

 Based on Cleanthes's poem, what are some of the beliefs of the Stoics? How do they differ from the beliefs of the Epicureans?

THE STOIC CLEANTHES (klee-AN-theez) (331–232 B.C.E.) succeeded Zeno as head of this school of philosophy. One historian of Hellenistic civilization has called this work by Cleanthes the greatest religious hymn in Greek literature. Certainly, it demonstrates that Stoicism, unlike Epicureanism, did have an underlying spiritual foundation. This poem has been compared to the great psalms of the Hebrews.

Cleanthes, *Hymn to Zeus*

No work is wrought apart from Thee, God,
Or in the world, or in the heaven above.

Or on the deep, save only what is done
By sinners in their folly. Nay, Thou can
Make the rough smooth, bring wondrous order forth
From chaos; in Thy sight unloveliness
Seems beautiful; for so Thou has fitted things
Together, good and evil, that there reigns
One everlasting Reason in them all.
The wicked heed not this, but suffer it
To slip, to their undoing; these are they
Who, yearning ever to secure the good,
Mark not nor hear the law of God, by wise
Obedience unto which they might attain
A nobler life, with Reason harmonized.

Source: *The Hymn of Cleanthes with Brief Introduction and Notes*, ed. by E. H. Blakeney (New York: Macmillan Company, 1921).

was by its very nature good. By accepting divine law, people mastered themselves and gained inner peace. Life's problems could not disturb such individuals, and they could bear whatever life offered (hence our word *stoic*).

Unlike Epicureans, Stoics did not believe in the need to separate oneself from the world and politics. Public service was regarded as noble. The real Stoic was a good citizen and could even be a good government official. Because Stoics believed that a divine principle was present throughout the universe, each human being also contained a divine spark. This led to a belief in the oneness of humanity. The world constituted a single society of equal human beings. Although humans were not equal in the outer world, the divine spark in each meant that all were free to follow divine will (what was best for each individual). All persons then, even slaves, though unfree in body, were equal at the level of the soul.

The Appeal of Epicureanism and Stoicism Epicureanism and especially Stoicism appealed to large numbers of people in the Hellenistic world. Both of these philosophies focused primarily on the problem of human happiness. Their popularity would suggest a fundamental change in the character of the Greek lifestyle. In the classical Greek world, the happiness of individuals and the meaning of life were closely associated with the life of the polis. One found fulfillment within the community. In the Hellenistic kingdoms, although the polis continued to exist, the sense that one could find satisfaction and fulfillment through life in the polis had weakened. As a result, individuals sought new philosophies that offered personal happiness. At the same time, in the cosmopolitan world of the Hellenistic states, with their mixtures of peoples, a new openness

to thoughts of universality could also emerge. For some people, Stoicism embodied this larger sense of community. The appeal of new philosophies in the Hellenistic era can also be explained by the apparent decline in certain aspects of traditional religion.

4-5 Religion in the Hellenistic World

 FOCUS QUESTION: Which religions were prominent during the Hellenistic period, and what does their popularity suggest about Hellenistic society?

When the Greeks spread throughout the Near East, they took their gods with them. Hellenistic cities increased the number of public festivals and celebrated them with great magnificence. But as time went on, there was a noticeable decline in the vitality of the traditional Greek Olympian religion. The civic cults based on the traditional gods no longer seemed sufficient to satisfy people's emotional needs.

This left Greeks receptive to the numerous religious cults of the eastern world. The Greeks were always tolerant of other existing religious institutions. Hence, in the Hellenistic cities of the Near East, the traditional civic cults of their own gods and foreign cults existed side by side. Alexandria had cults of the traditional Greek gods, Egyptian deities such as Isis and Horus, the Babylonian Astarte, and the Syrian Atargatis.

But for many people, the search for personal meaning remained unfulfilled. Among educated Greeks, the philosophies of Epicureanism and especially Stoicism offered help. Another source of solace came in the form of **mystery religions**.

4-5a Mystery Religions

Mystery cults, with their secret initiations and promises of individual salvation, were not new to the Greek world. They included the cult of Dionysus, which had mysteries associated with it, and the cult of the Cabeiri (gods of fertility) on the island of Samothrace. The Cabeiri were especially known for helping seafarers and attracted initiates who hoped thereby to avoid misfortune. But the Greeks of the Hellenistic era were also strongly influenced by eastern mystery cults, such as those of Egypt, which offered a distinct advantage over the Greek mystery religions. The latter had usually been connected to specific locations (such as Eleusis), which meant that a would-be initiate had to undertake a pilgrimage in order to participate in the rites. In contrast, the eastern mystery religions were readily available because temples to their gods and goddesses were located throughout the Greek cities of the east.

All of the mystery religions were based on the same fundamental premises. Individuals could pursue a path to salvation and achieve eternal life by being initiated into a union with a savior god or goddess who had died and risen again. The ritual of initiation, by which the seeker identified with the god or goddess, was no doubt a highly emotional experience.

The Egyptian cult of Isis was one of the most popular mystery religions. The cult of Isis was very ancient but became truly universal in Hellenistic times. Isis was the goddess of women, marriage, and children, as one of her hymns states: "I am she whom women call goddess. I ordained that women should be loved by men: I brought wife and husband together, and invented the marriage contract. I ordained that women should bear children."[11] Isis was also portrayed as the giver of civilization who had brought laws and letters to all humankind. The cult of Isis offered a precious commodity to its initiates—the promise of eternal life. After the Roman conquest of the Hellenistic world (see Chapter 5), mystery cults would find acceptance in the wider Roman world. And in many ways, the mystery religions of the Hellenistic era helped pave the way for Christianity.

4-5b The Jews in the Hellenistic World

In observing the similarities among their gods and goddesses, Greeks and easterners tended to assume that the deities were the same beings with different names, giving rise to a process of **syncretism**. But a special position in the Hellenistic world was occupied by the Jews, whose monotheistic religion was exclusive and did not permit this kind of fusion of spiritual beings.

The Jewish province of Judaea was ruled by the Ptolemies until it fell under the control of the Seleucids by 200 B.C.E. In the reign of the Seleucid king Antiochus IV (175–163 B.C.E.), conflict erupted in Judaea. Hellenistic monarchs were generally tolerant of all religions, but problems with Rome prompted Antiochus to try to impose more cultural and religious unity in Judaea. He sent troops to Jerusalem and seized the Second Temple, which had been built after the Jews in Babylonian captivity had

been allowed to return to Jerusalem by the Persian ruler Cyrus in 539 B.C.E. (see Chapter 2). In doing so, Antiochus sparked a Jewish uprising led eventually by Judas Maccabaeus (JOO-dus mak-uh-BEE-uss) (see Image 4.9). In 164 B.C.E., the rebels succeeded in recapturing the temple, a joyous event that has been celebrated every year since in the Jewish holiday of Hanukkah (HAH-nuh-kuh) (Hebrew for "rededication"). Although the conflict in Judaea continued, the Seleucids ultimately made concessions and allowed the Jews considerable freedom.

But since the Diaspora (see Chapter 2), large numbers of Jews no longer lived in Judaea. There was a large Jewish population in Egypt, particularly in Alexandria, as well as Jewish settlements throughout the cities of Asia Minor and Syria. In each city, Jews generally set up a synagogue and formed a private association for worship as other foreigners did. Some city authorities also allowed the Jews to form a political corporation that gave them greater rights than other resident aliens. Most importantly, they gained the privilege to live by their own laws and their own judicial system. The Jews were not really interested in citizenship in the cities in which they resided because full citizenship meant worship of the city's gods—anathema to Jews who believed only in Yahweh.

IMAGE 4.9 **The Victory of Judas Maccabeus.** Judas Maccabeus was the third son of a Jewish priest who led a revolt against the Seleucid ruler. After the death of his father in 166 B.C.E., Judas became leader of the revolt. He relied on guerrilla warfare but in the Battle of Emmaus defeated the Seleucid forces led by Nicanor. In this scene painted by the seventeenth-century Dutch painter Gerrit van Honthorst, Judas (in yellow) is seen after his victory over Nicator, but in seventeenth-century garb.

Q *Why do you think a seventeenth-century painter would want to paint this scene?*

Erich Lessing/Art Resource, NY

While the Greek city-states were pursuing their squabbles, to their north a new and powerful kingdom—Macedonia—emerged. Under King Philip II, the Macedonians undertook military reforms, defeated a Greek allied army in 338 B.C.E., and then consolidated their control over the Greek peninsula. Although the independent Greek city-states lost their freedom when they were conquered by the Macedonians, Greek culture did not die, and a new age, known as the Hellenistic era, eventually came into being.

The Hellenistic era began with the conquest of the Persian Empire by Alexander the Great, the young successor to his father, Philip II. Alexander, vowing to avenge the Persian attacks on Greece, crossed into Asia Minor with his army in 334 B.C.E. By 330, the Persian Empire had been defeated, but Alexander, never at rest, moved eastward into India, where a mutiny by his exhausted troops forced him to return to Babylon, where he died in 323 B.C.E. Though a great military leader, Alexander was not a good political administrator. He failed to establish any definite structure for the empire he had conquered, and four major Hellenistic kingdoms eventually emerged as his successors.

Within those kingdoms, the resulting society is known as *Hellenistic,* meaning Greek-like or "to imitate Greeks." The Greek language became dominant throughout the area as Greek ideas became influential. Greek merchants, artists, philosophers, and soldiers found opportunities and rewards throughout the Near East, now a world of kingdoms rather than independent city-states.

The Hellenistic period was, in its own way, a vibrant one. New cities rose and flourished. New philosophical doctrines—such as Epicureanism and Stoicism—captured the minds of many. Sculptors and architects found many opportunities under the patronage of kings and other wealthy individuals. Significant achievements occurred in literature and science, as is evident in the work of Polybius, Euclid, and Archimedes. Greek culture spread throughout the Near East and made an impact wherever it was carried. In some areas of the Hellenistic world, queens played an active role in political life, and many women found new avenues for expressing themselves. Commerce increased, and women often played significant roles in economic activities. Although the Hellenistic era achieved a degree of political stability, by the late third century B.C.E. signs of decline were beginning to multiply, and the growing power of Rome eventually endangered the Hellenistic world.

CHAPTER TIMELINE

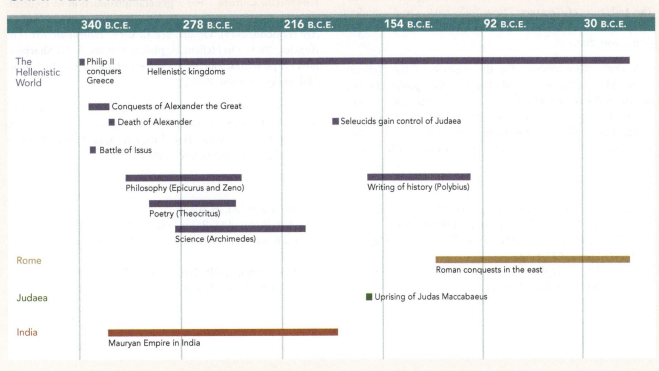

	340 B.C.E.	278 B.C.E.	216 B.C.E.	154 B.C.E.	92 B.C.E.	30 B.C.E.

The Hellenistic World
- Philip II conquers Greece
- Hellenistic kingdoms
- Conquests of Alexander the Great
- Death of Alexander
- Battle of Issus
- Seleucids gain control of Judaea
- Philosophy (Epicurus and Zeno)
- Writing of history (Polybius)
- Poetry (Theocritus)
- Science (Archimedes)

Rome
- Roman conquests in the east

Judaea
- Uprising of Judas Maccabaeus

India
- Mauryan Empire in India

CHAPTER REVIEW

Upon Reflection

Q How was the Hellenistic period different from the Greek classical age?

Q What role did Alexander the Great play in the creation of the Hellenistic kingdoms?

Q What were the main achievements of the Hellenistic kingdoms, and why did they fail to bring any lasting order to the lands of the Near East?

Q It can be said that the Hellenistic Age witnessed a shift from the *polis* to the *cosmopolis*. What does this mean, and what effects did it have on Greek life?

Key Terms

Hellenistic (p. 90)
gymnasium (p. 104)
Epicureanism (p. 108)

Stoicism (p. 108)
mystery religions (p. 110)

Full definitions also appear in the Glossary at the end of the book.

Suggestions for Further Reading

General Works For good introductions to the Hellenistic era, see **P. Green**, *The Hellenistic Age: A Short History* (New York, 2007); **G. Shipley**, *The Greek World After Alexander, 323–30 B.C.* (London, 2000); and **P. Thonemann**, *The Hellenistic Age: A Very Short Introduction* (New York, 2018). See also **R. M. Errington**, *A History of the Hellenistic World, 323–30 B.C.* (New York, 2008). On Macedonia, see **I. Worthington**, *By the Spear: Philip II, Alexander the Great and the Rise and Fall of the Macedonian Empire* (Oxford, 2014).

Alexander There are considerable differences of opinion on Alexander the Great. Good biographies include **P. Cartledge**, *Alexander the Great* (New York, 2004); **P. Freeman**, *Alexander the Great* (New York, 2011); and **G. M. Rogers**, *Alexander: The Ambiguity of Greatness* (New York, 2004). On Alexander's conquests, see **P. Briant**, *Alexander the Great and His Empire* (Princeton, 2010).

Hellenistic Monarchies On the creation of the Hellenistic world, see **R. Waterfield**, *Dividing the Spoils: The War for Alexander the Great's Empire* (Oxford, 2011). On the various Hellenistic monarchies, see the collection of essays in **C. Habicht**, *Hellenistic Monarchies* (Ann Arbor, Mich., 2006). The Seleucid kingdom is covered in **P. Kosmin**, *The Land of*

the Elephant Kings (Cambridge, Mass., 2014). On the Ptolemaic dynasty of Egypt, see **G. Hölbl**, *A History of the Ptolemaic Empire* (London, 2001). On warfare, see **A. Chaniotis**, *War in the Hellenistic World: A Social and Cultural History* (Oxford, 2005).

The Celts On the Celts, see the beautifully illustrated brief study by **J. Davies**, *The Celts* (London, 2000).

Hellenistic Women Hellenistic women are examined in two works by **S. B. Pomeroy**, *Goddesses, Whores, Wives, and Slaves: Women in Classical Antiquity*, 2nd edition (New York, 1995), pp. 120–148, and *Women in Hellenistic Egypt* (New York, 1984).

Hellenistic Culture For a general introduction to Hellenistic culture, see **J. Onians**, *Art and Thought in the Hellenistic Age* (London, 1979). On art, see **L. Birn**, *Hellenistic Art* (Los Angeles, 2005). On Hellenistic philosophy, see **R. W. Sharpies**, *Stoics, Epicureans, and Skeptics: An Introduction to Hellenistic Philosophy* (London, 1996).

Hellenistic Religion On various facets of Hellenistic religion, see **L. Martin**, *Hellenistic Religions: An Introduction* (New York, 1987), and **A. Tripolitis**, *Religions of the Hellenistic-Roman Age* (Ann Arbor, Mich., 2001).

Notes

1. Quoted in S. B. Pomeroy et al., *Ancient Greece: A Political, Social, and Cultural History* (Oxford, 1999), p. 390.
2. Polybius, *The Histories*, trans. W. R. Paton (Cambridge, Mass., 1960), 18.37.8–10.
3. Quoted in G. Shipley, *The Greek World After Alexander, 323–30 B.C.* (London, 2000), p. 53.

4. Quoted in ibid., p. 304.
5. M. B. Fant and M. R. Lefkowitz, *Women's Life in Greece and Rome: A Source Book in Translation* (Baltimore, 1992), no. 208.
6. R. S. Bagnall and P. Derow, *Greek Historical Documents: The Hellenistic Period* (Chico, Calif., 1981), p. 113.

7. Plutarch, *Life of Marcellus,* trans. John Dryden (New York, n.d.), p. 378.

8. Celsus, *De Medicina,* trans. W. G. Spencer (Cambridge, Mass., 1935), pp. 23–24.

9. *Epicurus: The Extant Remains,* trans. Cyril Bailey (Oxford, 1926), pp. 89–90, 115, 101.

10. Diogenes Laertius, *Life of Zeno,* vol. 2, trans. R. D. Hicks (London, 1925), p. 195.

11. Quoted in W. W. Tarn, *Hellenistic Civilization* (London, 1930), p. 324.

MindTap *Tips*

Highlight key text from your book, add notes and create custom flashcards with the MindTap reader. The StudyHub App in MindTap will track your notes, highlights and bookmarks as well as those from your instructor—keeping everything in one spot for ease of access. You can also use StudyHub to create a custom study guide covering any range of content you choose, with just a few mouse clicks!

CHAPTER 5

The Roman Republic

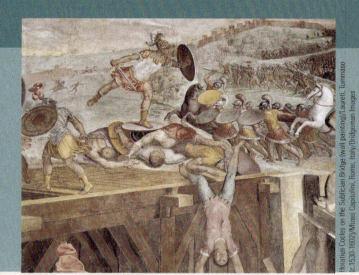

Horatius Cocles on the Sublician Bridge (wall painting)/Laureti, Tommaso (c.1530–1602)/Musei Capitolini, Rome, Italy/Bridgeman Images

IMAGE 5.1 **Horatius Defending the Bridge as Envisioned by Tommaso Laureti, a Sixteenth-Century Italian Painter**

CHAPTER OUTLINE AND FOCUS QUESTIONS

5-1 The Emergence of Rome

Q What impact did geography have on the history of Rome? What influence did the Greeks and Etruscans have on early Roman history?

5-2 The Roman Republic (ca. 509–264 B.C.E.)

Q What were the major political institutions of the Roman republic? How did Rome conquer Italy, and what policies and institutions help explain the Romans' success in conquering Italy?

5-3 The Roman Conquest of the Mediterranean (264–133 B.C.E.)

Q How did Rome achieve its empire from 264 to 133 B.C.E., and what is meant by the phrase "Roman imperialism"?

5-4 Society and Culture in the Roman Republic

Q How did the acquisition of an empire affect Roman religious, social, and economic institutions, values and attitudes, law, and art and literature?

5-5 The Decline and Fall of the Roman Republic (133–31 B.C.E.)

Q What were the main problems Rome faced during the last century of the republic, and how were they ultimately resolved? What was the role of powerful individuals?

CONNECTIONS TO TODAY

What lessons does the fall of the Roman republic offer to the United States today?

EARLY ROMAN HISTORY is filled with legendary tales of the heroes who made Rome great. One of the best known is the story of Horatius at the bridge. Threatened by attack from the neighboring Etruscans, Roman farmers abandoned their fields and moved into the city, where the walls protected them. One weak point in the Roman defenses, however, was a wooden bridge over the Tiber River. Horatius was on guard at the bridge when a sudden assault by the Etruscans caused many Roman troops to throw down their weapons and flee. Horatius urged them to make a stand at the bridge to protect Rome; when they hesitated, as a last resort he told them to destroy the bridge behind him while he held the Etruscans back. Astonished at the sight of a single defender, the confused Etruscans threw their spears at Horatius, who caught them on his shield and barred the way. By the time the Etruscans had regrouped and were about to overwhelm the lone defender, the Roman soldiers brought down the bridge. When Horatius heard the bridge crash into the river behind him, he dived fully armed into the water and swam safely to the other side through a hail of arrows. Rome had been saved by the courageous act of a Roman who knew his duty and was determined to carry it out. Courage, duty, determination—these qualities would also serve the many Romans who believed that it was their mission to rule nations and peoples.

In the first millennium B.C.E., a group of Latin-speaking people established a small community on the plain of Latium on the Italian peninsula. This community, called Rome, was one of numerous Latin-speaking communities in Latium, and the Latin speakers, in turn, constituted only some of the many peoples in Italy. Roman history is basically the story of the Romans' conquest of the plain of Latium, then Italy, and finally the entire Mediterranean world. Why were the Romans able to do this? The Romans made the right decisions at the right time; in other words, the Romans had political wisdom.

The Romans were also practical. Unlike the Greeks, who reserved their citizenship for small, select groups, the Romans often offered citizenship to the peoples they conquered, thus laying the groundwork for a strong, integrated empire. The Romans also did not hesitate to borrow ideas and culture from the Greeks. Roman strength lay in government, law, and engineering. The Romans knew how to govern people, establish legal structures, and construct the roads that took them to the ends of the known world. Throughout their empire, they carried their law, their political institutions, their engineering skills, and their Latin language. And even after the Romans were gone, those same gifts continued to play an important role in the continuing saga of Western civilization.

5-1 The Emergence of Rome

 FOCUS QUESTIONS: What impact did geography have on the history of Rome? What influence did the Greeks and Etruscans have on early Roman history?

Not much is known about the prehistoric peoples who lived in Italy. We do know that Indo-European peoples moved into Italy during the second half of the second millennium B.C.E. By the first millennium B.C.E., other peoples had also settled in Italy, the two most notable being the Greeks and the Etruscans (ih-TRUSS-kunz). Before examining these peoples, however, we need to consider the influence geography had on the historical development of the peoples on the Italian peninsula.

5-1a Geography of the Italian Peninsula

Geography had a major impact on Roman history. Italy is a narrow peninsula extending about 750 miles from north to south but averaging only about 120 miles across (see Map 5.1). The Apennine Mountains traverse the peninsula from north to south, forming a ridge down the middle that divides west from east. Nevertheless, Italy has some fairly large fertile plains that are ideal for farming, the most important of which at the time were the Po Valley in the north, probably the most fertile agricultural area; Latium (LAY-shee-um), on which Rome was located; and Campania (kam-PAH-nyuh) to the south of Latium. To the east of the Italian peninsula is the Adriatic Sea, and to the west, the

Tyrrhenian Sea and the large islands of Corsica and Sardinia. Sicily lies just west of the toe of the boot-shaped peninsula.

Although the Apennines bisect Italy, they are less rugged than the mountain ranges of Greece and so did not divide the peninsula into many small isolated communities. Italy also possessed considerably more productive farmland than Greece, enabling it to support a large population. Rome's location was favorable from a geographic point of view. Located 18 miles inland on the Tiber River, Rome had access to the sea but was far enough inland to be safe from pirates. Built on seven hills, it was easily defended, and because it was situated where the Tiber could be readily forded, Rome became a natural crossing point for north–south traffic in western Italy. All in all, Rome had a good central location in Italy from which to expand.

Moreover, the Italian peninsula juts into the Mediterranean Sea, making it an important crossroads between the western and eastern Mediterranean. Once Rome had unified Italy, involvement in Mediterranean affairs was natural. And after the Romans had conquered their Mediterranean empire, Italy's central location made their task of governing that empire considerably easier.

5-1b The Greeks

The Greeks arrived on the Italian peninsula in large numbers during the age of Greek colonization (750–550 B.C.E.; see Chapter 3). Initially, the Greeks settled in southern Italy. They founded Cumae on the Bay of Naples, Naples itself, and Tarentum and then crept around the coast and up the peninsula as far as Brindisi. They also occupied the eastern two-thirds of Sicily. In establishing their colonies, the Greeks planned permanent communities, secured the coastal plains for agriculture, and built walled cities with harbors to carry on trade. Ultimately, the Greeks had considerable influence on Rome. They cultivated the olive and the vine, passed on their alphabetic system of writing, and provided artistic and cultural models through their sculpture, architecture, and literature. Indeed, many historians view Roman culture as a continuation of Greek culture. While Greek influence initially touched Rome indirectly through the Etruscans, the Romans' conquest of southern Italy and Sicily brought them into direct contact with the Greeks.

HISTORIANS DEBATE ## 5-1c Who Were the Etruscans?

The initial development of Rome was influenced most by a people known as the Etruscans, who had settled north of Rome in Etruria (ih-TROOR-ee-uh). They were a city-dwelling people who established their towns in commanding positions and fortified them with walls. Numerous inscriptions in tombs show that the Etruscans adopted alphabetic writing from the Greeks before 600 B.C.E.

The origins of the Etruscans are not clear, but some historians believe that recent DNA analysis has confirmed the theory of the ancient Greek historian Herodotus (see Chapter 3) that the Etruscans emigrated from the region of Lydia (now western Turkey) and took over the lands of the native people known as Villanovans in the eighth century B.C.E. However, other scholars have argued that there is no archaeological evidence of attacks and that the Etruscans were simply descendants of the native Villanovans.

MAP 5.1 **Ancient Italy.** Ancient Italy was home to several peoples. Both the Etruscans in the north and the Greeks in the south had a major influence on the development of Rome.

Q *Once Rome had conquered the Etruscans, Sabines, Samnites, and other local groups, what aspects of the Italian peninsula helped make it defensible against outside enemies?*

In any case, after 650 B.C.E., the Etruscans expanded throughout Italy and became the dominant cultural and economic force in a number of areas (see Image 5.2). To the north, they moved into north-central Italy. To the south, according to Roman tradition and archaeological evidence, they controlled Rome and possibly all of Latium. From Latium they moved south into Campania, founded a settlement at Capua, and came into direct contact with Greek colonists in southern Italy. In the sixth century B.C.E., the Etruscans were at the height of their power. But by 480 B.C.E., their power had begun to decline, and by 400 B.C.E., they were again limited to Etruria itself. Later they were invaded by the Gauls and then conquered by the Romans. But by then the Etruscans had already made an impact. By transforming villages into towns and cities, they brought urbanization to northern and central Italy (the Greeks brought urbanization to southern Italy). Rome was, of course, the Etruscans' most famous creation.

5-1d Early Rome

In order to provide a noble ancestry for their city, the Romans created two significant legends. One was the story of Aeneas, the son of the goddess Venus and a mortal man. Aeneas was a Trojan hero who fought the Greeks and who had escaped from the sacking of Troy and eventually made his way to Italy. According to one version of the legend he founded the city of Rome, which he named after a Trojan woman. The legend reflects the desire of the Romans to connect Roman history to Greek history, and especially Greece's heroic age, an indication of the strong impact Greek culture made on the Romans.

The other legend is the story of Romulus and Remus, the twin sons of the god Mars and Rhea Silvia, a Vestal Virgin (see Chapter 6) who was punished for losing her virginity to Amulius, who had become king of Alba Longa by overthrowing her father. Her boys were set adrift on the Tiber River in a reed basket. They were found by a she-wolf who suckled them and were then raised by the family of a shepherd. When the boys became grown men they were told of their origins and avenged their mother and grandfather by killing Amulius and then founded the new city of Rome. According to legend, Romulus founded a new city on the Palatine Hill in 753 B.C.E., killed his brother in an argument, and then became the first king of Rome.

Of course, the Romans invented these stories to provide a noble ancestry for their city. Archaeologists have found, however, that by the eighth century there was a settlement consisting

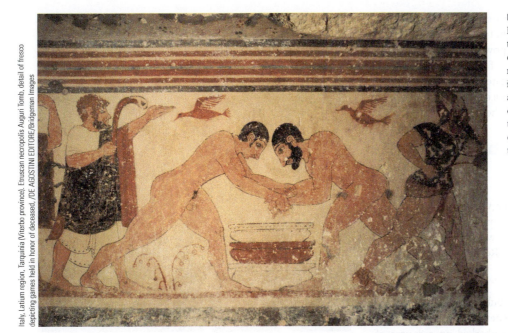

Italy, Latium region, Tarquinia (Viterbo province). Etruscan necropolis Auguri Tomb, detail of fresco depicting games held in honor of deceased, /DE AGOSTINI EDITORE/Bridgeman Images

IMAGE 5.2 The Tomb of the Augurs. Like the Egyptians, the Etruscans filled their tombs with furniture, bowls, and other objects of daily life, as well as murals showing diversions experienced in life and awaiting the dead in the afterlife. This tomb of the augurs from ca. 520 B.C.E. is carved out of bedrock at the Etruscan city of Tarquinia. This detail of a fresco shows games held in honor of the departed.

of huts on the tops of Rome's hills. The early Romans, basically a pastoral people, spoke Latin, which, like Greek, belongs to the Indo-European family of languages (see Table 1.3 in Chapter 1). The Roman historical tradition also maintained that early Rome (753–509 B.C.E.) had been under the control of seven kings and that two of the last three had been Etruscans. Some historians believe that the list of kings may have some historical accuracy. What is certain is that Rome did fall under the influence of the Etruscans for about one hundred years during the period of the kings.

By the beginning of the sixth century, under Etruscan influence, Rome began to emerge as a city (see Map 5.2). The Etruscans were responsible for an outstanding building program. They constructed the first roadbed of the chief street through Rome—the Sacred Way—before 575 B.C.E. and oversaw the development of temples, markets, shops, streets, and houses. By 509 B.C.E., supposedly when the monarchy was overthrown, a new Rome had emerged, essentially a product of the fusion of Etruscan and native Roman elements. After Rome had expanded over its seven hills and the valleys in between, the Servian Wall was built in the fourth century B.C.E. to surround the city.

The Etruscans had an impact on Roman civilization in numerous ways, both large and small. The Romans adopted Etruscan dress—the toga and short cloak. The insignia of the Etruscan kings became the insignia of Roman magistrates. Most impressive was the *fasces* (FAS-eez), an ax surrounded by a bundle of rods used as a symbol for the power to scourge and execute—hence to rule. The Romans

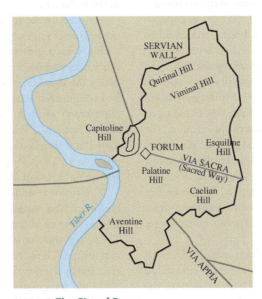

MAP 5.2 The City of Rome

were also indebted to the Etruscans for the alphabet. The Latin alphabet was a modification of the Etruscan alphabet derived from the Greeks.

The Romans traditionally associated the end of both monarchy and Etruscan domination with the rape of Lucretia, a Roman noblewoman of great virtue. Raped by a son of the king, Lucretia told her father, husband, and their friends what had happened and then committed suicide rather than be an example of "unchastity to other wives," as an ancient Roman historian put it. Lucretia became the model Roman woman: a faithful wife and a pure and courageous woman who chose death rather than be seen as lacking in virtue. According to Livy (LIV-ee), one of the chief ancient sources for the history of the Roman republic (see "Livy," in Section 6-1e), the nephew of the king, a man named Brutus, immediately sought revenge. He had a number of grievances against his uncle, including the execution of his brother by the king. After Lucretia's suicide, Brutus organized a group of noblemen and drove the king out of the city. According to Livy, Brutus made the people of Rome swear an oath to never again allow a king to rule Rome. Brutus is credited with establishing a republican form of government, which ushered in the era of the republic. According to the Romans of the late republic, all this occurred in 509 B.C.E.

Though interesting, Livy's account has little historical foundation. It is more likely that the overthrow of the monarchy was accomplished by nobles who experienced a loss of power because of the shift from cavalry to heavy-armed infantry during the reign of Servius Tullius

(SUR-vee-uss TUHL-ee-uss), the next-to-last king. The over-throw was not a patriotic uprising but an attempt by Roman nobles to maintain their position of power. Some scholars have even argued that the continuation of Etruscan influence in Rome into the fifth century necessitates dating the beginning of the Roman republic to around 475 B.C.E., but most historians remain committed to a date close to the traditional 509 B.C.E.

5-2 The Roman Republic (ca. 509–264 B.C.E.)

 FOCUS QUESTIONS: What were the major political institutions of the Roman republic? How did Rome conquer Italy, and what policies and institutions help explain the Romans' success in conquering Italy?

The transition from monarchy to republican government was not easy. Rome felt threatened by enemies from every direction and in meeting these threats embarked on a course of military expansion that led to the conquest of the entire Italian peninsula. During this period of expansion in Italy, the Roman republic developed political institutions that were in many ways determined by the social divisions that existed within the community.

5-2a The Roman State

In politics and law, as in conquest, the Romans took a practical approach and fashioned political institutions in response to problems as they arose. Hence, it is important to remember that the political institutions we will discuss evolved over a period of centuries.

Political Institutions The Romans had a clear concept of executive authority, embodied in their word **imperium** (im-PEE-ree-um), or "the right to command." Invested with imperium, the chief magistrates of the Roman state exercised a supreme power that was circumscribed only by extraneous means—officials held office for a limited term and could be tried for offenses committed in office once their term ended.

The chief executive officers of the Roman republic who possessed imperium were the consuls and praetors. Two **consuls** (KAHN-sulls), chosen annually, administered the government and led the Roman army into battle (see Image 5.3). In 366 B.C.E., a new office, that of the **praetor** (PREE-tur), was created. The praetor also possessed imperium and could govern Rome when the consuls were away from the city and lead armies. The praetor's primary function, however, was the execution of justice. He was in charge of the civil law as it applied to Roman citizens. In 242 B.C.E., reflecting Rome's growth, another praetor was added to adjudicate cases in which one or both parties were noncitizens.

As Rome expanded into the Mediterranean, additional praetors were established to govern the newly conquered provinces (two in 227, two more in 197 B.C.E.). But as the number of provinces continued to grow, the Romans devised

IMAGE 5.3 **Lictors with Fasces.** Pictured are lictors bearing the *fasces*, an ax surrounded by a bundle of rods tied with a red thong, an insignia borrowed from the Etruscan kings. The *fasces* was a symbol of the power to rule, and twelve lictors bearing the *fasces* always preceded the consuls, the chief executives of the Roman republic.

 What connection is there between the Roman use of the fasces and the use of the word fascism in twentieth-century Italy?

a new system in which ex-consuls and ex-praetors who had served their one-year terms were given the title of *proconsul* and *propraetor*, respectively, and sent out as provincial governors—demonstrating once again the Romans' practical solution to an immediate problem. It was reasonable to assume that officials with governmental experience would make good provincial administrators, although this was not always true in practice because of the opportunities for financial corruption in the provinces.

Periodically, the republic also created an extraordinary executive. In an emergency, the consuls would resign, and a **dictator** with unlimited power would be chosen to run the state. This office was supposed to last only for the duration of the emergency, the usual limit being six months. The Roman state also had administrative officials with specialized duties. **Quaestors** (KWE-sturs) assisted consuls and praetors in the administration of financial affairs. **Aediles** (EE-dylz) supervised the public games and watched over the grain supply of the city, a major problem for a rapidly growing urban community that came to rely on imported grain to feed its population.

The Roman **senate** came to hold an especially important position in the republic. The senate or council of elders was a select group of about three hundred men who served for life. The senate was not a legislative body and could only advise the magistrates. The advice of the senate was not taken lightly, however, and by the third century B.C.E. had virtually the force of law. No doubt the prestige of the senate's members furthered this development. But it also helped that the senate met continuously,

Alinari/Art Resource, NY

whereas the chief magistrates changed annually and the popular assemblies operated slowly and met only periodically.

The Roman republic possessed a number of popular assemblies. By far the most important was the **centuriate assembly**, essentially the Roman army functioning in its political role. Organized by classes based on wealth, it was structured in such a way that the wealthiest citizens always had a majority. The centuriate assembly elected the chief magistrates and passed laws. It is important to remember, however, that the Romans passed few statutory laws and simply left much governance to magisterial authority. As a result of the struggle between the orders, another assembly, the council of the plebs, came into being in 471 B.C.E. (see "The Struggle of the Orders," which follows).

The government of the Roman republic thus consisted of three major elements. Two consuls and later other elected officials served as magistrates and ran the state. An assembly of adult males (the centuriate assembly), controlled by the wealthiest citizens, elected these officials, while the senate, a small group of large landowners, advised them. Thus, the Roman state was an aristocratic republic controlled by a relatively small group of privileged people.

Social Organization The family was the basis of Roman society. At its head was the *paterfamilias* (pay-tur-fuh-MEEL-yus), who theoretically had unlimited power over his family. When a father died, his sons became heads of their own families. Families were often grouped into social units known as *gentes* (GEN-tayz) or clans, descended from the same ancestor and bearing the same family name.

In the early republic, a Roman citizen had two names, but three names became more common later in the republic. Each man had a *praenomen* (pree-NOH-mun), or forename, which was his personal name. There were only a limited number of personal names, such as Gaius or Marcus, and these were usually abbreviated in writing (C. for Gaius, from the earlier spelling Caius, or M. for Marcus). The praenomen was followed by the *nomen* (NOH-mun), which was the name of the group of families or clan (*gens*) to which the person belonged. Thus, the full name of the politician and writer Cicero was Marcus Tullius Cicero, Tullius referring to the clan Tullia. The third name, in this case Cicero, was the *cognomen* (kahg-NOH-mun), which was an extra personal name, sometimes even a nickname, by which the person was known. Eventually, the cognomen became a hereditary family name, enabling people to identify different branches of the same clan. Women usually had one name, the feminine form of the father's nomen. Thus, the daughter of Marcus Tullius Cicero was called Tullia. Names were important to the Romans because they signified a person's place in Roman society.

Closely associated with clan and family was the practice of clientage. Clients constituted a dependent class; they were people who did not have the means to protect themselves or their families without the assistance of a patron. The patron, usually a wealthy member of the upper classes, gave protection and especially legal assistance to his clients. In return, clients provided their patrons with certain services, such as field labor, military assistance, and, especially important in the republic, votes in the assemblies.

The most noticeable element in the social organization of early Rome was the division between two groups—the **patricians** and the **plebeians** (pleh-BEE-unz). The patrician class in Rome consisted of families who were descended from the original senators appointed during the period of the kings. Their initial prominence was probably due to their wealth as great landowners. Thus, the patricians constituted an aristocratic governing class. They alone could be consuls, other magistrates, and senators. Through their patronage of large numbers of dependent clients, they could control the centuriate assembly and many other facets of Roman life.

The plebeians constituted the considerably larger group of "independent, unprivileged, poorer, and vulnerable men" as well as nonpatrician large landowners, less wealthy landholders, artisans, merchants, and small farmers. Although they were citizens, the plebeians did not possess the same rights as the patricians, and at the beginning of the fifth century B.C.E., they began a struggle to rectify that situation.

The Struggle of the Orders Two major problems that existed in the fifth century B.C.E. probably fueled the struggle between the patricians and plebeians. Both patricians and plebeians could vote, but only the patricians could be elected to governmental offices. Both had the right to make legal contracts and marriages, but intermarriage between patricians and plebeians was forbidden. The wealthy plebeians wanted political equality with the patricians, namely the right to hold office, and social equality in the form of the right of intermarriage.

The plebeians' first success came in 494 B.C.E., when they withdrew physically from the state. The patricians, realizing that they could not defend Rome by themselves, were forced to compromise. Two new officials known as **tribunes of the plebs** were instituted (later the number was raised to five and then ten). These tribunes were given the power to protect plebeians against arrest by patrician magistrates. Moreover, after a new popular assembly for plebeians only, called the **council of the plebs**, was created in 471 B.C.E., the tribunes became responsible for convoking it and placing proposals before it. If adopted, these measures became *plebiscita* (pleb-i-SEE-tuh) ("it is the opinion of the plebs"), but they were binding only on the plebeians, not on the patricians. Nevertheless, the council of the plebs gave the plebeians considerable political leverage.

The next step for the plebeians involved the law. The plebeians came to realize that if they were to increase their power they needed knowledge of the law and the legal and governmental procedures carefully guarded by the patricians. Due to plebeian pressure, a special commission of ten officials was created with the task of regularizing and publishing the laws. This action resulted in the publication in 450 B.C.E. of the Twelve Tables of Law, which included the procedures for going to court; provisions on family, women, and divorce; regulations concerning private property; rules governing relationships and injuries to others; and a provision prohibiting intermarriage between patricians and plebeians. The Twelve Tables were not a comprehensive legal code and include very little on public, constitutional law, focusing primarily on practical matters (see Historical Voices, "The Twelve Tables," p. 120).

The Twelve Tables

 What do the selections from the Twelve Tables reveal about Roman society? In what ways do these points of law differ from those found in the Code of Hammurabi? In what ways are they similar?

THE TWELVE TABLES were the first formal codification of Roman laws and customs. The code was inscribed on bronze plaques that eventually were destroyed. These selections are taken from reconstructions of the code preserved in the works of later writers.

Selections from the Twelve Tables

Table III: Execution; Law of Debt

When a debt has been acknowledged, or judgment about the matter has been pronounced in court, thirty days must be the legitimate time of grace. After that, the debtor may be arrested by laying on of hands. Bring him into court. If he does not satisfy the judgment, or no one in court offers himself as surety in his behalf, the creditor may take the defaulter with him. He may bind him either in stocks or in fetters. . . .

Unless they make a settlement, debtors shall be held in bond for sixty days. During that time they shall be brought before the praetor's court in the meeting place on three successive market days, and the amount for which they are judged liable shall be announced; on the third market day they shall suffer capital punishment or be delivered up for sale abroad, across the Tiber.

Table IV: Rights of Head of Family

Quickly kill . . . a dreadfully deformed child.

If a father three times surrenders a son for sale, the son shall be free from the father.

A child born ten months after the father's death will not be admitted into legal inheritance.

Table V: Guardianship; Succession

Females shall remain in guardianship even when they have attained their majority.

If a man is raving mad, rightful authority over his person and chattels shall belong to his agnates [nearest male relatives] or to his clansmen.

A spendthrift is forbidden to exercise administration over his own goods. . . . A person who, being insane or a spendthrift, is prohibited from administering his own goods shall be under trusteeship of agnates.

Table VII: Rights Concerning Land

Branches of a tree may be lopped off all round to a height of more than 15 feet. . . . Should a tree on a neighbor's farm be bent crooked by a wind and lean over your farm, action may be taken for removal of that tree.

It is permitted to gather up fruit falling down on another man's farm.

Table VIII: Torts or Delicts

If any person has sung or composed against another person a song such as was causing slander or insult to another, he shall be clubbed to death.

If a person has maimed another's limb, let there be retaliation in kind unless he makes agreement for settlement with him.

Any person who destroys by burning any building or heap of corn deposited alongside a house shall be bound, scourged, and put to death by burning at the stake, provided that he has committed the said misdeed with malice aforethought, but if he shall have committed it by accident, that is, by negligence, it is ordained that he repair the damage, or, if he be too poor to be competent for such punishment, he shall receive a lighter chastisement.

Table IX: Public Law

The penalty shall be capital punishment for a judge or arbiter legally appointed who has been found guilty of receiving a bribe for giving a decision.

Table XI: Supplementary Laws

Intermarriage shall not take place between plebeians and patricians.

Source: From *Roman Civilization*, vol. I, by N. Lewis and M. Reinhold. © 1955. Reprinted with permission of Columbia University Press.

This publication of the laws led to further agitation from the plebeians between 450 and 445 because they could now see how disadvantaged they were. In particular, they demanded the right of intermarriage and admission to the chief magistracies, especially the consulship. In 445 B.C.E., the Canuleian law allowed patricians and plebeians to intermarry. Once this was permitted, the division between the two groups became

less important, and the solidarity of the patrician class against plebeian gains began to falter. In the fourth century B.C.E., the consulship was opened to plebeians.

The chief landmark in Roman constitutional history—and the climax of the struggle between the orders—came in 287 B.C.E. with the Hortensian law. Henceforth all plebiscita passed by the plebeian assembly had the force of law and

First secession of the plebeians; creation of tribunes of the plebs	494 B.C.E.
Creation of the council of the plebs	471 B.C.E.
Publication of the Twelve Tables of Law	450 B.C.E.
Canuleian law: right of plebeians to marry patricians	445 B.C.E.
Consulship opened to plebeians	300s B.C.E.
Hortensian law: laws passed by plebeian assembly are binding on all Romans	287 B.C.E.

were binding on the entire community, both plebeians and patricians. Moreover, unlike the laws passed by the centuriate assembly, these plebiscita did not need the approval of the senate.

The struggle between the orders therefore had a significant impact on the development of the Roman constitution. Plebeians could hold the highest offices of state, intermarry with the patricians, and help pass laws binding on the entire Roman community. Although the struggle had been long, the Romans had handled it by compromise, not violent revolution. Theoretically, by 287 B.C.E. all Roman citizens were equal under the law, and all could strive for political office. But in reality, as a result of the right of intermarriage, a select number of wealthy patrician and plebeian families formed a new senatorial aristocracy called the *nobiles* ("nobles") (no-BEE-layz), which came to dominate the political offices. The Roman republic had not become a democracy.

5-2b The Roman Conquest of Italy

At the beginning of the republic, Rome was surrounded by enemies, including the Etruscans to the north and the Sabines (SAY-bynz), Volscians (VOL-shunz), and Aequi (EYE-kwee *or* EE-kwy) to the east and south. The Latin communities on the plain of Latium posed an even more immediate threat. If we are to believe Livy (LIV-ee), Rome was engaged in almost continuous warfare with its neighbors for the next hundred years.

In his account of these years, Livy provided a detailed narrative of Roman efforts. Many of Livy's stories were legendary in character and indeed were modeled on events in Greek history. But Livy, writing in the first century B.C.E., used these stories to teach Romans the moral values and virtues that had made Rome great. As seen in the story of Cincinnatus (sin-suh-NAT-uss), these included tenacity, duty, courage, and especially discipline (see Historical Voices, "Cincinnatus Saves Rome," p. 122). Indeed, Livy recounted stories of military leaders who executed their own sons for leaving their place in battle, a serious offense because the success of the hoplite infantry depended on maintaining a precise order. These stories had little basis in fact, but like the story of George Washington and the cherry tree in American history, they provided mythic images to reinforce Roman patriotism.

By 338 B.C.E., Rome had crushed the Latin states in Latium. During the next fifty years, the Romans waged a fierce struggle with the Samnites (SAM-nyts), a hill people from the central Apennines, some of whom had settled in Campania, south of Rome. The conquest of the Samnites gave Rome considerable control over a large part of Italy and brought it into direct contact with the Greek communities of southern Italy. Soon the Romans were involved in hostilities with some of these Greek cities. The Greek communities were primarily commercial cities and had no standing armies. They were accustomed to hiring mercenaries to fight their battles for them. Consequently, they bought the aid of King Pyrrhus (PEER-uss) of Epirus (approximately modern-day Epirus in Greece), who crossed the Adriatic with 20,000 troops and defeated the Romans twice. In both battles, however, Pyrrhus experienced heavy losses, leading him to comment that "another such victory, and we shall be lost"—hence our phrase "Pyrrhic victory." After a diversion to Sicily, Pyrrhus came back for one more battle with the Romans and this time was decisively defeated. By 267 B.C.E., the Romans had completed their conquest of southern Italy. After crushing the remaining Etruscan states to the north, Rome had conquered all of Italy, except the extreme north, by 264 B.C.E.

To rule Italy, the Romans devised the Roman confederation in 338 B.C.E. Under this system, Rome allowed some peoples—especially the Latins—to have full Roman citizenship. Most of the remaining communities were made allies. They remained free to run their own local affairs but were required to provide soldiers for Rome. Moreover, the Romans made it clear that loyal allies could improve their status and even aspire to become Roman citizens. Thus, the Romans had found a way to give conquered states a stake in Rome's success.

In the course of their expansion throughout Italy, the Romans pursued consistent policies that help explain their success. The Romans excelled at making the correct diplomatic decisions; they were superb diplomats. Though firm and even cruel when necessary—rebellions were crushed without mercy—they were also shrewd in extending their citizenship and allowing autonomy in domestic affairs. Once at war, the Romans were not only good soldiers but also persistent ones. The loss of an army or a fleet did not cause them to quit but spurred them on to build new armies and new fleets. As one Roman poet wrote in the 130s B.C.E., "The Roman people has often been defeated by force and overcome in many battles, but never in an actual war on which everything depends."[1] And by granting citizenship to conquered peoples, Rome had achieved the ability to raise new armies following defeats. Finally, the Romans had a practical sense of strategy. As they conquered, they settled Romans and Latins in new communities outside Latium. By 264 B.C.E., the Romans had established colonies—fortified towns—at all strategic locations. By building roads to these settlements and connecting them, the Romans assured themselves of an impressive military and communications network that enabled them to rule effectively and efficiently (see Global Perspectives, "Roman and Chinese Roads," p. 123). By insisting on military service from new citizens and the allies in the Roman confederation, Rome essentially mobilized the entire military manpower of all Italy for its wars.

Cincinnatus Saves Rome: A Roman Morality Tale

 What values did Livy emphasize in his account of Cincinnatus? How important were those values to Rome's success? Why did Livy say he wrote his history?

THERE IS PERHAPS NO BETTER ACCOUNT of how the virtues of duty and simplicity enabled good Roman citizens to prevail during the travails of the fifth century B.C.E. than Livy's account of Cincinnatus (sin-suh-NAT-uss). He was chosen dictator, supposedly in 457 B.C.E., to defend Rome against the attacks of the Aequi. The position of dictator was a temporary expedient used only in emergencies; the consuls would resign, and a leader with unlimited power would be appointed for a limited period (usually six months). In this account, Cincinnatus did his duty, defeated the Aequi, and returned to his simple farm in just fifteen days.

Livy, *The Early History of Rome*

The city was thrown into a state of turmoil, and the general alarm was as great as if Rome herself were surrounded. Nautius was sent for, but it was quickly decided that he was not the man to inspire full confidence; the situation evidently called for a dictator, and, with no dissenting voice, Lucius Quinctius Cincinnatus was named for the post.

Now I would solicit the particular attention of those numerous people who imagine that money is everything in this world, and that rank and ability are inseparable from wealth: let them observe that Cincinnatus, the one man in whom Rome reposed all her hope of survival, was at that moment working a little three-acre farm . . . west of the Tiber, just opposite the spot where the shipyards are today. A mission from the city found him at work on his land—digging a ditch, maybe, or plowing. Greetings were exchanged, and he was asked—with a prayer for divine blessing on himself and his country—to put on his toga and hear the Senate's instructions. This naturally surprised him, and, asking if all were well, he told his wife Racilia to run to their cottage and fetch his toga. The toga was brought, and wiping the grimy sweat from his hands and face he put it on; at once the envoys from the city saluted him, with congratulations, as Dictator, invited him to enter Rome, and informed him of the terrible danger of Municius's army. A state vessel was waiting for him on the river, and on the city bank he was welcomed by his three sons who had come to meet him, then by other kinsmen and friends, and finally by nearly the whole body of senators. Closely attended by all these people and preceded by his lictors he was then escorted to his residence through streets lined with great crowds of common folk who, be it said, were by no means so pleased to see the new Dictator, as they thought his power excessive and dreaded the way in which he was likely to use it.

[Cincinnatus proceeds to raise an army, march out, and defeat the Aequi.]

In Rome the Senate was convened by Quintus Fabius the City Prefect, and a decree was passed inviting Cincinnatus to enter in triumph with his troops. The chariot he rode in was preceded by the enemy commanders and the military standards, and followed by his army loaded with its spoils. . . . Cincinnatus finally resigned after holding office for fifteen days, having originally accepted it for a period of six months.

Source: Livy, *The Early History of Rome: Books I–V of the History of Rome from Its Foundation*, trans. A. de Selincourt (London: Penguin Classics, 1960).

5-3 The Roman Conquest of the Mediterranean (264–133 B.C.E.)

 FOCUS QUESTION: How did Rome achieve its empire from 264 to 133 B.C.E., and what is meant by the phrase "Roman imperialism"?

After their conquest of the Italian peninsula, the Romans found themselves face to face with a formidable Mediterranean power—Carthage (KAR-thij). Founded around 800 B.C.E. by Phoenicians from Tyre, Carthage was located in a favorable position for commanding Mediterranean trade routes and had become an important commercial center (see Map 5.4).

In the sixth century B.C.E., Carthage was governed by two judges, who were elected annually. They were usually men of wealth from prominent families. Separately elected generals led the military forces, which consisted primarily of mercenaries recruited from different parts of the western Mediterranean. There was also a senate composed of several hundred prominent men chosen for life. Ordinary citizens had little power, although a group of 104 judges examined the activities of officials and generals and prevented anyone from either group from establishing a tyranny.

Carthage gradually became a strong military state. By the third century B.C.E., its empire included the coast of North Africa, southern Spain, Sardinia, Corsica, and western Sicily. With its monopoly of western Mediterranean trade, Carthage was the largest and richest state in the area. The presence of Carthaginians (kar-thuh-JIN-ee-unz) in Sicily made the Romans apprehensive about Carthaginian encroachment on the Italian coast. In 264 B.C.E., mutual suspicions drove the

Roman and Chinese Roads

Q *What was the importance of roads to the Roman and Han Empires?*

AS WE HAVE SEEN in the Assyrian and Persian Empires, roads were important means for rulers to keep abreast of developments in their empires and maintain control of far-flung provinces. At the beginning of the first millennium C.E., two great empires—the Roman Empire in the West and the Han Chinese Empire in the East—dominated large areas of the world. Both built elaborate systems of roads in order to rule efficiently.

The Romans constructed a remarkable system of roads. After laying a foundation with gravel, which allowed for drainage, the Roman builders placed flagstones that were fitted closely together. Unlike other peoples who built similar kinds of roads, the Romans did not follow the contours of the land but made their roads as straight as possible to facilitate communication and transportation, especially for military

purposes. Image 5.4a shows a view of the Via Appia (Appian Way), built in 312 B.C.E. under the leadership of the censor and consul Appius Claudius (Roman roads were often named after the great Roman families who encouraged their construction). The Via Appia (see location on Map 5.3) was constructed to make it easy for Roman armies to march from Rome to the newly conquered city of Capua, a distance of 152 miles. By the beginning of the fourth century C.E., the Roman Empire contained 372 major roads covering 50,000 miles.

Like the Roman Empire, the Han Empire relied on roads constructed with stone slabs for the movement of military forces (see Image 5.4b). The First Emperor of Qin was responsible for the construction of 4,350 miles of roads, and by the end of the second century C.E., China had almost 22,000 miles of roads. Although roads in both the Roman and Chinese empires were originally constructed for military purposes, they came to be used for communication and commercial traffic as well; however, unlike the Romans, the Han emperors used waterways for most of their transportation needs.

MAP 5.3 **Roman Roads**

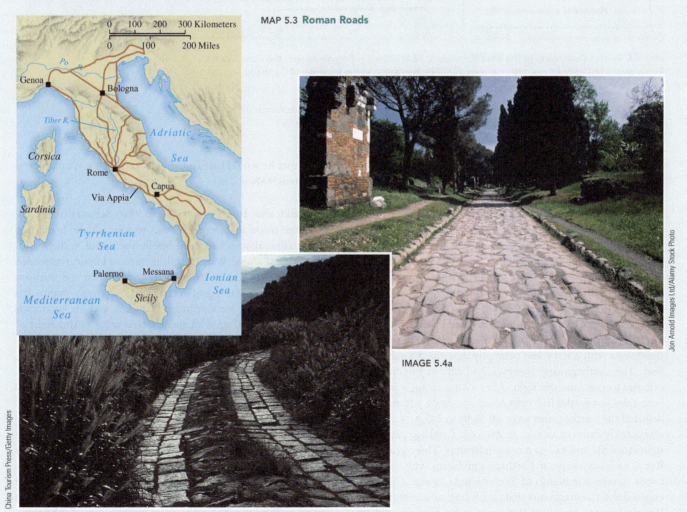

IMAGE 5.4a

Jon Arnold Images Ltd/Alamy Stock Photo

IMAGE 5.4b

China Tourism Press/Getty Images

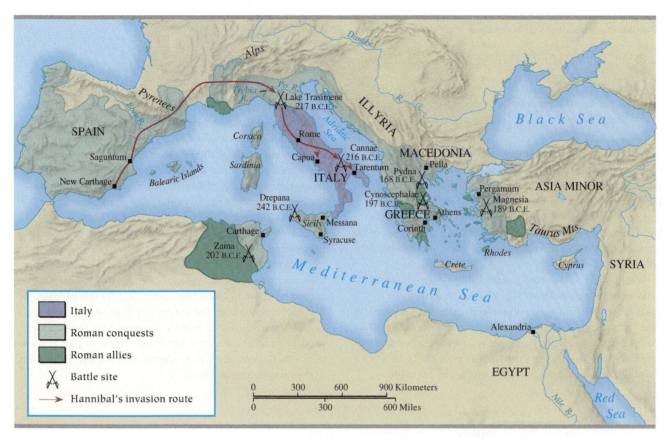

MAP 5.4 **Roman Conquests in the Mediterranean, 264–133 B.C.E.** Beginning with the Punic Wars, Rome expanded its holdings, first in the western Mediterranean at the expense of Carthage and later in Greece and western Asia Minor.

 What aspects of Mediterranean geography, combined with the territorial holdings and aspirations of Rome and the Carthaginians, made the Punic Wars more likely?

two powers into a lengthy struggle for control of the western Mediterranean.

5-3a The Struggle with Carthage

The First Punic (PYOO-nik) War (264–241 B.C.E.)—the Latin word for Phoenician was *Punicus*—began when the Romans decided to intervene in a struggle between two Sicilian cities and sent an army to Sicily. The Carthaginians, who considered Sicily within their own sphere of influence, regarded this as a just cause for war. In going to war, both sides determined on the conquest of Sicily. The Romans realized that the war would be long and drawn out if they could not supplement their land operations with a navy and promptly developed a substantial fleet. The Carthaginians, however, had difficulty finding mercenaries to continue the fight. After a long struggle in which both sides lost battles in North Africa and Sicily, a Roman fleet defeated the Carthaginian navy off Sicily in 242 B.C.E., and the war quickly came to an end. In 241 B.C.E. Carthage gave up all rights to Sicily and had to pay an indemnity. Three years later, Rome took advantage of Carthage's problems with its mercenaries to seize the islands of Sardinia and Corsica. This act so angered the Carthaginians that, according to one story, their leading general, Hamilcar Barca, made his nine-year-old son

swear that he would hate Rome ever after. The son's name was Hannibal (HAN-uh-bul).

Hannibal and the Second Punic War Between the wars, Carthage made an unexpected recovery under the leadership of the general who had been briefly successful in Sicily during the First Punic War, Hamilcar Barca. Hamilcar extended Carthage's domains in Spain to compensate for the territory lost to Rome. A major goal in creating the Spanish empire was to get manpower for Carthage. Hamilcar and his successors proceeded to build up a formidable land army in the event of a second war with Rome because they realized that Carthage's success depended on defeating Rome on land. In 221 B.C.E., Hamilcar's son Hannibal, now twenty-five, took over the direction of Carthaginian policy. Within three years, Rome and Carthage were again at war.

Carthage and Rome had agreed to divide Spain into respective spheres of influence. Although Saguntum was located in the Carthaginian sphere, Rome made an alliance with the city and encouraged its inhabitants in anti-Carthaginian activities. Thoroughly provoked by the Roman action, Hannibal attacked Saguntum, and the Romans declared war on Carthage in 218 B.C.E. This time the Carthaginian strategy aimed at bringing the war home to the Romans and defeating them in their own backyard. In an amazing march, Hannibal crossed the Alps with an army of 30,000 to 40,000 men and 6,000 horses and elephants and advanced into northern Italy. The Alps took a toll on the Carthaginian army, however, and most of the elephants did not survive the trip. After defeating the Romans at the Trebia River, Hannibal added thousands of Gauls to his army and proceeded into central Italy. At Lake Trasimene in Etruria, he again defeated the Romans. In desperation, the Romans elected as consul Quintus Fabius Maximus, who became known as the "Delayer" because of his tactics of following and delaying Hannibal's army without risking a pitched battle. Hannibal hoped to destroy the Roman confederation and win Italian cities away from Rome. The policy failed; virtually all remained loyal to Rome.

In 216 B.C.E., the Romans decided to meet Hannibal head-on. It was a serious mistake. At Cannae (KAN-nye or KAN-ee), Hannibal's forces devastated the Roman army, killing as many as 40,000 soldiers. At last, some of the southern Italian cities rebelled against Roman rule and went over to Hannibal. Rome seemed on the brink of disaster but refused to give up and raised yet another army.

Rome gradually recovered. Although Hannibal remained free to roam in Italy, he had neither the men nor the equipment to lay siege to the major cities, including Rome itself. The Romans began to reconquer some of the rebellious Italian cities. More importantly, the Romans pursued a Spanish strategy that aimed at undermining the Carthaginian empire in Spain. Publius Cornelius Scipio, later known as Scipio Africanus (SIP-ee-oh af-ree-KAY-nuss) the Elder, was given command of the Roman forces in Spain. A brilliant general who learned from Hannibal's tactics, he had pushed the Carthaginians out of Spain by 206 B.C.E.

The Romans then took the war directly to Carthage. Late in 204 B.C.E., Scipio led a Roman army from Sicily into North Africa and forced the Carthaginians to recall Hannibal from Italy. At the Battle of Zama (ZAH-muh) in 202 B.C.E., Scipio decisively defeated Hannibal and the Carthaginian forces, and the war was over. Hannibal eventually left Carthage and went to help Antiochus, the ruler of the Seleucid kingdom, in his struggle with Rome. After Antiochus made peace with the Romans, Hannibal fled to Bithynia, near the Black Sea. Pursued by the Romans, Hannibal killed himself saying, "Let us free Rome of her dread of one old man."

By the peace treaty signed in 201 B.C.E. by the Carthaginians and Romans, Carthage lost Spain, agreed to pay an indemnity, and promised not to go to war without Rome's permission. Spain, like Sicily, Corsica, and Sardinia earlier, was made into a Roman province. Rome had become the dominant power in the western Mediterranean.

The Destruction of Carthage But some Romans wanted even more. A number of prominent Romans, especially the conservative politician Cato, advocated the complete destruction of Carthage. Cato ended every speech he made to the senate with the words, "And I think Carthage must be destroyed." When the Carthaginians technically broke their peace treaty with Rome by going to war against one

of Rome's North African allies that had been encroaching on Carthage's home territory, the Romans declared war. Led by Scipio Aemilianus (SIP-ee-oh ee-mil-ee-AY-nuss) Africanus the Younger, Roman forces undertook their third and last war with Carthage (149–146 B.C.E.). This time, Carthage was no match for the Romans, who seized the opportunity to carry out its final destruction (see Historical Voices, "The Destruction of Carthage," p. 126). The territory of Carthage was made a province called Africa.

5-3b The Eastern Mediterranean

During the Punic Wars, Rome had become acutely aware of the Hellenistic states of the eastern Mediterranean when the king of Macedonia made an alliance with Hannibal after the Roman defeat at Cannae. But the Romans were preoccupied with the Carthaginians, and it was not until after the defeat of Carthage that Rome became involved in the world of Hellenistic politics as an advocate for the freedom of the Greek states. This support of the Greeks brought the Romans into conflict with both Macedonia and the kingdom of the Seleucids (see Chapter 4). Roman military victories and diplomatic negotiations rearranged the territorial boundaries of the Hellenistic kingdoms and achieved the freedom of the Greek states in 196 B.C.E. For fifty years, Rome tried to be a power broker in the affairs of the Greeks without direct control of their lands. When the effort failed, the Romans changed their policy.

Macedonia was made a Roman province in 148 B.C.E., and when some of the Greek states rose in revolt against Rome's restrictive policies, Rome acted decisively. The Romans destroyed the city of Corinth, leader of the revolt, in 146 B.C.E. to teach the Greeks a lesson, and the Roman governor of Macedonia took control of Greece. Thirteen years later, in 133 B.C.E., the king of Pergamum deeded his kingdom to Rome, giving Rome its first province in Asia. Rome was now master of the Mediterranean Sea.

5-3c The Nature of Roman Imperialism

Rome's empire was built in three stages: the conquest of Italy, the conflict with Carthage and expansion into the western Mediterranean, and the involvement with and domination of

CHRONOLOGY	The Roman Conquest of the Mediterranean
First Punic War	264–241 B.C.E.
Second Punic War	218–201 B.C.E.
Battle of Cannae	216 B.C.E.
Scipio completes seizure of Spain	206 B.C.E.
Battle of Zama	202 B.C.E.
Third Punic War	149–146 B.C.E.
Incorporation of Macedonia as a Roman province	148 B.C.E.
Destruction of Carthage	146 B.C.E.
Roman acquisition of Pergamum	133 B.C.E.

The Destruction of Carthage

 What does this description of Rome's destruction of Carthage reveal about the nature of Roman imperialism? What features seem more rhetorical than realistic? Why?

THE ROMANS USED A TECHNICAL BREACH of Carthage's peace treaty with Rome as a pretext to undertake a third and final war with Carthage (149–146 B.C.E.). Although Carthage posed no real threat to Rome's security, the Romans still remembered the traumatic experiences of the Second Punic War when Hannibal had ravaged much of their homeland. The hard-liners gained the upper hand in the senate and called for the complete destruction of Carthage. The city was razed, the survivors were sold into slavery, and the land was made a province of Rome. In this passage, the historian Appian of Alexandria describes the final destruction of Carthage by the Romans under the command of Scipio Aemilianus.

Appian, *Roman History*

Then came new scenes of horror. The fire spread and carried everything down, and the soldiers did not wait to destroy the buildings little by little, but pulled them all down together. So the crashing grew louder, and many fell with the stones into the midst dead. Others were seen still living, especially old men, women, and young children who had hidden in the inmost nooks of the houses, some of them wounded, some more or less burned, and uttering horrible cries. Still others, thrust out and falling from such a height with the stones, timbers, and fire, were torn asunder into all kinds of horrible shapes, crushed and mangled. Nor was this the end of their miseries, for the street cleaners, who were removing the rubbish with axes, mattocks, and boat-hooks, and making the roads passable, tossed with these instruments the dead and the living together into holes in the ground, sweeping them along like sticks and stones or turning them over with their iron tools, and man was used for filling up a ditch. Some were thrown in head foremost, while their legs, sticking out of

the ground, writhed a long time. Others fell with their feet downward and their heads above the ground. Horses ran over them, crushing their faces and skulls, not purposely on the part of the riders, but in their headlong haste. Nor did the street cleaners either do these things on purpose; but the press of war, the glory of approaching victory, the rush of the soldiery, the confused noise of heralds and trumpeters all round, the tribunes and centurions changing guard and marching the cohorts here and there—all together made everybody frantic and heedless of the spectacle before their eyes.

Six days and nights were consumed in this kind of turmoil, the soldiers being changed so that they might not be worn out with toil, slaughter, lack of sleep, and these horrid sights. . . .

Scipio, beholding this city, which had flourished 700 years from its foundation and had ruled over so many lands, islands, and seas, as rich in arms and fleets, elephants, and money as the mightiest empires, but far surpassing them in hardihood and high spirit . . . now come to its end in total destruction—Scipio, beholding this spectacle, is said to have shed tears and publicly lamented the fortune of the enemy. After meditating by himself a long time and reflecting on the inevitable fall of cities, nations, and empires, as well as of individuals, upon the fate of Troy, that once proud city, upon the fate of the Assyrian, the Median, and afterwards of the great Persian empire, and, most recently of all, of the splendid empire of Macedon, either voluntarily or otherwise the words of the poet [Homer, *Iliad*] escaped his lips:

> The day shall come in which our sacred Troy
> And Priam, and the people over whom
> Spear-bearing Priam rules, shall perish all.

Being asked by Polybius in familiar conversation (for Polybius had been his tutor) what he meant by using these words, Polybius says that he did not hesitate frankly to name his own country, for whose fate he feared when he considered the mutability of human affairs. And Polybius wrote this down just as he heard it.

Source: Appian, *Roman History*, trans. H. White (Cambridge, Mass.: Harvard University Press, 1912).

the Hellenistic kingdoms in the eastern Mediterranean. The Romans did not have a master plan for creating an empire. Much of their expansion was opportunistic; once involved in a situation that threatened their security, the Romans did not hesitate to act. And the more they expanded, the more threats to their security appeared on the horizon, involving them in yet more conflicts. Indeed, the Romans liked to portray themselves as declaring war only for defensive reasons or to protect allies. That is only part of the story, however. It is likely, as some

historians have suggested, that at some point a group of Roman aristocratic leaders emerged who favored expansion both for the glory it offered and for the economic benefits it provided. Certainly, by the second century B.C.E., aristocratic senators perceived new opportunities for lucrative foreign commands, enormous spoils of war, and an abundant supply of slave labor for their growing landed estates. And, in fact, it is likely that all levels of Roman society were attracted by sheer greed for the economic profits of victory.

At the same time, the Roman political system encouraged an imperialistic policy. There was an intense competition between families for the consulship (as we have seen, there were only two per year). Moreover, many Romans believed in outdoing the deeds of their ancestors. The combination of these factors helped lead upper-class Romans to seek glory and power by winning wars abroad.

By the second century B.C.E., as the destruction of Corinth and Carthage indicates, Roman imperialism had become more arrogant and brutal. Rome's foreign success also had enormous repercussions for the internal development of the Roman republic.

5-3d Evolution of the Roman Army

By the fourth century B.C.E., the Roman army consisted of four legions, each made up of 4,000 to 5,000 men; each legion had about 300 cavalry and the rest infantry. The infantry consisted of three lines of battle. The *hastati* (hahs-TAH-tee) (spearmen), made up of the youngest recruits, formed the front line; they were armed with heavy spears and short swords and protected by a large oval shield, helmet, breastplate, and greaves (shin guards) (see Image 5.5). The *principes* (PRIN-kih-payz *or* PRIN-sih-peez) (chief men), armed and protected like the hastati,

formed the second line. The third line of battle was formed by the *triarii* (trih-AR-ee-ee) (third-rank men), who knelt behind the first two lines, ready to move up and fill any gaps. A fourth group of troops, poor citizens who wore cloaks but no armor and were lightly armed, functioned as skirmishers who usually returned to the rear lines after their initial contact with the enemy to form backup reserves.

In the early republic, the army was recruited from citizens between the ages of eighteen and forty-six who had the resources to equip themselves for battle. Since most of them were farmers, they enrolled only for a year, campaigned during the summer months, and returned home in time for the fall harvest. Later, during the Punic Wars of the third century B.C.E., the period of service had to be extended, although this was resisted by farmers whose livelihoods could be severely harmed by a long absence. Nevertheless, after the disastrous Battle of Cannae in 216 B.C.E., the Romans had to recruit larger armies, and the number of legions rose to twenty-five.

The ancient historian Polybius believed that one of the reasons the Romans were so successful militarily was that in the early centuries of the republic the Roman army was basically a citizen army led by the republic's elected magistrates. An army of citizens defending their homeland would be braver

IMAGE 5.5a

IMAGE 5.5b

IMAGE 5.5 **Roman Legionaries.** Roman legionaries, famed for their courage and tenacity, made possible Roman domination of the Mediterranean Sea. At the time of the Punic Wars, a Roman legionary wore chain-mail armor and a plumed helmet and carried an oval shield, as in the bronze statue from the second or first century B.C.E. shown in Image 5.5a. Heavy javelins and swords were their major weapons. This equipment remained standard until the time of Julius Caesar. Image 5.5b shows a Roman legion on the march from Trajan's column, erected in the second century C.E.

Gianni Dagli Orti/Shutterstock.com

Roger-Viollet/The Image Works

and fight harder than hired mercenaries. Roman military success may also have been due to the aggressive behavior of the Roman military leaders, although this could be detrimental at sea. According to Polybius:

> The Romans, to speak generally, rely on force in all their enterprises, and think it is incumbent on them to carry out their projects in spite of all, and that nothing is impossible when they have once decided on it. They owe their success in many cases to this spirit, but sometimes they conspicuously fail by reason of it and especially at sea. For on land they are attacking men and the works of man and are usually successful, as there they are employing force against forces of the same nature. . . . But when they come to encounter the sea and the atmosphere and choose to fight them by force they meet with signal defeats.[2]

Major changes in the military would not come until the first century B.C.E. with the military reforms of Marius (see "5-5c Marius and the New Roman Army" later in this chapter).

5-4 Society and Culture in the Roman Republic

FOCUS QUESTION: How did the acquisition of an empire affect Roman religious, social, and economic institutions, values and attitudes, law, and art and literature?

One of the most noticeable aspects of Roman society and culture is the impact of the Greeks. The Romans had experienced Greek influence early on through the Greek cities in southern Italy. By the end of the third century B.C.E., however, Greek civilization played an ever-increasing role in Roman culture. Greek ambassadors, merchants, and artists traveled to Rome and spread Greek thought and practices. After their conquest of the Hellenistic kingdoms, Roman military commanders shipped Greek manuscripts and art back to Rome. Roman households used multitudes of educated Greek slaves. Greek models affected virtually every area of Roman life, from literature and philosophy to religion and education. Wealthy Romans hired Greek tutors and sent their sons to Athens to study. As the Roman poet Horace said, "Captive Greece took captive her rude conqueror." Greek thought captivated the less sophisticated Roman minds, and the Romans became willing transmitters of Greek culture—not, however, without some resistance from Romans who had nothing but contempt for Greek politics and feared the end of old Roman values. Even those who favored Greek culture blamed the Greeks for Rome's new vices, including luxury and homosexual practices.

5-4a Roman Religion

Every aspect of Roman society was permeated with religion. The official state religion focused on the worship of a pantheon of gods and goddesses, including Juno, the patron goddess of women; Minerva, the goddess of craftspeople; Mars, the god of war; and Jupiter Optimus Maximus (JOO-puh-tur AHP-tuh-muss

MAK-suh-muss) ("best and greatest"), who became the patron deity of Rome and assumed a central place in the religious life of the city (see Image 5.6). As Rome developed and came into contact with other peoples and gods, the community simply adopted new deities. Hence, the Greek Hermes became the Roman Mercury, and the Greek Demeter, Ceres. Eventually, a complete amalgamation of Greek and Roman religion occurred, giving the Romans and the Greeks essentially the same "Greco-Roman" religion.

The Importance of Ritual Unlike later religions that were concerned with personal salvation or morality, Roman religion focused on the worship of the gods for a very practical reason—human beings were thought to be totally dependent on them. The exact performance of ritual was crucial to establishing a right relationship with the gods. What was true for individuals was also valid for the state: it also had to observe correct ritual in order to receive its reward. Consequently, accurate performance of ritual was important, and the Romans established a college of priests or *pontiffs* to carry out that responsibility. Initially three in number, by the first century B.C.E., they had increased to sixteen. At the head of the pontiffs was the *pontifex maximus* (PAHN-ti-feks MAK-suh-muss) (chief pontiff), a powerful figure who controlled the state religion. First, Julius Caesar and later all emperors until 381 C.E. held this position. The pontifex maximus also chose six girls between the ages of six and ten to serve as Vestal Virgins (see Historical Voices, "The Vestal Virgins," p. 130).

The pontiffs were in charge of what the Romans called the divine law, maintaining the right relationship between the state and the gods. The pontiffs performed all public religious acts and supervised magistrates in the correct ritual for public political acts. If the rituals were performed correctly, the Romans would obtain the peace of the gods. The Romans' success in creating an empire was no doubt taken as confirmation of divine favor. As Cicero, the first-century B.C.E. politician and writer, claimed, "We have overcome all the nations of the world, because we have realized that the world is directed and governed by the gods."[3]

The Use of Omens In addition to the college of pontiffs, a college of *augurs* (AW-gurz) existed whose responsibility was to interpret the *auspices* (AWSS-puh-sizz)—signs or warnings that the gods gave to men through such phenomena as unusual changes in the weather or the migratory pattern of birds. Before every important act of state, a magistrate with imperium took the auspices to make sure the gods approved. The Romans attributed great importance to this—if the omens were unfavorable, the act was invalid or the planned action was not auspicious. As Cicero later commented, the augurs had "the highest and most important authority in the State" because "no act of any magistrate at home or in the field can have any validity for any person without their authority."[4] Auspices were taken by observing the flights of birds, lightning and other natural phenomena, and the behavior of certain animals.

Scala/Art Resource, NY

IMAGE 5.6a

DEA/A. DAGLI ORTI/Getty Images

IMAGE 5.6b

IMAGE 5.6 **Roman Religion.** The Romans considered the proper worship of the gods an important key to success. As one Roman official said, "The fact that we Romans have, absolutely and consistently, judged reverence toward the gods as of first importance is proved by the favor we have received from them on this account." Typical of Roman religious architecture was the small urban temple located in the midst of a crowded commercial center. Pictured in Image 5.6a is a rectangular temple built in Rome in the late second or early first century B.C.E. and dedicated to Portunus, the god of harbors. Image 5.6b shows a second-century C.E. Roman statue of Jupiter. Statues of Jupiter were found in major Roman temples.

 What role did religion play in Roman life?

Household Cults Just as the state had an official cult, so did families. Because the family was regarded as a small state within the state, it had its own household cults, including Janus, the spirit of the doorway; Vesta, the goddess of the hearth; and the Penates (puh-NAY-teez), the spirits of the storehouse. Here, too, proper ritual was important, and it was the responsibility of the paterfamilias as head of the family to ensure that the religious obligations were properly fulfilled.

One of the most important ceremonies involved purification. In his manual *On Agriculture*, Marcus Cato the Elder spelled out the proper ritual for purifying a landed estate. The ceremony included these words, addressed to Mars, the god of vegetation as well as war:

> Father Mars, I beg and entreat you to be of good will and favorable to me and to our house and household, for which purpose I have ordered the swine-sheep-bull procession to be led around my land and fields and farm. And [I beg] that you will check, thrust back, and avert diseases seen and unseen,

crop failure and crop destruction, sudden losses and storms, and that you will permit the annual crops, the grain crops, the vineyards, and tree and vine slips to grow and turn out well. And [that you] keep safe the shepherds and the flocks and give good health and strength to me and to our house and household: with these purposes in view . . . receive the honor of this suckling swine-sheep-bull sacrifice.[5]

Proper observance of the ritual was so crucial that any error necessitated a repetition of the entire ritual.

Religious Festivals Religious festivals were an important part of Roman religious practice. There were two kinds: public festivals ordained and paid for by the state and private festivals celebrated by individuals and families. By the middle of the second century B.C.E., six public festivals were celebrated annually, each lasting several days.

The practice of holding games also grew out of religious festivals. The games were inaugurated in honor of

The Vestal Virgins

 What was the importance of the Vestal Virgins? Why were any violations of the rules treated with such harsh punishments?

THE VESTAL VIRGINS GUARDED THE FIRE on the state hearth in the temple of Vesta (goddess of the hearth) in Rome. To the Romans, the extinguishing of the fire was a warning of the destruction of the city. It was also a sign that a Vestal Virgin had lost her virginity, an act that was punished harshly, as is explained in this selection from the historian Dionysius of Halicarnassus, a Greek who lived in Rome and published his *Roman Antiquities* near the end of the first century B.C.E.

Dionysius of Halicarnassus, *Roman Antiquities*

Originally there were four virgins who served the goddess Vesta. They were chosen by the king in accordance with the regulations which Numa established. Because of the numerous sacred duties which they perform, their number was increased to six, and six it has remained up to our own time. The virgins live in the sanctuary of the goddess, and no one can be prevented from entering there in the day if he so wishes, but it is forbidden for any man to stay there at night.

The priestesses remain pure and unmarried for 30 years, offering sacrifices, and performing other religious rituals in accordance with the law. They learn these rituals in the first ten years, and for the second ten years they perform them, and during the remaining ten years they must teach them to their successors. When the 30 years have been completed, nothing prohibits those who want to from putting aside their headbands and other insignia of their service and getting married. But only a few have done that, and their lives for their remaining years were neither enviable nor very happy. Therefore, taking what has happened to those unhappy few as a warning, the rest of the virgins remain in service to the goddess until their deaths, at which time another virgin is appointed by the priests to take the place of the one who has died.

They receive many splendid honors from the city, and therefore they do not want children or marriage. And anyway, there are heavy penalties for misbehavior. Misdeeds are investigated and punished by priests according to the law. They whip those who have committed some lesser offense, but those who have lost their virginity are sentenced to a shameful and pitiful death. While they are still alive they are carried in a funeral procession. Their friends and relatives join the procession and mourn for them as though for someone deceased. They are taken as far as the Colline gate, and interred (alive) in an underground cell which has been built within the walls of the gate. They are dressed in funeral clothes but they receive no monument or funeral offering or any of the other rites which are customary at funerals.

There are said to be many clues which indicate that a priestess who is performing a holy ritual is no longer a virgin, but the principal clue is that the fire goes out, something which the Romans fear more than all catastrophes, since they believe that whatever was the cause of the fire going out, it warns of the destruction of the city. They reintroduce the fire with many rituals of atonement.

Source: Dionysius, *Roman Antiquities*, trans. E. Cary (Cambridge, Mass.: Harvard University Press, 1937).

Jupiter Optimus Maximus but had become annual events by 366 B.C.E. In the late republic, both the number of games and number of days they lasted were increased. Originally, the games consisted of chariot racing in the Circus Maximus; later, animal hunts and theatrical performances were added. In the empire, gladiatorial contests would become the primary focus (see Chapter 6).

5-4b Education: The Importance of Rhetoric

The Romans did not possess a system of public education. In the early republic, the family provided training in the various skills needed by a Roman citizen. Boys were expected to master the basic elements of farming, develop the physical skills needed to be good soldiers, learn the traditions of the state through the legends of heroic Roman ancestors, and become acquainted with public affairs. Girls were supposed to learn the skills needed to be good wives and mothers. Every upper-class Roman boy or girl was expected to learn to read.

Through contact with the Greek world, Roman education took on new ideals in the third and second centuries B.C.E. The wealthy classes wanted their children exposed to Greek studies and were especially attracted to the training in **rhetoric** and philosophy that would prepare their sons for a successful public career. For upper-class males, rhetoric—the art of persuasive speaking—was an especially important part of their education (see Image 5.7). To pursue a public career, they needed to learn good speaking skills that would enable them to win elections and lawsuits in the courts. By winning lawsuits, a person could make a name for himself and build political support.

Since knowledge of Greek was a crucial ingredient in education, schools taught by professional teachers emerged to supply this need. Those who could afford to might provide Greek tutors for their children, but less well-endowed families could turn to private schools where most of the instructors were educated slaves or freedmen, usually of Greek origin. After several years of primary instruction, the aim of which was simply to teach

IMAGE 5.7 **Schoolmaster and Pupils.** In the third and second centuries B.C.E., wealthy Romans sought to prepare their sons for successful public careers with a thorough education in rhetoric and philosophy. Pictured here from a relief on a stele is a teacher with his two pupils, one of whom is reading from a papyrus scroll.

Q *What was the role of education in the Roman Republic?*

the basics of reading, writing, and arithmetic, the pupil went to a secondary school run by a *grammaticus*, or grammarian. These schools had a standard curriculum based on the liberal arts: literature, dialectic (logic), arithmetic, geometry, astronomy, and music. The core of the liberal arts and the curriculum, however, was Greek literature. As a result, by the second and first centuries B.C.E., educated Romans had become increasingly bilingual.

5-4c The Growth of Slavery

Slavery was a common institution throughout the ancient world, but no one possessed more slaves or relied so much on slave labor as the Romans eventually did. Before the third century B.C.E., a small Roman farmer might possess one or two slaves who would help farm his few acres and perform domestic chores. These slaves would most likely be from Italy and regarded as part of the family household.

The Roman conquest of the Mediterranean brought a drastic change in the use of slaves. Large numbers of foreign slaves were transported back to Italy. Thus, the chief source of slaves during the republic was from capture in war, followed by piracy. Of course, the children of slaves also became slaves. Although some Roman generals brought back slaves to be sold to benefit the public treasury, ambitious generals of the first century, such as Pompey and Caesar, made personal fortunes by treating slaves captured by their armies as private property.

Slaves were used in many ways in Roman society. The rich, of course, owned the most and the best. In the late republic, it became a badge of prestige to be attended by many slaves. Greeks were in much demand as tutors, musicians, doctors, and artists. Roman businessmen would employ them as shop assistants or artisans. Slaves were also used as farm laborers; huge gangs of

slaves living in pitiful conditions worked the large landed estates known as *latifundia* (lat-ih-FOON-dee-uh). Cato the Elder argued that it was cheaper to work slaves to death and then replace them than to treat them well. Many slaves of all nationalities were used as menial household workers, such as cooks, valets, waiters, cleaners, and gardeners. Contractors used slave labor to build roads, aqueducts, and other public facilities. The total number of slaves is difficult to judge—estimates range from one-fourth to one-half the number of free people. One historian has recently estimated that there were between 1.5 and 2 million slaves in Italy, constituting perhaps 20 percent of the total population.

It is also difficult to generalize about the treatment of Roman slaves. There are numerous instances of humane treatment by masters and situations when slaves even protected their owners from danger out of gratitude and esteem. But slaves were also subject to severe punishments, torture, abuse, and hard labor that drove some to run away or even revolt against their owners. The republic had stringent laws against aiding a runaway slave. The murder of a master by a slave usually meant the execution of all the other household slaves. Near the end of the second century B.C.E., large-scale slave revolts occurred in Sicily, where enormous gangs of slaves were subjected to horrible working conditions on large landed estates. Slaves were branded, beaten, fed inadequately, worked in chains, and housed at night in underground prisons. The most famous revolt on the Italian peninsula occurred in 73 B.C.E. Led by a Thracian gladiator named Spartacus (SPAR-tuh-kuss), the revolt broke out in southern Italy and involved 70,000 slaves. Spartacus managed to defeat several Roman armies before he was finally trapped and killed in southern Italy in 71 B.C.E. Six thousand of his followers were crucified, the traditional form of execution for slaves (see Movies & History, *Spartacus*, below).

MOVIES & HISTORY
Spartacus (1960)

Watch **Spartacus**, which tells the story of a gladiator who organized a revolt of a large number of escaped slaves who were able to create the semblance of a trained army and initially defeat a Roman army. Freedom is the key word and theme of the movie. Spartacus is portrayed as a man who dreamed of the end of slavery, thousands of years before its death (although he would be disappointed to know that it still survives in some corners of the world today).

 How accurate is the film's depiction of Spartacus and the Roman armies that opposed him? The film was released in 1960. Why were the speeches about freedom made such a central theme of the movie?

Cato the Elder on Women

 What particular actions of the women protesting the Oppian law have angered Cato? What more general concerns does he have about Roman women? What was Cato's attitude toward women? Compare and contrast this selection with the first selection by Xenophon in Chapter 3 (see p. 86).

DURING THE SECOND PUNIC WAR, the Romans enacted the Oppian law, which limited the amount of gold women could possess and restricted their dress. In 195 B.C.E., an attempt was made to repeal the law, and women demonstrated in the streets on behalf of the effort. According to the Roman historian Livy, the conservative Roman official Cato the Elder spoke against repeal and against the women favoring it. His words reflect a traditional male Roman attitude toward women.

Livy, *The History of Rome*

"If each of us, citizens, had determined to assert his rights and dignity as a husband with respect to his own spouse, we should have less trouble with the sex as a whole; as it is, our liberty, destroyed at home by female violence, even here in the Forum is crushed and trodden underfoot, and because we have not kept them individually under control, we dread them collectively. . . . But from no class is there not the greatest danger if you permit them meetings and gatherings and secret consultations. . . .

Our ancestors permitted no woman to conduct even personal business without a guardian to intervene in her behalf; they wished them to be under the control of fathers, brothers, husbands; we (Heaven help us!) allow them now even to interfere in public affairs, yes, and to visit the Forum and our informal and formal sessions. What else are they doing now on the streets and at the corners except urging the bill of the tribunes and voting for the repeal of the law? Give loose rein to their uncontrollable nature and to this untamed creature and expect that they will themselves set no bounds to their license. Unless you act, this is the least of the things enjoined upon women by custom or law and to which they submit with a feeling of injustice. It is complete liberty or rather, if we wish to speak the truth, complete license that they desire.

If they win in this, what will they not attempt? Review all the laws with which your forefathers restrained their license and made them subject to their husbands; even with all these bonds you can scarcely control them. What of this? If you suffer them to seize these bonds one by one and wrench themselves free and finally to be placed on a parity with their husbands, do you think you will be able to endure them? The moment they begin to be your equals, they will be your superiors. . . .

Now they publicly address other women's husbands, and, what is more serious, they beg for a law and votes, and from various men they get what they ask. In matters affecting yourself, your property, your children, you, Sir, can be importuned; once the law has ceased to set a limit to your wife's expenditures you will never set it yourself. Do not think, citizens, that the situation which existed before the law was passed will ever return."

Source: Livy, *History of Rome*, trans. B. O. Foster (Cambridge, Mass.: Harvard University Press, 1935).

Although Roman slavery could be as brutal as slavery in classical Greece, there was one noticeable difference between Roman and Greek slavery. Roman slaves, especially those doing domestic work, were often given their freedom or allowed to buy their freedom if they had managed to save enough cash. If their owners were Roman citizens, they also became Roman citizens. Some historians believe that by the second century C.E., most of the free citizens of the city of Rome were the descendants of former slaves.

5-4d The Roman Family

At the heart of the Roman social structure stood the family, headed by the paterfamilias—the dominant male. The household also included the wife, sons with their wives and children, unmarried daughters, and slaves. A family was virtually a small state within the state, and the power of the paterfamilias paralleled that of the state magistrates over citizens. He held absolute authority over his children; he could sell them or have them put to death. Like the Greeks, Roman males believed that the weakness of the female sex necessitated male guardians (see Historical Voices, "Cato the Elder on Women," above). The paterfamilias exercised that authority; on his death, sons or the nearest male relatives assumed the role of guardians. By the late republic, however, although the rights of male guardians remained legally in effect, many upper-class women had found numerous ways to circumvent the power of their guardians.

As in Greece, the proper role of a woman was to be faithful to her husband, produce children, manage the household, and weave clothes for the family. This epitaph, written in second century B.C.E., expresses well the expected role of women:

> Here is the unlovely grave of a lovely woman....She loved her husband with her heart. She bore two sons. One of these she leaves on earth, the other under the earth. She was graceful in her speech and elegant in her step. She kept the home. She made wool. That's what there is to say.[6]

Marriage Fathers arranged the marriages of daughters, although there are instances of mothers and daughters influencing the choice. In the republic, women married *cum manu* (koom MAH-noo), "with legal control" passing from father to husband. By the middle of the first century B.C.E., the dominant practice had changed to *sine manu* (SEE-nay MAH-noo), "without legal control," which meant that married daughters officially remained within their father's legal power. Since the fathers of most married women were dead, not being in "legal control" of a husband made possible independent property rights that forceful women could translate into considerable power within the household and outside it. Traditionally, Roman marriages were intended to be for life, but divorce was introduced in the third century and became relatively easy to obtain because either party could initiate it and no one needed to prove the breakdown of the marriage. Divorce became especially prevalent in the first century B.C.E.—a period of political turmoil—when marriages were used to cement political alliances.

Some upper-class parents provided education for their daughters. Some girls had private tutors, and others may have gone to primary schools. But at the age when boys were entering secondary schools, girls were pushed into marriage. The legal minimum age was twelve; fourteen was a more common age in practice. Although some Roman doctors warned that early pregnancies could be dangerous to young girls, early marriages persisted due to the desire to benefit from dowries as soon as possible and the reality of early mortality. A good example is Tullia, Cicero's beloved daughter. She was married at sixteen, widowed at twenty-two, remarried one year later, divorced at twenty-eight, remarried at twenty-nine, and divorced at thirty-three. She died at thirty-four, not unusual for females in Roman society.

Upper-Class Women In contrast to upper-class Athenian women, upper-class Roman women were not segregated from males in the home (see Image 5.8). Wives were appreciated as enjoyable company and were at the center of household social life. Women talked to visitors and were free to shop, visit friends, and go to games, temples, and theaters. Nevertheless, they were not allowed to participate in public life, although there are examples of women exerting considerable political influence through their husbands. In fact, while upper-class men served the government abroad or in the military, they depended on their wives and mothers to manage their estates and protect their political interests.

5-4e The Evolution of Roman Law

One of Rome's chief gifts to the Mediterranean world of its day and to succeeding generations of Western civilization was its development of law. The Twelve Tables of 450 B.C.E. were

IMAGE 5.8a

IMAGE 5.8 **Roman Women.** Roman women, especially those of the upper class, had more freedom than women in classical Athens despite the persistent male belief that women required guardianship. These depictions of Roman women are from frescoes on the wall of the Villa of the Mysteries in Pompeii dating from the first century B.C.E. The woman in Image 5.8a is serving food while the woman in Image 5.8b is pouring water from a pitcher.

IMAGE 5.8b

the first codification of Roman law, and although inappropriate for later times, they were never officially abrogated and were still memorized by schoolboys in the first century B.C.E. Civil law, or *ius civile* (YOOSS see-VEE-lay), derived from the Twelve Tables, proved inadequate for later Roman needs, however, and gave way to corrections and additions by the praetors. Upon taking office, a praetor issued an edict listing his guidelines for dealing with different kinds of legal cases. The praetors were knowledgeable in law, but they also relied on Roman jurists—amateur law experts—for advice in preparing their edicts. The interpretations of the jurists, often embodied in the edicts of the praetors, created a body of legal principles.

In 242 B.C.E., the Romans appointed a second praetor who was responsible for examining suits between a Roman and a non-Roman as well as between two non-Romans. The Romans found that although some of their rules of law could be used in these cases, special rules were often needed. These rules gave rise to a body of law known as the *ius gentium* (YOOSS GEN-tee-um)—the law of nations—defined by the Romans as "that part of the law which we apply both to ourselves and to foreigners." But the influence of Greek philosophy, primarily Stoicism, led Romans in the late republic to develop the idea of *ius naturale* (YOOSS nah-too-RAH-lay)—natural law—or universal divine law derived from right reason. The Romans came to view their law of nations as derived from or identical to this natural law, thus giving Roman jurists a philosophical justification for systematizing Roman law according to basic principles.

5-4f The Development of Literature

The Romans produced little literature before the third century B.C.E., and the Latin literature that emerged in that century was strongly influenced by Greek models. The demand for plays at public festivals eventually led to a growing number of native playwrights (see Image 5.9). One of the best known was Plautus (PLAW-tuss) (ca. 254–184 B.C.E.), who used plots from Greek New Comedy (see Chapter 4) for his own plays. The actors wore Greek costumes and masks and portrayed the same stock characters: dirty old men, clever slaves, prostitutes, and young men in love, whose pains are discussed in some detail.

Though indebted to the Greeks, Plautus managed to infuse his plays with his own earthy Latin quality, incorporating elements that appealed to the Romans: drunkenness, gluttony, and womanizing. Plautus wrote for the masses and became very popular in Rome.

A second playwright of distinction was Terence (185–159 B.C.E.), who was born in Carthage and brought to Rome as a slave by a Roman senator who freed him. Terence also used plots from Greek New Comedy, but his plays contained less slapstick than those of Plautus. Terence was more concerned with the subtle portrayal of character and the artistry of language. His refined Latin style appealed more to a cultivated audience than to the masses. In the prologue to *The Brothers*, he stated: "The author . . . takes it as a high compliment if he can win the approval of men who themselves find favor with you all and with the general public, men whose services in war, in peace, and in your private affairs, are given at the right moment, without ostentation, to be available for each one of you."[7] Terence wrote for Rome's aristocracy.

Actors rehearsing for a Satyr play, c.62-79 AD (mosaic) (see also 5035)/Roman Imperial Period (27 BC-476 AD)/Museo Archeologico Nazionale, Naples, Campania, Italy/ Bridgeman Images

IMAGE 5.9 **Roman Theater.** The eruption of Mount Vesuvius in 79 C.E. buried Pompeii under volcanic ash and preserved works of art that were later discovered when the city was excavated (see Chapter 6). This mosaic found at Pompeii shows Roman actors preparing to present a Greek play. The seated figure is the chorus master who observes two actors dancing to the music of a pipe. Plays were a popular form of entertainment in Pompeii, where the local theater could seat five thousand people.

Q *Do you see any differences between Greek and Roman theater?*

Latin prose developed later than poetry and playwriting and was often the product of Rome's ruling elite. These upper classes were interested in history as a means of exalting their ideals and in oratory because it could be an important instrument for effective statecraft. Hence, their emphasis in writing prose was on creating works of a practical value. This is a prominent feature of the oldest existing work of Latin prose, Cato the Elder's treatise *On Agriculture*.

Despite their attraction to the Greek world, Romans were generally repelled by much of Greek philosophy with the exception of Stoicism. The latter's emphasis on virtuous conduct and performance of duty (see Chapter 4) fit well with Roman ideals and the practical bent of the Roman character.

5-4g Roman Art

The Romans also depended on the Greeks for artistic inspiration. During the third and second centuries B.C.E., they adopted many features of the Hellenistic style of art (see Chapter 4). The Romans excelled in architecture, a highly practical art. In addition to their justly famous highways, they built sturdy bridges and aqueducts that made use of the arch. They also developed the technique of using concrete in construction projects, which enabled them to erect giant amphitheaters, public baths, and the high-rise tenement buildings that housed Rome's exploding population in the late second and first centuries B.C.E.

The Romans developed a taste for Greek statues, which they placed not only in public buildings but in their homes as well. When demand outstripped the supply of original works, reproductions of Greek statues became fashionable. The Romans' own portrait sculpture was characterized by an intense realism that included even unattractive physical details.

5-4h Values and Attitudes

The Romans were by nature a conservative people. They were very concerned about maintaining the *mos maiorum* (MOHSS my-YOR-um), the customs or traditions of their ancestors. The Romans emphasized parental authority and, above all, their obligations to the state. The highest virtue was *pietas* (PY-ih-tass *or* PEE-ih-tass)—the dutiful execution of one's obligations to one's fellow citizens, to the gods, and to the state.

By the second century B.C.E., however, the creation of an empire had begun to weaken the old values. The Romans began to focus more on affluence, status, and material possessions. Emphasis shifted toward individualism and away from collective well-being, the old public spirit that had served Rome so well. Romans who worried about the decline of the old values blamed it on different causes. Some felt that after the destruction of Carthage, the Romans no longer had any strong enemies to challenge them. Others believed that the Romans had simply been overwhelmed by the affluence created by the new empire. And finally, there were those who blamed everything on the Greeks for importing ideas and practices baneful to the Romans.

Of course, Romans responded differently to the changes brought by the creation of an empire. Two examples from the second century demonstrate this well. Marcus Cato the Elder (234–149 B.C.E.) was a Roman praetor, consul, and member of the ruling class. Cato scorned the "Greeklings"—people who followed Greek ways and read Greek philosophy and literature. He wrote to his son:

> I shall speak about those Greek fellows in their proper place, son Marcus, and point out the results of my inquiries at Athens, and convince you what benefit comes from dipping into their literature, and not making a close study of it. They are a quite worthless people, and an intractable one, and you must consider my words prophetic. When that race gives us its literature it will corrupt all things.[8]

But Cato was not stupid. He not only learned Greek himself but also allowed his own son to study in Athens. He knew only too well that, like it or not, Greek was becoming a necessity in Roman political life.

Scipio Aemilianus (185–129 B.C.E.) was a member of a patrician family and a brilliant general who easily achieved the top offices of the Roman state. Scipio was also concerned about traditional Roman values but was much more inclined to accept Rome's growing urbanization as it became the center of the Mediterranean world and was consequently more open to the Greeks as well. He was an admirer of Greek philosophy and literature. While desirous of maintaining old Roman virtues, Scipio was well aware that the acquisition of an empire had created a new world with new demands and values.

5-5 The Decline and Fall of the Roman Republic (133–31 B.C.E.)

 FOCUS QUESTIONS: What were the main problems Rome faced during the last century of the republic, and how were they ultimately resolved? What was the role of powerful individuals?

By the middle of the second century B.C.E., Roman domination of the Mediterranean Sea was well established. Yet the process of building an empire had weakened and threatened the internal stability of Rome. This internal instability characterizes the period of Roman history from 133 until 31 B.C.E., when Octavian defeated Mark Antony and stood supreme over the Roman world. By that time, the constitution of the Roman republic was in shambles.

5-5a Background: Social, Economic, and Political Problems

By the second century B.C.E., the senate had become the effective governing body of the Roman state. It had achieved this position through its own initiative—not through law, but by custom. As always, it comprised some three hundred men drawn primarily from the landed aristocracy who remained senators for life and held the chief magistracies of the republic. During the wars of the third and second centuries, the senate came to exercise enormous power. It directed the wars and took control of both foreign and domestic policy, including financial affairs. The advice of the senate to the consuls had come to have the force of law.

Moreover, a relatively select circle of wealthy and powerful families—both patrician and plebeian—called the *nobiles* increasingly controlled the magistracies and senate. The nobiles were essentially the men whose families were elected to the more important political offices of the republic. In the hundred years from 233 to 133 B.C.E., 80 percent of the consuls came from twenty-six families; 50 percent came from only ten families. Hence, the nobiles constituted a governing oligarchy that managed, through landed wealth, patronage, and intimidation, to maintain its hold over the magistracies and senate and thus guide the destiny of Rome while running the state in its own interests. When a new man—a *novus homo* (NOH-vuss HOH-moh)—did win a consulship, he and his descendants became members of this select oligarchy.

Division of the Aristocrats By the end of the second century B.C.E., two types of aristocratic leaders, called the *optimates* (ahp-tuh-MAH-tayz) ("the best men") and the *populares* (PAWP-oo-lahr-ayss) ("favoring the people"), became prominent. These were not political parties or even individual cliques but leaders who followed two different approaches to politics. Optimates and populares were terms of political rhetoric that were used by individuals within the aristocracy against fellow aristocratic rivals to distinguish one set of tactics from another. The optimates tended to be the nobiles who controlled the senate and wished to maintain their oligarchical privileges, whereas the populares were usually other ambitious aristocrats who used the people's assemblies, especially the council of the plebs, as instruments to break the domination of the optimates. The conflicts between these aristocratic leaders and their supporters engulfed the first century B.C.E. in political turmoil.

Role of the Equestrians Another social group in Rome also became entangled in this political turmoil—the *equites* (EK-wuh-teez), or **equestrians**, so called because they had once formed Rome's cavalry. Many equestrians had become extremely wealthy through a variety of means, often related to the creation of the empire. Some, for example, were private contractors who derived their wealth from government contracts for the collection of taxes, the outfitting of armies, and the construction of fleets and public works. In 218 B.C.E., the senate enacted a law that forbade senators to bid for state contracts or engage in commerce. The law effectively barred the equestrians from high office because they would have to give up their livelihoods to serve in the senate. By the end of the second century B.C.E., the equestrians were seeking real political power commensurate with their financial stake in the empire. They would play an important role in the political turmoil that brought an end to the republic.

The Land Problem Of course, equestrians and aristocrats together formed only a tiny minority of the Roman people. The backbone of the Roman state and army had traditionally been the small farmers who tilled their little plots of land and made up the chief source of recruits for the army. But economic changes that began in the period of the Punic Wars increasingly undermined the position of that group. This occurred for several reasons. Their lands had been severely damaged during the Second Punic War when Hannibal invaded Italy. Moreover, in order to win the wars, Rome had to increase the term of military service to six years. The Roman army was never meant to serve in distant wars but was called out for the "war season," after which the soldiers returned to their farms. Now when the soldiers returned home after many years of service abroad, they found their farms so deteriorated that they chose to sell out instead of remaining on the land. Landed aristocrats had been able to develop large estates (latifundia) by taking over state-owned land and by buying out small peasant owners. These large estates relied on slave and tenant labor and frequently concentrated on cash crops, such as grapes for wine, olives, and sheep for wool, which small farmers could not afford to do. Thus, the rise of latifundia contributed to the decline in the number of small citizen farmers. Since the latter group traditionally formed the basis of the Roman army—Rome conscripted only people with a financial stake in the community—the number of men available for military service declined. Many of the newly landless families stayed in the countryside, finding agricultural work as best they could. Some of them, however, drifted to the cities, especially Rome, where they formed a large class of day laborers who possessed no property. This new urban proletariat formed a highly unstable mass with the potential to create much trouble in depressed times.

5-5b The Reforms of Tiberius and Gaius Gracchus

Tiberius Gracchus (ty-BEER-ee-uss GRAK-us) (163–133 B.C.E.) was a member of the nobiles who ruled Rome. Although concerned with the immediate problem of a shortage of military recruits, Tiberius believed that the underlying cause of Rome's problems was the decline of the small farmers. He once described the men who fought Rome's wars as "masters of the world but have not a patch of earth to call their own." Tiberius was not a revolutionary, and his proposals for reform, drafted with the help of several prominent senators, were essentially conservative; he was looking back to what had constituted the foundation of Rome's greatness.

Tiberius Gracchus was elected one of the tribunes of the plebs in 133 B.C.E. Without consulting the senate, where he knew his rivals would oppose his proposal, Tiberius took his legislation directly to the council of the plebs, which passed his land-reform bill authorizing the government to reclaim public land held by large landowners and to distribute it to landless Romans. Many senators, themselves large landowners whose estates included large tracts of public land, were furious, and a group of them took the law into their own hands and assassinated Tiberius.

The efforts of Tiberius Gracchus were continued by his brother Gaius (GY-uss) (153–121 B.C.E.), who was elected tribune for both 123 and 122 B.C.E. Like Tiberius, Gaius pushed for the rapid distribution of land to displaced farmers, but he also broadened his reform program to appeal to more people disenchanted with the current senatorial leadership. To win the support of the equites, he replaced the senators on the jury courts that tried provincial governors accused of extortion with members of the equestrian order and opened the new province of Asia to equestrian tax collectors. Thus, Gaius gave the equites two instruments of public power: control over the jury courts that often tried provincial governors and control over provincial taxation. Fellow senators, hostile to Gaius's reforms and fearful of his growing popularity, made use of a constitutional innovation, a "final decree of the senate," which encouraged the consuls to do what was necessary to prevent any misfortune befalling the Republic. As a result, Gaius and many of his followers were killed in 121 B.C.E. The attempts of the Gracchus brothers to bring reforms had opened the door to more instability and violence.

5-5c Marius and the New Roman Army

In the closing years of the second century B.C.E., a series of military disasters gave rise to a fresh outburst of popular anger against the old leaders of the senate and resulted in the rise of Marius (MAR-ee-uss) (157–86 B.C.E.). Military defeats in North Africa under a senate-appointed general encouraged Marius—a "new man" from the equestrian order—to run for the consulship with "Win the War" as his campaign slogan. Marius won and became a consul for 107 B.C.E. The council of the plebs then voted to give Marius command of the army in Africa, a definite encroachment on the senate's right to conduct wars. Generals no longer needed to be loyal to the senate.

Marius brought the war in North Africa to a successful conclusion in 105 B.C.E. and was then called on to defeat the Celtic tribes (or Gauls, as the Romans called them), who threatened to invade Italy. Marius was made consul for five years, from 104 to 100 B.C.E., raised a new army, and decisively defeated the Celts, leaving him in a position of personal ascendancy in Rome.

In raising a new army, Marius initiated military reforms that proved to have drastic consequences. The Roman army had traditionally been a conscript army of small landholders—basically a citizen army, as described earlier. Marius recruited volunteers from both the urban and rural proletariat who possessed no property. These volunteers, who were now trained more thoroughly, swore an oath of loyalty to the general, not the senate, and thus inaugurated a professional-type army that might no longer be subject to the state. Moreover, to recruit these men, a general would promise them land, so generals had to play politics to get legislation passed that would provide the land for their veterans. Marius left a powerful legacy. He had created a new system of military recruitment that placed much power in the hands of the individual generals.

5-5d The Role of Sulla

After almost a decade of relative quiet, the Roman republic was threatened with another crisis—the Italian War (90–88 B.C.E.), also known as the Social War. This war resulted from Rome's unwillingness to deal constructively with the complaints of its Italian allies. These allies had fought loyally on Rome's side but felt they had not shared sufficiently in the lands and bonuses given to Roman veterans. In 90 B.C.E., the Italians rebelled and formed their own confederation, which they called Italia. Two years of bitter fighting took an enormous number of lives and left Italy devastated. The Romans managed to end the rebellion but only by granting full rights of Roman citizenship to all free Italians. "Rome was now Italy, and Italy Rome."[9] The influx of new voters into the popular assemblies drastically altered the voting power structure in favor of the populares, who had earlier favored enfranchising the Italians.

During this war, a new figure came to prominence—Lucius Cornelius Sulla (138–78 B.C.E.), a member of the nobiles. Sulla (SULL-uh) had been made a consul for 88 B.C.E. and given command by the senate of a war in Asia Minor. But when the council of the plebs, contradicting the senate's wishes, transferred command of this war to Marius, a civil war ensued between the forces of Marius and Sulla. Sulla won and seized Rome itself in 82 B.C.E. He forced the senate to grant him the title of dictator to reconstitute the Republic. After conducting a reign of terror to wipe out all opposition, Sulla revised the constitution to restore power to the senate. He eliminated most of the powers of the popular assemblies and the tribunes of the plebs and restored the senators to the jury courts. He also enlarged the senate by adding men of the equestrian order. In 79 B.C.E., believing that he had restored the traditional republic governed by a powerful senate, he resigned his office of dictator, retired, and soon died, leaving a power vacuum. But his real legacy was quite different from what he had intended. His example of using an army to seize power would prove most attractive to ambitious men.

5-5e The Death of the Republic

For the next fifty years, Roman history would be characterized by two important features: the jostling for power by a number of powerful individuals and the civil wars generated by their conflicts.

The Rise of Pompey Not long after Sulla's attempts to revive senatorial power, the senate made two extraordinary military appointments that raised to prominence two very strong personalities—Crassus (KRASS-uss) (ca. 112–53 B.C.E.) and Pompey (PAHM-pee) (106–48 B.C.E.). Crassus had fought for Sulla and had also become extremely rich—it was said that he "owned" most of Rome. In 73 B.C.E., the senate gave Crassus a military command against the slave rebellion led by Spartacus, which he successfully completed. Pompey had also fought for Sulla and was given an important military command in Spain in 77 B.C.E. When he returned six years later, he was hailed as a military hero.

Despite their jealousy, Pompey and Crassus joined forces and were elected consuls in 70 B.C.E. Although both men had been supporters of Sulla, they undid his work. They restored the power of the tribunes and helped put equites back on the jury courts, thereby reviving the populares as a path to political power.

With their power reestablished by this action, friendly plebeian tribunes now proposed legislation that gave two important military commands to Pompey. In 67 B.C.E., he cleared the Mediterranean Sea of the pirates who were harassing Roman commerce. After this success, he was put in charge of the campaign against Mithridates (mih-thruh-DAY-teez), who thought he could take advantage of Rome's internal troubles to pursue his plans of conquest in Asia Minor. Pompey defeated Mithridates and reorganized the east, winning immense success and prestige as well as enormous wealth. When he returned to Rome, he disbanded his army, expecting that the senate would automatically ratify his eastern settlement and give land to his veterans. But new forces and new personalities had risen to prominence during his absence, and his requests encountered complications.

The Role of Cicero Marcus Tullius Cicero (106–43 B.C.E.) was one of these new personalities (see Image 5.10). A novus homo from the equestrian order and the first of his family to achieve the consulship, Cicero (SIS-uh-roh) made a name for himself as a lawyer, using his outstanding oratorical skills to defend people accused of crimes and to prosecute others, including a corrupt provincial governor. He became consul in 63 B.C.E. and upheld the interests of the senate (see Historical Voices, "How to Win an Election," p. 139). Cicero was one of the few prominent politicians who attempted to analyze the problems of the republic systematically. He believed in a "concord of the orders," meaning the cooperation of the equestrians and senators. In effect, Cicero harked back to the days of collective rule, a time when political leaders were motivated to work together for the good of the Roman state. But collective rule was no longer meaningful to ambitious men seeking personal power. Cicero himself had few military skills and could not command an army. He realized that the senate needed the support of a powerful general if the concord of the orders was to be made a reality. In 62 B.C.E., he saw Pompey as that man. But a number

IMAGE 5.10 **Cicero.** The great orator Marcus Tullius Cicero, whose writings provide much information about politics and upper-class life, rose to the highest offices in the republic because of his oratorical skills. He supported the senate and wished to establish a "concord of the orders," cooperative rule by the equestrians and the senators. This realistic portrait, typical of republican Rome, gives a sense of Cicero's rigid character.

command in Gaul (modern France, Belgium, and parts of the Netherlands) for five years.

Caesar did so well in Gaul that Crassus and Pompey realized anew the value of military command. They became consuls again in 55 B.C.E. and garnered more benefits for the coalition: Caesar was given a five-year extension in Gaul; Crassus, a command in Syria; and Pompey, one in Spain. When Crassus was killed in battle in 53 B.C.E., his death left two powerful men with armies in direct competition. Caesar had used his time in Gaul to gain fame and military experience. He had waged numerous campaigns, costing the lives of hundreds of thousands of men, women, and children, according to estimates. As a military leader, Caesar had always been willing to face great personal danger. One ancient writer said that Caesar's soldiers were astonished that

> he should undergo toils beyond his body's apparent power of endurance . . . because he was of a spare habit, had soft and white skin, suffered from epileptic fits. . . . Nevertheless, he did not make his feeble health an excuse for soft living, but rather his military service a cure for his feeble health, since by wearisome journeys, simple diet, continuously sleeping in the open air, and enduring hardships he fought off his trouble and kept his body strong against its attacks.[10]

Caesar's wars had also enabled him to amass enough booty and slaves to pay off all of the debts he had accumulated in gaining political offices. Moreover, he now had an army of seasoned veterans who were loyal to him. No doubt most senators would

of senators felt that Pompey had become too powerful, and they now refused to grant his wishes after his return from the east. These same senators treated Julius Caesar in a similar fashion when he returned from Spain. That turned out to be a big mistake.

The Struggle Between Pompey and Caesar Julius Caesar (100–44 B.C.E.) had been a spokesman for the populares from the beginning of his political career, an alliance that ran in the family—Marius was his uncle by marriage. Caesar pursued political power by appealing to many of the same groups who had supported Marius. After serving as aedile and praetor, he sought a military command and was sent to Spain. He returned from Spain in 60 B.C.E. and requested a special dispensation so that he could both celebrate a triumph with his troops and run for the consulship, which would place him in the highest rank within the senate. Rival senators blocked his request. Consequently, Caesar joined with two fellow senators, Crassus and Pompey, who were also being stymied by the senate. Historians call their coalition the First Triumvirate (see Image 5.11). Though others had made political deals before, the combined wealth and power of these three men was enormous and enabled them to dominate the political scene. Caesar was elected consul in 59 B.C.E. and used the popular assemblies to achieve the basic aims of the triumvirs: Pompey received his eastern settlement and lands for his veterans, equestrian allies of Crassus were given a reduction on tax contracts for which they had overbid, and Caesar was granted a special military

IMAGE 5.11 **Caesar.** Conqueror of Gaul and member of the First Triumvirate, Julius Caesar is perhaps the best-known figure of the late republic. Caesar became dictator of Rome in 47 B.C.E. and after his victories in the civil war was made dictator for life. Some members of the senate who resented his power assassinated him in 44 B.C.E. Pictured is a marble copy of a bust of Caesar.

How to Win an Election

 What advice does Quintus Cicero give his brother for winning an election? How does his advice compare with the practices followed by politicians in our modern elections?

CICERO WAS A "NEW MAN" who had achieved the offices of quaestor and praetor. In the summer of 64 B.C.E., he decided to run for consul, although he knew that his lack of noble birth would make it difficult to win. To help him, his older brother Quintus penned some words of advice on how to win an election. This excerpt is taken from Quintus's pamphlet, although some historians question whether he was actually the author.

Quintus Tullius Cicero, *How to Win an Election*

To my brother Marcus,

Although you already have all the skills a man can possess through natural ability, experience, and hard work, because of the affection we have for one another I would like to share with you what I have been thinking about night and day concerning your upcoming campaign. . . .

There are three things that will guarantee votes in an election: favors, hope, and personal attachment. You must work to give these incentives to the right people. . . .

There are certain key men in every neighborhood and town who exercise power. These are diligent and wealthy people who, in spite of not backing you previously, can be persuaded to support you if they feel indebted to you or see you as useful to them. As you cultivate relationships with these men, make sure they realize that you know what you can expect from them, that you recognize what they have done for you, and that you will remember their work for you. . . .

Since I have been writing so much on the subject of friendship, I think now is the time to sound a note of caution. Politics is full of deceit, treachery, and betrayal. I'm not going to begin a long-winded discussion of how to separate true friends from false, but I do want to give you some simple advice. Your good nature has in the past led some men to feign friendship while they were in fact jealous of you, so remember the wise words . . . Don't trust people too easily. . . ."

I have said enough about developing political friendships, so now I would like to focus on impressing the voters at large. This is done by knowing who people are, being personable and generous, promoting yourself, being available, and never giving up. . . .

Now, my brother, you have many wonderful qualities, but those you lack you must acquire, and it must appear as if you were born with them. You have excellent manners and are always courteous, but you can be rather stiff at times. You desperately need to learn the art of flattery—a disgraceful thing in normal life but essential when you are running for office. If you use flattery to corrupt a man there is no excuse for it, but if you apply ingratiation as a way to make political friends, it is acceptable. For a candidate must be a chameleon, adapting to each person he meets, changing his expression and speech as necessary.

Source: Cicero, *How to Win an Election: An Ancient Guide for Modern Politicians*, trans. P. Freeman (Princeton, N.J.: Princeton University Press, 2012).

---

have preferred both Pompey and Caesar to lay down their commands and give up their armies. Since both refused, the leading senators fastened on Pompey as the less harmful to their cause and voted for Caesar to lay down his command and return as a private citizen to Rome. Such a step was intolerable to Caesar because it would leave him totally vulnerable to his enemies (see Opposing Viewpoints, "The End of the Republic," p. 140). He chose to keep his army and moved into Italy by crossing the Rubicon, the river that formed the southern boundary of his province, on January 10, 49 B.C.E. (The phrase "crossing the Rubicon" is still used today to mean being unable to turn back.) According to his ancient biographer Suetonius, Caesar said to his troops, "Even now we could turn back; but once we cross that tiny bridge, then everything will depend on armed force."[11]

Pompey and his followers fled to Greece, where they raised a new army. Meanwhile it took Caesar until the end of 49 to raise a fleet and ship his troops to Greece. The next spring, at the Battle of Pharsalus (far-SAY-luss), Caesar's veterans carried the day against Pompey's forces. The defeated Pompey fled to Egypt, where the king had Pompey killed. The war continued, however, because some of the senators on his side had recruited new troops. After victories in North Africa and Spain, Caesar returned triumphant to Rome in 45 B.C.E.

No doubt Caesar realized that the old order of unfettered political competition could not be saved. He was unwilling to take the title of king, which was intensely disliked by the Roman upper classes, but he had no intention of giving up his control. Caesar had officially been made dictator in 47 B.C.E., and in 44 B.C.E. he was made dictator for life. He continued to hold elections for offices but saw to it that his supporters chose the people he recommended. As Rome's new ruler, he quickly instituted a number of ambitious reforms, although he seems not to have had any long-term vision for governing Rome but was only responding to immediate issues. He increased the senate to nine hundred members by filling it with many of his followers. He granted citizenship to a number of people in the provinces who had provided assistance to him. By establishing colonies of Roman citizens in North Africa, Gaul, and Spain, he initiated a

The End of the Republic: Three Views

 How did Caesar view the steps he had taken to move into Italy with his troops? How did Cicero view those steps? What do the differences between Caesar and Cicero tell you about the end of the republic? How do the views of Caesar and Cicero give support to Sallust's argument? What do these three selections have in common in regard to the fall of the republic? How do they differ?

ALTHOUGH ROME STOOD SUPREME over the Mediterranean world by 133 B.C.E., the internal structure of the republic had begun to disintegrate. During the next hundred years, the republic would be afflicted with mob violence, assassinations, civil wars, and unscrupulous politicians who seized every opportunity to advance their own interests. The Roman historian Sallust (86–35 B.C.E.), who lived through many of these crises, reflected on the causes of Rome's problems. In the first selection that follows, he discusses the moral decline that set in after the destruction of Carthage in 146 B.C.E. Sallust presented a broad, philosophical view of the problem, but some figures directly involved in the struggles of the last century—namely, Caesar and Cicero—had their own ideas about the immediate crisis that led to the end of the republic. In the second selection, taken from *The Civil Wars*, Caesar presents a defense of his decision to move into Italy with his troops. In his letter to his friend Atticus, Cicero indicates what he thinks of Caesar's action.

Sallust, *The War with Catiline*

Good morals were cultivated at home and in the field; [in the early republic] there was the greatest harmony and little or no avarice; justice and honesty prevailed among them, thanks not so much to laws as to nature. Quarrels, discord, and strife were reserved for their enemies; citizen vied with citizen only for the prize of merit. They were lavish in their offerings to the gods, frugal in the home, loyal to their friends. By practicing these two qualities, boldness in warfare and justice when peace came, they watched over themselves and their country. . . .

But when our country had grown great through toil and the practice of justice, when great kings had been vanquished in war, savage tribes and mighty people subdued by force of arms, when Carthage, the rival of Rome's sway, had perished root and branch, and all seas and lands were open, then Fortune began to grow cruel and to bring confusion into all our affairs. Those who had found it easy to bear hardships and dangers, anxiety and adversity, found leisure and wealth, desirable under other circumstances, a burden and a curse. Hence the lust for power first, then for money, grew upon them; these were, I may say, the root of all evils.

For avarice destroyed honor, integrity, and all other noble qualities; taught in their place insolence, cruelty, to neglect the gods, to set a price on everything. Ambition drove many men to become false; to have one thought locked in the breast, another ready on the tongue; to value friendships and enmities not on their merits but by the standard of self-interest, and to show a good front rather than a good heart. At first these vices grew slowly; from time to time they were punished; finally, when the disease had spread like a deadly plague, the state was changed and a government second to none in justice and excellence became cruel and intolerable.

Caesar, *The Civil Wars*

Having called the senate together, he [Caesar, who refers to himself in the third person] recounts the wrongs done him by his personal enemies. He explains that he had sought no extraordinary office, but, waiting for the legitimate time of his consulship, had been content with privileges open to all the citizens. . . . He sets forth his own patience when under no pressure he had made the request about the disbandment of the armies, a point in which he was ready to make a personal sacrifice of dignity and position. He tells them of the bitterness of his foes who refused in his case what they demanded in the other, and preferred utter confusion to the surrender of military power and armed force. He tells of their injustice in robbing him of his legions, of their cruelty and insolence in infringing the rights of the tribunes; he enumerates the terms that he had offered, the conferences asked for and refused. On these considerations he exhorts and charges them to take up the burden of state and administer it with his help; but if they shrink through fear he will not burden them, and will administer the state himself. Envoys should be sent to Pompey to effect a settlement, nor was he afraid of the remark made by Pompey a little before in the senate, to the effect that undue influence is attributed to those to whom envoys are sent and fear argued on the part of those that send them. Such considerations seemed to belong to a poor and weak spirit. His own wish was to be superior to others in justice and equity as he had striven to surpass them in action.

Cicero, *Letter to Atticus*

Pray, what's all this? What is going on? I am in the dark. Is it a Roman general or Hannibal we are talking of? Deluded wretch, with never in his [Caesar's] life a glimpse of even the shadow of Good! And he says he is doing all this for his honor's sake! Where is honor without moral good? And is it good to have an army without public authority, to seize Roman towns by way of opening the road to the mother city, to plan debt cancellations, recall of exiles, and a hundred other villainies "all for that first of deities, Sole Power"? He is welcome to his greatness. I would rather a single hour with you, warming myself in that "bonus" sunshine of yours, than all such autocracies, or rather I had sooner die a thousand deaths than entertain one such thought.

Sources: Sallust, *The War with Catiline*, trans. J. C. Rolfe (Cambridge, Mass.: Harvard University Press, 1921); Caesar, *The Civil Wars* (Cambridge, Mass.: Harvard University Press, 1966); and Cicero, *Letter to Atticus*, ed. S. Bailey (Cambridge, Mass.: Harvard University Press, 1968).

process of Romanization in those areas. He tried to reorganize the administrative structures of cities in Italy in order to create some sense of rational order in their government.

Caesar was a generous victor and pardoned many of the republican leaders who had opposed him, allowing them to return to Rome. He also replaced the Roman calendar with the Egyptian solar year of 365 days (this so-called Julian calendar, with later changes made in 1582, became the basis of our modern calendar). He planned much more in the way of building projects and military adventures in the east but was not able to carry them out. In 44 B.C.E., a group of leading senators who resented his curtailment of their power assassinated him, believing that the old republican system would now return (see Historical Voices, "The Assassination of Julius Caesar," p. 142). In truth, however, they had set the stage for another civil war that delivered the death blow to the republic.

The Final Struggle: Octavian Versus Antony A new struggle for power soon ensued. Caesar's heir and adopted son, his grandnephew Octavian (ahk-TAY-vee-un), though only nineteen, took command of some of Caesar's legions. After forcing the senate to name him consul, he joined forces with Mark Antony, Caesar's ally and assistant, and Marcus Lepidus, who had been commander of Caesar's cavalry. Together the three formed the Second Triumvirate, which was legally empowered to rule Rome. Their first act was to restore Sulla's policy of proscription, as described by the ancient historian Appian:

> As soon as they were on their own, the three drew up a list of those who were to die. They put on the list, both then and later, those of whom they were suspicious because of their ability, as well as their personal enemies, trading with each other for the lives of their own relations and friends. They decreed death and confiscation of property for about 300 senators and 2,000 equestrians, among them their own brothers and uncles, as well as senior officers serving under them who had had cause to offend them or their own colleagues.[12]

In addition to proscribing their enemies at home (Cicero was one of those killed), the three commanders pursued Caesar's assassins, who had in the meantime raised an army, and defeated them at Philippi in Macedonia. Lepidus was soon shunted aside, and Octavian and Antony then divided the Roman world between them—Octavian taking the west and Antony the east. To seal their bargain, Antony married Octavia, Octavian's sister.

But the empire of the Romans, large as it was, was still too small for two masters, and Octavian and Antony eventually came into conflict. Antony abandoned Octavia and allied himself with the Egyptian queen Cleopatra VII. Julius Caesar had succumbed to her beauty when he went to Egypt in 48 in pursuit of Pompey. Her son by Caesar, known as Caesarion ("little Caesar"), was made co-regent of Egypt. Like Caesar before him, Antony also fell deeply in love with Cleopatra, fathering three children with her and giving her lands in the eastern Mediterranean. Octavian began a propaganda campaign, accusing Antony of catering to Cleopatra and giving away Roman territory to this "whore of the east." Finally, at the Battle of Actium in Greece in 31 B.C.E., Octavian's forces smashed the army and navy of Antony and Cleopatra. Both fled to Egypt, where, according to the Roman historian Florus, they committed suicide a year later:

> Antony was the first to commit suicide, by the sword. Cleopatra threw herself at Octavian's feet, and tried her best to attract his gaze: in vain, for his self-control was impervious to her beauty. It was not her life she was after, for that had already been granted, but a portion of her kingdom. When she realized this was hopeless and that she had been earmarked to feature in Octavian's triumph in Rome, she took advantage of her guard's carelessness to get herself into the mausoleum, as the royal tomb is called. Once there, she put

CHRONOLOGY	The Decline and Fall of the Roman Republic
Reforms of Tiberius Gracchus	133 B.C.E.
Reforms of Gaius Gracchus	123–122 B.C.E.
Marius: consecutive consulships	104–100 B.C.E.
Italian or Social War	90–88 B.C.E.
Sulla as dictator	82–79 B.C.E.
Pompey's command in Spain	77–71 B.C.E.
Consulship of Crassus and Pompey	70 B.C.E.
First Triumvirate (Caesar, Pompey, Crassus)	60 B.C.E.
Caesar in Gaul	59–49 B.C.E.
Crassus and Pompey as consuls	55 B.C.E.
Crassus killed in battle	53 B.C.E.
Caesar crosses the Rubicon	49 B.C.E.
Battle of Pharsalus; Pompey killed in Egypt	48 B.C.E.
Caesar as dictator	47–44 B.C.E.
Assassination of Caesar	44 B.C.E.
Second Triumvirate (Octavian, Antony, Marcus Lepidus); Cicero killed	43 B.C.E.
Caesar's assassins defeated at Philippi	42 B.C.E.
Octavian defeats Antony at Actium	31 B.C.E.

The Assassination of Julius Caesar

 What does this account of Caesar's assassination reveal about the character of Julius Caesar? Based on this selection, what lessons did classical historians intend their readers to take from their accounts of great and dramatic political events?

WHEN IT BECAME APPARENT that Julius Caesar had no intention of restoring the republic as they conceived it, about sixty senators, many of them his friends or pardoned enemies, formed a conspiracy to assassinate the dictator. It was led by Gaius Cassius and Marcus Brutus, who naively imagined that this act would restore the traditional republic. The conspirators set the Ides of March (March 15) of 44 B.C.E. as the date for the assassination. Caesar was in the midst of preparing for a campaign in the eastern part of the empire. Although warned about a plot against his life, he chose to disregard it. This account of Caesar's death is taken from his biography by the Greek writer Plutarch.

Plutarch, *Life of Caesar*

Fate, however, is to all appearance more unavoidable than unexpected. For many strange prodigies and apparitions are said to have been observed shortly before this event. . . . One finds it also related by many that a soothsayer bade him [Caesar] prepare for some great danger on the Ides of March. When this day was come, Caesar, as he went to the senate, met this soothsayer, and said to him mockingly, "The Ides of March are come," who answered him calmly, "Yes, they are come, but they are not past. . . ."

All these things might happen by chance. But the place which was destined for the scene of this murder, in which the senate met that day, was the same in which Pompey's statue stood, and was one of the edifices which Pompey had raised and dedicated with his theater to the use of the public, plainly showing that there was something of a supernatural influence which guided the action and ordered it to that particular place. Cassius, just before the act, is said to have looked toward Pompey's statue, and silently implored his assistance. . . . When Caesar entered, the senate stood up to show their respect to him, and of Brutus's confederates, some came about his chair and stood behind it, others met him, pretending to add their petitions to those of Tillius Cimber, in behalf of his brother, who was in exile; and they followed him with their joint applications till he came to his seat. When he sat down, he refused to comply with their requests, and upon their urging him further began to reproach them severely for their demand, when Tillius, laying hold of his robe with both his hands, pulled it down from his neck, which was the signal for the assault. Casca gave him the first cut in the neck, which was not mortal nor dangerous, as coming from one who at the beginning of such a bold action was probably very much disturbed; Caesar immediately turned about, and laid his hand upon the dagger and kept hold of it. And both of them at the same time cried out, he that received the blow, in Latin, "Vile Casca, what does this mean?" and he that gave it, in Greek to his brother, "Brother, help!" Upon this first onset, those who were not privy to the design were astonished, and their horror and amazement at what they saw were so great that they dared not fly nor assist Caesar, nor so much as speak a word. But those who came prepared for the business enclosed him on every side, with their naked daggers in their hands. Which way so ever he turned he met with blows, and saw their swords leveled at his face and eyes, and was encompassed like a wild beast in the toils on every side. For it had been agreed they should each of them make a thrust at him, and flesh themselves with his blood: for which reason Brutus also gave him one stab in the groin. Some say that he fought and resisted all the rest, shifting his body to avoid the blows, and calling out for help, but that when he saw Brutus's sword drawn, he covered his face with his robe and submitted, letting himself fall, whether it were by chance or that he was pushed in that direction by his murderers, at the foot of the pedestal on which Pompey's statue stood, and which was thus wetted with his blood. So that Pompey himself seemed to have presided, as it were, over the revenge done upon his adversary, who lay here at his feet, and breathed out his soul through his multitude of wounds, for they say he received three-and-twenty. And the conspirators themselves were many of them wounded by each other while they all leveled their blows at the same person.

Source: Plutarch, *The Lives of the Noble Grecians and Romans*, ed. A. H. Clough, trans. J Dryden.

on the royal robes which she was accustomed to wear, and lay down in a richly perfumed coffin beside her Antony. Then she applied poisonous snakes to her veins and passed into death as though into a sleep.[13]

Octavian, at the age of thirty-two, stood supreme over the Roman world (see Map 5.5). The civil wars had ended. And so had the republic.

5-5f Literature in the Late Republic

The last century of the Roman republic witnessed the completion of the union of Greek and Roman culture in a truly Greco-Roman civilization. Greek was now the language not just of Greece but of the entire Hellenistic world of the eastern Mediterranean, which Rome had conquered, and educated, upper-class Romans spoke it fluently. The influence of

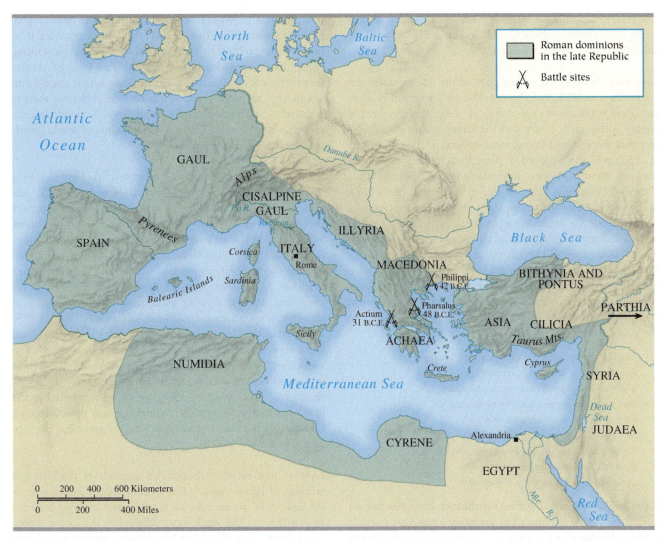

MAP 5.5 Roman Dominions in the Late Republic, 31 B.C.E. Rome expanded its empire not only in response to military threats on its borders but also for increased access to economic resources and markets, in addition to the vanity of conquest itself. For comparison, look back at Map 5.4.

 In what areas did the Romans gain the greatest amount of territory, and how?

Greece would continue to be felt in the development of Latin literature.

In the last century of the republic, the Romans began to produce a new poetry that was less dependent on epic themes and more inclined to personal expression. Latin poets now took to using various Greek forms to express their own feelings about people, social and political life, and love. The finest example is the work of Catullus (kuh-TULL-uss) (ca. 87–54 B.C.E.), the best lyric poet Rome produced and one of the greatest in world literature.

Catullus Like most of the great Roman writers of the first century B.C.E., Catullus was not from Rome. He grew up in northern Italy but moved to Rome, where he joined a group of carefree, youthful aristocrats. He became a master at adapting and refining Greek forms of poetry to express emotions. He wrote a variety of poems on, among other themes, political figures, social customs, the use of language, the death of his brother, and the travails of love. Catullus became infatuated with Clodia, the promiscuous sister of a tribune and wife of a provincial governor, and addressed a number of poems to her (he called her Lesbia) describing his passionate love and hatred for her (Clodia had many other lovers besides Catullus):

> You used to say that you wished to know only Catullus,
>   Lesbia, and wouldn't take even Jove before me!
> I didn't regard you just as my mistress then: I cherished you
>   as a father does his sons or his daughters' husbands.
> Now that I know you, I burn for you even more fiercely,
>   though I regard you as almost utterly worthless.
> How can that be, you ask? It's because such cruelty forces
>   lust to assume the shrunken place of affection.

Source: Martin, Charles, trans., *The Poems of Catullus*, p. 109. © 1979 Charles Martin. © 1990 The Johns Hopkins University Press. Reprinted with permission of Johns Hopkins University Press.

The ability of Catullus to express in simple fashion his intense feelings and curiosity about himself and his world had a noticeable impact on later Latin poets.

Lucretius Another important poet of the late republic was Lucretius (loo-KREE-shus) (ca. 94–55 B.C.E.), who followed an old Greek tradition of expounding philosophy in the form of poetry. Although Stoicism was the Greek school of philosophy that the Romans found most congenial, the philosophy of Epicurus also enjoyed a period of intense popularity between 60 and 40 B.C.E. Lucretius's lengthy poem *On the Nature of Things* played a role in furthering that philosophy. In this work, Lucretius attempted to set out poetically Epicurus's idea that the world and all its creatures had been created by an accidental combination of atoms and not by the operation of divine forces. Two themes are repeated: divine forces have no effect on us, and death is of no real consequence because the soul, like the body, is material and after death also dissolves into atoms. Lucretius was especially adept at using vivid imagery. Describing the movement of atoms in the void, he wrote:

> Consider the rays of the sun that are always stealing
> Into the shade of a house to pour their light.
> There in the void you'll notice many and sundry
> Dust flecks that mingle among the rays themselves,
> Stirring up in a sort of ceaseless strife
> Skirmishes, wars, realigning their squadrons, never
> Stopping for breath, assailed by alliance, secession;
> From this you can project how atoms are
> Constantly tossed along the gulf of space.[14]

If the gods and death are of no significance, how then are we to lead our lives? Lucretius's Epicurean argument that a simple life free of political worries was the highest good ran counter to Roman ideals but had an obvious appeal to Romans sick of the civil discord of the first century B.C.E.

Cicero The development of Roman prose was greatly aided by the practice of oratory. Romans had great respect for oratory because the ability to persuade people in public debate often led to success in politics. Oratory was brought to perfection in a literary fashion by Cicero, the best exemplar of the literary and intellectual interests of the elite of the late republic and, indeed, the greatest prose writer of that period. For Cicero, oratory was not simply skillful speaking. An orator was a statesman, a man who achieved his highest goal by pursuing an active life in public affairs.

Later, when the turmoil of the late republic forced him into semiretirement politically, Cicero turned his attention to writing philosophical treatises. He performed a valuable service for Roman society by popularizing and making understandable the works of Greek philosophers. In his philosophical works, Cicero, more than anyone else, transmitted the classical intellectual heritage to the Western world. Cicero's original contributions to Western thought came in the field of politics. His works *On the Laws* and *On the Republic* provided fresh insights into political thought, including the need for a mixed constitution: "A moderate and well-balanced form of government which is a combination of the three simple good forms (monarchy, aristocracy, and democracy) is preferable even to monarchy."[15] Centuries later his emphasis on the need to pursue an active life to benefit and improve humankind would greatly influence the Italian Renaissance.

Sallust Rome's upper classes continued to have a strong interest in history. The best-known historian of the late republic is Sallust (86–35 B.C.E.), who established an approach to historical studies that influenced later Roman historians. Sallust was on Caesar's side in the civil war and after Caesar's death went into retirement and turned to the writing of history. His two extant works are *War with Jugurtha*, which discusses Rome's war with an African king from 111 to 105 B.C.E., and *War with Catiline*, an account of the conspiracy of the disaffected aristocrat Catiline. Sallust modeled his style after that of the Greek historian Thucydides, whose historical work experienced a sudden wave of popularity in the 50s and 40s B.C.E. Sallust's works expressed his belief that the most important causative factor in Roman history was the moral degeneration of Roman society, which he attributed to the lack of a strong enemy after Carthage and the corrupting influence of the Greeks (see Opposing Viewpoints, "The End of the Republic," p. 140).

Caesar Brief mention should also be made of the historical writings of Julius Caesar. Most famous is his *Commentaries on the Gallic War*, an account of his conquest of Gaul between 58 and 51 B.C.E. The work was published in 51 B.C.E., at a time when Caesar was afraid that his political enemies would take advantage of his absence from Rome. Although the *Commentaries* served a partisan purpose by defending his actions in Gaul, Caesar presented his material in straightforward, concise prose. He referred to himself in the third person and, as the following passage indicates, was not averse to extolling his own bravery:

> Caesar saw that the situation was critical, and there was no reserve to throw in. He snatched a shield from a soldier in the rear—he had not brought one himself—and moved to the front line; he called upon the centurions by name, encouraged the men to advance, and directed them to open their lines out to give freer play to their swords. His coming inspired the men with hope and gave them new heart. Even in a desperate situation each man was anxious to do his utmost when his general was looking on, and the enemy's onset was somewhat slowed down.[16]

Caesar's work reminds us that some of the best prose of the late republic was written by politicians who were concerned with enhancing their own position in a world of civil conflict.

Sometime in the eighth century B.C.E., a group of Latin-speaking people built a small community called Rome on the Tiber River in Italy. Between 509 and 264 B.C.E., this city expanded and united almost all of Italy under its control. Diplomacy was as important as the Roman armies in this achievement, and the Romans made their rule acceptable by allowing local autonomy and gradually granting Roman citizenship to non-Romans. During this time of conquest, Rome also developed the political institutions of a republic ruled by an aristocratic oligarchy.

Although Rome had no master plan for expansion, its relationship with its neighbors outside Italy soon led to involvement in new wars. Its first challenge was Carthage and the Carthaginian Empire in Spain and Africa. Rome was victorious after the three long and bloody Punic Wars. In the east, Rome conquered Macedonia and took control of the Greek states. Thus, between 264 and 133 B.C.E., Rome expanded to the west and east and became master of the Mediterranean Sea.

Religion and law permeated Roman life. Ritual was at the focus of religion because it established the "correct" relationship with the gods, both for individuals and for the state. Roman law was among Rome's most enduring accomplishments. The early laws, written in the Twelve Tables, constituted civil law for Romans. As Rome expanded, the Romans developed a new body of law, the law of nations, that applied to Romans and non-Romans alike. Republican Rome was also influenced by Hellenistic Greece, especially in literature, art, and philosophy.

In the second century B.C.E., the conservative, traditional values of Rome declined as affluence and individualism increased. After 133 B.C.E., Rome's republican institutions proved inadequate for the task of ruling an empire. In the breakdown that ensued, ambitious individuals such as Pompey, Crassus, and Caesar saw opportunities for power unparalleled in Roman history and succumbed to

the temptations. The military reforms of Marius at the beginning of the first century had made possible the creation of professional armies that were loyal to the generals who recruited them rather than to the state. Bloody civil war ensued as powerful individuals jockeyed for power. Peace was finally achieved when Octavian defeated Antony and Cleopatra. Octavian, who came to be known by the title of Augustus, would soon create a new system of government that seemed to preserve the republic while establishing the basis for a new system that would rule the empire in an orderly fashion.

CHAPTER TIMELINE

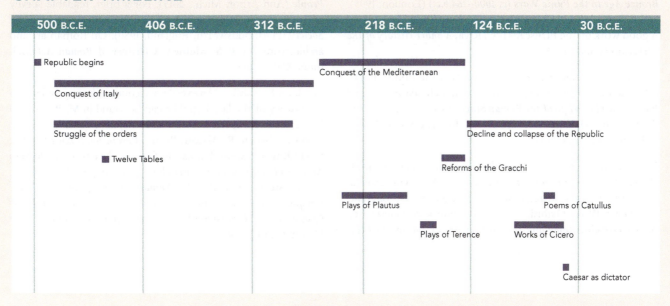

500 B.C.E.	406 B.C.E.	312 B.C.E.	218 B.C.E.	124 B.C.E.	30 B.C.E.

Republic begins

Conquest of the Mediterranean

Conquest of Italy

Struggle of the orders

Decline and collapse of the Republic

Twelve Tables

Reforms of the Gracchi

Plays of Plautus

Poems of Catullus

Plays of Terence

Works of Cicero

Caesar as dictator

CHAPTER REVIEW

Upon Reflection

Q What did the Roman poet Horace mean when he wrote, "Captive Greece took captive her rude conqueror"? What evidence supports the assertion?

Q How did Rome's contact with the Hellenistic world affect Roman civilization in the second and first centuries B.C.E.?

Q How did Rome achieve its empire from 264 to 133 B.C.E., and in the course of its expansion, what happened to the political structure and the political values of the Roman republic?

Q Was the fall of the Roman republic due to systemic institutional weaknesses or the personal ambitions of generals and politicians? Explain your answer.

Key Terms

imperium (p. 118)
consuls (p. 118)
praetor (p. 118)
dictator (p. 118)
quaestors (p. 118)
aediles (p. 118)
senate (p. 118)
centuriate assembly (p. 119)
paterfamilias (p. 119)
patricians (p. 119)

plebeians (p. 119)
tribunes of the plebs (p. 119)
council of the plebs (p. 119)
plebiscita (p. 119)
nobiles (p. 121)
rhetoric (p. 130)
latifundia (p. 131)
optimates (p. 135)
populares (p. 135)
equestrians (p. 136)

Full definitions also appear in the Glossary at the end of the book.

Suggestions for Further Reading

General Surveys   Good surveys of Roman history include **M. Beard**, *SPQR: A History of Ancient Rome* (New York, 2015); **G. Wolf**, *Rome: An Empire's Story* (Oxford, 2012); and **M. T. Boatwright, D. J. Gargola**, and **R. J. A. Talbert**, *The Romans: From Village to Empire* (New York, 2004). For a brief introduction to the Republic, see **P. Gwynn**, *The Roman Republic: A Short History* (New York, 2012).

Early Rome   The history of early Rome is well covered in **T. J. Cornell**, *The Beginnings of Rome: Italy and Rome from the Bronze Age to the Punic Wars (c. 1000–264 b.c.)* (London, 1995), and **A. Fraschetti**, *The Foundations of Rome* (Edinburg, 2006). A good work on the Etruscans is **C. Riva**, *A Short History of the Etruscans* (London, 2019).

Political and Social Structure   Aspects of the Roman political structure can be studied in **R. E. Mitchell**, *Patricians and Plebeians: The Origin of the Roman State* (Ithaca, N.Y., 1990). On the Roman social structure, see **G. Alfoldy**, *The Social History of Rome* (New York, 2014).

The Expansion of Rome   On the conquest of Italy, see **J.-M. David**, *The Roman Conquest of Italy*, trans. A. Nevill (Oxford, 1996). On Rome's struggle with Carthage, see **N. Bagnall**, *The Punic Wars* (Oxford, 2002). On Rome's conquests, see **N. Rosenstein**, *Rome and the Mediterranean 290 to 146 B.C.:*

The Imperial Republic (Edinburgh, 2012). On Roman military forces, see **A. Goldsworthy**, *The Complete Roman Army* (London, 2003).

Roman Society and Culture   Roman religion can be examined in **E. M. Orlin**, *Temples, Religion, and Politics in the Roman Republic* (New York, 2002). Roman women are examined in **Eve d'Ambra**, *Roman Women* (New York, 2006). On slavery, see **B. D. Shaw**, *Spartacus and the Slave Wars* (New York, 2001). On Roman law, see **C. Williamson**, *The Laws of the Roman People* (Ann Arbor, Mich., 2015). For a brief, readable survey of Latin literature, see **R. M. Ogilvie**, *Roman Literature and Society* (Harmondsworth, England, 1980). On Roman art and architecture, see **F. S. Kleiner**, *A History of Roman Art* (Belmont, Calif., 2006).

The Late Republic   An excellent account of basic problems in the history of the late Republic can be found in **M. Beard** and **M. H. Crawford**, *Rome in the Late Republic* (London, 1985). Also valuable are **R. Alston**, *Rome's Revolution* (Oxford, 2015); **E. Hildinger**, *Swords Against the Senate: The Rise of the Roman Army and the Fall of the Republic* (Cambridge, Mass., 2002); and **C. Steel**, *The End of the Roman Republic, 146 t0 44 B.C.: Conquest and Crisis* (Edinburgh, 2013). For a good biography of Caesar, see **A. Goldsworthy**, *Caesar: Life of a Colossus* (New Haven, Conn., 2006).

Notes

1. Quoted in Mary Beard, *SPQR: A History of Ancient Rome* (New York, 2015), p. 164.
2. Polybius. *The Histories*, trans. W. R. Paton (Cambridge, Mass., 1960), Book I, 37.7–37.10.
3. Quoted in C. Starr, *Past and Future in Ancient History* (Lanham, Md., 1987), pp. 38–39.
4. Cicero, *Laws*, trans. C. W. Keyes (Cambridge, Mass., 1966), 2.12.31.
5. Cato the Censor, *On Farming*, trans. E. Brehaut (New York, 1933), 141.
6. Quoted in M. Beard, SPQR: *A History of Ancient Rome*, p. 304
7. Terence, *The Comedies*, trans. Betty Radice (Harmondsworth, England, 1976), p. 339.
8. Pliny, *Natural History*, trans. W. H. S. Jones (Cambridge, Mass., 1963), 29.7.
9. M. Beard and M. Crawford, *Rome in the Late Republic* (London, 1985), p. 3.
10. Quoted in A. Goldsworthy, *Caesar: Life of a Colossus* (New Haven, Conn., 2006), p. 235.
11. Quoted in ibid., p. 358.
12. Appian, *Roman History: The Civil Wars*, trans. H. White (Cambridge, Mass., 1961), 4.2.149–151.
13. Florus, *Epitome of Roman History*, trans. E. S. Forster (Cambridge, Mass., 1960), 2.22.327.
14. Lucretius, *On the Nature of Things*, trans. A. M. Esolen (Baltimore, 1995), 2.115–123.
15. Quoted in A. Everitt, *Cicero* (New York, 2001), p. 181.
16. Caesar, *The Gallic War and Other Writings*, trans. Moses Hadas (New York, 1957), 2.25.

MindTap *Tips* You can access MindTap anytime via the Cengage Mobile App. The app provides a full, interactive ebook, readable online or off, study tools that empower anytime, anywhere learning and 24/7 course access, helping keep you focused and ready to study whenever it's convenient!

CHAPTER 6

The Roman Empire

IMAGE 6.1 **A Second-Century Roman Marble Bust of Hadrian**

CHAPTER OUTLINE AND FOCUS QUESTIONS

6-1 The Age of Augustus (31 B.C.E.–14 C.E.)

Q In his efforts to solve the problems Rome had faced during the late Republic, what changes did Augustus make in Rome's political, military, and social institutions? What was his primary goal in making these changes?

6-2 The Early Empire (14–180 C.E.)

Q What problems did the Roman Empire face in the first century C.E.? What were the chief features of the Roman Empire at its height during the second century?

6-3 Roman Culture and Society in the Early Empire

Q What were the chief intellectual, artistic, and social developments in the early Empire? How did these differ from the intellectual, artistic, and social developments of the Republic?

6-4 Transformation of the Roman World: Crises in the Third Century

Q What political, military, economic, and social problems did the Roman Empire face during the third century?

6-5 Transformation of the Roman World: The Rise of Christianity

Q What characteristics of Christianity enabled it to grow and ultimately to succeed? How did it transform the Roman world?

CONNECTIONS TO TODAY

What lessons can be learned from the history of the Roman Empire that apply to nation-states in the twentieth and twenty-first centuries?

WITH THE VICTORIES OF OCTAVIAN, peace finally settled on the Roman world. Although civil conflict still erupted occasionally, the new imperial state constructed by Octavian experienced a period of remarkable stability for the next two hundred years. The Romans imposed their peace on the largest empire established in antiquity. Indeed, Rome's writers proclaimed that "by heaven's will my Rome shall be capital of the world."[1] Rome's writers were not quite accurate, but few Romans were aware of the Han Empire, which flourished at the same time (202 B.C.E.–221 C.E.) and extended from Central Asia to the Pacific. Although there was little contact between them, the Han and Roman Empires had remarkable similarities: both lasted for centuries, both had considerable success in establishing centralized control, and both maintained their law and political institutions, their technical skills, and their languages throughout the empire.

To the Romans, their divine mission was clearly to rule nations and peoples. Hadrian (HAY-dree-un), one of the emperors of the second century C.E., was but one of many Roman rulers who believed in Rome's mission. He was a strong and intelligent ruler who took his responsibilities quite seriously. Between 121 and 132, he visited all of the provinces in the empire. According to his Roman biographer, Aelius Spartianus, hardly any emperor ever traveled so fast over so much territory. When he arrived in a province, Hadrian dealt firsthand with any problems

Bust of Emperor Hadrian (76-138 AD) (marble), Roman, (2nd century AD)/Galleria degli Uffizi, Florence, Italy/Bridgeman Images

and bestowed many favors on the local population. He also worked to establish the boundaries of the provinces and provide for their defense. New fortifications, such as the 80-mile-long Hadrian's Wall across northern Britain, were built to defend the borders. Hadrian insisted on rigid discipline for frontier armies and demanded that the soldiers be kept in training "just as if war were imminent." He also tried to lead by personal example; according to his biographer, he spent time with the troops and "cheerfully ate out of doors such camp food as bacon, cheese, and vinegar." Moreover, he "would walk as much as twenty miles fully armed." By the third century C.E., however, Rome's ability to rule nations and peoples began to weaken as the Roman Empire began to experience renewed civil war, economic chaos, and invasions. In the meantime, the growth of Christianity, one of the remarkable success stories of Western civilization, led to the emergence of a new and vibrant institution.

6-1 The Age of Augustus (31 B.C.E.–14 C.E.)

 FOCUS QUESTION: In his efforts to solve the problems Rome had faced during the late Republic, what changes did Augustus make in Rome's political, military, and social institutions? What was his primary goal in making these changes?

In 27 B.C.E., Octavian proclaimed that the republic had been restored. He understood that only traditional republican forms would satisfy the senatorial aristocracy. At the same time, Octavian was aware that the republic could not be fully restored and managed to arrive at a compromise that worked, at least during his lifetime. In 27 B.C.E., the senate awarded him the title of Augustus—"the revered one" (see Image 6.2). He preferred the title *princeps* (PRIN-keps *or* PRIN-seps), meaning chief citizen or first among equals. The system of rule that Augustus established is sometimes called the **principate**, conveying the idea of a constitutional monarch as co-ruler with the senate. But while Augustus worked to maintain this appearance, in reality, power was heavily weighted in favor of the princeps.

6-1a The New Order

In the new constitutional order that Augustus created, the basic governmental structure consisted of the princeps (Augustus) and an aristocratic senate. Augustus retained the senate as the chief deliberative body of the Roman state. Its decrees, screened in advance by the princeps, now had the effect of law. The title of princeps—first citizen of the state—carried no power in itself, but each year until 23 B.C.E., Augustus held the office of consul, which gave him *imperium*, or the right to command (see Chapter 5). When Augustus gave up the consulship in 23 B.C.E., he was granted *maius imperium* (MY-yoos im-PEE-ree-um)—greater imperium than all others. The consulship was now

IMAGE 6.2 **Augustus.** Octavian, Caesar's adopted son, emerged victorious from the civil conflict that racked the republic after Caesar's assassination. The senate awarded him the title Augustus. This marble statue from Prima Porta is an idealized portrait that is based on Greek rather than Roman models. It was meant to be a propaganda piece, depicting a youthful general addressing his troops. At the bottom stands Cupid, the son of Venus, goddess of love, as a reminder that the Julians, Caesar's family, claimed descent from Venus and thus that the ruler had a divine background. Augustus also claimed to be a direct descendant of Aeneas.

 Why would Augustus claim to be a descendant of Aeneas (see Chapter 5 and "Virgil," in Section 6-1e)?

unnecessary. Moreover, very probably in 23 B.C.E., Augustus was given the power of a tribune without actually holding the office itself; this power enabled him to propose laws and veto any item of public business. Although officials continued to be elected, Augustus's authority ensured that his candidates usually won. This situation caused participation in elections to decline. Consequently, the popular assemblies, shorn of any real role in elections and increasingly overshadowed by the senate's decrees, gradually declined in importance.

Why had Augustus succeeded in establishing a new order while Julius Caesar, his adoptive father, had failed? Caesar had defined himself as a dictator for life, thus raising suspicion

The Achievements of Augustus

 What were the achievements of Augustus? To what extent did these accomplishments create the "job" of being emperor? In what sense could this document be called a piece of propaganda?

THIS EXCERPT IS TAKEN FROM A TEXT written by Augustus and inscribed on a bronze tablet at Rome. Copies of the text in stone were displayed in many provincial capitals. Often called the most famous ancient inscription, the Res Gestae (RAYS GES-ty *or* REEZ JES-tee) of Augustus summarizes his accomplishments in three major areas: his offices, his private expenditures on behalf of the state, and his exploits in war and peace. Though factual in approach, it is a highly subjective account.

Augustus, *Res Gestae*

Below is a copy of the accomplishments of the deified Augustus by which he brought the whole world under the empire of the Roman people, and of the moneys expended by him on the state and the Roman people, as inscribed on two bronze pillars set up in Rome.

1. At the age of nineteen, on my own initiative and at my own expense, I raised an army by means of which I liberated the Republic, which was oppressed by the tyranny of a faction [Mark Antony and his supporters]. . . .
2. Those who assassinated my father [Julius Caesar, his adoptive father] I drove into exile, avenging their crime by due process of law; and afterwards when they waged war against the state, I conquered them twice on the battlefield.
3. I waged many wars throughout the whole world by land and by sea, both civil and foreign, and when victorious I spared all citizens who sought pardon. . . .

5. The dictatorship offered to me . . . by the people and the senate, both in my absence and in my presence, I refused to accept. . . .
17. Four times I came to the assistance of the treasury with my own money, transferring to those in charge of the treasury 150,000,000 sesterces. And in the consulship of Marcus Lepidus and Lucius Arruntius I transferred out of my own patrimony 170,000,000 sesterces to the soldiers' bonus fund, which was established on my advice for the purpose of providing bonuses for soldiers who had completed twenty or more years of service. . . .
22. I gave a gladiatorial show three times in my own name, and five times in the names of my sons or grandsons; at these shows about 10,000 fought. . . .
25. I brought peace to the sea by suppressing the pirates. In that war I turned over to their masters for punishment nearly 30,000 slaves who had run away from their owners and taken up arms against the state. . . .
26. I extended the frontiers of all the provinces of the Roman people on whose boundaries were peoples not subject to our empire. . . .
27. I added Egypt to the empire of the Roman people. . . .
28. I established colonies of soldiers in Africa, Sicily, Macedonia, in both Spanish provinces, in Achaea, Asia, Syria, Narbonese Gaul, and Pisidia. Italy, moreover, has twenty-eight colonies established by me, which in my lifetime have grown to be famous and populous. . . .
35. When I held my thirteenth consulship, the senate, the equestrian order, and the entire Roman people gave me the title of "father of the country" and decreed that this title should be inscribed in the vestibule of my house, in the Julian senate house, and in the Augustan Forum. . . . At the time I wrote this document I was in my seventy-sixth year.

Source: N. Lewis and M. Renhold, *Roman Civilization*, vol. I (New York: Columbia University Press, 1955).

among the Romans that he planned to become a king, a position that they strongly disliked. Cicero was clear that Caesar had been justly killed as a tyrant. Augustus was careful to present himself as an ordinary citizen and to exercise power by holding the traditional offices of the Roman republic.

Augustus proved highly popular. As the Roman historian Tacitus commented, "Indeed, he attracted everybody's goodwill by the enjoyable gift of peace. . . . Opposition did not exist."[2] The ending of the civil wars had greatly bolstered Augustus's popularity (see Historical Voices, "The Achievements of Augustus," above). At the same time, his continuing control of the army, while making possible the Roman peace, was a crucial source of his power.

6-1b The Army

As a result of the civil wars of the first century B.C.E., the Roman army had increased in size and had become more professional with legionaries who served a longer term. Under the empire, the shift to a professional army was completed when early emperors created a bureaucracy that could train and administer such an army. The peace of the Roman Empire depended on the army, and so did the security of the princeps. Though primarily responsible for guarding the frontiers of the empire, the army was also used to maintain domestic order within the provinces. Moreover, the army played an important social role. It was an agent of upward mobility for both officers and recruits. The colonies of veterans established by Augustus throughout the empire proved especially valuable in bringing Roman ways to the provinces.

Augustus maintained a standing army of twenty-eight legions. Since each legion at full strength numbered 5,400 soldiers, the Roman Empire had an army of about 150,000 men, certainly not large either by modern standards or in terms of the size of the empire itself (the population of the empire was probably close to 50 million). Roman legionaries served twenty years and were recruited only from the citizenry and, under Augustus, largely from Italy. Augustus also maintained a large contingent of auxiliary forces enlisted from the subject peoples. They served as both light-armed troops and cavalry and were commanded by Roman officers as well as tribal leaders. During the principate of Augustus, the **auxiliaries** numbered around 130,000. They were recruited only from noncitizens, served for twenty-four years, and along with their families received citizenship after their terms of service.

Augustus was also responsible for establishing the **praetorian guard** (see Image 6.3). These nine cohorts, roughly nine thousand men, had the important task of guarding the princeps. They were recruited from Roman citizens in Italy and served for sixteen years. Eventually, the praetorian guard would play an important role in making and deposing emperors.

The role of the princeps as military commander gave rise to a title by which this ruler eventually came to be known. When victorious, a military commander was acclaimed by his troops as *imperator* (im-puh-RAH-tur). Augustus was so acclaimed on a number of occasions. Imperator is our word *emperor*. Although such a title was applied to Augustus and his successors, Augustus still preferred to use the title princeps.

6-1c Roman Provinces and Frontiers

Augustus inaugurated a new system for governing the provinces. Under the republic, the senate had appointed the provincial governors. Now certain provinces were allotted to the princeps, who assigned deputies known as legates to govern them. These legates were from the senatorial class and held office as long as the emperor chose. The senate continued to designate the governors of the remaining provinces, but the authority of Augustus gave him the power to overrule the senatorial governors and thus to establish a unified imperial policy.

Since a governor had relatively few administrative officials to assist him, effective government of the provinces necessitated considerable cooperation from local authorities. By supporting the power of local elites—the upper classes—in return for their cooperation, Roman policy encouraged a substantial degree of self-government and local autonomy in the cities. By fostering municipal life, Rome essentially made cities and city-states the basic units of imperial administration. City councils of leading citizens made for stable local government, and leading city officials were rewarded for their administrative services with Roman citizenship.

Frontier Policy Augustus added more territory to the Roman Empire than any other single Roman. In the east, instead of creating new provinces, Augustus established client kingdoms, continuing a policy that had begun in the early second century B.C.E. with the conquest of Greece and parts of the Near East; this policy enabled him to minimize the Roman military presence in the east so that he could use his forces elsewhere. Augustus expended his greatest military efforts along the northern frontiers of the Roman Empire. He conquered the central and maritime Alps and then expanded Roman control of the Balkan peninsula up to the Danube River.

The extension of Roman power to the Danube now opened the door for Augustus's major military project—expansion into Germany. After 15 B.C.E., Roman forces advanced across the Rhine, and by 9 B.C.E. they had reached the Elbe River in eastern Germany. In 6 C.E., the Romans began another advance between the Elbe and the Danube but encountered a series

IMAGE 6.3 **The Praetorian Guard.** Augustus was responsible for setting up the praetorian guard as an imperial bodyguard of elite troops. Pictured in this second-century relief are members of the praetorian guard. Their body armor resembled that of the legionaries, although the cohort serving in the palace wore togas.

Q *What problems did the praetorian guard create for the Roman state?*

© RMN-Grand Palais/Art Resource, NY

of difficulties, including the great catastrophe of 9 C.E. when three Roman legions under Varus were massacred in the Teutoburg Forest by a coalition of German tribes led by Arminius, a German tribal leader who had served in the Roman auxiliary forces and had even received Roman citizenship. Roman historians blamed Varus for the disaster: "He [Varus] entertained the notion that the Germans were a people who were men only in voice and limbs. . . . With this purpose in mind, he entered the heart of Germany as though he were going among a people enjoying the blessings of peace."[3] The defeat severely dampened Augustus's enthusiasm for continued expansion in central Europe. Thereafter, the Romans were content to use the Rhine as a frontier between the Roman province of Gaul and the German tribes to the east. In fact, the difficulties had convinced Augustus that "the empire should not be extended beyond its present frontiers."[4] His defeats in Germany taught Augustus that Rome's power was limited. They also left him devastated; for months afterward he would beat his head against a door and shout, "Varus, give me back my legions!"

6-1d Augustan Society

Society in the early Roman Empire was characterized by a system of social stratification that had been inherited from the republic, in which Roman citizens were divided into three basic classes: senatorial, equestrian, and lower.

The Social Order Augustus had accepted the senatorial order as a ruling class for the empire. Senators filled the chief magistracies of the Roman government, held the most important military posts, and governed the provinces. One needed to possess property worth 1 million sesterces to belong to the senatorial order (an unskilled laborer in Rome received 3 sesterces a day; a Roman legionary, 900 sesterces a year in pay). When Augustus took charge, the senate had more than a thousand members. Augustus revised the senatorial list and reduced its size to six hundred but also added new men from wealthy families throughout Italy. Overall, Augustus was successful in winning the support of the senatorial class for his new order.

The equestrian order was expanded under Augustus and given a share of power in the new imperial state. The order was open to all Roman citizens of good standing who possessed property valued at 400,000 sesterces. They could now hold military and governmental offices, but the positions open to them were less important than those held by the senatorial order. At the end of his career, an equestrian might be rewarded by membership in the senatorial order.

Citizens not of the senatorial or equestrian orders belonged to the nonelite and lower classes, who made up the overwhelming majority of the free citizens. They varied considerably from middling types to the very poor. Most of the fifty million were peasant farmers whose survival and well-being depended on climatic conditions.

The diminution of the power of the Roman assemblies ended whatever political power the lower classes may have possessed earlier in the republic. Many of these people suffered extreme urban poverty and were provided with free grain and public spectacles to keep them from creating disturbances. Nevertheless, by gaining wealth and serving as lower officers in the Roman legions, it was sometimes possible for some of these people to advance to the equestrian order.

Augustus's Reforms Augustus was very concerned about certain aspects of Rome's social health. He believed that the civil strife of the first century B.C.E. had sapped the strength of public religion, which he considered the cornerstone of a strong state. Therefore, he restored traditional priesthoods that had fallen into disuse in the late republic, rebuilt many ruined temples and shrines, and constructed new ones to honor the Roman gods.

Augustus also instituted a new religious cult to strengthen the empire. Since the Roman state was intimately tied to Roman religion, an imperial cult served as a unifying instrument for the Roman world. Augustus did not claim to be a god, but he did permit the construction of temples to his deified adoptive father, Julius Caesar. Augustus also permitted the building of temples to Augustus and Roma, the personification of the Roman state. The worship of Augustus and Roma became the foundation of the imperial cult. Its development was furthered when Augustus was acclaimed as a god upon his death.

Augustus's belief that Roman morals had been corrupted during the late republic led him to initiate social legislation to arrest the decline. He thought that increased luxury had undermined traditional Roman frugality and simplicity and caused a decline in morals, evidenced by easy divorce, a falling birthrate among the upper classes, and lax behavior manifested in hedonistic parties and the love affairs of prominent Romans with fashionable women and elegant boys.

Through his new social legislation, Augustus hoped to restore respectability to the upper classes and reverse the declining birthrate as well. Expenditures for feasts were limited, and other laws made adultery a criminal offense. In fact, Augustus exiled his own daughter Julia for adultery. Augustus also revised the tax laws to penalize bachelors, widowers, and married persons who had fewer than three children.

6-1e A Golden Age of Latin Literature

The high point of Latin literature was reached in the time of Augustus. The literary accomplishments of the Augustan Age were such that the period has been called the golden age of Latin literature.

Virgil The most distinguished poet of the Augustan Age was Virgil (VUR-jul) (70–19 B.C.E.). The son of a small landholder in northern Italy, Virgil welcomed the rule of Augustus and wrote his greatest work in the emperor's honor. Virgil's masterpiece was *The Aeneid,* an epic poem clearly meant to rival the work of Homer. The poem makes an explicit connection between Troy and Rome. Aeneas (ih-NEE-uss), the son of Anchises of Troy, survives the destruction of Troy and eventually settles in Latium; thus, Roman civilization is linked to Greek history. The character of Aeneas is portrayed in terms that remind us of the ideal Roman—his virtues are duty, piety, and faithfulness. Virgil's overall purpose was to show that

Aeneas had fulfilled his mission to establish the Romans in Italy and thereby start Rome on its divine mission to rule the world:

> Let others fashion from bronze more lifelike, breathing
> Image—
> For so they shall—and evoke living faces from marble;
> Others excel as orators, others track with their
> instruments
> The planets circling in heaven and predict when stars
> will appear.
> But, Romans, never forget that government is your
> medium!
> Be this your art:—to practice men in the habit of
> peace,
> Generosity to the conquered, and firmness against
> aggressors.[5]

As Virgil expressed it, ruling was Rome's gift.

Horace Another prominent Augustan poet was Horace (HOR-uss) (65–8 B.C.E.), a friend of Virgil. Horace was a very sophisticated writer whose overriding concern seems to have been to point out to his contemporaries the follies and vices of his age. In the *Satires*, a medley of poems on a variety of subjects, Horace is revealed as a detached observer of human weaknesses. He directed his attacks against movements, not living people, and took on such subjects as sexual immorality, greed, and job dissatisfaction ("How does it happen, Maecenas, that no man alone is content with his lot?"[6]). Horace mostly laughs at the weaknesses of humankind and calls for forbearance: "Supposing my friend has got liquored and wetted my couch. . . . Is he for such a lapse to be deemed less dear as a friend, or because when hungry he snatched up before me a chicken from my side of the dish?"[7] In his final work, the *Epistles*, Horace used another Greek form—the imaginary letter in verse—to provide a portrait of the things he held most dear: a simple life, good friends, and his beloved countryside.

Ovid Ovid (AH-vid) (43 B.C.E.–18 C.E.) was the last of the great poets of the golden age. He belonged to a privileged group of Roman youths who liked to ridicule old Roman values. In keeping with the spirit of this group, Ovid wrote a frivolous series of love poems known as the *Amores*. Intended to entertain and shock, they achieved their goal. Ovid's most popular work was the *Metamorphoses*, a series of fifteen complex mythological tales involving transformations of shapes, such as the change of chaos into order. A storehouse of mythological information, the *Metamorphoses* inspired many Western painters, sculptors, and writers, including Shakespeare.

Another of Ovid's works was *The Art of Love*. This was essentially a takeoff on didactic poems. Whereas authors of earlier didactic poems had written guides to farming, hunting, or some such subject, Ovid's work was a handbook on the seduction of women (see Historical Voices, "Ovid and the Art of Love," p. 154). *The Art of Love* appeared to applaud the loose sexual morals of the Roman upper classes at a time when Augustus was trying to clean them up. The princeps was not pleased. Ovid chose to ignore the wishes of Augustus and paid a price for it. In 8 C.E., Ovid was implicated in a sexual scandal, possibly involving the emperor's daughter Julia. He was banished to a small town on the coast of the Black Sea and died in exile.

Livy The historian Livy (LIV-ee) (59 B.C.E.–17 C.E.) wrote the most famous Latin prose work of the golden age. His masterpiece was a history of Rome from the foundation of the city to 9 B.C.E. Although written in 142 books, only 35 have survived. Livy perceived history in terms of moral lessons. He stated in the preface:

> The study of history is the best medicine for a sick mind; for in history you have a record of the infinite variety of human experience plainly set out for all to see; and in that record you can find for yourself and your country both examples and warnings: fine things to take as models, base things, rotten through and through, to avoid.[8]

For Livy, human character was the determining factor in history.

Livy's history celebrated Rome's greatness. He built scene upon scene that not only revealed the character of the chief figures but also demonstrated the virtues that had made Rome great. Of course, he had serious weaknesses as a historian. He was not always concerned about the factual accuracy of his stories and was not overly critical of his sources. But he did tell a good tale, and his work remained the standard history of Rome for centuries.

6-1f Significance of the Augustan Age

The Augustan Age was a lengthy one. Augustus died in 14 C.E. after dominating the Roman world for forty-five years. He had created a new order while placating the old by restoring and maintaining traditional values, a fitting combination for a leader whose favorite maxim was "make haste slowly." By the time of his death, his new order was so well established that few Romans agitated for an alternative. Indeed, as the Roman historian Tacitus (TASS-i-tuss) pointed out, "Actium had been won before the younger men were born. Even most of the older generation had come into a world of civil wars. Practically no one had ever seen truly Republican government. . . . Political equality was a thing of the past; all eyes watched for imperial commands."[9] The republic was now only a memory and, given its last century of warfare, an unpleasant one at that. The new order was here to stay.

6-2 The Early Empire (14–180 C.E.)

FOCUS QUESTIONS: What problems did the Roman Empire face in the first century C.E.? What were the chief features of the Roman Empire at its height during the second century?

There was no serious opposition to Augustus's choice of successor, his stepson Tiberius (ty-BEER-ee-uss). By designating a family member as princeps, Augustus established the Julio-Claudian dynasty; the next four rulers were related either to his own family or to that of his wife, Livia.

Ovid and the Art of Love

 What were Ovid's principles of love? Why do you think Augustus found The Art of Love so offensive?

OVID HAS BEEN CALLED the last great poet of the Augustan golden age of literature. One of his most famous works was *The Art of Love,* a guidebook for the seduction of women. Unfortunately for Ovid, the work appeared at a time when Augustus was anxious to improve the morals of the Roman upper class. Augustus considered the poem offensive, and Ovid soon found himself in exile.

Ovid, *The Art of Love*

Now I'll teach you how to captivate and hold the woman of your choice. This is the most important part of all my lessons. Lovers of every land, lend an attentive ear to my discourse; let goodwill warm your hearts, for I am going to fulfill the promises I made you.

First of all, be quite sure that there isn't a woman who cannot be won, and make up your mind that you will win her. Only you must prepare the ground. Sooner would the birds cease their song in the springtime, or the grasshopper be silent in the summer . . . than a woman resist the tender wooing of a youthful lover. . . .

Now the first thing you have to do is to get on good terms with the fair one's maid. She can make things easy for you. Find out whether she is fully in her mistress's confidence, and if she knows all about her secret dissipations. Leave no stone unturned to win her over. Once you have her on your side, the rest is easy. . . .

In the first place, it's best to send her a letter, just to pave the way. In it you should tell her how you dote on her; pay her pretty compliments and say all the nice things lovers always say. . . . And promise, promise, promise. Promises will cost you nothing. Everyone's a millionaire where promises are concerned. . . .

If she refuses your letter and sends it back unread, don't give up; hope for the best and try again. . . .

Don't let your hair stick up in tufts on your head; see that your hair and your beard are decently trimmed. See also that your nails are clean and nicely filed; don't have any hair growing out of your nostrils; take care that your breath is sweet, and don't go about reeking like a billy-goat. . . .

When you find yourself at a feast where the wine is flowing freely, and where a woman shares the same couch with you, pray to that god whose mysteries are celebrated during the night, that the wine may not overcloud your brain. 'Tis then you may easily hold converse with your mistress in hidden words whereof she will easily divine the meaning. . . .

By subtle flatteries you may be able to steal into her heart, even as the river insensibly overflows the banks which fringe it. Never cease to sing the praises of her face, her hair, her taper fingers and her dainty foot. . . .

Tears, too, are a mighty useful resource in the matter of love. They would melt a diamond. Make a point, therefore, of letting your mistress see your face all wet with tears. Howbeit, if you can't manage to squeeze out any tears—and they won't always flow just when you want them to—put your finger in your eyes.

Source: *The Love Books of Ovid,* trans. J. L. May (New York: Rarity Press, 1930).

6-2a The Julio-Claudians (14–68 C.E.)

The Julio-Claudian rulers varied greatly in ability. Tiberius (r. 14–37 C.E.) was a competent general and an able administrator who tried initially to involve the senate in government. Caligula (kuh-LIG-yuh-luh) (r. 37–41) was a grandnephew of Tiberius and the great-grandson of Augustus. He exhibited tyrannical behavior and was extremely erratic. Claudius (KLAW-dee-uss) (r. 41–54) had been mistreated by his family because of a physical disability due to partial paralysis, but he was intelligent, well educated, and competent. He was followed by Nero (NEE-roh) (r. 54–68), who was only sixteen when he came to power. Nero's interest in the arts caused him to neglect affairs of state, especially the military, and that proved to be his undoing.

Several major tendencies emerged during the reigns of the four Julio-Claudians. In general, more and more of the responsibilities that Augustus had given to the senate tended to be taken over by the emperors. Moreover, Claudius instituted an imperial bureaucracy. He rationalized the central government by developing bureaucratic departments with talented freedmen as their chiefs. This practice further undermined the authority of the senators, who had previously shared in these responsibilities.

As the Julio-Claudian successors of Augustus began to behave openly like real rulers rather than "first citizens of the state," the opportunity for arbitrary and corrupt acts increased. Caligula, who became mentally unbalanced, wanted to be hailed as a god and neglected affairs of state while indulging his passions. Nero freely eliminated people he wanted out of the way, including his own mother, whom he had murdered. Without troops, the senators proved unable to oppose these excesses. Only the praetorian guard established by Augustus seemed capable of interfering with these rulers, but it did so in a manner that did not bode well for future stability. Caligula proved so unpredictable that the officers of the praetorian guard hatched a plot and assassinated him before he had ruled

The Fate of Cremona in the Year of the Four Emperors

 What does this selection from Tacitus tell you about the nature of the civil war in the Roman Empire? What were its results?

AFTER THE DEATH OF NERO in 68 C.E., a power struggle ensued that resulted in a year of confusion with four different emperors, each the leader of a field army. Galba replaced Nero and was succeeded by Otho, who was then defeated by Vitellius. Finally, Vespasian established a new dynasty. Some of the Italian cities suffered greatly in these struggles between Roman legions loyal to their commanders. This excerpt is from Tacitus's account of the destruction of Cremona by the forces that had declared for Vespasian.

Tacitus, *The Histories*

Forty thousand armed men forced their way into the city. . . . Neither rank nor years saved the victims from an indiscriminate orgy in which rape alternated with murder and murder with rape. Graybeards and frail old women, who had no value as loot, were dragged off to raise a laugh. But any full-grown girl or good-looking lad who crossed their path was pulled this way and that in a violent tug-of-war between the would-be captors, and finally drove them to destroy each other. A single looter trailing a hoard of money or temple-offerings of massive gold was often cut to pieces by others who were stronger. Some few turned up their noses at the obvious finds and inflicted flogging and torture on the owners in order to rummage after hidden valuables and dig for buried treasure. In their hands they held firebrands, which, once they had got their spoil away, they wantonly flung into the empty houses and rifled temples. It is not surprising that, in an army of varied tongues and conventions, including Romans, allies and foreigners [auxiliaries], there was a diversity of wild desires, differing conceptions of what was lawful, and nothing barred. Cremona lasted them four days. While all its buildings, sacred and secular, collapsed in flames, only the temple of Melitis [goddess of pestilential vapors] outside the walls remained standing, defended by its position or the power of the divinity.

Source: Tacitus, *The Histories*, trans. K. Wellesley (London: Penguin Classics, 1964; revised edition 1975).

---

for four complete years. Afterward, they chose Claudius, Caligula's uncle, as the next emperor and forced the senate to confirm their act, thereby demonstrating the power of the military units stationed around Rome.

The downfall of the Julio-Claudian dynasty came during the reign of Nero. His early reign had been quite successful. The young emperor worked hard and with the assistance of his childhood tutor, the philosopher Seneca (SEN-uh-kuh), gave the empire a sound government. But Nero soon tired of his duties and began to pursue other interests, including singing, acting, horse racing, and sexual excesses. After Seneca resigned his position in disgust in 62 C.E., Nero's rule deteriorated. His obsession with singing and acting in public was greeted with contempt by the senatorial class. At the same time, he aroused animosity by executing a number of prominent figures, including a popular general, on charges of treason. His actions finally led to a conspiracy, not by the praetorian guard, but by the Roman legions themselves. In 68, Galba (GAHL-buh), governor of one of the Spanish provinces, rose in revolt and secured the principate for himself. Nero, abandoned by his guards, committed suicide by stabbing himself in the throat after uttering his final words, "What an artist the world is losing in me."

6-2b The Flavians (69–96 C.E.)

Galba, however, was not readily accepted by the other provincial armies, which led to civil wars in 69 C.E., known as the year of the four emperors (see Historical Voices, "The Fate of Cremona," above). Finally, Vespasian (vess-PAY-zhun), commander of the legions in the east, established himself as sole ruler and his family as a new dynasty known as the Flavians. The significance of the year 69 was summed up precisely by the Roman historian Tacitus when he stated that "a well-hidden secret of the principate had been revealed: it was possible, it seemed, for an emperor to be chosen outside Rome"[10]—chosen, of course, by members of the Roman army.

The accession of Vespasian to the imperial power demonstrated that it was no longer necessary to be descended from an ancient aristocratic family to be emperor. In fact, the family of Vespasian (r. 69–79) was from the equestrian order. Once in control, he managed to reestablish the economy on a sound basis after the extravagances of Nero and the destruction wrought by the civil wars of 69. More important, Vespasian had no compunctions whatsoever about establishing the principle of dynastic succession for the principate. He was followed by his sons Titus (TY-tuss) (r. 79–81) and Domitian (doh-MISH-un) (r. 81–96). The Flavians, especially Domitian, dropped the pretense of the word princeps and began to use the title of imperator (emperor) freely. The emperor was rapidly becoming an absolute monarch.

6-2c The Five "Good Emperors" (96–180 C.E.)

Many historians see the **Pax Romana** (PAKS *or* PAHKS ro-MAH-nuh) ("Roman peace") and the prosperity it engendered as the chief benefits of Roman rule during the first and second centuries C.E. These benefits were especially noticeable during the reigns of the five so-called **good emperors**. These rulers treated the ruling classes with respect, cooperated with the senate, ended arbitrary executions, maintained peace in the empire, and supported domestic policies generally beneficial to the empire. Though absolute monarchs, they were known for their tolerance and diplomacy.

The first of the five good emperors was Nerva (NUR-vuh) (r. 96–98), chosen by the senate after the assassination of Domitian. By chance, Nerva and his next three successors had no sons and had to resort to adoption to obtain heirs. According to one Roman historian, "Nerva, therefore, finding himself held in such contempt by reason of his old age, ascended the Capitol and said in a loud voice: 'May good success attend the Roman senate and people and myself: I hereby adopt Marcus Ulpius Nerva Trajan.'"[11] Trajan (TRAY-jun) (r. 98–117) was a capable man who was also acceptable to the army, an increasingly important requirement. He had been born in Spain to an old Roman family and was the first emperor born outside Italy.

Trajan was succeeded by his second cousin Hadrian (r. 117–138), who spent years inspecting the provinces and restoring the military forces to good order. Hadrian adopted as his successor Antoninus Pius (an-tuh-NY-nuss PY-uss) (r. 138–161), who achieved a reputation as the most beneficent of the five good emperors. It was said of him that "one should behave in all things like a pupil of Antoninus: his energy on behalf of what was done in accord with reason, his equability everywhere, his serene expression, his sweetness, his disdain of glory, his ambition to grasp affairs."[12] Unlike Hadrian, who traveled extensively in the provinces, Antoninus Pius stayed in Rome and made even greater use of the senate. He in turn adopted Marcus Aurelius (MAR-kuss aw-REE-lee-uss) (r. 161–180), who has been viewed as a philosopher-king of the sort Plato envisioned (see Chapter 3). Highly influenced by Stoicism, Marcus Aurelius wrote his *Meditations*, reflecting on the ideal of Stoic duty as a religious concept.

Under the five good emperors, the powers of the emperor continued to expand at the expense of the senate. Increasingly, imperial officials appointed and directed by the emperor took over the running of the government. The five good emperors also extended the scope of imperial administration to areas previously untouched by the imperial government. Trajan established a program that provided state funds to assist poor parents in raising and educating their children. He was not motivated simply by benevolence, as he believed that such assistance would materially aid in creating a larger pool of young men in Italy eligible for military service.

The five good emperors were widely praised by their subjects for their extensive building programs. Trajan and Hadrian were especially active in constructing public works—aqueducts, bridges, roads, and harbor facilities—throughout the provinces and in Rome. Trajan built a new forum in Rome to provide a setting for his celebrated victory column. Hadrian's Pantheon, a temple of "all the gods," is one of the grandest ancient buildings surviving in Rome (see "6-3b Art in the Early Empire," later in this chapter).

While we are justified in praising the Roman Empire in the first and second centuries for its achievements, it is also important to remember its other side: the enormous gulf between rich and poor, the dependence upon enslaved or otherwise subject human beings, and the use of institutionalized terror to maintain the order for which the empire is so often praised.

Although we think of the Pax Romana as a time of peace and orderly government, there were rebellions against Roman rule. Revolts of Jews in Egypt and North Africa during the reign of Trajan in 115 C.E. were crushed. A revolt of native Egyptians in 139 was only suppressed after several years of fighting. Another Egyptian revolt during the reign of Marcus Aurelius in 172–173 was also suppressed but not without much damage to the economy. In 60 or 61, Boudica, the British queen of the Iceni tribe, revolted and led an attack against Roman rule that burned and destroyed several cities before Roman forces won out. Rebellions against Roman rule were crushed without mercy, leading one Scottish chieftain to say (according to the Roman author Tacitus) when rousing his troops to fight the Romans: "To robbery, slaughter, plunder, they give the lying name of empire; and where they make a solitude they call it peace" (see Historical Voices, "The Resistance to Rome," p. 157) Obviously, Roman imperialism had a negative as well as positive side. The chief source of resistance to the Roman authorities occurred with two Jewish revolts (66–70 and 132–135) to establish Jewish independence (see "6-5b The Jewish Background," later in this chapter).

6-2d The Roman Empire at Its Height: Frontiers and Provinces

At its height in the second century, the Roman Empire (see Map 6.1) covered about 3.5 million square miles and had a population, like that of Han China, estimated at more than 50 million. While the emperors and the imperial administration

CHRONOLOGY	Rulers of The Early Empire
Julio-Claudian Dynasty	
Augustus	31 B.C.E.–14 C.E.
Tiberius	14–37
Caligula	37–41
Claudius	41–54
Nero	54–68
Flavian Dynasty	
Vespasian	69–79
Titus	79–81
Domitian	81–96
Five Good Emperors	
Nerva	96–98
Trajan	98–117
Hadrian	117–138
Antoninus Pius	138–161
Marcus Aurelius	161–180

The Resistance to Rome: The Exhortations of Calgacus

 What was the purpose of Tactitus in creating this speech by Galgacus? How does Tacitus' view of Roman values, as seen in the speech of Calgacus, compare to those of Virgil in the Aeneid (see "Virgil," in Section 6-1e)?

THE FOLLOWING SELECTION is taken from the work of the Roman historian Tacitus (see "Tacitus," in Section 6-3a), who wrote a life of his father-in-law, Julius Agricola, a Roman general who undertook the invasion of Caledonia (the Roman name for what is now Scotland) in 80 C.E. In this work, Tacitus summarized the resistance of the Caledonians by creating a speech by the chieftain Calgacus urging his people to fight the Romans. Despite his exhortations, the Romans defeated the Caledonians at the battle of Mons Graupius in 84.

Tacitus, *The Life and Character of Julius Agricola*

For the Britons, indeed, in no way cowed by the result of the late engagement, had made up their minds to be either avenged or enslaved . . . and had . . . summoned forth the whole strength of all their state. More than 30,000 armed men were now to be seen, . . . men renowned in war. Meanwhile, among the many leaders, one superior to the rest in valor and in birth, Galgacus by name, is said to have thus harangued the multitude gathered around him and clamoring for battle:

"Whenever I consider the origin of this war and the necessities of our position, I have a sure confidence that this day, and this union of yours, will be the beginning of freedom to the whole of Britain. To all of us slavery is a thing unknown; there are no lands beyond us, and even the sea is not safe, menaced as we are by a Roman fleet. And

thus in war and battle, in which the brave find glory, even the coward will find safety. Former contests, in which, with varying fortune, the Romans were resisted, still left in us a last hope of succor, inasmuch as being the most renowned nation of Britain, dwelling in the very heart of the country, and out of sight of the shores of the conquered, we could keep even our eyes unpolluted by the contagion of slavery. To us who dwell on the uppermost confines of the earth, and of freedom, this remote sanctuary of Britain's glory has up to this time been a defense. Now, however, the furthest limits of Britain are thrown open, the unknown always passes for something peculiarly grand. But there are no tribes beyond us, nothing indeed but waves and rocks, and the yet more terrible Roman, from whose oppression escape is vainly sought by obedience and submission. Robbers of the world, having by their universal plunder exhausted the land, they rifle the deep. If the enemy be rich, they are rapacious; if he be poor, they lust for dominion; neither the east nor the west has been able to satisfy them. Alone among men they covet with equal eagerness poverty and riches. To robbery, slaughter, plunder they give the lying name of empire, and where they make a solitude they call it peace . . . .

All the incentives to victory are on our side. The Romans have no wives to kindle their courage, no parents to taunt them with flight; many have either no country or one far way. Few in number, dismayed by their ignorance, looking around upon a sky, a sea, and forests which are all unfamiliar to them; hemmed in, as it were, and enmeshed, the gods have delivered them into our hands . . . ."

They received his speech with enthusiasm, and as is usual among barbarians, with songs, shouts, and discordant cries.

Source: A. J. Church and W. J. Brodribb, trans. *The Agricola and Germany of Tacitus* (London, 1877), *The Agricola*, 29–33.

---

provided a degree of unity, considerable leeway was given to local customs, and the privileges of Roman citizenship were extended to many people throughout the empire. In 212 C.E., the emperor Caracalla (kar-uh-KAL-uh) completed the process by giving Roman citizenship to every free inhabitant of the empire. Since only citizens paid inheritance taxes, the emperor's gesture added an important source of revenue for the empire. Latin was the language of the western part of the empire, whereas Greek was used in the east. Although Roman culture spread to all parts of the empire, local languages persisted and many of the empire's residents spoke neither Latin nor Greek.

Roman Frontiers With the exception of Claudius's annexation of Britain, the first-century successors of Augustus had largely followed his advice to curb expansion and remain within

the natural frontiers of the empire—the ocean to the west, the rivers in the north, and the desert in the east and south.

Although Trajan broke with Augustus's policy of defensive imperialism by extending Roman rule into Dacia (modern Romania), Mesopotamia, and the Sinai peninsula, his conquests represent the high-water mark of Roman expansion. His successors recognized that the empire was overextended and pursued a policy of retrenchment. Hadrian withdrew Roman forces from much of Mesopotamia. Although he retained Dacia and Arabia, he went on the defensive in his frontier policy, reinforcing the fortifications along a line connecting the Rhine and Danube Rivers and building a defensive wall 80 miles long across northern Britain. By the end of the second century, the vulnerability of the empire had become apparent. Frontiers were stabilized, and the Roman forces were established in permanent bases behind the frontiers. But when one frontier was

MAP 6.1 **The Roman Empire from Augustus Through Trajan (14–117 C.E.).** Augustus and later emperors continued the expansion of the Roman Empire, adding more resources but also increasing the tasks of administration and keeping the peace. Compare this map with Map 5.4.

Q *Which territories were conquered by Augustus, and which were added by the end of Trajan's reign?*

attacked, troops had to be drawn from other frontiers, leaving them vulnerable. The empire lacked a real strategic reserve, and its weakness would become ever more apparent.

The Army The Roman army was the primary instrument for defending the Roman frontiers. In 14 C.E., it numbered twenty-eight legions but had increased to thirty by the time of Trajan. The auxiliaries were increased correspondingly, creating a Roman army of about 400,000 by the end of the second century. Since legionaries had to be Roman citizens, most recruits in Augustus's time were from Italy. Over the course of the first century, however, the Italians' reluctance to serve in the military led to the recruitment of citizens from the provinces. By 100, only one in five legionaries was Italian.

In addition to defense and protection, the Roman army also served as an important instrument for romanizing the provinces. Roman military camps became centers for the spread of the Latin language and Roman institutions and ways of

thought and conduct. The presence of large numbers of troops and their dependent women and slaves encouraged the development of trade and local production to meet the army's need for supplies. Urban centers developed around army bases or nearby colonies. Many cities along the Rhine had their roots in legionary bases or auxiliary forts (see Image 6.4). The city of Cologne, for example, grew out of the military colony the Romans called Colonia Agrippinensis. Since many veterans, when they retired, chose to remain in the new towns, establishing families and new businesses, the towns served to pass on Roman culture and attitudes to the people in the provinces.

HISTORIANS DEBATE **What Was Romanization?** Romanization is a controversial term. An earlier generation of historians used the term to describe a process of transformation in which the Roman governors of provinces imposed the Romans' "civilized" ways on conquered peoples. Many historians today reject that model and argue that becoming

Porta Nigra, Trier, Rhineland Palatinate, Germany 2nd century AD/Roman, (2nd century AD)/DE AGOSTINI EDITORE/Trier, Germany/Bridgeman Images

IMAGE 6.4 Rome in Germany. The Roman army helped bring Roman culture and institutions to the provinces. Local production and trade grew up around the military camps to meet the soldiers' needs, and cities often developed from the bases themselves or from colonies located nearby. Pictured are the remains of the Porta Nigra, or gateway to the Roman city of Augusta Treverorum (modern Trier). In the early empire, Trier became the headquarters of the imperial procurator of Belgica and the two Germanies. Its close location to Roman military camps along the Rhine enabled it to flourish as one of the most significant cities in the Western Roman Empire.

Roman—i.e., adopting its architecture, food, clothing, language, and religious policy—was a process initiated by local elites themselves who adopted the trappings of Roman civilization because being Roman was a means to power. Thus, the elites of the western provinces followed a policy of "self-romanization." The Roman historian Tacitus described the process in Roman Britain: "Hence, too, a liking sprang up for our style of dress, and the toga became fashionable. Step by step they were led to things which dispose to vice, the lounge, the bath, the elegant banquet. All this in their ignorance, they called civilization, when it was but a part of their servitude."[13]

The eastern part of the empire presented a different picture. The Greek language was dominant and the pre-Roman, Hellenistic culture survived. Instead of self-romanization, some historians use the term "culture of classicism" to refer to ways in the east. At the same time, although Roman and Greek culture spread to all parts of the empire, local languages persisted, and many of the empire's residents spoke neither Latin nor Greek.

Cities The administration and cultural life of the Roman Empire depended greatly on cities and towns. A provincial governor's staff was not large, so it was left to local city officials to act as Roman agents in carrying out many government functions, especially those related to taxes. Most towns and cities were not large by modern standards. The largest was Rome, but there were also some large cities in the east: Alexandria in Egypt numbered over 300,000 inhabitants, Ephesus in Asia Minor had 200,000, and Antioch in Syria had around 150,000. In the west, cities were usually small, with only a few thousand inhabitants. Cities were important in the spread of Roman culture, law, and the Latin language. They were also uniform in physical appearance, with similar temples, markets, amphitheaters, and other public buildings as rich men and women in the provinces sought the favor of the emperor by building a scaled-down version of the city of Rome.

Magistrates and town councillors chosen from the ranks of the wealthy upper classes directed municipal administration. Although these municipal offices were unsalaried, wealthy citizens were eager to hold them because they conferred prestige and power at the local level as well as Roman citizenship. Roman municipal policy effectively tied the upper classes to Roman rule and ensured that these classes would retain control over the rest of the population.

Significant changes also occurred in the governing classes of the empire. In the course of the first century, there was a noticeable decline in the number of senators from Italian families. By the end of the second century, Italian senators made up less than half the total. The Roman senate was increasingly being recruited from wealthy provincial equestrian families. The provinces also provided many of the legionaries for the Roman army and, beginning with Trajan, supplied many of the emperors.

As we have seen, however, the extent and speed of becoming Roman varied widely in different areas of the empire. In the western areas where Greeks and Phoenicians had established cities centuries earlier, such as Spain, Africa, and parts of Gaul, the process occurred quickly. Temples, aqueducts, amphitheaters, and the Latin language all became a regular part of life in these areas. In other parts of the empire, however, especially in Asia, towns and cities had their own traditions free of Roman influence. Their common language was Greek, not Latin, and many people outside the urban areas spoke neither Latin nor Greek. Even more important than geography in determining the degree of becoming Roman, however, was class status. By 200 C.E., the upper classes everywhere in the empire had come to share a common culture as well as similar economic and social interests.

Roman Law As Roman citizenship spread in the cities, the new citizens became subject to Roman law. The early empire experienced great progress in the study and codification of law. The second and third centuries C.E. witnessed the classical age of Roman law, a period in which a number of great jurists classified and compiled basic legal principles that have proved valuable to the Western world. Most jurists emphasized the emperor as the source of law: "What has pleased the emperor has the force of law."

During the classical age of Roman law, the identification of the law of nations with natural law led to a concept of natural rights. According to the jurist Ulpian (d. 228), natural rights implied that all men are born equal and should therefore be equal before the law. In practice, however, the principle was not applied.

The Romans did, however, establish standards of justice, applicable to all people, that included principles that we would immediately recognize. A person was considered innocent until proved otherwise. People accused of wrongdoing were allowed to defend themselves before a judge. A judge was expected to weigh evidence carefully before arriving at a decision. These principles lived on in Western civilization long after the fall of the Roman Empire.

For Roman citizens, Roman law provided a uniform system of principles by which they conducted their affairs and led their lives. After Roman citizenship was extended to all free persons in the empire in 212 C.E., Roman law became an even more significant factor in binding the entire empire together.

6-2e Prosperity in the Early Empire

The early empire was a period of considerable prosperity. Internal peace resulted in unprecedented levels of trade (see Map 6.2). Merchants from all over the empire came to the chief Italian ports of Puteoli on the Bay of Naples and Ostia at the mouth of the Tiber. The importation of large quantities of grain to feed the populace of Rome and an incredible quantity of luxury items for the wealthy upper classes in the west led to a steady drain of gold and silver coins from Italy and the west to the eastern part of the empire.

Long-distance trade beyond the Roman frontiers also flourished during the early empire. Developments in both the Roman and Chinese empires helped foster the growth of this trade. Although both empires built roads chiefly for military purposes, the roads also facilitated trade. Moreover, by creating large empires, the Romans and Chinese not only established internal stability but also pacified bordering territories, thus reducing the threat that bandits posed to traders. As a result, merchants developed a network of trade routes that brought these two great empires into commercial contact. Most important was the overland Silk Road, a regular caravan route between west and east (see Map 6.3).

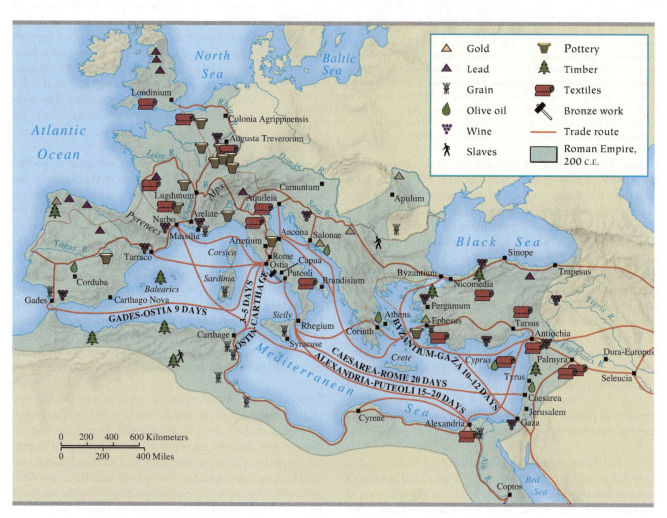

MAP 6.2 Trade Routes and Products in the Roman Empire, ca. 200 C.E. Although still primarily an agrarian economy, the Roman Empire provided the single currency and stable conditions necessary for an expansion of trade in various commodities and products. An extensive system of roads and shipping routes also facilitated trade.

Q *What truth is there to the statement that "all roads lead to Rome"?*

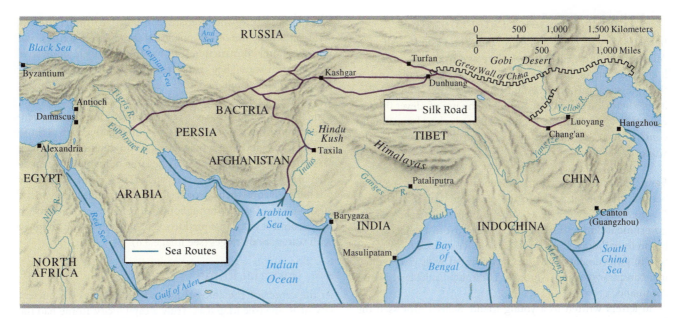

MAP 6.3 **The Silk Road**

The Silk Road received its name from the Chinese export of silk cloth, which became a popular craze among Roman elites, leading to a vast outpouring of silver from Rome to China and provoking the Roman emperor Tiberius to grumble that the ladies and their trinkets were transferring money to "foreigners." The silk trade also stimulated a degree of mutual curiosity between the two great civilizations, but not much mutual knowledge or understanding. There was little personal or diplomatic contact between the two civilizations, but Chinese sources do reveal that a delegation from the emperor Marcus Aurelius arrived in China in 166 and that a Roman merchant made it to the court of Emperor Wu in 226. After the takeover of Egypt in the first century C.E., Roman merchants also began an active trade with India, from where they received precious pearls as well as pepper and other spices used in the banquets of the wealthy. The Romans even established a trading post in southern India, where their merchants built warehouses and docks.

The increased trade helped stimulate manufacturing. The cities of the east still produced the items made in Hellenistic times (see Chapter 4). The first two centuries of the empire also witnessed the high point of industrial development in Italy. Some industries became concentrated in certain areas, such as bronze work in Capua and pottery in Arretium in Etruria. Other industries, such as brickmaking, were pursued in rural areas on large landed estates. Much industrial production remained small-scale and was done by individual artisans, usually freedmen or slaves. In the course of the first century, Italian centers of industry experienced increasing competition from the provinces.

Despite the extensive trade and commerce, agriculture remained the chief occupation of most people and the underlying basis of Roman prosperity. While the large landed estates called *latifundia* still dominated agriculture, especially in southern and central Italy, small peasant farms persisted, particularly in Etruria and the Po valley. Although large estates concentrating on sheep and cattle raising used slave labor, the lands of some latifundia were worked by free tenant farmers called *coloni* (kuh-LOH-nee). Coloni were essentially sharecroppers who paid rent in labor, produce, or sometimes cash.

In considering the prosperity of the Roman world, it is important to remember the enormous gulf between rich and poor underlying it. The development of towns and cities, so important to the creation of any civilization, is based to a large degree on the agricultural surpluses of the countryside. In ancient times, the margin of surplus produced by each farmer was relatively small. Therefore, the upper classes and urban populations had to be supported by the labor of a large number of agricultural producers who never found it easy to produce much more than enough for themselves. In lean years, when there were no surpluses, the townspeople often took what they wanted, leaving little for the peasants.

6-3 Roman Culture and Society in the Early Empire

 FOCUS QUESTIONS: What were the chief intellectual, artistic, and social developments in the early empire? How did these differ from the intellectual, artistic, and social developments of the republic?

The shift from republic to empire not only transformed the Roman political world but also affected its cultural and social life. Intellectuals found ways to accommodate the autocratic rule of emperors while Roman architects created massive buildings befitting an empire. Gladiatorial games and slavery increased dramatically during the early empire, while upper-class women acquired greater independence.

6-3a The Silver Age of Latin Literature

In the history of Latin literature, the century and a half after Augustus is often labeled the silver age to indicate that the literary efforts of the period, while good, were not equal to the high standards of the Augustan golden age. The popularity of rhetorical training encouraged the use of clever literary expressions, often at the expense of original and meaningful content. A good example of this trend can be found in the works of Seneca.

Seneca Educated in Rome, Seneca (ca. 4 B.C.E.–65 C.E.) became strongly attached to the philosophy of Stoicism (see Chapter 4). After serving as tutor to Nero, he helped run the government during the first five years of Nero's reign. Seneca began to withdraw from politics after Nero took a more active role in government. In 65, he was charged with involvement in a conspiracy against Nero and committed suicide at Nero's command.

In letters written to a young friend, Seneca expressed the basic tenets of Stoicism: living according to nature, accepting events dispassionately as part of the divine plan, and a universal love for all humanity. Thus, "the first thing philosophy promises us is the feeling of fellowship, of belonging to mankind and being members of a community. . . . Philosophy calls for simple living, not for doing penance, and the simple way of life need not be a crude one."[14] Viewed in retrospect, Seneca displays some glaring inconsistencies. While preaching the virtues of simplicity, he amassed a fortune and was ruthless at times in protecting it. His letters show humanity, benevolence, and fortitude, but his sentiments are often undermined by an attempt to be clever with words.

Tacitus The greatest historian of the silver age was Tacitus (ca. 56–120). His main works included the *Annals* and the *Histories*, which presented a narrative account of Roman history from the reign of Tiberius through the assassination of Domitian in 96. Tacitus believed that history had a moral purpose: "It seems to me a historian's foremost duty to ensure that merit is recorded, and to confront evil deeds and words with the fear of posterity's denunciations."[15] As a member of the senatorial class, Tacitus was disgusted with the abuses of power perpetrated by the emperors and was determined that the evil deeds of wicked men would not be forgotten. Many historians believe he went too far in projecting the evils of his own day back into his account of the past. Tacitus's work *Germania* is especially important as a source of information about the early Germans. But it too is colored by his attempt to show the Germans as noble savages in contrast to the decadent Roman upper classes.

6-3b Art in the Early Empire

The Romans contributed little that was original to painting and sculpture. Much work was done by Greek artists and craftspeople who adhered to the Roman desire for realism and attention to details. Wall paintings and frescoes in the houses of the rich realistically depicted landscapes, portraits, and scenes from mythological stories.

In architecture, the Romans continued to imitate Greek styles and made use of colonnades, rectangular structures, and post-and-lintel construction. But the Romans were innovative in their own way. They made considerable use of curvilinear forms: the arch, vault, and dome (see Image 6.5). The Romans were the first people in antiquity to use concrete on a massive scale. By combining concrete and curvilinear forms, they were able to construct massive buildings—public baths, such as those of Caracalla, and amphitheaters, the most famous of which was the Colosseum in Rome. These large buildings were made possible by Roman engineering skills. These same skills were put to use in constructing roads (the Romans built a network of 50,000 miles of roads throughout their empire), aqueducts (in Rome, almost a dozen aqueducts kept the population supplied with water), and bridges (see Image 6.6).

6-3c Imperial Rome

At the center of the colossal Roman Empire was the ancient city of Rome (see Map 6.4). Truly a capital city, Rome had the largest population of any city in the empire. It is estimated that its population was close to one million by the time of Augustus. For anyone with ambitions, Rome was the place to be. A magnet to many people, Rome was extremely cosmopolitan. Nationalities from all over the empire resided there, with entire neighborhoods inhabited by specific groups, such as Greeks and Syrians.

Rome was no doubt an overcrowded and noisy city. Because of the congestion, carts and wagons were banned from the streets during the day, but their noisy traffic at night often made sleep difficult. Evening pedestrian travel was dangerous. Although Augustus had organized a police force, lone travelers might be assaulted, robbed, or soaked by filth thrown out of the upper-story windows of Rome's massive apartment buildings.

An enormous gulf existed between rich and poor in the city of Rome. While the rich had comfortable villas, the poor lived in apartment blocks called *insulae* that might be six stories high. Constructed of concrete, they were often poorly built and prone to collapse. The use of wooden beams in the floors and movable stoves, torches, candles, and lamps for heat and light created a constant danger of fire. Once started, fires were extremely difficult to put out. The famous conflagration of 64, which Nero was unjustly accused of starting, devastated a large part of the city. In addition to the hazards of collapse and fire, living conditions were miserable. High rents forced entire families into one room. In the absence of plumbing and central heating, conditions were so uncomfortable that poorer Romans spent most of their time outdoors in the streets.

Fortunately for these people, Rome boasted public buildings unequaled anywhere in the empire. Its temples, forums, markets, baths, theaters, triumphal arches, governmental buildings, and amphitheaters gave parts of the city an appearance of grandeur and magnificence.

Though the center of a great empire, Rome was also a great parasite. Beginning with Augustus, the emperors accepted responsibility for providing food for the urban populace, with about 200,000 people receiving free grain. But even the free

IMAGE 6.5a

IMAGE 6.5 **The Pantheon.** Image 6.5a shows the exterior of the Pantheon, one of Rome's greatest buildings. Constructed of brick, six kinds of concrete, and marble, it was a stunning example of the Romans' engineering skills. The outside porch of the Pantheon contained eighteen Corinthian granite columns, quarried in Egypt, but it was the inside of the temple that amazed onlookers. The interior, shown in Image 6.5b, is a large circular space topped by a huge dome. A hole in the center of the roof was the only source of light. The dome, built up by layer after layer of concrete, weighs 5,000 tons. The walls holding the dome are almost 20 feet thick.

IMAGE 6.5b

grain did not relieve the grim conditions of the poor. Early in the second century c.e., a Roman doctor claimed that rickets was common among the city's children.

In addition to food, entertainment was provided on a grand scale for the inhabitants of Rome. The poet Juvenal said of the Roman masses: "Nowadays, with no vote to sell, their motto is 'Couldn't care less.' Time was when their vote elected generals, heads of state, commanders of legions: but now they've pulled in their horns, there's only two things that concern them: Bread and Circuses."[16] The emperor and other state officials provided public spectacles as part of the great festivals—most of them religious in origin—celebrated by the state. More than one hundred days a year were given over to these public holidays. The festivals included three major types of entertainment. At the Circus Maximus, horse and chariot races attracted hundreds of thousands, while dramatic and other performances were held in theaters. But the most famous of all the public spectacles were the gladiatorial shows.

IMAGE 6.6 **Roman Aqueduct.** The engineering skills of the Romans enabled them to build massive constructions, including aqueducts such as this one in southern France, known as the Pont du Gard. The Pont du Gard is a three-story bridge built of blocks of stone without cement; at the top was a channel that carried water. Nîmes received its water from a source 30 miles away. Since gravity kept the water flowing, the channels holding the water had to have a gradual decline from the source of the water to its final destination. The Pont du Gard, which crosses the Gardon River outside Nîmes, was built to the exact height needed to maintain the flow of water into the city.

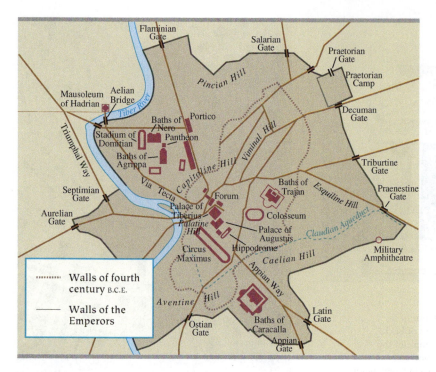

MAP 6.4 **Imperial Rome.** A large, overcrowded, and dirty city, Rome was the political, economic, social, and cultural hub of the Roman Empire. Squalid and desperate living conditions for the poor contrasted dramatically with the city's magnificent architectural works.

Q *How did roads from outside enter Rome, and what could possibly explain this?*

6-3d The Gladiatorial Shows

The gladiatorial shows were an integral part of Roman society. They took place in amphitheaters; the first permanent one was constructed in Rome in 29 B.C.E. Perhaps the most famous was the Flavian amphitheater, called the Colosseum, constructed in Rome under Vespasian and his son Titus to seat 50,000 spectators. Amphitheaters were constructed throughout the empire. They varied in size, with capacities ranging from a few thousand to tens of thousands. Considerable resources and ingenuity went into building them, especially in the arrangements for moving wild beasts efficiently into the arena. In most cities and towns, amphitheaters came to be the biggest buildings, rivaled only by the circuses for races and the public baths. As we shall see repeatedly in the course of Western civilization, where a society invests its money gives an idea of its priorities. Since the amphitheater was the primary location for the gladiatorial games, it is fair to say that public slaughter was an important part of Roman culture.

Gladiatorial games were held from dawn to dusk. Their main features were contests to the death between trained fighters. Most gladiators were slaves or condemned criminals who were trained for combat in special gladiatorial schools (see *Movies & History, Gladiator*).

Gladiatorial games included other forms of entertainment as well. Criminals of all ages and both genders were sent into the arena without weapons to face certain death from wild animals who would tear them to pieces. Numerous kinds of animal contests were also held: wild beasts against each other, such as bears against buffalo; staged hunts with men shooting safely from behind iron bars; and gladiators in the arena with bulls, tigers, and lions. Reportedly, five thousand beasts were killed in one day of games when the emperor

MOVIES & HISTORY
Gladiator (2000)

Watch **Gladiator**, a fictional story set in the Roman Empire near the end of the second century C.E. In the movie, Emperor Marcus Aurelius informs his son Commodus that he intends to turn over imperial power to his successful and respected general Maximus, setting off a violent chain of events. Although *Gladiator* shows little concern for historical facts, the movie became one of the highest earning films of 2000.

Q *Gladiator is a relatively exciting story, but how much of it is based on historical facts? Why do you think it was such a popular film?*

Titus inaugurated the Colosseum in 80 C.E. (see Image 6.7). Enormous resources were invested in capturing and shipping wild animals for slaughter, and whole species were hunted to extinction in parts of the empire.

These bloodthirsty spectacles were extremely popular with the Roman people. Tacitus reported, "Few indeed are to be found who talk of any other subjects in their homes, and whenever we enter a classroom, what else is the conversation of the youths."[17] But the gladiatorial games served a purpose beyond mere entertainment. Like the other forms of public entertainment, the games fulfilled both a political and a social function.

Thomas S. England/Science Source

IMAGE 6.7 **Interior of the Colosseum of Rome.** The Colosseum was a large amphitheater constructed under the emperor Vespasian and his son Titus. Such amphitheaters, in which gladiatorial contests were held, were built throughout the empire. They varied in size, but the one in Rome was the largest. The Colosseum was named after the Colossus of Nero, a large statue of the first-century C.E. emperor that stood nearby. The scene of many bloody gladiatorial combats, the Colosseum could be used for other spectacles as well. It was flooded for a spectacular naval battle when the emperor Titus held the first games there.

Certainly, the games served to divert the idle masses from political unrest. It was said of the emperor Trajan that he understood that although the distribution of grain and money satisfied the individual, spectacles were necessary for the contentment of the masses.

6-3e Disaster in Southern Italy

Humans contrived gladiatorial spectacles, but the Roman Empire also experienced some horrific natural spectacles. One of the greatest was the eruption of Mount Vesuvius (vuh-SOO-vee-uss) on August 24, 79 C.E. Although known to be a volcano, Vesuvius was thought to be extinct, its hillsides green with flourishing vineyards. Its eruption threw up thousands of tons of lava and ash. Toxic fumes killed many people, and the nearby city of Pompeii (pahm-PAY) was quickly buried under volcanic ash. To the west, Herculaneum and other communities around the Bay of Naples were submerged beneath a mud flow. Not for another 1,700 years were systematic excavations begun on the buried towns. The examination of their preserved remains has enabled archaeologists to reconstruct the everyday life and art of these Roman towns. Their discovery in the eighteenth century was an important force in stimulating both scholarly and public interest in classical antiquity and helped give rise to the neoclassical style of that century.

6-3f The Art of Medicine

Although early Romans had no professional physicians, they did possess an art of medicine. Early Roman medicine was essentially herbal. The *paterfamilias* would prepare various remedies to heal wounds and cure illnesses. Knowledge of the healing properties of plants was passed down from generation to generation. This traditional approach to medicine continued throughout the early empire.

As in other areas of Roman life, Greek influence was also felt in medicine. At the end of the third century B.C.E., scientific medicine entered the Roman world through professional practitioners from the Hellenistic world. Doctors became fashionable in Rome, although prejudice against them was never completely abandoned. Many were Greek slaves who belonged to the households of large aristocratic families. The first public doctors in Rome were attached to the Roman army. Military practices were then extended to imperial officials and their families in the provinces and included the establishment of public hospitals. Gladiatorial schools had their own resident doctors as well. In fact, one of the most famous physicians, the Greek Galen (129–199 C.E.), emerged from the ranks of gladiatorial doctors to become court physician to the emperor Marcus Aurelius. Roman scientific medicine also witnessed the development of numerous specialists. For example, Alcon, the famous surgeon of the Flavian age, specialized in bone diseases and hernia operations.

6-3g Slaves and Their Masters

The number of slaves had increased dramatically during the Roman republic as the empire expanded through warfare. Consequently, slaves were highly visible in the early empire. Slaves filled the residences of the rich. Possessing a large number of slaves was a status symbol; a single household might include dozens of slaves, serving as hairdressers, footmen, messengers, accountants, secretaries, carpenters, plumbers, librarians, goldsmiths, and doctors as well as ordinary domestic servants. The reliance on slaves, especially as skilled craftspeople, undoubtedly created unemployment among the free population. Some slaves worked at high-status jobs as architects and managers of businesses, while some imperial slaves held positions in the government bureaucracy. Slaves were also used on landed estates.

But the number of slaves probably peaked in the early empire. The defensive imperial policies pursued after Augustus led to a decline in the supply of slaves from foreign conquest. Manumission also contributed to the decline in the number of slaves. It had been customary in Rome for "good masters" to free their slaves, especially well-educated ones or good workers. Although freedmen became Roman citizens, they did not receive full rights of citizenship. They could vote but not run for office.

Many authors have commented on the supposed advance in humanitarian attitudes toward slaves in the early empire, especially in the second century. They argue that the philosophy of Stoicism, with its emphasis on the universality of humanity, had an influence in this direction. Seneca stressed the need for kindness to slaves. Very likely, however, the practical Romans were as much, if not more, concerned about the usefulness of their slaves as about any humanitarian attitudes. New laws in the second century moralized more than they actually improved the condition of slaves. Hadrian, for example, forbade the sale of slaves for immoral or gladiatorial purposes, but such laws had little impact on how masters actually treated their slaves. Despite the changes, there were still instances of slaves murdering their owners, and many Romans continued to live in fear of their slaves (see Historical Voices, "The Roman Fear of Slaves," p. 167).

6-3h The Upper-Class Roman Family

By the second century C.E., significant changes were occurring in the Roman family. The foundations of the authority of the paterfamilias over his family, which had already begun to weaken in the late Republic, were further undermined. The paterfamilias no longer had absolute authority over his children; he could no longer sell them into slavery or have them put to death (see Images of Everyday Life, "Children in the Roman World," p. 168). Moreover, the husband's absolute authority over his wife also disappeared, a process that had begun in the late republic (see Chapter 5). In the early empire, the idea of male guardianship continued to weaken significantly, and by the late second century, it had become a mere formality.

Upper-class Roman women in the early empire had considerable freedom and independence (see Global Perspectives, "Women in the Roman and Han Empires," on p. 169). They had acquired the right to own, inherit, and dispose of property. Upper-class women could attend races, the theater, and events in the amphitheater, although in the latter two places they were forced to sit in separate female sections. Moreover, ladies of rank were still accompanied by maids and companions when they went out. Some women operated businesses, such as shipping firms. Women still could not participate in politics, but the early empire saw a number of important women who influenced politics through their husbands or sons, including Livia, the wife of Augustus; Agrippina, the mother of Nero; and Plotina, the wife of Trajan.

At the end of the first century and beginning of the second, there was a noticeable decline in the number of children among the upper classes, a trend that had already begun in the late republic. Especially evident was an increase in childless marriages. Despite imperial laws aimed at increasing the number of children, the low birthrate persisted. Not only did **infanticide** continue to be practiced, but upper-class Romans also used contraception and abortion to limit their families. There were numerous techniques for contraception. Though highly touted, amulets, magical formulas, and potions to induce temporary sterility proved ineffective, as did the rhythm method, since Roman medical writers believed that a woman was most fertile just when menstruation was ending. A more dependable practice involved the use of oils, ointments, and soft wool to obstruct the opening of the uterus. Contraceptive techniques for males were also advocated. An early version of a condom used the bladder of a goat, but it was prohibitively expensive. Although the medical sources do not mention it, the Romans may also have used the ubiquitous coitus interruptus. Abortion was practiced with use of drugs or surgical instruments. Ovid chastises Corinna: "Ah, women, why will you thrust and pierce with the instrument, and give dire poisons to your children yet unborn?"[18]

Women also faced great dangers in childbirth. They gave birth at home with the assistance of a midwife and a few female relatives. Fathers-to-be and other males were not present. Although exact numbers are not available, we do know that many upper-class women between the ages of sixteen and thirty-five died in childbirth. Prominent women who died in childbirth or soon after due to complications include Cicero's daughter Tullia and Caesar's daughter Julia.

6-4 Transformation of the Roman World: Crises in the Third Century

 FOCUS QUESTION: What political, military, economic, and social problems did the Roman Empire face during the third century?

During the reign of Marcus Aurelius, the last of the five good emperors, a number of natural catastrophes struck Rome. Floods of the Tiber, famine, and plague brought back from the east by the army led to a considerable loss of the population and a shortage of military manpower. Some historians have estimated that after the plagues of the 160s–170s C.E. and the wars of Marcus Aurelius the population of the empire declined, possibly from its height in the second century C.E. of 65 million to 40 million. To many Romans, these natural disasters seemed to portend an ominous future for Rome. New problems arose soon after the death of Marcus Aurelius.

6-4a Political and Military Woes

Unlike the first four good emperors, who chose capable successors by adopting competent men as their sons, Marcus Aurelius allowed his own son, Commodus (KAHM-uh-duss) (r. 180–192), to become emperor. A cruel man, Commodus

The Roman Fear of Slaves

 What do these selections reveal about the practice of slavery in the Roman Empire? What were Roman attitudes toward the events discussed in these documents?

THE LOWEST STRATUM of the Roman population consisted of slaves. They were used extensively in households and the court, as craftspeople in industrial enterprises, as business managers, and in numerous other ways. Although some historians have argued that slaves were treated more humanely during the early empire, these selections by the Roman historian Tacitus and the Roman statesman Pliny indicate that slaves still rebelled against their masters because of mistreatment. Many masters continued to live in fear of their slaves, as witnessed by the saying "as many enemies as you have slaves."

Tacitus, *The Annals of Imperial Rome*

The City Prefect, Lucius Pedanius Secundus, was murdered by one of his slaves [in 61 C.E.]. Either Pedanius had refused to free the murderer after agreeing to a price, or the slave, in a homosexual infatuation, found competition from his master intolerable. After the murder, ancient custom required that every slave residing under the same roof must be executed. But a crowd gathered, eager to save so many innocent lives; and rioting began. The senate-house was besieged. Inside, there was feeling against excessive severity, but the majority opposed any change. Among the latter was Gaius Cassius Longinus, who when his turn came spoke as follows. . . .

"An ex-consul has been deliberately murdered by a slave in his own home. None of his fellow-slaves prevented or betrayed the murderer, though the senatorial decree threatening the whole household with execution still stands. Exempt them from the penalty if you like. But then, if the City Prefect was not important enough to be immune, who will be? Who will have enough slaves to protect him if

Pedanius's 400 were too few? Who can rely on his household's help if even fear for their own lives does not make them shield us?" [The sentence of death was carried out.]

Pliny, Letter to Acilius

An atrocious business this—and one deserving a better record than a mere letter—the treatment which Larcius Macedo, a man of praetorian rank, has suffered at the hands of his slaves. He was in general a haughty and cruel master, and one who did not sufficiently remember that his own father had been a slave, or rather who remembered it too well. He was bathing at his villa near Formiae, when all of a sudden his slaves surrounded him: one sprang at his throat, another struck him on the face, a third inflicted blows on his chest and belly, and even, horrible to relate, in his private parts. When they thought the breath was out of him, they threw him on the hot pavement, to ascertain whether he was still alive. On seeing him extended without motion—either because he was really senseless, or else pretended to be so—they were satisfied that they had done for him. Then, at last, they carried him out, under pretence that he had been suffocated by the heat. His more confidential servants received the body, and his mistresses ran up with wailings and shrieks. Whereupon, roused by the sound of voices, and refreshed by the coolness of the place, he showed that he was alive—he could do it safely now—by opening his eyes and by the movements of his body. The slaves fled, of whom the greater number have been arrested, and the remainder are being searched for. He himself, having been nursed with difficulty for some days, died, not without the satisfaction of seeing them punished, for he was avenged during his lifetime as persons usually are after they have been slain.

You see to what a number of dangers and affronts and mockeries we are exposed; nor has any one reason to feel secure on the ground of being easy-going and indulgent, for masters are assassinated, not upon a judgment of their conduct, but from sheer wickedness.

Source: *The Letters of the Younger Pliny*, translated by John Delaware Lewis, M.A. (London: Trubner & Co., 1879).

---

was a poor choice, and his assassination led to a brief renewal of civil war until Septimius Severus (sep-TIM-ee-uss se-VEER-uss) (r. 193–211), who was born in North Africa and spoke Latin with an accent, used his legions to seize power (see Image 6.9). One contemporary described him as "small of stature but powerful, ... mentally he was very keen and very vigorous." On his deathbed, Septimius advised his sons, "Agree among yourselves, enrich the soldiers, and despise all the others."[19] His advice set the tone for the new dynasty he established. The Severan rulers (r. 193–235) began to create a military monarchy. The army was expanded, soldiers' pay was increased, and military officers were appointed to important government positions. A new stability seemed at hand, but the increased power

of the military led new military leaders to aspire to become emperor. In 235, a senior army officer named Maximinus, who was described "by his birth and normal behavior" as a barbarian who possessed a "bloodthirsty temperament" murdered the teenage emperor Alexander Severus and his mother. Three years later Maximinus's own soldiers killed him and his son. The military monarchy of the Severan rulers ended with the beginning of military anarchy.

For the next fifty years (235–284), the empire was mired in the chaos of continual civil war. Contenders for the imperial throne found that bribing soldiers was an effective way to become emperor, and the Roman imperial throne became occupied by anyone who had the military strength to seize it.

Children in the Roman World

Q *What are the similarities and differences between the Greek (see Chapter 3) and Roman treatment of children?*

LIKE THE GREEKS, the Romans did not always raise all the children born into their families. Deformed children were exposed to die, and infant mortality rates were high—as many as half of all infants did not survive into adulthood. Nevertheless, upper-class families did take good care of their surviving children. The statue of a young boy shown in Image 6.8a reflects this concern. He is wearing a bulla (also seen in Image 6.8b), a golden amulet given to male children on the day they were named, nine days after birth, to protect them against evil spirits. As shown in Image 6.8c, boys were encouraged to engage in athletic games at a very young age. Image 6.8d shows a scene from a third-century sarcophagus, depicting an idealized version of an upper-class child's life: being breast-fed by his mother, being held by his father, playing in a small chariot pulled by a goat, and reciting to his father. The father was largely responsible for providing for the education of his children. Roman boys learned reading and writing, moral principles and family values, law, and physical training to prepare them to be soldiers. Girls learned at home what they needed to know to be good wives and mothers.

The end of childhood for Roman males came at the age of sixteen, when the young man gave up his bulla, exchanged his purple-edged toga for a plain white toga—the toga of manhood—and soon after began his career. For Roman girls, childhood ended at age fourteen, the common age of marriage. Lower-class children were put to work in their teens and often apprenticed to a craftsperson at the age of twelve. Slave children were expected to work when they were five.

Gianni Dagli Orti/The Art Archive at Art Resource, NY

IMAGE 6.8a

Chronicle/Alamy Stock Photo

IMAGE 6.8b

DeAgostini/Superstock

IMAGE 6.8c

Roman/Getty Images

IMAGE 6.8d

Women in the Roman and Han Empires

Q *What are the views of Gaius Musonius Rufus and Ban Zhao on the responsibilities of a woman? In what ways do they agree? In what ways do they disagree? How do you explain the differences? From your point of view, what are the strengths and weaknesses in each argument?*

AS WE SAW IN CHAPTER 4, two great empires existed at the same time, the Roman Empire in the west and the Han Chinese Empire in the east. The two excerpts below are taken from the works of writers from these two great empires: one is a male philosopher living in the Roman Empire and the other is from a female writer in Han China. Although they reflect different cultures, they have similar ideas about the role and education of women. Gaius Musonius Rufus was a philosopher who taught Stoicism in Rome in the first century c.e. His students wrote down some of his philosophical opinions. The excerpt here is taken from his thoughts on whether women should study philosophy. Ban Zhao was a well-educated woman from a prominent aristocratic family. She wrote *Admonitions for Women* as a guide for upper-class women in the proper performance of their wifely duties.

Gaius Musonius Rufus, "That Women Too Should Study Philosophy"

When he was asked whether women ought to study philosophy, he began to answer. . . . Women have received from the gods the same ability to reason that men have. . . . Likewise women have the same senses as men, sight, hearing, smell, and the rest. . . . Since that is so, why is it appropriate for men to seek out and examine how they might live well, that is, to practice philosophy, but not women? . . .

Let us consider in detail the qualities that a woman who seeks to be good must possess, for it will be apparent that she could acquire each of these qualities from the practice of philosophy.

In the first place a woman must run her household and pick out what is beneficial for her home and take charge of the household slaves. . . . Next a woman must be chaste, and capable of keeping herself free from illegal love affairs . . . and not enjoy quarrels, not be extravagant or occupied with her appearance. . . . There are still other requirements: she must control anger, and not be overcome by grief, and be stronger than every kind of emotion. . . .

[When asked if sons and daughters should be given the same education, he replied] There are not different sets of virtues for men and women. First, men and women both need to be sensible. . . . Second, both need to live just lives. . . . Third, a wife ought to be chaste, and so should a husband . . .

Well, then, suppose someone says, "Do you think that men ought to learn spinning like women and that women ought to practice gymnastics like men?" No, that is not what I suggest. I say that because in the case of the human race, the males are naturally stronger, and the women weaker, appropriate work ought to be assigned to each, and the heavier task be given to the stronger, and the lighter to the weaker. For this reason, spinning is more appropriate work for women than for men, and household management. Gymnastics are more appropriate for men than for women, and outdoor work likewise. . . . Some tasks are more appropriate for one nature, others for the other. For that reason some jobs are called men's work, and others women's. . . .

Without philosophy no man and no woman either can be well educated. I do not mean to say that women need to have clarity with or facility in argument, because they will use philosophy as women use it. . . . My point is that women ought to be good and noble in their characters, and that philosophy is no other than the training for that nobility.

Ban Zhao, *Admonitions for Women*

Let a woman modestly yield to others; let her respect others, let her put others first, herself last. Should she do something good, let her not mention it; should she do something bad, let her not deny it. Let her bear contempt; let her even endure when others speak or do evil to her. . . .

Let a woman retire late to bed, but rise early to her duties; let her not dread tasks by day or night. Let her not refuse to perform domestic duties whether easy or difficult. That which must be done, let her finish completely, tidily and systematically. . . .

Let a woman be composed in demeanor and upright in bearing in the service of her husband. Let her live in purity and quietness and keep watch over herself. Let her not love gossip and silly laughter. Let her cleanse, purify and arrange in order the wine and the food for the offerings to the ancestors. . . .

Now examine the gentlemen of the present age. They only know that wives must be controlled and that the husband's authority must be maintained. They therefore teach their boys to read books and study histories. . . . Yet only to teach men and not to teach women—is this not ignoring the reciprocal relation between them? Book learning begins at the age of eight, and at the age of fifteen one goes off to school. Why, however, should this principle not apply to girls as well as boys. . . .

In womanly behavior there are four things . . . womanly virtue, womanly speech, womanly appearance, and womanly work.

(continued)

(Continued)

To guard carefully her chastity, to control circumspectly her behavior, in every motion to exhibit modesty . . . this may be called womanly virtue.

To choose her words with care, to avoid vulgar language, to speak at appropriate times, and not to be offensive to others may be called womanly speech.

To wash and scrub dirt and grime, to keep clothes and ornaments fresh and clean, to wash the head and bathe the body regularly . . . may be called womanly appearance.

With wholehearted devotion to sew and weave, not to love gossip and silly laughter, to prepare the wine and food for serving guests may be called womanly work.

Sources: M. Rufus: M. R. Lefkowitz, and M. B. Fant, *Women's Life in Greece and Rome: A Source Book in Translation*, 2nd edition (Baltimore: Johns Hopkins University Press, 1992), pp. 50–54; W. T. de Bary and I. Bloom, editors, *Sources of Chinese Tradition*, 2nd edition (New York: Columbia University Press, 1999), pp. 821–824.

In these five decades, there were twenty-seven emperors, only four of whom did not meet a violent end.

At the same time, the empire was beset by a series of invasions, no doubt encouraged by the internal turmoil. In the east, the Sassanid Persians made inroads into Roman territory. A fitting symbol of Rome's crisis was the capture of the Roman emperor himself, Valerian (r. 253–260), by the Persians and his death in captivity, an event unprecedented in Roman history. Valerian's body was displayed in the chief towns of Persia. Germanic tribes also poured into the empire. The Goths overran the Balkans and moved into Greece and Asia Minor. The Franks advanced into Gaul and Spain. In 267, a group known as Heruli, a migrant people who originated in Scandinavia, laid waste to Athens. Not until the reign of Aurelian (aw-REEL-yun) (r. 270–275) were most of the boundaries restored. Although he abandoned the Danubian province of Dacia, Aurelian reconquered Gaul and reestablished order in the east and along the Danube. He also built a new defensive wall around Rome to defend the city against invaders. Grateful citizens hailed him as "restorer of the world."

As civil wars and invasions wore down the central government, provinces began to break away from the empire. A military commander named Postumus seized control of Gaul and then gained the support of Britain and Spain. He defended his "Gallic empire" until he was killed by his own soldiers in 269. In the east, Zenobia (zuh-NOH-bee-uh), the wife of the ruler of Syria, seized power after his death and compared herself to the former Egyptian ruler Cleopatra. In 270 she extended her control over Egypt and much of Asia Minor. In 272, Emperor Aurelian ended this threat to imperial power by defeating Zenobia and her forces in Syria.

Antikensammlung, Staatliche Museen, Berlin, Germany/Art Resource, NY

IMAGE 6.9 **Septimius Severus and His Family.** This portrait, which was painted on wood about 200 C.E. and found in Egypt, is the only existing painted likeness of a Roman emperor. The emperor is portrayed with gray hair and beard in memory of Marcus Aurelius. To legitimize his authority, Septimius Severus had himself adopted into the Antonine dynasty, calling himself the son of Marcus Aurelius. The emperor stands next to his wife with their two sons in front of them. The face of his son Geta has been blotted out, no doubt by order of the other son standing next to him, Caracalla. Upon his succession to the throne, Caracalla had his brother killed.

6-4b Economic and Social Problems

Invasions, civil wars, and a recurrence of the plague created new problems for the Roman Empire in the third century. The population declined drastically, possibly by as much as one-third. There was a significant decline in trade and small industry. The manpower shortage created by the plagues at the end of the second century C.E. had affected both military recruiting and the economy. Farm production deteriorated as fields were ravaged by barbarians and even more often by the defending Roman armies. Many farmers complained that Roman commanders and their soldiers were confiscating produce and livestock. Provincial governors seemed powerless to stop these depredations, and some even joined in the frenzy. Recent research has indicated, however, that these problems were not present throughout the empire.

The monetary system began to show signs of collapse as a result of debased coinage and the onset of serious inflation. Gold coins disappeared from circulation, and silver coins were diluted. The standard coin, the denarius, was now worth less than half of its first-century value. After further decline, it was replaced by new coins of even less value. Goods began to replace money as a medium of exchange.

Armies were needed more than ever, but financial strains made it difficult to enlist and pay the necessary soldiers. Short of cash, the imperial government paid its soldiers with produce, causing bitter resentment. Whereas in the second century the Roman army had been recruited among the inhabitants of frontier provinces, by the middle of third century the state had to rely on hiring barbarians to fight under Roman commanders. These soldiers had no understanding of Roman traditions and no real attachment to either the empire or the emperors. By the end of the third century, a new form of political structure would emerge (see Chapter 7).

6-5 Transformation of the Roman World: The Rise of Christianity

FOCUS QUESTION: What characteristics of Christianity enabled it to grow and ultimately to succeed? How did it transform the Roman world?

The advent of Christianity marks a fundamental break with the dominant values of the Greco-Roman world. Christian views of God, human beings, and the world were quite different from those of the Greeks and Romans. Nevertheless, to understand the rise of Christianity, we must first examine both the religious environment of the Roman world and the Jewish background from which Christianity emerged.

6-5a The Religious World of the Roman Empire

Augustus had taken a number of steps to revive the Roman state religion, which had declined during the turmoil of the late republic. The official state religion focused on the worship of a pantheon of Greco-Roman gods and goddesses, including Jupiter, Juno, Minerva, and Mars. Observance of proper ritual by state priests theoretically brought the Romans into proper relationship with the gods and guaranteed security, peace, and prosperity. The polytheistic Romans were extremely tolerant of other religions. The Romans allowed the worship of native gods and goddesses throughout their provinces and even adopted some of the local gods. In addition, the imperial cult of Roma and Augustus was developed to bolster support for the emperors. After Augustus, deceased emperors deified by the Roman senate were included in the official imperial cult.

The desire for a more emotional spiritual experience led many people to the mystery religions of the Hellenistic east, which flooded into the western Roman world during the early empire. The mystery religions offered secret teachings that supposedly brought special benefits. They promised their followers advantages unavailable through Roman religion: an entry into a higher world of reality and the promise of a future life superior to the present one. They also featured elaborate rituals with deep emotional appeal. By participating in their ceremonies and performing their rites, an adherent could achieve communion with spiritual beings and undergo purification that opened the door to life after death.

Many mystery cults vied for the attention of the Roman world. The cults of Cybele (the Great Mother) and the Egyptian Isis had many followers, especially among the urban poor, who gained little from the prosperity of the early empire. The cult of Isis, an Egyptian mother goddess, had become especially widespread throughout the empire by the first century C.E. Isis, seen in her role as the loving mother of Horus, appealed especially to women. Initiation into the cult of Isis came with a promise of immortality after death.

Perhaps the most important mystery cult was Mithraism. Mithra was the chief agent of Ahuramazda, the supreme god of light in Persian Zoroastrianism (see Chapter 2). In the Roman world, Mithra came to be identified with the sun-god and was known by his Roman title "Unconquered Sun." Mithraism had spread rapidly in Rome and the western provinces by the second century C.E. and was especially favored by soldiers, who viewed Mithra as their patron deity. It was a religion for men only and featured an initiation ceremony in which devotees were baptized in the blood of a sacrificed bull. Mithraists paid homage to the sun on the first day of the week (Sunday), commemorated the sun's birthday around December 25, and celebrated ceremonial meals.

6-5b The Jewish Background

Christianity emerged out of Judaism, and so it is to the Jewish political-religious world that we must turn to find the beginnings of Christianity. In Hellenistic times, the Jewish people had enjoyed considerable independence under their Seleucid rulers (see Chapter 4). Roman involvement with the Jews began in 63 B.C.E., and by 6 C.E. Judaea had been made a province and placed under the direction of a Roman procurator. But unrest continued, augmented by divisions among the Jews themselves. The Sadducees favored a rigid adherence to Hebrew law, rejected the possibility of personal immortality, and favored cooperation with the Romans. The Pharisees adhered strictly to Jewish ritual and, although they wanted Judaea to be free from Roman control, did not advocate violent means for achieving this goal. The Essenes were a Jewish sect that lived in a religious community near the Dead Sea. As revealed in the Dead Sea Scrolls, a collection of documents first discovered in 1947, the Essenes, like many other Jews, awaited a Messiah who would save Israel from oppression, usher in the kingdom of God, and establish a paradise on earth. A fourth group, the Zealots, were militant extremists who advocated the violent overthrow of Roman rule.

Despite their differences, discontent with Roman rule led many Jews in Judaea to rise in revolt in 66 C.E. Jewish forces massacred the Roman garrison in Jerusalem, defeated a Roman force sent from Syria, and set up a new government. It was not until 70 C.E. that Roman forces recaptured the city of Jerusalem, killing many of its inhabitants and destroying the Jewish temple. Roman power once more stood supreme in Judaea.

Another Jewish revolt against Roman rule occurred in 132 when the emperor Hadrian attempted to set up a new Roman colony on the site of Jerusalem. Although Jewish forces under the leadership of Simon bar Kokhba, who was viewed by many Jews as a Messiah, were initially successful, the Roman legions gradually wore down the Jewish forces and captured Jerusalem in 135. Judaea, now renamed Syria-Palaestina, was a wasteland, and Jews were forbidden to enter Jerusalem. The Jews, driven by their religious uniqueness, had tried and failed to maintain an independent state. Another Jewish state would not arise until after World War II with the creation of modern Israel.

6-5c The Origins of Christianity

Jesus of Nazareth (ca. 6 B.C.E.–30 C.E.) was a Palestinian Jew who grew up in Galilee, an important center of the militant Zealots (see Image 6.10). He began his itinerant public preaching as a young adult amid the confusion and conflict in Judaea. Jesus's message was basically simple. He reassured his fellow Jews that he did not plan to undermine their traditional religion: "Do not think that I have come to abolish the Law or the Prophets; I have not come to abolish them but to fulfill them."[20] According to Jesus, what was important was not strict adherence to the letter of the law and attention to rules and prohibitions but the transformation of the inner person: "So in everything, do to others what you would have them do to you, for this sums up the Law and the Prophets."[21] God's command was simply to love God and one another: "Love the Lord your God with all your heart and with all your soul and with all your mind and with all your strength. The second is this: Love your neighbor as yourself."[22] In the Sermon on the Mount (see Historical Voices, "Christian Ideals," p. 173), Jesus presented the ethical concepts—humility, charity, and brotherly love—that would form the basis for the value system of medieval Western civilization. As we have seen, these were not the values of classical Greco-Roman civilization.

Although some Jews welcomed Jesus as the Messiah who would save Israel from oppression and establish God's kingdom on earth, Jesus spoke of a heavenly kingdom, not an earthly one: "My kingdom is not of this world."[23] Consequently, he disappointed the radicals. At the same time, conservative religious leaders believed Jesus was another false Messiah who was undermining respect for traditional Jewish religion. To the Roman authorities of Palestine and their local allies, Jesus was a potential revolutionary who might transform Jewish expectations of a messianic kingdom into a revolt against Rome. Therefore, Jesus found himself denounced on many sides and was given over to the Roman authorities. The procurator Pontius Pilate ordered his crucifixion. But that did not solve the problem. A few loyal disciples of Jesus spread the story, common to mystery cults (see Chapter 4), that he had overcome death, been resurrected, and then ascended into heaven. The belief in Jesus's resurrection became an important tenet of Christian doctrine. Jesus was now hailed by his followers as the "anointed one" (*Christ* in Greek), the Messiah who would return and usher in the kingdom of God on earth.

Scala/Art Resource, NY

IMAGE 6.10 **Jesus and His Apostles.** Pictured is a fourth-century fresco from a Roman catacomb depicting Jesus and his apostles. Catacombs were underground cemeteries where early Christians buried their dead. Christian tradition holds that in times of imperial repression, Christians withdrew to the catacombs to pray and hide.

Q *What was the appeal of Christianity?*

Christian Ideals: The Sermon on the Mount

 What were the ideals of early Christianity? How do they differ from the values and principles of classical Greco-Roman civilization?

CHRISTIANITY WAS SIMPLY ONE OF MANY religions competing for attention in the Roman Empire during the first and second centuries. The rise of Christianity marked a fundamental break with the value system of the upper-class elites who dominated the world of classical antiquity. As these excerpts from the Sermon on the Mount in the Gospel of Matthew illustrate, Christians emphasized humility, charity, brotherly love, and a belief in the inner being and a spiritual kingdom superior to this material world. These values and principles were not those of classical Greco-Roman civilization as exemplified in the words and deeds of its leaders.

The Gospel According to Matthew

Now when he saw the crowds, he went up on a mountainside and sat down. His disciples came to him, and he began to teach them saying:

> *Blessed are the poor in spirit: for theirs is the
>   kingdom of heaven.*
> *Blessed are those who mourn: for they will be
>   comforted.*
> *Blessed are the meek: for they will inherit the earth.*
> *Blessed are those who hunger and thirst for
>   righteousness: for they will be filled.*
> *Blessed are the merciful: for they will be shown mercy.*
> *Blessed are the pure in heart: for they will see God.*

> *Blessed are the peacemakers: for they will be called
> sons of God.*
> *Blessed are those who are persecuted because of
>   righteousness: for theirs is the kingdom of
>   heaven. . . .*

You have heard that it was said, "Eye for eye, and tooth for tooth." But I tell you, Do not resist an evil person. If someone strikes you on the right cheek, turn to him the other also. . . .

You have heard that it was said, "Love your neighbor, and hate your enemy." But I tell you, Love your enemies and pray for those who persecute you. . . .

Do not store up for yourselves treasures on earth, where moth and rust destroy, and where thieves break in and steal. But store up for yourselves treasures in heaven, where moth and rust do not destroy, and where thieves do not break in and steal. For where your treasure is, there your heart will be also. . . .

No one can serve two masters. Either he will hate the one and love the other, or he will be devoted to the one and despise the other. You cannot serve both God and Money.

Therefore I tell you, do not worry about your life, what you will eat or drink; or about your body, what you will wear. Is not life more important than food, and the body more important than clothes? Look at the birds of the air; they do not sow or reap to store away in barns, and yet your heavenly Father feeds them. Are you not much more valuable than they? . . . So do not worry, saying, What shall we eat? or What shall we drink? or What shall we wear? For the pagans run after all these things, and your heavenly Father knows that you need them. But seek first his kingdom and his righteousness, and all these things will be given to you as well.

Source: The Holy Bible, New International Version (Colorado Springs, Colo.: Biblica, 1973).

The Importance of Paul Christianity began, then, as a religious movement within Judaism and was viewed that way by Roman authorities for many decades. Although tradition holds that one of Jesus's disciples, Peter, founded the Christian church at Rome, the most important figure in early Christianity after Jesus was Paul of Tarsus (ca. 5–67 C.E.). Paul reached out to non-Jews and transformed Christianity from a Jewish sect into a broader religious movement.

Called the second founder of Christianity, Paul was a Jewish Roman citizen who had been strongly influenced by Hellenistic Greek culture. He believed that the message of Jesus should be preached not only to Jews but to Gentiles (non-Jews) as well. Paul was responsible for founding Christian communities throughout Asia Minor and along the shores of the Aegean.

It was Paul who provided a universal foundation for the spread of Jesus's ideas. He taught that Jesus was, in effect, a savior-god, the son of God, who had come to earth to save all humans, who were basically sinners as a result of Adam's original sin of disobedience against God. By his death, Jesus had atoned for the sins of all humans and made it possible for all men and women to experience a new beginning with the potential for individual salvation. By accepting Jesus as their savior, they, too, could be saved.

The Spread of Christianity At first, Christianity spread slowly. Although the teachings of early Christianity were mostly disseminated by the preaching of convinced Christians, written materials also appeared. Paul had written a series of letters, or epistles, outlining Christian beliefs for different Christian communities. Some of Jesus's disciples may also have preserved some of the sayings of the master in writing and would have passed on personal memories that became the basis of the written gospels— the "good news" concerning Jesus of Matthew, Mark, Luke, and John—which eventually became the authoritative record of Jesus's life and teachings and formed the core of the New Testament. Controversy over the legitimate gospels, however, continued well into the fourth century. Recently, some scholars have argued that other gospels, such as that of Thomas, were rejected because they deviated from the beliefs about Jesus held by the emerging church leaders. In the first few centuries after Jesus's death, who was a Christian and what Christianity was remained open to discussion, leading some historians to speak of multiple christianities rather than one Christianity in the early centuries.

Although Jerusalem was the first center of Christianity, its destruction by the Romans in 70 C.E. left individual Christian churches with considerable independence. By 100, Christian churches had been established in most of the major cities of the east and in some places in the western part of the empire. Many early Christians came from the ranks of Hellenized Jews and the Greek-speaking populations of the east. But in the second and third centuries, an increasing number of followers were Latin-speaking people. A Latin translation of the Greek New Testament that appeared soon after 200 aided this process.

Early Christian Communities Early Christian groups met in private homes in the evening to share a common meal called an *agape* (ah-GAH-pay) or love feast and to celebrate what became known as the sacrament of the **Eucharist** (YOO-kuh-rist), or Lord's Supper—the communal celebration of Jesus's Last Supper:

> While they were eating, Jesus took bread, gave thanks and
> broke it, and gave it to the disciples, saying, Take and eat; this
> is my body. Then he took the cup, gave thanks, and offered it
> to them, saying, Drink from it, all of you. This is my blood of
> the covenant, which is poured out for many for the forgiveness
> of sins.[24]

Early Christian communities were loosely organized, with both men and women playing significant roles. Some women held important positions, often as preachers. Local churches were under the leadership of boards of elders (*presbyters*), but by the beginning of the second century officials known as *bishops* came to exercise considerable authority over the presbyters. These bishops based their superior position on apostolic succession—as the successors to Jesus's original twelve apostles (disciples), they were living representatives of Jesus's power. As Ignatius of Antioch wrote in 107, "It is clear that we must regard a bishop as the Lord Himself. . . . Your clergy . . . are attuned to their bishop like the strings of a harp, and the result is a hymn of praise to Jesus Christ from minds that are in unison."[25] Bishops were invariably men, a clear indication that by the second century C.E., most Christian communities were following the views of Paul that Christian women should be subject to Christian men.

Although some of the fundamental values of Christianity differed markedly from those of the Greco-Roman world, the Romans initially did not pay much attention to the Christians, whom they regarded at first as simply another sect of Judaism. The structure of the Roman Empire itself aided the growth of Christianity. Christian missionaries, including some of Jesus's original twelve apostles, used Roman roads to travel throughout the empire spreading their "good news."

The Changing Roman View of Christianity As the popular appeal of Christianity grew, the Roman attitude toward it began to change. As we have seen, the Romans were tolerant of other religions except when they threatened public order or public morals. Many Romans came to view Christians as harmful to the order of the Roman state. These views were often based on misperceptions. The celebration of the Lord's Supper, for example, led to rumors that Christians practiced horrible crimes, such as the ritualistic murder of children. Although we know these rumors are untrue, some Romans believed them and used them to incite people against the Christians during times of crisis. Moreover, because Christians held their meetings in secret and seemed to be connected to Christian groups in distant areas, the government could view them as potentially dangerous to the state.

Some Romans felt that Christians were overly exclusive and hence harmful to the community and public order. The Christians did not recognize other gods and therefore abstained from public festivals honoring the popular deities. Finally, Christians refused to participate in the worship of the state gods and the imperial cult. Since the Romans regarded these as important to the state, the Christians' refusal seemed to undermine the security of the state and hence constituted an act of treason, punishable by death. It was also proof of atheism (disbelief in the gods) and subject to punishment on those grounds. But to the Christians, who believed there was only one real God, the worship of state gods and the emperors was idolatry and would endanger their own salvation.

Roman persecution of Christians in the first and second centuries was never systematic but only sporadic and local. Persecution began during the reign of Nero. After the fire that destroyed much of Rome, the emperor used the Christians as scapegoats, accusing them of arson and hatred of the human race and subjecting them to cruel deaths in Rome. In the second century, Christians were often ignored as harmless (see Opposing Viewpoints, "Roman Authorities and a Christian on Christianity," p. 175). By the end of the reigns of the five good emperors, Christians still represented a small minority, but one of considerable strength. That strength lay in their conviction of the rightness of their path, a conviction that had been reinforced by the willingness of the first Christians to become martyrs for their faith.

Christian Martyrs From its beginning, Christianity was characterized by the willingness of many of its followers to accept death for their faith. In 177 C.E., a group of fifty Christians in Lyon were sacrificed to wild beasts. In Asia, Polycarp, the bishop of Smyrna, when told to renounce his faith, replied, "I have served [Christ] for eighty-six years and he has done me no wrong. How can I blaspheme my king and my savior?" Polycarp, who had played an important role in spreading Christian teachings in Asia, was burned at the stake as "an offering ready and acceptable to God." In Africa, in 180, a small group of Christian men and women from near Carthage were put on trial and condemned to die: "having confessed that they live according to the Christian religion, since they obstinately persisted when given the opportunity of returning to Roman

Roman Authorities and a Christian on Christianity

 What were Pliny's personal opinions of Christians? Why was he willing to execute them? What was Trajan's response, and what were its consequences for the Christians? What major points did Origen make about the benefits of the Christian religion? Why did the Roman authorities consider these ideas dangerous to the Roman state?

AT FIRST, ROMAN AUTHORITIES were uncertain how to deal with the Christians. In the second century, as seen in the following exchange between Pliny the Younger and the emperor Trajan, Christians were often viewed as harmless and yet were subject to persecution if they persisted in being Christians. Pliny was governor of the province of Bithynia in northwestern Asia Minor (present-day Turkey). He wrote to the emperor for advice about how to handle people accused of being Christians. Trajan's response reflects the general approach toward Christians by the emperors of the second century. The final selection is taken from *Against Celsus*, written about 246 C.E. by Origen of Alexandria. In it, Origen defended the value of Christianity against Celsus, a philosopher who had written an attack on Christians and their teachings.

An Exchange Between Pliny and Trajan
Pliny to Trajan

It is my custom to refer to you all matters on which I am in doubt. Who, indeed, is better able, either to direct my scruples or to instruct my ignorance?

I have never been present at trials of Christians, and consequently do not know for what reasons, or how far, punishment is usually inflicted or inquiry made in their case. . . .

Meanwhile, in the case of those who have been brought before me in the character of Christians, my course has been as follows: I put it to themselves whether they were or were not Christians. To such as professed that they were, I inquire a second and a third time, with a warning of the punishment awaiting them. Those who persisted, I ordered to execution. For, indeed, I could not doubt, whatever might be the nature of that which they professed, that their pertinacity, at any rate, and inflexible obstinacy, ought to be punished. There were others afflicted with like madness, with regard to whom, as they were Roman citizens, I made a memorandum that they were to be sent to Rome for trial.

Soon, the very handling of this matter causing, as often happens, the area of the charge to spread, many fresh examples occurred. An anonymous paper was put forth containing the names of many persons. . . .

Therefore, I have had recourse to your counsels. Indeed, the matter seemed to me a proper one for consultation, chiefly on account of the number of persons endangered. For many of all ages and all ranks, and of both sexes, are being called, and will be called, into danger. Nor are cities only permeated by the contagion of this superstition, but villages and country parts as well; yet it seems possible to stop it and cure it. It is in truth sufficiently evident that the temples, which were almost entirely deserted, have begun to be frequented, that the customary religious rites which had long been interrupted are being resumed, and that there is a sale for the food of sacrificial beasts, for which hitherto very few buyers indeed could be found. From all this it is easy to form an opinion as to the great number of persons who may be reclaimed, if they be given the chance to repent.

Trajan to Pliny

You have followed the right mode of procedure, my dear Pliny, in investigating the cases of those who had been brought before you as Christians. For, indeed, it is not possible to establish any universal rule in a fixed form. These people should not be searched for; if they are informed against and convicted they should be punished; yet, so that he who shall deny being a Christian, and shall make this plain in action, that is by worshipping our gods, even though suspected on account of his past conduct, shall obtain pardon by his penitence. Anonymous pamphlets, however, ought not to be allowed a standing in any kind of charge; a course which would not only form the worst of precedents, but which is not in accordance with the spirit of our time.

Origen, *Against Celsus*

He [Celsus] says that Christians perform their rites and teach their doctrines in secret, and they do this with good reason to escape the death penalty that hangs over them. He compares the danger to the risks encountered for the sake of philosophy as by Socrates. . . . I reply to this that in Socrates's case the Athenians at once regretted what they had done, and cherished no grievance against him. . . . But in the case of the Christians the Roman Senate, the contemporary emperors, the army . . . and the relatives of believers fought against the gospel and would have hindered it; and it would have been defeated by the combined force of so many unless it had overcome and risen above the opposition by divine power, so that it has conquered the whole world that was conspiring against it. . . .

He [also] ridicules our teachers of the gospel who try to elevate the soul in every way to the Creator of the universe. . . . He compares them [Christians] to wool-workers in houses, cobblers, laundry-workers, and the most obtuse yokels, as if they called children quite in infancy and women to evil practices,

(continued)

telling them to leave their father and teachers and to follow them. But let Celsus . . . tell us how we make women and children leave noble and sound teaching, and call them to wicked practices. But he will not be able to prove anything of any kind against us. On the contrary, we deliver women from licentiousness and from perversion caused by their associates, and from all mania for theaters and dancing, and from superstition, while we make boys self-controlled when they come to the age of puberty and burn with desires for sexual pleasure, showing them not only the disgrace of their sins, but also what a state these pleasures produce in the souls of bad men, and what penalties they will suffer and how they will be punished.

Source: *The Letters of the Younger Pliny*, translated by John Delaware Lewis, M.A. (London: Trubner & Co., 1879). Origen, *Against Celsus*. From Origen, *Contra Celsum*. Trans Henry Chadwick. Copyright © 1953. Reprinted with the permission of Cambridge University Press.

ways, [they] are to be executed by the sword." The Christians responded, "We give thanks to God."[26]

For many Christians, martyrdom meant achieving salvation by following the example of Jesus's sacrificial suffering and death on the cross. Indeed, Tertullian (tur-TULL-yun) (ca. 160–225), a Christian writer from Carthage, declared that Christian martyrs were "witnesses to the Grace of God." By imitating Jesus, the Christian martyrs established a model to be followed by other Christians. Said Tertullian, "No one would want to be killed unless possessed of the truth," making the blood of martyrs "the seed of the church."[27] Witnessing Christian martyrs die may well have encouraged others to convert to Christianity.

6-5d The Growth of Christianity

The sporadic persecution of Christians by the Romans in the first and second centuries did nothing to stop the growth of Christianity. In fact, it served to strengthen Christianity as an institution in the second and third centuries by causing it to shed the loose structure of the first century and move toward a more centralized organization of its various church communities. Crucial to this change was the emerging role of the bishops. Though still chosen by the community, bishops began to assume more control, with the bishop serving as leader and the presbyters emerging as clergy subject to the bishop's authority. By the third century, bishops were nominated by the clergy, simply approved by the congregation, and then officially ordained into office. The Christian church was creating a well-defined hierarchical structure in which the bishops and clergy were salaried officers separate from the laity or regular church members.

Christianity and Greco-Roman Culture Many early Christians expressed considerable hostility toward the pagan culture of the Classical world. Tertullian had proclaimed: "What has Jerusalem to do with Athens, the Church with the Academy, the Christian with the heretic? . . . After Jesus Christ we have no need of speculation, after the Gospel no need of research."[28] To many early Christians, the Bible contained all the knowledge anyone needed.

Others, however, thought it was not possible to separate Christian theological thought from classical traditions and education and encouraged Christians to absorb the classical heritage. As it spread in the eastern Roman world, Christianity adopted Greek as its language. The New Testament was written in Greek. Christians also turned to Greek thought for help in expressing complicated theological concepts. An especially important influence was Neoplatonism, a revival of Platonic thought that reached its high point in the third century C.E. Neoplatonists believed that one could use reason (the Intellect) to perceive the link between the invisible spiritual world and the visible material world. Christian theologians used Neoplatonic concepts to explain doctrines on Jesus, especially the distinction between his human and divine natures. In many ways, then, Christianity served to preserve Greco-Roman culture.

The Appeal of Christianity Christianity grew slowly in the first century, took root in the second, and had spread widely by the third. Why was Christianity able to attract so many followers? Historians are not really sure but have offered several answers. Certainly, the Christian message had much to offer the Roman world. The promise of salvation, made possible by Jesus's death and resurrection, had immense appeal in a world full of suffering and injustice. Christianity seemed to imbue life with a meaning and purpose beyond the simple material things of everyday reality. Second, Christianity was not entirely unfamiliar. It could be viewed as simply another eastern mystery religion, offering immortality as the result of the sacrificial death of a savior-god. At the same time, it offered advantages that the other mystery religions lacked. Jesus had been a human figure, not a mythological one, such as Isis or Mithra. Moreover, Christianity had universal appeal. Unlike Mithraism, it was not restricted to men. Furthermore, it did not require a difficult or expensive initiation rite as other mystery religions did. Initiation was accomplished simply by baptism—a purification by water—by which one entered into direct communion with Jesus. In addition, Christianity gave new meaning to life and offered what the Roman state religions could not—a personal relationship with God and a link to higher worlds.

Finally, Christianity fulfilled the human need to belong. Christians formed communities bound to one another in which people could express their love by helping each other and offering assistance to the poor, sick, widows, and orphans. Christianity satisfied the need to belong in a way that the huge, impersonal, and remote Roman Empire could never do.

Christianity proved attractive to all classes. The promise of eternal life was for all—rich, poor, aristocrats, slaves, men, and women. As Paul stated in his Epistle to the Colossians: "And [you] have put on the new self, which is being renewed in knowledge in the image of its Creator. Here there is no Greek nor Jew, circumcised or uncircumcised, barbarian, Scythian, slave or free, but Christ is all, and is in all."[29] Although it did not call for revolution or social upheaval, Christianity emphasized a sense of spiritual equality for all people.

Women and Early Christianity
As we have seen, first-century c.e. Christian communities had allowed both men and women to play significant roles. By the second century, however, men had gained control of church organization and restricted women to secondary roles. Women, as Paul had argued, should be subject to men.

Nevertheless, many women found that Christianity offered them new roles and new forms of companionship with other women. Christian women fostered the new religion in their own homes and preached their convictions to other people in their towns and villages. Many also died for their faith. Perpetua (d. 203 c.e.) was an aristocratic woman who converted to Christianity. Her pagan family begged her to renounce her new faith, but she refused. Arrested by the Roman authorities, she chose instead to die for her faith and was one of a group of Christians who were slaughtered by wild beasts in the arena at Carthage on March 7, 203.

Persecution
As the Christian church became more organized, two emperors in the third century responded with more systematic persecutions. The emperor Decius (DEE-she-uss) (r. 249–251) blamed the Christians for the disasters befalling the Roman Empire in the terrible third century: their refusal to acknowledge the state gods had brought the gods' retribution against the Romans. Moreover, as the administrative organization of the church grew, Christianity appeared to Decius even more like a state within a state that was undermining the empire. Accordingly, he initiated the first systematic persecution of Christians. All citizens were required to appear before their local magistrates and offer animal sacrifices to the Roman gods. Christians, of course, refused to do so. But Decius's scheme failed to work. Not only did local officials fail to cooperate, but Decius's reign was not very long. The last great persecution was by Diocletian (dy-uh-KLEE-shun) at the beginning of the fourth century (see Chapter 7), but by then it was too late. Christianity had become too strong to be eradicated by force.

CHAPTER SUMMARY

The Roman republic had created one of the largest empires in antiquity, but its republican institutions had proved inadequate for the task of ruling an empire. After a series of bloody civil wars, Augustus created a new order that began the Roman Empire. Although he never declared the republic dead and continued to give the senate a role in governing, most political power remained in the hands of the *princeps,* or chief citizen, as he called himself. Significantly, the army swore loyalty to him, and the restoration of peace soon made the new political order acceptable to most people in the empire.

Augustus established the Julio-Claudian dynasty, which lasted until 68. In 69, Vespasian, a successful general, founded the Flavian dynasty after a year of civil war. This dynasty began to openly use the title of *imperator,* or emperor. In the second century, the five "good emperors" maintained a period of peace and prosperity in which trade flourished and the provinces were governed efficiently. Within their empire, the Romans were responsible for a remarkable series of achievements that were bequeathed to the future.

These achievements were fundamental to the development of Western civilization, a civilization that would arise for the most part in the lands in Europe conquered by the Romans, where Roman culture and political ideals were gradually spread. The Romance languages of today (French, Italian, Spanish, Portuguese, and Romanian) are based on Latin. Western practices of impartial justice and trial by jury owe much to Roman law.

As great builders, the Romans left monuments to their skills throughout Europe, some of which, including aqueducts and roads, are still in use today. Other monuments provided models for public buildings in the West for hundreds of years. Aspects of Roman administrative practices survived in the Western world for centuries. The Romans also preserved the intellectual heritage of the Greco-Roman world of antiquity.

By the third century, however, the Roman world was suffering an era of decline. Generals fought each other in civil wars. Between the years 235 and 284 c.e., there were twenty-seven emperors, and only four of them did not suffer a violent end. German tribes and Persian armies invaded the empire. There were plagues, population decline, and economic problems. At the same time, a new religion—Christianity—was spreading throughout the empire. Beginning among the followers of Jesus of Nazareth, Christianity, with its promise of salvation, its similarity to many mystery religions, and its universality as a religion for all—rich and poor, men and women, Greek and Roman—slowly gained acceptance. As we shall see in the next chapter, the response to the crises of the third century and the rise of Christianity would gradually bring a transformation of the Roman Empire in the fourth and fifth centuries.

CHAPTER TIMELINE

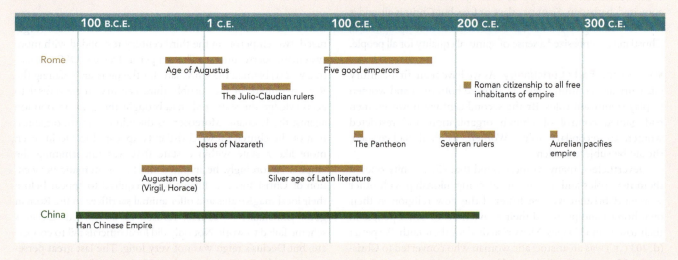

	100 B.C.E.	1 C.E.	100 C.E.	200 C.E.	300 C.E.

Rome
- Age of Augustus
- The Julio-Claudian rulers
- Five good emperors
- Roman citizenship to all free inhabitants of empire
- Jesus of Nazareth
- The Pantheon
- Severan rulers
- Aurelian pacifies empire
- Augustan poets (Virgil, Horace)
- Silver age of Latin literature

China
- Han Chinese Empire

CHAPTER REVIEW

Upon Reflection

Q How did changes in the composition and character of the Roman military affect the Roman Empire?

Q Was Augustus the last of the republicans or the first of the emperors? Why do you think so?

Q In what ways was the rule of the Roman emperors in the first and second centuries C.E. an improvement over the republic of the first century B.C.E.? In what ways was their rule not an improvement over the last century of the republic?

Q How do you explain the spread of Christianity in the Roman Empire?

Key Terms

principate (p. 149)
auxiliaries (p. 151)
praetorian guard (p. 151)
Pax Romana (p. 155)

good emperors (p. 156)
coloni (p. 161)
infanticide (p. 166)
Eucharist (p. 174)

Full definitions also appear in the Glossary at the end of the book.

Suggestions for Further Reading

General Histories of the Roman Empire   For an overview of the Roman Empire, see **G. Woolf**, *Rome: An Empire's Story* (New York, 2012). A good survey of the early empire is **M. Goodman**, *The Roman World, 44 B.C. – A.D. 180,* 2nd ed. (London, 2012). Also useful are **C. Kelly**, *The Roman Empire: A Very Short Introduction* (Oxford, 2006), and **P. Garnsey and R. Saller**, *The Roman Empire: Economy, Society and Culture,* 2nd ed. (Oakland, CA., 2015). On the crises of the third century, see **D. S. Potter**, *The Roman Empire at Bay, A.D. 180–395* (New York, 2004).

Roman Emperors   Studies of Roman emperors of the first and second centuries include **A. Goldsworthy**, *Augustus: First Emperor of Rome* (New Haven, 2014); **A. Everitt**, *Hadrian and the Triumph of Rome* (New York, 2009); and **P. Matyszak**, *The Sons of Caesar: Imperial Rome's First Dynasty* (London, 2006) on the Julio-Claudian rulers.

Roman Army and Provinces   On warfare, see **A. Goldsworthy**, *Roman Warfare* (New York, 2005). On the provinces and Roman foreign policy, see **B. Isaac**, *The Limits of Empire: The Roman Empire in the East* (Oxford, 1990), and **S. L. Dyson**, *The Creation of the Roman Frontier* (Princeton, N.J., 1985). On the governing of the empire, see **J. E. Lendon**, *Empire of Honor: The Art of Government in the Roman Empire* (New York, 2007).

Roman Culture   A survey of Roman art can be found in **F. S. Kleiner**, *A History of Roman Art* (Belmont, Calif., 2006). Architecture is covered in the standard work by **J. B. Ward-Perkins**, *Roman Imperial Architecture* (Harmondsworth, England, 1992). On the importance of concrete in Roman architecture, see **L. C. Lancaster**, *Concrete Vaulted Construction in Imperial Rome* (Cambridge, 2005).

Roman Society Various aspects of Roman society are covered in **J. Carcopino, *Daily Life in Ancient Rome: The People and the City at the Height of the Empire***, 2nd ed. (New Haven, 2003). On the gladiators, see **F. Meijer, *The Gladiators: History's Most Deadly Sport*** (Boston, 2005). On Roman women, see **S. Dixon, *Reading Roman Women*** (London, 2001).

Early Christianity For a general introduction to early Christianity, see **J. Court** and **K. Court, *The New Testament World*** (Cambridge, 1990). On Christian women, see **R. Kraemer, *Her Share of the Blessings: Women's Religion Among the Pagans, Jews and Christians in the Graeco-Roman World*** (Oxford, 1995). On the controversies surrounding the Christian gospels in the early history of Christianity, see **D. Brakke, *The Gnostics: Myth, Ritual and Diversity in Early Christianity*** (Cambridge, Mass., 2012). On the divisions in Christianity in the first few centuries C.E., see **B. Ehrman, *Lost Christianities: The Battles for Scripture and the Faiths We Never Knew*** (Oxford, 2005).

Notes

1. Livy, *The Early History of Rome,* trans. A. de Sélincourt (Harmondsworth, England, 1960), p. 35.
2. Tacitus, *The Annals of Imperial Rome,* trans. M. Grant (Harmondsworth, England, 1956), p. 30.
3. Velleius Paterculus, *Compendium of Roman History,* trans. Frederick Shipley (Cambridge, Mass., 1967), 2.117.
4. Tacitus, *Annals of Imperial Rome,* p. 37.
5. Virgil, *The Aeneid,* trans. C. Day Lewis (Garden City, N.Y., 1952), p. 154.
6. Horace, *Satires,* in *The Complete Works of Horace,* trans. Lord Dunsany and M. Oakley (London, 1961), 1.1.
7. Ibid., 1.3.
8. Livy, *Early History of Rome,* p. 18.
9. Tacitus, *Annals of Imperial Rome,* p. 31.
10. Tacitus, *The Histories,* trans. K. Wallesley (Harmondsworth, England, 1964), p. 23.
11. Quoted in M. Goodman, *The Roman World, 44 B.C. – A.D. 180* (London, 1997), p. 67.
12. Quoted in ibid., p. 72.
13. Tacitus, *Agricola,* p. 21.
14. Seneca, *Letters from a Stoic,* trans. R. Campbell (Harmondsworth, England, 1969), letter 5.
15. Tacitus, *Annals of Imperial Rome,* p. 147.
16. Juvenal, *The Sixteen Satires,* trans. P. Green (Harmondsworth, England, 1967), satire 10, p. 207.
17. Tacitus, *A Dialogue on Oratory,* in *The Complete Works of Tacitus,* trans. A. Church and W. Brodribb (New York, 1942), p. 758.
18. Ovid, *The Amores,* trans. G. Showerman (Cambridge, Mass., 1963), 2.14.26–27.
19. Dio Cassius, *Roman History,* Vol. 9, tr. E. Cary (Cambridge, Mass., 1925), 77.15.
20. Matthew 5:17.
21. Matthew 7:12.
22. Mark 12:30–31.
23. John 18:36.
24. Matthew 26:26–28.
25. *Early Christian Writings* (Harmondsworth, England, 1968), pp. 76–77.
26. These lines and the one by Polycarp are quoted in C. Wells, *The Roman Empire* (Stanford, Calif., 1984), pp. 263–264.
27. Quotations by Tertullian can be found in D. Chidester, *Christianity: A Global History* (New York, 2000), pp. 74, 79, 82.
28. Tertullian, "The Prescriptions Against the Heretics," in *The Library of Christian Classics,* vol. 5: *Early Latin Theology,* ed. and trans. S. L. Greenslade (Philadelphia, 1956), p. 36.
29. Colossians 3:10–11.

MindTap *Tips* Be sure to check out the Primary Source Writing Activities at the end of each chapter in MindTap. These activities will help you develop crucial skills for larger writing assignments and research. You'll practice developing a thesis and defending it with an argument that draws support from multiple primary sources.

CHAPTER 7

Late Antiquity and the Emergence of the Medieval World

IMAGE 7.1 **A Fifteenth-Century Manuscript Illustration of Clovis, His Wife Clotilde, and Their Four Sons**

CHAPTER OUTLINE AND FOCUS QUESTIONS

7-1 The Late Roman Empire

Q What reforms did Diocletian and Constantine institute, and to what extent were the reforms successful? What brought about the end of the Roman empire in the west?

7-2 The Germanic Kingdoms

Q What changes did the Germanic kingdoms make to the political, economic, and social conditions of the Western Roman Empire? What were the main features of Germanic law and society, and how did they differ from those of the Romans?

7-3 Development of the Christian Church

Q How and why did the organization of the Christian church and its relations with the state change during the fourth and fifth centuries? What was the role of the pope in the western Christian church? What were the chief characteristics of Benedictine monasticism? What role did monks play in both the conversion of Europe to Christianity and the intellectual life of the Germanic kingdoms?

7-4 The Byzantine Empire

Q How did the Byzantine Empire that had emerged by the eighth century differ from the empire of Justinian and from the Germanic kingdoms in the west?

7-5 The Rise of Islam

Q What was the basic message of Islam, and how does it compare to Judaism and Christianity? Why was Islam able to expand so successfully?

CONNECTIONS TO TODAY

In what ways are developments in the seventh and eighth centuries related to problems in the world in the early twenty-first century?

BY THE THIRD CENTURY, the Roman Empire was experiencing a number of problems as well as witnessing the growth of a new religion—Christianity. To restore the empire, the emperors Diocletian and Constantine (KAHN-stun-teen) initiated a number of reforms that created the so-called late empire. Constantine also converted to Christianity, starting a process that gave the late empire a new state religion.

After Constantine, the empire survived, but in the west it increasingly faced incursions of Germanic tribes. By the second half of the fifth century, new political arrangements were taking shape that brought the collapse of the old imperial structure in the west and the emergence of a series of Germanic kingdoms in western Europe that would form the basis of a new civilization. In these kingdoms, the Christian church also played a role as it converted these Germanic tribes to its faith.

The conversion to Christianity of the pagan leaders of the Germanic tribes was sometimes dramatic, at least as reported by the sixth-century historian Gregory of Tours. Clovis (KLOH-viss), leader of the Franks, married Clotilde, daughter of the king of the Burgundians. She was a Christian, but Clovis refused her pleas to become a Christian, telling her, "Your god can do nothing." But during a battle with the Alemanni, when Clovis's army was close to utter destruction, "he saw the danger; his heart was stirred; and he raised his eyes to heaven, saying,

'Jesus Christ, I beseech the glory of your aid. If you shall grant me victory over these enemies, I will believe in you and be baptized in your name.'"[1] When he had uttered these words, the Alemanni began to flee. Clovis soon became a Christian.

While the Germanic kingdoms were putting down roots in the west, the eastern part of the old Roman Empire, increasingly Greek in culture, continued as the Byzantine Empire. Serving as a buffer between Europe and the peoples to the east, the Byzantine (or Eastern Roman) Empire also preserved the intellectual and legal accomplishments of Greek and Roman antiquity. At the same time, a new culture centered on Islam emerged in the east; it spread through large parts of the old Roman Empire, preserved much of Greek culture, and created its own flourishing civilization. This chapter, then, concerns the transformation of the Roman world in late antiquity, the heirs of the Roman Empire, and the medieval world they began to create.

7-1 The Late Roman Empire

 FOCUS QUESTIONS: What reforms did Diocletian and Constantine institute, and to what extent were the reforms successful? What brought about the end of the Roman Empire in the west?

At the end of the third century and beginning of the fourth, the Roman Empire gained a new lease on life through the efforts of two strong emperors, Diocletian and Constantine, who restored order and stability. The empire was virtually transformed into a new state, the Late Roman Empire, which included a new governmental structure, a rigid economic and social system, and a new state religion—Christianity.

7-1a The Reforms of Diocletian and Constantine

At the end of the troubled third century, a new emperor—Diocletian (r. 284–305 C.E.)—began the process of restoring the strength of the Roman Empire. Diocletian had risen through the ranks to become a prominent military leader, and after the murder of the emperor Numerian by his praetorian prefect, Diocletian executed the prefect and was then hailed as emperor by his soldiers. Diocletian's own rise to power led him to see the need for a new system for ruling the Roman Empire.

Political Reforms Diocletian created a new administrative system for a restructured empire. The number of provinces was increased to almost one hundred by creating smaller districts superintended by more officials. The provinces were in turn grouped into twelve dioceses, each headed by an official called a vicar. The twelve dioceses were grouped into four prefectures (see Map 7.1), and the entire Roman Empire was divided into two parts: east and west. Each part contained two prefectures and was ruled by an "Augustus." Diocletian ruled the east, and Maximian (mak-SIM-ee-un), a strong military commander, the west. Each Augustus was assisted by a chief lieutenant or "vice-emperor" called a "Caesar," who theoretically would eventually succeed to the position of Augustus. This new system was called **tetrarchy** (rule by four). Diocletian had obviously come to believe that one man was not capable of ruling such an enormous empire, especially in view of the barbarian invasions of the third century. Each of the four tetrarchs—two Augusti and two Caesars—resided in a different administrative capital. Diocletian, for example, established his base at Nicomedia in Bithynia. Despite the appearance of four-man rule, however, it is important to note that Diocletian's military seniority enabled him to claim a higher status and hold the ultimate authority.

In his attempt to save the empire, Diocletian also instituted a policy that all Romans should participate in the imperial cult (worship of the emperor) and worship of the state gods as a unifying force in Roman society. When Christians refused, Diocletian launched the Great Persecution, burning Christian churches and books and killing thousands of Christians, often by having them thrown into arenas where they were mauled by wild animals. Diocletian's persecution, although motivated by political reasons, failed to stop the growth of Christianity and often created more converts to the faith by the acts of bravery demonstrated by Christian martyrs who went to their deaths singing hymns of praise for their God.

Soon after Diocletian's retirement in 305 C.E., a new struggle for power ensued. The victory of Constantine (r. 306–337) in 312 led to his control of the entire west, although he continued to share imperial authority with Licinius (ly-SIN-ee-uss), a fellow emperor. Twelve years later, in 324, Constantine's army routed Licinius's forces, and Constantine established himself as the sole ruler of a unified empire.

Constantine continued and even expanded the autocratic policies of Diocletian. Under these two rulers, the Roman Empire was transformed into a system in which the emperor had far more personal power than Augustus, Trajan, or any of the other emperors had had during the *Pax Romana*. The emperor was now viewed as a supreme leader, "whose authority was limitless, universal, and divine," as one historian has put it. To retain the new order, Constantine returned to the practice of giving power to his family. His son Constantius succeeded him as emperor when he died in 337.

The emperor, now clothed in jewel-bedecked robes of gold and blue, was seen as a divinely sanctioned monarch whose will was law. Government officials were humble servants required to kneel before the emperor and kiss his robe. The Roman senate was stripped of any power and became merely the city council for Rome.

Diocletian and Constantine greatly strengthened and enlarged the administrative bureaucracies of the Roman Empire. Henceforth, civil and military bureaucracies were sharply separated. Each contained a hierarchy of officials who exercised control at the various levels. The emperor presided over both hierarchies and served as the only link between them. New titles of nobility—such as *illustres* (ee-loo-STRAYSS)

MAP 7.1 **Divisions of the Late Roman Empire, ca. 300 C.E.** Diocletian imposed order and a new economic and administrative structure on the late empire. He divided the Roman Empire into four regions, each ruled by either an "Augustus" or a "Caesar," although Diocletian retained supreme power.

Q *Compare this map with Map 6.1. How much territory had been lost by the time of Diocletian?*

("illustrious ones") and *illustrissimi* (ee-loo-STREE-see-mee) ("most illustrious ones")—were instituted to dignify the holders of positions in the civil and military bureaucracies.

Military Reforms Additional military reforms were also instituted. The army was enlarged to 400,000 men, including units filled with Germans. By the end of Constantine's reign, the army also had a new organization. Military forces were divided between garrison troops, which were located on the frontiers to serve as a first line of defense against invaders, and field army or mobile units, which were based behind the frontier but could be quickly moved to support frontier troops when the borders were threatened. This system gave the empire greater flexibility in responding to invasion. Constantine enhanced the separation between the mobile or field army soldiers and border troops begun under Diocletian. The field army soldiers were paid more and served directly under the command of the emperor.

Economic and Social Trends The political and military reforms of Diocletian and Constantine greatly enlarged two institutions—the army and the civil service—that drained most of the public funds. Although more revenues were needed to pay for the military and the bureaucracy, the population was not growing, so the tax base could not be expanded. Diocletian and Constantine devised new economic and social policies to deal with these financial burdens. Like their political policies, these economic and social policies were all based on coercion and loss of individual freedom.

To fight **inflation**, Diocletian resorted to issuing an edict in 301 C.E. that established maximum wages and prices for the entire empire. It was applied mostly in the east, but despite severe penalties, like most wage and price controls, was largely unenforceable. The decline in the coins in circulation forced Diocletian to collect taxes and make government payments in produce. Constantine, however, managed to introduce a new gold coin, the solidus, and new silver coins that remained in circulation during his reign.

In the third century, the city councils, which had formed one of the most important administrative units of the empire, had begun to decline. Since the *curiales* (KUR-ee-all-ayss) (the city councillors) were forced to pay expenses out of their own pockets when the taxes they collected were insufficient, the wealthy no longer wanted to serve in these positions. Diocletian and Constantine responded by issuing edicts that forced the rich to continue in their posts as curiales, making the positions virtually hereditary. Some curiales realized that their fortunes would be wiped out and fled the cities to escape the clutches of the imperial bureaucracy. If caught, however, they were returned to their cities like runaway slaves and forced to resume their duties.

Coercion also came to form the underlying basis for numerous occupations in the late Roman Empire. To maintain the tax base and keep the empire going despite the shortage of labor, the emperors issued edicts that forced people to remain in their designated vocations. Hence, basic jobs, such as bakers and shippers, became hereditary.

Free tenant farmers—the *coloni*—continued to decline and increasingly found themselves bound to the land as large landowners took advantage of the depressed agricultural conditions to enlarge their landed estates. To guarantee their supply of labor, the landlords obtained the government's cooperation in attaching the tenant farmers to the estates. One imperial edict stated: "And as for *coloni* themselves, it will be proper for such as contemplate flight to be bound with chains to a servile status, so that by virtue of such condemnation to servitude they may be compelled to fulfill the duties that befit free men."[2]

In addition to facing increased restrictions on their freedom, the lower classes were burdened with enormous taxes because the wealthiest classes in the late Roman Empire were either exempt from paying taxes or evaded them by bribing the tax collectors. These tax pressures undermined lower-class support for the regime. A fifth-century writer reported that the Roman peasants welcomed the Visigothic invaders of southern Gaul as liberators because they were more lenient than the tax collectors.

In general, the economic and social policies of Diocletian and Constantine were based on an unprecedented degree of control and coercion. Though temporarily successful, in the long run such authoritarian policies stifled the very vitality the late empire needed to revive its sagging fortunes.

Constantine's Building Program Constantine engaged in extensive building programs despite the strain they placed on the budget. Many of them took place in the provinces, as Rome had become merely a symbolic capital. It was considered too far from the frontiers to serve as an imperial administrative center.

Between 324 and 330 C.E., Constantine carried out his biggest project, the construction of a new capital city in the east, on the site of the Greek city of Byzantium (bih-ZAN-tee-um), on the shores of the Bosporus. Named the "city of Constantine," or Constantinople (modern Istanbul), it was developed for defensive reasons; it had an excellent strategic location. Calling it his "New Rome," Constantine endowed the city with a forum, large palaces, and a vast amphitheater. It

IMAGE 7.2 **The Emperor Constantine.** Constantine played an important role in restoring order and stability to the Roman Empire at the beginning of the fourth century. This marble head of Constantine, which is 8 feet 6 inches high, was part of an enormous 30-foot-tall seated statue of the emperor in the New Basilica in Rome. Constantine used these awe-inspiring statues throughout the empire to build support for imperial policies by reminding his subjects of his position as an absolute ruler with immense power. Being depicted with his eyes cast up toward heaven also emphasized Constantine's special relationship with God.

was officially dedicated on May 11, 330, "by the commandment of God," and in the following years, many Christian churches were built there.

Constantine did not entirely forget Rome. Earlier he was responsible for building public baths and the triumphal Arch of Constantine, erected between 312 and 315. Constantine was also the first emperor to build churches at state expense for the Christian faith in Rome, including the first basilica dedicated to Saint Peter, built on the supposed site of Saint Peter's burial. These acts by Constantine are a reminder of the new role Christianity was beginning to play in the Late Empire (see Image 7.2).

7-1b The Empire's New Religion

In the fourth century, Christianity flourished as never before, and the emperor Constantine played an important role in its new status.

The Conversion of Constantine Constantine's support for Christianity supposedly began in 312 C.E., when his army was about to fight a crucial battle against the forces of Maxentius (mak-SEN-shuss) at the Milvian Bridge, which crossed the Tiber River just north of Rome. According to the traditional story, before the battle, Constantine had a vision of a Christian cross with the words "In this sign you will conquer." Having won the battle, the story goes, Constantine was convinced of the power of the Christian God and converted to Christianity. In 313 he issued the famous Edict of Milan, which officially tolerated the existence of Christianity.

After the defeat of Licinius in 324, Constantine began to have a sense of mission in converting the empire to Christianity. In a speech in 325, he said, "We strive to the best of our ability to fill those who are uninitiated in such [Christian] teachings with good hope, having summoned God to assist us in the endeavor."[3] Two years after the speech, on May 22, 337, he died but not before he had been formally baptized into the Christian faith.

After Constantine, all of the emperors were Christian with the exception of Julian (r. 360–363), who tried briefly to restore the traditional Greco-Roman polytheistic religion. But he died in battle, and his reign was too short to make a difference. Under Theodosius (thee-uh-DOH-shuss) I "the Great" (r. 379–395), Christianity was made the official religion of the Roman Empire. Once in control, Christian leaders used their influence and power to condemn and outlaw pagan religious practices.

Organization and Religious Disputes By the fourth century C.E., the Christian church had developed a system of government based on a territorial plan borrowed from Roman administration. The Christian community in each city was headed by a bishop whose area of jurisdiction was known as a bishopric or diocese. The bishoprics of each Roman province were clustered together under the direction of an archbishop. The bishops of four great cities—Rome, Jerusalem, Alexandria, and Antioch—held positions of special power in church affairs because the churches in these cities all asserted that they had been founded by the original apostles sent out by Jesus.

One reason the church needed a more formal organization was the problem of **heresy**. As Christianity developed and spread, contradictory interpretations of important doctrines emerged. Heresy came to be viewed as a teaching different from the official "catholic" or universal beliefs of the church, hence the name Catholic Christians or Catholics. For people deeply concerned about salvation, the question of whether Jesus's nature is divine or human—a study that became known as **Christology**—took on great significance. These doctrinal differences also became political issues, creating political factions that warred with one another. It is unlikely that ordinary people understood the issues in these debates.

One of the major heresies of the fourth century was **Arianism** (AR-ee-uh-niz-um), which was a product of the followers of Arius (AR-ee-uss), a priest from Alexandria in Egypt. Arius postulated that Jesus had been human and thus not truly God. Arius was opposed by Athanasius (ath-uh-NAY-shuss), a bishop of Alexandria, who argued that Jesus was human but also truly God. Emperor Constantine, disturbed by the controversy, called the first ecumenical council of the church, a meeting composed of representatives from the entire Christian community. The Council of Nicaea (ny-SEE-uh), held in 325 C.E., condemned Arianism and stated that Jesus was of the same substance as God: "We believe in one God the Father Allsovereign, maker of all things visible and invisible; And in one Lord Jesus Christ, the Son of God, begotten of the Father, onlybegotten, that is, of the substance of the Father, God of God, Light of Light, true God of true God, begotten not made, of one substance with the Father."[4]

The Council of Nicaea did not end the controversy, however; not only did Arianism persist in some parts of the Roman Empire for many years, but even more important, many of the Germanic Goths who established states in the west converted to Arian Christianity (see "7-2 The Germanic Kingdoms," later in this chapter). As a result of these fourth-century religious controversies, the Roman emperor came to play an increasingly important role in church affairs, especially by taking responsibility for calling church councils.

7-1c The End of the Western Empire

After Constantine's death, the empire began to divide into western and eastern parts as fighting erupted on a regular basis between elements of the Roman army backing the claims of rival emperors. By 395 C.E., the western and eastern parts of the empire had become virtually two independent states. In the course of the fifth century, while the empire in the east remained intact under the Roman emperor in Constantinople (see "7-4 The Byzantine Empire," later in this chapter), the administrative structure of the empire in the west collapsed and was replaced by an assortment of Germanic kingdoms. The process was a gradual one, involving the movement of Germans into the empire, military failures, struggles for power on the part of both Roman and German military leaders, and the efforts of wealthy aristocrats to support whichever side seemed to offer them greater security.

The Germans During the first and second centuries C.E., the Romans had established the Rhine and Danube Rivers as the empire's northern boundary. The Romans called all the peoples to the north of the rivers "Germans" and regarded them as uncivilized barbarians. In fact, the Germans comprised many different groups with their own customs and identities. Organized into clans or extended families, several clans might coalesce into larger tribes, but these constantly changed as tribes broke up and came together in new configurations. At times they formed larger confederations under strong warrior leaders. The Roman historian Tacitus explained that it was a disgrace when battle was joined for the chieftain to be surpassed in courage or for his followers not to live up to his standard. Warfare thus became an important part of German life, as warriors competed to exert their power.

The Germans lived by herding and farming and traded with people living along the northern frontiers of the Roman Empire. Their proximity to the Romans also led to some of the tribes adopting Roman ways. They were familiar with the Roman use of coins rather than barter and also gained some knowledge of both the Latin language and Roman military matters.

Contacts between Romans and Germans were common across the boundaries established along the Rhine and Danube Rivers. In fact, for some time, the Romans had hired Germanic tribes to fight other Germanic tribes that threatened Rome and enlisted groups of Germans to fight for Rome. Until the fourth century, the empire had proved capable of absorbing these people without harm to its political structure. As that century wore on, however, the situation began to change as the Germanic tribes came under new pressures from invaders.

German Migrations

In the late fourth century C.E., the Huns, a fierce tribe of nomads from Asia (see Opposing Viewpoints, "Two Views of the Huns," p. 186), began moving into the Black Sea region and forced the Germanic inhabitants westward. In 376, one of the largest groups, which came to be known as the Visigoths (VIZ-uh-gahthz), asked the Roman emperor Valens (VAY-linz) (r. 364–378) to allow them to cross the Danube and farm in the Balkans in return for providing troops for the Roman military. But the Roman military commanders mistreated them, as one ancient German historian recounted:

> Soon famine and want came upon them. . . . Their leaders . . . begged the Roman commanders to open a market. But to what will not the "cursed lust for gold" compel men to assent? The generals, swayed by greed, sold them at a high price not only the flesh of sheep and oxen, but even the carcasses of dogs and unclean animals. . . . When their goods and chattels failed, the greedy traders demanded their sons in return for the necessities of life. And the parents consented even to this.[5]

Outraged at this treatment, the Visigoths revolted. In 378, Emperor Valens and an army of 40,000 soldiers confronted the Visigoths at Adrianople. The emperor was killed, and two-thirds of the Roman soldiers were left dead on the battlefield.

The loss was not fatal, although the new emperor, Theodosius I, resettled the Visigoths and incorporated many of their soldiers into the Roman army. Some of the Visigoths even became army leaders. By the second half of the fourth century, Roman policy allowed Roman army units to be composed entirely of Germanic tribes, known as **federates**, or allies of Rome.

The Threat of the Germans

The existence of such military groups proved dangerous to the late empire. This was especially evident after Alaric (AL-uh-rik) became the leader of the Visigoths. Between 395 and 401 C.E., Alaric and his soldiers moved through the Balkans and then into Italy, seeking food and cash payments from Roman officials. When the city of Rome refused his demands in 408, Alaric marched to the gates and besieged the city, causing the senate of Rome to agree to pay 5,000 pounds of gold and 30,000 pounds of silver for his withdrawal. Two years later, frustrated in his demand that the Visigoths be given part of northern Italy, Alaric and his forces sacked Rome for three days. Alaric died soon after, and his Visigothic followers left Italy, crossed the Alps, and moved into Spain and southern Gaul as Roman allies (see Map 7.2).

By this time, other Germanic tribes were also entering the Roman Empire and settling down. As one contemporary observer noted, "the barbarians, detesting their swords, turned to their plows and now cherish the Romans as comrades and friends."[6] In the early fifth century, the Burgundians arrived in southern Gaul, while the Franks moved into northern Gaul. Another group, the Vandals, under their leader Gaiseric (GY-zuh-rik), moved through Gaul and Spain, crossed the Strait of Gibraltar into North Africa, and seized Carthage, the capital city, in 439.

As the Germanic tribes moved into the empire and settled down, Roman forces were often withdrawn from the provinces, effectively reducing the central authority of the emperors. In 410, for example, the emperor Honorius (hoh-NOR-ee-uss) recalled the last Roman legions from Britain. As one ancient commentator remarked, "Honorius sent letters to the cities in Britain, urging them to fend for themselves."[7] With the withdrawal, the Saxons, who had arrived earlier as Roman allies, now expanded their control in Britain. Within another decade, both Spain and Gaul had also become free of imperial authority.

Role of Masters of the Soldiers

By the middle of the fifth century C.E., the western provinces of the Roman Empire had been taken over by Germanic peoples who were in the process of creating independent kingdoms. At the same time, a semblance of imperial authority remained in Rome, although the real power behind the throne tended to rest in the hands of important military officials known as Masters of the Soldiers.

These military commanders controlled the government and dominated the imperial court. The three most prominent in the fifth century were Stilicho (STIL-i-koh), Aetius (ay-EE-shuss), and Ricimer (RISS-uh-mur). Stilicho and Ricimer were both Germans, whereas Aetius was a Roman. Although all three propped up emperors to maintain the fiction of imperial rule, they were also willing to cooperate with the Germans to maintain their power. But even the Masters of the Soldiers were never safe in the bloody world of fifth-century Roman political life. Stilicho was executed by the guards of Emperor Honorius. Aetius was killed by Emperor Valentinian (val-en-TIN-ee-un) III, who was in turn assassinated by two of Aetius's German bodyguards,

CHRONOLOGY	The Late Roman Empire
Diocletian	284–305 C.E.
Constantine	306–337
Edict of Milan	313
Construction of Constantinople	324–330
Valens	364–378
Battle of Adrianople	378
Theodosius I "the Great"	379–395
Division of the empire	395
Alaric and Visigoths sack Rome	410
Vandals sack Rome	455
Odoacer deposes Romulus Augustulus	476

Two Views of the Huns

 What motives may have prompted Ammianus Marcellinus to describe the Huns so harshly? How does the account of Priscus differ, and do you detect any strategies of the Huns to impress and overawe foreigners? How reliable do you think these descriptions of the Huns are? Why?

THE FIRST SELECTION is a description of the Huns by Ammianus Marcellinus (am-ee-AY-nuss mar-suh-LY-nuss) (ca. 330–393 C.E.), who has been called the last great Roman historian. Ammianus wrote a history of Rome from 96 C.E. to his own day. Only the chapters that deal with the period from 354 to 378 have survived. Historians believe that his account of the Huns is largely based on stereotypes. The second selection is taken from an account by Priscus, an envoy from the Eastern Roman Empire to the court of Attila (uh-TILL-uh or AT-ih-luh), king of the Huns from 434 to 453. His description of the Huns in 448 is quite different from that of Ammianus Marcellinus.

Ammianus Marcellinus, *The Later Roman Empire*

The Huns . . . are quite abnormally savage. From the moment of their birth they make deep gashes in their children's cheeks, so that when in due course hair appears its growth is checked by the wrinkled scars. . . . They have squat bodies, strong limbs, and thick necks, and are so prodigiously ugly and bent that they might be two-legged animals. . . . Still, their shape, however disagreeable, is human; but their way of life is so rough that they have no use for fire or seasoned food, but live on the roots of wild plants and the half-raw flesh of any sort of animal, which they warm a little by placing it between their thighs and the backs of their horses. They have no buildings to shelter them . . . not so much as a hut thatched with reeds is to be found among them. . . . They wear garments of linen or of the skins of field-mice stitched together, and there is no difference between their clothing whether they are at home or abroad. Once they have put their necks in some dingy shirt they never take it off or change it till it rots and falls to pieces from incessant wear. They have round caps of fur on their heads, and protect their hairy legs with goatskins. Their shapeless shoes . . . make it hard to walk easily. In consequence they are ill-fitted to fight on foot, and remain glued to their

horses, hardy but ugly beasts, on which they sometimes sit like women to perform their everyday business. Buying or selling, eating or drinking, are all done by day or night on horseback, and they even bow forward over their beasts' narrow necks to enjoy a deep and dreamy sleep. . . .

They sometimes fight by challenging their foes to single combat, but when they join battle they advance in packs, uttering their various warcries. Being lightly equipped and very sudden in their movements they can deliberately scatter and gallop about at random, inflicting tremendous slaughter; their extreme nimbleness enables them to force a rampart or pillage an enemy's camp before one catches sight of them. . . . None of them plows or ever touches a plow-handle. They have no fixed abode, no home or law or settled manner of life, but wander like refugees with the wagons in which they live. In these their wives weave their filthy clothing, mate with their husbands, and give birth to their children, and rear them to the age of puberty.

Priscus, "An Account of the Court of Attila the Hun"

[We were invited to a banquet with Attila.] When the hour arrived we went to Attila's palace, along with the embassy from the western Romans, and stood on the threshold of the hall in the presence of Attila. The cupbearers gave us a cup, according to the national custom, that we might pray before we sat down. Having tasted the cup, we proceeded to take our seats, all the chairs being ranged along the walls of the room on either side. Attila sat in the middle on a couch; a second couch was set behind him, and from it steps led up to his bed, which was covered with linen sheets and coverlets. . . .

[First the king and his guests pledged one another with the wine.] When this ceremony was over the cupbearers retired and tables, large enough for three or four, or even more, to sit at, were placed next to the table of Attila, so that each could take of the food on the dishes without leaving his seat. The attendant of Attila first entered with a dish full of meat, and behind him came the other attendants with bread and other dishes, which they laid on the tables. A luxurious meal, served on silver plate, had been made ready for us and the other guests, but Attila ate nothing but meat on a wooden platter. In everything else, too, he showed himself temperate; his cup was of wood, while to the guests were given goblets of gold and silver. His dress, too, was quite simple, affecting only to be clean.

Sources: Ammianus Marcellinus, *The Later Roman Empire*, trans. W. Hamilton (London: Penguin Classics, 1986). Priscus, "An Account of the Court of Attila the Hun," in *Fragmenta Historicorum Graecorum*, trans. J. B. Bury (Didot, 1868).

who sought to avenge their betrayed leader. Ricimer died a natural death, an unusual event in fifth-century Rome. No doubt, the constant infighting at the center of the Western Empire added to the instability of imperial rule.

By the middle of the fifth century, imperial authority in the west was still operating only in Italy and small parts of Gaul. Even Rome itself was not safe. In 455, after the Romans broke a treaty that they had made with Gaiseric, leader of the Vandals,

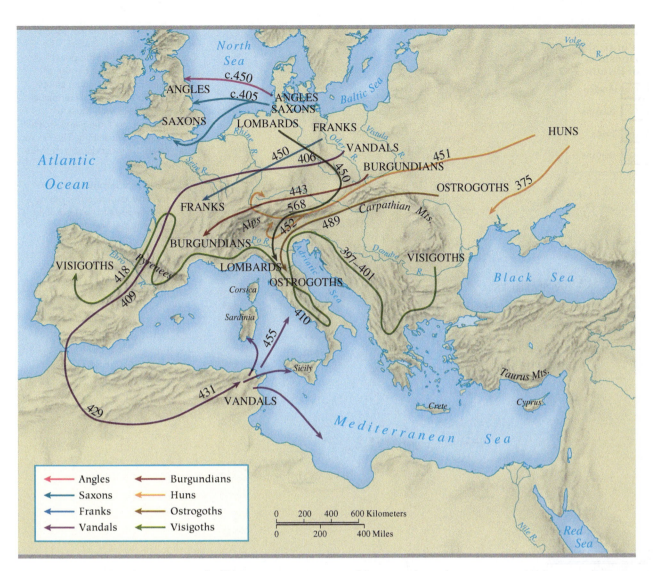

MAP 7.2 German Migration Routes. In the fifth century, various groups of Germans migrated throughout the Western Roman Empire. Pressure from Huns in the east forced some tribes to move west into the empire, and many tribes already in the empire became involved in conflicts. Some fought the Roman forces, while others were induced to move to the empire's far regions.

 How far did the Vandals travel and in what period of time?

Gaiseric sent a Vandal fleet to Italy and sacked the undefended city. Twenty-one years later, in 476, Odoacer (oh-doh-AY-sur), a new Master of the Soldiers, himself of German origin, deposed the Roman emperor, the boy Romulus Augustulus (RAHM-yuh-luss ow-GOOS-chuh-luss). To many historians, the deposition of Romulus signaled the end of the Roman Empire. Of course, this is only a symbolic date, since much of direct imperial rule had already been lost in the course of the fifth century. Even then the empire remained, as Odoacer presented himself as a German king obedient in theory to the Roman emperor Zeno (ZEE-noh) in Constantinople.

By the end of the fifth century, Roman imperial authority in the west had ceased. Nevertheless, the intellectual, governmental, and cultural traditions of the late Roman Empire continued to live on in the new Germanic kingdoms.

7-2 The Germanic Kingdoms

FOCUS QUESTIONS: What changes did the Germanic kingdoms make to the political, economic, and social conditions of the Western Roman Empire? What were the main features of Germanic law and society, and how did they differ from those of the Romans?

By 500 C.E., the Western Roman Empire was being replaced politically by a series of kingdoms ruled by German kings (see Map 7.3). Although the Germans now ruled, they were greatly outnumbered by the Romans, who still controlled most of the economic resources. Both were Christian, but many of the Germans were Arian Christians, considered heretics by

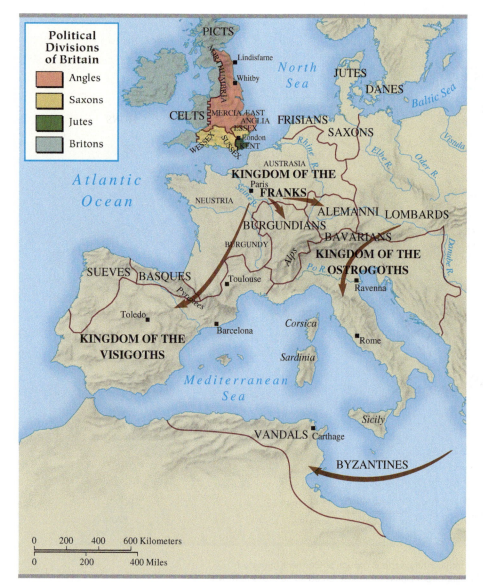

Political Divisions of Britain

🟥	Angles
🟨	Saxons
🟩	Jutes
⬜	Britons

MAP 7.3 The Germanic Kingdoms of the Old Western Empire. The Germanic tribes filled the power vacuum created by the demise of the Roman Empire, building states that blended elements of Germanic customs and laws with those of Roman culture, including large-scale conversions to Christianity. The Franks established the most durable of these Germanic states.

 How did the movements of the Franks during this period correspond to the borders of present-day France?

Romans who belonged to the Christian church in Rome, which had become known as the Roman Catholic Church. Gradually, the two groups merged into a common culture, although the pattern of settlement and the fusion of the Romans and Germans took different forms in the various Germanic kingdoms.

7-2a The Ostrogothic Kingdom of Italy

Zeno, the Roman emperor in Constantinople, was not pleased with Odoacer's actions and plotted to unseat him. In his desire to act against the German leader, Zeno brought another German tribe, the Ostrogoths (AHSS-truh-gahthss), into Italy. The Ostrogoths had recovered from a defeat by the Huns in the fourth century and under their king Theodoric (thee-AHD-uh-rik) (r. 493–526 C.E.) had attacked Constantinople. To divert them, Emperor Zeno invited Theodoric to act as his deputy to defeat Odoacer and bring Italy back into the empire. Theodoric accepted the challenge, marched into Italy, killed Odoacer, and then, contrary to Zeno's wishes, established himself as ruler of Italy in 493.

Theodoric's Rule More than any other Germanic state, the Ostrogothic kingdom of Italy managed to maintain the Roman tradition of government. Theodoric had received a Roman education while a hostage in Constantinople. After taking control of Italy, he was eager to synthesize Ostrogothic and Roman practices. In addition to maintaining the entire structure of Roman imperial government, he established separate systems of rule for the Ostrogoths and Romans. The Romans lived under Roman law administered by Roman officials. The Ostrogoths were governed by their own customs and officials. Nevertheless, although the Roman administrative system was kept intact, it was the Ostrogoths alone who controlled the army. Despite the apparent success of this "dual approach," Theodoric's system made possible a degree of stability by encouraging the living together of Germans and Romans.

In religion, too, Theodoric initially sought accommodation. Theodoric and his followers were Arian Christians but allowed Catholic Christians to worship and even provided funds for both groups to build new churches. Later, however, he abruptly

Church of San Juan Bautista, oldest church in Spain, erected in 661 by King Recceswinth, near Palencia, Castile and Leon, Spain/DE AGOSTINI EDITORE/Bridgeman Images

IMAGE 7.3 A Visigothic Church.
The church of St. John the Baptist is typical of Visigothic architecture in Spain. The Visigothic king Recceswinth, who had a very successful reign, had it built in 661 in gratitude for having been cured after bathing in the waters there. Modeled after Roman architecture, it is built in the style of a basilica with a central nave and aisles with a rounded horseshoe arch.

 What does the size of the church tell us about the Visigothic kingdom?

changed policies and was less tolerant of Catholics. Theodoric's rule grew ever harsher as discontent with Ostrogothic authority deepened.

End of the Ostrogothic Kingdom After Theodoric's death in 526 C.E., it quickly became apparent that much of his success had been due to the force of his own personality. His successors soon found themselves facing opposition from the imperial forces of the Eastern Roman Empire. Under Emperor Justinian (juh-STIN-ee-un) (r. 527–565) (see "7-4a The Reign of Justinian," later in this chapter), Eastern Roman armies reconquered Italy between 535 and 552, devastating much of the peninsula in the process and destroying Rome as one of the great urban centers of the Mediterranean world. The Eastern Roman reconquest proved ephemeral, however. Another German tribe, the Lombards, invaded Italy in 568 and conquered much of northern and central Italy. Unlike the Ostrogoths, the Lombards were harsh rulers and cared little for Roman structures and traditions. Their fondness for fighting each other enabled the Eastern Romans to retain control of some parts of Italy, especially the area around Ravenna, which became the capital of imperial government in the west.

7-2b The Visigothic Kingdom of Spain

The Visigoths had first settled in southern Gaul (France) in 418 C.E., but after the Vandals had migrated from Spain to North Africa, they moved into Spain and established another Germanic kingdom.

The Visigothic kingdom in Spain demonstrated a number of parallels to the Ostrogothic kingdom of Italy, and in fact, was initially dependent on Theodoric's Ostrogoths, with whom they made an alliance. Both favored coexistence between the Roman and German populations, both featured a warrior caste

dominating a larger native population, and both continued to maintain much of the Roman structure of government while largely excluding Romans from power. There were also noticeable differences, however. Perceiving that their Arianism was a stumbling block to good relations, in the late sixth century the Visigothic rulers converted to Latin or Catholic Christianity (see Image 7.3) and ended the tension caused by this heresy. Laws preventing intermarriage were dropped, and the Visigothic and Hispano-Roman peoples began to fuse together. A new body of law common to both peoples also developed.

The kingdom possessed one fatal weakness, however—the Visigoths fought constantly over the kingship. The Visigoths did not have a hereditary monarchy and lacked any established procedure for choosing new rulers. Church officials tried to help develop a sense of order, as this canon from the Fourth Council of Toledo in 633 illustrates: "No one of us shall dare to seize the kingdom; no one shall arouse sedition among the citizenry; no one shall think of killing the king." Church decrees failed to stop the feuds, however, and assassinations remained a way of life in Visigothic Spain. In 711, Muslim invaders destroyed the Visigothic kingdom itself (see "7-5 The Rise of Islam," later in this chapter).

7-2c The Frankish Kingdom

Only one of the German states on the European continent proved long-lasting—the kingdom of the Franks. The establishment of a Frankish kingdom was the work of Clovis (r. ca. 482–511 C.E.), the leader of one group of Franks who eventually became king of them all.

The Rule of Clovis Around 500 C.E., Clovis became a Catholic Christian. He was not the first German king to convert to Christianity, but the others had joined the Arian sect of Christianity. The Roman Catholic Church regarded the Arians as heretics, people who believed in teachings that departed from the official church doctrine on Christology. Clovis found that his conversion to Catholic Christianity gained him the support of the Roman Catholic Church, which was only too eager to obtain the friendship of a major Germanic ruler who was a Catholic Christian. The conversion of the king also paved the way for the conversion of the Frankish peoples. Finally, Clovis could pose as a defender of the orthodox Catholic faith in order to justify his expansion at the beginning of the sixth century. He defeated the Alemanni (al-uh-MAH-nee) in southwest Germany and the Visigoths in southern Gaul. By 510, Clovis had established a powerful new Frankish kingdom stretching from the Pyrenees in the west to German lands in the east (modern-day France and western Germany).

Clovis was thus responsible for establishing a Frankish kingdom under the Merovingian (meh-ruh-VIN-jee-un) dynasty, a name derived from Merovech, their semi-legendary ancestor. Clovis came to rely on his Frankish followers to rule in the old Roman city-states under the title of count. Often these officials were forced to share power with the Gallo-Roman Catholic bishops, producing a gradual fusion of Latin and German cultures, with the church serving to preserve the Latin culture. Clovis spent the last years of his life ensuring the survival of his dynasty by killing off relatives who were leaders of other groups of Franks.

The Successors of Clovis After the death of Clovis, his sons divided the newly created kingdom, as was the Frankish custom. During the sixth and seventh centuries C.E., the once-united Frankish kingdom came to be partitioned into three major areas: Neustria (NOO-stree-uh) in northern Gaul; Austrasia (aw-STRAY-zhuh), consisting of the ancient Frankish lands on both sides of the Rhine; and the former kingdom of Burgundy. All three were ruled by members of the Merovingian dynasty. Within the three territories, members of the dynasty were assisted by powerful nobles. Frankish society possessed a ruling class that gradually intermarried with the old Gallo-Roman senatorial class to form a new nobility. These noble families took advantage of their position to expand their own lands and wealth at the expense of the monarchy. Within the royal household, the position of *major domus* (my-YOR DOH-moos), or mayor of the palace, the chief officer of the king's household, began to overshadow the king. Essentially, both nobles and mayors of the palace were expanding their power at the expense of the kings.

At the beginning of the eighth century, the most important political development in the Frankish kingdom was the rise of Charles Martel, who served as mayor of the palace of Austrasia beginning in 714. Charles Martel led troops that defeated the Muslims near Poitiers (pwah-TYAY) in 732 and by the time of his death in 741 had become virtual ruler of the three Merovingian kingdoms. Though he was not king, Charles Martel's dynamic efforts put his family on the verge of creating a new dynasty that would establish an even more powerful Frankish state (see Chapter 8).

CHRONOLOGY	The Germanic Kingdoms
Theodoric establishes an Ostrogothic kingdom in Italy	493 C.E.
Clovis, king of the Franks, converts to Christianity	ca. 500
Reconquest of Italy by Byzantines	535–552
Lombards begin conquest of Italy	568
Muslims shatter Visigoth kingdom in Spain	711
Charles Martel defeats Muslims	732

During the sixth and seventh centuries, the Frankish kingdom witnessed a process of fusion between Gallo-Roman and Frankish cultures and peoples, a process accompanied by a significant decline in Roman standards of civilization and commercial activity. The Franks were warriors and did little to encourage either urban life or trade. Commerce declined in the interior, though seacoast towns maintained some activity. By 750, Frankish Gaul was basically an agricultural society in which the old Roman estates of the late empire continued unimpeded. Institutionally, however, Germanic concepts of kingship and customary law replaced the Roman governmental structure.

7-2d Anglo-Saxon England

The barbarian pressures on the Western Roman Empire had forced the emperors to withdraw the Roman armies and abandon Britain by the beginning of the fifth century C.E. This opened the door to the Angles and Saxons, Germanic tribes from Denmark and northern Germany. Although these same peoples had made plundering raids for a century, the withdrawal of the Roman armies enabled them to make settlements instead. They met with resistance from the Celtic Britons, however, who still controlled the western regions of Cornwall, Wales, and Cumberland at the beginning of the seventh century (see Map 7.3). The German invaders eventually succeeded in carving out small kingdoms throughout the island, such as Mercia, Northumberland, and Kent. This wave of German invaders would eventually be converted to Christianity by new groups of Christian missionaries (see "The Conversion of England" in Section 7-3e).

7-2e The Society of the Germanic Kingdoms

As the Germans infiltrated the Roman Empire, they were influenced by the Roman society they encountered. Consequently, the Germanic peoples of the fifth, sixth, and seventh centuries were probably quite different from the Germans that the forces of Augustus encountered in the first century C.E. Moreover, there was a meaningful fusion of Roman and German upper classes in the new kingdoms. In Merovingian Frankish lands, upper-class Gallo-Romans intermarried with Frankish nobles to produce a new ruling class. Each influenced the other.

Franks constructed Roman-style villas; Gallo-Romans adopted Frankish weapons.

The crucial social bond among the Germanic peoples was the family, especially the extended or patriarchal family of husbands, wives, children, brothers, sisters, cousins, and grandparents. In addition to working the land together and passing it down to succeeding generations, the extended family provided protection, which was sorely needed in the violent atmosphere of Merovingian times.

Germanic Law The German conception of family and kinship affected the way Germanic law treated the problem of crime and punishment. In the Roman system, as in our own, a crime such as murder was considered an offense against society or the state and was handled by a court that heard evidence and arrived at a decision. Germanic law tended to be personal. An injury by one person against another could lead to a blood feud in which the family of the injured party took revenge on the kin of the wrongdoer. Feuds could result in savage acts of revenge—hands or feet might be hacked off, eyes gouged out, or ears and noses sliced off. Since this system had a tendency to get out of control and allow mayhem to multiply, an alternative system arose that made use of a fine called *wergeld* (WURR-geld). This was the amount paid by a wrongdoer to the family of the person who had been injured or killed. Wergeld, which means "money for a man," was the value of a person in monetary terms. That value varied considerably according to social status. The law of the Salic Franks, which was first written down under Roman influence at the beginning of the sixth century, stated: "If any one shall have killed a free Frank, or a barbarian living under the Salic law, and it have been proved on him, he shall be sentenced to 8,000 denars. . . . But if any one has slain a man who is in the service of the king, he shall be sentenced to 24,000 denars."[8] An offense against a noble obviously cost considerably more than one against a free person or a slave.

Under German customary law, compurgation and the ordeal were the two most commonly used procedures for determining whether an accused person was guilty and should have to pay wergeld. Compurgation was the swearing of an oath by the accused person, backed up by a group of "oathhelpers," numbering twelve or twenty-five, who would also swear that the accused person should be believed. The ordeal functioned in a variety of ways, all of which were based on the principle of divine intervention; divine forces (whether pagan or Christian) would not allow an innocent person to be harmed (see Historical Voices, "Germanic Customary Law," p. 192).

The Frankish Family and Marriage For the Franks, like other Germanic peoples of the early Middle Ages, the extended family was at the center of social organization. The Frankish family structure was quite simple. Males were dominant and made all the important decisions. A woman obeyed her father until she married and then fell under the legal domination of her husband. A widow, however, could hold property without a male guardian. In Frankish law, the wergeld of a wife

of childbearing age—of value because she could produce children—was considerably higher than that of a man. The Salic law stated: "If any one killed a free woman after she had begun bearing children, he shall be sentenced to 24,000 denars. . . . After she can have no more children, he who kills her shall be sentenced to 8,000 denars."[9]

Since marriage affected the extended family group, fathers or uncles could arrange marriages for the good of the family without considering their children's wishes. Most important was the engagement ceremony in which a prospective son-in-law made a payment symbolizing the purchase of paternal authority over the bride. The essential feature of the marriage itself involved placing the married couple in bed to achieve their physical union. In first marriages, it was considered important that the wife be a virgin to ensure that any children would be the husband's. A virgin symbolized the ability of the bloodline to continue. For this reason, adultery was viewed as pollution of the woman and her offspring, poisoning the future. Adulterous wives were severely punished (an adulterous woman could be strangled or even burned alive); adulterous husbands were not. Divorce was relatively simple and was initiated primarily by the husband. Divorced wives simply returned to their families.

For most women in the new Germanic kingdoms, their legal status reflected the material conditions of their lives. Archaeological evidence suggests that most women had life expectancies of only thirty or forty years and that about 10 to 15 percent of women died in their childbearing years, no doubt due to complications associated with childbirth.

For most women, life consisted of domestic labor: providing food and clothing for the household, caring for the children, and assisting with numerous farming chores. This labor was crucial to the family economy. In addition to clothing and feeding their own families, women could sell or barter clothes and food for additional goods. Of all the duties of women, the most important was childbearing because it was crucial to the maintenance of the family and its properties.

7-3 Development of the Christian Church

FOCUS QUESTIONS: How and why did the organization of the Christian church and its relations with the state change during the fourth and fifth centuries? What was the role of the pope in the western Christian church? What were the chief characteristics of Benedictine monasticism? What role did monks play in both the conversion of Europe to Christianity and the intellectual life of the Germanic kingdoms?

By the end of the fourth century C.E., Christianity had become the predominant religion of the Roman Empire. As the official Roman state disintegrated, the Christian church played an increasingly important role in the new civilization built on the ruins of the old Roman Empire.

Germanic Customary Law: The Ordeal

 What was the purpose of the ordeal of hot water? What does it reveal about the nature of the society that used it? What conception of justice do you think was held by this society?

IN GERMANIC CUSTOMARY LAW, the ordeal came to be a means by which accused persons might clear themselves. Although the ordeal took different forms, all involved a physical trial of some sort, such as holding a red-hot iron. It was believed God would protect the innocent and allow them to come through the ordeal unharmed. This sixth-century account by Gregory of Tours (TOOR) describes an ordeal by hot water.

Gregory of Tours, *An Ordeal of Hot Water* (ca. 580 C.E.)

An Arian priest disputing with a deacon of our religion made venomous assertions against the Son of God and the Holy Ghost, as is the habit of that sect [the Arians]. But when the deacon had discoursed a long time concerning the reasonableness of our faith and the heretic, blinded by the fog of unbelief, continued to reject the truth . . . the former said: "Why weary ourselves with long discussions? Let acts approve the truth; let a kettle be heated over the fire and someone's ring be thrown into the boiling water. Let him who shall take it from the heated liquid be approved as a follower of the truth, and afterward let the other party be converted to the knowledge of the truth. And do you also understand, O heretic, that this our party will fulfill the conditions with the aid of the Holy Ghost; you shall confess that there is no discordance, no dissimilarity in the Holy Trinity [belief that God, Jesus (son of God), and Holy Spirit (Ghost) are three manifestations of the same unique Deity]." The heretic consented to

the proposition and they separated after appointing the next morning for the trial. But the fervor of faith in which the deacon had first made this suggestion began to cool through the instigation of the enemy. Rising with the dawn he bathed his arm in oil and smeared it with ointment. But nevertheless he made the round of the sacred places and called in prayer on the Lord. . . . About the third hour they met in the marketplace. The people came together to see the show. A fire was lighted, the kettle was placed upon it, and when it grew very hot the ring was thrown into the boiling water. The deacon invited the heretic to take it out of the water first. But he promptly refused, saying, "You who did propose this trial are the one to take it out." The deacon all of a tremble bared his arm. And when the heretic saw it besmeared with ointment he cried out: "With magic arts you have thought to protect yourself, that you have made use of these salves, but what you have done will not avail." While they were thus quarreling there came up a deacon from Ravenna named Iacinthus and inquired what the trouble was about. When he learned the truth he drew his arm out from under his robe at once and plunged his right hand into the kettle. Now the ring that had been thrown in was a little thing and very light so that it was thrown about by the water as chaff would be blown about by the wind; and searching for it a long time he found it after about an hour. Meanwhile the flame beneath the kettle blazed up mightily so that the greater heat might make it difficult for the ring to be followed by the hand; but the deacon extracted it at length and suffered no harm, protesting rather that at the bottom the kettle was cold while at the top it was just pleasantly warm. When the heretic beheld this he was greatly confused and audaciously thrust his hand into the kettle saying, "My faith will aid me." As soon as his hand had been thrust in all the flesh was boiled off the bones clear up to the elbow. And so the dispute ended.

Source: *Translations and Reprints from the Original Sources of European History*, vol. 4., trans. A. C. Howland (Philadelphia: University of Pennsylvania Press, 1898).

7-3a The Church Fathers

A number of intellectuals in the early church who wrote in Latin profoundly influenced the development of Christian thought in the west. They came to be known as the Latin Fathers of the Catholic Church. They include Augustine, Jerome, Ambrose, and Gregory the Great (the last two are discussed in "Church and State" and "Pope Gregory the Great" later in this chapter).

The Work of Augustine Saint Augustine (AW-guh-steen) (354–430 C.E.) was the most prominent of the Latin Fathers. His work provides one of the best examples of how Christian theologians used pagan culture in the service of Christianity.

Born in North Africa, Augustine was reared by his mother, an ardent Christian. He eventually became a professor of rhetoric at Milan in 384. But two years later, after experiencing a profound and moving religious experience, Augustine gave up his teaching position and went back to North Africa, where he served as bishop of Hippo from 396 until his death in 430.

Augustine's two most famous works are the *Confessions* and *The City of God*. Written in 397, the *Confessions* was a self-portrait not of Augustine's worldly activities but of the "history of a heart," an account of his own personal and spiritual experiences, written to help others with their search. Augustine describes how he struggled throughout his early life to find God until in his thirty-second year he

The *Confessions* of Augustine

 What was the nature of Augustine's conversion experience? How did it affect his life and teaching?

SAINT AUGUSTINE'S SPIRITUAL and intellectual autobiography is a revealing self-portrait of the inner struggles of one of the intellectual giants of early Christianity. The first excerpt is taken from Book 8, in which Augustine describes how he heard a voice from heaven and was converted from his old habits. In the second excerpt, from Book 9, Augustine expresses joy and gratitude for his conversion.

Augustine, *Confessions*
From Book 8

So was I speaking and weeping in the most bitter contrition of my heart, when, lo! I heard from a neighboring house a voice as of boy or girl, I know not, chanting, and oft repeating, "Take up and read; Take up and read." Instantly, my countenance altered, I began to think most intently whether children were wont in any kind of play to sing such words: nor could I remember ever to have heard the like. So checking the torrent of my tears, I arose; interpreting it to be no other than a command from God to open the book, and read the first chapter I should find. For I had heard of Antony, that coming in during the reading of the Gospel, he received the admonition, as if what was being read was spoken to him:

Go, sell all that you have, and give to the poor, and you shall have treasure in heaven, and come and follow me: and by such oracle he was forthwith converted unto You. Eagerly then I returned to the place where Alypius was sitting; for there I had laid the volume of the Apostle [Paul] when I arose thence. I seized, opened, and in silence read that section on which my eyes first fell: Not in rioting and drunkenness, not in chambering and wantonness, not in strife and envying; but put you on the Lord Jesus Christ, and make not provision for the flesh. . . . No further would I read; nor need I: for instantly at the end of this sentence, by a light as it were of serenity infused into my heart, all the darkness of doubt vanished away.

From Book 9

O Lord I am your servant; I am your servant, and the son of your handmaid: You have broken my bonds in sunder. I will offer to You the sacrifice of praise. Let my heart and my tongue praise You; yea, let all my bones say, O Lord, who is like unto You? Let them say, and answer You me, and say unto my soul, I am your salvation. Who am I, and what am I? What evil have not been either my deeds, or if not my deeds, my words, or if not my words, my will? But You, O Lord, are good and merciful, and your right hand had respect unto the depth of my death, and from the bottom of my heart emptied that abyss of corruption.

Source: *The Confessions of St. Augustine*, trans. E. B. Pusey (New York: P. F. Collier & Son, 1838).

experienced a miraculous conversion (see Historical Voices, "The Confessions of Augustine," above).

The City of God, Augustine's other major work, was a profound expression of a Christian philosophy of government and history. In it, Augustine theorized on the ideal relations between two kinds of societies existing throughout time—the City of God and the City of the World. Those who loved God would be loyal to the City of God, whose ultimate location was the kingdom of heaven. Earthly society would always be insecure because of human beings' imperfect nature and inclination to violate God's commandments. And yet the City of the World was still necessary, for it was the duty of rulers to curb the depraved instincts of sinful humans and maintain the peace necessary for Christians to live in the world. Hence, Augustine posited that secular government and authority were necessary for the pursuit of the true Christian life on earth; in doing so, he provided a justification for secular political authority that would play an important role in medieval thought.

Augustine was also important in establishing the Christian church's views on theological issues. Only faith alone in Jesus, he believed, imparted by divine grace, could save undeserving humans from the damnation they merited. Augustine also posited the belief that only God knew who would be saved and who would be damned, a doctrine of predestination that would play an important role in the Reformation of the sixteenth century (see Chapter 13). Augustine was also influential in determining a Christian view of sexual desire. Many early Christians had seen **celibacy** (SELL-uh-buh-see), or complete abstinence from sexual activity, as the surest way to holiness. Augustine, too, believed Christians should reject sex, but he maintained that many Christians were unable to do so. For them, marriage was a good alternative, but with the understanding that even in marriage, sex between a man and woman had to serve a purpose—the procreation of children. It was left to the clergy of the church to uphold the high ideal of celibacy. Augustine's active role as bishop of Hippo also provided a model for later bishops.

Jerome and the Bible Another Latin Father was Jerome (345–420 C.E.), who pursued literary studies in Rome and became a master of Latin prose. Jerome had mixed feelings about his love for liberal studies, however, and like Augustine, experienced a spiritual conversion, after which he tried to dedicate himself more fully to Jesus. He had a dream in which Jesus appeared as his judge:

> Asked who and what I was, I replied: "I am a Christian." But He who presided said: "You lie, you are a follower of Cicero, not of Christ. For where your treasure is, there will your heart be also." Instantly, I became dumb. . . . Accordingly I made oath and called upon His name, saying: "Lord, if ever again I possess worldly books [the classics], or if ever again I read such, I have denied You."

After this dream, Jerome determined to "read the books of God with a zeal greater than I had previously given to the books of men."[10]

Ultimately, Jerome found a compromise by purifying the literature of the pagan world and then using it to further the Christian faith. Jerome was the greatest scholar among the Latin Fathers, and his extensive knowledge of both Hebrew and Greek enabled him to translate the Old and New Testaments into Latin. In the process, he created the so-called Latin Vulgate, or common text, of the Scriptures that became the standard edition for the Catholic Church in the Middle Ages.

7-3b The Power of the Pope

In the early centuries of Christianity, the churches in the larger cities had great influence in the administration of the church. It was only natural, then, that the bishops of those cities would also exercise considerable power. One of the far-reaching developments in the history of the Christian church was the emergence of one bishop—that of Rome—as the recognized leader of the western Christian church.

The doctrine of **Petrine supremacy**, based on the belief that the bishops of Rome occupied a preeminent position in the church, was grounded in Scripture. According to the Gospel of Matthew, when Jesus asked his disciples, "Who do you say I am?" Simon Peter answered:

> You are the Christ, the Son of the living God. Jesus replied, Blessed are you, Simon, son of Jonah, for this was not revealed by man, but by my Father in heaven. And I tell you that you are Peter, and on this rock I will build my church, and the gates of hell will not overcome it. I will give you the keys of the kingdom of heaven; whatever you bind on earth will be bound in heaven; and whatever you loose on earth will be loosed in heaven.[11]

According to church tradition, Jesus had given the keys to the kingdom of heaven to Peter, who was considered the chief apostle and the first bishop of Rome. Subsequent bishops of Rome were considered Peter's successors and later the "vicars of Christ" on earth. Though this exalted view of the bishops of Rome was by no means accepted by all early Christians, Rome's position as the traditional capital of the Roman Empire served to buttress this claim.

By the end of the fourth century C.E., the bishops of Rome were using the title of *papa*, "father" (which became the English *pope*). Pope Leo I (440–461) was especially energetic in systematically expounding the doctrine of Petrine supremacy. He portrayed himself as the heir of Peter, whom Jesus had chosen to be head of the Christian church. Pope Leo is also known for stopping the advance of Attila and the Huns as they prepared to attack and sack the city of Rome (see Historical Voices, "Pope Leo Meets Attila the Hun," p. 195). After a meeting with the pope, Attila and his troops turned back.

7-3c Church and State

Although the popes claimed authority over the Christian church, state authorities were also claiming some power over the church. Once the Roman emperors became Christians, they came to play a significant role in the affairs of the church. Christian emperors viewed themselves as God's representatives on earth. They not only built churches and influenced the structure of the church's organization but also became involved in church government and doctrinal controversies.

While emperors were busying themselves in church affairs, the spiritual and political vacuum left by the disintegration of the Roman state allowed bishops to play a more active role in imperial government. Increasingly, they served as advisers to Christian Roman emperors. Moreover, as imperial authority declined, bishops often played a noticeably independent political role. Ambrose (ca. 339–397 C.E.) of Milan was an early example of a strong and independent bishop. Through his activities and writings, which brought him recognition as another of the four Latin Fathers of the Catholic Church, Ambrose created an image of the ideal Christian bishop. Among other things, this ideal bishop would defend the independence of the church against the tendency of imperial officials to oversee church policy: "Exalt not yourself, but if you would reign the longer, be subject to God. It is written, God's to God and Caesar's to Caesar. The palace is the Emperor's, the Churches are the Bishop's."[12] When Emperor Theodosius I ordered the massacre of many citizens of Thessalonika for refusing to obey his commands, Ambrose denounced the massacre and refused to allow the emperor to take part in church ceremonies. Theodosius finally agreed to do public penance in the cathedral of Milan for his dastardly deed. Ambrose proved himself a formidable advocate of the position that spiritual authority should take precedence over temporal power, at least in spiritual matters.

The weakness of the political authorities on the Italian peninsula also contributed to the church's independence in that area. In the Germanic kingdoms, the kings controlled both churches and bishops. But in Italy, a different tradition prevailed, fed by semi-legendary accounts of papal deeds. For example, as we have seen, Pope Leo I supposedly caused Attila the Hun to turn away from Rome in 452. Popes, then, played significant political roles in Italy, which only added to their claims of power vis-à-vis the secular authorities. As Pope Gelasius (juh-LAY-shuss) I (492–496) wrote to the emperor at Constantinople:

> There are two powers, august Emperor, by which this world is ruled from the beginning: the consecrated authority of the bishops, and the royal power. In these matters the priests bear the heavier burden because they will render account, even for rulers of men, at the divine judgment. Besides, most gracious son, you are aware that, although you in your office are the ruler of the human race, nevertheless you devoutly bow your head before those who are leaders in things divine and look to them for the means of your salvation.[13]

HISTORICAL VOICES

Pope Leo Meets Attila the Hun

 According to this account, why did Attila withdraw from his planned attack of Rome? What do you think motivated this author's account of the encounter?

THE ACCOUNT OF POPE LEO'S ENCOUNTER with Attila the Hun was first written down by Prosper, a Christian chronicler, in 455 C.E. and later turned into a miraculous tale by an unknown Christian author. The excerpt that follows is taken from the latter. Modern historians argue that Attila and his force withdrew after Pope Leo promised food and supplies to the disease-ridden Hun army.

An Account of the Encounter of Pope Leo and Attila the Hun

Attila, the leader of the Huns, who was called the scourge of God, came into Italy, inflamed with fury, after he had laid with most savage frenzy [many regions of Europe]. He was utterly cruel in inflicting torture, greedy in plundering, insolent in abuse. . . . He . . . razed to the ground those regal cities, Pavia and Milan; he laid waste many other towns, and was rushing down upon Rome.

Then Leo had compassion on the calamity of Italy and Rome, and with one of the consuls and a large part of the Roman senate he went to meet Attila. The old man of harmless simplicity, venerable in his gray hair and his majestic garb, ready of his own will to give himself entirely for the defense of his flock, went forth to meet the tyrant who was destroying all things. He met Attila, it is said, in the neighborhood of the river Mincio, and he spoke to the grim monarch, saying: "The senate and the people of Rome, once conquerors of the world, now indeed vanquished, come before you as suppliants. We pray for mercy and deliverance. O Attila, you king of kings, you could have no greater glory to see suppliant at your feet this people before whom once all peoples and kings lay suppliant. You have subdued, O Attila, the whole circle of the lands which it was granted to the Romans, victors over all peoples, to conquer. Now we pray that you, who hast conquered others should conquer yourself. The people have felt your scourge; now as suppliants they would feel your mercy."

As Leo said these things, Attila stood looking upon his venerable garb and aspect, silent, as if thinking deeply. And lo, suddenly there were seen the apostles Peter and Paul, clad like bishops, standing by Leo, the one on the right hand, the other on the left. They held swords stretched out over his head, and threatened Attila with death if he did not obey the pope's command. Wherefore Attila was appeased by Leo's intercession . . . he who had raged as one mad. He straightway promised a lasting peace and withdrew beyond the Danube.

Source: J. H. Robinson, *Readings in European History*, vol. 1 (Boston: Ginn and Company, 1914), pp. 50–51.

According to Gelasius, though there were two ruling powers, spiritual and temporal, with different functions, the church was ultimately the higher authority because all men, including emperors, must look to the church "for the means of . . . salvation."

7-3d Pope Gregory the Great

Although eventually western Christians came to accept the bishop of Rome as head of the church, there was no unanimity on the extent of the powers the pope possessed as a result of his position. Nevertheless, the emergence in the sixth century C.E. of a strong pope, Gregory I, known as Gregory the Great, the last of the Latin Fathers, set the papacy and the Roman Catholic Church on an energetic path that enabled the church in the seventh and eighth centuries to play an increasingly prominent role in civilizing the Germans and aiding the emergence of a distinctly new European civilization (see Image 7.4).

As pope, Gregory I (590–604) assumed direction of Rome and its surrounding territories, which had suffered enormously from the Ostrogothic-Byzantine struggle and the Lombard invasion of the sixth century. Gregory described the conditions in a sermon to the people of Rome:

What Rome herself, once deemed the Mistress of the World, has now become, we see—wasted away with afflictions grievous and many, with the loss of citizens, the assaults of enemies, the frequent fall of ruined buildings. . . . Where is the Senate? Where is the people? The bones are all dissolved, the flesh is consumed, all the pomp of the dignities of this world is gone.[14]

Gregory took charge and made Rome and its surrounding area into an administrative unit that eventually came to be known as the Papal States. Although historians disagree about Gregory's motives in establishing papal temporal power, no doubt Gregory was probably only doing what he felt needed to be done: provide for the defense of Rome against the Lombards, establish a government for Rome, and feed the people. Gregory remained loyal to the empire and continued to address the Byzantine emperor as the rightful ruler of Italy.

Gregory also pursued a policy of extending papal authority over the Christian church in the west, although few people in Europe at this time looked to the pope as the church's ruler. He intervened in ecclesiastical conflicts throughout Italy and corresponded with the Frankish rulers, urging them to reform the church in Gaul. He successfully initiated the efforts of missionaries to convert England to Christianity and was especially

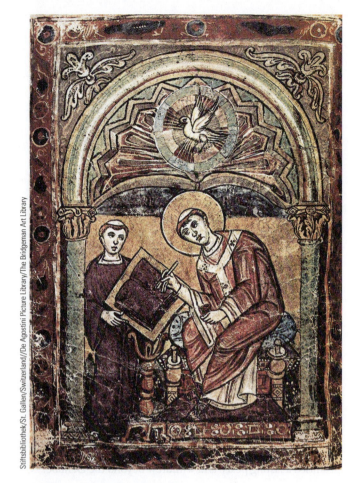

Stiftsbibliothek/St. Gallen/Switzerland//De Agostini Picture Library/The Bridgeman Art Library

IMAGE 7.4 Pope Gregory I. Pope Gregory the Great became one of the most important popes of the early Middle Ages. As a result of his numerous writings, he is considered the last of the Latin Fathers of the church. This ninth-century manuscript illustration shows Gregory working on a manuscript, assisted by a monk. Above Gregory's head is a dove, symbol of the Holy Spirit, which is providing divine inspiration for what he is writing.

active in converting the pagan peoples of Germanic Europe. His primary instrument was the monastic movement.

7-3e The Monks and Their Missions

A **monk** (Latin *monachus*, meaning "someone who lives alone") was a man who sought to live a life divorced from the world, cut off from ordinary human society, in order to pursue an ideal of godliness or total dedication to the will of God. Christian **monasticism**, which developed first in Egypt, was initially based on the model of the solitary hermit who forsakes all civilized society to pursue spirituality. Saint Anthony (ca. 250–350 C.E.) was a prosperous Egyptian peasant who decided to follow Jesus's injunction in the Gospel of Mark: "Go your way, sell whatsoever you have, and give to the poor, and you shall have treasure in heaven: and come, take up the cross, and follow me."[15] Anthony gave his three hundred acres of land to the poor and went into the desert to pursue his ideal of holiness (see Historical Voices, "The Life of Saint Anthony," p. 197). Others did likewise, often to extremes. Saint Simeon the Stylite lived for three decades in a basket atop a pillar more than 60 feet high. These spiritual

gymnastics established a new ideal for Christianity. Whereas the early Christian model had been the martyr who died for the faith and achieved eternal life in the process, the new ideal was the monk who died to the world and achieved spiritual life through denial, asceticism, and mystical experience of God.

These early monks, however, soon found themselves unable to live in solitude. Their feats of holiness attracted followers on a wide scale, and as the monastic ideal spread throughout the east, a new form of monasticism, based on the practice of communal life, soon became the dominant form. Monastic communities soon came to be seen as the ideal Christian society that could provide a moral example to the wider society around them.

Benedictine Monasticism Saint Benedict of Nursia (ca. 480–543 C.E.), who founded a monastic house and wrote a set of rules for it sometime between 520 and 530, established the fundamental form of monastic life in the western Christian church (see Image 7.5). Benedict's rules largely rejected the ascetic ideals of eastern monasticism, which had tended to emphasize such practices as fasting and self-inflicted torments (such as living atop pillars for thirty years), in favor of an ideal of moderation. In Chapter 40 of the rules, on the amount of drink a monk should imbibe, this sense of moderation becomes apparent:

> "Every man has his proper gift from God, one after this manner, another after that." And therefore it is with some misgiving that we determine the amount of food for someone else. Still, having regard for the weakness of some brothers, we believe that a hemina [a quarter liter] of wine per day will suffice for all. Let those, however, to whom God gives the gift of abstinence, know that they shall have their proper reward. But if either the circumstances of the place, the work, or the heat of summer necessitates more, let it lie in the discretion of the abbot to grant it. But let him take care in all things lest satiety or drunkenness supervene.

St. Benedict delivering his Rule/BRITISH LIBRARY/British Library, London, UK/Bridgeman Images

IMAGE 7.5 Saint Benedict Delivering His Rule. Benedict was the author of a set of rules that was instrumental in the development of monastic groups in the Catholic Church. In this twelfth-century Latin manuscript miniature, Saint Benedict is shown delivering his rule to Saint Maurus and other monks of his order.

The Life of Saint Anthony

 Based on this account by Athanasius, how would you characterize the ascetic ideals of early Christian monks? How important were those ideals to the growth of early Christianity? What do you think would be the broader cultural effects of a Christian hatred of the human body?

IN THE THIRD AND EARLY FOURTH CENTURIES, the lives of martyrs had provided important models for early Christianity. But in the course of the fourth century C.E., monks who attempted to achieve spiritual perfection through asceticism, the denial of earthly life, and the struggle with demons became the new spiritual ideal for Christians. Consequently, spiritual biographies of early monks became a significant new form of Christian literature. Especially noteworthy was *The Life of Saint Anthony* by Saint Athanasius, the defender of Catholic orthodoxy against the Arians. His work had been translated into Latin before 386. This excerpt describes how Anthony fought off the temptations of Satan.

Athanasius, *The Life of Saint Anthony*

Now when the Enemy [Satan] saw that his craftiness in this matter was without profit, and that the more he brought temptation into Saint Anthony, the more strenuous the saint was in protecting himself against him with the armor of righteousness, he attacked him by means of the vigor of early manhood which is bound up in the nature of our humanity. With the goadings of passion he sued to trouble him by night, and in the daytime also he would vex him and pain him with the same to such an extent that even those who saw him knew from his appearance that he was waging war against the Adversary. But the more the Evil One brought unto him filthy and maddening thoughts, the more Saint Anthony took refuge in prayer and in abundant supplication, and amid them all he remained wholly chaste. And the Evil One was working upon him every shameful deed according to his wont, and at length he even appeared unto Saint Anthony in the form of a woman; and other things which resembled this he performed with ease, for such things are a subject for boasting to him.

But the blessed Anthony knelt down upon his knees on the ground, and prayed before Him who said, "Before you criest unto Me, I will answer you," and said, "O my Lord, this I entreat you. Let not Your love be blotted out from my mind, and behold, I am, by Your grace, innocent before You." And again the Enemy multiplied in him the thoughts of lust, until Saint Anthony became as one who was being burned up, not through the Evil One, but through his own lusts; but he girded himself about with the threat of the thought of the Judgment, and of the torture of Gehenna [Hell], and of the worm which does not die. And while meditating on the thoughts which could be directed against the Evil One, he prayed for thoughts which would be hostile to him. Thus, to the reproach and shame of the Enemy, these things could not be performed; for he who imagined that he could be God was made a mock of by a young man, and he who boasted over flesh and blood was vanquished by a man who was clothed with flesh.

Source: A. Freemantle, *A Treasury of Early Christianity* (Denver, Colo.: Mentor Books, 1953).

At the same time, moderation did not preclude a hard and disciplined existence based on the ideals of stability (staying in the monastery for life), fidelity (accepting the routine of the monastery), and obedience (to the abbot as head of the monastery).

Benedict's rules divided each day into a series of activities with primary emphasis on prayer and manual labor. Physical work of some kind was required of all monks for several hours a day because "idleness is the enemy of the soul." At the very heart of community practice was prayer, the proper "work of God." While this included private meditation and reading, all monks gathered together seven times during the day for common prayer and chanting of psalms. A Benedictine life was a communal one; monks ate, worked, slept, and worshiped together.

Each Benedictine monastery was strictly ruled by an **abbot**, or "father" of the monastery, who had complete authority over the monks, who bent unquestioningly to the will of the abbot. Each Benedictine monastery owned lands that enabled it to be a self-sustaining community, isolated from and independent of the world surrounding it. Within the monastery, however, monks were to fulfill an ideal of poverty: "Let all things be common to all, as it is written, lest anyone should say that anything is his own or arrogate it to himself."[16] By the eighth century, Benedictine monasticism had spread throughout the west.

Women, too, sought to withdraw from the world to dedicate themselves to God. Already in the third century, groups of women abandoned the cities to form communities in the deserts of Egypt and Syria. The first monastic rules for western women were produced by Caesarius of Arles for his sister in the fifth century. They strongly emphasized a rigid cloistering of female religious, known as **nuns**, to preserve them from dangers. Later in the west, in the seventh and eighth centuries, the growth of double monasteries allowed monks and nuns to reside close by and follow a common set of rules. Not all women pursued the celibate life in the desert, however. In a number of cities in the fourth century, women organized religious communities in their own homes.

Irish Monasticism and the Penitential

 What does the penitential of Cummean reveal about the nature of Irish monasticism? What do you think was the theory of human sexuality held by early Irish Christianity?

IRISH MONASTICISM BECAME WELL KNOWN for its ascetic practices. It emphasized careful examination of conscience to determine whether one had committed a sin against God. To facilitate this examination, penitentials were developed that listed possible sins with appropriate penances. Penance usually meant fasting—taking only bread and water—for a number of days each week. Although these penitentials were eventually used throughout Christendom, they were especially important in Irish Christianity. This excerpt from the penitential of Cummean, an Irish abbot, was written about 650 C.E. and demonstrates a distinctive feature of the penitentials, an acute preoccupation with sexual sins.

The Penitential of Cummean

A bishop who commits fornication shall be degraded and shall do penance for twelve years.

A priest or a deacon who commits natural fornication, having previously taken the vow of a monk, shall do penance for seven years. He shall ask pardon every hour; he shall perform a special fast during every week except in the days between Easter and Pentecost.

He who defiles his mother shall do penance for three years, with perpetual pilgrimage.

So shall those who commit sodomy do penance every seven years.

He who merely desires in his mind to commit fornication, but is not able, shall do penance for one year, especially in the three forty-day periods.

He who is willingly polluted during sleep shall arise and sing nine psalms in order, kneeling. On the following day, he shall live on bread and water.

A cleric who commits fornication once shall do penance for one year on bread and water; if he begets a son he shall do penance for seven years as an exile; so also a virgin.

He who loves any woman, but is unaware of any evil beyond a few conversations, shall do penance for forty days.

He who is in a state of matrimony ought to be continent during the three forty-day periods and on Saturday and on Sunday, night and day, and in the two appointed week days [Wednesday and Friday], and after conception, and during the entire menstrual period.

After a birth he shall abstain, if it is a son, for thirty-three [days]; if a daughter, for sixty-six [days].

Boys talking alone and transgressing the regulations of the elders [in the monastery], shall be corrected by three special fasts.

Children who imitate acts of fornication, twenty days; if frequently, forty.

But boys of twenty years who practice masturbation together and confess [shall do penance] twenty or forty days before they take communion.

Source: J. T. McNeilland and H. M. Garner, eds., *Medieval Handbooks of Penance* (New York: Columbia University Press, 1990).

Monasticism played an indispensable role in early medieval civilization. Monks became the new heroes of Christian civilization. Their dedication to God became the highest ideal of Christian life. Moreover, the monks played an increasingly significant role in spreading Christianity to all of Europe.

Irish Monks As Missionaries Ireland had remained a Celtic outpost beyond the reach of the Roman Empire and the Germanic invaders. The most famous of the Christian missionaries to Ireland in the fifth century C.E. was Saint Patrick (ca. 390–461). Son of a Romano-British Christian, Patrick was kidnapped as a young man by Irish raiders and kept as a slave in Ireland. After his escape to Gaul, he became a monk and chose to return to Ireland to convert the Irish to Christianity. Irish tradition ascribes to Patrick the title of "founder of Irish Christianity," a testament to his apparent success.

Since Ireland had not been part of the Roman world and was fairly isolated from the European continent even after its conversion, Irish Christianity tended to develop along lines somewhat different from Roman Christianity. Whereas Catholic ecclesiastical structure had followed Roman government models, the absence of these models in Ireland led to a different pattern of church organization. Rather than bishoprics, monasteries became the fundamental units of church organization, and abbots, the heads of the monasteries, exercised far more control over the Irish church than bishops did.

By the sixth century, Irish monasticism was a flourishing institution with its own striking characteristics. It was strongly ascetic. Monks performed strenuous fasts, prayed and meditated frequently under extreme privations, and confessed their sins on a regular basis to their superiors. In fact, Irish monasticism gave rise to the use of penitentials or manuals that provided a guide for examining one's life to see what offenses against the will of God had been committed (see Historical Voices, "Irish Monasticism and the Penitential," above).

A great love of learning also characterized Irish monasticism. The Irish eagerly absorbed both Latin and Greek culture and fostered education as a major part of their monastic life.

Anglo-Saxon kingdom of Northumbria. Lindisfarne in turn became a training center for monks who spread out to different parts of Anglo-Saxon England. Meanwhile, other Irish monks traveled to the European mainland. New monasteries founded by the Irish became centers of learning wherever they were located.

The Conversion of England At the same time the Irish monks were busy bringing their version of Christianity to the Anglo-Saxons of Britain, Pope Gregory the Great had set in motion his own effort to convert England to Roman Christianity. His most important agent was Augustine, a monk from a monastery in Rome, who arrived in England in 597 C.E. England at that time had a number of Anglo-Saxon kingdoms. Augustine went first to Kent, where he converted King Ethelbert, whereupon most of the king's subjects followed suit. Pope Gregory's conversion techniques emphasized persuasion rather than force, and as seen in this excerpt from one of his letters, he was willing to assimilate old pagan practices in order to coax the pagans into the new faith:

> We wish you [Abbot Mellitus] to inform him [Augustine] that we have been giving careful thought to the affairs of the English, and have come to the conclusion that the temples of the idols among that people should on no account be destroyed. The idols are to be destroyed, but the temples themselves are to be sprinkled with holy water, altars set up in them, and relics deposited there. For if these temples are well-built, they must be purified from the worship of demons and dedicated to the service of the true God. In this way, we hope that the people, seeing that their temples are not destroyed, may abandon their error and, flocking more readily to their accustomed resorts, may come to know and adore the true God.[17]

Freed of their pagan past, temples became churches, as one Christian commentator noted with joy: "The dwelling place of demons has become a house of God. The saving light has come to shine, where shadows covered all. Where sacrifices once took place and idols stood, angelic choirs now dance. Where God was angered once, now God is made content."[18]

Likewise, old pagan feasts were given new names and incorporated into the Christian calendar. No doubt Gregory was aware that early Christians had done the same. The Christian feast of Christmas, for example, was held on December 25, the day of the pagan celebration of the winter solstice.

As Roman Christianity spread northward in Britain, it encountered Irish Christianity moving southward. Soon arguments arose over the differences between Irish and Roman Christianity, especially over different calendar days for the feast of Easter and matters of discipline. At the Synod of Whitby, held in the kingdom of Northumbria in 664, the king of Northumbria accepted the arguments of the representatives of Roman Christianity and decided the issue in favor of Roman practices. A gradual fusion of Irish and Roman Christianity now ensued. Despite its newfound unity and loyalty to Rome, the English church retained some Irish features.

© The Board of Trinity College, Dublin Ireland/The Bridgeman Art Library

IMAGE 7.6 **The Book of Kells.** Art historians use the term *Hiberno-Saxon* (Hibernia was the ancient name for Ireland) or *Insular* to refer to works produced primarily in the monasteries of the British Isles, especially Ireland. The best example of Hiberno-Saxon art is *The Book of Kells*, a richly decorated illuminated manuscript of the Christian gospels. Though owned by the monastery of Kells, the work was produced by the monks of Iona, who combined Celtic and Anglo-Saxon abstract designs with elaborate portrayals of human figures and animals. A twelfth-century priest who viewed it observed: "Look . . . keenly at it and you . . . will make out intricacies, so delicate and subtle, so exact and compact, so was the work of an angel, and not of a man." This introductory page from the Gospel of Matthew shows Jesus with four angels.

 Why do you think the monks of Iona used such abstract designs?

Irish monks were preserving classical Latin at the same time spoken Latin was being corrupted on the continent into new dialects that eventually became the Romance languages, such as Italian, French, and Spanish. Irish monasteries produced extraordinary illuminated manuscripts illustrated with abstract geometric patterns (see Image 7.6).

The emphasis on asceticism led many Irish monks to go into voluntary exile. This "exile for the love of God" was not into isolation, however, but into missionary activity. Irish monks became fervid missionaries. Saint Columba (521–597) left Ireland in 565 as a "pilgrim for Christ" and founded a highly influential monastic community off the coast of Scotland on the island of Iona. From there Irish missionaries went to northern England to begin the process of converting the Angles and Saxons. Aidan of Iona, for example, founded the island monastery of Lindisfarne (LIN-dis-farn) in the

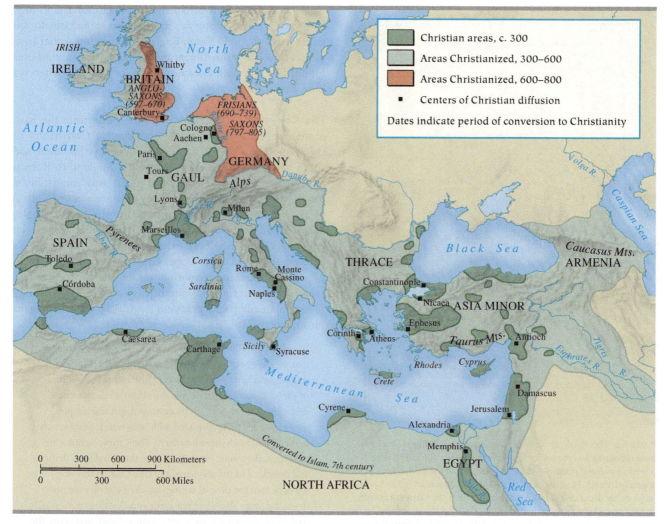

Legend

■ (dark green)	Christian areas, c. 300
■ (light green)	Areas Christianized, 300–600
■ (orange)	Areas Christianized, 600–800
■	Centers of Christian diffusion

Dates indicate period of conversion to Christianity

MAP 7.4 The Spread of Christianity, 400–800 c.e. The Christian church had penetrated much of the Roman Empire by the end of the fifth century. After the fall of the empire, the church emerged as a major base of power and pushed its influence into new areas through the activities of missionaries.

 What aspects of geography help explain the relatively late conversions of the Anglo-Saxons in Britain and the Frisians and Saxons east of the Rhine River?

Most important was the concentration on monastic culture with special emphasis on learning and missionary work. By 700, the English clergy had become the best trained and most learned in western Europe.

Following the Irish example, English monks journeyed to the European continent to carry on the work of conversion (see Map 7.4). Most important was Boniface (ca. 675–754), who undertook the conversion of pagan Germans in Frisia, Bavaria, and Saxony. By 740, Saint Boniface, the "Apostle of the Germans," had become the most famous churchman in Europe. Fourteen years later, he was killed while trying to convert the pagan Frisians. Boniface was a brilliant example of the numerous Irish and English monks whose tireless efforts made Europe the bastion of the Roman Catholic faith.

Women and Monasticism Women, too, played an important role in the monastic missionary movement and the conversion of the Germanic kingdoms. Double monasteries, where monks and nuns lived in separate houses but attended church services together, were found in both the English and Frankish kingdoms. The monks and nuns followed common rules under a common head—frequently an **abbess** rather than an abbot. Many of these abbesses belonged to royal houses, especially in Anglo-Saxon England. In the kingdom of Northumbria, for example, Saint Hilda founded the monastery of Whitby in 657 c.e. As abbess, she was responsible for giving learning an important role in the life of the monastery; five future bishops were educated under her tutelage (see Historical Voices, "An Anglo-Saxon Abbess," p. 201). For female intellectuals, monasteries offered opportunities for learning not found elsewhere in the society of their day.

Nuns of the seventh and eighth centuries were not always as heavily cloistered as they once had been and were therefore able to play an important role in the spread of Christianity. The great English missionary Boniface relied on nuns in England for books and money. He also asked the abbess of Wimborne

An Anglo-Saxon Abbess: Hilda of Whitby

 Q *What kind of portrait does Bede present of Hilda? What moral lessons is he trying to teach?*

HILDA, ABBESS OF THE MONASTERY of Whitby, is a good example of the abbesses from royal families in Anglo-Saxon England who played important roles in English monastic institutions. Hilda was especially known for her exemplary life and high regard for learning. This account of her life is taken from Bede, considered by many the first major historian of the Middle Ages.

Bede, *The Ecclesiastical History of the English People*

In the following year, that is the year of our Lord 680, Hilda, abbess of the monastery of Whitby, a most religious servant of Christ, passed away to receive the reward of eternal life on the seventeenth of November at the age of sixty-six, after a life full of heavenly deeds. Her life fell into two equal parts, for she spent thirty-three years most nobly in secular occupations, and dedicated the remainder of her life even more nobly to our Lord in the monastic life. She was nobly born, the daughter of Hereric, nephew to King Edwin, with whom she received the Faith and sacraments of Christ through the preaching of Paulinus of blessed memory, first bishop of the Northumbrians, and she preserved this Faith inviolate until she was found worthy to see him in heaven. . . .

When she had ruled this monastery (Heruteu) for some years, constantly occupied in establishing the regular life, she further undertook to found or organize a monastery at a place known as Streaneshalch, and carried out this appointed task with great energy. She established the same regular life as in her former monastery, and taught the observance of justice, devotion, purity, and other virtues, but especially in peace and charity. After the example of the primitive Church, no one there was rich or poor, for everything was held in common, and none possessed any personal property. So great was her prudence that not only ordinary folk, but kings and princes used to come and ask her advice in their difficulties. Those under her direction were required to make a thorough study of the Scriptures and occupy themselves in good works, in order that many might be found fitted for Holy Orders and the service of God's altar. Subsequently, five bishops were chosen from this monastery—Bosa, Hedda, Oftfor, John, and Wilfrid—all of them men of outstanding merit and holiness. . . .

Christ's servant Abbess Hilda, whom all her acquaintances called Mother because of her wonderful devotion and grace, was not only an example of holy life to members of her own community, for she also brought about the amendment and salvation of many living far distant, who heard the inspiring story of her industry and goodness. . . . When Hilda ruled this monastery for many years, it pleased the Author of our salvation to try her holy soul by a long sickness, in order that, like the Apostle, her strength might be perfected in weakness. She was attacked by a burning fever that racked her continually for six years; but during all this time she never ceased to give thanks to her Maker, or to instruct the flock committed to her both privately and publicly. For her own example taught them all to serve God rightly when in health, and to render thanks to him faithfully when in trouble or bodily weakness. In the seventh year of her illness she suffered interior pains, and her last day came. About dawn she received holy Communion, and when she had summoned all the servants of Christ in the monastery, she urged them to maintain the gospel peace among themselves and with others. And while she was still speaking, she joyfully welcomed death, and in the words of our Lord, passed from death to life.

Source: Bede, *The Ecclesiastical History of the English People*, trans. L. Sherley-Price (London: Penguin Classics, 1955; revised edition 1968, 1990).

to send groups of nuns to establish convents in newly converted German lands. A nun named Leoba established the first convent in Germany at Bischofsheim.

The Path of Celibacy The monastic movement enabled some women to pursue a new path to holiness. Cloisters for both men and women offered the ideal place to practice the new Christian ideal of celibacy. This newfound emphasis on abstaining from sexual relations, especially evident in the emphasis on virginity, created a new image of the human body in late antiquity. To many Greeks and Romans, the human body had been a source of beauty, joy, and pleasure, an attitude evident in numerous works of art. Many Christians, however, viewed the body as a hindrance to a spiritual connection with God. The refusal to have sex was a victory over the desires of the flesh and thus an avenue to holiness.

In the fourth and fifth centuries C.E., a cult of virginity also moved beyond the walls of monasteries and convents. Throughout the Mediterranean world, groups of women met together to study the importance and benefits of celibacy. In Rome, a woman named Marcella supported a group of aristocratic women who studied the teachings about celibacy and also aided Jerome, the church father, with his work in translating the Bible into Latin.

The Growing Wealth of Monasteries Beginning in the sixth century C.E., monasteries and local churches became the beneficiaries of grants of land from kings, bishops, and aristocrats.

These gifts reached a high point in the eighth century. In fact, one historian has estimated that by the end of the eighth century, one-third of the land of Italy and the kingdom of the Franks was owned by church establishments. Those who gave these gifts did so in large part for religious favors, such as prayers and assurances of salvation. As a result of the gifts, however, individual monasteries sometimes became as wealthy as landed aristocrats and thus also served as instruments of political power.

7-3f Christian Intellectual Life in the Germanic Kingdoms

Although the Christian church came to accept classical culture, it was not easy to do so in the new Germanic kingdoms. Nevertheless, some Christian scholars managed to keep learning alive.

Cassiodorus Most prominent was Cassiodorus (ca. 490–585 C.E.), who came from an aristocratic Roman family and served as an official of the Ostrogothic king Theodoric. The conflicts that erupted after the death of Theodoric led Cassiodorus to withdraw from public life and retire to his landed estates in southern Italy, where he wrote his final work *Divine and Human Readings*, a compendium of the literature of both Christian and pagan antiquity. Cassiodorus accepted the advice of earlier Christian intellectuals to make use of classical works while treasuring the Scriptures above all else.

Cassiodorus continued the tradition of late antiquity of classifying knowledge according to certain subjects. In assembling his compendium of authors, he followed the works of late ancient authors in placing all secular knowledge into the categories of the seven **liberal arts**, which were divided into two major groups: the *trivium* (TRIV-ee-um), consisting of grammar, rhetoric, and dialectic or logic, and the *quadrivium* (kwah-DRIV-ee-um), consisting of arithmetic, geometry, astronomy, and music. The seven liberal arts would remain the cornerstone of Western education for nearly twelve hundred years.

Bede The Venerable Bede (BEED) (ca. 672–735 C.E.) was a scholar and product of Christian Anglo-Saxon England. He entered a monastery at Jarrow as a small boy and remained there most of the rest of his life. His *Ecclesiastical History of the English People*, completed in 731, was a product of the remarkable flowering of English ecclesiastical and monastic culture in the eighth century. His history of England begins with the coming of Christianity to Britain. Although Bede shared the credulity of his age in regard to stories of miracles, he had a remarkable sense of history. He used his sources so judiciously that they remain our chief source of information about early Anglo-Saxon England (see Historical Voices, "An Anglo-Saxon Abbess," p. 201). His work was a remarkable accomplishment for a monk from a small corner of England and reflects the high degree of intellectual achievement in England in the eighth century.

7-4 The Byzantine Empire

FOCUS QUESTION: How did the Byzantine Empire that had emerged by the eighth century differ from the empire of Justinian and from the Germanic kingdoms in the west?

As noted earlier, in the fourth century C.E., a separation between the western and eastern parts of the Roman Empire began to occur. Even as the Germans moved into the western part of the empire and established various kingdoms over the course of the fifth century, the Late Roman Empire in the east, centered in Constantinople, solidified and prospered.

7-4a The Reign of Justinian (527–565 C.E.)

In the sixth century, the empire in the east came under the control of one of its most remarkable rulers, the emperor Justinian (see Image 7.7). As the nephew and heir of the previous emperor, Justinian had been well trained in imperial administration. As he stated, he was determined to reestablish the Roman Empire in the entire Mediterranean world: "We are inspired with the hope that God will grant us rule over the rest of what, subject to the ancient Romans to the limits of both seas, they later lost by their neglect."[19] He began his attempt to reconquer the west in 533.

Justinian's army under Belisarius (bell-uh-SAH-ree-uss), probably the best general of the late Roman world, presented a formidable force. Belisarius sailed to North Africa and quickly destroyed the Vandals in two major battles. From North Africa, he led his forces onto the Italian peninsula after occupying Sicily in 535. But it was not until 552 that the Ostrogoths were finally defeated. The struggle devastated Italy, which suffered more from Justinian's reconquest than from all of the previous barbarian invasions.

Justinian has been criticized for overextending his resources and bankrupting the empire. Historians now think, however, that a devastating plague in 542 and long-term economic changes were far more damaging to the Eastern Roman Empire than Justinian's conquests. Before he died, Justinian appeared to have achieved his goals. He had restored the imperial Mediterranean world; his empire included Italy, part of Spain, North Africa, Asia Minor, Palestine, and Syria (see Map 7.5). But the conquest of the Western Empire proved fleeting. Only three years after Justinian's death, the Lombards entered Italy. Although the Eastern Empire maintained the fiction of Italy as a province, its forces were limited to southern and central Italy, Sicily, and coastal areas, such as the territory around Ravenna.

The Codification of Roman Law Though his conquests proved short-lived, Justinian made a lasting contribution to Western civilization through his codification of Roman law. The Eastern Empire was heir to a vast quantity of materials connected to the development of Roman law. These included laws passed by the senate and assemblies, legal commentaries of jurists, decisions of praetors, and the edicts of emperors.

Atlantic
Ocean

FRANKS

LOMBARDS
ALEMANNI
BURGUNDIANS   Alps   OSTROGOTHS
SUEVES   Pyrenees   Milon
VISIGOTHS   Ravenna
              Corsica   Rome
              Sardinia   Naples
                      Sicily
              Carthage
VANDALS   Mediterranean   Sea

AVARS
SLAVS
BULGARS

BYZANTINE
Constantinople
        EMPIRE
Athens

Black   Sea

Caucasus Mts.

ARMENIA
        Manzikert
PERSIAN
EMPIRE

Taurus Mts.
        Antioch
Cyprus   SYRIA
             Damascus
Crete

Jerusalem   ARABIA
Alexandria

Red
Sea

Rhine R.
Danube R.
Euphrates R.
Tigris R.
Nile R.

 Empire before Justinian
Territory gained by Justinian
FRANKS Groups of people

0   200   400   600 Kilometers
0   200   400 Miles

MAP 7.5 The Eastern Roman Empire in the Time of Justinian. The Eastern Roman emperor Justinian briefly restored much of the Mediterranean portion of the old Roman Empire. His general Belisarius quickly conquered the Vandals in North Africa but wrested Italy from the Ostrogoths only after a long and devastating struggle.

Q *Look back at Map 6.1. What former Roman territories remained outside Justinian's control?*

Justinian had been well trained in imperial government and was thoroughly acquainted with Roman law. He wished to codify and simplify this mass of materials.

To accomplish his goal, Justinian authorized the jurist Trebonian to make a systematic compilation of imperial edicts. The result was the Code of Law, the first part of the *Corpus Iuris Civilis* (KOR-pus YOOR-iss see-VIL-liss) ("Body of Civil Law"), completed in 529 c.e. Four years later, two other parts of the *Corpus* appeared: the *Digest*, a compendium of writings of Roman jurists, and the *Institutes*, a brief summary of the chief principles of Roman law that could be used as a textbook on Roman law. The fourth part of the *Corpus* was the *Novels*, a compilation of the most important new edicts issued during Justinian's reign.

Justinian's codification of Roman law became the basis of imperial law in the Byzantine Empire until its end in 1453. More important, however, since it was written in Latin (it was, in fact, the last product of eastern Roman culture to be written in Latin, which was soon replaced by Greek), it was also eventually used in the west and became the basis of the legal system of all of continental Europe.

Intellectual Life Under Justinian The intellectual life of the Eastern Roman Empire was highly influenced by the traditions of classical civilization. Scholars actively strived to preserve the works of the ancient Greeks and Romans while basing a great deal of their own literature on classical models. Later, when the empire collapsed with the capture of Constantinople in 1453 c.e., Byzantine emigrants to Italy brought a wealth of ancient works with them, adding to the growth of the Renaissance in Italy (see Chapter 12).

Initially, however, the most outstanding literary achievements of the Eastern Empire were historical and religious works. The best known of the historians was Procopius (pruh-KOH-pee-uss) (ca. 500–562), court historian during the reign of Justinian. Procopius served as secretary to the great general Belisarius and accompanied him on his wars on behalf of Justinian. Procopius's best historical work, the *Wars*, is a firsthand account of Justinian's wars of reconquest in the western Mediterranean and his wars against the Persians in the east. Deliberately modeled after the work of his hero, the Greek historian Thucydides (see Chapter 3), Procopius's narrative features vivid descriptions of battle scenes, clear judgment, and noteworthy objectivity.

Scala/Art Resource, NY

IMAGE 7.7 **The Emperor Justinian and His Court.** As the seat of Byzantine power in Italy, the town of Ravenna was adorned with many examples of Byzantine art. The Church of San Vitale at Ravenna contains some of the finest examples of sixth-century Byzantine mosaics. Small pieces of colored glass were set in mortar on the wall to form these figures and their surroundings. The emperor is seen as both head of state (he wears a jeweled crown and a purple robe) and head of the church (he carries a gold bowl symbolizing the body of Jesus).

Procopius also wrote a work that many historians consider mostly scandalous gossip, his infamous *Secret History*. At the beginning of this work, Procopius informed his readers that "what I shall write now follows a different plan, supplementing the previous formal chronicle with a disclosure of what really happened throughout the Roman Empire."[20] What he revealed constituted a scathing attack on Justinian and his wife Theodora for their alleged misdeeds.

The Empress Theodora Theodora (thee-uh-DOR-uh) was the daughter of the "keeper of bears" for the games at Constantinople, who died when she was a child. Theodora followed in her mother's footsteps by becoming an actress, which at that time was considered a lowborn activity. Often actresses also worked as prostitutes, and Theodora was no exception. At the age of twenty-five, she met Justinian, who was forty. His uncle, the emperor Justin, had to change the law to allow an aristocratic senator to marry a woman who had been an actress. After his uncle died in 527 C.E., Justinian became emperor and Theodora empress, a remarkable achievement for a woman from the lower classes (see Image 7.8).

Justinian and Theodora were close and loving companions. She also influenced her husband in both church and state affairs. A strong-willed and intelligent woman, she proved especially valuable in 532, when the two factions of charioteer supporters in Constantinople joined forces and rioted against the emperor. The riots soon became a revolt as the rioters burned and looted the center of the city, shouting *"Nika!"* ("win"), a word normally used to cheer on their favorite chariot teams. Justinian seemed ready to flee, but Theodora strengthened his resolve by saying, "My opinion then is that the present time, above all others, is inopportune for flight, even though it bring safety. . . . For one who has been emperor it is unendurable to be a fugitive . . . and may I not live that day on which those who meet me shall not address me as mistress."[21] On hearing her words, Justinian resolved to stay and fight. Many of the protesters were killed as the so-called Nika Revolt was suppressed.

The Emperor's Building Program After the riots destroyed much of Constantinople, Justinian rebuilt the city and gave it the appearance it would keep for almost a thousand years (see Map 7.6). Earlier, Emperor Theodosius II (r. 408–450 C.E.) had constructed an enormous defensive wall to protect the city on its land side. The city was dominated by an immense palace complex, a huge arena known as the Hippodrome, and hundreds of churches. No residential district was particularly fashionable; palaces, tenements, and slums ranged alongside one another. Justinian added many new buildings. His public works projects included roads, bridges, walls, public baths, law courts, and colossal underground reservoirs to hold the city's water supply. He also built hospitals, schools, monasteries, and churches. Churches were his special passion, and in Constantinople alone he built or rebuilt thirty-four of them. His greatest achievement was the famous Hagia Sophia (HAG-ee-uh soh-FEE-uh), the Church of the Holy Wisdom.

Completed in 537, Hagia Sophia was designed by a Greek architect who departed radically from the simple, flat-roofed basilica of Western architecture. The center of Hagia Sophia consisted of four huge piers crowned by an enormous dome, which seemed to be floating in space (see Image 7.9). This effect was emphasized by Procopius, the court historian, who, at Justinian's request, wrote a treatise on the emperor's building projects: "From the lightness of the building, it does not appear to rest upon a solid foundation, but to cover the place beneath as though it were suspended from heaven by the fabled golden chain." In part, this impression was created by putting forty-two windows around the base of the dome, which allowed an incredible play of light within the cathedral. Light served to remind the worshipers of God; as Procopius commented:

> Whoever enters there to worship perceives at once that it is
> not by any human strength or skill, but by the favor of God
> that this work has been perfected; his mind rises sublime
> to commune with God, feeling that He cannot be far off,
> but must especially love to dwell in the place which He has

IMAGE 7.8 **The Empress Theodora and Her Attendants.** This mosaic, located on the south wall of the apse of the Church of San Vitale (Justinian is on the north wall), depicts Theodora and her attendants. At the bottom of her robe is a scene of the Three Wise Men, an indication that Theodora was special enough to have belonged in the company of the three kings who visited the newborn Jesus.

Q *Considering the role of women in late antiquity, why was Theodora placed on the wall of the Church of San Vitale?*

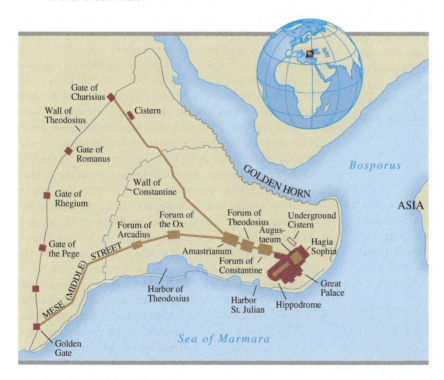

MAP 7.6 **Constantinople.** Constantinople was the largest city in Europe, and until the twelfth century, it was the nexus of trade between east and west. Emperor Justinian oversaw a massive building program that produced important architectural monuments such as Hagia Sophia.

Q *What natural and human-built aspects of the city helped protect it from invasion?*

chosen; and this takes place not only when a man sees it for the first time, but it always makes the same impression upon him, as though he had never beheld it before.[22]

As darkness is illumined by invisible light, so too, it was believed, the world is illumined by invisible spirit.

The royal palace complex, Hagia Sophia, and the Hippodrome were the three greatest buildings in Constantinople. The last was a huge amphitheater, constructed of brick covered by marble, that could hold as many as 60,000 spectators. Although gladiator fights were held there, the main events were

IMAGE 7.9 **Interior View of Hagia Sophia.** Pictured here is the interior of the Church of the Holy Wisdom in Constantinople (modern Istanbul), constructed under Justinian by Anthemius of Tralles (an-THEE-mee-uss of TRAL-leez) and Isidore of Miletus (IH-zuh-dor of mih-LEE-tuss). Some of the stones used in the construction of the church had been plundered from the famous Temple of Diana, near Ephesus, in Asia Minor. This view gives an idea of how the windows around the base of the dome produced a special play of light within the cathedral. The pulpits and plaques bearing inscriptions from the Qur'an were introduced when the Turks converted this church to a mosque in the fifteenth century.

the chariot races; twenty-four would usually be presented in one day. The citizens of Constantinople were passionate fans of chariot racing. Successful charioteers were acclaimed as heroes and honored with public statues. Crowds in the Hippodrome also took on political significance. Being a member of the two chief factions of charioteers—the Blues or the Greens—was the only real outlet for political expression. Even emperors had to be aware of their demands and attitudes: the loss of a race in the Hippodrome frequently resulted in bloody riots that could threaten the emperor's power.

7-4b From Eastern Roman to Byzantine Empire

Justinian's accomplishments had been spectacular, but when he died, he left the Eastern Roman Empire with serious problems: too much distant territory to protect, an empty treasury, a smaller population after the plague, and renewed threats to the frontiers. In the first half of the seventh century C.E., during the reign of Heraclius (he-ruh-KLY-uss *or* huh-RAK-lee-uss) (r. 610–641), the empire faced attacks from the Persians to the east and the Slavs to the north.

The empire was left exhausted by these struggles. In the midst of them, it had developed a new system of defense by creating a new administrative unit, the *theme*, which combined civilian and military offices in the hands of the same person. Thus, the civil

governor was also the military leader of the area. Although this innovation helped the empire survive, it also fostered an increased militarization of the empire. By the mid-seventh century, it had become apparent that a restored Mediterranean empire was simply beyond the resources of the Eastern Empire, which now increasingly turned its back on the Latin west.

The most serious challenge to the Eastern Roman Empire came from the rise of Islam, which unified the Arab tribes and created a powerful new force that swept through the east (see "7-5 The Rise of Islam," later in this chapter). The empire lost the provinces of Syria and Palestine after the Arabs defeated an eastern Roman army at Yarmuk (yahr-MOOK) in 636. The Arabs also moved into the old Persian Empire and conquered it. An Arab attempt to besiege Constantinople failed, in large part due to the use of Greek fire against the Arab fleets. Greek fire was a petroleum-based compound containing quicklime and sulfur. Because it would burn under water, the eastern Romans created the equivalent of modern flamethrowers by using tubes to blow Greek fire onto wooden ships, with frightening effect. Arabs and eastern Roman forces now faced each other along a frontier in southern Asia Minor.

Problems also arose along the northern frontier, especially in the Balkans, where an Asiatic people known as the Bulgars had arrived earlier in the sixth century. In 679, the Bulgars defeated the eastern Roman forces and took possession of the lower Danube valley, setting up a strong Bulgarian kingdom.

By the beginning of the eighth century, the Eastern Roman Empire was greatly diminished in size, consisting only of the eastern Balkans and Asia Minor. It was now an eastern Mediterranean state (see Map 7.7). These external challenges had important internal repercussions as well. By the eighth century, the Eastern Roman Empire had been transformed into what historians call the Byzantine Empire, a civilization with its own unique character that would last until 1453 (Constantinople was built on the site of an older city named Byzantium—hence the term *Byzantine*).

MAP 7.7 **The Byzantine Empire, ca. 750** C.E.

The Byzantine Empire in the Eighth Century The Byzantine Empire was both a Greek and a Christian state. Increasingly, Latin fell into disuse as Greek became both the common and the official language of the empire. The Byzantine Empire was also built on a faith in Jesus that was shared in a profound way by almost all its citizens. An enormous amount of artistic talent was poured into the construction of churches, church ceremonies, and church decoration. Spiritual principles deeply permeated Byzantine art. The importance of religion to the Byzantines explains why theological disputes took on an exaggerated form. The most famous of these disputes, the so-called iconoclastic controversy, threatened the stability of the empire in the first half of the eighth century C.E.

Beginning in the sixth century, the use of religious images, especially in the form of icons or pictures of sacred figures, became so widespread that charges of idolatry, the worship of images, began to be heard. The use of images or icons had been justified by the argument that icons were not worshiped but were simply used to help illiterate people understand their religion. This argument failed to stop the **iconoclasts**, as the opponents of icons were called.

Iconoclasm was not unique to the Byzantine Empire. In the neighboring Islamic empire (see "7-5 The Rise of Islam," later in the chapter), religious art did not include any physical representations of Muhammad. Iconoclasm would also play a role among some of the new religious groups that emerged in the Protestant Reformation in sixteenth-century Europe (see Chapter 13).

Beginning in 730, the Byzantine emperor Leo III (r. 717–741) outlawed the use of icons. Strong resistance ensued, especially from monks. Leo also used the iconoclastic controversy to add to the prestige of the patriarch of Constantinople, the highest church official in the east and second in dignity only to the bishop of Rome. The Roman popes were opposed to the iconoclastic edicts, and their opposition created considerable dissension between the popes and the Byzantine emperors. Late in the eighth century, the Byzantine rulers reversed their stand on the use of images, but not before considerable damage had been done to the unity of the Christian church. Although the final separation between Roman Catholicism and Greek Orthodoxy (as the Christian church in the Byzantine Empire was called) did not occur until 1054, the iconoclastic controversy was important in moving both sides in that direction.

The Byzantine Emperor The emperor occupied a crucial position in the Byzantine state. Portrayed as chosen by God, the Byzantine emperor was crowned in sacred ceremonies, and his subjects were expected to prostrate themselves in his presence. The wives of the emperors also played significant roles in the court rituals that upheld imperial authority.

Court ritual could be very complicated and included a variety of activities. Everyday rituals included the daily opening of the imperial palace: imperial officials, all arranged in order of rank, waited until the palace doors were officially opened; then they marched into the palace in a procession. A similar ceremony was held for the opening of the palace in the afternoon. In addition to these regular daily ceremonies, special ceremonies involving specific rituals were held on many occasions,

including the emperor's birthday, the promotion of officials, imperial marriages, and commemorations of important military battles. The emperor was also required to participate in the ceremonies held regularly in the churches on important saints' days and during church festivals.

The power of the Byzantine emperor was considered absolute and was limited in practice only by deposition or assassination. Because the emperor appointed the patriarch, he also exercised control over both church and state. The Byzantines believed that God had commanded their state to preserve the true Christian faith. Emperor, clergy, and civic officials were all bound together in service to this ideal. It can be said that spiritual values truly held the Byzantine state together.

Because of their many foreign enemies, Byzantine emperors spent considerable energy on war and preparations for war. Byzantine literature included many manuals on war, instructing people in the ways of fighting (see Historical Voices, "A Byzantine Emperor Gives Military Advice," p. 208). Byzantine armies, often led by the emperors, were well trained and well equipped with the latest weapons. The Byzantines, however, often preferred to use diplomacy rather than fight. Our word *byzantine*—often defined as "extremely complicated or carried on by underhand methods"—stems from the complex and crafty instructions that Byzantine rulers sent to their envoys.

By 750, it was apparent that two of Rome's heirs, the Germanic kingdoms and the Byzantine Empire, were moving in different directions. Nevertheless, Byzantine influence on the Western world was significant. The images of a Roman imperial state that continued to haunt the west lived on in Byzantium. The legal system of the west came to owe much to Justinian's codification of Roman law. In addition, the Byzantine Empire served in part as a buffer state, protecting the west for a long time from incursions from the east. Although the Byzantine Empire would continue to influence the west until its demise in 1453, it went its own unique way.

Life in Constantinople: The Importance of Trade With a population estimated in the hundreds of thousands, Constantinople was the largest city in Europe during the Middle Ages. It viewed itself as the center of an empire and a special Christian city. The Byzantines believed that the city was under the protection of God and the Virgin Mary. One thirteenth-century

CHRONOLOGY	The Byzantine Empire
Protective walls of Theodosius II	408–450 C.E.
Justinian codifies Roman law	529–533
Reconquest of Italy by Justinian's army	535–552
Completion of Hagia Sophia	537
Attacks on the empire during reign of Heraclius	610–641
Defeat by the Arabs at Yarmuk	636
Defeat by the Bulgars; losses in the Balkans	679

A Byzantine Emperor Gives Military Advice

 According to Maurice, what are the strengths and weaknesses of the Germanic peoples? Based on his analysis of their traits, what advice does he give his military forces in the event that they face the Germans in battle?

TO AN EMPIRE SURROUNDED BY ENEMIES on all sides, military prowess was an absolute necessity. Both the Byzantine emperors and the ruling elite, however, also realized that military forces alone would not suffice, and consequently they fostered the art of diplomacy and military intelligence. This document is from an early seventh-century work entitled the *Strategikon* (stra-TEE-jih-kahn), a manual of strategy written by the emperor Maurice (r. 582–602 C.E.), himself an experienced general who led his troops into battle. The work is based on the assumption that a detailed knowledge of the habits and fighting skills of their enemies would give the Byzantines an advantage if they had to fight.

Maurice, *Strategikon*

The light-haired races [Germanic peoples] place great value on freedom. They are bold and undaunted in battle. Daring and impetuous as they are, they consider any timidity and even a short retreat as a disgrace. They calmly despise death as they fight violently in hand-to-hand combat either on horseback or on foot. If they are hard pressed in cavalry actions, they dismount at a single prearranged sign and line up on foot. Although only a few against many horsemen, they do not shrink from the fight. They are armed with shields, lances, and short swords slung from their shoulders. They prefer fighting on foot and rapid charges.

Whether on foot or horseback, they draw up for battle, not in any fixed measure and formation, or in regiments or divisions, but according to tribes, their kinship with one another, and common interest. Often, as a result, when things are not going well and their friends have been killed, they will risk their lives fighting to avenge them. In combat they make the front of their battle line even and dense. Either on horseback or on foot they are impetuous and undisciplined in charging, as if they were the only people in the world who are not cowards. They are disobedient to their leaders. They are not interested in anything that is at all complicated and pay little attention to external security and their own advantage. They despise good order, especially on horseback. They are easily corrupted by money, greedy as they are.

They are hurt by suffering and fatigue. . . . When it comes to a cavalry battle, they are hindered by uneven and wooded terrain. They are easily ambushed along the flanks and to the rear of their battle line, for they do not concern themselves at all with scouts and other security measures. Their ranks are easily broken by a simulated flight and a sudden turning back against them. . . .

Above all, therefore, in warring against them one must avoid engaging in pitched battles, especially in the early stages. Instead, make use of well-planned ambushes, sneak attacks, and stratagems. Delay things and ruin their opportunities. Pretend to come to agreements with them. Aim at reducing their boldness and zeal by shortage of provisions or the discomfort of heat or cold. This can be done when our army has pitched camp on rugged and difficult ground. On such terrain this enemy cannot attack successfully because they are using lances.

Source: *Maurice's Strategikon: Handbook of Byzantine Military Strategy*, Book 11, trans. G. T. Dennis (Philadelphia: University of Pennsylvania Press, 1984), pp. 118–119.

Byzantine said: "About our city you shall know: until the end she will fear no nation whatsoever, for no one will entrap or capture her, not by any means, for she has been given to the Mother of God and no one will snatch her out of Her hands. Many nations will break their horns against her walls and withdraw with shame."[23]

Until the twelfth century C.E., Constantinople was Europe's greatest commercial center. The city was the chief entrepôt for the exchange of products between west and east, and trade formed the basis for its fabulous prosperity. This trade, however, was largely carried on by foreign merchants. As one contemporary said:

> All sorts of merchants come here from the land of Babylon, from . . . Persia, Media, and all the sovereignty of the land of Egypt, from the lands of Canaan, and from the empire of

Russia, from Hungaria, Kharzaria, and the land of Lombardy and Sepharad. It is a busy city, and merchants come to it from every country by sea or land, and there is none like it in the world except Baghdad, the great city of Islam.[24]

Highly desired in western Europe were the products of the east: silk from China, spices from Southeast Asia and India, jewelry and ivory from India (the latter used by artisans for church items), wheat and furs from southern Russia, and flax and honey from the Balkans. Many of these eastern goods were shipped from Constantinople to the Mediterranean and northern Europe. Despite the Germanic incursions, European trade did not entirely end.

Moreover, imported raw materials were used in Constantinople for local industries. During Justinian's reign, two Christian monks smuggled silkworms from China to begin a silk industry. The state had a monopoly on the production of silk cloth, and the workshops themselves were housed in Constantinople's royal palace complex. European demand for silk cloth made it the city's most lucrative product. It is interesting to note that the upper classes, including emperors and empresses, were not discouraged from making money through trade and manufacturing. Indeed, one empress even manufactured perfumes in her bedroom.

7-5 The Rise of Islam

 FOCUS QUESTION: What was the basic message of Islam, and how does the religion compare with Judaism and Christianity? Why was Islam able to expand so successfully?

The Arabs were a Semitic-speaking people of southwestern Asia with a long history. In Roman times, the Arabian peninsula came to be dominated by Bedouin (BED-oo-un *or* BED-wuhn) nomads who moved constantly to find water and food for their animals. In early times, the Bedouins had supported themselves primarily by sheepherding or by raiding passing caravans, but after the domestication of the camel during the second millennium B.C.E., the Bedouins began to participate in the caravan trade themselves and became major carriers of goods between the Persian Gulf and the Mediterranean Sea.

Although these early Arabs were polytheistic, there was a supreme God named Allah (AH-lah) (Arabic for "God") who ruled over the other gods. There was no priesthood; all members of the tribe were involved in the practice of the faith. Allah was symbolized by a sacred stone, and each tribe had its own stone. All tribes, however, worshiped a massive black meteorite—the Black Stone—which had been placed in a central shrine called the *Ka'aba* (KAH-buh) in the city of Mecca.

In the fifth and sixth centuries C.E., the Arabian peninsula took on new importance. As a result of political disorder in Mesopotamia and Egypt, the usual trade routes in the region began to change. A new trade route—from the Mediterranean through Mecca to Yemen and then by ship across the Arabian Sea and the Indian Ocean—became more popular, and communities in that part of the Arabian peninsula, including Mecca, began to prosper from this caravan trade. As a result, tensions arose between the Bedouins in the desert and the increasingly wealthy merchant classes in the towns. Into this intense world came Muhammad (moh-HAM-mud *or* moo-HAM-mud).

7-5a Muhammad

Born in Mecca to a merchant family, Muhammad (ca. 570–632 C.E.) was orphaned at the age of five. He grew up to become a caravan manager and

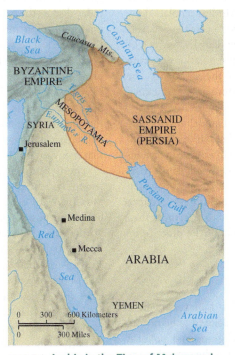

MAP 7.8 Arabia in the Time of Muhammad

eventually married a rich widow who was also his employer. In his middle years, he began to experience visions that he believed were inspired by Allah. Muhammad believed that although Allah had already revealed himself in part through Moses and Jesus—and thus through the Hebrew and Christian traditions—the final revelations were now being given to him. Out of these revelations, which were eventually written down, came the Qur'an (kuh-RAN *or* kuh-RAHN) or Koran, which contained the guidelines by which followers of Allah were to live. Muhammad's teachings formed the basis for the religion known as Islam, which means "submission to the will of Allah." Allah was the all-powerful being who had created the universe and everything in it. Humans must subject themselves to Allah if they wished to achieve everlasting life. His followers were called Muslims, meaning "practitioners of Islam."

After receiving the revelations, Muhammad set out to convince the people of Mecca that the revelations were true. At first, many thought he was insane, and others feared that his attacks on the corrupt society around him would upset the established social and political order. Discouraged by the failure of the Meccans to accept his message, in 622 Muhammad and some of his closest supporters left the city and moved north to the rival city of Yathrib, later renamed Medina (muh-DEE-nuh) ("city of the Prophet"). The year of the journey to Medina, known in history as the *Hegira* (hee-JY-ruh *or* HEH-juh-ruh) ("departure"), became year 1 in the official calendar of Islam (see Map 7.8).

Muhammad, who had been invited to the town by a number of prominent residents, soon began to win support from people in Medina as well as from members of Bedouin tribes in the surrounding countryside. From these groups, he formed the first Muslim community. Muslims saw no separation between political and religious authority; submission to the will of Allah meant submission to Muhammad, his Prophet. Muhammad soon became both a religious and a political leader. His political and military skills enabled him to put together a reliable military force, with which he returned to Mecca in 630, conquering the city and converting the townspeople to the new faith. From Mecca, Muhammad's ideas spread quickly across the Arabian peninsula and within a relatively short time had resulted in both the religious and the political unification of Arab society.

7-5b The Teachings of Islam

At the heart of Islam was its sacred book, the Qur'an, with its basic message that there is no God but Allah, and Muhammad is his Prophet. Essentially, the Qur'an contains Muhammad's revelations of a heavenly book written down by secretaries. Consisting of 114 chapters, the Qur'an recorded the beliefs of the Muslims and served as their code of ethics and law.

Islam was a direct and simple faith, emphasizing the need to obey the will of Allah. This meant following a basic ethical code consisting of the **Five Pillars of Islam**: belief in Allah and Muhammad as his Prophet; standard prayer five times a day and public prayer on Friday at midday to worship Allah; observance of the holy month of Ramadan (RAH-muh-dan) (the ninth month on the Muslim calendar) with fasting from dawn to sunset (see Image 7.10); making a pilgrimage—known as the *hajj* (HAJ)—to Mecca in one's lifetime, if possible; and giving alms to the poor and unfortunate. The faithful who observed the law were guaranteed a place in an eternal paradise.

Islam was not just a set of religious beliefs but a way of life as well. After the death of Muhammad, Muslim scholars drew up a law code called *Shari'a* (shah-REE-uh) to provide believers with a set of prescriptions to regulate their daily lives. Much of the shari'a was drawn from existing legal regulations or from the Hadith (hah-DEETH), a collection of the sayings of the Prophet that was used to supplement the revelations contained in the holy scriptures.

Believers are subject to strict behavioral guidelines. In addition to the Five Pillars, Muslims were forbidden to gamble, to eat pork, to drink alcoholic beverages, and to engage in dishonest behavior. Sexual practices were also strictly regulated. Marriages were to be arranged by parents, and contacts between unmarried men and women were discouraged. In accordance with Bedouin custom, males were permitted to have more than one wife, but Muhammad attempted to limit the practice by restricting the number of wives to four.

7-5c The Spread of Islam

The death of Muhammad presented his followers with a dilemma. Although Muhammad had not claimed to be divine, Muslims saw no separation between religious and political authority. Submission to the will of Allah was the same thing as

submission to his Prophet, Muhammad. He had never named a successor, and although he had several daughters, he left no sons. In a male-oriented society, who would lead the community of the faithful? Shortly after Muhammad's death, a number of his closest followers selected Abu Bakr (ah-boo BAHK-ur), a wealthy merchant who was Muhammad's father-in-law, as **caliph** (KAY-liff), or temporal leader, of the Islamic community. He was also considered, in general terms, to be a religious leader, or imam (lih-MAHM).

Muhammad and the early caliphs who succeeded him took up the Arab tribal custom of the *razzia,* or raid in the struggle against their enemies. When historians of the Middle East today discuss the expansion of Islam after the death of Muhammad, the Arabic term *jihad* (ji-HAHD) is often used to describe the process. The word appears in the Qur'an on several occasions, and it appears to have had multiple meanings. Sometimes jihad is used in the sense of "striving in the way of the Lord" to achieve personal betterment. In other cases, however, it has been translated as "holy war," justifying hostile action against the enemies of Islam. Islamic terrorist movements of the present day clearly view jihad in the latter sense, an interpretation that many other Muslims vigorously reject.

The Byzantines and the Persians were the first to feel the strength of the newly united Arabs. At Yarmuk in 636 C.E., the Muslim Arabs defeated the Byzantine army, and by 640, they had taken possession of the province of Syria (see Map 7.9). To the east, the Arabs went on to conquer the entire Persian Empire by 650. In the meantime, Egypt and other areas of North Africa had been added to the new Muslim empire. Led by a series of brilliant generals, the Arabs had put together a large and highly motivated army, whose valor was enhanced by the belief that Muslim warriors were guaranteed a place in paradise if they died in battle.

Early caliphs, ruling from Medina, organized their newly conquered territories into taxpaying provinces. Officially,

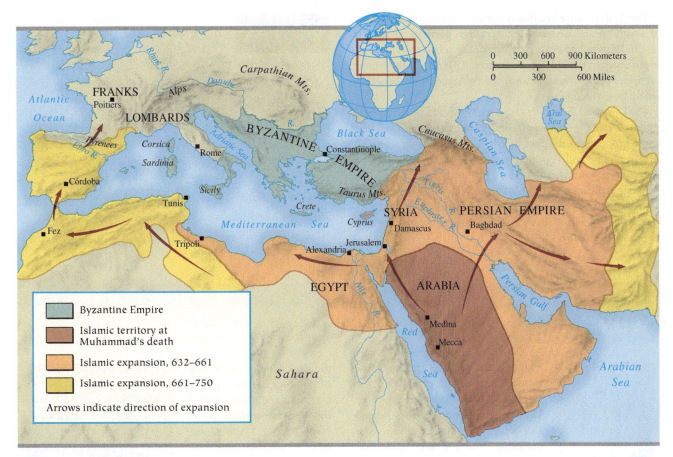

MAP 7.9 **The Expansion of Islam.** Muhammad, the prophet of Islam, engaged in warfare against neighboring tribes. Militaristic expansion continued with great zeal under the Prophet's successors. Islamic rule spread rapidly in the decades after Muhammad's death, stopped finally by the Byzantine Empire and the Franks.

 Why was the continued existence of the Byzantine Empire a key factor in stopping the spread of Islam into Europe?

conversion to Islam was voluntary, in accordance with the maxim in the Qur'an that "there shall be no compulsion in religion." Those who chose not to convert, however, were required to submit to Muslim rule and to pay a head tax in return for exemption from military service, which was required of all Muslim males.

By the mid-seventh century, problems arose again over the succession to the Prophet until Ali, Muhammad's son-in-law, was assassinated and the general Muawiya (moo-AH-wee-yah), the governor of Syria and one of Ali's chief rivals, became caliph in 661. Muawiya was known for one outstanding virtue: he used force only when necessary. As he said, "I never use my sword when my whip will do, nor my whip when my tongue will do."[25] Muawiya moved quickly to make the caliphate hereditary in his own family, thus establishing the Umayyad (oo-MY-ad) dynasty. As one of their first actions, the Umayyads moved the capital of the Muslim empire from Medina to Damascus in Syria. This internal dissension over the caliphate created a split in Islam between the **Shi'ites** (SHEE-yts), or those who accepted only the descendants of Ali, Muhammad's son-in-law, as the true rulers, and

the **Sunnis** (SOO-nees), who claimed that the descendants of the Umayyads were the true caliphs. This seventh-century split in Islam has persisted until the present day, as is evident in the current struggle in the Middle East between Sunni Saudi Arabia and Shi'ite Iran.

Internal dissension, however, did not stop the expansion of Islam. After sweeping across North Africa, the Muslims crossed the Strait of Gibraltar and moved into Spain around 710. The Visigothic kingdom collapsed, and by 725, most of Spain had become a Muslim state with its center at Córdoba. In 732, a Muslim army, making a foray into southern France, was defeated at the Battle of Tours near Poitiers. Muslim expansion in Europe came to a halt.

Meanwhile, in 717, another Muslim force had launched a naval attack on Constantinople with the hope of destroying the Byzantine Empire. In the spring of 718, the Byzantines destroyed the Muslim fleet and saved the Byzantine Empire and indirectly Christian Europe, because the fall of Constantinople would no doubt have opened the door to Muslim invasion of eastern Europe. The Byzantine Empire and Islam now established an uneasy frontier in southern Asia Minor.

The Arab advance had finally come to an end, but not before the southern and eastern Mediterranean portions of the old Roman Empire had been conquered. Islam had truly become heir to much of the old Roman Empire. That part of the empire had been a prosperous one, and the new Arab Empire benefited greatly from its conquest.

The Umayyad dynasty at Damascus now ruled an enormous empire. While expansion had conveyed untold wealth and new ethnic groups into the fold of Islam, it also brought contact with Byzantine and Persian civilizations. As a result, the new Arab Empire would be influenced by Greek culture as well as the older civilizations of the ancient Near East. The children of the conquerors would be educated in new ways and produce a brilliant culture that would eventually influence western Europe intellectually.

CHRONOLOGY	The Rise of Islam	
Birth of Muhammad		ca. 570 C.E.
Muhammad's flight from Mecca (*Hegira*)		622
Death of Muhammad		632
Defeat of Byzantines at Yarmuk		636
Defeat of Persians		637–650
Seizure of Byzantine provinces of Syria and Egypt		640–642
Invasion of Spain		ca. 710
Arab failure to capture Constantinople		717–718
Defeat of Muslims near Poitiers		732

CHAPTER SUMMARY

The period from the middle of the third century to the middle of the eighth was both chaotic and creative. During late antiquity, the Roman world of the Mediterranean was gradually transformed. Diocletian and Constantine restored an aura of stability to the late empire by increasing the size of the bureaucracy and the army, establishing price controls, raising taxes, and making occupations hereditary. Nevertheless, even their efforts ultimately proved to be in vain as the empire stumbled along. With fewer resources and little resolve, the government was less able to repel the German migrants who moved into the western part of the empire. In 476, the last western emperor was deposed.

As the western part of the Roman Empire disintegrated, a new civilization slowly emerged, formed by the coalescence of three major elements: the Germanic peoples who moved into the western part of the empire and established new kingdoms, the continuing attraction of the Greco-Roman cultural legacy, and the Christian church. Politically, the Roman Empire in the west was replaced by a new series of Germanic kingdoms, including the Ostrogoths in Italy, the Visigoths in Spain, several Anglo-Saxon kingdoms in Britain, and a Frankish kingdom in Gaul. Each of these kingdoms fused Roman and Germanic elements to create a new society.

Beginning in the fourth century, Christianity had become the official religion of the Roman Empire. The Christian church (or Roman Catholic Church, as it came to be called in the west) played a crucial role in the growth of a new civilization. The church developed an organized government under

the leadership of the bishop of Rome, who became known as the pope. One of the most significant popes was Gregory I the Great, who established claims to both religious and political power. The church also assimilated the classical tradition and through its clergy brought Christianized civilization to the Germanic tribes. Especially important were the monks and nuns who led the way in converting the Germanic peoples in Europe to Christianity.

But the Germanic kingdoms were not the only heir to Roman civilization. In the east, Greek and eastern elements of late antiquity were of more consequence as the Eastern Roman Empire was transformed into the Byzantine Empire. Although the Germanic kingdoms of the west and the Byzantine civilization of the east came to share a common bond in Christianity, it proved incapable of keeping them in harmony politically as the two civilizations continued to move apart.

The rise of Islam, Rome's third heir, resulted in the loss of the southern and eastern Mediterranean portions of the old Roman Empire to a religious power that was neither Roman nor Christian. The new Islamic empire forced Europe proper back upon itself, and slowly, a new civilization emerged that became the heart of what we know as Western civilization.

CHAPTER TIMELINE

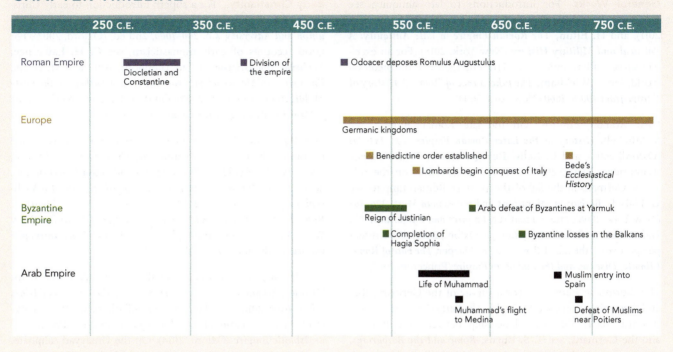

	250 C.E.	350 C.E.	450 C.E.	550 C.E.	650 C.E.	750 C.E.

Roman Empire — Diocletian and Constantine; Division of the empire; Odoacer deposes Romulus Augustulus

Europe — Germanic kingdoms; Benedictine order established; Lombards begin conquest of Italy; Bede's *Ecclesiastical History*

Byzantine Empire — Reign of Justinian; Completion of Hagia Sophia; Arab defeat of Byzantines at Yarmuk; Byzantine losses in the Balkans

Arab Empire — Life of Muhammad; Muhammad's flight to Medina; Muslim entry into Spain; Defeat of Muslims near Poitiers

CHAPTER REVIEW

Upon Reflection

Q In what ways were the Byzantine and Islamic civilizations different from the civilization developing in western Europe? In what ways were they similar?

Q What role did monks and nuns play in early medieval society?

Q What contributions did the Germanic peoples make to the political, economic, and social conditions of early medieval society?

Q What impact did Christianity have on the intellectual life of early medieval society?

Key Terms

tetrarchy (p. 181)
inflation (p. 182)
curiales (p. 183)
heresy (p. 184)
Arianism (p. 184)
Christology (p. 184)
federates (p. 185)
major domus (p. 190)
wergeld (p. 191)
celibacy (p. 193)
Petrine supremacy (p. 194)
monk (p. 196)
monasticism (p. 196)

abbot (p. 197)
nuns (p. 197)
abbess (p. 200)
liberal arts (p. 202)
trivium (p. 202)
quadrivium (p. 202)
iconoclasts (p. 207)
iconoclasm (p. 207)
Five Pillars of Islam (p. 210)
caliph (p.210)
jihad (p. 210)
Shi'ites (p. 211)
Sunnis (p. 211)

Full definitions also appear in the Glossary at the end of the book.

Suggestions for Further Reading

General Works   For introductions to late antiquity, see **G. Clark**, *Late Antiquity: A Very Short Introduction* (Oxford, 2011), and **H. Elton**, *The Roman Empire in Late Antiquity: A Political and Military History* (New York, 2018). For an excellent survey of late antiquity and the emergence of the medieval world, see **C. Wickham**, *The Inheritance of Rome: A History of Europe from 400 to 1000* (New York, 2009).

Late Roman Empire   On the late Roman Empire, see **S. Mitchell**, *History of the Later Roman Empire, A.D. 284–641* (Oxford, 2006), and **C. Kelly**, *Ruling the Later Roman Empire* (Cambridge, Mass., 2006). For new perspectives on the role of the Germans in the fall of the Western Roman Empire, see **G. Halsall**, *Barbarian Migrations and the Roman West, 376–568* (New York, 2008), and **P. Heather**, *Empires and Barbarians: The Fall of Rome and the Birth of Europe* (Oxford, 2009). For a recent perspective on the fall of Rome, see **K. Harper**, *The Fate of Rome: Climate, Disease, and the End of an Empire* (Princeton, 2017).

The Germanic Peoples   For a survey of the German tribes and their migrations, see **M. Todd**, *The Early Germans*, 2nd ed. (Oxford, 2004). On the relationship between the Romans and the Germans, see **T. S. Burns**, *Rome and the Barbarians, 100 B.C.–A.D. 400* (Baltimore, 2003), and **M. Kulikowski**, *Rome's Gothic Wars* (New York, 2007).

Early Christianity   For a superb introduction to early Christianity, see **P. Brown**, *The Rise of Western Christendom: Triumph and Adversity, A.D. 200–1000*, 2nd ed. (Oxford, 2002). For good accounts of early monasticism, see **C. H. Lawrence**, *Medieval Monasticism*, 3rd ed. (London, 2000), and **M. Dunn**, *Emergence of Monasticism: From the Desert Fathers to the Early Middle Ages* (New York, 2003). On Pope Gregory the Great, see **J. Moorhead**, *Gregory the Great* (London, 2005).

The Byzantine Empire   Good introductions to Byzantine history can be found in **A. Cameron**, *The Byzantines* (Oxford, 2006); **W. Treadgold**, *A Concise History of Byzantium* (London, 2001); and **J. Herrin**, *Byzantium, The Surprising Life of a Medieval Empire* (Princeton, 2007). On Justinian, see **P. Heather**, *Rome Resurgent: War and Empire in the Age of Justinian* (New York, 2018). On Constantinople, see **J. Harris**, *Constantinople: Capital of Byzantium* (London, 2007).

The Islamic Middle East   On the rise of Islam, see **F. M. Donner**, *Muhammad and the Believers: At the Origins of Islam* (New York, 2010). On the expansion of Islam, see **R. G. Hoyland**, *In God's Path: The Arab Conquests and the Creation of an Islamic Empire* (Oxford, 2014). On the Umayyad caliphate, see **G. R. Hawting**, *The First Dynasty of Islam: The Umayyad Caliphate, A.D. 661–750*, 2nd ed. (New York, 2005).

Notes

1. Quoted in Gregory Bishop of Tours, *History of the Franks* (New York, 1969), pp. 38–40.
2. N. Lewis and M. Reinhold, eds., *Roman Civilization*, vol. 2 (New York, 1955), p. 191.
3. Quoted in B. Strauss, *Ten Caesars: Roman Emperors from Augustus to Constantine* (New York, 2019), p. 301.
4. "The Creed of Nicaea," in H. Bettenson, ed., *Documents of the Christian Church* (London, 1963), p. 35.
5. C. C. Mierow, trans., *The Gothic History of Jordanes* (Princeton, N.J., 1915), pp. 88–89.
6. Quoted in C. Wickham, *The Inheritance of Rome: A History of Europe from 400 to 1000* (New York, 2009), p. 82.
7. Quoted in A. Cameron, *The Mediterranean World in Late Antiquity* (London, 1993), p. 37.
8. E. F. Henderson, *Selected Historical Documents of the Middle Ages* (London, 1892), p. 182.
9. Ibid., p. 181.
10. A. Fremantle, ed., *A Treasury of Early Christianity* (New York, 1953), p. 91.
11. Matthew 16:15–19.
12. R. C. Petry, ed., *A History of Christianity: Readings in the History of Early and Medieval Christianity* (Englewood Cliffs, N.J., 1962), p. 70.
13. B. Pullan, ed., *Sources for the History of Medieval Europe* (Oxford, 1966), p. 46.
14. Quoted in S. Painter and B. Tierney, *Western Europe in the Middle Ages, 300–1475* (New York, 1983), p. 106.
15. Mark 10:21.
16. N. F. Cantor, ed., *The Medieval World, 300–1300* (New York, 1963), pp. 104, 101, 108, 103.
17. Bede, *A History of the English Church and People*, trans. L. Sherley-Price (Harmondsworth, England, 1968), pp. 86–87.
18. Quoted in P. Brown, *The Rise of Western Christendom: Triumph and Adversity, A.D. 200–1000* (Oxford, 1997), p. 98.
19. Quoted in P. Heather, *Rome Resurgent: War and Empire in the Age of Justinian* (Oxford, 2018), p. 114.
20. Procopius, *Secret History*, trans. R. Atwater (Ann Arbor, Mich., 1963), p. 3.
21. H. B. Dewing, trans., *Procopius*, vol. 1 (Cambridge, Mass., 1914), p. 48.
22. Procopius, *Buildings of Justinian* (London, 1897), pp. 9, 6–7, 11.
23. Quoted in J. Harris, *Constantinople: Capital of Byzantium* (New York, 2007), p. 40.
24. Quoted in ibid., p. 118.
25. Quoted in A. Goldschmidt Jr., *A Concise History of the Middle East*, 7th ed. (Boulder, Colo., 2001), p. 60.

 **MindTap** *Tips*   Look for the extensive multimedia assets available throughout MindTap. Lesson readings include links to Google Arts & Culture websites for deeper explorations of places, people and events. Readings also include links to online videos that bring history to life.

CHAPTER 8

European Civilization in the Early Middle Ages, 750–1000

IMAGE 8.1 **A Fifteenth-Century French Manuscript Illustration of the Coronation of Charlemagne by Pope Leo III**

CONNECTIONS TO TODAY

What is the relationship between events in eastern Europe and the eastern Mediterranean world in the early Middle Ages and the situation in those areas today?

IN 800 C.E., CHARLEMAGNE, the king of the Franks, journeyed to Rome to help Pope Leo III, who was barely clinging to power in the face of rebellious Romans. On Christmas Day, Charlemagne (SHAR-luh-mayn) and his family, attended by Romans, Franks, and visitors from the Byzantine Empire, crowded into Saint Peter's Basilica to hear Mass. One Frankish writer explained that quite unexpectedly, as the king rose from praying before the tomb of the apostle Peter, Pope Leo placed a "golden crown on his head." In keeping with ancient tradition, the people in the church shouted, "Long life and victory to Charles Augustus, crowned by God the great and pacific Emperor of the Romans." Seemingly, the Roman Empire in the west had been reborn, and Charles had become its first western emperor since 476. But this "Roman emperor" was actually a German king, and he had been crowned by the head of the western Christian church. In truth, the coronation of Charlemagne was a sign not of the rebirth of the Roman Empire but of the emergence of a new civilization.

By the year of Charlemagne's coronation, the contours of this new civilization were beginning to emerge in western Europe. Increasingly, Europe would become the focus and center of Western civilization. Building on a fusion of Germanic, Greco-Roman, and Christian elements, the medieval European world first became visible in the Carolingian Empire of Charlemagne. The agrarian foundations of the eighth and ninth centuries proved inadequate to maintain a large monarchical system, however, and a new political and military order based on the decentralization of political power subsequently evolved to become an integral part of the political world of the Middle Ages.

European civilization began on a shaky and uncertain foundation, however. In the ninth century, Vikings, Magyars, and Muslims posed threats that could easily have stifled the new society. But the Vikings and Magyars were assimilated, and recovery slowly began to set in. By 1000, European civilization was ready to embark on a period of dazzling vitality and expansion.

8-1 Europeans and the Environment

 FOCUS QUESTION: What were the main features of the physical environment of the early Middle Ages?

The number of people in early medieval Europe is a matter of considerable uncertainty. In all probability, the population of the eighth century still had not recovered from the losses caused by the plagues of the sixth and seventh centuries. Historians generally believe that in the early Middle Ages, Europe was a sparsely populated landscape dotted with villages and clusters of villages of farmers and warriors. Although rivers, such as the Loire, Seine, Rhine, Elbe, and Oder, served as major arteries of communication, villages were still separated from one another by forests, swamps, and mountain ridges. Forests, which provided building and heating materials as well as game, covered the European landscape. In fact, it has been estimated that less than 10 percent of the land was cultivated, a figure so small that some economic historians believe that Europe had difficulty feeding even its modest population. Thus, hunting and fishing were necessary to supplement the European diet.

8-1a Farming

The cultivation of new land proved especially difficult in the early Middle Ages. Given the crude implements of the time, it was not easy to clear forests and prepare the ground for planting. Moreover, German tribes had for centuries considered trees sacred and resisted cutting them down to make room for farms. Even conversion to Christianity did not entirely change these attitudes. In addition, the heavy soils of northern Europe were not easily plowed. Agricultural methods also worked against significant crop yields. Land was allowed to lie fallow

(unplanted) every other year to regain its fertility, but even so it produced low yields. Evidence indicates that Frankish estates yielded incredibly low ratios of two measures of grain to one measure of seed.

8-1b The Climate

Climatic patterns show that European weather began to improve around 700 C.E. after several centuries of wetter and colder conditions. Nevertheless, natural disasters were always a threat, especially since the low yields meant that little surplus could be saved for bad times. Drought or too much rain could mean meager harvests, famine, and dietary deficiencies that made people susceptible to a wide range of diseases. This was a period of low life expectancy. One study of Hungarian graves found that of every five skeletons, one was a child below the age of one, and two were children between one and fourteen; more than one in five was a woman below the age of twenty. Overall, then, the picture of early medieval Europe is of a relatively small population subsisting on the basis of a limited agricultural economy and leading, in most cases, a precarious existence.

8-2 The World of the Carolingians

 FOCUS QUESTIONS: How was the government of Charlemagne organized? What was the significance of Charlemagne's coronation as emperor? In what ways did the political, intellectual, and daily life in the Carolingian Empire represent a fusion of Gallo-Roman, Germanic, and Christian practices?

By the eighth century C.E., the Merovingian dynasty was losing its control of the Frankish lands. Charles Martel, the Carolingian mayor of the palace of Austrasia, became the virtual ruler of these territories. When Charles Martel died in 741, his son, Pepin (PEP-in *or* pay-PANH), deposed the Merovingians and assumed the kingship of the Frankish state for himself and his family. Pepin's actions, which were approved by the pope, created a new form of Frankish kingship. Pepin (r. 751–768) was crowned king and formally anointed by a representative of the pope with holy oil in imitation of an Old Testament practice. The anointing not only symbolized that the king had been entrusted with a sacred office but also provides yet another example of how a Germanic institution fused with a Christian practice in the early Middle Ages.

8-2a Charlemagne and the Carolingian Empire (768–814 C.E.)

Pepin's death in 768 brought to the throne of the Frankish kingdom his son, a dynamic and powerful ruler known to history as Charles the Great or Charlemagne (*Carolus magnus* in Latin—hence our word *Carolingian*). Charlemagne was a determined and decisive man, intelligent and inquisitive. A fierce warrior, he was also a wise patron of learning and a resolute statesman (see Historical Voices, "The Achievements of Charlemagne," p. 217). He greatly expanded the territory of the Carolingian Empire during his lengthy rule.

The Achievements of Charlemagne

 Based on Einhard's account, discuss the strengths and weaknesses of Charlemagne. Which characteristics help explain Charlemagne's success as a ruler? Does Einhard exaggerate Charlemagne's strengths? What might motivate him to do that?

EINHARD (YN-hart), THE BIOGRAPHER OF CHARLEMAGNE, was born in the valley of the Main River in Germany about 775 C.E. Raised and educated in the monastery of Fulda, an important center of learning, he arrived at the court of Charlemagne in 791 or 792. Although he did not achieve high office under Charlemagne, he served as private secretary to Louis the Pious, Charlemagne's son and successor. Einhard's *Life of Charlemagne*, written between 817 and 830, was modeled on *Lives of the Caesars* by the Roman author Suetonius (swee-TOH-nee-uss), especially his biography of Augustus. In this selection, Einhard discusses some of Charlemagne's accomplishments.

Einhard, *Life of Charlemagne*

Such are the wars, most skillfully planned and successfully fought, which this most powerful king waged during the forty-seven years of his reign. He so largely increased the Frank kingdom, which was already great and strong when he received it at his father's hands, that more than double its former territory was added to it. . . . He subdued all the wild and barbarous tribes dwelling in Germany between the Rhine and the Vistula, the Ocean and the Danube, all of which speak very much the same language, but differ widely from one another in customs and dress. . . .

He added to the glory of his reign by gaining the good will of several kings and nations; so close, indeed, was the alliance that he contracted with Alfonso, King of Galicia and Asturias, that the latter, when sending letters or ambassadors to Charles, invariably styled himself his man. . . . The Emperors of Constantinople [the Byzantine emperors] sought friendship and alliance with Charles by several embassies; and even when the Greeks [the Byzantines] suspected him of designing to take the empire from them, because of his assumption of the title Emperor, they made a close alliance with him, that

he might have no cause of offense. In fact, the power of the Franks was always viewed with a jealous eye, whence the Greek proverb, "Have the Frank for your friend, but not for your neighbor."

This King, who showed himself so great in extending his empire and subduing foreign nations, and was constantly occupied with plans to that end, undertook also very many works calculated to adorn and benefit his kingdom, and brought several of them to completion. Among these, the most deserving of mention are the basilica of the Holy Mother of God at Aix-la-Chapelle [Aachen], built in the most admirable manner, and a bridge over the Rhine River at Mainz, half a mile long, the breadth of the river at this point. . . . Above all, sacred buildings were the object of his care throughout his whole kingdom; and whenever he found them falling to ruin from age, he commanded the priests and fathers who had charge of them to repair them, and made sure by commissioners that his instructions were obeyed. . . . Thus did Charles defend and increase as well as beautify his kingdom. . . .

He cherished with the greatest fervor and devotion the principles of the Christian religion, which had been instilled into him from infancy. Hence it was that he built the beautiful church at Aix-la-Chapelle, which he adorned with gold and silver and lamps, and with rails and doors of solid brass. He had the columns and marbles for this structure brought from Rome and Ravenna, for he could not find such as were suitable elsewhere. He was a constant worshiper at this church as long as his health permitted, going morning and evening, even after nightfall, besides attending Mass. . . .

He was very forward in caring for the poor, so much so that he not only made a point of giving in his own country and his own kingdom, but when he discovered that there were Christians living in poverty in Syria, Egypt, and Africa, at Jerusalem, Alexandria, and Carthage, he had compassion on their wants, and used to send money over the seas to them. . . . He sent great and countless gifts to the popes, and throughout his whole reign the wish that he had nearest at heart was to reestablish the ancient authority of the city of Rome under his care and by his influence, and to defend and protect the Church of St. Peter, and to beautify and enrich it out of his own store above all other churches.

Source: Einhard, *The Life of Charlemagne*, trans. S. E. Turner (New York: Harper & Brothers, 1880).

Expansion of the Carolingian Empire In the tradition of Germanic kings, Charlemagne was a determined warrior who undertook fifty-four military campaigns. Even though the Frankish army was relatively small—only eight thousand men gathered each spring for campaigning—supplying it and transporting it to distant areas could still present serious problems.

The Frankish army comprised mostly infantry, with some cavalry armed with swords and spears.

Charlemagne's campaigns took him to many areas of Europe. In 773 C.E., he led his army into Italy, crushed the Lombards, and took control of the Lombard state. Although his son was crowned king of Italy, Charlemagne was its real ruler. Four years after subduing Italy, Charlemagne and his forces advanced into northern Spain. This campaign proved disappointing; not only did the Basques harass his army as it crossed the Pyrenees on the way home, but they also ambushed and annihilated his rear guard.

Charlemagne was considerably more successful with his eastern campaigns into Germany, especially against the Saxons, who had settled between the Elbe River and the North Sea. As Einhard, Charlemagne's biographer, recounted it:

> No war ever undertaken by the Frank nation was carried on with such persistence and bitterness, or cost so much labor, because the Saxons, like almost all the tribes of Germany, were a fierce people, given to the worship of devils, and hostile to our religion, and did not consider it dishonorable to transgress and violate all law, human and divine.[1]

Charlemagne's insistence that the Saxons convert to Christianity simply fueled their resistance. Not until 804, after eighteen campaigns, was Saxony finally pacified and added to the Carolingian domain.

Charlemagne invaded the lands of the Bavarians in southeastern Germany in 787 and had incorporated them into his empire by the following year, an expansion that brought him into contact with the southern Slavs and the Avars. The latter disappeared from history after their utter devastation at the hands of Charlemagne's army. Now at its height, Charlemagne's empire covered much of western and central Europe (see Map 8.1); not until the time of Napoleon in the nineteenth century would an empire of this size be seen again in Europe (see Image 8.2).

MAP 8.1 The Carolingian Empire. Charlemagne inherited the Frankish kingdom from his father, Pepin. He expanded his territories in several directions, creating an empire that would not be rivaled in size until the conquests of Napoleon in the early nineteenth century.

Q *How might Charlemagne's holdings in northern Italy have influenced his relationship with the pope?*

IMAGE 8.2 **Bronze Equestrian Statue of Charlemagne.** This small bronze statue is believed to represent the emperor Charles the Great, although some scholars believe it is his grandson, Charles the Bald. The figure dates from the ninth century, but the horse is a sixteenth-century restoration. The attire on the figure accords with Einhard's account of how Charlemagne dressed. The imperial crown rests on his head, and in his left hand he grasps a globe, a symbol of world power and a reminder that the power of the Roman Empire had been renewed.

Governing the Empire Charlemagne continued the efforts of his father in organizing the Carolingian kingdom. Because there was no system of public taxation, Charlemagne depended upon the royal estates for the resources he needed to govern his empire. Food and goods derived from these lands provided support for the king, his household staff, and officials. To keep the nobles in his service, Charlemagne granted part of the royal lands as lifetime holdings to nobles who assisted him.

In addition to the household staff, the administration of the empire depended on counts, who were the king's chief representatives in local areas, although in dangerous border districts officials known as margraves (literally, *mark graf*, count of the border district) were used. Counts were members of the nobility who had already existed under the Merovingians. They had come to control public services in their own lands and thus acted as judges, military leaders, and agents of the king. Gradually, as the rule of the Merovingian kings weakened, many counts had simply attached the royal lands and services performed on behalf of the king to their own family possessions.

In an effort to gain greater control over his kingdom, Charlemagne attempted to limit the power of the counts. They were required to serve outside their own family lands and were moved about periodically rather than being permitted to remain in a county for life. By making the offices appointive, Charlemagne tried to prevent the counts' children from automatically inheriting their offices. Moreover, as another check on the counts, Charlemagne instituted the *missi dominici* (MISS-ee doh-MIN-i-chee) ("messengers of the lord king"), two men, one lay lord, and one church official, who were sent out to local districts to ensure that the counts were executing the king's wishes. They had the power to remove counts if they were abusing their power, thus making the *missi* an important instrument in bolstering royal power.

Important to Charlemagne's reign and Carolingian government in general was the role of assemblies—annual gatherings of the most important men in the kingdom. In these assemblies, gifts were made to the king and issues involving the political community were settled. Beginning in 779, decisions made by the king in consultation with the assemblies were written down, known as capitularies. These capitularies were then copied and sent out to local districts for implementation. The *missi dominici*, who were often important local people, were one group that was responsible for seeing that they were executed.

Charlemagne also realized that the Catholic Church could provide valuable assistance in governing his kingdom. By the late seventh century, the system of ecclesiastical government within the Christian church that had been created in the late Roman Empire had largely disintegrated. Many church offices were not filled or were held by grossly unqualified relatives of the royal family. Both Pepin and his son Charlemagne took up the cause of church reform by creating new bishoprics and archbishoprics, restoring old ones, and seeing to it that the clergy accepted the orders of their superiors and executed their duties.

Charlemagne as Emperor As Charlemagne's power grew, so did his prestige as the most powerful Christian ruler; one monk even wrote of his empire as the "kingdom of Europe." Charlemagne acquired a new title—emperor of the Romans—in 800 C.E., but substantial controversy surrounds this event, and it can only be understood within the context of the relationship between the papacy and the Frankish monarchs.

Already during the reign of Pepin, a growing alliance had emerged between the kingdom of the Franks and the papacy. The popes welcomed this support, and in the course of the second half of the eighth century, they severed more and more of their ties with the Byzantine Empire and drew closer to the Frankish kingdom. Charlemagne encouraged this development. In 799, after a rebellion against his authority, Pope Leo III (795–816) managed to escape from Rome and flee to safety at Charlemagne's court. Charlemagne offered assistance, and when he went to Rome in November 800 to settle affairs, he was received by the pope like an emperor. On Christmas Day in 800, after Mass, Pope Leo placed a crown on Charlemagne's head and proclaimed him emperor of the Romans.

What Was the Significance of Char-lemagne? The significance of this imperial coronation has been much debated by historians. We are not even sure whether the pope or Charlemagne initiated the idea when they met in the summer of 799 in Paderborn in German lands or whether Charlemagne was pleased or displeased. His biographer Einhard claimed that "at first [he] had such an aversion that he declared that he would not have set foot in the Church the day that [it was] conferred, although it was a great feast-day, if he could have foreseen the design of the Pope."[2] But Charlemagne also perceived the usefulness of the imperial title; after all, he was now on a level of equality with the Byzantine emperor. Moreover, the papacy now had a defender of great stature, although later popes in the Middle Ages would become involved in fierce struggles with emperors over who possessed the higher power.

In any case, Charlemagne's coronation as Roman emperor certainly demonstrated the strength, even after three hundred years, of the concept of an enduring Roman Empire. More important, it symbolized the fusion of Roman, Christian, and Germanic elements. Did this fusion constitute the foundations of European civilization? A Germanic king had been crowned emperor of the Romans by the spiritual leader of western Christendom. Charlemagne had created an empire that stretched from the North Sea in the north to Italy in the south, and from France in western Europe to Vienna in central Europe. This empire differed significantly from the Roman Empire, which encompassed much of the Mediterranean world. Had a new civilization emerged? And should Charlemagne be seen, as one recent biographer has argued, as the "father of Europe"?[3] Other historians disagree and argue that there was only a weak sense of community in Europe before 1000. As one has stated, "Europe was not born in the early Middle Ages. . . . There was no common European culture, and certainly not any Europe-wide economy."[4]

8-2b The Carolingian Intellectual Renewal

Charlemagne had a strong desire to revive learning in his kingdom, an attitude that stemmed from his own intellectual curiosity as well as the need to provide educated clergy for the church and literate officials for the government. His efforts led to a revival of learning and culture that some historians have labeled the Carolingian Renaissance, or "rebirth" of learning. But Charlemagne also had a deeper purpose (see Historical Voices, "Charlemagne's Goal of Learning," p. 221). He expressed this in a letter to bishops in 800 C.E.: "We exhort you not only not to neglect the study of letters but also with most humble and God-pleasing application to learn zealously for a purpose, namely, that you may be able the more easily… to penetrate the mysteries of divine scripture."[5]

For the most part, the revival of classical studies and the efforts to preserve Latin culture took place in the monasteries, many of which had been established by the Irish and English missionaries of the seventh and eighth centuries C.E. (see Chapter 7). By the ninth century, the work required of Benedictine monks was the copying of manuscripts. Monasteries established **scriptoria** (skrip-TOR-ee-uh), or writing rooms, where monks copied not only the works of early Christianity, such as the Bible and the treatises of the church fathers, but also the works of classical Latin authors (see Image 8.3), which included the works of Cicero, Horace, Tacitus, Suetonius, and Livy among others (see Chapters 5 and 6).

Mary Evans Picture Library/The Image Works

IMAGE 8.3 The Monk as Copyist. The copying of manuscripts was a major task of monastic establishments in the Middle Ages. The work took place in a scriptorium, or writing room. This medieval manuscript illustration from the fourteenth century shows a monk at work in the scriptorium of a monastery. To copy an entire book was considered a work of special spiritual merit. Copying the Bible was especially important because it was considered a sacred object. The monk in this illustration had the benefit of wearing eyeglasses, first introduced in the thirteenth century and refined in the fourteenth.

Q *What was the importance of copying manuscripts?*

CHRONOLOGY	The Carolingian Empire	
Pepin crowned king of the Franks	751 C.E.
Reign of Charlemagne	768–814
Campaign in Italy	773–774
Campaign in Spain	778
Conquest of Bavarians	787–788
Charlemagne crowned emperor	800
Final conquest of Saxons	804
Reign of Louis the Pious	814–840
Treaty of Verdun divides Carolingian Empire	843

Charlemagne's Goal of Learning

 Why was Charlemagne attracted to the two Scots? What did they help Charlemagne to achieve? What does this story tell you about the purpose of the Carolingian Renaissance?

CHARLEMAGNE HAD A CLEAR GOAL in reviving learning in his kingdom. Notker Balbulus (the Stammerer), a monk in what is now Switzerland, explained this goal in his The Deeds of Charlemagne, a work that he wrote at the end of the ninth century C.E. for Charles the Fat, Charlemagne's great-great grandson. Notker told the following story.

Notker the Stammerer, *The Deeds of Charlemagne*

When he [Charlemagne] had begun to rule alone in the western parts of the world, and the study of letters was everywhere almost forgotten, so that the worship of the true God was weak, it happened that two Scots from Ireland [Scotia was the name for Ireland] came with British traders to the coast of Gaul, and they were men most wonderfully instructed both in secular and in sacred texts. When they displayed nothing for sale, they used to shout to the crowds who had come to buy things: "If anyone is eager for wisdom, let him come to us and receive it, for that is what we have for sale." They claimed that

they had it for sale because they saw that the people were trading in what was priced rather than what was free, so they could either spur them to buy wisdom just like the other things they were buying; or else, as subsequent events proved, by such an announcement they provoked wonder and amazement. They proclaimed these things for such a long time that finally the onlookers, thinking them crazy, brought the matter to the ears of King Charles, who was always a most greedy lover of wisdom. He summoned them to his presence with the utmost speed and asked them if it was true, as rumor had it, that they had brought wisdom with them. They said: "Yes indeed we have it, and in the name of the Lord we are ready to give to those who seek it in a proper way." When he had asked them what they wanted for it, they replied: "We only ask for a suitable place and talented minds and food and clothing, without which our pilgrimage cannot be accomplished." When he received this answer [Charlemagne] was filled with great joy and first he kept them both with him for a short time. Later, when he was compelled to go on military campaigns he ordered one of them to live in Gaul, and he entrusted to him many boys very noble and middling and wretched, and ordered that they be fed and given suitable places to live. The second was sent to Italy and granted the monastery of St. Augustine near the city of Pavia so that whoever wished might gather there to be taught by him.

Source: David Ganz, ed. and trans., Notker the Stammerer, *The Deeds of Charlemagne* (Penguin Classics, 2008), pp. 55–56.

But even more important was the emphasis in the Carolingian Renaissance on the works of early Christianity. Much stress was put on making the correct versions of the Old and New Testaments, which had been "corrupted by the ignorance of the copyists," according to Charlemagne, In addition to the Bible, Carolingian scholars sought the correct versions of the early Church Fathers, as well as the liturgy for the mass, canon law, and sermons. And the emphasis on correct Latin in old Roman texts was to be put to use in perfecting Christian texts. Moreover, Carolingian scholars produced a body of original Christian literature, including commentaries on the Bible, works on theology, and histories of bishoprics.

Following the example of the Irish and English monks, their Carolingian counterparts developed new ways of producing books. Their texts were written on pages made of parchment or sheepskin rather than papyrus and then bound in covers decorated with jewels and precious metals. The use of parchment made books very expensive; making a Bible required an entire herd of sheep. (Papyrus was no longer available because Egypt was in Muslim hands, and the west could no longer afford to import it.) Carolingian monastic scribes also developed a new writing style called the Carolingian minuscule (see Image 8.5b on p. 227). This was really hand printing rather than cursive writing and was far easier to read than the Merovingian script.

The manuscripts, some of them illustrated, that were produced in Carolingian monastic scriptoria were crucial in preserving the ancient legacy. About eight thousand manuscripts survive from Carolingian times. Some 90 percent of the ancient Roman works that we have today exist because they were copied by Carolingian monks.

Charlemagne personally promoted learning by establishing a palace school and encouraging scholars from all over Europe to come to the Carolingian court. These included men of letters from Italy, Spain, Germany, and Ireland. Best known was Alcuin (AL-kwin), from the famous school at York, founded as part of the great revival of learning in the Anglo-Saxon kingdom of Northumbria. From 782 to 796, while serving at Charlemagne's court as an adviser on ecclesiastical affairs, Alcuin also provided the leadership for the palace school. He concentrated on teaching classical Latin and adopted Cassiodorus's sevenfold division of knowledge known as the liberal arts (see Chapter 7), which became the basis for all later medieval education. Charlemagne also encouraged monasteries and bishoprics to establish schools for children; many of these students later became well known in public life and the church. The goal in education was "to inculcate Christian learning and understanding."

Charlemagne's official seal carried the words "renewal of the Roman Empire." For Charlemagne, who made a number of visits to Italy, this included a revival of the arts, which meant looking to Italy for inspiration. Charlemagne encouraged his own artists and architects to look to the arts of ancient Rome and the Byzantine Empire. The chapel he built at Aachen was modeled after the Church of San Vitale in Ravenna, a church that had been built by the emperor Justinian after his reconquest of much of Italy (see Chapter 7). All in all, the Carolingian Renaissance played an important role in keeping the classical heritage alive as well as strengthening the Christian faith by spreading the basic works on which that faith was rooted.

8-2c Life in the Carolingian World

In daily as well as intellectual life, the Europe of the Carolingian era witnessed a fusion of Roman, Germanic, and Christian practices. The last in particular seem to have exercised an ever-increasing influence.

The Family and Marriage By Carolingian times, the Catholic Church had begun to make a significant impact on Frankish family life and marital and sexual attitudes. Fathers or uncles arranged marriages in Frankish society to meet the needs of the extended family. Although wives were expected to be faithful to their husbands, Frankish aristocrats often kept concubines, either slave girls or free women from their estates. Even the "most Christian king" Charlemagne had a number of concubines.

To limit such sexual license, the church increasingly emphasized its role in marriage and attempted to Christianize it. Although marriage was a civil arrangement, priests tried to add their blessings and strengthen the concept of a special marriage ceremony.

To stabilize marriages, the church also began to emphasize **monogamy** and permanence. A Frankish church council in 789 C.E. stipulated that marriage was "indissoluble" and condemned concubinage and easy divorce. During the reign of Emperor Louis the Pious (r. 814–840), the church formally prohibited divorce. Now a husband was expected to remain with his wife "even though she were sterile, deformed, old, dirty, drunken, a frequenter of bad company, lascivious, vain, greedy, unfaithful, quarrelsome, abusive . . . for when that man was free, he freely engaged himself."[6] This change was not easily accepted, however, and it was not until the thirteenth century that divorce was largely stamped out among both the common people and the nobility.

The acceptance and spread of the Catholic Church's views on the indissolubility of marriage encouraged the development of the **nuclear family** at the expense of the extended family. Although kinship was still an influential social and political force, the conjugal unit came to be seen as the basic unit of society. The new practice of young couples establishing their own households had a significant impact on women. In the extended family, the oldest woman controlled all the other female members; in the nuclear family, the wife was still dominated by her husband, but at least she now had control of her own household and children. In aristocratic families, women had even more opportunity to play independent roles (see Historical Voices, "Advice from a Carolingian Mother," p. 223). The wives of Carolingian aristocrats were often entrusted with the management of the household and even the administration of extensive landed estates while their husbands were absent in the royal service or on a military campaign.

Christianity and Sexuality The early church fathers had stressed that celibacy and complete abstinence from sexual activity constituted an ideal state superior to marriage. Subsequently, the early church gradually developed a case for clerical celibacy, although it proved impossible to enforce in the early Middle Ages.

The early fathers had also emphasized, however, that not all people had the self-discipline to remain celibate. It was thus permissible to marry, as Paul had indicated in his first epistle to the Corinthians: "It is good for a man not to touch a woman. Nevertheless, to avoid fornication, let every man have his own wife, and let every woman have her own husband. . . . I say therefore to the unmarried and widows, it is good for them if they abide even as I. But if they cannot contain, let them marry: for it is better to marry than to burn [with passion]."[7] The church thus viewed marriage as the lesser of two evils; it was a concession to human weakness and fulfilled the need for companionship, sex, and children. Although marriage was the subject of much debate in the early medieval church, it was generally agreed that marriage gave the right to indulge in sexual intercourse. Sex, then, was permissible within marriage, but only so long as it was used for the purpose of procreation, or the begetting of children, not for pleasure.

Because the church developed the tradition that sexual relations between man and wife were legitimate only if engaged in for procreation, it condemned all forms of contraception. The church accepted only one way to limit children: abstinence from intercourse, either periodic or total. The church also strongly condemned abortion, although its prohibition failed to stop the practice. Various herbal potions, whose formulas appear in writings from Roman and Byzantine doctors, were available to prevent conception or cause abortion.

The church's condemnation of sexual activity outside marriage also included homosexuality. Neither Roman religion nor Roman law had recognized any real difference between homosexual and heterosexual eroticism, and the Roman Empire had taken no legal measures against the practice of homosexuality between adults. Later, however, in 538 C.E. the Byzantine emperor Justinian condemned homosexuality, claiming that it brought down the wrath of God ("we have provoked Him to anger") and endangered the welfare of the state: "For because of such crimes, there are famines, earthquakes, and pestilences; wherefore we admonish men to abstain from the aforesaid unlawful acts, that they may not lose their souls."[8] Justinian recommended that the guilty parties be punished by castration. Although the early medieval church similarly condemned homosexuality, it also pursued a flexible policy in its treatment of homosexuals. In the early Middle Ages, homosexuals were treated less harshly than married couples who practiced contraception.

New Attitudes Toward Children The Catholic Church also had an impact on another aspect of family life—children. The ancient Romans had limited their family size through infanticide, done primarily by the exposure of unwanted children, which was accepted in classical society. The Romans then

Advice from a Carolingian Mother

 What advice does Dhuoda of Septimania give her son? What does this selection tell us about aristocratic women in the early Middle Ages and their relationship with power?

IN ADDITION TO HER OTHER RESPONSIBILITIES, the wife of a Carolingian aristocrat was expected to bear large numbers of children and to supervise their upbringing. This selection by Dhuoda (doo-OH-duh), wife of Bernard, marquis of Septimania (in southern France), is taken from a manual she wrote to instruct her son on his duties to his new lord, King Charles the Bald (r. 840–877).

Dhuoda, *Handbook for William*

Direction on your comportment toward your lord.

You have Charles as your lord; you have him as lord because, as I believe, God and your father, Bernard, have chosen him for you to serve at the beginning of your career, in the flower of your youth. Remember that he comes from a great and noble lineage on both sides of his family. Serve him not only so that you please him in obvious ways, but also as one clearheaded in matters of both body and soul. Be steadfastly and completely loyal to him in all things. . . .

This is why, my son, I urge you to keep this loyalty as long as you live, in your body and in your mind. For the advancement that it brings you will be of great value both to you and to those who in turn serve you. May the madness of treachery never, not once, make you offer an angry insult. May it never give rise in your heart to the idea of being disloyal to your lord. There is harsh and shameful talk about men who act in this fashion. I do not think that such will befall you or those who fight alongside you because such an attitude has never shown itself among your ancestors. It has not been seen among them, it is not seen now, and it will not be seen in the future.

Be truthful to your lord, my son William, child of their lineage. Be vigilant, energetic, and offer him ready assistance as I have said here. In every matter of importance to royal power take care to show yourself a man of good judgment—in your own thoughts and in public—to the extent that God gives you strength. Read the sayings and the lives of the holy Fathers who have gone before us. You will there discover how you may serve your lord and be faithful to him in all things. When you understand this, devote yourself to the faithful execution of your lord's commands. Look around as well and observe those who fight for him loyally and constantly. Learn from them how you may serve him. Then, informed by their example, with the help and support of God, you will easily reach the celestial goal I have mentioned above. And may your heavenly Lord God be generous and benevolent toward you. May he keep you safe, be your kind leader and your protector. May he deign to assist you in all your actions and be your constant defender.

Source: Dhuoda, "A Carolingian Woman's Counsel for Her Son," *Handbook for William: A Carolingian Woman's Counsel for Her Son*, trans. C. Neel (Lincoln: University of Nebraska Press, 1991).

---

paid much attention to the children chosen to survive, as is especially evident in the education of upper-class children. In the emerging early medieval world, German practices of child rearing became influential. As we saw in Chapter 7, the Germanic law codes listed *wergelds*, whose size represented a crude evaluation of a person's importance. According to a Visigothic code of the mid-seventh century, for example, male children were valued at 60 solidi. At the age of twenty, when they had become warriors, the wergeld increased fivefold to 300 solidi, where it remained until the adult male reached fifty, after which it again declined. The value of females was only half that of males, although it also jumped tremendously (to 250 solidi) for women between the ages of fifteen and forty because of their importance as bearers of children.

Although the Christian church condemned infanticide, it was not able to eliminate the practice, especially among the poor and among victims of seduction who did not want to keep their illegitimate offspring. Nevertheless, priests tried to discourage such practices by urging people to abandon unwanted children in churches. Often such children were taken in by monasteries and convents and raised to be monks and nuns. Following the example of Jesus's love for children, monks and nuns tended to respect and preserve the virtues of childhood. As children grew older, however, it was thought necessary to use strict discipline to control what was considered the natural inclination of children to sin, especially by disobeying their elders.

Travel and Hospitality Monasteries served another important function in the early medieval world as providers of hospitality. Both monasteries and aristocratic households were expected to provide a place to stay for weary travelers, who were ever at risk from thieves or violence of many kinds. Indeed, Burgundian law stipulated that "anyone who refused to offer a visitor shelter and warmth shall pay a fine of three solidi."[9] Hospitality, then, was a sacred duty, and monasteries were especially active in providing it. It was customary for monasteries to have two guest houses, one for the rich and another for the poor. The plan for the monastery of Saint Gall, for example, provided pilgrims and paupers with a house containing benches, two dormitories, and outbuildings. For travelers of high rank, there was a separate guest house with two heated rooms, servants' bedrooms, and stables for horses. One could not always be sure of hospitality in the early Middle Ages, however. The famous English missionary to Germany, Saint Boniface, reported that female pilgrims to Rome had been forced to become prostitutes in every town along their route in order to obtain their sustenance and reach their goal. The church responded by forbidding females to go on such pilgrimages.

Diet For both rich and poor, the main staple of the Carolingian diet was bread. The aristocratic classes, as well as the monks, consumed it in large quantities. Ovens at the monastery of Saint Gall were able to bake a thousand loaves of bread. Sometimes a gruel made of barley and oats was substituted for bread in the peasant diet.

The upper classes in Carolingian society enjoyed a much more varied diet than the peasants. Pork was the primary meat. Domestic pigs, allowed to run wild in the forests to find their own food, were collected and slaughtered in the fall, then smoked and salted to be eaten during the winter months. Because Carolingian aristocrats were especially fond of roasted meat, hunting wild game became one of their favorite activities. They ate little beef or mutton, however, because cattle were kept as dairy cows and oxen to draw plows, and sheep were raised for wool.

Dairy products were also important in the Carolingian diet. Milk, which spoiled rapidly, was made into cheese and butter. Chickens were raised for their eggs. Vegetables also formed a crucial part of the diet of both rich and poor. These included legumes, such as beans, peas, and lentils, and roots, such as garlic, onions, and carrots.

The Carolingian diet, especially of the upper classes, was also heavily dependent on honey and spices. Honey was used as a sweetener, both for foods and for many drinks, including wine and ale. Spices and herbs included domestic varieties that were grown in home gardens, such as thyme, sage, and chives, and more exotic—and outrageously expensive—varieties imported from the East, such as pepper, cumin, cloves, and cinnamon. Aristocrats enjoyed spicy dishes, not just for their taste but as a sign of prestige and wealth; spices were also believed to aid the digestion.

Gluttony and drunkenness were vices shared by many people in Carolingian society. Monastic rations were greatly enlarged in the eighth century to include a daily allotment of 3.7 pounds of bread (nuns were permitted 3 pounds), 11.2 quarts of wine or ale, 2 or 3 ounces of cheese, and 8 ounces of vegetables (4 ounces for nuns). These rations provided 6,000 calories a day, and since only heavy, fatty foods—bread, milk, and cheese—were considered nourishing, we begin to understand why some Carolingians were known for their potbellies. Malnutrition, however, remained a widespread problem for common people.

Everyone in Carolingian society, including abbots and monks, drank heavily and often to excess. Taverns became a regular feature of life and were found everywhere: in marketplaces, at pilgrimage centers, and on royal, episcopal, and monastic estates. Drinking contests were not unusual; one penitential stated: "Does drunken bravado encourage you to attempt to outdrink your friends? If so, thirty days' fast."

The aristocrats and monks favored wine above all other beverages, and much care was lavished on its production, especially by monasteries. Although ale was considered inferior in some quarters, it was especially popular in the northern and eastern parts of the Carolingian world. Water was also drunk as a beverage, but much care had to be taken to obtain pure sources from wells or clear streams.

Water was also used for bathing. Although standards of personal hygiene were not high, medieval people did not ignore cleanliness. A royal palace, such as Charlemagne's, possessed both hot and cold baths. Carolingian aristocrats changed clothes and bathed at least once a week, on Saturdays. The Saturday bath was also a regular practice in many Carolingian monasteries. To monks, bathing more than once a week seemed an unnecessary luxury; to aristocrats, it often seemed desirable.

Health Medical practice in Carolingian times stressed the use of medicinal herbs (see Historical Voices, "Medical Practices in the Early Middle Ages," p. 225) and bleeding (see Image 8.4). Although the latter was practiced regularly, moderation was

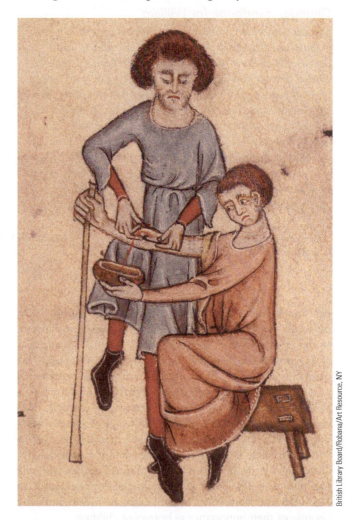

IMAGE 8.4 **Bloodletting in Early Medieval Medicine.** Bleeding was a regular part of medieval medical practice. It involved the withdrawing of blood from a person in the belief that doing so would bring balance to the body and thus heal a diseased condition. This fourteenth-century manuscript illustration shows a physician bleeding his patient with a cut in the arm. As the physician squeezes the arm, the blood spurts into a bowl; the patient seems to be quite anxious about the procedure.

British Library Board/Robana/Art Resource, NY

Medical Practices in the Early Middle Ages

 What were the basic medical remedies used by Anglo-Saxon physicians? How do these medical practices compare with those of the Romans? What notable similarities and differences do you find?

A NUMBER OF MEDICAL MANUSCRIPTS written in Old English have survived from Anglo-Saxon England. Although most of the medical texts date from the tenth to twelfth centuries, scholars believe that they include copies of earlier works and contain older influences as well. As the following selections from three of these treatises illustrate, herbs were the basic materials of the Anglo-Saxon physicians (or *leeches*, as they were called), and treatments consequently focused almost entirely on botanical remedies. The identity of many of the plants used remains unknown.

The Anglo-Saxon Herbal
Cress (Nasturtium)

1. In case a man's hair falls out, take juice of the plant which one names nasturtium and by another name cress, put it on the nose, the hair shall grow.
2. This plant is not sown but it is produced of itself in springs and in brooks; also it is written that in some lands it will grow against walls.
3. For a sore head, that is for scurf [dandruff] and for itch, take the seed of this same plant and goose grease, pound together, it draws from off the head the whiteness of the scurf.
4. For soreness of the body [indigestion], take this same plant nasturtium and pennyroyal, soak them in water and give to drink; the soreness and the evil departs.

Source: S. Rubin, *English Medieval Medicine* (New York: Barnes & Noble, 1974), pp. 49, 60, 66–67.

The Leechbook of Bald

Here are wound salves for all wounds and drinks and cleansings of every sort, whether internally or externally. Waybroad beaten and mixed with old lard, the fresh is of no use. Again, a wound salve: take waybroad seed, crush it small, shed it on the wound and soon it will be better.

For a burn, if a man be burned with fire only, take woodruff and lily and brooklime; boil in butter and smear therewith. If a man be burned with a liquid, let him take elm rind and roots of the lily, boil them in milk, smear thereon three times a day. For sunburn, boil in butter tender ivy twigs and smear thereon.

The Peri-Didaxeon
For a Broken Head

For a broken or wounded head which is caused by the humors of the head. Take betony and pound it and lay it on the wound and it will relieve all the pain.

For Sleep

Thus must one do for the man who cannot sleep; take wormwood and rub it into wine or warm water and let the man drink it and soon it will be better with him.

For Sore Hands

This leechcraft is good for sore hands and for sore fingers which is called chilblains. Take white frankincense and silver cinders and brimstone and mingle together, then take oil and add it into this mixture, then warm the hands and smear them with the mixture thus made. Wrap up the hands in a linen cloth.

---

frequently recommended. Some advised carefulness as well: "Who dares to undertake a bleeding should see to it that his hand does not tremble."

Physicians were also available when people faced serious illnesses. Many were clerics, and monasteries trained their own. Monastic libraries kept medical manuscripts copied from ancient works and grew herbs to provide stocks of medicinal plants. Carolingian medical manuscripts contained scientific descriptions of illnesses, recipes for medical potions, and even gynecological advice, although monks in particular expended little effort on female medical needs. Some manuals even included instructions for operations, especially for soldiers injured in battle. Some sources clearly demonstrate that there were accurate techniques for amputating gangrenous limbs:

If you must cut off an unhealthy limb from a healthy body, then do not cut to the limit of the healthy flesh, but cut further into the whole and quick flesh, so that a better and quicker cure may be obtained. When you set fire on the man [i.e., cauterize], take leaves of tender leek and grated salt, overlay the places so that the heat of the fire be more quickly drawn away.[10]

Although scholars are not sure whether anesthesia was used for such operations, medieval manuals recommended poppy, mandrake, and henbane for their narcotic properties.

Physicians of the early Middle Ages supplemented their medicines and natural practices with appeals for otherworldly help. Magical rites and influences were carried over from pagan times; the Germanic tribes had used magical medicine for centuries. Physicians recommended that patients wear amulets and charms around their bodies to ward off diseases:

> Procure a little bit of the dung of a wolf, preferably some which contains small bits of bone, and pack it in a tube which the patient may easily wear as an amulet.
>
> For epilepsy take a nail of a wrecked ship, make it into a bracelet and set therein the bone of a stag's heart taken from its body whilst alive; put it on the left arm; you will be astonished at the result.[11]

But as pagans were converted to Christianity, miraculous healing through the intervention of God, Jesus, or the saints soon replaced pagan practices. Medieval chronicles abound with accounts of people healed by touching a saint's body. The use of Christian prayers, written down and used as amulets, however, reminds us that for centuries Christian and pagan medical practices survived side by side.

8-3 Disintegration of the Carolingian Empire

 FOCUS QUESTIONS: Why did the Carolingian Empire disintegrate? What impact did the Vikings have on the history and culture of medieval Europe?

The Carolingian Empire began to disintegrate soon after Charlemagne's death. Charlemagne was succeeded by his son Louis the Pious. Though a decent man, Louis was not a strong ruler and was unable to control either the Frankish aristocracy or his own four sons, who fought continually. In 843 C.E., after their father's death, the three surviving brothers signed the Treaty of Verdun, which divided the Carolingian Empire among them into three major sections (see Map 8.2): Charles the Bald (r. 843–877) obtained the western Frankish lands, which formed the core of the eventual kingdom of France (see Image 8.5); Louis the German (r. 843–876) took the eastern lands, which became Germany; and Lothar (r. 840–855) received the title of emperor and a "Middle Kingdom" extending from the North Sea to the Mediterranean, including the Netherlands, the Rhineland, and northern Italy. The territories of the Middle Kingdom became a source of incessant struggle between the other two Frankish rulers and their heirs. Indeed, France and Germany would fight over the territories of this Middle Kingdom for centuries.

Although this division of the Carolingian Empire was made for political reasons (dividing a kingdom among the male heirs was a traditional Frankish custom), two different cultures began to emerge. By the ninth century, inhabitants of the western

Frankish area were speaking a Romance language derived from Latin that became French. Eastern Franks spoke a Germanic dialect. The later kingdoms of France and Germany did not yet exist, however. In the ninth century, the frequent struggles among the numerous heirs of the sons of Louis the Pious led to further disintegration of the Carolingian Empire. In the meantime, while powerful aristocrats acquired even more power in their own local territories at the expense of the squabbling Carolingian rulers, external attacks on different parts of the old Carolingian world added to the process of disintegration.

8-3a Invasions of the Ninth and Tenth Centuries

In the ninth and tenth centuries C.E., western Europe was beset by a wave of invasions by several non-Christian peoples—one old enemy, the Muslims, and two new ones, the Magyars (MAG-yarz) and the Vikings (see Map 8.3). The Muslims began a new series of attacks in the Mediterranean in the ninth century. They raided the southern coasts of Europe, especially Italy, and even threatened Rome in 843. Their invasion of Sicily in 827 eventually led to a successful occupation of the island. Muslim forces also destroyed the Carolingian defenses in northern Spain and conducted forays into southern France.

The Magyars were a people from West Asia who moved into eastern and central Europe by the end of the ninth century. They established themselves on the plains of Hungary and from there made raids into western Europe. The Magyars were finally crushed at the Battle of Lechfeld (LEK-feld) in Germany in 955. At the end of the tenth century, they were converted to Christianity and settled down to establish the kingdom of Hungary.

The Vikings By far the most devastating and far-reaching attacks came from the Northmen or Norsemen of Scandinavia, also known to us as the Vikings. The Vikings were a Germanic people based in Scandinavia and constitute, in a sense, the final wave of Germanic migration. Why they began to move is not very clear to historians. One common explanation focuses on overpopulation, although recent research indicates that this may have been true only in western Norway. Other reasons have included the Vikings' great love of adventure and their search for wealth and new avenues of trade.

Two features of Viking society help explain what the Vikings accomplished. First of all, they were warriors. Second, they were superb shipbuilders and sailors. Their ships were the best of the period. Long and narrow with beautifully carved arched prows, the Viking dragon ships carried about fifty men. They had banks of

MAP 8.2 **Division of the Carolingian Empire by the Treaty of Verdun,** 843 C.E.

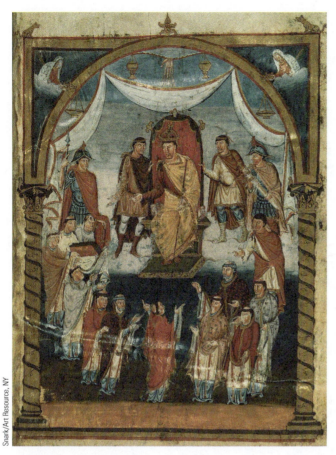

IMAGE 8.5a

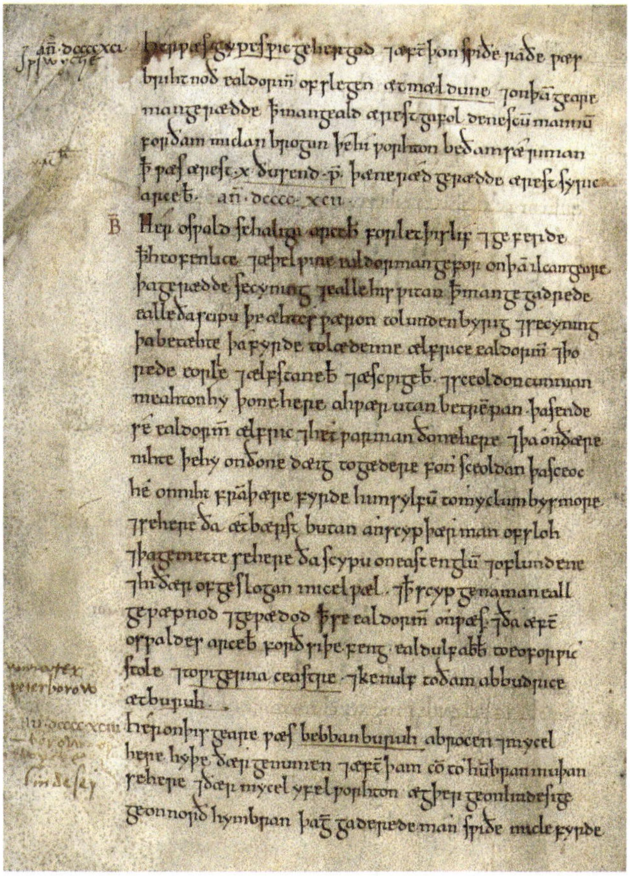

IMAGE 8.5b

IMAGE 8.5 **The First Bible of Charles the Bald.** Charles the Bald, who took control of the western Frankish lands, is pictured in Image 8.5a in an illustration from his first Bible, which dates from between 843 and 851 C.E. Illustrated Bibles were one of the finest achievements of Carolingian art. Also pictured in Image 8.5b is a page from a ninth-century chronicle, showing the Carolingian minuscule style of writing.

 What was the advantage of the minuscule style of writing?

oars as well as a single great sail (see Image 8.6). Their shallow draft enabled them to sail up European rivers and attack places at some distance inland. Although Viking raids in the eighth century tended to be small-scale and sporadic, they became more regular and more devastating in the ninth (see Historical Voices, "The Vikings Invade England," p. 230). Vikings sacked villages and towns, destroyed churches, and easily defeated small local armies. Viking attacks frightened people and led many a clergyman to exhort his parishioners to change their behavior to appease God's anger, as in this sermon by an English archbishop in 1014:

> Things have not gone well now for a long time at home or abroad, but there has been devastation and persecution in every district again and again, and the English have been for a long time now completely defeated and too greatly disheartened through God's anger; and the pirates [Vikings] so strong with God's consent that often in battle one puts to flight ten, and sometimes less, sometimes more, all because of

our sins. . . . We pay them continually and they humiliate us daily; they ravage and they burn, plunder, and rob and carry on board; and lo, what else is there in all these events except God's anger clear and visible over this people?[12]

Because there were different groups of Scandinavians, Viking expansion varied a great deal. Norwegian Vikings moved into Ireland and western England; Danes attacked eastern England, Frisia, and the Rhineland and navigated rivers to enter western Frankish lands. Swedish Vikings dominated the Baltic Sea and progressed into the Slavic areas to the east. Moving into northwestern Russia, they went down the rivers of Russia to Novgorod and Kiev and established fortified ports throughout these territories. There they made contact with the Byzantine Empire, either as traders or as invaders. They also made contact with Arab traders on the Volga River and the Sea of Azov.

Early Viking raids had been carried out largely in the summer; by the mid-ninth century, however, the Norsemen had

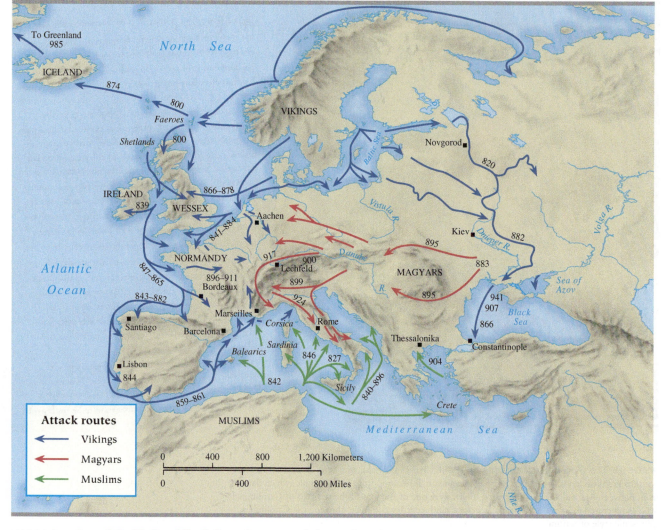

MAP 8.3 Invasions of the Ninth and Tenth Centuries C.E. Attacks by invading Vikings, Magyars, and Muslims terrorized much of Europe in the ninth and tenth centuries, disrupting economic activity and spurring the development of fief-holding. The Vikings were the biggest problem, but they eventually formed settlements, converted to Christianity, and were assimilated.

Q *Why was it important for the marauding Vikings to build sound boats and develop good seafaring skills?*

begun to establish winter settlements in Europe from which they could make expeditions to conquer and settle new lands. By 850 C.E., groups of Norsemen had settled in Ireland, and the Danes occupied an area known as the Danelaw in northeastern England by 878. Agreeing to accept Christianity, the Danes were eventually assimilated into a larger Anglo-Saxon kingdom. Beginning in 911, the ruler of the western Frankish lands gave one band of Vikings land at the mouth of the Seine River, forming a section of France that ultimately came to be known as Normandy. This policy of settling the Vikings and converting them to Christianity was a deliberate one, since the new inhabitants served as protectors against additional Norseman attacks.

The Vikings were also daring explorers. After 860, they sailed westward in their long ships across the North Atlantic Ocean,

reaching Iceland in 874. Erik the Red, a Viking exiled from Iceland, traveled even farther west and discovered Greenland in 985. A Viking site has also been found in Newfoundland in North America.

Trade was also an important component of Viking activity. Vikings were not only warriors but merchants, and when they left their homeland in the late eighth century many sought to discover or open new trade routes in different regions. One area was along the Black Sea as far as Constantinople, to which they brought furs and honey from the Russian forests (see "8-6c Eastern Slavs," later in this chapter). Others traded along Europe's coast and even set up trade enters in Dublin, Ireland, and York, England. Vikings also captured slaves in their raids and traded them in the markets of Constantinople.

IMAGE 8.6 The Vikings Attack England. In Image 8.6a, an illustration from an eleventh-century English manuscript depicts a group of armed Vikings invading England. Two ships have already reached the shore, and a few Vikings are shown walking down a long gangplank onto English soil. Image 8.6b shows a replica of a well-preserved Viking ship found at Oseberg, Norway. The Oseberg ship was one of the largest Viking ships in its day.

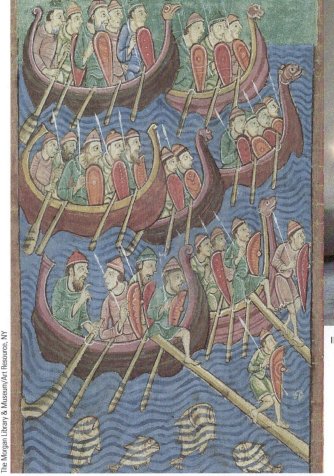

The Morgan Library & Museum/Art Resource, NY

IMAGE 8.6a

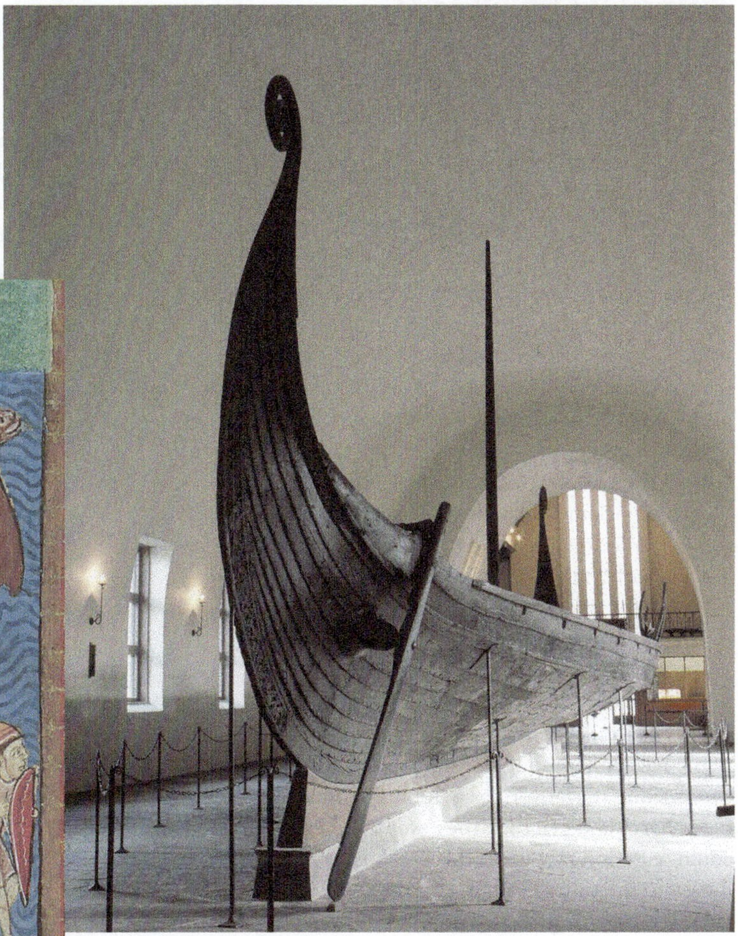

The Oseberg Ship/WERNER FORMAN ARCHIVE/Bridgeman Images

IMAGE 8.6b

By the tenth century, Viking expansion was drawing to a close. Greater control by the monarchs of Denmark, Norway, and Sweden over their inhabitants and the increasing Christianization of the Scandinavian kings and peoples tended to inhibit Viking expansion, but not before Viking settlements had been established in many parts of Europe. Like the Magyars, the Vikings were assimilated into European civilization. Once again, Christianity proved a decisive civilizing force. Europe and Christianity were becoming virtually synonymous.

The Viking raids and settlements also had important political repercussions. The inability of royal authorities to stem these incursions caused local populations to turn instead to local aristocrats for protection. As a result, the landed aristocrats not only increased their strength and prestige but also assumed even more of the functions of local government that had previously belonged to the kings; over time these developments led to a new political and military order.

8-4 The Emerging World of Lords and Vassals

FOCUS QUESTION: What was fief-holding, and how was it related to manorialism?

The renewed invasions and the disintegration of the Carolingian Empire led to the emergence of a new type of relationship between free individuals. When governments ceased to be able to defend their subjects, it became important to find some powerful lord who could offer protection in exchange for service. The contract sworn between a lord and his subordinate is the basis of a form of social organization that later generations of historians called *feudalism*, but feudalism was never a system, and many historians today prefer to avoid using the term. Some historians have also argued recently that it was not the disintegration of the

The Vikings Invade England

 What do you think were the tactics of the Viking invaders? How would you know from these accounts that the Chronicle was written by monks?

NEAR THE END OF THE NINTH CENTURY, a number of monks in England began to compile a series of chronicles, or yearly records of events. Although there are several chronicles, they have come to be known as the *Anglo-Saxon Chronicle*, Although much of the chronicle focuses on politics, there are also numerous accounts of events of immediate concern to the monks, such as the death of a bishop or inclement weather conditions. This selection from the *Anglo-Saxon Chronicle* focuses on the Danish Viking invasions of England. These selections, taken from the accounts for the years 994, 997, 998, 999, and 1003, show how regular and devastating the Viking invasions were.

Anglo-Saxon Chronicle

994. Olaf and Swein came to London, on the Nativity of St. Mary, with ninety-four ships, fighting constantly the city, and they meant, moreover, to set it on fire. But they there suffered more harm and evil than they ever believed any town-dwellers could have done them. In this God's holy mother showed her mercy to the town-dwellers and delivered them from their enemies; then they went from there, and wrought the most evil that any force had ever done, in burning, ravaging and killing, both along the seacoast, in Essex, and in Kent, Sussex and Hampshire; finally they seized horses for themselves, and rode as widely as they would, working unspeakable evil.

997. The Danes went around Devonshire into the mouth of the Severn, and there ravaged in Cornwall, Wales and Devon. Then they put in at Watchet and did much evil by burning and slaughtering. After that, they went around Land's End again on the south side, and went into the mouth of the Tamar, continuing up until they came to Lydford, burning or killing each thing they met—they burnt down Ordulf's monastery at Tavistock, and brought with them to their ships indescribable plunder.

998. The force went eastward again into the mouth of the Frome, and went inland as widely as they pleased into Dorset. Troops were often gathered against them, but as soon as they should have come together, always, in some way, flight was ordered, and they always had the victory in the end. Another time they settled themselves on the Isle of Wight, and fed themselves from Hampshire and Sussex.

999. The force came again into the Thames, and went up along Medway to Rochester; there the Kentish troops came against them, and they came together resolutely. But alas, they moved too quickly, and fled because they had not the help they should have had—then the Danes had the power of the battlefield, seized horses, and rode as widely as they pleased. They ravaged and destroyed nearly all West Kent.

1003. Exeter was ruined, because of the Frankish peasant Hugh, whom the lady had set up as her reeve [local official]; the Danish force destroyed the town completely, and took much booty. A very great army was gathered from Wiltshire and Hampshire, and went very resolutely against the force. The ealdorman [town official] Aelfric should have led the army, but he displayed his old wiles. As soon as they were close enough to look on one another, he feigned sickness, and began retching to vomit, and said that he was taken ill; so he betrayed the people he should have led, as it is said: "When the war-leader weakens, all the army is greatly hindered." When Swein saw that they were not resolute, and all scattering, he led his force into Wilton, ravaged and burnt the borough, went to Salisbury, and from there went back to the sea, where he knew his wave-coursers were.

Source: *The Anglo-Saxon Chronicle*, trans. A. Savage (New York: St. Martin's, 1982).

Carolingian Empire but a result of processes released by Carolingian reform that led to a new pattern of social organization.

8-4a Vassalage

The practice of **vassalage** was derived from Germanic society, in which warriors swore an oath of loyalty to their leader. They fought for their chief, and he in turn took care of their needs. By the eighth century C.E., an individual who served a lord in a military capacity was known as a *vassal*.

Both the breakdown of governments, which allowed powerful nobles to take control of large areas of land, and a change in fighting techniques contributed to this process. The Frankish army had originally consisted of foot soldiers, dressed in coats of mail and armed with swords. But with the introduction of larger horses and the stirrup in the eighth century, a military change began to occur. Earlier, horsemen had been throwers of spears. Now they wore armored coats of mail (the larger horse could carry the weight) and wielded long lances that enabled them to act as battering rams (the stirrups kept the riders on their horses) (see Image 8.7). For almost five hundred years, warfare in Europe would be dominated by heavily armored cavalry, or *knights*, as they came to be called.

IMAGE 8.7 A Knight's Equipment Showing Saddle and Stirrups.
In return for his fighting skills, a knight received a piece of land from his lord that provided for his economic support. Pictured here is a charging knight with his equipment. The introduction of the high saddle, stirrup, and larger horses allowed horsemen to wear heavier armor and to wield long lances, vastly improving the fighting ability of the cavalry.

Of course, a horse, armor, and weapons were expensive to purchase and maintain, and learning to wield these instruments skillfully from horseback took much time and practice. Consequently, lords who wanted men to fight for them had to grant each vassal a piece of land that provided for the support of the vassal and his family. In return for the land, the vassal provided his lord with one major service, his fighting skills. Each needed the other. In the society of the early Middle Ages, where there was little trade and wealth was based primarily on land ownership, land became the most important gift a lord could give to a vassal in return for military service.

The relationship between lord and vassal was made official by a public ceremony. To become a vassal, a man performed an act of homage to his lord, as described in this passage from a medieval treatise on law:

> The man should put his hands together as a sign of humility, and place them between the two hands of his lord as a token that he vows everything to him and promises faith to him; and the lord should receive him and promise to keep faith with him. Then the man should say: "Sir, I enter your homage and faith and become your man by mouth and hands [i.e., by taking the oath and placing his hands between those of the lord], and

I swear and promise to keep faith and loyalty to you against all others, and to guard your rights with all my strength.[13]

As in the earlier Germanic band, loyalty to one's lord was the chief virtue (see Global Perspectives, "Lords, Vassals, and Samurai in Europe and Japan," p. 232).

8-4b Fief-Holding

The land or some other type of income granted to a vassal in return for military service came to be known as a **fief** (FEEF). In time, many vassals who held such grants of land came to exercise rights of jurisdiction or political and legal authority within their fiefs. As the Carolingian world disintegrated politically under the impact of dissension within and invasions from without, an increasing number of powerful lords arose. Instead of a single government, many people were now responsible for keeping order. In some areas of France, for example, some lords—called *castellans*—constructed castles and asserted their authority to collect taxes and dispense justice to the local population. Lack of effective central control led to ever-larger numbers of castles and castellans.

Fief-holding also became increasingly complicated as **subinfeudation** developed. The vassals of a king, who were themselves great lords, might also have vassals who would owe them military service in return for a grant of land from their estates. Those vassals, in turn, might likewise have vassals, who at such a level would be simple knights with barely enough land to provide their equipment. The lord-vassal relationship, then, bound together both greater and lesser landowners. Historians used to speak of a hierarchy with the king at the top, greater lords on the next level, lesser lords on the next, and simple knights at the bottom; this was only a model, however, and rarely reflected reality. Such a hierarchy implies a king at the top. The reality in the tenth-century west Frankish kingdom was that the Capetian kings (see "8-4c New Political Configurations in the Tenth Century," later in this chapter) actually controlled only the region around Paris. They possessed little real power over the great lords who held fiefs throughout France.

The lord–vassal relationship at all levels always constituted an honorable relationship between free men and did not imply any sense of servitude. Since kings could no longer provide security in the midst of the breakdown created by the invasions of the ninth century, subinfeudation became ever more widespread. With their rights of jurisdiction, fiefs gave lords virtual possession of the rights of government.

The new practice of lordship was basically a product of the Carolingian world, but it also spread to England, Germany, and central Europe, and in modified form to Italy. Fief-holding came to be characterized by a set of practices worked out in the course of the tenth century, although they became more prominent after 1000. These practices included a series of mutual obligations of lord toward vassal and vassal toward lord, but it is crucial to remember that such obligations varied considerably from place to place and even from fief to fief. As usual, practice almost always diverged from theory.

Mutual Obligations Because the basic objective of fief-holding was to provide military support, it is no surprise to

Lords, Vassals, and Samurai in Europe and Japan

> **Q** *According to Bishop Fulbert, what were the mutual obligations of lords and vassals? Why were these important in the practice of fief-holding? The lord–vassal relationship was based on loyalty. What differences and similarities do you see in the loyalty owed by vassals and samurai in Europe and Japan?*

EUROPE WAS NOT THE ONLY PART of the world where a form of social organization based on lords and vassals emerged. In Japan, a social order much like that found in Europe developed between 800 and 1500 C.E. The samurai (SAM-uh-ry) was the Japanese equivalent of the medieval European knight. Like the knights, the samurai fought on horseback and were expected to adhere to a strict moral code. The first selection is the classic statement by Bishop Fulbert (ful-BEHR) of Chartres in 1020 on the mutual obligations of lord and vassals. The second selection is taken from *The Way of the Samurai*, a document written in the 1500s, although the distinct mounted warrior class described here had already emerged in Japan by the tenth century.

Bishop Fulbert of Chartres

Asked to write something concerning the form of fealty, I have noted briefly for you, on the authority of the books, the things which follow. He who swears fealty to his lord ought always to have these six things in memory: what is harmless, safe, honorable, useful, easy, practicable. *Harmless*, that is to say, that he should not injure his lord in his body; *safe*, that he should not injure him by betraying his secrets or the defenses upon which he relies for safety; *honorable*, that he should not injure him in his justice or in other matters that pertain to his honor; *useful*, that he should not injure him in his possessions; *easy* and *practicable*, that that good which his lord is able to do easily he make not difficult, nor that which is practicable he make not impossible to him.

That the faithful vassal should avoid these injuries is certainly proper, but not for this alone does he deserve his holding; for it is not sufficient to abstain from evil, unless what is good is done also. It remains, therefore, that in the same six things mentioned above he should faithfully counsel and aid his lord, if he wishes to be looked upon as worthy of his benefice [fief] and to be safe concerning the fealty which he has sworn.

The lord also ought to act toward his faithful vassal reciprocally in all these things. And if he does not do this, he will be justly considered guilty of bad faith, just as the former, if he should be detected in avoiding or consenting to the avoidance of his duties, would be perfidious and perjured.

The Way of the Samurai

The business of the samurai consists in reflecting on his own station in life, in discharging loyal service to his master if he has one, in deepening his fidelity in associations with friends, and with due consideration of his own position, in devoting himself to duty above all. . . . The samurai dispenses with the business of the farmer, artisan, and merchant [the three classes of the common people] and confines himself to practicing this Way. . . . Outwardly he stands in physical readiness for any call to service, and inwardly he strives to fulfill the Way of the lord and subject, friend and friend, father and son, older and younger brother, and husband and wife. Within his heart he keeps to the ways of peace, but without he keeps his weapons ready for use. The three classes of the common people make him their teacher and respect him. By following his teachings, they are enabled to understand what is fundamental and what is secondary.

Herein lies the Way of the samurai, the means by which he earns his clothing, food, and shelter, and by which his heart is put at ease, and he is enabled to pay back at length his obligation to his lord and the kindness of his parents. Were there no such duty, it would be as though one were to steal the kindness of one's parents, greedily devour the income of one's master, and make one's whole life a career of robbery and brigandage. This would be very grievous.

Sources: J. H. Robinson, *Readings in European History*, vol. 1 (Lexington, Mass.: Ginn and Co., 1904); W. T. de Bary, C. Gluck, and A. E. Tiedemann, *Sources of Japanese Tradition* (New York: Columbia University Press, 2005).

learn that the major obligation of a vassal to his lord was to perform military service. In addition to his own personal service, a great lord was also responsible for providing a group of knights for the king's army. Moreover, vassals had to furnish suit at court; this meant that a vassal was obliged to appear at his lord's court when summoned, either to give advice to the lord or to sit in judgment in a legal case, since the important vassals of a lord were peers, and only they could judge each other. Many vassals were also obliged to provide hospitality for their lord when he stayed at a vassal's castle. This obligation was especially important to medieval kings because they tended to be itinerant. Finally, vassals were responsible for aids, or financial payments, to the lord on a number of occasions, including the knighting of the lord's eldest son, the marriage of his eldest daughter, and the ransom of the lord's person if he was held captive.

In turn, a lord had responsibilities toward his vassals. His major obligation was to protect his vassal, either by defending him militarily or by taking his side in a court of law if necessary.

The lord was also responsible for the maintenance of the vassal, usually by granting him a fief.

As this system of mutual obligations between lord and vassal evolved, certain practices became common. If a lord acted improperly toward his vassal, the bond between them could be dissolved. Likewise, if a vassal failed to fulfill his vow of loyalty, he was subject to forfeiture of his fief. Upon a vassal's death, his fief theoretically reverted to the lord, since it had been granted to the vassal for use, not as a possession. In practice, however, by the tenth century fiefs tended to be hereditary. Following the principle of primogeniture (pry-muh-JEN-ih-chur), the eldest son inherited the father's fief. If a vassal died without heirs, the lord could reclaim the fief.

8-4c New Political Configurations in the Tenth Century

In the tenth century, Europe began to recover from the invasions of the century before. The disintegration of the Carolingian Empire and the emergence of great and powerful lords soon produced new political configurations.

The Eastern Franks In the east Frankish kingdom, the last Carolingian king died in 911 C.E., whereupon local rulers, especially the powerful dukes (the title of *duke* is derived from the Latin word *dux*, meaning "leader") of the Saxons, Swabians, Bavarians, Thuringians, and Franconians, who exercised much power in their large dukedoms, elected one of their own number, Conrad of Franconia, to serve as king of Germany (as we think of it) or of the eastern Franks (as contemporaries thought of it). But Conrad did not last long, and after his death, the German dukes chose Henry the Fowler, duke of Saxony, as the new king of Germany (r. 919–936). The first of the Saxon dynasty of German kings, Henry was not particularly successful in creating a unified eastern Frankish kingdom because he lacked the resources to impose effective rule over the entire area.

The best known of the Saxon kings of Germany was Henry's son, Otto I (r. 936–973). He defeated the Magyars at the Battle of Lechfeld in 955 and encouraged an ongoing program of Christianization of both the Slavic and the Scandinavian peoples. Even more than his father, he relied on bishops and abbots in governing his kingdom. This practice was in part a response to the tendency of the lay lords to build up their power at the expense of the king. Since the clergy were theoretically celibate, bishops and abbots could not make their offices hereditary, thus allowing the king to maintain more control over them.

Otto also intervened in Italian politics and for his efforts was crowned emperor of the Romans by the pope in 962, reviving a title that had fallen into disuse with the disintegration of Charlemagne's empire. Once again, a pope had conferred the Roman imperial title on a king of the Franks, even though he was a Saxon king of the eastern Franks. Otto's creation of a new "Roman Empire" in the hands of the eastern Franks (or Germans) added a tremendous burden to the kingship of Germany. To the difficulties of governing Germany was appended the onerous task of ruling Italy as well. It proved a formidable and ultimately impossible task.

The Western Franks In the ninth and tenth centuries, the Carolingian kings had little success in controlling the great lords of the western Frankish kingdom. The counts, who were supposed to serve as the chief administrative officials, often paid little attention to the wishes of the Carolingian kings. In 987, when the Carolingian king died, the western Frankish nobles and chief prelates of the church chose Hugh Capet (YOO ka-PAY), count of Orléans and Paris, as the new king (r. 987–996).

The nobles who elected Hugh Capet did not intend to establish a new royal dynasty. After all, although Hugh was officially king of the western Franks and overlord of the great nobles of the kingdom, his own family controlled only the Île-de-France (eel-duh-FRAHNS), the region around Paris. Other French nobles possessed lands equal to or greater than those of the Capetians and assumed that the king would be content to live off the revenues of his personal lands and not impose any burdensome demands on the nobility. Hugh Capet did succeed in making his position hereditary, however. He asked the nobles, and they agreed, to choose his eldest son, Robert, as his anointed associate in case Hugh died on a campaign to Spain in 987. And although Hugh Capet could not know it then, the Capetian (kuh-PEE-shun) dynasty would rule the western Frankish kingdom, or France, as it eventually came to be known, for centuries. In the late tenth century, however, the territory that would become France was not a unified kingdom but a loose alliance of powerful lords who treated the king as an equal. They assisted him only when it was in their own interests to do so.

Anglo-Saxon England England's development in the ninth and tenth centuries took a course somewhat different from that of the Frankish kingdoms. The long struggle of the Anglo-Saxon kingdoms against the Viking invasions ultimately produced a unified kingdom. Alfred the Great, king of Wessex (r. 871–899 C.E.), played a crucial role. He defeated a Danish army in 879, according to an account by Asser, his adviser, who wrote a biography of the king:

CHRONOLOGY	New Political Configurations of the Tenth Century
Eastern Franks	
Conrad of Franconia	911–918 C.E.
Saxon dynasty: Henry I	919–936
Otto I	936–973
Defeat of Magyars	955
Coronation as emperor	962
Western Franks	
Election of Hugh Capet as king	987
Anglo-Saxon England	
Alfred the Great, king of Wessex	871–899
Peace with the Danes	886
Reign of King Edgar	959–975

[Alfred] gained the victory through God's will. He destroyed the Vikings with great slaughter, and pursued those who fled as far as the stronghold, hacking them down; he seized everything which he found outside the stronghold—men (whom he killed immediately), horses and cattle—and boldly made camp in front of the gate of the Viking stronghold with all his army. When he had been there for fourteen days the Vikings, thoroughly terrified by hunger, cold and fear, and in the end by despair, sought peace.[14]

Alfred eventually made peace with the Danes in 886 after strengthening his army and creating a navy.

Alfred also believed in the power of education. He invited scholars to his court and encouraged the translation of the works of such church fathers as Augustine and Gregory the Great from Latin into Anglo-Saxon (Old English), the vernacular, or the language spoken by the people. Old English was also soon used for official correspondence as well. Alfred's successors reconquered the remaining areas occupied by the Danes and established a unified Anglo-Saxon monarchy. By the time of King Edgar (r. 959–975), Anglo-Saxon England had a well-developed and strong monarchical government. Although the kingship was elective, only descendants of Alfred were chosen for the position. In the counties or *shires*, the administrative units into which England was divided, the king was assisted by an agent appointed and controlled by him, the shire-reeve or sheriff. An efficient chancery or writing office was responsible for issuing writs (or royal letters) conveying the king's orders to the sheriffs.

8-4d The Manorial System

The landholding class of nobles and knights comprised a military elite whose ability to function as warriors depended on having the leisure time to pursue the arts of war. Landed estates worked by a dependent peasant class provided the economic sustenance that made this way of life possible. A **manor** (see Map 8.4) was simply an agricultural estate operated by a lord and worked by peasants. Lords provided protection; peasants gave up their freedom, became tied to the lord's land, and provided labor services for him.

Manorialism grew out of the unsettled circumstances of the early Middle Ages, when small farmers often needed protection or food in a time of bad harvests. Free peasants gave up their freedom to the lords of large landed estates in return for protection and use of the lord's land. Although a large class of free peasants continued to exist, increasing numbers of them became bound to the land as serfs. Unlike slaves, **serfs** could not be bought and sold, but they were subservient to their lords in a variety of ways. Serfs were required to provide labor services, pay rents, and be subject to the lord's jurisdiction. By the ninth century, probably 60 percent of the population of western Europe had become serfs.

A serf's labor services consisted of working the lord's **demesne** (duh-MAYN *or* duh-MEEN), the land retained by the lord, which might encompass one-third to one-half of the cultivated lands scattered throughout the manor (the rest would have been allotted to the serfs for their maintenance), as well as building barns and digging ditches (see Image 8.8). Although labor requirements varied from manor to manor and person to person, a common work obligation was three days a week.

The serfs paid rent by giving their lord a share of every product they raised. Serfs also paid the lord for the use of the manor's common pasturelands, streams, ponds, and surrounding woodlands. For example, if tenants fished in the pond or stream on a manor, they turned over part of the catch to their lord. For grazing a cow in the common pasture, a serf paid a rent in cheese produced from the cow's milk. Serfs were also obliged to pay a **tithe** (a tenth of their produce) to their local village church.

Lords also possessed a variety of legal rights over their serfs. Serfs were legally bound to the lord's land; they could not leave without his permission. Although free to marry, serfs could not marry anyone outside their manor without the lord's approval. Moreover, lords sometimes exercised public rights or political

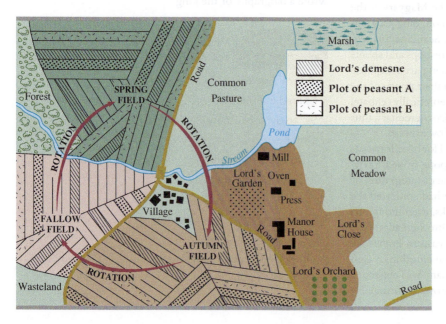

MAP 8.4 **A Typical Manor.** The manorial system created small, tightly knit communities in which peasants were economically and physically bound to their lord. Crops were rotated, with roughly one-third of the fields lying fallow at any one time, which helped replenish soil nutrients (see Chapter 9).

Q *How does the area of the lord's manor house, other buildings, garden, and orchard compare with that of the peasant holdings in the village?*

British Library Board/Robana/Art Resource, NY

IMAGE 8.8 **Peasants in the Manorial System.** In the manorial system, peasants were required to provide labor services for their lord. This thirteenth-century illustration shows a group of English peasants harvesting grain. Overseeing their work is a bailiff, or manager, who supervised the work of the peasants.

authority on their lands. This gave the lord the right to try serfs in his own court, although only for lesser crimes (called "low justice"). In fact, the lord's manorial court provided the only law that most serfs knew. Finally, the lord's political authority enabled him to establish monopolies on certain services that provided additional revenues. Serfs could be required to bring their grain to the lord's mill and pay a fee to have it ground into flour. Thus, the rights a lord possessed on his manor gave him virtual control over both the lives and the property of his serfs.

The administration of manors varied considerably. If the lord of a manor was a simple knight, he would probably live on the estate and supervise it in person. Great lords possessed many manors and relied on a steward or bailiff to run each estate. Note that manors were controlled not only by lay lords but also by monasteries and cathedral churches. Monasteries tended to be far more conscientious about keeping accurate records of their manorial estates than lay lords, and their surveys provide some of the best sources of information on medieval village life. The relationship between manors and villages was highly variable. A single village might constitute a manor, or a large manor might encompass several villages.

In the early Middle Ages, the vast majority of men and women, free or unfree—possibly as many as 90 percent—worked the land. This period had witnessed a precipitous decline in trade. Coins and jewelry were often hoarded, and at the local level, goods were frequently bartered because so few coins were in circulation. But trade never entirely disappeared. Even in an agrarian society, surplus products could be exchanged at local markets. More significant, however, was that both aristocrats and wealthy clerics desired merchandise not produced locally, such as spices, silk cloth, wine, and gold and silver jewelry, and it took trade to obtain these items.

Much of the trade in luxury goods, especially beginning in the ninth century, was conducted with the Byzantine Empire, particularly the city of Constantinople, and the Islamic caliphs of Baghdad. Products from the west included iron, timber, furs, and slaves (many from eastern Europe, including captured Slavs, from whom the modern word *slave* is derived). Traders, often Jews, carried goods by boat on European rivers or on caravans with horses or mules. An Arab geographer of the ninth century left this account of Jewish traders from southern France:

> [They] speak Arabic, Persian, Greek, Frankish, Spanish, and Slavonic. They travel from west to east and from east to west, by land and by sea. From the west they bring eunuchs, slave-girls, boys, brocade, marten and other furs, and swords. They take ship from Frankland in the western Mediterranean sea and land at Farama, whence they take their merchandise on camel-back to Qulzum. . . . Then they sail on the eastern [Red] sea from Qulzum, and onward to India and China. From China they bring back musk, aloes, camphor, cinnamon, and other products of those parts, and return to Qulzum. Then they transport them to Farama and sail again on the western sea. Some sail with their goods to Constantinople and sell them to the Greeks, and some take them to the king of the Franks and sell them there.[15]

By 900 C.E., Italian merchants, especially the Venetians, were entering the trade picture. Overall, however, compared with the Byzantine Empire or Muslim caliphates, western Europe in the early Middle Ages was an underdeveloped, predominantly agrarian society and could not begin to match the splendor of either of the other heirs of the Roman Empire.

8-5 The Zenith of Byzantine Civilization

 FOCUS QUESTION: What were the chief developments in the Byzantine Empire between 750 and 1000?

In the seventh and eighth centuries, the Byzantine Empire had lost much of its territory to Slavs, Bulgars, and Muslims. By 750 C.E., the empire consisted only of Asia Minor, some lands in the Balkans, and the southern coast of Italy. Although Byzantium was beset with internal dissension and invasions in the ninth century, it was able to deal with them and not only endured but even expanded, reaching its high point in the tenth century, which some historians have called the golden age of Byzantine civilization.

During the reign of Michael III (r. 842–867), the Byzantine Empire began to experience a revival. Iconoclasm was finally abolished in 843, and reforms were made in education, church life, the military, and the peasant economy. There was a noticeable intellectual renewal. But the Byzantine Empire under Michael was still plagued by persistent problems. The Bulgars mounted new attacks, and the Arabs continued to harass the empire. Moreover, a new church problem with political repercussions erupted over differences between the pope as leader of the western Christian church and the patriarch of Constantinople as leader of the eastern (or Orthodox) Christian church. Patriarch Photius (FOH-shuss) condemned the pope as a heretic for accepting a revised form of the Nicene Creed stating that the Holy Spirit proceeded from the Father and the Son instead of "the Holy Spirit, who proceeds from the Father." A council of eastern bishops followed Photius's wishes and excommunicated the pope, creating the so-called Photian schism. Although the differences were later papered over, this controversy served to further the division between the eastern and western Christian churches.

8-5a The Macedonian Dynasty

The problems that arose during Michael's reign were effectively dealt with by a new dynasty of Byzantine emperors known as the Macedonians (r. 867–1056). This dynastic line managed to hold off the external enemies, go over to the offensive, and reestablish domestic order. Supported by the church, the emperors thought of the Byzantine Empire as a continuation of the Christian Roman Empire of late antiquity. Although for diplomatic reasons they occasionally recognized the imperial title of western emperors, such as Charlemagne, they still regarded them as little more than barbarian parvenus.

The Macedonian emperors could boast of a remarkable number of achievements in the late ninth and tenth centuries. They worked to strengthen the position of the free farmers, who felt threatened by the attempts of landed aristocrats to expand their estates at the expense of the farmers. The emperors were well aware that the free farmers made up the rank and file of the Byzantine cavalry and provided the military strength of the empire. The Macedonian emperors also fostered a burst of economic prosperity by expanding trade relations with western Europe, especially by selling silks and metalwork. Thanks to this prosperity, the city of Constantinople flourished. Foreign visitors continued to be astounded by its size, wealth, and physical surroundings. To western Europeans, it was the stuff of legends and fables (see Historical Voices, "A Western View of the Byzantine Empire," p. 237).

In the midst of this prosperity, Byzantine cultural influence expanded due to the active missionary efforts of eastern Byzantine Christians. Eastern Orthodox Christianity was spread to eastern European peoples, such as the Bulgars and Serbs. Perhaps the greatest missionary success occurred when the prince of Kiev in Russia converted to Christianity in 987.

Under the Macedonian rulers, Byzantium enjoyed a strong civil service, talented emperors, and military advances. The Byzantine civil service was staffed by well-educated, competent

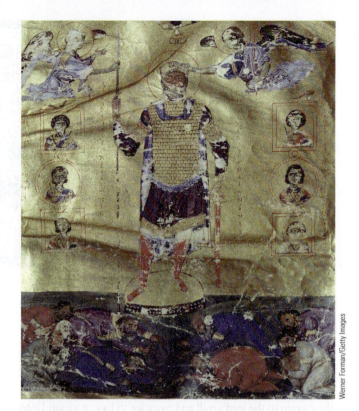

Werner Forman/Getty Images

IMAGE 8.9 **Basil the Bulgar-Slayer.** Basil II became known as the Bulgar-slayer after his devastating victory over the Bulgars in 1014. This frontispiece illustration from a religious prayer book shows the warrior Basil standing on top of bodies of the conquered Bulgarians. Both angels and warrior-saints are shown protecting the emperor.

 Why were military ideals important to the Byzantine Empire?

aristocrats from Constantinople who oversaw the collection of taxes, domestic administration, and foreign policy. At the same time, the Macedonian dynasty produced some truly outstanding emperors skilled in administration and law, including Leo VI (r. 886–912), who systemized rules for regulating both trade and court officials and arranged for a new codification of Byzantine law. In the tenth century, competent emperors combined with a number of talented generals to mobilize the empire's military resources and take the offensive. Especially important was Basil II (r. 976–1025), who defeated the Bulgars and annexed both the eastern and western parts of Bulgaria to the empire (see Image 8.9). The Byzantines went on to add the islands of Crete and Cyprus to the empire and defeat the Muslim forces in Syria, expanding the empire to the upper Euphrates. By the end of the reign of Basil II in 1025, the Byzantine Empire was the largest it had been since the beginning of the seventh century (see Map 8.5).

8-5b Women in Byzantium

In Byzantium, as in western Europe, women were regarded as inferior to men, and at times, even considered to be the instrument of the devil. In general, women were expected to remain at home. They could leave to shop, visit parents, and take part in civic celebrations, but they were supposed to wear veils on these occasions.

A Western View of the Byzantine Empire

 Q *What impressions of the Byzantine court do you receive from Liudprand of Cremona's account? What is the modern meaning of the word* byzantine*? How does this account help explain the modern meaning of the word?*

BISHOP LIUDPRAND (leh-OOD-prand) **OF CREMONA** undertook diplomatic missions to Constantinople on behalf of two western kings, Berengar of Italy and Otto I of Germany. This selection is taken from the bishop's description of his mission to the Byzantine emperor Constantine VII as an envoy for Berengar, king of Italy from 950 C.E. until his overthrow by Otto I of Germany in 964. Liudprand had mixed feelings about Byzantium: admiration, yet also envy and hostility because of its superior wealth.

Liudprand of Cremona, *Antapodosis*

Next to the imperial residence at Constantinople there is a palace of remarkable size and beauty which the Greeks call Magnavra . . . the name being equivalent to "fresh breeze." In order to receive some Spanish envoys, who had recently arrived, as well as myself . . . Constantine gave orders that his palace should be got ready. . . .

Before the emperor's seat stood a tree, made of bronze gilded over, whose branches were filled with birds, also made of gilded bronze, which uttered different cries, each according to its varying species. The throne itself was so marvelously fashioned that at one moment it seemed a low structure, and at another it rose high into the air. It was of immense size and was guarded by lions, made either of bronze or of wood covered over with gold, who beat the ground with their tails and gave a dreadful roar with open mouth and quivering tongue. Leaning upon the shoulders of two eunuchs I was brought into the emperor's presence. At my approach the lions began to roar and the birds to cry out, each according to its kind; but I was neither terrified nor surprised, for I had previously made enquiry about all these things from people who were well acquainted with them. So after I had three times made obeisance to the emperor with my face upon the ground, I lifted my head, and behold! the man whom just before I had seen sitting on a moderately elevated seat had now changed his raiment and was sitting on the level of the ceiling. How it was done I could not imagine, unless perhaps he was lifted up by some such sort of device as we use for raising the timbers of a wine press. On that occasion he did not address me personally . . . but by the intermediary of a secretary he enquired about Berengar's doings and asked after his health. I made a fitting reply and then, at a nod from the interpreter, left his presence and retired to my lodging.

It would give me some pleasure also to record here what I did then for Berengar. . . . The Spanish envoys . . . had brought handsome gifts from their masters to the emperor Constantine. I for my part had brought nothing from Berengar except a letter and that was full of lies. I was very greatly disturbed and shamed at this and I began to consider anxiously what I had better do. In my doubt and perplexity it finally occurred to me that I might offer the gifts, which on my account I had brought for the emperor, as coming from Berengar, and trick out my humble present with fine words. I therefore presented him with nine excellent curaisses, seven excellent shields with gilded bosses, two silver gilt cauldrons, some swords, spears and spits, and what was more precious to the emperor than anything, four carzimasia; that being the Greek name for young eunuchs who have had both their testicles and their penis removed. This operation is performed by traders at Verdun, who take the boys into Spain and make a huge profit.

Source: The Works of Liudprand of Cremona, trans. F. A. Wright (London: Routledge and Sons, 1930).

Women were generally expected to fulfill three major functions: to marry and bear children, to maintain the household, and to weave clothes for their families. Thus, a good wife was seen as a special gift to her husband. Contrary to these ideal female roles, some women in the Byzantine world worked outside the home as artisans and sellers, especially of foodstuffs, in the markets of Constantinople. Others served as midwives, bakers, cooks, or dancers, although some dancers also worked as prostitutes.

MAP 8.5 The Byzantine Empire in 1025

Upper-class women had greater opportunities to play important roles in the empire. Some aristocratic wives funded the establishment of monasteries, occupied important positions at court, and patronized the arts. Imperial wives could exercise considerable political power as regents for their sons; some even became empresses in their own right. Irene, for example, was married to the Byzantine emperor Leo IV. After the death of her husband, she served as regent for her son until 797 C.E. when she blinded and deposed him. She then ruled briefly in her own right as emperor until a group of officials deposed her and exiled her to the island of Lesbos, where she died in 803. She was responsible for restoring the use of icons to the Byzantine world and patronizing many monasteries.

8-6 The Slavic Peoples of Central and Eastern Europe

 FOCUS QUESTION: What patterns of development occurred in central and eastern Europe as a result of the Slavic peoples?

North of Byzantium and east of the Carolingian Empire lay a spacious plain through which a number of Asiatic nomads, including the Huns, Bulgars, Avars, and Magyars, had pushed their way westward, terrorizing and plundering the settled peasant communities. Eastern Europe was ravaged by these successive waves of invaders, who found it relatively easy to create large empires that were in turn overthrown by the next invaders. Over a period of time, the invaders themselves were largely assimilated by the native Slavic peoples of the area.

The Slavic peoples were originally a single people in central and eastern Europe who through mass migrations and nomadic invasions were gradually divided into three major groups: the western, southern, and eastern Slavs (see Map 8.6).

8-6a Western Slavs

In the region east of the eastern Frankish or Germanic kingdom emerged the Polish and Bohemian kingdoms of the western Slavs. The Germans assumed responsibility for the conversion of these Slavic peoples because German emperors considered it their duty to spread Christianity to the "barbarians." Of course, it also gave them the opportunity to extend their political authority. German missionaries had converted the Czechs in Bohemia by the end of the ninth century, and a bishopric eventually occupied by a Czech bishop was established at Prague in the tenth century. The Slavs in Poland were not converted until the reign of Prince Mieszko (MYESH-koh) (r. ca. 960–992 C.E.). In 1000, an independent Polish archbishopric was set up at Gniezno by the pope. The non-Slavic kingdom of Hungary, which emerged after the Magyars settled down after their defeat at Lechfeld in 955, was also converted to Christianity by German missionaries. Saint Stephen, king of Hungary from 997 to 1038, facilitated the acceptance of Christianity by his people. The Poles, Czechs, and Hungarians all accepted Catholic or western Christianity and became closely tied to the Roman Catholic Church and its Latin culture.

8-6b Southern Slavs

The southern and eastern Slavic populations largely took a different path because of their proximity to the Byzantine Empire. Two Byzantine missionary brothers, Cyril and Methodius, who began their activities in 863 C.E., converted the southern Slavic peoples to the Eastern Orthodox Christianity of the Byzantine Empire. They created a Slavonic (Cyrillic) alphabet, translated the Bible

MAP 8.6 The Migrations of the Slavs. Originally from east-central Europe, the Slavic people broke into three groups. The western Slavs converted to Catholic Christianity, while the eastern Slavs and southern Slavs, under the influence of the Byzantine Empire, embraced the Eastern Orthodox faith.

 What connections do these Slavic migrations have with what we today characterize as eastern Europe?

A Muslim's Description of the Rus

 What was Ibn Fadlan's impression of the Rus? Why do you think he was so critical of their behavior?

DESPITE THE DIFFICULTIES that travel presented, early medieval civilization did witness some contact among the various cultures. This might occur through trade, diplomacy, or the conquest and migration of peoples. This document is a description of the Swedish Rus who eventually merged with the native Slavic peoples to form the principality of Kiev, commonly regarded as the first Russian state. This account was written by Ibn Fadlan, a Muslim diplomat sent from Baghdad in 921 C.E. to a settlement on the Volga River. His comments on the filthiness of the Rus reflect the Muslim emphasis on cleanliness.

Ibn Fadlan, *Description of the Rus*

I saw the Rus folk when they arrived on their trading-mission and settled at the river Atul (Volga). Never had I seen people of more perfect physique. They are tall as date-palms, and reddish in color. They wear neither coat nor kaftan, but each man carried a cape which covers one half of his body, leaving one hand free. No one is ever parted from his ax, sword, and knife. Their swords are Frankish in design, broad, flat, and fluted. Each man has a number of trees, figures, and the like from the fingernails to the neck. Each woman carried on her bosom a container made of iron, silver, copper or gold—its size and substance depending on her man's wealth. . . .

They [the Rus] are the filthiest of God's creatures. They do not wash after discharging their natural functions, neither do they wash their hands after meals. They are as lousy as donkeys. They arrive from their distant river, and there they build big houses on its shores. Ten or twenty of them may live together in one house, and each of them has a couch of his own where he sits and diverts himself with the pretty slave girls whom he had brought along for sale. He will make love with one of them while a comrade looks on; sometimes they indulge in a communal orgy, and, if a customer should turn up to buy a girl, the Rus man will not let her go till he has finished with her.

They wash their hands and faces every day in incredibly filthy water. Every morning the girl brings her master a large bowl of water in which he washes his hands and face and hair, then blows his nose into it and spits into it. When he has finished the girl takes the bowl to his neighbor—who repeats the performance. Thus, the bowl goes the rounds of the entire household. . . .

If one of the Rus folk falls sick they put him in a tent by himself and leave bread and water for him. They do not visit him, however, or speak to him, especially if he is a serf. Should he recover he rejoins the others; if he dies they burn him. But if he happens to be a serf they leave him for the dogs and vultures to devour. If they catch a robber they hang him to a tree until he is torn to shreds by wind and weather.

Source: From *The Vikings* by Johannes Brøndsted, translated by Kalle Skov (Penguin Books, 1965) copyright © Johannes Brøndsted, 1960, 1965. Reproduced by permission of Penguin Books Ltd.

---

into Slavonic, and developed Slavonic church services. Although the southern Slavic peoples accepted Christianity, a split eventually developed between the Croats, who accepted the Roman church, and the Serbs, who remained loyal to eastern Christianity.

Although the Bulgars were originally an Asiatic people who conquered much of the Balkan peninsula, they were eventually absorbed by the larger native southern Slavic population. Together, by the ninth century, they formed a largely Slavic Bulgarian kingdom. Although the conversion to Christianity of this state was complicated by the rivalry between the Roman Catholic and Eastern Orthodox Churches, the Bulgarians eventually accepted the latter. By the end of the ninth century, they embraced the Slavonic church services earlier developed by Cyril and Methodius. The acceptance of Eastern Orthodoxy by the southern Slavic peoples, the Serbs and Bulgarians, meant that their cultural life was also linked to the Byzantine state.

8-6c Eastern Slavs

The eastern Slavic peoples, from whom the modern Russians, White Russians (Byelorussians), and Ukrainians are descended, had settled in the territory of present-day Ukraine and European Russia. There, beginning in the late eighth century C.E., they began to contend with Viking invaders. Swedish Vikings, known to the eastern Slavs as Varangians, moved down the extensive network of rivers into the lands of the eastern Slavs in search of booty and new trade routes. After establishing trading links with the Byzantine state, the Varangians built trading settlements, became involved in the civil wars among the Slavic peoples, and eventually came to dominate the native peoples, just as their fellow Vikings were doing in parts of western Europe. According to the traditional version of the story, the semi-legendary Rurik (ROO-rik) secured his ruling dynasty in the Slavic settlement of Novgorod (NAHV-guh-rahd) in 862. Rurik and his fellow Vikings were called the Rus (ROOSS *or* ROOSH), from which the name that eventually became attached to the state they founded, Russia, is derived (see Historical Voices, "A Muslim's Description of the Rus," above). Although much about Rurik is unclear, it is certain that his follower Oleg (r. ca. 873–913) took up residence in Kiev (KEE-yev) and created the Rus state, a union of eastern Slavic territories known as the principality of Kiev. Oleg's successors extended their control over the eastern Slavs and expanded the territory of Kiev until it encompassed the lands between the Baltic and Black Seas and the Danube and Volga Rivers. By marrying Slavic wives, the Viking ruling class was gradually assimilated into the Slavic population, a process confirmed by their assumption of Slavic names.

The growth of the principality of Kiev attracted religious missionaries, especially from the Byzantine Empire. One Rus ruler, Vladimir (r. ca. 980–1015), married the Byzantine emperor's sister and officially accepted Christianity for himself and his people in 987. His primary motive was probably not spiritual. By all accounts, Vladimir was a cruel and vicious man who believed an established church would be helpful in developing an organized state. From the end of the tenth century on, Byzantine Christianity became the model for Russian religious life, just as Byzantine imperial ideals came to influence the outward forms of Russian political life.

8-6d Women in the Slavic World

As in western Europe, women in central and eastern Europe were subordinated to men and expected to focus their lives on their families, nurturing their children, providing food and clothing, and helping their husbands and fathers. Female labor thus made up a significant part of the early medieval economy in the Slavic world. In the centuries after 1000 C.E., more opportunities for women became available, especially for aristocratic women. Beginning in the eleventh century, for example, noble women in Russia could administer the household and the family's property.

8-7 The Expansion of Islam

 FOCUS QUESTION: What were the chief developments in the Islamic world between 750 and 1000?

The Umayyad dynasty of caliphs had established Damascus as the center of an Islamic empire created by Muslim Arab expansion in the seventh and eighth centuries. But Umayyad rule aroused resentment, and the Umayyads' corrupt behavior also helped bring about their end. One caliph, for example, supposedly swam in a pool of wine and drank enough of it to lower the wine level considerably. Finally, in 750 C.E., Abu al-Abbas (uh-BOO al-uh-BUSS), a descendant of the uncle of Muhammad, brought an end to the Umayyad dynasty and established the Abbasid (uh-BAH-sid *or* AB-uh-sid) dynasty, which lasted until 1258.

8-7a The Abbasid Dynasty

The Abbasid rulers brought much change to the world of Islam. They tried to break down the distinctions between Arab and non-Arab Muslims. All Muslims, regardless of their ethnic background, could now hold both civil and military offices. This helped open Islamic life to the influences of the civilizations the Arabs had conquered. Many Arabs now began to intermarry with the peoples they had conquered.

In 762 C.E., the Abbasids built a new capital city, Baghdad, on the Tigris River far to the east of Damascus. The new capital was well placed. It took advantage of river traffic to the Persian Gulf and at the same time was located on the caravan route from the Mediterranean to Central Asia. The move eastward allowed Persian influence to come to the fore, encouraging a new cultural orientation. Under the Abbasids, judges, merchants, and government officials, rather than warriors, were viewed as the ideal citizens.

The new Abbasid dynasty experienced a period of splendid rule well into the ninth century. Best known of the caliphs of the time was Harun al-Rashid (huh-ROON al-rah-SHEED) (r. 786–809), whose reign is often described as the golden age of the Abbasid caliphate. His son al-Ma'mun (al-muh-MOON) (r. 813–833) was a great patron of learning. He founded an astronomical observatory and created a foundation for translating classical Greek works. This was also a period of growing economic prosperity. The Arabs had conquered many of the richest provinces of the old Roman Empire, and they now controlled the trade routes to the east. Baghdad became the center of an enormous trade empire that extended into Europe, Asia, and Africa, greatly adding to the wealth of the Islamic world (see Map 8.7).

Despite the prosperity, all was not quite well in the empire of the Abbasids. There was much fighting over the succession to the caliphate. When Harun al-Rashid died, his two sons fought to succeed him in a struggle that almost destroyed the city of Baghdad. As the tenth-century Muslim historian al-Mas'udi wrote: "Mansions were destroyed, most remarkable monuments obliterated; prices soared. . . . Brother turned his sword against brother, son against father, as some fought for Amin, others for Ma'mun. Houses and palaces fueled the flames; property was put to the sack."[16]

Vast wealth also gave rise to financial corruption. By awarding important positions to court favorites, the Abbasid caliphs began to undermine the foundations of their own power and soon became figureheads. Rulers of the provinces of the empire broke away from the control of the caliphs and established their own independent dynasties. In the eighth century, Spain had already established its own caliphate when Abd al-Rahman (AHB-d al-rahkh-MAHN) of the Umayyad dynasty had fled there. In 756, he seized control of southern Spain and then expanded his power into the center of the peninsula. He took the title of *emir*, or commander, and set up the emirate of al-Andalus (the Arabic name for Spain—Europeans called it Andalusia) with its center at Córdoba (KOR-duh-buh). In 929, Abd al-Rahman III (r. 912–961) proclaimed himself caliph. Al-Andalus became part of a vast trade network that stretched all the way from the Strait of Gibraltar to the Red Sea and beyond. The rulers of al-Andalus also developed a unique society in which all religions were tolerated. The court also supported writers and artists, creating a brilliant and flourishing culture.

Unfortunately, the primacy of al-Andalus as a cultural center was short-lived. By the end of the tenth century, factionalism was beginning to undermine the foundations of the emirate. In 1009, the royal palace at Córdoba was totally destroyed in a civil war. Twenty years later, the caliphate itself disappeared as the emirate dissolved into a patchwork of city-states. In the

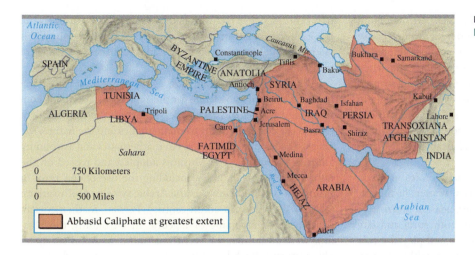

MAP 8.7 **The Abbasid Caliphate at the Height of Its Power**

meantime, the Christian kingdoms that had managed to establish themselves in the north of the Iberian Peninsula were consolidating their position and beginning to expand southward (see Chapter 10).

Elsewhere the fragmentation of the Islamic empire had accelerated in the tenth century. The Fatimid (FAT-i-mid) family established a caliphate in Egypt in 973, and an independent dynasty also operated in North Africa. Despite the political disunity of the Islamic world, however, there was an underlying Islamic civilization based on two common bonds, the Qur'an and the Arabic language.

CHRONOLOGY	Byzantium, the Slavs, and the Islamic World
Byzantine Empire	
Michael III	842–867 c.e.
Macedonian dynasty	867–1056
Leo VI	886–912
Basil II	976–1025
Slavic Peoples of Central and Eastern Europe	
Cyril and Methodius begin to convert Moravian Slavs	863
Oleg creates principality of Kiev	ca. 873–913
Reign of Prince Mieszko; Slavs in Poland converted to Christianity	ca. 960–992
Vladimir's conversion to Christianity	987
Saint Stephen, king of Hungary	997–1038
World of Islam	
Overthrow of Umayyad dynasty by Abbasids	750
Harun al-Rashid	786–809
al-Ma'mun	813–833
Creation of caliphate of al-Andalus	929
Establishment of Fatimid caliphate, Egypt	973

8-7b Islamic Civilization

From the beginning of their empire, Muslim Arabs had demonstrated a willingness to absorb the culture of their conquered territories. The Arabs were truly heirs to the remaining Greco-Roman culture of the Roman Empire. Just as readily, they assimilated Byzantine and Persian culture. In the eighth and ninth centuries, numerous Greek, Syrian, and Persian scientific and philosophical works were translated into Arabic. As the chief language in the southern Mediterranean and the Near East and the required language of Muslims, Arabic became a truly international tongue.

The Muslims created a brilliant urban culture at a time when western Europe was predominantly a rural world of farming villages. This can be seen in such new cities as Baghdad and Cairo, but also in Córdoba, the capital of the Umayyad caliphate in Spain. With a population of possibly 100,000, Córdoba was Europe's largest city after Constantinople. It had seventy public libraries, and the number of manuscripts in the caliph's private library reached 400,000. One caliph, al-Hakem (r. 961–976), collected books from different parts of the world and then had them translated into Arabic and Latin. These included works on geography that later proved valuable to Western sailors and merchants. Schools were also established, and the Great Mosque of Córdoba became a center for scholars from all over the Islamic world. Large numbers of women served as teachers and librarians in Córdoba.

Islamic cities had a distinctive physical appearance due to their common use of certain architectural features, such as the pointed arch and traceried windows, and specific kinds of buildings. The latter included palaces and public buildings with fountains and secluded courtyards, mosques for worship, public baths, and bazaars or marketplaces. Muslims embellished their buildings with a unique decorative art that avoided representation of living things because their religion prohibited the making of graven images.

Women in the Islamic World Although the Qur'an instructed men to treat women with respect, the male was dominant in Muslim society. Women were to be good mothers and wives by raising their children and caring for their husbands. Islamic custom required that women be secluded in their homes and kept from social contacts with males outside their own families. One jurist wrote that "a woman should leave her house on three occasions only: when she is conducted to the house of her bridegroom, on the deaths of her parents, and when she goes to her own grave."[17] The custom of requiring women to cover virtually all parts of their bodies when appearing in public was common in the cities and is still practiced today in many Islamic societies. It should be noted, however, that these customs owed more to traditional Arab practice than to the Qur'an.

Some women, however, also played active roles in medieval Islamic society. Although upper-class women in the cities were kept in seclusion in their homes, peasant women or female domestic servants were active in both rural and city life. Many upper-class women were literate and played a role in cultural and intellectual pursuits. Some wealthy women established salons where scholars and poets could meet, while some women wrote poetry. Women also had the right to own and inherit property and could pass on their property to female family members.

The Culture of Islam During the first few centuries of the Arab Empire, it was the Islamic world that saved and spread the scientific and philosophical works of ancient civilizations. At a time when the ancient Greek philosophers were largely unknown in Europe, key works by Plato and Aristotle were translated into Arabic (see Image 8.10). They were put in a library called the House of Wisdom in Baghdad, where they were read and studied by Muslim scholars. Texts on mathematics were brought from India. The use of paper aided the preservation of ancient texts. The making of paper was introduced from China in the eighth century, and by the end of

that century, paper factories had been established in Baghdad. Booksellers and libraries soon followed. European universities later benefited from this scholarship when these works were translated from Arabic into Latin.

Although Islamic scholars are rightly praised for preserving much of classical knowledge for the West, they also made considerable advances of their own. Nowhere is this more evident than in their contributions to mathematics and the natural sciences. The list of achievements in mathematics and astronomy alone is impressive. The Muslims adopted and passed on the numerical system of India, including the use of the zero. In Europe, it became known as the Arabic system. Al-Khwarizmi (al-KHWAR-iz-mee), a ninth-century Persian mathematician, developed the discipline of algebra. In astronomy, the Muslims were aware that the earth was round, and they set up an observatory at Baghdad to study the stars, many of which they named. They also perfected the astrolabe, an instrument used by sailors to determine their location by observing the positions of heavenly bodies. It was the astrolabe that made it possible for Europeans to sail to the Americas.

Muslim scholars also made discoveries in chemistry and developed medicine as a field of scientific study. Especially renowned was Ibn Sina (ib-un SEE-nuh) (980–1037), known as Avicenna (av-i-SENN-uh) in the West, who wrote a medical encyclopedia that, among other things, stressed the contagious nature of certain diseases and showed how they could be spread by contaminated water supplies. After its translation into Latin, Avicenna's work became a basic medical textbook for medieval European university students. Avicenna was but one of many Muslim scholars whose work was translated into Latin and contributed to the development of intellectual life in Europe in the twelfth and thirteenth centuries.

IMAGE 8.10 Preserving Greek Literature. After the collapse of the Western Roman Empire, the philosophical works of ancient Greece were virtually forgotten in Europe. It was thanks to Muslim scholars, who stored copies and translations in libraries in the Arab world, that many classical Greek writings survived. Here young Muslim scholars are being trained in the Greek language so that they can translate classical Greek literature into Arabic. Later the works were translated back into Latin and served as a catalyst for an intellectual revival in medieval and Renaissance Europe.

At the end of the eighth century C.E., a new kingdom—the Carolingian Empire—came to control much of western and central Europe, especially during the reign of Charlemagne. The coronation of Charlemagne, descendant of a Germanic tribe converted to Christianity, as Roman emperor in 800 symbolized the fusion of the three chief components of a new European civilization: the German tribes, the classical tradition, and Christianity. In the long run, the creation of a western empire fostered the idea of a distinct European identity and marked a shift of power from the south to the north. Italy and the Mediterranean had been the center of the Roman Empire. The lands north of the Alps now became the political center of Europe, and increasingly, Europe emerged as the focus and center of Western civilization.

The Carolingian Empire was well governed but was held together primarily by personal loyalty to a strong king. The economy of the eighth and ninth centuries was based almost entirely on farming, which proved inadequate to maintain a large monarchical system. As a result, a new political and military order, known as fief-holding, subsequently evolved to become an integral part of the political world of the Middle Ages. Fief-holding was characterized by a decentralization of political power, in which lords exercised legal, administrative, and military power. This transferred public power into many private hands and seemed to provide the security sorely lacking in a time of weak central government and invasions by Muslims, Magyars, and Vikings. In eastern Europe, the Slavic kingdoms of Poland and Bohemia were established. Catholic missionaries converted their peoples to Christianity, while the eastern and southern Slavs adopted Orthodox Christianity.

While Europe struggled, the Byzantine and Islamic worlds continued to prosper and flourish. The tenth century was the golden age of Byzantine civilization. Under the Macedonian dynasty, trade flourished, the Bulgars were defeated, Muslim armies were repelled, and Byzantine territory was increased.

The Umayyad dynasty of caliphs had established Damascus as the center of an Islamic empire created by Arab Muslim expansion in the seventh and eighth centuries. In the eighth century, the new Abbasid dynasty moved the capital east to Baghdad, where Persian influence was more pronounced. Greek and Persian scientific and philosophical writings were translated into Arabic, and the Muslims created a brilliant urban culture.

The brilliance of the urban cultures of both the Byzantine Empire and the Islamic world stood in marked contrast to the underdeveloped rural world of Europe. By 1000, however, that rural world had not only recovered but was beginning to expand in ways undreamed of by previous generations. Europe stood poised for a giant leap.

CHAPTER TIMELINE

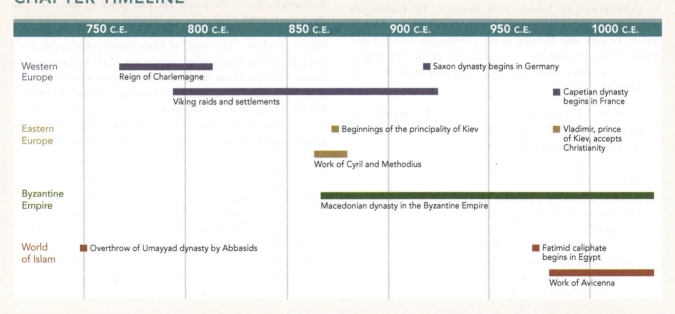

CHAPTER REVIEW

Upon Reflection

Q What did Islamic societies and those in western Europe have in common during the ninth and tenth centuries? How did they differ?

Q Of what significance was the Carolingian intellectual renaissance to western European civilization and to the government of the Carolingian empire?

Q What role did the Vikings play in the history of medieval Europe?

Q Why does the author use the title "The Zenith of Byzantine Civilization" to describe Byzantine civilization in the ninth and tenth centuries?

Key Terms

scriptoria (p. 220)
monogamy (p. 222)
nuclear family (p. 222)
vassalage (p. 230)
fief (p. 231)

subinfeudation (p. 231)
manor (p. 234)
serfs (p. 234)
demesne (p. 234)
tithe (p. 234)

Full definitions also appear in the Glossary at the end of the book.

Suggestions for Further Reading

General Histories A good general history of the entire medieval period can be found in **C. Wickham,** *Medieval Europe* (New Haven, Conn., 2016). See also **J. M. Riddle,** *A History of the Middle Ages, 300–1500* (Lanham, Md., 2008). For a good general survey of the social history of the Middle Ages, see **C. B. Bouchard,** *Life and Society in the West: Antiquity and the Middle Ages* (San Diego, Calif., 1988). For an excellent history of the period covered in this chapter, see **C. Wickham,** *The Inheritance of Rome: A History of Europe from 400 to 1000* (New York, 2009). See also **L. Olson,** *The Early Middle Ages* (New York, 2007).

The Carolingian World On Charlemagne, see **A. Barbero,** *Charlemagne: Father of a Continent,* trans. A. Cameron (Berkeley, Calif., 2004), and **J. Fried, trans. P. Lewis,** *Charlemagne* (Cambridge, Mass., 2016). On the Carolingian world, see **M. Costambeys, M. Innes,** and **S. Maclean,** *The Carolingian World* (New York, 2011). On Carolingian culture, see **R. McKitterick,** *History and Memory in the Carolingian World* (Cambridge, 2004). On one aspect of social life in the Carolingian world, see **L. Bitel,** *Women in Early Medieval Europe, 400–1100* (Cambridge, 2002).

The Vikings The Vikings are examined in **M. Arnold,** *The Vikings: Culture and Conquest* (London, 2006), and **R. Hall,** *The World of the Vikings* (New York, 2007).

Fief-Holding For an important revisionist view, see **S. Reynolds,** *Fiefs and Vassals* (Oxford, 1994). See also the recent work by **C. West,** *Reframing the Feudal Revolution* (Cambridge, 2013). Works on the new political configurations that emerged in the tenth century are cited in Chapter 9.

Economic History For the economic history of the early Middle Ages, see **G. A. Hodgett,** *A Social and Economic History of Medieval Europe* (London, 2006), and **A. E. Verhulst,** *The Carolingian Economy* (Cambridge, 2002).

Byzantine Empire and Slavic Peoples Byzantine civilization in this period is examined in **W. Treadgold,** *The Byzantine Revival, 780–842* (Stanford, Calif., 1991). See also **J. Herrin,** *Byzantium: The Surprising Life of a Medieval Empire* (Princeton, 2007). On the Slavic peoples of central and eastern Europe, see **S. Franklin** and **J. Shepard,** *The Emergence of Rus, 750–1200* (New York, 1996).

World of Islam The world of Islam in this period is discussed in **H. Kennedy,** *The Prophet and the Age of the Caliphates: The Islamic Near East from the Sixth to the Eleventh Century,* 2nd ed. (London, 2004); **H. Kennedy,** *When Baghdad Ruled the Muslim World: The Rise and Fall of Islam's Greatest Dynasty* (New York, 2006); and **P. Crone** and **M. Hinds,** *God's Caliph: Religious Authority in the First Centuries of Islam* (New York, 2003).

Notes

1. Einhard, *The Life of Charlemagne,* trans. Samuel Turner (Ann Arbor, Mich., 1960), p. 30.
2. Ibid., p. 57.
3. A. Barbero, *Charlemagne: Father of a Continent,* trans. Allan Cameron (Berkeley, Calif., 2004), p. 4.
4. C. Wickham, *The Inheritance of Rome: A History of Europe from 400 to 1000* (New York, 2009), p. 4.
5. R. McKitterick, "The Carolingian Renaissance of Culture and Learning," in J. Story, ed., *Charlemagne: Empire and Society* (Manchester: University of Manchester Press, 2005), p. 153.
6. Quoted in P. Riché, *Daily Life in the World of Charlemagne,* trans. J. A. McNamara (Philadelphia, 1978), p. 56.
7. 1 Corinthians 7:1–2, 8–9.

8. Quoted in D. Bailey, *Homosexuality and the Western Christian Tradition* (London, 1955), p. 73.

9. Quoted in P. Veyne, ed., *A History of Private Life*, vol. 1: *From Pagan Rome to Byzantium*, trans. A. Goldhammer (Cambridge, Mass., 1987), p. 440.

10. S. Rubin, *Medieval English Medicine* (New York, 1974), p. 136.

11. Quoted in B. Inglis, *A History of Medicine* (New York, 1965), p. 51.

12. Quoted in S. Keynes, "The Vikings in England, c. 790–1016," in Peter Sawyer, ed., *The Oxford Illustrated History of the Vikings* (Oxford, 1997), p. 81.

13. Quoted in O. Thatcher and E. McNeal, *A Source Book for Medieval History* (New York, 1905), p. 363.

14. S. Keynes and M. Lapidge, *Alfred the Great: Asser's "Life of King Alfred" and Other Contemporary Sources* (Harmondsworth, England, 1983), pp. 84–85.

15. Quoted in B. Lewis, *The Arabs in History* (London, 1958), p. 90.

16. al-Mas'udi, *The Meadows of Gold: The Abbasids*, eds. Paul Lunde and Caroline Stone (London, 1989), p. 151.

17. Quoted in A. Hourani, *A History of the Arab People* (Cambridge, Mass., 1991), p. 120.

MindTap *Tips* Your entire textbook, or any part of it, can be read out loud to you for on-the-go studying. Just click the Readspeaker App in the app dock. Choose from a variety of reading speeds and accents!

CHAPTER 9

The Recovery and Growth of European Society in the High Middle Ages

IMAGE 9.1 **A Town Street Scene in Thirteenth-Century England**

CHAPTER OUTLINE AND FOCUS QUESTIONS

9-1 Land and People in the High Middle Ages

Q What new agricultural practices arose in the High Middle Ages? What roles did peasants and aristocrats play in the civilization of the High Middle Ages?

9-2 The New World of Trade and Cities

Q What developments contributed to the revival of trade during the High Middle Ages, and what areas were the primary beneficiaries of the revival? How do you explain the growth of cities in the High Middle Ages? What were the major features of medieval cities?

9-3 The Intellectual and Artistic World of the High Middle Ages

Q What were the major intellectual achievements of European civilization in the High Middle Ages? What were the major developments in architecture, and how did Romanesque and Gothic buildings differ?

CONNECTIONS TO TODAY

What is the relationship between the economic developments of the High Middle Ages and current economic developments?

THE NEW EUROPEAN CIVILIZATION that had emerged in the ninth and tenth centuries began to come into its own in the eleventh and twelfth centuries as Europeans established new patterns that reached their zenith in the thirteenth century. The High Middle Ages (1000–1300) was a period of recovery and growth for Western civilization, characterized by a greater sense of security and a burst of energy and enthusiasm. New agricultural practices that increased the food supply helped give rise to a commercial and urban revival that, accompanied by a rising population, created new dynamic elements in a formerly static society.

Townspeople themselves were often great enthusiasts for their new way of life. In the twelfth century, William Fitz-Stephen spoke of London as one of the noble cities of the world: "It is blessed in the wholesomeness of its air, in its reverence for the Christian faith, in the strength of its bulwarks, the nature of its [site], the honor of its citizens, the chastity of its [women]; . . . most merry in its sports; and fruitful of noble men." To Fitz-Stephen, London offered myriad opportunities and pleasures. Fairs and markets were held regularly, and "and those that ply their several trades, the vendors of each several thing, the hirers out of their several sorts of labor are found every morning each in their separate quarters and each engaged upon his own peculiar task." Moreover, "to this city, from every nation that is under heaven, merchants rejoice to bring their trade in ships." Then, too, there are the happy inhabitants of the city: "The citizens of London are everywhere regarded as illustrious and renowned beyond those of all other cities for the elegance of their fine manners." Sporting events and leisure activities are available in every season of the year: "In Easter holidays [they fight battles on water]." In summer, "the youths exercise themselves in leaping, archery and wrestling, putting the stone, . . . and fighting with sword and buckler." In winter, "when the great marsh that washes the northern walls of the city is frozen, dense throngs of youth go forth to disport themselves upon the ice, some gathering speed by a run, glide sidelong, with feet set well apart, over a vast space of ice . . ." To Fitz-Stephen, every convenience for human pleasure was "at hand in London."[1] One would hardly know from his cheerful description that medieval cities faced overcrowded conditions, foul smells from rotting garbage and raw sewage, and the constant threat of epidemics and fires.

By the twelfth and thirteenth centuries, both the urban centers and the urban population of Europe were experiencing dramatic expansions. New forms of cultural and intellectual expression also arose in this new urban world. Although European society in the High Middle Ages remained overwhelmingly agricultural, the growth of trade and cities along with the development of a money economy and new commercial practices and institutions constituted a veritable commercial revolution that affected most of Europe.

9-1 Land and People in the High Middle Ages

 FOCUS QUESTIONS: What new agricultural practices arose in the High Middle Ages? What roles did peasants and aristocrats play in the civilization of the High Middle Ages?

The period from 1000 to 1300 witnessed an improvement in climate as a small but nevertheless significant rise in temperature made for longer and better growing seasons. At the same time, the European population experienced a dramatic increase, virtually doubling from 38 to 74 million people between 1000 and 1300. The rate of growth tended to vary from region to region (see Table 9.1). This rise in population was physically evident in the growth of agricultural villages, towns, and cities and the increase in arable land.

What accounted for this dramatic increase in population? Obviously, fertility rates increased sufficiently to gradually outstrip the relatively high mortality rates of medieval society, which were especially acute in infancy and the childhood years. Traditionally, historians have cited two factors to explain the population increase: increased security stemming from more settled and peaceful conditions after the invasions of the early Middle Ages had stopped, and a dramatic increase in agricultural production capable of sustaining a larger population.

9-1a The New Agriculture

During the High Middle Ages, significant changes occurred in the way Europeans farmed. Although the warmer climate played an underlying role by improving growing conditions, another factor contributing to the increased production of food

TABLE 9.1	Population Estimates (in millions), 1000 and 1340	
AREA	**1000**	**1340**
Mediterranean		
Greece and Balkans	5	6
Italy	5	10
Iberia	7	9
Total	17	25
Western and Central Europe		
France and Low Countries	6	19
British Isles	2	5
Germany and Scandinavia	4	11.5
Total	12	35.5
Eastern Europe		
Russia	6	8
Poland	2	3
Hungary	1.5	2
Total	9.5	13
Grand total	38.5	73.5

Source: J. C. Russell, *The Control of Late Ancient and Medieval Population* (Philadelphia: American Philosophical Society, 1985), p. 36. Demographic specialists caution that these are merely estimates. Some figures, especially those for eastern Europe, could be radically revised by new research.

was the expansion of arable land, achieved chiefly by clearing forested areas for cultivation (see Historical Voices, "The Elimination of Medieval Forests," p. 248). Eager for land, peasants cut down trees, drained swamps, and in the Netherlands even began to reclaim land from the sea. By the thirteenth century, the total acreage available for farming in Europe was greater than at any time before or since.

Technological Changes Technological changes also furthered the expansion of agriculture. Many of these depended on the use of iron, which was mined in various areas of Europe and traded to places where it was not found. Iron was in demand to make swords and armor as well as scythes, ax heads, new types of farming implements such as hoes, and saws, hammers, and nails for building purposes. It was crucial for making the heavy, wheeled plow, the carruca (kuh-ROO-kuh), which made an enormous impact on medieval agriculture north of the Alps.

The plow of the Mediterranean and Near Eastern worlds had been the *aratrum* (uh-RAH-trum), a nonwheeled, light scratch plow made mostly of wood that was sufficient to break the top layer of the light soils of those areas. It could be pulled by a single donkey, ox, or horse. But such a light plow was totally ineffective in the heavy clay soils north of the Alps. The carruca, a heavy, wheeled plow with an iron plowshare, came into widespread use by the tenth century (see Image 9.2). It could turn over heavy soils and allow them to drain. Because the carruca was so heavy, six or eight oxen were needed to pull

The Elimination of Medieval Forests

 Q *What does Suger's search for wooden beams reveal about the environmental problems of the Middle Ages? How do they compare to those of today?*

ONE OF THE INTERESTING environmental changes of the Middle Ages was the elimination of millions of acres of forest to create new areas of arable land and to meet the demand for timber. Timber was used as fuel and to build houses, mills of all kinds, bridges, fortresses, and ships. Incredible quantities of wood were burned to make charcoal for the iron forges. The clearing of the forests caused the price of wood to skyrocket by the thirteenth century. This document from 1140 illustrates the process. Suger (soo-ZHAYR), the abbot of Saint-Denis (san-duh-NEE), needed 35-foot beams for the construction of a new church. His master carpenters told him that there were no longer any trees big enough in the area around Paris and that he would have to go far afield to find such tall trees. This selection recounts his efforts.

Suger's Search for Wooden Beams

On a certain night, when I had returned from celebrating Matins [a prayer service], I began to think in bed that I myself should go through all the forests of these parts. . . . Quickly disposing of all duties and hurrying up in the early morning, we hastened with our carpenters, and with the measurements of the beams, to the forest called Iveline. When we traversed our possession in the Valley of Chevreuse we summoned . . . the keepers of our own forests as well as men who know about the other woods, and questioned them under oath whether we would find there, no matter with how much trouble, any timbers of that measure. At this they smiled, or rather would have laughed at us if they had dared; they wondered whether we were quite ignorant of the fact that nothing of the kind could be found in the entire region, especially since Milon, the Castellan of Chevreuse . . . had left nothing unimpaired or untouched that could be used for palisades and bulwarks while he was long subjected to wars both by our Lord the King and Amaury de Montfort. We however—scorning whatever they might say—began, with the courage of our faith as it were, to search through the woods; and toward the first hour we found one timber adequate to the measure. Why say more? By the ninth hour or sooner, we had, through the thickets, the depths of the forest and the dense, thorny tangles, marked down twelve timbers (for so many were necessary) to the astonishment of all.

Source: E. Panofsky, ed., trans., *Abbot Suger on the Abbey Church of St. Denis and Its Art Treasures* (Princeton, N.J.: Princeton University Press, 1946).

it, but oxen were slow. Two new inventions for the horse made it possible to plow faster. In the tenth century, a new horse collar appeared that distributed the weight around the shoulders and chest rather than the throat and could be used to hitch up a series of horses, enabling them to pull the new heavy plow faster and cultivate more land. The use of horseshoes, iron shoes nailed to a horse's hooves, produced greater traction and better protection against the rocky and heavy clay soils of northern Europe.

The use of the heavy, wheeled plow also led to cooperative agricultural villages. Because iron was expensive, the plow had to be purchased by the entire community. Similarly, an individual family could not afford a team of animals, so villagers shared their beasts. Moreover, the plow's size and weight made it hard to maneuver, so land was cultivated in long strips to minimize the amount of turning that would have to be done.

People in the High Middle Ages also learned to harness the power of water and wind to do jobs formerly done by humans or animals. Although the watermill had been invented as early as the second century B.C.E., it did not come into widespread use until the High Middle Ages. In one area of central France, the number of watermills increased from 14 in the eleventh century to over 200 in the thirteenth century. Mills, located along streams and powered by the rushing water, were used to grind grain to produce flour and to pulverize olives to make

oil. Often dams were built to increase the force of the water. The development of the cam enabled millwrights to mechanize entire industries; waterpower was used in certain phases of cloth production and to run trip-hammers for the working of metals. The Chinese had made use of the cam in operating trip-hammers for hulling rice by the third century C.E. but had apparently not extended its use to other industries.

Europeans also developed windmills to capture the power of the wind. Historians are uncertain whether windmills were imported into Europe (they were invented in Persia) or designed independently by Europeans. In either case, by the end of the twelfth century, they were beginning to dot the European landscape. The windmill had obvious advantages over the watermill: they could operate in areas without rushing water and were not affected by freezing weather. Nevertheless, both the watermill and windmill were important devices for harnessing power before the invention of the steam engine in the eighteenth century.

The Three-Field System The shift from a two-field system to a three-field system of crop rotation also contributed to the increase in agricultural production. In the early Middle Ages, farmers commonly planted one field while allowing another of equal size to lie fallow to regain its fertility. Now estates were divided into three parts. One field was planted in the fall with

Add 18855 October: ploughting and sowing, from a Book of Hours, c.1540 (vellum), Bening, Simon (c.1483-1561)/Victoria & Albert Museum, London, UK/Bridgeman Images

IMAGE 9.2 **The Heavy, Wheeled Plow.** The heavy, wheeled plow was an important invention that enabled peasants to turn over the heavy clay soils of northern Europe. This sixteenth-century illustration shows a heavy, wheeled plow pulled by draft horses with collars.

grains such as rye and wheat, while spring-sown grains, such as oats and barley, and legumes, such as peas, beans, or lentils, were planted in the second field. The third was allowed to lie fallow. By rotating their use, only one-third, rather than one-half, of the land lay fallow at any time. The rotation of crops also prevented the soil from being exhausted so quickly, especially since legumes improve soil fertility because their roots fix nitrogen in the soil. Grain yields increased as well.

By the thirteenth century, the growing demand for agricultural produce in the towns and cities led to higher food prices. This encouraged lords to try to grow more food for profit. One way to do so was to lease their demesne land to their serfs and to transform labor services into money payments or fixed rents, thereby converting many serfs into free peasants. Although many peasants still remained economically dependent on their lords, they were no longer legally tied to the land. Lords, in turn, became collectors of rents rather than operators of manors with political and legal privileges. The political and legal powers formerly exercised by lords were increasingly reclaimed by the monarchical states.

9-1b The Life of the Peasantry

The seasons of the year largely determined peasant activities (see Image 9.3). Each season brought a new round of tasks appropriate for the time, although some periods, especially summer and fall, were considerably more hectic than others. The basic

staple of the peasant diet was bread, so an adequate harvest of grains was crucial to survival in the winter months. A new cycle began in October when peasants prepared the ground for the planting of winter crops. In November came the slaughter of excess livestock because there was usually insufficient fodder to keep animals all winter. The meat would be salted to preserve it for winter use. In February and March, the land was plowed for spring crops—oats, barley, peas, beans, and lentils. Early summer was a comparatively relaxed time, although weeding and sheep-shearing still had to be done. In every season, the serfs worked not only their own land but also the lord's demesne. They also tended the gardens adjacent to their dwellings where they grew the vegetables and fruits that made up part of their diet.

Holidays and the Village Church But peasants did not face a life of constant labor thanks to the feast days or holidays of the Catholic Church, which commemorated the great events of the Christian faith or the lives of Christian saints or holy persons. The three great feasts of the Catholic Church were Christmas (celebrating the birth of Jesus), Easter (celebrating the resurrection of Jesus), and Pentecost (celebrating the descent of the Holy Spirit on Jesus's disciples fifty days after his resurrection). Numerous other feasts dedicated to saints or the Virgin Mary, the mother of Jesus, were also celebrated, making a total of more than fifty holidays.

Religious feast days, Sunday Mass, baptisms, marriages, and funerals all brought peasants into contact with the village church, a crucial part of manorial life. In the village church, the peasant was baptized as an infant, confirmed in the faith, sometimes married, and given the sacrament of Holy Communion; before death, the peasant would receive the last rites of the church. The village priest instructed the peasants in the basic elements of Christianity so that they might attain the Christian's ultimate goal—salvation. But village priests were often barely literate peasants themselves, and it is hard to know how much church doctrine the peasants actually understood. Very likely, they regarded God as an all-powerful force who needed to be appeased by prayer to bring good harvests.

The Peasant Household Peasant dwellings were very simple. The cottages were built with wood frames with walls made of laths or sticks; the spaces between the laths were stuffed with straw and rubble and then plastered over with clay. Roofs were often thatched with reeds or straw. In timber-poor areas, peasants built their houses out of stone. The houses of poorer peasants consisted of a single room, but others had at least two rooms—a main room for cooking, eating, and other activities and another room for sleeping. There was little privacy in a medieval household. A hearth in the main room was used for heating and cooking; the smoke from fires in the hearth went out a hole in the roof or gable.

Family and the Role of Women Surveys of monastic manors reveal that the typical peasant household consisted of a husband and wife with two or three children. Infant mortality rates were high. Peasant women occupied both an important and a difficult position in manorial society. They were expected

© RMN-Grand Palais/Art Resource, NY

IMAGE 9.3 **Peasant Activities.** The seasons of the year largely determined the life of the European peasant. The kind of work that peasants did was dictated by the month and the season. This French calendar from 1460 shows a number of medieval farming activities, including sowing seeds, harvesting crops, pruning plants, shearing sheep, threshing, pressing grapes, and taking care of animals.

Q *What do these images tell you about the quality of life of the peasants?*

to carry and bear children, as well as provide for their socialization and religious training. Peasant women also did the spinning and weaving that provided the household's clothes, tended the family's vegetable garden and chickens, and cooked the meals. A woman's ability to manage the household might determine whether her family would starve or survive in difficult times. In addition to managing the household, peasant women often worked with men in the fields, especially at harvest time. Indeed, as one historian has noted, peasant marriage was an "economic partnership" in which both husbands and wives contributed their own distinctive labor.

The Peasant Diet Though simple, a peasant's daily diet was potentially nutritious when food was available. The basic staple of the peasant diet, and the medieval diet in general, was bread. Women made the dough for the bread, but the loaves were usually baked in community ovens, which were a monopoly of the lord of the manor. Peasant bread was made of the cheaper grains (rye, barley, millet, and oats) rather than expensive wheat. It was dark and had a very heavy, hard texture. Bread was supplemented by legumes (peas and beans) from the household gardens, bacon from the family pig, cheese from cow's or goat's milk, and where available, wild game and fish from hunting and fishing. Manorial lords tended to regulate fishing, however, and were especially reluctant to allow peasants to hunt for fear that insufficient game would remain for the nobility. Woodlands also provided nuts, berries, and a foraging area for pigs. Fruits, such as apples, pears, and cherries, were also available. Chickens provided eggs and occasionally meat. Peasants usually ate fresh meat only on the great feast days, such as Christmas, Easter, and Pentecost.

Grains were important not only for bread but also for making ale. In many northern European countries, ale was the most common drink of the poor. If records are accurate, enormous quantities of ale were consumed. A monastery in the twelfth century recorded a daily allotment of three gallons a day to each monk, far above the weekend consumption of many present-day college students. Peasants in the field undoubtedly consumed even more. This high consumption of alcohol might explain the large number of fights and accidents recorded in medieval court records.

9-1c The Aristocracy of the High Middle Ages

In the High Middle Ages, a group of men whose primary preoccupation was warfare dominated European society. King Alfred of England had said that a "well-peopled land" must have men of prayer, men of war, and men of work, and medieval ideals held to a tripartite division of society into these three basic groups. The men of war were the **aristocracy** who came to form a distinct social group, albeit one with considerable variation in wealth among its members. Nevertheless, they, along with their wives and children, shared a common ethos and a distinctive lifestyle.

The Significance of the Aristocracy King Alfred's men of war were the lords and vassals of medieval society. The lords were the kings, dukes, counts, barons, and viscounts (and even bishops and archbishops) who held extensive lands and considerable political power. They formed an aristocracy or nobility that consisted of people who held real political, economic, and social power. Nobles relied for military help on knights, mounted warriors who fought for them in return for weapons and daily sustenance. Knights initially were by no means the social equals of nobles; many knights in fact possessed little more than peasants. But in the course of the twelfth and thirteenth centuries, knights improved their social status and joined the ranks of the nobility. In the process, *noble* and *knight* came to mean much the same thing, and warfare likewise tended to become a distinguishing characteristic of the nobleman. The great lords and knights came to form a common caste. Although social divisions based on extremes of wealth and landholdings persisted, they were all warriors united by the institution of knighthood.

The Men of War Medieval theory maintained that the warlike qualities of the nobility were justified by their role as defenders of society. Knights, however, were also notorious for fighting each other. The Catholic Church intervened, and though it could not stop the incessant bloodletting, it did at least try to limit it by instituting the "Peace of God." Beginning in the eleventh century, the church encouraged knights to take an oath to respect churches and pilgrimage centers and to refrain from attacking noncombatants, such as clergy, poor people, merchants, and women. It was, of course, permissible to continue killing each other. At the same time, the church initiated the "Truce of God," which forbade fighting on Sundays and the primary feast days.

In addition to trying to diminish fighting, the church also worked to redirect the nobility's warlike energy into different channels, such as the Crusades against the Muslims (see Chapter 10), and was quite willing to justify violence when used against peace-breakers and especially against non-Christians. Hence, being a warrior on behalf of God easily vindicated the nobles' love of war and in fact justified their high social status as the defenders of Christian society. The church furthered this process by steeping knighthood in Christian symbols. A knight formally received his arms in a religious ceremony, and a priest blessed his weapons for Christian service. Throughout the Middle Ages, a constant tension existed between the ideals of a religion founded on the ideal of peace and the ethos of a nobility based on the love of war.

Castles The growth of the European nobility in the High Middle Ages was made visible by an increasing number of castles scattered across the landscape (see Image 9.4). Although castle architecture varied considerably, castles did possess two common features: they were permanent residences for the noble family, its retainers, and servants, and they were defensible fortifications. For defensive purposes, castles were surrounded by open areas and large stone walls. At the heart of the castle was the keep, a large, multistoried building that housed kitchens, stables, and storerooms; numerous rooms for sleeping and living; and a great hall for visitors, dining, and administrative business. The growing wealth of the High Middle Ages made it possible for the European nobility to build more secure castles with thicker walls and more elaborately decorated interiors. With their sturdier construction, castles were easier to defend and harder to seize by force.

Buyenlarge/Getty Images

IMAGE 9.4 **Castle and Aristocrats.** This illustration is from the *Très Riches Heures* (Very Sumptuous Hours) of Jean, duke of Berry. The three Limbourg brothers created this book of hours, which was a book containing prayers to be recited at different times each day. This scene depicts the Château d'Étampes and its surrounding lands. In the foreground, elaborately dressed aristocratic men and women carrying falcons are going hunting while in the background peasants are working and swimming in the river.

Q *How does this image show the social differences of the High Middle Ages?*

Aristocratic Women Although women could legally hold and inherit property, most women remained under the control of men—their fathers until they married and their husbands after they married. Nevertheless, aristocratic women had numerous opportunities to play important roles. Because the lord was often away at war, on a crusade, or at court, the lady of the castle had to manage the estate, a considerable responsibility in view of the fact that households, even of lesser aristocrats, could include large numbers of officials and servants. Supervising financial accounts, both for the household and for the landed estate, alone required considerable financial knowledge. The lady of the castle was also often responsible

Women in Medieval Thought

 What do these two documents reveal about male attitudes toward women in the Middle Ages? How do the authors justify these attitudes?

WHETHER A NUN OR THE WIFE of an aristocrat, townsman, or peasant, a woman in the Middle Ages was considered inferior to a man and subject to a man's authority. Although there are a number of examples of strong women who ignored such attitudes, church teachings also reinforced these notions. The first selection from Gratian (GRAY-shee-un or GRAY-shun), the twelfth-century jurist who wrote the first systematic work on canon law (church law), supports this view. The second selection was written in the 1390s by a wealthy fifty-year-old Parisian who wanted to instruct his fifteen-year-old bride on how to be a good wife.

Gratian, *Decretum*

Women should be subject to their men. The natural order for mankind is that women should serve men and children their parents, for it is just that the lesser serve the greater.

The image of God is in man and it is one. Women were drawn from man, who has God's jurisdiction as if he were God's vicar, because he has the image of one God. Therefore woman is not made in God's image.

Woman's authority is nil; let her in all things be subject to the rule of man. . . . And neither can she teach, nor be a witness, nor give a guarantee, nor sit in judgment.

Adam was beguiled by Eve, not she by him. It is right that he whom woman led into wrongdoing should have her under his direction, so that he may not fail a second time through female levity.

A Merchant of Paris, *On Marriage*

I entreat you to keep his linen clean, for this is up to you. Because the care of outside affairs is men's work, a husband must look after these things, and go and come, run here and there in rain, wind, snow, and hail—sometimes wet, sometimes dry, sometimes sweating, other times shivering, badly fed, badly housed, badly shod, badly bedded—and nothing harms him because he is cheered by the anticipation of the care his wife will take of him on his return—of the pleasures, joys, and comforts she will provide, or have provided for him in her presence: to have his shoes off before a good fire, to have his feet washed, to have clean shoes and hose, to be well fed, provided with good drink, well served, well honored, well bedded in white sheets and white nightcaps, well covered with good furs, and comforted with other joys and amusements, intimacies, affections, and secrets about which I am silent. And on the next day fresh linen and garments. . . .

Also keep peace with him. Remember the country proverb that says there are three things that drive a good man from his home: a house with a bad roof, a smoking chimney, and a quarrelsome woman. I beg you, in order to preserve your husband's love and good will, be loving, amiable, and sweet with him. . . . Thus protect and shield your husband from all troubles, give him all the comfort you can think of, wait on him, and have him waited on in your home. . . . If you do what is said here, he will always have his affection and his heart turned toward you and your service, and he will forsake all other homes, all other women, all other help, and all other households.

Source: J. O'Faolaln and L. Martines, *Not in God's Image: Women in History from the Greeks to Victorians* (New York: Harper & Row, 1973).

---

for overseeing the food supply and maintaining all other supplies for the smooth operation of the household.

Childhood ended early for the daughters of aristocrats. Since aristocratic girls were married in their teens (usually at the age of fifteen or sixteen) and were expected by their husbands to assume their responsibilities immediately, the training of girls in a large body of practical knowledge could never start too early. Sent at a young age to the castles of other nobles to be brought up, girls were trained as ladies-in-waiting. The lady of the castle taught them how to sew and weave and instructed them in all the skills needed for running an estate. They also learned how to read and write, dance, sing, and play musical instruments.

Although women were expected to be subservient to their husbands (see Historical Voices, "Women in Medieval Thought," above), there were many strong women who advised and sometimes even dominated their husbands. Perhaps the most famous was Eleanor of Aquitaine (ca. 1122–1204), heiress to the duchy of Aquitaine in southwestern France. Married first to King Louis VII of France (r. 1137–1180), Eleanor even accompanied her husband on a crusade, but her failure to bear sons led Louis to have their marriage annulled. Eleanor then married Henry, count of Anjou (AHN-zhoo), who became King Henry II of England (r. 1154–1189) and duke of Normandy. She bore him both sons and daughters and took an active role in politics, even assisting her sons in rebelling against Henry in 1173–1174. Imprisoned by her husband for her activities, after Henry's death she again assumed an active political life, providing both military and political support for her sons.

Blanche of Castile (1188–1252) was another powerful medieval queen. She became regent while her son Louis IX was a boy and ruled France with a powerful hand during much of the 1220s and 1230s. She repelled the attempt of some rebellious

French nobles to seize her son, the young king, and defeated Henry III of England when he tried to incite an uprising in France in order to reconquer Normandy. Blanche's political sense was so astute that even when Louis IX came of age, he continued to rely on her as his chief adviser. One medieval chronicler gave her the highest compliment he could think of: "she ruled as a man."

The Way of the Warrior At the age of seven or eight, aristocratic boys were sent either to a clerical school to pursue a religious career or to another nobleman's castle, where they prepared for the life of a noble. The chief lessons for those learning to be nobles were military; they learned how to joust, hunt, ride, and handle weapons properly. Occasionally, aristocrats' sons might also learn the basic fundamentals of reading and writing. After his apprenticeship in knighthood, at about the age of twenty-one, a young man formally entered the adult world in the ceremony of "knighting." A sponsor girded a sword on the young candidate and struck him on the cheek or neck with an open hand (or later touched him three times on the shoulder with the blade of a sword), possibly signifying the passing of the sponsor's military valor to the new knight.

In the eleventh and twelfth centuries, under the influence of the church, an ideal of civilized behavior called **chivalry** gradually evolved among the nobility. Chivalry represented a code of ethics that knights were supposed to uphold. In addition to defending the church and the defenseless, knights were expected to treat captives as honored guests instead of throwing them in dungeons. Chivalry also implied that knights should fight only for glory, but this account of a group of English knights by a medieval writer reveals another motive for battle: "The whole city was plundered to the last farthing, and then they proceeded to rob all the churches throughout the city . . . and seizing gold and silver, cloth of all colors, women's ornaments, gold rings, goblets, and precious stones. . . . They all returned to their own lords rich men."[2] Apparently, not all chivalric ideals were taken seriously.

After his formal initiation into the world of warriors, a young man returned home to find himself once again subject to his parents' authority. Young men were discouraged from marrying until their fathers died, at which time they could marry and become lords of the castle. Trained to be warriors but with no adult responsibilities, young knights naturally gravitated toward military activities and often furthered the private warfare endemic to the noble class.

British Library Board/Robana/Art Resource, NY

IMAGE 9.5a

Ms 527 f.5v Teaching Knights to Joust, from 'Roman du Saint Graal' (vellum), French School, (15th century)/Bibliotheque Municipale, Dijon, France/Bridgeman Images

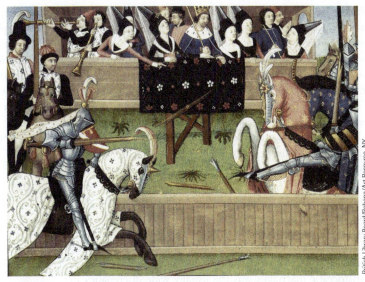

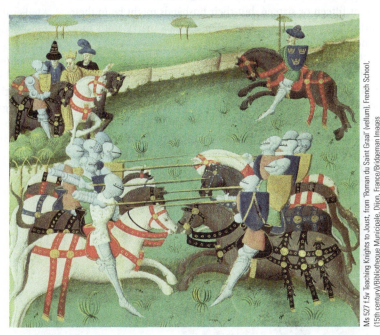

IMAGE 9.5b

IMAGE 9.5 **The Tournament and the Joust.** The tournament arose as a socially acceptable alternative to the private warfare that plagued the nobility in the Middle Ages, and jousts eventually became the main events of the tournament. The fifteenth-century English illustration in Image 9.5a shows a joust between two heavily armored knights while a crowd of royal and noble onlookers watches. A wooden barrier separates the knights, whose lances have both been broken. The fifteenth-century French illustration in Image 9.5b shows a group of knights being taught how to joust.

The Role of Tournaments In the twelfth century, tournaments began to appear as an alternative to the socially destructive fighting that the church was trying to curb (see Image 9.5). Initially, tournaments consisted of the "melee," in which warriors on horseback fought with blunted weapons in free-for-all combat. The goal was to take prisoners who would then be ransomed, making success in tournaments a path to considerable wealth. Within an eight-month span, the English knight William Marshall made a tour of the tournament circuit, defeated 203 knights, and made so much money that he had to hire two clerks to take care of it.

By the late twelfth century, the melee was preceded by the joust, or individual combat between two knights. Gradually, jousts became the main part of the tournament. No matter how much the church condemned tournaments, knights themselves continued to see them as an excellent way to train for war. As one knight explained: "A knight cannot distinguish himself in that [war] if he has not trained for it in tourneys. He must have seen his blood flow, heard his teeth crack under fist blows, felt his opponent's weight bear down upon him as he lay on the ground and, after being twenty times unhorsed, have risen twenty times to fight."[3]

Marriage Patterns of the Aristocracy Aristocratic marriages were expected to establish alliances with other families, bring new wealth, and provide heirs to carry on the family line (see Image 9.6). Parents therefore supervised the choice of spouses for their children. One of the most noticeable features of aristocratic marriages was the usually wide discrepancy in the ages of the marital partners. Daughters of the nobles married at fifteen or sixteen, but their husbands might be in their thirties or even forties, since men did not marry until they came into their inheritances.

By the twelfth century, the efforts of the church since Carolingian times to end divorce (see Chapter 8) had borne much fruit. As a sacrament, marriage was intended to last for a lifetime and could not be dissolved. In certain cases, however, the church allowed married persons to separate by granting them an annulment or official recognition that their marriage had not been valid in the first place. If it could be established that the couple had not consented to the marriage, that one or the other suffered from a sexual incapacity that prevented the consummation of the marriage, or that the couple were related by blood (more closely than sixth or, after 1215, third cousins), the church would approve an annulment of their marriage, and the partners would be free to marry again.

9-2 The New World of Trade and Cities

FOCUS QUESTIONS: What developments contributed to the revival of trade during the High Middle Ages, and what areas were the primary beneficiaries of the revival? How do you explain the growth of cities in the High Middle Ages? What were the major features of medieval cities?

Medieval Europe was an overwhelmingly agrarian society with most people living in small villages. In the eleventh and twelfth centuries, however, new elements were introduced that began to transform the economic foundation of Western civilization: a revival of trade, considerable expansion in the circulation of money, the emergence of specialized craftspeople and artisans, and the growth and development of towns. These changes were made possible by the new agricultural practices and subsequent increase in food production, which freed some European families from the need to produce their own food. Merchants and craftspeople could now buy their necessities. The increase in agricultural production also had an impact on the development of trade. Crop surpluses made possible the export of food and the development of local markets and eventually regional markets to handle new trade possibilities.

9-2a The Revival of Trade

The revival of commercial activity was a gradual process. During the chaotic conditions of the early Middle Ages, large-scale trade had declined in western Europe except for Byzantine contacts with Italy and the Jewish traders who moved back and forth between the Muslim and Christian worlds. By the end of the tenth century, however, people with both the skills and the products for commercial activity were emerging in Europe.

Cities in Italy assumed a leading role in the revival of trade (see Map 9.1). By the end of the eighth century, Venice, on the northeastern coast, had emerged as a town with close trading ties to the Byzantine Empire. Venice developed a trading fleet and by the end of the tenth century had become the chief western trading center for Byzantine and Islamic commerce. Venice sent wine, grain, and timber to Constantinople in exchange for silk cloth, which was then peddled to other communities. Other coastal communities in western Italy, such as Genoa and Pisa, also opened new trade routes. By 1100, Italian merchants began to benefit from the

IMAGE 9.6 **Marriage.** Marriage festivities for members of the aristocracy were usually quite elaborate. As seen in this illustration of the marriage of Renaud de Montaubon and Clarisse, daughter of the ruler of Gascogne, after the festivities, the wedding party would accompany the new couple to their bedroom to prepare them for the physical consummation of their marriage. Only after physical union was a medieval marriage considered valid.

Why did the Catholic Church move to end the practice of divorce?

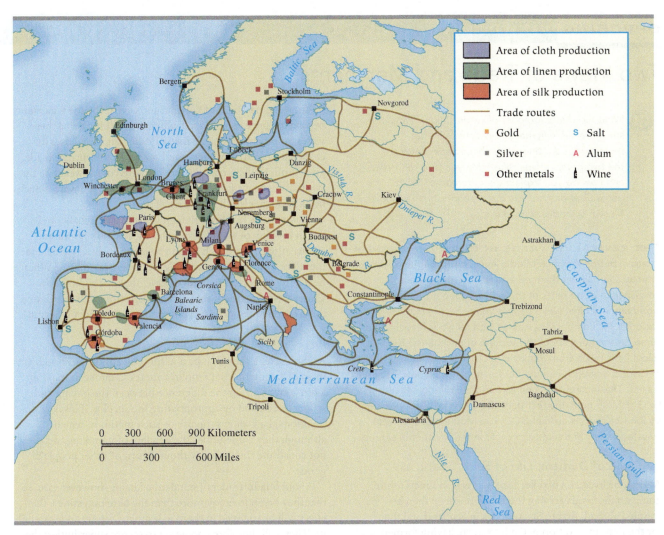

MAP 9.1 **Medieval Trade Routes.** Italian cities and Flanders were the centers of gradually expanding trade in Europe. They fostered the exchange of goods from the Byzantine Empire and the Far East with those of various regions of Europe. The decline in the level of violence over time greatly helped trade.

 Look back at Map 6.2. In what areas had trade expanded since 200 c.e., and how can you account for this?

Crusades (see Chapter 10) and were able to establish new trading centers in eastern ports. There the merchants obtained silks, sugar, and spices, which they subsequently carried back to Italy and the West.

In the High Middle Ages, Italian merchants became even more daring in their trade activities. They established trading posts in Cairo, Damascus, and a number of Black Sea ports, where they acquired goods brought by Muslim merchants from India, China, and Southeast Asia. A few Italian merchants even journeyed to India and China in search of trade.

While the northern Italian cities were busy trading in the Mediterranean, the towns of Flanders were doing likewise

MAP 9.2 **Flanders as a Trade Center**

in northern Europe. Flanders, the area along the coast of present-day Belgium and northern France, was known for the production of a much desired high-quality woolen cloth. Flanders's location made it a logical entrepôt for the traders of northern Europe (see Map 9.2). Merchants from England, Scandinavia, France, and Germany converged there to trade their wares for woolen cloth. Flanders prospered in the eleventh and twelfth centuries, and Flemish towns such as Bruges (BROOZH) and Ghent became centers for the trade and manufacture of woolen cloth.

By the twelfth century, it was almost inevitable that a regular exchange of goods would develop between Flanders and Italy.

Two Views of Trade and Merchants

Q *What did the biographer of Godric and Ibn Khaldun see as valuable in mercantile activity? What reservations did they have about trade? How are the two perspectives alike? How are they different, and how do you explain the differences? What generalizations can you make about Christian and Muslim attitudes toward trade?*

THE REVIVAL OF TRADE IN EUROPE was a gradual process, but by the High Middle Ages, it had begun to expand dramatically. During the medieval period, trade already flourished in other parts of the world, especially in the Islamic world and in China. Nevertheless, many people in these societies, including rulers, nobles, and religious leaders, had some reservations about the success of merchants. The first selection is taken from Reginald of Durham's account of the life of Godric, a twelfth-century European merchant who became a saint. The second selection is from the *Prolegomena* (proh-lih-GAHM-uh-nuh), the first part of a universal history written by Ibn Khaldun (ib-un kahl-DOON), a Muslim historian who traveled widely in the Muslim world in the fourteenth century.

Reginald of Durham, *Life of Saint Godric*

At first, he lived as a peddler for four years in Lincolnshire, going on foot and carrying the smallest wares; then he traveled abroad, first to St. Andrews in Scotland and then for the first time to Rome. On his return, having formed a familiar friendship with certain other young men who were eager for merchandise, he began to launch upon bolder courses, and to coast frequently by sea to the foreign lands that lay around him. Thus, sailing often to and fro between Scotland and Britain, he traded in many divers wares and, amid these occupations, learned much worldly wisdom. . . .

   Thus aspiring ever higher and higher, and yearning upward with his whole heart, at length his great labors and cares bore much fruit of worldly gain. For he labored not only as a merchant but also as a shipman . . . to Denmark and to Flanders and Scotland; in all which lands he found certain rare, and therefore more precious, wares, which he carried to other parts wherein

he knew them to be least familiar, and coveted by the inhabitants beyond the price of gold itself; wherefore he exchanged these wares for others coveted by men of other lands; and thus he chaffered [traded] most freely and assiduously. Hence he made great profit in all his bargains, and gathered much wealth in the sweat of his brow; for he sold dear in one place the wares which he had bought elsewhere at a small price.

   And now he had lived sixteen years as a merchant, and began to think of spending on charity, to God's honor and service, the goods which he had so laboriously acquired. He therefore took the cross as a pilgrim to Jerusalem. . . . [When he had returned to England] Godric, that he might follow Christ the more freely, sold all his possessions and distributed them among the poor [and began to live the life of a hermit].

Ibn Khaldun, *Prolegomena*

As for Trade, although it be a natural means of livelihood, yet most of the methods it employs are tricks aimed at making a profit by securing the difference between the buying and selling prices, and by appropriating the surplus. This is why [religious] Law allows the use of such methods, which, although they come under the heading of gambling, yet do not constitute the taking without return of other people's goods. . . .

   Should their [traders'] standard of living, however, rise, so that they begin to enjoy more than the bare necessities, the effect will be to breed in them a desire for repose and tranquility. They will therefore cooperate to secure superfluities; their food and clothing will increase in quantity and refinement; they will enlarge their houses and plan their towns for defense. A further improvement in their conditions will lead to habits of luxury, resulting in extreme refinement in cooking and the preparation of food; in choosing rich clothing of the finest silk; in raising lofty mansions and castles and furnishing them luxuriously, and so on. At this stage the crafts develop and reach their height. Lofty castles and mansions are built and decorated sumptuously, water is drawn to them and a great diversity takes place in the way of dress, furniture, vessels, and household equipment. Such are the townsmen, who earn their living in industry or trade.

Sources: Reginald of Durham, *Life of St. Godric*, in G. G. Coulton, ed., *Social Life in Britain from the Conquest to the Reformation* (Cambridge: Cambridge University Press, 1918), pp. 415–420; Ibn Khaldun, *Prolegomena*, in C. Issawi, ed., trans., *An Arab Philosophy of History* (New York: Darwin Press, 1987).

To encourage this trade, the counts of Champagne in northern France devised a series of six fairs held annually in the chief towns of their territory. The fairs of Champagne became the largest commercial marketplace in western Europe where the goods of northern Europe could be exchanged for the goods of southern Europe and the East. Northern merchants brought the furs, woolen cloth, tin, hemp, honey, and other foodstuffs of northern Europe and exchanged them for the cloth and swords of northern Italy and the silks, sugar, and spices of the East (see Opposing Viewpoints, "Two Views of Trade and Merchants," above). The prosperity of the Champagne fairs caused lords everywhere to follow their example and establish trading fairs.

The thirteenth century also witnessed an enormous expansion of trade. Historians speak of a Commercial Revolution to indicate not only the increased volume of goods traded but also the development of new commercial practices and institutions, many of which were pioneered by Italian merchants.

The Italian merchants discovered that their growing trade required new ways of raising capital and new commercial practices. Slowly, a money economy began to emerge. They created partnerships in order to raise capital for ships and goods in overseas journeys. New methods of credit, such as bills of exchange or notes on credit, were utilized to circumvent the problem of insufficient reserves of money or the inconvenience of exchanging coins for large transactions. It should be noted, however, the Italians also minted new gold coins that became standards in western Europe. The gold florin of Florence was first struck in 1252, the Venetian gold ducat in 1284. New techniques, including double-entry bookkeeping, commercial contracts, and insurance, also appeared to facilitate the expansion of businesses. All of these new practices were part of a commercial revolution based on the growth of **capitalism**, an economic system in which commerce and industry are controlled by private owners who invest in trade and goods in order to make profits.

9-2b The Growth of Cities

The revival of trade led to a revival of cities. Merchants needed places where they could live and build warehouses to store their goods. Towns had greatly declined in the early Middle Ages, especially in Europe north of the Alps. Old Roman cities continued to exist but had dwindled in size and population.

With the revival of trade, merchants began to settle in these old cities, followed by craftworkers or artisans, people who had developed skills on manors or elsewhere and now perceived the opportunity to ply their trade producing objects that could be sold by the merchants. In the course of the eleventh and twelfth centuries, the old Roman cities came alive with new residents. By 1100, the old areas of these cities had been repopulated; soon the population outgrew the walls, necessitating the construction of new city walls outside the old.

In the Mediterranean world, cities had survived in a more visible fashion. Spain's Islamic cities had a flourishing urban life, and southern Italy still possessed such thriving cities as Bari, Salerno, Naples, and Amalfi. Although greatly reduced in size, Rome, the old capital of the Roman world, had survived as the center of papal administration. In northern Italy, Venice had already emerged as a town by the end of the eighth century because of its commercial connections to the Byzantine Empire.

Founding of New Cities and Towns Beginning in the late tenth century, many new cities or towns were founded, particularly in northern Europe. Usually, a group of artisans and merchants established a settlement near some fortified stronghold, such as a castle or monastery. Castles were particularly favored because they were usually located along major routes of transportation or at the intersection of two trade routes; the lord of the castle also offered protection. If the settlement prospered and expanded, walls were built to protect it (see Image 9.7). The original meaning of the English *borough* or *burgh* and the German *Burg* as a fortress or walled enclosure is

IMAGE 9.7 **Fortified Town of Carcassonne.** The expansion of commerce and industry led to an ongoing growth of towns and cities in the High Middle Ages. As seen in this picture of the French town of Carcassonne, medieval towns were surrounded by walls strengthened by defensive towers and punctuated by gates. As is evident here, medieval urban skylines were dominated by towers of all kinds.

still evident in the names of many cities, such as Edinburgh and Hamburg. The merchants and artisans of these boroughs and burghs came to be called burghers or **bourgeoisie**.

Most towns were closely tied to their surrounding territories because they were dependent on the countryside for their food supplies. In addition, they were often part of the territory belonging to a lord and were subject to his jurisdiction. Although lords wanted to treat towns and townspeople as they would their vassals and serfs, cities had totally different needs and a different perspective. Townspeople needed mobility to trade. Consequently, the merchants and artisans of the towns constituted a revolutionary group who needed their own unique laws to meet their requirements. Since the townspeople were profiting from the growth of trade and sales of their products, they were willing to pay for the right to make their own laws and govern themselves. In many instances, lords and kings saw the potential for vast new sources of revenues and were willing to grant (or more accurately, sell) to the townspeople the liberties they were beginning to demand.

The Rights of Townspeople By 1100, townspeople were obtaining charters of liberties from their territorial lords that granted them the privileges they wanted, including the right to bequeath goods and sell property, freedom from military obligation to the lord, written urban law that guaranteed their freedom, and the right for serfs to become free after residing a year and a day in the town. The last provision made it possible for a runaway serf who could avoid capture to become a free person in a city. Almost all new urban communities gained these elementary liberties, but only some towns obtained the right to govern themselves by choosing their own officials and administering their own courts of law. Where townspeople experienced difficulty in obtaining privileges, they often swore an oath, forming an association called a **commune**, and resorted to force against their lay or ecclesiastical lords.

Communes appeared first in Italy, where urban communities existed even in the early Middle Ages. In northern Italy, in the regions called Tuscany and Lombardy, towns were governed by their bishops, but the nobles whose lands surrounded the towns took an active interest in them. Bishops were usually supported by the emperors, who used them as their chief administrators. In the eleventh century, city residents rebelled against the rule of the bishops, swore communal associations with the bishops' noble vassals, and overthrew the authority of the bishops by force. The alliance between town residents and rural nobles was overwhelming, and in the course of the eleventh and twelfth centuries, bishops were shorn of their authority. Communes took over the rights of government and created new offices, such as consuls and city councils, for self-rule. Pisa, Milan, Arezzo, and Genoa all attained self-government by the end of the eleventh century.

Although communes were also sworn in northern Europe, especially in France and Flanders, townspeople did not have the support of rural nobles. Revolts against lay lords were usually brutally suppressed; those against bishops, as in Laon (LAHn) at the beginning of the twelfth century (see Historical Voices, "A Communal Revolt," p. 259), were more frequently successful.

When they succeeded, communes received the right to choose their own officials, hold their own courts, and run their own cities. Unlike the towns in Italy, however, where the decline of the emperor's authority ensured that the northern Italian cities could function as self-governing republics, towns in France and England did not become independent city-states but remained ultimately subject to royal authority.

Medieval cities, then, possessed varying degrees of self-government, depending on the amount of control retained over them by the lord or king in whose territory they were located. Nevertheless, all towns, regardless of the degree of outside control, evolved institutions of government for running the affairs of the community.

City Governments Medieval cities defined citizenship narrowly and accorded it only to males who had been born in the city or who had lived there for some time. In many cities, citizens elected members of a city council that bore primary responsibility for running the affairs of the city. City councillors (known as *consuls* in Italy and southern France) not only enacted legislation but also served as judges and city magistrates. The electoral process was carefully engineered to ensure that only members of the wealthiest and most powerful families, who came to be called the *patricians*, were elected. They kept the reins of government in their hands despite periodic protests from lesser merchants and artisans. In the twelfth and thirteenth centuries, cities added some kind of sole executive leader, even if he was only a figurehead. Although the title varied from town to town, this executive officer was frequently called a *mayor*.

City governments kept close watch over the activities of their community. To care for the welfare and safety of the community, a government might regulate air and water pollution; provide water barrels and delegate responsibility to people in every section of the town to fight fires, which were an ever-present danger; construct warehouses to stockpile grain in the event of food emergencies; and establish and supervise the standards of weights and measures used in the various local trades and industries.

Crime was not a major problem in the towns of the High Middle Ages because the relatively small size of communities made it difficult for criminals to operate openly. Nevertheless, medieval urban governments did organize town guards to patrol the streets by night and the city walls by day. People caught committing criminal acts were quickly tried for their offenses. Serious offenses, such as murder, were punished by execution, usually by hanging. Lesser crimes were punished by fines, flogging, branding, public exposure (as in the pillory), or expulsion.

Medieval cities remained relatively small in comparison with either ancient or modern cities. A large trading city would number about 5,000 inhabitants. By 1300, London was the largest city in England, with 80,000 people or more. Otherwise, north of the Alps, only a few great commercial urban centers, such as Bruges and Ghent, had a population close to 40,000. Italian cities tended to be larger, with Venice, Florence, Genoa, Milan, and Naples numbering almost 100,000. Even the largest European

A Communal Revolt

 What does this communal revolt reveal about new social and political problems in the High Middle Ages? How did the rise of cities change or complicate an older medieval balance of power between rich and poor, countryside and city?

THE GROWTH OF TOWNS AND CITIES was a major aspect of economic life in the High Middle Ages. When townspeople were unable to gain basic liberties for themselves from the lord in whose territory their town was located, they sometimes swore a "commune" to gain these privileges by force. This selection by a contemporary abbot describes the violence that accompanied the formation of a commune at Laon in France in 1116. The bishop of Laon, lord of the town, had granted privileges to the townspeople in return for a large payment. Later he rescinded his grant but kept the money, thereby angering the citizens.

The Autobiography of Guibert, Abbot of Nogent-sous-Coucy

All the efforts of the prelate and nobles in these days were reserved for fleecing their inferiors. But those inferiors were no longer moved by mere anger, but goaded into a murderous lust for the death of the bishop and his accomplices and bound themselves by oath to effect their purpose. Now they say that 400 took the oath. Such a mob could not be secret and when it came to the ears of Anselm [the bishop's assistant] toward evening of the holy Sabbath, he sent word to the bishop, as he was retiring to rest, not to go out to the early morning service, knowing that if he did he must certainly be killed. But he, infatuated with excessive pride, said, "Fie, surely I shall not perish at the hands of such." . . .

The next day, . . . as he [the bishop] was engaged in business with Archdeacon Walter, . . . behold there arose a disorderly noise throughout the city, men shouting "Commune!" and . . . citizens now entered the bishop's court with swords, battle-axes, bows and hatchets, and carrying clubs and spears, a very great company.

Next the outrageous mob attacking the bishop and howling before the walls of his palace, he with some who were aiding him fought them off by hurling of stones and shooting of arrows. . . . [But] being unable to stand against the reckless assaults of the people, he put on the clothes of one of his servants and flying to the vaults of the church hid himself in a cask, shut up in which with the head fastened on by a faithful follower he thought himself safely hidden. And as they ran hither and thither demanding where, not the bishop, but the hangdog, was, they seized one of his pages, but through his faithfulness could not get what they wanted. Laying hands on another, they learned from the traitor's nod where to look for him. Entering the vaults therefore, and searching everywhere, at last they found [him]. . . .

[The bishop] therefore, . . . was dragged forth from the cask by the hair, beaten with many blows and brought out into the open. . . . And as he piteously implored them, ready to take oath that he would henceforth cease to be their bishop, that he would leave the country, and as they with hardened hearts jeered at him, one named Bernard . . . lifting his battle-ax brutally dashed out the brains of that sacred, though sinner's, head, and he, slipping between the hands of those who held him, was dead before he reached the ground stricken by another thwart blow under the eye-sockets and across the middle of the nose. There brought to his end, his legs were cut off and many another wound inflicted. But Thibaut seeing the ring on the finger of the erstwhile prelate and not being able to draw it off, cut off the dead man's finger and took it. And so stripped to his skin he was thrown into a corner in front of his chaplain's house.

Source: *The Autobiography of Guibert, Abbot of Nogent-sous-Coucy*, trans. C. C. S. Bland (London: George Routledge, 1925).

city, however, seemed insignificant alongside the Byzantine capital of Constantinople or the Arab cities of Damascus, Baghdad, and Cairo (see Global Perspectives, "Medieval Cities in the West and East," p. 260). For a long time to come, Europe remained predominantly rural, but in the long run the rise of towns and the growth of trade laid the foundation for the eventual transformation of Europe from a rural agricultural society to an urban industrial one.

Life in the Medieval City Medieval towns were surrounded by stone walls that were expensive to build, so the space within was precious and tightly filled. This gave medieval cities their characteristic appearance of narrow, winding streets with houses crowded against each other. Until the thirteenth century, streets were generally left unpaved, and buildings fronted directly on them. To gain more space, inhabitants frequently added balconies or built the second and third stories of their dwellings out over the streets. Since dwellings were crowded so closely together and candles and wood fires were used for light and heat, the danger of fire was great.

A medieval urban skyline was dominated by the towers of castles and town halls, but especially of churches, whose number could be staggering. At the beginning of the thirteenth century, London had 120 monastic and parish churches. If a city

Medieval Cities in the West and East

 Based on a comparison of these medieval cities, which of these civilizations do you think was the most advanced? Why?

THE EXCHANGE OF GOODS BETWEEN SOCIETIES was a feature of both the ancient and medieval worlds. Trade routes crisscrossed the lands of the medieval world, and with increased trade came the growth of cities. In Europe, towns had dwindled after the collapse of the Western Roman Empire, but with the revival of trade in the eleventh and twelfth centuries, the cities came back to life. This revival occurred first in the old Roman cities, but soon new cities arose as merchants and artisans sought additional centers for their activities. As cities grew, so did the number of fortified houses, town halls, and churches whose towers punctuated the urban European skyline. Nevertheless, in the Middle Ages, cities in western Europe, especially north of the Alps, remained relatively small. Even the larger cities of Italy, such as Florence and Venice, with populations of 100,000, seemed insignificant in comparison with Constantinople and the great cities of the Middle East and China.

With a population of possibly 300,000 people, Constantinople, the capital city of the Byzantine Empire, was the largest city in Europe in the High Middle Ages, and until the twelfth century, it was Europe's greatest commercial center, an important crossroads for the exchange of goods between West and East. In addition to palaces, cathedrals, and monastic buildings, Constantinople also had numerous gardens and orchards that occupied large areas inside its fortified walls. Despite the extensive open and cultivated spaces, the city was not self-sufficient and relied on imports of food under close government direction.

As trade flourished in the Islamic world, cities prospered. When the Abbasids were in power, Baghdad, with a population close to 700,000, was probably the largest city in the empire and one of the greatest cities in the world. Islamic cities had a distinctive physical appearance. Usually, the most impressive urban buildings were the palaces for the caliphs or the local governors and the great mosques for worship. There were also public buildings with fountains and secluded courtyards, public baths, and bazaars. The bazaar, a covered market, was a crucial part of every Muslim settlement and an important trading center where goods from all the known world were available. Food prepared for sale at the market was carefully supervised. A rule in one Muslim city stated that grilled meats should only be made with fresh meat and not with meat that came from a sick animal and purchased for its cheapness. The merchants were among the greatest beneficiaries of the growth of cities in the Islamic world.

During the medieval period, cities in China were the largest in the world. The southern port of Hangzhou had at least a million residents by 1000, and a number of other cities, including Chang'an and Kaifeng, may also have reached that size. Chinese cities were known for their broad canals and wide, tree-lined streets. They were no longer administrative centers dominated by officials and their families but now included a broader mix of officials, merchants, artisans, and entertainers. The prosperity of Chinese cities was well known. Marco Polo, in describing Hangzhou to unbelieving Europeans in the late thirteenth century, reported that so many pleasures can be found that one "fancies himself to be in Paradise."

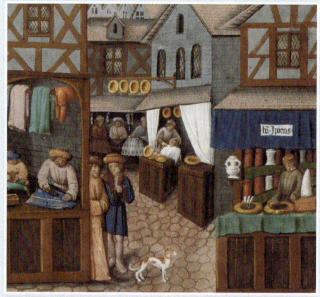

Snark/Art Resource, NY

IMAGE 9.8a Shops in a European Medieval Town. Most urban residents were merchants involved in trade and artisans who manufactured a wide variety of products. Master craftsmen had their workshops in the ground-level rooms of their homes. In this illustration, two well-dressed burghers are touring the shopping district of a French town. Tailors, furriers, a barber, and a grocer (from left to right) are visible at work in their shops.

IMAGE 9.8b A Baghdad Bazaar. Pictured here in this thirteenth-century painting is a bazaar in Baghdad, showing (from left to right) shops for jewelers, herbalists, butchers, and bakers. Bazaars were a common feature of Muslim communities.

Scene from the only known illustrated manuscript of the poem, the Romance of Varqa and Gulshah, by Urwa b/ WERNER FORMAN ARCHIVE/Bridgeman Images

Pollution in a Medieval City

 What does the king's command to Boutham illustrate about the physical environment of medieval cities? What factors or human habits contributed to the degradation of the medieval urban environment?

ENVIRONMENTAL POLLUTION is not new. Medieval cities and towns had their own problems with filthy living conditions. This excerpt is taken from an order sent by the king of England to the town of Boutham, a suburb of York, which was then being used by the king as his headquarters in a war with the Scots. It demands rectification of the town's pitiful physical conditions.

The King's Command to Boutham

To the bailiffs of the abbot of St. Mary's, York, at Boutham. Whereas it is sufficiently evident that the pavement of the said town of Boutham is so very greatly broke up that all and singular passing and going through that town sustain immoderate damages and grievances, and in addition the air is so corrupted and infected by the pigsties situated in the king's highways and in the lanes of that town and by the swine feeding and frequently wandering about in the streets and lanes and by dung and dunghills and many other foul things placed in the streets and lanes, that great repugnance overtakes the king's ministers staying in that town and also others there dwelling and passing through; the advantage of more wholesome air is impeded; the state of men is grievously injured, and other unbearable inconveniences and many other injuries are known to proceed from such corruption, to the nuisance of the king's ministers aforesaid and of others there dwelling and passing through, and to the peril of their lives. . . . The king, being unwilling longer to tolerate such great and unbearable defects there, orders the bailiffs to cause the pavement to be suitably repaired within their liberty before All Saints next, and to cause the pigsties, aforesaid streets and lanes to be cleansed from all dung and dunghills, and to cause proclamation to be made throughout their bailiwick forbidding any one, under pain of grievous forfeiture, to cause or permit their swine to feed or wander outside his house in the king's streets or the lanes aforesaid.

Source: H. Rothwell, ed., *English Historical Documents III* (London: Methuen, 1975).

---

was the center of a bishop's see, a large cathedral would dominate the other buildings and be visible for miles outside the city.

Most of the people who lived in the cities were merchants involved in trade and artisans engaged in manufacturing of some kind. Sometimes merchants and artisans had their own sections in a city. The merchant area included warehouses, inns, and taverns. Artisan sections were usually divided along craft lines, and each craft might have its own street where its activity was pursued.

The physical environment of medieval cities was not pleasant. They were often dirty and rife with smells from animal and human waste deposited in backyard privies or on the streets (see Historical Voices, "Pollution in a Medieval City," above). In some places, city governments required citizens to periodically collect garbage and waste and cart it outside the town. Atmospheric pollution was also a fact of life, not only from the ubiquitous wood fires but also from the use of coal, a cheap fuel that was used industrially by lime-burners, brewers, and dyers. Burning coal emitted foul-smelling, noxious fumes and was sometimes prohibited under pain of fine.

Cities were also unable to stop water pollution, especially from the animal-slaughtering and tanning industries. Butchers dumped blood and other waste products from their butchered animals into the river, while tanners unloaded tannic acids, dried blood, fat, hair, and the other waste products of their operations. Forcing both industries to locate downstream to avoid polluting the water used by the city upstream was only partly effective. Tanneries and slaughterhouses existed in every medieval town, so the river could rapidly become polluted from other towns' wastes.

Because of the pollution, cities were not inclined to use the rivers for drinking water but relied instead on wells. Occasionally, communities repaired the system of aqueducts or conduits left over from Roman times and sometimes even constructed new ones. Private and public baths also existed in medieval towns. Paris, for example, had thirty-two public baths for men and women. City laws did not allow lepers and people with "bad reputations" to use them, but such measures did not prevent the public baths from being known for permissiveness due to public nudity. One contemporary commented on what occurred in public bathhouses: "Shameful things. Men make a point of staying all night in the public baths and women at the break of day come in and through 'ignorance' find themselves in the men's rooms."[4] Authorities came under increasing pressure to close the baths down, and the great plague of the fourteenth century sealed their fate. The standards of medieval hygiene broke down, and late medieval and early modern European society would prove to be remarkably dirty.

Because of the limited space in medieval towns, houses were narrow, built next to one another, and usually multi-storied. In many houses, the shops or workrooms of merchants and craftspeople occupied the ground floor. Inhabitants, who might include husband and wife, children, servants, and apprentices, would live upstairs.

Women in Medieval Cities For most ordinary merchants and artisans, then, home life and work life were closely intertwined. Merchants and artisans taught their trades to their children and their wives and apprentices, or their children might be apprenticed to another merchant or artisan. Married women, in addition to supervising the household, purchasing food and preparing meals, washing clothes, managing the family finances, and bearing and taking care of children, were also often expected to help their husbands in their trades. While men produced goods at home, their wives often peddled them at markets or fairs.

Single women and widows had little alternative but to become involved in activities to generate income in order to provide for themselves financially. Some women earned money by practicing a trade, such as brewing ale, manufacturing glass, or making hats and cloth. Other women became midwives, innkeepers, or prostitutes. A widow often carried on her husband's trade. Some women in medieval towns were thus able to lead lives of considerable independence and made important contributions to the market economy. Nevertheless, women often earned less than men and faced obstacles that kept them from more rewarding opportunities. For example, women in textile production usually were given the most menial jobs. Many were forced to become domestic servants and received room and board in return for cooking, cleaning, and other domestic services.

9-2c Industry in Medieval Cities

The revival of trade enabled cities and towns to become important centers for manufacturing a wide range of goods, such as cloth, metalwork, shoes, and leather goods. A host of crafts were carried on in houses along the narrow streets of the medieval cities. From the twelfth century on, merchants and artisans began to organize themselves into **guilds**, which came to play a leading role in the economic life of the cities.

By the thirteenth century, virtually every group of craftspeople, such as tanners, carpenters, and bakers, had their own guild, and specialized groups of merchants, such as dealers in silk, spices, wool, or banking, had their separate guilds as well. Florence alone had fifty different guilds. Some communities were so comprehensive in covering all trades that they even had guilds for prostitutes.

Craft guilds directed almost every aspect of the production process. They set standards for the articles produced, specified the methods of production to be used, and even fixed the price at which the finished goods could be sold. Guilds also determined the number of individuals who could enter a specific trade and the procedure they must follow to do so.

A person who wanted to learn a trade first became an apprentice to a master craftsman, usually at around the age of ten. Apprentices were not paid but did receive room and board from their masters. After five to seven years of service, during which they learned their craft, apprentices became journeymen (or journeywomen, although most were male) who then worked for wages for other masters. Journeymen aspired to become masters as well. To do so, a journeyman had to produce a "masterpiece," a finished piece in his craft that allowed

the master craftsmen of the guild to judge whether the journeyman was qualified to become a master and join the guild.

Craft guilds continued to dominate manufacturing in industries where raw materials could be acquired locally and the products sold locally. But in industries that required raw materials from outside the local area to produce high-quality products for growing markets abroad, a new form of industry dependent on large concentrations of capital and unskilled labor began to emerge. It was particularly evident in the "putting-out" or domestic system used in the production of woolen cloth in both Flanders and northern Italy. An entrepreneur, whose initial capital outlay probably came from commercial activities, bought raw wool and distributed it to workers who carried out the various stages of carding, spinning, weaving, dyeing, and fulling to produce a finished piece of woolen cloth. These laborers worked in their own homes and were paid wages. As wage earners, they were dependent on their employers and the fluctuations in prices that occurred periodically in the international market for the finished goods. The entrepreneur collected the final products and sold the finished cloth, earning a profit that could then be invested in more production. Woolen industries operated by capitalist entrepreneurs in seventeen principal centers in northern Europe, mostly in Flanders, produced most of the woolen cloth used in northern Europe. An Italian chronicler at the beginning of the fourteenth century estimated that the woolen industry in Florence produced 80,000 pieces of cloth a year and employed 30,000 men, women, and children, usually at pitiful wages.

9-3 The Intellectual and Artistic World of the High Middle Ages

FOCUS QUESTIONS: What were the major intellectual achievements of European civilization in the High Middle Ages? What were the major developments in architecture, and how did Romanesque and Gothic buildings differ?

The High Middle Ages was a time of tremendous intellectual and artistic vitality. The period witnessed the growth of educational institutions, a rebirth of interest in ancient culture, a quickening of theological thought, a revival of law, the development of a vernacular literature, and a burst of activity in art and architecture. Although monks continued to play an important role in intellectual activity, increasingly the secular clergy, cities, and courts, whether of kings, princes, or high church officials, began to exert a newfound influence. Especially significant were the new cultural expressions that emerged in towns and cities.

9-3a The Rise of Universities

The university as we know it with faculty, students, and degrees was a product of the High Middle Ages. The word *university* is derived from the Latin word *universitas* (yoo-nee-VAYR-see-tahss), meaning a corporation or guild, and referred to either a guild of teachers or a guild of students. Medieval universities were educational guilds or corporations that produced educated and trained individuals.

The Origins of Universities Education in the early Middle Ages rested primarily with the clergy, especially the monks. Although monastic schools were the centers of learning from the ninth century, they were surpassed in the course of the eleventh century by the cathedral schools organized by the secular (nonmonastic) clergy. Cathedral schools, like the cities in which they were located, expanded rapidly in the eleventh century. There were twenty of them in 900, but by 1100 the number had grown to at least two hundred since every cathedral city felt compelled to establish one. The most famous were Chartres, Reims, Paris, Laon, and Soissons, all in France, which was the intellectual center of Europe by the twelfth century (see Map 9.3). Although the primary purpose of cathedral schools was to educate priests to be more literate men of God, they also attracted other individuals who desired some education but did not want to become priests. Many university administrators today carry titles, such as chancellor, provost, and dean, that were originally used for the officials of cathedral chapters.

The first European university appeared in Bologna, Italy, and coincided with the revival of interest in Roman law, especially the rediscovery of Justinian's *Corpus Iuris Civilis* (see "9-3d The Revival of Roman Law," later in this chapter). In the twelfth century, Irnerius (1088–1125), a great teacher of Roman law

in Bologna (buh-LOHN-yuh), attracted students from all over Europe. Most of them were laymen, usually older individuals who served as administrators to kings and princes and were eager to learn more about law so that they could apply it in their jobs. To protect themselves, students at Bologna formed a guild, or *universitas*, which was recognized by Emperor Frederick Barbarossa and given a charter in 1158. Although the faculty also organized itself as a group, the universitas of students at Bologna was far more influential. It obtained a promise of freedom for students from local authorities, regulated the price of lodging, and determined the curriculum, fees, and standards for their masters. Teachers were fined if they missed a class or began their lectures late. The University of Bologna remained the greatest law school in Europe throughout the Middle Ages.

In northern Europe, the University of Paris became the first recognized university. A number of teachers or masters who had received licenses to teach from the cathedral school of Notre-Dame in Paris began to take on extra students for a fee. By the end of the twelfth century, these masters teaching at Paris had formed a universitas (guild) of masters. By 1200, the king of France, Philip Augustus, granted a charter for what became the University of Paris.

The University of Oxford in England, organized on the Paris model, first appeared in 1208. A migration of scholars from Oxford in 1209 led to the establishment of Cambridge University. In the Late Middle Ages, kings, popes, and princes vied to found new universities as they realized their importance,

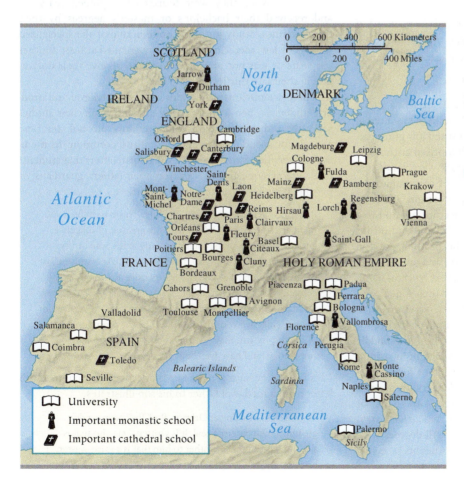

MAP 9.3 Intellectual Centers of Medieval Europe. Products of the High Middle Ages, universities provided students with a basic liberal arts education and the opportunity to pursue further studies in law, medicine, or theology. Courses were taught in Latin, primarily by professors reading from books. There were no exams in individual courses, but students had to pass a comprehensive oral exam to gain a degree.

Q *In what ways did France qualify as the intellectual capital of Europe?*

IMAGE 9.9 **University Classroom.** This illustration shows a university classroom in fourteenth-century Germany. As was customary in medieval classrooms, the master is lecturing from a text. The students vary considerably in age and in the amount of attention they are giving the lecturer.

Q *What are the notable similarities and differences in this classroom and classrooms in twenty-first-century American universities?*

such as the one created by Holy Roman Emperor Frederick II at Naples in 1224. By the end of the Middle Ages, there were eighty universities in Europe, most of them located in France, Italy, Germany, and England.

Teaching in the Medieval University A student's initial studies at a medieval university centered around the traditional liberal arts curriculum. The *trivium* consisted of grammar, rhetoric, and logic, and the *quadrivium* comprised arithmetic, geometry, astronomy, and music. All classes were conducted in Latin, which provided a common means of communication for students, regardless of their country of origin. Basically, medieval university instruction used the lecture method (see Image 9.9). The word *lecture* is derived from Latin and means "to read." Before the development of the printing press in the fifteenth century, books were expensive, and few students could afford them, so masters read from a text (such as a collection of laws when the subject was law) and then added commentaries, which came to be known as glosses. No exams were given after a series of lectures, but when a student applied for a degree, he (women did not attend universities in the Middle Ages) was given a comprehensive oral examination by a committee of teachers. These exams were taken after a four- or six-year period of study. The first degree a student could earn was an A.B., the *artium baccalaureus* (ar-TEE-um bak-uh-LAR-ee-uss), or bachelor of arts; later he might receive an A.M., *artium magister* (ar-TEE-um muh-GISS-ter), master of arts. All degrees were technically licenses to teach, although most students receiving them did not become teachers.

After completing the liberal arts curriculum, a student could go on to study law, medicine, or theology, which was the most highly regarded subject of the medieval curriculum. The study of law, medicine, or theology was a long process that could take a decade or more. A student who passed his final oral examinations was granted a doctor's degree, which officially enabled him to teach his subject. Most students who pursued advanced degrees received their master's degrees first and taught the arts curriculum while continuing to pursue their advanced degrees. Students who received degrees from medieval universities could pursue other careers besides teaching that were much more lucrative. A law degree was deemed essential for those who wished to serve as advisers to kings and princes. The growing administrative bureaucracies of popes and kings also demanded a supply of clerks with a university education who could keep records and draw up official documents.

Students in the Medieval University Students at medieval universities stemmed predominantly from the middle groups of medieval society, the families of lesser knights, merchants, and artisans. All were male; many were poor but ambitious and upwardly mobile. Many students started when they were fourteen to eighteen years old and received their bachelor's or master's degrees by their early twenties. Study for a doctorate in one of the specialized schools of law, medicine, or theology entailed at least another ten years. It was not unusual for men to receive their doctorates in their late thirties or early forties.

There are obvious similarities between medieval and modern students. Then as now, many students took their studies seriously and worked hard. Then as now, alcohol, sex, and appeals for spending money were all too common. In medieval universities, handbooks provided form letters that students could use in requesting money from their fathers, guardians, or patrons. This is an example from Oxford:

B. to his venerable master A., greeting. This is to inform you that I am studying at Oxford with the greatest of diligence, but the matter of money stands greatly in the way of my promotion, as it is now two months since I have spent the last of what you sent me. The city is expensive and makes many demands; I have to rent lodgings, buy necessaries, and provide for many other things which I cannot now specify. Wherefore I respectfully beg your paternity that by the promptings of divine pity you may assist me, so that I may be able to complete what I have well begun.[5]

Lack of studiousness is not just a modern phenomenon, as this letter from a medieval father to his son illustrates:

To his son G. residing at Orleans, P. of Besançon sends greetings with paternal zeal. It is written, "He also that is slothful in his work is brother to him that is a great waster." I have recently discovered that you live dissolutely and slothfully,

University Students and Violence at Oxford

 Who do you think was responsible for this conflict between town and gown? Why? Why do you think the king supported the university?

MEDIEVAL UNIVERSITIES shared in the violent atmosphere of their age. Town-and-gown quarrels often resulted in bloody conflicts, especially during the universities' formative period. This selection is taken from an anonymous description of a student riot at Oxford at the end of the thirteenth century.

A Student Riot at Oxford

They [the townsmen] seized and imprisoned all scholars on whom they could lay hands, invaded their inns [halls of residence], made havoc of their goods and trampled their books under foot. In the face of such provocation the proctors [university officials] sent their assistants about the town, forbidding the students to leave their inns. But all commands and exhortations were in vain. By nine o'clock next morning, bands of scholars were parading the streets in martial array. If the proctors failed to restrain them, the mayor was equally powerless to restrain his townsmen. The great bell of St. Martin's rang out an alarm; oxhorns were sounded in the

streets; messengers were sent into the country to collect rustic allies. The clerks [students and teachers], who numbered 3,000 in all, began their attack simultaneously in various quarters. They broke open warehouses in the Spicery, the Cutlery and elsewhere. Armed with bow and arrows, swords and bucklers, slings and stones, they fell upon their opponents. Three they slew, and wounded fifty or more. One band . . . took up a position in High Street between the Churches of St. Mary and All Saints', and attacked the house of a certain Edward Hales. This Hales was a longstanding enemy of the clerks. There were no half measures with him. He seized his crossbow, and from an upper chamber sent an unerring shaft into the eye of the pugnacious rector. The death of their valiant leader caused the clerks to lose heart. They fled, closely pursued by the townsmen and countryfolk. Some were struck down in the streets, and others who had taken refuge in the churches were dragged out and driven mercilessly to prison, lashed with thongs and goaded with iron spikes.

Complaints of murder, violence, and robbery were lodged straightway with the king by both parties. The townsmen claimed 3,000 pounds' damage. The commissioners, however, appointed to decide the matter, condemned them to pay 200 marks, removed the bailiffs, and banished twelve of the most turbulent citizens from Oxford.

Source: C. Headlam, *The Story of Oxford*, 1907.

---

preferring license to restraint and play to work and strumming a guitar while the others are at their studies, whence it happens that you have read but one volume of law while your more industrious companions have read several. Wherefore I have decided to exhort you herewith to repent utterly of your dissolute and careless ways, that you may no longer be called a waster and your shame may be turned to good repute.[6]

We have no idea whether the letter convinced the student to change his ways.

Medieval universities shared in the violent atmosphere of the age. Records from courts of law reveal numerous disturbances at European universities. One German professor was finally dismissed for stabbing one too many of his colleagues in faculty meetings. A student in Bologna was attacked in the classroom by another student armed with a sword. Oxford regulations attempted to dampen the violence by forbidding students to bring weapons to class. Not uncommonly, town and gown struggles (*gown* refers to the academic robe worn by teachers and students) escalated into bloody riots between townspeople and students (see Historical Voices, "University Students and Violence at Oxford," above).

Despite the violence, universities proved important to medieval civilization, not only for the growth of learning, which, after

all, is the main task of the university, but also by providing a mechanism for training the personnel who served as teachers, administrators, lawyers, and doctors in an increasingly specialized society.

9-3b A Revival of Classical Antiquity

Another aspect of the intellectual revival of the High Middle Ages was a resurgence of interest in the works of classical antiquity—the works of the Greeks and Romans. In the twelfth century, western Europe was introduced to a large number of Greek scientific and philosophical works, including those of Galen and Hippocrates on medicine, Ptolemy on geography and astronomy, and Euclid on mathematics. Above all, the West now had available the complete works of Aristotle. During the second half of the twelfth century, the majority of Aristotle's scientific works were translated into Latin, which served as an international language for both speaking and writing in the West. This great influx of Aristotle's works had an overwhelming impact on the West. He came to be viewed as the "master of those who know," the man who seemed to have understood every field of knowledge.

The recovery of Greek scientific and philosophical works was not a simple process, however. Little knowledge of Greek had survived in Europe. Thus, it was through the Muslim world that the West recovered Aristotle and other Greek works. The translation of Greek works into Arabic had formed but one aspect of a brilliant Muslim civilization. In the twelfth century, these writings were now translated from Arabic into Latin, making them available to the West. Wherever Muslim and Christian cultures met—in the Norman kingdom of Sicily, southern Italy, and above all Spain—the work of translation was carried on by both Arabic and Jewish scholars.

The Islamic world had more to contribute intellectually to the West than translations, however. Scientific work in the ninth and tenth centuries had enabled it to forge far ahead of the Western world, and in the twelfth and thirteenth centuries, Arabic works on physics, mathematics, medicine, and optics became available to the West in Latin translations. Adelard of Bath (1090–1150) was one source of these works. Having traveled throughout the Mediterranean region, he later translated an Arabic version of Euclid's *Elements* (see Chapter 4) into Latin, as well as the mathematical works of al-Khwarizmi (see Chapter 8). Adelard also introduced to Europeans the astrolabe, an Arabic astronomical instrument that proved valuable to sailors.

When Aristotle's works arrived in the West, they were accompanied by commentaries written by outstanding Arabic and Jewish philosophers. One example was Ibn-Rushd (ib-un-RUSHT or ib-un-RUSH-ed), or Averroës (uh-VERR-oh-eez) (1126–1198), who lived in Córdoba and composed a systematic commentary on virtually all of Aristotle's surviving works. The works of Arabic philosophers proved highly influential to Western intellectuals.

The West was also receptive to the works of Jewish scholars living in the Islamic world. Perhaps the best known is Moses ben Maimon, or Maimonides (my-MAH-nuh-deez) (1135–1204), who also lived in Córdoba. He was conversant with Greek and Arabic traditions and interested in the problem of reconciling faith and reason. In his *Guide for the Perplexed*, written in Arabic, Maimonides attempted to harmonize the rational and natural philosophy of Aristotle with the basic truths of Judaism. Although it was attacked by some Orthodox Jews, Western scholars in the thirteenth century paid close attention to it after its translation into Latin.

9-3c The Development of Scholasticism

Christianity's importance in medieval society probably made it inevitable that theology would play a central role in the European intellectual world. Whether in monastic or cathedral schools or the new universities, theology, the formal study of religion, reigned as "queen of the sciences."

Beginning in the eleventh century, the effort to apply reason or logical analysis to the church's basic theological doctrines had a significant impact on the study of theology. The philosophical and theological system of the medieval schools is known as **scholasticism**. A primary preoccupation of scholasticism was the attempt to reconcile faith and reason, to demonstrate that what was accepted on faith was in harmony with what could be learned by reason. The scholastic method came to be the basic instructional mode of the universities. In essence, this method consisted of posing a question, presenting contradictory authorities on that question, and then arriving at conclusions. It was a system that demanded rigorous analytical thought and

had its beginnings in the theological world of the eleventh and twelfth centuries, especially in the work of Abelard.

Abelard Peter Abelard (1079–1142) studied in northern France but scorned his teachers as insignificant and took up the teaching of theology in Paris. Possessed of a colorful personality, Abelard was a very popular teacher who attracted many students. A man with a strong ego, he became known for the zest with which he entered into arguments with fellow students as well as for his affair with his student Heloise. Heloise bore a child by Abelard and secretly married him. But her uncle, who had hired Abelard as a tutor for his niece, sought revenge, as Abelard related in an account of his life titled *History of My Misfortunes*: "One night they took from me a most cruel and shameful vengeance, as I was resting and sleeping in the inner room of my lodging. . . . For they cut off those parts of my body, by which I had committed the deed which sorrowed them."[7]

Above all others, Abelard was responsible for furthering the new scholastic approach to theology. In his most famous work, *Sic et Non* (Yes and No), he listed passages from Scripture and the church fathers that stood in direct contradiction to one another and stressed the need to use logic or dialectical reasoning to reconcile the apparent differences systematically. He summed up his method thus: "By doubting we come to inquiry, through inquiry to the truth."

The Problem of Universals Beginning in the twelfth century, a major controversy—the problem of universals—began to occupy many theologians. The basic issue involved the nature of reality itself: What constitutes what is real? Theologians were divided into two major schools of thought reflecting the earlier traditions of Greek thought, especially the divergent schools of Plato and Aristotle.

Following Plato, the scholastic **realists** took the position that the individual objects that we perceive with our senses, such as trees, are not real but merely manifestations of universal ideas ("treeness") that exist in the mind of God. All knowledge, then, is based on the ideas implanted in human reason by the creator. To the realists, truth can be discovered only by contemplating universals. The **nominalists** were adherents of Aristotle's ideas and believed that only individual objects are real. In their view, universal ideas and concepts were simply names (Latin *nomina*, hence *nominalism*). Truth could be discovered only by examining individual objects.

By the thirteenth century, the scholastics were confronting a new challenge—how to harmonize Christian revelation with the work of Aristotle. The great influx of Aristotle's works into the West in the High Middle Ages threw many theologians into consternation. Aristotle was so highly regarded that he was called "the Philosopher," yet he had arrived at his conclusions by rational thought, not revelation, and some of his doctrines, such as the eternal universe, contradicted the teachings of the church. The most famous attempt to reconcile Aristotle and the doctrines of Christianity was that of Saint Thomas Aquinas (uh-KWY-nuss).

Aquinas Thomas Aquinas (1225–1274) studied theology at Cologne and Paris and taught at both Naples and Paris, and it was at the latter that he worked on his famous *Summa Theologica* (SOO-muh tay-oh-LOG-jee-kuh) (A *Summa of Theology*—a

The Dialectical Method of Thomas Aquinas

 Based on this excerpt, how would you describe the dialectical method of the scholastic philosophers? What do you learn about Aquinas's view of women?

IN HIS MASTERPIECE of scholastic theology, the *Summa Theologica*, Thomas Aquinas attempted to resolve some six hundred theological issues by the dialectical method. This method consisted of posing a question, stating the objections to it, and then replying to the objections. This selection from the *Summa Theologica* focuses on Article 4 of Question 92, "The Production of the Woman."

Thomas Aquinas, *Summa Theologica*
Question 92: The Production of the Woman (in Four Articles)

We must next consider the production of the woman. Under this head there are four points of inquiry: (1) Whether the woman should have been made in that first production of things? (2) Whether the woman should have been made from man? (3) Whether of man's rib? (4) Whether the woman was made immediately by God? . . .

Fourth Article: Whether the Woman Was Formed Immediately by God?

We proceed thus to the Fourth Article:—

Objection 1. It would seem that the woman was not formed immediately by God. For no individual is produced immediately by God from another individual alike in species. But the woman was made from a man who is of the same species. Therefore she was not made immediately by God.

Objection 2. Further, Augustine says that corporeal things are governed by God through the angels. But the woman's body was formed from corporeal matter. Therefore it was made through the ministry of the angels, and not immediately by God.

Objection 3. Further, those things which preexist in creatures as to their causal virtues are produced by the power of some creature, and not immediately by God. But the woman's body was produced in its causal virtues among the first created works, as Augustine says. Therefore it was not produced immediately by God.

On the contrary, Augustine says, in the same work: *God alone, to Whom all nature owes its existence, could form or build up the woman from the man's rib.*

I answer that, as was said above, the natural generation of every species is from some determinate matter. Now the matter whence man is naturally begotten is the human semen of man or woman. Wherefore from any other matter an individual of the human species cannot naturally be generated. Now God alone, the Author of nature, can produce an effect into existence outside the ordinary course of nature. Therefore God alone could produce either a man from the slime of the earth, or a woman from the rib of a man.

Reply Objection 1. This argument is verified when an individual is begotten, by natural generation, from that which is like it in the same species.

Reply Objection 2. As Augustine says, we do not know whether the angels were employed by God in the formation of the woman; but it is certain that, as the body of man was not formed by the angels from the slime of the earth, so neither was the body of the woman formed by them from the man's rib.

Reply Objection 3. As Augustine says, the first creation of things did not demand that woman should be made thus; it made it possible for her to be thus made.

Therefore the body of the woman did indeed preexist in these causal virtues, in the things first created; not as regards active potentiality, but as regards a potentiality passive in relation to the active potentiality of the Creator.

Source: St. Thomas Aquinas, *Summa Theologica*, vol. 1, trans. Fathers of the English Dominican Province (Allen, TX: Christian Classics, 1948).

summa was a compendium of knowledge that attempted to bring together all the received learning of the preceding centuries on a given subject into a single whole). Aquinas's masterpiece was organized according to the dialectical method of the scholastics. Aquinas first posed a question, then cited sources that offered opposing opinions on the question, and finally resolved the issue by arriving at his own conclusions. In this fashion, Aquinas raised and discussed some six hundred articles or issues (see Historical Voices, "The Dialectical Method of Thomas Aquinas," above).

Aquinas's reputation derives from his masterful attempt to reconcile faith and reason. He took it for granted that there were truths derived by reason and truths derived by faith. He was certain, however, that the two truths could not be in conflict with each other:

> The light of faith that is freely infused into us does not destroy the light of natural knowledge [reason] implanted in us naturally. For although the natural light of the human mind is insufficient to show us these things made manifest by faith, it is nevertheless impossible that these things which the divine principle gives us by faith are contrary to these implanted in us by nature [reason]. Indeed, were that the case, one or the other would have to be false, and since both are given to us by God, God would have to be the author of untruth, which is impossible. . . .
>
> It is impossible that those things which are of philosophy can be contrary to those things which are of faith.[8]

The natural mind, unaided by faith, could arrive at truths concerning the physical universe. Without God's help, however, unaided reason alone could not grasp spiritual truths, such as the Trinity (the belief that God, Jesus, and the Holy Spirit are three manifestations of the same unique deity) or the Incarnation (the belief that Jesus in his lifetime was God in human form).

9-3d The Revival of Roman Law

A systematic approach to knowledge was also expressed in the area of law. Of special importance was the rediscovery of the great legal work of Justinian, the *Corpus Iuris Civilis*, known to the medieval West before 1100 only at second hand. Initially, teachers of law, such as Irnerius of Bologna, were content merely to explain the meaning of Roman legal terms to their students. Gradually, they became more sophisticated so that by the mid-twelfth century, doctors of law had developed commentaries and systematic treatises on the legal texts. Italian cities, above all Pavia and Bologna, became prominent centers for the study of Roman law. By the thirteenth century, Italian jurists were systematizing the various professional commentaries on Roman law into a single commentary known as the ordinary gloss. Study of Roman law at the universities came to consist of learning the text of the law along with this gloss.

This revival of Roman law occurred in a world dominated by a body of law quite different from that of the Romans. European law comprised a hodgepodge of Germanic law codes, feudal customs, and urban regulations. The desire to know a more orderly world, already evident in the study of theology, perhaps made it inevitable that Europeans would enthusiastically welcome the more systematic approach of Roman law.

The training of students in Roman law at medieval universities led to further application of its principles as these students became judges, lawyers, scribes, and councillors for the towns and monarchies of western Europe. By the beginning of the thirteenth century, the old system was being replaced by a rational, decision-making process based on the systematic collection and analysis of evidence, a clear indication of the impact of Roman law on the European legal system.

9-3e Literature in the High Middle Ages

Latin was the universal language of medieval civilization. Used in the church and schools, it enabled learned people to communicate anywhere in Europe. The intellectual revival of the High Middle Ages included an outpouring of Latin literature. Much of medieval Latin poetry was religious verse, but there was also a large body of Latin verse dedicated to themes of love and nature. Many of these poems constitute the so-called Goliardic (gohl-YAR-dik) poetry (see Historical Voices, "Goliardic Poetry: The Archpoet," p. 269).

While Latin continued to be used for literary purposes, by the twelfth century much creative literature was being written in the **vernacular** (the local language, such as Spanish, French, English, or German). Throughout the Middle Ages, there had been a popular vernacular literature, especially manifest in the Germanic, Celtic, Old Icelandic, and Slavonic sagas. But a new market for vernacular literature appeared in the twelfth century when educated laypeople at courts and in the new urban society sought fresh avenues of entertainment.

Troubadour Poetry Perhaps the most popular vernacular literature of the twelfth century was *troubadour poetry*, chiefly the product of nobles and knights. This poetry focused on themes of courtly love, the love of a knight for a lady, generally a married noble lady, who inspires him to become a braver knight and a better poet. A good example is found in the laments of Jaufre Rudel (zhoh-FRAY roo-DEL), a crusading noble who cherished a dream lady from afar whom he said he would always love but feared he would never meet:

> Sad and grievous shall I leave,
> If I don't see this distant love.
> But I don't know when I shall ever see her,
> Since our lands are so far apart. . . .
> Yet I shall never enjoy love
> Unless it be this distant love.
> I know of no better love
> Whether near or far away.
> So precious and noble are her virtues
> That I would be a captive in the lands of the Muslims,
> Far away, if she could just see me.[9]

Although it originated in southern France, troubadour poetry also spread to northern France, Italy, and Germany.

The Heroic Epic Another type of vernacular literature was the **chanson de geste** (shahn-SAWNH duh ZHEST), or heroic epic. The earliest and finest example is the *Chanson de Roland (The Song of Roland)*, which appeared around 1100 and was written in a dialect of French, a Romance language derived from Latin. The *chansons de geste* were written for a male-dominated society. The chief events described in these poems, as in *Chanson de Roland*, are battles and political contests. Their world is one of combat in which knights fight courageously for their kings and lords. Women play little or no role in this literary genre.

The Courtly Romance Although *chansons de geste* were still written in the twelfth century, a different kind of long poem, the *courtly romance*, also became popular. It was composed in rhymed couplets and dwelt on romantic subjects: brave knights, virtuous ladies, evil magicians, bewitched palaces, fairies, talking animals, and strange forests. The story of King Arthur, the legendary king of the fifth-century Britons, became a popular subject for the courtly romance. The best versions of the Arthurian legends survive in the works of Chrétien de Troyes (kray-TYEN duh TRWAH), a French writer in the second half of the twelfth century, whose courtly romances were viewed by contemporaries as the works of a master storyteller.

9-3f Romanesque Architecture: "A White Mantle of Churches"

The eleventh and twelfth centuries witnessed an explosion of building, both private and public. The construction of castles and churches absorbed most of the surplus resources of

Goliardic Poetry: The Archpoet

 Q *What groups of people in medieval society would be attracted to Goliardic poetry? Why?*

THE GOLIARDS (GOHL-yurds *or* GOHL-yards) were a group of Latin writers who wrote poems satirizing the hypocrisy of the church while celebrating the joys of wine, women, and song. Although it was once thought that the Goliards were wandering scholars—vagabond students and teachers—many historians today believe that they were established poets living at courts or in monasteries. One of these poets was a German known only as the Archpoet, who was probably from the knightly order and was in service at the court of the archbishop of Cologne. This selection is from his most famous work, *The Confession of Golias.*

The Archpoet, *The Confession of Golias*

Dull and dour sobriety
   Never takes my money,
Give me loose society
   Where the jokes are funny;
Love will bring variety,
   Toil that's sweet as honey.
Pillars of propriety,
   Have you hearts as sunny?
Down the primrose path I
   post Straight to Satan's grotto,
Shunning virtue, doing most
   Things that I ought not to;

Little hope of heaven I boast,
   Charmed by pleasure's otto [fragrance]:
Since the soul is bound to roast
   Save the skin's my motto. . . .
Much too hard it is, I find,
   So to change my essence
As to keep a virgin mind
   In a virgin's presence.
Rigid laws can never bind
   Youth to acquiescence;
Light o' loves must seek their kind,
   Bodies take their pleasance. . . .
Next, I'm called in terms precise
   Monstrous fond of gaming;
Losing all my clothes at dice
   Gains me this worth naming:
While outside I'm cool as ice,
   Inwardly I'm flaming,
Then with daintiest device
   Poems and songs I'm framing. . . .
My intention is to die
   In the tavern drinking;
Wine must be at hand, for I
   Want it when I'm sinking.
Angels when they come shall cry,
   At my frailties winking:
"Spare this drunkard, God, he's high,
   Absolutely stinking!"

Source: By George F. Whicher, from the original by the Archpoet of Cologne, from *The Goliard Poets*, copyright ©1949 by George F. Whicher. Reprinted by permission of New Directions Publishing Corp.

---

medieval society and at the same time reflected its basic preoccupations, warfare and God. The churches were by far the most conspicuous of the public buildings. As a chronicler of the eleventh century commented:

> [After the] year of the millennium, which is now about three years past, people all over the world, but especially in Italy and France, began to rebuild their churches. Although most of them were well built and in little need of alterations, Christian nations were rivaling each other to have the most beautiful edifices. One might say the world was shaking herself, throwing off her old garments, and robing herself with a white mantle of churches. Then nearly all the cathedrals, the monasteries dedicated to different saints, and even the small village chapels were reconstructed more beautifully by the faithful.[10]

Hundreds of new cathedrals and abbey and pilgrimage churches, as well as thousands of parish churches in rural villages, were built in the eleventh and twelfth centuries. This building spree reflected both the revived religious culture and the increased wealth of the period produced by agriculture, trade, and the growth of cities.

The cathedrals of the eleventh and twelfth centuries were built in a truly international style, the **Romanesque** (roh-man-ESK). The construction of churches required the services of professional master builders, whose employment throughout Europe guaranteed an international unity in basic features. Prominent examples of Romanesque churches can be found in Germany, France, and Spain.

Romanesque churches were normally built in the rectangular basilica shape used in the construction of churches in the Late Roman Empire. Romanesque builders made a significant innovation by replacing the earlier flat wooden ceiling with a long, round stone vault called a barrel vault or a cross vault where two barrel vaults intersected (a vault is simply a curved roof made of masonry). The latter was used when a transept

IMAGE 9.10 **Barrel Vaulting.** The eleventh and twelfth centuries witnessed an enormous amount of church construction. Utilizing the basilica shape, master builders replaced flat wooden roofs with long, round stone vaults known as barrel vaults. As this illustration of a Romanesque church in Vienne, France, indicates, the barrel vault limited the size of a church and left little room for windows.

was added to create a church plan in the shape of a cross (see Image 9.10). Although barrel and cross vaults were technically difficult to construct, they were considered aesthetically pleasing and technically proficient and had fine acoustics.

Because stone vaults were extremely heavy, Romanesque churches required massive pillars and walls to hold them up. This left little space for windows, making Romanesque churches notoriously dark on the inside. Their massive walls and pillars gave the churches a sense of solidity and almost the impression of a fortress. Indeed, massive walls and slit windows were also characteristic of the castle architecture of the period.

9-3g The Gothic Cathedral

Begun in the twelfth century and brought to perfection in the thirteenth, the **Gothic** cathedral remains one of the greatest artistic triumphs of the High Middle Ages. Soaring skyward, almost as if to reach heaven, it was a fitting symbol for medieval people's preoccupation with God (see Image 9.11). This religious enthusiasm in building these churches is evident in the words of a French bishop:

> [T]he construction of new churches everywhere heightened people's zeal. And so the bishop, seeing his own church at Auxerre, which was of ancient and crude construction, suffering from neglect and old age, while others all around were lifting their heads in marvelous beauty, determined to provide it with a new building so that it might not be inferior to these others in form and treatment.[11]

Two fundamental innovations of the twelfth century made Gothic cathedrals possible. The combination of ribbed vaults and pointed arches replaced the barrel vault of Romanesque churches and enabled builders to make Gothic churches higher than their Romanesque counterparts. The use of pointed arches and ribbed vaults created an impression of upward movement, a sense of weightless upward thrust that implied the energy of God (see Image 9.12). Another technical innovation, the flying buttress, a heavy arched pier of stone built onto the outside of the walls, made it possible to distribute the weight of the church's vaulted ceilings outward and downward and thereby eliminate the heavy walls used in Romanesque churches to hold the weight of the massive barrel vaults. Thus, Gothic cathedrals could be built with thin walls that were filled with magnificent stained-glass windows, which created a play of light inside that varied with the sun at different times of the day.

Medieval craftspeople of the twelfth and thirteenth centuries perfected the art of stained glass. Small pieces of glass were stained in glowing colors like jewels (see Image 9.13). The colored light that filled Gothic cathedrals was not accidental but was achieved by people inspired by the belief that natural light was a symbol of the divine light of God. Light is invisible but enables people to see; so too is God invisible, but the existence of God allows the world of matter to be. Those impressed by the mystical significance of light were also impressed by the mystical significance of number. The proportions of Gothic cathedrals were based on mathematical ratios that their builders believed were derived from

View of the Cathedral from the Seine, 1163-1345 (photo) (see also 98568)/French School/Notre Dame, Paris, France/Bridgeman Images

IMAGE 9.11 **The Gothic Cathedral.** The Gothic cathedral was one of the great artistic triumphs of the High Middle Ages. Seen here from the Seine River is the cathedral of Notre-Dame in Paris. Begun in 1163, it was not completed until the beginning of the fourteenth century.

trade and industries, as well as from kings and nobles. Master masons who were both architects and engineers designed the cathedrals. They drew up the plans and supervised the work of construction. Stonemasons and other craftspeople were paid a daily wage and provided the skilled labor to build the cathedrals. Indeed, these buildings were the first monumental structures of consequence built by free, salaried labor.

The building of cathedrals often became highly competitive as communities vied with one another to build the highest tower, a rivalry that sometimes ended in disaster. The cathedral of Beauvais in northern France collapsed in 1284 after reaching the height of 157 feet. Gothic cathedrals also depended on a community's faith. After all, it often took two or more generations to complete a cathedral, and the first generation of builders must have begun with the knowledge that they would not live to see the completed project. Most important, a Gothic cathedral symbolized the chief preoccupation of a medieval Christian community, its dedication to a spiritual ideal. As we have observed before, the largest buildings of an era reflect the values of its society. The Gothic cathedral, with its towers soaring toward heaven, gave witness to an age when a spiritual impulse still underlay most of existence.

IMAGE 9.12 **Interior of a Gothic Cathedral.** The use of ribbed vaults and pointed arches gave the Gothic cathedral a feeling of upward movement. Moreover, due to the flying buttress, the cathedral could have thin walls with stained-glass windows that filled the interior with light. The flying buttress was a heavy pier of stone built onto the outside of the walls to bear the brunt of the weight of the church's vaulted ceiling. The flying buttresses are visible at the right in the photograph of the cathedral of Notre-Dame in Image 9.11 on p. 270.

 What are the major differences and similarities between Romanesque and Gothic cathedrals?

the ancient Greek school of Pythagoras and expressed the intrinsic harmony of the world as established by its creator.

The first fully Gothic church was the abbey church of Saint-Denis near Paris, which was built between 1140 and 1150 at the inspiration of Suger, the famous abbot of the monastery from 1122 to 1151. Although the Gothic style was the product of northern France, by the mid-thirteenth century French Gothic architecture had spread to England, Spain, Germany—indeed, to virtually all of Europe. This French Gothic style was seen most brilliantly in cathedrals in Paris (Notre-Dame), Reims, Amiens, and Chartres.

A Gothic cathedral was the work of an entire community. All classes contributed to its construction. Money was raised from wealthy townspeople who had profited from the new

IMAGE 9.13 **Chartres Cathedral: Stained-Glass Window.** The stained glass of Gothic cathedrals is remarkable for the beauty and variety of its colors. Stained-glass windows depicted a remarkable variety of scenes. The windows of Chartres Cathedral, for example, present the saints, views of the everyday activities of ordinary men and women, and, as in this panel, scenes from the life of Jesus.

 What was the purpose of the stained-glass windows in Gothic cathedrals?

The new European civilization that had emerged in the ninth and tenth centuries began to come into its own in the eleventh and twelfth centuries, as Europeans established new patterns that reached their high point in the thirteenth century. The High Middle Ages (1000–1300) was a period of recovery and growth for Western civilization, characterized by a greater sense of security and a burst of energy and enthusiasm. Climatic improvements that produced better growing conditions, an expansion of cultivated land, and technological and agricultural changes combined to enable Europe's food supply to increase significantly after 1000. This increase in agricultural production helped sustain a dramatic rise in population that was physically apparent in the expansion of towns and cities.

The development of trade and the rise of cities added a dynamic new element to the civilization of the High Middle Ages. Trading activities flourished first in northern Italy and Flanders and then spread outward from these centers. In the late tenth and eleventh centuries, this renewal of commercial life led to a revival of cities. Old Roman cities came back to life, and new towns arose at major crossroads or natural harbors favorable to trading activities. By the twelfth and thirteenth centuries, both the urban centers and the urban population of Europe were experiencing a dramatic expansion. The revival of trade, the expansion of towns and cities, and the development of a money economy did not mean the end of a predominantly rural European society, but they did open the door to new ways to make a living and new opportunities for people to expand and enrich their lives. Eventually, they created the foundations for the development of a predominantly urban industrial society.

The High Middle Ages also gave birth to an intellectual and artistic revival. The intellectual revival led to a rediscovery of important aspects of the classical heritage, including the works of Aristotle, who came to be viewed as the "master of those who know." New centers of learning emerged in the universities, where reason was used to systematize the study of theology and law. In addition to Latin literature, a vernacular literature emerged that appealed both to knights and to townspeople.

An artistic revival was especially evident in architecture, where Romanesque cathedrals, with their barrel vaults and massive pillars and walls with little space for windows gave way in the twelfth century to Gothic cathedrals. Ribbed vaults and pointed arches made it possible to build higher cathedrals, and flying buttresses, by redistributing the weight, allowed for thin walls and stained-glass windows. A cathedral's construction took decades, but it was a community's act of faith in an age when a spiritual ideal still underlay most of existence.

CHAPTER TIMELINE

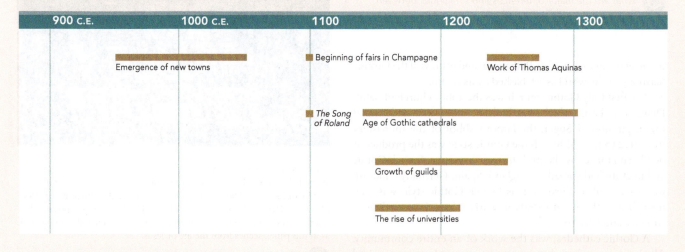

900 C.E.	1000 C.E.	1100	1200	1300

Emergence of new towns

Beginning of fairs in Champagne

Work of Thomas Aquinas

The Song of Roland

Age of Gothic cathedrals

Growth of guilds

The rise of universities

CHAPTER REVIEW

Upon Reflection

Q What is the relationship between economic and social changes and intellectual and artistic developments in the High Middle Ages?

Q How did the revival of trade and cities affect the economy and society of Europe in the High Middle Ages?

Q What were the causes and the consequences of the development of medieval universities?

Q In what ways did the artistic and literary culture of the High Middle Ages reflect the religious preoccupations and problems of medieval society?

Key Terms

aristocracy (p. 250)
chivalry (p. 253)
capitalism (p. 257)
bourgeoisie (p. 258)
commune (p. 258)
guilds (p. 262)
scholasticism (p. 266)

realists (p. 266)
nominalists (p. 266)
vernacular (p. 268)
chanson de geste (p. 268)
Romanesque (p. 269)
Gothic (p. 270)

Full definitions also appear in the Glossary at the end of the book.

Suggestions for Further Reading

General Histories For a good introduction to this period, see **W. C. Jordan,** *Europe in the High Middle Ages* (New York, 2003).

The New Agriculture On peasant life, see **R. Fossier,** *The Axe and the Oath: Ordinary Life in the Middle Ages* (Princeton, N.J., 2010). Technological changes are discussed in **J. Langdon,** *Horses, Oxen, and Technological Innovation* (New York, 2002).

The Aristocracy On the function and activities of the nobility in the High Middle Ages, see **S. Reynolds,** *Kingdoms and Communities in Western Europe, 900–1300,* 2nd ed. (Oxford, 1997). On tournaments, see **D. Crouch,** *Tournament* (London, 2005).

Women in the High Middle Ages On women, see **J. Ward,** *Women in Medieval Europe, 1200–1500* (London, 2003). For an excellent reference work, see **M. C. Schaus,** *Women and Gender in Medieval Europe: An Encyclopedia* (London, 2006).

Revival of Trade and Cities For a general introduction, see **S. Epstein,** *An Economic and Social History of Medieval Europe* (Cambridge, 2009). On the revival of trade, see **R. S. Lopez,** *The*

Commercial Revolution of the Middle Ages, 950–1350 (New York, 2005). Urban history is covered in **D. Nicholas,** *The Growth of the Medieval City: From Late Antiquity to the Early Fourteenth Century* (New York, 1997). On daily life, see **C. Frugoi,** *A Day in a Medieval City,* trans. **W. McCuaig** (Chicago, 2006). On women in the cities, see **M. P. P. Cosman,** *Women at Work in Medieval Europe* (New York, 2001).

Intellectual Life A basic work on medieval intellectual life is **M. L. Colish,** *Medieval Foundations of the Western Intellectual Tradition, 400–1400* (New Haven, Conn., 1997). The development of universities is covered in **S. Ferruolo,** *The Origin of the University* (Stanford, Calif., 1985). Various aspects of the intellectual and literary developments of the High Middle Ages are examined in **M. Haren,** *Medieval Thought,* 2nd ed. (London, 1994).

Art and Architecture A good introduction to Romanesque style is **A. Petzold,** *Romanesque Art,* rev. ed. (New York, 2003). On the Gothic movement, see **M. Camille,** *Gothic Art: Glorious Visions,* rev. ed. (New York, 2003).

Notes

1. Quoted in William Fitz Stephen, "A Description of London" in *Norman London* (New York, 1990), pp. 48, 50, 52, 54, 57–58.
2. Quoted in J. Gies and F. Gies, *Life in a Medieval Castle* (New York, 1974), p. 175.
3. Quoted in R. Delort, *Life in the Middle Ages,* trans. R. Allen (New York, 1972), p. 218.
4. Quoted in J. Gimpel, *The Medieval Machine* (Harmondsworth, England, 1976), p. 92.
5. Quoted in C. H. Haskins, *The Rise of Universities* (Ithaca, N.Y., 1957), pp. 77–78.
6. Ibid., pp. 79–80.
7. Quoted in D. Herlihy, *Medieval Culture and Society* (New York, 1968), p. 204.

8. Quoted in J. H. Mundy, *Europe in the High Middle Ages, 1150–1309* (New York, 1973), pp. 474–475.

9. Author's translation of the third and fourth verses of Jaufre Rudel's poem, "Languan li jorn son lonc e may," ("When the days are long in May").

10. Quoted in J. W. Baldwin, *The Scholastic Culture of the Middle Ages, 1000–1300* (Lexington, Mass., 1971), p. 15.

11. Quoted in K. Slocum, *Medieval Civilization* (Belmont, Calif., 2005), p. 386.

 MindTap *Tips*   MindTap can help you connect your knowledge of history to current events! Check out the Analyzing Recent World Events and Global Issues activity for a look at the contemporary world.

CHAPTER 10

The Rise of Kingdoms and the Growth of Church Power

IMAGE 10.1 **A Medieval Abbot and His Monks**

CHAPTER OUTLINE AND FOCUS QUESTIONS

10-1 The Emergence and Growth of European Kingdoms, 1000–1300

Q What steps did the rulers of England and France take during the High Middle Ages to reverse the decentralizing tendencies of fief-holding? What were the major political and religious developments in Spain, the Holy Roman Empire, and northern and eastern Europe during the High Middle Ages? What role did the Mongols play in Europe?

10-2 The Recovery and Reform of the Catholic Church

Q What was the importance of the Cluniac reform movement? What was at issue in the Investiture Controversy, and what effect did it have on the church and on Germany? What did the reform of the papacy accomplish?

10-3 Christianity and Medieval Civilization

Q What were the characteristics of the papal monarchy and the new religious orders of the High Middle Ages, and what role did women play in the religious life of the period? What was the church's attitude toward heretics and Jews during the High Middle Ages?

10-4 The Crusades

Q What were the reasons for the Crusades, and who or what benefited the most from the experience of the Crusades?

CONNECTIONS TO TODAY

What, if any, is the relationship between the Crusades in the Middle Ages and contemporary events in the Middle East, including the Persian Gulf War and the activities of al-Qaeda and the Islamic State of Iraq and the Levant (ISIL)?

THE RECOVERY AND GROWTH of European civilization in the High Middle Ages also affected the state and the church. Both lords and vassals and the Catholic Church recovered from the invasions and internal dissension of the early Middle Ages. Although lords and vassals seemed forever mired in endless petty conflicts, some medieval kings began to exert a centralizing authority and inaugurated the process of developing new kinds of monarchical states. By the thirteenth century, European monarchs were solidifying their governmental institutions in pursuit of greater power.

The recovery of the Catholic Church produced a reform movement that led to exalted claims of papal authority. This increase in church power, coupled with the rise of monarchical states, made it almost inevitable that there would be conflicts between church and state. At the same time, vigorous papal leadership combined with new dimensions of religious life to make the Catholic Church a forceful presence in every area of life. The role of the church in the new European civilization was quite evident in the career of a man named Samson, who became abbot, or head, of the great English abbey of Bury St. Edmunds in 1182. According to Jocelyn of Brakelond, a monk who assisted him, Abbot Samson was a devout man who wore

275

undergarments of horsehair and a horsehair shirt. He loved virtue and hated liars, drunkards, and "talkative folk." His primary concern was the spiritual well-being of his monastery, but he spent much of his time working on problems in the world beyond the abbey walls. The monastery had fallen into debt under his predecessors, and Abbot Samson toiled tirelessly to recoup the abbey's fortunes by carefully supervising its manors. He also rounded up murderers to stand trial in St. Edmunds and provided knights for the king's army. But his actions were not always tolerant or beneficial. He was instrumental in driving the Jews from the town and was not above improving the abbey's possessions at the expense of his neighbors. By building up the bank of a fish-pond for the service of a new mill, he caused his neighbors to lose their gardens and orchards. The abbot's worldly cares weighed heavily on him, but he had little choice if his abbey were to flourish and fulfill its spiritual and secular functions. But he did have regrets and confided to Jocelyn that if he could do it over, he would never "have become a monk or an abbot."

10-1 The Emergence and Growth of European Kingdoms, 1000–1300

 FOCUS QUESTIONS: What steps did the rulers of England and France take during the High Middle Ages to reverse the decentralizing tendencies of fief-holding? What were the major political and religious developments in Spain, the Holy Roman Empire, and northern and eastern Europe during the High Middle Ages? What role did the Mongols play in Europe?

The domination of society by the nobility reached its apex in the High Middle Ages. During this time, however, kings began the process of extending their power in more effective ways. Out of this growth in the monarchies would eventually come the European states that dominated much of later European history.

In theory, kings were regarded as the heads of their kingdoms and were expected to lead their vassals and subjects into battle. The king's power, however, was strictly limited. As we saw in Chapter 8, he had to honor the rights and privileges of his vassals, and if he failed to observe his vassals' rights, they could and did rebel. Weak kings were overthrown or, like the later Carolingians, replaced by another ruling dynasty.

Nevertheless, kings did possess some sources of power that other lords did not. Kings were anointed by holy oil in ceremonies reminiscent of Old Testament precedents; thus, their positions seemed sanctioned by divine favor. War and marriage alliances enabled them to increase their power, and their conquests enabled them to reward their followers with grants of land and bind powerful nobles to them. In the High Middle

Ages, kings found ways to strengthen governmental institutions and consequently to extend their powers. The revival of commerce, the growth of cities, and the emergence of a money economy eventually enabled monarchs to hire soldiers and officials and to rely less on their vassals.

10-1a England in the High Middle Ages

At the beginning of the eleventh century, Anglo-Saxon England had fallen subject to Scandinavian control after a successful invasion by the Danes in 1016. King Canute (kuh-NOOT) (r. 1016–1035) continued English institutions and laws and even supported the Catholic Church. His dynastic line proved unable to maintain itself, however, and in 1042, the Anglo-Saxon line of kings was restored in the person of Edward the Confessor (r. 1042–1066). After his death, the kingship was taken by Harold Godwinson, who belonged to one of England's greatest noble families.

A cousin of Edward the Confessor, William of Normandy, however, laid claim to the throne of England. William crossed the English Channel with his forces in late September. The Anglo-Saxon forces of Harold Godwinson were in northern England, where they had defeated an invading Viking army, and had to return quickly to the south to face the new invaders. The Anglo-Saxon and Norman forces met on October 14, 1066, at Hastings, in one of the most famous battles in English history. Both forces numbered about 7,000 men. The Anglo-Saxon army, consisting mostly of foot soldiers armed with shields, swords, and battle-axes, created a shield wall at the top of a hill. Opposing them were the Norman forces of archers and the heavily armed knights that were a product of the fief-holding order that we examined in Chapter 8. Exhausted from their march from the north, the Anglo-Saxon forces fought bravely but were gradually worn down by the charges of the Norman knights (see Image 10.2). The battle lasted almost the entire day, but after the death of Harold Godwinson on the battlefield, the Anglo-Saxon forces fled. William then began his advance to London, where he was crowned king of England at Christmastime.

William of Normandy After his conquest, William (r. 1066–1087) treated all of England as a royal possession. Based on the Domesday (DOOMZ-day) Book, which William commissioned in 1086 by sending out royal officials to ascertain who owned or held land in tenancy, modern historians have estimated that the Norman royal family took possession of about one-fifth of the land in England as the royal demesne (domain). The remaining English land was held by nobles or the church as fiefs from the king; each of these vassals was in turn responsible for supplying a quota of knights for the royal army. The great landed nobles were allowed to divide their lands among their subvassals as they wished. In 1086, however, by the Oath of Salisbury Plain, William required all subvassals to swear loyalty to him as their king and liege lord. Henceforth, all subvassals owed their primary loyalty to the king rather than to their immediate lords.

Thus, the Norman conquest of England had brought a dramatic change. In Anglo-Saxon England, the king had only limited lands while great families controlled large stretches of

IMAGE 10.2a

IMAGE 10.2b

DEA/M. SEEMULLER/Getty Images

IMAGE 10.2 **Norman Conquest of England.** The Bayeux (bah-YUH) tapestry, a wall hanging of woolen embroidery on a linen backing, was made by English needlewomen before 1082 for Bayeux Cathedral. It depicts scenes from the Norman invasion of England. The first segment (Image 10.2a) shows the Norman fleet beginning its journey to England. The second segment (Image 10.2b) shows the Norman cavalry charging the shield wall of the Saxon infantry during the Battle of Hastings.

Q *What can you learn about medieval warfare from these images?*

Duke William Exhorts his Troops to Prepare Themselves Wisely Like Men for the Battle Against the English Army, detail from the Bayeux Tapestry, before 1082 (wool embroidery on linen), French School, (11th century)/Musée de la Tapisserie, Bayeux, France/With special authorisation of the city of Bayeux/ Bridgeman Images

territory and acted rather independently of the king. In contrast, the Normans established a hierarchy of nobles holding land as fiefs from the king. William of Normandy had created a strong, centralized monarchy. Gradually, a process of fusion between the victorious Normans and the defeated Anglo-Saxons created a new England. Although the Norman ruling class spoke French, Anglo-Saxon and French gradually merged into a new English language as the Norman-French intermarried with the Anglo-Saxon nobility.

William maintained the Anglo-Saxon administrative system in which counties (shires) were divided into hundreds (groups of villages). Within each shire, the sheriff was the chief royal officer responsible for leading the military forces of the county, collecting royal tolls, and presiding over the county court. William retained the office but replaced the Anglo-Saxon sheriffs with Normans. William also more fully developed the system of taxation and royal courts begun by the Anglo-Saxon and Danish kings of the tenth and eleventh centuries.

The Norman conquest of England had repercussions in France as well. Because the new king of England was still the duke of Normandy, he was both a king (of England) and at the same time a vassal to a king (of France), but a vassal who was now far more powerful than his lord. This connection with France kept England heavily involved in Continental affairs throughout the High Middle Ages.

A New Dynasty In the twelfth century, the power of the English monarchy increased substantially during the reign of Henry II (r. 1154–1189), the founder of the new Plantagenet (plan-TAJ-uh-net) dynasty (see Movies & History, *The Lion in Winter*, p. 278). Although Henry had considerable trouble controlling his wife, Eleanor of Aquitaine (see Chapter 9), he was particularly successful in developing administrative and legal institutions that strengthened the royal government. He continued the development of the **exchequer** (EKS-chek-ur), or permanent royal treasury. Royal officials, known as "barons of the exchequer," received taxes collected by the sheriffs while seated around a table covered by a checkered cloth that served as a counting device. (*Exchequer* is derived from the French word for chessboard.) The barons gave receipts to the sheriffs, while clerks recorded the accounts on sheets of parchment that were then rolled up. These so-called pipe rolls have been an important source of economic and social information for historians.

MOVIES & HISTORY
The Lion in Winter (1968)

Watch *The Lion in Winter*, a film based on a play by James Goldman. The action takes place in a castle in Chinon, France, in 1183. The powerful but world-weary King Henry II, ruler of England and a number of French lands (the "Angevin Empire"), wants to establish his legacy and plans a Christmas gathering to decide which of his sons should succeed him. In contemporary terms, Henry and Eleanor are a dysfunctional married couple, and their family is acutely dysfunctional.

 In what ways is this film an accurate portrayal of a royal family's Christmas gathering? How realistic are the depictions of Henry II and his wife Eleanor?

Perhaps even more significant than Henry's financial reforms were his efforts to strengthen the royal courts. Henry expanded the number of criminal cases tried in the king's courts and also devised ways of taking property cases from local courts to the royal courts. Henry's goals were clear: expanding the jurisdiction of the royal courts extended the king's power and, of course, brought revenues into his coffers. Moreover, because the royal courts were now found throughout England, a body of **common law** (law that was common to the whole kingdom) began to replace the local law codes, which varied from place to place.

Henry was less successful at imposing royal control over the church. The king claimed the right to punish clergymen in the royal courts, but Thomas à Becket, archbishop of Canterbury and thus the highest-ranking English cleric, claimed that only church courts could try clerics. Attempts at compromise failed, and in 1170 the angry king publicly expressed the desire to be rid of Becket: "Who will free me of this priest?" he screamed. Four knights took the challenge, went to Canterbury, and murdered the archbishop in the cathedral. Faced with public outrage, Henry was forced to allow the right of appeal from English church courts to the papal court.

King John and Magna Carta Many English nobles came to resent the ongoing growth of royal power and rose in rebellion during the reign of Henry's son, King John (r. 1199–1216). Following in his father's footsteps, John continued the effort to strengthen royal power and proved particularly ingenious at finding novel ways to levy taxes. The barons of England came to resent him deeply. By 1205, John had lost the duchy of Normandy, Maine, Anjou, and Touraine to the French king, Philip Augustus; when John's attempt to reconquer the duchy ended in a devastating defeat, many of the English barons rose in rebellion. At Runnymede (RUHN-ee-meed) in 1215, John was forced to assent to Magna Carta, the "great charter" of feudal liberties. Much of Magna Carta was aimed at limiting government practices that affected the relations between the king and his vassals on the one hand and between the king and the church on the other (see Historical Voices, "Magna Carta," p. 279).

Despite later interpretations and efforts to broaden its principles, Magna Carta remains, above all, a feudal document. Feudal custom had always recognized that the relationship between king and vassals was based on mutual rights and obligations. Magna Carta gave written recognition to that fact and was used in subsequent years to underscore the concept that the monarch should be limited rather than absolute.

Edward I and the Emergence of Parliament In the late thirteenth century, a very talented and powerful monarch ascended the throne in the person of Edward I (r. 1272–1307). He began the process of uniting all of the British Isles into a single kingdom. Although Wales was eventually conquered and pacified, his attempt to subdue Scotland failed. Edward managed merely to begin a lengthy conflict between England and Scotland that lasted for centuries.

Edward was successful in reestablishing monarchical rights after a period of baronial control. During his reign, the role of the English Parliament, an institution of great importance in the development of representative government, began to be defined.

Originally, the word *parliament* was applied to meetings of the king's Great Council in which the greater barons and chief prelates of the church met with the king's judges and principal advisers to deal with judicial affairs. But in need of money in 1295, Edward I invited two knights from every county and two residents (known as burgesses) from each city and town to meet with the Great Council to consent to new taxes. This was the first Parliament.

The English Parliament, then, came to be composed of two knights from every county and two burgesses from every town or city, as well as the barons and ecclesiastical lords. Eventually, the barons and church lords formed the House of Lords; the knights and burgesses, the House of Commons. The Parliaments of Edward I granted taxes, discussed politics, passed laws, and handled judicial business. Although not yet the important body it would eventually become, the English Parliament had clearly emerged as an institution by the end of the thirteenth century. The law of the realm was beginning to be determined not by the king alone but by the king in consultation with representatives of various groups that constituted the community. By the beginning of the fourteenth century, England had begun to develop a unique system of national monarchy.

10-1b The Growth of the French Kingdom

The Capetian dynasty of French kings had emerged at the end of the tenth century. Although they bore the title of king, the Capetians had little real power. They controlled as the royal domain (the lands of the king) only the lands around Paris known as the Île-de-France (eel-duh-FRAHNS). As kings of France, the Capetians were formally the overlords of the great lords of France, such as the dukes of Normandy, Brittany, Burgundy, and Aquitaine. In reality, however, many of the dukes

Magna Carta

 What are the major principles of Magna Carta as seen in this excerpt? Why has Magna Carta been considered such an important historical document?

AFTER THE DISMAL DEFEAT of King John at the hands of the French king, some of the English barons rebelled against their king. At Runnymede in 1215, King John agreed to seal Magna Carta, the "great charter" of liberties regulating the relationship between the king and his vassals. Magna Carta was, above all, a feudal document but was used in later years to strengthen the concept of limited monarchy.

Magna Carta

John, by the Grace of God, king of England, lord of Ireland, duke of Normandy and Aquitaine, count of Anjou, to the archbishops, bishops, abbots, earls, barons, justiciars, foresters, sheriffs, reeves, servants, and all bailiffs and his faithful people greeting.

1. In the first place we have granted to God, and by this our present charter confirmed, for us and our heirs forever, that the English church shall be free, and shall hold its rights entire and its liberties uninjured. . . . We have granted moreover to all free men of our kingdom for us and our heirs forever all the liberties written below, to be had and holden by themselves and their heirs from us and our heirs.

2. If any of our earls or barons, or others holding from us in chief by military service shall have died, and when he had died his heir shall be of full age and owe relief, he shall have his inheritance by the ancient relief; that is to say, the heir or heirs of an earl for the whole barony of an earl a hundred pounds; the heir or heirs of a baron for a whole barony a hundred pounds; the heir or heirs of a knight, for a whole knight's fee, a hundred shillings at most; and who owes less let him give less according to the ancient custom of fiefs.

3. If moreover the heir of any one of such shall be under age, and shall be in wardship, when he comes of age he shall have his inheritance without relief and without a fine. . . .

12. No scutage or aid shall be imposed in our kingdom except by the common council of our kingdom, except for the ransoming of our body, for the making of our oldest son a knight, and for once marrying our oldest daughter, and for these purposes it shall be only a reasonable aid. . . .

13. And the city of London shall have all its ancient liberties and free customs, as well by land as by water. Moreover, we will and grant that all other cities and boroughs and villages and ports shall have all their liberties and free customs.

14. And for holding a common council of the kingdom concerning the assessment of an aid otherwise than in the three cases mentioned above, or concerning the assessment of a scutage we shall cause to be summoned the archbishops, bishops, abbots, earls, and greater barons by our letters under seal; and besides we shall cause to be summoned generally, by our sheriffs and bailiffs, all those who hold from us in chief, for a certain day, that is at the end of forty days at least, and for a certain place; and in all the letters of that summons, we will express the cause of the summons, and when the summons has thus been given, the business shall proceed on the appointed day, on the advice of those who shall be present, even if not all of those who were summoned have come. . . .

39. No free man shall be taken or imprisoned or dispossessed, or outlawed, or banished, or in any way destroyed, nor will we go upon him, nor send upon him, except by the legal judgment of his peers or by the law of the land. . . .

60. Moreover, all those customs and franchises mentioned above in which we have conceded in our kingdom, and which are to be fulfilled, as far as pertains to us, in respect to our men; all men of our kingdom, as well as clergy as laymen, shall observe as far as pertains to them, in respect to their men.

Source: Magna Carta, University of Pennsylvania Translation and Reprints, trans. E. P. Cheyney (Philadelphia: University of Pennsylvania Press, 1897), pp. 6–16.

---

were considerably more powerful than the Capetian kings. It would take the Capetian dynasty hundreds of years to create a truly centralized monarchical authority in France.

The Conquests of Philip II The reign of King Philip II Augustus (r. 1180–1223) was an important turning point. He perceived that the power of the French monarch would never be extended until the Plantagenets' power was defeated. After all, Henry II and his sons were not only kings of England but also rulers of the French territories of Normandy, Maine, Anjou, and Aquitaine. Accordingly, Philip II waged war against

King John of England and was successful in wresting control of Normandy, Maine, Anjou, and Touraine from the English king (see Map 10.1). Through these conquests, Philip II quadrupled the income of the French monarchy and greatly enlarged its power. To administer justice and collect royal revenues in his new territories, Philip appointed new royal officials, thus inaugurating a French royal bureaucracy.

The Saintly Louis IX Capetian rulers after Philip II continued to add lands to the royal domain. Although Philip had used military force, other kings used both purchase and marriage

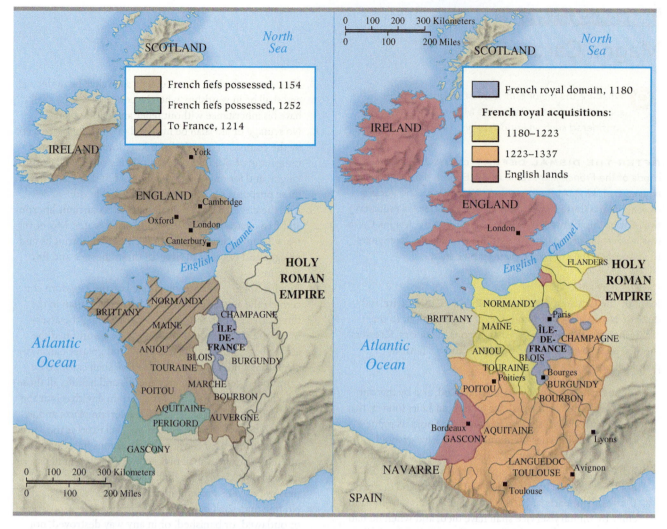

MAP 10.1 **England and France (1154–1337): (left) England and Its French Holdings; (right) Growth of the French State.** King Philip II Augustus of France greatly expanded the power of the Capetian royal family through his victories over the Plantagenet monarchy of England, which enabled Philip to gain control over much of north-central France.

 How could the presence of the English Channel have made it more difficult for the English kings to rule their French possessions?

to achieve the same end. Much of the thirteenth century was dominated by Louis IX (r. 1226–1270), one of the most celebrated of the medieval French kings. A deeply religious man, he was later canonized as a saint by the church, an unusual action regardless of the century. Louis was known for his attempts to bring justice to his people and ensure their rights. He sent out royal agents to check on the activities of royal officials after hearing complaints that they were abusing their power. Sharing in the religious sentiments of his age, Louis played a major role in two of the later Crusades (see "10-4 The Crusades," later in this chapter). Both were failures, and he met his death during an invasion of North Africa.

Philip IV and the Estates-General One of Louis's successors, Philip IV the Fair (r. 1285–1314), was particularly effective in strengthening the French monarchy. The machinery of government became even more specialized. French kings

going back to the early Capetians had possessed a household staff for running their affairs. In effect, the division and enlargement of this household staff produced the three major branches of royal administration: a council for advice; a chamber of accounts for finances; and the *Parlement* (par-luh-MAHNH), or royal court (the French *Parlement* was not the same as the English Parliament). By the beginning of the fourteenth century, the Capetians had established an efficient royal bureaucracy.

Philip IV also brought a French parliament into being by summoning representatives of the three estates, or classes—the clergy (First Estate), the nobles (Second Estate), and the townspeople (Third Estate)—to meet with him. They did so in 1302, inaugurating the Estates-General, the first French parliament. The Estates-General came to function as an instrument to bolster the king's power because he could ask representatives of the major French social classes to change the laws or grant new taxes. By the end of the thirteenth century, France was the largest, wealthiest, and best-governed monarchial state in Europe.

10-1c Christian Reconquest: The Spanish Kingdoms

Much of Spain had been part of the Islamic world since the eighth century. Muslim Spain had flourished in the early Middle Ages. Córdoba became a major urban center with a population exceeding 300,000 people. Agriculture prospered, and Spain became known for excellent leather, wool, silk, and paper. Beginning in the tenth century, however, the most noticeable feature of Spanish history was the weakening of Muslim power and the beginning of a Christian reconquest that lasted until the final expulsion of the Muslims at the end of the fifteenth century. The *Reconquista* (ray-con-KEES-tuh), as the Spaniards called it, became over a period of time a sacred mission to many of the Christian rulers and inhabitants of the peninsula.

The Reconquest By the eleventh century, a number of small Christian kingdoms in northern Spain—Leon, Castile (ka-STEEL), Navarre, Aragon, and Catalonia—were ready to take the offensive against the Muslims. Rodrigo Diaz de Vivar, known as El Cid ("The Master"), was the most famous military adventurer of the time. Unlike the Christian warriors of France, El Cid (ell SID or ell THEED) fought under either Christian or Muslim rulers. He carved out his own kingdom of Valencia in 1094 but failed to create a dynasty when it was reconquered by the Muslims after his death.

By the end of the twelfth century, the Christian reconquest of Spain had slowed considerably. The northern half had been consolidated into the Christian kingdoms of Castile, Navarre, Aragon, and Portugal, which had emerged by 1179 as a separate kingdom (see Map 10.2). The southern half of Spain remained under the control of the Muslims.

In the thirteenth century, Christian rulers again took the offensive against the Muslims. Aragon and Castile had become the two strongest Spanish kingdoms, and Portugal had reached its modern boundaries. All three states made significant conquests of Muslim territory. Castile subdued most of Andalusia in the south, down to the Atlantic and the Mediterranean; at the same time, Aragon conquered Valencia. The crucial battle occurred in 1212 at Las Navas de Tolosa (lahss nah-vahss day toh-LOH-suh). Alfonso VIII of Castile (r. 1158–1214) had amassed an army of 60,000 men and crushed the Muslim forces, leading to Christian victories over the next forty years. By the mid-thirteenth century, the Muslims held only the kingdom of Granada, along the southeastern edge of the Iberian peninsula.

As the Christian armies moved down the peninsula, the rulers followed a policy known as *repartimiento* (ray-par-tuh-my-EN-toh). They distributed houses, land, and property in the countryside to individuals who had made the conquests and new Christian colonists. The former—consisting of nobles, important churchmen, high-ranking soldiers, and royal officials—often received the best lands. The colonists, some of them ordinary foot soldiers, also received land. Muslims who were not expelled or killed and chose to stay under Christian rule were known as *mudejares* (moo-theh-KHAH-rayss); most of them continued to work in small industrial enterprises or as farmers.

To encourage other settlers to move into the newly conquered regions, Spanish kings issued written privileges that guaranteed rule in accordance with the law for most of the communities in their kingdoms. These privileges, or *fueros* (FWYA-rohss), stipulated the punishments for crimes committed within community boundaries and the means for resolving civil disputes. They also established a procedure for acquiring citizenship in the community, rules for service in the local militia, and laws protecting the rights of women and children living in the towns. By the thirteenth century, kings were increasingly required to swear that they would respect these community customs before they were confirmed in office by assemblies of their leading citizens.

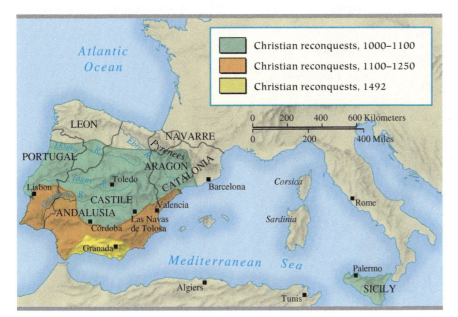

MAP 10.2 **Christian Reconquests in the Western Mediterranean.** Muslims seized most of Spain in the eighth century, near the end of the period of rapid Islamic expansion. In the eleventh century, small Christian kingdoms in the north began the *Reconquista*, finally conquering the last Moors near the end of the fifteenth century.

Q *How do you explain the roughly north-to-south conquest of the Muslim lands in Spain?*

The Spanish kingdoms followed no consistent policy in the treatment of the conquered Muslim population. Muslim farmers continued to work the land but were forced to pay very high rents in Aragon. In Castile, King Alfonso X (r. 1252–1284), who called himself the "King of Three Religions," encouraged the continued development of a cosmopolitan culture shared by Christians, Jews, and Muslims.

10-1d The Lands of the Holy Roman Empire: Germany and Italy

The Saxon kings of the tenth century had strengthened their hold over the German kingdom and revived the empire of Charlemagne. A new dynasty, known as the Salian kings, began in 1024 with the election of Conrad II (r. 1024–1039) of Franconia (see Map 10.3). Both Conrad and his successors, Henry III (r. 1039–1056) and Henry IV (r. 1056–1106), managed to create a strong German monarchy and a powerful empire by leading armies into Italy. The great lords of Germany took advantage of the early death of Henry III and the minority of Henry IV to extend their own power at the expense of the latter. The elective nature of the German monarchy posed a problem for the German kings. Although some dynasties were strong enough for their members to be elected regularly, the great lords who were the electors did at times deliberately choose otherwise. It was to their advantage to select a weak king.

To compensate for their weaknesses, German kings came to rely on their ability to control the church and select bishops and abbots whom they could then use as royal administrators. But the struggle between church and state during the reign of Henry IV weakened the king's ability to use church officials in this way (see "The Investiture Controversy," in Section 10-2c).

Involvement in Italy The German kings also tried to bolster their power by using their position as emperors to exploit the resources of Italy. Italy seemed a likely area for intervention because it had no central political authority. While important nobles struggled to dominate northern Italy, central Italy remained under the control of the Papal States. In southern Italy, the Lombard dukes, Muslims, and Byzantines seemed to be in constant conflict.

In the latter half of the eleventh century, a group of Norman adventurers led by Robert Guiscard (gees-KAR) ("the cunning") conquered much of southern Italy. Robert's brother Roger subdued Muslim Sicily in 1091 after a thirty-year struggle. In 1130, Roger II, the son of Roger of Sicily, was crowned king of Sicily. By the end of the twelfth century, the Norman kingdom was one of the most powerful in Europe as well as one of the most fascinating. A melting pot of Christian, Jewish, and Muslim culture, the state issued its official documents in Latin, Greek, and Arabic.

The Norman kingdom in southern Italy was beyond any claims of the German kings, but the wealthy cities of northern Italy, which by the twelfth century had become virtually independent after overthrowing the rule of their bishops, were

MAP 10.3 The Lands of the Holy Roman Empire in the Twelfth Century.
The Hohenstaufen rulers Frederick I and Frederick II sought to expand the Holy Roman Empire to include all of Italy. Frederick II had only fleeting success: after his death, several independent city-states arose in northern Italy, while in Germany, the nobles had virtually free rein within their domains.

Q *Why did the territorial conquests of the Holy Roman Emperors cause alarm in the papacy?*

a tempting prize to the German kings, who never entirely gave up their dreams of a restored empire. No German dynasty proved more susceptible to the allure of this dream than the Hohenstaufens (hoh-en-SHTOW-fenz).

Frederick I Both Frederick I (r. 1152–1190) and Frederick II (r. 1212–1250) tried to create a foundation for a new kind of empire. Frederick I, known as Barbarossa (bar-buh-ROH-suh) (Redbeard) to the Italians, was a powerful lord from the house of Hohenstaufen when he was elected king. Previous German kings had focused on building a strong German kingdom, to which Italy might be added as an appendage. Frederick I, however, planned to get his chief revenues from northern Italy as the center of a "holy empire," as he called it—the Holy Roman Empire. But his attempt to conquer northern Italy ran into severe difficulties. The pope opposed him, fearful that the emperor wanted to incorporate Rome and the Papal States into his empire. The cities of northern Italy, which had become used to their freedom, were also not willing to be Frederick's subjects. An alliance of these northern Italian cities, with the support of the papacy, defeated the forces of the Emperor Frederick at Legnano (leh-NYAH-noh) in 1176.

Later Frederick returned to Italy and arranged a settlement with the northern Italian cities by which they retained their independence in return for an annual payment to the emperor. Frederick now had the financial base he had sought. Moreover, by marrying his son (who became Henry VI, r. 1190–1197) to the heiress of the Norman kingdom of southern Italy, Frederick seemed to be creating the foundation for making the Holy Roman Empire a reality and for realizing the pope's nightmare: the encirclement of Rome and the Papal States. After Frederick's death, Henry VI's control of Germany and both northern and southern Italy made him the strongest European ruler since Charlemagne. Henry's empire soon collapsed, however, for he died prematurely, leaving as his heir a son only two years old.

Frederick II The son, Frederick II, grew up to become the most brilliant of the Hohenstaufen rulers. King of Sicily in 1198, king of Germany in 1212, and crowned emperor in 1220 (see Image 10.3), Frederick II was a truly brilliant man who awed his contemporaries (see Historical Voices, "The Deeds of Emperor Frederick II," p. 284). Frederick was raised in Sicily, with its diverse peoples, languages, and religions. His court there brought together a brilliant array of lawyers, poets, artists, and scientists, and he himself took a deep interest in their work.

Until he was crowned emperor, Frederick spent much time in Germany; once he left in 1220, though, he rarely returned. He gave the German princes full control of their territories, voluntarily surrendering any real power over Germany in exchange for revenues while he pursued his main goal, the establishment of a strong centralized state in Italy dominated by his kingdom in Sicily. Frederick's major task was to gain control of northern Italy. In reaching to extend his power in Italy, he became involved in a deadly struggle with the popes, who realized that a single ruler of northern and southern Italy meant the end of papal secular power in central Italy. The northern Italian cities

IMAGE 10.3 **The Coronation of Frederick II.** Shown here is the coronation of Frederick II of Germany as Holy Roman Emperor by Pope Honorius II in Rome on November 22, 1220. The pope agreed to the coronation after Frederick promised to lead a Crusade to the Holy Land, a promise that he took years to fulfill. This scene is taken from a fifteenth-century French manuscript on the monarchs of Europe.

were also unwilling to give up their freedom. Frederick waged a bitter struggle in northern Italy, winning many battles but ultimately losing the war.

Frederick's preoccupation with the creation of an empire in Italy left Germany in confusion and chaos until 1273, when the major German princes, serving as electors, chose an insignificant German noble, Rudolf of Habsburg (HAPS-burg), as the new German king. In choosing a weak king, the princes were ensuring that the German monarchy would remain impotent and incapable of reestablishing a centralized monarchical state. The failure of the Hohenstaufens had led to a situation in which his exalted majesty, the German king and Holy Roman Emperor, had no real power over either Germany or Italy. Unlike France and England, neither Germany nor Italy created a unified national monarchy in the Middle Ages. Both became geographic designations for loose confederations of hundreds of petty independent states under the vague direction of king or emperor. In fact, neither Germany nor Italy would become united until the nineteenth century.

Following the death of Frederick II, Italy fell into political confusion. While the papacy remained in control of much of central Italy, the defeat of imperial power left the cities and towns of northern Italy independent of any other authority. Gradually, the larger ones began to emerge as strong city-states.

The Deeds of Emperor Frederick II

 According to Salimbene de Adam, what were Frederick II's idiosyncrasies? Do you think Salimbene was fair in his judgment of Frederick II? Why or why not?

FREDERICK II, KING OF GERMANY AND SICILY and would-be ruler of all Italy, was viewed even by contemporaries as one of the most unusual rulers of his time. This account of his "idiosyncrasies" is by Salimbene (SAL-im-bay-nee) de Adam, a Franciscan friar whose *Chronicle* is one of the richest sources of information about medieval life in thirteenth-century Italy. He was, however, also known to be notoriously biased against Frederick II.

Salimbene de Adam, *Chronicle*

Note that Frederick almost always enjoyed having discord with the Church and fighting her on all sides, although she had nourished him, defended him, and raised him up. He held the true faith to be worthless. He was a cunning, crafty man, avaricious, lecherous, and malicious, easily given to wrath.

At times, however, Frederick was a worthy man, and when he wished to show his good, courtly side, he could be witty, charming, urbane, and industrious. He was adept at writing and singing, and was well-versed in the art of writing lyrics and songs. He was a handsome, well-formed man of medium height. I myself saw him and, at one time, loved him. For he once wrote Brother Elias, Minister General of the Friars Minor, on my behalf asking him to return me to my father. He also could speak many and various languages. In short, if he had been a good Catholic and had loved God, the Church, and his own soul, he would scarcely have had an equal as an emperor in the world. . . .

Now, it is necessary to speak of Frederick's idiosyncrasies.

His first idiosyncrasy is that he had the thumb of a certain notary cut off because he had written his name in a way different from the way the Emperor desired. . . .

His second idiosyncrasy was that he wanted to discover what language a child would use when he grew up if he had never heard anyone speak. Therefore, he placed some infants in the care of wet-nurses, commanding them to bathe and suckle the children, but by no means ever to speak to or fondle them. For he wanted to discover whether they would speak Hebrew, the first language, or Greek, Latin, Arabic, or the language of their parents. But he labored in vain, because all of the infants died. . . .

Furthermore, Frederick had many other idiosyncrasies: idle curiosity, lack of faith, perversity, tyranny, and accursedness, some of which I have written about in another chronicle. Once, for example, he sealed up a live man in a cask and kept him there until he died in order to prove that the soul totally perished with the body. . . . For Frederick was an Epicurean, and so he and the learned men of his court searched out whatever Biblical passage they could find to prove that there is no life after death. . . .

This sixth example of Frederick's idiosyncrasy and idle curiosity . . . was that he fed two men a fine meal, and he sent one to bed to sleep, the other out hunting. And that evening he had both men disemboweled in his presence, in order to determine which one had digested his food the best. The decisions by his doctors went to the man who had slept after the meal. . . .

I have heard and known many other idiosyncrasies of Frederick, but I keep quiet for the sake of brevity, and because reporting so many of the Emperor's foolish notions is tedious to me.

Source: *Chronicle of Salimbene de Adam*, vol. 40, trans. J. F. Baird (Binghamton, N.Y.: State University of New York, 1986), pp. 350–356.

Florence assumed the leadership of Tuscany, while Milan, under the guidance of the Visconti family, took control of the Lombard region. With its great commercial wealth, the republic of Venice dominated the northeastern part of the peninsula.

10-1e New Kingdoms in Northern and Eastern Europe

The Scandinavian countries of northern Europe had little political organization before 1000, and it was not until the second half of the tenth century and the first half of the eleventh that the three Scandinavian kingdoms—Denmark, Norway, and Sweden (see Map 10.4)—emerged with a noticeable political structure. At the same time, the three kingdoms were converted to Christianity by kings who believed that an organized church was a necessary accompaniment to an organized state.

The adoption of Christianity, however, did not eliminate the warlike tendencies of the Scandinavians. Not only did the three kingdoms fight each other in the eleventh and twelfth centuries, but rival families were in regular conflict over the throne in each state. This period also witnessed the growth of a powerful noble landowning class.

To the south, in eastern Europe, Hungary, which had been a Christian state since 1000, remained relatively stable throughout the High Middle Ages, but the history of Poland and Russia was more turbulent. In the thirteenth century, eastern Europe was beset by two groups of invaders, the Teutonic Knights from the west and the Mongols from the east.

In the eleventh century, a Polish kingdom existed as a separate state but with no natural frontiers. Consequently, German settlers encroached on its territory on a regular basis, leading to considerable intermarriage between Slavs and Germans.

MAP 10.4 **Northern and Eastern Europe ca. 1150.** Acceptance of Christianity gave many northern and eastern European kingdoms greater control over their subjects. Warfare was common in the region: dynastic struggles occurred in Scandinavia, and the Teutonic Knights, based in East Prussia, attacked pagan Slavs.

 Which areas of northern and eastern Europe had large Slavic populations? (Look back at Map 8.6.)

During the thirteenth century, relations between the Germans and the Slavs of eastern Europe worsened due to the aggression of the Teutonic Knights. The Teutonic Knights had been founded near the end of the twelfth century to protect the Christian Holy Land. In the early thirteenth century, however, these Christian knights found greater opportunity to the east of Germany, where they attacked the pagan Slavs. East Prussia was given to the military order in 1226, and five years later the knights moved into the lands beyond the Vistula River, where they waged war against the Slavs for another thirty years (see Map 10.5). By the end of the thirteenth century, Prussia had become German and Christian as the pagan Slavs were forced to convert.

Central and eastern Europe had periodically been subject to invasions from

MAP 10.5 **Settlements of the Teutonic Knights, ca. 1230**

fierce Asiatic nomads, such as the Huns, Avars, Bulgars, and Magyars. In the thirteenth century, the Mongols exploded onto the scene, causing far more disruption than earlier invaders.

10-1f Impact of the Mongol Empire

The Mongols rose to power in Asia with stunning speed. A pastoral people in the region of modern-day Mongolia, they were loosely organized into clans and tribes that were often warring with each other. This changed when one leader, Temuchin (TEM-yuh-jin), unified the Mongol tribes and gained the title of Genghis Khan (ca. 1162–1227), which means "universal ruler." From that time on, Genghis Khan (GENG-uss *or* JING-uss KAHN) created a powerful military force and devoted himself to fighting. "Man's highest joy," Genghis Khan remarked, "is in victory: to conquer one's enemies, to pursue them, to deprive them of their possessions, to make their beloved weep, to ride on their horses, and to embrace their wives and daughters."[1] Genghis Khan was succeeded by equally dedicated sons and grandsons.

The Mongols burst onto the scene in the thirteenth century. They advanced eastward, eventually conquering China and Korea. One of Genghis Khan's grandsons, Khubilai Khan (KOO-bluh KAHN), completed the conquest of China and established a new Chinese dynasty of rulers known as the Yuan (YOO-enn *or* YWAHN). In 1279, Khubilai Khan moved the capital of China northward to Khanbaliq (kahn-bah-LEEK) ("city of the khan"), which would later be known by the Chinese name Beijing (bay-ZHING).

The Mongols also moved westward against the Islamic empire. Persia fell by 1233, and by 1258, they had conquered Baghdad and destroyed the Abbasid caliphate. Beginning in the 1230s, the Mongols moved into Europe. They conquered Russia, advanced into Poland and Hungary, and destroyed a force of Poles and Teutonic Knights in Silesia in 1241 (see Map 10.6). Europe then seemingly got lucky when the Mongol hordes turned back because of internal fighting; western and southern Europe thus escaped the wrath of the Mongols. Overall, the Mongols had little impact in Europe, although their occupation of Russia had some residual effects.

10-1g The Development of Russia

The Kievan Rus state, which had formally become Christian in 987 C.E., prospered considerably afterward, reaching its high point in the first half of the eleventh century. Kievan society was dominated by a noble class of landowners known as the **boyars** (boh-YARS). Kievan merchants maintained regular trade with Scandinavia to the northwest and the Islamic and Byzantine worlds to the south. But destructive civil wars and new invasions by Asiatic nomads caused the principality of Kiev to disintegrate into a number of constituent parts, and the sack of Kiev by north Russian princes in 1169 brought an inglorious end to the first Russian state.

MAP 10.6 **The Mongol Empire in the Thirteenth Century.** Beginning with the exploits of Genghis Khan, the Mongols used unorthodox but effective military tactics to establish an empire that stretched from Russia to China and included parts of India and South Asia. The empire was divided into khanates. The Golden Horde, the khanate in Russia, was eventually overwhelmed by princes of Moscow who went on to establish the Russian state.

 Why would it be difficult for one khan to effectively rule the entire Mongol Empire?

The fundamental civilizing and unifying force of early Russia was the Christian church. The Russian church imitated the liturgy and organization of the Byzantine Empire, whose Eastern Orthodox priests had converted the Kievan Rus to Christianity at the end of the tenth century. The Russian church became known for its rigid religious orthodoxy. Although Christianity provided a common bond between Russian and European civilization, Russia's religious development guaranteed an even closer affinity between Russian and Byzantine civilization.

In the thirteenth century, the Mongols conquered Russia and cut it off even more from western Europe. The Mongols were not numerous enough to settle the vast Russian lands but were content to rule directly an area along the lower Volga and north of the Caspian and Black Seas to Kiev and rule indirectly elsewhere. In the latter territories, Russian princes were required to pay tribute to the Mongol overlords.

One Russian prince soon emerged as more visible and powerful than the others. Alexander Nevsky (NYEF-skee) (ca. 1220–1263), prince of Novgorod, defeated a German invading army at Lake Peipus in northwestern Russia in 1242. His cooperation with the Mongols, which included denouncing his own brother and crushing native tax revolts, won him their favor. The khan, the acknowledged leader of the western part of the Mongol Empire, rewarded Alexander Nevsky with the title of grand-prince, enabling his descendants to become the princes of Moscow and eventually leaders of all Russia.

10-2 The Recovery and Reform of the Catholic Church

 FOCUS QUESTIONS: What was the importance of the Cluniac reform movement? What was at issue in the Investiture Controversy, and what effect did the controversy have on the church and on Germany? What did the reform of the papacy accomplish?

In the early Middle Ages, the Catholic Church had played a leading role in converting and civilizing first the Germanic invaders and later the Vikings and Magyars. Although highly successful, this had not been accomplished without challenges that undermined the spiritual life of the church itself.

10-2a The Problems of Decline

Since the eighth century, the popes had come to exercise control over the territories in central Italy known as the Papal States; this kept the popes involved in political matters, often at the expense of their spiritual obligations. At the same time,

CHRONOLOGY	Growth of the European Kingdoms

England

Battle of Hastings	1066
William the Conqueror	1066–1087
Henry II, first of the Plantagenet dynasty	1154–1189
Murder of Thomas à Becket	1170
John	1199–1216
Magna Carta	1215
Edward I	1272–1307
First Parliament	1295

France

Philip II Augustus	1180–1223
Louis IX	1226–1270
Philip IV	1285–1314
First Estates-General	1302

Spain

El Cid in Valencia	1094–1099
Alfonso VIII of Castile	1155–1214
Battle of Las Navas de Tolosa	1212
Alfonso X of Castile	1252–1284

Germany, the Holy Roman Empire, and Italy

Henry IV	1056–1106
Frederick I Barbarossa	1152–1190
Lombard League defeats Frederick at Legnano	1176
Henry VI	1190–1197
Frederick II	1212–1250
Election of Rudolf of Habsburg as king of Germany	1273

Eastern Europe

East Prussia given to the Teutonic Knights	1226
Genghis Khan and the rise of the Mongols	ca. 1162–1227
Mongol conquest of Russia	1230s
Alexander Nevsky, prince of Novgorod	ca. 1220–1263
Defeat of the Germans	1242

the church became increasingly entangled in the evolving lord–vassal relationships. High officials of the church, such as bishops and abbots, came to hold their offices as fiefs from nobles. As vassals, they were obliged to carry out the usual duties, including military service. Of course, lords assumed the right to choose their vassals, even when those vassals included bishops and abbots. Because lords often selected their vassals from other noble families for political reasons, these bishops and abbots were often worldly figures who cared little about their spiritual responsibilities.

The monastic ideal had also suffered during the early Middle Ages. Benedictine monasteries had sometimes been exemplary centers of Christian living and learning, but the invasions of Vikings, Magyars, and Muslims wreaked havoc with many monastic establishments. Discipline declined, and with it the monastic reputation for learning and holiness. At the same time, a growing number of monasteries fell under the control of local lords, as did much of the church. A number of people believed that the time for reform had come.

10-2b The Cluniac Reform Movement

Reform of the Catholic Church began in Burgundy in eastern France in 910 c.e. when Duke William of Aquitaine founded the abbey of Cluny (kloo-NEE). The monastery began with a renewed dedication to the highest spiritual ideals of the Benedictine rule and was fortunate in having a series of abbots in the tenth century who maintained these ideals. Cluny was deliberately kept independent from secular control. As Duke William stipulated in his original charter, "It has pleased us also to insert in this document that, from this day, those same monks there congregated shall be subject neither to our yoke, nor to that of our relatives, nor to the sway of the royal might, nor to that of any earthly power."[2] The new monastery at Cluny tried to eliminate some of the abuses that had crept into religious communities by stressing the need for work, replacing manual labor with the copying of manuscripts, and demanding more community worship and less private prayer.

The Cluniac reform movement sparked an enthusiastic response, first in France and eventually in all of western and central Europe. Hundreds of new monasteries were founded on Cluniac ideals, and existing monasteries rededicated themselves by adopting the Cluniac program. The movement also began to reach beyond monasticism and into the papacy itself, which was in dire need of help.

10-2c Reform of the Papacy

By the eleventh century, a movement for change, led by a series of reforming popes, was sweeping through the Catholic Church. One of the reformers' primary goals was to free the church from the interference of lords in the election of church officials. This issue was dramatically taken up by the greatest of the reform popes of the eleventh century, Gregory VII (1073–1085).

Pope Gregory VII and Reform Elected pope in 1073, Gregory was absolutely certain that he had been chosen by God to reform the church. In pursuit of those aims, Gregory claimed that he—the pope—was God's "vicar on Earth" and that the pope's authority extended over all of Christendom and included the right to depose emperors if they disobeyed his wishes. Gregory sought nothing less than the elimination of **lay investiture** (both interference by nonmembers of the clergy in elections and their participation in the installation of prelates). Only then could the church regain its freedom, by which Gregory meant the right of the church to appoint

The "Gregorian Revolution": Papal Claims

 What was Gregory VII's position in his conflict with Henry IV? How do you think Gregory viewed himself vis-à-vis the monarch?

IN THE ELEVENTH CENTURY, a dynamic group of reformers pushed for the "freedom of the church." This came to mean not only papal control over the affairs of the church but also the elimination of lay investiture. The reformers saw the latter as the chief issue at the heart of lay control of the church. In trying to eliminate it, Gregory VII extended papal claims to include the right to oversee the secular authorities and, in particular, to depose rulers under certain circumstances. The following selection is from a document that was entered in the papal register in 1075. It consists of twenty-seven assertions that probably served as headings, or a table of contents, for a collection of ecclesiastical writings that supported the pope's claims.

The Dictates of the Pope

1. That the Roman church was founded by God alone.
2. That the Roman pontiff alone can with right be called universal.
3. That he alone can depose or reinstate bishops.
4. That, in a council, his legate, even if a lower grade, is above all bishops, and can pass sentence of deposition against them.
5. That the pope may depose the absent.
6. That, among other things, we ought not to remain in the same house with those excommunicated by him. . . .
8. That he alone may use the imperial insignia.
9. That of the pope alone all princes shall kiss the feet.
10. That his name alone shall be spoken in the churches.
11. That this is the only name in the world.
12. That it may be permitted to him to depose emperors.
13. That he may be permitted to transfer bishops if need be. . . .
17. That no chapter and no book shall be considered canonical without his authority.
18. That a sentence passed by him may be retracted by no one; and that he himself, alone of all, may retract it.
19. That he himself may be judged by no one.
20. That no one shall dare to condemn one who appeals to the apostolic chair.
21. That to the latter should be referred the more important cases of every church.
22. That the Roman church has never erred; nor will it err to all eternity, the Scripture bearing witness.
23. That the Roman pontiff, if he have been canonically ordained, is undoubtedly made a saint by the merits of St. Peter. . . .
25. That he may depose and reinstate bishops without assembling a synod.
26. That he who is not at peace with the Roman church shall not be considered catholic.
27. That he may absolve subjects from their fealty to wicked men.

Source: E. F. Henderson, *Select Historical Documents of the Middle Ages* (London: George Bell & Sons, 1896).

its own clergy and run its own affairs. If rulers did not accept these "divine" commands, they could be deposed by the pope in his capacity as the vicar of Christ (see Historical Voices, "The 'Gregorian Revolution': Papal Claims," above). Gregory VII soon found himself in conflict with the king of Germany over these claims. (The king of Germany was also the emperor-designate since it had been accepted by this time that only kings of Germany could be emperors, but they did not officially use the title "emperor" until they were crowned by the pope.)

King Henry IV of Germany was just as determined as the pope. For many years, German kings had appointed high-ranking clerics, especially bishops, as their vassals in order to use them as administrators. Without them, the king could not hope to maintain his own power vis-à-vis the powerful German nobles. In 1075, Pope Gregory issued a decree forbidding important clerics from receiving investiture from an emperor or king or any lay person. Henry had no intention of obeying a decree that challenged the very heart of his administration.

The Investiture Controversy The immediate cause of the so-called Investiture Controversy was a disputed election to the bishopric of Milan in northern Italy, an important position because the bishop was also the ruler of the city. Control of the bishopric was crucial if the king wished to reestablish German power in northern Italy. Since Milan was considered second only to Rome in importance as a bishopric, papal interest in the office was also keen. Pope Gregory VII and King Henry IV backed competing candidates for the position.

To gain acceptance of his candidate, the pope threatened the king with **excommunication**. Excommunication is a censure by which a person is deprived of receiving the sacraments of the church. To counter this threat, the king called a synod or assembly of German bishops, all of whom he had appointed, and had them depose the pope.

Pope Gregory VII responded by excommunicating the king and freeing his subjects from their allegiance to him. The latter was a clever move. The German nobles were only too eager to diminish the power of a centralized monarchy because of the threat it posed to their own power, and they welcomed this opportunity to rebel against the king. Both the nobles and the bishops of Germany agreed to hold a meeting in Germany with the pope to solve the problem, possibly by choosing a new king. Gregory set out for Germany. Henry, realizing the threat to his power, forestalled the pope by traveling to northern Italy, where he met the pope at Canossa, a castle belonging to Countess Matilda of Tuscany, an avid supporter of the papal reform program. There, in January 1077, the king admitted his transgressions and begged for forgiveness and absolution. Although he made the king wait three days, the pope was constrained by his priestly responsibility to grant absolution to a penitent sinner and lifted the ban of excommunication. This did not end the problem, however. Within three years, pope and king were again locked in combat.

The struggle continued until 1122, when a new German king and a new pope achieved a compromise called the Concordat of Worms (WURMZ *or* VORMPS). Under this agreement, a bishop in Germany was first elected by church officials. After election, the nominee paid homage to the king as his secular lord, who in turn invested him with the symbols of temporal office. A representative of the pope then invested the new bishop with the symbols of his spiritual office.

This struggle between church and state was an important element in the history of Europe in the High Middle Ages. In the early Middle Ages, popes had been dependent on emperors and had allowed them to exercise considerable authority over church affairs. But a set of new ideals championed by activist reformers in the eleventh century now supported the "freedom of the church," which meant not only the freedom of the church to control its own affairs but also extreme claims of papal authority. Not only was the pope superior to all other bishops, but popes now claimed the right to depose kings under certain circumstances. Such papal claims ensured further church-state confrontations.

10-3 Christianity and Medieval Civilization

 FOCUS QUESTIONS: What were the characteristics of the papal monarchy and the new religious orders of the High Middle Ages, and what role did women play in the religious life of the period? What was the church's attitude toward heretics and Jews during the High Middle Ages?

Christianity was an integral part of the fabric of medieval European society and the consciousness of Europe. Papal directives affected the actions of kings and princes alike, while Christian teaching and practices touched the economic, social, intellectual, cultural, and daily lives of all Europeans.

10-3a Growth of the Papal Monarchy

The popes of the twelfth century did not abandon the reform ideals of Gregory VII, but they were less dogmatic and more inclined to consolidate their power and build a strong administrative system. By the twelfth century, the Catholic Church possessed a clearly organized, hierarchical structure. The pope and **papal curia** (KYUR-ee-uh) were at the apex of the administrative structure. The curia was staffed by a bevy of officials led by high church officials known as cardinals, who served as major advisers and administrators to the popes; at the pope's death, the college of cardinals, as they were collectively called, elected the new pope. Below the pope and cardinals were the archbishops, each of whom controlled a large region called an archdiocese. Each archdiocese was divided into smaller units called dioceses, each headed by a bishop. Each diocese was divided into parishes, each headed by a priest. Theoretically, the bishop chose all priests in his diocese, administered his diocese, and was responsible only to the pope.

The Pontificate of Innocent III In the thirteenth century, the Catholic Church reached the height of its political, intellectual, and secular power. The papal monarchy extended its sway over both ecclesiastical and temporal affairs, as was especially evident during the papacy of Pope Innocent III (1198–1216) (see Image 10.4). At the beginning of his pontificate, in a letter to a priest, Innocent made a clear statement of his views on papal supremacy:

> As God, the creator of the universe, set two great lights in the firmament of heaven, the greater light to rule the day, and the lesser light to rule the night, so He set two great dignities in the firmament of the universal church . . . the greater to rule the day, that is, souls, and the lesser to rule the night, that is, bodies. These dignities are the papal authority and the royal power. And just as the moon gets her light from the sun, and is inferior to the sun . . . so the royal power gets the splendor of its dignity from the papal authority.[3]

Innocent's actions were those of a man who believed that he, the pope, was the supreme judge of European affairs. He forced King Philip II Augustus of France to take back his wife and queen after Philip had tried to have the marriage annulled. The pope intervened in German affairs and installed his candidate as emperor. He compelled King John of England to accept the papal choice for the position of archbishop of Canterbury. To achieve his political ends, Innocent did not hesitate to use the spiritual weapons at his command, especially the **interdict**, which forbade priests to dispense the **sacraments** of the church in the hope that the people, deprived of the comforts of religion, would exert pressure against their ruler. Pope Innocent's interdict was so effective that it caused King Philip Augustus to restore his wife to her rightful place as queen of France.

10-3b New Religious Orders and Spiritual Ideals

In the second half of the eleventh century and the first half of the twelfth, a wave of religious enthusiasm seized Europe, leading to a spectacular growth in the number of monasteries and the emergence of new monastic orders. Most important was the Cistercian (sis-TUR-shun) order, founded in 1098 by a group of monks dissatisfied with the lack of strict discipline at their Benedictine monastery. Cistercian monasticism spread rapidly from southern France into the rest of Europe.

IMAGE 10.4 **Pope Innocent III.** Innocent III was an active and powerful pope during the High Middle Ages. He approved the creation of the Franciscan and Dominican religious orders and inaugurated the Fourth Crusade. He is shown here with the papal bull he issued to establish the monastery of Sacro Speco in Subiaco, Italy.

Q *What is a papal bull?*

The Cistercians were strict. They ate a simple diet and possessed only a single robe apiece. All decorations were eliminated from their churches and monastic buildings. More time for prayer and manual labor was provided by shortening the number of hours spent at religious services. The Cistercians played a major role in developing a new activist spiritual model for twelfth-century Europe. A Benedictine monk often spent hours in prayer to honor God. The Cistercian ideal had a different emphasis: "Arise, soldier of Christ, arise! Get up off the ground and return to the battle from which you have fled! Fight more boldly after your flight, and triumph in glory!"[4] These were the words of Saint Bernard of Clairvaux (klair-VOH) (1090–1153), who more than any other person embodied the new spiritual ideal of Cistercian monasticism, He has been called the most widely respected holy man of the twelfth century. Bernard was an outstanding preacher, wholly dedicated to the service of God. His reputation reportedly influenced many young men to join the Cistercian order.

Bernard also gave religious piety a more personal touch when he portrayed Christ, the Virgin Mary, and the saints in more human fashion. In the early Middle Ages, these holy figures were most often presented in a majestic, triumphant manner and viewed as remote from people's lives. Achieving salvation seemed difficult since Christ was portrayed as a stern judge. In his sermons and writings, Bernard pictured these sacred figures as living human beings to whom people could relate directly. He encouraged an emotional love for Jesus and for the mother of Christ, the Virgin Mary, whom he portrayed as a gentle, loving, kindly intercessor with her Son.

Women in Religious Orders Not only men were susceptible to the religious fervor of the twelfth century; women were also active participants in the spiritual movements of the age. The image of women, in fact, was steadily changing in both religious thought and secular imagery. The cult of the Virgin Mary spread dramatically throughout Europe, while the poetry of courtly love (see Chapter 9) made women objects of adoration. At the same time, the number of women joining religious houses grew perceptibly with the growth of the new orders of the twelfth century.

By that time, female monasticism was already hundreds of years old. Medieval monasticism however, always remained an overwhelmingly male phenomenon. Even in 1200, after a century of growth, there were only about 3,000 nuns in England compared to 14,000 monks. In the High Middle Ages, most nuns were from the ranks of the landed aristocracy. Convents were convenient for families unable or unwilling to find husbands for their daughters and for aristocratic women who did not wish to marry. Female intellectuals found them a haven for their activities. Most of the learned women of the Middle Ages, especially in Germany, were nuns. One of the most distinguished was Hildegard of Bingen (HIL-duh-gard of BING-un) (1098–1179), who became abbess of a convent at Disibodenberg in western Germany.

Hildegard shared in the religious enthusiasm of the twelfth century (see Movies & History, *Vision*, p. 291). Soon after becoming abbess, she began to write an account of the mystical visions she had experienced for years. She stated that a great flash of light from heaven pierced her brain, which left her mind

MOVIES & HISTORY
Vision (2009)

Watch *Vision*, a cinematic reconstruction of the life of the twelfth-century nun and mystic Hildegard of Bingen.

© Zeitgeist Films/Courtesy Everett Collection

The movie follows her life from her initial entry as a young girl into a Benedictine monastery at Disibodenberg in western Germany through her career as abbess of a convent at Rupertsberg. The film is a realistic portrayal of Hildegard's life and her many accomplishments.

 What accomplishments of Hildegard are presented in the film? Why is she presented as a forerunner of the modern, liberated woman and as early practitioner of holistic medicine? How realistic is the film's portrayal of the twelfth-century religious world?

filled with the meaning of the "sacred books." Eventually, she produced three books based on her visions. In one of them, she presented the universe as a living cosmology in which nature, humanity, divinity, and the cosmos were all interconnected in a harmonious whole. The macrocosm (universe) was one with the microcosm (humankind). Humans, she wrote, were "completely the image of God," and she urged them to be "co-creators" with God. Hildegard also gained considerable renown as a mystic and prophet, and popes, emperors, kings, dukes, and bishops eagerly sought her advice.

Hildegard of Bingen was also one of the first important female composers and a major contributor to the body of music known as Gregorian chant or plainsong. Gregorian chant was basically monophonic—a single line of unaccompanied vocal music—set to Latin texts and chanted by a group of monks or nuns during church services. Hildegard's work is especially remarkable because she succeeded at a time when music in general, and sacred music in particular, was almost exclusively the domain of men.

Living the Gospel Life In the early thirteenth century, two religious leaders, Saint Francis and Saint Dominic, founded two new religious orders whose members did not remain in the cloister like the monks of the contemplative orders, such as the Benedictines and Cistercians, but rather went out into the secular arena of the towns to preach the word of God. By their example, the new orders strove to provide a more personal religious experience for ordinary people. The new orders were known as mendicant ("begging") orders because their members adopted lives of deliberate poverty in order to imitate the lives of Jesus's original apostles, who lived in poverty. They were also reacting against the growing wealth of the High Middle Ages, especially evident in the cities, which they considered harmful to a Christian's soul. After all, Jesus had stated in the New Testament: "How hard it is for a rich man to enter the kingdom of God! Indeed, it is easier for a camel to go through the eye of a needle than for a rich man to enter the kingdom of God."[5]

Saint Francis of Assisi (1182–1226) was born to a wealthy Italian merchant family, but as a young man he abandoned all worldly goods and began to live and preach in poverty after a series of dramatic spiritual experiences. His simplicity, joyful nature, and love for others soon attracted a band of followers, all of whom took vows of absolute poverty, agreeing to reject all property and live by working and begging for their food. Francis drew up a simple rule for his followers that focused on the need to preach and the importance of poverty. He sought approval for his new rule from Pope Innocent III, who confirmed the new order as the Order of Friars Minor, more commonly known as the Franciscans. The Franciscans struck a responsive chord among many Europeans and became very popular. The Franciscans lived among the people, preaching repentance and aiding the poor. Their calls for a return to the simplicity and poverty of the early church, reinforced by their own example, were especially effective. The Franciscans had a female branch as well, known as the Poor Clares, which was founded by Saint Clare, an aristocratic lady of Assisi who was a great admirer of Francis.

The second new religious order of the early thirteenth century arose out of the desire to defend orthodox church teachings from heresy. The Order of Preachers, popularly known as the Dominicans, was created through the efforts of a Spanish priest, Dominic de Guzmán (DAH-muh-nik duh gooz-MAHN) (1170–1221). Unlike Francis, Dominic was an intellectual who was particularly appalled by the recent growth of heretical movements. He came to believe that a new religious order of men who lived lives of poverty but were learned and capable of preaching effectively would best be able to attack heresy. With the approval of Pope Innocent III, the Dominicans became an order of mendicant friars in 1215. The Dominicans soon became the chief officials in the papal Inquisition (see "Voices of Protest and Intolerance," later in this chapter).

In addition to the friars, the thirteenth century witnessed the development of yet another kind of religious order. Known as Beguines (bay-GEENZ), these were communities of women dwelling together in poverty. Devout and dedicated to prayer, they begged for their daily support or worked as laundresses in hospitals or at other menial tasks. They did not take religious vows and were free to leave the community at will. Although the Beguines originated in the Low Countries, they eventually became quite strong in the Rhineland area of Germany as well.

Monasticism and Social Services Monastic life in all of its different forms was the most important component of religious life in the Middle Ages. Monks and nuns performed a remarkable variety of tasks, including praying for themselves and others, copying manuscripts, maintaining libraries and schools, acting as missionaries to the heathen, preaching to the poor, and fighting heresy. But in an age unlike our own, when governments provide basic social services, monks and nuns also worked for society by providing a number of social welfare services (see Global Perspectives, "Medieval Monasteries in the West and East," p. 292).

Monasteries often provided both food and clothing for the poor. Otto of Freising, a German writer of history in the twelfth century, declared that there was always a pious

Medieval Monasteries in the West and East

Q *What are the similarities and differences between Christian and Buddhist monasticism?*

MANY OF THE WORLD'S RELIGIONS have monastic groups—men or women living in communities dedicated to the worship of God and service. In the West, monastic ideals begun by the Benedictines were then promoted and embellished by new monastic orders in the eleventh, twelfth, and thirteenth centuries. In Images 10.5a and 10.5b, we see some of the activities of monks and nuns in Europe in the High Middle Ages. Image 10.5a shows at the left a group of nuns welcoming a novice (dressed in white) to their order. At the right a nun receives a sick person on a stretcher for the order's hospital care. Image 10.5b shows Cistercian monks, one at prayer and others at work. The Cistercians restored strict ideals of monastic living and initiated their own activist spiritual model. By cutting the number of hours spent at religious services, Cistercians were able to spend more hours at manual labor and preaching to laypeople.

Image 10.5c—a ninth-century wall painting from the Shikshen monastery in Karabar, China—shows a group of Buddhist monks in prayer. Buddhist monasteries were first established in India around the fourth century B.C.E. Although the first groups wandered from town to town seeking alms and dispensing their teachings, monks and nuns eventually became grounded in monastic communities. In India, Buddhist monasteries developed into centers of learning.

With the spread of Buddhism to China and Japan, Buddhist monasteries were also established. During the Tang Dynasty (618–907), monasteries sprang up throughout China. Some Buddhist monks even served as advisers at the imperial court. Like some monasteries in the West, some Buddhist monasteries in the east were simple communities where monks and nuns found a refuge but also became consumers of luxury goods provided by rich patrons.

The reception of a novice and welcoming a patient, from 'Le Livre de Vie Active de l'Hotel Dieu de Paris' by Jean Henry, c.1482 (vellum) (detail of 236791), French School, (15th century)/Musée de l'Assistance Publique, Hopitaux de Paris, France/Archives Charmet/Bridgeman Images

IMAGE 10.5a

Erich Lessing/Art Resource, NY

IMAGE 10.5b

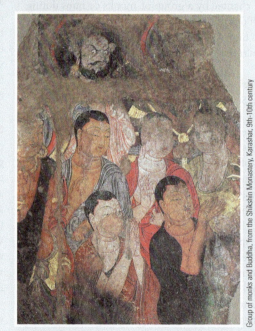

Group of monks and Buddha, from the Shikshin Monastery, Karashar, 9th-10th century (fragment of a painting), Xinjiang/Hermitage, St. Petersburg, Russia/Bridgeman Images

IMAGE 10.5c

The Miraculous Power of the Sacraments

 What do these two stories tell us about popular religious beliefs in the thirteenth century?

IN THE MIDDLE AGES, the sacraments of the Catholic Church came to be associated with miraculous occurrences. Many stories emerged, telling of the wondrous workings of the sacraments. Wandering priests then spread these tales to laypeople. The first excerpt below is taken from a collection called *The Dialogues Concerning Miracles*, put together by a Cistercian monk in the thirteenth century. The second excerpt is taken from the work of a Dominican priest in the thirteenth century.

Caesar of Heisterbach

In Hemmenrode a certain aged priest, Henry by name, died a few years ago. He was a holy and just man, and had been for many years sacristan in that monastery. When he was celebrating the mass one day at the altar of St. John the Baptist, in the choir of the lay brethren, a certain one of the lay brethren standing near saw, in the hands of the priest, the Saviour (Jesus) in the form of a man. Nevertheless the priest himself did not see it. One of the elders of that convent related this to me.

Stephen of Bourbon

I have heard that a certain rustic, wishing to become wealthy and having many hives of bees, asked certain evil men how he could get rich and increase the number of his bees. He was told by some one that if he retained the sacred host [sacrament of the Eucharist or Lord's Supper] on Easter and placed it in some one of his hives, he would entice away all of his neighbor's bees, which, leaving their own hives, would come to the place where the body of our Lord was and there would make honey. So he did this.

Then all the bees came to the hive where the body of Christ was, and just as if they felt sorrow for the irreverence done to it, by their labor they began to construct a little church and to erect foundations, and bases, and columns, and an altar; then with the greatest reverence they place the body of our Lord upon the altar. And within their little beehive they formed the little church with wonderful and most beautiful workmanship. The bees of the vicinity, leaving their hives, came to that one; and over that work they sang in their own manner certain wonderful melodies like hymns.

The rustic, hearing this, marveled. But waiting until the fitting time for collecting the honey, he found nothing in his hives. Finding himself impoverished through the means by which he had expected to be enriched, he went to the hive where he had placed the host, and where he saw the bees had come together. But when he approached, just as if they wished to vindicate the insult to our Savior, the bees rushed upon the rustic and stung him so severely that he escaped with difficulty and in great agony. Going to the priest, he related all that he had done, and what the bees had done.

The priest, by the advice of the bishop, collected his parishioners and made a procession to that place. Then the bees, leaving the hive, rose in the air, making sweet melody. Raising the hive, they found inside the noble structure of that little church and the body of our Lord placed upon the altar. Then, returning thanks, they bore to their own church that little church of the bees, constructed with such skill and elegance, and place it on the altar.

By this deed those who do not reverence, but offer insult instead, to the sacred body of Christ, or the sacred place where it is, ought to be put to great confusion.

Source: J. H. Robinson, *Readings in European History* (Boston: Ginn & Company, 1904), pp. 355–356.

friar sitting at the gate receiving all arriving guests, pilgrims, and poor people, "as friendly and kind-hearted as Christ himself." Due to a shortage of inns, monasteries also provided hospitality for pilgrims and other travelers, as the Rule of St. Benedict noted that all who arrive as guests were to be "welcomed like Christ." Monks and nuns also took care of the sick. They planted herb gardens so that they could prepare the herbal remedies that were commonly used in medieval medicine. In addition, monks and nuns ran hospitals, especially for poor people who could not receive care elsewhere. Unlike modern-day hospitals, medieval hospitals were primarily residences for the elderly, the terminally ill, or the blind. Separate quarters were provided for lepers. There were about two thousand leper houses in France in the thirteenth century, a good indication of the widespread nature of the disease.

10-3c Popular Religion in the High Middle Ages

We have witnessed the actions of popes, bishops, monks, and nuns. But what of ordinary clergy and laypeople? What were their religious hopes and fears? What were their spiritual aspirations?

The sacraments of the Catholic Church ensured that the church was an integral part of people's lives, from birth to death. There were (and still are) seven sacraments—the Eucharist (the Lord's Supper), baptism, marriage, penance, extreme unction, holy orders, and confirmation—administered only by the clergy. The sacraments were viewed as outward symbols of an inward grace (grace was God's freely given gift that enabled humans to be saved) and were considered imperative for a Christian's salvation (see Historical Voices, "The Miraculous Power of the Sacraments," above).

Therefore, the clergy were seen to have a key role in the attainment of salvation.

The Importance of Saints Other church practices were also important to ordinary people. Saints, it was believed, were men and women who, through their holiness, had achieved a special position in heaven, enabling them to act as intercessors before God. The saints' ability to protect poor souls enabled them to take on great importance at the popular level. Jesus's apostles were recognized throughout Europe as saints, but there were also numerous local saints that were of special significance to the area. New cults rapidly developed, particularly in the intense religious atmosphere of the eleventh and twelfth centuries. The English introduced Saint Nicholas, the patron saint of children, who remains instantly recognizable today through his identification with Santa Claus.

Of all the saints, the Virgin Mary, the mother of Jesus, occupied the foremost position in the High Middle Ages. Mary was viewed as the most important mediator with her son Jesus, the judge of all sinners. Moreover, from the eleventh century on, a fascination with Mary as Jesus's human mother became more evident. A sign of Mary's growing importance was the number of churches all over Europe that were dedicated to "Our Lady" in the twelfth and thirteenth centuries, including the cathedral of Notre-Dame in Paris (see Chapter 9).

The Use of Relics Emphasis on the role of the saints was closely tied to the use of **relics**, which also increased noticeably in the High Middle Ages. Relics were usually the bones of saints or objects intimately connected to saints that were considered worthy of veneration by the faithful. A twelfth-century English monk began his description of the abbey's relics by saying, "There is kept there a thing more precious than gold . . . the right arm of St. Oswald. . . . This we have seen with our own eyes and have kissed, and have handled with our own hands. . . . There are kept here also part of his ribs and of the soil on which he fell."[6] The monk went on to list additional purported relics possessed by the abbey, including two pieces of Jesus's swaddling clothes, pieces of Jesus's manger, and parts of the five loaves of bread with which Jesus miraculously fed five thousand people. Because the holiness of the saint was considered to be inherent in his relics, these objects were believed to be capable of healing people or producing other miracles.

In the High Middle Ages, it became a regular practice of the church to attach **indulgences** to these relics. Indulgences brought a remission of time spent in **purgatory**. Purgatory was believed to be a place of punishment in which the soul of the departed could be purified before ascending to heaven. The living could ease that suffering through Masses and prayers offered on behalf of the deceased or through indulgences. Indulgences were granted for good works such as charitable contributions and viewing the relics of saints. The church specified the number of years and days of each indulgence, enabling the soul to spend less time in purgatory.

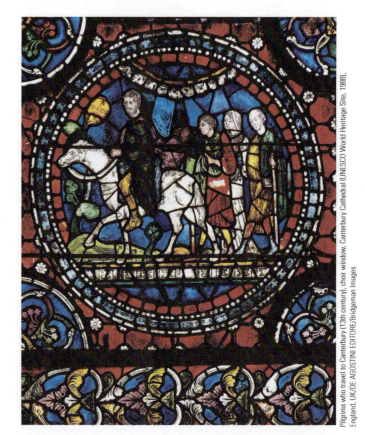

Pilgrims who travel to Canterbury (13th century), choir window, Canterbury Cathedral (UNESCO World Heritage Site, 1988), England, UK/DE AGOSTINI EDITORE/Bridgeman Images

IMAGE 10.6 **The Pilgrimage.** The pilgrimage has been called the "most characteristic mode of travel" in the High Middle Ages. Travel of this kind was often dangerous, and the pilgrim had to be strongly committed to undertake it. This illustration shows a thirteenth-century stained-glass window in Canterbury cathedral that portrays a group on pilgrims on their way to the tomb of Thomas á Becket in Canterbury, a popular pilgrimage site in England.

Q *Why was the tomb of Thomas á Becket such a popular pilgrimage site in England?*

The Pilgrimage Medieval Christians believed that a pilgrimage to a holy shrine was of particular spiritual benefit (see Image 10.6). The greatest shrine but the most difficult to reach was the Holy City of Jerusalem (see Map 10.7). On the European continent, two pilgrim centers were especially popular in the High Middle Ages: Rome, which contained the relics of Saints Peter and Paul, and the town of Santiago de Compostela, supposedly the site of the tomb of the Apostle James. Local attractions, such as shrines dedicated to the Virgin Mary, also became pilgrimage centers.

10-3d Voices of Protest and Intolerance

The desire for more personal and deeper religious experience, which characterized the spiritual revival of the High Middle Ages, also led people into directions hostile to the institutional church. From the twelfth century on, heresy, the holding of religious doctrines different from the orthodox teachings of the church as determined by church authorities, became a serious problem for the Catholic Church.

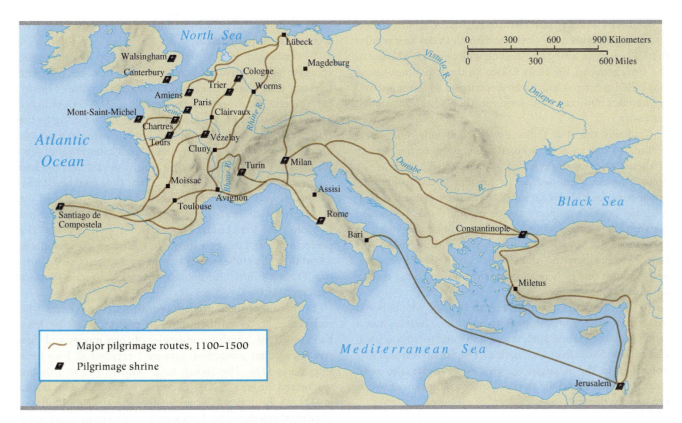

MAP 10.7 **Pilgrimage Routes in the Middle Ages.** Some Christians sought spiritual solace by traveling to pilgrimage sites. Many went to local shrines honoring the Virgin Mary, but Jerusalem, Rome, and Santiago de Compostela were the most desired locations.

Q *Roughly how far would a pilgrim from Lübeck have to travel to reach Jerusalem, and how long would the journey take if he walked 20 miles per day?*

The best-known heresy of the twelfth and thirteenth centuries was Catharism (KA-thuh-riz-um). The Cathars (the word *Cathar* means "pure") were often called Albigensians (al-buh-JEN-see-unz) after the city of Albi, one of their strongholds in southern France. They believed in a dualist system in which good and evil were separate and distinct. Things of the spirit were good because they were created by God, the source of light; things of the world were evil because they were created by Satan, the prince of darkness. Humans, too, were enmeshed in **dualism**. Their souls, which were good, were trapped in material bodies, which were evil. According to the Cathars, the Catholic Church, itself a materialistic institution, had nothing to do with God and was essentially evil. There was no need to follow its teachings or recognize its authority. The Cathar movement gained valuable support from important nobles in southern France and northern Italy.

The spread of heresy in southern France alarmed the church authorities. Pope Innocent III appealed to the nobles of northern France for a **crusade** (a military campaign in defense of Christendom) against the heretics. The crusade against the Albigensians, which began in the summer of 1209 and lasted for almost two decades, was a bloody one. Thousands of heretics (and the innocent) were slaughtered, including entire populations of some towns (see Image 10.7). In Beziers, for example, seven thousand men, women, and children were massacred when they took refuge in the local church.

Cott Nero E II pt2 f.20v The expulsion of the Albigensians from Carcassonne: Catharist heretics of the 12th and 13th centuries, from 'The Chronicles of France, from Priam King of Troy until the crowning of Charles VI', 15th century, Boucicaut Master, (fl.1390-1430) (and workshop)/British Library, London, UK/© British Library Board. All Rights Reserved/Bridgeman Images

IMAGE 10.7 **Expulsion of Albigensian Heretics.** In 1209, Pope Innocent III authorized a crusade against the heretical Albigensians. In this medieval illustration, French knights are shown expelling Albigensian heretics from the town of Carcassonne near Albi, an Albigensian stronghold in southern France.

Q *What do you think was the fate of these expelled Albigensians?*

Southern France was devastated, but Catharism persisted, which caused the Catholic Church to devise a regular method for discovering and dealing with heretics. This led to the emergence of the Holy Office, as the papal Inquisition was called, a formal court whose job it was to ferret out and try heretics. Officials who were mostly Dominicans staffed the court.

Gradually, the Holy Office developed its inquisitorial procedure. Anyone could be accused of heresy since the identity of the accuser was not revealed to the indicted heretic. If the accused heretic confessed, he or she was forced to perform public penance and was subjected to punishment, such as flogging; the heretic's property was then confiscated and divided between the secular authorities and the church. Beginning in 1252, those not confessing voluntarily were subjected to torture. Relapsed heretics—those who confessed, did penance, and then reverted to heresy—were turned over to the secular authorities for execution.

To the Christians of the thirteenth century, who believed that there was only one path to salvation, heresy was a crime against God and against humanity, and force was justified to save Souls from damnation. The fanaticism and fear unleashed in the struggle against heretics were also used against others, especially the best-known outgroup of Western society, the Jews.

Persecution of the Jews The Jews were the only religious minority in Christian Europe that was allowed to practice a non-Christian religion. In the early Middle Ages, Jews were actively involved in trade and crafts. Later, after being excluded from practicing most trades by the guild system, some Jews turned to money-lending as a way to survive.

There is little certainty about the number of Jews in Europe. England had relatively few Jews, probably 2,500 to 3,000, or one of every thousand inhabitants. Larger numbers lived in southern Italy, Spain, France, and Germany. In southern Europe, Jews served an important function as cultural and intellectual intermediaries between the Muslim and Christian worlds.

The religious enthusiasm of the High Middle Ages produced an outburst of intolerance against the supposed enemies of Christianity. Although this was evident in the Crusades against the Muslims (see "10-4 The Crusades," later in this chapter), Christians also took up the search for enemies at home, persecuting Jews in France and the Rhineland at the time of the First Crusades. Jews in Speyer, Worms, Mainz, and Cologne were all set upon by bands of Christian crusaders. A contemporary chronicler described how a band of English crusaders who stopped at Lisbon, Portugal, en route to the Holy Land "drove away the pagans and Jews, servants of the king, who dwelt in the city and plundered their property and possessions, and burned their houses; and they then stripped their vineyards, not leaving them so much as a grape or a cluster."[7] Even people who tried to protect the Jews were in danger. When the archbishop of Mainz provided shelter for the Jews, a mob stormed his palace and forced him to flee. Popes also came to the Jews' defense by issuing decrees ordering that Jews were not to be persecuted.

Nevertheless, in the thirteenth century, in the supercharged religious atmosphere created by the struggle with heretics, Jews were persecuted more and more (see Historical Voices, "Treatment of the Jews," p. 297). Friars urged action against these "murderers of Christ," referring to the traditional Christian view of the Jews as being responsible for the death of Jesus, and organized public burnings of Jewish books. The Fourth Lateran Council in 1215 decreed that Jews must wear special clothing so that they could be distinguished from Christians. The same council encouraged the development of Jewish ghettos, or walled enclosures, not to protect the Jews but to isolate them from Christians. The persecutions and the new image of the hated Jew stimulated a tradition of anti-Semitism that proved to be one of Christian Europe's most insidious contributions to the Western heritage.

By the end of the thirteenth century, European kings, who had earlier portrayed themselves as protectors of the Jews, had fleeced the Jewish communities of their money and then renounced their protection. Edward I expelled all Jews from England in 1290. The French king followed suit in 1306 but readmitted the Jews in 1315. They then left of their own accord in 1322. As the policy of expulsion spread into central Europe, most northern European Jews were forced to move into Poland as a last refuge.

Intolerance and Homosexuality The climate of intolerance that characterized thirteenth-century attitudes toward Muslims, heretics, and Jews was also evident toward homosexuals. Although the church had condemned homosexuality in the early Middle Ages, it had not been overly concerned with homosexual behavior, an attitude also prevalent in the secular world. By the thirteenth century, however, these tolerant attitudes had altered drastically. Some historians connect this change to the century's climate of fear and intolerance against any group that deviated from the standards of the majority. A favorite approach of the critics was to identify homosexuals with other detested groups. Homosexuality was portrayed as a regular practice of Muslims and such notorious heretics as the Albigensians. Between 1250 and 1300, what had been tolerated in most of Europe became a criminal act deserving of death.

The legislation against homosexuality commonly referred to it as a "sin against nature." This is precisely the argument developed by Thomas Aquinas (see Chapter 9), who formed Catholic opinion on the subject for centuries to come. In his *Summa Theologica*, Aquinas argued that because the purpose of sex was procreation, it could legitimately take place only in ways that did not exclude this possibility. Hence, homosexuality was "contrary to nature" and a deviation from the natural order established by God. This argument and laws prohibiting homosexual activity on pain of severe punishment remained the norm in Europe and elsewhere in the Christian world until the twentieth century.

Treatment of the Jews

 Q *What do these documents reveal about Christian attitudes toward the Jews?*

THE NEW RELIGIOUS SENSIBILITIES that emerged in the High Middle Ages also had a negative side, the turning of Christians against their supposed enemies. Although the Crusades provide the most obvious example, Christians also turned on the "murderers of Christ," the Jews. As a result, Jews suffered increased persecution. These three documents show different sides of the picture. The first is Canon 68 of the decrees of the Fourth Lateran Council called by Pope Innocent III in 1215. The decree specifies the need for special dress, one of the ways Christians tried to separate Jews from their community. The second selection is a chronicler's account of the most deadly charge levied against the Jews—that they were guilty of the ritual murder of Christian children to obtain Christian blood for the Passover service. This charge led to the murder of many Jews. The third document, taken from a list of regulations issued by the city of Avignon, France, illustrates the contempt Christian society held for the Jews.

Canon 68

In some provinces a difference in dress distinguishes the Jews or Saracens [Muslims] from the Christians, but in certain others such a confusion has grown up that they cannot be distinguished by any difference. Thus it happens at times that through error Christians have relations with the women of Jews or Saracens, and Jews or Saracens with Christian women. Therefore, that they may not, under pretext of error of this sort, excuse themselves in the future for the excesses of such prohibited intercourse, we decree that such Jews and Saracens of both sexes in every Christian province and at all times shall be marked off in the eyes of the public from other peoples through the character of their dress. . . . Moreover, during the last three days before Easter and especially on Good Friday,

they shall not go forth in public at all, for the reason that some of them on these very days, as we hear, do not blush to go forth better dressed and are not afraid to mock the Christians who maintain the memory of the most holy Passion by wearing signs of mourning.

An Accusation of the Ritual Murder of a Christian Child by Jews

[The eight-year-old boy] Harold, who is buried in the Church of St. Peter the Apostle, at Gloucester . . . is said to have been carried away secretly by Jews, in the opinion of many, on Feb. 21, and by them hidden till March 16. On that night, on the sixth of the preceding feast, the Jews of all England coming together as if to circumcise a certain boy, pretend deceitfully that they are about to celebrate the feast [Passover] appointed by law in such case, and deceiving the citizens of Gloucester with the fraud, they tortured the lad placed before them with immense tortures. It is true no Christian was present, or saw or heard the deed, nor have we found that anything was betrayed by any Jew. But a little while after when the whole convent of monks of Gloucester and almost all the citizens of that city, and innumerable persons coming to the spectacle, saw the wounds of the dead body, scars of fire, the thorns fixed on his head, and liquid wax poured into the eyes and face, and touched it with the diligent examination of their hands, those tortures were believed or guessed to have been inflicted on him in that manner. It was clear that they had made him a glorious martyr to Christ, being slain without sin, and having bound his feet with his own girdle, threw him into the river Severn.

The Regulations of Avignon, 1243

Likewise, we declare that Jews or whores shall not dare to touch with their hands either bread or fruit put out for sale, and that if they should do this they must buy what they have touched.

Source: J. Jacobs, *The Jews of Angevin England* (London: David Nutt, 1893), p. 45.

10-4 The Crusades

 Q FOCUS QUESTION: What were the reasons for the Crusades, and who or what benefited the most from the experience of the Crusades?

Another manifestation of the wave of religious enthusiasm that seized Europe in the High Middle Ages was the series of Crusades mounted against the Muslims. The Crusades gave the revived papacy of the High Middle Ages yet another

opportunity to demonstrate its influence over European society. The Crusades were a curious mix of God and warfare, two of the chief concerns of the Middle Ages.

10-4a Background to the Crusades

Although European civilization developed in relative isolation, it had never entirely lost contact with the lands and empires of the east. At the end of the eleventh century, that contact increased, in part because developments in the Islamic and Byzantine worlds prompted the first major attempt of the new European civilization to expand beyond Europe proper.

Islam and the Seljuk Turks By the mid-tenth century, the Islamic empire led by the Abbasid caliphate in Baghdad was disintegrating. An attempt was made in the tenth century to unify the Islamic world under the direction of a Shi'ite dynasty known as the Fatimids. Their origins lay in North Africa, but they managed to conquer Egypt and establish the new city of Cairo as their capital. In establishing a Shi'ite caliphate, they became rivals to the Sunni caliphate of Baghdad and divided the Islamic world.

Nevertheless, the Fatimid dynasty prospered and surpassed the Abbasid caliphate as the dynamic center of Islam. Benefiting from their position in the heart of the Nile delta, the Fatimids played a major role in the regional trade passing from the Mediterranean to the Red Sea and beyond. They were tolerant in matters of religion and created a strong army by using nonnative peoples as mercenaries. One of these peoples, the Seljuk (SEL-jook) Turks, soon posed a threat to the Fatimids themselves.

The Seljuk Turks were a nomadic people from Central Asia who had been converted to Islam and flourished as military mercenaries for the Abbasid caliphate. Moving gradually into Persia and Armenia, their numbers grew until by the eleventh century they were able to take over the eastern provinces of the Abbasid empire. In 1055, a Turkish leader captured Baghdad and assumed command of the Abbasid empire with the title of **sultan** ("holder of power"). While the Abbasid caliph remained the chief representative of Sunni religious authority, the real military and political power of the state was in the hands of the Seljuk Turks. In Europe and within the Muslim world itself, the Turks were initially regarded as a disaster. They were viewed as barbarians who destroyed civilizations and oppressed populations. In many respects, however, Turkish rule in the Middle East was probably beneficial by bringing an end to the squabbles between Sunni and Shi'ite Muslims while supporting the Sunnis. The Turks also put their energies into revitalizing Islamic law and institutions.

By the latter part of the eleventh century, the Seljuk Turks were exerting military pressure on Egypt and the Byzantine Empire. When the Byzantine emperor foolishly challenged the Turks, the latter routed the Byzantine army at Manzikert in 1071. In dire straits, the Byzantines looked west for help, setting in motion the papal pleas that led to the Crusades. To understand the complexities of the situation, however, we need to look first at the Byzantine Empire.

The Byzantine Empire The Macedonian dynasty of the tenth and eleventh centuries had restored much of the power of the Byzantine Empire; its incompetent successors, however, reversed most of the gains. After the Macedonian dynasty was extinguished in 1056, the empire was beset by internal struggles for power between ambitious military leaders and aristocratic families who attempted to buy the support of the great landowners of Anatolia by allowing them greater control over their peasants. This policy was self-destructive, however,

because the peasant-warrior was the traditional backbone of the Byzantine state.

The growing division between the Catholic Church of the West and the Eastern Orthodox Church of the Byzantine Empire also weakened the Byzantine state. The Eastern Orthodox Church was unwilling to accept the pope's claim that he was the sole head of the church. This dispute reached a climax in 1054 when Pope Leo IX and Patriarch Michael Cerularius (seer-oo-LAR-ee-uss), head of the Byzantine church, formally excommunicated each other, initiating a schism between the two great branches of Christianity that has not been healed to this day.

The Byzantine Empire faced external threats to its security as well. The greatest challenge came from the Seljuk Turks who had moved into Asia Minor—the heartland of the empire and its main source of food and manpower (see Map 10.8). After defeating the Byzantine forces at Manzikert in 1071, the Turks advanced into Anatolia, where many peasants, already disgusted by their exploitation at the hands of Byzantine landowners, readily accepted Turkish control.

A new dynasty, however, soon breathed new life into the Byzantine Empire. The Comneni, under Alexius I Comnenus (kahm-NEE-nuss) (r. 1081–1118), were victorious on the Greek Adriatic coast against the Normans, defeated the Pechenegs in the Balkans, and stopped the Turks in Anatolia. Lacking the resources to undertake additional campaigns against the Turks, Emperor Alexius I turned to the West for military assistance. The positive response to the emperor's request led to the Crusades. The Byzantine Empire lived to regret it.

10-4b The Early Crusades

The Crusades were based on the idea of a holy war against the infidels or unbelievers. The wrath of Christians was directed against the Muslims and had already found some expression

Frontier between the Byzantine and Abbasid empires, c. 930

Areas of Anatolia occupied by the Abbasids in 1070

Areas of Anatolia occupied by the Seljuk Turks in the early twelfth century

MAP 10.8 **The Seljuk Turks and the Byzantines**

in the attempt to reconquer Spain from the Muslims and the success of the Normans in reclaiming Sicily. At the end of the eleventh century, Christian Europe found itself with a glorious opportunity to attack the Muslims.

The immediate impetus for the Crusades came when the Byzantine emperor, Alexius I, asked Pope Urban II (1088–1099) for help against the Seljuk Turks. The pope saw a golden opportunity to provide papal leadership for a great cause: to rally the warriors of Europe for the liberation of Jerusalem and the Holy Land from the infidel. As we have seen, the Holy City of Jerusalem—where Jesus had lived and died—had long been the object of Christian pilgrimages. At the Council of Clermont in southern France near the end of 1095, Urban challenged Christians to take up their weapons against the infidel and join in a holy war to recover the Holy Land (see Historical Voices, "Pope Urban Proclaims a Crusade," p. 300). The pope promised remission of sins: "All who die by the way, whether by land or by sea, or in battle against the pagans, shall have immediate remission of sins. This I grant them through the power of God with which I am invested."[8]

The initial response to Urban's speech reveals how appealing many people found this combined call to military arms and religious fervor. The First Crusade was preceded by an exercise in religious fanaticism and futility. A self-appointed leader, Peter the Hermit, who preached of his visions of the Holy City of Jerusalem, convinced a large mob, most of them poor and many of them peasants, to undertake a Crusade to the east. One person who encountered Peter described him in these words: "Outdoors he wore a woolen tunic, which revealed his ankles, and above it a hood; he wore a cloak to cover his upper body, a bit of his arms, but his feet were bare. He drank wine and ate fish, but scarcely ever ate bread. This man, partly because of his reputation, partly because of his preaching, [assembled] a very large army."[9]

This "Peasants' Crusade," or "Crusade of the Poor," comprised a ragtag rabble that moved through the Balkans, terrorizing the natives and looting food and supplies. Their misplaced religious enthusiasm led to another tragic by-product as well, the persecution of the Jews, long depicted by the church as the murderers of Christ. As a contemporary chronicler put it, "they persecuted the hated race of the Jews wherever they were found." Two bands of peasant crusaders, led by Peter the Hermit, managed to reach Constantinople. Emperor Alexius wisely shipped them over to Asia Minor where the Turks massacred the undisciplined and poorly armed rabble.

HISTORIANS DEBATE **What Motivated the Crusaders?** Pope Urban II did not share the wishful thinking of the peasant crusaders but was more inclined to trust knights who had been well trained in the art of war. The warriors of western Europe, particularly France, formed the first crusading armies. But was Urban motivated by a desire to free Jerusalem from the infidels in a just war? One historian maintains that the pope thought of the crusade as "an attempt to consolidate papal empowerment and expand Rome's sphere of influence," in order to "meet the needs of the papacy." Some historians have also suggested that Urban might have welcomed the invitation of the Byzantine emperor in order to heal the schism between the Catholic and the Greek Orthodox churches that had occurred in 1054.

Historians have long debated the motives of the Crusaders. Many historians today maintain that the knights who made up this first serious crusading host were motivated by religious fervor and an opportunity to gain salvation—had the pope not offered a full remission of sins for those who participated in these "armed pilgrimages"? But were there other attractions as well? Some historians argue that we cannot preclude other possibilities for some of the Crusaders—including that they sought adventure and welcomed a legitimate opportunity to pursue their favorite pastime (fighting), as well as an opportunity to gain territory, riches, status, and possibly a title. An older generation of historians had believed that from the perspective of the pope and European monarchs, the Crusades offered a way to rid Europe of contentious young nobles who disturbed the peace and wasted lives and energy fighting each other. The Catholic Church had tried earlier with the "Peace of God" and "Truce of God" to limit the ongoing bloodletting, but without a great deal of success (see Chapter 9). Historians recently, however, have made a strong case against this old argument and maintain that the Crusaders were wealthy and pious nobles who even risked their wealth to pursue a just cause of helping their fellow Christians in the east. Then, too, the older perspective that merchants in many Italian cities relished the prospect of new trading opportunities in Muslim lands has also been rejected. Instead, many scholars have emphasized that many Italians also were motivated by the pursuit of a just cause to help their fellow Christians.

The First Crusade In the First Crusade, begun in 1096, three organized bands of noble warriors, most of them French, made their way to the east (see Map 10.9). The crusading army probably numbered several thousand cavalry and as many as 10,000 foot soldiers. After the capture of Antioch in 1098, much of the crusading host proceeded down the coast of Palestine, evading the garrisoned coastal cities, and reached Jerusalem in June 1099 (see Image 10.8). After a five-week siege, the Holy City was taken amid a massacre of the inhabitants (see Opposing Viewpoints, "The Siege of Jerusalem: Christian and Muslim Perspectives," p. 302).

After further conquest of Palestinian lands, the crusaders ignored the wishes of the Byzantine emperor (who believed the crusaders were working on his behalf) and organized four crusader states (Edessa, Antioch, Tripoli, and Jerusalem). Because Muslim enemies surrounded the crusader states, they grew increasingly dependent on the Italian commercial cities for supplies from Europe. Some Italian cities, such as Genoa, Pisa, and especially Venice, benefitted in the process.

The Second Crusade At first, Muslim rulers in the Middle East were taken aback by the invading crusaders, whose armored cavalry presented a new challenge to local warriors, and their response was ineffectual. The Seljuk Turks by that

Pope Urban II Proclaims a Crusade

 How did Urban II appeal to his audience? How well did he understand his audience?

TOWARD THE END OF THE ELEVENTH CENTURY, the Byzantine emperor Alexius I sent Pope Urban II a request for aid against the Seljuk Turks. At the Council of Clermont, Urban II appealed to a large crowd to take up weapons and recover Palestine from the Muslims. This description of Urban's appeal is taken from an account by Fulcher of Chartres.

Pope Urban II

Pope Urban II . . . addressed them [the French] in a very persuasive speech, as follows: "O race of the Franks, O people who live beyond the mountain [that is, north of the Alps], O people loved and chosen of God, as is clear from your many deeds, distinguished over all nations by the situation of your land, your catholic faith, and your regard for the holy church, we have a special message and exhortation for you. For we wish you to know what a grave matter has brought us to your country. The sad news has come from Jerusalem and Constantinople that the people of Persia, an accursed and foreign race [the Seljuk Turks], enemies of God . . . have invaded the lands of those Christians and devastated them with the sword, rapine, and fire. Some of the Christians they have carried away as slaves, others they have put to death. The churches they have either destroyed or turned into mosques. They desecrate and overthrow the altars. They circumcise the Christians and pour the blood from the circumcision on the altars or in the baptismal fonts. Some they kill in a horrible way by cutting open the abdomen, taking out a part of the entrails and tying them to a stake; they then beat them and compel them to walk until all their entrails are drawn out and they fall to the ground. Some they use as targets for their arrows. They compel some to stretch out their necks and then they try to see whether they can cut off their heads with one strike of the sword. It is better to say nothing of their horrible treatment of the women. They have taken from the Greek empire a tract of land so large that it takes more than two months to walk through it. Whose duty is to avenge this and recover that land, if not yours? For to you more than to any other nations the Lord has given the military spirit, courage, agile bodies, and the bravery to strike down those who resist you. Let your minds be stirred to bravery by the deeds of your forefathers, and by the efficiency and greatness of Karl the Great [Charlemagne] . . . and of the other kings who have destroyed Turkish kingdoms, and established Christianity in their lands. You should be moved especially by the holy grave of our Lord and Savior which is now held by unclean peoples, and by the holy places which are treated with dishonor and irreverently befouled with their uncleanness. . . .

"O bravest of knights, descendants of unconquered ancestors, do not be weaker than they, but remember their courage. . . . Set out on the road to the holy sepulchre, take the land from that wicked people, and make it your own. . . . Jerusalem is the best of all lands, more fruitful than all others. . . . This land our Savior made illustrious by his birth, beautiful with his life, and sacred with his suffering. . . . This royal city is now held captive by her enemies, and made pagan by those who know not God. She asks and longs to be liberated and does not cease to beg you to come to her aid. . . . Set out on this journey and you will obtain the remission of your sins and be sure of the incorruptible glory of the kingdom of heaven."

When Pope Urban had said this and much more of the same sort, all who were present were moved to cry out with one accord, "It is the will of God, it is the will of God." When the pope heard this he raised his eyes to heaven and gave thanks to God, and commanding silence with a gesture of his hand, he said: "My dear brethren, today there is fulfilled in you that which the Lord says in the Gospel, 'Where two or three are gathered together in my name, there am I in the midst.' For unless the Lord God had been in your minds you would not all have said the same thing. . . . So I say unto you, God, who put those words into your hearts, has caused you to utter them. Therefore let these words be your battle cry, because God caused you to speak them. Whenever you meet the enemy in battle, you shall all cry out, 'It is the will of God, it is the will of God. . . .' Whoever therefore shall determine to make this journey and shall make a vow to God and shall offer himself as a living sacrifice, holy, acceptable to God, shall wear a cross on his brow or on his breast. And when he returns after having fulfilled his vow he shall wear the cross on his back."

Source: O. J. Thatcher and E. H. McNeal, *A Sourcebook for Mediaeval History* (New York: Charles Scribner's Sons, 1905).

---

time were preoccupied with events taking place farther to the east and took no action themselves. But the crusader states soon foundered, and by the 1120s, the Muslims were striking back. In 1144, Edessa became the first of the four Latin states to be recaptured. Its fall led to renewed calls for another Crusade, especially from the monastic firebrand Saint Bernard of Clairvaux, who exclaimed, "Now, on account of our sins, the sacrilegious enemies of the cross have begun to show their faces. . . . What are you doing, you servants of the cross? Will you throw to the dogs that which is most holy? Will you cast pearls before swine?"[10] Bernard aimed his message at knights and even managed to enlist two powerful rulers, King Louis VII of France and Emperor Conrad III of Germany. Their Second Crusade, however, proved to be a total failure.

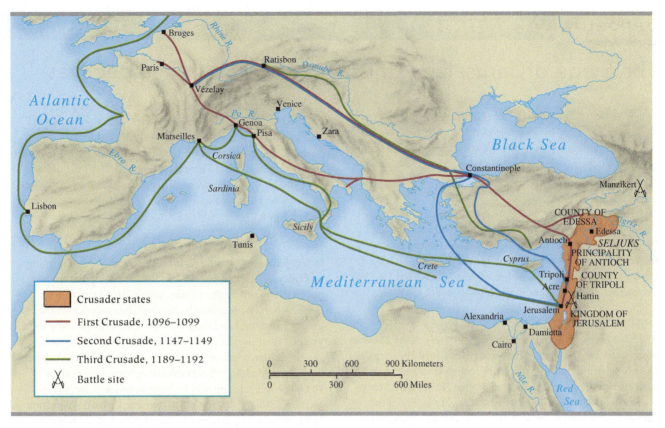

MAP 10.9 **The Early Crusades.** Pope Urban II launched the Crusades to recapture the Holy Land from the "enemies of God," a call met with great enthusiasm in Europe. The fighters of the First Crusade massacred the inhabitants of Jerusalem and established the crusader states.

Q *In the Third Crusade, which countries sent crusaders by land and which by sea, and why would they choose these methods of travel?*

IMAGE 10.8 **The First Crusade: The Capture of Jerusalem.** Recruited from the noble class of western Europe, the first crusading army had taken Antioch by 1098. Working down the coast of Palestine, the crusaders captured Jerusalem in 1099. Shown here in a fifteenth-century manuscript illustration is a fanciful re-creation of the looting of Jerusalem after its capture by the Christian crusaders.

Q *Despite its fanciful nature, what does this image reveal about the motives of some of the crusaders?*

Jean de Courcy/Getty Images

The Siege of Jerusalem: Christian and Muslim Perspectives

 What happened to the inhabitants of Jerusalem when the Christian knights captured the city? How do you explain the extreme intolerance and brutality of the Christian knights? How do these two accounts differ, and how are they similar?

DURING THE FIRST CRUSADE, Christian knights laid siege to Jerusalem in June 1099. The first excerpt is taken from an account by Fulcher of Chartres, who accompanied the crusaders to the Holy Land. The second selection is by a Muslim writer, Ibn al-Athir, whose account of the First Crusade can be found in his history of the Muslim world.

Fulcher of Chartres, *Chronicle of the First Crusade*

Then the Franks entered the city magnificently at the noonday hour on Friday, the day of the week when Christ redeemed the whole world on the cross. With trumpets sounding and with everything in an uproar, exclaiming: "Help, God!" they vigorously pushed into the city, and straightway raised the banner on the top of the wall. All the heathen, completely terrified, changed their boldness to swift flight through the narrow streets of the quarters. The more quickly they fled, the more quickly they put to flight.

Count Raymond and his men, who were bravely assailing the city in another section, did not perceive this until they saw the Saracens [Muslims] jumping from the top of the wall. Seeing this, they joyfully ran to the city as quickly as they could, and helped the others pursue and kill the wicked enemy.

Then some, both Arabs and Ethiopians, fled into the Tower of David; others shut themselves in the Temple of the Lord and of Solomon, where in the halls a very great attack was made on them. Nowhere was there a place where the Saracens could escape swordsmen.

On the top of Solomon's Temple, to which they had climbed in fleeing, many were shot to death with arrows and cast down headlong from the roof. Within this Temple, about ten thousand were beheaded. If you had been there, your feet would have been stained up to the ankles with the blood of the slain. What more shall I tell? Not one of them was allowed to live. They did not spare the women and children.

Account of Ibn al-Athir

In fact Jerusalem was taken from the north on the morning of Friday 22 Sha'ban 492/15 July 1099. The population was put to the sword by the Franks, who pillaged the area for a week. A band of Muslims barricaded themselves into the Oratory of David and fought on for several days. They were granted their lives in return for surrendering. The Franks honored their word, and the group left by night for Ascalon. In the Masjid al-Aqsa the Franks slaughtered more than 70,000 people, among them a large number of Imams and Muslim scholars, devout and ascetic men who had left their homelands to live lives of pious seclusion in the Holy Place. The Franks stripped the Dome of the Rock of more than forty silver candelabra, each of them weighing 3,600 drams, and a great silver lamp weighing forty-four Syrian pounds, as well as a hundred and fifty smaller candelabra and more than twenty gold ones, and a great deal more booty. Refugees from Syria reached Baghdad in Ramadan, among them the qadi Abu sa'd al-Harawi. They told the Caliph's ministers a story that wrung their hearts and brought tears to their eyes. On Friday they went to the Cathedral Mosque and begged for help, weeping so that their hearers wept with them as they described the sufferings of the Muslims in that Holy City: the men killed, the women and children taken prisoner, the homes pillaged. Because of the terrible hardships they had suffered, they were allowed to break the fast.

Sources: E. Peters, ed., *The Chronicle of Fulcher of Chartres and Other Source Materials*, 2nd ed. (Philadelphia: University of Pennsylvania Press, 1998), pp. 90–91; E. J. Costello, ed., trans., *Arab Historians of the Crusades* (Berkeley: University of California Press, 1969).

The Third Crusade In 1169, Sunni Muslims under the leadership of Saladin (SAL-uh-din) brought an end to the Fatimid dynasty in Egypt. Proclaiming himself sultan, Saladin succeeded in establishing his control over both Egypt and Syria and began to confront the Christian states in the area with united Muslim power on two fronts. In 1187, Saladin's army invaded the kingdom of Jerusalem and destroyed the Christian forces there. Further operations reduced Christian occupation in the area to a handful of fortresses along the northern coast. Unlike the Christians of the First Crusade, who had slaughtered much of the population of Jerusalem when they captured the city, Saladin did not permit a massacre of the civilian population and even tolerated Christian religious services in conquered territories. For a time, Christian occupation forces even carried on a lively trade with Muslim communities in the region.

The fall of the Holy City of Jerusalem, however, set all of Christendom ablaze with calls for a new Crusade. Three major monarchs agreed to lead the Third Crusade in person: Emperor Frederick Barbarossa of Germany, King Richard I the Lion-hearted of England (r. 1189–1199), and Philip II Augustus, king of France. Some of the crusaders finally arrived in the Middle East by 1189 only to encounter problems. Frederick Barbarossa drowned while swimming in a local river, and his army quickly fell apart. The English and French arrived by sea and met with success against the coastal cities, where they had the support of their fleets, but when they moved inland, they failed miserably. Eventually, after Philip went home, Richard negotiated a settlement whereby Saladin agreed to allow Christian pilgrims free access to Jerusalem.

10-4c The Crusades of the Thirteenth Century

After the death of Saladin in 1193, Pope Innocent III initiated the Fourth Crusade. On its way to the Holy Land, the crusading army became involved in a dispute over the succession to the Byzantine throne. Although some historians believe the Venetian leaders of the Fourth Crusade saw an opportunity to neutralize their greatest commercial competitor, the Byzantine Empire, it is more likely that a series of unfortunate circumstances and misunderstandings led the western Crusaders to sack the great capital city in 1204 and create a new Latin Empire of Constantinople. Not until 1261 did a Byzantine army recapture Constantinople. The Byzantine Empire had been saved, but it was no longer a great Mediterranean power. The restored empire now comprised only the city of Constantinople and its surrounding territory as well as some lands in Asia Minor. Though reduced in size, the empire limped along for another 190 years until its weakened condition finally enabled the Ottoman Turks to conquer it in 1453.

Despite the failures, the crusading ideal was not yet completely lost. In Germany in 1212, a youth known as Nicholas of Cologne announced that God had inspired him to lead the so-called Children's Crusade to the Holy Land. Thousands of young people joined Nicholas and made their way down the Rhine and across the Alps to Italy, where the pope told them to go home. Most tried to do so. The next Crusade of adult warriors was hardly more successful. The Fifth Crusade (1219–1221) attempted to recover the Holy Land by way of the powerful Muslim state of Egypt. The Crusade achieved some early successes, but its ultimate failure marked an end to papal leadership of the western crusaders.

The Sixth Crusade, which was led by the German emperor Frederick II, took place without papal support because the emperor had been excommunicated by the pope for starting late. In 1228, Frederick marched into Jerusalem and accepted the crown as king of Jerusalem after he had made an agreement with the sultan of Egypt. The Holy City had been taken without a fight and without papal support. However, the city fell once again ten years later, this time to a group of Turks allied with the sultan of Egypt. The last two major Crusades, although well organized by the pious king of France, Louis IX, were complete failures. Soon the remaining Christian possessions in the Middle East were retaken. Acre, the last foothold

CHRONOLOGY	The Crusades
Pope Urban II's call for a Crusade at Clermont	1095
First Crusade	1096–1099
Fall of Edessa	1144
Second Crusade	1147–1149
Saladin's conquest of Jerusalem	1187
Third Crusade	1189–1192
Fourth Crusade—sack of Constantinople	1204
Latin Empire of Constantinople	1204–1261
Children's Crusade	1212
Fifth Crusade	1219–1221
Frederick II occupies Jerusalem (Sixth Crusade)	1228
First Crusade of Louis IX (Seventh Crusade)	1248–1254
Second Crusade of Louis IX (Eighth Crusade)	1270
Surrender of Acre and end of Christian presence in the Holy Land	1291

of the crusaders, surrendered in 1291. All in all, the Crusades had failed to accomplish their primary goal of holding the Holy Land for the Christian West.

HISTORIANS DEBATE 10-4d **What Were the Effects of the Crusades?**

Whether the Crusades had much effect on European civilization is debatable. The crusaders made little long-term impact on the Middle East, where the only visible remnants of their conquests were their castles. There may have been some broadening of perspective that comes from the exchange between two cultures, but the interaction of Christian Europe with the Muslim world was actually both more intense and more meaningful in Spain and Sicily than in the Holy Land. Nevertheless, some historians believe that there was some influence of the Crusades on Europe's intellectual development with the absorption of the advanced science and learning of the Islamic world.

Did the Crusades help stabilize European society by removing large numbers of young warriors who would have fought each other in Europe? Some historians think so and believe that Western monarchs established their control more easily as a result. However, as we have seen, historians today doubt this and argue that it was the wealthy and pious nobles who risked their lives and fortunes to help their fellow Christians. Taking the cross as a religious incentive was important to many nobles. As one prayed, "Lord, take me from wars between Christians in which I have spent much of my life; let me die in your service so I may share your kingdom in Paradise."[11]

There is no doubt that the Crusades did contribute to the economic growth of the Italian port cities, especially Genoa, Pisa, and Venice. But it is important to remember that the growing wealth and population of twelfth-century Europe had made the Crusades possible in the first place. The Crusades may have enhanced Italian trade in the Mediterranean, but they certainly did not cause the revival of trade. Even without the Crusades, Italian merchants would have pursued new trade contacts with the eastern world. Moreover, there was little economic gain for many Crusaders, most of whom did not settle in the east but returned home after their initial success. Many faced economic ruin after selling their lands to finance their expeditions.

Did the Crusades have side effects that would haunt European society for generations? The Crusades did not lead, as some historians have suggested, to the decline of the Muslim world, which had little interest in the Crusades during the Middle Ages; after all, once united, the Muslim world had ended the crusader states in the Middle East. Not until the twentieth century, after believers in Western imperialism redefined the Crusades as the first effort of Western colonialism, did many in the Islamic world begin to view the Crusades as the first attempt of Western powers to colonize the Middle East, helping to lead to the troubled relationship between the Muslim world and the West today.

Another possible side effect is more apparent. The first widespread attacks on the Jews began with the Crusades. As some Christians argued, to undertake holy wars against infidel Muslims while the "murderers of Christ" ran free at home was unthinkable. With the crusades, the massacre of Jews became a regular feature of medieval European life.

CHAPTER SUMMARY

During the High Middle Ages, European society was dominated by a landed aristocracy whose primary function was to fight. These nobles built innumerable castles that gave a distinctive look to the countryside. Although lords and vassals seemed forever mired in endless petty conflicts, over time medieval kings began to exert a centralizing authority and inaugurated the process of developing new kinds of monarchical states. By the thirteenth century, European monarchs were solidifying their governmental institutions in pursuit of greater power. The nobles, who rationalized their warlike attitudes by calling themselves the defenders of Christian society, continued to dominate the medieval world politically, economically, and socially. But quietly and surely, within this world of castles and private power, kings gradually began to extend their public powers and developed the machinery of government that would enable them to become the centers of political authority in Europe. The actions of these medieval monarchs laid the foundation for the European kingdoms that in one form or another have dominated the European political scene ever since.

The power of both nobles and kings, however, was often overshadowed by the authority of the Catholic Church, perhaps the dominant institution of the High Middle Ages. The church shared in the challenge of new growth by reforming itself and striking out on a path toward greater papal power, both within the church and over European society.

The High Middle Ages also witnessed a spiritual renewal that led to numerous and even divergent paths: expanded papal leadership, especially evident in the reign of Pope Innocent III, the development of centralized administrative machinery within the church that buttressed papal authority, and new dimensions to the religious life of the clergy and laity. A wave of religious enthusiasm in the twelfth and thirteenth centuries led to the formation of new religious orders that worked to provide for the needs of the people, especially their concern for achieving salvation. But there were also seeds of discontent and change. Dissent from church teaching and practices grew, leading to a climate of fear and intolerance as the church responded with inquisitorial procedures to enforce conformity to its teachings.

At the same time, the spiritual renewal of the High Middle Ages also gave rise to the crusading "holy warrior" who killed for God, thereby creating an animosity between Christians and Muslims that still has repercussions to this day. The economic, political, and religious growth of the High Middle Ages had given European society a new confidence that enabled it to look beyond its borders to the lands and empires of the east. Only a confident Europe could have undertaken the Crusades, the military effort to recover the Holy Land of the Near East from the Muslims. The Crusades gave the revived papacy of the High Middle Ages yet another opportunity to demonstrate its influence over European society. And yet, the Crusades ended ignominiously with the fall of the last crusading foothold in the east in 1291. By that time, more and more signs of trouble were appearing. As we shall see in the next chapter, the fourteenth century would prove to be a time of crisis for European civilization.

CHAPTER TIMELINE

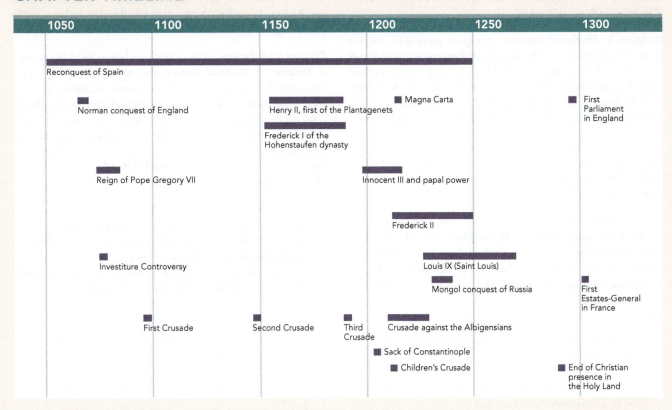

1050	1100	1150	1200	1250	1300

Reconquest of Spain

Norman conquest of England

Henry II, first of the Plantagenets

Magna Carta

First Parliament in England

Frederick I of the Hohenstaufen dynasty

Reign of Pope Gregory VII

Innocent III and papal power

Frederick II

Investiture Controversy

Louis IX (Saint Louis)

Mongol conquest of Russia

First Estates-General in France

First Crusade

Second Crusade

Third Crusade

Crusade against the Albigensians

Sack of Constantinople

Children's Crusade

End of Christian presence in the Holy Land

CHAPTER REVIEW

Upon Reflection

Q What factors contributed to the development of centralized kingdoms in some parts of Europe but not in others?

Q What are the similarities and dissimilarities in the development of England, France, and the German empire?

Q The medieval Catholic Church developed in the High Middle Ages at two levels, an institutional level and a popular religion level. What are the most important features of each level?

Q What were the motivations of the crusaders, and how successful were they?

Key Terms

exchequer (p. 277)
common law (p. 278)
Reconquista (p. 281)
boyars (p. 285)
lay investiture (p. 287)
excommunication (p. 288)
papal curia (p. 289)
interdict (p. 289)

sacraments (p. 289)
relics (p. 294)
indulgences (p. 294)
purgatory (p. 294)
dualism (p. 295)
crusade (p. 295)
sultan (p. 298)

Full definitions also appear in the Glossary at the end of the book.

Suggestions for Further Reading

The Medieval States There are numerous works on the different medieval states. On England, see **R. Frame, *The Political Development of the British Isles, 1100–1400*,** 2nd ed. (Oxford, 1995). On France, see **M. Bull, *France in the Central Middle Ages, 900–1200*** (Oxford, 2003). On Spain, see **B. F. Reilly, *The Medieval Spains*** (Cambridge, 2010). On Germany, see **B. Arnold,**

Princes and Territories in Medieval Germany, 2nd ed. (Cambridge, 2005). On Italy, see **P. Jones**, *The Italian City-State: From Commune to Signoria* (Oxford, 1997).

Religion in Medieval Europe   For good surveys of religion in medieval Europe, see **B. Hamilton**, *Religion in the Medieval West*, 2nd ed. (London, 2003), and **F. D. Logan**, *A History of the Church in the Middle Ages* (London, 2002). Also see **M. Rubin** and **W. Simons**, eds., *Cambridge History of Christianity, Vol. 4, Christianity in Western Europe, c. 1100–c. 1500* (Cambridge, 2009).

The Papacy   On the papacy in the High Middle Ages, see the general survey by **I. S. Robinson**, *The Papacy* (Cambridge, 2003). The papacy of Innocent III is covered in **J. C. Moore**, *Pope Innocent III* (New York, 2003).

Monasticism and Popular Religion   On monasticism see **C. H. Lawrence**, *Medieval Monasticism*, 3rd ed. (London, 2000), a good general account. On Saint Francis, see **A. House**, *Francis of Assisi: A Revolutionary Life* (London, 2001). **S. Flanagan**, *Hildegard of Bingen*, 2nd ed. (London, 1998), is a

good account of the twelfth-century mystic. For an introduction to popular religion in the eleventh and twelfth centuries, see **R. Brooke** and **C. N. L. Brooke**, *Popular Religion in the Middle Ages* (London, 1985).

Dissent and Heresy   On dissent and heresy, see **J. K. Deane**, *A History of Medieval Heresy and Inquisition* (New York, 2011). On the Inquisition, see **C. C. Ames**, *Righteous Persecution: Inquisition, Dominicans, and Christianity in the Middle Ages* (Philadelphia, 2008). On the Albigensians, see **M. Pegg**, *A Most Holy War: The Albigensian Crusade and the Battle for Christendom* (Oxford, 2008). The persecution of Jews in the thirteenth century can be examined in **R. Chazan**, *The Jews of Medieval Western Christendom* (Cambridge, 2006).

The Crusades   For a detailed survey of the Crusades, see **C. Tyerman**, *God's War: A New History of the Crusades* (Cambridge, Mass., 2006). On the First Crusade, see **T. Asbridge**, *The First Crusade: A New History* (Oxford, 2004). The disastrous Fourth Crusade is examined in **J. Phillips**, *The Fourth Crusade and the Sack of Constantinople* (New York, 2004).

Notes

1. Quoted in J. K. Fairbank, E. O. Reischauer, and A. M. Craig, *East Asia: Tradition and Transformation* (Boston, 1973), p. 164.
2. E. F. Henderson, ed., *Selected Historical Documents of the Middle Ages* (London, 1892), p. 332.
3. O. J. Thatcher and E. H. McNeal, eds., *A Source Book for Medieval History* (New York, 1905), p. 208.
4. Quoted in R. H. C. Davis, *A History of Medieval Europe from Constantine to Saint Louis*, 2nd ed. (New York, 1988), p. 252.
5. Luke 18:23–25.
6. Quoted in R. Brooke and C. N. L. Brooke, *Popular Religion in the Middle Ages* (London, 1984), p. 19.
7. H. T. Riley, ed., *Memorials of London and London Life in the Thirteenth, Fourteenth, and Fifteenth Centuries* (London, 1868), vol. 2, pp. 148–149.
8. Thatcher and McNeal, *Source Book for Medieval History*, p. 517.
9. Quoted in T. Asbridge, *The First Crusade: A New History* (Oxford, 2004), pp. 79–80.
10. Quoted in H. E. Mayer, *The Crusades*, trans. John Gillingham (New York, 1972), pp. 99–100.
11. Quoted in C. Tyerman, *God's War: A New History of the Crusades* (Cambridge, Mass., 2006), p. 921.

MindTap *Tips*   Be sure to check out the Cengage Western Civilization playlist on YouTube—a curated collection of interesting videos on topics from the ancient world to the present day. You'll find the link in the Course Videos, Images, Maps, and Classroom Activities Unit in MindTap.

CHAPTER 11

The Later Middle Ages: Crisis and Disintegration in the Fourteenth Century

IMAGE 11.1 **A Medieval Illustration of Death as a Reaper During the Black Death**

CONNECTIONS TO TODAY

What similarities and differences do you see in the responses to natural disasters in the fourteenth and twenty-first centuries?

AS A RESULT OF THEIR CONQUESTS in the thirteenth and fourteenth centuries, the Mongols created a vast empire stretching from Russia in the west to China in the east. Mongol rule brought stability to the Eurasian trade routes; increased trade brought prosperity but also avenues for the spread of flea-infested rats that carried bubonic plague to both East Asia and Europe. The mid-fourteenth century witnessed one of the most destructive natural disasters in history—the Black Death. One contemporary observer named Henry Knighton, a canon of Saint Mary of the Meadow Abbey in Leicester, England, was simply overwhelmed by the magnitude of the catastrophe. Knighton began his account of the great plague with these words: "In this year [1348] and in the following one there was a general mortality of people throughout the whole world." Few were left untouched; the plague struck even isolated monasteries: "At Montpellier, there remained out of a hundred and forty friars only seven." Animals, too, were devastated: "During this same year, there was a great mortality of sheep everywhere in the kingdom; in one place and in one pasture, more than five thousand sheep died and became so putrefied that neither beast nor bird wanted to touch them." Knighton was also stunned by the economic and social consequences of the Black Death. Prices dropped: "And the price of everything was cheap, because of the fear of death; there were very few who took any care for their wealth, or for anything else." Meanwhile laborers were scarce, so their wages increased: "In the following autumn, one could not hire a reaper at a lower wage than eight pence with food, or a mower at less than twelve pence with food. Because of this, much grain rotted in the fields for lack of harvesting." So many people died that some towns were deserted and some villages disappeared altogether: "Many small villages and hamlets were completely deserted; there was not one house left in them, but all those who had lived in them were dead."[1] Some people thought the end of the world was at hand.

Plague was not the only disaster in the fourteenth century. Signs of disintegration were everywhere: famine, economic depression, war, social upheaval, a rise in crime and violence, and a decline in the power of the universal Catholic Church. Periods of disintegration, however, are often fertile ground for change and new developments. Out of the dissolution of medieval civilization came a rebirth of culture that many historians have labeled the Renaissance.

11-1 A Time of Troubles: Black Death and Social Crisis

 FOCUS QUESTION: What was the Black Death, and what impact did it have on the society and economy of Europe?

Well into the thirteenth century, Europe had experienced good harvests and an expanding population. By the end of the century, however, a period of disastrous changes had begun.

11-1a Famine and Population

For one thing, there were noticeable changes in weather patterns as Europe entered a "little ice age." Shortened growing seasons and disastrous weather conditions, including severe storms and constant rain, led to widespread famine and hunger. The great famine of 1315–1317 in northern Europe resulted in extreme hunger and starvation. The great famine expanded to other parts of Europe in an all-too-familiar pattern, as is evident in this scene described by a contemporary chronicler:

> We saw a large number of both sexes, not only from nearby places but from as much as five leagues away, barefooted and maybe even, except for women, in a completely nude state, together with their priests coming in procession at the Church of the Holy Martyrs, their bones bulging out, devoutly carrying bodies of saints and other relics to be adorned hoping to get relief.[2]

Some historians estimate that famine killed 10 percent of the European population in the first half of the fourteenth century.

Europe had experienced a great increase in population in the High Middle Ages. By 1300, however, indications are that Europe had reached the upper limit in the number of people who could be supported by existing agricultural production and technology. Virtually all productive land was being farmed, including many marginal lands that needed intensive cultivation and proved easily susceptible to changing weather patterns.

There was also a movement from overpopulated rural areas to urban locations. Eighteen percent of the people in the village of Broughton in England, for example, migrated between 1288 and 1340. There is no certainty that these migrants found better economic opportunities in urban areas. We might in fact conclude the opposite, based on the reports of increasing numbers of poor people in the cities. In 1330, for example, one chronicler estimated that of the 100,000 inhabitants of Florence, 17,000 were paupers. Moreover, evidence suggests that because of the growing population, by 1300 individual peasant holdings were shrinking in size to an acreage that could no longer support a peasant family. Europe seemed to have reached an upper limit to population growth, and the number of poor appeared to have increased noticeably.

Some historians have pointed out that famine may have led to chronic malnutrition, which in turn contributed to increased infant mortality, lower birthrates, and higher susceptibility to disease because malnourished people are less able to resist infection. This, they argue, helps explain the high mortality of the great plague known as the Black Death.

11-1b The Black Death: From Asia to Europe

In the mid-fourteenth century, the disaster known as the **Black Death** struck Asia, North Africa, and Europe. Although there were several types of plague, the most common and most important form in the diffusion of the Black Death was bubonic plague, which was spread by black rats infested with fleas who were host to the deadly bacterium *Yersinia pestis*.

Role of the Mongols This great plague originated in Asia. After disappearing from Europe and the Middle East in the Middle Ages, bubonic plague continued to haunt areas of southwestern China. In the early 1300s, rats accompanying Mongol troops spread the plague into central China and by 1331 to northeastern China. In one province near Beijing, it was reported that 90 percent of the population died. Overall, China's population may have declined from 120 million in the mid-fourteenth century to 80 million by 1400.

In the thirteenth century, the Mongols had brought much of the Eurasian landmass under a single rule, which in turn facilitated long-distance trade, particularly along the Silk Road (see Chapter 6), now dominated by Muslim merchants from Central Asia. The movement of people and goods throughout this Eurasian landmass also facilitated the spread of the plague.

In the 1330s, there were outbreaks of plague in Central Asia; by 1339, it had reached Samarkand, a caravan stop on the Silk Road. From Central Asia, trading caravans carried the plague westward, to Caffa, on the Black Sea, in 1346, and Constantinople by 1347. Its arrival in the Byzantine Empire was noted by Emperor John VI, who lost a son: "Upon arrival in Constantinople she [the empress] found Andronikos, the youngest born, dead from the invading plague, which . . . attacked almost all the seacoasts of the world and killed most of their people."[3] By 1348, the plague had spread to Mecca and Damascus as well as to other parts of the Middle East. It also spread to North Africa. Between 1347 and 1349, Egypt was heavily hit, perhaps losing one-third of its population. Cairo alone lost almost 300,000 out of a population of one and one-half million.

Causes of the Black Death: Contemporary Views

Q *What were the different explanations for the causes of the Black Death? How do you explain the differences, and what do these explanations tell you about the level of scientific knowledge in the later Middle Ages? Why do you think Jews became scapegoats?*

THE BLACK DEATH was the most terrifying natural calamity of the Middle Ages and affected wide areas of Europe, North Africa, and Asia. People were often baffled by the plague, especially its causes, and gave widely different explanations. The first selection is taken from the preface to the *Decameron* by the fourteenth-century Italian writer Giovanni Boccaccio. The other selections are from contemporary treatises that offered widely different explanations for the great plague.

Giovanni Boccaccio, *Decameron*

In the year of Our Lord 1348 the deadly plague broke out in the great city of Florence, most beautiful of Italian cities. Whether through the operation of the heavenly bodies or because of our own iniquities which the just wrath of God sought to correct, the plague had arisen in the East some years before, causing the death of countless human beings. It spread without stop from one place to another, until, unfortunately, it swept over the West. Neither knowledge nor human foresight availed against it, though the city was cleansed of much filth by chosen officers in charge and sick persons were forbidden to enter it, while advice was broadcast for the preservation of health. Nor did humble supplications serve. Not once but many times they were ordained in the form of processions and other ways for the propitiation of God by the faithful, but, in spite of everything, toward the spring of the year the plague began to show its ravages.

On Earthquakes as the Cause of Plague

There is a fourth opinion, which I consider more likely than the others, which is that insofar as the mortality arose from natural causes its immediate cause was a corrupt and poisonous earthy exhalation, which infected the air in various parts of the world and, when breathed in by people, suffocated them and suddenly snuffed them out. . . .

It is a matter of scientific fact that earthquakes are caused by the exhalation of fumes enclosed in the bowels of the earth. When the fumes batter against the sides of the earth, and cannot get out, the earth is shaken and moves. I say that it is the vapor and corrupted air which has been vented—or so to speak purged—in the earthquake which occurred on St. Paul's day, 1347, along with the corrupted air vented in other earthquakes and eruptions, which has infected the air above the earth and killed people in various parts of the world; and I can bring various reasons in support of this conclusion.

Herman Gigas on Well Poisoning

In 1347 there was such a great pestilence and mortality throughout almost the whole world that in the opinion of well-informed men scarcely a tenth of mankind survived. . . . Some say that it was brought about by the corruption of the air; others that the Jews planned to wipe out all the Christians with poison and had poisoned wells and springs everywhere. And many Jews confessed as much under torture: that they had bred spiders and toads in pots and pans, and had obtained poison from overseas; and that not every Jew knew about this wickedness, only the more powerful ones, so that it would not be betrayed. As evidence of this heinous crime, men say that the bags full of poison were found in many wells and springs, and as a result, in cities, towns and villages throughout Germany, and in fields and woods too, almost all the wells and springs have been blocked up or built over, so that no one can drink from them or use the water for cooking, and men have to use rain or river water instead. God, the lord of vengeance, has not suffered the malice of the Jews to go unpunished. Throughout Germany, in all but a few places, they were burnt. For fear of that punishment many accepted baptism and their lives were spared. This action was taken against the Jews in 1349, and it still continues unabated, for in a number of regions many people, noble and humble alike, have laid plans against them and their defenders which they will never abandon until the whole Jewish race has been destroyed.

Sources: Giovanni Boccaccio, *Decameron*, trans. F. Winwar (New York: Limited Editions, 1930), pp. xxii–xxiv, xxviii–xxix; "On Earthquakes as the Cause of Plague" and "Herman Gigas on Well Poisoning," in *The Black Death*, R. Horrox, ed., trans. (Manchester, U.K.: Manchester University Press).

11-1c The Black Death in Europe

The Black Death of the mid-fourteenth century was the most devastating natural disaster in European history, ravaging Europe's population and causing economic, social, political, and cultural upheaval (see Opposing Viewpoints, "Causes of the Black Death: Contemporary Views," above). Contemporary chroniclers lamented that parents attempted to flee, abandoning their children; one related the words of a child left behind: "Oh father, why have you abandoned me? . . . Mother where have you gone?"[4] People were horrified by an evil force they could not understand and by the subsequent breakdown of all normal human relations.

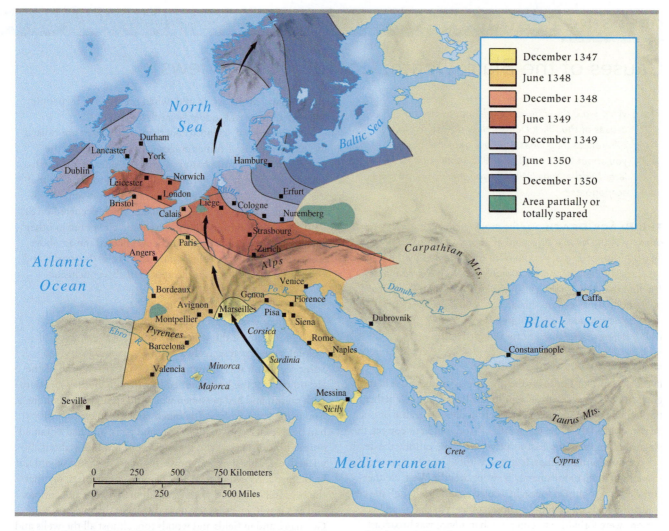

MAP 11.1 **Spread of the Black Death.** The plague entered Europe by way of Sicily in 1347 and within three years had killed between one-quarter and one-half of the population. Outbreaks continued into the early eighteenth century, and the European population took two hundred years to return to the level it had reached before the Black Death.

Q *Is there a general pattern between distance from Sicily and the elapsed time before a region was infected with the plague?*

Symptoms of bubonic plague included high fever, aching joints, swelling of the lymph nodes, and dark blotches caused by bleeding beneath the skin. Bubonic plague was actually the least virulent form of plague but nevertheless killed 50 to 60 percent of its victims. In pneumonic plague, the bacterial infection spread to the lungs, resulting in severe coughing, bloody sputum, and the relatively easy spread of the bacillus from human to human by coughing.

The plague reached Europe in October 1347 when Genoese merchants brought it from Caffa to the island of Sicily off the coast of Italy. One contemporary wrote: "As it happened, among those who escaped from Caffa by boat, there were a few sailors who had been infected with the poisonous disease. Some boats were bound for Genoa, others went to Venice and other Christian areas. When the sailors reached these places and mixed with the people there, it was as if they had brought evil spirits with them."[5] The plague spread quickly, reaching southern Italy

and southern France and Spain by the end of 1347 (see Map 11.1). Usually, the diffusion of the Black Death followed commercial trade routes. In 1348, the plague spread through France and the Low Countries and into Germany. By the end of that year, it had moved to England, ravaging it in 1349. By the end of 1349, the plague had expanded to northern Europe and Scandinavia. Eastern Europe and Russia were affected by 1351, although mortality rates were never as high in eastern Europe as they were in western and central Europe (see Image 11.2).

Mortality figures for the Black Death were incredibly high. Italy was hit especially hard. As the commercial center of the Mediterranean, Italy possessed scores of ports where the plague could be introduced. Italy's crowded cities, whether large, such as Florence, Genoa, and Venice, with populations near 100,000, or small, such as Orvieto and Pistoia, suffered losses of 50 to 60 percent. France and England were also particularly devastated. In northern France, farming villages suffered mortality

Snark/Art Resource, NY

IMAGE 11.2 **Mass Burial of Plague Victims.** The Black Death had spread to northern Europe by the end of 1348. Shown here is a mass burial of victims of the plague in Tournai, located in modern Belgium. As is evident in the illustration, at this stage of the plague, there was still time to make coffins for the victims' burial. Later, as the plague intensified, the dead were thrown into open pits.

rates of 30 percent, while cities such as Rouen were more severely affected and experienced losses as high as 40 percent. In England and Germany, entire villages simply disappeared. In Germany, of approximately 170,000 inhabited locations, only 130,000 were left by the end of the fourteenth century.

It has been estimated that the European population declined by 25 to 50 percent between 1347 and 1351. If we accept the recent scholarly assessment of a European population of 75 million in the early fourteenth century, this means a death toll of 19 to 38 million people in four years. And the plague did not end in 1351. There were major outbreaks again in 1361–1362 and 1369 and then recurrences every five or six to ten or twelve years, depending on climatic and ecological conditions, until the end of the fifteenth century. The European population thus did not begin to recover until around 1500 and took several generations after that to reattain thirteenth-century levels.

Life and Death: Reactions to the Plague Natural disasters of the magnitude of the great plague produce extreme psychological reactions. Knowing they could be dead in a matter of days, people began to live for the moment; some threw themselves with abandon into sexual and alcoholic orgies. The fourteenth-century Italian writer Giovanni Boccaccio (joe-VAH-nee boh-KAH-choh) gave a classic description of this kind of reaction to the plague in Florence in the preface to his famous *Decameron*:

> [Some people] held that plenty of drinking and enjoyment, singing and free living and the gratification of the appetite in every possible way, letting the devil take the hindmost, was the best preventative . . . and as far as they could, they suited the action to the word. Day and night they went from one tavern to another drinking and carousing unrestrainedly. At the least inkling of something that suited them, they ran wild in other people's houses, and there was no one to prevent them, for everyone had abandoned all responsibility for his belongings as well as for himself, considering his days numbered.[6]

Wealthy and powerful people fled to their country estates, as Boccaccio recounted: "Still others . . . maintained that no

remedy against plagues was better than to leave them miles behind. Men and women without number . . . caring for nobody but themselves, abandoned the city, their houses and estates, their own flesh and blood even, and their effects, in search of a country place."[7]

The attempt to explain the Black Death and mitigate its harshness led to extreme sorts of behavior. To many people, the plague had either been sent by God as a punishment for humans' sins or been caused by the devil. Some resorted to extreme asceticism to cleanse themselves of sin and gain God's forgiveness. Such were the flagellants (FLAJ-uh-lunts), whose movement became popular in 1348, especially in Germany. Groups of flagellants, both men and women, wandered from town to town, flogging themselves with whips to win the forgiveness of God, whom they believed had sent the plague to punish humans for their sinful ways (see Image 11.3). One contemporary chronicler described a flagellant procession:

> The penitents went about, coming first out of Germany. They were men who did public penance and scourged themselves with whips of hard knotted leather with little iron spikes. Some made themselves bleed very badly between the shoulder blades and some foolish women had cloths ready to catch the blood and smear it on their eyes, saying it was miraculous blood. While they were doing penance, they sang very mournful songs about the nativity and the passion of Our Lord. The object of this penance was to put a stop to the mortality.[8]

The flagellants attracted attention and created mass hysteria wherever they went. The Catholic Church, however, became alarmed when flagellant groups began to kill Jews and attack clergy who opposed them. Some groups also developed a millenarian aspect, anticipating the imminent end of the world, the return of Jesus, and the establishment of a thousand-year kingdom under his governance. Pope Clement VI condemned the flagellants in October 1349 and urged the public authorities to crush them. By the end of 1350, most of the flagellant movement had been destroyed.

The Cremation of the Strasbourg Jews

 What charges were made against the Jews in regard to the Black Death? Can it be said that these charges were economically motivated? Why or why not?

IN THEIR ATTEMPT TO EXPLAIN the widespread horrors of the Black Death, medieval Christian communities looked for scapegoats. As at the time of the Crusades, the Jews were blamed for poisoning wells and thereby spreading the plague. This selection by a contemporary chronicler, written in 1349, gives an account of how Christians in the town of Strasbourg in the Holy Roman Empire dealt with their Jewish community. It is apparent that financial gain was also an important motive in killing the Jews.

Jacob von Konigshofen, "The Cremation of the Strasbourg Jews"

In the year 1349 there occurred the greatest epidemic that ever happened. Death went from one end of the earth to the other. . . . And from what this epidemic came, all wise teachers and physicians could only say that it was God's will. . . . This epidemic also came to Strasbourg in the summer of the above-mentioned year, and it is estimated that about sixteen thousand people died.

In the matter of this plague the Jews throughout the world were reviled and accused in all lands of having caused it through the poison which they are said to have put into the water and the wells—that is what they were accused of—and for this reason the Jews were burnt all the way from the Mediterranean into Germany. . . .

[The account then goes on to discuss the situation of the Jews in the city of Strasbourg.]

On Saturday . . . they burnt the Jews on a wooden platform in their cemetery. There were about two thousand people of them. Those who wanted to baptize themselves were spared. [About one thousand accepted baptism.] Many small children were taken out of the fire and baptized against the will of their fathers and mothers. And everything that was owed to the Jews was canceled, and the Jews had to surrender all pledges and notes that they had taken for debts. The council, however, took the cash that the Jews possessed and divided it among the working-men proportionately. The money was indeed the thing that killed the Jews. If they had been poor and if the lords had not been in debt to them, they would not have been burnt. . . .

Thus were the Jews burnt at Strasbourg, and in the same year in all the cities of the Rhine, whether Free Cities or Imperial Cities or cities belonging to the lords. In some towns they burnt the Jews after a trial, in others, without a trial. In some cities the Jews themselves set fire to their houses and cremated themselves.

It was decided in Strasbourg that no Jew should enter the city for 100 years, but before 20 years had passed, the council and magistrates agreed that they ought to admit the Jews again into the city for 20 years. And so the Jews came back again to Strasbourg in the year 1368 after the birth of our Lord.

Source: J. R. Marcus, *The Jew in the Medieval World* (Pittsburgh: The Hebrew Union College Press, 1972).

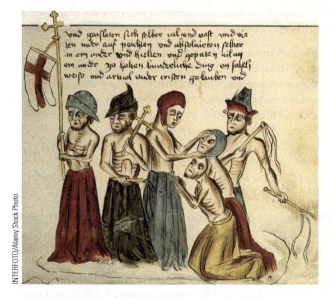

IMAGE 11.3 The Flagellants. Reactions to the plague were extreme at times. Believing that asceticism could atone for humanity's sins and win God's forgiveness, flagellants wandered from town to town flogging themselves and each other with whips, as in this illustration from a fifteenth-century German manuscript.

An outbreak of virulent attacks on Jews also accompanied the Black Death. Jews were accused of causing the plague by poisoning town wells. Although Jews were persecuted in Spain, the worst organized massacres, or **pogroms** (POH-grums), against this helpless minority were carried out in Germany; more than sixty major Jewish communities in Germany had been exterminated by 1351 (see Historical Voices, "The Cremation of the Strasbourg Jews," above). Many Jews fled eastward to Russia and especially to Poland, where the king offered them protection. Eastern Europe became home to large Jewish communities.

The prevalence of death because of the plague and its recurrences affected people in profound ways. Some survivors apparently came to treat life as something cheap and transient. Violence and violent death appeared to be more common after the plague than before. Post-plague Europe also demonstrated a morbid preoccupation with death. In their sermons, priests reminded parishioners that each night's sleep might be their last. Tombstones were decorated with macabre scenes of naked corpses in various stages of decomposition with snakes entwined in their bones and their innards filled with worms.

Art and the Black Death The Black Death made a visible impact on art. For one thing, it wiped out entire guilds of artists. At the same time, survivors, including the newly rich who patronized artists, were no longer so optimistic. Some were more guilty about enjoying life and more concerned about gaining salvation. Post-plague art began to concentrate on pain and death. A fairly large number of artistic works came to be based on the *ars moriendi* (AHRS moh-ree-EN-dee), the art of dying. A morbid concern with death is especially evident in the fresco *The Triumph of Death* by Francesco Traini (frahn-CHES-koh TRAY-nee) in Pisa (see Image 11.4). On the left side of the fresco, several young nobles encounter three coffins containing decomposing bodies, while on the right young aristocrats engage in pleasant pursuits but are threatened by a grim figure of Death in the form of a witch flying through the air swinging a large scythe. Beneath her lie piles of dead citizens and clergy cut down in the prime of life.

11-1d Economic Dislocation and Social Upheaval

The population collapse of the fourteenth century had dire economic and social consequences. Economic dislocation was accompanied by social upheaval. Between 1000 and 1300, Europe had been relatively stable. The division of society into the three estates of clergy (those who pray), nobility (those who fight), and laborers (those who work) had already begun to disintegrate in the thirteenth century, however. In the fourteenth century, a series of urban and rural revolts rocked European society.

Noble Landlords and Peasants The demographic crisis of the fourteenth century affected both peasants and noble landlords. Most noticeably, Europe experienced a serious labor shortage that caused a dramatic rise in the price of labor. At Cuxham manor in England, for example, a farm laborer who had received two shillings a week in 1347 was paid seven in 1349 and almost eleven by 1350. At the same time, the decline in population depressed or held stable the demand for agricultural produce, resulting in stable or falling prices for output (although in England prices remained high until the 1380s). The chronicler Henry Knighton observed: "And the price of everything was cheap. . . . A man could buy a horse for half a mark [six shillings], which before was worth forty shillings."[9] Because landlords were having to pay more for labor at the same time that their rents or incomes were declining, they began to experience considerable adversity and lower standards of living. In England, aristocratic incomes dropped more than 20 percent between 1347 and 1353.

Landed aristocrats responded by seeking to lower the wage rate. The English Parliament passed the Statute of Laborers (1351), which attempted to limit wages to pre-plague levels and forbid the mobility of peasants as well. Although such laws proved largely unworkable, they did keep wages from rising as high as they might have in a free market. Overall, the position of landlords continued to deteriorate during the late fourteenth and early fifteenth centuries. At the same time, conditions for peasants improved, though not uniformly throughout Europe.

The decline in the number of peasants after the Black Death accelerated the process of converting labor services to rents, freeing peasants from the obligations of servile tenure and weakening the system of manorialism. But there were limits to how much the peasants could advance. Not only did they face the same economic hurdles as the lords, but the latter attempted to impose wage restrictions and reinstate old forms of labor service. New governmental taxes also hurt. Peasant complaints became widespread and soon gave rise to rural revolts.

IMAGE 11.4 **Francesco Traini, *The Triumph of Death*.** The plague led to a morbid fascination with death that is visible in the art of the period. Shown here is the left side of Francesco Traini's fresco, which depicts a group of young aristocrats on a hunt encountering three decaying corpses in coffins. One of the nobles is shown gagging at the smell of the decomposing bodies.

 How has social change in the twenty-first century been reflected in the world of contemporary art?

Erich Lessing/Art Resource, NY

Peasant Revolt in France In 1358, a peasant revolt, known as the *Jacquerie* (zhahk-REE), broke out in northern France. The destruction of normal order by the Black Death and the subsequent economic dislocation were important factors in causing the revolt, but the ravages created by the Hundred Years' War also affected the French peasantry (see "11-2 War and Political Instability," later in this chapter). Both the French and English forces followed a deliberate policy of laying waste to peasants' fields while bands of mercenaries lived off the land by taking peasants' produce as well.

Growing class tensions also exacerbated peasant anger. Landed nobles were eager to hold on to their politically privileged position and felt increasingly threatened in the new post-plague world of higher wages and lower prices. Many aristocrats looked on peasants with utter contempt. A French tale told to upper-class audiences contained this remarkable passage:

> Tell me, Lord, if you please, by what right or title does a villein [peasant] eat beef? . . . Should they eat fish? Rather let them eat thistles and briars, thorns and straw and hay on Sunday and peapods on weekdays. They should keep watch without sleep and have trouble always; that is how villeins should live. Yet each day they are full and drunk on the best wines, and in fine clothes. The great expenditures of villeins come as a high cost, for it is this that destroys and ruins the world. It is they who spoil the common welfare. From the villein comes all unhappiness. Should they eat meat? Rather should they chew grass on the heath with the horned cattle and go naked on all fours.[10]

The peasants reciprocated this contempt for their so-called social superiors.

The outburst of peasant anger led to savage confrontations. Castles were burned and nobles murdered (see Historical Voices, "A Revolt of French Peasants," p. 315). Such atrocities did not go unanswered, however. The *Jacquerie* soon failed as the privileged classes closed ranks, savagely massacred the rebels, and ended the revolt (see Image 11.5).

An English Peasant Revolt The English Peasants' Revolt of 1381 was the most prominent of all. It was a product not of desperation but of rising expectations. After the Black Death, the condition of the English peasants had improved as they enjoyed greater freedom and higher wages or lower rents. Aristocratic landlords had fought back with legislation to depress wages and attempted to reimpose old feudal dues. The most immediate cause of the revolt, however, was the monarchy's attempt to raise revenues by imposing a poll tax or a flat charge on each adult member of the population. Peasants in eastern England, the wealthiest part of the country, refused to pay the tax and expelled the collectors forcibly from their villages.

This action sparked a widespread rebellion of both peasants and townspeople led by a well-to-do peasant called Wat Tyler and a preacher named John Ball. The latter preached an effective message against the noble class, as recounted by the French chronicler Jean Froissart (ZHAHNH frwah-SAR):

> Good people, things cannot go right in England and never will, until goods are held in common and there are no more villeins and gentlefolk, but we are all one and the same. . . . If we all spring from a single father and mother, Adam and Eve, how can they claim or prove that they are lords more than us, except by making us produce and grow the wealth which they spend?[11]

The revolt was initially successful as the rebels burned down the manor houses of aristocrats, lawyers, and government officials and murdered several important officials, including

IMAGE 11.5 **Peasant Rebellion.** The fourteenth century witnessed a number of revolts of the peasantry against noble landowners. Although the revolts often met with initial success, they were soon crushed. This fifteenth-century illustration shows nobles during the French *Jacquerie* of 1358 massacring the rebels in the town of Meaux, in northern France.

Art Media/HIP/The Image Works

A Revolt of French Peasants

 Why did the peasants react so strongly against their aristocratic lords? Do you think this is an unbiased account? Why or why not?

IN 1358, FRENCH PEASANTS ROSE UP in a revolt known as the *Jacquerie*. The relationship between aristocrats and peasants had degenerated as a result of the social upheavals and privations caused by the Black Death and the Hundred Years' War. This excerpt from the chronicle of an aristocrat paints a horrifying picture of the barbarities that occurred during the revolt.

Jean Froissart, *Chronicles*

There were very strange and terrible happenings in several parts of the kingdom of France. . . . They began when some of the men from the country towns came together in the Beauvais region. They had no leaders and at first they numbered scarcely 100. One of them got up and said that the nobility of France, knights and squires, were disgracing and betraying the realm, and that it would be a good thing if they were all destroyed. . . .

They banded together and went off, without further deliberation and unarmed except for pikes and knives, to the house of a knight who lived nearby. They broke in and killed the knight, with his lady and his children, big and small, and set fire to the house. . . .

They did similar things in a number of castles and big houses, and their ranks swelled until there were a good 6,000 of them. Wherever they went their numbers grew, for all the men of the same sort joined them. The knights and squires fled before them with their families. They took their wives and daughters many miles away to put them in safety, leaving their houses open with their possessions inside. And those evil men, who had come together without leaders or arms, pillaged and burned everything and violated and killed all the ladies and girls without mercy, like mad dogs. . . . Never did men commit such vile deeds. They were such that no living creature ought to see, and the men who committed the most were admired and had the highest places among them. I could never bring myself to write down the horrible and shameful things which they did to the ladies. But, among other brutal excesses, they killed a knight, put him on a spit, and turned him at the fire and roasted him before the lady and her children. After about a dozen of them had violated the lady, they tried to force her and the children to eat the knight's flesh before putting them cruelly to death.

Source: Froissart, *Chronicles*, trans. G. Brereton (London: Penguin Classics, 1968; revised 1978).

the archbishop of Canterbury. After the peasants marched on London, the young King Richard II, age fifteen, promised to accept the rebels' demands if they returned to their homes. They accepted the king's word and dispersed, but the king reneged and with the assistance of the aristocrats arrested hundreds of the rebels. The poll tax was eliminated, however, and in the end most of the rebels were pardoned.

Revolts in the Cities Revolts also erupted in the cities. Commercial and industrial activity suffered almost immediately from the Black Death. An oversupply of goods and an immediate drop in demand led to a decline in trade after 1350. Some industries suffered greatly. Florence's woolen industry, one of the giants, produced 70,000 to 80,000 pieces of cloth in 1338; in 1378, it was yielding only 24,000 pieces. Bourgeois merchants and manufacturers responded to the decline in trade and production by attempting to restrict competition and resist the demands of the lower classes.

In urban areas, where capitalist industrialists paid low wages and managed to prevent workers from forming organizations to help themselves, industrial revolts broke out throughout Europe. Ghent experienced one in 1381, Rouen in 1382. Most famous, however, was the revolt of the *ciompi* (CHAHM-pee) in Florence in 1378. The *ciompi* were wool workers in Florence's most prominent industry. In the 1370s, not only was the woolen industry

depressed, but the wool workers saw their real wages decline when the coinage in which they were paid was debased. Their revolt won them some concessions from the municipal government, including the right to form guilds and be represented in the government. But their newly won rights were short-lived; authorities ended *ciompi* participation in the government by 1382.

Although the peasant and urban revolts sometimes resulted in short-term gains for the participants, the uprisings were quickly crushed and their gains lost. Accustomed to ruling, the established classes easily formed a united front and quashed dissent. Nevertheless, the rural and urban revolts of the fourteenth century ushered in an age of social conflict that characterized much of later European history.

11-2 War and Political Instability

 FOCUS QUESTIONS: What major problems did European states face in the fourteenth century? What impact did the Hundred Years' War have on England and France?

Famine, plague, economic turmoil, social upheaval, and violence were not the only problems of the fourteenth century. War and political instability must also be added to the list. Of all the struggles that ensued in the fourteenth century, the Hundred Years' War was the most famous and the most violent.

11-2a Causes of the Hundred Years' War

In 1259, the English king, Henry III, had relinquished his claims to all the French territories previously held by the English monarchy except for one relatively small possession known as the duchy of Gascony. As duke of Gascony, the English king pledged loyalty as a vassal to the French king. But this territory gave rise to numerous disputes between the kings of England and France. By the thirteenth century, the Capetian monarchs had greatly increased their power over their more important vassals, the great lords of France. Royal officials interfered regularly in the affairs of the vassals' fiefs, especially in matters of justice. Although this policy irritated all the vassals, it especially annoyed the king of England, who considered himself the peer of the French king.

A dispute over the right of succession to the French throne also complicated relations between the French and the English. In the fourteenth century, the Capetian dynasty failed to produce a male heir for the first time in almost four hundred years. In 1328, the last son of King Philip IV died without a male heir. The closest male relative in line to the throne was King Edward III of England (r. 1327–1377), whose mother was Isabella, the daughter of Philip IV (see Chart 11.1). Known for her strong personality (she was nicknamed the "she-wolf of France"), Isabella, with the assistance of her lover, led a revolt against her husband, King Edward II, overthrew him, and ruled England until her teenage son, Edward III, took sole control of the throne in 1330. As the son of the daughter of King Philip IV,

King Edward III of England had a claim to the French throne, but the French nobles, angered by the thought of an English king on the throne, argued that the inheritance of the monarchy could not pass through the female line and chose a cousin of the Capetians, Philip, duke of Valois (val-WAH), as King Philip VI (r. 1328–1350).

11-2b Conduct and Course of the War

The Hundred Years' War began in a burst of knightly enthusiasm. Trained to be warriors, knights viewed the clash of battle as the ultimate opportunity to demonstrate their fighting abilities. But this struggle would change the nature of warfare, for as it dragged on, it was not knights but peasant foot soldiers who increasingly determined the outcomes of battles. The French army of 1337, with its heavily armed noble cavalry, resembled its twelfth- and thirteenth-century forebears. The noble cavalrymen considered themselves the fighting elite and looked with contempt on the foot soldiers and crossbowmen, their social inferiors.

The English army, however, had evolved differently and had included peasants as paid foot soldiers since at least Anglo-Saxon times. Armed with pikes, many of these foot soldiers had also adopted the longbow. The longbow was first used by the Welsh, but the English, recognizing the power of the longbow used against them, soon adopted its use. English archery laws in the thirteenth and fourteenth centuries also decreed that all English men should possess a bow and arrow and practice on Sundays and holidays. A well-trained longbowman could shoot ten to twelve arrows per minute, a more rapid speed of fire than the more powerful crossbow. And the arrows could pierce the armor of a knight at ranges of more than 250 yards. Although the English made use of heavily armed cavalry, they relied even more on large numbers of foot soldiers.

Early Phases of the War Edward III's early campaigns in France achieved little. When Edward renewed his efforts in 1346 with an invasion of Normandy, Philip responded by raising a large force to crush the English army and met Edward's forces at Crécy (kray-SEE), just south of Flanders. Recent estimates are a French army of 30,000 warriors meeting an English army of 15,000 men. The larger French army followed no battle plan but simply attacked the English lines in a disorderly fashion. The arrows of the English archers devastated the French

CHART 11.1

Philip III
king of France (1270–1285)

Philip IV
(1285–1314)

Charles of Valois
(d. 1325)

Louis X
(1314–1316)

Philip V
(1316–1322)

Charles IV
(1322–1328)

Isabella = Edward II
king of England
(1307–1327)

Philip VI
king of France
(1328–1350)

John I
(1316)

(daughters)

(daughters)

Edward III
king of England
(1327–1377)

John II
king of France
(1350–1364)

CHART 11.1 Background to the Hundred Years' War: Kings of France and England. The immediate cause of the war between France and England was yet another quarrel over Gascony. In 1337, when Edward III, the king of England and duke of Gascony, refused to do homage to Philip VI for Gascony, the French king seized the duchy. Edward responded by declaring war on Philip, the "so-called king of France." There is no doubt that the personalities of the two monarchs also had much to do with the outbreak of the Hundred Years' War. Both Edward and Philip loved luxury and shared a desire for the glory and prestige that came from military engagements. Both were only too willing to use their respective nation's resources to satisfy their own desires. Moreover, for many nobles, the promise of plunder and territorial gain was an incentive to follow the disruptive path of their rulers.

IMAGE 11.6 **Battle of Crécy.** This fifteenth-century manuscript illustration depicts the Battle of Crécy, the first of several military disasters suffered by the French in the Hundred Years' War, and shows why the English preferred the longbow to the crossbow. At left, the French crossbowmen have to stop shooting and prime their weapons by cranking the handle, while the English archers continue to shoot their longbows (a skilled archer could launch ten to twelve arrows a minute).

 How did the battles of the Hundred Years' War change the nature of warfare in the fourteenth century?

Bibliotheque Nationale, Paris, France/Bridgeman Images

cavalry. It was a stunning victory for the English. The Battle of Crécy (see Image 11.6) determined that the six-foot longbow would become a dominant battlefield weapon at the time. Edward followed up by capturing the French port of Calais (ka-LAY) to serve as a staging ground for future invasions.

The Battle of Crécy was not decisive, however. The English simply did not possess the resources to subjugate all of France. Truces, small-scale hostilities, and some major operations were combined in an orgy of seemingly incessant struggle. The English campaigns were waged by Edward III and his son Edward, the prince of Wales, known as the Black Prince. The Black Prince's campaigns in France were devastating. Avoiding pitched battles, his forces deliberately ravaged the land, burning crops and entire unfortified villages and towns and stealing anything of value. In 1356, at the Battle of Poitiers (pwah-TYAY), the Black Prince and the English were again victorious. This Battle of Poitiers ended the first phase of the Hundred Years' War and was followed by several temporary truces. But the first phase of the war made it clear that despite their victories, the English were not really strong enough to subdue all of France and make Edward III's claim to the French monarchy a reality.

Monarchs, however, could be slow learners. In the next phase of the war, the French went on the offensive and by 1374 had recovered their lost lands, although France itself continued to be plagued by "free companies" of mercenaries who, no longer paid by the English, simply lived off the land by plunder and ransom. Nevertheless, for the time being, the war seemed over, especially when a twenty-year truce was negotiated in 1396.

Renewal of the War In 1415, however, the English king, Henry V (r. 1413–1422), renewed the war at a time when the French were enduring civil war as the dukes of Burgundy and Orléans (or-lay-AHN) competed to control the weak French king, Charles VI (r. 1380–1422). In the summer of 1413, Paris

exploded with bloody encounters. Taking advantage of the chaos, Henry V invaded France in 1415. At the Battle of Agincourt (AH-zhen-koor) (1415), the French suffered a disastrous defeat, and 1,500 French nobles died when the heavy, armor-plated French knights attempted to attack across a field turned to mud by heavy rain. Altogether, French losses were 6,000 dead; the English lost only three hundred men.

Henry went on to reconquer Normandy and forge an alliance with the duke of Burgundy, which led Charles VI to agree to the Treaty of Troyes (TRWAH) in 1420. By this treaty, Henry V was married to Catherine, daughter of Charles VI, and recognized as the heir to the French throne. By 1420, the English were masters of northern France (see Map 11.2).

The seemingly hopeless French cause fell into the hands of Charles the dauphin (DAH-fin *or* doh-FAN) (heir to the throne), the son of Charles VI, who, despite being disinherited by the Treaty of Troyes, still considered himself the real heir to the French throne. The dauphin governed the southern two-thirds of French lands from Bourges. Charles was weak and timid and was unable to rally the French against the English, who in 1428 had turned south and were besieging the city of Orléans to gain access to the valley of the Loire. The French monarch was saved, quite unexpectedly, by a French peasant woman.

Joan of Arc Joan of Arc was born in 1412 to well-to-do peasants from the village of Domrémy in Champagne. Deeply religious, Joan experienced visions and came to believe that her favorite saints had commanded her to free France and have the dauphin crowned as king. In February 1429, Joan made her way to the dauphin's court, where her sincerity and simplicity persuaded Charles to allow her to accompany a French army to Orléans. Apparently inspired by the faith of the peasant girl, the French armies found new confidence in themselves and liberated Orléans, changing the course of

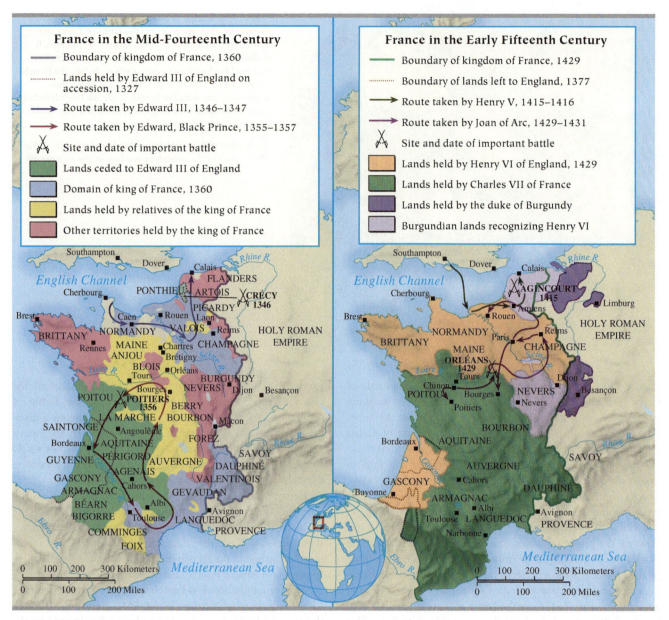

France in the Mid-Fourteenth Century

— Boundary of kingdom of France, 1360

······· Lands held by Edward III of England on accession, 1327

→ Route taken by Edward III, 1346–1347

→ Route taken by Edward, Black Prince, 1355–1357

⚔ Site and date of important battle

▇ Lands ceded to Edward III of England

▇ Domain of king of France, 1360

▇ Lands held by relatives of the king of France

▇ Other territories held by the king of France

France in the Early Fifteenth Century

— Boundary of kingdom of France, 1429

········· Boundary of lands left to England, 1377

→ Route taken by Henry V, 1415–1416

→ Route taken by Joan of Arc, 1429–1431

⚔ Site and date of important battle

▇ Lands held by Henry VI of England, 1429

▇ Lands held by Charles VII of France

▇ Lands held by the duke of Burgundy

▇ Burgundian lands recognizing Henry VI

MAP 11.2 The Hundred Years' War. This long, exhausting struggle began in 1337 and dragged on until 1453. The English initially gained substantial French territory, but in the later phases of the war, France turned the tide, eventually expelling the English from all Continental lands except the port of Calais.

 What gains had the English made by 1429, and how do they correlate to proximity to England and the ocean?

the war (see Image 11.7). Within a few weeks, the entire Loire valley had been freed of the English. In July 1429, fulfilling Joan's other task, the dauphin was crowned king of France and became Charles VII (r. 1422–1461). In accomplishing the two commands of her angelic voices, Joan had brought the war to a decisive turning point.

Joan did not live to see the war concluded, however. She was captured by the Burgundian allies of the English in 1430. Wishing to eliminate the "Maid of Orléans" for obvious political reasons, the English turned Joan over to the Inquisition on charges of witchcraft. In the fifteenth century, spiritual visions were thought to be inspired by either God or the devil. Because

Joan dressed in men's clothing, it was easy for her enemies to believe she was in league with the "prince of darkness." She was condemned to death as a heretic and burned at the stake in 1431, at the age of nineteen. To the end, as the flames engulfed her, she declared that her voices came from God and had not deceived her (see Movies & History, *Joan of Arc*, p. 319). Twenty-five years later, a church court exonerated her of these charges. To a contemporary French writer, Christine de Pizan (kris-TEEN duh pee-ZAHN), who penned *The Poem of Joan of Arc* in 1429, Joan was a heroine (see "Christine de Pizan" later in Section 11-4a). In 1920, Joan of Arc was made a saint of the Roman Catholic Church.

IMAGE 11.7 **Joan of Arc.** Pictured here in an early sixteenth-century French manuscript entitled "Lives of Celebrated Women" is Joan of Arc in a suit of armor. There are no known portraits of Joan made from life.

MOVIES & HISTORY
Joan of Arc (1948) and
*The Messenger: The Story
of Joan of Arc* (1999)

Watch *Joan of Arc* and *The
Messenger: The Story of Joan of
Arc*, two films on one of history's
best-known figures. The 1948 film
version of Joan's story follows
the main historical facts that are
known about Joan. Joan's
voices are accepted as
an important part of a
spiritually determined
young woman. *The
Messenger* presents
a more contemporary
and fictionalized approach to Joan. The brutality of war
is rendered in realistically bloody detail, and the movie
introduces revenge as a possible motive by having Joan
witness the rape and murder of her sister by an English
mercenary—she must kill the English to avenge her
sister's death. After this traumatic incident, her voices
become more strident.

Q *What are the significant differences in the
approaches of these two films? What impact does
the years in which the films were made have on
these approaches? Which one is a more accurate
rendering of Joan's life?*

End of the War Joan of Arc's accomplishments proved decisive. The war dragged on for another two decades, during which time the devastation of France continued (see Historical Voices, "The Hundred Years' War," p. 320). However, defeats of English armies in Normandy and Aquitaine ultimately led to French victory. Important to the French success was the use of the cannon, a new weapon made possible by the invention of gunpowder. The Chinese had invented gunpowder in the eleventh century and devised a simple cannon by the thirteenth century. The Mongols greatly improved this technology, developing more accurate cannons and cannonballs; both spread to the Middle East and Europe by the thirteenth century.

The deaths of England's best commanders and the instability of the English government under King Henry VI (r. 1422–1471) also contributed to England's defeat. By 1453, the only part of France that was left in English hands was the coastal town of Calais, which remained English for another century.

11-2c Political Instability

The fourteenth century was a period of adversity for the internal political stability of European governments. Although government bureaucracies grew ever larger, at the same time the question of who should control the bureaucracies led to internal conflict and instability. Like the lord–serf relationship, the

CHRONOLOGY	The Hundred Years' War
Outbreak of hostilities	1337
Battle of Crécy	1346
Battle of Poitiers	1356
Peace of Brétigny	1359
Death of Edward III	1377
Twenty-year truce declared	1396
Henry V (1413–1422) renews the war	1415
Battle of Agincourt	1415
Treaty of Troyes	1420
French recovery under Joan of Arc	1429–1431
End of the war	1453

lord–vassal relationship based on land and military service was being replaced by a contract based on money. Especially after the Black Death, money payments called **scutage** (SKYOO-tij) were increasingly substituted for military service. Monarchs welcomed this development because they could now hire professional soldiers, who tended to be more reliable anyway.

The Hundred Years' War

 What do these accounts reveal about the nature of late medieval warfare and its impact on civilian populations?

THE FOLLOWING EXCERPTS are taken from a collection of letters and other sources from the Hundred Years' War. They provide an excellent account of how noncombatants fared during the war. Included in the destruction were numerous churches and monasteries.

Accounts of the Hundred Years' War

The count of Arundel, John Fitz-Alain, attacked Millé and its church with fire. The women, boys, and old men took refuge in the tower of the church, but were soon surrounded by flames. The lead of the roof melted and fell in burning drops on the miserable folk below, and even the molten metal of the bells ran down upon all. All but two perished. The fire not only destroyed the church, but all the houses within a wide circuit to the number of more than seven hundred. The wretched inhabitants and the cultivators of the soil were ordered to be hung.

Out of one thousand churches in the region of Quercy, when the war with the English was done there were scarce three or four hundred left in which services could be held, so completely was everything devastated and consumed. Certain parishes . . . were entirely deserted by their former inhabitants, so that the bishop of Bourges was forced to give the lands belonging to his temporalities as fiefs to those living at a distance.

Charles VI, being dead, Charles VII succeeded to his father in the kingdom, in the year of our Lord 1422, when he was about twenty-two years of age. In his time, owing to the long wars which had raged within and without, the lethargy and cowardliness of the officers and commanders who were under him, the destruction of all military disciple and order, the rapacity of the troopers, and general dissolution into which all things has fallen, such destruction had been wrought that from the river Loire to the Seine—even to the Somme—the farmers were dead or had fled, and almost all the fields had for many years lain without cultivation or anyone to cultivate them. A few districts might indeed be excepted, where if any agriculture remained, it was because they were far from cities, towns, or castles, and in consequence the constant excursions of the despoilers could not be extended to them. . . .

We have ourselves beheld vast regions . . . well-nigh deserted, untilled, without husbandmen, grown up to weeds and briers. In many places where fruit trees could flourish these had grown up into dense forests. The vestiges of such ruin, unless the divine clemency shall aid mere human endeavor, will, it is to be feared, last for long years to come.

Source: J. H. Robinson, *Readings in European History*, vol. 1 (Boston: Ginn & Company, 1904), pp. 474–475.

As lord–vassal relationships became less personal and less important, new relationships based on political advantage began to be formed, creating new avenues for political influence—and for corruption as well. Especially noticeable as the landed aristocrats suffered declining rents and social uncertainties with the new relationships was the formation of factions of nobles who looked for opportunities to advance their power and wealth at the expense of other noble factions and of their monarchs as well. Other nobles went to the royal courts, offering to serve the kings.

The kings had their own problems, however. By the mid-fifteenth century, reigning monarchs in many European countries were not the direct descendants of the rulers of 1300. The founders of these new dynasties had to struggle for position as factions of nobles vied to gain material advantages for themselves. As the fifteenth century began, there were two claimants to the throne of France, two aristocratic factions fighting for control of England, and three German princes struggling to be recognized as Holy Roman Emperor.

Fourteenth-century monarchs of old dynasties and new ones faced financial problems as well. The shift to using mercenary soldiers left monarchs perennially short of cash. Traditional revenues, especially rents from property, increasingly proved insufficient to meet their needs. Monarchs attempted to generate new sources of revenues, especially through taxes, which often meant going through parliaments. This opened the door for parliamentary bodies to gain more power by asking for favors first. Although unsuccessful in most cases, the parliaments simply added another element of uncertainty and confusion to fourteenth-century politics. Turning now to a survey of western and central European states (eastern Europe and the Ottoman Empire will be examined in Chapter 12), we can see how these disruptive factors worked.

11-2d The Growth of England's Political Institutions

The fifty-year reign of Edward III (r. 1327–1377) was important for the evolution of English political institutions in the fourteenth century. Parliament increased in prominence and developed its basic structure and functions during Edward's reign. Due to his constant need for money to fight the Hundred Years' War, Edward came to rely on Parliament to levy new taxes. In return for regular grants, Edward made several concessions, including a commitment to levy no direct tax without Parliament's consent and to allow Parliament to examine the government accounts to ensure that the money was being spent properly. By the end of Edward's reign, Parliament had become an important component of the English governmental system.

During this same period, Parliament began to assume the organizational structure it has retained to this day. The Great Council of barons became the House of Lords and evolved into a body composed of the chief bishops and abbots of the realm and aristocratic peers whose position in Parliament was hereditary. The representatives of the shires and boroughs, who were considered less important than the lay and ecclesiastical lords, held collective meetings and soon came to be regarded as the House of Commons. Together, the House of Lords and House of Commons constituted Parliament. Although the House of Commons did little beyond approving measures proposed by the Lords, during Edward's reign the Commons did begin the practice of drawing up petitions, which, if accepted by the king, became law.

After Edward III's death, England began to experience the internal instability of aristocratic factionalism that was racking other European countries. The early years of the reign of Edward's grandson, Richard II (r. 1377–1399), began inauspiciously with the peasant revolt that ended only when the king made concessions. Richard's reign was troubled by competing groups of nobles who sought to pursue their own interests. One faction, led by Henry of Lancaster, defeated the king's forces and then deposed and killed him. Henry of Lancaster became King Henry IV (r. 1399–1413). In the fifteenth century, factional conflict would lead to a devastating series of civil wars.

11-2e The Problems of the French Kings

At the beginning of the fourteenth century, France was the most prosperous monarchy in Europe. By the end of the century, much of its wealth had been dissipated, and rival factions of aristocrats had made effective monarchical rule virtually impossible.

The French monarchical state had always had an underlying inherent weakness that proved its undoing in difficult times. Although the Capetian monarchs had found ways to enlarge their royal domain and extend their control by developing a large and effective bureaucracy, the various territories that made up France still maintained their own princes, customs, and laws. The parliamentary institutions of France provide a good example of France's basic lack of unity. The French parliament, known as the Estates-General and composed of representatives of the clergy, the nobility, and the **Third Estate** (everyone else), usually represented only the north of France, not the entire kingdom. The southern provinces had their own estates, and local estates existed in other parts of France. Unlike the English Parliament, which was evolving into a crucial part of the English government, the French Estates-General was simply one of many such institutions.

When Philip VI (r. 1328–1350) became involved in the Hundred Years' War with England, he found it necessary to devise new sources of revenue, including a tax on salt known as the *gabelle* (gah-BELL) and a hearth tax eventually called the *taille* (TY). These taxes weighed heavily on the French peasantry and middle class. Consequently, when additional taxes were needed to pay for the ransom of King John II after his capture at the Battle of Poitiers, the middle-class inhabitants of the towns tried to use the Estates-General to reform the French government and tax structure.

At the meeting of the Estates-General in 1357, under the leadership of the Parisian provost Étienne Marcel (ay-TYEN mahr-SEL), representatives of the Third Estate granted taxes in exchange for a promise from King John's son, the dauphin Charles, not to tax without the Estates-General's permission and to allow the Estates-General to meet on a regular basis and participate in important political decisions. After Marcel's movement was crushed in 1358, this attempt to make the Estates-General a functioning part of the French government collapsed. The dauphin became King Charles V (r. 1364–1380) and went on to recover much of the land lost to the English. His military successes underscored his efforts to reestablish strong monarchical powers. He undermined the role of the Estates-General by getting it to grant him taxes with no fixed time limit. Charles's death in 1380 soon led to a new time of troubles for the French monarchy, however.

The insanity of Charles VI (r. 1380–1422), which first became apparent in 1392, opened the door to rival factions of French nobles aspiring to power and wealth. The dukes of Burgundy and Orléans competed to control Charles and the French monarchy. Their struggles created chaos for the French government and the French people. Many nobles supported the Orléanist faction, while Paris and other towns favored the Burgundians. By the beginning of the fifteenth century, France seemed hopelessly mired in a civil war. When the English renewed the Hundred Years' War in 1415, the Burgundians supported the English cause and the English monarch's claim to the throne of France.

11-2f The German Monarchy

England and France had developed strong national monarchies in the High Middle Ages. Nevertheless, by the end of the fourteenth century, they seemed in danger of disintegrating due to dynastic problems and the pressures generated by the Hundred Years' War. In contrast, the Holy Roman Empire, whose core consisted of the lands of Germany, had already begun to fall apart in the High Middle Ages (see Map 11.3). Northern Italy, which the German emperors had tried to include in their medieval empire, had been free from any real imperial control since the end of the Hohenstaufen dynasty in the thirteenth century. In Germany itself, the failure of the Hohenstaufens ended any chance of centralized monarchical authority, and Germany became a land of hundreds of states that varied in size and power. These

MAP 11.3 **The Holy Roman Empire in the Fourteenth Century**

included princely states, such as the duchies of Bavaria and Saxony; free imperial city-states (self-governing cities directly under the control of the Holy Roman Emperor rather than a German territorial prince), such as Nuremberg; modest territories of petty imperial knights; and ecclesiastical states, such as the archbishopric of Cologne, in which an ecclesiastical official, such as a bishop, archbishop, or abbot, served in a dual capacity as an administrative official of the Catholic Church and as secular lord over the territories of the state. Although all of the rulers of these different states had some obligations to the German king and Holy Roman Emperor, more and more they acted independently.

Electoral Nature of the German Monarchy Because of its unique pattern of development in the High Middle Ages, the German monarchy had become established on an elective rather than a hereditary basis. The Golden Bull issued in 1356 by Emperor Charles IV (r. 1346–1378) standardized this principle of election. This document stated that four lay princes (the count palatine of the Rhine, the duke of Saxony, the margrave of Brandenburg, and the king of Bohemia) and three ecclesiastical rulers (the archbishops of Mainz, Trier, and Cologne) would serve as electors with the legal power to elect the "king of the Romans and future emperor, to be ruler of the world and of the Christian people."[12] "King of the Romans" was the official title of the German king; after his imperial coronation, he would also have the title of emperor.

In the fourteenth century, the electoral principle further ensured that kings of Germany were generally weak. Their ability to exercise effective power depended on the extent of their own family possessions. At the beginning of the fifteenth century, three emperors claimed the throne. Although the dispute was quickly settled, Germany entered the fifteenth century in a condition that verged on anarchy. Princes fought princes and leagues of cities. The emperors were virtually powerless to control any of them.

11-2g The States of Italy

Italy, too, had failed to develop a centralized monarchical state by the fourteenth century. Papal opposition to the rule of the Hohenstaufen emperors in northern Italy had virtually guaranteed that. Moreover, southern Italy was divided into the kingdom of Naples, ruled by the French house of Anjou, and Sicily, whose kings came from the Spanish house of Aragon (see Map 11.4). The center of the peninsula remained under the rather shaky control of the papacy. Lack of centralized authority had enabled numerous city-states in northern Italy to remain independent of any political authority.

In fourteenth-century Italy, two general tendencies can be discerned: the replacement of republican

MAP 11.4 **The States of Italy in the Fourteenth Century**

governments by tyrants and the expansion of the larger city-states at the expense of the less powerful ones. Nearly all the cities of northern Italy began their existence as free communes with republican governments. But in the fourteenth century, intense internal strife led city-states to resort to temporary expedients, allowing rule by one man with dictatorial powers. Limited rule, however, soon became long-term despotism as tyrants proved willing to use force to maintain themselves in power. Eventually, such tyrants tried to legitimize their power by purchasing titles from the emperor (still nominally the ruler of northern Italy as Holy Roman Emperor). In this fashion, the Visconti became the dukes of Milan and the d'Este, the dukes of Ferrara.

The other change of great significance was the development of larger, regional states as the larger states conquered the smaller ones. To fight their battles, city-states came to rely on mercenary soldiers, whose leaders, called **condottieri** (kahn-duh-TYAY-ree), sold the services of their bands to the highest bidder (see Image 11.8). These mercenaries wreaked havoc on the countryside, living by blackmail and looting when they were not actively engaged in battles. Many were foreigners who flocked to Italy during the periods of truce in the Hundred Years' War. By the end of the fourteenth century, three major states came to dominate northern Italy: the despotic state of Milan and the republican states of Florence and Venice.

Duchy of Milan Located in the fertile Po valley, at the intersection of the chief trade routes from Italian coastal cities to the Alpine passes, Milan was one of the richest city-states in Italy. Politically, it was also one of the most agitated until the Visconti family established themselves as the hereditary despots of Milan in 1322. Giangaleazzo Visconti (jahn-gah-lay-AH-tsoh vees-KOHN-tee), who ruled from 1385 to 1402, transformed this despotism into a hereditary duchy by purchasing the title of duke from the emperor in 1395. Under Giangaleazzo's direction, the duchy of Milan extended its power over all of Lombardy and even threatened to conquer much of northern Italy until the duke's untimely death before the gates of Florence in 1402.

Republic of Florence Florence, like the other Italian towns, was initially a free commune dominated by a patrician class of nobles known as the *grandi* (GRAHN-dee). But the rapid expansion of Florence's economy made possible the development of a wealthy merchant-industrialist class known as the *popólo grasso* (PAWP-oo-loh GRAH-soh)—literally the "fat people." In 1293, the popólo grasso assumed a dominant role in government by establishing a new constitution known as the Ordinances of Justice. It provided for a republican

in the government after their revolt in 1378. Only four years later, however, a counterrevolution brought the "fat people" back into virtual control of the government. After 1382, the Florentine government was controlled by a small merchant oligarchy that manipulated the supposedly republican government. By that time, Florence had also been successful in a series of wars against its neighbors. It had conquered most of Tuscany and established itself as a major territorial state in northern Italy.

Republic of Venice The other major northern Italian state was the republic of Venice, which had grown rich from commercial activity throughout the eastern Mediterranean and into northern Europe, Moreover, Venice had begun trading with the Islamic world in the ninth century and continued to do so into the sixteenth century. As a result, a large number of merchant families became extremely wealthy. In the constitution of 1297, these patricians took control of the republic. In this year, the Great Council, the source of all political power, was closed to all but the members of about two hundred families. Since all other magistrates of the city were chosen either from or by this council, these families now formed a hereditary patriciate that completely dominated the city. Although the doge (DOHJ) (or duke) had been the executive head of the republic since the early Middle Ages, by 1300 he had become largely a figurehead. Actual power was vested in the hands of the Great Council and the legislative body known as the Senate, while an extraordinary body known as the Council of Ten,

IMAGE 11.8 **A Famous Condottiere.** Many of the *condottieri* who fought in Italy were foreigners. One of the most prominent was Sir John Hawkwood, who went to Italy after fighting on the English side in the Hundred Years' War. There he led a band of mercenary soldiers in many battles and was known for his brutality—he murdered the entire population of Cesena. Hawkwood, known to the Italians as Giovanni Acuto, ended his career in the early 1390s fighting for the city of Florence. To honor him, the city commissioned this fresco by Paolo Uccello (PAH-oh-loh oo-CHELL-oh), which can still be seen today in the cathedral of Florence.

 What circumstances created the condottieri?

government controlled by the seven major guilds of the city, which represented the interests of the wealthier classes. Executive power was vested in the hands of a council of elected priors. Around the mid-fourteenth century, revolutionary activity by the *popólo minuto*, the small shopkeepers and artisans, won them a share in the government. Even greater expansion occurred briefly when the *ciompi*, or industrial wool workers, were allowed to be represented

CHRONOLOGY	The States of Western and Central Europe	
England		
Edward III		1327–1377
Richard II		1377–1399
Henry IV		1399–1413
France		
Philip IV		1328–1350
John II		1350–1364
Capture at Poitiers		1356
Charles V		1364–1380
Charles VI		1380–1422
German Monarchy		
Golden Bull		1356
Italy		
Florence		
Ordinances of Justice		1293
Venice		
Closing of Great Council		1297
Milan		
Visconti establish themselves as rulers of Milan		1322

first formed in 1310, came to be the real executive power of the state. Contemporaries respected the Venetian government for its stability. A sixteenth-century Italian historian noted that Venice had "the best government of any city not only in our own times but also in the classical world."[13]

In the fourteenth century, Venice also embarked on a policy of expansion. By the end of the century, it had created a commercial empire by establishing colonies and trading posts in the eastern Mediterranean and Black Sea as well as continuing its commercial monopolies in the Byzantine Empire. At the same time, Venice began to conquer the territory adjoining it in northern Italy.

11-3 The Decline of the Church

 FOCUS QUESTION: How and why did the authority and prestige of the papacy decline in the fourteenth century?

The papacy of the Roman Catholic Church reached the height of its power in the thirteenth century. Theories of papal supremacy included a doctrine of "fullness of power" as the spiritual head of Christendom and claims to universal temporal authority over all secular rulers. But papal claims of temporal supremacy were increasingly out of step with the growing secular monarchies of Europe and ultimately brought the papacy into a conflict with the territorial states that it was unable to win.

11-3a Boniface VIII and the Conflict with the State

The struggle between the papacy and the monarchies began during the pontificate of Pope Boniface VIII (1294–1303). One major issue appeared to be at stake between the pope and King Philip IV (r. 1285–1314) of France. In his desire to acquire new revenues, Philip claimed the right to tax the French clergy.

Boniface VIII responded that the clergy of any state could not pay taxes to their secular ruler without the pope's consent (see Image 11.9). Underlying this issue, however, was a basic conflict between the claims of the papacy to universal authority over both church and state, which necessitated complete control over the clergy, and the claims of the king that all subjects, including the clergy, were under the jurisdiction of the crown and subject to the king's authority on matters of taxation and justice. In short, the fundamental issue was the universal sovereignty of the papacy versus the royal sovereignty of the monarch.

Boniface VIII asserted his position in a series of papal bulls or letters, the most important of which was *Unam Sanctam* (OO-nam SAHNK-tahm), issued in 1302. It was the strongest statement ever made by a pope on the supremacy of the spiritual authority over the temporal authority (see Historical Voices, "Boniface VIII's Defense of Papal Supremacy," p. 325). When it became apparent that the pope had decided to act on his principles by excommunicating Philip IV, the latter sent a small contingent of French forces to capture Boniface and bring him back to France for trial. The pope was captured in Anagni, although Italian nobles from the surrounding countryside soon rescued him. The shock of this experience, however, soon led to the pope's death. Philip's strong-arm tactics had produced a clear victory for the national monarchy over the papacy, and no later pope has dared renew the extravagant claims of Boniface VIII.

To ensure his position and avoid any future papal threat, Philip IV brought enough pressure to bear on the college of cardinals to achieve the election of a Frenchman as pope in 1305. Using the excuse of turbulence in the city of Rome, the new pope, Clement V (1305–1314), took up residence in Avignon (ah-veen-YOHN) on the east bank of the Rhône River (see Map 11.5). Although Avignon was located in the Holy Roman Empire and was not a French possession, it lay just across the river from the territory of King Philip IV. Clement may have intended to return

IMAGE 11.9 **Pope Boniface VIII.** The conflict between church and state in the Middle Ages reached its height in the struggle between Pope Boniface VIII and Philip IV of France. This fourteenth-century manuscript miniature depicts Boniface VIII promulgating his decrees.

Boniface VIII's Defense of Papal Supremacy

 What claims did Boniface VIII make in Unam Sanctam? *To what extent were these claims a logical continuation of the development of the papacy in the Middle Ages? If you were a monarch, why would you object to this papal bull?*

ONE OF THE MOST REMARKABLE DOCUMENTS of the fourteenth century was the exaggerated statement of papal supremacy issued by Pope Boniface VIII in 1302 in the heat of his conflict with the French king Philip IV. Ironically, this strongest statement ever made of papal supremacy was issued at a time when the rising power of the monarchies made it increasingly difficult for its premises to be accepted.

Pope Boniface VIII, *Unam Sanctam*

We are compelled, our faith urging us, to believe and to hold—and we do firmly believe and simply confess—that there is one holy catholic and apostolic church, outside of which there is neither salvation nor remission of sins. . . . In this church there is one Lord, one faith and one baptism. . . . Therefore, of this one and only church there is one body and one head . . . Christ, namely, and the vicar of Christ, St. Peter, and the successor of Peter. For the Lord himself said to Peter, feed my sheep. . . .

We are told by the word of the gospel that in this His fold there are two swords—a spiritual, namely, and a temporal. . . . Both swords, the spiritual and the material, therefore, are in the power of the church; the one, indeed, to be wielded for the church, the other by the church; the one by the hand of the priest, the other by the hand of kings and knights, but at the will and sufferance of the priest. One sword, moreover, ought to be under the other, and the temporal authority to be subjected to the spiritual. . . .

Therefore if the earthly power err it shall be judged by the spiritual power; but if the lesser spiritual power err, by the greater. But if the greatest, it can be judged by God alone, not by man, the apostle bearing witness. A spiritual man judges all things, but he himself is judged by no one. This authority, moreover, even though it is given to man and exercised through man, is not human but rather divine, being given by divine lips to Peter and founded on a rock for him and his successors through Christ himself whom he has confessed; the Lord himself saying to Peter: "Whatsoever you shall bind, etc." Whoever, therefore, resists this power thus ordained by God, resists the ordination of God. . . .

Indeed, we declare, announce and define, that it is altogether necessary to salvation for every human creature to be subject to the Roman pontiff.

Source: E. F. Henderson, *Select Historical Documents of the Middle Ages* (London: George Bell & Sons, 1896).

---

to Rome, but he and his successors remained in Avignon for the next seventy-two years, thereby creating yet another crisis for the church.

11-3b The Papacy at Avignon (1305–1377)

The residency of the popes in Avignon for most of the fourteenth century led to a decline in papal prestige and growing antipapal sentiment. The city of Rome was the traditional capital of the universal church. The pope was the bishop of Rome, and his position was based on being the successor to the Apostle Peter, traditionally considered the first bishop of Rome. It was unseemly that the head of the Catholic Church should reside elsewhere. In the 1330s, the popes began to construct a stately palace in Avignon, a clear indication that they intended to stay for some time.

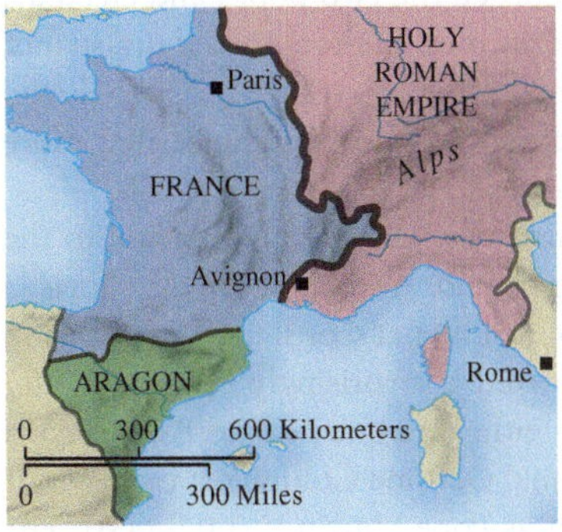

MAP 11.5 Avignon

Other factors also contributed to the decline in papal prestige during the Avignonese residency. It was widely believed that the popes at Avignon were captives of the French monarchy. Although questionable, since Avignon did not belong to the French monarchy, it was easy to believe in view of Avignon's proximity to French lands. The Italian scholar Petrarch (see "11-4a The Development of Vernacular Literature," later in this chapter) labeled this period as the Babylonian Captivity of the church, comparing the French holding the church in captivity to the exile of the Jews into captivity in Babylon in the sixth century B.C.E. (see Chapter 2). Moreover, during the seventy-two years of the Avignonese papacy, of the 134 new cardinals created by the popes, 113 were French. The papal residency at Avignon was also an important turning point in the church's attempt to adapt to the changing economic and political conditions of Europe. Like the growing monarchical states, the popes centralized their administration by developing a specialized bureaucracy. In fact, the papal bureaucracy in the fourteenth century under the leadership of the pope and college of cardinals became the most sophisticated administrative system in the medieval world.

At the same time, the popes attempted to find new sources of revenue to compensate for their loss of income from the

Papal States and began to impose new taxes on the clergy. Furthermore, the splendor in which the pope and cardinals were living in Avignon led to highly vocal criticism of both clergy and papacy in the fourteenth century. Avignon had become a powerful symbol of abuses within the church, and many people began to call for the pope's return to Rome.

One of the most prominent calls came from Catherine of Siena (ca. 1347–1380), whose saintly demeanor and claims of visions from God led the city of Florence to send her on a mission to Pope Gregory XI (1370–1378) in Avignon. She told the pope, "Because God has given you authority and because you have accepted it, you ought to use your virtue and power; if you do not wish to use it, it might be better for you to resign what you have accepted; it would give more honor to God and health to your soul."[14]

11-3c The Great Schism

Catherine of Siena's admonition seemed to be heeded in 1377, when at long last Pope Gregory XI, perceiving the disastrous decline in papal prestige, returned to Rome. He died soon afterward, however, in the spring of 1378. When the college of cardinals met in conclave to elect a new pope, the citizens of Rome, fearful that the French majority would choose another Frenchman who would return the papacy to Avignon, threatened that the cardinals would not leave Rome alive unless they elected a Roman or at least an Italian as pope. Indeed, the guards of the conclave warned the cardinals that they "ran the risk of being torn in pieces" if they did not choose an Italian. Wisely, the terrified cardinals duly elected the Italian archbishop of Bari, who was subsequently crowned as Pope Urban VI (1378–1389) on Easter Sunday. Following his election, Urban VI made clear his plans to reform the papal curia and even to swamp the college of cardinals with enough new Italian cardinals to eliminate the French majority. After many of the cardinals (the French ones) withdrew from Rome in late summer and were finally free of the Roman mob, they issued a manifesto, saying that they had been coerced by the mob and that Urban's election was therefore null and void. The dissenting cardinals thereupon chose one of their number, a Frenchman, who took the title of Clement VII and promptly returned to Avignon. Since Urban remained in Rome, there were now two popes, initiating what has been called the **Great Schism** of the church.

Europe's loyalties soon became divided: France, Spain, Scotland, and southern Italy supported Clement, while England, Germany, Scandinavia, and most of Italy supported Urban. These divisions generally followed political lines and reflected the bitter division between the English and the French in the Hundred Years' War. Because the French supported the Avignonese pope, so did their allies; their enemies, particularly England and its allies, supported the Roman pope. The need for political support caused both popes to subordinate their policies to the policies of these states.

The Great Schism lasted for nearly forty years and had a baleful effect on the Catholic Church and Christendom in general. The schism greatly aggravated the financial abuses that had developed within the church during the Avignonese papacy. Two papal administrative systems (with only half the

accustomed revenues) worked to increase taxation. At the same time, the schism badly damaged the faith of Christian believers in the institution of the Catholic Church as its leader. The pope was widely believed to be the leader of Christendom and, as Boniface VIII had pointed out, held the keys to the kingdom of heaven. Since each line of popes denounced the other as the Antichrist, such a spectacle could not help but undermine the institution that had become the very foundation of the church.

11-3d New Thoughts on Church and State and the Rise of Conciliarism

As dissatisfaction with the papacy grew, so did the calls for a revolutionary approach to solving the church's institutional problems. One of the most systematic was provided by Marsiglio of Padua (mar-SIL-yoh of PAD-juh-wuh) (ca. 1270–1342), rector of the University of Paris and author of a remarkable book, *Defender of the Peace*. Marsiglio denied that the temporal authority was subject to the spiritual authority, as many popes had maintained. Instead, he argued that the church was only one element of society and must confine itself solely to spiritual functions. Furthermore, Marsiglio argued, the church is a community of the faithful in which all authority is ultimately derived from the entire community. The clergy hold no special authority from God but serve only to administer the affairs of the church on behalf of all Christians. Thus, final authority in spiritual matters must reside not with the pope but with a general church council representing all members.

The Conciliar Movement The Great Schism led large numbers of churchmen to take up this theory, known as **conciliarism**, in the belief that only a general council of the church could end the schism and bring reform to the church in its "head and members." The only serious issue left to be decided was who should call the council. Church law held that only a pope could convene a council. Professors of theology argued, however, that since the competing popes would not do so, either members of the church hierarchy or even secular princes, especially the Holy Roman Emperor, could convene a council to settle all relevant issues.

In desperation, a group of cardinals from both camps finally convened a general council on their own. This Council of Pisa, which met in 1409, deposed the two popes and elected a new one, Alexander V. The council's action proved disastrous, however, when the two deposed popes refused to step down. There were now three popes, and the church seemed more hopelessly divided than ever.

Leadership in convening a new council now passed to the Holy Roman Emperor, Sigismund. As a result of his efforts, a new ecumenical church council met at Constance from 1414 to 1418. Ending the schism proved a surprisingly easy task: after the three competing popes either resigned or were deposed, a new conclave elected Cardinal Oddone Colonna, a member of a prominent Roman family, as Pope Martin V (1417–1431). The Great Schism had finally been ended.

11-3e Popular Religion in an Age of Adversity

The seeming preoccupation of the popes and leading clerics with finances and power during the struggles of Boniface VIII, the Avignonese papacy, and the Great Schism could not help but lead to a decline in prestige and respect for the institutional church, especially the papacy. At the same time, in the fourteenth century, the Black Death and its recurrences made an important impact on the religious life of ordinary Christians by heightening their preoccupation with death and salvation. The church often failed to provide sufficient spiritual comfort as many parish priests fled from the plague.

Christians responded in different ways to the adversities of the fourteenth century. First of all, there was a tendency to stress the performance of good works, including acts of charity, as a means of ensuring salvation. Bequests to hospitals and other charitable foundations increased. Family chapels were established, served by priests whose primary responsibility was to say Mass for the good of the souls of deceased family members. These chapels became even more significant as the importance of purgatory rose. Purgatory was defined by the church as the place where souls went after death to be purged of punishment for sins committed in life. In effect, the soul was purified in purgatory before it ascended into heaven. It was believed that like indulgences, prayers and private Masses for the dead could shorten the amount of time souls spent in purgatory.

Chalking up good deeds to ensure salvation was done in numerous ways but was nowhere more evident than in the growing emphasis on indulgences. We should also note that pilgrimages, which became increasingly popular, and charitable contributions were good works that could be accomplished without the involvement of clerics, a reflection of the loss of faith in the institutional church and its clergy and another noticeable feature of popular religious life. At the same time, interest in Christian faith itself did not decline; if anything, it increased (see Global Perspectives, "Religious Imagery in the Medieval World," p. 328). Indeed, people sought to play a more active role in their own salvation. This is particularly evident in the popularity of mysticism and lay piety in the fourteenth century.

Mysticism and Lay Piety The mysticism of the fourteenth century was certainly not new, for Christians throughout the Middle Ages had claimed to have had mystical experiences. Simply defined, **mysticism** is the immediate experience of oneness with God. It is this experience that characterized the teaching of Meister Eckhart (MY-stur EK-hart) (1260–1327), who sparked a mystical movement in western Germany. Eckhart was a well-educated Dominican theologian who wrote learned Latin works on theology, but he was also a popular preacher whose message on the union of the soul with God was typical of mysticism. According to Eckhart, such a union was attainable by all who pursued it wholeheartedly.

Eckhart's movement spread from Germany into the Low Countries, where it took on a new form, called the **Modern Devotion**, founded by Gerard Groote (GROH-tuh) (1340–1384). After a religious conversion, Groote entered a monastery for several years of contemplation before reentering the world. His messages were typical of a practical mysticism. To achieve true spiritual communion with God, people must imitate Jesus and lead lives dedicated to serving the needs of their fellow human beings. Groote emphasized a simple inner piety and morality based on Scripture and an avoidance of the complexities of theology.

Eventually, Groote attracted a group of followers who came to be known as the Brothers of the Common Life. From this small beginning, a movement developed that spread through the Netherlands and back into Germany. Houses of the Brothers, as well as separate houses for women (Sisters of the Common Life), were founded in one city after another. The Sisters and Brothers of the Common Life did not constitute regular religious orders. They were laypeople who took no formal monastic vows but were nevertheless regulated by rules that they imposed on their own communities. They also established schools throughout Germany and the Netherlands in which they stressed their message of imitating the life of Jesus by serving others. The Brothers and Sisters of the Common Life attest to the vitality of spiritual life among lay Christians in the fourteenth century.

Unique Female Mystical Experiences A number of female mystics had their own unique spiritual experiences. For them, fasting and receiving the Eucharist (the communion wafer that, according to Roman Catholic doctrine, contains the body of Jesus) became the mainstay of their religious practices. Catherine of Siena, for example, gave up eating any solid food at the age of twenty-three and thereafter lived only on cold water and herbs that she sucked and then spat out. Her primary nourishment, however, came from the Eucharist. She wrote: "The immaculate lamb [Christ] is food, table, and servant. . . . And we who eat at that table become like the food [that is, Christ], acting not for our own utility but for the honor of God and the salvation of neighbor."[15] For Catherine and a number of other female mystics, reception of the Eucharist was their primary instrument in achieving a mystical union with God.

11-3f Changes in Theology

The fourteenth century presented challenges not only to the institutional church but also to its theological framework, especially evident in the questioning of the grand synthesis

Religious Imagery in the Medieval World

Q *How is the importance of religious imagery in the Middle Ages evident in these three illustrations?*

THE MIDDLE AGES WAS A GOLDEN AGE of religious art, reflecting the important role of religion itself in medieval society. These three illustrations show different aspects of medieval religious imagery. In Europe, much Christian art appeared in illuminated manuscripts. Image 11.10a shows a page depicting the figure of Jesus from *The Book of Kells*, a richly decorated manuscript of the Christian gospels produced by the monks of Iona in the British Isles. Byzantine art was also deeply religious, as was especially evident in icons. Image 11.10b is an icon of the Virgin and Child (Mary and Jesus) from the monastery of Saint Catherine at Mount Sinai in Egypt dating to around the year 600. Painted on wood, this icon shows the enthroned Virgin and Child between Saints Theodore and George with two angels behind them looking upward to a beam of light containing the hand of God. The figures are not realistic; the goal of the icon was to bridge the gap between the divine and the outer material world. Artists in the Muslim world faced a

different challenge—Muslims warned against imitating God by creating pictures of living beings, thus effectively prohibiting the representation of humans, especially Muhammad. Islamic religious artists therefore used decorative motifs based on geometric patterns and the Arabic script. The scriptural panel in Image 11.10c is an artistic presentation of a verse from the Qur'an, thus blending the spiritual and artistic spheres.

IMAGE 11.10b

IMAGE 11.10a

IMAGE 11.10c

Art Resource, NY

Erich Lessing/Art Resource, NY

Vanni Archive/ Art Resource, NY

attempted by Thomas Aquinas. In the thirteenth century, differences with Aquinas were kept within a framework of commonly accepted scholastic thought. In the fourteenth century, however, the philosopher William of Occam (1285–1329) posed a severe challenge to the scholastic achievements of the High Middle Ages.

Occam posited a radical interpretation of nominalism. He asserted that all universals or general concepts were simply names and that only individual objects perceived by the senses were real. Although the mind was capable of analyzing individual objects, it could not establish any truths about the nature of external, higher reality. Reason could not be used to substantiate spiritual truths. It could not, for example, prove the statement "God exists." For William of Occam as a Christian believer, this did not mean that God did not exist, however. It simply indicated that the truths of religion could only be known by an act of faith and were not demonstrable by reason. The acceptance of Occam's nominalist philosophy at the University of Paris brought an element of uncertainty to late medieval theology by seriously weakening the synthesis of faith and reason that had characterized the theological thought of the High Middle Ages. Nevertheless, Occam's emphasis on using reason to analyze the observable phenomena of the world had an important impact on the development of physical science by creating support for rational and scientific analysis. Some late medieval theologians came to accept the compatibility of rational analysis of the material world with mystical acceptance of spiritual truths.

11-4 The Cultural World of the Fourteenth Century

 FOCUS QUESTION: What were the major developments in literature and art in the fourteenth century?

The cultural life of the fourteenth century was also characterized by ferment. In literature, several writers used their vernacular languages to produce notable works. In art, in addition to the morbid themes inspired by the Black Death and other problems of the century, the period also produced Giotto, whose paintings expressed a new realism that would be developed further by the artists of the next century.

11-4a The Development of Vernacular Literature

Although Latin remained the language of the church liturgy and the official documents of both church and state throughout Europe, the fourteenth century witnessed the rapid growth of vernacular literature, especially in Italy. The development of an Italian vernacular literature was mostly the result of the efforts of three writers in the fourteenth century: Dante, Petrarch (PEE-trark *or* PET-trark), and Boccaccio. Their use of the Tuscan dialect common in Florence and its surrounding countryside ensured that it would prevail as the basis of the modern Italian language.

Dante Dante Alighieri (DAHN-tay al-lih-GAIR-ee) (1265–1321) came from an old Florentine noble family that had fallen on hard times. Although he had held high political office in republican Florence, factional conflict led to his exile from the city in 1302. Until the end of his life, Dante hoped to return to his beloved Florence, but his wish remained unfulfilled.

Dante's masterpiece in the Italian vernacular was the *Divine Comedy*, written between 1313 and 1321. Cast in a typical medieval framework, the *Divine Comedy* is basically the story of the soul's progression to salvation, a fundamental medieval preoccupation. The lengthy poem was divided into three major sections corresponding to the realms of the afterworld: hell, purgatory, and heaven or paradise. In the "Inferno" (see Historical Voices, "Dante's Vision of Hell," p. 330), Dante is led by his guide, the classical author Virgil, who is a symbol of human reason. But Virgil (or reason) can lead the poet only so far on his journey. At the end of "Purgatory," Beatrice (the true love of Dante's life), who represents revelation—which alone can explain the mysteries of heaven—becomes his guide into "Paradise." Here Beatrice presents Dante to Saint Bernard, a symbol of mystical contemplation. The saint turns Dante over to the Virgin Mary, since grace is necessary to achieve the final step of entering the presence of God, where one beholds "the love that moves the sun and the other stars."[16]

Petrarch Like Dante, Francesco Petrarca, known as Petrarch (1304–1374), was a Florentine who spent much of his life outside his native city. Petrarch's role in the revival of the classics made him a seminal figure in the literary Italian Renaissance (see Chapter 12). His primary contribution to the development of the Italian vernacular was made in his sonnets. He is considered one of the greatest European lyric poets. His sonnets were inspired by his love for a married lady named Laura, whom he had met in 1327. Though honoring an idealized female figure was a long-standing medieval tradition, Laura was very human and not just an ideal. She was a real woman with whom Petrarch was involved for a long time. He poured forth his lamentations in sonnet after sonnet:

> I weary me alway with questions keen
> How, why my thoughts ne'er turn from you away,
> Wherefore in life they still prefer to stay,
> When they might flee this sad and painful scene,
> And how of the fine hair, the lovely mien,
> Of the bright eyes which all my feelings sway,
> Calling on your dear name by night and day,
> My tongue ne'er silent in their praise has been,
> And how my feet not tender are, nor tired,
> Pursuing still with many a useless pace
> Of your fair footsteps the elastic trace;
> And whence the ink, the paper whence acquired,
> Fill'd with your memories: if in this I err,
> Not art's defect but Love's own fault it were.[17]

In analyzing every aspect of the unrequited lover's feelings, Petrarch appeared less concerned to sing his lady's praise than to immortalize his own thoughts. This interest in his own personality reveals a sense of individuality stronger than in any previous medieval literature.

Dante's Vision of Hell

 How does Dante's vision of hell reflect medieval religious thought? Why were there Florentines in hell? What lessons do you think this work was intended to teach its readers?

THE *DIVINE COMEDY* OF DANTE ALIGHIERI is regarded as one of the greatest literary works of all time. Many consider it the supreme summary of medieval thought. It combines allegory with a remarkable amount of contemporary history. Indeed, forty-three of the seventy-nine people consigned to hell in the "Inferno" were Florentines. This excerpt is taken from canto 18 of the "Inferno," in which Dante and Virgil visit the eighth circle of hell, which is divided into ten trenches containing the souls of people who had committed malicious frauds on their fellow human beings.

Dante, "Inferno," *Divine Comedy*

Now as we were standing where the narrow path
Crosses the second mound, and of it makes
Support to bear it to the other arch.

Here, then, we felt the woeful groans of those
In the other gorge, sputtering with nose and mouth,
And themselves striking with their open palms.

The banks were crusted with a moldy paste,
Born of the breath below, and here it stuck,
Causing to eyes and nostrils rank offense.

So deep the depth, it needed we should mount,
If we would see the place, upon the arch,
Where to the highest point the rock rose up;

And there we came, and looking there, we saw
A crowd below in a dung pool immersed,
From human privies seemingly derived.

And while I looked beneath with searching eye,
There I saw one with head so foul with filth,
Cleric or lay person, which one I could not say

He cried to me, "Wherefore so eager you
Me more than the other filthy ones to scan?"
I answered him, "Because if memory holds,

Already have I seen you with dry hair,
[You are] Alessio Interminelli da Lucca.
Therefore I mark you more than all the rest."

Then, while he struck his head, again he spoke,
"Those flatteries have plunged me here below,
Of which my tongue no [excess] never knew."

Soon after this, my leader spoke, and said,
"A little further thrust you forth your face,
That with its eyes it may the features note

Of that disheveled [whore] foul and vile,
Who tears her body with her filthy nails;
Now lounging low, now on her feet upright.

Thais it is—the harlot who, when asked
Once by her lover, 'Do you give me great thanks?'
Answered him thus, 'Thanks marvelous indeed.'"

And now our eyes enough of this had seen.

Source: David Johnston, *A Translation of Dante's Inferno* (Bath, U.K.: Chronicle Office, 1867), pp. 104–105.

Boccaccio Although he too wrote poetry, Giovanni Boccaccio (1313–1375) is known primarily for his prose. Another Florentine, he also used the Tuscan dialect. While working for the Bardi banking house in Naples, he fell in love with a noble lady, and under her inspiration, he began to write prose romances. His best-known work, the *Decameron*, however, was not written until after he had returned to Florence. The *Decameron* is set at the time of the Black Death. Ten young people flee to a villa outside Florence to escape the plague and decide to while away the time by telling stories. Although the stories are not new and still reflect the acceptance of basic Christian values, Boccaccio does present the society of his time from a secular point of view. It is the seducer of women, not the knight or philosopher or pious monk, who is the real hero. Perhaps, as some historians have argued, the *Decameron* reflects the immediate easygoing, cynical post-plague values. Boccaccio's later work certainly became gloomier and more pessimistic; as he grew older, he

even rejected his earlier work as irrelevant. He commented in a 1373 letter, "I am certainly not pleased that you have allowed the illustrious women in your house to read my trifles. . . . You know how much in them is less than decent and opposed to modesty, how much stimulation to wanton lust, how many things that drive to lust even those most fortified against it."[18]

Chaucer Another leading vernacular author was Geoffrey Chaucer (ca. 1340–1400), who brought a new level of sophistication to the English vernacular language in his famous *Canterbury Tales*. His beauty of expression and clear, forceful language were important in transforming his East Midland dialect into the chief ancestor of the modern English language. *The Canterbury Tales* is a collection of stories told by a group of twenty-nine pilgrims journeying from the London suburb of Southwark to the tomb of Saint Thomas à Becket at Canterbury. This format gave Chaucer the chance to portray an entire range of English society, both high- and low-born. Among others, he presented the Knight, the Yeoman, the Prioress, the Monk, the Merchant, the Student, the Lawyer, the Carpenter, the Cook, the Doctor, the Plowman, and, "A Good Wife was there from beside the city of Bath—a little deaf, which was a pity." The stories these pilgrims told to while away the time on the journey were just as varied as the storytellers themselves: knightly romances, fairy tales, saints' lives, sophisticated satires, and crude anecdotes.

Chaucer also used some of his characters to criticize the corruption of the church in the late medieval period. His portrayal of the Friar leaves no doubt of Chaucer's disdain for the corrupt practices of clerics. Of the Friar, he says:

> He knew the taverns well in every town.
> The barmaids and innkeepers pleased his mind
> Better than beggars and lepers and their kind.[19]

And yet Chaucer was still a pious Christian, never doubting basic Christian doctrines and remaining optimistic that the church could be reformed.

Christine de Pizan One of the extraordinary vernacular writers of the age was Christine de Pizan (ca. 1364–1430) (see Image 11.11). Because of her father's position at the court of Charles V of France, she received a good education. Her husband died when she was only twenty-five (they had been married for ten years), leaving her with little income and three small children and her mother to support. Christine took the unusual step of becoming a writer in order to earn her living. Her poems

IMAGE 11.11 Christine de Pizan. Christine de Pizan was one of the extraordinary vernacular writers of the late fourteenth and early fifteenth centuries. In this fifteenth-century French illustration from the *Works of Christine de Pizan*, she is shown giving instructions to an assistant.

Q *How does this image reflect a reversal of traditional medieval norms?*

were soon in demand, and by 1400 she had achieved financial security.

Christine de Pizan is best known, however, for her French prose works written in defense of women. In *The Book of the City of Ladies*, written in 1404, she denounced the many male writers who had argued that women needed to be controlled by men because women by their very nature were prone to evil, unable to learn, and easily swayed. With the help of Reason, Righteousness, and Justice, who appear to her in a vision, Christine refutes these antifemale attacks. Women, she argues, are not evil by nature, and they could learn as well as men if they were permitted to attend the same schools: "Should I also tell you whether a woman's nature is clever and quick enough to learn speculative sciences as well as to discover them, and likewise the manual arts. I assure you that women are equally well-suited and skilled to carry them out and to put them to sophisticated use once they have learned them."[20] Much of the book includes a detailed discussion of women from the past and present who have distinguished themselves as leaders, warriors, wives, mothers, and martyrs for their religious faith. She ends by encouraging women to defend themselves against the attacks of men, who are incapable of understanding them.

11-4b A New Art: Giotto

The fourteenth century produced an artistic outburst in new directions as well as a large body of morbid work influenced by the Black Death and the recurrences of the plague. The city of Florence witnessed the first dramatic break with medieval tradition in the work of Giotto (JOH-toh) (1266–1337), often considered a forerunner of Italian Renaissance painting. Born into a peasant family, Giotto acquired his painting skills in a workshop in Florence. Although he worked throughout Italy, his most famous works were done in Padua and Florence.

Coming out of the formal Byzantine school, Giotto transcended it with a new kind of realism, a desire to imitate nature that Renaissance artists later identified as the basic component of classical art. Giotto's figures were solid and rounded; placed realistically in relationship to each other and their background, they conveyed three-dimensional depth (see Image 11.12). The expressive faces and physically realistic bodies gave his sacred figures human qualities with which spectators could identify. Although Giotto had no direct successors, Florentine painting in the early fifteenth century pursued even more dramatically the new direction his work represents.

11-5 Society in an Age of Adversity

 FOCUS QUESTIONS: How did the adversities of the fourteenth century affect urban life and medical practices? What new inventions and patterns emerged in the fourteenth century?

In the midst of disaster, the fourteenth century proved creative in its own way. New inventions made an impact on daily life at the same time that the effects of the plague were felt in many areas of medieval urban life.

SCIENCE SOURCE/Science Source

IMAGE 11.12 **Giotto, Lamentation.** The work of Giotto marked the first clear innovation in fourteenth-century painting, making him a forerunner of the early Renaissance. This fresco was part of a series done on the walls of the Arena Chapel in Padua begun in 1305. Giotto painted thirty-eight scenes on three levels: the lives of Mary, the mother of Jesus, and her parents (top panel); the life and work of Jesus (middle panel); and his passion, crucifixion, and resurrection (bottom panel). Shown here from the bottom panel is the *Lamentation*. A group of Jesus's followers, including his mother and Mary Magdalene, mourn over the body of Jesus before it is placed in its tomb. The solidity of Giotto's human figures gives them a three-dimensional sense. He also captured the grief and despair felt by the mourners.

11-5a Changes in Urban Life

One immediate by-product of the Black Death was greater regulation of urban activities by town governments. Authorities tried to keep cities cleaner by enacting new ordinances against waste products in the streets. Viewed as unhealthy places, bathhouses were closed down, leading to a noticeable decline in personal cleanliness. Efforts at regulation also affected the practice of female prostitution.

Medieval society had tolerated prostitution as a lesser evil: it was better for males to frequent prostitutes than to seduce virgins or married women. Since many males in medieval towns married late, the demand for prostitutes was high and was met by a regular supply, derived no doubt from the need of many poor girls and women to survive. The recession of the fourteenth century probably increased the supply of prostitutes, while the new hedonism prevalent after the Black Death also increased demand. As a result, cities intensified their regulation of prostitution.

By organizing brothels, city authorities could supervise as well as tax prostitutes. Officials granted charters to citizens who were allowed to set up brothels, provided they were located only in certain areas of town. Prostitutes were also expected to wear special items of clothing—such as red hats—to distinguish them from other women. It was assumed that the regulation of prostitution made it easier to supervise and hence maintained public order.

Family Life and Gender Roles in Late Medieval Cities The basic unit of the late medieval town was the nuclear family of husband, wife, and children (see Images of Everyday Life, "Entertainment in the Middle Ages," p. 333). Especially in wealthier families, there might also be servants, apprentices, and other relatives, including widowed mothers and the husband's illegitimate children.

Before the Black Death, late marriages were common for urban couples. It was not unusual for husbands to be in their late thirties or forties and wives in their early twenties. The expense of setting up a household probably necessitated the delay in marriage. But the situation changed dramatically after the plague, reflecting new economic opportunities for the survivors and a new reluctance to postpone living in the presence of so much death.

The economic difficulties of the fourteenth century also tended to strengthen the development of gender roles. Based on the authority of Aristotle, Thomas Aquinas and other scholastic theologians had advanced the belief that according to the natural order, men were active and domineering while women were passive and submissive. As more and more lawyers, doctors, and priests, who had been trained in universities where these notions were taught, entered society, these ideas about the different natures of men and women became widely accepted. This was evident in legal systems, many of which limited the legal capacity of women. Increasingly, women were expected to give up any active functions in society and remain subject to direction from males (see Historical Voices, "A Liberated Woman in the Fourteenth Century," p. 334). A fourteenth-century Parisian provost commented that among glass cutters, "no master's widow who keeps working at his craft after her husband's death may take on apprentices, for the men of the craft do not believe that a woman can master it well enough to teach a child to master it, for the craft is a very delicate one."[21] Although this statement suggests that some women were, in fact, running businesses, it also reveals that they were viewed as incapable of undertaking all of men's activities. Europeans in the fourteenth century imposed a division of labor roles between men and women that persisted until the Industrial Revolution.

In practice, however, some women in the fourteenth century benefited from the effects of the Black Death. The

Entertainment in the Middle Ages

Q *What are the similarities and differences in the forms of entertainment in the Middle Ages and today?*

MEDIEVAL PEOPLE engaged in a variety of activities for entertainment. City dwellers enjoyed feast days and holidays, when minstrels and jugglers amused people with their arts and tricks. Castle life had its courtly feasts, featuring tournaments accompanied by banquets, music, and dancing. Games were popular at all levels of society; castle dwellers played backgammon, checkers, and chess. Image 11.13a, from a fifteenth-century fresco, shows a group of ladies and gentlemen playing cards.

Like children in all ages, medieval children joined with other children in playing a variety of games. A number of writers on children saw play as a basic symbol of childhood itself. Images 11.13b and 11.13c are illustrations from medieval manuscripts depicting children catching butterflies and playing with a spinning top, and playing a game of blind man's bluff.

IMAGE 11.13a

Palazzo Borromeo, Milan//Scala/Art Resource, NY

IMAGE 11.13b

British Library Board/Bridgeman Art Library

IMAGE 11.13c

Gianni Dagli Orti/Shutterstock.com

deaths of many male workers in cities opened up new jobs for women, such as metalworkers and stevedores. In cloth making, women were allowed to assume better-paying jobs as weavers. Brewing became an all-female profession by 1450. Widows also occasionally carried on their husbands' shops or businesses.

Medieval Children Parents in the High and later Middle Ages invested considerable resources and affection in rearing their children. The dramatic increase in specialized roles that accompanied the spread of commerce and the growth of cities demanded a commitment to educating children in the marketable skills needed for the new occupations. Philip of

A Liberated Woman in the Fourteenth Century

 Q *Why were the views of Grazida Lizier on religion and sexuality so unusual? Did her Cathar background have any impact on her views?*

DURING THE HIGH AND LATER MIDDLE AGES, women were increasingly viewed as weak beings who were unable to play independent roles. One exception in the fourteenth century was Grazida Lizier, a peasant woman of Cathar background who lived in the village of Montaillou in France. She expressed some radical views on religion and sexuality, as recorded by a Catholic inquisitor who was questioning her about her potentially heretical views.

The Testimony of Grazida Lizier

When I was married and made love with the priest Pierre, it did not seem more proper to make love with my husband—all the same it seemed to me, and I still believe, it was as little sin with Pierre as with my husband. Did I have any qualms at the time, or think that such deeds might displease God? No, I had none, and did not think my lying with Pierre should displease any living being, since it gave joy to us both.

If my husband had forbidden it? Supposing he had—even though he never did—I still would not have thought it a sin, because of the shared joy of love. If any man whatever lies with any women (unless she is related to him by blood), whether she's a virgin or has been seduced, whether in marriage or outside it—all such coupling of men and women gives displeasure to God, and yet I still do not think the partners sin, insofar as their joy is mutual. . . .

I don't know but I've heard it said there is a paradise, and I believe it; I've also heard there is a hell, but that I don't believe, though I won't urge it is untrue. I believe there is a paradise, for it is something good, as I've heard tell; I don't believe in hell (though I don't argue against it), for that is something evil, as people say. I've often heard that we shall rise again after death—I don't believe that, though I don't discredit it.

I still believe it is no sin when love-making brings joy to both partners. I have believed that ever since Pierre first knew me. No one taught me these ideas except myself. I haven't taught them to others—no one has ever asked me about them.

Source: E. Delamotte, N. Meeker, and J. O'Barr, *Women Imagine Change* (New York: Routledge, 1977), p. 53.

Navarre noted in the twelfth century that boys ought to be taught a trade "as soon as possible. Those who early become and long remain apprentices ought to be the best masters."[22] Some cities provided schools to educate the young. A chronicler in Florence related that between 8,000 and 10,000 boys and girls between the ages of six and twelve attended the city's grammar schools, a figure that probably represented half of all school-aged children. Although grammar school completed education for girls, some 1,100 boys went on to six secondary schools that prepared them for business careers, while another 600 studied Latin and logic in four other schools that readied them for university training and a career in medicine, law, or the church. In the High Middle Ages, then, urban communities demonstrated a commitment to training the young.

As a result of the devastating effects of the plague and its recurrences, these same communities became concerned about investing in the survival and health of children. A number of hospitals existed in both Florence and Rome in the fourteenth century, and in the 1420s and 1430s, hospitals were established that catered only to the needs of foundlings, supporting them until boys could be taught a trade and girls could marry.

11-5b New Directions in Medicine

The medical community comprised a number of functionaries. At the top of the medical hierarchy were the physicians, who received their education in the universities, where they studied ancient authorities, such as Hippocrates and Galen. As a result, physicians were highly trained in theory but had little or no clinical practice. By the fourteenth century, they were educated in six chief medical schools—Salerno, Montpellier, Bologna, Oxford, Padua, and Paris. Bologna and Padua were regarded as the most prestigious.

The pre-plague medicine of university-trained physicians was theoretically grounded in the classical Greek theory of the "four humors," each connected to a particular organ: blood (from the heart), phlegm (from the brain), yellow bile (from the liver), and black bile (from the spleen). Because the four humors corresponded in turn to the four elemental qualities of the universe—air (blood), water (phlegm), fire (yellow bile), and earth (black bile)—a human being was considered a microcosm of the cosmos. Good health resulted from a perfect balance of the four humors; sickness meant that the humors were out of balance. The task of the medieval physician was to restore proper order through a number of remedies, such as rest, diet, herbal medicines, or bloodletting.

Beneath the physicians in the hierarchy of the medical profession stood the surgeons, whose activities included performing operations, setting broken bones, and bleeding patients. Their knowledge was based largely on practical experience. Below surgeons were midwives, who delivered babies, and barber-surgeons, who were less trained than surgeons and performed menial tasks such as bloodletting and setting simple bone fractures. Barber-surgeons supplemented their income by shaving and cutting hair and pulling teeth. Apothecaries also constituted part of the medical establishment. They filled herbal prescriptions recommended by physicians and also prescribed drugs on their own authority.

All of these medical practitioners proved unable to deal with the plague. When King Philip VI of France requested the opinion of the medical faculty of the University of Paris on the plague, their advice proved worthless. This failure to understand the Black Death, however, produced a crisis in medieval medicine that resulted in some new approaches to health care.

One result was the rise of surgeons to greater prominence because of their practical knowledge. Surgeons were now recruited by universities, which placed them on an equal level with physicians and introduced a greater emphasis on practical anatomy into the university curriculum. Connected to this was a burgeoning of medical textbooks, often written in the vernacular and stressing practical, how-to approaches to medical and surgical problems.

Finally, as a result of the plague, cities, especially in Italy, gave increased attention to public health and sanitation. Public health laws were instituted, and municipal boards of health came into being. The primary concern of the latter was to prevent plague, but gradually they came to control almost every aspect of health and sanitation. Boards of public health, consisting of medical practitioners and public officials, were empowered to enforce sanitary conditions, report on and attempt to isolate epidemics by quarantine (rarely successful), and regulate the activities of doctors.

11-5c Inventions and New Patterns

Despite its problems, the fourteenth century witnessed a continuation of the technological innovations that had characterized the High Middle Ages.

The Clock The most extraordinary of these inventions, and one that made a visible impact on European cities, was the clock. The mechanical clock was invented at the end of the thirteenth century but not perfected until the fourteenth. The time-telling clock was actually a by-product of a larger astronomical clock. The best-designed one was constructed by Giovanni di Dondi in the mid-fourteenth century. Dondi's clock contained the signs of the zodiac but also struck on the hour. Since clocks were expensive, they were usually installed only in the towers of churches or municipal buildings. The first clock striking equal hours was in a church in Milan; in 1335, a chronicler described it as "a wonderful clock, with a very large clapper which strikes a bell twenty-four times according to the twenty-four hours of the day and night and thus at the first hour of the night gives one sound, at the second two strikes . . . and so distinguishes one hour from another, which is of greatest use to men of every degree."[23]

Clocks revolutionized how people thought about and used time. Throughout most of the Middle Ages, time was determined by natural rhythms (daybreak and nightfall) or church bells that were rung at more or less regular three-hour intervals, corresponding to the ecclesiastical offices of the church. Clocks made it possible for people to plan their day and organize activities around the regular striking of bells. This brought a new regularity into the lives of workers and merchants, defining urban existence and enabling merchants and bankers to see the value of time in a new way.

Eyeglasses and Paper Like clocks, eyeglasses were introduced in the thirteenth century but not refined until the fourteenth. Even then they were not particularly effective by modern standards and were still extremely expensive. The high cost of parchment forced people to write in extremely small script; eyeglasses made it more readable. At the same time, a significant change in writing materials occurred in the fourteenth century when parchment was supplemented by much cheaper paper made from cotton rags. Although it was more subject to insect and water damage than parchment, medieval paper was actually superior to modern papers made of high-acid wood pulp.

Gunpowder and Cannons Invented earlier by the Chinese, gunpowder also made its appearance in the West in the thirteenth century. The use of gunpowder eventually brought drastic changes to European warfare. Its primary use was in cannons, although early cannons were prone to blow up, making them as dangerous to the people firing them as to the enemy. Even as late as 1460, an attack on a castle using an enormous Flemish cannon called the "Lion" proved disastrous for the Scottish king James II when the "Lion" blew up, killing the king and a number of his retainers. Continued improvement in the construction of cannons, however, soon made them extremely valuable in reducing both castles and city walls. Gunpowder made castles, city walls, and armored knights obsolete.

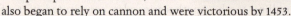

CHAPTER SUMMARY

In the eleventh, twelfth, and thirteenth centuries, European civilization developed many of its fundamental features. Territorial states, parliaments, capitalist trade and industry, banks, cities, and vernacular literature were all products of that fertile period. During the same time, the Catholic Church under the direction of the papacy reached its apogee.

Fourteenth-century European society, however, was challenged by an overwhelming number of crises that led to the disintegration of medieval civilization. At mid-century, one of the most destructive natural disasters in history erupted—the Black Death, a devastating plague that wiped out at least one-third of the European population, with even higher mortality rates in urban areas. Reactions varied. Some people escaped into alcohol, sex, and crime. Others, such as the flagellants, believing the Black Death to be a punishment from God, attempted to atone for people's sins through self-inflicted pain. In many areas, the Jews became scapegoats. Economic crises and social upheavals, including a decline in trade and industry, bank failures, and peasant revolts pitting the lower classes against the upper classes, followed in the wake of the Black Death.

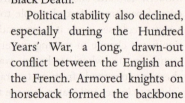

Political stability also declined, especially during the Hundred Years' War, a long, drawn-out conflict between the English and the French. Armored knights on horseback formed the backbone of medieval armies, but English peasants using the longbow began to change the face of war. After numerous defeats, the French cause was saved by Joan of Arc, a young peasant woman whose leadership inspired the French, who also began to rely on cannon and were victorious by 1453.

The Catholic Church, too, experienced a crisis. The confrontation between Pope Boniface VIII and Philip IV of France led to a loss of papal power and the removal of the papacy to Avignon on France's border in 1305. The absence of the popes from Rome created a new crisis, but the return of the papacy to Rome in 1377 only led to new problems with the Great Schism, which witnessed the spectacle of two competing popes condemning each other as the Antichrist. A new conciliar movement based on the belief that church councils, not popes, should rule the church finally ended the Great Schism in 1417.

All of these crises seemed to overpower Europeans in this calamitous fourteenth century. Not surprisingly, much of the art of the period depicted the Four Horsemen of the Apocalypse described in the New Testament Book of Revelation: Death, Famine, Pestilence, and War. No doubt, to some people, the last days of the world appeared to be at hand. European society, however, proved remarkably resilient. Already in the fourteenth century new ideas and practices were beginning to emerge, as often happens in periods of crisis. As we shall see in the next chapter, the pace of change began to quicken as Europe experienced a rebirth of classical culture that some historians have called the Renaissance.

CHAPTER TIMELINE

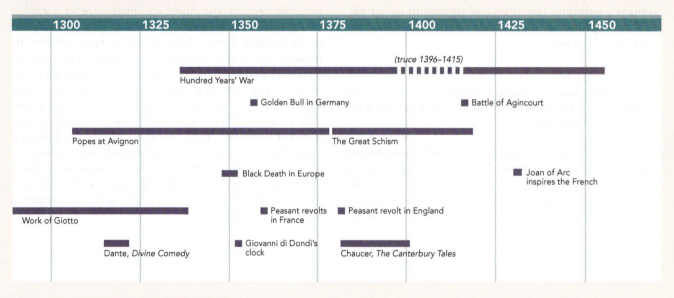

CHAPTER REVIEW

Upon Reflection

Q Make an argument either for or against the idea that climate and disease played a major role in producing social, economic, and political changes in the fourteenth century.

Q What were the chief factors that led to the urban and rural revolts of the fourteenth century?

Q What were the causes of the Hundred Years' War, and what were the results of the war in the fourteenth century for France and England?

Q What impact did the adversities of the fourteenth century have on Christian practices?

Key Terms

Black Death (p. 308)
pogroms (p. 312)
scutage (p. 319)
Third Estate (p. 321)
condottieri (p. 322)

Great Schism (p. 326)
conciliarism (p. 326)
mysticism (p. 327)
Modern Devotion (p. 327)

Full definitions also appear in the Glossary at the end of the book.

Suggestions for Further Reading

General Works   For a general introduction to the fourteenth century, see **D. P. Waley** and **P. Denley**, *Later Medieval Europe*, 3rd ed. (London, 2001), and **J. Aberth**, *From the Brink of the Apocalypse: Confronting Famine, War, Plague, and Death in the Later Middle Ages* (London, 2001).

The Black Death   On the Black Death, see **O. J. Benedictow**, *The Black Death: The Complete History* (Suffolk, 2008), and **J. Kelly**, *The Great Mortality* (New York, 2005).

Hundred Years' War   Good accounts of the Hundred Years' War include **A. Curry**, *The Hundred Years' War*, 2nd ed. (New York, 2004), and **R. H. Neillands**, *The Hundred Years' War*, 2nd ed. (New York, 2001). On Joan of Arc, see **H. Carter**, *Joan of Arc* (New York, 2015).

Political History   On the political history of the period, see **B. Guenee**, *States and Rulers in Later Medieval Europe*, trans. **J. Vale** (Oxford, 1985). On medieval mercenaries, see **W. Urban**, *Medieval Mercenaries* (London, 2006). On the social revolts of the period, see **S. K. Cohn**, *Lust for Liberty: The Politics of Social Revolt in Medieval Europe, 1200–1425* (Cambridge, Mass., 2008).

Catholic Church   A good general study of the church in the fourteenth century can be found in **F. P. Oakley**, *The Western*

Church in the Later Middle Ages (Ithaca, N.Y., 1980). On female mystics in the later Middle Ages, see **D. Elliott**, *Proving Woman: A Female Spirituality and Inquisitorial Culture in the Later Middle Ages* (Princeton, N.J., 2004). On late medieval religious practices, see **R. N. Swanson**, *Religion and Devotion in Europe, c. 1215–1515* (Cambridge, 1995).

Culture   A classic work on the life and thought of the later Middle Ages is **J. Huizinga**, *The Autumn of the Middle Ages*, trans. **R. J. Payton** and **U. Mammitzsch** (Chicago, 1996). On Dante, see **B. Reynolds**, *Dante: The Poet, the Political Thinker, the Man* (London, 2006). The best work on Christine de Pizan is **C. C. Willard**, *Christine de Pizan: Her Life and Works* (New York, 1984).

Social History   For an introduction, see **S. Epstein**, *An Economic and Social History of Later Medieval Europe, 1000–1500* (New York, 2009). On women in the later Middle Ages, see **S. Shahar**, *The Fourth Estate: A History of Women in the Middle Ages*, trans. **C. Galai**, rev. ed. (London, 2003). On childhood, see **N. Orme**, *Medieval Children* (New Haven, Conn., 2001). For a general introduction to the changes in medicine, see **N. G. Siraisi**, *Medieval and Early Renaissance Medicine* (Chicago, 1990).

Notes

1. Quoted in James B. Ross and Mary M. McLaughlin, *The Portable Medieval Reader* (New York, 1949), pp. 216–221.
2. Quoted in H. S. Lucas, "The Great European Famine of 1315, 1316, and 1317," *Speculum* 5 (1930): 359.
3. Quoted in C. S. Bartsocas, "Two Fourteenth-Century Descriptions of the 'Black Death,'" *Journal of the History of Medicine* (October 1966): 395.
4. Quoted in D. Herlihy, *The Black Death and the Transformation of the West*, ed. S. K. Cohn Jr. (Cambridge, Mass., 1997), p. 9.
5. Quoted in R. Horrox, ed., *The Black Death* (Manchester, U.K., 1994), pp. 18–19.
6. Giovanni Boccaccio, *Decameron*, trans. F. Winwar (New York, 1955), p. xxv.
7. Ibid., p. xxvi.
8. Jean Froissart, *Chronicles*, Geoffrey Brereton, ed., trans. (Harmondsworth, U.K., 1968), p. 111.
9. Quoted in J. B. Ross and M. M. McLaughlin, *The Portable Medieval Reader*, pp. 218–219.

10. Quoted in B. W. Tuchman, *A Distant Mirror* (New York, 1978), p. 175.

11. Froissart, *Chronicles*, p. 212.

12. O. J. Thatcher and E. H. McNeal, eds., *A Source Book for Medieval History* (New York, 1905), p. 288.

13. Quoted in D. S. Chambers, *The Imperial Age of Venice, 1380–1580* (London, 1970), p. 30.

14. Quoted in R. Coogan, *Babylon on the Rhône: A Translation of Letters by Dante, Petrarch, and Catherine of Siena* (Washington, D.C., 1983), p. 115.

15. Quoted in C. W. Bynum, *Holy Feast and Holy Fast: The Religious Significance of Food to Medieval Women* (Berkeley, Calif., 1987), p. 180.

16. Dante Alighieri, *Divine Comedy*, trans. D. Sayers (New York, 1962), "Paradise," canto 33, line 145.

17. Sonnet LIV from *The Sonnets, Triumphs, and Other Poems of Petrarch*, edited by Thomas Campbell (London: George Bell and Sons, 1879), p. 78. Accessed at: http://www.gutenberg.org/files/17650/17650-h/17650-h.htm.

18. Quoted in M. Meiss, *Painting in Florence and Siena After the Black Death* (Princeton, N.J., 1951), p. 161.

19. Geoffrey Chaucer, *The Canterbury Tales*, in T. Morrison, ed., *The Portable Chaucer* (New York, 1949), p. 67.

20. Christine de Pizan, *The Book of the City of Ladies*, trans. E. J. Richards (New York, 1982), pp. 83–84.

21. Quoted in S. M. Stuard, "The Dominion of Gender, or How Women Fared in the High Middle Ages," in R. Bridenthal, C. Koonz, and S. Stuard, eds., *Becoming Visible: Women in European History*, 3rd ed. (Boston, 1998), p. 147.

22. Quoted in D. Herlihy, "Medieval Children," in B. K. Lackner and K. R. Philp, eds., *Essays on Medieval Civilization* (Austin, Tex., 1978), p. 121.

23. Quoted in J. Gimpel, *The Medieval Machine* (New York, 1976), p. 168.

MindTap Tips

"When everything that you need is in one place, things tend to go much more smoothly. MindTap is a comprehensive study tool that gives you everything you need to succeed—e–textbooks, quizzes, assignments, flashcards, a dictionary if you get stuck on a word — it's all there! MindTap is the whole package." — Erica, student

CHAPTER 12

Recovery and Rebirth: The Age of the Renaissance

IMAGE 12.1 **Michelangelo's** *Creation of Adam* **on the Sistine Chapel Ceiling**

CHAPTER OUTLINE AND FOCUS QUESTIONS

12-1 Meaning and Characteristics of the Italian Renaissance

Q What characteristics distinguish the Renaissance from the Middle Ages? What are the continuities between the Middle Ages and Renaissance?

12-2 The Making of Renaissance Society

Q What major economic and social changes occurred during the Renaissance?

12-3 The Italian States in the Renaissance

Q How important was the role of the city-state in Italy? How did Machiavelli's works reflect the political realities of Renaissance Italy?

12-4 The Intellectual Renaissance in Italy

Q What was humanism, and what effect did it have on philosophy, education, attitudes toward politics, the writing of history, and women?

12-5 The Artistic Renaissance

Q What were the chief characteristics of Renaissance art, and how did it differ in Italy and northern Europe? Choose any three artists and explain their importance to the development of art in the Renaissance.

12-6 The European State in the Renaissance

Q Why do historians sometimes refer to the monarchies of the late fifteenth century as "new monarchies" or

"Renaissance states"? What states provide the best examples? Why?

12-7 The Church in the Renaissance

Q How were the problems of heresy and reform resolved? What were the policies of the Renaissance popes, and what impact did those policies have on the Catholic Church?

CONNECTIONS TO TODAY

How does the concept of the Renaissance have relevance to the early twenty-first century?

WERE THE FOURTEENTH AND FIFTEENTH CENTURIES a continuation of the Middle Ages or the beginning of a new era? Both positions can be defended. Although the disintegrative patterns of the fourteenth century continued into the fifteenth, at the same time there were elements of recovery that made the fifteenth century a period of significant political, economic, artistic, and intellectual change. The humanists or intellectuals of the age called their period (from the mid-fourteenth to the mid-sixteenth century) an age of rebirth, believing that they had restored arts and letters to new glory after they had been "neglected" or "dead" for centuries. The humanists also saw their age as one of accomplished individuals who dominated the landscape of their time.

Michelangelo, the great Italian artist of the early sixteenth century, and Pope Julius II, the "warrior

339

pope," were two such titans. The artist's temperament and the pope's temper led to many lengthy and often loud quarrels between the two. The pope had hired Michelangelo to paint the ceiling of the Sistine Chapel in Rome, a difficult task for a man long accustomed to being a sculptor. Michelangelo undertook the project but refused for a long time to allow anyone, including the pope, to see his work. Julius grew anxious, pestering Michelangelo on a regular basis about when the ceiling would be finished. Exasperated by the pope's requests, Michelangelo once replied, according to Giorgio Vasari, his contemporary biographer, that the ceiling would be completed when it satisfied him "as an artist." The pope responded by threatening Michelangelo that if he did not finish the ceiling quickly, the pope would have him thrown down from the scaffolding. Fearing the pope's anger, Michelangelo began doing "all that was wanted" and quickly completed the ceiling, one of the great masterpieces in the history of Western art.

The humanists' view of their age as a rebirth of the classical civilization of the Greeks and Romans ultimately led historians to use the French word *Renaissance* to identify this age. Although recent historians have emphasized the many elements of continuity between the Middle Ages and the Renaissance, the latter age was also distinguished by its own unique characteristics.

12-1 Meaning and Characteristics of the Italian Renaissance

 FOCUS QUESTIONS: What characteristics distinguish the Renaissance from the Middle Ages? What are the continuities between the Middle Ages and the Renaissance?

Renaissance means "rebirth." Many people who lived in Italy between 1350 and 1550 believed that they had witnessed a rebirth of antiquity or Greco-Roman civilization, marking a new age. To them, the thousand or so years between the end of the Roman Empire and their own era constituted a middle period (the "Middle Ages"), characterized by darkness because of its lack of classical culture. Historians of the nineteenth century later used similar terminology to describe this period in Italy. The Swiss historian and art critic Jacob Burckhardt (YAK-ub BOORK-hart) created the modern concept of the **Renaissance** in his celebrated book *The Civilization of the Renaissance in Italy*, published in 1860. He portrayed Italy in the fourteenth and fifteenth centuries as the birthplace of the modern world (the Italians were "the firstborn among the sons of modern Europe") and saw the revival of antiquity, the "perfecting of the individual," and secularism ("worldliness of the Italians") as its distinguishing features. Burckhardt exaggerated the individuality and secularism of the Renaissance and failed to recognize the depths of its religious sentiment; nevertheless, he established the framework for all modern interpretations of the period. Although contemporary scholars do not believe that the Renaissance represents a sudden or dramatic cultural break with the Middle Ages, as Burckhardt argued—there was, after all, much continuity in economic, political, and social life—the Renaissance can still be viewed as a distinct period of European history that manifested itself first in Italy and then spread to the rest of Europe.

Renaissance Italy was largely an urban society. As a result of its commercial preeminence and political evolution, northern Italy by the mid-fourteenth century was mostly a land of independent cities that dominated the country districts around them. These city-states became the centers of Italian political, economic, social, and cultural life. Within this new urban society, a secular spirit emerged as increasing wealth created new possibilities for the enjoyment of worldly things (see Historical Voices, "A Renaissance Banquet," p. 341).

Above all, the Renaissance was an age of recovery from the calamitous fourteenth century, a time for the slow process of recuperating from the effects of the Black Death, political disorder, and economic recession. This recovery was accompanied by a rediscovery of the culture of classical antiquity. Increasingly aware of their own historical past, Italian intellectuals became intensely interested in the Greek and Roman culture of the ancient Mediterranean world. This revival of classical antiquity (the Middle Ages had in fact preserved much of ancient Latin culture) affected activities as diverse as politics and art and led to new attempts to reconcile the pagan philosophy of the Greco-Roman world with Christian thought, as well as new ways of viewing human beings.

A revived emphasis on individual ability became a characteristic of the Italian Renaissance. As the fifteenth-century Florentine architect Leon Battista Alberti (LAY-un buh-TEESS-tuh al-BAYR-tee) expressed it, "Men can do all things if they will."[1] A high regard for human dignity and worth and a realization of individual potentiality created a new social ideal of the well-rounded personality or universal person—*l'uomo universale* (LWOH-moh OO-nee-ver-SAH-lay)—who was capable of achievements in many areas of life.

These general features of the Italian Renaissance were not characteristic of all Italians but were primarily the preserve of the wealthy upper classes, who constituted a small percentage of the total population. The achievements of the Italian Renaissance were the product of an elite, rather than a mass, movement. Nevertheless, indirectly it did have some impact on ordinary people, especially in the cities, where so many of the intellectual and artistic accomplishments of the period were most visible.

12-2 The Making of Renaissance Society

 FOCUS QUESTION: What major economic and social changes occurred during the Renaissance?

After the severe economic reversals and social upheavals of the fourteenth century, the European economy gradually recovered as the volume of manufacturing and trade increased.

A Renaissance Banquet

 What kinds of people would be present at a banquet where these foods would be served? What does this menu tell you about the material culture of the Renaissance and the association of food with social status?

AS IN GREEK AND ROMAN SOCIETY, a banquet during the Renaissance was an occasion for good food, interesting conversation, music, and dancing. In Renaissance society, it was also a symbol of status and an opportunity to impress people with the power and wealth of one's family. Banquets were held to celebrate public and religious festivals, official visits, anniversaries, and weddings. The following menu lists the foods served at a grand banquet given by Pope Pius V in the sixteenth century.

A Sixteenth-Century Banquet

First Course
Cold Delicacies from the Sideboard

Pieces of marzipan and marzipan balls
Neapolitan spice cakes
Malaga wine and Pisan biscuits
Fresh grapes
Prosciutto cooked in wine, served with capers and grape pulp
Salted pork tongues cooked in wine, sliced
Spit-roasted songbirds, cold, with their tongues sliced
  over them
Sweet mustard

Second Course
Cold Hot Foods from the Kitchen, Roasts

Fried veal sweetbreads and liver
Spit-roasted skylarks with lemon sauce
Spit-roasted quails with sliced eggplants

Stuffed spit-roasted pigeons with capers sprinkled over them
Spit-roasted rabbits, with sauce and crushed pine nuts
Partridges larded and spit-roasted, served with lemon
Heavily seasoned poultry with lemon slices
Slices of veal, spit-roasted, with a sauce made from the juices
Leg of goat, spit-roasted, with a sauce made from the juices
Soup of almond paste, with the flesh of three pigeons to
  each serving

Third Course
Hot Foods from the Kitchen, Boiled Meats and Stews

Stuffed fat geese, boiled Lombard style and covered with
  sliced almonds
Stuffed breast of veal, boiled, garnished with flowers
Very young calf, boiled, garnished with parsley
Almonds in garlic sauce
Turkish-style rice with milk, sprinkled with cinnamon
Stewed pigeons with mortadella sausage and whole onions
Cabbage soup with sausages
Poultry pie, two chickens to each pie
Fricasseed breast of goat dressed with fried onions
Pies filled with custard cream
Boiled calves' feet with cheese and egg

Fourth Course
Delicacies from the Sideboard

Bean tarts
Quince pastries
Pear tarts, the pears wrapped in marzipan
Parmesan cheese and Riviera cheese
Fresh almonds on vine leaves
Chestnuts roasted over the coals and served with
  salt and pepper
Milk curds
Ring-shaped cakes
Wafers made from ground grain

Source: R. Tannahill, *Food in History*. Copyright © 1973 The Estate of Reay Tannahill. Reprinted by permission of The London Library.

12-2a Economic Recovery

By the fourteenth century, Italian merchants were carrying on a flourishing commerce throughout the Mediterranean and had also expanded their lines of trade north along the Atlantic seaboard. The great galleys of the Venetian Flanders Fleet maintained a direct sea route from Venice to England and the Netherlands, where Italian merchants came into contact with the increasingly powerful Hanseatic League of merchants. Hard hit by the plague, the Italians lost their commercial preeminence while the Hanseatic League continued to prosper.

Expansion of Trade As early as the thirteenth century, a number of North German coastal towns had formed a commercial and military association known as the Hansa, or Hanseatic League. The city of Lübeck took the lead and became a major trading center for northern Europe and the chief city of the Hanseatic League (see Image 12.2). By 1500, more than eighty cities belonged to the League, which created its own armies for mutual protection and established settlements and commercial bases in many cities in England and northern Europe, including the chief towns of Denmark, Norway, and Sweden. For almost two hundred years, the Hansa had a monopoly on northern

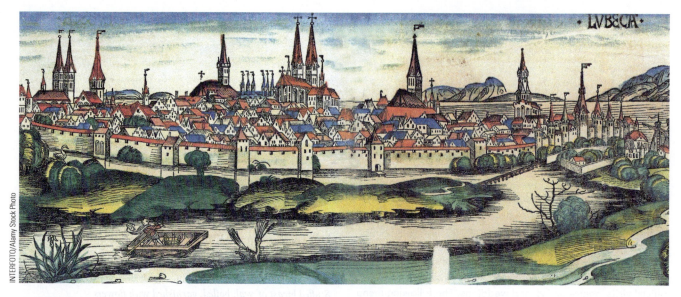

INTERFOTO/Alamy Stock Photo

IMAGE 12.2 Lübeck and the Hanseatic League. The Hanseatic League, or Hansa, was an economic and military alliance of northern European trading cities that established a monopoly on trade from the Baltic to the North Sea. The city of Lübeck in northern Germany played a major role in the founding of the Hanseatic League and became known as the "Queen of the Hansa." This colored woodcut by Michael Wohlgemut in Hartmann Schedel's *Chronicle of the World* presents a panoramic view of this prosperous German city.

 What are the outstanding features of Lübeck as seen from this perspective? How do these compare to the photograph of Carcassonne in Chapter 9 (Image 9.7)? What does the comparison tell you about medieval and Renaissance cities?

European trade in timber, fish, grain, metals, honey, and wines. Its southern outlet in Flanders, the port city of Bruges, became the economic crossroads of Europe in the fourteenth century, serving as the meeting place between Hanseatic merchants and the Flanders Fleet of Venice. In the fifteenth century, however, silting of the port caused Bruges to enter a slow decline. So did the Hanseatic League, which was increasingly unable to compete with the developing larger territorial states.

Overall, trade recovered dramatically from the economic contraction of the fourteenth century. The Italians and especially the Venetians, despite new restrictive pressures on their eastern Mediterranean trade from the Ottoman Turks (see "12-6f The Ottoman Turks and the End of the Byzantine Empire," later in this chapter), continued to maintain a wealthy commercial empire. Not until the sixteenth century, when transatlantic discoveries gave new importance to the states along the ocean, did the petty Italian city-states begin to suffer from the competitive advantages of the ever-growing and more powerful national territorial states.

Industries Old and New The economic depression of the fourteenth century also affected patterns of manufacturing. The woolen industries of Flanders and the northern Italian cities had been particularly devastated. By the beginning of the fifteenth century, however, the Florentine woolen industry had begun to recover. At the same time, the Italian cities began to develop and expand luxury industries, especially silk, glassware, and handworked items in metal and precious stones.

Other new industries, especially printing, mining, and metallurgy, began to rival the textile industry in importance in the fifteenth century. New machinery and techniques for digging deeper mines and for separating metals from ore and purifying them were devised, and entrepreneurs quickly developed large mining operations to produce copper, iron, and silver. Especially valuable were the rich mineral deposits in central Europe. Expanding iron production and new skills in metalworking in turn contributed to the development of firearms that were more effective than the crude weapons of the fourteenth century.

Banking and the Medici The city of Florence regained its preeminence in banking in the fifteenth century, due primarily to the Medici (MED-ih-chee) family. The Medici had expanded from cloth production into commerce, real estate, and banking. In its best days (in the fifteenth century), the House of Medici was the greatest bank in Europe, with branches in Venice, Milan, Rome, Avignon, Bruges, London, and Lyons. Moreover, the family had controlling interests in industrial enterprises for wool, silk, and the mining of alum, used in the dyeing of textiles. Except for a brief period, the Medici were also the principal bankers for the papacy, a position that produced big profits and influence at the papal court. Despite its great success in the early and middle part of the fifteenth century, the Medici bank suffered a rather sudden decline at the end of the century due to poor leadership and a series of bad loans, especially uncollectible loans to rulers. In 1494, when the French expelled the Medici from Florence and confiscated their property, the Medici financial edifice collapsed.

12-2b Social Changes in the Renaissance

The Renaissance inherited its social structure from the Middle Ages. Society remained fundamentally divided into three **estates**: the First Estate, the clergy, whose preeminence was grounded in the belief that people should be guided to spiritual ends; the Second Estate, the nobility, whose privileges were based on the principle that the nobles provided security and justice for society; and the Third Estate, which consisted of the peasants and inhabitants of the towns and cities. This social order experienced certain adaptations in the Renaissance, which we can see by examining the Second and Third Estates (the clergy will be examined in Chapter 13).

The Nobility Throughout much of Europe, the landholding nobles faced declining real incomes during the greater part of the fourteenth and fifteenth centuries. Nevertheless, many members of the old nobility survived, and new blood infused their ranks. A reconstruction of the aristocracy was well under way by 1500. As a result of this reconstruction, the nobles, old and new, who constituted between 2 and 3 percent of the population in most countries, managed to dominate society as they had done in the Middle Ages, serving as military officers and holding important political posts as well as advising the king. In the sixteenth century, members of the aristocracy increasingly pursued education as the means to maintain their role in government.

By 1500, certain ideals came to be expected of the noble or aristocrat. These ideals were best expressed in *The Book of the Courtier* by the Italian Baldassare Castiglione (bal-duh-SAH-ray ka-steel-YOH-nay) (1478–1529). First published in 1528, Castiglione's work soon became popular throughout Europe and remained a fundamental handbook for European aristocrats for centuries.

In his book, Castiglione described the three basic attributes of the perfect courtier. First, nobles should possess fundamental native endowments, such as impeccable character, grace, talents, and noble birth. The perfect courtier must also cultivate certain achievements. Primarily, he should participate in military and bodily exercises, because the principal profession of a courtier was bearing arms. But unlike the medieval knight, who had been required only to have military skill, the Renaissance courtier was also expected to have a classical education and to adorn his life with the arts by playing a musical instrument, drawing, and painting. In Castiglione's hands, the Renaissance ideal of the well-developed personality became a social ideal of the aristocracy. Finally, the aristocrat was expected to follow a certain standard of conduct. Nobles were to make a good impression; while remaining modest, they should not hide their accomplishments but show them with grace.

What was the purpose of these courtly standards? Castiglione wrote:

> I think that the aim of the perfect Courtier, which we have not spoken of up to now, is so to win for himself, by means of the accomplishments ascribed to him by these gentlemen, the favor and mind of the prince whom he serves that he may be able to tell him, and always will tell him, the truth

about everything he needs to know, without fear or risk of displeasing him; and that when he sees the mind of his prince inclined to a wrong action, he may dare to oppose him . . . so as to dissuade him of every evil intent and bring him to the path of virtue.[2]

The aim of the perfect noble, then, was to serve his prince in an effective and honest way. Nobles would adhere to these principles for hundreds of years while they continued to dominate European life socially and politically.

Peasants and Townspeople Peasants made up the overwhelming mass of the Third Estate and continued to constitute 85 to 90 percent of the European population, except in the highly urbanized areas of northern Italy and Flanders. The most noticeable trend produced by the economic crisis of the fourteenth century was the decline of the manorial system and the continuing elimination of serfdom. This process had already begun in the twelfth century when the introduction of a money economy made possible the conversion of servile labor dues into rents paid in money, although they also continued to be paid in kind or labor. The contraction of the peasantry after the Black Death simply accelerated this process, since lords found it convenient to deal with the peasants by granting freedom and accepting rents. The lords' lands were then tilled by hired workers or rented out. By the end of the fifteenth century, serfdom was declining in western Europe, and more and more peasants were becoming legally free.

The remainder of the Third Estate centered around the inhabitants of towns and cities, originally the merchants and artisans who formed the bourgeoisie. The Renaissance town or city of the fifteenth century actually was home to a multitude of townspeople widely separated socially and economically.

At the top of urban society were the patricians, whose wealth from capitalistic enterprises in trade, industry, and banking enabled them to dominate their urban communities economically, socially, and politically. Below them were the petty burghers—the shopkeepers, artisans, guildmasters, and guild members, who were largely concerned with providing goods and services for local consumption. Below these two groups were the propertyless workers earning pitiful wages and the unemployed, living squalid and miserable lives; these people constituted 30 to 40 percent of the population living in cities. In many places in Europe in the late fourteenth and fifteenth centuries, urban poverty increased dramatically. One rich merchant of Florence wrote:

> Those that are lazy and indolent in a way that does harm to the city, and who can offer no just reason for their condition, should either be forced to work or expelled from the Commune. The city would thus rid itself of that most harmful part of the poorest class. . . . If the lowest order of society earn enough food to keep them going from day to day, then they have enough.[3]

But even this large group was not at the bottom of the social scale; beneath them were the slaves, especially in the Italian cities.

Slavery in the Renaissance Agricultural slavery existed in the early Middle Ages but had declined for economic reasons and been replaced by serfdom by the ninth century. Although some domestic slaves remained, slavery in European society had largely disappeared by the eleventh century. It reappeared first in Spain, where both Christians and Muslims used captured prisoners as slaves during the lengthy *Reconquista*. In the second half of the fourteenth century, the shortage of workers after the Black Death led Italians to introduce slavery on a fairly large scale.

In the Italian cities, slaves were used as skilled workers, making handcrafted goods for their masters, or as household workers. Girls served as nursemaids and boys as playmates. Fiammetta Adimari wrote to her husband in 1469: "I must remind you that when Alfonso is weaned we ought to get a little slave-girl to look after him, or else one of the black boys to keep him company."[4] Most slaves, though, were females, many of them young girls. In Florence, wealthy merchants might own two or three slaves. Often men of the household took slaves as concubines, which sometimes led to the birth of illegitimate children. In 1392, the wealthy merchant Francesco Datini fathered an illegitimate daughter by Lucia, his twenty-year-old slave. His wife, Margherita, who was unable to bear any children, reluctantly agreed to raise the girl as their own daughter. Many illegitimate children were not as fortunate.

Slaves for the Italian market were obtained primarily from the eastern Mediterranean and the Black Sea region and included Tartars, Russians, Albanians, and Dalmatians. There were also slaves from Africa, either Moors or Ethiopians, and Muslims from Spain. Because of the lucrative nature of the slave trade, Italian merchants became involved in the transportation of slaves. Between 1414 and 1423, ten thousand slaves were sold on the Venetian market.

By the end of the fifteenth century, slavery had declined dramatically in the Italian cities. Many slaves had been freed by their owners for humanitarian reasons, and the major source of slaves dried up as the Black Sea slave markets were closed to Italian traders after the Turks conquered the Byzantine Empire. Moreover, a general feeling had arisen that slaves—the "domestic enemy," as they were called—were dangerous and not worth the effort. By the sixteenth century, slaves were in evidence only at princely courts, where they were kept as curiosities; this was especially true of black slaves.

In the fifteenth century, the Portuguese had imported increasing numbers of African slaves for southern European markets. It has been estimated that between 1444 and 1505, some 140,000 slaves were shipped from Africa. The presence of blacks in European society was not entirely new. Saint Maurice, a Christian martyr of the fourth century, was portrayed by medieval artists as a black knight and became the center of a popular cult in the twelfth and thirteenth centuries. The number of blacks in Europe was small, however, until their importation as slaves.

12-2c The Family in Renaissance Italy

The family played an important role in Renaissance Italy (see Images of Everyday Life, "Family and Marriage in Renaissance Italy," p. 345). Family meant, first of all, the extended household of parents, children, and servants (if the family was wealthy) and could also include grandparents, widowed mothers, and even unmarried sisters. Families that were related and bore the same surname often lived near each other and might dominate an entire urban district. Old family names—Strozzi (STRAWT-see), Rucellai (roo-CHELL-eye), Medici—conferred great status and prestige. The family bond was a source of great security in a dangerous and violent world, and its importance helps explain the vendetta in the Italian Renaissance. A crime committed by one family member fell on the entire family, ensuring that retaliation by the offended family would be a bloody affair involving large numbers of people.

Marriage To maintain the family, parents gave careful attention to arranging marriages, often to strengthen business or family ties. Details were worked out well in advance, sometimes when children were only two or three years old, and reinforced by a legally binding marriage contract (see Historical Voices, "Marriage Negotiations," p. 346). The important aspect of the contract was the amount of the dowry, money presented by the wife's family to the husband upon marriage. The dowry could involve large sums and was expected of all families. The size of the dowry was an indication of whether the bride was moving upward or downward in society. With a large dowry, a daughter could marry a man of higher social status, thereby enabling her family to move up in society; if the daughter married a man of lower social status, however, her dowry would be smaller because the reputation of her family would raise the status of her husband's family.

The father-husband was the center of the Italian family. He gave it his name, was responsible for it in all legal matters, managed all finances (his wife had no share in his wealth), and made the crucial decisions that determined his children's lives. A father's authority over his children was absolute until he died or formally freed his children. In Renaissance Italy, children did not become adults on reaching a certain age; adulthood came only when the father went before a judge and formally emancipated them. The age of emancipation varied from early teens to late twenties.

Children The wife managed the household, a position that gave women a certain degree of autonomy in their daily lives. Women of the upper and middle classes, however, were expected to remain at home, under the supervision of their father or husband. Moreover, most wives knew that their primary function was to bear children. Upper-class wives were frequently pregnant; Alessandra Strozzi of Florence, for example, who had been married at the age of sixteen, bore eight children in ten years. Poor women did not conceive at the same rate because they nursed their own babies. Wealthy women gave their infants out to wet nurses, which enabled them to become pregnant more quickly after the birth of a child.

For women in the Renaissance, childbirth was a fearful occasion. Not only was it painful, but it could be deadly; as many as 10 percent of mothers died in childbirth. In his memoirs, the Florentine merchant Gregorio Dati recalled that three of his

Family and Marriage in Renaissance Italy

Q *What was the importance of marriage in Renaissance Italy?*

THE FAMILY WAS AN IMPORTANT UNIT in Renaissance Italy. For the upper classes, family meant an extended household of parents, children, and servants, as is evident in the portrait of the Gonzaga family by Andrea Mantegna (ahn-DRAY-uh mahn-TEN-yah) in Image 12.3a. Ludovico Gonzaga, marquis of Mantua, is shown at the left listening to a messenger. To his right are his wife Barbara, two sons, and two daughters, as well as servants. In the lower-right corner is a dwarf. Dwarfs were common at Italian Renaissance courts, where they were kept as a source of entertainment.

In the upper classes, parents arranged marriages to reinforce business or family connections. As seen in the painting in Image 12.3b, the marriage ceremony involved an exchange of vows and the placing of a ring (see inset) by the bridegroom on the bride's hand. The ring was a sign of affection and a symbol of the union of the two families. The church encouraged the presence of a priest, but it was not necessary. The wedding was then recorded in a marriage contract that was considered a crucial part of the marital arrangements. So was a wedding feast, as seen in the painting by Sandro Botticelli in Image 12.3c. It shows the wedding banquet that celebrated the marriage of Nastagio degli Onesti and the daughter of Paulo Traversaro in Florence. After the feast, the couple retired to a bedroom, usually in the house of the bride, where they physically consummated their marriage. Later, the husband introduced his bride to his household, usually on Sunday, in order to make it public knowledge that the marriage had been consummated.

Scala/Art Resource, NY

IMAGE 12.3a

Museum Of London/ Shutterstock.com

DEA/G. DAGLI ORTI/De Agostini/Getty Images

IMAGE 12.3b

Private Collection/Bridgeman Images

IMAGE 12.3c

Marriage Negotiations

 What were the most important considerations in marriage negotiations? Why were they so important?

MARRIAGES WERE SO IMPORTANT in maintaining families in Renaissance Italy that much energy was put into arranging them. Parents made the choices for their children, most often for considerations that had little to do with the modern notion of love. This selection is taken from the letters of a Florentine matron of the illustrious Strozzi family to her son Filippo in Naples. The family's considerations were complicated by the fact that the son was in exile.

Alessandra Strozzi to Her Son Filippo in Naples

[April 20, 1464] . . . Concerning the matter of a wife [for you], it appears to me that if Francesco di Messer Tanagli wishes to give his daughter, that it would be a fine marriage. . . . Francesco Tanagli has a good reputation, and he has held office, not the highest, but still he has been in office.

[July 26, 1465] . . . Francesco is a good friend of Marco [Parenti, Alessandra's son-in-law] and he trusts him. On S. Jacopo's day, he spoke to him discreetly and persuasively, saying that for several months he had heard that we were interested in the girl and . . . that when we had made up our minds, she will come to us willingly. [He said that] you were a worthy man, and that his family had always made good marriages, but that he had only a small dowry to give her, and so he would prefer to send her out of Florence to someone of worth, rather than to give her to someone here, from among those who were available, with little money. . . . We have information that she is affable and competent. She is responsible for a large family (there are twelve children, six boys and six girls), and the mother is always pregnant and isn't very competent. . . .

[August 31, 1465] . . . I have recently received some very favorable information [about the Tanagli girl] from two individuals. . . . They are in agreement that whoever gets her will be content. . . . Concerning her beauty, they told me what I had already seen, that she is attractive and well-proportioned. Her face is long, but I couldn't look directly into her face, since she appeared to be aware that I was examining her . . . and so she turned away from me like the wind. . . . She reads quite well . . . and she can dance and sing. . . .

So yesterday I sent for Marco and told him what I had learned. And we talked about the matter for a while, and decided that he should say something to the father and give him a little hope, but not so much that we couldn't withdraw, and find out from him the amount of the dowry. . . . May God help us to choose what will contribute to our tranquility and to the consolation of us all.

[September 13, 1465] . . . Marco came to me and said that he had met with Francesco Tanagli, who had spoken very coldly, so that I understand that he had changed his mind.

[Filippo Strozzi eventually married Fiametta di Donato Adimari in 1466.]

Source: G. Brucker, ed., *The Society of Renaissance Florence* (Toronto: University of Toronto Press, 1971).

---

four wives had died in childbirth. His third wife, after bearing eleven children in fifteen years, "died in childbirth after lengthy suffering, which she bore with remarkable strength and patience."[5] Nor did the tragedies end with childbirth. Surviving mothers often faced the death of their children. In Florence in the fifteenth century, for example, almost 50 percent of the children born to merchant families died before the age of twenty. Given these mortality rates, many upper-class families sought to have as many children as possible to ensure that there would be a surviving male heir to the family fortune. This concern is evident in the Florentine humanist Leon Battista Alberti's treatise *On the Family*, where one of the characters remarks, "How many families do we see today in decadence and ruin! . . . Of all these families not only the magnificence and greatness but the very men, not only the men but the very names are shrunk away and gone. Their memory . . . is wiped out and obliterated."[6]

Sexual Norms Considering that marriages were arranged, marital relationships ran the gamut from deep emotional attachments to purely formal ties. The lack of emotional attachment in arranged marriages did encourage extramarital relationships, especially among groups whose lifestyle offered special temptations. Although sexual license for males was the norm for princes and their courts, women were supposed to follow different guidelines. The first wife of Duke Filippo Maria Visconti of Milan had an affair with the court musician and was executed for it.

The great age difference between husbands and wives in Italian Renaissance marriage patterns also encouraged the tendency to seek sexual outlets outside marriage. In Florence in 1427–1428, the average difference was thirteen years. Though females married between the ages of sixteen and eighteen, factors of environment, wealth, and demographic trends favored relatively late ages for the first marriages of males, who were usually in their thirties or even early forties. The existence of large numbers of young, unmarried males encouraged extramarital sex as well as prostitution. Prostitution was viewed as a necessary vice; since it could not be eliminated, it should be regulated. In Florence in 1415, the city fathers established communal brothels:

> Desiring to eliminate a worse evil by means of a lesser one, the lord priors . . . have decreed that the priors . . . may authorize the establishment of two public brothels in the city of Florence, in addition to the one which already exists. . . . [They are to be located] in suitable places or in places where the exercise of such scandalous activity can best be concealed, for the honor of the city.[7]

A prostitute in Florence was required to wear a traditional garb of "gloves on her hands and a bell on her head."

Sexual regulation was also directed against males participating in homosexual activity. To some observers, the revival of Greek and Roman antiquity led in part to a renewed interest in "Greek love," that is, love between two males, especially by the intellectual elite. In any case, in Florence, males engaging in same-sex activity became quite common, especially among late adolescents of the upper classes. Venice also had a significant homosexual subculture.

Between 1300 and 1400, both cities passed statutes that levied harsh punishments against "sodomites," whose activities, they argued, put the city in danger of being "punished by God." In the fourteenth century, punishments included being burned at the stake as well as castration. By the beginning of the fifteenth century, punishments were being severely reduced to fines and brief imprisonment.

12-3 The Italian States in the Renaissance

FOCUS QUESTIONS: How important was the role of city-state in Italy? How did Machiavelli's works reflect the political realities of Renaissance Italy?

By the fifteenth century, five major powers dominated the Italian peninsula: Milan, Venice, Florence, the Papal States, and Naples (see Map 12.1).

12-3a The Five Major States

Northern Italy was divided between the duchy of Milan and the republic of Venice. After the death of the last Visconti ruler of Milan in 1447, Francesco Sforza (frahn-CHESS-koh SFORT-sah), one of the leading *condottieri* of the time (see Chapter 11), turned on his Milanese employers, conquered the city, and became its new duke. Both the Visconti and the Sforza rulers worked to create a highly centralized territorial state. They were especially successful in devising systems of taxation that generated enormous revenues for the government. The maritime republic of Venice remained an extremely stable political entity governed by a small oligarchy of merchant-aristocrats. Its commercial empire brought in enormous revenues and gave it the status

MAP 12.1 Renaissance Italy. Italy in the late fourteenth century was a land of five major states and numerous independent city-states. Increased prosperity and a supportive intellectual climate helped create the atmosphere for the middle and upper classes to "rediscover" Greco-Roman culture. Modern diplomacy was also a product of Renaissance Italy.

 Could the presence of several other powers within easy marching distance make it more likely that a ruler would recognize the importance of diplomacy?

of an international power. At the end of the fourteenth century, Venice embarked on the conquest of a territorial state in northern Italy to protect its food supply and its overland trade routes. Although expansion on the mainland made sense to the Venetians, it frightened Milan and Florence, which worked to curb what they perceived as the expansionary designs of the Venetians.

The republic of Florence dominated the region of Tuscany. By the beginning of the fifteenth century, Florence was governed by a small merchant oligarchy that manipulated the apparently republican government. In 1434, Cosimo de' Medici took control of this oligarchy. Although the wealthy Medici family maintained republican forms of government for appearances' sake, it ran the government from behind the scenes. Through lavish patronage and careful courting of political allies, Cosimo (1434–1464) and later his grandson, Lorenzo the Magnificent (1469–1492), were successful in dominating the city at a time when Florence was the center of the cultural Renaissance.

To some Florentines, Florence was the ideal city. One city official at the beginning of the fifteenth century exclaimed:

> What city not merely in Italy, but in all the world, is more securely placed within its walls, more proud in its palazzi, more bedecked with churches, more beautiful in its architecture, more imposing in its gates, richer in piazzas, happier in its wide streets, greater in its people, more glorious in its citizenry, more inexhaustible in wealth, more fertile in its fields?[8]

But as one historian has recently noted, official praise of the city failed to note the ugly side of Renaissance Florence: the gross inequality between rich and poor; poverty that was common to a majority of Florentines, begging that was widespread, and both crime and disease that were rampant.

The Papal States lay in central Italy. Although these lands were nominally under the political control of the popes, papal residence in Avignon and the Great Schism had enabled individual cities and territories, such as Urbino (ur-BEE-noh), Bologna (buh-LOHN-yuh), and Ferrara, to become independent of papal authority. The Renaissance popes of the fifteenth century directed much of their energy toward reestablishing their control over the Papal States (see "12-7b The Renaissance Papacy," later in this chapter).

The kingdom of Naples, which encompassed most of southern Italy and usually the island of Sicily, was fought over by the French and the Aragonese until the latter established their domination in the mid-fifteenth century. Throughout the Renaissance, the kingdom of Naples remained a backward monarchy with a population consisting largely of poverty-stricken peasants dominated by unruly nobles. It shared little in the cultural glories of the Renaissance.

12-3b Independent City-States

Besides the five major states, there were a number of independent city-states under the control of powerful ruling families that became brilliant centers of Renaissance culture in the fifteenth century (see Historical Voices, "The Problems of Renaissance City Governments," p. 349). These included Mantua (MAN-choo-uh), under the enlightened rule of the Gonzaga (gun-DZAH-gah) lords; Ferrara, governed by the flamboyant d'Este (DESS-tay) family; and perhaps the most famous, Urbino, ruled by the Montefeltro dynasty.

Urbino Federigo da Montefeltro (fay-day-REE-goh dah mahn-tuh-FELL-troh), who ruled Urbino from 1444 to 1482, received a classical education typical of the famous humanist school in Mantua run by Vittorino da Feltre (vee-tor-EE-noh dah FELL-tray) (1378–1446) (see "12-4b Education in the Renaissance," later in this chapter). He also learned the skills of fighting, since the Montefeltro family compensated for the poverty of Urbino by hiring themselves out as condottieri. Federigo was not only a good ruler but also a rather unusual condottiere by fifteenth-century standards (see Image 12.4). Although not a

IMAGE 12.4 *Piero della Francesca, Duke and Duchess of Urbino.* Federigo da Montefeltro and his wife, Battista Sforza, ruled the small central Italian principality of Urbino. These profile portraits by Piero della Francesca gave a realistic rendering of the two figures. Visible in the background are the hills and valleys of Urbino, over which they ruled.

Q *Why do you think these rulers are shown against a background of the lands they ruled?*

Alinari/Art Resource, NY

The Problems of Renaissance City Governments

 Based on the two concerns described here, what other problems would you expect Renaissance cities to have? How do these compare to the concerns of modern American cities?

AMONG OTHERS, TWO PROBLEMS IN URBAN LIFE in Renaissance Italy necessitated government action, which urban governments were quick to provide. These excerpts from official actions in Venice and Florence deal with the practice of infanticide and the plague.

Judges in Florence Act in a Case of Infanticide

WE CONDEMN MONNA FRANCESCA . . . a most cruel woman and murderess . . . During the past year, Francesca . . . had conversations with a certain Jacopo…who told her that he wanted to take her for his wife. So Francesca . . . became pregnant by Jacopo . . . Then Francesca, knowing herself to be pregnant, promised to marry Cecco Arrighi . . . and after their wedding they had intercourse together, as is proper between husband and wife, Cecco did not realize that Francesca was pregnant by Jacopo . . . In the month of March of the present year, Francesca was approaching the time of delivery and with God's help, she gave birth to a healthy male child in the house of her husband Cecco . . . But inspired by an evil spirit and so

that no one would know that she had given birth to that child, she threw him in the river . . . and as a result this son and creature of God was drowned. [Francesca confessed and was burned at the stake]

Venetian Health Office Acts Against the Possibility of Plague

ORDINANCES TO BE OBSERVED when plague is discovered in the city, that steps may be taken to ensure that, by God's grace, it does not spread further. When the [Health] Office has been notified that a death has occurred in the city . . . the doctor of the Office must be sent to view the body . . . to see if there is an abscess, carbuncle or other symptom . . . If plague is found, the whole house must immediately be placed under a ban. . . . Then the notary and an attendant at the Office must be sent to examine the inhabitants on oath and under threat of punishment. . . . The notary must take special care to ask if the sick or dead person has been in any house where anyone has died; whether foreigners have lodged with him . . . for how many days he has been ill . . . whether any relative or friend has been there to visit and how many times . . . whether any of the neighbors has come in to help around the house, as often happens; whether any goods have been taken out of the house, and where, and to whom.

Sources: G. Brucker, *The Society of Renaissance Florence* (New York: Harper and Row, 1971), pp. 146–147; D. Chambers and B. Pullan, eds., *Venice: A Documentary History, 1450–1630* (Oxford: Blackwell, 1992), p. 111.

brilliant general, he was reliable and honest. He did not break his promises, even when urged to do so by a papal legate. At the same time, Duke Federigo was one of the greatest patrons of Renaissance culture. Under his direction, Urbino became a well-known cultural and intellectual center. Though a despot, Federigo was also benevolent. It was said of him that he could walk safely through the streets of Urbino unaccompanied by a bodyguard, a feat few Renaissance rulers dared to emulate.

The Role of Women A noticeable feature of these smaller Renaissance courts was the important role played by women. Battista Sforza (buh-TEESS-tuh SFORT-sah), niece of the ruler of Milan, was the wife of Federigo da Montefeltro (see Image 12.4). The duke called his wife "the delight of both my public and my private hours." An intelligent woman, she was well versed in both Greek and Latin and did much to foster art and letters in Urbino. As a prominent condottiere, Federigo was frequently absent, and like the wives of medieval lords, Battista Sforza was respected for governing the state "with firmness and good sense."

Perhaps the most famous of the Renaissance ruling women was Isabella d'Este (1474–1539), daughter of the duke of Ferrara, who married Francesco Gonzaga, marquis of Mantua. Their court was another important center of art and learning in the Renaissance. Educated at the brilliant court of Ferrara, Isabella was known for her intelligence and political wisdom. Called the "first lady of the world," she attracted artists and intellectuals to the Mantuan court and was responsible for amassing one of the finest libraries in all of Italy. Her numerous letters to friends, family, princes, and artists all over Europe reveal her political acumen as well as her good sense of humor (see Historical Voices, "The Letters of Isabella d'Este," p. 350). Both before and after the death of her husband, she effectively ruled Mantua and won a reputation as a clever negotiator.

12-3c Warfare in Italy

The fragmented world of the Italian territorial states gave rise to a political practice that was later used on a larger scale by competing European states. This was the concept of a balance of power, designed to prevent the aggrandizement of any one

The Letters of Isabella d'Este

 What do these letters reveal about Isabella's character and about the attributes and strategies of expression on which noble women had to rely in order to participate effectively in high politics?

MANY ITALIAN AND EUROPEAN RULERS at the beginning of the sixteenth century regarded Isabella d'Este as an important political figure. These excerpts from her letters reveal Isabella's political skills and her fierce determination. After her husband was taken prisoner by the Venetians in 1509, she refused to accept the condition for his release—namely, that her son Federico be kept as a hostage by the Venetians or the Holy Roman Emperor. She wrote to both the emperor and her husband, refusing to do as they asked.

Letter of Isabella d'Este to the Imperial Envoy

As to the demand for our dearest first-born son Federico, besides being a cruel and almost inhuman thing for anyone who knows the meaning of a mother's love, there are many reasons which render it difficult and impossible. Although we are quite sure that his person would be well cared for and protected by His Majesty [the Holy Roman Emperor], how could we wish him to run the risk of this long and difficult journey, considering the child's tender and delicate age? And you must know what comfort and solace, in his father's present unhappy condition, we find in the presence of this dear son, the hope and joy of all our people and subjects. To deprive us of him, would be to deprive us of life itself, and of all we count good and precious. If you take Federico away you might as well take away our life and state. . . . Once [and] for all, we will suffer any loss rather than part from our son, and this you may take to be our deliberate and unchanging resolution.

Letter of Isabella d'Este to Her Husband, Who Had Ordered Her to Send the Boy to Venice

If in this matter Your Excellency were to despise me and deprive me of your love and grace, I would rather endure such harsh treatment, I would rather lose our State, than deprive us of our children. I am hoping that in time your own prudence and kindness will make you understand that I have acted more lovingly toward you than you have to yourself.

Have patience! You can be sure that I think continuously of your liberation and when the time comes I will not fail you, as I have not relaxed my efforts. As witness I cite the Pope, the Emperor, the King of France, and all the other reigning heads and potentates of Christendom. Yes, and the infidels as well [she had written to the Turkish sultan for help]. If it were *really* the only means of setting you free, I would not only send Federico but all the other children as well. I will do everything imaginable. Some day I hope I can make you understand. . . .

Pardon me if this letter is badly written and worse composed, but I do not know if I am dead or alive.

Isabella, who desires the best for Your Excellency, written with her own hand

[Isabella's husband was not pleased with her response and exclaimed angrily: "That whore of my wife is the cause of it all. Send me into battle alone, do what you like with me. I have lost in one blow my state, my honor, and my freedom. If she does not obey, I'll cut her vocal cords."]

Source: The Letters of Isabella d'Este, *The Bed and the Throne*, ed. G. R. Marek (New York: HarperCollins, 1976).

---

state at the expense of the others. This system was especially evident after 1454 when the Italian states signed the Peace of Lodi (LAH-dee), which ended almost a half-century of war and inaugurated a relatively peaceful forty-year era in Italy. An alliance system (Milan, Florence, and Naples versus Venice and the papacy) was created that led to a workable balance of power within Italy. It failed, however, to establish lasting cooperation among the major powers.

The growth of powerful monarchical states (see "12-6 The European State in the Renaissance," later in this chapter) led to trouble for the Italians. Italy soon became a battlefield for the great power struggle between the French and Spanish monarchies. Italian wealth and splendor would probably have been inviting to its northern neighbors under any circumstances, but it was actually the breakdown of the Italian balance of power that encouraged the invasions and began the Italian wars.

Feeling isolated, Ludovico Sforza, the duke of Milan, foolishly invited the French to intervene in Italian politics. The French king Charles VIII (r. 1483–1498) was eager to do so, and in 1494, with an army of 30,000 men, he advanced through Italy and occupied the kingdom of Naples. Other Italian states turned to the Spanish for help, and Ferdinand of Aragon indicated his willingness to intervene. For the next fifteen years, the French and Spanish competed to dominate Italy. After 1510, the war was continued by a new generation of rulers, Francis I of France and Charles I of Spain (see Chapter 13). This war was part of a long struggle for power throughout Europe between the Valois and Habsburg dynasties. Italy was only a pawn for the two great powers, a convenient arena for fighting battles. The terrible sack of Rome in 1527 by the armies of the Spanish king Charles I brought a temporary end to the Italian wars. Thereafter, the Spaniards dominated Italy.

Although some Italians had differentiated between Italians and "barbarians" (all foreigners), few Italians conceived of creating an alliance or confederation of states that could repel foreign invaders. Italians remained fiercely loyal to their own petty states, making invasion a fact of life in Italian history for all too long. Italy would not achieve unification and nationhood until 1870.

12-3d The Birth of Modern Diplomacy

The modern diplomatic system was a product of the Italian Renaissance. There were ambassadors in the Middle Ages, but they were used only on a temporary basis. Moreover, an ambassador, regardless of whose subject he was, regarded himself as the servant of all Christendom, not just of his particular employer. As a treatise on diplomacy stated, "An ambassador is sacred because he acts for the general welfare." Since he was the servant of all Christendom, "the business of an ambassador is peace."[9]

This concept of an ambassador changed during the Italian Renaissance because of the political situation in Italy. A large number of states existed, many so small that their neighbors easily threatened their security. To survive, the Italian states began to send resident diplomatic agents to each other to ferret out useful information. During the Italian wars, the practice of resident diplomats spread to the rest of Europe, and in the course of the sixteenth and seventeenth centuries, Europeans developed the diplomatic machinery still in use today, such as the rights of ambassadors in host countries and the proper procedures for conducting diplomatic business.

With the use of permanent resident agents or ambassadors, the conception of the purpose of an ambassador also changed. A Venetian diplomat attempted to define an ambassador's function in a treatise written at the end of the fifteenth century. He wrote, "The first duty of an ambassador is exactly the same as that of any other servant of a government, that is, to do, say, advise, and think whatever may best serve the preservation and aggrandizement of his own state."[10] An ambassador was now an agent only of the territorial state that sent him, not the larger body of Christendom. He could use any methods that were beneficial to the political interests of his own state. We are at the beginning of modern politics when the interests of the state supersede all other considerations.

12-3e Machiavelli and the New Statecraft

No one gave better expression to the Renaissance preoccupation with political power than Niccolò Machiavelli (nee-koh-LOH mahk-ee-uh-VEL-ee) (1469–1527) (see Image 12.5). He entered the service of the Florentine republic in 1498, four years after the Medici family had been expelled from the city. As a secretary to the Florentine Council of Ten, he made numerous diplomatic missions, including trips to France and Germany, and saw the workings of statecraft at first hand. Machiavelli's political activity occurred during the period of tribulation and devastation for Italy that followed the French invasion in 1494. In 1512, French defeat and Spanish victory led to the reestablishment of Medici power in Florence. Staunch republicans, including Machiavelli, were sent into exile. Forced to give up politics, the great love of his life, Machiavelli now reflected on political power and wrote books, including *The Prince* (1513), one of the most famous treatises on political power in the Western world.

The Prince Machiavelli's ideas on politics stemmed from two major sources, his knowledge of ancient Rome and his preoccupation with Italy's political problems. As a result of his experiences, Machiavelli fully realized that the small Italian states were no match for the larger monarchical states outside Italy's borders and that Italy itself had become merely a battleground for the armies of foreign states. His major concerns in *The Prince* were the acquisition and expansion of political power as the means to

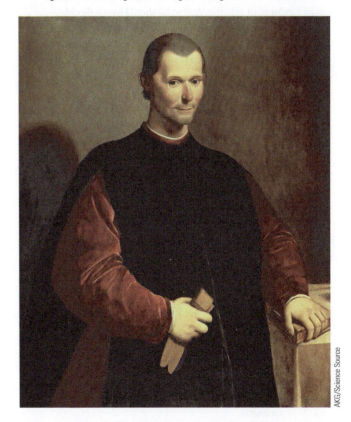

IMAGE 12.5 **Niccolò Machiavelli.** In *The Prince*, Machiavelli gave concrete expression to the Renaissance preoccupation with political power. This slender volume remains one of the most famous and most widely read Western treatises on politics. Machiavelli is seen here in a portrait by Santi di Tito.

AKG/Science Source

restore and maintain order in his time. In the Middle Ages, many political theorists stressed the ethical side of a prince's activity—how a ruler ought to behave based on Christian moral principles. Machiavelli bluntly contradicted this approach:

> But since my intention is to say something that will prove of practical use to the inquirer, I have thought it proper to represent things as they are in real truth, rather than as they are imagined. . . . [For] the gulf between how one should live and how one does live is so wide that a man who neglects what is actually done with what should be done learns the way to self-destruction rather [than] self-preservation.[11]

Machiavelli considered his approach far more realistic than that of his medieval forebears.

In Machiavelli's view, a prince's attitude toward power must be based on an understanding of human nature, which he perceived as basically self-centered: "One can make this generalization about men: they are ungrateful, fickle, liars, and deceivers, they shun danger and are greedy for profit." Political activity, therefore, could not be restricted by moral considerations. The prince acts on behalf of the state and for the sake of the state must be willing to let his conscience sleep. As Machiavelli put it:

> You must realize this: that a prince, and especially a new prince, cannot observe all those things which give men a reputation for virtue, because in order to maintain his state he is often forced to act in defiance of good faith, of charity, of kindness, of religion. And so he should have a flexible disposition, varying as fortune and circumstances dictate. As I said above, he should not deviate from what is good if that is possible, but he should know how to do evil, if that is necessary.[12]

Machiavelli found a good example of the new Italian ruler in Cesare Borgia (CHAY-zah-ray BOR-juh), the son of Pope Alexander VI, who used ruthless measures to achieve his goal of carving out a new state in central Italy. As Machiavelli said: "So a new prince cannot find more recent examples than those set by the duke, if he thinks it necessary to secure himself against his enemies, win friends, conquer either by force or by stratagem, make himself both loved and feared by his subjects."[13] Machiavelli was among the first to abandon morality as the basis for the analysis of political activity (see Opposing Viewpoints, "The Renaissance Prince: The Views of Machiavelli and Erasmus," p. 353).

12-4 The Intellectual Renaissance in Italy

 FOCUS QUESTION: What was humanism, and what effect did it have on philosophy, education, attitudes toward politics, the writing of history, and women?

Individualism and **secularism**—two characteristics of the Italian Renaissance—were most noticeable in the intellectual and artistic realms. Italian culture had matured by the fourteenth

century. For the next two centuries, Italy was the cultural leader of Europe. This new Italian culture was primarily the product of a relatively wealthy, urban lay society. The most important literary movement associated with the Renaissance was **humanism**.

12-4a Italian Renaissance Humanism

Renaissance humanism was an intellectual movement based on the study of the classical literary works of Greece and Rome. Humanists examined the *studia humanitatis* ("the studies of humanity")—grammar, rhetoric, poetry, moral philosophy or ethics, and history—all based on the writings of ancient Greek and Roman authors. These are the subjects we call the humanities.

The central importance of literary preoccupations in Renaissance humanism is evident in the professional status or occupations of the humanists. Some of them were teachers of the humanities in secondary schools and universities, where they either gave occasional lectures or held permanent positions, often as professors of rhetoric. Others served as secretaries in the chancelleries of Italian city-states or at the courts of princes or popes. All of these occupations were largely secular, and most humanists were laymen rather than members of the clergy.

The Emergence of Humanism Petrarch (1304–1374) has often been called the father of Italian Renaissance humanism (see Chapter 11 on his use of the Italian vernacular). Petrarch rejected his father's desire that he become a lawyer and took up a literary career instead. Although he lived in Avignon for a time, most of his last decades were spent in Italy as the guest of various princes and city governments. With his usual lack of modesty, Petrarch once exclaimed, "Some of the greatest kings of our time have loved me and cultivated my friendship. . . . When I was their guest it was more as if they were mine."[14]

Petrarch did more than any other individual in the fourteenth century to foster the development of Renaissance humanism. He was the first intellectual to characterize the Middle Ages as a period of darkness, promoting the mistaken belief that medieval culture was ignorant of classical antiquity. Petrarch's interest in the classics led him on a quest for forgotten Latin manuscripts and set in motion a ransacking of monastic libraries throughout Europe. In his preoccupation with the classics and their secular content, Petrarch worried at times that he might not be sufficiently attentive to spiritual ideals. His qualms, however, did not prevent him from inaugurating the humanist emphasis on the use of pure classical Latin, making it fashionable for humanists to use Cicero as a model for prose and Virgil for poetry. As Petrarch said, "Christ is my God; Cicero is the prince of the language."

Humanism in Fifteenth-Century Italy In Florence, the humanist movement took a new direction at the beginning of the fifteenth century when it became closely tied to Florentine civic spirit and pride, giving rise to what one modern scholar has labeled **civic humanism**. Fourteenth-century humanists such as Petrarch had described the intellectual life as one of solitude. They rejected family and a life of action in the

The Renaissance Prince: The Views of Machiavelli and Erasmus

 What does Machiavelli have to say about being loved rather than feared? How does this view contrast with that of Erasmus on the characteristics of a good ruler? Which viewpoint do you consider more modern? Why? Which viewpoint do you think is correct? Why?

AT THE BEGINNING OF THE SIXTEENTH CENTURY, two writers produced very different views of political power and how a ruler should conduct affairs of state. In 1513, Niccolò Machiavelli wrote a short treatise on political power that, justly or unjustly, has given him a reputation as a political opportunist. In this selection from Chapter 17 of *The Prince*, Machiavelli analyzes whether it is better for a ruler to be loved than to be feared. Three years later the Dutch intellectual Erasmus, leader of the Christian humanists (see Chapter 13), also wrote a treatise on political power, entitled *Education of a Christian Prince*. As is evident in this excerpt from his treatise, Erasmus followed in the footsteps of medieval theorists on power by insisting that a true prince should think only of his moral obligations to the people he rules.

Machiavelli, *The Prince* (1513)

This leads us to a question that is in dispute: Is it better to be loved than feared, or vice versa? My reply is one ought to be both loved and feared; but, since it is difficult to accomplish both at the same time, I maintain it is much safer to be feared than loved, if you have to do without one of the two. For of men one can, in general, say this: They are ungrateful, fickle, deceptive and deceiving, avoiders of danger, eager to gain. As long as you serve their interests, they are devoted to you. They promise you their blood, their possessions, their lives, and their children, as I said before, so long as you seem to have no need of them. But as soon as you need help, they turn against you. Any ruler who relies simply on their promises and makes no other preparations, will be destroyed. For you will find that those whose support you buy, who do not rally to you because they admire your strength of character and nobility of soul, these are people you pay for, but they are never yours, and in the end you cannot get the benefit of your investment. Men are less nervous of offending someone who makes himself lovable, than someone who makes himself frightening. For love attaches men by ties of obligation, which, since men are wicked, they break whenever their interests are at stake. But fear restrains men because they are afraid of punishment, and this fear never leaves them. Still, a ruler should make himself feared in such a way that, if he does not inspire love, at least he does not provoke hatred. For it is perfectly possible to be feared and not hated. You will only be hated if you seize the property or the women of your subjects and citizens. Whenever you have to kill someone, make sure that you have a suitable excuse and an obvious reason; but, above all else, keep your hands off other people's property; for men are quicker to forget the death of their father than the loss of their inheritance. Moreover, there are always reasons why you might want to seize people's property; and he who begins to live by plundering others will always find an excuse for seizing other people's possessions; but there are fewer reasons for killing people, and one killing need not lead to another.

When a ruler is at the head of his army and has a vast number of soldiers under his command, then it is absolutely essential to be prepared to be thought cruel; for it is impossible to keep an army united and ready for action without acquiring a reputation for cruelty.

Erasmus, *Education of a Christian Prince* (1516)

Follow the right, do violence to no one, plunder no one, sell no public office, be corrupted by no bribes. . . . As you would rather stand for an injury than avenge it at great loss to the state, perchance you will lose a little something of your empire. Bear that; consider that you have gained a great deal because you have brought hurt to fewer than you would otherwise have done. . . . If you cannot defend . . . your realm without violating justice, without wanton loss of human life, without great loss to religion, give up and yield to the importunities of the age! . . .

A good prince . . . is a living likeness of God, who is at once good and powerful. His goodness makes him want to help all; his power makes him able to do so. On the other hand, an evil prince, who is like a plague to his country, is the incarnation of the devil, who has great power joined with his wickedness. All his resources to the very last, he uses for the undoing of the human race. . . .

[A good prince is one] who holds the life of each individual dearer than his own; who works and strives night and day for just one end—to be the best he can for everyone; with whom rewards are ready for all good men . . . for so much does he want to be of real help to his people, without thought of recompense, that if necessary he would not hesitate to look out for their welfare at great risk to himself; who considers his wealth to lie in the advantage of his country; who is ever on the watch so that everyone else may sleep deeply; who grants no leisure to himself so that he may spend his life in the peace of his country; who worries himself with continual cares so that his subjects may have peace and quiet. . . . He does everything and allows everything that will bring everlasting peace to his country, for he realizes that war is the source of all misfortunes to the state.

Sources: Machiavelli, *The Prince* (1513), trans. D. Wootton (Indianapolis: Hackett Publishing Company, 1995), pp. 51–52; Erasmus, *Education of a Christian Prince* (1516), trans. L. K. Born (New York: Columbia University Press, 1936).

community. In the busy civic world of Florence, however, intellectuals began to take a new view of their role as intellectuals. The classical Roman statesman and intellectual Cicero became their model. Leonardo Bruni (leh-ah-NAHR-doh BROO-nee) (1370–1444), a humanist, Florentine patriot, and chancellor of the city, wrote a biography of Cicero titled *The New Cicero*, in which he waxed enthusiastic about the fusion of political action and literary creation in Cicero's life. From Bruni's time on, Cicero served as the inspiration for the Renaissance ideal that intellectuals had a duty to live an active life for their state. An individual only "grows to maturity—both intellectually and morally—through participation" in the life of the state. Civic humanism reflected the values of the urban society of the Italian Renaissance. Humanists came to believe that their study of the humanities should be put to the service of the state. It is no accident that humanists served the state as chancellors, councillors, and advisers.

Also evident in the humanism of the first half of the fifteenth century was a growing interest in classical Greek civilization. Bruni was one of the first Italian humanists to gain a thorough knowledge of Greek. He became an enthusiastic pupil of the Byzantine scholar Manuel Chrysoloras (man-WEL kris-uh-LAHR-uss), who taught in Florence from 1396 to 1400. Humanists eagerly perused the works of Plato as well as those of Greek poets, dramatists, historians, and orators, such as Euripides, Sophocles, and Thucydides, all of whom had been ignored by the scholastics of the High Middle Ages as irrelevant to the theological questions they were examining.

By the fifteenth century, a consciousness of being humanists had emerged. This was especially evident in the career of Lorenzo Valla (1407–1457). Valla was brought up in Rome and educated in both Latin and Greek. Eventually, he achieved his chief ambition of becoming a papal secretary. Valla's major work, *The Elegances of the Latin Language*, was an effort to purify medieval Latin and restore Latin to its proper position over the vernacular. The treatise examined the proper use of classical Latin and created a new literary standard. Early humanists had tended to take as classical models any author (including Christians) who had written before the seventh century c.e. Valla identified different stages in the development of the Latin language and accepted only the Latin of the last century of the Roman Republic and the first century of the empire.

Humanism and Philosophy

In the second half of the fifteenth century, a dramatic upsurge of interest in the works of Plato occurred, especially evident among the members of an informal discussion group known as the Florentine Platonic Academy. Cosimo de' Medici, the de facto ruler of Florence, encouraged this development by commissioning a translation of Plato's dialogues by Marsilio Ficino (mar-SIL-yoh fee-CHEE-noh) (1433–1499), one of the academy's leaders. Ficino dedicated his life to the translation of Plato and the exposition of the Platonic philosophy known as **Neoplatonism**.

In two major works, Ficino undertook the synthesis of Christianity and Platonism into a single system. His Neoplatonism was based on two primary ideas, the Neoplatonic hierarchy of substances and a theory of spiritual love. The former

postulated the idea of a hierarchy of substances, or great chain of being, from the lowest form of physical matter (plants) to the purest spirit (God), in which humans occupied a central or middle position. They were the link between the material world (through the body) and the spiritual world (through the soul), and their highest duty was to ascend toward that union with God that was the true end of human existence. Ficino's theory of spiritual or Platonic love maintained that just as all people are bound together in their common humanity by love, so too are all parts of the universe held together by bonds of sympathetic love.

Renaissance Hermeticism

Hermeticism was another product of the Florentine intellectual environment of the late fifteenth century. At the request of Cosimo de' Medici, Ficino translated into Latin a Greek work titled *Corpus Hermeticum* (KOR-pus hur-MET-i-koom). The Hermetic manuscripts contained two kinds of writings. One type stressed the occult sciences, with an emphasis on astrology, alchemy, and magic; the other focused on theological and philosophical beliefs and speculations. Some Hermetic writings espoused **pantheism**, seeing divinity embodied in all aspects of nature and in the heavenly bodies as well as in earthly objects. As Giordano Bruno (jor-DAHN-oh BROO-noh), one of the most prominent sixteenth-century Hermeticists, stated, "God as a whole is in all things."[15]

For Renaissance intellectuals, the Hermetic revival offered a new view of humankind. They believed that human beings had been created as divine beings endowed with divine creative power but had freely chosen to enter the material world (nature). Humans could recover their divinity, however, through a regenerative experience or purification of the soul. Thus regenerated, they became true sages or magi, as the Renaissance called them, who had knowledge of God and of truth. In regaining their original divinity, they reacquired an intimate knowledge of nature and the ability to employ the powers of nature for beneficial purposes.

In Italy, the most prominent magi in the late fifteenth century were Ficino and his friend and pupil, Giovanni Pico della Mirandola (PEE-koh DELL-uh mee-RAN-doh-lah) (1463–1494). Pico produced one of the most famous pieces of writing of the Renaissance, the *Oration on the Dignity of Man*. Pico combed diligently through the works of many philosophers of different backgrounds for the common "nuggets of universal truth" that he believed were all part of God's revelation to humanity. In the *Oration* (see Historical Voices, "Pico della Mirandola and the Dignity of Man," p. 355), Pico offered a ringing statement of unlimited human potential: "To him it is granted to have whatever he chooses, to be whatever he wills."[16] Like Ficino, Pico took an avid interest in Hermetic philosophy, accepting it as the "science of the Divine," which "embraces the deepest contemplation of the most secret things, and at last the knowledge of all nature."[17]

The works of Ficino and Pico show that Italian Renaissance humanism was not just a secular movement but also had a strong spiritual component. In the treatises of Ficino and Pico, Renaissance humanism sought to illuminate the relationship

HISTORICAL VOICES

Pico della Mirandola and the Dignity of Man

 What does Pico mean by the "dignity of man"? Why would Pico be regarded as one of the Renaissance magi?

GIOVANNI PICO DELLA MIRANDOLA was one of the foremost intellects of the Italian Renaissance. Pico boasted that he had studied all schools of philosophy, which he tried to demonstrate by drawing up nine hundred theses for public disputation at the age of twenty-four. As a preface to his theses, he wrote his famous *Oration on the Dignity of Man*, in which he proclaimed the unlimited potentiality of human beings.

Pico della Mirandola, *Oration on the Dignity of Man*

At last the best of artisans [God] ordained that that creature to whom He had been able to give nothing proper to himself should have joint possession of whatever had been peculiar to each of the different kinds of being. He therefore took man as a creature of indeterminate nature, and assigning him a place in the middle of the world, addressed him thus: "Neither a fixed abode nor a form that is yours alone nor any function peculiar to yourself have we given you, Adam, to the end that according to your longing and according to your judgment you may have and possess what abode, what form, and what functions you yourself desire. The nature of all other beings is limited and constrained within the bounds of laws prescribed by Us. You, constrained by no limits, in accordance with your own free will, in whose hand We have placed you, shall ordain for yourself the limits of your nature. We have set you at the world's center that you may from there more easily observe whatever is in the world. We have made you neither of heaven nor of earth, neither mortal nor immortal, so that with freedom of choice and with honor, as though the maker and molder of yourself, you may fashion yourself in whatever shape you shall prefer. You shall have the power to degenerate into the lower forms of life, which are brutish. You shall have the power, out of your soul's judgment, to be reborn into the higher forms, which are divine."

O supreme generosity of God the Father, O highest and most marvelous felicity of man! To him it is granted to have whatever he chooses, to be whatever he wills. Beasts as soon as they are born bring with them from their mother's womb all they will ever possess. Spiritual beings, either from the beginning or soon thereafter, become what they are to be for ever and ever. On man when he came into life the Father conferred the seeds of all kinds and the germs of every way of life. Whatever seeds each man cultivates will grow to maturity and bear in him their own fruit. If they be vegetative, he will be like a plant. If sensitive, he will become brutish. If rational, he will grow into a heavenly being. If intellectual, he will be an angel and the son of God.

Source: E. Cassirer, P. Kristeller, and J. Randall Jr., *The Renaissance Philosophy of Man* (Chicago: University of Chicago Press, 1948).

---

between humans and God and to define humans not only as physical beings but divinely inspired beings as well.

12-4b Education in the Renaissance

The humanist movement had a profound effect on education. Renaissance humanists believed that human beings could be dramatically changed by education. They wrote books on education and developed secondary schools based on their ideas. Most famous was the school founded in 1423 by Vittorino da Feltre at Mantua, where the ruler of that small Italian state, Gian Francesco I Gonzaga, wished to provide a humanist education for his children. Vittorino based much of his educational system on the ideas of classical authors, particularly Cicero and Quintilian.

At the core of humanist schools were the "liberal studies." A treatise on education called *Concerning Character* by Pietro Paolo Vergerio (PYAY-troh PAH-oh-loh vur-JEER-ee-oh) (1370–1444) especially influenced the Renaissance view of the value of the liberal arts. This work stressed the importance of liberal studies as the key to true freedom, enabling individuals to reach their full potential. According to Vergerio, "We call those studies liberal which are worthy of a free man; those studies by which we attain and practice virtue and wisdom; that education which calls forth, trains, and develops those highest gifts of body and mind which ennoble men."[18] The liberal studies included history, moral philosophy, eloquence (rhetoric), letters (grammar and logic), poetry, mathematics, astronomy, and music. The purpose of a liberal education was thus to produce individuals who followed a path of virtue and wisdom and possessed the rhetorical skills with which to persuade others to do the same. Following the Greek precept of a sound mind in a sound body, Vittorino's school at Mantua also stressed physical education. Pupils were taught the skills of javelin throwing, archery, and dancing and encouraged to run, wrestle, hunt, and swim.

Humanist education was thought to be a practical preparation for life. Its aim was not to create great scholars but rather to produce complete citizens who could participate in the civic life of their communities. As Vittorino said, "Not everyone is obliged to excel in philosophy, medicine, or the law, nor are all equally favored by nature; but all are destined to live in society and to practice virtue."[19] Humanist schools, combining the classics and Christianity, provided the model for the basic education of the European ruling classes until the twentieth century.

Although a small number of children from the lower classes received free educations, humanist schools such as Vittorino's were primarily geared for the education of an elite, the ruling classes of their communities. Also largely absent from such schools were females. Vittorino's only female pupils were the two daughters of the Gonzaga ruler of Mantua. Though these few female students studied the classics and were encouraged to know some history and to ride, dance, sing, play the lute, and appreciate poetry, they were discouraged from learning mathematics and rhetoric. In the educational treatises of the time, religion and morals were thought to "hold the first place in the education of a Christian lady."

HISTORIANS DEBATE **Was There a Renaissance for Women?** Historians have disagreed over the benefits of the Renaissance for women. Some maintain that during the Middle Ages upper-class women in particular had greater freedom to satisfy their emotional needs and that upper-class women in the Renaissance experienced a contraction of both social and personal options as they became even more subject to male authority and patterns. Other historians have argued that although conditions remained bleak for most women, some women, especially those in courtly, religious, and intellectual environments, found ways to develop a new sense of themselves as women. This may be especially true of three women who were educated in the humanist fashion and went on to establish their own literary careers.

Isotta Nogarola (ee-ZAHT-uh NOH-guh-roll-uh), born to a noble family in Verona, mastered Latin and wrote numerous letters and treatises that brought her praise from male Italian intellectuals. Cassandra Fedele (FAY-duh-lee) of Venice, who learned both Latin and Greek from humanist tutors hired by her family, became well known in Venice for her orations. In one of these, she proclaimed: "And when I meditate on the idea of marching forth in life with the lowly and execrable weapons of the little woman—the needle and the distaff—even if the study of literature offers women no rewards or honors, I believe women must nonetheless pursue and embrace such studies alone for the pleasure and enjoyment they contain."[20] Laura Cereta (say-REE-tuh) was educated in Latin by her father, a physician from Brescia. Cereta dedicated her life to humanist learning after the death of her husband and defended the ability of women to pursue scholarly pursuits (see Historical Voices, "A Woman's Defense of Learning," p. 357).

12-4c Humanism and History

Humanism had a strong impact on the writing of history. Influenced by Roman and Greek historians, the humanists approached the writing of history differently from the chroniclers of the Middle Ages. The humanists' belief that classical civilization had been followed by an age of barbarism (the Middle Ages), which had in turn been succeeded by their own age, with its rebirth of the study of the classics, enabled them to think in terms of the passage of time, of the past as past. Their division of the past into ancient world, dark ages, and their own age provided a new sense of chronology or periodization in history.

The humanists were also responsible for secularizing the writing of history. Humanist historians reduced or eliminated the role of miracles in historical interpretation, not because they were anti-Christian but because they took a new approach to sources. They wanted to use documents and exercised their newly developed critical skills in examining them. Greater attention was paid to the political events and forces that affected their city-states or larger territorial units. Thus, Leonardo Bruni wrote the *History of the Florentine People*. The new emphasis on secularization was also evident in the humanists' conception of causation in history. Medieval historical literature often portrayed historical events as being caused by God's active involvement in human affairs. Humanists de-emphasized divine intervention in favor of human motives, stressing political forces or the role of individuals in history.

Guicciardini The high point of Renaissance historiography was achieved at the beginning of the sixteenth century in the works of Francesco Guicciardini (frahn-CHESS-koh gwee-char-DEE-nee) (1483–1540). To many historians, his *History of Italy* and *History of Florence* represent the beginning of "modern analytical historiography." To Guicciardini, the purpose of writing history was to teach lessons, but he was so impressed by the complexity of historical events that he felt those lessons were not always obvious. From his extensive background in government and diplomatic affairs, he developed the skills that enabled him to analyze political situations precisely and critically. Emphasizing political and military history, his works relied heavily on personal examples and documentary sources.

12-4d The Impact of Printing

The Renaissance witnessed the invention of printing, one of the most important technological innovations of Western civilization. The art of printing made an immediate impact on European intellectual life and thought. Printing from hand-carved wooden blocks had been done in the West since the twelfth century and in China even before that. What was new to Europe in the fifteenth century was multiple printing with movable metal type. The development of printing from movable type was a gradual process that culminated between 1445 and 1450; Johannes Gutenberg (yoh-HAH-nuss GOO-ten-bayrk) of Mainz played an important role in bringing the process to completion. Gutenberg's Bible, completed in 1455 or 1456, was the first true book in the West produced from movable type.

The new printing spread rapidly throughout Europe in the second half of the fifteenth century. Printing presses were established throughout the Holy Roman Empire in the 1460s

A Woman's Defense of Learning

 How does Cereta explain her intellectual interests and accomplishments? Why were Renaissance women rarely taken seriously when they sought educational opportunities and recognition for their intellectual talents? Were any of those factors unique to the Renaissance era?

AS A YOUNG WOMAN, LAURA CERETA was proud of her learning but was condemned by a male world that found it unseemly for women to be scholars. One monk said to her father, "She gives herself to things unworthy of her—namely, the classics." Before being silenced, Laura Cereta wrote a series of letters, including one to a male critic who had argued that her work was so good it could not have been written by a woman.

Laura Cereta, *Defense of the Liberal Instruction of Women*

My ears are wearied by your carping. You brashly and publicly not merely wonder but indeed lament that I am said to possess as fine a mind as nature ever bestowed upon the most learned man. You seem to think that so learned a woman has scarcely before been seen in the world. You are wrong on both counts. . . .

I would have been silent. . . . But I cannot tolerate your having attacked my entire sex. For this reason my thirsty soul seeks revenge, my sleeping pen is aroused to literary struggle, raging anger stirs mental passions long chained by silence. With just cause I am moved to demonstrate how great a reputation for learning and virtue women have won by their inborn excellence, manifested in every age as knowledge. . . .

Only the question of the rarity of outstanding women remains to be addressed. The explanation is clear: women have been able by nature to be exceptional, but have chosen lesser goals. For some women are concerned with parting their hair correctly, adorning themselves with lovely dresses, or decorating their fingers with pearls and other gems. Others delight in mouthing carefully composed phrases, indulging in dancing, or managing spoiled puppies. Still others wish to gaze at lavish banquet tables, to rest in sleep, or, standing at mirrors, to smear their lovely faces. But those in whom a deeper integrity yearns for virtue, restrain from the start their youthful souls, reflect on higher things, harden the body with sobriety and trials, and curb their tongues, open their ears, compose their thoughts in wakeful hours, their minds in contemplation, to letters bonded to righteousness. For knowledge is not given as a gift, but [is gained] with diligence. The free mind, not shirking effort, always soars zealously toward the good, and the desire to know grows ever more wide and deep. It is because of no special holiness, therefore, that we [women] are rewarded by God the Giver with the gift of exceptional talent. Nature has generously lavished its gifts upon all people, opening to all the doors of choice through which reason sends envoys to the will, from which they learn and convey its desires. The will must choose to exercise the gift of reason. . . .

I have been praised too much; showing your contempt for women, you pretend that I alone am admirable because of the good fortune of my intellect. . . . Do you suppose, O most contemptible man on earth, that I think myself sprung [like Athena] from the head of Jove? I am a school girl, possessed of the sleeping embers of an ordinary mind. Indeed I am too hurt, and my mind, offended, too swayed by passions, sighs, tormenting itself, conscious of the obligation to defend my sex. For absolutely everything—that which is within us and that which is without—is made weak by association with my sex.

Source: Laura Cereta, "Defense of the Liberal Instruction of Women," in *Her Immaculate Hand: Selected Works by and about the Women Humanists of Quattrocentro Italy*, eds. M. King and A. Rabil (Asheville, N.C.: Pegasus Press, 2000).

and within ten years had spread to both western and eastern Europe. Especially well known as a printing center was Venice, home by 1500 to almost one hundred printers who had produced almost 2 million volumes.

By 1500, there were more than a thousand printers in Europe who had published almost 40,000 titles (between 8 million and 10 million copies). Probably 50 percent of these books were religious—Bibles and biblical commentaries, books of devotion, and sermons. Next in importance were the Latin and Greek classics, medieval grammars, legal handbooks, works on philosophy, and an ever-growing number of popular romances.

Printing became one of the largest industries in Europe, and its effects were soon felt in many areas of European life. The printing of books encouraged the development of scholarly research and the desire to attain knowledge. Moreover, printing facilitated cooperation among scholars and helped produce standardized and definitive texts. Printing also stimulated the development of an ever-expanding lay reading public, a development that had an enormous impact on European society. Indeed, without the printing press, the new religious ideas of the Reformation would never have spread as rapidly as they did in the sixteenth century.

12-5 The Artistic Renaissance

Q FOCUS QUESTION: What were the chief characteristics of Renaissance art, and how did it differ in Italy and northern Europe? Choose any three artists and explain their importance to the development of art in the Renaissance.

Leonardo da Vinci (dah VEEN-chee), one of the great Italian Renaissance artists, once explained: "Hence the painter will produce pictures of small merit if he takes for his standard the pictures of others, but if he will study from natural objects he will bear good fruit. . . . Those who take for their standard anyone but nature . . . weary themselves in vain."[21] Renaissance artists considered the imitation of nature their primary goal. Their search for naturalism became an end in itself: to persuade onlookers of the reality of the object or event they were portraying. At the same time, the new artistic standards reflected a new attitude of mind as well, one in which human beings became the focus of attention, the "center and measure of all things," as one artist proclaimed.

12-5a Art in the Early Renaissance

Leonardo and other Italians maintained that it was Giotto in the fourteenth century (see Chapter 11) who began the imitation of nature. But what Giotto had begun was not taken up again until the work of Masaccio (muh-ZAH-choh) (1401–1428) in Florence. Masaccio's cycle of frescoes in the Brancacci Chapel has long been regarded as the first masterpiece of Early Renaissance art (see Image 12.6). With his use of monumental figures, a more realistic relationship between figures and landscape, and visual representation of the laws of perspective, a new realistic style of painting was born. Onlookers become aware of a world of reality that appears to be a continuation of their own world. Masaccio's massive, three-dimensional human figures provided a model for later generations of Florentine artists.

During the fifteenth century, other Florentine painters absorbed and modified this new Renaissance style. Especially important was the development of an experimental trend that took two directions. One emphasized the mathematical side of painting, the working out of the laws of perspective and the organization of outdoor space and light by geometry and perspective. In the work of Paolo Uccello (PAH-oh-loh oo-CHELL-oh) (1397–1475), figures became mere stage props to show off his mastery of the laws of perspective. The other aspect of the experimental trend involved the investigation of movement and anatomical structure. *The Martyrdom of Saint Sebastian* by Antonio Pollaiuolo (pohl-ly-WOH-loh) (ca. 1432–1498) revels in classical motifs and attempts to portray the human body under stress. Indeed, the realistic portrayal of the human nude became one of the foremost preoccupations of Italian Renaissance art. The fifteenth century, then, was a period of experimentation and technical mastery.

IMAGE 12.6 **Masaccio, *Tribute Money*.** With the frescoes of Masaccio, regarded by many as the first great works of Early Renaissance art, a new realistic style of painting was born. *Tribute Money* was one of a series of frescoes that Masaccio painted in the Brancacci Chapel of the Church of Santa Maria del Carmine in Florence. In *Tribute Money*, Masaccio depicted the biblical story of Jesus's confrontation by a tax collector at the entrance to the town of Capernaum (seen at the center). Jesus sent Peter to collect a coin from the mouth of a fish from Lake Galilee (seen at the left); Peter then paid the tax collector (seen at the right). In illustrating this story from the Bible, Masaccio used a rational system of perspective to create a realistic relationship between the figures and their background; the figures themselves are realistic. As one Renaissance observer said, "The works made before Masaccio's day can be said to be painted, while his are living, real, and natural."

Q *Compare this image with Image 11.12 of Giotto's Lamentation in Chapter 11. What are the similarities and what are the differences between the two? Based on your analysis, why is Giotto considered only a forerunner of Italian Renaissance art?*

Scala/Art Resource, NY

IMAGE 12.7 **Donatello,** *David.* Donatello's *David* first stood in the courtyard of the Medici Palace. On its base was an inscription praising Florentine heroism and virtue, leading art historians to believe that the statue was meant to commemorate the victory of Florence over Milan in 1428. David's pose and appearance are reminiscent of the nude statues of antiquity.

IMAGE 12.8 **Filippo Brunelleschi, Dome of the Duomo.** Brunelleschi was first commissioned to design the dome for the unfinished cathedral of Florence in 1417, but work did not begin until 1420. Although Brunelleschi would have preferred the Roman hemispheric dome, for practical reasons he was forced to elevate the center of the dome and then lessen the weight of the structure by building a thin double shell around a structure of twenty-four ribs. The most important ribs were placed on the outside of the dome (four of them are visible in this photograph).

The revolutionary achievements of Florentine painters in the fifteenth century were matched by equally stunning advances in sculpture and architecture. Donato di Donatello (doh-NAH-toh dee doh-nuh-TELL-oh) (1386–1466) spent time in Rome studying and copying the statues of antiquity. His subsequent work in Florence reveals how well he had mastered the essence of what he saw. Among his numerous works was a statue of David, which is the first known life-size, freestanding bronze nude in European art since antiquity (see Image 12.7). With the severed head of the giant Goliath beneath David's feet, Donatello's statue may have celebrated Florentine heroism in the triumph of Florence over the Milanese in 1428. Like Donatello's other statues, *David* also radiated a simplicity and strength that reflected the dignity of humanity.

Filippo Brunelleschi (fee-LEE-poh BROO-nuh-LESS-kee) (1377–1446), a friend of Donatello's, accompanied the latter to Rome. Brunelleschi drew much inspiration from the architectural monuments of Roman antiquity, and when he returned to Florence, he poured his new insights into the creation of a new architecture. His first project involved the challenge of building a dome for the unfinished cathedral of Florence (the Duomo).

The cathedral had been started in 1296, but it was Brunelleschi who devised new building techniques and machinery to create a dome, built between 1420 and 1436, that spanned a 140-foot opening (see Image 12.8).

An even better example of Brunelleschi's new Renaissance architectural style is evident in the Church of San Lorenzo. When the Medici commissioned him to design the church, Brunelleschi, inspired by Roman models, created a church interior very different from that of the great medieval cathedrals. San Lorenzo's classical columns, rounded arches, and coffered ceiling created an environment that did not overwhelm the worshiper materially and psychologically, as Gothic cathedrals did, but comforted as a space created to fit human, not divine, measurements (see Image 12.9). Like painters and sculptors, Renaissance architects sought to reflect a human-centered world.

The new assertion of human individuality, evident in Early Renaissance art, was also reflected in the new emphasis on portraiture. Patrons appeared in the corners of sacred pictures, and monumental tombs and portrait statues honored many of Florence's prominent citizens. By the mid-fifteenth century, artists were giving an accurate rendering of their subjects' facial

12-5b The Artistic High Renaissance

By the end of the fifteenth century, Italian painters, sculptors, and architects had created a new artistic environment. Many artists had mastered the new techniques for a scientific observation of the world around them and were now ready to move into individualistic forms of creative expression. This final stage of Renaissance art, which flourished between 1480 and 1520, is called the High Renaissance. The shift to the High Renaissance was marked by the increasing importance of Rome as a new cultural center of the Italian Renaissance.

The High Renaissance was dominated by the work of three artistic giants: Leonardo da Vinci (1452–1519), Raphael (1483–1520), and Michelangelo (1475–1564). Leonardo represents a transitional figure in the shift to High Renaissance principles. He carried on the fifteenth-century experimental tradition by studying everything and even dissecting human bodies to see more clearly how nature worked. But Leonardo stressed the need to advance beyond such realism and initiated the High Renaissance's preoccupation with the idealization of nature, or the attempt to generalize from realistic portrayal to an ideal form.

Leonardo's *Last Supper*, painted in Milan, is a brilliant summary of fifteenth-century trends in its organization of space and use of perspective to depict subjects three-dimensionally in a two-dimensional medium (see Image 12.10). But it is also more. The figure of Philip is idealized, and the work embodies profound psychological dimensions. The words of Jesus that "one of you shall

IMAGE 12.9 **Brunelleschi, Interior of San Lorenzo.** Cosimo de' Medici contributed massive amounts of money to the rebuilding of the Church of San Lorenzo. As seen in this view of the nave and choir of the church, Brunelleschi's architectural designs were based on the basilica plan borrowed by early Christians from pagan Rome. San Lorenzo's simplicity, evident in its rows of slender Corinthian columns, created a human-centered space.

Q *Compare this interior with that of a Gothic cathedral (Image 9.12 on p. 271). What are the noticeable differences, and what do they reveal about medieval and Renaissance architecture?*

features while revealing the inner qualities of their personalities. The portraits of the duke and duchess of Urbino by Piero della Francesca (ca. 1410–1492) provide accurate representations as well as a sense of both the power and the wealth of the rulers of Urbino (see Image 12.4 on p. 348).

IMAGE 12.10 **Leonardo da Vinci, *The Last Supper*.** Leonardo da Vinci was the impetus behind the High Renaissance concern for the idealization of nature, moving from a realistic portrayal of the human figure to an idealized form. Evident in Leonardo's *Last Supper* is his effort to depict a person's character and inner nature by the use of gesture and movement. Unfortunately, Leonardo used an experimental technique in this fresco, which soon led to its physical deterioration.

betray me" are experienced directly as each of the apostles reveals his personality and his relationship to Jesus. Through gestures and movement, Leonardo hoped to reveal a person's inner life.

Raphael (RAFF-ee-ul) blossomed as a painter at an early age; at twenty-five, he was already regarded as one of Italy's best painters. Raphael was acclaimed for his numerous madonnas, in which he attempted to achieve an ideal of beauty far surpassing human standards. He is well known for his frescoes in the Vatican Palace; his *School of Athens* reveals a world of balance, harmony, and order—the underlying principles of the art of the classical world of Greece and Rome (see Image 12.11).

Michelangelo (my-kuh-LAN-juh-loh), an accomplished painter, sculptor, and architect, was another giant of the High Renaissance. Fiercely driven by his desire to create, he worked with great passion and energy on a remarkable number of projects. Michelangelo was influenced by Neoplatonism, especially evident in his figures on the ceiling of the Sistine Chapel in Rome. In 1508, Pope Julius II had called Michelangelo to Rome and commissioned him to decorate the chapel ceiling. This colossal project was not completed until 1512.

Michelangelo attempted to tell the story of the Fall of Man by depicting nine scenes from the biblical book of Genesis. In his *Creation of Adam* (see Image 12.1, at the beginning of this chapter), the well-proportioned figure of Adam awaits the divine spark. Adam, like the other muscular figures on the ceiling, reveals an ideal type of human being with perfect proportions. In good Neoplatonic fashion, the beauty of these figures is meant to be a reflection of divine beauty; the more beautiful the body, the more God-like the figure.

Another manifestation of Michelangelo's search for ideal beauty was his *David*, a colossal marble statue commissioned by the Florentine government in 1501 and completed in 1504 (see Image 12.12). Michelangelo maintained that the form of a statue already resided in the uncarved piece of stone: "I only take away the surplus, the statue is already there."[22] Out of a piece of marble that had remained unused for fifty years, Michelangelo created a 14-foot-high figure, the largest sculpture in Italy since the time of Rome. An awe-inspiring hero, Michelangelo's *David* proudly proclaims the beauty of the human body and the glory of human beings.

Erich Lessing/Art Resource, NY

IMAGE 12.11 **Raphael, *School of Athens*.** Raphael arrived in Rome in 1508 and began to paint a series of frescoes commissioned by Pope Julius II for the papal apartments at the Vatican. In *School of Athens*, painted in 1510 or 1511, Raphael created an imaginary gathering of ancient philosophers. In the center stand Plato and Aristotle. At the left is Pythagoras, showing his system of proportions on a slate. At the right is Ptolemy, holding a celestial globe.

Q *What is the significance of the hand gestures of Plato and Aristotle (see Chapter 4)?*

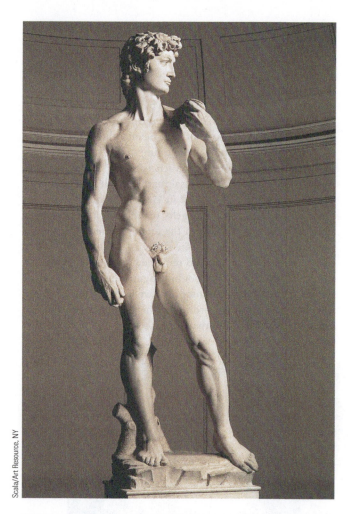

Scala/Art Resource, NY

IMAGE 12.12 Michelangelo, *David*. This statue of David, cut from an 18-foot-high piece of marble, exalts the beauty of the human body and is a fitting symbol of the Italian Renaissance's affirmation of human power. Completed in 1504, *David* was moved by Florentine authorities to a special location in front of the Palazzo Vecchio, the seat of the Florentine government.

Q *Compare this David with that of Donatello's David on p. 359. What are the noticeable differences, and what does this tell you about the development of Renaissance art over a period of time?*

The High Renaissance was also evident in architecture, especially in the work of Donato Bramante (doh-NAH-toh brah-MAHN-tay) (1444–1514). He came from Urbino but took up residence in Rome, where he designed a small temple on the supposed site of Saint Peter's martyrdom. The Tempietto, or little temple, with its Doric columns surrounding a sanctuary enclosed by a dome, summarized the architectural ideals of the High Renaissance. Columns, dome, and sanctuary form a monumental and harmonious whole. Inspired by antiquity, Bramante had recaptured the grandeur of ancient Rome.

12-5c The Artist and Social Status

Early Renaissance artists began their careers as apprentices to masters in craft guilds. Apprentices with unusual talent might eventually become masters and run their own workshops. As in the Middle Ages, artists were still largely viewed as artisans. Since guilds depended on commissions for their projects, patrons played an important role in the art of the Early Renaissance. The wealthy upper classes determined both the content and the purpose of the paintings and pieces of sculpture they commissioned.

By the end of the fifteenth century, a transformation in the position of the artist had occurred. Especially talented individuals, such as Leonardo, Raphael, and Michelangelo, were no longer regarded as artisans but as artistic geniuses with creative energies akin to the divine (see Historical Voices, "The Genius of Michelangelo," p. 363). Artists were heroes, individuals who were praised more for their creativity than for their competence as craftspeople. Michelangelo, for example, was frequently addressed as "Il Divino"—the Divine One. As society excused their eccentricities and valued their creative genius, the artists of the High Renaissance became the first to embody the modern concept of the artist.

As respect for artists grew, so did their ability to profit economically from their work and to rise on the social scale. Now welcomed as equals into the circles of the upper classes, they mingled with the political and intellectual elite of their society and became more aware of new intellectual theories, which they then embodied in their art. The Platonic Academy and Renaissance Neoplatonism had an especially important impact on Florentine painters.

12-5d The Northern Artistic Renaissance

In trying to provide an exact portrayal of their world, the artists of the north (especially the Low Countries) and Italy took different approaches. In Italy, the human form became the primary vehicle of expression as Italian artists sought to master the technical skills that allowed them to portray humans in realistic settings. The large wall spaces of Italian churches had given rise to the art of fresco painting, but in the north, the prevalence of Gothic cathedrals with their stained-glass windows resulted in more emphasis on illuminated manuscripts and wooden panel painting for altarpieces. The space available in these works was limited, and great care was required to depict each object, leading northern painters to become masters at rendering details.

The most influential northern school of art in the fifteenth century was centered in Flanders. Jan van Eyck (YAHN vahn YK *or* van AYK) (ca. 1390–1441) was among the first to use oil paint, a medium that enabled the artist to use a varied range of colors and create fine details. In the famous *Giovanni Arnolfini and His Bride*, van Eyck's attention to detail is staggering: precise portraits, a glittering chandelier, and a mirror reflecting the objects in the room (see Image 12.13). Although each detail was rendered as observed, it is evident that van Eyck's comprehension of perspective was still uncertain. His work is truly indicative of northern Renaissance painters, who, in their effort to imitate nature, did so not by mastery of the laws of perspective and proportion but by empirical observation of visual reality and the accurate portrayal of details. Moreover, northern painters placed great emphasis on the emotional intensity of religious feeling and created great works of devotional art, especially in their altarpieces. Michelangelo summarized the

The Genius of Michelangelo

 How do you think Vasari's comments on Michelangelo fostered the image of the Renaissance artist as a "creative genius with almost divine qualities"?

DURING THE RENAISSANCE, artists came to be viewed as creative geniuses with almost divine qualities. One individual who helped create this image was himself a painter. Giorgio Vasari (JOR-joh vuh-ZAHR-ee) was an avid admirer of Italy's great artists and wrote a series of brief biographies of them. This excerpt is taken from his account of Michelangelo.

Giorgio Vasari, *Lives of the Artists*

Michelangelo was much inclined to the labors of art, seeing that everything, however difficult, succeeded with him, he having had from nature a genius very apt and ardent in the noble arts of design. Moreover, in order to be entirely perfect, innumerable times he made anatomical studies, dissecting men's bodies in order to see the principles of their construction and the arrangement of the bones, muscles, veins and nerves; the various movements and all the postures of the human body; and not of men only, but also of animals, and particularly of horses . . . Of all these he desired to learn the principles and laws in so far as touched his art, and this knowledge he so demonstrated in the works that fell to him to handle that those who attend to no

other study than this do now know more. He so executed his works, whether with the brush or with the chisel, that they are almost inimitable, and he gave to his labors such grace and loveliness that he surpassed and vanquished the ancients. He was able to wrest things out of the greatest difficulties with such facility that they do not appear wrought with effort, although whoever draws his works after him finds it very hard to imitate them.

The genius of Michelangelo was recognized in his lifetime, and not, as happens to many, after death, for several of the popes always wished to have him near them, and also Suleiman, emperor of the Turks, Francis of Valois, king of France, the emperor Charles V, the signory of Venice, and finally Duke Cosimo de' Medici. All offered him honorable salaries, for no other reason but to avail themselves of his great genius. This does not happen except to men of great worth, such as he was. It is well known that all the three arts of painting, sculpture, and architecture were so perfect in him, that it is not found that among persons ancient or modern, in all the many years that the sun had been whirling round, God has granted this to any other but Michelangelo. He had imagination of such a kind, and so perfect, and the things conceived by him in idea were such, that often, through not being able to express with the hands conceptions so terrible and grand, he abandoned his works—nay, destroyed many of them.

Source: H. Webster, *Readings in Medieval and Modern History* (Boston: D.C. Heath & Co., 1917), pp. 191–192.

---

difference between northern and Italian Renaissance painting in these words:

In Flanders, they paint, before all things, to render exactly and deceptively the outward appearance of things. The painters choose, by preference, subjects provoking transports of piety, like the figures of saints or of prophets. But most of the time they paint what are called landscapes with plenty of figures. Though the eye is agreeably impressed, these pictures have neither choice of values nor grandeur. In short, this art is without power and without distinction; it aims at rendering minutely many things at the same time, of which a single one would have sufficed to call forth a man's whole application.[23]

By the end of the fifteenth century, however, artists from the north began to study in Italy and were visually influenced by what artists were doing there.

One northern artist of this later period who was greatly affected by the Italians was Albrecht Dürer (AHL-brekht DOO-rur) (1471–1528) from Nuremberg. Dürer made two trips to Italy and absorbed most of what the Italians could teach, as is evident in his mastery of the laws of perspective and Renaissance theories

of proportion. He wrote detailed treatises on both subjects. At the same time, as in his famous *Adoration of the Magi*, Dürer did not reject the use of minute details characteristic of northern artists. He did try, however, to integrate those details more harmoniously into his works and, like the Italian artists of the High Renaissance, to achieve a standard of ideal beauty by a careful examination of the human form. Dürer was also the first northern Renaissance artist to provide an account of his life through his letters, a diary, and his self-portraits (see Image 12.14).

Hieronymus Bosch (ca. 1450–1516), a contemporary of Dürer who lived in the Netherlands, occupies a special place in the Northern High Renaissance. In his *Garden of Earthly Delights*, Bosch continued the Northern Renaissance style of naturalistic detail but combined it with a personal style of symbolic fantasies. Art historians have provided many interpretations, but it is probable that the major theme is sin and its consequences. The left wing of the triptych (a work of art divided in three panels hinged together side by side, often used as an altarpiece) focused on the creation of Adam and Eve, the center on the activities that condemn humans (see Image 12.15), and the right on the Last Judgment with the condemned in Hell.

National Gallery, London/Art Resource, NY

Self Portrait at the Age of Twenty-Eight, 1500 (oil on panel)/Dürer or Duerer, Albrecht (1471-1528)/Alte Pinakothek, Munich, Germany/Bridgeman Images

IMAGE 12.13 **Van Eyck, *Giovanni Arnolfini and His Bride.***
Northern painters took great care in depicting each object and became masters at rendering details. This emphasis on a realistic portrayal is clearly evident in this oil painting, supposedly a portrait of Giovanni Arnolfini, an Italian merchant who had settled in Bruges, and his wife, Giovanna Cenami.

IMAGE 12.14 **Dürer, *Self-Portrait.*** By the end of the fifteenth century, northern artists had begun to study in Italy and to adopt many of the techniques used by Italian painters. Albrecht Dürer masterfully incorporated the laws of perspective and the ideals of proportion into his works. At the same time, he did not abandon the preoccupation with detail typical of northern artists, as seen in this self-portrait done in 1500. Reflecting the Italian Renaissance view of the artist as a genius inspired by God, Dürer presents himself here as a Christlike figure.

Masterpics/Alamy Stock Photo

IMAGE 12.15 **Bosch, *Garden of Earthly Delights.***
Shown here in the central panel of Bosch's *Garden of Earthly Delights* are the extravagant activities of human beings. Bosch was an orthodox Catholic, and it is possible that the sensual and bizarre delights depicted here showed, in Bosch's eyes, that some forms of human activity were subject to damnation.

12-5e Music in the Renaissance

For much of the fifteenth century, an extraordinary cultural environment was fostered in the domains of the dukes of Burgundy in northern Europe. The court of the dukes attracted some of the best artists and musicians of the time. Among them was Guillaume Dufay (gee-YOHM doo-FAY) (ca. 1400–1474), perhaps the most important composer of his era. Born in northern France, Dufay lived for a few years in Italy and was thus well suited to combine the late medieval style of France with the early Renaissance style of Italy. One of Dufay's greatest contributions was a change in the composition of the Mass. He was the first to use secular tunes to replace Gregorian chants as the fixed melody that served as the basis for the Mass. Dufay also composed a number of secular songs, an important reminder that during the Renaissance, music ceased to be used chiefly in the service of God and moved into the secular world of courts and cities. In Italy and France, the chief form of secular music was the madrigal.

The Renaissance madrigal was a poem set to music, and it originated in the fourteenth-century Italian courts. The texts were usually twelve-line poems written in the vernacular, and their theme was emotional or erotic love. By the mid-sixteenth century, most madrigals were written for five or six voices and employed a technique called text painting, in which the music tried to portray the literal meaning of the text. Thus, the melody would rise for the word *heaven* or use a wavelike motion to represent the word *water*. By the mid-sixteenth century, the madrigal had also spread to England, where the most popular form was characterized by the *fa-la-la* refrain like that found in the English carol "Deck the Halls."

12-6 The European State in the Renaissance

FOCUS QUESTIONS: Why do historians sometimes refer to the monarchies of the late fifteenth century as "new monarchies" or "Renaissance states"? What states provide the best examples? Why?

In the first half of the fifteenth century, European states continued the disintegrative patterns of the previous century. In the second half of the century, however, recovery set in, and attempts were made to reestablish the centralized power of monarchical governments. To characterize the results, some historians have used the label "Renaissance states"; others have spoken of the "**new monarchies**," especially those of France, England, and Spain at the end of the fifteenth century (see Map 12.2). Although monarchs in western Europe succeeded to varying degrees at extending their political authority, rulers in central and eastern Europe were often weak and unable to impose their authority.

12-6a The Growth of the French Monarchy

The Hundred Years' War had left France prostrate. Depopulation, desolate farmlands, ruined commerce, and independent and unruly nobles had made it difficult for the kings to assert their authority. But the war had also developed a strong degree of French national feeling toward a common enemy that the kings could use to reestablish monarchical power. The need to prosecute the war provided an excuse to strengthen the authority of the king, already evident in the policies of Charles VII (r. 1422–1461) after he was crowned king at Reims. With the consent of the Estates-General, Charles established a royal army composed of cavalry and archers. The Estates-General also granted him the right to levy the *taille*, an annual direct tax usually on land or property, without any need for further approval from the Estates-General. Losing control of the purse meant less power for this parliamentary body.

The process of developing a French territorial state was greatly advanced by King Louis XI (r. 1461–1483), known as the Spider because of his wily and devious ways. By retaining the taille as a permanent tax imposed by royal authority, Louis secured a sound, regular source of income. Louis was not, however, completely successful in repressing the French nobility, whose independence posed a threat to his own state building. A major problem was his supposed vassal, Charles the Bold, duke of Burgundy (r. 1467–1477). Charles attempted to create a middle kingdom between France and Germany, stretching from the Low Countries to Switzerland. Louis opposed his efforts, and when Charles was killed in 1477 fighting the Swiss, Louis added part of Charles's possessions, the duchy of Burgundy, to his own lands. Three years later, the provinces of Anjou, Maine, Bar, and Provence were brought under royal control. Many historians believe that Louis created a base for the later development of a strong French monarchy.

12-6b England: Civil War and a New Monarchy

The Hundred Years' War had also strongly affected the other protagonist in that conflict. The cost of the war in its final years and the losses in manpower strained the English economy. Moreover, even greater domestic turmoil came to England when a period of civil wars broke out in the 1450s. These wars pitted the ducal house of Lancaster against the ducal house of York. (The wars are popularly known as the "Wars of the Roses" because Shakespeare a hundred years later created the fiction that a white rose symbolized the Yorkists and a red rose, the Lancasters.) Many aristocratic families of England were drawn into the conflict. Finally, in 1485, Henry Tudor, duke of Richmond, defeated the last Yorkist king, Richard III (r. 1483–1485), at Bosworth Field and established the new Tudor dynasty.

As the first Tudor king, Henry VII (r. 1485–1509) worked to reduce internal dissension and establish a strong monarchical government. Henry ended the private wars of the nobility by abolishing "livery and maintenance," the practice by which wealthy aristocrats maintained private armies of followers dedicated to the service of their lord. Since England, unlike France and Spain, did not possess a standing army, the king relied on special commissions to trusted nobles to raise troops for a specific campaign, after which the troops were disbanded. Henry also controlled the irresponsible activity of the nobles by establishing the Court of Star Chamber, which did not use juries and allowed torture to be used to extract confessions.

MAP 12.2 **Europe in the Second Half of the Fifteenth Century.** By the second half of the fifteenth century, states in western Europe, particularly France, Spain, and England, had begun the process of modern state building. With varying success, they reined in the power of the church and nobles, increased the ability to levy taxes, and established effective government bureaucracies.

 What aspects of Europe's political boundaries help explain why France and the Holy Roman Empire were often at war with each other?

Henry VII was particularly successful in extracting income from the traditional financial resources of the English monarch, such as the crown lands, judicial fees and fines, and customs duties. By using diplomacy to avoid wars, which are always expensive, the king avoided having to call Parliament on any regular basis to grant him funds. By not overburdening the landed gentry and middle class with taxes, Henry won their favor, and they provided much support for his monarchy. Henry's policies enabled him to leave England with a stable and prosperous government and an enhanced status for the monarchy itself.

12-6c The Unification of Spain

During the Middle Ages, several independent Christian kingdoms had emerged in the course of the long reconquest of the Iberian peninsula from the Muslims. Aragon and Castile were the strongest Spanish kingdoms; in the west was the independent monarchy of Portugal; in the north, the small kingdom of Navarre, oriented toward France; and in the south, the Muslim

kingdom of Granada (see Map 12.3). Few people at the beginning of the fifteenth century could have predicted the unification of the Iberian kingdoms.

A major step in that direction was taken with the marriage of Isabella of Castile (r. 1474–1504) and Ferdinand of Aragon (r. 1479–1516) in 1469. This was a dynastic union of two rulers, not a political union. Both kingdoms maintained their own parliaments (Cortes), courts, laws, coinage, speech, customs, and political organs. Nevertheless, the two rulers worked to strengthen royal control of government, especially in Castile. The royal council, which was supposed to supervise local administration and oversee the implementation of government policies, was stripped of aristocrats and filled primarily with middle-class lawyers. Trained in the principles of Roman law, these officials operated on the belief that the monarchy embodied the power of the state.

Seeking to replace the undisciplined feudal levies they had inherited with a more professional royal army, Ferdinand and

MAP 12.3 **The Iberian Peninsula.** The marriage of Isabella of Castile to Ferdinand of Aragon laid the foundation for the unification of Spain and its rise as a major European power. The two monarchs instituted military and bureaucratic reforms and forced Jews and Muslims to flee the country.

 What aspects of Portugal's geography help explain why it became a major seafaring nation, with little overland trade with Europe?

Isabella reorganized the military forces of Spain. The development of a strong infantry force as the heart of the new Spanish army made it the best in Europe by the sixteenth century.

Because of its vast power and wealth, Ferdinand and Isabella recognized the importance of controlling the Catholic Church. They secured from the pope the right to select the most important church officials in Spain, virtually guaranteeing the creation of a Spanish Catholic Church in which the clergy became an instrument for the extension of royal power. The monarchs also used their authority over the church to institute reform. Isabella's chief minister, the able and astute Cardinal Ximenes (khee-MAY-ness), restored discipline and eliminated immorality among the monks and secular clergy.

The religious zeal exhibited in Cardinal Ximenes's reform program was also evident in the policy of strict religious uniformity pursued by Ferdinand and Isabella. Of course, it served a political purpose as well: to create unity and further bolster royal power. Spain possessed two large religious minorities, the Jews and Muslims, both of which had generally been tolerated in medieval Spain. Although anti-Semitism had become a fact of life in medieval Europe, Spain had largely remained tolerant. In some areas of Spain, Jews exercised much influence in economic and intellectual affairs. During the fourteenth century, however, increased persecution led the majority of Spanish Jews to convert to Christianity. Although many of these converted Jews came to play important roles in Spanish society, complaints that they were secretly reverting to Judaism prompted Ferdinand and Isabella to ask the pope to introduce the Inquisition into Spain in 1478. Under royal control, the Inquisition worked with cruel efficiency to guarantee the orthodoxy of the converts but had no authority over practicing Jews. Consequently, in 1492, flush with the success of their conquest of Muslim Granada, Ferdinand and Isabella took the drastic step of expelling all professed Jews from Spain. It is estimated that 150,000 out of possibly 200,000 Jews fled.

Ferdinand and Isabella also pursued a policy of battling the Muslims by attacking the kingdom of Granada. The war against this remaining Muslim kingdom lasted eleven years until the final bastion of the city of Granada fell in 1492. Muslims were now "encouraged" to convert to Christianity, and in 1502 Isabella issued a decree expelling all professed Muslims from her kingdom. To a very large degree, the "Most Catholic" monarchs had achieved their goal of absolute religious orthodoxy as a basic ingredient of the Spanish state. To be Spanish was to be Catholic, a policy of uniformity enforced by the Inquisition. It was no accident that Spain became a staunch pillar of the Catholic Church during the era of the Reformation in the sixteenth century (see Chapter 13).

12-6d The Holy Roman Empire: The Success of the Habsburgs

Unlike France, England, and Spain, the Holy Roman Empire failed to develop a strong monarchical authority. After 1438, the position of Holy Roman Emperor remained in the hands of the Habsburg dynasty. Having gradually acquired a number of possessions along the Danube, known collectively as Austria, the house of Habsburg had become one of the wealthiest landholders in the empire and by the mid-fifteenth century began to play an important role in European affairs.

Much of the Habsburg success in the fifteenth century was due not to military success but to a well-executed policy of dynastic marriages. As the old Habsburg motto said, "Leave the waging of wars to others! But you, happy Austria, marry; for the realms which Mars [god of war] awards to others, Venus [goddess of love] transfers to you." By marrying his son Maximilian to Mary, the daughter of Duke Charles the Bold of Burgundy, Emperor Frederick III (r. 1440–1493) gained Franche-Comté in east-central France, Luxembourg, and a large part of the Low Countries. The addition of these territories made the Habsburg dynasty an international power and brought it the undying opposition of the French monarchy because the rulers of France feared they would be surrounded by the Habsburgs.

Much was expected of the flamboyant Maximilian I (r. 1493–1519) when he became emperor. Through the Reichstag, the imperial diet or parliament, Maximilian attempted to centralize the administration by creating new institutions common to the entire empire. Opposition from the German princes doomed these efforts, however. Maximilian's only real success lay in his marriage alliances. Philip of Burgundy, the son of Maximilian's marriage to Mary, was married to Joanna, the daughter of Ferdinand and Isabella. Philip and Joanna produced a son, Charles, who, through a series of unexpected deaths, became heir to all three lines, the Habsburg, Burgundian, and Spanish, making him the leading monarch of his age (see Chapter 13).

12-6e The Struggle for Strong Monarchy in Eastern Europe

In eastern Europe, rulers struggled to achieve the centralization of their territorial states but faced serious obstacles. Although the population was mostly Slavic, there were islands of other ethnic groups that caused untold difficulties. Religious differences also troubled the area, as Roman Catholics, Greek Orthodox Christians, and pagans confronted each other.

Much of Polish history revolved around a bitter struggle between the crown and the landed nobility until the end of the fifteenth century, when the preoccupation of Poland's rulers with problems in Bohemia and Hungary, as well as war with the Russians and Turks, enabled the aristocrats to reestablish their power. Through their control of the Sejm (SAYM) or national diet, the magnates reduced the peasantry to serfdom by 1511 and established the right to elect their kings. The Polish kings proved unable to establish a strong royal authority.

Bohemia, Poland's neighbor, was part of the Holy Roman Empire, but distrust of the Germans and close ethnic ties to the Poles and Slovaks encouraged the Czechs of Bohemia to associate with their northeastern Slavic neighbors. The Hussite wars (see "12-7a The Problems of Heresy and Reform," later in this chapter) led to further dissension and civil war. Because of a weak monarchy, the Bohemian nobles increased their authority and wealth at the expense of both crown and church.

The history of Hungary had been closely tied to that of central and western Europe by its conversion to Roman Catholicism by German missionaries. The church became a large and prosperous institution. Wealthy bishops, along with the great territorial lords, became powerful, independent political figures. For a brief while, Hungary developed into an important European state, the dominant power in eastern Europe. King Matthias Corvinus (muh-THY-uss kor-VY-nuss) (1458–1490) broke the power of the wealthy lords and created a well-organized bureaucracy. Like a typical Renaissance prince, he patronized the new humanist culture, brought Italian scholars and artists to his capital at Buda, and made his court one of the most brilliant outside Italy. After his death, however, Hungary returned to weak rule, and the work of Corvinus was largely undone.

Since the thirteenth century, Russia had been under the domination of the Mongols. Gradually, the princes of Moscow rose to prominence by using their close relationship to the Mongol khans to increase their wealth and expand their possessions.

CHRONOLOGY	Europe in the Renaissance
France	
Charles VII	1422–1461
Louis XI the Spider	1461–1483
England	
"War of the Roses"	1450s–1485
Henry VII	1485–1509
Spain	
Isabella of Castile	1474–1504
Ferdinand of Aragon	1479–1516
Marriage of Ferdinand and Isabella	1469
Introduction of Inquisition	1478
Expulsion of the Jews	1492
Expulsion of the Muslims	1502
Holy Roman Empire	
Frederick III	1440–1493
Maximilian I	1493–1519
Eastern Europe	
Battle of Kosovo	1389
Fall of Constantinople and Byzantine Empire	1453
Hungary: Matthias Corvinus	1458–1490
Russia: Ivan III	1462–1505

In the reign of the great prince Ivan III (r. 1462–1505), a new Russian state—the principality of Moscow—was born. Ivan III annexed other Russian principalities and took advantage of dissension among the Mongols to throw off their yoke by 1480.

12-6f The Ottoman Turks and the End of the Byzantine Empire

The steadily advancing Ottoman Turks increasingly threatened Eastern Europe (see Map 12.4). The Byzantine Empire had, of course, served as a buffer between the Muslim Middle East and the Latin West for centuries, but it had been severely weakened by the sack of Constantinople in 1204 and its occupation by the West. Although the Palaeologus dynasty (1260–1453) had tried to reestablish Byzantine power in the Balkans after the overthrow of the Latin empire, the threat from the Turks finally doomed the long-lasting empire.

Beginning in northeastern Asia Minor in the thirteenth century, the Ottoman Turks spread rapidly, seizing the lands of the Seljuk Turks and the Byzantine Empire. In 1345, they bypassed Constantinople and moved into the Balkans. Under Sultan Murad (moo-RAHD), Ottoman forces moved through Bulgaria and into the lands of the Serbs, who provided a strong center of opposition under King Lazar (lah-ZAR). But in 1389, at the Battle of Kosovo (KAWSS-suh-voh), Ottoman

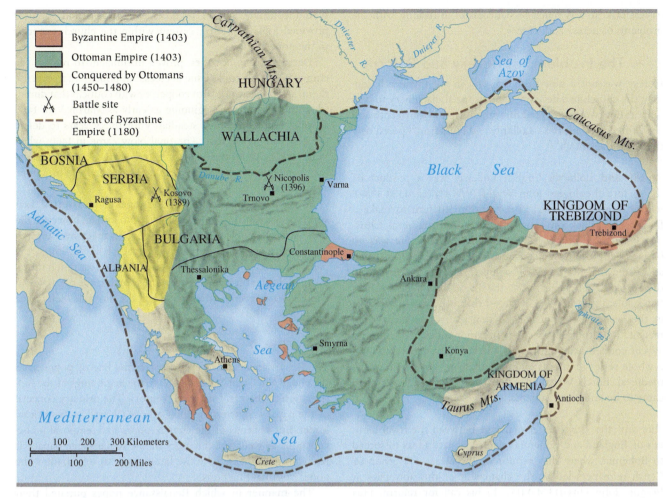

MAP 12.4 **The Ottoman Empire and Southeastern Europe.** Long a buffer between Christian Europe and the Muslim Middle East, the Byzantine Empire quickly waned in power and territory after crusaders sacked Constantinople in 1204. The Ottoman Turks slowly gained Byzantine territory and ended the thousand-year empire with the fall of Constantinople in 1453.

 Why would the Byzantine Empire have found it difficult to make alliances by 1403?

forces defeated the Serbs; both King Lazar and Sultan Murad perished in the battle. Kosovo became a battlefield long revered and remembered by the Serbs. Not until 1480 were Bosnia, Albania, and the rest of Serbia added to the Ottoman Empire in the Balkans.

In the meantime, in 1453, the Ottomans completed the demise of the Byzantine Empire. With 80,000 troops ranged against only 7,000 defenders, Sultan Mehmet II (meh-MET) laid siege to Constantinople. In their attack on the city, the Turks made use of massive cannons with 26-foot barrels that could launch stone balls weighing up to 1,200 pounds each. Finally, the walls were breached; the Byzantine emperor died in the final battle. Mehmet II, standing before the palace of the emperor, paused to reflect on the passing nature of human glory.

After their conquest of Constantinople, the Ottoman Turks tried to complete their conquest of the Balkans, where they had been established since the fourteenth century. Although they were successful in taking the Romanian territory of Wallachia (wah-LAY-kee-uh) in 1476, the resistance of the Hungarians

initially kept the Turks from advancing up the Danube valley. Until the end of the fifteenth century, internal problems and the need to consolidate their eastern frontiers kept the Turks from any further attacks on Europe. But at the beginning of the sixteenth century, the Ottomans would renew their offensive against the West, challenging Hungary, Austria, Bohemia, and Poland and threatening to turn the Mediterranean into a Turkish lake.

12-7 The Church in the Renaissance

 FOCUS QUESTIONS: How were the problems of heresy and reform resolved? What were the policies of the Renaissance popes, and what impact did those policies have on the Catholic Church?

As a result of the efforts of the Council of Constance, the Great Schism had finally been brought to an end in 1417 (see Chapter 11). The ending of the schism proved to be the council's easiest task; it was much less successful in dealing with the problems of heresy and reform.

12-7a The Problems of Heresy and Reform

Heresy was not a new problem, and in the thirteenth century, the church had developed inquisitorial machinery to deal with it. But two widespread movements in the fourteenth and early fifteenth centuries—Lollardy and Hussitism—posed new threats to the church.

Wyclif and Lollardy English Lollardy was a product of the Oxford theologian John Wyclif (WIK-lif) (ca. 1328–1384), whose disgust with clerical corruption led him to make a far-ranging attack on papal authority and medieval Christian beliefs and practices. Wyclif alleged that there was no basis in Scripture for papal claims of temporal authority and advocated that the popes be stripped of their authority and their property. Believing that the Bible should be a Christian's sole authority, Wyclif urged that it be made available in the vernacular languages so that every Christian could read it. Rejecting all practices not mentioned in Scripture, Wyclif condemned pilgrimages, the veneration of saints, and a whole series of rituals and rites that had developed in the medieval church. Wyclif attracted a number of followers who came to be known as Lollards.

Hus and the Hussites A marriage between the royal families of England and Bohemia enabled Lollard ideas to spread to Bohemia, where they reinforced the ideas of a group of Czech reformers led by the chancellor of the university at Prague, John Hus (1374–1415). In his call for reform, Hus urged the elimination of the worldliness and corruption of the clergy and attacked the excessive power of the papacy within the Catholic Church. Hus's objections fell on receptive ears, for the Catholic Church, as one of the largest landowners in Bohemia, was already widely criticized. Moreover, many clergymen were German, and the native Czechs' strong resentment of the Germans who dominated Bohemia also contributed to Hus's movement.

The Council of Constance attempted to deal with the growing problem of heresy by summoning John Hus to the council. Granted safe conduct by Emperor Sigismund, Hus went in the hope of a free hearing of his ideas. Instead he was arrested, condemned as a heretic (by a narrow vote), and burned at the stake in 1415. This action turned the unrest in Bohemia into revolutionary upheaval, and the resulting Hussite wars racked the Holy Roman Empire until a truce was arranged in 1436.

Reform of the Church The efforts of the Council of Constance to reform the church were even less successful than its attempt to eradicate heresy. The council passed two reform decrees. *Sacrosancta* (sak-roh-SANK-tuh) stated that a general council of the church received its authority from God; hence, every Christian, including the pope, was subject to its authority. The decree *Frequens* (FREE-kwens) provided for the regular holding of general councils to ensure that church reform would continue. Taken together, *Sacrosancta* and *Frequens* provided for a legislative system within the church superior to the popes.

Decrees alone, however, proved insufficient to reform the church. Councils could issue decrees, but popes had to execute them, and popes would not cooperate with councils that diminished their authority. Beginning as early as Martin V in 1417, successive popes worked steadfastly for thirty years to defeat the conciliar movement. The final blow came in 1460, when Pope Pius II issued the papal bull *Execrabilis* (ek-suh-KRAB-uh-liss), condemning appeals to a council over the head of a pope as heretical.

By the mid-fifteenth century, the popes had reasserted their supremacy over the Catholic Church. No longer, however, did they have any possibility of asserting supremacy over temporal governments as the medieval papacy had. Although the papal monarchy had been maintained, it had lost much moral prestige. In the fifteenth century, the Renaissance papacy contributed to an even further decline in the moral leadership of the popes.

12-7b The Renaissance Papacy

The Renaissance papacy encompasses the line of popes from the end of the Great Schism (1417) to the beginnings of the Reformation in the early sixteenth century. The primary concern of the papacy is governing the Catholic Church as its spiritual leader. But as heads of the church, popes had temporal preoccupations as well, and the story of the Renaissance papacy is really an account of how the latter came to overshadow the popes' spiritual functions.

The manner in which Renaissance popes pursued their interests in the Papal States and Italian politics, especially their use of intrigue and even bloodshed, seemed shocking. Of all the Renaissance popes, Julius II (1503–1513) was most involved in war and politics. The fiery "warrior-pope" personally led armies against his enemies, much to the disgust of pious Christians, who viewed the pope as a spiritual leader. As one intellectual wrote, "How, O bishop standing in the room of the Apostles, dare you teach the people the things that pertain to war?"

To further their territorial aims in the Papal States, the popes needed loyal servants. Because they were not hereditary monarchs, popes could not build dynasties over several generations and came to rely on the practice of **nepotism** to promote their families' interests. Pope Sixtus IV (1471–1484), for example, made five of his nephews cardinals and gave them an abundance of church offices to build up their finances (the word *nepotism* is in fact derived from the Latin *nepos*, meaning "nephew"). Alexander VI (1492–1503), a member of the Borgia family who was known for his debauchery and sensuality, raised one son, one nephew, and the brother of one mistress to the cardinalate. A Venetian envoy stated that Alexander, "joyous by nature, thought of nothing but the aggrandizement of his children." Alexander scandalized the church by encouraging his son Cesare to carve out a state for himself from the territories of the Papal States in central Italy.

The Renaissance popes were great patrons of Renaissance culture, and their efforts made Rome a cultural leader at the beginning of the sixteenth century. For the warrior-pope Julius II, the patronage of Renaissance culture was mostly a matter of policy as he endeavored to add to the splendor of his pontificate by tearing down the Basilica of Saint Peter, which had been built by the emperor Constantine, and beginning construction of the greatest building in Christendom, the present Saint Peter's Basilica.

Julius's successor, Leo X (1513–1521), was also a patron of Renaissance culture, not as a matter of policy but as a deeply involved participant (see Image 12.16). Such might be expected of the son of Lorenzo de' Medici. Made an archbishop at the age of eight and a cardinal at thirteen, he acquired a refined taste in art, manners, and social life among the Florentine Renaissance elite. He became pope at the age of thirty-seven, reportedly remarking to the Venetian ambassador, "Let us enjoy the papacy, since God has given it to us." Raphael was commissioned to do paintings, and the construction of Saint Peter's was accelerated as Rome became the literary and artistic center of the Renaissance.

Scala/Ministero per i Beni e le Attività culturali/Art Resource, NY

IMAGE 12.16 A Renaissance Pope: Leo X. The Renaissance popes allowed secular concerns to overshadow their spiritual duties. Shown here is the Medici pope Leo X. Raphael portrays the pope as a collector of books, looking up after examining an illuminated manuscript with a magnifying glass. At left is the pope's cousin Guilio, a cardinal. Standing behind the pope is Luigi de' Rossi, another relative who had also been made a cardinal.

 Compare this portrait with that of Image 12.14 on p. 364. What are the noticeable similarities and differences, and what do they tell you about the differences between Italian and Northern Renaissance painting?

CHRONOLOGY	The Church in the Renaissance
Council of Constance	1414–1418
Burning of John Hus	1415
End of the Great Schism	1417
Pius II issues the papal bull Execrabilis	1460
The Renaissance papacy	
Sixtus IV	1471–1484
Alexander VI	1492–1503
Julius II	1503–1513
Leo X	1513–1521

CHAPTER SUMMARY

Beginning in Italy, the Renaissance was an era that rediscovered and was influenced by the culture of ancient Greece and Rome. It was also a time of recovery from the difficulties of the fourteenth century as well as a period of transition that witnessed a continuation of the economic, political, and social trends that had begun in the High Middle Ages.

The Renaissance was also a movement in which intellectuals and artists proclaimed a new vision of humankind and raised fundamental questions about the value and importance of the individual. The humanists or intellectuals of the age called their period (from the mid-fourteenth to the mid-sixteenth century)

an age of rebirth, believing that they had restored arts and letters to new glory. Humanism was an intellectual movement based on the study of the classical literary works of Greece and Rome. The goal of a humanist education was to produce individuals of virtue and wisdom. Civic humanism posited that the ideal citizen was not only an intellectual but also an active participant in the life of the state.

The Renaissance is perhaps best known for its artistic brilliance. Renaissance artists in Italy sought not only to persuade onlookers of the reality of the object they were portraying, but also to focus attention on human beings as "the center and

Chapter Summary ◼ 371

measure of all things." This new Renaissance style was developed, above all, in Florence, but at the end of the fifteenth century, Renaissance art moved into a new phase in which Rome became the new cultural center. In the works of Leonardo da Vinci, Raphael, and Michelangelo, the High Renaissance ideal of beauty was convincingly portrayed.

The Renaissance in Europe was also an era of "new monarchies," best seen in England, France, and Spain. Monarchs in these countries limited the private armies of the aristocracy, raised taxes, created professional armies, and in the process were able to reestablish the centralized power of monarchical governments. At the same time, the Renaissance popes

became increasingly mired in political and temporal concerns that overshadowed their spiritual responsibilities.

Of course, the intellectuals and artists of the Renaissance wrote and painted for the upper classes, and the brilliant intellectual, cultural, and artistic accomplishments of the Renaissance were products of and for the elite. The ideas of the Renaissance did not have a broad base among the masses of the people. The Renaissance did, however, raise new questions about medieval traditions. In advocating a return to the early sources of Christianity and criticizing current religious practices, the humanists

raised fundamental issues about the Catholic Church, which was still an important institution. In the sixteenth century, as we shall see in the next chapter, the intellectual renaissance of the fifteenth century gave way to a religious renaissance that touched the lives of people, including the masses, in new and profound ways.

CHAPTER TIMELINE

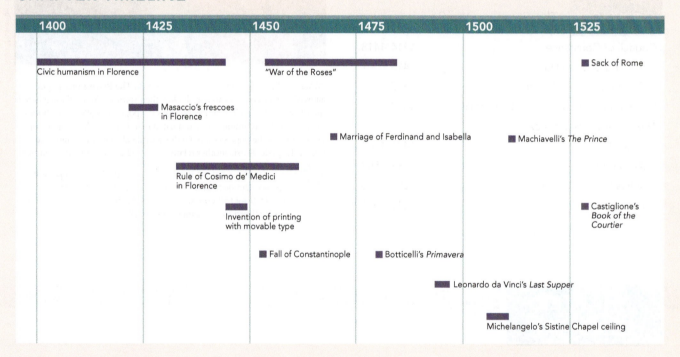

1400	1425	1450	1475	1500	1525

Civic humanism in Florence

"War of the Roses"

Sack of Rome

Masaccio's frescoes in Florence

Marriage of Ferdinand and Isabella

Machiavelli's *The Prince*

Rule of Cosimo de' Medici in Florence

Castiglione's *Book of the Courtier*

Invention of printing with movable type

Fall of Constantinople

Botticelli's *Primavera*

Leonardo da Vinci's *Last Supper*

Michelangelo's Sistine Chapel ceiling

CHAPTER REVIEW

Upon Reflection

Q How did Renaissance art and the humanist movement reflect the political, economic, and social developments of the period?

Q What was the pattern of political development in Renaissance Italy? What new political practices (statecraft) did the Italians contribute to Europe, and how were these new political practices reflected in the work of Machiavelli?

Q What was the relationship between Italian Renaissance humanism and Italian Renaissance art?

Q What impact did the policies of the Renaissance popes have on the Catholic Church?

Key Terms

Renaissance (p. 340)
estates (p. 343)
individualism (p. 352)
secularism (p. 352)
humanism (p. 352)
civic humanism (p. 352)

Neoplatonism (p. 354)
Hermeticism (p. 354)
pantheism (p. 354)
new monarchies (p. 365)
nepotism (p. 370)

Full definitions also appear in the Glossary at the end of the book.

Suggestions for Further Reading

General Works on the Renaissance General works on the Renaissance in Europe include **M. L. King,** *The Renaissance in Europe* (New York, 2005), and **J. Brotton,** *The Renaissance: A Very Short Introduction* (Oxford, 2005). See also **E. S. and T. Y. Cohen,** *Daily Life in Renaissance Italy* (London, 2001); **T. K. Rabb,** *The Last Days of the Renaissance* (New York, 2006); and **Alexander Lee,** *The Ugly Renaissance: Sex, Greed, Violence and Depravity in an Age of Beauty* (New York, 2013).

Family and Marriage On family and marriage, see **C. Klapisch-Zuber,** *Women, Family, and Ritual in Renaissance Italy* (Chicago, 1985). On women, see **M. L. Brown** and **K. B. McBride,** *Women's Roles During the Renaissance* (New York, 2005).

Italian City-States For studies of the Italian city-states, see **J. M. Najemy, ed.,** *Italy in the Age of the Renaissance, 1300–1550* (Oxford, 2004). There is an enormous literature on Renaissance Florence. A good introduction is **J. M. Najemy,** *History of Florence, 1200–1575* (London, 2006). Machiavelli's life can be examined in **R. King,** *Machiavelli: Philosopher of Power* (New York, 2007).

Renaissance Humanism A brief introduction to Renaissance humanism can be found in **C. G. Nauert Jr.,** *Humanism and the Culture of Renaissance Europe,* 2nd ed. (Cambridge, 2006). See also **R. Mackenny,** *Renaissances: The Cultures of Italy, c. 1300–c. 1600* (New York, 2004).

Renaissance Art Good surveys of Renaissance art include **J. T. Paoletti** and **G. M. Radke,** *Art, Power, and Patronage in Renaissance Italy,* 3rd ed. (Upper Saddle River, N.J., 2003); **C. Bucci** and **S. Buricchi,** *Renaissance Art* (New York, 2007); **R. Turner,** *Renaissance Florence: The Invention of a New Art* (New York, 1997); and **P. F. Brown,** *Art and Life in Renaissance Venice* (Upper Saddle River, N.J., 2005).

Political Developments On the political development of Europe in the Renaissance, see **C. Mulgan,** *The Renaissance Monarchies, 1469–1558* (Cambridge, 1998).

The Church in the Renaissance The Renaissance papacy can be examined in **G. Noel,** *The Renaissance Popes* (New York, 2006).

Notes

1. Quoted in J. Burckhardt, *The Civilization of the Renaissance in Italy,* trans. S. G. C. Middlemore (London, 1960), p. 81.
2. Baldassare Castiglione, *The Book of the Courtier,* trans. C. S. Singleton (Garden City, N.Y., 1959), pp. 288–289.
3. Quoted in D. L. Jensen, *Renaissance Europe* (Lexington, Mass., 1981), p. 94.
4. Quoted in I. Origo, "The Domestic Enemy: The Eastern Slaves in Tuscany in the Fourteenth and Fifteenth Centuries," *Speculum* 30 (1955): 333.
5. Quoted in G. Brucker, ed., *Two Memoirs of Renaissance Florence* (New York, 1967), p. 132.
6. Quoted in M. L. King, *Women of the Renaissance* (Chicago, 1991), p. 3.
7. Quoted in G. Brucker, ed., *The Society of Renaissance Florence* (New York, 1971), p. 190.
8. Quoted in A. Lee, *The Ugly Renaissance: Sex, Greed, Violence and Depravity in an Age of Beauty* (New York, 2013), p. 25.
9. Quoted in G. Mattingly, *Renaissance Diplomacy* (Baltimore, 1964), p. 42.
10. Ibid., p. 95.
11. Niccolò Machiavelli, *The Prince,* trans. G. Bull (New York, 1991), pp. 90–91.
12. Ibid., pp. 96, 101.
13. Ibid., p. 60.
14. Petrarch, "Epistle to Posterity," *Letters from Petrarch,* trans. M. Bishop (Bloomington, Ind., 1966), pp. 6–7.
15. Quoted in F. Yates, *Giordano Bruno and the Hermetic Tradition* (Chicago, 1964), p. 211.
16. Giovanni Pico della Mirandola, *Oration on the Dignity of Man,* in E. Cassirer, P. O. Kristeller, and J. H. Randall Jr., eds., *The Renaissance Philosophy of Man* (Chicago, 1948), p. 225.
17. Ibid., pp. 247, 249.
18. Quoted in W. H. Woodward, *Vittorino da Feltre and Other Humanist Educators* (Cambridge, 1897), p. 102.
19. Quoted in I. Origo, *The Light of the Past* (New York, 1959), p. 136.
20. Quoted in M. L. King, *The Renaissance in Europe* (London, 2005), p. 89.

21. Quoted in Elizabeth G. Holt, ed., *A Documentary History of Art* (Garden City, N.Y., 1957), vol. 1, p. 286.
22. Quoted in R. M. Letts, *The Cambridge Introduction to Art: The Renaissance* (Cambridge, 1981), p. 86.
23. Quoted in J. Huizinga, *The Waning of the Middle Ages* (Garden City, N.Y., 1956), p. 265.

MindTap *Tips*   MindTap can help you improve skills that will apply beyond your history course. Writing activities in MindTap give you plenty of opportunities to strengthen these essential skills, and extensive primary source analysis activities will help you enhance critical thinking skills.

CHAPTER 13

Reformation and Religious Warfare in the Sixteenth Century

IMAGE 13.1 **A Nineteenth-Century Engraving Showing Luther Before the Diet of Worms**

CHAPTER OUTLINE AND FOCUS QUESTIONS

13-1 Prelude to Reformation

Q What were the chief ideas of the Christian humanists, and how did they differ from the ideas of the Protestant reformers?

13-2 Martin Luther and the Reformation in Germany

Q What were Martin Luther's main disagreements with the Roman Catholic Church, and what political, economic, and social conditions help explain why the movement he began spread so quickly across Europe?

13-3 The Spread of the Protestant Reformation

Q What were the main tenets of Lutheranism, Zwinglianism, Anabaptism, and Calvinism, and how did they differ from each other and from Catholicism? What impact did political, economic, and social conditions have on the development of these four reform movements? In what ways was the Reformation in England different from these reform movements?

13-4 The Social Impact of the Protestant Reformation

Q What impact did the Protestant Reformation have on the family, education, and popular religious practices in the sixteenth century?

13-5 The Catholic Reformation

Q What measures did the Roman Catholic Church take to reform itself and to combat Protestantism in the sixteenth century?

13-6 Politics and the Wars of Religion in the Sixteenth Century

Q What role did politics, economic and social conditions, and religion play in the European wars of the sixteenth century? What is the significance of Montaigne?

CONNECTIONS TO TODAY

How are the religious controversies of the sixteenth century related to religious and social conditions in the Western world today?

ON APRIL 18, 1521, a lowly monk stood before the emperor and princes of Germany in the city of Worms. He had been called before this august gathering to answer charges of heresy, charges that could threaten his very life. The monk was confronted with a pile of his books and asked if he wished to defend them all or reject a part. Courageously, Martin Luther defended them all and asked to be shown where any part was in error on the basis of "Scripture and plain reason." The emperor was outraged by Luther's response and made his own position clear the next day: "Not only I, but you of this noble German nation, would be forever disgraced if by our negligence not only heresy but the very suspicion of heresy were to survive. After having heard yesterday the obstinate defense of Luther, I regret that I have so long delayed in proceeding against him and his false teaching. I will have no more to do with him."[1] Luther's appearance at Worms set the stage for a serious challenge to the authority of the Catholic Church. This was by no means the first crisis in the church's fifteen-hundred-year history, but its consequences were more far-reaching than anyone at Worms in 1521 could have imagined.

Throughout the Middle Ages, the Christian church had continued to assert its primacy of position. It had overcome defiance of its temporal authority by emperors and kings, and challenges to its doctrines had been crushed by the Inquisition and combated by new religious orders that carried its message of salvation to all the towns and villages of medieval Europe. The growth of the papacy had paralleled the growth of the church, but by the end of the Middle Ages, challenges to papal authority from the rising power of monarchical states had resulted in a loss of papal temporal authority. An even greater threat to papal authority and church unity arose in the sixteenth century when the Reformation shattered the unity of Christendom.

The movement begun by Martin Luther when he made his dramatic stand quickly spread across Europe, a clear indication of dissatisfaction with Catholic practices. Within a short time, new forms of religious practices, doctrines, and organizations, including Zwinglianism, Calvinism, Anabaptism, and Anglicanism, were attracting adherents all over Europe. Although seemingly helpless to stop the new Protestant churches, the Catholic Church also underwent a reformation and managed to revive its fortunes by the mid-sixteenth century. All too soon, the doctrinal divisions between Protestants and Catholics led to a series of religious wars that dominated the history of western Europe in the second half of the sixteenth century.

13-1 Prelude to Reformation

 FOCUS QUESTION: What were the chief ideas of the Christian humanists, and how did they differ from the ideas of the Protestant reformers?

Martin Luther's reform movement was by no means the first. During the second half of the fifteenth century, the new classical learning that was part of Italian Renaissance humanism spread to northern Europe and spawned a movement called **Christian (northern Renaissance) humanism** whose major goal was the reform of Christianity.

13-1a Christian or Northern Renaissance Humanism

Like their Italian counterparts, northern humanists cultivated knowledge of the classics, the bond that united all humanists into a kind of international fellowship. In returning to the writings of antiquity, northern humanists (also called Christian humanists because of their profound preoccupation with religion) focused on the sources of early Christianity, the Holy Scriptures and the writings of such church fathers as Augustine, Ambrose, and Jerome. In these early Christian writings, they discovered a simple religion that they came to feel had been distorted by the complicated theological arguments of the Middle Ages.

The most important characteristic of northern humanism was its reform program. Convinced of the ability of human beings to reason and improve themselves, the northern humanists felt that through education in the sources of classical, and especially Christian, antiquity, they could instill a true inner piety or an inward religious feeling that would bring about a reform of the church and society. For this reason, Christian humanists supported schools, brought out new editions of the classics, and prepared new editions of the Bible and writings of the church fathers. In the preface to his edition of the Greek New Testament, the famous humanist Erasmus wrote:

> I disagree very much with those who are unwilling that Holy Scripture, translated into the vulgar tongue, be read by the uneducated, as if Christ taught such intricate doctrines that they could scarcely be understood by very few theologians, or as if the strength of the Christian religion consisted in men's ignorance of it. . . . I would that even the lowliest women read the Gospels and the Pauline Epistles. And I would that they were translated into all languages so that they could be read and understood not only by Scots and Irish but also by Turks and Saracens. . . . Would that, as a result, the farmer sing some portion of them at the plow, the weaver hum some parts of them to the movement of his shuttle, the traveler lighten the weariness of the journey with stories of this kind![2]

This belief in the power of education would remain an important characteristic of European civilization. Like later intellectuals, Christian humanists believed that to change society, they must first change the human beings who compose it. Although some critics have called the Christian humanists naive, they were in fact merely optimistic. The turmoil of the Reformation, however, shattered much of this intellectual optimism, as the lives and careers of two of the most prominent Christian humanists, Desiderius Erasmus and Thomas More, illustrate.

Erasmus The most influential of all the Christian humanists was Desiderius Erasmus (dez-ih-DEER-ee-uss ih-RAZZ-mus) (1466–1536), who formulated and popularized the reform program of Christian humanism. Born in Holland, Erasmus was educated at one of the schools of the Brothers of the Common Life (see Chapter 11). He wandered to France, England, Italy, Germany, and Switzerland, conversing everywhere in the classical Latin that might be called his mother tongue (see Image 13.2). Erasmus was a strong believer in the value of classical antiquity but sought a synthesis between the pagan literature of antiquity and Christian civilization. He saw the classics as preparation for the Christian Gospel. In one of his dialogues, he had a character say, "Saint Socrates, pray for me."

The *Handbook of the Christian Knight*, printed in 1503, reflected his preoccupation with religion. He called his conception of religion "the philosophy of Christ," by which he meant that Christianity should be a guiding philosophy for the direction of daily life rather than the system of dogmatic beliefs and practices that the medieval church seemed to stress. In other words, he emphasized inner piety and de-emphasized the external forms

IMAGE 13.2 **Erasmus.** Desiderius Erasmus was the most influential of the northern Renaissance humanists. He sought to restore Christianity to the early simplicity found in the teachings of Jesus. This portrait of Erasmus was painted in 1523 by Hans Holbein the Younger, who had formed a friendship with the great humanist while they were both in Basel.

of religion (such as the sacraments, pilgrimages, fasts, veneration of saints, and relics). To return to the simplicity of the early church, people needed to understand the original meaning of the Scriptures and the writings of the early church fathers. Because Erasmus thought that the standard Latin edition of the Bible, known as the Vulgate, contained errors, he edited the Greek text of the New Testament from the earliest available manuscripts and published it, along with a new Latin translation, in 1516. Erasmus also wrote *Annotations*, a detailed commentary on the Vulgate Bible itself. In his day, Erasmus's work on the New Testament was considered his most outstanding achievement, and Martin Luther himself would use Erasmus's work as the basis for his German translation of the New Testament.

To Erasmus, the reform of the church meant spreading an understanding of the philosophy of Jesus, providing enlightened education in the sources of early Christianity, and making common-sense criticisms of the abuses in the church. This last is especially evident in *The Praise of Folly*, written in 1509, in which Erasmus engaged in humorous yet effective criticism of the most corrupt practices of his own society. He was especially harsh on the abuses within the ranks of the clergy (see Historical Voices, "Erasmus: In Praise of Folly," p. 378).

In another satirical work, *Julius Excluded from Heaven*, Erasmus pilloried the Renaissance papacy in the person of Julius II, the "warrior pope" (see Chapter 12). When Julius dies, he appears before the gates of heaven, expecting a quick entry. When St. Peter denies him entrance because of Julius' misdeeds, Julius threatens to raise an army and storm heaven itself.

Erasmus's program did not achieve the reform of the church that he so desired. His moderation and his emphasis on education were quickly overwhelmed by the passions of the Reformation. Undoubtedly, though, his work helped prepare the way for the Reformation; as contemporaries proclaimed, "Erasmus laid the egg that Luther hatched." Yet Erasmus eventually disapproved of Luther and the Protestant reformers. He had no intention of destroying the unity of the medieval Christian church; rather, his whole program was based on reform within the church. But was Erasmus influential in a later age, as one scholar has recently argued? Did his emphasis on education, tolerance, and the use of reason by humans to improve themselves have an impact on the Enlightenment thinkers of the eighteenth century (see Chapter 17)?

Thomas More The son of a London lawyer, Thomas More (1478–1535) received the benefits of a good education. Although trained in the law, he took an avid interest in the new classical learning and became proficient in both Latin and Greek. Like the Italian humanists, who believed in putting their learning at the service of the state, More embarked on a public career that ultimately took him to the highest reaches of power as lord chancellor of England.

His career in government service, however, did not keep More from the intellectual and spiritual interests that were so dear to him. He was well acquainted with other English humanists and became an intimate friend of Erasmus. He made translations from Greek authors and wrote both prose and poetry in Latin. A devout man, he spent many hours in prayer and private devotions. Contemporaries praised his household as a shining model of Christian family life.

More's most famous work, and one of the most controversial of his age, was *Utopia*, written in 1516. This literary masterpiece is an account of the idealistic life and institutions of the community of Utopia (Greek for "nowhere"), an imaginary island in the vicinity of the recently discovered New World. It reflects More's own concerns with the economic, social, and political problems of his day. He presented a new social system in which cooperation and reason replaced power and fame as the proper motivating agents for human society. Utopian society, therefore, was based on communal ownership rather than private property. All residents of Utopia worked nine hours a day, regardless of occupation, and were rewarded according to their needs. Possessing abundant leisure time and relieved of competition and greed, Utopians were free to lead wholesome and enriching lives.

In serving King Henry VIII, More came face to face with the abuses and corruption he had criticized in *Utopia*. But he did not allow idealism to outweigh his own ultimate realism, and in *Utopia* itself he justified his service to the king:

> If you can't completely eradicate wrong ideas, or deal with
> inveterate vices as effectively as you could wish, that's no
> reason for turning your back on public life altogether. . . . On
> the other hand, it's no use attempting to put across entirely

Erasmus: In Praise of Folly

Q *What are Erasmus's main criticisms of monks? What do you think he hoped to achieve by this satirical attack on monastic practices? How do you think the circulation of many printed copies of such attacks would have affected popular attitudes toward the Catholic Church?*

THE PRAISE OF FOLLY is one of the most famous pieces of literature produced in the sixteenth century. Erasmus, who wrote it in a short time during a visit to the home of Thomas More, considered it a "little diversion" from his "serious work." Yet both contemporaries and later generations have appreciated "this laughing parody of every form and rank of human life." In this selection, Erasmus belittles one of his favorite objects of scorn, the monks. They were, however, merely one of the many groups he disparaged.

Erasmus, *The Praise of Folly*

Those who are the closest to these [the theologians] in happiness are generally called "the religious" or "monks," both of which are deceiving names, since for the most part they stay as far away from religion as possible and frequent every sort of place. I [Folly] cannot, however, see how any life could be more gloomy than the life of these monks if I did not assist them in many ways. Though most people detest these men so much that accidentally meeting one is considered to be bad luck, the monks themselves believe that they are magnificent creatures. One of their chief beliefs is that to be illiterate is to be of a high state of sanctity, and so they make sure that they are not able to read. Another is that when braying out their gospels in church they are making themselves very

pleasing and satisfying to God, when in fact they are uttering these psalms as a matter of repetition rather than from their hearts. . . .

Moreover, it is amusing to find that they insist that everything be done in fastidious detail, as if employing the orderliness of mathematics, a small mistake in which would be a great crime. Just so many knots must be on each shoe and the shoelace may be of only one specified color; just so much lace is allowed on each habit; the girdle must be of just the right material and width; the hood of a certain shape and capacity; their hair of just so many fingers' length; and finally they can sleep only the specified number of hours per day. Can they not understand that, because of a variety of bodies and temperaments, all this equality of restrictions is in fact very unequal? Nevertheless, because of all this detail that they employ they think that they are superior to all other people. And what is more, amid all their pretense of Apostolic charity, the members of one order will denounce the members of another order clamorously because of the way in which the habit has been belted or the slightly darker color of it. . . .

Many of them work so hard at protocol and at traditional fastidiousness that they think one heaven hardly a suitable reward for their labors; never recalling, however, that the time will come when Christ will demand a reckoning of that which he had prescribed, namely charity, and that he will hold their deeds of little account. One monk will then exhibit his belly filled with every kind of fish; another will profess a knowledge of over a hundred hymns. Still another will reveal a countless number of fasts that he has made, and will account for his large belly by explaining that his fasts have always been broken by a single large meal. Another will show a list of church ceremonies over which he has officiated so large that it would fill seven ships.

Source: Erasmus, "The Praise of Folly," in *The Essential Erasmus*, trans. J. P. Dolan (New York: Dutton Signet, 1964).

---

new ideas, which will obviously carry no weight with people who are prejudiced against them. You must go to work indirectly. You must handle everything as tactfully as you can, and what you can't put right you must try to make as little wrong as possible. For things will never be perfect, until human beings are perfect—which I don't expect them to be for quite a number of years.[3]

More's religious devotion and belief in the universal Catholic Church ultimately proved even more important than his service to the king, however. While in office, More's intolerance of heresy led him to advocate persecution of those who would fundamentally change the Catholic Church. Moreover, always the man of conscience, More willingly gave up his life opposing England's break with the Roman Catholic Church over the divorce of King Henry VIII.

13-1b Church and Religion on the Eve of the Reformation

Corruption in the Catholic Church was another factor that spurred people to want reform. No doubt the failure of the Renaissance popes to provide spiritual leadership had affected the spiritual life of all Christendom. The papal court's preoccupation with finances had an especially strong impact on the clergy. So did the economic changes of the fourteenth and fifteenth centuries. Increasingly, nobles or wealthy members of the bourgeoisie held the highest positions among the clergy. Moreover, to increase their revenues, high church officials (bishops, archbishops, and cardinals) took over more than one church office. This so-called **pluralism** led in turn to absenteeism: church officeholders ignored their duties and hired underlings who sometimes lacked the proper qualifications.

Complaints about the ignorance and ineptness of parish priests became widespread in the fifteenth century.

The Search for Salvation While many of the leaders of the church were failing to meet their responsibilities, ordinary people were clamoring for meaningful religious expression and certainty of salvation. As a result, for some the salvation process became almost mechanical. As more and more people sought certainty of salvation through veneration of relics, collections of such objects grew. Frederick the Wise, elector of Saxony and Martin Luther's prince, had amassed more than 19,000 relics to which were attached indulgences that could reduce one's time in purgatory by nearly 2 million years. (An indulgence, you will recall, is a remission, after death, of all or part of the punishment for sin.) Other people sought certainty of salvation in the popular mystical movement known as the Modern Devotion, which downplayed religious dogma and stressed the need to follow the teachings of Jesus. Thomas à Kempis, author of *The Imitation of Christ*, wrote that "truly, at the day of judgment we shall not be examined by what we have read, but what we have done; not how well we have spoken, but how religiously we have lived."

What is striking about the revival of religious piety in the fifteenth century—whether expressed through such external forces as the veneration of relics and the buying of indulgences or the mystical path—was its adherence to the orthodox beliefs and practices of the Catholic Church. The agitation for certainty of salvation and spiritual peace occurred within the framework of the "holy mother Church." But disillusionment grew as the devout experienced the clergy's inability to live up to their expectations. The deepening of religious life, especially in the second half of the fifteenth century, found little echo among the worldly-wise clergy, and this environment helps explain the tremendous and immediate impact of Luther's ideas.

Calls for Reform At the same time, several sources of reform were already at work within the Catholic Church at the end of the fifteenth and the beginning of the sixteenth century. Especially noticeable were the calls for reform from the religious orders of the Franciscans, Dominicans, and Augustinians. Members of these groups put particular emphasis on preaching to laypeople. One of the popular preachers was Johannes Geiler of Kaisersberg (KY-zerz-bayrk), who denounced the corruption of the clergy.

The Oratory of Divine Love, first organized in Italy in 1497, was not a religious order but an informal group of clergy and laymen who worked to foster reform by emphasizing personal spiritual development and outward acts of charity. The "philosophy of Christ," advocated by the Christian humanist Erasmus, was especially appealing to many of them. The Oratory's members included a number of cardinals who favored church reform. A Spanish archbishop, Cardinal Ximenes, was especially active in using Christian humanism to reform the church. To foster spirituality among the people, he had a number of religious writings, including Thomas à Kempis's *The Imitation of Christ*, translated into Spanish.

13-2 Martin Luther and the Reformation in Germany

 FOCUS QUESTION: What were Martin Luther's main disagreements with the Roman Catholic Church, and what political, economic, and social conditions help explain why the movement he began spread so quickly across Europe?

The Protestant Reformation began with a typical medieval question: What must I do to be saved? Martin Luther, a deeply religious man, found an answer that did not fit within the traditional teachings of the late medieval church. Ultimately, he split with that church, destroying the religious unity of western Christendom. That other people were concerned with the same question is evident in the rapid spread of the Reformation. But religion was so entangled in the social, economic, and political forces of the period that the Protestant reformers' hope of transforming the church quickly proved illusory.

13-2a The Early Luther

Martin Luther was born in Germany on November 10, 1483. His father wanted him to become a lawyer, so Luther enrolled at the University of Erfurt, where he received his bachelor's degree in 1502. Three years later, after becoming a master in the liberal arts, the young man began to study law. But Luther was not content, not in small part due to his long-standing religious inclinations. That summer, while returning to Erfurt after a brief visit home, he was caught in a ferocious thunderstorm and vowed that if he survived unscathed, he would become a monk. He then entered the monastic order of the Augustinian Hermits in Erfurt, much to his father's disgust. In the monastery, Luther focused on his major concern, the assurance of salvation. The traditional beliefs and practices of the church seemed unable to relieve his obsession with this question, especially evident in his struggle with the sacrament of penance or **confession**. The sacraments were a Catholic's chief means of receiving God's grace; confession offered the opportunity to have one's sins forgiven. Luther spent hours confessing his sins, but he was always doubtful. Had he remembered all of his sins? Even more, how could a hopeless sinner be acceptable to a totally just and all-powerful God? Luther threw himself into his monastic routine with a vengeance:

> I was indeed a good monk and kept my order so strictly that I could say that if ever a monk could get to heaven through monastic discipline, I was that monk. . . . And yet my conscience would not give me certainty, but I always doubted and said, "You didn't do that right. You weren't contrite enough. You left that out of your confession." The more I tried to remedy an uncertain, weak and troubled conscience with human traditions, the more I daily found it more uncertain, weaker and more troubled.[4]

Despite his strenuous efforts, Luther achieved no certainty.

To help overcome his difficulties, his superiors recommended that the monk study theology. He received his doctorate in 1512 and then became a professor in the theological faculty at the University of Wittenberg (VIT-ten-bayrk), lecturing on the Bible. Sometime between 1513 and 1516, through his study of the Bible, he arrived at an answer to his problem.

Catholic doctrine had emphasized that both faith and good works were required for a Christian to achieve personal salvation. In Luther's eyes, human beings, weak and powerless in the sight of an almighty God, could never do enough good works to merit salvation. Through his study of the Bible, especially his work on Paul's Epistle to the Romans, Luther rediscovered another way of viewing this problem. To Luther, humans are saved not through their good works but through faith in the promises of God, made possible by the sacrifice of Jesus on the cross. The doctrine of salvation or justification by grace through faith alone became the primary doctrine of the Protestant Reformation (**justification** is the act by which a person is made deserving of salvation). Because Luther had arrived at this doctrine from his study of the Bible, the Bible became for Luther, as for all other Protestants, the chief guide to religious truth. Justification by faith and the Bible as the sole authority in religious affairs were the twin pillars of the Protestant Reformation.

The Indulgence Controversy Luther did not see himself as either a revolutionary innovator or a heretic, but his involvement in the indulgence controversy propelled him into an open confrontation with church officials and forced him to see the theological implications of justification by faith alone. In 1517, Pope Leo X had issued a special jubilee indulgence to finance the ongoing construction of Saint Peter's Basilica in Rome. Johann Tetzel, a rambunctious Dominican, hawked the indulgences in Germany with the slogan "As soon as the coin in the coffer rings, the soul from purgatory springs."

Greatly distressed by the sale of indulgences, Luther was certain that people who relied on these pieces of paper to assure themselves of salvation were guaranteeing their eternal damnation instead. Angered, he issued his Ninety-Five Theses, although scholars are unsure whether he nailed them to a church door in Wittenberg, as is traditionally alleged, or mailed them to his ecclesiastical superior. In either case, his theses were a stunning indictment of the abuses in the sale of indulgences (see Historical Voices, "Luther and the Ninety-Five Theses," p. 381). It is doubtful that Luther intended any break with the church over the issue of indulgences. If the pope had clarified the use of indulgences, as Luther wished, he would probably have been satisfied, and the controversy would have ended. But Pope Leo X did not take the issue seriously and is even reported to have said that Luther was simply "some drunken German who will amend his ways when he sobers up." Thousands of copies of a German translation of the Ninety-Five Theses were quickly printed and were received sympathetically in a Germany that had a long tradition of dissatisfaction with papal policies and power.

Of course, Luther was not the first theologian to criticize the powers of the papacy. As we saw in Chapter 12, John Wyclif at the end of the fourteenth century and John Hus at the beginning of the fifteenth century had attacked the excessive power of the papacy. Luther was certainly well aware of John Hus's fate at the Council of Constance, where he was burned at the stake on charges of heresy.

The Quickening Rebellion The controversy reached an important turning point with the Leipzig Debate in July 1519. In Leipzig, Luther's opponent, the capable Catholic theologian Johann Eck, forced Luther to move beyond indulgences and deny the authority of popes and councils. During the debate, Eck also identified Luther's ideas with those of John Hus, the condemned heretic. Luther was now compelled to see the consequences of his new theology. At the beginning of 1520, he proclaimed: "Farewell, unhappy, hopeless, blasphemous Rome! The Wrath of God has come upon you, as you deserve. We have cared for Babylon, and she is not healed: let us then, leave her, that she may be the habitation of dragons, spectres, and witches."[5] At the same time, Luther was convinced that he was doing God's work and had to proceed regardless of the consequences.

In three pamphlets published in 1520, Luther moved toward a more definite break with the Catholic Church. The *Address to the Nobility of the German Nation* was a political tract written in German in which Luther called on the German princes to overthrow the papacy in Germany and establish a reformed German church. The *Babylonian Captivity of the Church*, written in Latin for theologians, attacked the sacramental system as the means by which the pope and church had held the real meaning of the Gospel captive for a thousand years. Luther called for the reform of monasticism and for the clergy to marry. Though virginity is good, he argued, marriage is better, and freedom of choice is best. *On the Freedom of a Christian Man* was a short treatise on the doctrine of salvation. It is faith alone, not good works, that justifies, frees, and brings salvation through Jesus. Being saved and freed by his faith in Jesus, however, does not free the Christian from doing good works. Rather, he performs good works out of gratitude to God. "Good works do not make a good man, but a good man does good works."[6]

Unable to accept Luther's forcefully worded dissent from traditional Catholic teachings, the church excommunicated him in January 1521. He was also summoned to appear before the Reichstag (RYKHSS-tahk), the imperial diet of the Holy Roman Empire, in Worms (WURMZ *or* VORMPS), convened by the recently elected Emperor Charles V (1519–1556). Expected to recant the heretical doctrines he had espoused, Luther refused and made the famous reply that became the battle cry of the Reformation:

> Since then Your Majesty and your lordships desire a simple reply, I will answer without horns and without teeth. Unless I am convicted by Scripture and plain reason—I do not accept the authority of popes and councils, for they have contradicted each other—my conscience is captive to the Word of God. I cannot and I will not recant anything, for to go against conscience is neither right nor safe. Here I stand, I cannot do otherwise. God help me. Amen.[7]

Emperor Charles was outraged at Luther's audacity and gave his opinion that "a single friar who goes counter to all Christianity for a thousand years must be wrong." By the Edict of Worms, Martin Luther was made an outlaw within the empire. His works were to be burned, and Luther himself was to be captured and delivered to the emperor. Instead, Luther's prince, the Elector of Saxony, sent him into hiding at the Wartburg (VART-bayrk) Castle, where he remained for nearly a year (see Movies & History, *Luther*, p. 381).

Luther and the Ninety-Five Theses

Q *What were the major ideas of Luther's Ninety-Five Theses? Why did they have such a strong appeal in Germany?*

TO MOST HISTORIANS, the publication of Luther's Ninety-Five Theses marks the beginning of the Reformation. To Luther, they were simply a response to what he considered Johann Tetzel's blatant abuses in selling indulgences. Although written in Latin, Luther's statements were soon translated into German and disseminated widely across Germany. They made an immense impression on Germans already dissatisfied with the ecclesiastical and financial policies of the papacy.

Martin Luther, Selections from the Ninety-Five Theses

5. The Pope has neither the will nor the power to remit any penalties, except those which he has imposed by his own authority, or by that of the canons [canon law].

20. Therefore the Pope, when he speaks of the plenary remission of all penalties, does not mean simply of all, but only of those imposed by himself.

21. Thus those preachers of indulgences are in error who say that, by the indulgences of the Pope, a man is loosed and saved from all punishment.

27. They preach man [It is mere human talk], who say that the soul flies out of purgatory as soon as the money thrown into the chest rattles.

28. It is certain, that, when the money rattles in the chest, avarice and gain may be increased, but the suffrage of the Church depends on the will of God alone.

50. Christians should be taught, that, if the Pope were acquainted with the exactions of the preachers of pardons, he would prefer that the Basilica of St. Peter should be burnt to ashes, than that it should be built up with the skin, flesh, and bones of his sheep.

81. This license in the preaching of pardons makes it no easy thing, even for learned men, to protect the reverence due to the Pope against the calumnies, or, at all events, the keen questionings, of the laity;

82. As, for instance: Why does not the Pope empty purgatory for the sake of most holy charity and of the supreme necessity of souls,—this being the most just of all reasons,—if he redeems an infinite number of souls for the sake of that most fatal thing, money, to be spent on building a basilica—this being a slight reason?

86. Again: Why does not the Pope, whose riches are at this day more ample than those of the wealthiest of the wealthy, build the one Basilica of St. Peter with his own money, rather than with that of poor believers?

90. To repress these scruples and arguments of the laity by force alone, and not to solve them by giving reasons, is to expose the Church and the Pope to the ridicule of their enemies, and to make Christian men unhappy.

94. Christians should be exhorted to strive to follow Christ their head through pains, deaths, and hells;

95. And thus trust to enter heaven through many tribulations, rather than in the security of peace.

Source: P. Schaff, *History of the Christian Church*, vol. VI (New York: Charles Scribner's Sons, 1916), pp. 161–166.

MOVIES & HISTORY
Luther (2003)

Photo 12/Alamy Stock Photo

Watch *Luther*, which depicts the early life and career of Martin Luther, largely from a Lutheran point of view. The movie focuses on some of the major events in Luther's early life, such as his years in a monastery, his study for a doctorate in theology at the University of Wittenberg, the writing of his Ninety-Five Theses, and his dramatic stand at the Diet of Worms. The movie is based more on legends about Luther than on a strict adherence to the historical facts.

Q *What historical errors can you find in this portrayal of Luther's career? Does the film reveal what made Luther a rebel? Why or why not?*

13-2b The Rise of Lutheranism

At the beginning of 1522, Luther returned to Wittenberg in Electoral Saxony and began to organize a reformed church. While at the Wartburg Castle, Luther's foremost achievement was his translation of the New Testament into German. Within twelve years, his German New Testament had sold almost 200,000 copies. Lutheranism had wide appeal and spread rapidly, but not primarily through the written word since only 4 to 5 percent of people in Germany were literate. And most of these were in urban areas.

Instead, the primary means of disseminating Luther's ideas was the sermon. The preaching of evangelical sermons, based on a return to the original message of the Bible, found favor throughout Germany. In city after city, the arrival of preachers presenting Luther's teachings was soon followed by a public debate in which the new preachers proved victorious. State authorities then instituted a reform of the church.

Also useful to the spread of the Reformation were pamphlets illustrated with vivid woodcuts portraying the pope as a hideous Antichrist and titled with catchy phrases such as "I Wonder Why There Is No Money in the Land" (which, of course, was an attack on papal greed) (see Image 13.3). Luther also insisted on the use of music as a means to teach the Gospel, and his own composition, "A Mighty Fortress Is Our God," became the battle hymn of the Reformation:

With our power nothing is done.
  We are soon lost.
But for us fights the mighty one
  Whom God himself has chosen.
You ask, who is this?
He is called Jesus Christ
The Lord God of hosts.
And there is no other God.
He must hold the field forever.[8]

The Spread of Luther's Ideas Lutheranism spread to both princely and ecclesiastical states in northern and central Germany as well as to two-thirds of the free imperial cities, especially those of southern Germany, where prosperous burghers, for both religious and secular reasons, became committed to Luther's cause. Nuremberg, where an active city council led by the dynamic city secretary Lazarus Spengler (SCHPEN-ler) brought about a conversion as early as 1525, was the first imperial city to convert to Lutheranism. Luther had visited the city in 1518 and made a number of friends and supporters

there, including some prominent men. Albrecht Dürer, the artist (see Chapter 12) said, "In my opinion, it is exactly here that Luther has helped to clarify the situation by making it a point to trust God more than oneself, worldly works, and the laws of human beings."[9] At its outset, the Reformation in Germany was largely an urban phenomenon. Three-fourths of the early converts to the reform movement were from the clergy, many of them from the upper classes, which made it easier for them to work with the ruling elites in the cities.

A series of crises in the mid-1520s made it apparent, however, that spreading the word of God was not as easy as Luther had originally envisioned—the usual plight of most reformers. Luther experienced dissent within his own ranks in Wittenberg from people such as Andreas Carlstadt (KARL-shtaht), who wished to initiate a more radical reform by abolishing all relics, images, and the Mass. Luther had no sooner dealt with them than he began to face opposition from the Christian humanists. Many had initially supported Luther, believing that he shared their goal of reforming the abuses within the church. But when it became apparent that Luther's movement threatened the unity of Christendom, the older generation of Christian humanists, including Erasmus, broke with the reformer. In a letter to Luther, Erasmus wrote, "I do not concede that your passion for the purity of the gospel is more sincere than my own," but "I see many desperate and disloyal men taking advantage of the present situation. I see humane letters and good learning tumbling into ruin. I see old friendships broken, and I fear a bloody conflict is about to break out."[10]

Scala/Art Resource, NY

IMAGE 13.3 **Woodcut: Luther versus the Pope.** In the 1520s, after Luther's return to Wittenberg, his teachings began to spread rapidly, ending ultimately in a reform movement supported by state authorities. Pamphlets containing picturesque woodcuts were important in the spread of Luther's ideas. In the woodcut shown here, the crucified Jesus attends Luther's service on the left, while on the right the pope is at a table selling indulgences.

Q *As seen in this image, how did woodcuts serve to spread Luther's ideas?*

Luther and the "Robbing and Murdering Hordes of Peasants"

 What does this passage tell you about the political interests and sympathies of key religious reformers like Luther? Were the reformers really interested in bringing about massive social changes to accompany their religious innovations?

THE PEASANTS' WAR OF 1524–1525 encompassed a series of uprisings by German peasants who were suffering from economic changes they did not comprehend. Led by radical religious leaders, the revolts quickly became entangled with the religious revolt set in motion by Luther's defiance of the church. But it was soon clear that Luther himself did not believe in any way in social revolution. This excerpt is taken from Luther's pamphlet written in May 1525 at the height of the peasants' power but not published until after their defeat.

Martin Luther, *Against the Robbing and Murdering Hordes of Peasants*

The peasants have taken on themselves the burden of three terrible sins against God and man, by which they have abundantly merited death in body and soul. In the first place they have sworn to be true and faithful, submissive and obedient, to their rulers, as Christ commands, when he says, "Render unto Caesar the things that are Caesar's," and in Romans XIII, "Let everyone be subject unto the higher powers." Because they are breaking this obedience, and are setting themselves against the higher powers, willfully and with violence, they have forfeited body and soul, as faithless, perjured, lying, disobedient knaves and scoundrels are wont to do. . . .

In the second place, they are starting a rebellion, and violently robbing and plundering monasteries and castles which are not theirs, by which they have a second time deserved death in body and soul, if only as highwaymen and murderers. . . . For rebellion is not simple murder, but is like a great fire, which attacks and lays waste a whole land. . . . Therefore, let everyone who can, smite, slay and stab, secretly or openly, remembering that nothing can be more poisonous, hurtful or devilish than a rebel. . . .

In the third place, they cloak this terrible and horrible sin with the Gospel, call themselves "Christian brothers," receive oaths and homage, and compel people to hold with them to these abominations. Thus, they become the greatest of all blasphemers of God and slanderers of his holy Name, serving the devil, under the outward appearance of the Gospel, thus earning death in body and soul ten times over. . . . It does not help the peasants, when they pretend that, according to Genesis I and II, all things were created free and common, and that all of us alike have been baptized. . . . For baptism does not make men free in body and property, but in soul; and the Gospel does not make goods common. . . . Since the peasants, then, have brought both God and man down upon them and are already so many times guilty of death in body and soul . . . I must instruct the worldly governors how they are to act in the matter with a clear conscience.

First, I will not oppose a ruler who, even though he does not tolerate the Gospel, will smite and punish these peasants without offering to submit the case to judgment. For he is within his rights, since the peasants are not contending any longer for the Gospel, but have become faithless, perjured, disobedient, rebellious murderers, robbers and blasphemers, whom even heathen rulers have the right and power to punish; nay, it is their duty to punish them, for it is just for this purpose that they bear the sword, and are "the ministers of God upon him that doeth evil."

Source: E. G. Rupp and B. Drewery, *Martin Luther: Documents of Modern History* (London: Palgrave Macmillan, 1970).

A younger generation of Christian humanists, however, played a significant role in Lutheranism. When Philip Melanchthon (muh-LANK-tun) (1497–1560) arrived in Wittenberg in 1518 at the age of twenty-one to teach Greek and Hebrew, he was immediately attracted to Luther's ideas and became a staunch supporter.

The Peasants' War Luther's greatest challenge in the mid-1520s, however, came from the Peasants' War. Peasant dissatisfaction in Germany stemmed from several sources. Many peasants had not been touched by the gradual economic improvement of the early sixteenth century. In some areas, especially southwestern Germany, influential local lords continued to abuse their peasants, and new demands for taxes and other services caused them to wish for a return to "the good old days." Social discontent soon became entangled with religious revolt as peasants looked to Martin Luther, believing that he would support them. It was not Luther, however, but one of his ex-followers, the radical Thomas Müntzer (MOON-tsur), himself a pastor, who inflamed the peasants against their rulers with his fiery language: "Strike while the iron is hot!" Revolt first erupted in southwestern Germany in June 1524 and spread northward and eastward.

Luther reacted quickly and vehemently against the peasants. In his pamphlet *Against the Robbing and Murdering Hordes of Peasants*, he called on the German princes to "smite, slay and stab" the stupid and stubborn peasantry (see Historical Voices, "Luther and the 'Robbing and Murdering Hordes of Peasants,'" above).

CHRONOLOGY	Luther's Reform Movement	
Ninety-Five Theses		1517
Leipzig Debate		1519
Diet and Edict of Worms		1521
Peasants' War		1524–1525

Luther, who knew how much his reformation of the church depended on the full support of the German princes and magistrates, supported the rulers, although he also blamed them for helping to set off the rebellion by their earlier harsh treatment of the peasants. To Luther, the state and its rulers were ordained by God and given the authority to maintain the peace and order necessary for the spread of the Gospel. It was the duty of princes to put down all revolts. By May 1525, the German princes had ruthlessly suppressed the peasant hordes. By this time, Luther found himself ever more dependent on state authorities for the growth and maintenance of his reformed church.

13-2c Organizing the Church

Justification by faith alone was the starting point for most of Protestantism's major doctrines. Since Luther downplayed the role of good works in salvation, the sacraments also had to be redefined. No longer regarded as merit-earning works, they were now viewed as divinely established signs signifying the promise of salvation. Based on his interpretation of scriptural authority, Luther kept only two of the Catholic Church's seven sacraments—baptism and the Lord's Supper. Baptism signified rebirth through grace. Regarding the Lord's Supper, Luther denied the Catholic doctrine of **transubstantiation**, which taught that the substance of the bread and wine consumed in the rite is miraculously transformed into the body and blood of Jesus. Yet he continued to insist on the real presence of Jesus's body and blood in the bread and wine given as a testament to God's forgiveness of sin.

Luther's emphasis on the importance of Scripture led him to reject the Catholic belief that the authority of Scripture must be supplemented by the traditions and decrees of the church. The word of God as revealed in the Bible was sufficient authority in religious affairs. A hierarchical priesthood was thus unnecessary since all Christians who followed the word of God were their own priests, constituting a "priesthood of all believers." Even though Luther thus considered the true church to be an invisible entity, the difficulties of actually establishing a reformed church led him to believe that a tangible, organized church was needed. Since the Catholic ecclesiastical hierarchy had been scrapped, Luther came to rely increasingly on the princes or state authorities to organize and guide the new Lutheran reformed churches. He had little choice. Secular authorities in Germany, as elsewhere, were soon playing an important role in church affairs. By 1530, in the German states that had converted to Lutheranism, both princes and city councils appointed officials who visited churches in their territories and regulated matters of worship. The Lutheran churches in Germany (and later in Scandinavia) quickly became territorial or state churches in which the state supervised and disciplined church members.

As part of the development of these state-dominated churches, Luther also instituted new religious services to replace the Mass. These featured a worship service consisting of a vernacular liturgy that focused on Bible reading, preaching the word of God, and song. Following his own denunciation of clerical celibacy, Luther married a former nun, Katherina von Bora (kat-uh-REE-nuh fun BOH-rah), in 1525 (see Image 13.4). His union provided a model of married and family life for the new Protestant minister.

IMAGE 13.4 **Martin Luther and Katherina von Bora.** This double portrait of Martin Luther and his wife was done by Lucas Cranach the Elder in 1529. By this time, Luther's reforms had begun to make an impact in many parts of Germany. Luther married Katherina von Bora in 1525, thus creating a new model of family life for Protestant ministers.

 What message was Lucas Cranach the Elder presenting in painting this double portrait?

bpk, Berlin/Kupferstichkabinett, SMB/Jörg P. Anders//Art Resource, NY

13-2d Germany and the Reformation: Religion and Politics

From its very beginning, the fate of Luther's movement was closely tied to political affairs. In 1519, Charles I, king of Spain and grandson of Emperor Maximilian (see Chart 13.1), was elected Holy Roman Emperor as Charles V (see Image 13.5). Charles ruled over an immense empire, consisting of Spain and its overseas possessions, the traditional Austrian Habsburg lands, Bohemia, Hungary, the Low Countries, and the kingdom of Naples in southern Italy (see Map 13.1). The extent of his possessions was reflected in the languages he used. He said once that he spoke Spanish to God, Italian to women, French to men, and German to his horse. Politically, Charles wanted to maintain his dynasty's control over his enormous empire; religiously, he hoped to preserve the unity of the Catholic faith throughout his empire. Despite Charles's strengths, his empire was overextended, and he spent a lifetime in futile pursuit of his goals. Four major problems—the French, the papacy, the Turks, and Germany's internal situation—cost him both his dream and his health. At the same time, the emperor's problems gave Luther's movement time to grow and organize before facing the concerted onslaught of the Catholic forces.

The French and the Papacy Charles V's chief political concern was his rivalry with the Valois king of France, Francis I (r. 1515–1547). Encircled by the possessions of the Habsburg empire, Francis became embroiled in a series of conflicts with Charles over disputed territories in southern France, the Netherlands, the Rhineland, northern Spain, and Italy. These conflicts, known as the Habsburg–Valois Wars, were fought intermittently for twenty-four years (1521–1544), preventing Charles from concentrating on the Lutheran problem in Germany.

Meanwhile, Charles faced two other enemies. The Habsburg emperor expected papal cooperation in dealing with the Lutheran heresy. Papal policy, however, was guided by political considerations, not religious ones, a clear indication that, like the Catholic king of France, a pope could act against his religious interests because of the political situation. Fearful of Charles's power in Italy, Pope Clement VII (1523–1534) joined the side of

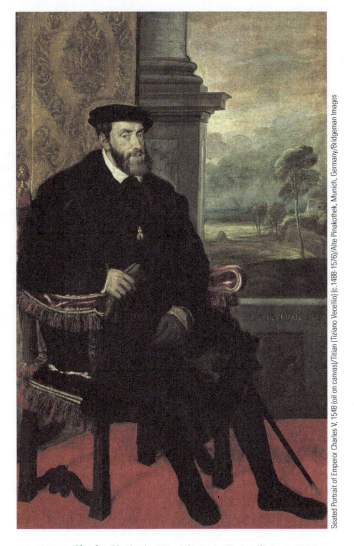

Seated Portrait of Emperor Charles V, 1548 (oil on canvas)/Titian (Tiziano Vecellio) (c.1488-1576)/Alte Pinakothek, Munich, Germany/Bridgeman Images

IMAGE 13.5 Charles V. Charles V sought to maintain religious unity throughout his vast empire by keeping all his subjects within the bounds of the Catholic Church. Due to his conflict with Francis I of France and his difficulties with the Turks, the papacy, and the German princes, Charles was never able to check the spread of Lutheranism. This portrait of Charles V is by the Venetian painter Titian.

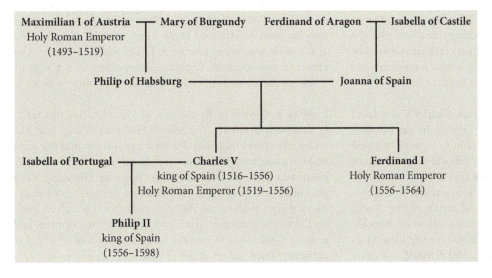

CHART 13.1 The Habsburgs as Holy Roman Emperors and Kings of Spain

Maximilian I of Austria — Mary of Burgundy   Ferdinand of Aragon — Isabella of Castile
Holy Roman Emperor
(1493–1519)

Philip of Habsburg ——————— Joanna of Spain

Isabella of Portugal ——— Charles V   Ferdinand I
                          king of Spain (1516–1556)   Holy Roman Emperor
                          Holy Roman Emperor (1519–1556)   (1556–1564)

Philip II
king of Spain
(1556–1598)

MAP 13.1 **The Empire of Charles V.** Charles V spent much of his reign fighting wars in Italy, against France and the Ottoman Empire, and within the borders of the Holy Roman Empire. He failed in his main goal to secure Europe for Catholicism: the Peace of Augsburg in 1555 recognized the equality of Catholicism and Lutheranism and let each German prince choose his realm's religion.

Q *Why would France feel threatened by the empire of Charles V?*

Francis I in the second Habsburg–Valois War (1527–1529), with catastrophic results. In April 1527, the Spanish-imperial army of Charles V went berserk while attacking Rome and gave the capital of Catholicism a fearful and bloody sacking. Sobered by the experience, Clement came to terms with the emperor, and by 1530, Charles V stood supreme over much of Italy.

The Ottoman Empire In the meantime, Charles V also faced problems in the eastern part of his empire. In the fifteenth century, the Ottoman Turks had overrun Constantinople and established control over much of the Balkans in southeastern Europe (see Chapter 12). Now, in the first decades of the sixteenth century, the Ottomans posed a new threat to Europe. Ottoman armies had taken control of much of the North African coast and captured the Christian island of Rhodes. Under their new leader, Suleiman (SOO-lay-mahn) the Magnificent (r. 1520–1566), Ottoman forces had defeated and killed

King Louis of Hungary, Charles's brother-in-law, at the Battle of Mohács (MOH-hach) in 1526. Subsequently, the Ottomans overran most of Hungary, moved into Austria, and advanced as far as Vienna, where they were finally repulsed in 1529. The emperor and much of Christian Europe breathed a sigh of relief but still remained fearful of another Ottoman attack.

Politics in Germany By the end of 1529, Charles was ready to deal with Germany. The second Habsburg–Valois War had ended, the Turks had been defeated temporarily, and the pope had been subdued. The internal political situation in the Holy Roman Empire was not in his favor, however. Germany was a land of several hundred territorial states: princely states, ecclesiastical principalities, and free imperial cities. Though all owed loyalty to the emperor, Germany's medieval development had enabled these states to become quite independent of imperial authority. They had no desire to have a strong emperor.

Charles's attempt to settle the Lutheran problem at the Diet of Augsburg in 1530 proved completely inadequate, and the emperor wound up demanding that the Lutherans return to the Catholic Church by April 15, 1531. In February 1531, fearful of Charles's intentions, eight princes and eleven imperial cities—all Lutheran—formed a defensive alliance known as the Schmalkaldic League. These Protestant German states vowed to assist each other "whenever any one of us is attacked on account of the Word of God and the doctrine of the Gospel." Religion was dividing the empire into two armed camps.

The renewed threat of the Turks against Vienna forced Charles once again to seek compromise instead of war with the Protestant authorities. From 1532 to 1535, Charles was forced to fight off an Ottoman, Arab, and Barbary attack on the Mediterranean coasts of Italy and Spain. Two additional Habsburg–Valois Wars (1535–1538 and 1542–1544) soon followed and kept Charles preoccupied with military campaigns in southern France and the Low Countries. Finally, Charles made peace with Francis in 1544 and the Turks in 1545. Fifteen years after the Diet of Augsburg, Charles was finally free to resolve his problem in Germany.

By the time of Luther's death in February 1546, all hopes of a peaceful compromise had faded. Charles brought a sizable imperial army of German, Dutch, Italian, and Spanish troops to do battle with the Protestants. In the first phase of the Schmalkaldic Wars (1546–1547), the emperor's forces decisively defeated the Lutherans at the Battle of Mühlberg (MOOL-bayrk). Charles V was at the zenith of his power, and the Protestant cause seemed doomed.

Appearances proved misleading, however. The Schmalkaldic League was soon reestablished, and the German Protestant princes allied themselves with the new French king, Henry II (r. 1547–1559)—a Catholic—to revive the war in 1552. This time Charles was less fortunate and had to negotiate a truce. Exhausted by his efforts to maintain religious orthodoxy and the unity of his empire, Charles abandoned German affairs to his brother Ferdinand, abdicated all of his titles in 1556, and retired to his country estate in Spain to spend the remaining two years of his life in solitude.

An end to religious warfare in Germany came in 1555 with the Peace of Augsburg, which marked an important turning point in the history of the Reformation. The agreement formally acknowledged the division of Christianity, with Lutheranism granted equal legal standing with Catholicism. Moreover, the peace settlement accepted the right of each German ruler to determine the religion of his subjects (but not the right of the subjects to choose their religion). Charles's hope for a united empire had been completely dashed, and the ideal of medieval Christian unity was irretrievably lost. The rapid proliferation of new Protestant groups served to underscore that new reality.

13-3 The Spread of the Protestant Reformation

 FOCUS QUESTIONS: What were the main tenets of Lutheranism, Zwinglianism, Anabaptism, and Calvinism, and how did they differ from each other and from Catholicism? What impact did political, economic, and social conditions have on the development of these four reform movements? In what ways was the Reformation in England different from these reform movements?

For both Catholics and Protestant reformers, Luther's heresy raised the question of what constituted the correct interpretation of the Bible. The inability to agree on this issue led not only to theological confrontations but also to bloody warfare as each Christian group was unwilling to admit that it could be wrong.

13-3a Lutheranism in Scandinavia

In 1397, the Union of Kalmar had brought about the unification of Denmark, Norway, and Sweden under the rule of one monarch, the king of Denmark. This union, however, failed to achieve any real social or political unification of the three states, particularly since the independent-minded landed nobles worked to frustrate any increase in monarchical centralization. By the beginning of the sixteenth century, the union was on the brink of disintegration. In 1520, Christian II (r. 1513–1523) of Denmark, ruler of the three Scandinavian kingdoms, was overthrown by Swedish barons led by Gustavus Vasa. Three years later, Vasa became king of an independent Sweden (r. 1523–1560) and took the lead in establishing a Lutheran Reformation in his country, and by the 1530s he had created a Swedish Lutheran National Church.

Meanwhile, the Danish nobility had also deposed Christian II as the king of Denmark. He was succeeded by his uncle, who became Frederick I (r. 1523–1533). Frederick encouraged Lutheran preachers to spread their evangelical doctrines and to introduce a Lutheran liturgy into the Danish church service. In the 1530s, under Frederick's successor, Christian III (r. 1534–1559), a Lutheran state church was installed with the king as the supreme authority in all ecclesiastical affairs. Christian was also instrumental in spreading Lutheranism to Norway. By the 1540s, Scandinavia had become a Lutheran stronghold. Like the German princes, the Scandinavian monarchs had been the dominant force in establishing state-run churches.

CHRONOLOGY	Politics and the German Reformation	
First Habsburg–Valois War	1521–1525
Second Habsburg–Valois War	1527–1529
Defeat of the Turks at Vienna	1529
Diet of Augsburg	1530
Third Habsburg–Valois War	1535–1538
Fourth Habsburg–Valois War	1542–1544
Schmalkaldic Wars	1546–1555
Peace of Augsburg	1555

13-3b The Zwinglian Reformation

In the sixteenth century, the Swiss Confederation was a loose association of thirteen self-governing states called cantons (see Map 13.2). Theoretically part of the Holy Roman Empire, they had become virtually independent in 1499. The six forest cantons were democratic republics; the seven urban cantons, which included Zürich, Bern, and Basel, were for the most part governed by city councils controlled by narrow oligarchies of wealthy citizens.

Ulrich Zwingli (OOL-rikh TSFING-lee) (1484–1531) was a product of the Swiss forest cantons (see Image 13.6). The precocious son of a relatively prosperous peasant, the young Zwingli eventually obtained both bachelor of arts and master of arts degrees. During his university education at Vienna and Basel, Zwingli was strongly influenced by Christian humanism. Ordained a priest in 1506, he accepted a parish post in rural Switzerland until his appointment as a cathedral priest in the Great Minster of Zürich

MAP 13.2 **The Swiss Cantons**

in 1518. Through his preaching there, Zwingli began the Reformation in Switzerland.

Zwingli's preaching of the Gospel caused such unrest that in 1523 the city council held a public disputation or debate in the town hall. The disputation became a standard method for spreading the Reformation to many cities. It gave an advantage to reformers, since they had the power of new ideas and Catholics were not used to defending their teachings. The victory went to Zwingli's party, and the council declared that "Mayor, Council and Great Council of Zürich, in order to do away with disturbance and discord, have upon due deliberation and consultation decided and resolved that Master Zwingli should continue as heretofore to proclaim the Gospel and the pure sacred Scripture."[11]

Reforms in Zürich Over the next two years, a city council strongly influenced by Zwingli promulgated evangelical reforms in Zürich. Zwingli looked to the state to supervise the church. He declared that a church without the magistrate is "mutilated and incomplete." The city council abolished relics and images and removed all paintings and decorations from the churches, replacing them with whitewashed walls. As Zwingli remarked, "The images are not to be endured; for all that God has forbidden, there can be no compromise."[12] A new liturgy consisting of Scripture reading, prayer, and sermons replaced the Mass, and music was eliminated from the service as a distraction from the pure word of God. Monasticism, pilgrimages, the veneration of saints, clerical celibacy, and the pope's authority were all abolished as remnants of papal Christianity. Zwingli's movement soon spread to other cities in Switzerland, including Bern in 1528 and Basel in 1529.

A Futile Search for Unity By 1528, Zwingli's reform movement faced a serious political problem as the forest cantons remained staunchly Catholic. Zürich feared that they would ally with the Habsburgs. To counteract this danger, Zwingli attempted to build a league of evangelical cities by seeking an agreement with Luther and the German reformers. An alliance between them seemed possible, since the Reformation had spread to the southern German cities, especially Strasbourg, where Martin Bucer (1491–1551) had instituted a moderate reform movement containing characteristics of both Luther's and Zwingli's movements. Both the German and the Swiss reformers realized the need for unity to defend against imperial and conservative opposition.

Protestant political leaders, especially Landgrave Philip of Hesse, fearful that Charles V would take advantage of the division between the reformers, attempted to promote an alliance of the Swiss and German reformed churches by persuading

Gianni Dagli Orti/The Art Archive at Art Resource, NY

IMAGE 13.6 **Zwingli.** Ulrich Zwingli began the Reformation in Switzerland through his preaching in Zürich. Zwingli's theology was accepted in Zürich and soon spread to other Swiss cities. This portrait of Zwingli was done by an unknown artist in the early sixteenth century.

A Reformation Debate: Conflict at Marburg

Q *How did the positions of Zwingli and Luther on the sacrament of the Lord's Supper differ? What was the purpose of this debate? Based on this example, why do you think Reformation debates led to further hostility rather than compromise and unity between religious and sectarian opponents? What implications did this have for the future of the Protestant Reformation?*

DEBATES PLAYED A CRUCIAL ROLE in the Reformation period. They were a primary instrument in introducing the Reformation into innumerable cities as well as a means of resolving differences among like-minded Protestant groups. This selection contains an excerpt from the vivacious and often brutal debate between Luther and Zwingli over the sacrament of the Lord's Supper at Marburg in 1529. The two protagonists failed to reach agreement.

The Marburg Colloquy, 1529

THE HESSIAN CHANCELLOR FEIGE: My gracious prince and lord [Landgrave Philip of Hesse] has summoned you for the express and urgent purpose of settling the dispute over the sacrament of the Lord's Supper. . . . Let everyone on both sides present his arguments in a spirit of moderation, . . . Now then, Doctor Luther, you may proceed.

LUTHER: Noble prince, gracious lord! Undoubtedly the colloquy is well intentioned. . . . Although I have no intention of changing my mind, which is firmly made up, I will nevertheless present the grounds of my belief and show where the others are in error. . . . Your basic contentions are these: In the last analysis you wish to prove that a body cannot be in two places at once, and you produce arguments about the unlimited body which are based on natural reason. I do not question how Christ can be God and man and how the two natures can be

joined. For God is more powerful than all our ideas, and we must submit to his word.

Prove that Christ's body is not there where the Scripture says, "This is my body!" Rational proofs I will not listen to. It is God who commands, "Take, eat, this is my body." I request, therefore, valid scriptural proof to the contrary.

ZWINGLI: I insist that the words of the Lord's Supper must be figurative. This is ever apparent, and even required by the article of faith: "taken up into heaven, seated at the right hand of the Father." Otherwise, it would be absurd to look for him in the Lord's Supper at the same time that Christ is telling us that he is in heaven. One and the same body cannot possibly be in different places. . . .

LUTHER: I call upon you as before: your basic contentions are shaky. Give way, and give glory to God!

ZWINGLI: And we call upon you to give glory to God and to quit begging the question. The issue at stake is this: Where is the proof of your position? . . . You're trying to outwit me. I stand by this passage in the sixth chapter of John, verse 63, and shall not be shaken from it. You'll have to sing another tune.

LUTHER: You're being obnoxious.

ZWINGLI: (*excitedly*) Don't you believe that Christ was attempting in John 6 to help those who did not understand?

LUTHER: You're trying to dominate things! You insist on passing judgment . . . It is your point that must be proved, not mine. But let us stop this sort of thing. It serves no purpose.

ZWINGLI: It certainly does! It is for you to prove that the passage in John 6 speaks of a physical repast.

LUTHER: You express yourself poorly and make about as much progress as a cane standing in a corner. You're going nowhere.

ZWINGLI: No, no, no! This is the passage that will break your neck!

LUTHER: Don't be so sure of yourself. Necks don't break this way. You're in Hesse, not Switzerland.

Source: "The Marburg Colloquy," in *Great Debates of the Reformation*, ed. D. Ziegler (New York: Modern Library, 1969).

the leaders of both groups to attend a colloquy (conference) at Marburg to resolve their differences. Able to agree on virtually everything else, the gathering splintered over the interpretation of the Lord's Supper (see Opposing Viewpoints, "A Reformation Debate: Conflict at Marburg," above). Zwingli believed that the scriptural words "This is my body" and "This is my blood" should be taken symbolically, not literally. To Zwingli, the Lord's Supper was only a meal of remembrance, and he refused to accept Luther's insistence on the real presence of

the body and blood of Jesus "in, with, and under the bread and wine." The Marburg Colloquy of 1529 produced no agreement and no evangelical alliance. It was a foretaste of the issues that would divide one reform group from another and lead to the creation of different Protestant groups.

In October 1531, war erupted between the Swiss Protestant and Catholic cantons. Zürich's army was routed, and Zwingli was found wounded on the battlefield. His enemies killed him, cut up his body, burned the pieces, and scattered the ashes. This

Swiss civil war of 1531 provided an early indication of what religious passions would lead to in the sixteenth century. Unable to find peaceful ways to agree on the meaning of the Gospel, the disciples of Christianity resorted to violence and decision by force. When he heard of Zwingli's death, Martin Luther, who had not forgotten the confrontation at Marburg, is supposed to have remarked that Zwingli "got what he deserved."

13-3c The Radical Reformation: The Anabaptists

Although many reformers were ready to allow the state to play an important, if not dominant, role in church affairs, some people rejected this kind of magisterial reformation and favored a far more radical reform movement. Collectively called the Anabaptists, these radicals were actually members of a large variety of groups who shared some common characteristics. Anabaptism was especially attractive to the peasants, weavers, miners, and artisans who had been adversely affected by the economic changes of the age.

The Ideas of the Anabaptists Anabaptists everywhere held certain ideas in common. All felt that the true Christian church was a voluntary association of believers who had undergone spiritual rebirth and had then been baptized into the church. Anabaptists advocated adult rather than infant baptism. No one, they believed, should be forced to accept the truth of the Bible. They also tried to return literally to the practices and spirit of early Christianity. Adhering to the accounts of early Christian communities in the New Testament, they followed a strict sort of democracy in which all believers were considered equal. Each church chose its own minister, who might be any member of the community, since all Christians were considered priests (though women were often excluded). Those chosen as ministers had the duty to lead services, which were very simple and contained nothing not found in the early church. Like early Christians, Anabaptists, who called themselves "Christians" or "Saints," accepted that they would have to suffer for their faith. Anabaptists rejected theological speculation in favor of simple Christian living according to what they believed was the pure word of God. The Lord's Supper was interpreted as a remembrance, a meal of fellowship celebrated in the evening in private houses according to Jesus's example.

Unlike the Catholics and other Protestants, most Anabaptists believed in the complete separation of church and state. Not only was government to be excluded from the realm of religion, but it was not even supposed to exercise political jurisdiction over real Christians. Human law had no power over those whom God had saved. Anabaptists refused to hold political office or bear arms because many took the commandment "Thou shall not kill" literally, although some Anabaptist groups did become quite violent. Their political beliefs as much as their religious beliefs caused the Anabaptists to be regarded as dangerous radicals who threatened the very fabric of sixteenth-century society. Indeed, the chief thing Protestants and Catholics could agree on was the need to stamp out the Anabaptists.

Varieties of Anabaptists One early group of Anabaptists known as the Swiss Brethren arose in Zürich. Their ideas, especially adult baptism, frightened Zwingli, and they were expelled from the city in 1523. Because the first members of the Swiss Brethren who were baptized as adults had already been baptized as children (in the Catholic Church), their opponents labeled them Anabaptists or Rebaptists. Under Roman law, such people were subject to the death penalty.

As the teachings of the Swiss Brethren spread through southern Germany, the Austrian Habsburg lands, and Switzerland, Anabaptists suffered ruthless persecution, especially after the Peasants' War of 1524–1525, when the upper classes resorted to repression. Virtually eradicated in Germany, Anabaptist survivors emerged in Moravia and Poland, and in the Netherlands, Anabaptism took on a strange form.

In the 1530s, the city of Münster, in Westphalia in northwestern Germany near the Dutch border, was the site of an Anabaptist uprising that determined the fate of Dutch Anabaptism. Seat of a powerful Catholic prince-bishop, Münster had experienced severe economic disasters, including crop failure and plague. Although converted to Lutheranism in 1532, Münster experienced a more radical mass religious hysteria that led to legal recognition for the Anabaptists. Soon Münster became a haven for Anabaptists from the surrounding neighborhood, especially the more wild-eyed variety known as Melchiorites, who adhered to a vivid **millenarianism**. They believed that the end of the world was at hand and that they would usher in the kingdom of God with Münster as the New Jerusalem. By the end of February 1534, these millenarian Anabaptists had taken control of the city, driven out everyone they considered godless or unbelievers, burned all books except the Bible, and proclaimed communal ownership of all property. Eventually, the leadership of this New Jerusalem fell into the hands of one man, John of Leiden, who proclaimed himself king of the New Jerusalem. As king, he would lead the elect from Münster out to cover the entire world and purify it of evil by the sword in preparation for Jesus's Second Coming and the creation of a New Age. In this new kingdom, John of Leiden believed, all goods would be held in common and the saints would live without suffering.

But it was not to be. As the Catholic prince-bishop of Münster gathered a large force and laid siege to the city, the new king repeatedly had to postpone the ushering forth from Münster. Finally, after many inhabitants had starved, a joint army of Catholics and Lutherans recaptured the city in June 1535 and executed the radical Anabaptist leaders in gruesome fashion. The New Jerusalem had ceased to exist.

Purged of its fantasies and its more extreme elements, Dutch Anabaptism reverted to its pacifist tendencies, especially evident in the work of Menno Simons (1496–1561), the man most responsible for rejuvenating Dutch Anabaptism. A popular leader, Menno dedicated his life to the spread of a peaceful, evangelical Anabaptism that stressed separation from the world in order to truly emulate the life of Jesus. Simons imposed strict discipline on his followers and banned those who refused to conform to the rules. The Mennonites, as his followers were called, spread from the Netherlands into northwestern Germany and eventually into Poland and Lithuania as well as the New World. Both the Mennonites and the Amish, who are also descended from the Anabaptists, maintain communities in the United States and Canada today.

13-3d The Reformation in England

The English Reformation was initiated by King Henry VIII (r. 1509–1547), who wanted to divorce his first wife, Catherine of Aragon, because she had failed to produce a male heir (see Image 13.7). Furthermore, Henry had fallen in love with Anne Boleyn (BUH-lin *or* buh-LIN), a lady-in-waiting to [Queen Catherine. Anne's unwillingness to be only the king's mistress and the king's desire to have a legitimate male heir made their marriage imperative, but the king's first marriage stood in the way.

Henry relied on Cardinal Wolsey, the highest-ranking English church official and lord chancellor to the king, to obtain from Pope Clement VII an annulment of the king's marriage. Normally, the pope might have been willing to oblige, but the sack of Rome in 1527 had made the pope dependent on the Holy Roman Emperor Charles V, who happened to be the nephew of Queen Catherine. Discretion dictated delay in granting the English king's request. Impatient with the process, Henry dismissed Wolsey in 1529.

Two new advisers now became the king's agents in fulfilling his wishes. These were Thomas Cranmer (1489–1556), who became archbishop of Canterbury in 1532, and Thomas Cromwell (1485–1540), the king's principal secretary after the fall of Wolsey. They advised the king to obtain an annulment of his marriage in England's own ecclesiastical courts. The most important step toward this goal was an act of Parliament cutting off all appeals from English church courts to Rome, a piece of legislation that essentially abolished papal authority in England. Henry no longer needed the pope to obtain his annulment. He was now in a hurry because Anne Boleyn had become pregnant and he had

secretly married her in January 1533 to legitimize the expected heir. In May, as archbishop of Canterbury and head of the highest ecclesiastical court in England, Thomas Cranmer ruled that the king's marriage to Catherine was "null and absolutely void" and then validated Henry's marriage to Anne. At the beginning of June, Anne was crowned queen. Three months later, a child was born. Much to the king's disappointment, the baby was a girl, whom they named Elizabeth.

In 1534, Parliament completed the break of the Church of England with Rome by passing the Act of Supremacy, which declared that the king was "taken, accepted, and reputed the only supreme head on earth of the Church of England." This meant that the English monarch now controlled the church in all matters of doctrine, clerical appointments, and discipline. In addition, Parliament passed the Treason Act, making it punishable by death to deny that the king was the supreme head of the church.

One who challenged the new order was Thomas More, the humanist and former lord chancellor, who saw clearly to the heart of the issue: loyalty to the pope in Rome was now treason in England. More refused to support the new laws and was duly tried for treason. At his trial, he asked, rhetorically, what the effect of the actions of the king and Parliament would be: "Therefore am I not bound . . . to conform my conscience to the Council of one realm [England] against the general Council of Christendom?"[13] Because his conscience could not accept the victory of the national state over the church, nor would he, as a Christian, bow his head to a secular ruler in matters of faith, More was beheaded in London on July 6, 1535.

IMAGE 13.7 **Henry VIII.** This portrait by the German artist Hans Holbein the Younger gives us a picture of the English king at the height of his power at the age of 49, seven years before his death. Hans Holbein the Younger was a Northern Renaissance painter and regarded as one of the great portrait painters of the sixteenth century. Beginning in 1535, he became King's Painter in England, in which position he did portraits and festive decorations.

 What features of this portrait indicate that Holbein was a Northern Renaissance artist (see Chapter 12)?

Portrait of Henry VIII aged 49, 1540 (oil on panel)/Holbein the Younger, Hans (1497/8-1543)/Palazzo Barberini, Gallerie Nazionali Barberini Corsini, Rome, Italy/Bridgeman Images

Recent research that emphasizes the strength of Catholicism in England suggests that Thomas More was not alone in his view of the new order. In fact, one historian has argued that Catholicism was vibrant in England in both the fifteenth and sixteenth centuries; in his view, the English Reformation was alien to many English people.

The New Order Thomas Cromwell worked out the details of the Tudor government's new role in church affairs based on the centralized power exercised by the king and Parliament. Cromwell also came to his extravagant king's financial rescue with a daring plan for the dissolution of the monasteries. About four hundred religious houses were closed in 1536, and the king confiscated their lands and possessions. Many were sold to nobles, gentry, and some merchants. The king added enormously to his treasury and also to his ranks of supporters, who now had a stake in the new Tudor order.

Although Henry VIII had broken with the papacy, little change occurred in matters of doctrine, theology, and ceremony. Some of his supporters, such as Archbishop Thomas Cranmer, wished to have a religious reformation as well as an administrative one, but Henry was unyielding. Nevertheless, some clergymen ignored Henry on the matter of priestly celibacy and secretly married.

The final decade of Henry's reign was preoccupied with foreign affairs, factional intrigue, and a continued effort to find the perfect wife. Henry soon tired of Anne Boleyn and had her beheaded in 1536 on a charge of adultery. His third wife, Jane Seymour, produced the long-awaited male heir but died twelve days later. His fourth marriage, to Anne of Cleves, a German princess, was arranged for political reasons. Henry relied on a painted portrait of Anne when he made the arrangements, but he was disappointed at her physical appearance when he saw her in person and soon divorced her. His fifth wife, Catherine Howard, was more attractive but less moral. When she committed adultery, Henry had her beheaded. His last wife was Catherine Parr, who married the king in 1543 and outlived him. Henry was succeeded by the underage and sickly Edward VI (r. 1547–1553), the son of his third wife.

Since the new king was only nine years old at the time of his accession to the throne, real control of England passed to a council of regency. During Edward's reign, Archbishop Cranmer and others inclined toward Protestant doctrines were able to move the Church of England in a more Protestant direction. New acts of Parliament instituted the right of the clergy to marry, eliminated images, and authorized a revised Protestant liturgy that was elaborated in a new prayer book and liturgical guide known as the Book of Common Prayer. These rapid changes in doctrine and liturgy aroused much opposition and prepared the way for the reaction that occurred when Mary, Henry's first daughter by Catherine of Aragon, came to the throne.

Reaction Under Mary Mary (r. 1553–1558) was a Catholic who fully intended to restore England to the Roman Catholic fold. But her restoration of Catholicism, achieved by joint action of the monarch and Parliament, aroused opposition. There was widespread antipathy to Mary's unfortunate marriage to Philip II, son of Charles V and the future king of Spain. Philip was strongly disliked in England, and Mary's foreign policy of alliance with Spain aroused further hostility, especially when her forces lost Calais, the last English possession in France after the Hundred Years' War. The burning of more than three hundred Protestant heretics aroused further ire against "bloody Mary." As a result of her policies, Mary managed to achieve the opposite of what she had intended: England was more Protestant by the end of her reign than it had been at the beginning. When she came to power, Protestantism had become identified with church destruction and religious anarchy. Now people identified it with English resistance to Spanish interference. Mary's death in 1558 ended the restoration of Catholicism in England.

13-3e John Calvin and Calvinism

Of the second generation of Protestant reformers, one stands out as the systematic theologian and organizer of the Protestant movement—John Calvin (1509–1564) (see Image 13.8). Calvin received a remarkably diverse education in humanistic studies and law in his

IMAGE 13.8 **John Calvin.** After a conversion experience, John Calvin abandoned his life as a humanist and became a reformer. In 1536, Calvin began working to reform the city of Geneva, where he remained until his death in 1564. This is a seventeenth-century portrait of Calvin done by a member of the Swiss school.

Q *What do you think this seventeenth-century artist was trying to portray about John Calvin in this painting?*

native France. He was also influenced by Luther's writings, which were being circulated and read by French intellectuals as early as 1523. In 1533, Calvin experienced a religious crisis that determined the rest of his life's work. He described it in these words:

> God, by a sudden conversion, subdued and brought my mind to a teachable frame, which was more hardened in such matters than might have been expected from one at my early period of life. Having thus received some taste and knowledge of true godliness, I was immediately inflamed with so intense a desire to make progress therein, although I did not leave off other studies, I yet pursued them with less ardor.[14]

Calvin's conversion was solemn and straightforward. He was so convinced of the inner guidance of God that he became the most determined of all the Protestant reformers.

After his conversion and newfound conviction, Calvin was no longer safe in Paris, since King Francis I periodically persecuted Protestants. Eventually, Calvin made his way to Basel, where in 1536 he published the first edition of the *Institutes of the Christian Religion*, a masterful synthesis of Protestant thought that immediately secured his reputation as one of the new leaders of Protestantism.

Calvin's Ideas On most important doctrines, Calvin stood very close to Luther. He adhered to the doctrine of justification by faith alone to explain how humans achieved salvation. Calvin also placed much emphasis on the absolute sovereignty of God or the "power, grace, and glory of God." Thus, "God asserts his possession of omnipotence, and claims our acknowledgment of this attribute; not such as is imagined by sophists, vain, idle, and almost asleep, but vigilant, efficacious, operative and engaged in continual action."[15]

One of the ideas derived from his emphasis on the absolute sovereignty of God—**predestination**—gave a unique cast to Calvin's teachings, although Luther also believed in this principle. This "eternal decree," as Calvin called it, meant that God had predestined some people to be saved (the elect) and others to be damned (the reprobate). According to Calvin, "He has once for all determined, both whom he would admit to salvation, and whom he would condemn to destruction."[16] Calvin identified three tests that might indicate possible salvation: an open profession of faith, a "decent and godly life," and participation in the sacraments of baptism and communion. In no instance did Calvin ever suggest that worldly success or material wealth was a sign of election. Significantly for the future of Calvinism, although Calvin himself stressed that there could be no absolute certainty of salvation, some of his followers did not always make this distinction. The practical psychological effect of predestination was to give some later Calvinists an unshakable conviction that they were doing God's work on earth. It is no accident that Calvinism became the activist international form of Protestantism.

To Calvin, the church was a divine institution responsible for preaching the word of God and administering the sacraments. Calvin kept the same two sacraments as other Protestant reformers, baptism and the Lord's Supper. Baptism was a sign of the remission of sins. Calvin believed in the real presence of Jesus in the sacrament of the Lord's Supper, but only in a spiritual sense. Jesus's body is at the right hand of God and thus cannot be in the sacrament, but to the believer, Jesus is spiritually present in the Lord's Supper.

Calvin's Geneva Before 1536, John Calvin had essentially been a scholar. But in that year, he took up a ministry in Geneva that lasted, except for a brief exile (1538–1541), until his death in 1564. Calvin achieved a major success in 1541 when the city council accepted his new church constitution, known as the Ecclesiastical Ordinances.

This document created a church government that used both clergy and laymen in the service of the church. The Consistory, a special body for enforcing moral discipline, was set up as a court to oversee the moral life and doctrinal purity of Genevans (see Historical Voices, "Calvin's Rules for the Church in Geneva," p. 394). As its power increased, the Consistory went from "fraternal corrections" to the use of public penance and excommunication. More serious cases could be turned over to the city council for punishments greater than excommunication. During Calvin's last years, stricter laws against blasphemy were enacted and enforced with banishment and public whippings.

Calvin's success in Geneva enabled the city to become a vibrant center of Protestantism. John Knox, the Calvinist reformer of Scotland, called it "the most perfect school of Christ on earth." Following Calvin's lead, missionaries trained in Geneva were sent to all parts of Europe. Calvinism became established in France, the Netherlands, Scotland, and central and eastern Europe. By the mid-sixteenth century, Calvinism had replaced Lutheranism as the international form of Protestantism, and Calvin's Geneva stood as the fortress of the Reformation.

CHRONOLOGY	New Reform Movements	
The Zwinglian Reformation		
Zwingli made cathedral priest at Zürich	1518	
Reform adopted in Zürich	1523	
Marburg Colloquy	1529	
The Anabaptists		
Anabaptists expelled from Zürich	1523	
New Jerusalem in Münster	1534–1535	
The Reformation in England		
Henry VIII	1509–1547	
Act of Supremacy	1534	
Edward VI	1547–1553	
Mary	1553–1558	
Calvin and Calvinism		
Institutes of the Christian Religion	1536	
Calvin begins ministry in Geneva	1536	
Ecclesiastical Ordinances	1541	

Calvin's Rules for the Church in Geneva

 Why did Calvin and Geneva put so much emphasis on the role of the Consistory? What specific Catholic practices did Calvin and Geneva wish to stop?

JOHN CALVIN HAD EMPHASIZED in his reform movement that the church should have the ability to enforce proper behavior. Consequently, the Ecclesiastical Ordinances of 1541, the constitution of the church in Geneva, provided for an order of elders whose function was to cooperate with the pastors in maintaining discipline—"to watch over the conduct of every individual," as Calvin expressed it. These selections from Calvin's plan demonstrate the organization of the elders and some of the rules that were expected to be followed in Geneva.

Plan for the Elders and Consistory and Rules for the Church in Geneva

The office of the elders is to watch over the conduct of every individual, to admonish lovingly those whom they see doing wrong or leading an irregular life. When there is need, they should lay the matter before the body deputed to inflict paternal disciple [that is, the Consistory] of which they are members. As the Church is organized, it is best that the elders be chosen, two from the small council, four from the council of sixty, and six from the council of two hundred [the councils constituted the government of the city of Geneva]; they should be men of good life and honest, without reproach and beyond suspicion, above all, God-fearing without reproach and endowed with spiritual prudence. And they should be so chosen they be distributed in each quarter of the city, so that they can have an eye on everything. . . .

The elders, who have been described, shall assemble once a week with the ministers, namely Thursday morning, to see if there be any disorders in the Church and discuss together such remedies as shall be necessary. . . . If any one shall in contempt refuse to appear before them, it shall be their duty to inform the council, so that it may supply a remedy. . . .

Those who are found to have rosaries or idols to adore, let them be sent before the consistory, and in addition to the reproof they receive there, let them be sent before the council. Let the same be done with those who go on a pilgrimage. Those who observe feasts or [Catholic] fasts should only be admonished. Those who go to mass shall, besides being admonished, be sent before the council, and it shall consider the propriety of punishing the offenders by imprisonment or special fines, as it judges best.

He who blasphemes, swearing by the body or blood of our Lord, or in like manner, shall kiss the earth for the first offense, pay five sous for the second and ten for the third. He who contradicts the word of God shall be sent before the consistory for reproof, or before the council for punishment, as the case may require. If any one sings indecent songs, or dances or otherwise, he shall be kept in prison three days and then sent to the council.

Source: J. H. Robinson, *Readings in European History*, vol. 2 (Boston: Ginn & Company, 1906), pp. 133–134.

13-4 The Social Impact of the Protestant Reformation

 FOCUS QUESTION: What impact did the Protestant Reformation have on family, education, and popular religious practices in the sixteenth century?

Because Christianity was such an integral part of European life, it was inevitable that the Reformation would have an impact on the family, education, and popular religious practices.

13-4a The Family

For centuries, Catholicism had praised the family and sanctified its existence by making marriage a sacrament. But the Catholic Church's high regard for abstinence from sex as the surest way to holiness made the celibate state of the clergy preferable to marriage. Nevertheless, because not all men could remain chaste, marriage offered the best means to control sexual intercourse and give it a purpose, the procreation of children. To some extent, this attitude persisted among the Protestant reformers; Luther, for example, argued that sex in marriage allowed one to "make use of this sex in order to avoid sin," and Calvin advised that every man should "abstain from marriage only so long as he is fit to observe celibacy." If "his power to tame lust fails him," then he must marry.

But the Reformation did bring some change to the conception of the family. Both Catholic and Protestant clergy preached sermons advocating a more positive approach to family relationships. The Protestants were especially important in developing this new view of the family. Because Protestantism had eliminated any idea of special holiness for celibacy, abolishing both monasticism and a celibate clergy, the family could be placed at the center of human life, and a new stress on "mutual love between man and wife" could be extolled. But were doctrine and reality the same? For more radical religious groups, at times they were (see Historical Voices, "A Protestant Woman," p. 395). One Anabaptist wrote to his wife before his execution, "My faithful helper, my loyal

A Protestant Woman

 What was Katherine Zell's argument against Ludwig Rabus? Of what Protestant sect do you think she was a member?

IN THE INITIAL ZEAL of the Protestant Reformation, women were frequently allowed to play unusual roles. Katherine Zell of Germany (ca. 1497–1562) first preached beside her husband in 1527. After the deaths of her two children, she devoted the rest of her life to helping her husband and their reform faith. This selection is taken from one of her letters to the city of Strasbourg to defend herself against Ludwig Rabus, a Lutheran minister who had criticized her activities.

A Letter to the Whole Citizenship of the City of Strasbourg from Katherine Zell

So that you, dear Strasbourg, may know why I have first introduced this long speech about how I was loved in my youth and marriage (a speech that should be unnecessary!) so read now also what disrespect and judgment I have received in my old age. Therefore I have put here the letter that Mr. Ludwig sent to me. See how he ascribes to me insult, dishonor and godlessness together with all errors and heresies before God and human beings. He hands me over to the devil, with whom (God be praised) I have nothing to do forever, but I belong to my Lord Jesus Christ, who with His own blood redeemed me from the devil. So besides showing Rabus's letter I also seek to give a full accounting of my faith to anyone who wants it.

In this account you may see whether my good husband's faith and mine are alike or unlike or whether my confidence and faith in the Lord Jesus have changed or not. However, I will clearly show Rabus that he and others have not kept to the pure knowledge of Jesus Christ as the old architects of our church taught us, . . .

Well then, this is now enough. However, if Mr. Ludwig is not satisfied with his injudicious condemnation of me, a poor solitary women, then I want to take God as my helper and further recount my dear husband's and my faith, teaching and life, and let anyone who wants to do so judge who has fallen away or climbed out of the right way! Now, dear Strasbourg, read this letter that Mr. Ludwig Rabus sent to me and judge without any favor and ill humor toward him or me. If I am owed this and have behaved as he describes, then I will gladly bear my punishment. But I believe that no Jew would give me such a testimony and bring such a judgment on me. I am also assured in my heart that I stand before my Lord Christ and His heavenly Father in a fitting way through the power of His Spirit; I stand before Him through the great and high merit of Christ in whom I believe, who also will bring to light this wicked letter or witness by Mr. Ludwig (which lies about me) on the great day of His glorious appearance, when all the books of the conscience with stand open. Yes, here I stand also before many people who know me, who know my life story and have seen me from youth: as a young woman in my father's house, in my marriage, and now in my grieving widowhood—let them also judge this matter between Mr. Ludwig and me.

Source: Elsie McKee, *Church Mother: The Writings of a Protestant Reformer in Sixteenth-Century Germany* (Chicago: University of Chicago Press, 2006), pp. 230–231.

friend. I praise God that he gave you to me, you who have sustained me in all my trial."[17] But more often reality reflected the traditional roles of husband as the ruler and wife as the obedient servant whose chief duty was to please her husband. Luther stated it clearly:

> The rule remains with the husband, and the wife is compelled to obey him by God's command. He rules the home and the state, wages war, defends his possessions, tills the soil, builds, plants, etc. The woman on the other hand is like a nail driven into the wall . . . so the wife should stay at home and look after the affairs of the household, as one who has been deprived of the ability of administering those affairs that are outside and that concern the state. She does not go beyond her most personal duties.[18]

Obedience to her husband was not a wife's only role; her other important duty was to bear children. To Calvin and Luther, this function of women was part of the divine plan. God punishes women for the sins of Eve by the burdens of procreation and feeding and nurturing their children, but, said Luther, "it is a gladsome punishment if you consider the hope of eternal life and the honor of motherhood which had been left to her."[19] Although the Protestant reformers sanctified this role of woman as mother and wife, viewing it as a holy vocation, Protestantism also left few alternatives for women. Because monasticism had been destroyed, life as a nun was no longer available; for most Protestant women, family life was their only destiny. At the same time, by emphasizing the father as "ruler" and hence the center of household religion, Protestantism even removed the woman from her traditional role as controller of religion in the home.

Protestant reformers called on men and women to read the Bible and participate in religious services together. In this way, the reformers did provide a stimulus for the education of girls so that they could read the Bible and other religious literature. The city council of Zwickau, for example, established a girls' school in 1525. But these schools were designed to encourage proper moral values rather than intellectual development and really did little to improve the position of women in society. Likewise, when women attempted to take more active roles in religious life, reformers—Lutheran and Calvinist alike—shrank back in horror. To them, the equality of the Gospel did not mean overthrowing the inequality of social classes or the sexes. Calvin also made clear what he thought of women rulers: "the government of women . . . is utterly at variance with the legitimate order of nature. . . . For a female rule badly organized is like a tyranny, and is to be tolerated until God sees fit to overthrow it."[20] Overall, the Protestant Reformation did not noticeably transform women's subordinate place in society.

13-4b Education in the Reformation

The Reformation had an important effect on the development of education in Europe. Renaissance humanism had significantly altered the content of education, and Protestant educators were very successful in implementing and using humanist methods in Protestant secondary schools and universities. Unlike the humanist schools, however, which had been mostly for an elite, the sons and a few daughters of the nobility and wealthier bourgeoisie, Protestant schools were aimed at a much wider audience. Protestantism created an increased need for at least a semiliterate body of believers who could read the Bible for themselves.

While adopting the classical emphasis of humanist schools, Protestant reformers broadened the base of the people being educated. Convinced of the need to provide the church with good Christians and good pastors as well as the state with good administrators and citizens, Martin Luther advocated that all children should have the opportunity of an education provided by the state. To that end, he urged the cities and villages of Saxony to establish schools paid for by the public. Luther's ideas were shared by his Wittenberg co-worker Philip Melanchthon, whose educational efforts earned him the title of *Praecepter Germaniae* (PREE-sep-tur gayr-MAHN-ee-ee), the Teacher of Germany. In his scheme for education in Saxony, Melanchthon divided students into three classes or divisions based on their age or capabilities.

Following Melanchthon's example, the Protestants in Germany were responsible for introducing the gymnasium, or secondary school, where the humanist emphasis on the liberal arts based on instruction in Greek and Latin was combined with religious instruction (see Image 13.9). Most famous was the school in Strasbourg founded by Johannes Sturm in 1538, which served as a model for other Protestant schools. John Calvin's Genevan Academy, founded in 1559, was organized in two distinct parts. The "private school" or gymnasium was divided into seven classes for young people who were taught Latin and Greek grammar and literature as well as logic. In the "public school," students were taught philosophy, Hebrew, Greek, and theology. The Genevan Academy, which eventually became a university, came to concentrate on preparing ministers to spread the Calvinist view of the Gospel.

13-4c Religious Practices and Popular Culture

The Protestant reformers' attacks on the Catholic Church led to radical changes in religious practices. The Protestant Reformation abolished or severely curtailed such customary practices as indulgences, the veneration of relics and saints, pilgrimages, monasticism, and clerical celibacy. The elimination of saints put an end to the numerous celebrations of religious holy days and changed a community's sense of time. Thus,

Öffentliche Kunstsammlung, Basel/Giraudon/Bridgeman Images

IMAGE 13.9 **A Sixteenth-Century Classroom.** Protestants in Germany developed secondary schools that combined instruction in the liberal arts with religious education. This scene from a painting by Ambrosius Holbein shows a schoolmaster instructing a pupil in the alphabet while his wife helps a little girl.

 Based on this image, what educational practices were used in a sixteenth-century classroom?

in Protestant communities, religious ceremonies and imagery, such as processions and statues, tended to be replaced with individual private prayer, family worship, and collective prayer and worship at the same time each week on Sunday.

In addition to abolishing saints' days and religious carnivals, some Protestant reformers even tried to eliminate customary forms of entertainment. The Puritans (as English Calvinists were called), for example, attempted to ban drinking in taverns, dramatic performances, and dancing. Dutch Calvinists denounced the tradition of giving small presents to children on the feast of Saint Nicholas, in early December. Many of these Protestant attacks on popular culture were unsuccessful, however. The importance of taverns in English social life made it impossible to eradicate them, and celebrating at Christmastime persisted in the Dutch Netherlands.

13-5 The Catholic Reformation

 FOCUS QUESTION: What measures did the Roman Catholic Church take to reform itself and to combat Protestantism in the sixteenth century?

By the mid-sixteenth century, Lutheranism had become established in parts of Germany and Scandinavia, and Calvinism in parts of Switzerland, France, the Netherlands, and eastern Europe (see Map 13.3). In England, the split from Rome had resulted in the creation of a national church. The situation in Europe did not look particularly favorable for the Roman Catholic Church. Yet constructive, positive forces were already at work within the Catholic Church.

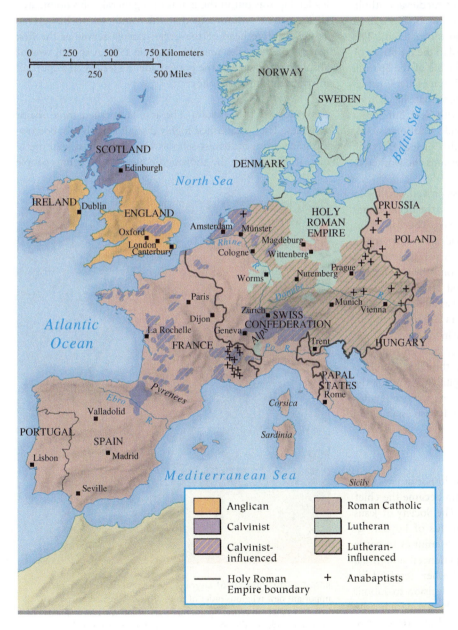

MAP 13.3 Catholics and Protestants in Europe by 1560. The Reformation continued to evolve beyond the basic split of the Lutherans from the Catholics. Several Protestant sects broke away from the teachings of Martin Luther, each with a separate creed and different ways of worship. In England, Henry VIII broke with the Catholic Church for political and dynastic reasons.

 Which areas of Europe were solidly Catholic, which were solidly Lutheran, and which were neither?

13-5a Catholic Reformation or Counter-Reformation?

There is no doubt that the Catholic Church underwent a revitalization in the sixteenth century. But was this reformation a **Catholic Reformation** or a Counter-Reformation? Some historians prefer to call it a "Counter-Reformation" to focus on the aspects that were a direct reaction against the Protestant movement. Historians who prefer to use "Catholic Reformation" point out that elements of reform were already present in the Catholic Church at the end of the fifteenth century and the beginning of the sixteenth, and that by the mid-sixteenth century, they came to be directed by a revived and reformed papacy, giving the church new strength.

No doubt, both positions on the nature of the reformation of the Catholic Church contain elements of truth. The Catholic Reformation revived the best features of medieval Catholicism and then adjusted them to meet new conditions, as is most apparent in the revival of mysticism and monasticism. The emergence of a new mysticism, closely tied to the traditions of Catholic piety, was especially evident in the life of the Spanish mystic Saint Teresa of Avila (1515–1582). A nun of the Carmelite order, Teresa experienced mystical visions that she claimed resulted in the ecstatic union of her soul with God. But Teresa also believed that mystical experience should lead to an active life of service on behalf of her Catholic faith. Consequently, she founded a new order of barefoot Carmelite nuns and worked to foster their mystical experiences.

The regeneration of religious orders also proved valuable to the reform of Catholicism. Old orders, such as the Benedictines and Dominicans, were reformed and renewed. The Capuchins emerged when a group of Franciscans decided to return to the simplicity and poverty of Saint Francis of Assisi, the medieval founder of the Franciscan order. In addition to caring for the sick and the poor, the Capuchins focused on preaching the Gospel directly to the people and emerged as an effective force against Protestantism. New religious orders and brotherhoods were also created. The Theatines, founded in 1524, placed their emphasis on reforming the secular clergy and encouraging those clerics to fulfill their duties among the laity. The Theatines also founded orphanages and hospitals to care for the victims of war and plague. The Ursulines, a new order of nuns founded in Italy in 1535, focused their attention on establishing schools for the education of girls.

13-5b The Society of Jesus

Of all the new religious orders, the most important was the Society of Jesus, known as the Jesuits, who became the chief instrument of the Catholic Reformation. The Society of Jesus was founded by a Spanish nobleman, Ignatius of Loyola (ig-NAY-shuss of loi-OH-luh) (1491–1556), whose injuries in battle cut short his military career. Loyola experienced a spiritual torment similar to Luther's but, unlike Luther, resolved his problems not by a new doctrine but by a decision to submit his will to the will of the church. Unable to be a real soldier, he vowed to be a soldier of God. Over a period of twelve years, Loyola prepared for his lifework by prayer, pilgrimages, going to school, and working out a spiritual program in his brief but powerful book, *The Spiritual Exercises*. This was a training manual for spiritual development emphasizing exercises by which the human will could be strengthened and made to follow the will of God as manifested through his instrument, the Catholic Church (see Historical Voices, "Loyola and Obedience to 'Our Holy Mother, the Hierarchical Church,'" p. 399).

Loyola gathered together a small group of individuals who were eventually recognized as a religious order, the Society of Jesus, by a papal bull in 1540 (see Image 13.10). The new order was grounded on the principles of absolute obedience to the papacy, a strict hierarchical order for the society, the use of education to achieve its goals, and a dedication to engage in "conflict for God." The Jesuits' organization came to resemble the structure of a military command. A two-year novitiate weeded out all but the most dedicated adherents. Executive leadership was put in the hands of a general, who nominated all important positions in the order and was to be revered as the absolute head of the order. Loyola served as the first general of the order until his death in 1556. A special vow of absolute obedience to the pope made the Jesuits an important instrument for papal policy.

Activities of the Jesuits The Jesuits pursued three major activities. They established highly disciplined schools, borrowing freely from humanist schools for their educational methods. To the Jesuits, the thorough education of young people

IMAGE 13.10 **Ignatius of Loyola.** The Jesuits became the most important new religious order of the Catholic Reformation. Shown here in a sixteenth-century painting by an unknown artist is Ignatius of Loyola, founder of the Society of Jesus. Loyola is seen kneeling before Pope Paul III, who officially recognized the Jesuits in 1540.

Scala/Art Resource, NY

Loyola and Obedience to "Our Holy Mother, the Hierarchical Church"

 Q *What are the fundamental assumptions that inform Loyola's rules for "thinking with the church"? What do these assumptions tell you about the nature of the Catholic reform movement?*

IN HIS SPIRITUAL EXERCISES, Ignatius of Loyola developed a systematic program for "the conquest of self and the regulation of one's life" for service to the hierarchical Catholic Church. Ignatius's supreme goal was the commitment of the Christian to active service under Jesus's banner in the Church of Christ (the Catholic Church). In the final section of *The Spiritual Exercises,* Loyola explained the nature of that commitment in a series of "Rules for Thinking with the Church."

Ignatius of Loyola, "Rules for Thinking with the Church"

The following rules should be observed to foster the true attitude of mind we ought to have in the Church militant.

1. We must put aside all judgment of our own, and keep the mind ever ready and prompt to obey in all things the true Spouse of Jesus Christ, our holy Mother, the hierarchical Church.
2. We should praise sacramental confession, the yearly reception of the Most Blessed Sacrament [the Lord's Supper], and praise more highly monthly reception, and still more weekly Communion. . . .
3. We ought to praise the frequent hearing of Mass, the singing of hymns, psalmody, and long prayers whether in the church or outside. . . .
4. We must praise highly religious life, virginity, and continency; and matrimony ought not be praised as much as any of these.

5. We should praise vows of religion, obedience, poverty, chastity, and vows to perform other works of supererogation conducive to perfection. . . .
6. We should show our esteem for the relics of the saints by venerating them and praying to the saints. We should praise visits to the Station Churches, pilgrimages, indulgences, jubilees, the lighting of candles in churches.
7. We must praise the regulations of the Church, with regard to fast and abstinence, for example, in Lent, on Ember Days, Vigils, Fridays, and Saturdays.
8. We ought to praise not only the building and adornment of churches, but also images and veneration of them according to the subject they represent.
9. Finally, we must praise all the commandments of the Church, and be on the alert to find reasons to defend them, and by no means in order to criticize them.
10. We should be more ready to approve and praise the orders, recommendations, and way of acting of our superiors than to find fault with them. Though some of the orders, etc., may not have been praiseworthy, yet to speak against them, either when preaching in public or in speaking before the people, would rather be the cause of murmuring and scandal than of profit. As a consequence, the people would become angry with their superiors, whether secular or spiritual. But while it does harm in the absence of our superiors to speak evil of them before the people, it may be profitable to discuss their bad conduct with those who can apply a remedy. . . .
13. If we wish to proceed securely in all things, we must hold fast to the following principle: What seems to me white, I will believe black if the hierarchical Church so defines. For I must be convinced that in Christ our Lord, the bridegroom, and in His spouse the Church, only one Spirit holds sway, which governs and rules for the salvation of souls.

Source: Ignatius of Loyola, "Rules for Thinking with the Church," in *The Spiritual Exercises of St. Ignatius of Loyola,* trans. L. J. Puhl (Baltimore: Loyola University Press, 1951).

---

was crucial to combating the advance of Protestantism. In the course of the sixteenth century, the Jesuits took over the premier academic posts in Catholic universities, and by 1600, they were the most famous educators in Europe.

Another prominent Jesuit activity was the propagation of the Catholic faith among non-Christians. Francis Xavier (ZAY-vee-ur) (1506–1552), one of the original members of the Society of Jesus, carried the message of Catholic Christianity to the East. After converting tens of thousands in India, he traveled to Malacca and the Moluccas before reaching Japan in 1549. He

spoke highly of the Japanese: "They are a people of excellent morals—good in general and not malicious."[21] Thousands of Japanese, especially in the southernmost islands, became Christians. In 1552, Xavier set out for China but died of a fever before he reached the mainland.

Although conversion efforts in Japan proved short-lived, Jesuit activity in China, especially that of the Italian Matteo Ricci (ma-TAY-oh REE-chee) (1552–1610), was more long-lasting. Recognizing the Chinese pride in their own culture, the Jesuits attempted to draw parallels between Christian and Confucian concepts and to show the similarities between Christian morality and Confucian ethics. For their part, the missionaries were impressed with many aspects of Chinese civilization, and reports of their experiences heightened European curiosity about this great society on the other side of the world.

The Jesuits were also determined to carry the Catholic banner and fight Protestantism. Jesuit missionaries succeeded in restoring Catholicism to parts of Germany and eastern Europe. Poland was largely won back for the Catholic Church through Jesuit efforts.

13-5c A Revived Papacy

The involvement of the Renaissance papacy in dubious finances and Italian political and military affairs had given rise to numerous sources of corruption. The meager steps taken to control corruption left the papacy still in need of serious reform, and it took the jolt of the Protestant Reformation to bring it about.

The pontificate of Pope Paul III (1534–1549) proved to be a turning point in the reform of the papacy. Raised in the lap of Renaissance luxury, Paul III continued Renaissance papal practices by appointing his nephews as cardinals, involving himself in politics, and patronizing arts and letters on a lavish scale. Nevertheless, he perceived the need for change and expressed it decisively. He made advocates of reform, such as Gasparo Contarini (GAHS-puh-roh kahn-tuh-REE-nee) and Gian Pietro Caraffa (JAHN PYAY-troh kuh-RAH-fuh), cardinals. In 1535, Paul took the audacious step of appointing a reform commission to study the condition of the church. The commission's report in 1537 blamed the church's problems on the corrupt policies of popes and cardinals. Paul III also formally recognized the Jesuits and summoned the Council of Trent (see Section 13-5d).

A decisive turning point in the direction of the Catholic Reformation and the nature of papal reform came in the 1540s. In 1541, a colloquy had been held at Regensburg in a final attempt to settle the religious division peacefully. Here Catholic moderates, such as Cardinal Contarini, who favored concessions to Protestants in the hope of restoring Christian unity, reached a compromise with Protestant moderates on a number of doctrinal issues. When Contarini returned to Rome with these proposals, Cardinal Caraffa and other hardliners, who regarded all compromise with Protestant innovations as heresy, accused him of selling out to the heretics. It soon became apparent that the conservative reformers were in the ascendancy when Caraffa was able to persuade Paul III to establish the Roman Inquisition or Holy Office in 1542 to ferret out doctrinal errors. There was to be no compromise with Protestantism.

When Cardinal Caraffa was chosen pope as Paul IV (1555–1559), he so increased the power of the Inquisition that even liberal cardinals were silenced. This "first true pope of the Catholic Counter-Reformation," as he has been called, also created the Index of Forbidden Books, a list of books that Catholics were not allowed to read. It included all the works of Protestant theologians as well as authors considered "unwholesome,"

a category general enough to include the works of Erasmus. Rome, the capital of Catholic Christianity, was rapidly becoming Fortress Rome; any hope of restoring Christian unity by compromise was fast fading. The activities of the Council of Trent made compromise virtually impossible.

13-5d The Council of Trent

In 1542, Pope Paul III took the decisive step of calling for a general council of Christendom to resolve the religious differences created by the Protestant revolt. It was not until March 1545, however, that a group of cardinals, archbishops, bishops, abbots, and theologians met in the city of Trent on the border between Germany and Italy and initiated the Council of Trent. But a variety of problems, including an outbreak of plague, war between France and Spain, and the changing of popes, prevented the council from holding regular annual meetings. Nevertheless, the council met intermittently in three major sessions between 1545 and 1563. Moderate Catholic reformers hoped that the council would make compromises in formulating doctrinal definitions that would encourage Protestants to return to the church. Conservatives, however, favored an uncompromising restatement of Catholic doctrines in strict opposition to Protestant positions. After a struggle, the latter group won.

The final doctrinal decrees of the Council of Trent reaffirmed traditional Catholic teachings in opposition to Protestant beliefs. The council affirmed Scripture and tradition as equal authorities in religious matters; only the church could interpret Scripture. Other decrees declared both faith and good works to be necessary for salvation and upheld the seven sacraments, the Catholic doctrine of transubstantiation, and clerical celibacy. The council also affirmed the belief in purgatory and in the efficacy of indulgences, although it prohibited the hawking of indulgences. Of the reform decrees that were passed, the most important established theological seminaries in every diocese for the training of priests.

After the Council of Trent, the Roman Catholic Church possessed a clear body of doctrine and a unified church under the acknowledged supremacy of the popes, who had triumphed over bishops and councils. The Roman Catholic Church had become one Christian denomination among many with an organizational framework and doctrinal pattern that would not be significantly altered for four hundred years. With renewed confidence, the Catholic Church entered a new phase of its history.

CHRONOLOGY	The Catholic Reformation
Pope Paul III	1534–1549
Papal recognition of Society of Jesus (Jesuits)	1540
Establishment of Roman Inquisition (Holy Office)	1542
Council of Trent	1545–1563
Pope Paul IV	1555–1559

13-6 Politics and the Wars of Religion in the Sixteenth Century

 FOCUS QUESTIONS: What role did politics, economic and social conditions, and religion play in the European wars of the sixteenth century? What is the significance of Montaigne?

By the middle of the sixteenth century, Calvinism and Catholicism had become activist religions dedicated to spreading the word of God as they interpreted it. Although this struggle for the minds and hearts of Europeans is at the heart of the religious wars of the sixteenth century, economic, social, and political forces also played an important role in these conflicts. Of the sixteenth-century religious wars, none were more momentous or shattering than the French civil wars known as the French Wars of Religion.

13-6a The French Wars of Religion (1562–1598)

Religion was the engine that drove the French civil wars of the sixteenth century. Concerned by the growth of Calvinism, the French kings tried to stop its spread by persecuting Calvinists but had little success. **Huguenots** (HYOO-guh-nots), as the French Calvinists were called, came from all levels of society: artisans and shopkeepers hurt by rising prices and a rigid guild system, merchants and lawyers in provincial towns whose local privileges were tenuous, and members of the nobility. Possibly 40 to 50 percent of the French nobility became Huguenots, including the house of Bourbon (boor-BOHN), which stood next to the Valois (val-WAH) in the royal line of succession and ruled the southern French kingdom of Navarre (nuh-VAHR). The conversion of so many nobles made the Huguenots a potentially dangerous political threat to monarchical power. Though the Calvinists constituted only about 10 percent of the population, they were a strong-willed and well-organized minority.

The Catholic majority greatly outnumbered the Calvinist minority. The Valois monarchy was staunchly Catholic, and its control of the Catholic Church gave it little incentive to look on Protestantism favorably. When King Henry II was killed accidentally in a tournament in 1559, he was succeeded by a series of weak and neurotic sons, two of whom were dominated by their mother, Catherine de' Medici (1519–1589). As regent for her sons, the moderate Catholic Catherine looked to religious compromise as a way to defuse the political tensions but found to her consternation that both sides possessed their share of religious fanatics unwilling to make concessions. The extreme Catholic party—known as the ultra-Catholics—favored strict opposition to the Huguenots and was led by the Guise (GEEZ) family. Possessing the loyalty of Paris and large sections of northern and northwestern France through their client-patronage system, the Guises could recruit and pay for large armies and received support abroad from the papacy and Jesuits who favored the family's uncompromising Catholic position.

But religion was not the only factor contributing to the French civil wars. Resentful of the growing power of monarchical centralization, towns and provinces were only too willing to join a revolt against the monarchy. This was also true of the nobility, and because so many of them were Calvinists, they formed an important base of opposition to the crown. The French Wars of Religion, then, presented a major constitutional crisis for France and temporarily halted the development of the French centralized territorial state. The claim of the state's ruling dynasty to a person's loyalties was temporarily superseded by loyalty to one's religious belief. For some people, the unity of France was less important than religious truth. But there also emerged in France a group of public figures who placed politics before religion and believed that no religious truth was worth the ravages of civil war. These **politiques** (puh-lee-TEEKS) ultimately prevailed, but not until both sides were exhausted by bloodshed.

Course of the Struggle The wars erupted in 1562 when the powerful duke of Guise massacred a peaceful congregation of Huguenots at Vassy. In the decade of the 1560s, the Huguenots held their own. Though too small a group to conquer France, their armies were so good at defensive campaigns that they could not be defeated either, despite the infamous Saint Bartholomew's Day massacre.

This massacre of Huguenots occurred in August 1572 at a time when the Catholic and Calvinist parties had apparently been reconciled through the marriage of the sister of the reigning Valois king, Charles IX (r. 1560–1574), and Henry of Navarre, the Bourbon ruler of Navarre. Henry was the son of Jeanne d'Albret (ZHAHN dahl-BRAY), queen of Navarre, who had been responsible for introducing Calvinist ideas into her kingdom. Henry was also the acknowledged political leader of the Huguenots, and many Huguenots traveled to Paris for the wedding.

But the Guise family persuaded the king and his mother, Catherine de' Medici, that this gathering of Huguenots posed a threat to them. Charles and his advisers decided to eliminate the Huguenot leaders with one swift blow. According to one French military leader, Charles and his advisers believed that civil war would soon break out anyway and that "it was better to win a battle in Paris, where all the leaders were, than to risk it in the field and fall into a dangerous and uncertain war."[22]

The massacre began early in the day on August 24 when the king's guards sought out and killed some prominent Huguenot leaders (see Image 13.11). These murders soon unleashed a wave of violence that gripped the city of Paris. For three days, frenzied Catholic mobs roamed the streets of Paris, killing Huguenots in an often cruel and bloodthirsty manner. According to one eyewitness account: "Then they took her [Françoise Lussault] and dragged her by the hair a long way through the streets, and spying the gold bracelets on her arms, without having the patience to unfasten them, cut off her wrists."[23] Three days of killing left three thousand Huguenots dead, although not Henry of Navarre, who saved his life by promising to turn Catholic. Thousands more were killed in provincial towns. The massacre boomeranged, however, because it discredited the Valois dynasty without ending the conflict.

Musée Cantonal des Beaux-Arts, Lausanne//De Agostini Picture Library/G. Dagli Orti/Bridgeman Images

IMAGE 13.11 **The Saint Bartholomew's Day Massacre.** Although the outbreak of religious war seemed unlikely in France, the collapse of the strong monarchy with the death of Henry II unleashed forces that led to a series of civil wars. Pictured here is the Saint Bartholomew's Day massacre of 1572. This contemporary painting by the Huguenot artist François Dubois vividly depicts a number of the incidents of that day when approximately three thousand Huguenots were murdered in Paris.

The fighting continued. The Huguenots rebuilt their strength, and in 1576, the ultra-Catholics formed a "Holy League," vowing to exterminate heresy and seat a true Catholic champion—Henry, duke of Guise—on the French throne in place of the ruling king, Henry III (r. 1574–1589), who had succeeded his brother Charles IX. The turning point in the conflict came in the War of the Three Henries in 1588–1589. Henry, duke of Guise, in the pay of Philip II of Spain, seized Paris and forced King Henry III to make him chief minister. To rid himself of Guise influence, Henry III assassinated the duke of Guise and then joined with Henry of Navarre (who meanwhile had returned to Calvinism), who was next in line to the throne, to crush the Catholic Holy League and retake the city of Paris. Although successful, Henry III was assassinated in 1589 by a monk who was repelled by the spectacle of a Catholic king cooperating with a Protestant. Henry of Navarre now claimed the throne. Realizing, however, that Catholic France would never accept him, Henry took the logical way out and converted once again to Catholicism. With his coronation in 1594, the French Wars of Religion finally came to an end.

Nevertheless, the religious problem persisted until the Edict of Nantes (NAHNT) was issued in 1598. The edict acknowledged Catholicism as the official religion of France but guaranteed the Huguenots the right to worship in selected places in every district and allowed them to retain a number of fortified towns for their protection. In addition, Huguenots were allowed to enjoy all political privileges, including the holding of public offices. Although the Edict of Nantes recognized the rights of the Protestant minority and ostensibly the principle of religious toleration, it did so only out of political necessity, not out of conviction.

CHRONOLOGY	The French Wars of Religion (1562–1598)	
Duke of Guise massacres Huguenot congregation at Vassy		1562
Saint Bartholomew's Day massacre		1572
Henry III		1574–1589
Formation of the Holy League		1576
War of the Three Henries		1588–1589
Assassination of Henry III		1589
Coronation of Henry IV		1594
Edict of Nantes		1598

13-6b Philip II and Militant Catholicism

The greatest advocate of activist Catholicism in the second half of the sixteenth century was King Philip II of Spain (r. 1556–1598), the son and heir of Charles V. Philip's reign ushered in an age of Spanish greatness, both politically and culturally (see Image 13.12).

The first major goal of Philip II was to consolidate and secure the lands he had inherited from his father. These included Spain, the Netherlands, and possessions in Italy (see Map 13.4) and the New World. For Philip, this meant strict conformity to

Scala/Art Resource, NY

IMAGE 13.12 **Philip of Spain.** This portrait by Titian depicts Philip II of Spain. The king's attempts to make Spain a great power led to large debts and crushing taxes, and his military actions in defense of Catholicism ended in failure and misfortune in both France and the Netherlands.

Q *What does this portrait of Philip II and that of Henry VIII (see Image 13.7) tell you about sixteenth-century monarchs and their relationship to prominent artists?*

Catholicism, enforced by aggressive use of the Spanish Inquisition, and the establishment of strong, monarchical authority. The latter was not an easy task because Philip had inherited a governmental structure in which each of the various states and territories of his empire stood in an individual relationship to the king. Philip did manage, however, to expand royal power in Spain by making the monarchy less dependent on the traditional landed aristocracy. Philip tried to be the center of the whole government and supervised the work of all departments, even down to the smallest details. Unwilling to delegate authority, he failed to distinguish between important and trivial matters and fell weeks behind on state correspondence, where he was inclined to make marginal notes and even correct spelling. One Spanish official said, "If God used the Escorial [the royal palace where Philip worked] to deliver my death sentence, I would be immortal."

One of Philip's aims was to make Spain a dominant power in Europe. To a great extent, Spain's preeminence depended on a prosperous economy fueled by its importation of gold and silver from its New World possessions, its agriculture, its commerce, and its industry, especially in textiles, silk, and leather goods. The importation of silver also had detrimental effects, however, as it helped set off a spiraling inflation that disrupted the Spanish economy, eventually hurting both textile production and agriculture. Moreover, the expenses of war, especially after 1580, proved devastating to the Spanish economy. American gold and silver never constituted more than 20 percent of the royal revenue, leading the government to impose a crushing burden of direct and indirect taxes. Even then the government was forced to borrow. Philip repudiated his debts seven times; still, two-thirds of state income went to pay interest on the debt by the end of his reign. The attempt to make Spain a great power led to its decline after Philip's reign.

Crucial to an understanding of Philip II is the importance of Catholicism to the Spanish people and their ruler. Driven by a heritage of crusading fervor, the Spanish had little difficulty seeing themselves as a nation of people divinely chosen to save Catholic Christianity from the Protestant heretics. Philip II, the "Most Catholic King," became the champion of Catholicism throughout Europe, a role that led to spectacular victories and equally spectacular defeats for the Spanish king. Spain's leadership of a holy league against Turkish encroachments in the Mediterranean, especially the Muslim attack on the island of Cyprus, resulted in a stunning victory over the Turkish fleet at the Battle of Lepanto (LEH-pahn-toh *or* LIH-pan-toh) in 1571. Philip's greatest misfortunes came from his attempt to crush the revolt in the Netherlands and his tortured relations with Queen Elizabeth of England.

13-6c Revolt of the Netherlands

As one of the richest parts of Philip's empire, the Spanish Netherlands was of great importance to the Most Catholic King. The Netherlands consisted of seventeen provinces (the modern Netherlands, Belgium, and Luxembourg). The seven northern provinces were largely Germanic in culture and Dutch speaking, while the French- and Flemish-speaking southern provinces were closely tied to France. Situated at the commercial

MAP 13.4 **The Height of Spanish Power Under Philip II.** Like his father, Charles V, Philip II, the "Most Catholic King," was a champion of the Catholic cause against Protestantism. He sought to maintain Habsburg control in the Netherlands by combating a Protestant revolt, a rebellion eventually supported by Queen Elizabeth of England. Spain's attempt to invade England in 1588 ended in disaster.

 Why would England feel threatened by Spanish territory in the Netherlands?

crossroads of northwestern Europe, the Netherlands had become prosperous through commerce and a flourishing textile industry. Because of its location, the Netherlands was open to the religious influences of the age. Though some inhabitants had adopted Lutheranism or Anabaptism, by the time of Philip II, Calvinism was also making inroads. These provinces had no real political bond holding them together except their common ruler, and that ruler was Philip II, a foreigner who was out of touch with the local situation.

Philip II hoped to strengthen his control in the Netherlands, regardless of the traditional privileges of the separate provinces. This was strongly opposed by the nobles, towns, and provincial states, which stood to lose politically if their jealously guarded privileges and freedoms were weakened. Resentment against Philip increased when the residents of the Netherlands realized that the taxes they paid were being used for Spanish interests. Finally, religion became a major catalyst for rebellion when Philip attempted to crush Calvinism. Violence erupted in 1566 when Calvinists—especially nobles—began to destroy statues and stained-glass windows in Catholic churches. Philip responded by sending the duke of Alva with 10,000 veteran Spanish and Italian troops to crush the rebellion.

The repressive policies of the duke proved counterproductive. The levying of a permanent sales tax alienated many

merchants and commoners, who now joined the nobles and Calvinists in the struggle against Spanish rule. A special tribunal, known as the Council of Troubles (nicknamed the Council of Blood by the Dutch), inaugurated a reign of terror in which even powerful aristocrats were executed. As a result, the revolt now became organized, especially in the northern provinces, where William of Nassau, the prince of Orange, also known as William the Silent, and Dutch pirates known as the "Sea Beggars" mounted growing resistance. In 1573, Philip removed the duke of Alva and shifted to a more conciliatory policy to bring an end to the costly revolt.

William of Orange wished to unify all seventeen provinces, a goal seemingly realized in 1576 with the Pacification of Ghent. This agreement stipulated that all the provinces would stand together under William's leadership, respect religious differences, and demand that the Spanish troops be withdrawn. But religious differences proved too strong for any lasting union. When the duke of Parma, the next Spanish leader, arrived in the Netherlands, he astutely played on the religious differences of the provinces and split their united front. The southern provinces formed a Catholic union—the Union of Arras—in 1579 and accepted Spanish control. To counter this, William of Orange organized the seven northern, Dutch-speaking states into a Protestant union—the Union of Utrecht—determined to

CHRONOLOGY	Philip II and Militant Catholicism	
Philip II		1556–1598
Outbreak of revolt in the Netherlands		1566
Battle of Lepanto		1571
Spanish armada		1588
Twelve-year truce (Spain and Netherlands)		1609
Independence of the United Provinces		1648

Europe, laid the foundations for a world empire, and experienced a cultural renaissance (see Image 13.13).

The daughter of King Henry VIII and Anne Boleyn, Elizabeth had had a difficult early life. During Mary's reign, she had even been imprisoned for a while and had learned early to hide her true feelings from both private and public sight. Intelligent, cautious, and self-confident, she moved quickly to solve the difficult religious problem she had inherited from Mary, who had become extremely unpopular when she tried to return England to the Catholic fold.

oppose Spanish rule. The Netherlands was now divided along religious, geographic, and political lines into two hostile camps. The struggle dragged on until 1609, when a twelve-year truce ended the war, virtually recognizing the independence of the northern provinces. These "United Provinces" soon emerged as the Dutch Republic, although the Spanish did not formally recognize them as independent until 1648. The ten southern provinces remained a Spanish possession (see Map 13.4).

13-6d The England of Elizabeth

After the death of Queen Mary in 1558, her half-sister Elizabeth (r. 1558–1603) ascended the throne of England. During Elizabeth's reign, England rose to prominence as the relatively small island kingdom became the leader of the Protestant nations of

Religious Policy Elizabeth's religious policy was based on moderation and compromise. As a ruler, she wished to prevent England from being torn apart over matters of religion. Parliament cooperated with the queen in initiating the Elizabethan religious settlement in 1559. The Catholic legislation of Mary's reign was repealed, and the new Act of Supremacy designated Elizabeth as "the only supreme governor of this realm, as well in all spiritual or ecclesiastical things or causes, as temporal." She used this title rather than "supreme head of the church," which had been used by both Henry VIII and Edward VI, because she did not want to upset the Catholics, who considered the pope the supreme head, or radical Protestants, who thought that Christ alone was head of the church. The Act of Uniformity restored the church service of the Book of Common Prayer from the reign of Edward VI with some revisions to make it more acceptable to Catholics. The

IMAGE 13.13 **Procession of Queen Elizabeth I.** Intelligent and learned, Elizabeth Tudor was familiar with Latin and Greek and spoke several European languages. Served by able administrators, Elizabeth ruled for nearly forty-five years and generally avoided open military action against any major power. This picture, painted near the end of her reign, shows the queen in a ceremonial procession with her courtiers.

Queen Elizabeth I: "I Have the Heart of a King"

 What qualities evident in Elizabeth's speech would have endeared her to her listeners? How was her popularity connected to the events of the late sixteenth century?

QUEEN ELIZABETH RULED ENGLAND from 1558 to 1603 with a consummate skill that contemporaries considered unusual in a woman. Though shrewd and paternalistic, Elizabeth, like other sixteenth-century monarchs, depended for her power on the favor of her people. When England faced the threat of an invasion by the Spanish armada of Philip II in 1588, Elizabeth sought to rally her troops with a speech at Tilbury, a town on the Thames River. This selection is taken from her speech.

Queen Elizabeth I, Speech to the Troops at Tilbury

My loving people, we have been persuaded by some, that are careful of our safety, to take heed how we commit ourselves to armed multitudes, for fear of treachery; but I assure you, I do not desire to live to distrust my faithful and loving people. Let tyrants fear; I have always so behaved myself that, under God, I have placed my chiefest strength and safeguard in the loyal hearts and good will of my subjects. And therefore I am come amongst you at this time, not as for my recreation or sport, but being resolved, in the midst and heat of the battle, to live or die amongst you all; to lay down, for my God, and for my kingdom, and for my people, my honor and my blood, even in the dust. I know I have but the body of a weak and feeble woman; but I have the heart of a king, and of a king of England, too; and think foul scorn that Parma or Spain, or any prince of Europe, should dare to invade the borders of my realm: to which, rather than any dishonor should grow by me, I myself will take up arms; I myself will be your general, judge, and rewarder of every one of your virtues in the field. I know already, by your forwardness, that you have deserved rewards and crowns; and we do assure you, on the word of a prince, they shall be duly paid you. In the mean my lieutenant general shall be in my stead, than whom never prince commanded a more noble and worthy subject; not doubting by your obedience to my general, by your concord in the camp and by your valor in the field, we shall shortly have a famous victory over the enemies of my God, of my kingdom, and of my people.

Source: Elizabeth I's Speech to the Troops at Tilbury in 1588.

Thirty-Nine Articles, a new confession of faith, defined theological issues midway between Lutheranism and Calvinism. Elizabeth's religious settlement was basically Protestant, but it was a moderate Protestantism that avoided overly subtle distinctions and extremes.

The new religious settlement worked, at least to the extent that it smothered religious differences in England in the second half of the sixteenth century. Two groups, however, the Catholics and the Puritans, continued to oppose it. One of Elizabeth's greatest challenges came from her Catholic cousin, Mary, queen of Scots, who was next in line to the English throne. Mary was ousted from Scotland by rebellious Calvinist nobles in 1568 and fled for her life to England. There Elizabeth placed her under house arrest and for fourteen years tolerated her involvement in a number of ill-planned Catholic plots designed to kill Elizabeth and replace her on the throne with the Catholic Mary. Finally, in 1587, after Mary became embroiled in a far more serious plot, Elizabeth had her cousin beheaded to end the threats to her regime.

Potentially more dangerous to Anglicanism in the long run were the **Puritans**. The word *Puritan* first appeared in 1564 when it was used to refer to Protestants within the Anglican Church who, inspired by Calvinist theology, wanted to remove any trace of Catholicism from the Church of England. Elizabeth managed to keep the Puritans in check during her reign.

Elizabeth proved as adept in government and foreign policy as in religious affairs (see Historical Voices, "Queen Elizabeth: 'I Have the Heart of a King,'" above). She was well served administratively by the principal secretary of state. The talents of Sir William Cecil and Sir Francis Walsingham, who together held the office for thirty-two years, ensured much of Elizabeth's success in foreign and domestic affairs. Elizabeth also handled Parliament with much skill; it met only thirteen times during her entire reign.

Foreign Policy Caution, moderation, and expediency also dictated Elizabeth's foreign policy. Fearful of other countries' motives, Elizabeth realized that war could be disastrous for her island kingdom and her own rule. Unofficially, however, she encouraged English seamen to raid Spanish ships and colonies. Francis Drake was especially adept at plundering Spanish fleets loaded with gold and silver from Spain's New World empire. While encouraging English piracy and providing clandestine aid to French Huguenots and Dutch Calvinists to weaken France and Spain, Elizabeth pretended

MOVIES & HISTORY
Elizabeth (1998)

Watch *Elizabeth*, which opens with Queen Mary pursuing her dream of restoring Catholicism to England as she contemplates signing a death warrant for her Protestant half-sister Elizabeth. But she refuses to do so before dying in 1558. Elizabeth becomes queen and is portrayed in her early years of rule as an uncertain monarch who "rules from the heart instead of the mind," as one adviser tells her. The strength of the movie, which contains numerous historical inaccuracies, is the performance of Cate Blanchett, who captures some of the characteristics of Queen Elizabeth I.

 What historical inaccuracies do you find in the movie? What is convincing about the portrait of Queen Elizabeth?

complete aloofness and avoided alliances that would force her into war with any major power (see Movies & History, *Elizabeth*, above). Gradually, however, Elizabeth was drawn into more active involvement in the Netherlands. This move accelerated the already mounting friction between Spain and England. After years of resisting the idea of invading England as impractical, Philip II of Spain was finally persuaded to do so by advisers who assured him that the people of England would rise against their queen when the Spaniards arrived. Moreover, Philip was easily convinced that the revolt in the Netherlands would never be crushed as long as England provided support for it. In any case, a successful invasion of England would mean the overthrow of heresy and the return of England to Catholicism, surely an act in accordance with the will of God. Accordingly, Philip ordered preparations for a fleet of warships that would rendezvous with the army of the duke of Parma in Flanders and escort his troops across the English Channel for the invasion.

The Spanish Armada The armada proved to be a disaster. The Spanish fleet that finally set sail had neither the ships nor the troops that Philip had planned to send. A conversation between a papal emissary and an officer of the Spanish fleet before the armada departed reveals the fundamental flaw:

> "And if you meet the English armada in the Channel, do you expect to win the battle?" "Of course," replied the Spaniard.
>
> "How can you be sure?" [asked the emissary].
>
> "It's very simple. It is well known that we fight in God's cause. So, when we meet the English, God will surely arrange matters so that we can grapple and board them, either by sending some strange freak of weather or, more likely, just

by depriving the English of their wits. If we can come to close quarters, Spanish valor and Spanish steel (and the great masses of soldiers we shall have on board) will make our victory certain. But unless God helps us by a miracle the English, who have faster and handier ships than ours, and many more long-range guns, and who know their advantage just as well as we do, will never close with us at all, but stand aloof and knock us to pieces with their culverins [cannons], without our being able to do them any serious hurt. So," concluded the captain, and one fancies a grim smile, "we are sailing against England in the confident hope of a miracle."[24]

The hoped-for miracle never materialized. The Spanish fleet, battered by a number of encounters with the English, sailed back to Spain by a northward route around Scotland and Ireland, where it was further battered by storms. Although the English and Spanish would continue their war for another sixteen years, the defeat of the Spanish armada guaranteed for the time being that England would remain a Protestant country. Although Spain made up for its losses within a year and a half, the defeat was a psychological blow to the Spaniards.

13-6e Response to the Wars of Religion: Michel de Montaigne

In a world beset by religious strife leading to violence and chaos, one French intellectual stands out as he urged Europeans to take a more peaceful path. Born into a wealthy family, Michel de Montaigne (1533–1592) received a humanist education before becoming a lawyer. After practicing law for many years, the wealthy Montaigne chose to retire to his family's country estate. As he stated, "In . . . 1571, at the age of thirty-eight . . . Michel de Montaigne, long weary of the servitude of the court and of public employments . . . retired to [his country estate], where in calm and freedom from all cares he will spend what little remains of his life, now more than half run out."[25] However, as a recent biographer has argued, Montaigne did not really retire but continued with his political ambitions, becoming mayor of Bordeaux and serving as a negotiator between Henry III and Henry of Navarre (see "13-6a The French Wars of Religion," above).

Nevertheless, beginning in his country retreat and continuing thereafter, Montaigne wrote a series of essays in which he rejected the discord of his age and adopted the ancient doctrine of skepticism. Arguing that humans can never be certain about anything, he wrote, "What do I know? Nothing." Thus, he rejected both the Catholic and Protestant certainty of their doctrines that had led to French civil war. He also denounced the labeling of recently discovered New World natives as barbarians, stating, "[E]veryone gives the title of barbarism to everything that is not in his own country. As, indeed, we have no other level of truth and reason, than the example and idea of the opinions and customs of the place wherein we live."[26] Montaigne's clear voice of reason in an era of religious fanaticism helped create a movement toward secularism that would eventually dominate European civilization.

When the Augustinian monk Martin Luther burst onto the scene with a series of theses on indulgences, few people suspected that his observations would eventually split all of Europe along religious lines. But the yearning for reform of the church and meaningful religious experiences caused a seemingly simple dispute to escalate into a powerful movement.

Martin Luther established the twin pillars of the Protestant Reformation: the doctrine of justification by faith alone and the Bible as the sole authority in religious affairs. Although Luther felt that his revival of Christianity based on his interpretation of the Bible should be acceptable to all, others soon appeared who also read the Bible but interpreted it in different ways. Protestantism fragmented into different sects—Zwinglianism, Calvinism, Anglicanism, Anabaptism—which, though united in their dislike of Catholicism, were themselves divided over the interpretation of the sacraments and religious practices. As reform ideas spread, religion and politics became ever more intertwined.

Although the peace of Augsburg in 1555 legally acknowledged Lutheranism in the Holy Roman Empire, it had lost much of its momentum and outside of Scandinavia had scant ability to attract new supporters. Its energy was largely replaced by the new Protestant form of Calvinism, which had a clarity of doctrine and a fervor that made it attractive to a

whole new generation of Europeans. But while Calvinism's activism enabled it to spread across Europe, Catholicism was also experiencing its own revival. New religious orders based on reform, a revived and reformed papacy, and the Council of Trent, which reaffirmed traditional Catholic doctrine, gave the Catholic Church a renewed vitality.

By the middle of the sixteenth century, it was apparent that the religious passions of the Reformation era had brought an end to the religious unity of medieval Europe. The religious division (Catholics versus Protestant) was instrumental in beginning a series of religious wars that were complicated by economic, social, and political forces that also played a role. The French Wars of Religion, the revolt of the Netherlands against Philip II of Spain, and the conflict between Philip II and Elizabeth of England, which led to the failed attempt of the Spanish armada to invade England, were the major struggles in the sixteenth-century religious wars.

That people who were disciples of the Apostle of Peace would kill each other over their beliefs aroused skepticism about Christianity itself. As one German writer put it, "Lutheran, popish, and Calvinistic, we've got all these beliefs here, but there is some doubt about where Christianity has got."[27] It is surely no accident that the search for a stable, secular order of politics and for order in the universe through natural laws would come to play important roles. Before we look at this search for order in the seventeenth century, however, we need first to look at the adventures that plunged Europe into its new role in the world.

CHAPTER TIMELINE

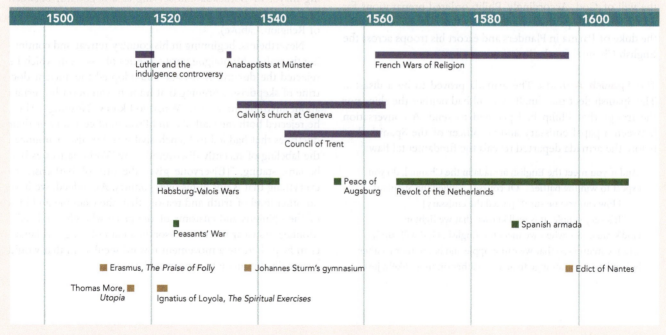

1500	1520	1540	1560	1580	1600

Luther and the indulgence controversy

Anabaptists at Münster

French Wars of Religion

Calvin's church at Geneva

Council of Trent

Habsburg-Valois Wars

Peace of Augsburg

Revolt of the Netherlands

Peasants' War

Spanish armada

Erasmus, *The Praise of Folly*

Johannes Sturm's gymnasium

Edict of Nantes

Thomas More, *Utopia*

Ignatius of Loyola, *The Spiritual Exercises*

CHAPTER REVIEW

Upon Reflection

Q Where and how did the reform movements take hold, and how did the emergence of these reform movements affect the political and social realms where they were adopted?

Q If attempts at reform of the Catholic Church were unsuccessful in the fifteenth century, why did they succeed during the sixteenth-century Reformation?

Q What role did politics play in the establishment of Lutheranism and Anglicanism?

Q Elizabeth of England and Philip II of Spain were two of Europe's most famous monarchs in the second half of the sixteenth century. Compare and contrast their methods of ruling and their foreign policy. Which was a more successful ruler? Why?

Key Terms

Christian (northern Renaissance) humanism (p. 376)
pluralism (p. 378)
confession (p. 379)
justification (p. 380)
transubstantiation (p. 384)
millenarianism (p. 390)

predestination (p. 393)
Catholic Reformation (p. 398)
Huguenots (p. 401)
politiques (p. 401)
Puritans (p. 406)

Full definitions also appear in the Glossary at the end of the book.

Suggestions for Further Reading

The Reformation For a general history of the era of the Reformation, see **M. Greengrass, *Christendom Destroyed: Europe 1517–1648*** (New York, 2014). Basic surveys of the Reformation period include **C. Eire, *Reformations: The Early Modern World, 1450–1650*** (New Haven, Conn., 2016); **J. D. Tracy, *Europe's Reformations, 1450–1650*,** 2nd ed. (Oxford, 2006); and **D. MacCulloch, *The Reformation*** (New York, 2003).

Northern Renaissance Humanism The development of humanism outside Italy is examined in **C. G. Nauert Jr., *Humanism and the Culture of Renaissance Europe*,** 2nd ed. (Cambridge, 2006).

Luther and Lutheranism On Martin Luther's life, see **L. Roper, *Martin Luther: Renegade and Prophet*** (New York, 2017), and the brief biography by **M. Marty, *Martin Luther*** (New York, 2004). For a dual biography of Erasmus and Luther, see **M. Massing, *Fatal Discord: Erasmus, Luther, and the Fight for the Western Mind*** (New York, 2018). On the role of Charles V, see **G. Parker, *A New Life of Charles V*** (New Haven, Conn., 2019).

Spread of the Protestant Reformation **W. P. Stephens's** *Zwingli* (Oxford, 1994) is an important study of the man's ideas. The most comprehensive account of the various groups and individuals who are called Anabaptists is **G. H. Williams, *The***

Radical Reformation, 2nd ed. (Kirksville, Mo., 1992). On the English Reformation, see **N. L. Jones, *English Reformation: Religion and Cultural Adaptation*** (London, 2002). On Calvinism, see **W. G. Naphy, *Calvin and the Consolidation of the Genevan Reformation*** (Philadelphia, 2003).

Social Impact of the Reformation On the impact of the Reformation on the family, see **J. F. Harrington, *Reordering Marriage and Society in Reformation Germany*** (New York, 1995). On women, see **K. Stjerna, *Women and the Reformation*** (New York, 2008).

Catholic Reformation A good introduction to the Catholic Reformation can be found in **M. A. Mullett, *The Catholic Reformation*** (London, 1999). Also valuable is **R. P. Hsia, *The World of Catholic Renewal, 1540–1770*,** 2nd ed. (Cambridge, 2006).

Wars of Religion For a good introduction to the French Wars of Religion, see **R. J. Knecht, *The French Wars of Religion, 1559–1598*,** 3rd ed. (New York, 2010). On Philip II, see **G. Parker, *Imprudent King: A New Life of Philip II*** (New Haven, Conn., 2014). Elizabeth's reign can be examined in **D. Loades, *Elizabeth I*** (New York, 2006).

Response to the Wars of Religion For a good biography of Montaigne, see **P. Desan, *Montaigne: A Life*** (Princeton, N.J., 2017).

Notes

1. Quoted in R. Bainton, *Here I Stand: A Life of Martin Luther* (Nashville, 1978), p. 183.
2. Desiderius Erasmus, *The Paraclesis*, in *Christian Humanism and the Reformation: Selected Writings of Erasmus*, 3rd ed., J. Olin, ed. (New York, 1987), p. 101.
3. Thomas More, *Utopia*, trans. Paul Turner (Harmondsworth, U.K., 1965), p. 76.
4. Quoted in A. E. McGrath, *Reformation Thought: An Introduction* (Oxford, 1988), p. 72.

5. Quoted in G. Rupp, *Luther's Progress to the Diet of Worms* (New York, 1964), p. 82.

6. Martin Luther, *On the Freedom of a Christian Man*, quoted in E. G. Rupp and B. Drewery, eds., *Martin Luther* (New York, 1970), p. 50.

7. Quoted in R. Bainton, *Here I Stand: A Life of Martin Luther*, pp. 181–182.

8. Author's translation of Martin Luther's lyrics, second verse of *Ein feste Burg ist unser Gott*.

9. Quoted in A. Dürer, *The Writings of Albrecht Dürer*, ed. and trans. (New York, 1958), p. 157.

10. Quoted in M. Massing, *Fatal Discord: Erasmus, Luther, and the Fight for the Western Mind* (New York: HarperCollins, 2018), p. 605.

11. Quoted in D. L. Jensen, *Reformation Europe* (Lexington, Mass., 1981), p. 83.

12. Quoted in L. P. Wandel, *Voracious Idols and Violent Hands: Iconoclasm in Reformation Zürich, Strasbourg, and Basel* (New York, 1995), p. 81.

13. Quoted in A. G. Dickens and D. Carr, eds., *The Reformation in England to the Accession of Elizabeth I* (New York, 1968), p. 72.

14. Quoted in L. W. Spitz, *The Renaissance and Reformation Movements* (Chicago, 1971), p. 414.

15. John Calvin, *Institutes of the Christian Religion*, trans. J. Allen (Philadelphia, 1936), vol. 1, p. 220.

16. Ibid., vol. 1, p. 228; vol. 2, p. 181.

17. Quoted in R. Bainton, *Women of the Reformation in Germany and Italy* (Minneapolis, 1971), p. 154.

18. Quoted in B. S. Anderson and J. P. Zinsser, *A History of Their Own: Women in Europe from Prehistory to the Present* (New York, 1988), vol. 1, p. 259.

19. Quoted in J. A. Phillips, *Eve: The History of an Idea* (New York, 1984), p. 105.

20. Quoted in J. Zophy, *A Short History of Renaissance and Reformation Europe*, 3rd ed. (Upper Saddle River, N.J., 2003), p. 227.

21. Quoted in J. O'Malley, *The First Jesuits* (Cambridge, Mass., 1993), p. 76.

22. Quoted in R. J. Knecht, *The French Wars of Religion, 1559–1598*, 2nd ed. (New York, 1996), p. 47.

23. Quoted in M. P. Holt, *The French Wars of Religion, 1562–1629* (Cambridge, 1995), p. 86.

24. Quoted in G. Mattingly, *The Armada* (Boston, 1959), pp. 216–217.

25. Quoted in D. Hollier, ed., *A New History of French Literature* (Cambridge, Mass., 1995), p. 249.

26. Quoted in C. Cotton, trans., *The Essays of Michel de Montaigne* (New York, 1893), p. 210.

27. Quoted in T. Schieder, *Handbuch der Europäischen Geschichte* (Stuttgart, 1979), vol. 3, p. 579.

MindTap *Tips*   MindTap makes forgotten due dates a thing of the past by ensuring current and upcoming assignments appear front-and-center at log in. An at-a-glance view of individual performance shows how you're doing at any given time. The Cengage Mobile App provides you with due date notifications as well.

CHAPTER 14

Europe and the World: New Encounters, 1500–1800

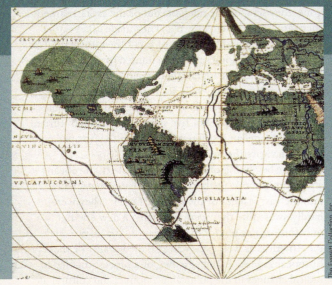

IMAGE 14.1 **A 1536 Mercator Projection Map Showing the Route of Ferdinand Magellan's First Circumnavigation of the World**

CHAPTER OUTLINE AND FOCUS QUESTIONS

14-1 On the Brink of a New World

Q Why did Europeans begin to embark on voyages of discovery and expansion at the end of the fifteenth century? What made their voyages possible?

14-2 New Horizons: The Portuguese and Spanish Empires

Q How did Portugal and Spain acquire their overseas empires, and how did their empires differ? How did Spain administer its empire?

14-3 New Rivals on the World Stage

Q How did the arrival of the Dutch, British, and French on the world scene in the seventeenth and eighteenth centuries affect Africa, Southeast Asia, India, China, and Japan? What were the main features of the African slave trade, and what effects did it have on Africa?

14-4 The Impact of European Expansion

Q How did European expansion affect the native populations and places that the Europeans conquered? For the Europeans who conquered the New World, how were their lives different from their Old World European counterparts?

14-5 Toward a World Economy

Q What was mercantilism, and what was its relationship to colonial empires? How did joint-stock companies change global trade?

CONNECTIONS TO TODAY

Considering both the benefits and the consequences, what are the similarities and differences between the overseas trade that developed in the seventeenth and eighteenth centuries and the global trade of the twenty-first century?

WHILE MANY EUROPEANS were occupied with the problems of dynastic expansion and religious reform, others were taking voyages that propelled Europeans far beyond the medieval walls in which they had been enclosed for almost a thousand years. One of these adventurers was the Portuguese explorer Ferdinand Magellan. Convinced that he could find a sea passage to Asia through America, Magellan persuaded the king of Spain to finance an exploratory voyage. On August 10, 1519, Magellan set sail on the Atlantic with five ships and a Spanish crew of 277 men. After a stormy and difficult crossing of the Atlantic, Magellan's fleet moved down the coast of South America, searching for the elusive strait that would take him through. His Spanish ship captains thought he was crazy: "The fool is obsessed with his search for a strait," one remarked. "On the flame of his ambition he will crucify us all." At last, in October 1520, he found it, passing through a narrow waterway (later named the Strait of Magellan) and emerging into an unknown ocean that he called the Pacific Sea. Magellan reckoned that it would then be a short distance to the Spice Islands of the East, but he was badly mistaken. Week after week, he and his crew sailed on across the Pacific as their food supplies dwindled. According to one account, "When their last biscuit had

411

gone, they scraped the maggots out of the casks, mashed them and served them as gruel. They made cakes out of sawdust soaked with the urine of rats—the rats themselves, as delicacies, had long since been hunted to extinction." At last they reached the islands that would later be called the Philippines (after King Philip II of Spain), where Magellan met his death at the hands of the natives. Although only one of his original fleet of five ships survived and returned to Spain, Magellan is still remembered as the first person to circumnavigate the world.

At the beginning of the sixteenth century, European adventurers like Magellan had begun launching small fleets into the vast reaches of the Atlantic Ocean. They were hardly aware that they were beginning a new era, not only for Europe, but for the peoples of Asia, Africa, and the Americas as well. Nevertheless, the voyages of these Europeans marked the beginning of a process that led to radical changes in the political, economic, and cultural life of the entire world.

Between 1500 and 1800, European power engulfed the world. In the Americas, Europeans established colonies that spread their laws, religions, and cultures. In the island regions of Southeast Asia, Europeans firmly established their rule. In other parts of Asia and in Africa, their activities ranged from trading goods to trafficking in humans, permanently altering the lives of the local peoples. In all regions touched by European expansion, the indigenous peoples faced exposure to new diseases, alteration of their religions and customs, and the imposition of new laws.

14-1 On the Brink of a New World

 FOCUS QUESTIONS: Why did Europeans begin to embark on voyages of discovery and expansion at the end of the fifteenth century? What made their voyages possible?

Nowhere has the dynamic and even ruthless energy of Western civilization been more apparent than in its expansion into the rest of the world. By the late sixteenth century, the Atlantic seaboard had become the center of a commercial activity that raised Portugal and Spain and later the Dutch Republic, England, and France to prominence. The age of expansion was a crucial factor in the European transition from the agrarian economy of the Middle Ages to a commercial and industrial capitalistic system. Expansion also brought Europeans into new and lasting contacts with non-European peoples that inaugurated a new age of world history in the sixteenth century.

14-1a The Motives for Expansion

For almost a millennium, Catholic Europe had been confined to one geographic area. Its one major attempt to expand beyond those frontiers, the Crusades, had largely failed. Of course, Europe had never completely lost touch with the outside world: the goods of Asia and Africa made their way into medieval castles, the works of Muslim philosophers were read in medieval universities, and in the ninth and tenth centuries, the Vikings had even made their way to the eastern fringes of North America. But in all cases, contacts with non-European civilizations remained limited until the end of the fifteenth century, when Europeans embarked on a remarkable series of overseas journeys. What caused Europeans to undertake such dangerous voyages to the ends of the earth?

Fantastic Lands Europeans had long felt the lure of lands outside Europe as a result of a large body of fantasy literature about "other worlds" that blossomed in the Middle Ages. In the fourteenth century, the author of *The Travels of John Mandeville* spoke of realms (which he had never seen) filled with precious stones and gold. Other lands were more frightening and considerably less appealing. In one country, "the folk be great giants of twenty-eight foot long, or thirty foot long. . . . And they eat more gladly man's flesh than any other flesh." Farther north was a land inhabited by "full cruel and evil women. And they have precious stones in their eyes. And they be of that kind that if they behold any man with wrath they slay him at once with the beholding."[1] Other writers, however, enticed Europeans with descriptions of mysterious Christian kingdoms: the magical kingdom of Prester John in Africa and a Christian community in southern India that was supposedly founded by Thomas, an apostle of Jesus.

Economic Motives Although Muslim control of Central Asia cut Europe off from the countries farther east, the Mongol conquests in the thirteenth century had reopened the doors. The most famous medieval travelers to the East were the Polos of Venice. Niccolò and Maffeo, merchants from Venice, accompanied by Niccolò's son Marco, undertook the lengthy journey to the court of the great Mongol ruler Khubilai Khan (r. 1259–1294) in 1271. An account of Marco's experiences, the *Travels*, was the most informative of all the descriptions of Asia by medieval European travelers (see Historical Voices, "Marco Polo's Travels," p. 413). Others followed the Polos, but in the fourteenth century, the conquests of the Ottoman Turks and then the breakup of the Mongol Empire reduced Western traffic to the East. With the closing of the overland routes, a number of people in Europe became interested in the possibility of reaching Asia by sea to gain access to the spices and other precious items of the region. Christopher Columbus had a copy of Marco Polo's *Travels* in his possession when he began to envision his epoch-making voyage across the Atlantic Ocean.

An economic motive thus loomed large in European expansion in the Renaissance. Merchants, adventurers, and government officials had high hopes of finding new areas of trade, especially more direct access to the spices of the East. These continued to come to Europe via Arab intermediaries but were outrageously expensive. In addition to the potential profits to be made from the spice trade, many European explorers and conquerors did not hesitate to express their desire for material gain in the form of gold and other precious metals.

Marco Polo's Travels

 What does this description of the city of Kinsay tell us about Europe in the late thirteenth century? Why would Asia appeal to European merchants who read Marco Polo's account?

ONE OF THE MOST POPULAR TEXTS in late medieval Europe was *The Travels of Marco Polo,* in which the Venetian merchant Marco Polo recounted the story of his journeys throughout East and South Asia. His description of the city of Kinsay—modern Hangzhou (HAHNG-joh) in eastern China—heavily influenced Europeans' conception of Asia.

Marco Polo, "Description of the Great City of Kinsay"

When you have left the city of Changan and have traveled for three days through a splendid country, passing a number of towns and villages, you arrive at the most noble city of Kinsay, a name which is as much as to say in our tongue "The City of Heaven," as I told you before. . . .

First and foremost, then, the document stated the city of Kinsay to be so great that it hath a hundred miles of compass. And there are in it twelve thousand bridges of stone, for the most part so lofty that a great fleet could pass beneath them. . . .

The document aforesaid also stated that the number and wealth of the merchants, and the amount of goods that passed through their hands, was so enormous that no man could form a just estimate thereof. . . .

All the streets are paved with stone or brick, as indeed are all the highways throughout Manzi, so that you ride and travel in every direction without inconvenience. . . .

There is another thing I must tell you. It is the custom for every burgess of this city, and in fact for every description of person in it, to write over his door his own name, the name of his wife, and those of his children, his slaves, and all the inmates of his house, and also the number of animals that he keeps. And if any one dies in the house then the name of that person is erased, and if any child is born its name is added. So in this way the sovereign is able to know exactly the population of the city. . . .

In this part [of the city] are ten principal markets, though besides these there are a vast number of others in the different parts of the town. . . . In each of the squares is held a market three days in the week, frequented by 40,000 or 50,000 persons, who bring thither for sale every possible necessary of life, so that there is always an ample supply of every kind of meat and game, as of roebuck, red-deer, fallow-deer, hares, rabbits, partridges, pheasants, francolins, quails, fowls, capons, and of ducks and geese an infinite quantity; for so many are bred on the Lake that for a Venice groat of silver you can have a couple of ducks. . . .

Those markets make a daily display of every kind of vegetables and fruits; and among the latter there are in particular certain pears of enormous size, weighing as much as ten pounds apiece. . . .

To give you an example of the vast consumption in this city let us take the article of *pepper*; and that will enable you in some measure to estimate what must be the quantity of victual, such as meat, wine, groceries, which have to be provided for the general consumption. Now Messer Marco heard it stated by one of the Great Khan's officers of customs that the quantity of pepper introduced daily for consumption into the city of Kinsay amounted to 43 loads, each load being equal to 223 lbs.

The houses of the citizens are well built and elaborately finished; and the delight they take in decoration, in painting and in architecture, leads them to spend in this way sums of money that would astonish you.

Source: H. Yule, ed., trans., *The Book of Ser Marco Polo,* vol. 1 (London: John Murray, 1903), pp. 185–193, 200–208.

One Spanish conquistador (kahn-KEESS-tuh-dor) explained that the purpose of their mission to the New World was to "serve God and His Majesty, to give light to those who were in darkness, and to grow rich, as all men desire to do."[2]

Religious Zeal The conquistador's statement expressed another major reason for the overseas voyages—religious zeal. A crusading mentality was particularly strong in Portugal and Spain, where the Muslims had largely been driven out in the Middle Ages. Contemporaries of Prince Henry the Navigator of Portugal (see "14-2a The Development of a Portuguese Maritime Empire," later in this chapter) said that he was motivated by "his great desire to make increase in the faith of our Lord Jesus Christ and to bring him all the souls that should be saved." Although most scholars believe that the religious motive was secondary to economic considerations, it would be foolish to overlook the genuine desire of explorers and conquistadors, let alone missionaries, to convert the heathen to Christianity. Hernàn Cortés (hayr-NAHN kor-TAYSS *or* kor-TEZ), the conqueror of Mexico, asked his Spanish rulers if it was not their duty to ensure that the native Mexicans "are introduced into and instructed in the holy Catholic faith" and predicted that if "the devotion, trust and hope which they now have in their idols turned so as to repose with the divine power of the true God . . . they would work many miracles."[3] Spiritual and secular affairs were closely intertwined in the sixteenth century. No doubt, the desire for grandeur and glory as well as plain intellectual curiosity and a spirit of adventure also played some role in European expansion.

14-1b The Means for Expansion

If "God, glory, and gold" were the primary motives, what made the voyages possible? First of all, the expansion of Europe was connected to the growth of centralized monarchies during the Renaissance. Although historians still debate the degree of that centralization, the reality is that Renaissance expansion was a state enterprise. By the second half of the fifteenth century, European monarchies had increased both their authority and their resources and were in a position to turn their energies beyond their borders. For France, that meant the invasion of Italy, but for Portugal, a state not strong enough to pursue power in Europe, it meant going abroad. The Spanish monarchy was strong enough by the sixteenth century to pursue power both in Europe and beyond.

Maps At the same time, Europeans had achieved a level of wealth and technology that enabled them to make a regular series of voyages beyond Europe. Although the highly schematic and symbolic medieval maps were of little help to sailors, the *portolani* (pohr-tuh-LAH-nee), or charts made by medieval navigators and mathematicians in the thirteenth and fourteenth centuries, were more useful. With details on coastal contours, distances between ports, and compass readings, these charts proved of great value for voyages in European waters. But because the portolani were drawn on a flat scale and took no account of the curvature of the earth, they were of little use for longer overseas voyages. Only when seafarers began to venture beyond the coast of Europe did they begin to accumulate information about the actual shape of the earth. By the end of the fifteenth century, cartography had developed to the point that Europeans possessed fairly accurate maps of the known world.

One of the most important world maps available to Europeans at the end of the fifteenth century was that of Ptolemy (TAHL-uh-mee), an astronomer of the second century C.E. Ptolemy's work, the *Geography*, had been known to Arab geographers as early as the eighth century, but it was not until the fifteenth century that a Latin translation was made of the work. Printed editions of Ptolemy's *Geography*, which contained his world map, became available from 1477 on. Ptolemy's map (see Image 14.2) showed the world as spherical with three major landmasses—Europe, Asia, and Africa—and only two oceans. In addition to showing the oceans as considerably smaller than the landmasses, Ptolemy had also drastically underestimated the circumference of the earth, which led Columbus and other adventurers to believe that it would be feasible to sail west from Europe to reach Asia.

Ships and Sailing Europeans had also developed remarkably seaworthy ships as well as new navigational techniques. European shipbuilders had mastered the use of the axial rudder (an import from China) and had learned to combine the use of lateen sails with a square rig. With these innovations, they could construct ships mobile enough to sail against the wind and engage in naval warfare and also large enough to mount heavy cannons and carry a substantial amount of goods over long distances. Previously, sailors had used a quadrant and their knowledge of

IMAGE 14.2 **Ptolemy's World Map.** Contained in the Latin translation of Ptolemy's *Geography* was this world map, which did not become available to Europeans until the late 1400s. Scholars quickly accepted it as the most accurate map of its time. The twelve "wind faces," meant to show wind currents around the earth, were a fifteenth-century addition to the ancient map.

Huntington Library/SuperStock

the position of the Pole Star to ascertain their latitude. Below the equator, however, this technique was useless. Only with the assistance of new navigational aids such as the compass and the astrolabe were they able to explore the high seas with confidence.

A final spur to exploration was the growing knowledge of the wind patterns in the Atlantic Ocean. The first European fleets sailing southward along the coast of West Africa had found their efforts to return hindered by the strong winds that blew steadily from the north along the coast. By the late fifteenth century, however, sailors had learned to tack out into the ocean, where they were able to catch westerly winds in the vicinity of the Azores that brought them back to the coast of western Europe. Christopher Columbus used this technique in his voyages to the Americas, and others relied on their new knowledge of the winds to round the continent of Africa in search of the Spice Islands.

14-2 New Horizons: The Portuguese and Spanish Empires

 FOCUS QUESTIONS: How did Portugal and Spain acquire their overseas empires, and how did their empires differ? How did Spain administer its empire?

Portugal took the lead in the European age of expansion when it began to explore the coast of Africa under the sponsorship of Prince Henry the Navigator (1394–1460). His motives were a blend of seeking a Christian kingdom as an ally against the Muslims, acquiring trade opportunities for Portugal, and spreading Christianity.

14-2a The Development of a Portuguese Maritime Empire

In 1419, Prince Henry founded a school for navigators on the southwestern coast of Portugal. Shortly thereafter, Portuguese fleets began probing southward along the western coast of Africa in search of gold, which had been carried northward from south of the Atlas Mountains in central Morocco for centuries. In 1441, Portuguese ships reached the Senegal River, just north of Cape Verde, and brought home a cargo of black Africans, most of whom were then sold as slaves to wealthy buyers elsewhere in Europe. Within a few years, an estimated one thousand slaves were shipped annually from the area back to Lisbon.

Through regular expeditions, the Portuguese gradually crept down the African coast, and in 1471, they discovered a new source of gold along the southern coast of the hump of West Africa (an area that would henceforth be known to Europeans as the Gold Coast). A few years later, they established contact with the state of Bakongo, near the mouth of the Zaire (Congo) River in Central Africa. To facilitate trade in gold, ivory, and slaves (some slaves were brought back to Lisbon, while others were bartered to local merchants for gold), the Portuguese leased land from local rulers and built stone forts along the coast.

The Portuguese in India Hearing reports of a route to India around the southern tip of Africa, Portuguese sea captains

continued their probing. In 1488, Bartholomeu Dias (bar-toh-loh-MAY-oo DEE-ush) (ca. 1450–1500) took advantage of westerly winds in the South Atlantic to round the Cape of Good Hope, but he feared a mutiny from his crew and returned (see Map 14.1). Ten years later, a fleet under the command of Vasco da Gama (VAHSH-koh dah GAHM-uh) (ca. 1460–1524) rounded the cape and stopped at several ports controlled by Muslim merchants along the coast of East Africa. Da Gama's fleet then crossed the Arabian Sea and reached the port of Calicut, on the southwestern coast of India, on May 18, 1498. On arriving in Calicut, da Gama announced to his surprised hosts that he had come in search of "Christians and spices." He found no Christians, but he did find the spices he sought. Although he lost two ships en route, da Gama's remaining vessels returned to Europe with their holds filled with ginger and cinnamon, a cargo that earned the investors a profit of several thousand percent.

Portuguese fleets returned annually to the area, seeking to destroy Arab shipping and establish a monopoly in the spice trade. In 1509, a Portuguese armada defeated a combined fleet

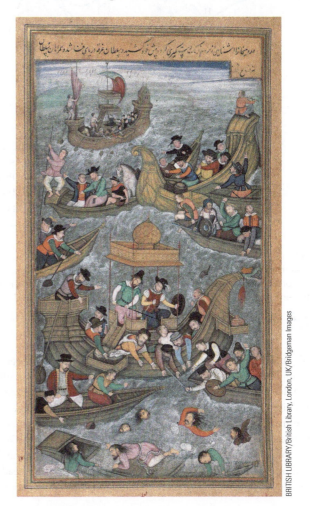

IMAGE 14.3 **Portuguese in India.** The Portuguese continued their exploration of India after gaining control of Goa in 1509 by moving northward into the territory of Gujarat. This painting by a Mughal artist portrays the killing of Bahadur Shah, leader of the Gujarat sultanate, by a Portuguese convoy in 1537 after Bahadur Shah had formed an alliance with the Portuguese in an attempt to regain control of his sultanate after it was conquered by the Mughals.

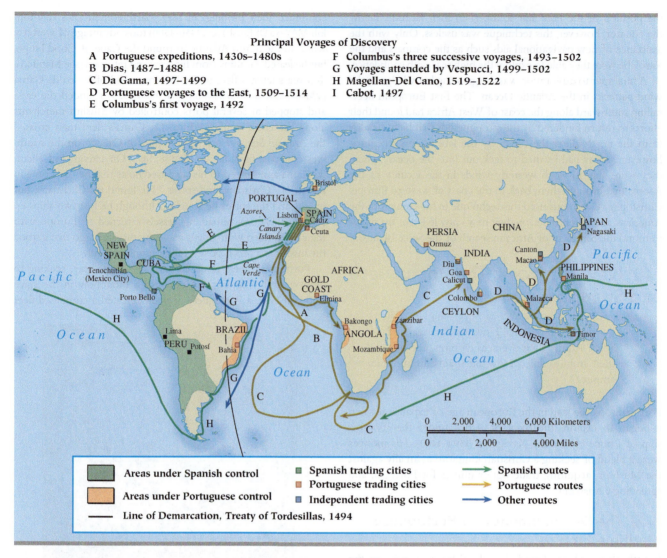

Principal Voyages of Discovery

A Portuguese expeditions, 1430s–1480s
B Dias, 1487–1488
C Da Gama, 1497–1499
D Portuguese voyages to the East, 1509–1514
E Columbus's first voyage, 1492

F Columbus's three successive voyages, 1493–1502
G Voyages attended by Vespucci, 1499–1502
H Magellan–Del Cano, 1519–1522
I Cabot, 1497

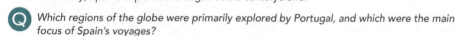

▬ Areas under Spanish control	▪ Spanish trading cities	→ Spanish routes
▬ Areas under Portuguese control	▪ Portuguese trading cities	→ Portuguese routes
— Line of Demarcation, Treaty of Tordesillas, 1494	▪ Independent trading cities	→ Other routes

MAP 14.1 Discoveries and Possessions in the Fifteenth and Sixteenth Centuries. Desire for wealth was the main motivation of the early explorers, though spreading Christianity was also an important factor. Portugal under Prince Henry the Navigator initiated the first voyages in the early fifteenth century; Spain's explorations began at the century's end.

Q *Which regions of the globe were primarily explored by Portugal, and which were the main focus of Spain's voyages?*

of Turkish and Indian ships off the coast of India and began to impose a blockade on the entrance to the Red Sea to cut off the flow of spices to Muslim rulers in Egypt and the Ottoman Empire. The following year, seeing the need for a land base in the area, Admiral Afonso de Albuquerque (ah-FAHN-soh day AL-buh-kur-kee) (ca. 1462–1515) set up port facilities at Goa (GOH-uh), on the western coast of India south of present-day Mumbai (Bombay) (see Image 14.3). Goa henceforth became the headquarters for Portuguese operations throughout the entire region.

In Search of Spices In the early sixteenth century, the Portuguese expanded their search for spices (see Images of Everyday Life, "Spices and World Trade," p. 417). In 1511, Albuquerque sailed into the harbor of Malacca (muh-LAK-uh) on the Malay peninsula. Its Muslim rulers had transformed Malacca into a thriving port and a major stopping point in the spice trade. After

a short but bloody battle, the Portuguese seized the city and massacred the local population, which consisted of many different South, Southeast, and East Asian groups. This slaughter initiated a fierce and brutal struggle between the Portuguese and Malays. According to one account, "To enhance the terror of his name he [Albuquerque] always separated Arabs from the other inhabitants of a captured city, and cut off the right hand of the men, and the noses and ears of the women."[4] By seizing Malacca, the Portuguese had not only weakened Muslim control of the spice trade but obtained a major port en route to the Moluccas (muh-LUHK-uhz), then known as the Spice Islands.

From Malacca, the Portuguese launched expeditions farther east, to China and the Spice Islands. There they signed a treaty with a local ruler for the purchase and export of cloves to the European market. The new trading empire was now complete. Within a few years, the Portuguese had managed to seize

IMAGES OF EVERYDAY LIFE

Spices and World Trade

Q *In what ways did the spice trade impact the lives of explorers, Venetians, and the people of Ceylon?*

PEPPER, CINNAMON, NUTMEG, and other spices from the East had long been a part of European life. Image 14.4a from a fifteenth-century French manuscript depicts pepper being harvested in Malabar, in southwestern India. Europeans' interest in finding a direct route to the Spice Islands intensified after the fall of Constantinople in 1453, which led to a thirtyfold increase in the price of pepper. The Venetians played a dominant role in the spice trade via Constantinople, as is evident in the Venetian fresco shown in Image 14.4b. The fresco portrays a spice seller's shop with a wide variety of spices for sale. Vasco da Gama's success in locating a route to the East by sailing around Africa shifted much of the control over the spice trade into Portuguese hands. In 1518, the Portuguese established a fort in Ceylon (present-day Sri Lanka). Ceylon became the center of cinnamon production, enabling the Portuguese to dominate Europe's cinnamon trade. Image 14.4c shows a portrait of Vasco da Gama from circa 1600. The artist chose to depict da Gama with a large cinnamon stick in his right hand, an indication of the significance of the spice to his legacy and its role in his expeditions. Without the desire for spices, men such as da Gama and Christopher Columbus might not have ventured around Africa or across the Atlantic Ocean, thereby opening and forever altering European trade.

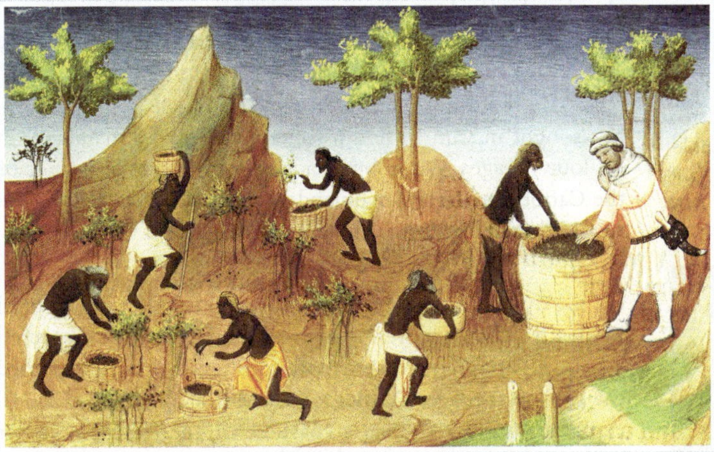

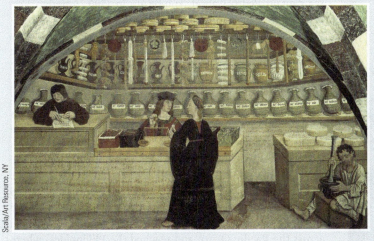

Bibliothe'que Nationale, Paris/Archives Charmet/The Bridgeman Art Library

IMAGE 14.4a

Scala/Art Resource, NY

IMAGE 14.4b

Gianni Dagli Orti/The Art Archive at Art Resource, NY

IMAGE 14.4c

control of the spice trade from Muslim traders and had garnered substantial profits for the Portuguese monarchy. Nevertheless, the Portuguese Empire remained limited, consisting only of trading posts on the coasts of India and China. The Portuguese lacked the power, the population, and the desire to colonize the Asian regions.

Why were the Portuguese so successful? Basically, their success was a matter of guns and seamanship. The first Portuguese fleet to arrive in Indian waters was relatively modest in size, consisting of three ships and twenty guns, a force sufficient for self-defense and intimidation but not for serious military operations. Later Portuguese fleets, which began to arrive with regularity early in the sixteenth century, were more heavily armed and were able not only to intimidate but also to inflict severe defeats if necessary on local naval and land forces. The Portuguese by no means possessed a monopoly on the use of

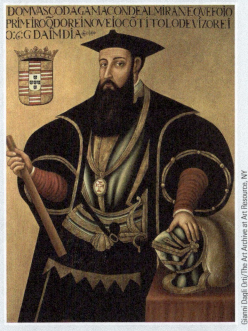

firearms and explosives, but their effective use of naval technology, their heavy guns that could be mounted in the hulls of their sturdy vessels, and their tactics gave them military superiority over lightly armed rivals that they were able to exploit until the arrival of other European forces several decades later.

14-2b Voyages to the New World

While the Portuguese were seeking access to the spice trade of the Indies by sailing eastward through the Indian Ocean, the Spanish were attempting to reach the same destination by sailing westward across the Atlantic. Although the Spanish came to overseas discovery and exploration after the initial efforts of Henry the Navigator, their greater resources enabled them to establish a far grander overseas empire than that of the Portuguese—and one that was quite different.

The Voyages of Columbus An important figure in the history of Spanish exploration was an Italian known as Christopher Columbus (1451–1506) (see Image 14.5). Knowledgeable Europeans were aware that the world was round but had little understanding of its circumference or the extent of the

Ian Woolcock/SuperStock

IMAGE 14.5 **Christopher Columbus.** Columbus was an Italian explorer who worked for the queen of Spain. He has become a symbol for two entirely different perspectives. To some, he was a great and heroic explorer who discovered the New World; to others, especially in Latin America, he was responsible for beginning a process of invasion that led to the destruction of an entire way of life. Because Columbus was never painted during his lifetime, the numerous portraits of him are more fanciful than accurate. The portrait shown here was probably done by the Italian painter Ridolfo Ghirlandaio.

 Why would an artist paint a portrait of a person he had never seen?

continent of Asia. Convinced that the circumference of the earth was less than contemporaries believed and that Asia was larger than people thought, Columbus felt that Asia could be reached by sailing west instead of around Africa. After being rejected by the Portuguese, he persuaded Queen Isabella of Spain to finance his exploratory expedition.

With a crew of ninety men and three ships, the *Santa María*, the *Niña*, and the *Pinta*, Columbus set sail on August 3, 1492. On October 12, he reached the Bahamas and then went on to explore the coastline of Cuba and the northern shores of Hispaniola (present-day Haiti and the Dominican Republic). Columbus believed that he had reached Asia, and in his reports to Queen Isabella and King Ferdinand upon his return to Spain, he assured them not only that he would eventually find gold but also that they had a golden opportunity to convert the natives—whom Columbus persisted in calling "Indians"—to Christianity (see Historical Voices, "Columbus Lands in the New World," p. 419). In three subsequent voyages (1493, 1498, 1502), Columbus sought in vain to find a route to the Asian mainland. In his four voyages, Columbus landed on all the major islands of the Caribbean and the mainland of Central America, still convinced that he had reached the Indies in Asia.

New Voyages Although Columbus clung to his belief until his death, other explorers soon realized that he had discovered a new frontier altogether. State-sponsored explorers joined the race to the New World. A Venetian seaman, John Cabot, explored the New England coastline of the Americas under a license from King Henry VII of England. The continent of South America was discovered accidentally by the Portuguese sea captain Pedro Cabral (kuh-BRAL) in 1500. Amerigo Vespucci (ahm-ay-REE-goh vess-POO-chee), a Florentine, accompanied several voyages and wrote a series of letters describing the geography of the New World. The publication of these letters led to the use of the name "America" (after Amerigo) for the new lands.

The first two decades of the sixteenth century witnessed numerous overseas voyages that explored the eastern coasts of both North and South America. Vasco Nuñez de Balboa (VAHS-koh NOON-yez day bal-BOH-uh) (1475–1519), a Spanish explorer, led an expedition across the Isthmus of Panama and reached the Pacific Ocean in 1513. Perhaps the most dramatic of all these expeditions was the journey of Ferdinand Magellan (1480–1521) in 1519. After passing through the strait named after him at the southern tip of South America, he sailed across the Pacific Ocean and reached the Philippines, where he was killed by the natives. Although only one of his fleet of five ships completed the return voyage to Spain, Magellan's name is still associated with the first known circumnavigation of the earth.

The Europeans referred to the newly discovered territories as the New World, even though they held flourishing civilizations populated by millions of people. But the Americas were indeed new to the Europeans, who quickly saw opportunities for conquest and exploitation. The Spanish, in particular, were interested because the 1494 Treaty of Tordesillas (tor-day-SEE-yass) had divided up the newly discovered world into separate

Columbus Lands in the New World

 What evidence in Columbus's comments suggests that his remarks were made mainly for public consumption and not just for the Spanish court? What elements in society might have responded to his statements, and why?

ON RETURNING FROM AMERICA, which he believed was the coast of Asia, Christopher Columbus wrote about his experience. In this passage from a letter describing his first voyage, he tells of his arrival on the island of Hispaniola (Haiti). Historians believe that Columbus wrote this letter for public consumption.

Letter to Raphael Sanchez, Treasurer to the King and Queen of Spain

Thirty-three days after my departure from Cadiz I reached the Indian sea, where I discovered many islands, thickly peopled, of which I took possession without resistance in the name of our most illustrious Monarch, by public proclamation and with unfurled banners. To the first of these islands, I gave the name of the blessed Savior (San Salvador), relying upon whose protection I had reached this as well as the other islands; to each of these I also gave a name. . . .

The inhabitants of both sexes in this island, and in all the others which I have seen, or of which I have received information, go always naked as they were born, with the exception of some of the women, who use the covering of a leaf, or small bough, or an apron of cotton which they prepare for that purpose. None of them are possessed of any iron, neither have they weapons, being unacquainted with, and indeed incompetent to use them, not from any deformity of body (for they are well-formed), but because they are timid and full of fear. . . . As soon however as they see that they are safe, and have laid aside all fear, they are very simple and honest, and exceedingly liberal with all they have; none of them refusing any thing he may possess when he is asked for it. . . . They also give objects of great value for trifles, and content themselves with very little or nothing in return.

I however forbade that these trifles and articles of no value (such as pieces of dishes, plates, and glass, keys, and leather straps) should be given to them, although if they could obtain them, they imagined themselves to be possessed of the most beautiful trinkets in the world. . . . Thus, they bartered, like idiots, cotton and gold for fragments of bows, glasses, bottles, and jars. . . .

In all these islands there is no difference of physiognomy, of manners, or of language, but they all clearly understand each other, a circumstance very propitious for the realization of what I conceive to be the principal wish of our most serene King, namely, the conversion of these people to the holy faith of Christ, to which indeed, as far as I can judge, they are very favorable and well-disposed. . . .

Finally, to compress into a few words the entire summary of my voyage and speedy return, and of the advantages derivable there from, I promise, that with a little assistance afforded me by our most invincible sovereigns, I will procure them as much gold as they need, and as great a quantity of spices and cotton. . . . Let Christ rejoice on earth, as he rejoices in heaven in the prospect of the salvation of the souls of so many nations hitherto lost. Let us also rejoice as well on account of the exaltation of our faith as on account of the increase of our temporal prosperity, of which not only Spain but all Christendom will be partakers.

Source: R. H. Major, ed., trans., *Letters by Christopher Columbus* (London: Hakluyt Society, 1843), pp. 35–43.

Portuguese and Spanish spheres of influence, and it turned out that most of South America (except for the eastern hump) fell within the Spanish sphere (see Map 14.1 on p. 416). Hereafter the route east around the Cape of Good Hope was to be reserved for the Portuguese while the route across the Atlantic was assigned to Spain.

14-2c The Spanish Empire in the New World

The Spanish conquerors known as **conquistadors** were hardy individuals motivated by a typical sixteenth-century blend of glory, greed, and religious crusading zeal. Although authorized by the Castilian crown, these groups were financed and outfitted privately, not by the government. Their superior weapons, organizational skills, and determination brought the conquistadors incredible success. They also benefited from rivalries among the native peoples and the decimation of the native peoples by European diseases (see "14-2d Disease in the New World," later in this chapter).

Early Civilizations in Mesoamerica Before the Spaniards arrived in the New World, Mesoamerica (modern Mexico and Central America) had already hosted a number of flourishing civilizations. Beginning around 300 C.E., on the Yucatán peninsula a people known as the Maya (MY-uh) had built one of the most sophisticated civilizations in the Americas (see Map 14.2). The Maya built splendid temples and pyramids, were accomplished artists, and developed a sophisticated calendar, as accurate as any in existence in the world at that time. The Maya were an agrarian people who cleared the dense rain forests, developed farming, and built a patchwork of city-states. Mayan

MAP 14.2 **The Maya**

MAP 14.3 **The Aztecs**

civilization came to include much of Central America and southern Mexico. For unknown reasons, Mayan civilization began to decline around 800 and had collapsed less than a hundred years later.

Sometime during the early twelfth century C.E., a people known as the Aztecs began a long migration that brought them to the Valley of Mexico (see Map 14.3). They established their capital at Tenochtitlán (tay-nawch-teet-LAHN) between 1325 and 1345 on an island in the middle of Lake Texcoco (now the location of Mexico City). For the next hundred years, the Aztecs built their city, constructing temples, other public buildings, houses, and causeways of stone across Lake Texcoco to the north, south, and west, linking the many islands to the mainland. At the beginning of the fifteenth century, they built an aqueduct to bring fresh water from a spring 4 miles away. Tenochtitlán benefited from commercial routes that brought goods from as far away as the Gulf of Mexico and the Inca Empire in northern South America. By 1500, flourishing trade and agricultural growth supported cities of over 80,000 inhabitants, with some estimates as high as 200,000 inhabitants, larger than most European cities of the time.

The Aztecs were outstanding warriors, and while they were building their capital city, they also set out to bring the entire area around the city under their control. By the early fifteenth century, they had become the leading city-state in the lake region. For the remainder of the fifteenth century, the Aztecs consolidated their rule over much of what is modern Mexico, from the Atlantic to the Pacific Ocean and as far south as the Guatemalan border. The new kingdom was not a centralized state but a collection of semi-independent territories governed by local lords. The

Aztec ruler confirmed these rulers in their authority in return for the payment of tribute. This loose political organization would later contribute to the downfall of the Aztec Empire.

Spanish Conquest of the Aztec Empire In 1519, a Spanish expedition under the command of Hernán Cortés (1485–1547) landed at Veracruz, on the Gulf of Mexico. He marched to the city of Tenochtitlán (see the Historical Voices, "The Spanish Conquistador," p. 421) at the head of a small contingent of troops (550 soldiers and 16 horses); as he went, he made alliances with city-states that had tired of the oppressive rule of the Aztecs. Especially important was Tlaxcala (tuh-lah-SKAH-lah), a state that the Aztecs had not been able to conquer. In November, Cortés arrived at Tenochtitlán, where he received a friendly welcome from the Aztec monarch Moctezuma (mahk-tuh-ZOO-muh) (often called Montezuma). At first, Moctezuma believed that his visitor was a representative of Quetzalcoatl (KWET-sul-koh-AHT-ul), the god who had departed from his homeland centuries before and had promised that he would return. Riddled with fears, Moctezuma offered gifts of gold to the foreigners and gave them a palace to use while they were in the city.

But the Spaniards quickly wore out their welcome. They took Moctezuma hostage and proceeded to pillage the city. In the fall of 1520, one year after Cortés had arrived, the local population revolted and drove the invaders from the city. Many of the Spaniards were killed, but the Aztecs soon experienced new disasters. As one Aztec related, "At about the time that the Spaniards had fled from Mexico, there came a great sickness, a pestilence, the smallpox." With no natural immunity to the diseases of the Europeans, many Aztecs fell sick and died (see "14-2d Disease in the New World," later in this chapter). Meanwhile, Cortés received fresh soldiers from his new allies; the state of Tlaxcala alone provided 50,000 warriors. After four months, the city capitulated.

The Spaniards then embarked on a new wave of destruction. The pyramids, temples, and palaces were leveled, and the stones were used to build Spanish government buildings and churches. The rivers and canals were filled in. The mighty Aztec Empire on mainland Mexico was no more. Between 1531 and 1550, the Spanish gained control of northern Mexico.

The Inca In the late fourteenth century, the Inca were a small community in the area of Cuzco (KOOS-koh), a city located at an altitude of 10,000 feet in the mountains of southern Peru (see Map 14.4). In the 1440s, however,

MAP 14.4 **The Inca**

The Spanish Conquistador: Cortés and the Conquest of Mexico

 What does Cortés focus on in his description of this Aztec city? What are his justifications for overthrowing the Aztec Empire?

HERNÁN CORTÉS WAS A MINOR SPANISH NOBLEMAN who came to the New World in 1504 to seek his fortune. Contrary to his superior's orders, Cortés waged an independent campaign of conquest and overthrew the Aztec Empire in Mexico (1519–1522). Cortés wrote a series of five reports to Emperor Charles V to justify his action. The second report includes a description of Tenochtitlán, the capital of the Aztec Empire. The Spanish conquistador and his men were obviously impressed by this city, awesome in its architecture yet built by people who lacked European technology, such as wheeled vehicles and tools of hard metal.

Cortés's Description of Tenochtitlán

The great city Tenochtitlán is built in the midst of this salt lake, and it is two leagues from the heart of the city to any point on the mainland. Four causeways lead to it, all made by hand and some twelve feet wide. The city itself is as large as Seville or Cordoba. The principal streets are very broad and straight, the majority of them being of beaten earth, but a few and at least half of the smaller thoroughfares are waterways along which they pass in their canoes. Moreover, even the principal streets have openings at regular distances so that the water can freely pass from one to another, and these openings which are very broad are spanned by great bridges of huge beams, very stoutly put together, so firm indeed that over many of them ten horsemen can ride at once. . . .

The city has many open squares in which markets are continuously held and the general business of buying and selling proceeds. One square in particular is twice as big as that of Salamanca and completely surrounded by arcades where there are daily more than 60,000 folk buying and selling. Every kind of merchandise such as may be met with in every land is for sale there, whether of food and victuals, or ornaments of gold and silver, or lead, brass, copper, tin, precious stones, bones, shells, snails and feathers; limestone for building is likewise sold there, stone both rough and polished, bricks burnt and unburnt, wood of all kinds and in all stages of preparation. . . . There are houses as it were of apothecaries where they sell medicines made from these herbs, both for drinking and for use as ointments and salves. There are barbers' shops where you may have your hair washed and cut. There are other shops where you may obtain food and drink. . . .

Finally, to avoid being wordy in telling all the wonders of this city, I will simply say that the manner of living among the people is very similar to that in Spain, and considering that this is a barbarous nation shut off from a knowledge of the true God or communication with enlightened nations, one may well marvel at the orderliness and good government which is everywhere maintained.

The actual service of Montezuma and those things which call for admiration by their greatness and state would take so long to describe that I assure your Majesty I do not know where to begin with any hope of ending. For as I have already said, what could there be more astonishing than that a barbarous monarch such as he should have reproductions made in gold, silver, precious stones, and feathers of all things to be found in his land, and so perfectly reproduced that there is no goldsmith or silversmith in the world who could better them, nor can one understand what instrument could have been used for fashioning the jewels. . . .

Source: J. H. Parry, *The European Reconnaissance: Selected Documents* (New York: Harper & Row, 1968).

---

under the leadership of their powerful ruler Pachakuti (pah-chah-KOO-tee), the Inca launched a campaign of conquest that eventually brought the entire region under their control. Pachakuti created a highly centralized state. Cuzco, the capital, was transformed from a city of mud and thatch into an imposing city of stone. Under Pachakuti and his immediate successors, Topa Inca and Huayna Inca (the word *Inca* means "ruler"), the boundaries of the Inca Empire were extended as far as Ecuador, central Chile, and the edge of the Amazon basin. The empire included perhaps 12 million people.

Pachakuti divided his realm into four quarters, each ruled by a governor. The quarters were in turn divided into provinces, each also ruled by a governor. The governors were usually chosen from relatives of the royal family. Each province was supposed to contain about 10,000 residents. At the top of the entire system was the emperor, who was believed to be descended from the sun god.

The Inca were great builders. One major project was a system of 24,800 miles of roads that extended from the border of modern-day Colombia to a point south of modern-day Santiago, Chile. Two major roadways extended in a north–south direction, one through the Andes Mountains and the other along the coast, with connecting routes between them. Rest houses, located a day's walk apart, and storage depots were placed along the roads. The Inca also built various types of bridges, including some of the finest examples of suspension bridges in premodern times, over the ravines and waterways.

Spanish Conquest of the Inca Empire The Inca Empire was still flourishing when the first Spanish expeditions arrived in the area. In December 1530, Francisco Pizarro (frahn-CHESS-koh puh-ZAHR-oh) (ca. 1475–1541) landed on the Pacific coast of South America with a band of about 180 men, but like Cortés, he had steel weapons, gunpowder, and horses, none of which were familiar to his hosts. Pizarro was also lucky because the Inca Empire had already succumbed to an epidemic of smallpox. Like the Aztecs, the Inca had no immunities to European diseases, and all too soon, smallpox was devastating entire villages. In another stroke of good fortune for Pizarro, the Incan ruler had fallen victim to the disease. Following the death of the Incan ruler, a civil war ensued between his two sons. Pizarro capitalized on the internal turmoil and sought negotiations with Atahualpa (ah-tuh-WAHL-puh), whose forces had just defeated his brother's. Atahualpa agreed to meet with Pizarro in Cajamarca, a city in the northern Andes mountains. Pizarro arrived before Atahualpa and hid his cavalry forces. Atahualpa had left most of his armed soldiers outside of the city and was accompanied by a small band of 5,000 to 6,000 lightly armed soldiers and servants. The Incan forces were no match for Pizarro's cavalry as they charged the defenseless formation. Most of the Incan forces perished in the skirmish. Pizarro executed Atahualpa after holding him captive for eight months. Following the execution of Atahulpa, Pizarro and his men marched to the Incan capital of Cuzco and captured it. By 1535, Pizarro had finalized his conquest by establishing a capital at Lima for a new colony of the Spanish Empire.

Administration of the Spanish Empire Spanish policy toward the Indians of the New World was a combination of confusion, misguided paternalism, and cruel exploitation. Whereas the conquistadors made decisions based on expediency and their own interests, Queen Isabella declared the native peoples to be subjects of Castile and instituted the Spanish *encomienda* (en-koh-MYEN-dah), an economic and social system that permitted the conquering Spaniards to collect tribute from the Indians and use them as laborers. In return, the holders of an encomienda were supposed to protect the Indians, pay them wages, and supervise their spiritual needs. In practice, this meant that the settlers were free to implement the paternalistic system of the government as they pleased. Three thousand miles from Spain, Spanish settlers largely ignored their government and brutally used the Indians to pursue their own economic interests. The largest *encomiendas* were held by the earliest conquistadors. Cortés held an *encomienda* totaling 115,000 Indians, and Pizarro assigned himself 20,000 tributaries for his reward of capturing Peru. Indians were put to work on plantations and in the lucrative gold and silver mines. In Peru, the Spanish made use of the mita, a system that allowed authorities to enact compulsory labor service by drafting native labor to work in the silver mines.

Forced labor, starvation, and especially disease took a fearful toll of Indian lives. Voices were raised to protest the harsh treatment of the Indians, especially by Dominican friars. In a 1510 sermon, Antón Montecino startled churchgoers in Santo Domingo by saying:

> And you are heading for damnation . . . for you are destroying an innocent people. For they are God's people, these innocents, whom you destroyed. By what right do you make them die? Mining gold for you in your mines or working for you in your fields, by what right do you unleash enslaving wars upon them? They lived in peace in this land before you came, in peace in their own homes. They did nothing to harm you to cause you to slaughter them wholesale.[5]

In 1542, largely in response to the publications of Bartolomé de Las Casas (bahr-toh-loh-MAY day lahs KAH-sahs), a Dominican friar who championed the Indians (see Historical Voices, "Las Casas and the Spanish Treatment of the American Natives," p. 423), the government abolished the encomienda system and provided more protection for the natives.

In the New World, Spanish nobles recreated the urban cities of Spain by constructing towns built around a central plaza. The Spanish built their first town, Santo Domingo, in 1501 on the island of Hispaniola; by 1580, they had constructed 240 towns, with Mexico City and Lima being the largest. By 1600, over 250,000 Spanish émigrés had arrived from Spain to fill their streets.

The Spanish developed an administrative system based on viceroys to administer their new territories. Spanish possessions were initially divided into two major administrative units: New Spain (Mexico, Central America, and the Caribbean islands), with its center in Mexico City, and Peru (western South America), governed by a **viceroy** in Lima. According to legislation of 1542, "the kingdoms of New Spain and Peru are to be ruled and governed by viceroys, who shall represent our royal person, hold the superior government, do and administer justice equally to all our subjects and vassals, and concern themselves

CHRONOLOGY	The Portuguese and Spanish Empires in the Sixteenth Century
Bartholomeu Dias sails around the tip of Africa	1488
The voyages of Columbus	1492–1502
Treaty of Tordesillas	1494
Vasco da Gama lands at Calicut in India	1498
Portuguese seize Malacca	1511
Landing of Portuguese ships in southern China	1514
Magellan's voyage around the world	1519–1522
Spanish conquest of Mexico	1519–1522
Pizarro's conquest of the Inca	1530–1535

Las Casas and the Spanish Treatment of the American Natives

 In what ways did this account help create the image of the Spaniards as "cruel and murderous fanatics"? What motives may have prompted Las Casas to make this critique, and how might his opinions have affected the broader standing of Spain in the global politics of the age?

BARTOLOMÉ DE LAS CASAS (1474–1566) participated in the conquest of Cuba and received land and Indians in return for his efforts. But in 1514 he underwent a radical transformation and came to believe that the Indians had been cruelly mistreated by his fellow Spaniards. He became a Dominican friar and spent the remaining years of his life (he lived to the age of ninety-two) fighting for the Indians. This selection is taken from his most influential work, which is known to English readers as *The Tears of the Indians*. This work was largely responsible for the "black legend" of the Spanish as inherently "cruel and murderous fanatics." Most scholars feel that Las Casas may have exaggerated his account in order to shock his contemporaries into action.

Bartolomé de Las Casas, *The Tears of the Indians*

There is nothing more detestable or more cruel, than the tyranny which the Spaniards use toward the Indians for the getting of pearl. Surely the infernal torments cannot much exceed the anguish that they endure, by reason of that way of cruelty; for they put them under water some four or five ells [15 to 18 feet] deep, where they are forced without any liberty of respiration, to gather up the shells wherein the pearls are; sometimes they come up again with nets full of shells to take breath, but if they stay any while to rest themselves, immediately comes a hangman row'd in a little boat, who as soon as he has well beaten them, drags them again to their labor. Their food is nothing but filth, and the very same that contains the pearl, with a small portion of that bread which that country affords; in the first where of there is little nourishment; and as for the latter, it is made with great difficulty, besides that they have not enough of that neither for sustenance; they lie upon the ground in fetters, lest they should run away; and many times they are drown'd in this labor, and are never seen again till they swim upon the top of the waves: oftentimes they also are devoured by certain sea monsters, that are frequent in those seas. Consider whether this hard usage of the poor creatures be consistent with the precepts which God commands concerning charity to our neighbor, by those that cast them so undeservedly into the dangers of a cruel death, causing them to perish without any remorse or pity, or allowing them the benefit of the sacraments, or the knowledge of religion; it being impossible for them to live any time under the water; and this death is so much the more painful, by reason that by the constricting of the breast, while the lungs strive to do their office, the vital parts are so afflicted that they die vomiting the blood out of their mouths. Their hair also, which is by nature black, is hereby changed and made of the same color with that of the sea wolves; their bodies are also so besprinkled with the froth of the sea, that they appear rather like monsters than men.

Source: Bartolomé de Las Casas, *The Tears of the Indians* (Williamstown, Mass.: The John Lilburne Company Publishers, 1970).

with everything that will promote the calm, peace, ennoblement and pacification of those provinces."[6] Each viceroy served as the king's chief civil and military officer and was aided by advisory groups called *audiencias* (ow-dee-en-SEE-uss), which also functioned as supreme judicial bodies.

By papal agreement, the Catholic monarchs of Spain were given extensive rights over ecclesiastical affairs in the New World. They could appoint all bishops and clergy, build churches, collect fees, and supervise the various religious orders that sought to convert the heathen. Catholic missionaries converted and baptized hundreds of thousands of Indians in the early years of the conquest.

The mass conversion of the Indians brought the organizational and institutional structures of Catholicism to the New World. Dioceses, parishes, cathedrals, schools, and hospitals—all the trappings of civilized European society—soon appeared in the Spanish Empire. So, too, did the Spanish Inquisition, established first in Peru in 1570 and in Mexico the following year.

14-2d Disease in the New World

When Columbus reached the Caribbean island of Hispaniola in 1492, he brought more than gunpowder, horses, attack dogs, and soldiers to the shores of the New World. With no natural resistance to European diseases, the Indians of America were ravaged by smallpox, influenza, measles, and pneumonic plague, and later by typhus, yellow fever, and cholera.

Smallpox, a highly contagious disease, was spread through droplets in the air or direct contact with contaminated objects, such as clothing. In 1518, a smallpox epidemic erupted and quickly spread along trade routes from the Caribbean to Mesoamerica, killing a third of the Indian population (see Image 14.6). The disease ultimately reached Tenochtitlán and helped make possible its conquest by Hernán Cortés. When the Spaniards reentered

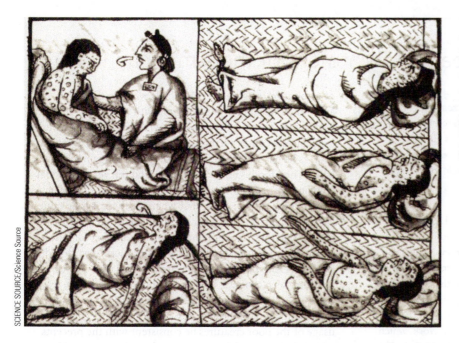

SCIENCE SOURCE/Science Source

IMAGE 14.6 **Aztec Victims of Smallpox.** The indigenous populations of the New World had no immunities to the diseases of the Old World. By 1520, smallpox had spread throughout the Caribbean and Mesoamerica. This sixteenth-century drawing by a Franciscan friar portrays Native Americans afflicted with the disease. The pustules that often covered the body are clearly depicted. The figure at the lower right twists in agony, reflecting the immense pain experienced by those who contracted the disease.

the city in 1521, they found an appalling scene, as reported by Bernal Díaz (ber-NAHL DEE-ass), who accompanied Cortés:

> We could not walk without treading on the bodies and heads of dead Indians. I have read about the destruction of Jerusalem, but I do not think the mortality was greater there than here in Mexico, where most of the warriors who had crowded in from all the provinces and subject towns had died. As I have said, the dry land and the stockades were piled with corpses. Indeed, the stench was so bad that no one could endure it. . . . Even Cortés was ill from the odors which assailed his nostrils.[7]

Smallpox ravaged the Aztecs. The Inca suffered a similar fate from smallpox and measles as well.

Throughout the sixteenth century, outbreaks of Old World diseases continued to spark epidemics that killed off large portions of the local populations. By 1630, smallpox had reached New England. The ferocity of the epidemics left few survivors to tend the crops, leading to widespread starvation and higher mortality rates. Although scholarly estimates vary drastically, approximately 30 to 40 percent of the local population died from Old World diseases. On Hispaniola alone, out of an initial population of 100,000 Indians when Columbus arrived in 1492, only 300 survived by 1570. The population of central Mexico, estimated at roughly 11 million in 1519, had declined to 6.5 million by 1540 and 2.5 million by the end of the sixteenth century.

The high mortality rates among the native populations resulted in a shortage of workers for the Europeans, which led them to turn to Africa for the labor needed for the silver mines and sugar plantations (see "14-3a Africa: The Slave Trade," which follows). Despite the Europeans' technological advantages, the biological weapons that they brought with them from the Old World proved to have an even greater impact on the Americas.

14-3 New Rivals on the World Stage

 FOCUS QUESTIONS: How did the arrival of the Dutch, British, and French on the world scene in the seventeenth and eighteenth centuries affect Africa, Southeast Asia, India, China, and Japan? What were the main features of the African slave trade, and what effects did it have on Africa?

Portugal and Spain had been the first Atlantic nations to take advantage of the age of exploration, starting in the late fifteenth century, and both had become great colonial powers. In the seventeenth century, however, their European neighbors to the north—first the Dutch and then the French and English—moved to replace the Portuguese and Spanish and create their own colonial empires. The new rivals and their rivalry soon had an impact on much of the rest of the world—in Africa, Asia, and the Americas.

14-3a Africa: The Slave Trade

Although the primary objective of the Portuguese in sailing around Africa was to find a sea route to the Spice Islands, they soon discovered that profits could be made in Africa itself. So did other Europeans.

The Portuguese built forts on both the western and eastern coasts of Africa and tried, above all, to dominate the trade in gold. During the mid-seventeenth century, however, the Dutch seized a number of Portuguese forts along the West African coast and at the same time took control of much of the Portuguese trade across the Indian Ocean.

The Dutch East India Company, a trading company established in 1602 under government sponsorship, also set up a settlement in southern Africa, at the Cape of Good Hope, to serve as a base to supply food and other provisions to Dutch ships en route to the Spice Islands. Eventually, however, it developed into a permanent colony. Dutch farmers, known as Boers, began to settle in areas outside the city of Cape Town. The area's moderate climate and freedom from tropical diseases made it attractive for Europeans to settle there.

The European exploration of the African coastline did not affect most Africans living in the interior of the continent, but for peoples living on or near the coast, the impact was great indeed. As the trade in slaves increased during the sixteenth through the eighteenth centuries, thousands and then millions of Africans were removed from their homes and forcibly shipped to plantations in the New World.

Origins of the Slave Trade Traffic in slaves was not new. As in other areas of the world, slavery had been practiced in Africa since ancient times. In the fifteenth century, it continued at a fairly steady level. The primary market for African slaves was the Middle East, where most were used as domestic servants. Slavery also existed in many European countries, where some slaves from Africa or war captives from the regions north of the Black Sea were used as household help or agricultural workers.

At first, the Portuguese simply replaced European slaves with African ones. During the second half of the fifteenth century, about a thousand slaves were taken to Portugal each year. Most ended up serving as domestic servants for affluent families in Europe. But the discovery of the Americas in the 1490s and the planting of sugarcane in South America and the islands of the Caribbean changed the situation drastically.

Cane sugar had first been introduced to Europeans from the Middle East during the Crusades. At the end of the fifteenth century, the Portuguese set up sugar plantations worked by African laborers on an island off the central coast of Africa. During the sixteenth century, sugarcane plantations were set up along the eastern coast of Brazil and on several islands in the Caribbean, reaching 195 in number by 1600. The sugar plantation more than any other part of the colonial economy rested on slave labor. The new plantations required more workers than could be provided by the small number of remaining American Indians. Since the climate and soil of much of West Africa were not conducive to the cultivation of sugar, African slaves began to be shipped to Brazil and the Caribbean to work on the plantations. The first were sent from Portugal, but in 1518, a Spanish ship carried the first boatload of African slaves directly from Africa to the New World.

Growth of the Slave Trade During the next two centuries, the trade in slaves grew dramatically and became part of the **triangular trade** connecting Europe, Africa, and the American continents that characterized the new Atlantic economy (see Map 14.5). European merchant ships (primarily those of England, France, Spain, Portugal, and the Dutch Republic) carried European manufactured goods, such as guns, gin, and cloth, to Africa, where they were traded for a

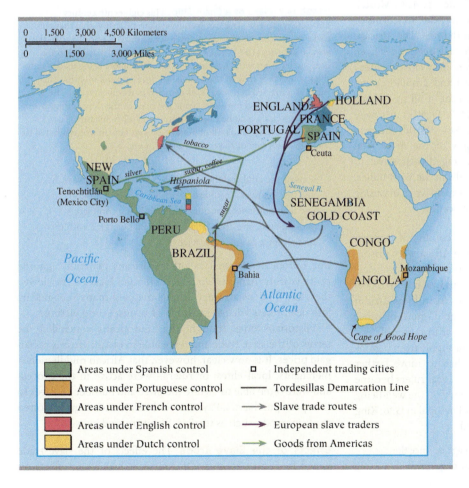

MAP 14.5 **Triangular Trade Route in the Atlantic Economy.** As the trade in slaves grew, it became part of the triangular trade route that characterized the Atlantic economy, involving the exchange of goods and slaves between the western coast of Europe, the slave depots on the African coast, and the ports of North and South America.

 What were the important source regions for slaves, and where were most of the slaves taken?

cargo of slaves. The slaves were then shipped to the Americas and sold. European merchants then bought tobacco, molasses, sugar, rum, coffee, and raw cotton and shipped them back to Europe to be sold in European markets.

An estimated 275,000 enslaved Africans were exported to other countries during the sixteenth century, with 2,000 going annually to the Americas alone. The total climbed to over a million in the seventeenth century and jumped to 6 million in the eighteenth century, when the trade spread from West and Central Africa to East Africa. Even during the nineteenth century, when Great Britain and other European countries tried to end the slave trade, nearly 2 million were exported. After 1770, half of the slaves went to Cuba to provide labor for the sugar plantations. The Portuguese colony of Brazil, however, imported the greatest number of slaves; by 1810, more than 2.5 million slaves had entered Brazilian ports. Altogether, as many as 10 million African slaves were transported to the Americas between the sixteenth and nineteenth centuries. About half were transported in British ships, with the rest divided among French, Dutch, Portuguese, Danish, and later, American ships.

One reason for the astonishing numbers of slaves, of course, was the high death rate. The journey of slaves from Africa to the Americas became known as the **Middle Passage**, the middle leg of the triangular trade route. African slaves were closely packed into cargo ships, 300 to 450 per ship, and chained in holds without sanitary facilities or room to stand up; there they remained during the voyage to America, which took at least 100 days (see Historical Voices, "The Atlantic Slave Trade," p. 427). Mortality rates averaged 10 percent; longer journeys due to storms or adverse winds resulted in even higher death rates. The Africans who survived the journey were subject to high death rates from diseases to which they had little or no immunity and dysentery from poor sanitation. Overall, between 1 and 2 million men, women, and children—more than 10 percent of all slaves leaving Africa—died in transit (see Image 14.7). Death rates were lower for slaves born and raised in the New World: the new generation developed immunity to many of the more fatal diseases. Owners, however, rarely encouraged their slaves to have children. Many slave owners, especially in the West Indies, believed that buying a new slave was less expensive than raising a child from birth to working age at adolescence.

Conduct of the Slave Trade Before the coming of Europeans in the fifteenth century, most slaves in Africa were prisoners of war. Many served as domestic servants or as wageless workers for the local ruler. When Europeans first began to take part in the slave trade, they bought slaves from local African merchants at slave markets in return for gold, guns, or other European goods such as textiles or copper or iron utensils.

At first, local slave traders obtained their supply from regions nearby, but as demand increased, they had to move farther inland to find their victims. In a few cases, local rulers became concerned about the impact of the slave trade on the well-being of their societies. In a letter to the king of Portugal in 1526, King Affonso of Congo (Bakongo) complained:

And we cannot reckon how great the damage is, since the mentioned merchants are taking every day our natives,

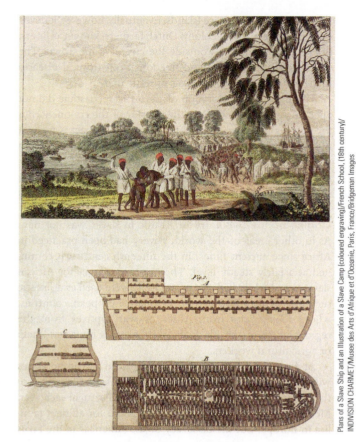

IMAGE 14.7 **Plans of a Slave Ship.** This eighteenth-century illustration shows a slave camp and the plans of a slave ship that will make the journey with African slaves across the Atlantic Ocean in the voyage known as the "Middle Passage." Slaves were marched to the coast, where they were held in small barracks before being loaded onto ships where they may have remained for up to several months. The Africans remained below deck, as depicted in the illustration. The only air came from small portholes along the sides of the ship. During storms these portholes would be closed, shutting off all ventilation. The close proximity of slaves and lack of ventilation and sanitation contributed to the high death rate of slaves during the voyage.

sons of the land and the sons of our noblemen and vassals and our relatives . . . and so great, Sir, is the corruption and licentiousness that our country is being completely depopulated, and Your Highness should not agree with this nor accept it as in your service.[8]

But Europeans as well as other Africans generally ignored protests from Africans. As a general rule, local rulers viewed the slave trade as a source of income, and many sent raiders into defenseless villages in search of unsuspecting victims.

Historians once thought that Europeans controlled the terms of the slave trade and were able to obtain victims at bargain prices. It is now clear, however, that African middlemen—merchants, local elites, or rulers—were active in the process and were often able to dictate the price and number of slaves to European purchasers. Payment to the slave merchant was often made in goods, such as textiles, furniture, and guns.

Effects of the Slave Trade The effects of the slave trade varied from area to area. Of course, it had tragic effects on

Plans of a Slave Ship and an Illustration of a Slave Camp (coloured engraving)/French School, (18th century)/ INDIVISION CHARMET/Musée des Arts d'Afrique et d'Océanie, Paris, France/Bridgeman Images

The Atlantic Slave Trade

 What does this account reveal about the nature of the slave trade and white attitudes toward blacks in the eighteenth century?

ONE OF THE MOST ODIOUS PRACTICES of early modern Western society was the Atlantic slave trade, which reached its height in the eighteenth century. Blacks were transported in densely packed cargo ships from the western coast of Africa to the Americas to work as slaves in the plantation economy. Not until late in the eighteenth century did a rising chorus of voices raise serious objections to this trade in human beings. This excerpt presents a criticism of the slave trade from an anonymous French writer.

Diary of a Citizen

As soon as the ships have lowered their anchors off the coast of Guinea, the price at which the captains have decided to buy the captives is announced to the Negroes who buy prisoners from various princes and sell them to Europeans. Presents are sent to the sovereign who rules over that particular part of the coast, and permission to trade is given. Immediately the slaves are brought by inhuman brokers like so many victims dragged to a sacrifice. White men who covet that portion of the human race receive them in a little house they have erected on the shore, where they have entrenched themselves with two pieces of cannon and twenty guards. As soon as the bargain is concluded, the Negro is put in chains and led aboard the vessel, where he meets his fellow sufferers. . . .

The vessel sets sail for the Antilles, and the Negroes are chained in a hold of the ship. . . . Twice a day some disgusting food is distributed to them. Their consuming sorrow and the sad state to which they are reduced would make them commit suicide if they were not deprived of all the means for an attempt upon their lives. Without any kind of clothing it would be difficult to conceal from the watchful eyes of the sailors in charge any instrument apt to alleviate their despair. The fear of a revolt, such as sometimes happens on the voyage from Guinea, is the basis of a common concern and produces as many guards as there are men in the crew. The slightest noise or a secret conversation among two Negroes is punished with utmost severity. All in all, the voyage is made in a continuous state of alarm on the part of the white men, who fear a revolt, and in a cruel state of uncertainty on the part of the Negroes, who do not know the fate awaiting them.

When the vessel arrives at a port in the Antilles, they are taken to a warehouse where they are displayed, like any merchandise, to the eyes of buyers. The plantation owner pays according to the age, strength, and health of the Negro he is buying. He has him taken to his plantation, and there he is delivered to an overseer who then and there becomes his tormentor. In order to domesticate him, the Negro is granted a few days of rest in his new place, but soon he is given a hoe and a sickle and made to join a work gang. Then he ceases to wonder about his fate; he understands that only labor is demanded of him. But he does not know yet how excessive this labor will be. As a matter of fact, his work begins at dawn and does not end before nightfall; it is interrupted for only two hours at dinnertime. The food a full-grown Negro is given each week consists of two pounds of salt beef or cod and two pots of tapioca meal. . . .

Source: R. Foster and E. Foster, eds., *European Society in the Eighteenth Century* (New York: Walker & Co., 1969).

---

the lives of the slaves and their families. There was also an economic price as the importation of cheap manufactured goods from Europe undermined local cottage industries and forced countless families into poverty. The slave trade also led to the depopulation of some areas and deprived many African communities of their youngest and strongest men and women.

The political effects of the slave trade were also devastating. The need to maintain a constant supply of slaves led to increased warfare and violence as African chiefs and their followers, armed with guns acquired from the trade in slaves, increased their raids and wars on neighboring peoples. A few Europeans lamented what they were doing to traditional African societies. One Dutch slave trader remarked, "From us they have learned strife, quarreling, drunkenness, trickery, theft, unbridled desire for what is not one's own, misdeeds unknown to them before, and the accursed lust for gold."[9] Nevertheless, the slave trade continued, with devastating effects for some African states.

Despite a rising chorus of humanitarian sentiments from European intellectuals, the use of black slaves remained largely acceptable to Western society. Europeans continued to view blacks as inferior beings fit primarily for slave labor. Not until the Society of Friends, known as the Quakers, began to criticize slavery in the 1770s and exclude from their church any member adhering to slave trafficking did European sentiment for the abolition of slavery begin to build. Even then, it was not until the radical stage of the French Revolution in the 1790s that the French abolished slavery. The British followed suit in 1807. Despite the elimination of the African source, slavery continued in the newly formed United States until the Civil War of the 1860s.

14-3b The West in Southeast Asia

Portugal's efforts to dominate the trade of Southeast Asia were never totally successful. The Portuguese lacked both the numbers and the wealth to overcome local resistance and colonize the Asian regions. Portugal's empire was simply too large and Portugal too small to maintain it. One Portuguese chronicler lamented, "My country, oh my country. Too heavy is the task that has been laid on your shoulders. Day after day I watch the ships leaving your shores filled always with your best and bravest men. And too many do not return. . . . Who then is left to till the fields, to harvest the grapes, to keep the enemy on our frontiers at bay?"[10] By the end of the sixteenth century, new European rivals had entered the fray.

One of them was Spain. The Spanish had established themselves in the region when Magellan landed in the Philippines. Although he was killed there, the Spanish were able to gain control over the Philippines, which eventually became a major Spanish base in the trade across the Pacific. Spanish ships carried silk and other luxury goods to Mexico in return for silver from the mines of Mexico.

The primary threat to the Portuguese Empire in Southeast Asia, however, came with the arrival of the Dutch and the English, who were better financed than the Portuguese. The shift in power began in the early seventeenth century when the Dutch seized a Portuguese fort in the Moluccas and then gradually pushed the Portuguese out of the spice trade. During the next fifty years, the Dutch occupied most of the Portuguese coastal forts along the trade routes throughout the Indian Ocean, including the island of Ceylon (today's Sri Lanka), and seized Malacca in 1641. The aggressive Dutch drove the English traders out of the spice market as well, eventually restricting the English to a single port on the southern coast of Sumatra.

The Dutch also began to consolidate their political and military control over the entire area. On the island of Java, where they had established a fort at Batavia (buh-TAY-vee-uh) (modern Jakarta) in 1619, the Dutch found that it was necessary to bring the inland regions under their control to protect their position. On Java and the neighboring island of Sumatra, the Dutch East India Company established pepper plantations, which soon became the source of massive profits for Dutch merchants in Amsterdam. By the end of the eighteenth century, the Dutch had succeeded in bringing almost the entire Indonesian archipelago under their control (see Image 14.8).

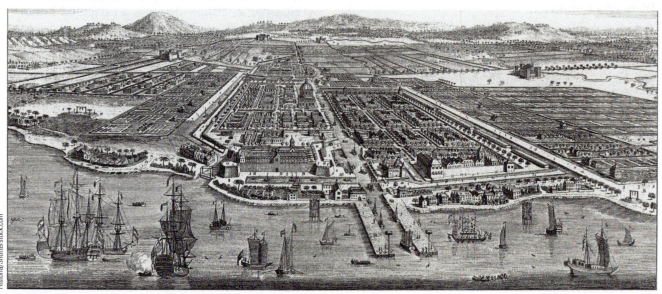

IMAGE 14.8a

IMAGE 14.8b

IMAGE 14.8 **Europe in Asia.** Europeans not only brought goods to the territories where they traded, they soon reproduced the port cities of Europe. As Europeans began to move into parts of Asia, they reproduced many of the physical surroundings of their homeland in the port cities they built there. This is evident in comparing these two scenes. Image 14.8a is a seventeenth-century view of Batavia, present-day Jakarta, which the Dutch built as their headquarters for the Dutch East India Company on the northern coast of Java in 1619. Batavia is built around three main canals; similar to the canal system found in Amsterdam. Image 14.8b is from a sixteenth-century map of Amsterdam. This Dutch city had become the financial and commercial capital of Europe. It was also the chief port for the ships of the Dutch East India Company, which brought the spices of the East to Europe.

Q *Why do you think the Dutch constructed canals for their port cities?*

The arrival of the Europeans had less impact on mainland Southeast Asia, where strong monarchies in Burma—now Myanmar (MYAN-mahr)—Thailand, and Vietnam resisted foreign encroachment (see Map 14.6). In the sixteenth century, the Portuguese established limited trade relations with several mainland states, including Thailand, Burma, Vietnam, and the remnants of the old Angkor kingdom in Cambodia. By the early seventeenth century, other nations had followed and had begun to compete actively for trade and missionary privileges. To obtain economic advantages, the Europeans soon became involved in local factional disputes. In general, however, these states were able to unite and drive the Europeans out.

In Vietnam, the arrival of Western merchants and missionaries coincided with a period of internal conflict among ruling groups in the country. Expansion had led to a civil war that temporarily divided the country into two separate states, one in the south and one in the north. After their arrival in the mid-seventeenth century, the European powers began to take sides in local politics, with the Portuguese and the Dutch supporting rival factions. The Europeans also set up trading posts for their merchants, but by the end of the seventeenth century, when it became clear that economic opportunities were limited, most of them were abandoned. French missionaries attempted to remain, but their efforts were blocked by the authorities, who viewed converts to Catholicism as a threat to the prestige of the Vietnamese emperor (see Global Perspectives, "West Meets East: An Exchange of Royal Letters," p. 430).

Why were the mainland states better able to resist the European challenge than the states in the Malay world? One factor, no doubt, was the cohesive nature of these states. The mainland states in Burma, Thailand, and Vietnam had begun to define themselves as distinct political entities. The Malay states had less cohesion. Moreover, the Malay states were victims of their own resources. The spice trade was enormously profitable. European merchants and rulers were determined to gain control of the sources of the spices, and that determination led them to take direct control of the Indonesian archipelago.

14-3c The French and British in India

When a Portuguese fleet arrived at the port of Calicut in the spring of 1498, the Indian subcontinent was divided into a number of Hindu and Muslim kingdoms. But it was on the verge of a new era of unity that would be brought about by a foreign dynasty called the Mughals (MOO-guls).

The Mughal Empire The founders of the Mughal Empire were not natives of India but came from the mountainous region north of the Ganges River valley. The founder of the dynasty, Babur (BAH-burr) (1483–1530), had an illustrious background. His father was descended from the great Asian conqueror Tamerlane; his mother, from the Mongol conqueror Genghis Khan. It was Akbar (AK-bar) (r. 1556–1605), Babur's grandson, however, who brought Mughal rule to most of India, creating the greatest Indian empire since the Mauryan dynasty nearly two thousand years earlier (see Map 14.7).

By the mid-seventeenth century, however, wars of succession and declining revenue led to the collapse of the Mughal Empire as Mughal nobles asserted their control over various territories. By the mid-eighteenth century the Mughals controlled little more territory than Delhi and its surrounding area. The vacuum of power created by the demise of the Mughals opened the door for European trading companies seeking to capitalize on the lucrative trade between India and Europe.

The Impact of the Western Powers As we have seen, the first Europeans to arrive in India were the Portuguese. At first, Portugal dominated regional trade in the Indian Ocean, but at the end of the sixteenth century, the English and the Dutch arrived on the scene. Soon both powers were competing with Portugal, and with each other, for trading privileges in the region.

MAP 14.6 **Southeast Asia, ca. 1700**

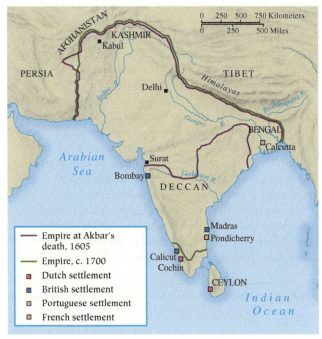

MAP 14.7 **The Mughal Empire**

Legend:
— Empire at Akbar's death, 1605
— Empire, c. 1700
□ Dutch settlement
■ British settlement
□ Portuguese settlement
□ French settlement

West Meets East: An Exchange of Royal Letters

 What are the underlying beliefs and approaches of these two rulers? How are they alike? How are they different? What is King Tonkin's justification for refusing Louis XIV's request? What is the significance of the way the two rulers date their letters?

ECONOMIC GAIN was not the only motivation of Western rulers who wished to establish a European presence in the East. In 1681, King Louis XIV of France wrote a letter to the king of Tonkin (the Trinh family head, then acting as viceroy to the Vietnamese emperor) asking permission for Christian missionaries to proselytize in Vietnam. The king of Tonkin politely declined the request.

A Letter to the King of Tonkin from Louis XIV

Most high, most excellent, most mighty and most magnanimous Prince, our very dear and good friend, may it please God to increase your greatness with a happy end!

We hear from our subjects who were in your Realm what protection you accorded them. We appreciate this all the more since we have for you all the esteem that one can have for a prince as illustrious through his military valor as he is commendable for the justice which he exercises in his Realm. We have even been informed that you have not been satisfied to extend this general protection to our subjects but, in particular, that you gave effective proofs of it to Messrs. Deydier and de Bourges. We would have wished that they might have been able to recognize all the favors they received from you by having presents worthy of you offered you; but since the war which we have had for several years, in which all of Europe had banded together against us, prevented our vessels from going to the Indies, at the present time, when we are at peace after having gained many victories and expanded our Realm through the conquest of several important places, we have immediately given orders to the Royal Company to establish itself in your kingdom as soon as possible, and have commanded Messrs. Deydier and de Bourges to remain with you in order to maintain a good relationship between our subjects and yours, also to warn us on occasions that might present themselves when we might be able to give you proofs of our esteem and of our wish to concur with your satisfaction as well as with your best interests.

By way of initial proof, we have given orders to have brought to you some presents which we believe might be agreeable to you. But the one thing in the world which we desire most, both for you and for your Realm, would be to obtain for your subjects who have already embraced the law of the only true God of heaven and earth, the freedom to profess it, since this law is the highest, the noblest, the most sacred and especially the most suitable to have kings reign absolutely over the people.

We are even quite convinced that, if you knew the truths and the maxims which it teaches, you would give first of all to your subjects the glorious example of embracing it. We wish you this incomparable blessing together with a long and happy reign, and we pray God that it may please Him to augment your greatness with the happiest of endings.

Written at Saint-Germain-en-Laye, the 10th day of January, 1681,

> Your very dear and good friend,
> Louis

Answer from the King of Tonkin to Louis XIV

The King of Tonkin sends to the King of France a letter to express to him his best sentiments, saying that he was happy to learn that fidelity is a durable good of man and that justice is the most important of things. Consequently practicing of fidelity and justice cannot but yield good results. Indeed, though France and our Kingdom differ as to mountains, rivers, and boundaries, if fidelity and justice reign among our villages, our conduct will express all of our good feelings and contain precious gifts. Your communication, which comes from a country which is a thousand leagues away, and which proceeds from the heart as a testimony of your sincerity, merits repeated consideration and infinite praise. Politeness toward strangers is nothing unusual in our country. There is not a stranger who is not well received by us. How then could we refuse a man from France, which is the most celebrated among the kingdoms of the world and which for love of us wishes to frequent us and bring us merchandise? These feelings of fidelity and justice are truly worthy to be applauded. As regards your wish that we should cooperate in propagating your religion, we do not dare to permit it, for there is an ancient custom, introduced by edicts, which formally forbids it. Now, edicts are promulgated only to be carried out faithfully; without fidelity nothing is stable. How could we disdain a well-established custom to satisfy a private friendship? . . .

We beg you to understand well that this is our communication concerning our mutual acquaintance. This then is my letter. We send you herewith a modest gift, which we offer you with a glad heart.

This letter was written at the beginning of winter and on a beautiful day.

Source: H. J. Benda and J. A. Larkin, eds. *The World of Southeast Asia: Selected Historical Readings* (New York: Harper & Row, 1967).

During the first half of the seventeenth century, the English presence in India steadily increased. The English captured a Portuguese ship filled with high-quality textiles and realized India's economic potential. By 1650, English trading posts had been established at Surat (a thriving port along the northwestern coast of India), Fort William (now the great city of Calcutta) near the Bay of Bengal, and Madras (now Chennai) on the southeastern coast. From Madras, English ships carried Indian-made cotton goods to the East Indies, where they were bartered for spices, which were shipped back to England. By the 1660s the British-owned East India Company was importing over four million square meters of cloth with a total value of nearly three-quarters of a million pounds. (The East India Company had been founded as a joint-stock company in 1600—see "14-5b The Growth of Commercial Capitalism," later in this chapter.) The EIC (East India Company) sold the cloth at London auctions, but English weavers protested in the 1690s, leading the British to impose protective tariffs on Asian textiles. By the early eighteenth century the British permitted the EIC to import only high-quality Indian calico cloth.

English success in India attracted rivals, including the Dutch and the French. The Dutch abandoned their interests to concentrate on the spice trade in the middle of the seventeenth century, but the French were more persistent and established their own forts on the east coast. For a brief period, the French competed successfully with the British, even capturing the British fort at Madras.

But the British were saved by the military genius of Sir Robert Clive (CLYV), an aggressive British empire-builder who eventually became the chief representative of the East India Company in India. The British were aided as well by the refusal of the French government to provide financial support for French efforts in far-off India. Eventually, the French were restricted to the fort at Pondicherry and a handful of small territories on the southeastern coast.

In the meantime, Clive began to consolidate British control in Bengal, where the local ruler had attacked Fort William and imprisoned the local British population in the "Black Hole of Calcutta" (an underground prison for holding the prisoners, many of whom died in captivity). In 1757, a small British force numbering about three thousand defeated a Mughal-led army more than ten times its size in the Battle of Plassey (PLASS-ee). As part of the spoils of victory, the British East India Company received from the now-decrepit Mughal court the authority to impose and collect taxes from over 20 million people in the area surrounding Calcutta. During the Seven Years' War (1756–1763), the British forced the French to withdraw completely from India (see Chapter 18).

To officials of the East India Company, the expansion of their authority into the interior of the subcontinent probably seemed like a simple economic decision. It made sense to seek regular revenues that would pay for increasingly expensive military operations in India. In a letter to the company's directors in London, Clive described the potential of the East India Company's future in India:

> I can assert with some degree of confidence that this rich and flourishing kingdom may be totally subdued by so small a force as two thousand Europeans . . . [The Indians are] indolent, luxurious, ignorant and cowardly beyond all conception . . . [They] attempt everything by treachery rather than force . . . What is it, then, can enable us to secure our present acquisitions or improve upon them but such a force as leaves nothing to the power of treachery and ingratitude?[11]

To historians, it marks a major step in the gradual transfer of all of the Indian subcontinent to the British East India Company and later, in 1858, to the British crown (see Chapter 24).

14-3d China

In 1514, a Portuguese fleet dropped anchor off the coast of China. It was the first direct contact between the Chinese Empire and Europe since the journeys of Marco Polo two hundred years earlier. At the time, the Chinese thought little of the event. China appeared to be at the height of its power as the most magnificent civilization on earth. Its empire stretched from the steppes of Central Asia to the China Sea, from the Gobi Desert to the tropical rain forests of Southeast Asia. From the lofty perspective of the imperial throne in Beijing, the Europeans could only be seen as an unusual form of barbarian. To the Chinese ruler, the rulers of all other countries were simply "younger brothers" of the Chinese emperor, who was regarded as the Son of Heaven.

The Ming and Qing Dynasties By the time the Portuguese fleet arrived off the coast of China, the Ming dynasty, which ruled from 1369 to 1644, had already begun a new era of greatness in Chinese history. Under a series of strong rulers, China extended its rule into Mongolia and Central Asia. The Ming even briefly reconquered Vietnam. Along the northern frontier, they strengthened the Great Wall and made peace with the nomadic tribesmen who had troubled China for centuries.

But the days of the Ming dynasty were numbered. In the 1630s, a major epidemic devastated the population in many areas. The suffering caused by the epidemic helped spark a peasant revolt led by Li Zicheng (lee zee-CHENG). In 1644, Li and his forces occupied the capital of Beijing. The last Ming emperor committed suicide by hanging himself from a tree in the palace gardens.

The overthrow of the Ming dynasty created an opportunity for the Manchus, a farming and hunting people who lived northeast of China in the area known today as Manchuria. The Manchus conquered Beijing, and Li Zicheng's army fell. The victorious Manchus then declared the creation of a new dynasty with the reign title of the Qing ("Pure") (see Map 14.8).

The Qing (CHING) were blessed with a series of strong early rulers who pacified the country, corrected the most serious social and economic ills, and restored peace and prosperity. Two Qing monarchs, Kangxi (KAHNG-shee) and Qian-long (CHAN-loong), ruled China for well over a century, from the middle of the seventeenth century to the end of the eighteenth. They were responsible for much of the greatness of Manchu China.

Western Inroads Although China was at the height of its power and glory in the mid-eighteenth century, the first signs of internal decay in the Qing dynasty were beginning to appear. Military campaigns along the frontier were expensive and placed heavy demands on the treasury. At the same time, increasing pressure on the land because of population growth led to economic hardship for many peasants and even rebellion.

Unfortunately for China, the decline of the Qing dynasty occurred just as Europe was increasing pressure for more trade. The first conflict had come from the north, where Russian traders sought skins and furs. Formal diplomatic relations between China and Russia were established in 1689 and provided for regular trade between the two countries.

Dealing with the foreigners who arrived by sea was more difficult. By the end of the seventeenth century, the English had replaced the Portuguese as the dominant force in European trade. Operating through the East India Company, which served as both a trading unit and the administrator of English territories in Asia, the English established their first trading post at Canton in 1699.

Over the next several decades, trade with China, notably the export of tea and silk to England, increased rapidly. To limit contacts between Europeans and Chinese, the Qing government confined all European traders to a small island just outside the city walls of Canton and permitted them to reside there only from October through March.

For a while, the British accepted this system, which brought considerable profit to the East India Company. But by the end of the eighteenth century, some British traders had begun to demand access to other cities along the Chinese coast and insist that the country be opened to British manufactured goods. In 1793, a British mission under Lord Macartney visited Beijing to press for liberalization of trade restrictions. But Emperor Qian-long expressed no interest in British products (see Historical Voices, "An Imperial Edict to the King of England," p. 433). An exasperated Macartney compared the Chinese Empire to "an old, crazy, first-rate man-of-war" that had once awed its neighbors "merely by her bulk and appearance" but was now destined under incompetent leadership to be "dashed to pieces on the shore." The Chinese would later pay for their rejection of the British request (see Chapter 24).

14-3e Japan

At the end of the fifteenth century, Japan was at a point of near anarchy, but in the course of the sixteenth century, a number of powerful individuals achieved the unification of Japan. One of them, Tokugawa Ieyasu (toh-koo-GAH-wah

MAP 14.8 **The Qing Empire**

ee-yeh-YAH-soo) (1543–1616), took the title of shogun ("general") in 1603, an act that initiated the most powerful and longest lasting of all the Japanese shogunates. The Tokugawa rulers completed the restoration of central authority and remained in power until 1868.

Opening to the West Portuguese traders had landed on the islands of Japan in 1543, and in a few years, Portuguese ships began stopping at Japanese ports on a regular basis to take part in the regional trade between Japan, China, and Southeast Asia. The first Jesuit missionary, Francis Xavier, arrived in 1549 and had some success in converting the local population to Christianity.

Initially, the visitors were welcomed. Tobacco, clocks, eyeglasses, and other European goods fascinated the curious Japanese, and local nobles were interested in purchasing all types of European weapons and armaments. Japanese rulers found the new firearms especially helpful in defeating their enemies and unifying the islands. The effect on Japanese military architecture was especially striking, as local lords began to erect castles in stone on the European model.

The success of the Catholic missionaries, however, provoked a strong reaction against the presence of Westerners. When the missionaries interfered in local politics, Tokugawa Ieyasu, newly come to power, expelled all missionaries. Japanese Christians were now persecuted. When a group of Christian peasants on the island of Kyushu revolted in 1637, they were bloodily suppressed.

The European merchants were the next to go. The government closed the two major foreign trading posts on the island of Hirado and at Nagasaki (nah-gah-SAH-kee). Only a small Dutch community in Nagasaki was allowed to remain in Japan (see Image 14.9). The Dutch, unlike the Spanish and Portuguese, had not allowed missionary activities to interfere with their trade interests. But the conditions for staying were strict. Dutch ships were allowed to dock at Nagasaki harbor just once a year and could remain for only two or three months.

14-3f The Americas

In the sixteenth century, Spain and Portugal had established large colonial empires in the Americas. Portugal continued to profit from its empire in Brazil. The Spanish also maintained an enormous South American empire, but Spain's importance as a commercial power declined rapidly in the seventeenth century because of a drop in the output of the silver mines and the poverty of the Spanish monarchy. By the beginning of the

An Imperial Edict to the King of England

> **Q** *What reasons does Qian-long give for denying Britain's request to open diplomatic and trading relations with China? Do his comments indicate any ignorance about the West at the end of the eighteenth century? If he had known more, would his response have been different? Why or why not?*

IN 1793, THE BRITISH EMISSARY Lord Macartney visited the Qing Empire to request the opening of trading relations between his country and China. Emperor Qian-long's reply, addressed to King George III of England, illustrates how the imperial court in Beijing viewed the world. King George cannot have been pleased.

An Imperial Edict to the King of England

You, O King, are so inclined toward our civilization that you have sent a special envoy across the seas to bring to our Court your memorial of congratulations on the occasion of my birthday and to present your native products as an expression of your thoughtfulness. On perusing your memorial, so simply worded and sincerely conceived, I am impressed by your genuine respectfulness and friendliness and greatly pleased.

As to the request made in your memorial, O King, to send one of your nationals to stay at the Celestial Court to take care of your country's trade with China, this is not in harmony with the state system of our dynasty and will definitely not be permitted. Traditionally people of the European nations who wished to tender some service under the Celestial Court have been permitted to come to the capital. But after their arrival they are obliged to wear Chinese court costumes, are placed in a certain residence and are never allowed to return to their own countries. This is the established rule of the Celestial Dynasty with which presumably you, O King, are familiar. Now you, O King, wish to send one of your nationals to live in the capital, but he is not like the Europeans, who come to Beijing as Chinese employees, live there and never return home again, nor can he be allowed to go and come and maintain any correspondence. This is indeed a useless undertaking. . . .

The Celestial Court has pacified and possessed the territory within the four seas. Its sole aim is to do its utmost to achieve good government and to manage political affairs, attaching no value to strange jewels and precious objects. The various articles presented by you, O King, this time are accepted by my special order to the office in charge of such functions in consideration of the offerings having come from a long distance with sincere good wishes. As a matter of fact, the virtue and prestige of the Celestial Dynasty having spread far and wide, the kings of the myriad nations come by land and sea with all sorts of precious things. Consequently there is nothing we lack, as your principal envoy and others have themselves observed. We have never set much store on strange objects, nor do we need any more of your country's manufactures.

Source: S. Teng and J. K. Fairbank, *China's Response to the West: A Documentary Survey* (Cambridge, Mass.: Harvard University Press, 1982).

IMAGE 14.9 The Portuguese Arriving at Nagasaki. Portuguese traders landed accidentally in Japan in 1543. In a few years, they arrived regularly, taking part in a regional trade network involving Japan, China, and Southeast Asia. In these panels, done in black lacquer and gold leaf, we see a late-sixteenth-century Japanese interpretation of the first Portuguese landing at Nagasaki.

seventeenth century, both Portugal and Spain found themselves with new challenges to their American empires from the Dutch, English, and French, who increasingly sought to create their own colonial empires in the New World.

West Indies Both the French and English colonial empires in the New World included large parts of the West Indies (see Map 14.9).

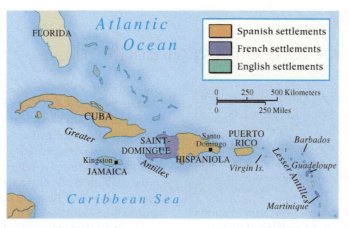

MAP 14.9 **The West Indies**

The English held Barbados, Jamaica, and Bermuda, and the French possessed Saint-Domingue, Martinique, and Guadeloupe. On these tropical islands, both the English and the French developed plantation economies, worked by African slaves, which produced tobacco, cotton, coffee, and sugar, all products increasingly in demand in Europe.

The "sugar factories," as the sugar plantations in the Caribbean were called, played an especially prominent role. Sugar and bullion (metals) were the most important colonial exports. Sugar prices remained steady throughout the seventeenth century, reinforcing the Atlantic triangle trade of slave exports from Africa, colonial sugar production in the colonies, and sugar exports to Europe. No other product contributed to the European imperial and local colonial economies like sugar. By the early eighteenth century, sugar was Britain's main export from its American colonies. By the last two decades of the century, the British colony of Jamaica, one of Britain's most important, was producing 50,000 tons of sugar annually with the slave labor of 200,000 blacks. The French colony of Saint-Domingue (later Haiti) had 500,000 slaves working on

three thousand plantations (see Image 14.10). This colony produced 100,000 tons of sugar a year, but at the expense of a high death rate from the brutal treatment of the slaves. It is not surprising that Saint-Domingue was the site of the first successful slave uprising in 1793 (see Chapter 19).

British North America Although Spain claimed all of North America as part of its American overseas empire, other nations largely ignored its claim. The British argued that "prescription without possession availeth nothing." The Dutch were among the first to establish settlements on the North American continent. Their activities began after 1609 when Henry Hudson, an English explorer hired by the Dutch, discovered the river that bears his name. Within a few years, the Dutch had established the mainland colony of New Netherland, which stretched from the mouth of the Hudson River as far north as Albany, New York. Present-day names such as Staten Island and Harlem remind us that it was the Dutch who initially settled the Hudson River valley. In the second half of the seventeenth century, competition from the English and French and years of warfare with those rivals led to the decline of the Dutch commercial empire. In 1664, the English seized the colony of New Netherland and renamed it New York; soon afterward, the Dutch West India Company went bankrupt.

In the meantime, the English had begun to establish their own colonies in North America. The first permanent English settlement in America was Jamestown, founded in 1607 in

IMAGE 14.10 **A Sugar Mill in the West Indies.** Cane sugar was one of the most valuable products produced in the West Indies. By 1700, sugar was replacing honey as a sweetener for increasing numbers of Europeans. This seventeenth-century French illustration shows the operation of a sugar mill in the French West Indies.

Q *Why do you think sugar plantations required large amounts of slave labor?*

modern Virginia. It barely survived, making it evident that the colonizing of American lands was not necessarily conducive to quick profits. But the desire to practice one's own religion, combined with economic interests, could lead to successful colonization, as the Massachusetts Bay Company demonstrated. The Massachusetts colony had 4,000 settlers in its early years but by 1660 had swelled to 40,000. By the end of the seventeenth century, the English had established control over most of the eastern seaboard of the present United States.

British North America came to consist of thirteen colonies. They were thickly populated, containing about 1.5 million people by 1750, and were also prosperous. Supposedly run by the British Board of Trade, the Royal Council, and Parliament, these thirteen colonies had legislatures that tended to act independently. Merchants in such port cities as Boston, Philadelphia, New York, and Charleston resented and resisted regulation from the British government.

The British colonies in both North America and the West Indies were assigned roles in keeping with mercantilist theory (see "14-5c Mercantilism," later in this chapter). They provided raw materials, such as cotton, sugar and tobacco, for the mother country while buying the latter's manufactured goods. Navigation acts regulated what could be taken from and sold to the colonies. Theoretically, the system was supposed to provide a balance of trade favorable to the mother country.

French North America The French also established a colonial empire in North America. Already in 1534, the French explorer Jacques Cartier (ZHAK kar-TYAY) had discovered the Saint Lawrence River and laid claim to Canada as a French possession. It was not until 1608, however, when Samuel de Champlain (shahm-PLAN *or* SHAM-playn) established a settlement at Quebec that the French began to take a more serious interest in Canada as a colony. In 1663, Canada was made the property of the French crown and administered by a French governor like a French province.

French North America was run autocratically as a vast trading area, where valuable furs, leather, fish, and timber were acquired. The inability of the French state to get its people to emigrate to its Canadian possessions, however, left the territory thinly populated. By the mid-eighteenth century, there were only about 15,000 French Canadians, most of whom were hunters, trappers, missionaries, or explorers. The French failed to provide adequate men or money, allowing their European wars to take precedence over the conquest of the North American continent. Already in 1713, by the Treaty of Utrecht, the French began to cede some of their American possessions to their British rival. As a result of the Seven Years' War, they would surrender the rest of their Canadian lands in 1763 (see Chapter 18).

British and French rivalry was also evident in the Spanish and Portuguese colonial empires in Latin America. The decline of Spain and Portugal had led these two states to depend even more on resources from their colonies, and they imposed strict mercantilist rules to keep others out. Spain, for example, tried to limit all trade with its colonies to Spanish ships. But the British and French were too powerful to be excluded. The British cajoled the Portuguese into allowing them into the lucrative

Portuguese traders land in Japan	1543
British East India Company formed	1600
Dutch East India Company formed	1602
English settlement at Jamestown	1607
Champlain establishes settlement at Quebec	1608
Dutch fort established at Batavia	1619
Dutch seize Malacca from the Portuguese	1641
English seize New Netherland	1664
English establish trading post at Canton	1699
Battle of Plassey	1757
French cede Canada to British	1763
British mission to China	1793

Brazilian trade. The French, however, were the first to break into the Spanish Latin American market when the French Bourbons became kings of Spain at the beginning of the eighteenth century. Britain's first entry into Spanish American markets came in 1713, when the British were granted the privilege, known as the *asiento* (ah-SYEN-toh), of transporting 4,500 slaves a year to Spanish Latin America.

14-4 The Impact of European Expansion

FOCUS QUESTIONS: How did European expansion affect the native populations and places that the Europeans conquered? For the Europeans who conquered the New World, how were their lives different than their Old World European counterparts?

Between 1500 and 1800, the Atlantic nations of Europe moved into all parts of the world. The first had been Spain and Portugal, the two great colonial powers of the sixteenth century, followed by the Dutch, who built their colonial empire in the seventeenth century as Portugal and Spain declined. The Dutch were soon challenged by the British and French, who outstripped the others in the eighteenth century while becoming involved in a bitter rivalry. By the end of the eighteenth century, it appeared that Great Britain would become the great European imperial power. European expansion had a great impact on both the conquered and the conquerors.

14-4a The Conquered

Different regions experienced different effects from the European expansion. The native American civilizations, which had their own unique qualities and a degree of sophistication not much appreciated by Europeans, were virtually destroyed. In addition to devastating losses of population from European diseases, ancient social and political structures were ripped up and replaced by European institutions, religion, language, and culture. In Africa, the real demographic impact of the slave trade is uncertain due to a lack of records; however, estimates of the population in West Africa suggest that the slave trade negated any population growth, rather than causing a decline. Politically and socially, the slave trade encouraged the growth of territories in West Africa, such as Dahomey and Benin, where the leaders waged internal wars to secure more slaves to trade for guns and gunpowder. Without the slave trade, these territories became susceptible to European control in the nineteenth century. The Portuguese trading posts in the East had little direct impact on native Asian civilizations, although Dutch control of the Indonesian archipelago was more pervasive. China and Japan were still little affected by Westerners, although India was subject to ever-growing British encroachment.

In Central and South America, a new civilization arose that we have come to call Latin America. It was a multiracial society. Spanish and Portuguese settlers who arrived in the Western Hemisphere were few in number relative to the native Indians; many of the newcomers were males who not only used female natives for their sexual pleasure but married them as well. Already by 1501, Spanish rulers had authorized intermarriage between Europeans and native American Indians, whose offspring became known as mestizos (mess-TEE-zohz). Another group of people brought to Latin America were the Africans. Over a period of three centuries, possibly as many as 8 million slaves were brought to Spanish and Portuguese America to work the plantations. Africans also contributed to Latin America's multiracial character. Mulattoes (muh-LAH-toh)—the offspring of Africans and whites—joined mestizos and descendants of whites, Africans, and native Indians to produce a unique society in Latin America. Unlike Europe, and unlike British North America, which remained a largely white offshoot of Europe, Latin America developed a multiracial society with less rigid attitudes about race.

The European presence also affected the ecology of the conquered areas. Europeans brought horses, sheep, goats, pigs and cattle to the Americas, which revolutionized the life of the Indians. The Americas were well suited for the European animals. Since they had few predators and plenty of land to roam, the new animals rapidly increased in number. Explorer Hernando De Soto arrived in Florida in 1539 with thirteen pigs; they increased to 700 by 1542. Cattle farming supplanted the Indian agricultural practice of growing maize (Indian corn), eventually leading to the development of large estates for raising cattle. South America would later become a great exporter of beef. Europeans also brought new crops, such as wheat and cane sugar, to be cultivated on large plantations by native or imported slave labor. In their trips to other parts of the world, Europeans also carried New World plants with them. Thus, Europeans introduced sweet potatoes and maize to Africa in the sixteenth century.

Catholic Missionaries Although there were some Protestant missionaries in the world outside Europe, Catholic missionaries were far more active in spreading Christianity. From the beginning of their conquest of the New World, Spanish and Portuguese rulers were determined to Christianize the native peoples. This policy gave the Catholic Church an important role to play in the New World, one that added considerably to church power. Catholic missionaries—especially the Dominicans, Franciscans, and Jesuits—fanned out to different parts of the Spanish Empire (see Historical Voices, "The Mission," p. 437).

To facilitate their efforts, missionaries brought Indians together into villages, where they could be converted, taught trades, and encouraged to grow crops. These missions enabled the missionaries to control the lives of the Indians and helped ensure that they would remain docile members of the empire (see Movies & History, *The Mission*, below). Missions generally benefited the missionaries more than the Indians. In frontier districts such as California and Texas, missions also served as military barriers to foreign encroachment.

The Catholic Church constructed hospitals, orphanages, and schools. Monastic schools instructed Indian students in the rudiments of reading, writing, and arithmetic. The Catholic Church also provided outlets for women other than marriage. Nunneries were places of prayer and quiet contemplation, but women in religious orders, many of them of aristocratic background, often lived well and worked outside their establishments by running schools and hospitals. Indeed, one of these nuns, Sor Juana Inés de la Cruz (SAWR HWAH-nuh ee-NAYSS day lah KROOZ) (1651–1695), was one of seventeenth-century Latin America's best-known literary figures. She wrote poetry and prose and promoted the education of women.

Christian missionaries also made the long voyage to China on European merchant ships. The Jesuits were among the most active and the most effective. Many of the early Jesuit missionaries to China were highly educated men who were familiar with European philosophical and scientific developments. They brought along clocks and various other instruments

MOVIES & HISTORY
The Mission (1986)

Watch *The Mission*, a cinematic reconstruction of San Carlos, a Jesuit mission in Spanish territory on the border of Paraguay, led by the compelling Father Gabriel. The film follows the activities of Father Gabriel, who has been able to win over the Guaraní Indians and establish a community based on communal livelihood and property. *The Mission* depicts the tragic end of the Jesuit missionaries after Spain agrees to turn over the Guaraní territory in Paraguay to Portugal.

© Warner Brothers/Courtesy Everett Collection

Q *How accurately does the film portray Indian life under Jesuit control? How does the film portray Europeans and their interaction with the native civilizations?*

The Mission

 How were the missions organized to enable the missionaries to control most aspects of the Indians' lives? Why was this deemed necessary?

IN 1609, TWO JESUIT PRIESTS EMBARKED on a missionary calling with the Guaraní Indians in eastern Paraguay. Eventually, the Jesuits established more than thirty missions in the region. Well organized and zealous, the Jesuits transformed their missions into profitable businesses. This description of a Jesuit mission in Paraguay was written by Félix de Azara, a Spanish soldier and scientist.

Félix de Azara, Description and History of Paraguay and Rio de la Plata

Having spoken of the towns founded by the Jesuit fathers, and of the manner in which they were founded, I shall discuss the government which they established in them. . . . In each town resided two priests, a curate and a subcurate, who had certain assigned functions. The subcurate was charged with all the spiritual tasks, and the curate with every kind of temporal responsibility. . . .

The curate allowed no one to work for personal gain; he compelled everyone, without distinction of age or sex, to work for the community, and he himself saw to it that all were equally fed and dressed. For this purpose the curates placed in storehouses all the fruits of agriculture and the products of industry, selling in the Spanish towns their surplus of cotton, cloth, tobacco, vegetables, skins, and wood, transporting them in their own boats down the nearest rivers, and returning with implements and whatever else was required.

From the foregoing one may infer that the curate disposed of the surplus funds of the Indian towns, and that no Indian could aspire to own private property. This deprived them of any incentive to use reason or talent, since the most industrious, able, and worthy person had the same food, clothing, and pleasures as the most wicked, dull, and indolent. It also follows that although this form of government was well designed to enrich the communities it also caused the Indian to work at a languid pace, since the wealth of his community was of no concern to him.

It must be said that although the Jesuit fathers were supreme in all respects, they employed their authority with a mildness and a restraint that command admiration. They supplied everyone with abundant food and clothing. They compelled the men to work only half a day, and did not drive them to produce more. Even their labor was given a festive air, for they went in procession to the fields, to the sound of music . . . and the music did not cease until they had returned in the same way they had set out. They gave them many holidays, dances, and tournaments, dressing the actors. . . . in the most costly European garments, but they permitted the women to act only as spectators.

They likewise forbade the women to sew; this occupation was restricted to the musicians, sacristans, and acolytes. But they made them spin cotton; and the cloth that the Indians wove, after satisfying their own needs, they sold together with the surplus cotton in the Spanish towns, as they did with the tobacco, vegetables, wood, and skins. The curate and . . . subcurate had their own plain dwellings, and they never left them except to take the air in the great enclosed yard of their college. They never walked through the streets of the town or entered the house of any Indian or let themselves be seen by any woman—or indeed, by any man, except for those indispensable few through whom they issued their orders.

Source: B. Keen, ed., *Latin American Civilization*, vol. I (Boston: Houghton Mifflin, 1974), pp. 223–224.

---

that impressed Chinese officials and made them more open to Western ideas.

The Jesuits used this openness to promote Christianity. To make it easier for the Chinese to accept Christianity, the Jesuits pointed to similarities between Christian morality and Confucian ethics. The Italian priest Matteo Ricci described the Jesuit approach:

In order that the appearance of a new religion might not arouse suspicion among the Chinese people, the Jesuit Fathers did not speak openly about religious matters when they began to appear in public. . . . They did, however, try to teach this pagan people in a more direct way, namely, by virtue of their example and by the sanctity of their lives. In this way they attempted to win the good will of the people and little by little to dispose their minds to receive what they could not be persuaded to accept by word of mouth. . . . From the time of their entrance they wore the ordinary Chinese outer garment, which was somewhat similar to their own religious habits; a long robe reaching down to the heels and with very ample sleeves, which are much in favor with the Chinese.[12]

The efforts of the Christian missionaries reached their height in the early eighteenth century. Several hundred Chinese officials became Catholics, as did an estimated 300,000 ordinary Chinese. But ultimately squabbling among the religious orders themselves undermined the Christian effort. To make it easier for the Chinese to convert, the Jesuits had allowed the new Catholics to continue the practice of ancestor worship. Jealous Dominicans and Franciscans complained to the pope, who condemned the practice. Soon Chinese authorities began to suppress Christian activities throughout China.

The Jesuits also had some success in Japan, where they converted a number of local nobles. By the end of the sixteenth century, thousands of Japanese on the southernmost islands of Kyushu and Shikoku had become Christians. But the Jesuit practice of destroying local idols and shrines and turning some temples into Christian schools or churches caused a severe reaction. When a new group of Spanish Franciscans continued the same policies, the government ordered the execution of nine missionaries and a number of their Japanese converts. When missionaries continued to interfere in local politics, Tokugawa Ieyasu expelled all missionaries. After Ieyasu's death in 1616, the anti-Christian movement intensified with strict orders barring all Japanese from converting to Christianity. By 1622, Japanese and foreign Christians were executed in high numbers. One English trader described the scene of foreign priests and Christians being burned at the stake: "I saw fifty-five of them martyred at one time at Miyako. Among them were little children of five or six years, burned alive in the arms of their mothers, who cried 'Jesus, receive their souls!' There are many in prison who hourly await death, for very few return to their idolatry."[13] By 1635, the persecution had eradicated most Japanese and foreign Christians.

14-4b The Conquerors

For some Europeans, expansion abroad brought the possibility of obtaining land, riches, and social advancement. One Spaniard commented in 1572 that many "poor young men" had left Spain for Mexico, where they hoped to acquire landed estates and call themselves "gentlemen." Although some wives accompanied their husbands abroad, many ordinary European women found new opportunities for marriage in the New World because of the lack of white women. Indeed, as one commentator bluntly put it, even "a whore, if handsome, [can] make a wife for some rich planter."[14] In the violence-prone world of early Spanish America, a number of women also found themselves rich after their husbands were killed unexpectedly. In one area of Central America, women owned about 25 percent of the landed estates by 1700.

European expansion also had other economic effects on the conquerors. Wherever they went in the New World, Europeans looked for sources of gold and silver. One Aztec commented that the Spanish conquerors "longed and lusted for gold. Their bodies swelled with greed, and their hunger was ravenous; they hungered like pigs for that gold."[15] Rich silver deposits were found and exploited in Mexico and southern Peru (modern Bolivia). When the mines at Potosí in Peru opened in 1545, the value of precious metals imported into Europe quadrupled. Between 1503 and 1650, an estimated 16 million kilograms (more than 35 million pounds) of silver and 185,000 kilograms (407,000 pounds) of gold entered the port of Seville and set off a price revolution that affected the Spanish economy.

But gold and silver were only two of the products that became part of the exchange between the New World and the Old. Historians refer to the reciprocal importation and exportation of plants and animals between Europe and the Americas as the **Columbian Exchange** (see Map 14.10). While Europeans were bringing horses, cattle, and wheat to the New World,

they were taking new agricultural products such as potatoes, chocolate, corn, tomatoes, and tobacco back to Europe. Potatoes became especially popular as a dietary staple in some areas of Europe. High in carbohydrates and rich in vitamins A and C, potatoes could be easily stored for winter use and enabled more people to survive on smaller plots of land. This improvement in nutrition was soon reflected in a rapid increase in population. Other products, such as cochineal, a red dye discovered in Mexico, gave European artists and artisans a "perfect red" for their paintings and cloth.

The European lifestyle was greatly affected by new products from abroad. In addition to new foods, new drinks also appeared in Europe. Chocolate, which had been brought to Spain from Aztec Mexico, became a common drink by 1700. The first coffee and tea houses opened in London in the 1650s and spread rapidly to other parts of Europe. In the eighteenth century, a craze for Chinese furniture and porcelain spread among the upper classes. Chinese ideas would also have an impact on intellectual attitudes (see Chapter 17).

European expansion, which was in part a product of European rivalries, also deepened that competition and increased the tensions among European states. Bitter conflicts arose over the cargoes coming from the New World and Asia. The Anglo–Dutch trade wars and the British–French rivalry over India and North America became part of a new pattern of worldwide warfare in the eighteenth century (see Chapter 18). Bitter rivalries also led to state-sponsored piracy as governments authorized private captains to attack enemy shipping and keep part of the proceeds for themselves.

In the course of their expansion, Europeans also came to have a new view of the world. When the travels began in the fifteenth century, Europeans were dependent on maps that were often fanciful and inaccurate. Their explorations helped them create new maps that gave a more realistic portrayal of the world, as well as new techniques called map projections that allowed them to represent the round surface of a sphere on a flat piece of paper. The most famous of these is the Mercator projection, the work of a Flemish cartographer, Gerardus Mercator (juh-RAHR-dus mur-KAY-tur) (1512–1594). A Mercator projection is what mapmakers call a conformal projection. It tries to show the true shape of landmasses, but only in a limited area. On the Mercator projection, the shapes of lands near the equator are quite accurate, but the farther away from the equator they lie, the more exaggerated their size becomes. For example, the island of Greenland on a Mercator projection appears to be larger than the continent of South America. In fact, Greenland is about one-ninth the size of South America. Nevertheless, the Mercator projection was valuable to ship captains (see Image 14.11). Every straight line on a Mercator projection is a line of true direction, whether north, south, east, or west. For four centuries, ship captains were very grateful to Mercator.

The psychological impact of colonization on the colonizers is difficult to evaluate but hard to deny. Europeans were initially startled by the discovery of new peoples in the Americas. Some deemed them inhuman and thus fit to be exploited for labor. Others, however, found them to be refreshingly natural and as yet untouched by European corruption. But even the latter

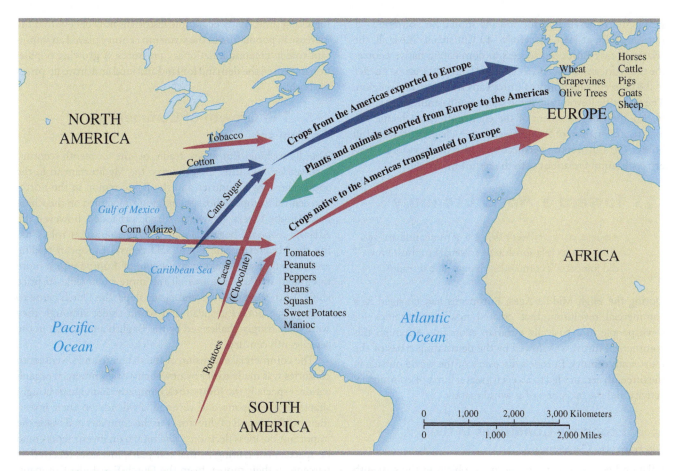

MAP 14.10 **The Columbian Exchange.** In addition to their diseases, which killed vast numbers of indigenous inhabitants of the Americas, Europeans transplanted many of their crops and domestic animals to the New World. Europeans also imported plants from the New World that improved food production and nutrition in Europe.

Q *Where were the main source regions for native plants imported into Europe?*

IMAGE 14.11 **A Seventeenth-Century World Map.** This beautiful world map was prepared in 1630 by Henricus Hondius. The four portraits are of Caesar, the Roman statesman; Ptolemy, the second-century astronomer; Mercator, the Flemish cartographer whose map projection Hondius followed; and Hondius himself.

Q *Compare this map with the map created by Ptolemy in Image 14.2 (p. 414). How much had Europeans learned about the shape of the world by the seventeenth century?*

The Huntington Library, San Marino, CA/SuperStock

group still believed that the Indians should be converted—if not forcefully, at least peacefully—to Christianity. Overall, the relatively easy European success in dominating native peoples (be they Africans or Indians) reinforced Christian Europe's belief in the inherent superiority of European civilization and religion. The Scientific Revolution of the seventeenth century (see Chapter 16), the Enlightenment of the eighteenth (see Chapter 17), and the imperialism of the nineteenth (see Chapter 24) would all bolster this Eurocentric perspective, which has pervaded Western civilization's relations with the rest of the world.

14-5 Toward a World Economy

 FOCUS QUESTIONS: What was mercantilism, and what was its relationship to colonial empires? How did joint-stock companies change global trade?

During the High Middle Ages, Europeans had engaged in a commercial revolution that created new opportunities for townspeople in a basically agrarian economy. Although this commercial thrust was slowed by the devastating crises of the fourteenth century, Europe's discovery of the world outside in the fifteenth century led to an even greater burst of commercial activity and the inception of a world market.

14-5a Economic Conditions in the Sixteenth Century

Inflation became a major economic problem in the sixteenth and early seventeenth centuries. This so-called **price revolution** was a Europe-wide phenomenon, although it affected different areas at different times. Though the inflation rate was probably a relatively low 2 to 3 percent a year, it was noticeable in a Europe accustomed to stable prices. Foodstuffs were most subject to price increases, especially evident in the price of wheat. An upward surge in wheat prices was first noticed in the Mediterranean area—in Spain, southern France, and Italy—and reached its peak there in the 1590s.

Although precise data are lacking, economic historians believe that as a result of the price revolution, wages failed to keep up with price increases. Wage earners, especially agricultural laborers and salaried workers in urban areas, saw their standard of living drop. At the same time, landed aristocrats, who could raise rents, managed to prosper. Commercial and industrial entrepreneurs also benefited from the price revolution because of rising prices, expanding markets, and relatively cheaper labor costs. Some historians regard this profit inflation as a valuable stimulus to investment and the growth of capitalism, helping to explain the economic expansion and prosperity of the sixteenth century. Governments were likewise affected by inflation. They borrowed heavily from bankers and imposed new tax burdens on their subjects, often stirring additional discontent.

The causes of the price revolution are a subject of much historical debate. Already in the 1560s, European intellectuals associated the rise in prices with the great influx of precious metals from the New World. Although this view was accepted for a long time, many economic historians now believe that the increase in population in the sixteenth century played an important role in creating inflationary pressures. A growing population increased the demand for land and food and drove up prices for both.

14-5b The Growth of Commercial Capitalism

The flourishing European trade of the sixteenth century revolved around three major areas: the Mediterranean in the south, the Low Countries and the Baltic region in the north, and central Europe, whose inland trade depended on the Rhine and Danube Rivers. As overseas trade expanded, however, the Atlantic seaboard began to play a more important role, linking the Mediterranean, Baltic, and central European trading areas together and making the whole of Europe into a more integrated market that was all the more vulnerable to price shifts. With their cheaper and faster ships, the Dutch came to monopolize both European and world trade, although they were increasingly challenged by the English and French in the seventeenth century.

The commercial expansion of the sixteenth and seventeenth centuries was made easier by new forms of commercial organization, especially the **joint-stock company**. Individuals bought shares in a company and received dividends on their investment while a board of directors ran the company and made the important business decisions. The return on investments could be spectacular. During its first ten years, investors received 30 percent on their money from the Dutch East India Company, which opened the Spice Islands and Southeast Asia to Dutch activity. The joint-stock company made it easier to raise large amounts of capital for world trading ventures.

Enormous profits were also being made in shipbuilding and in mining and metallurgy, where technological innovations, such as the use of pumps and new methods of extracting metals from ores, proved highly successful. The mining industry was closely tied to sixteenth-century family banking firms. In exchange for arranging large loans to Charles V, Jacob Fugger (YAH-gawp FOO-gurr) was given a monopoly over silver, copper, and mercury mines in the Habsburg possessions of central Europe that produced profits in excess of 50 percent per year. Though these close relationships between governments and entrepreneurs could lead to stunning successes, they could also be precarious. The House of Fugger went bankrupt at the end of the sixteenth century when the Habsburgs defaulted on their loans.

By the seventeenth century, the traditional family banking firms were no longer able to supply the numerous services needed for the expanding commercial capitalism. New institutions arose to take their place. The city of Amsterdam created the Bank of Amsterdam in 1609 as both a deposit and a transfer institution and the Amsterdam Bourse, or Exchange, where the trading of stocks replaced the exchange of goods. By the first half of the seventeenth century, the Amsterdam Exchange had emerged as the hub of the European business world, just as Amsterdam itself had replaced Antwerp as the greatest commercial and banking center of Europe.

Despite the growth of commercial capitalism, most of the European economy still depended on an agricultural system that had experienced few changes since the thirteenth century. At least 80 percent of Europeans still worked on the land. Almost all of the peasants of western Europe were free of serfdom, although many still owed a variety of feudal dues to the nobility. Despite the expanding markets and rising prices, European peasants saw little or no improvement in their lot as they faced increased rents and fees and higher taxes imposed by the state. In eastern Europe, the peasants' position even worsened as they were increasingly tied to the land in a new serfdom enforced by powerful landowners (see Chapter 15).

14-5c Mercantilism

In the seventeenth century, a set of economic tendencies that historians call **mercantilism** came to dominate economic practices. Fundamental to mercantilism was the belief that the total volume of trade was unchangeable. Therefore, states protected their economies by following certain practices: hoarding precious metals, implementing protectionist trade policies, promoting colonial development, increasing shipbuilding, supporting trading companies, and encouraging the manufacturing of products to be used in trade.

According to the mercantilists, the prosperity of a nation depended on a plentiful supply of bullion (gold and silver). For this reason, it was desirable to achieve a favorable balance of trade in which goods exported were of greater value than those imported, promoting an influx of gold and silver payments that would increase the quantity of bullion. Furthermore, to encourage exports, governments should stimulate and protect export industries and trade by granting trade monopolies, encouraging investment in new industries through subsidies, importing foreign artisans, and improving transportation systems by building roads, bridges, and canals. By imposing high tariffs on foreign goods, they could be kept out of the country and prevented from competing with domestic industries. Colonies were also deemed valuable as sources of raw materials and markets for finished goods.

The mercantilists also focused on the role of the state, believing that state intervention in some aspects of the economy was desirable for the sake of the national good. Government regulations to ensure the superiority of export goods, the construction of roads and canals, and the granting of subsidies to create trade companies were all predicated on government involvement in economic affairs.

14-5d Overseas Trade and Colonies: Movement Toward Globalization

Mercantilist theory on the role of colonies was matched in practice by Europe's overseas expansion. With the development of colonies and trading posts in the Americas and the East, Europeans embarked on an adventure in international commerce in the seventeenth century. Although some historians speak of a nascent world economy, we should remember that local, regional, and intra-European trade still predominated. At the end of the seventeenth century, for example, English imports totaled 360,000 tons, but only 5,000 tons came from the East Indies. About one-tenth of English and Dutch exports were shipped across the Atlantic; slightly more went to the East. What made the transoceanic trade rewarding, however, was not the volume but the value of its goods. Dutch, English, and French merchants were bringing back products that were still consumed largely by the wealthy but were beginning to make their way into the lives of artisans and merchants. Pepper and spices from the Indies, West Indian and Brazilian sugar, and Asian coffee and tea were becoming more readily available to European consumers.

Trade within Europe remained strong throughout the eighteenth century as wheat, timber, and naval stores from the Baltic, wines from France, wool and fruit from Spain, and silk from Italy were exchanged along with a host of other products. But this trade increased only slightly while overseas trade boomed. From 1716 to 1789, total French exports quadrupled; intra-European trade, which constituted 75 percent of these exports in 1716, accounted for only 50 percent of the total in 1789. This increase in overseas trade has led some historians to proclaim the emergence of a truly global economy in the eighteenth century. Trade patterns now interlocked Europe, Africa, the East, and the Americas.

CHAPTER SUMMARY

At the end of the fifteenth century, Europeans sailed out into the world in all directions. Beginning in the mid-fifteenth century with a handful of Portuguese ships that ventured southward along the West African coast, bringing back slaves and gold, the process of European expansion accelerated with the epochal voyages of Christopher Columbus to the Americas and Vasco da Gama to the Indian Ocean in the 1490s. The Portuguese Empire was based on trade; Portugal's population was too small for it to establish large colonies. But Spain had greater resources: Spanish conquistadors overthrew both the Aztec and Inca Empires, and Spain created two major administrative units in New Spain and Peru that subjected the native population to Spanish control. Catholic missionaries, under the control of the Spanish crown, brought Christianity, including cathedrals and schools.

Soon a number of other European peoples, including the Dutch, British, and French, had joined in the process of

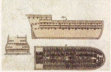

expansion, and by the end of the eighteenth century, they had created a global trade network dominated by Western ships and Western power. Although originally less prized than gold and spices, slaves became a major object of trade, and by the nineteenth century 10 million African slaves had been shipped to the Americas. Slavery was common in Africa, and the African terminus of the trade was in the hands of the Africans, but the insatiable demand for slaves led to increased warfare on that unfortunate continent. It was not until the late 1700s that slavery came under harsh criticism in Europe.

In less than three hundred years, the European age of exploration had changed the shape of the world. In some areas, such as the Americas and the Spice Islands in Asia, it led to the destruction of indigenous

civilizations and the establishment of European colonies. In others, such as Africa, India, and mainland Southeast Asia, it left native regimes intact but had a strong impact on local societies and regional trade patterns. Japan and China were least affected.

At the time, many European observers viewed the process in a favorable light. They believed that it not only expanded wealth through world trade and exchanged crops and discoveries between the Old World and the New but also introduced "heathen peoples" to the message of Jesus. No doubt, the conquest of the Americas and expansion into the rest of the world brought out the worst and some of the best of European civilization. The greedy plundering of resources and the brutal repression and enslavement were hardly balanced by attempts to create new institutions, convert others to Christianity, and foster the rights of the indigenous peoples. In any event, Europeans had begun to change the face of the world and increasingly saw their culture, with its religion, languages, and technology, as a coherent force to be exported to all corners of the world.

CHAPTER TIMELINE

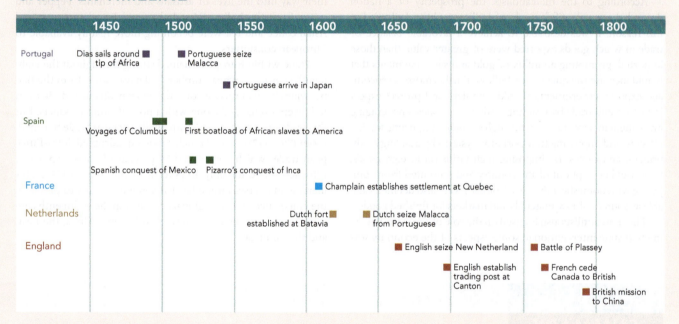

	1450	1500	1550	1600	1650	1700	1750	1800
Portugal	Dias sails around tip of Africa	Portuguese seize Malacca / Portuguese arrive in Japan						
Spain	Voyages of Columbus / Spanish conquest of Mexico	First boatload of African slaves to America / Pizarro's conquest of Inca						
France				Champlain establishes settlement at Quebec				
Netherlands			Dutch fort established at Batavia	Dutch seize Malacca from Portuguese				
England				English seize New Netherland / English establish trading post at Canton		Battle of Plassey / French cede Canada to British / British mission to China		

CHAPTER REVIEW

Upon Reflection

Q What was the relationship between European overseas expansion and political, economic, and social developments in Europe?

Q How did the experiences of the Spanish and Portuguese during the age of exploration differ from those of their French, Dutch, and English counterparts?

Q What role did religion play as a motivation in the age of exploration? Was it as important a motive as economics? Why or why not?

Q Why and how did Japan succeed in keeping Europeans largely away from its territory in the seventeenth century?

Key Terms

portolani (p. 414)
conquistadors (p. 419)
encomienda (p. 422)
viceroy (p. 422)
audiencias (p. 423)
triangular trade (p. 425)

Middle Passage (p. 426)
Columbian Exchange (p. 438)
price revolution (p. 440)
joint-stock company (p. 440)
mercantilism (p. 441)

Full definitions also appear in the Glossary at the end of the book.

Suggestions for Further Reading

General Works For general accounts of European discovery and expansion, see **T. H. Parsons**, *The Rule of Empires: Those Who Built Them, Those Who Endured Them, and Why They Always Fall* (Oxford, 2010); **D. Arnold**, *Age of Discovery*, 2nd ed. (London, 2002); **R. Fritze**, *New Worlds: The Great Voyages of Discovery, 1400–1600* (Westport, Conn., 2002); **G. J. Ames**, *The Globe Encompassed: The Age of European Discovery, 1500–1700* (Upper Saddle River, N.J., 2007); **P. Morgan** and **N. Canny**, eds., *The Oxford Handbook of the Atlantic World, 1450–1850* (New York, 2011); and **A. Suranyi**, *The Atlantic Connection: A History of the Atlantic World, 1450–1900* (New York, 2015).

Portuguese and Spanish Expansion On Portuguese expansion, see **R. Crowley**, *Conquerors: How Portugal Forged the First Global Empire* (New York, 2015). On Columbus, see **W. D. Phillips** and **C. R. Phillips**, *The Worlds of Christopher Columbus* (Cambridge, 1992). On the Spanish Empire in the New World, see **H. Kamen**, *Empire: How Spain Became a World Power, 1492–1763* (New York, 2003), and **R. Goodwin**, *Spain: The Centre of the World, 1519–1682* (New York, 2015). For a revisionist view of the Spanish conquest of the Americas, see **M. Restall**, *Seven Myths of the Spanish Conquest* (Oxford, 2003).

Mercantile Empires and Worldwide Trade The subject of mercantile empires and worldwide trade is covered in **J. H. Elliott**, *Empires of the Atlantic World* (New Haven, Conn., 2006), and **M. J. Seymour**, *Transformation of the North Atlantic World, 1492–1763* (Westport, Conn., 2004). On the African slave trade, see **J. K. Thornton**, *Africa and Africans in the Making of the Atlantic World, 1400–1800* (Cambridge, 1998). On slavery in the New World see **D. B. Davis**, *Inhuman Bondage: The Rise and Fall of Slavery in the New World* (New York, 2008).

Impact of Expansion The impact of expansion on European consciousness is explored in **A. Pagden**, *European Encounters with the New World: From Renaissance to Romanticism* (New Haven, Conn., 1993). On the impact of disease, see **N. D. Cook**, *Born to Die: Disease and the New World* (New York, 1998). The human and ecological effects of the interaction of New World and Old World cultures are examined thoughtfully in **A. W. Crosby**, *Ecological Imperialism: The Biological Expansion of Europe* (New York, 1986).

Economic Dimensions of Expansion On mercantilism, see **L. Magnusson**, *Mercantilism: The Shaping of an Economic Language* (New York, 1994). On the concept of a world economy, see **A. K. Smith**, *Creating a World Economy: Merchant Capital, Colonialism, and World Trade, 1400–1825* (Boulder, Colo., 1991).

Notes

1. Quoted in J. R. Hale, *Renaissance Exploration* (New York, 1968), p. 32.
2. Quoted in J. H. Parry, *The Age of Reconnaissance: Discovery, Exploration, and Settlement, 1450 to 1650* (New York, 1963), p. 33.
3. Quoted in R. B. Reed, "The Expansion of Europe," in R. D. Molen, ed., *The Meaning of the Renaissance and Reformation* (Boston, 1974), p. 308.
4. Quoted in I. Cameron, *Explorers and Exploration* (New York, 1991), p. 42.
5. Quoted in J. H. Parry and R. G. Keith, eds., *New Iberian World*, vol. 2 (New York, 1984), pp. 309–310.
6. Quoted in J. H. Elliott, *Empires of the Atlantic World* (New Haven, Conn., 2006), p. 125.
7. B. Diaz, *The Conquest of New Spain* (New York, 1963), pp. 405–406.
8. Quoted in A. Andrea and J. H. Overfield, *The Human Record: Sources of Global History*, 3rd ed. (Boston, 1998), p. 460.
9. Quoted in B. Davidson, *Africa in History: Themes and Outlines* (New York, 1991), p. 198.
10. Quoted in Cameron, *Explorers and Exploration*, p. 42.
11. Quoted in N. Ferguson, *Empire: The Rise and Demise of the British World Order and the Lessons for Global Power* (New York, 2002), p. 43.

12. Quoted in L. J. Gallagher, ed., trans., *China in the Sixteenth Century: The Journals of Matthew Ricci* (New York, 1953), p. 154.

13. Quoted in G. Sansom, *A History of Japan, 1615–1867* (Stanford, 1963), p. 43.

14. Quoted in G. V. Scammell, *The First Imperial Age: European Overseas Expansion, c. 1400–1715* (London, 1989), p. 62.

15. M. Leon-Portilla, ed., *The Broken Spears: The Aztec Account of the Conquest of Mexico* (Boston, 1969), p. 51.

MindTap *Tips*   Does your instructor encourage you to "think like a historian?" MindTap can help! Begin with the Critical Thinking Tutorial in the History Skills Tutorials folder, where you will be introduced to some of the skills that historians apply in their work.

CHAPTER 15

State Building and the Search for Order in the Seventeenth Century

IMAGE 15.1 Nicolas-René Jollain the Elder's Portrait of Louis XIV Captures the King's Sense of Royal Grandeur

CHAPTER OUTLINE AND FOCUS QUESTIONS

15-1 Social Crises, War, and Rebellions

Q What economic, social, and political crises did Europe experience in the first half of the seventeenth century?

15-2 The Practice of Absolutism: Western Europe

Q What was absolutism in theory, and how did its actual practice in France and Spain reflect or differ from the theory?

15-3 Absolutism in Central, Eastern, and Northern Europe

Q What developments enabled Brandenburg-Prussia, Austria, and Russia to emerge as major powers in the seventeenth century? What were the major developments in the Northern states and Ottoman Empire? What were the limits of absolutism?

15-4 Limited Monarchy and Republics

Q Why were Poland and the Dutch Republic exceptions to the growth of absolutism? What were the main issues in the struggle between king and Parliament in seventeenth-century England, and how were they resolved?

15-5 The Flourishing of European Culture

Q What were the major artistic and literary achievements of this era, and how did they reflect the political and economic developments of the period?

CONNECTIONS TO TODAY

How does the exercise of state power in the seventeenth century compare with the exercise of state power in the twenty-first century? What, if anything, has changed?

BY THE END OF THE SIXTEENTH CENTURY, Europe was beginning to experience a decline in religious passions and a growing secularization that affected both the political and the intellectual worlds (on the intellectual effects, see Chapter 16). Some historians like to speak of the seventeenth century as a turning point in the evolution of a modern state system in Europe. The ideal of a united Christian Europe gave way to the practical realities of a system of secular states in which matters of state took precedence over the salvation of subjects' souls. By the seventeenth century, the credibility of Christianity had been so weakened through religious wars that more and more Europeans came to think of politics in secular terms.

One response to the religious wars and other crises of the time was a yearning for order. As the internal social and political rebellions and revolts died down, it became apparent that the privileged classes of society—the aristocrats—remained in control, although the various states exhibited important differences in political forms. The most general trend saw an extension of monarchical power as a stabilizing force. This development, which historians have called absolute monarchy or absolutism, was most evident in France during the flamboyant reign of Louis XIV, regarded by some as the perfect embodiment of an absolute monarch. In his memoirs, the duc de Saint-Simon (dook duh san-see-MOHN), who had firsthand experience of French court life, said that Louis was "to the manner born, for he stood out like a king bee because of his height, grace, and beauty (even in the tone of his voice), and because of his princely bearing which was better than good looks." The king's natural grace gave him a special charm as well. He spoke well and learned quickly. He was naturally kind and "he loved glory; he desired peace and good government. He was born prudent, temperate, master of his emotions and his tongue . . . he was born good and just." His life was orderly, and his self-control was impeccable. But even absolute monarchs had imperfections, and Saint-Simon had the courage to point them out: "the king's intelligence was below the average. . . . Praise, or better, adulation pleased him so much that the most fulsome was welcome and the most servile even more delectable." Indeed, "he acquired a pride so colossal that, truly, had not God implanted in his heart the fear of the devil . . . he would have allowed himself to be worshipped."[1]

But absolutism was not the only response to the search for order in the seventeenth century. Other states, such as England, reacted differently to domestic crisis, and another very different system emerged in which monarchs were limited by the power of their representative assemblies. Absolute and limited monarchy were the two poles of seventeenth-century state building.

15-1 Social Crises, War, and Rebellions

 FOCUS QUESTION: What economic, social, and political crises did Europe experience in the first half of the seventeenth century?

The inflation-fueled prosperity of the sixteenth century showed signs of slackening by the beginning of the seventeenth. Economic contraction was evident in some parts of Europe in the 1620s. In the 1630s and 1640s, as imports of silver from the Americas declined, economic recession intensified, especially in the Mediterranean area. Once the industrial and financial center of Europe in the Renaissance, Italy was now becoming an economic backwater. Spain's economy was also seriously failing by the 1640s.

Population trends of the sixteenth and seventeenth centuries also reveal Europe's worsening conditions. The sixteenth century was a period of expanding population, possibly related to a warmer climate and increased food supplies. It has been estimated that the population of Europe increased from 60 million in 1500 to 85 million by 1600, the first major recovery of the European population since the devastation of the Black Death in the mid-fourteenth century. Records also indicate a leveling off of the population by 1620, however, and even a decline by 1650, especially in central and southern Europe. Only the Dutch, English, and French grew in number in the first half

of the seventeenth century. Europe's longtime adversaries—war, famine, and plague—continued to affect population levels. After the middle of the sixteenth century, another "little ice age," when average temperatures fell, affected harvests and caused famines. These problems created social tensions that came to a boil in the witchcraft craze.

15-1a The Witchcraft Craze

Hysteria over witchcraft affected the lives of many Europeans in the sixteenth and seventeenth centuries. Witchcraft trials were held in England, Scotland, Switzerland, Germany, some parts of France and the Low Countries, and even in New England in America.

Witchcraft was not a new phenomenon. Its practice had been part of traditional village culture for centuries, but it came to be viewed as both sinister and dangerous when the medieval church began to connect witches to the activities of the devil, thereby transforming witchcraft into a heresy that had to be wiped out. After the establishment of the Inquisition in the thirteenth century, some people were accused of a variety of witchcraft practices and, following the biblical injunction "Thou shalt not suffer a witch to live," were turned over to secular authorities for burning at the stake or, in England, hanging.

The Spread of Witchcraft What distinguished witchcraft in the sixteenth and seventeenth centuries from these previous developments was the increased number of trials and executions of presumed witches. Perhaps more than 100,000 people throughout Europe were prosecuted on charges of witchcraft. Although larger cities were affected first, the trials spread to smaller towns and rural areas as the hysteria persisted well into the seventeenth century (see Historical Voices, "A Witchcraft Trial in France," p. 447).

The accused witches usually confessed to a number of practices, most often after intense torture. Many said that they had sworn allegiance to the devil and attended sabbats or nocturnal gatherings where they feasted, danced, and even copulated with the devil in sexual orgies. More common, however, were admissions of using evil incantations and special ointments and powders to wreak havoc on neighbors by killing their livestock, injuring their children, or raising storms to destroy their crops.

A number of contributing factors have been suggested to explain why the witchcraft frenzy became so widespread in the sixteenth and seventeenth centuries. Religious uncertainties clearly played some part. Many witchcraft trials occurred in areas where Protestantism had recently been victorious or in regions, such as southwestern Germany, where Protestant–Catholic controversies still raged. As religious passions became inflamed, accusations of being in league with the devil became common on both sides. After all, both Martin Luther and John Calvin had described their personal battles with Satan.

Recently, however, historians have emphasized the importance of social conditions, especially the problems of a society in turmoil, in explaining the witchcraft hysteria. At a time when the old communal values that stressed working together for the good of the community were disintegrating before the onslaught of a new economic ethic that emphasized looking out for oneself, property owners became more fearful of the

A Witchcraft Trial in France

 Why were women, particularly older women, especially vulnerable to accusations of witchcraft? What "proofs" are offered that Suzanne Gaudry had consorted with the devil? What does this account tell us about the spread of witchcraft accusations in the seventeenth century?

PERSECUTIONS FOR WITCHCRAFT reached their high point in the sixteenth and seventeenth centuries when tens of thousands of people were brought to trial. In this excerpt from the minutes of a trial in France in 1652, we can see why the accused witch stood little chance of exonerating herself.

The Trial of Suzanne Gaudry

28 May, 1652. . . . Interrogation of Suzanne Gaudry, prisoner at the court of Rieux. . . . [During interrogations on May 28 and May 29, the prisoner confessed to a number of activities involving the devil.]

Deliberation of the Court—June 3, 1652

The undersigned advocates of the Court have seen these interrogations and answers. They say that the aforementioned Suzanne Gaudry confesses that she is a witch, that she had given herself to the devil, that she had renounced God, Lent, and baptism, that she has been marked on the shoulder, that she has cohabited with the devil and that she has been to the dances. . . .

Third Interrogation—June 27

This prisoner being led into the chamber, she was examined to know if things were not as she had said and confessed at the beginning of her imprisonment.

—Answers no, and that what she has said was done so by force.

Pressed to say the truth, that otherwise she would be subjected to torture . . .

—Answers that she is not a witch. . . .

She was placed in the hands of the officer in charge of torture. . . .

The Torture

This prisoner, before being strapped down, was admonished to maintain herself in her first confessions. . . .

—Says that she denies everything she has said. . . . Feeling herself being strapped down, says that she is not a witch . . . and being a little stretched [on the rack] screams ceaselessly that she is not a witch. . . .

Asked if she did not confess that she had been a witch for twenty-six years.

—Says that she said it, that she retracts it, crying that she is not a witch. . . .

The mark having been probed . . . it was adjudged by the aforesaid doctor and officer truly to be the mark of the devil.

Being more tightly stretched upon the torture-rack, urged to maintain her confessions.

—Said that it was true that she is a witch. Asked how long she has been in subjugation to the devil.

—Answers that it was twenty years ago that the devil appeared to her, being in her lodgings in the form of a man dressed in a little cow-hide and black breeches. . . .

Verdict

July 9, 1652. In the light of the interrogations, answers and investigations made into the charge against Suzanne Gaudry . . . seeing by her own confessions that she is said to have made a pact with the devil, received the mark from him . . . and that following this, she had renounced God, Lent, and baptism and had let herself be known carnally by him. . . . Also, seeing that she is said to have been a part of nocturnal carols and dances.

For expiation of which the advice of the undersigned is that the office of Rieux can legitimately condemn the aforesaid Suzanne Gaudry to death, tying her to a gallows, and strangling her to death, then burning her body and burying it here in the environs of the woods.

Source: A. C. Kors and E. Peters, eds., *Witchcraft in Europe, 1100–1700: A Documentary History* (Philadelphia: University of Pennsylvania Press, 1972).

growing numbers of poor in their midst and transformed them psychologically into agents of the devil. Old women were particularly susceptible to suspicion. Many of them, no longer the recipients of the local charity available in traditional society, may even have tried to survive by selling herbs, potions, or secret remedies for healing. When problems arose—and there were many in this crisis-laden period—these people were handy scapegoats. Of special concern was the fear that witches harmed mothers and their households or caused male impotence and thus disrupted the social order.

That women were most often the victims of the witch-hunt has led some scholars to argue that the witch hunt was really a woman hunt or "genderized mass murder," arguing that men hunted witches because they caused disorder and were sexual beings in a patriarchal society. Other scholars have rejected this approach and argue first, that men were also accused of witchcraft, and second, that women accused other women of witchcraft. These scholars believe that people in the sixteenth and seventeenth century believed in witchcraft as a constant threat in their society.

Despite scholarly differences about the nature of the witch hunts, there is no doubt that women were the primary victims. Current estimates are that there were 100,000 to 110,000 witch trials between 1450 and 1750 with about 50 percent of the trials leading to executions. Of those executed, 75 to 80 percent were women, many of them older women. A study of the Würzburg, Germany, witch trials reveals that of the 255 executed, 190 were women, 140 were women over forty, and 112 were over fifty.

That women should be the chief victims of witchcraft trials was hardly accidental. Nicholas Rémy, a witchcraft judge in France in the 1590s, found it "not unreasonable that this scum of humanity [witches] should be drawn chiefly from the feminine sex." To another judge, it came as no surprise that witches would confess to sexual experiences with Satan: "The Devil uses them so, because he knows that women love carnal pleasures, and he means to bind them to his allegiance by such agreeable provocations."[2] Of course, witch hunters were not the only ones who held women in such low esteem. Most theologians, lawyers, and philosophers in early modern Europe believed in the natural inferiority of women and thus would have found it plausible that women would be more susceptible to witchcraft.

Decline By the mid-seventeenth century, the witchcraft hysteria began to subside. The destruction caused by the religious wars had forced people to accept at least a grudging toleration, tempering religious passions. Moreover, as governments began to stabilize after the period of crisis, fewer magistrates were willing to accept the unsettling and divisive conditions generated by the trials of witches. Finally, by the turn of the eighteenth century, more and more educated people were questioning traditional attitudes toward religion and finding it contrary to reason to believe in the old view of a world haunted by evil spirits.

15-1b The Thirty Years' War

Although many Europeans responded to the upheavals of the second half of the sixteenth century with a desire for peace and order, the first fifty years of the seventeenth century continued to be plagued by crises. A devastating war that affected much of Europe and rebellions seemingly everywhere protracted the atmosphere of disorder and violence.

Background to the War Religion, especially the struggle between Catholicism and Calvinism, played an important role in the outbreak of the Thirty Years' War (1618–1648), often called the "last of the religious wars." As the war progressed, however, it became increasingly clear that secular, dynastic-nationalist considerations were far more important. Although much of the fighting during the Thirty Years' War took place in the Germanic lands of the Holy Roman Empire, it became a Europe-wide struggle (see Map 15.1). In fact, some historians view it as part of a larger conflict for European leadership between the Bourbon dynasty of France and the Habsburg dynasties of Spain and the Holy Roman Empire and date it from 1609 to 1659.

The Peace of Augsburg in 1555 had brought an end to religious warfare between German Catholics and Lutherans. Religion, however, continued to play a divisive role in German life as Lutherans and Catholics persisted in vying for control of various principalities. In addition, although the treaty had not recognized the rights of Calvinists, a number of German states had adopted Calvinism as their state church. At the beginning of the seventeenth century, the Calvinist ruler of the Palatinate (puh-LAT-uh-nuht *or* puh-LAT-uh-nayt), the Elector Palatine (PAL-uh-tyn) Frederick IV, assumed the leadership in forming a league of German Protestant states called the Protestant Union. To counteract it, Duke Maximilian of the south German state of Bavaria organized the Catholic League of German states. By 1609, then, Germany was dividing into two armed camps in anticipation of religious war.

A constitutional issue exacerbated the religious division. The desire of the Habsburg emperors to consolidate their authority in the Holy Roman Empire was resisted by the princes, who fought for their "German liberties," their constitutional rights and prerogatives as individual rulers. To pursue their policies, the Habsburg emperors looked to Spain (ruled by another branch of the family) for assistance while the princes turned to the enemies of Spain, especially France, for help against the emperors. The divisions in the Holy Roman Empire and Europe made it almost inevitable that if war did erupt, it would be widespread and difficult to stop.

The Bohemian Phase Historians have traditionally divided the Thirty Years' War into four major phases. The Bohemian phase (1618–1625) began in one of the Habsburgs' own territories. In 1617, the Bohemian Estates (primarily the nobles) accepted the Habsburg Archduke Ferdinand as their king but soon found themselves unhappy with their choice. Though many of the nobles were Calvinists, Ferdinand was a devout Catholic who began a process of re-Catholicizing Bohemia and strengthening royal power. The Protestant nobles rebelled against Ferdinand in May 1618 and proclaimed their resistance by throwing two of the Habsburg governors and a secretary out of a window in the royal castle in Prague, the seat of Bohemian government. The Catholic side claimed that their seemingly miraculous escape from death in the 70-foot fall from the castle was due to the intercession of the Virgin Mary, while Protestants pointed out that they fell into a manure pile. The Bohemian rebels now seized control of Bohemia, deposed Ferdinand, and elected as his replacement the Protestant ruler of the Palatinate, Elector Frederick V, who was also the head of the Protestant Union.

Ferdinand, who in the meantime had been elected Holy Roman Emperor, refused to accept his deposition. Realizing that the election of Frederick V, if allowed to stand, could upset the balance of religious and political power in central Europe and give the Protestant forces greater control of the Holy Roman Empire, Ferdinand sought the aid of the imposing forces of Duke Maximilian of Bavaria and the Catholic League. With their help, the imperial forces defeated Frederick and the Bohemian nobles at the Battle of White Mountain outside Prague on November 8, 1620. Spanish troops took advantage

MAP 15.1 The Thirty Years' War. The conflict began in the German states as Europe's major powers backed either the northern Protestant Union or the southern Catholic League. As the war progressed, religion receded in importance, replaced by a dynastic struggle between the French Bourbons and the Spanish and Austrian Habsburgs.

 Compare this map with Map 13.2. Which countries engaged in the war were predominantly Protestant, which were predominantly Catholic, and which were mixed?

of Frederick's predicament by invading the Palatinate and conquering it by the end of 1622. The unfortunate Frederick fled into exile in the United Provinces. Reestablished as king of Bohemia, Emperor Ferdinand declared Bohemia a hereditary Habsburg possession, confiscated the land of the Protestant nobles, and established Catholicism as the sole religion. The Spanish renewed their attack on the Dutch, and the forces of Catholicism seemed on the road to victory. But the war was far from over.

The Danish Phase The second phase of the war, the Danish phase (1625–1629), began when King Christian IV of Denmark (r. 1588–1648), a Lutheran, intervened on behalf of the Protestant cause by leading an army into northern Germany. Christian had made an anti-Habsburg and anti-Catholic alliance with the United Provinces and England. He also wanted,

however, to gain possession of some Catholic territories in northern Germany to benefit his family.

In the meantime, Ferdinand had gained a new commander for the imperial forces in Albrecht von Wallenstein (AWL-brekht fun VAHL-en-shtyn). A brilliant and enigmatic commander, Wallenstein was a Bohemian nobleman who had taken advantage of Ferdinand's victory to become the country's wealthiest landowner. Wallenstein's forces defeated a Protestant army at Dessau and then continued to operate in northern Germany. The forces of Christian IV, despite substantial aid from their allies, were defeated in 1626 by an army of the Catholic League under Count Tilly and then suffered an even more devastating loss to Wallenstein's forces the following year. Wallenstein now occupied parts of northern Germany, including the Baltic ports of Hamburg, Lübeck, and Bremen. Christian IV's defeat meant the end of Danish supremacy in the Baltic.

After the success of the imperial armies, Emperor Ferdinand II was at the height of his power and took this opportunity to issue the Edict of Restitution in March 1629. His proclamation prohibited Calvinist worship and restored all property taken by Protestant princes or cities during the past seventy-five years to the Catholic Church. But this sudden growth in the power of the Habsburg emperor frightened many German princes, who feared for their independent status and reacted by forcing the emperor to dismiss Wallenstein.

The Swedish Phase The Swedish phase (1630–1635) marked the entry of Gustavus Adolphus (goo-STAY-vus uh-DAHL-fuss), king of Sweden (r. 1611–1632), into the war. Gustavus Adolphus was responsible for reviving Sweden and transforming it into a great Baltic power. A military genius, he brought a disciplined and well-equipped Swedish army to northern Germany. He was also a devout Lutheran who felt compelled to aid his coreligionists in Germany.

Gustavus's army swept the imperial forces out of the north and moved into the heart of Germany. In desperation, the imperial side recalled Wallenstein, who was given command of the imperial army that met Gustavus's troops near Leipzig. At the Battle of Lützen (LOOT-sun) in 1632, the Swedish forces prevailed but paid a high price for the victory when the Swedish king was killed in the battle. Although the Swedish forces remained in Germany, they proved much less effective. Despite the loss of Wallenstein, who was assassinated in 1634 on the orders of Emperor Ferdinand, the imperial army decisively defeated the Swedes at the Battle of Nördlingen at the end of 1634 and drove them out of southern Germany. This imperial victory guaranteed that southern Germany would remain Catholic. The emperor used this opportunity to make peace with the German princes by agreeing to annul the Edict of Restitution of 1629. But peace failed to come to war-weary Germany. The Swedes wished to continue, while the French, under the direction of Cardinal Richelieu (REESH-uh-lyoo), the chief minister of King Louis XIII, entered the war directly, beginning the fourth and final phase of the war, the Franco-Swedish phase (1635–1648).

The Franco-Swedish Phase By this time, religious issues were losing their significance. The Catholic French were now supporting the Protestant Swedes against the Catholic Habsburgs of Germany and Spain. The Battle of Rocroi (roh-KRWAH) in 1643 proved decisive as the French beat the Spanish and brought an end to Spanish military greatness. The French then moved on to victories over the imperialist-Bavarian armies in southern Germany. By this time, all parties were ready for peace, and after five years of protracted negotiations, the Peace of Westphalia in 1648 officially ended the war in Germany. The war between France and Spain, however, continued until the Peace of the Pyrenees in 1659. By that time, Spain had become a second-class power, and France had emerged as the dominant nation in Europe.

Outcomes of the War What were the results of what one historian has called a "basically meaningless conflict"? The

CHRONOLOGY	The Thirty Years' War
Protestant Union	1608
Catholic League	1609
Election of Habsburg Archduke Ferdinand as king of Bohemia	1617
Bohemian revolt against Ferdinand	1618
Bohemian phase	1618–1625
Battle of White Mountain	1620
Danish phase	1625–1629
Edict of Restitution	1629
Swedish phase	1630–1635
Battle of Lützen	1632
Battle of Nördlingen	1634
Franco-Swedish phase	1635–1648
Battle of Rocroi	1643
Peace of Westphalia	1648
Peace of the Pyrenees	1659

Peace of Westphalia ensured that all German states, including the Calvinist ones, were free to determine their own religion. Territorially, France gained parts of western Germany, part of Alsace, and the three cities of Metz, Toul, and Verdun, giving the French control of the Franco-German border area. While Sweden and the German states of Brandenburg and Bavaria gained some territory in Germany, the Austrian Habsburgs did not really lose any but did see their authority as rulers of Germany further diminished. The more than three hundred states that made up the Holy Roman Empire were recognized as virtually independent, since each received the power to conduct its own foreign policy. The Habsburg emperor had been reduced to a figurehead in the Holy Roman Empire. The Peace of Westphalia also made it clear that religion and politics were now separate. The pope was completely ignored in all decisions at Westphalia, and political motives became the guiding forces in public affairs as religion moved closer to becoming primarily a matter of personal conviction and individual choice. Some historians also argue that the Peace of Westphalia marks the beginning of a modern international order in which sovereign states began to operate as equals within a secular framework.

The economic and social effects of the Thirty Years' War on Germany are still debated. Some areas of Germany were completely devastated (see Image 15.2), but others remained relatively untouched and even experienced economic growth. The most recent work pictures a damaged economy and a population decline of 15 to 20 percent in the Holy Roman Empire. Although historians may debate the degree of devastation, many people in Germany would have understood this description by a traveler journeying along the Main River in 1636:

> [We] came to a wretched little village called Neukirchen,
> which we found quite uninhabited yet with one house on

Soldiers Plundering a Farm during the Thirty Years' War, 1620 (oil on wood)/Vrancx, Sebastian (1573-1647)/DEUTSCHES HISTORISCHES MUSEUM/Deutsches Historisches Museum, Berlin, Germany/Bridgeman Images

IMAGE 15.2 The Thirty Years' War: Soldiers Plundering a Farm. This 1620 painting shows a group of soldiers running amok and plundering a farm. This scene was typical of many that occurred during the Thirty Years' War, especially in Germany, where the war caused enormous destruction.

fire. Here, since it was now late, we were obliged to stay all night, for the nearest town was four miles away; but we spent that night walking up and down with guns in our hands, and listening fearfully to the sound of shots in the woods around us. . . . Early next morning, His Excellency went to inspect the church and found it had been plundered and that the pictures and the altar had been desecrated. In the churchyard we saw a dead body, scraped out of the grave, while outside the churchyard we found another dead body.[3]

The Thirty Years' War was undoubtedly the most destructive conflict Europeans had yet experienced (see Historical Voices, "The Destruction of Magdeburg in the Thirty Years' War," p. 452).

HISTORIANS DEBATE 15-1c **Was There a Military Revolution?**

By the seventeenth century, war played an increasingly important role in European affairs. Military power was considered essential to a ruler's reputation and power; thus, the pressure to build an effective military machine was intense. Some historians

believe that the changes that occurred in the science of warfare between 1560 and 1660 warrant the title of military revolution.

Medieval warfare, with its mounted knights and supplementary archers, had been transformed in the Renaissance by the employment of infantry armed with pikes and halberds (long-handled weapons combining an axe with a spike) and arranged in massed rectangles known as squadrons or battalions. The use of firearms required adjustments to the size and shape of the massed infantry and made the cavalry less effective.

It was Gustavus Adolphus, the king of Sweden, who developed the first standing army of conscripts, notable for the flexibility of its tactics. The infantry brigades of Gustavus's army were composed of equal numbers of musketeers and pikemen, standing six men deep. They employed the salvo, in which all rows of the infantry fired at once instead of row by row. These salvos of fire, which cut up the massed ranks of the opposing infantry squadrons, were followed by a pike charge, giving the infantry a primarily offensive deployment. Gustavus also used his cavalry in a more mobile fashion. After shooting a pistol volley, they charged the enemy with their swords. Additional flexibility was obtained by using lighter artillery pieces that were

The Destruction of Magdeburg in the Thirty Years' War

 Q *What does this document reveal about the effect of war on ordinary Europeans? Compare this description with the descriptions of the treatment of civilians in other wars. Does this author exaggerate, or is this description similar to the others?*

AFTER GUSTAVUS ADOLPHUS entered the war, he was finally joined by German Protestant forces after the fall of the Protestant city of Magdeburg to the imperial forces. In this excerpt, a writer of this period gives a vivid description of what happened to Magdeburg and its inhabitants.

An Account of the Destruction of Magdeburg

Thus it came about that the city and all its inhabitants fell into the hands of the enemy, whose violence and cruelty were due in part to their common hatred of the adherents of the Augsburg Confession [Lutherans], and in part to their being embittered by the chain shot which had been fired at them and by the derision and insults that the Magdeburgers had heaped upon them from the ramparts.

Then was there naught but beating and burning, plundering, torture, and murder. Most especially was every one of the enemy bent on securing much booty. When a marauding party entered a house, if its master had anything to give he might thereby purchase respite and protection for himself and his family till the next man, who also wanted something should come along. It was only when everything had been brought forth and there was nothing left to give that the real trouble commenced. Then, what with blows and threats of shooting, stabbing, and hanging, the poor people were so terrified that if they had had anything left they would have brought it forth if it had been buried in the earth or hidden away in a thousand castles. In this frenzied rage, the great and splendid city that had stood like a fair princess in the land was now, in its hour of direct need and unutterable distress and woe, given over to the flames, and thousands of innocent men, women, and children, in the midst of a horrible din of heartrending shrieks and cries, were tortured and put to death in so cruel and shameful a manner that no words would suffice to describe, nor no tears to bewail it . . .

Thus, in a single day this noble and famous city, the pride of the whole country, went up in fire and smoke; and the remnant of its citizens, with their wives and children, were taken prisoner and driven away by the enemy with a noise of weeping and wailing that could be heard from afar, while the cinders and ashes from the town were carried by the wind to . . . distant places . . .

In addition to all this, quantities of sumptuous and irreplaceable house furnishings and movable property of all kinds, such as books, manuscripts, paintings, memorials of all sorts . . . which money could not buy, were either burned or carried away by the soldiers as booty. The most magnificent garments, hangings, silk stuffs, gold and silver lace, linen of all sorts, and other household goods were bought by the army soldiers for a mere song and peddled about by the cart load all throughout the archbishopric of Magdeburg. . . . Gold chains and rings, jewels, and every kind of gold and silver utensils were to be bought from the common soldiers for a tenth of their real value . . .

Source: J. H. Robinson, *Readings in European History*, vol. 2 (Boston: Ginn & Company, 1906), pp. 211–212.

---

more easily moved during battle. All of these changes required coordination, careful training, and better discipline, forcing rulers to move away from undisciplined mercenary forces. Naturally, the success of Gustavus Adolphus led to imitation.

Some historians have questioned the use of the phrase "military revolution" to describe the military changes from 1560 to 1660, arguing instead that military developments were gradual. In any case, for the rest of the seventeenth century, warfare continued to change. Standing armies, based partly on conscription, grew ever larger and more expensive. Standing armies necessitated better-disciplined and better-trained soldiers and led to the education of officers in military schools. Armies also introduced the use of linear rather than square formations to provide greater flexibility and mobility in tactics. There was also an increased use of firearms as the musket with attached bayonet increasingly replaced the pike in the ranks of the infantry. A naval arms race in the seventeenth century led to more and bigger warships or capital ships known as "ships of the line." By the end of the seventeenth century, most of these had two or three decks and were capable of carrying between fifty and one hundred heavy cannon.

Larger armies and navies could be maintained only by levying heavier taxes, making war a greater economic burden and an ever more important part of the early modern European state. The creation of large bureaucracies to supervise the military resources of the state led to growth in the power of state governments.

15-1d Rebellions

Before, during, and after the Thirty Years' War, a series of rebellions and civil wars stemming from the discontent of both nobles and commoners rocked the domestic stability of many European governments. To increase their power, monarchs attempted to extend their authority at the expense of traditional powerful elements who resisted the rulers' efforts. At the same time, to fight their battles, governments increased taxes and created such hard-ships that common people also rose in opposition.

Between 1590 and 1640, peasant and lower-class revolts erupted in central and southern France, Austria, and Hungary. In the decades of the 1640s and 1650s, even greater unrest occurred. Portugal and Catalonia rebelled against the Spanish government in 1640. The common people in Naples and Sicily revolted against both the government and the landed nobility in 1647. Russia, too, was rocked by urban uprisings in 1641, 1645, and 1648. Nobles rebelled in France from 1648 to 1652 in an effort to halt the growth of royal power. The northern states of Sweden, Denmark, and the United Provinces were not immune from upheavals involving clergy, nobles, and mercantile groups. The most famous and widest-ranging struggle, however, was the civil war and rebellion in England, commonly known as the English Revolution (see "15-4c England and the Emergence of Constitutional Monarchy," later in this chapter).

15-2 The Practice of Absolutism: Western Europe

 FOCUS QUESTION: What was absolutism in theory, and how did its actual practice in France and Spain reflect or differ from the theory?

Absolute monarchy or **absolutism** meant that the sovereign power or ultimate authority in the state rested in the hands of a king who claimed to rule by divine right. But what did sovereignty mean? The late-sixteenth-century political theorist Jean Bodin (ZHAHN boh-DAN) believed that sovereign power consisted of the authority to make laws, tax, administer justice, control the state's administrative system, and determine foreign policy. These powers made a ruler sovereign.

One of the chief theorists of **divine-right monarchy** in the seventeenth century was the French theologian and court preacher Bishop Jacques Bossuet (ZHAHK baw-SWAY) (1627–1704), who expressed his ideas in a book titled *Politics Drawn from the Very Words of Holy Scripture.* Bossuet argued first that government was divinely ordained so that humans could live in an organized society. God established kings and through them reigned over all the peoples of the world. Since kings received their power from God, their authority was absolute. They were responsible to no one (including parliaments) except God. For Bossuet, though, his last point was especially important. Because God would hold a king accountable for his actions, Bossuet believed that kings faced serious responsibilities as well as real limits on their power. There was also a large gulf between the theory of absolutism as expressed by Bossuet and the practice of absolutism. A monarch's absolute power was often limited greatly by practical realities.

15-2a Absolute Monarchy in France

France during the reign of Louis XIV (r. 1643–1715) has traditionally been regarded as the best example of the practice of absolute monarchy in the seventeenth century. French culture, language, and manners influenced all levels of European society. French

diplomacy and wars shaped the political affairs of western and central Europe. The court of Louis XIV seemed to be imitated everywhere in Europe. Of course, the stability of Louis's reign was magnified by the instability that had preceded it.

Foundations of French Absolutism: Cardinal Richelieu In the half century before Louis XIV came to power, royal and ministerial governments struggled to avoid the breakdown of the French state. The line between order and anarchy was often a narrow one. The situation was complicated by the fact that both Louis XIII (r. 1610–1643) and Louis XIV were only boys when they succeeded to the throne in 1610 and 1643, respectively, leaving the government dependent on royal ministers. Two especially competent ministers played crucial roles in maintaining monarchical authority.

Cardinal Richelieu, Louis XIII's chief minister from 1624 to 1642, initiated policies that eventually strengthened the power of the monarchy (see Image 15.3). By eliminating the political and military rights of the Huguenots while preserving their

IMAGE 15.3 **Cardinal Richelieu.** A key figure in the emergence of a strong monarchy in France was Cardinal Richelieu, pictured here in a portrait by Philippe de Champaigne. Chief minister to Louis XIII, Richelieu strengthened royal authority by eliminating the private armies and fortified cities of the Huguenots and by crushing aristocratic conspiracies.

 What could you learn about the character of Richelieu from this portrait?

religious privileges, Richelieu transformed the Huguenots into more reliable subjects. Richelieu acted more cautiously in "humbling the pride of the great men," the important French nobility. He understood the influential role played by the nobles in the French state. The dangerous ones were those who asserted their territorial independence when they were excluded from participating in the central government. Proceeding slowly but determinedly, Richelieu developed an efficient network of spies to uncover noble plots and then crushed the conspiracies and executed the conspirators, thereby eliminating a major threat to royal authority.

To reform and strengthen the central administration, initially for financial reasons, Richelieu sent out royal officials called **intendants** (anh-tahnh-DAHNHZ or in-TEN-dunts) to the provinces to execute the orders of the central government. As the functions of the intendants grew, they came into conflict with provincial governors. Since the intendants were victorious in most of these disputes, they further strengthened the power of the crown. Richelieu proved less capable in financial matters, however. Not only was the basic system of state finances corrupt, but so many people benefited from the system's inefficiency and injustice that the government faced strong resistance when it tried to institute reforms. The *taille* (TY) (an annual direct tax usually levied on land or property) was increased—in 1643 it was two and a half times what it had been in 1610. Richelieu's foreign policy goal of confronting the growing power of the Habsburgs in the Thirty Years' War, however, led to ever-increasing expenditures, which soon outstripped the additional revenues. French debt continued its upward spiral under Richelieu.

Cardinal Mazarin Richelieu died in 1642, followed five months later by King Louis XIII, who was succeeded by his son Louis XIV, then but four years old. This necessitated a regency under Anne of Austria, the mother of Louis XIV. But she allowed Cardinal Mazarin (maz-uh-RANH), Richelieu's trained successor, to dominate the government. An Italian who had come to France as a papal legate and then become naturalized, Mazarin attempted to carry on Richelieu's policies until his death in 1661.

The most important event during Mazarin's rule was a revolt of the nobles known as the Fronde (FROHND). As a foreigner, Mazarin was greatly disliked by all elements of the French population. The nobles, who particularly resented the centralized administrative power being built up at the expense of the provincial nobility, temporarily allied with the members of the Parlement (par-luh-MAHNH) of Paris, who opposed the new taxes levied by the government to pay the costs of the Thirty Years' War (Mazarin continued Richelieu's anti-Habsburg policy), and with the people of Paris, who were also angry at the additional taxes. The Parlement of Paris was the most important court in France, with jurisdiction over half of the kingdom, and its members formed the nobles of the robe, the service nobility of lawyers and administrators. These nobles of the robe led the first Fronde (1648–1649), which broke out in Paris and was ended by compromise. The second Fronde, begun in 1650, was led by the nobles of the sword, who were descended from the medieval nobility. They were interested in overthrowing Mazarin for their own purposes: to secure their positions and increase their own power. The second Fronde was crushed by 1652, a task made easier when the nobles began fighting each other instead of Mazarin. With the end of the Fronde, the vast majority of the French concluded that the best hope for stability in France lay in the crown. When Mazarin died in 1661, the greatest of the seventeenth-century monarchs, Louis XIV, took over supreme power.

15-2b The Reign of Louis XIV (1643–1715)

The day after Cardinal Mazarin's death, Louis XIV, age twenty-three, expressed his determination to be a real king and the sole ruler of France:

> Up to this moment I have been pleased to entrust the government of my affairs to the late Cardinal. It is now time that I govern them myself. You [secretaries and ministers of state] will assist me with your counsels when I ask for them. I request and order you to seal no orders except by my command. . . . I order you not to sign anything, not even a passport . . . without my command; to render account to me personally each day and to favor no one.[4]

His mother, who was well aware of Louis's proclivity for fun and games and getting into the beds of the maids in the royal palace, laughed aloud at these words. But Louis was quite serious.

Louis proved willing to pay the price of being a strong ruler. He established a conscientious routine from which he seldom deviated. Louis met with his different ministers for two or three hours each morning and afternoon. In addition, he also worked alone, dealing with numerous issues as they arose. He wrote, "I have always considered the satisfaction that is to be found in doing one's duty as the sweetest pleasure in the world."[5] Eager for glory (in the French sense of achieving what was expected of one in an important position), Louis created a grand and majestic spectacle at the court of Versailles (vayr-SY). Consequently, Louis and his court came to set the standard for monarchies and aristocracies all over Europe. Just a few decades after the king's death, the great French writer Voltaire dubbed the period from 1661 to 1715 the "Age of Louis XIV," and historians have tended to call it that ever since.

Although Louis may have believed in the theory of absolute monarchy and consciously fostered the myth of himself as the Sun King, the source of light for all of his people and an image, as Louis said, that should "represent the duties of a prince and inspire me always to fulfill them" (see Global Perspectives, "Sun Kings, West and East," p. 455), historians are quick to point out that the realities fell far short of the aspirations. Despite the centralizing efforts of Cardinals Richelieu and Mazarin, seventeenth-century France still possessed a bewildering system of overlapping authorities. Provinces had their own regional courts, their own local Estates (parliaments), their own sets of laws. Members of the high nobility, with their huge estates and clients among the lesser nobility, still exercised much authority. Both towns and provinces possessed privileges and powers seemingly from time immemorial that they would not easily relinquish.

Sun Kings, West and East

Q *Although these two rulers practiced very different religions, why did they justify their powers in such a similar fashion?*

AT THE END OF THE SEVENTEENTH CENTURY, two powerful rulers held sway in kingdoms that dominated the affairs of the regions around them. Both rulers saw themselves as favored by divine authority—Louis XIV of France as a divine-right monarch (Image 15.4a) and Kangxi (GANG-zhee) of China (Image 15.4b) as possessing the mandate of Heaven. Thus, both rulers saw themselves not as divine beings but as divinely ordained beings whose job was to govern organized societies. Louis, who ruled France from 1643 to 1715, is seen in a portrait by Hyacinthe Rigaud (ee-ah-SANT ree-GOH) that captures the king's sense of royal dignity and grandeur. One person at court said of the king: "Louis XIV's vanity was without limit or restraint." Kangxi, who ruled China from 1661 to 1722, is seen in a portrait that shows him seated in majesty on his imperial throne. A dedicated ruler, Kangxi once wrote, "One act of negligence may cause sorrow all through the country, and one moment of negligence may result in trouble for hundreds and thousands of generations."

IMAGE 15.4a

IMAGE 15.4b

Administration of the Government One of the keys to Louis's power was that he was able to restructure the central policy-making machinery of government because it was part of his own court and household. The royal court located outside the city of Paris at Versailles was an elaborate structure that served different purposes: it was the personal household of the king, the location of central governmental machinery, and the place where powerful subjects came to find favors and offices for themselves and their clients as well as the main arena where rival aristocratic factions jostled for power (see Image 15,5).

IMAGE 15.5 **The Palace of Versailles.** Louis XIV spent untold sums of money on the construction of a new palace at Versailles. As is evident from this exterior view, the palace was enormous—more than a quarter of a mile long. In addition to being the royal residence, it also housed the members of the king's government and served as home for thousands of French nobles. As the largest royal residence in Europe, Versailles impressed foreigners and became a source of envy for other rulers.

Q *How did the palace of Versailles support Louis's view of himself?*

The greatest danger to Louis's personal rule came from the very high nobles and princes of the blood (the royal princes), who considered it their natural function to assert the policy-making role of royal ministers. Louis eliminated this threat by removing them from the royal council, the chief administrative body of the king and overseer of the central machinery of government, and enticing them to his court, where he could keep them preoccupied with court life and out of politics. Instead of using the high nobility and royal princes, Louis relied on other nobles for his ministers. His ministers were expected to be subservient; Louis said that he had no intention of "sharing my authority with them."

Louis's domination of his ministers and secretaries gave him control of the central policy-making machinery of government and thus authority over the traditional areas of monarchical power: the formulation of foreign policy, the making of war and peace, the assertion of the secular power of the crown against any religious authority, and the ability to levy taxes to fulfill these functions. Louis had considerably less success with the internal administration of the kingdom, however. The traditional groups and institutions of French society—the nobles, officials, town councils, guilds, and representative Estates in some provinces—were simply too powerful for the king to have direct control over the lives of his subjects. Consequently,

control of the provinces and the people was achieved largely by bribing the individuals responsible for executing the king's policies. Nevertheless, local officials could still obstruct the execution of policies they disliked, indicating clearly that a so-called absolute monarch was not always absolute. A recent study of Louis's relationship with the **parlements**, however, asserts that he was able to exercise both political and economic control over these provincial law courts, which were responsible for registering new laws sent to them by the king.

Religious Policy The maintenance of religious harmony had long been considered an area of monarchical power. The desire to keep it brought Louis into conflict with the French Huguenots. Louis XIV did not want to allow Protestants to practice their faith in largely Catholic France. Perhaps he was motivated by religion, but it is more likely that Louis, who believed in the motto "One king, one law, one faith," felt that the existence of this minority undermined his own political authority. In October 1685, Louis issued the Edict of Fontainebleau (fawnh-ten-BLOH). In addition to revoking the Edict of Nantes, the new edict provided for the destruction of Huguenot churches and the closing of Protestant schools. It is estimated that 200,000 Huguenots defied the prohibition against their leaving France and sought asylum in England, the

United Provinces, and the German states. Although it was once believed that this exodus weakened the French economy, others maintain that an influx of English and Irish political and religious refugees into France offset the loss. Support for the expulsion of the Protestants came from Catholic lay-people, who rejected Protestant legal rights, banned them from government meetings, and destroyed Protestant churches in an effort to regain Catholic control of heavily populated Protestant regions.

Financial Issues The cost of building Versailles and other palaces, maintaining his court, and pursuing his wars made finances a crucial issue for Louis XIV. He was most fortunate in having the services of Jean-Baptiste Colbert (ZHAHNH-bah-TEEST kohl-BAYR) (1619–1683) as controller general of finances. Colbert sought to increase the wealth and power of France through general adherence to mercantilism, which stressed government regulation of economic activities to benefit the state. To decrease the need for imports and increase exports, Colbert founded new luxury industries, such as the royal tapestry works at Beauvais; invited Venetian glass-makers and Flemish clothmakers to France; drew up instructions regulating the quality of goods produced; oversaw the training of workers; and granted special privileges, including tax exemptions, loans, and subsidies, to individuals who established new industries. To improve communications and the transportation of goods internally, he built roads and canals. To decrease imports directly, Colbert raised tariffs on foreign manufactured goods and created a merchant marine to carry French goods.

Although Colbert's policies are given much credit for fostering the development of manufacturing in France, some historians are dubious about the usefulness of many of his mercantilistic policies and question whether Colbert stuck to rigid mercantilistic convictions. Regulations were often evaded, and the imposition of high tariffs brought foreign retaliation. French trading companies entered the scene too late to be really competitive with the English and the Dutch. And above all, Colbert's economic policies, which were geared to making his king more powerful, were ultimately self-defeating. The more revenue Colbert collected to enable the king to make war, the faster Louis depleted the treasury. At the same time, the burden of taxes fell increasingly on the peasants, who still constituted the overwhelming majority of the French population. Nevertheless, some historians argue that although Louis bankrupted the treasury in order to pay for his wars, the economic practices implemented under Colbert, including investment in the shipping and textile industries and improvements in transportation facilities, allowed for greater economic growth in the eighteenth century.

Daily Life at the Court of Versailles The court of Louis XIV at Versailles set a standard that was soon followed by other European rulers. In 1660, Louis decided to convert a hunting lodge at Versailles, not far from the capital city of Paris, into a chateau. Not until 1688, after untold sums of money had been spent and tens of thousands of workers had labored incessantly, was construction completed on the enormous palace.

Versailles served many purposes. It was the residence of the king, a reception hall for state affairs, an office building for the members of the king's government, and the home of thousands of royal officials and aristocratic courtiers. Versailles also served a practical political purpose. It became home to the high nobility and princes of the blood. By keeping them involved in the myriad activities that made up daily life at the court of Versailles, Louis excluded them from real power while allowing them to share in the mystique of power as companions of the king. Versailles became a symbol for the French absolutist state and the power of the Sun King, Louis XIV. As a visible manifestation of France's superiority and wealth, this lavish court was intended to overawe subjects and impress foreign powers (see Image 15.6).

Life at Versailles became a court ceremony with Louis XIV at the center of it all. The king had little privacy; only when he visited his wife or mother or mistress or met with ministers was he free of the noble courtiers who swarmed about the palace. Most daily ceremonies were carefully staged, such as those attending Louis's rising from bed, dining, praying, attending Mass, and going to bed. A mob of nobles aspired to assist the king in carrying out these solemn activities. It was considered a great honor for a noble to be chosen to hand the king his shirt while dressing (see Historical Voices, "The King's Day Begins," p. 459). But why did nobles participate in so many ceremonies, some of which were so obviously demeaning? Active involvement in the activities at Versailles was the king's prerequisite for obtaining the offices, titles, and pensions that only he could grant. This policy reduced great nobles and ecclesiastics, the "people of quality," to a plane of equality, allowing Louis to exercise control over them and prevent them from interfering in the real lines of power. To maintain their social prestige, the "people of quality" were expected to adhere to rigid standards of court etiquette appropriate to their rank.

Indeed, court etiquette became a complex matter. Nobles and royal princes were arranged in an elaborate order of seniority and expected to follow certain rules of precedence. Who could sit down and on what kind of chair was a subject of much debate. When Philip of Orléans, the king's brother, and his wife Charlotte sought to visit their daughter, the duchess of Lorraine, they encountered problems with Louis. Charlotte explained why in one of her letters:

> The difficulty is that the Duke of Lorraine claims that he is entitled to sit in an armchair in the presence of Philip and myself because the Emperor gives him an armchair. To this the King [Louis] replied that the Emperor's ceremonial is one thing and the King's another, and that, for example, the Emperor gives the cardinals armchairs, whereas here they may never sit at all in the King's presence.[6]

Louis refused to compromise; the duke of Lorraine was only entitled to a stool. The duke balked, and Philip and Charlotte canceled their visit.

Daily life at Versailles also included numerous forms of entertainment. Walks through the gardens, boating trips, performances of tragedies and comedies, ballets, and concerts

IMAGE 15.6 **Interior of Versailles: The Hall of Mirrors.** Pictured here is the exquisite Hall of Mirrors at Versailles. Located on the second floor, the hall overlooks the park below. Three hundred and fifty-seven mirrors were placed on the wall opposite the windows to create an illusion of even greater width. Careful planning went into every detail of the interior decoration. Even the doorknobs were specially designed to reflect the magnificence of Versailles. This photo shows the Hall of Mirrors after the restoration work that was completed in June 2007, a project that took three years, cost 12 million euros (more than $16 million), and included the restoration of the Bohemian crystal chandeliers.

all provided sources of pleasure. Three evenings a week, from seven to ten, Louis also held an *appartement* (uh-par-tuh-MAHNH) where he was "at home" to his court. The appartement was characterized by a formal informality. Relaxed rules of etiquette even allowed people to sit down in the presence of their superiors. The evening's entertainment began with a concert, followed by games of billiards or cards, and ended with a sumptuous buffet.

The Wars of Louis XIV Both the increase in royal power that Louis pursued and his desire for military glory led the king to wage war. Under the secretary of war, François-Michel Le Tellier (frahnh-SWAH-mee-SHEL luh tel-YAY), the marquis of Louvois (loo-VWAH), France developed a professional army numbering 100,000 men in peacetime and 400,000 in time of war. Louis made war an almost incessant activity of his reign. To achieve the prestige and military glory befitting the Sun King as well as to ensure the domination of his Bourbon dynasty over European affairs, Louis waged four wars between 1667 and 1713 (see Map 15.2).

In 1667, Louis began his first war by invading the Spanish Netherlands to his north and Franche-Comté to the east. But the Triple Alliance of the Dutch, English, and Swedes forced Louis to sue for peace in 1668 and accept a few towns in the Spanish Netherlands for his efforts. He never forgave the Dutch for arranging the Triple Alliance, and in 1672, after isolating the Dutch, France invaded the United Provinces with some initial success. Louis did not believe that he had to justify his action for posterity. He said, "Ambition and glory are always pardonable in a prince, and particularly in a prince so young and so well treated by fortune as I was."[7] But the French victories led Brandenburg, Spain, and the Holy Roman Empire to form a new coalition that forced Louis to end the Dutch War by making peace at Nijmegen (NIM-vay-gun) in 1678. While Dutch territory remained intact, France received Franche-Comté from Spain, which served merely to stimulate Louis's appetite for even more land.

This time, Louis moved eastward against the Holy Roman Empire, which he perceived from his previous war as feeble and unable to resist. The gradual annexation of the provinces of Alsace and Lorraine was followed by the occupation of the city

The King's Day Begins

 What were the message and purpose of the royal waking and dressing ceremony for both the nobles and the king? Do you think this account might be biased? Why?

THE DUC DE SAINT-SIMON (1675–1755) was one of many noble courtiers who lived at Versailles and had firsthand experience of court life there. In his *Memoirs,* he left a controversial and critical account of Louis XIV and his court. In this selection, Saint-Simon describes the scene in Louis's bedroom at the beginning of the day.

Duc de Saint-Simon, *Memoirs*

At eight o'clock the chief valet of the room on duty, who alone had slept in the royal chamber, and who had dressed himself, awoke the King. The chief physician, the chief surgeon, and the nurse (as long as she lived) entered at the same time. The latter kissed the King; the others rubbed and often changed his shirt, because he was in the habit of sweating a great deal. At the quarter, the grand chamberlain was called (or, in his absence, the first gentleman of the chamber), and those who had what was called the grandes entrées [grand entry]. The chamberlain (or chief gentleman) drew back the curtains which had been closed again, and presented the holy water

from the vase, at the head of the bed. These gentlemen stayed but a moment, and that was the time to speak to the King, if any one had anything to ask of him; in which case the rest stood aside. When, contrary to custom, nobody had anything to say, they were there but for a few moments. He who had opened the curtains and presented the holy water, presented also a prayer-book. Then all passed into the cabinet [a small room] of the council. A very short religious service being over, the King called, they reentered. The same officer gave him his dressing-gown; immediately after, other privileged courtiers entered, and then everybody, in time to find the King putting on his shoes and stockings, for he did almost everything himself and with address and grace. Every other day we saw him shave himself; and he had a little short wig in which he always appeared, even in bed, and on medicine days. . . .

As soon as he was dressed, he prayed to God, at the side of his bed, where all the clergy present knelt, the cardinals without cushions, all the laity remaining standing; and the captain of the guards came to the balustrade during the prayer, after which the king passed into his cabinet.

He found there, or was followed by all who had the entrée, a very numerous company, for it included everybody in any office. He gave orders to each for the day; thus within a half a quarter of an hour it was known what he meant to do; and then all this crowd left directly.

Source: B. St. John, trans., *The Memoirs of the Duke of Saint-Simon on the Reign of Louis XIV and the Regency*, vol. 3, 8th ed. (London: George Allen, 1913), pp. 221–222.

of Strasbourg, a move that led to widespread protest and the formation of a new coalition. The creation of this League of Augsburg, consisting of Spain, the Holy Roman Empire, the United Provinces, Sweden, and England, led to Louis's third war, the War of the League of Augsburg (1689–1697). This bitterly contested eight-year struggle brought economic depression and famine to France. The Treaty of Ryswick (RYZ-wik) ending the war forced Louis to give up most of his conquests in the empire, although he was allowed to keep Strasbourg and part of Alsace. The gains were hardly worth the bloodshed and the misery he had caused the French people.

Louis's fourth war, the War of the Spanish Succession (1702–1713), was over bigger stakes, the succession to the Spanish throne. Charles II, the sickly and childless Habsburg ruler, left the throne of Spain in his will to a grandson of Louis XIV. When the latter became King Philip V of Spain after Charles's death, the suspicion that Spain and France would eventually be united in the same dynastic family caused the formation of a new coalition, determined to prevent a Bourbon hegemony that would mean the certain destruction of the European balance of power. This coalition of England, the United Provinces, Habsburg Austria, and German states opposed France and Spain

in a war that dragged on in Europe and the colonial empires in North America for eleven years. In a number of battles, including the memorable defeat of the French forces at Blenheim (BLEN-im) in 1704 by allied troops led by the English commander, John Churchill, duke of Marlborough, the coalition wore down Louis's forces. An end to the war finally came with the Peace of Utrecht in 1713 and of Rastatt in 1714. Although these peace treaties confirmed Philip V as the Spanish ruler, initiating a Spanish Bourbon dynasty that would last into the twentieth century, they also affirmed that the thrones of Spain and France were to remain separated. The Spanish Netherlands, Milan, and Naples were given to Austria, and the emerging state of Brandenburg-Prussia gained additional territories. The real winner at Utrecht, however, was England, which received Gibraltar as well as the French possessions of Newfoundland, Hudson Bay Territory, and Nova Scotia in America. Though France, by its sheer size and position, remained a great power, England had emerged as a formidable naval force.

Only two years after the treaty, the Sun King was dead, leaving France in debt and surrounded by enemies. On his deathbed, the seventy-six-year-old monarch seemed remorseful when he told his successor:

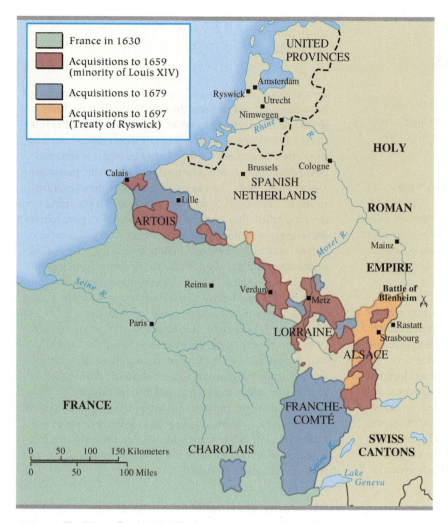

Map legend:
- France in 1630
- Acquisitions to 1659 (minority of Louis XIV)
- Acquisitions to 1679
- Acquisitions to 1697 (Treaty of Ryswick)

MAP 15.2 The Wars of Louis XIV. The Sun King instigated several wars in his efforts to expand the power of France and the Bourbon dynasty. A coalition of European states met each military thrust, however, so Louis's gains were minimal despite the amount of blood spilled and capital spent.

 At the expense of what countries did Louis XIV make most of his territorial acquisitions?

Soon you will be King of a great kingdom. I urge you not to forget your duty to God; remember that you owe everything to Him. Try to remain at peace with your neighbors. I loved war too much. Do not follow me in that or in overspending. Take advice in everything; try to find the best course and follow it. Lighten your people's burden as soon as possible, and do what I have had the misfortune not to do myself.[8]

Did Louis mean it? Did Louis ever realize how tarnished the glory he had sought had become? Ten years before the end of his reign one of his subjects wrote: "Even the people . . . who have so much loved you, and have placed such trust in you, begin to lose their love, their trust, and even their respect. . . . They believe you have no pity for their sorrows, that you are devoted only to your power and your glory."[9] In any event, the advice to his successor was probably not remembered; his great-grandson was only five years old.

15-2c The Decline of Spain

At the beginning of the seventeenth century, Spain possessed the most populous empire in the world, controlling almost all of South America and a number of settlements in Asia and Africa. To most Europeans, Spain still seemed the greatest power of the age, but the reality was quite different. The treasury was empty; Philip II went bankrupt in 1596 from excessive expenditures on war, and his successor, Philip III, did the same in 1607 by spending a fortune on his court. The armed forces were out-of-date, the government was inefficient, and the commercial class was weak in the midst of a suppressed peasantry, a luxury-loving class of nobles, and an oversupply of priests and monks. Spain continued to play the role of a great power, but appearances were deceiving.

During the reign of Philip III (r. 1598–1621), many of Spain's weaknesses became apparent. Interested only in court luxury or miracle-working relics, Philip III allowed his first minister, the greedy duke of Lerma, to run the country. The aristocratic Lerma's primary interest was accumulating power and wealth for himself and his family. As important offices were filled with his relatives, crucial problems went unsolved.

The Reign of Philip IV The reign of Philip IV (r. 1621–1665) seemed to offer hope for a revival of Spain's energies, especially in the capable hands of his chief minister, Gaspar de Guzman (gahs-PAR day goos-MAHN), the count of Olivares (oh-lee-BAH-rayss). This clever, hardworking, and power-hungry statesman dominated the king's every move and worked to revive the interests of the monarchy. A flurry of domestic reform decrees, aimed at curtailing the power of the Catholic Church and the landed aristocracy, was soon followed by a political reform program whose purpose was to further centralize the government of all Spain and its possessions in monarchical hands. All of these efforts met with little real success, however, because both the number (estimated at one-fifth of the population) and the power of the Spanish aristocrats made them too strong to curtail in any significant fashion.

At the same time, most of the efforts of Olivares and Philip were undermined by their desire to pursue Spain's imperial glory and by a series of internal revolts. Spain's involvement in the Thirty Years' War led to a series of frightfully expensive military campaigns that incited internal revolts and years of civil war. Unfortunately for Spain, the campaigns also failed

France	
Louis XIII	1610–1643
Cardinal Richelieu as chief minister	1624–1642
Ministry of Cardinal Mazarin	1642–1661
First Fronde	1648–1649
Second Fronde	1650–1652
Louis XIV	1643–1715
First war (versus Triple Alliance)	1667–1668
Dutch War	1672–1678
Edict of Fontainebleau	1685
War of the League of Augsburg	1689–1697
War of the Spanish Succession	1702–1713
Spain	
Philip III	1598–1621
Philip IV	1621–1665

to produce victory. As Olivares wrote to King Philip IV, "God wants us to make peace; for He is depriving us visibly and absolutely of all the means of war."[10] At the Battle of Rocroi in 1643, much of the Spanish army was destroyed.

The defeats in Europe and the internal revolts of the 1640s ended any illusions about Spain's greatness. The actual extent of Spain's economic difficulties is still debated, but there is no question about its foreign losses. The Peace of Westphalia formally recognized Dutch independence in 1648, and the Peace of the Pyrenees with France in 1659 meant the surrender of Artois and the outlying defenses of the Spanish Netherlands as well as certain border regions that went to France.

15-3 Absolutism in Central, Eastern, and Northern Europe

 FOCUS QUESTIONS: What developments enabled Brandenburg-Prussia, Austria, and Russia to emerge as major powers in the seventeenth century? What were the major developments in the Northern states and Ottoman Empire? What were the limits of absolutism?

During the seventeenth century, a development of great importance for the modern Western world took place in central and eastern Europe, as three new powers made their appearance: Prussia, Austria, and Russia.

15-3a The German States

The Peace of Westphalia, which officially ended the Thirty Years' War in 1648, left each of the states in the Holy Roman Empire virtually autonomous and sovereign. Properly speaking, there was no longer a German state but rather more than three hundred little Germanies. Of these, two emerged as great European powers in the seventeenth and eighteenth centuries.

The Rise of Brandenburg-Prussia The evolution of Brandenburg into a powerful state was largely the work of the Hohenzollern (hoh-en-TSULL-urn) dynasty, which in 1415 had come to rule the insignificant principality in northeastern Germany. In 1609, the Hohenzollerns inherited some lands in the Rhine valley in western Germany; nine years later, they received the duchy of Prussia (East Prussia). By the seventeenth century, then, the dominions of the house of Hohenzollern, now called Brandenburg-Prussia, consisted of three disconnected masses in western, central, and eastern Germany; only the person of the Hohenzollern ruler connected them (see Map 15.3).

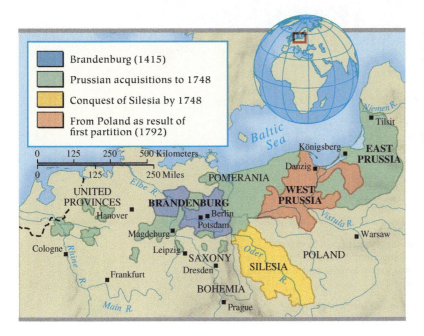

MAP 15.3 The Growth of Brandenburg-Prussia. Frederick William the Great Elector laid the foundation for a powerful state when he increased the size and efficiency of the army, raised taxes and created an efficient bureaucracy to collect them, and gained the support of the landed aristocracy. Later rulers added more territory.

 Why were the acquisitions of Pomerania and West Prussia important for Brandenburg-Prussia's continued rise to power?

Frederick William the Great Elector (r. 1640–1688), who came to power in the midst of the Thirty Years' War, laid the foundation for the Prussian state. Realizing that Brandenburg-Prussia was a small, open territory with no natural frontiers for defense, Frederick William built a competent and efficient standing army. By 1678, he possessed a force of 40,000 men that absorbed more than 50 percent of the state's revenues. To sustain the army and his own power, Frederick William established the General War Commissariat to levy taxes for the army and oversee its growth and training. The Commissariat soon evolved into an agency for civil government as well. Directly responsible to the elector, the new bureaucratic machine became his chief instrument for governing the state. Many of its officials were members of the Prussian landed aristocracy, the Junkers (YOONG-kers), who also served as officers in the all-important army.

The nobles' support for Frederick William's policies derived from the tacit agreement that he made with them. In order to eliminate the power that the members of the nobility could exercise in their provincial Estates-General, Frederick William made a deal with the nobles. In return for a free hand in running the government (in other words, for depriving the provincial Estates of their power), he gave the nobles almost unlimited power over their peasants, exempted the nobles from taxation, and awarded them the highest ranks in the army and the Commissariat with the understanding that they would not challenge his political control. As for the peasants, the nobles were allowed to appropriate their land and bind

them to the soil as serfs. Serfdom was not new to Brandenburg-Prussia, but Frederick William reinforced it through his concessions to the nobles.

To build Brandenburg-Prussia's economy, Frederick William followed the fashionable mercantilist policies, constructing roads and canals and using high tariffs, subsidies, and monopolies for manufacturers to stimulate domestic industry. At the same time, however, he continued to favor the interests of the nobility at the expense of the commercial and industrial middle classes in the towns.

Frederick William laid the groundwork for the Prussian state. His son Frederick III (r. 1688–1713) made one further significant contribution: in return for aiding the Holy Roman Emperor, he was officially granted the title of king-in-Prussia. Thus was Elector Frederick III transformed into King Frederick I, ruler of an important new player on the European stage.

The Emergence of Austria The Austrian Habsburgs had long played a significant role in European politics as Holy Roman Emperors, but by the end of the Thirty Years' War, the Habsburg hopes of creating an empire in Germany had been dashed. In the seventeenth century, the house of Austria made an important transition; the German empire was lost, but a new empire was created in eastern and southeastern Europe.

The nucleus of the new Austrian Empire remained the traditional Austrian hereditary possessions: Lower and Upper Austria, Carinthia, Carniola, Styria, and Tyrol (see Map 15.4).

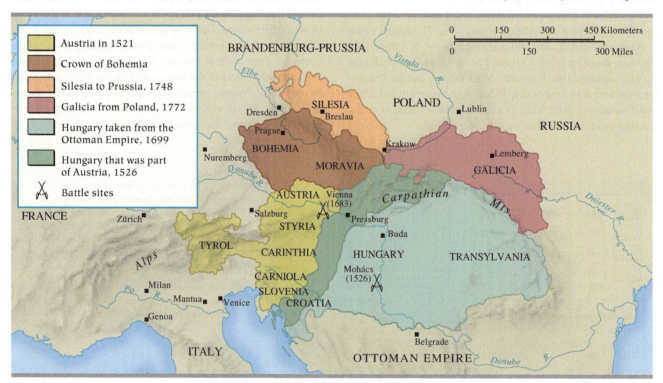

MAP 15.4 **The Growth of the Austrian Empire.** The Habsburgs had hoped to establish a German empire, but the results of the Thirty Years' War crushed that dream. So Austria expanded to the east and the south, primarily at the expense of the Ottoman Empire, and also gained the Spanish Netherlands and former Spanish territories in Italy.

Q In which areas did the Austrian Empire have access to the Mediterranean Sea, and why would that potentially be important?

To these had been added the kingdom of Bohemia and parts of northwestern Hungary in the sixteenth century.

In the seventeenth century, Leopold I (r. 1658–1705) encouraged the eastward movement of the Austrian Empire, but he was sorely challenged by the revival of Ottoman power. Having moved into Transylvania, the Ottomans eventually pushed westward and laid siege to Vienna in 1683. A European army, led by the Austrians, counterattacked and decisively defeated the Ottomans in 1687. By the Treaty of Karlowitz (KARL-oh-vits) in 1699, Austria took control of Hungary, Transylvania, Croatia, and Slovenia, thus establishing an Austrian Empire in southeastern Europe. At the end of the War of the Spanish Succession, Austria gained the Spanish Netherlands and received formal recognition of its occupation of the Spanish possessions in Italy, namely, Milan, Mantua, Sardinia, and Naples. By the beginning of the eighteenth century, the house of Austria had acquired an empire of considerable size.

The Austrian monarchy, however, never became a highly centralized, absolutist state, primarily because it included so many different national groups. The Austrian Empire remained a collection of territories held together by a personal union. The Habsburg emperor was archduke of Austria, king of Bohemia, and king of Hungary. Each of these territories had its own laws, Estates-General, and political life. The landed aristocrats throughout the empire were connected by a common bond of service to the house of Habsburg, as military officers or government bureaucrats, but no other common sentiment tied the regions together. Nevertheless, by the beginning of the eighteenth century, Austria was a populous empire in central Europe of great potential military strength.

15-3b Italy: From Spanish to Austrian Rule

By 1530, Emperor Charles V had managed to defeat the French armies in Italy and become the arbiter of Italy (see Chapter 13). Initially, he was content to establish close ties with many native Italian rulers and allowed them to rule, provided that they recognized his dominant role. But in 1540, he gave the duchy of Milan to his son Philip II and transferred all imperial rights over Italy to the Spanish monarchy.

From the beginning of Philip II's reign in 1556 until 1713, the Spanish presence was felt everywhere in Italy. Only Florence, the Papal States, and Venice managed to maintain relatively independent policies. At the same time, the influence of the papacy became oppressive in Italy as the machinery of the Catholic Counter-Reformation—the Inquisition, the Index, and the Jesuits—was used to stifle all resistance to the Catholic orthodoxy created by the Council of Trent (see Chapter 13).

At the beginning of the eighteenth century, Italy suffered further from the struggles between France and Spain. But it was Austria, not France, that benefited the most from the War of the Spanish Succession. By gaining Milan, Mantua, Sardinia, and Naples, Austria supplanted Spain as the dominant power in Italy.

15-3c Russia: From Fledgling Principality to Major Power

A new Russian state had emerged in the fifteenth century under the leadership of the principality of Moscow and its grand dukes (see Chapter 12). In the sixteenth century, Ivan IV the Terrible (r. 1533–1584), who was the first ruler to take the title of tsar ("Caesar"), expanded the territories of Russia eastward after finding westward expansion blocked by the powerful Swedish and Polish states. Ivan also extended the autocracy of the tsar by crushing the power of the Russian nobility, known as the **boyars** (boh-YARS). Ivan's dynasty came to an end in 1598 and was followed by a resurgence of aristocratic power in a period of anarchy known as the Time of Troubles. It did not end until the Zemsky Sobor (ZEM-skee suh-BOR), or national assembly, chose Michael Romanov (ROH-muh-nahf) (r. 1613–1645) as the new tsar, beginning a dynasty that lasted until 1917.

In the seventeenth century, Muscovite society was highly stratified. At the top was the tsar, who claimed to be a divinely ordained autocratic ruler. Russian society was dominated by an upper class of landed aristocrats who, in the course of the seventeenth century, managed to bind their peasants to the land. An abundance of land and a shortage of peasants made serfdom desirable to the landowners. Townspeople were also controlled. Many merchants were not allowed to move from their cities without government permission or to sell their businesses to anyone outside their class. In the seventeenth century, merchant and peasant revolts as well as a schism in the Russian Orthodox Church created very unsettled conditions. In the midst of these political and religious upheavals, seventeenth-century Moscow was experiencing more frequent contacts with the West, and Western ideas were beginning to penetrate a few Russian circles. Nevertheless, Russia remained largely outside the framework of the West: the Renaissance, the Reformation, and the geographic discoveries of the sixteenth and seventeenth centuries made little impact on Russia. At the end of the seventeenth century, Peter the Great (r. 1689–1725) noticeably accelerated the westernizing process.

The Reign of Peter the Great (1689–1725) Peter the Great was an unusual character. A strong man, towering 6 feet 9 inches tall, Peter was coarse in his tastes and rude in his behavior. He enjoyed a low kind of humor—belching contests, crude jokes, comical funerals—and vicious punishments, including floggings, impalings, roastings, and beard burnings (see Historical Voices, "Peter the Great Deals with a Rebellion," p. 464). Peter gained a firsthand view of the West when he made a trip there in 1697–1698 and returned to Russia with a firm determination to westernize—that is, Europeanize—his realm (see Image 15.7). He admired European technology and gadgets and desired to transplant these to Russia. Only this kind of modernization could give him the army and navy he needed to make Russia a great power.

As could be expected, one of Peter's first priorities was the reorganization of the army and the creation of a navy. Employing both Russians and Europeans as officers, he conscripted peasants for twenty-five-year stints of service to build a standing

Peter the Great Deals with a Rebellion

 How did Peter the Great deal with the revolt of the Streltsy? What does his approach to this problem tell us about the tsar?

DURING HIS FIRST VISIT TO THE WEST in 1697–1698, Peter received word that the Streltsy, an elite military unit stationed in Moscow, had revolted against his authority. Peter hurried home and crushed the revolt in a very savage fashion. This selection is taken from an Austrian account of how Peter dealt with the rebels.

Peter and the Streltsy

How sharp was the pain, how great the indignation, to which the tsar's Majesty was mightily moved, when he knew of the rebellion of the Streltsy, betraying openly a mind panting for vengeance! He was still tarrying at Vienna, quite full of the desire of setting out for Italy; but, fervid as was his curiosity of rambling abroad, it was, nevertheless, speedily extinguished on the announcement of the troubles that had broken out in the bowels of his realm. Going immediately to Lefort . . . he thus indignantly broke out: "Tell me, Francis, how I can reach Moscow by the shortest way, in a brief space, so that I may wreak vengeance on this great perfidy of my people, with punishments worthy of their abominable crime. Not one of them shall escape with impunity. Around my royal city, which, with their impious efforts, they planned to destroy, I will have gibbets and gallows set upon the walls and ramparts, and each and every one of them will I put to a direful death." Nor did he long delay the plan for his justly excited wrath; he took the quick post, as his ambassador suggested, and in four weeks' time he had got over about 300 miles without accident, and arrived the 4th of September, 1698—a monarch for the well disposed, but an avenger for the wicked.

His first anxiety after his arrival was about the rebellion— in what it consisted, what the insurgents meant, who dared to instigate such a crime. And as nobody could answer accurately upon all points, and some pleaded their own ignorance, others the obstinacy of the Streltsy, he began to have suspicions of everybody's loyalty. . . . No day, holy or profane, were the inquisitors idle; every day was deemed fit and lawful for torturing. There was as many scourges as there were accused, and every inquisitor was a butcher. . . . The whole month of October was spent in lacerating the backs of culprits with the knout and with flames; no day were those that were left alive exempt from scourging or scorching; or else they were broken upon the wheel, or driven to the gibbet, or slain with the ax. . . .

To prove to all people how holy and inviolable are those walls of the city which the Streltsy rashly meditated scaling in a sudden assault, beams were run out from all the embrasures in the walls near the gates, in each of which two rebels were hanged. This day beheld about two hundred and fifty die that death. There are few cities fortified with as many palisades as Moscow has given gibbets to her guardian Streltsy.

Source: J. H. Robinson, *Readings in European History*, vol. 2 (Boston: Ginn & Co., 1906).

army of 210,000 men. Peter has also been given credit for forming the first Russian navy.

Peter also reorganized the central government, partly along Western lines. In 1711, he created the Senate to supervise the administrative machinery of the state while he was away on military campaigns. In time, the Senate became something like a ruling council, but its ineffectiveness caused Peter to borrow the Western institution of "colleges," or boards of administrators entrusted with specific functions, such as foreign affairs, war, and justice. To impose the rule of the central government more effectively throughout the land, Peter divided Russia into eight provinces, and later, in 1719, into fifty. Although he hoped to create a "police state," by which he meant a well-ordered community governed in accordance with law, few of his bureaucrats shared his concept of honest service and duty to the state. Peter hoped for a sense of civic duty, but his own forceful personality created an atmosphere of fear that prevented it. He wrote to one administrator, "According to these orders act, act, act. I won't write more, but you will pay with your head if you interpret orders again."[11]

To further his administrative aims, Peter demanded that all members of the landholding class serve in either military or civil offices. Moreover, in 1722, Peter instituted the Table of Ranks to create opportunities for nonnobles to serve the state and join the nobility. He had all civil offices ranked according to fourteen levels and created a parallel list of fourteen grades for all military offices. Every official was then required to begin at level one and work his way up the ranks. When a nonnoble reached the eighth rank, he acquired noble status. Peter's successors did not continue his attempt to create a new nobility based on merit, however.

To obtain the enormous amount of money needed for an army and navy that absorbed as much as four-fifths of the state revenue, Peter adopted Western mercantilistic policies to stimulate economic growth. He tried to increase exports and develop new industries while exploiting domestic resources like the iron mines in the Urals. But his military needs were endless, and he came to rely on the old expedient of simply raising taxes, imposing additional burdens on the hapless peasants, who were becoming ever more oppressed in Peter's Russia.

Peter the Great, Tsar of Russia, 1698 (oil on canvas)/Kneller, Godfrey (1646-1723)/ROYAL COLLECTION/ Royal Collection Trust © Her Majesty Queen Elizabeth II, 2019/Bridgeman Images

IMAGE 15.7 Peter the Great. Peter the Great wished to westernize Russia, especially in the realm of technical skills. His goal was the creation of a strong army and navy and the acquisition of new territory in order to make Russia a great power. Godfrey Kneller, a German artist who studied with Rembrandt and worked in England as a portrait artist, painted this portrait of Peter for King William III while the tsar was in England. Peter was on his "Grand Embassy" to the more advanced countries of Western Europe and was especially fascinated with the ship-building techniques of the English and Dutch; Kneller portrayed ships on maneuver through a window to the right of the tsar.

Peter also sought to establish state control over the Russian Orthodox Church. In 1721, he abolished the position of patriarch and created a body called the Holy Synod to make decisions for the church. At its head stood a **procurator**, a layman who represented the interests of the tsar and assured Peter of effective domination of the church.

Shortly after his return from the West in 1698, Peter had begun to introduce Western customs, practices, and manners into Russia. He ordered the preparation of the first Russian book of etiquette to teach Western manners. Among other things, it pointed out that it was not polite to spit on the floor or to scratch oneself at dinner. Because Europeans at that time did not wear beards or traditional long-skirted coats, Russian beards had to be shaved and coats shortened, a reform Peter personally enforced at court by shaving off his nobles' beards

and cutting their coats at the knees with his own hands. Outside the court, barbers and tailors planted at town gates enforced the edicts by cutting the beards and cloaks of those who entered or left. Many Russians, as a result, according to one observer, regarded the tsar as a tyrant, "and there were many old Russians who, after having their beards shaved off, saved them preciously, in order to have them placed in their coffins, fearing that they would not be allowed to enter heaven without their beards."[12]

One group of Russians benefited greatly from Peter's cultural reforms—women. Having watched women mixing freely with men in Western courts, Peter shattered the seclusion of upper-class Russian women and demanded that they remove the traditional veils that covered their faces. Peter also decreed that social gatherings be held three times a week in the large houses of Saint Petersburg where men and women could mix for conversation, card games, and dancing, which Peter had learned in the West. The tsar also now insisted that women could marry of their own free will.

Russia as a Military Power The object of Peter's domestic reforms was to make Russia into a great state and a military power. His primary goal was to "open a window to the West," meaning a port easily accessible to Europe. This could only be achieved on the Baltic, but at that time the Baltic coast was controlled by Sweden, the most important power in northern Europe. Desirous of these lands, Peter, with the support of Poland and Denmark, attacked Sweden in the summer of 1700 believing that the young king of Sweden, Charles XII, could easily be defeated. Charles, however, proved to be a brilliant general. He smashed the Danes, flattened the Poles, and with a well-disciplined force of only 8,000 men, routed the Russian army of 40,000 at the Battle of Narva (1700). The Great Northern War (1701–1721) soon ensued.

But Peter fought back. He reorganized his army along western lines and at the Battle of Poltava (pul-TAH-vuh) in 1709 defeated Charles's army decisively. Although the war dragged on for another twelve years, the Peace of Nystadt (NEE-shtaht) in 1721 gave formal recognition to what Peter had already achieved: the acquisition of Estonia, Livonia, and Karelia (see Map 15.5). Sweden had become a second-rate power, and Russia was now the great European state Peter had wanted. And he was building it a fine capital. Early in the war, in the northern marshlands along the Baltic, Peter had begun to construct a new city, Saint Petersburg, his window on the West and a symbol that Russia was looking westward to Europe. Though its construction cost the lives of thousands of peasants, Peter completed the city during his lifetime. It remained the Russian capital until 1917.

Peter modernized and westernized Russia to the extent that it became a great military power and, by his death in 1725, an important member of the European state system. But his policies were also detrimental to Russia. Westernization was a bit of a sham because Western culture reached only the upper classes, and the real object of the reforms, the creation of a strong military, only added more burdens to the masses of the Russian people. The forceful way in which Peter the Great imposed westernization led his people to distrust Europe and Western civilization rather than embrace them.

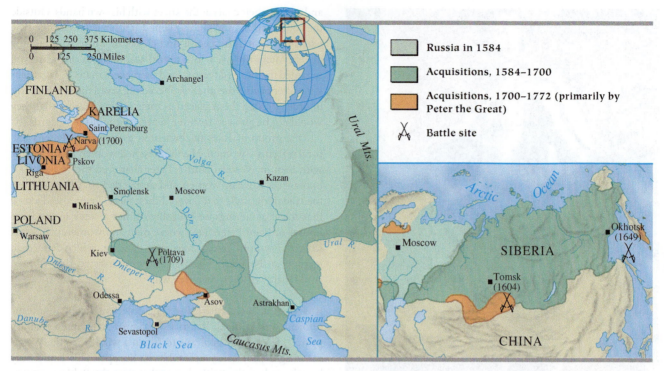

MAP 15.5 **Russia: From Principality to Nation-State.** Russia had expanded its territory since its emergence in the fifteenth century. Peter the Great modernized the country, instituting administrative and tax reforms and building up the military. He won territory on the Baltic from Sweden, enabling Russia to have a port at Saint Petersburg.

 Why would the westward expansion of Russia during Peter's reign affect the international balance of power in Europe?

15-3d The Great Northern States

As the economic thoroughfare for the products of eastern Europe and the West, the Baltic Sea bestowed special importance on the lands surrounding it. In the sixteenth century, Sweden had broken its ties with Denmark and emerged as an independent state (see Chapter 13). Despite their common Lutheran religion, Denmark's and Sweden's territorial ambitions in northern Europe kept them in almost constant rivalry during the seventeenth century.

Denmark Under Christian IV (r. 1588–1648), Denmark seemed a likely candidate for expansion, but it met with little success. The system of electing monarchs forced the kings to share their power with the Danish nobility, who exercised strict control over the peasants who worked their lands. Danish ambitions for ruling the Baltic were severely curtailed by the losses they sustained in the Thirty Years' War and later in the so-called Northern War (1655–1660) with Sweden.

Danish military losses led to a constitutional crisis in which a meeting of Denmark's Estates brought to pass a bloodless revolution in 1660. The power of the nobility was curtailed, a hereditary monarchy was reestablished, and a new absolutist constitution was proclaimed in 1665. Under Christian V (r. 1670–1699), a centralized administration was instituted with the nobility as the chief officeholders.

Sweden Compared with Denmark, Sweden seemed a relatively poor country, and historians have had difficulty explaining why it played such a large role in European affairs in the seventeenth century (see Map 15.6). Sweden's economy was weak, and the monarchy was still locked in conflict with the powerful Swedish nobility. During the reign of Gustavus Adolphus (r. 1611–1632), his wise and dedicated chief minister, Axel Oxenstierna (AHK-sul OOK-sen-shur-nah), persuaded the king to adopt a new policy in which the nobility formed a "First Estate" occupying the bureaucratic positions of an expanded central government. This created a stable monarchy and freed the king to raise a formidable army and participate in the Thirty Years' War, only to be killed in battle in 1632.

Sweden entered a period of severe political crisis after the death of Gustavus Adolphus. His daughter Christina (r. 1633–1654) proved to be far more interested in philosophy and religion than ruling. Her tendency to favor the interests of the nobility caused the other estates of the Riksdag (reeks-TAGH), Sweden's parliament—the burghers, clergy, and peasants—to protest. In 1654, tired of ruling and wishing to become a Catholic, which was forbidden in Sweden, Christina abdicated in favor of her cousin, who became King Charles X (r. 1654–1660). His accession to the throne defused a potentially explosive peasant revolt against the nobility.

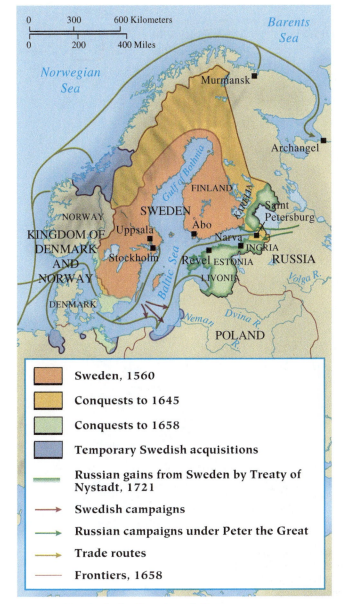

MAP 15.6 Sweden in the Seventeenth Century

Charles X reestablished domestic order, but it was his successor, Charles XI (r. 1660–1697), who did the painstaking work of building the Swedish monarchy along the lines of an absolute monarchy. By retaking control of the crown lands and the revenues attached to them from the nobility, Charles managed to weaken the independent power of the nobles. He built up a bureaucracy, subdued both the Riksdag and the church, improved the army and navy, and left to his son, Charles XII (r. 1697–1718), a well-organized Swedish state that dominated northern Europe. In 1693, he and his heirs were acclaimed as "absolute, sovereign kings, responsible for their actions to no man on earth."

Charles XII was primarily interested in military affairs. Though he was energetic and regarded as a brilliant general, his grandiose plans and strategies, which involved Sweden in conflicts with Poland, Denmark, and Russia, proved to be Sweden's undoing. By the time he died in 1718, Charles XII had lost much

of Sweden's northern empire to Russia, and Sweden was no longer a first-class northern power.

15-3e The Ottoman Empire

After conquering Constantinople in 1453, the Ottoman Turks tried to complete their conquest of the Balkans, where they had been established since the fourteenth century (see Map 15.7). Although they were successful in taking the Romanian territory of Wallachia in 1476, the resistance of the Hungarians kept them from advancing up the Danube valley. From 1480 to 1520, internal problems and the need to consolidate their eastern frontiers kept the Turks from any further attacks on Europe. The reign of Sultan Suleiman (SOO-lay-mahn) I the Magnificent (r. 1520–1566), however, brought the Turks back to Europe's attention. Advancing up the Danube, the Turks seized Belgrade in 1521 and Hungary by 1526, although their attempts to conquer Vienna in 1529 were repulsed. At the same time, the Turks extended their power into the western Mediterranean, threatening to turn it into a Turkish lake until the Spanish destroyed a large Turkish fleet at Lepanto (in modern-day Greece) in 1571. Despite the defeat, the Turks continued to hold nominal control over the southern shores of the Mediterranean.

Although Europeans frequently spoke of new Christian Crusades against the "infidel" Turks, by the beginning of the seventeenth century European rulers seeking alliances and trade concessions were treating the Ottoman Empire like another European power. The Ottoman Empire possessed a highly effective governmental system, especially when it was led by strong sultans or powerful grand viziers (prime ministers). The splendid capital, Constantinople, had a population far larger than that of any European city. Nevertheless, Ottoman politics periodically degenerated into bloody intrigues as factions fought each other for influence and the throne. In one particularly gruesome practice, a ruling sultan would murder his brothers to avoid challenges to his rule. Despite the periodic bouts of civil chaos, a well-trained bureaucracy of civil servants continued to administer state affairs efficiently.

A well-organized military system also added to the strength of the Ottoman Empire. Especially outstanding were the **Janissaries** (JAN-nih-say-reez), composed of Christian boys who had been taken from their parents, converted to the Muslim faith, and subjected to rigid military discipline to form an elite core of 8,000 troops personally loyal to the sultan.

In the first half of the seventeenth century, the Ottoman Empire was a "sleeping giant." Occupied by domestic bloodletting and severely threatened by a challenge from Persia, the Ottomans were content with the status quo in eastern Europe. But under a new line of grand viziers in the second half of the seventeenth century, the Ottoman Empire again took the offensive. By 1683, the Ottomans had marched through the Hungarian plain and laid siege to Vienna. Repulsed by a mixed army of Austrians, Poles, Bavarians, and Saxons, the Turks retreated and were pushed out of Hungary by a new European coalition. Although they retained the core of their empire, the Ottoman Turks would never again be a threat to Europe.

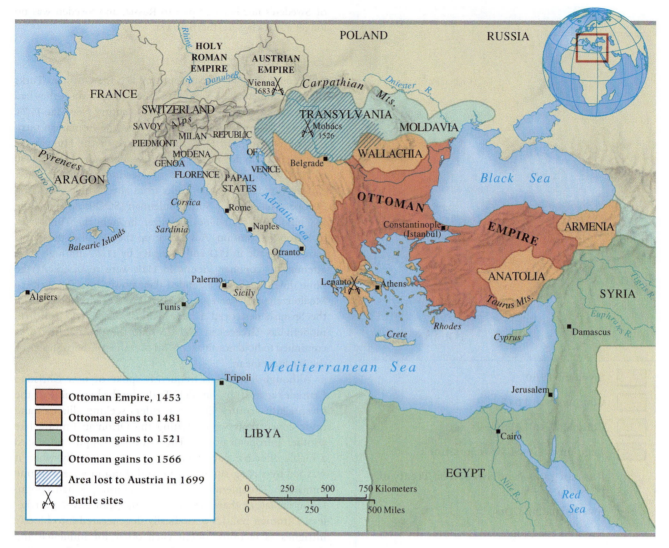

MAP 15.7 **The Ottoman Empire.** In the sixteenth and seventeenth centuries, the Ottoman Empire possessed an effective bureaucracy and military. During this period, it conquered much of the Balkans and made inroads into eastern Europe; by 1699, however, it had lost the farthest reaches of its European territory and would never again pose a serious threat to Europe.

Q *In what region did the Ottomans make the greatest territorial gains in the sixteenth century?*

15-3f The Limits of Absolutism

In recent decades, historical studies of local institutions have challenged the traditional picture of absolute monarchs. We now recognize that their power was far from absolute, and it is misleading to think that they actually controlled the lives of their subjects. In 1700, government for most people still meant the local institutions that affected their lives: local courts, local tax collectors, and local organizers of armed forces. Kings and ministers might determine policies and issue guidelines, but they still had to function through local agents and had no guarantee that their wishes would be carried out. A mass of urban and provincial privileges, liberties, and exemptions (including from taxation) and a whole host of corporate bodies and interest groups—provincial and national Estates, clerical officials, officeholders who had bought or inherited their positions, and provincial nobles—limited what monarchs could achieve. The most successful rulers were not those who tried to destroy the old system but rather those like Louis XIV, who knew how to use the old system to their advantage. Above all other considerations stood the landholding nobility. Everywhere in the seventeenth century, the landed aristocracy played an important role in the European monarchical system. As military officers, judges, officeholders, and landowners in control of vast, untaxed estates, their power remained immense. In some places, their strength put severe limits on how effectively even absolute monarchs could rule.

Brandenburg Prussia	
Hohenzollerns established in Brandenburg	1415
Hohenzollerns acquire East Prussia	1618
Frederick William the Great Elector	1640–1688
Elector Frederick III (King Frederick I)	1688–1713
Austrian Empire	
Leopold I	1658–1705
Turkish siege of Vienna	1683
Treaty of Karlowitz	1699
Russia	
Ivan IV the Terrible	1533–1584
Time of Troubles	1598–1613
Michael Romanov	1613–1645
Peter the Great	1689–1725
First trip to the West	1697–1698
Great Northern War	1701–1721
Construction of Saint Petersburg begins	1703
Battle of Poltava	1709
Denmark	
Christian IV	1588–1648
Christian V	1670–1699
Sweden	
Gustavus Adolphus	1611–1632
Christina	1633–1654
Charles X	1654–1660
Charles XI	1660–1697
Charles XII	1697–1718

15-4 Limited Monarchy and Republics

FOCUS QUESTIONS: Why were Poland and the Dutch Republic exceptions to the growth of absolutism? What were the main issues in the struggle between king and Parliament in seventeenth-century England, and how were they resolved?

Almost everywhere in Europe in the seventeenth century, kings and their ministers were in control of central governments that sought to impose order by strengthening their powers. But not all European states followed the pattern of absolute monarchy. In eastern Europe, the Polish aristocracy controlled a virtually powerless king. In western Europe, two great states—the Dutch Republic and England—successfully resisted the power of hereditary monarchs.

15-4a The Weakness of the Polish Monarchy

Much of Polish history revolved around the bitter struggle between the crown and the landed nobility. The dynastic union of Jagiello (yahg-YEL-oh), grand prince of Lithuania, with the Polish queen Jadwiga (yahd-VEE-guh) resulted in a large Lithuanian-Polish state in 1386, although it was not until 1569 that a formal merger occurred between the two crowns. The union of Poland and Lithuania under the Jagiello dynasty had created the largest kingdom in Christendom at the beginning of the fifteenth century. As a result, Poland-Lithuania played a major role in eastern Europe in the fifteenth century and also ruled much of Ukraine by the end of the sixteenth cen-

MAP 15.8 **Poland in the Seventeenth Century**

tury (see Map 15.8). Poland-Lithuania had a rather unique governmental system in that assemblies of nobles elected the king and carefully limited royal power. The power of the nobles also enabled them to keep the Polish peasantry in a state of serfdom.

In 1572, when the Jagiello dynasty came to an end, a new practice arose of choosing outsiders as kings, with the idea that they would bring in new alliances. When the throne was awarded to the Swede Sigismund III (r. 1587–1631), the new king dreamed of creating a vast Polish empire that would include Russia and possibly Finland and Sweden. Poland not only failed to achieve this goal but by the end of the seventeenth century had become a weak, decentralized state.

It was the elective nature of the Polish monarchy that reduced it to impotence. The Sejm (SAYM), or Polish diet, was a two-chamber assembly in which landowners completely dominated the few townspeople and lawyers who were also members. To be elected to the kingship, prospective monarchs had to agree to share power with the Sejm (in effect with the nobles) in matters of taxation, foreign and military policy, and the appointment of state officials and judges. The power of the Sejm had disastrous results for central monarchical authority, for the real aim of most of its members was to ensure that central authority would not affect their local interests. The acceptance of the liberum veto in 1652, whereby the meetings of the Sejm could be stopped by a single dissenting member, reduced government to virtual chaos.

Poland, then, was basically a confederation of semi-independent estates of landed nobles. By the late seventeenth century, it had also become a battleground for foreign powers, who found the nation easy to invade but difficult to rule.

15-4b The Golden Age of the Dutch Republic

The seventeenth century has often been called the golden age of the Dutch Republic as the United Provinces held center stage as one of Europe's great powers. Like France and England, the

United Provinces was an Atlantic power, underlining the importance of the shift of political and economic power from the Mediterranean basin to the countries on the Atlantic seaboard. As a result of the sixteenth-century revolt of the Netherlands, the seven northern provinces, which began to call themselves the United Provinces of the Netherlands in 1581, became the core of the modern Dutch state. The Peace of Westphalia officially recognized the new state in 1648.

With independence came internal dissension. There were two chief centers of political power in the new state. Each province had an official known as a stadholder (STAD-hohl-dur) who was responsible for leading the army and maintaining order. Beginning with William of Orange and his heirs, the house of Orange occupied the stadholderate in most of the seven provinces and favored the development of a centralized government with themselves as hereditary monarchs. The States General, an assembly of representatives from every province, opposed the Orangist ambitions and advocated a decentralized or republican form of government. For much of the seventeenth century, the republican forces were in control. But in 1672, burdened with war against both France and England, the United Provinces turned to William III (r. 1672–1702) of the house of Orange to establish a monarchical regime. But his death in 1702 without a direct heir enabled the republican forces to gain control once more, although the struggle persisted throughout the eighteenth century.

Underlying Dutch prominence in the seventeenth century was economic prosperity, fueled by the role of the Dutch as carriers of European trade. But warfare proved disastrous to the Dutch Republic. Wars with France and England placed heavy burdens on Dutch finances and manpower. English shipping began to challenge what had been Dutch commercial supremacy, and by 1715, the Dutch were experiencing a serious economic decline.

Life in Seventeenth-Century Amsterdam By the beginning of the seventeenth century, Amsterdam had replaced Antwerp as the financial and commercial capital of Europe. In 1570, Amsterdam had 30,000 inhabitants; by 1610, that number had doubled as refugees poured in, especially from the Spanish Netherlands. In 1613, this rapid growth caused the city government to approve an "urban expansion plan" that increased the city's territory from 500 to 1,800 acres through the construction of three large concentric canals. Builders prepared plots for the tall, narrow-fronted houses that were characteristic of the city by hammering wooden columns through the mud to the firm sand underneath. The canals in turn made it possible for merchants and artisans to use the upper stories of their houses as storerooms for their goods. Wares carried by small boats were hoisted to the top windows of these dwellings by block and tackle beams fastened to the gables of the roofs. Amsterdam's physical expansion was soon matched by its population as the city grew to 200,000 by 1660.

The exuberant expansion of Amsterdam in the seventeenth century owed much to the city's role as the commercial and financial center of Europe. But what had made this possible? For one thing, Amsterdam merchants possessed vast fleets of ships, many of which were used for the lucrative North Sea herring catch. Amsterdam-based ships were also important carriers for the products of other countries. The Dutch invention of the *fluyt* (FLYT), a shallow-draft ship of large capacity, enabled them to transport enormous quantities of cereals, timber, and iron.

Amsterdam merchants unloaded their cargoes at Dam Square, and the city soon became a crossroads for the exchange of many of Europe's chief products. Amsterdam was also, of course, the chief port for the Dutch West Indian and East Indian trading companies. Moreover, city industries turned imported raw materials into finished goods, making Amsterdam an important producer of woolen cloth, refined sugar and tobacco products, glass, beer, paper, books, jewelry, and leather goods. Some of the city's great wealth came from war profits: by 1700, Amsterdam was the principal supplier of military goods in Europe; its gun foundries had customers throughout the Continent.

Another factor in Amsterdam's prosperity was its importance as a financial center. Trading profits provided large quantities of capital for investment. The city's financial role was greatly facilitated by the foundation in 1609 of the Exchange Bank of Amsterdam, long the greatest public bank in northern Europe. The city also founded the Amsterdam Stock Exchange for speculating in commodities.

At the very top of Amsterdam's society stood a select number of very prosperous manufacturers, shipyard owners, and merchants whose wealth enabled them to control the city's government. In the first half of the seventeenth century, the Calvinist background of the wealthy Amsterdam burghers led them to adopt a simple lifestyle. They wore dark clothes and lived in substantial but simply furnished houses known for their steep, narrow stairways. The oft-quoted phrase that "cleanliness is next to godliness" was literally true for these self-confident Dutch burghers. Their houses were spotless and orderly (see Images of Everyday Life, "Dutch Domesticity," p. 471); foreigners often commented that Dutch housewives always seemed to be scrubbing. But in the second half of the seventeenth century, the wealthy burghers began to reject their Calvinist heritage, a transformation that is especially evident in their more elaborate and colorful clothes.

15-4c England and the Emergence of Constitutional Monarchy

One of the most prominent examples of resistance to absolute monarchy came in seventeenth-century England, where king and Parliament struggled to determine the role each should play in governing the nation. But a deep and profound religious controversy complicated the struggle over this political issue. With the victory of Parliament came the foundation for constitutional monarchy by the end of the seventeenth century.

King James I and Parliament Upon the death of Queen Elizabeth in 1603, the Tudor dynasty became extinct, and the Stuart line of rulers was inaugurated with the accession to the throne of Elizabeth's cousin, King James VI of Scotland (son of Mary, queen of Scots), who became James I (r. 1603–1625) of England. Although used to royal power as king of Scotland,

Dutch Domesticity

> **Q** How do these three images demonstrate the Dutch obsession with order and cleanliness? How would you explain that obsession?

DURING THE GOLDEN AGE of the Dutch Republic, Dutch painters delighted in painting scenes of domestic life, especially the lives of the wealthy burghers who prospered from trade, finance, and manufacturing. The Dutch painter Pieter de Hooch (PEE-ter duh HOHKH) specialized in painting pictures of Dutch interiors, as can be seen in three of his paintings. In *The Mother* (Image 15.8a), de Hooch portrays a tranquil scene of a mother with her infant and small daughter. The spotless, polished floors reflect the sunlight streaming in through the open door. The rooms are clean and in good order. Household manuals such as The *Experienced and Knowledgeable Hollands Householder* provided detailed outlines of the cleaning tasks that should be performed each day of the week. In *The Linen Cupboard* (Image 15.8b), a Dutch mother, assisted by her daughter, is shown storing her clean sheets in an elegant cupboard in another well-polished Dutch room. The Chinese porcelain on top of the cupboard and the antique statue indicate that this is the residence of a wealthy family. In *Two Women Teach a Child to Walk* (Image 15.8c), the artist again shows a well-furnished and

spotless interior. A small girl is learning to walk, assisted by a servant holding straps attached to a band around the girl's head to keep her from falling.

IMAGE 15.8b

IMAGE 15.8a

IMAGE 15.8c

James understood little about the laws, institutions, and customs of the English. He espoused the divine right of kings, the belief that kings receive their power directly from God and are responsible to no one except God. This viewpoint alienated Parliament, which had grown accustomed under the Tudors to act on the premise that monarch and Parliament together ruled England as a "balanced polity." Parliament expressed its displeasure with James's claims by refusing his requests for additional monies needed by the king to meet the increased cost of government. Parliament's power of the purse proved to be its trump card in its relationship with the king.

James's religious policy also alienated some members of Parliament. The Puritans—Protestants in the Anglican Church inspired by Calvinist theology—wanted James to eliminate the episcopal system of church organization used in the Church of England (in which the bishop, or *episcopos*, played the major administrative role) in favor of a Presbyterian model (used in Scotland and patterned after Calvin's church organization in Geneva, where ministers and elders—also called presbyters—played an important governing role). James refused because he realized that the Anglican Church, with its bishops appointed by the crown, was a major support of monarchical authority. But the Puritans were not easily cowed and added to the rising chorus of opposition to the king. Many of England's **gentry**, mostly well-to-do landowners below the level of the nobility, had become Puritans, and these Puritan gentry not only formed an important and substantial part of the House of Commons, the lower house of Parliament, but also held important positions locally as justices of the peace and sheriffs. It was not wise to alienate them.

Charles I and the Move Toward Revolution

The conflict that had begun during the reign of James came to a head during the reign of his son, Charles I (r. 1625–1649). In 1628, Parliament passed the Petition of Right, which the king was supposed to accept before being granted any tax revenues. This petition prohibited taxation without Parliament's consent, arbitrary imprisonment, the quartering of soldiers in private houses, and the declaration of martial law in peacetime. Although he initially accepted it, Charles later reneged on the agreement because of its limitations on royal power. In 1629, Charles decided that since he could not work with Parliament, he would not summon it to meet. From 1629 to 1640, Charles pursued a course of personal rule, which forced him to find ways to collect taxes without the cooperation of Parliament. One expedient was a tax called ship money, a levy on seacoast towns to pay for coastal defense, which was now collected annually by the king's officials throughout England and used to finance other government operations besides defense. This use of ship money aroused opposition from middle-class merchants and landed gentry, who objected to the king's attempts to tax without Parliament's consent.

The king's religious policy also proved disastrous. His marriage to Henrietta Maria, the Catholic sister of King Louis XIII of France, aroused suspicions about the king's own religious inclinations. Even more important, however, the efforts of Charles and William Laud, the archbishop of Canterbury, to introduce more ritual into the Anglican Church struck the Puritans as a return to Catholic popery. Grievances mounted. Charles might have survived unscathed if he could have avoided calling Parliament, which alone could provide a focus for the many cries of discontent throughout the land. But when the king and Archbishop Laud attempted to impose the Anglican Book of Common Prayer on the Scottish Presbyterian Church, the Scots rose up in rebellion against the king. Financially strapped and unable to raise troops to defend against the Scots, the king was forced to call Parliament into session. Eleven years of frustration welled up to create a Parliament determined to deal the king his due.

In its first session, from November 1640 to September 1641, the so-called Long Parliament (because it lasted in one form or another from 1640 to 1660) took a series of steps that placed severe limitations on royal authority. These included the abolition of arbitrary courts; the abolition of taxes that the king had collected without Parliament's consent, such as ship money; and the passage of the revolutionary Triennial Act, which specified that Parliament must meet at least once every three years, with or without the king's consent. By the end of 1641, one group in Parliament was prepared to go no further, but a group of more radical parliamentarians pushed for more change, including the elimination of bishops in the Anglican Church. When the king tried to take advantage of the split by arresting some members of the more radical faction in Parliament, a large group in Parliament led by John Pym and his fellow Puritans decided that the king had gone too far. England slipped into civil war.

Civil War in England Parliament proved victorious in the first phase of the English Civil War (1642–1646) (see Map 15.9). Most important to Parliament's success was the creation of the New Model Army, which was composed primarily of more extreme Puritans known as the Independents, who believed they were doing battle for the Lord. It is striking to read in the military reports of Oliver Cromwell (1599–1658), one of the group's leaders, such statements as "Sir, this is none other but the hand of God; and to Him alone belongs the glory." We might also attribute some of the credit to Cromwell himself, since his crusaders were well disciplined and trained in the latest military tactics (see Image 15.9). Supported by the New Model Army, Parliament ended the first phase of the civil war with the capture of King Charles I in 1646.

A split now occurred in the parliamentary forces. A Presbyterian majority wanted to disband the army and restore Charles I with a Presbyterian state church. The army, composed mostly of the more radical Independents, who opposed an established Presbyterian church, marched on London in 1647 and began negotiations with

MAP 15.9 **Civil War in England**

Portrait of Oliver Cromwell (1599-1658), c.1649 (oil on canvas) (see also 4592, 26907, 1229888, 140052)/Walker, Robert (1607-60) (studio of)/PHILIP MOULD LTD/Private Collection/Bridgeman Images

IMAGE 15.9 **Oliver Cromwell.** Oliver Cromwell was a dedicated Puritan who helped form the New Model Army and defeat the forces supporting King Charles I. Unable to work with Parliament, he came to rely on military force to rule England. Cromwell is pictured here in 1649, on the eve of his military campaign in Ireland.

the king. Charles took advantage of this division to flee and seek help from the Scots. Enraged by the king's treachery, Cromwell and the army engaged in a second civil war (1648) that ended with Cromwell's victory and the capture of the king. This time, Cromwell was determined to achieve a victory for the army's point of view. The Presbyterian members of Parliament were purged, leaving a Rump Parliament of fifty-three members of the House of Commons who then tried and condemned the king on a charge of treason and adjudged that "he, the said Charles Stuart, as a tyrant, traitor, murderer, and public enemy to the good people of this nation, shall be put to death by the severing of his head from his body." On January 30, 1649, Charles was beheaded, a most uncommon act in the seventeenth century. The revolution had triumphed, and the monarchy in England had been destroyed, at least for the moment.

Cromwell and New Governments After the death of the king, the Rump Parliament abolished the monarchy and the House of Lords and proclaimed England a republic or commonwealth (1649–1653). This was not an easy period for Cromwell. As commander in chief of the army, he had to crush a Catholic uprising in Ireland, which he accomplished with a brutality that earned him the eternal enmity of the Irish people. In Ireland, he had set an example early on in Drogheda (DRAW ih-duh) by killing most of the defending soldiers as well as members of

Catholic religious orders. Cromwell justified the violence by stating, "The enemy were filled with much terror. And truly I believe this bitterness will save much effusion of blood, through the goodness of God."[13] Cromwell's forces also crushed an uprising in Scotland on behalf of the son of Charles I.

Cromwell also faced opposition at home, especially from more radically minded groups who took advantage of the upheaval in England to push their agendas. The Levellers, for example, advocated such advanced ideas as freedom of speech, religious toleration, and a democratic republic, arguing for the right to vote for all male householders over the age of twenty-one. The Levellers also called for annual Parliaments, women's equality with men, and government programs to care for the poor. As one Leveller said, "The poorest he that is in England has a life to live as the greatest he." To Cromwell, a country gentleman, only people of property had the right to participate in the affairs of state, and he warned in a fit of rage: "I tell you . . . you have no other way to deal with these men but to break them or they will break you; and make void all that work that, with so many years' industry, toil, and pains, you have done . . . I tell you again, you are necessitated to break them."[14] And break them he did; Cromwell smashed the radicals by force. More than a century would pass before their ideas of democracy and equality became fashionable.

At the same time that Cromwell was dealing with the Levellers, he also found it difficult to work with the Rump Parliament and finally dispersed it by force. As the members of Parliament departed (in April 1653), he shouted after them, "It's you that have forced me to do this. . . . I have sought the Lord night and day that He would slay me rather than put upon me the doing of this work."[15] With the certainty of one who is convinced he is right, Cromwell had destroyed both king and Parliament (see Opposing Viewpoints, "Oliver Cromwell: Three Perspectives," p. 474).

The army provided a new government when it drew up the Instrument of Government, England's first and only written constitution. Executive power was vested in the Lord Protector (a position held by Cromwell) and legislative power in a reconstituted Parliament. But the new system failed to work. Cromwell found it difficult to work with Parliament, especially when its members debated his authority and advocated once again the creation of a Presbyterian state church. In 1655, Cromwell dissolved Parliament and divided the country into eleven regions, each ruled by a major general who served virtually as a military governor. To meet the cost of military government, Cromwell levied a 10 percent land tax on all former Royalists. Unable to establish a constitutional basis for a working government, Cromwell had resorted to military force to maintain the rule of the Independents, ironically using even more arbitrary policies than those of Charles I.

Oliver Cromwell died in 1658. After floundering for eighteen months, the military establishment decided that arbitrary rule by the army was no longer feasible and reestablished the monarchy in the person of Charles II, the eldest son of Charles I (see Chart 15.1, p. 475). The restoration of the Stuart monarchy ended England's time of troubles, but it was not long before yet another constitutional crisis arose.

Oliver Cromwell: Three Perspectives

 What motivated Cromwell's political and military actions? What was Edmund Ludlow's criticism of Cromwell, and how did Cromwell respond? In what ways did Edward Hyde see both good and bad features in Cromwell? How do you explain the differences in these three perspectives?

OLIVER CROMWELL WAS A STRONG LEADER with firm religious convictions. The first selection, taken from a letter written after the defeat of the king's forces at Naseby in 1645, reveals Cromwell's feelings about the reasons for his military victory. The next selection, also by Cromwell, is taken from his comments after his army's massacre of Catholic forces at Drogheda in Catholic Ireland. The third selection is by Edmund Ludlow, a general on Cromwell's side who broke with Cromwell after the latter had become Lord Protector. The final selection, by Edward Hyde, the first earl of Clarendon and a supporter of King Charles I and later Charles II, presents a royalist view of Cromwell.

Oliver Cromwell on the Victory at Naseby

Sir, this is none other but the hand of God; and to Him alone belongs the glory, wherein none are to share with Him. The general [Fairfax] served you with all faithfulness and honor: and the best commendations I can give him is, that I dare say he attributes all to God, and would rather perish than assume to himself. Which is an honest and a thriving way, and yet as much for bravery may be given to him, in this action, as to a man.

Cromwell on the Massacre at Drogheda

The next day, the other two towers were summoned, in one of which was about six or seven score; but they refused to yield themselves, and we knowing that hunger must compel them, set only good guards to secure them from running away until their stomachs were come down. From one of the said towers, notwithstanding their condition, they killed and wounded some of our men. When they submitted, their officers were knocked on the head, and every tenth man of the soldiers killed, and the rest shipped for the Barbados. The soldiers in the other tower were all spared, as to their lives only, and shipped likewise for the Barbados.

I am persuaded that this is a righteous judgment of God upon these barbarous wretches, who have imbrued their hands in so much innocent blood; and that it will tend to prevent the effusion of blood for the future, which are the satisfactory grounds to such actions, which otherwise cannot but work remorse and regret.

Edmund Ludlow, *Memoirs*

Then I drew near to the council-table, where Cromwell charged me with dispersing treasonable books in Ireland, and with endeavoring to render the officers of the army disaffected, by discoursing to them concerning new models of Government. I acknowledged that I had caused some papers to be dispersed in Ireland, but denied that they justly could be called treasonable. . . .

"You do well," said he, "to reflect on our fears. . . . I now require you to give assurance not to act against the Government." I desired to be excused in that particular, reminding him of the reasons I had formerly given him for my refusal, adding that I was in his power, and that he might use me as he thought fit. "Pray then," said he, "what is it that you would have? May not every man be as good as he will? What can you desire more than you have?" "It were easy," said I, "to tell what we would have." "What is that, I pray?" said he. "That which we fought for," said I, "that the nation might be governed by its own consent." "I am," said he, "as much for a government by consent as any man; but where shall we find that consent? Amongst the Prelatical, Presbyterian, Independent, Anabaptist, or Leveling Parties?" I answered, "Amongst those of all sorts who had acted with fidelity and affection to the public."

Lord Clarendon, *The History of the Rebellion and Civil Wars in England*

He was one of those men . . . whom his very enemies could not condemn without commending him at the same time: for he could never have done half that mischief without great parts of courage, industry, and judgment. He must have had a wonderful understanding in the natures and humors of men, and as great a dexterity in applying them; who, from a private and obscure birth (though of a good family), without interest or estate, alliance or friendship, could raise himself to such a height, and compound and knead such opposite and contradictory tempers, humors, and interests into a consistence, that contributed to his designs, and to their own destruction; whilst himself grew insensibly powerful enough to cut off those by whom he had climbed, in the instant that they projected to demolish their own building. What [a Roman writer] said of Cinna [a Roman politician] may very justly be said of him: he attempted those things which no good man dared have ventured on; and achieved those in which none but a valiant and great man could have succeeded. Without doubt, no man with more wickedness ever attempted any thing, or brought to pass what he desired more wickedly, more in the face and contempt of religion, and moral honesty; yet wickedness as great as his could never have accomplished those trophies, without the assistance of a great spirit, an admirable circumspection and sagacity, and a most magnanimous resolution.

Sources: Oliver Cromwell on the Victory at Naseby and on the Massacre at Drogheda, in T. Carlyle, ed., *The Letters and Speeches of Oliver Cromwell*, Vols. 1 and 3 (New York: G.P. Putnam's Sons, 1904); E. Ludlow, *Memoirs*, in C. H. Firth, *The Memoirs of Edmund Ludlow*, Vol. 2 (Oxford: Oxford University Press, 1894); Lord Clarendon, *The History of the Rebellion and Civil Wars in England*, Vol. 6 (Oxford: Oxford University Press, 1839).

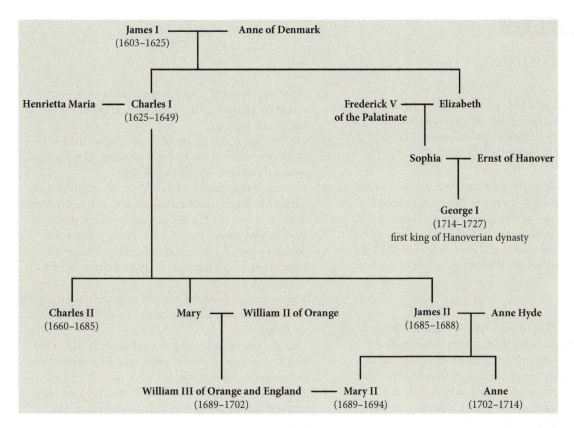

CHART 15.1 A Simplified Look at the Stuart Dynasty

Family tree diagram:

James I (1603–1625) — Anne of Denmark

Henrietta Maria — Charles I (1625–1649)

Frederick V of the Palatinate — Elizabeth

Sophia — Ernst of Hanover

George I (1714–1727) first king of Hanoverian dynasty

Charles II (1660–1685)

Mary — William II of Orange

James II (1685–1688) — Anne Hyde

William III of Orange and England (1689–1702) — Mary II (1689–1694)

Anne (1702–1714)

Restoration of the Monarchy After eleven years of exile, Charles II (r. 1660–1685) returned to England. As he entered London amid the acclaim of the people, he remarked cynically, "I never knew that I was so popular in England." The restoration of the monarchy and the House of Lords did not mean, however, that the work of the English Revolution was undone. Parliament kept much of the power it had won: its role in government was acknowledged, the necessity for its consent to taxation was accepted, and arbitrary courts were still abolished. Yet Charles continued to push his own ideas, some of which were clearly out of step with many of the English people. A serious religious problem disturbed the tranquility of Charles II's reign. After the restoration of the monarchy, a new Parliament (the Cavalier Parliament) met in 1661 and restored the Anglican Church as the official church of England. In addition, laws were passed to force everyone, particularly Catholics and Puritan Dissenters, to conform to the Anglican Church. Charles, however, was sympathetic to and perhaps even inclined toward Catholicism. Moreover, Charles's brother James, heir to the throne, did not hide the fact that he was a Catholic. Parliament's suspicions were therefore aroused in 1672 when Charles took the audacious step of issuing the Declaration of Indulgence, which suspended the laws that Parliament had passed against Catholics and Puritans. Parliament would have none of it and induced the king to suspend the declaration. Propelled by a strong anti-Catholic sentiment, Parliament then passed the Test Act of 1673, specifying that only Anglicans could hold military and civil offices.

A purported Catholic plot to assassinate King Charles and place his brother James on the throne, though soon exposed as imaginary, inflamed Parliament to attempt to pass a bill that would have barred James from the throne as a professed Catholic. Although these attempts failed, the debate over the bill created two political groupings: the Whigs, who wanted to exclude James and establish a Protestant king with toleration of Dissenters, and the Tories, who supported the king, despite their dislike of James as a Catholic, because they believed that Parliament should not tamper with the lawful succession to the throne. To foil these efforts, Charles dismissed Parliament in 1681, relying on French subsidies to rule alone. When he died in 1685, his Catholic brother came to the throne.

The accession of James II (r. 1685–1688) virtually guaranteed a new constitutional crisis for England. An open and devout Catholic, his attempt to further Catholic interests made religion once more a primary cause of conflict between king and Parliament. Contrary to the Test Act, James named Catholics to high positions in the government, army, navy, and universities. In 1687, he issued a new Declaration of Indulgence, which suspended all laws barring Catholics and Dissenters from office. Parliamentary outcries against James's policies stopped short of rebellion because members knew that he was an old man and that his successors were his Protestant daughters Mary and Anne, born to his first wife. But on June 10, 1688, a son was born to James II's second wife, also a Catholic. Suddenly, the specter of a Catholic hereditary monarchy loomed large.

The Bill of Rights

 How did the Bill of Rights lay the foundation for a constitutional monarchy? What key aspects of this document testify to the exceptional nature of English state politics in the seventeenth century?

IN 1688, THE ENGLISH EXPERIENCED yet another revolution, a bloodless one in which the Stuart king James II was replaced by Mary, James's daughter, and her husband, William of Orange. After William and Mary had assumed power, Parliament passed the Bill of Rights, which specified the rights of Parliament and laid the foundation for a constitutional monarchy.

The Bill of Rights

Whereas the said late King James II having abdicated the government, and the throne being thereby vacant, his Highness the prince of Orange (whom it has pleased Almighty God to make the glorious instrument of delivering this kingdom from popery and arbitrary power) did (by the device of the lords spiritual and temporal, and diverse principal persons of the Commons) cause letters to be written to the lords spiritual and temporal, being Protestants, and other letters to the several counties, cities, universities, boroughs, and Cinque Ports, for the choosing of such persons to represent them, as were of right to be sent to parliament, to meet and sit at Westminster upon the two and twentieth day of January, in this year 1689, in order to such an establishment as that their religion, laws, and liberties might not again be in danger of being subverted; upon which letters elections have been accordingly made.

And thereupon the said lords spiritual and temporal and Commons, pursuant to their respective letters and elections, being now assembled in a full and free representation of this nation, taking into their most serious consideration the best means for attaining the ends aforesaid, do in the first place (as their ancestors in like case have usually done), for the vindication and assertion of their ancient rights and liberties, declare:

1. That the pretended power of suspending laws, or the execution of laws, by regal authority, without consent of parliament is illegal.
2. That the pretended power of dispensing with the laws, or the execution of law by regal authority, as it has been assumed and exercised of late, is illegal.
3. That the commission for erecting the late court of commissioners for ecclesiastical causes, and all other commissions and courts of like nature, are illegal and pernicious.
4. That levying money for or to the use of the crown by pretense of prerogative, without grant of parliament, for longer time or in other manner than the same is or shall be granted, is illegal.
5. That it is the right of the subjects to petition the king, and all commitments and prosecutions for such petitioning are illegal.
6. That the raising or keeping a standing army within the kingdom in time of peace, unless it be with consent of parliament, is against law.
7. That the subjects which are Protestants may have arms for their defense suitable to their conditions, and as allowed by law.
8. That election of members of parliament ought to be free.
9. That the freedom of speech, and debates or proceedings in parliament, ought not to be impeached or questioned in any court or place out of parliament.
10. That excessive bail ought not to be required, nor excessive fines imposed, nor cruel and unusual punishments inflicted.
11. That jurors ought to be duly impaneled and returned, and jurors which pass upon men in trials for high treason ought to be freeholders.
12. That all grants and promises of fines and forfeitures of particular persons before conviction are illegal and void.
13. And that for redress of all grievances, and for the amending, strengthening, and preserving of the laws, parliament ought to be held frequently.

Source: *The Statutes: Revised Edition*, vol. 2 (London: Eyre and Spottiswoode, 1871), pp. 10–12.

A Glorious Revolution A group of seven prominent English noblemen invited William of Orange, husband of James's daughter Mary, to invade England. William and Mary raised an army and invaded England while James, his wife, and their infant son fled to France. With almost no bloodshed, England had embarked on a "Glorious Revolution," not over the issue of whether there would be a monarchy but rather over who would be monarch.

The events of late 1688 set the Glorious Revolution in motion. The far more important part was the Revolution Settlement, which confirmed William and Mary as monarchs. In January 1689, the Convention Parliament asserted that James had tried to subvert the constitution "by breaking the original contract between king and people" and declared the throne of England vacant. It then offered the throne to William and Mary, who accepted it along with the provisions of a declaration of rights, later enacted into law as the Bill of Rights in 1689 (see Historical Voices, "The Bill of Rights," above). The Bill of Rights affirmed Parliament's right to make laws and levy taxes and made it impossible for kings to oppose or do without Parliament by stipulating that standing armies could be raised only with the consent of Parliament. Both elections of members and debates in Parliament had to be free, meaning that the king could not interfere. The rights of citizens to petition the sovereign, keep arms, have a jury trial, and not be subject to excessive bail were also confirmed. The Bill of Rights helped fashion a system of government based on the rule of law and a freely elected Parliament, thus laying the foundation for a constitutional monarchy.

The Bill of Rights did not settle the religious questions that had played such a large role in England's troubles in the seventeenth century. The Toleration Act of 1689 granted Puritan Dissenters the right of free public worship (Catholics were still excluded), although they did not yet have full civil and political equality since the Test Act was not repealed. Although the Toleration Act did not mean complete religious freedom and equality, it marked a departure in English history: few people would ever again be persecuted for religious reasons.

Many historians have viewed the Glorious Revolution as the end of the seventeenth-century struggle between king and Parliament. By deposing one king and establishing another, Parliament had demolished the divine-right theory of kingship (William was, after all, king by grace of Parliament, not God) and confirmed its right to participate in the government. Parliament did not have complete control of the government, but it now had an unquestioned role in affairs of state. Over the next century, it would gradually prove to be the real authority in the English system of constitutional monarchy.

Responses to Revolution The English revolutions of the seventeenth century prompted very different responses from two English political thinkers—Thomas Hobbes and John Locke. Thomas Hobbes (1588–1679), who lived during the English Civil War, was alarmed by the revolutionary upheavals in his contemporary England. Hobbes's name has since been associated with the state's claim to absolute authority over its subjects, a topic that he elaborated in his major treatise on political thought known as the *Leviathan* (luh-VY-uh-thun), published in 1651.

Hobbes claimed that in the state of nature, before society was organized, human life was "solitary, poor, nasty, brutish, and short." Humans were guided not by reason and moral ideals but by animalistic instincts and a ruthless struggle for self-preservation. To save themselves from destroying each other (the "war of every man against every man"), people contracted to form a commonwealth, which Hobbes called "that great Leviathan (or rather, to speak more reverently, that mortal god) to which we owe our peace and defense." This commonwealth placed its collective power into the hands of a sovereign authority, preferably a single ruler, who served as executor, legislator, and judge. This absolute ruler possessed unlimited power. In Hobbes's view, subjects may not rebel; if they do, they must be suppressed.

John Locke (1632–1704) viewed the exercise of political power quite differently from Hobbes and argued against the absolute rule of one man. Locke's experience of English politics during the Glorious Revolution was incorporated into a political work called *Two Treatises of Government*. Like Hobbes, Locke began with the state of nature before human existence became organized socially. But unlike Hobbes, Locke believed that humans lived then in a state of equality and freedom rather than a state of war. In this state of nature, humans had certain inalienable natural rights—to life, liberty, and property. Like Hobbes, Locke did not believe all was well in the state of nature. Since there was no impartial judge in the state of nature, people found it difficult to protect these rights. So they mutually agreed to establish a government to ensure the protection of their rights. This agreement established mutual obligations: government would protect the rights of the people while the people would act reasonably toward government. But if a government broke this agreement—for example, if a monarch failed to live up to his obligation to protect the people's rights or claimed absolute authority and made laws without the consent of the community—the people might form a new government. For Locke, however, the community of people was primarily the landholding aristocracy who were represented in Parliament, not the landless masses. Locke was hardly an advocate of political democracy, but his ideas proved important to both the Americans and the French in the eighteenth century and were used to support demands for constitutional government, the rule of law, and the protection of rights.

CHRONOLOGY	Limited Monarchy and Republics
Poland	
Merger of Poland and Lithuania	1569
Sigismund III	1587–1631
Beginning of liberum veto	1652
United Provinces	
Official recognition of United Provinces	1648
House of Orange	
William III	1672–1702
England	
James I	1603–1625
Charles I	1625–1649
Petition of Right	1628
First Civil War	1642–1646
Second Civil War	1648
Execution of Charles I	1649
Commonwealth	1649–1653
Death of Cromwell	1658
Restoration of monarchy	1660
Charles II	1660–1685
Cavalier Parliament	1661
Declaration of Indulgence	1672
Test Act	1673
James II	1685–1688
Declaration of Indulgence	1687
Glorious Revolution	1688
Bill of Rights	1689

15-5 The Flourishing of European Culture

FOCUS QUESTION: What were the major artistic and literary achievements of this era, and how did they reflect the political and economic developments of the period?

In the midst of religious wars and the growth of absolutism, European culture continued to flourish. The era was blessed with a number of prominent artists and writers.

15-5a The Changing Faces of Art

After the Renaissance, European art passed through a number of stylistic stages. The artistic Renaissance came to an end when a new movement called Mannerism emerged in Italy in the 1520s and 1530s.

Mannerism The Reformation's revival of religious values brought much political turmoil. Especially in Italy, the worldly enthusiasm of the Renaissance gave way to anxiety, uncertainty, suffering, and a yearning for spiritual experience. **Mannerism** reflected this environment in its deliberate attempt to break down the High Renaissance principles of balance, harmony, and moderation (the term *Mannerism* derives from critics who considered their contemporary artists to be second-rate imitators, painting "in the manner of" Michelangelo's late style). Italian Mannerist painters deliberately distorted the rules of proportion by portraying elongated figures that conveyed a sense of suffering and a strong emotional atmosphere filled with anxiety and confusion.

Mannerism spread from Italy to other parts of Europe and perhaps reached its apogee in the work of El Greco (1541–1614). Doménikos Theotocópoulos (called "the Greek"—El Greco) was from Crete, but after studying in Venice and Rome, he moved in the 1570s to Spain, where he became a church painter in Toledo. El Greco's elongated and contorted figures, portrayed in unusual shades of yellow and green against an eerie background of turbulent grays, reflect the artist's desire to create a world of intense emotion (see Image 15.10).

The Baroque Period A new movement—the **Baroque** (buh-ROHK)—eventually replaced Mannerism. The Baroque began in Italy in the last quarter of the sixteenth century and spread to the rest of Europe, where it was most wholeheartedly embraced by the Catholic reform movement, and especially at the Catholic courts of the Habsburgs in Madrid, Prague, Vienna, and Brussels. Although it was resisted in France, England, and the Netherlands, eventually the Baroque style spread to all of Europe and to Latin America.

Baroque artists sought to bring together the classical ideals of Renaissance art with the spiritual feelings of the sixteenth-century religious revival. The Baroque painting style was known for its use of dramatic effects to arouse the emotions. In large part, though, Baroque art and architecture reflected the search for power that was so important to the seventeenth-century ethos. Baroque churches and palaces were magnificent and richly detailed. Kings and princes wanted other kings and princes as well as their subjects to be in awe of their power.

IMAGE 15.10 **El Greco, *Laocoön*.** Mannerism reached its height in the work of El Greco. Born in Crete, trained in Venice and Rome, and settling finally in Spain, El Greco worked as a church painter in Toledo. Pictured here is his version of the *Laocoön*, a Hellenistic sculpture discovered in Rome in 1506. The elongated, contorted bodies project a world of suffering, while the somber background scene of the city of Toledo and the threatening sky add a sense of terror and doom.

 Compare this painting with the painting by Raphael in Chapter 12 (Image 12.11). What are the significant similarities and differences? How do you explain them?

 4X5 Collection/SuperStock

Baroque painting was known for its use of dramatic effects to heighten emotional intensity. This style was especially evident in the works of the Flemish master Peter Paul Rubens (1577–1640), a prolific artist and an important figure in the spread of the Baroque from Italy to other parts of Europe (see Image 15.11). In his artistic masterpieces, bodies in violent motion, heavily fleshed nudes, a dramatic use of light and shadow, and rich, sensuous pigments converge to express intense emotions. The restless forms and constant movement blend together into a dynamic unity.

Perhaps the greatest figure of the Baroque was the Italian architect and sculptor Gian Lorenzo Bernini (ZHAHN loh-RENT-zoh bur-NEE-nee) (1598–1680), who completed Saint Peter's Basilica at the Vatican and designed the vast colonnade enclosing the piazza in front of it. Action, exuberance, profusion, and dramatic effects mark the work of Bernini in the interior of Saint Peter's, where his *Throne of Saint Peter* hovers in midair, held by the hands of the four great doctors of the Catholic Church. Above the chair, rays of golden light drive a mass of clouds

and angels toward the spectator. In his most striking sculptural work, the *Ecstasy of Saint Theresa*, Bernini depicts a moment of mystical experience in the life of the sixteenth-century Spanish saint (see Image 15.12). The elegant draperies and the expression on her face create a sensuously real portrayal of physical ecstasy.

Less well known than the male artists who dominated the art world of seventeenth-century Italy but prominent in her own right was Artemisia Gentileschi (ar-tuh-MEE-zhuh jen-tuh-LESS-kee) (1593–1653). Born in Rome, she studied painting under her father's direction. In 1616, she moved to Florence and began a successful career as a painter. At the age of twenty-three, she became the first woman to be elected to the Florentine Academy of Design. Although she was known internationally in her day as a portrait painter, her fame now rests on a series of pictures of heroines from the Old Testament. Most famous is *Judith Beheading Holofernes*, a dramatic rendering of the biblical scene in which Judith slays the Assyrian general Holofernes to save her besieged town from the Assyrian army (see Image 15.13).

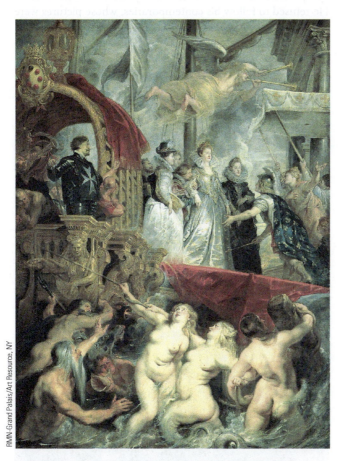

RMN-Grand Palais/Art Resource, NY

IMAGE 15.11 **Peter Paul Rubens, *The Landing of Marie de'Medici at Marseilles*.** Peter Paul Rubens played a key role in spreading the Baroque style from Italy to other parts of Europe. In *The Landing of Marie de' Medici at Marseilles*, Rubens made dramatic use of light and color, bodies in motion, and luxurious nudes to heighten the emotional intensity of the scene. This was one of a cycle of twenty-one paintings dedicated to the queen mother of France.

 Using only Image 15.11, what would you describe as the chief elements in the Baroque artistic style?

Cornaro Chapel, S. Maria della Vittoria, Rome/Scala/Art Resource, Inc.

IMAGE 15.12 **Gian Lorenzo Bernini, *Ecstasy of Saint Theresa*.** One of the great artists of the Baroque period was the Italian sculptor and architect Gian Lorenzo Bernini. The *Ecstasy of Saint Theresa*, created for the Cornaro Chapel in the Church of Santa Maria della Vittoria in Rome, was one of Bernini's most famous sculptures. Bernini sought to convey visually Theresa's mystical experience when, according to her description, an angel pierced her heart repeatedly with a golden arrow.

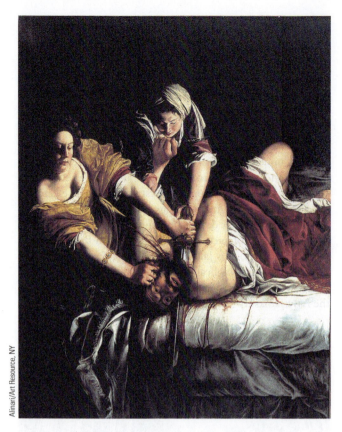

Alinari/Art Resource, NY

IMAGE 15.13 **Artemisia Gentileschi, *Judith Beheading Holofernes.*** Artemisia Gentileschi painted a series of pictures portraying scenes from the lives of courageous Old Testament women. In this painting, a determined Judith, armed with her victim's sword, struggles to saw off the head of Holofernes. Gentileschi realistically and dramatically shows the gruesome nature of Judith's act.

French Classicism In the second half of the seventeenth century, France replaced Italy as the cultural leader of Europe. Rejecting the Baroque style as overly showy and impassioned, the French remained committed to the classical values of the High Renaissance. French late classicism, with its emphasis on clarity, simplicity, balance, and harmony of design, was a rather austere version of the High Renaissance style. Its triumph reflected the shift in seventeenth-century French society from chaos to order. Though it rejected the emotionalism and high drama of the Baroque, French classicism continued the Baroque's conception of grandeur in the portrayal of noble subjects, especially those from classical antiquity.

Dutch Realism A brilliant flowering of Dutch painting paralleled the supremacy of Dutch commerce in the seventeenth century. Wealthy patricians and burghers of Dutch urban society commissioned works of art for their guild halls, town halls, and private dwellings. The subject matter of many Dutch paintings reflected the interests of this burgher society: portraits of themselves, group portraits of their military companies and guilds, landscapes, seascapes, genre scenes, still lives, and the interiors of their residences. Neither classical nor Baroque, Dutch painters were primarily interested in the realistic portrayal of secular everyday life.

This interest in painting scenes of everyday life is evident in the work of Judith Leyster (LESS-tur) (ca. 1609–1660), who established her own independent painting career, a remarkable occurrence in seventeenth-century Europe (see Image 15.14). Leyster became the first female member of the painting Guild of Saint Luke in Haarlem, which enabled her to set up her own workshop and take on three male pupils. Musicians playing their instruments, women sewing, children laughing while playing games, and actors performing all form the subject matter of Leyster's paintings of everyday Dutch life.

The finest product of the golden age of Dutch painting was Rembrandt van Rijn (REM-brant vahn RYN) (1606–1669). During his early career, Rembrandt painted opulent portraits and grandiose scenes that were often quite colorful (see Image 15.15). He was prolific and successful, but he turned away from materialistic success to follow his own artistic path; in the process, he lost public support and died bankrupt.

Although Rembrandt shared the Dutch predilection for realistic portraits, he became more introspective as he grew older. He refused to follow his contemporaries, whose pictures were largely secular; half of his own paintings depicted scenes from biblical tales. Since the Protestant tradition of hostility to religious pictures had discouraged artistic expression, Rembrandt stands out as the one great Protestant painter of the seventeenth century.

Art Reserve/Alamy Stock Photo

IMAGE 15.14 **Judith Leyster, *Self-Portrait.*** Although Judith Leyster was a well-known artist to her Dutch contemporaries, her fame diminished soon after her death. In the late nineteenth century, a Dutch art historian rediscovered her work. In Leyster's *Self-Portrait*, painted in 1635, she is seen pausing in her work painting one of the scenes of daily life that made her such a popular artist in her own day.

IMAGE 15.15 **Rembrandt van Rijn, *The Night Watch*.** The Dutch enjoyed a golden age of painting during the seventeenth century. The burghers and patricians of Dutch urban society commissioned works of art, and these quite naturally reflected the burghers' interests. In his painting *The Night Watch*, Rembrandt portrays the two leaders and sixteen members of a civic militia preparing for a parade in the city of Amsterdam.

15-5b A Wondrous Age of Theater

In England and Spain, writing reached new heights between 1580 and 1640. All of these impressive new works were written in the vernacular. Except for academic fields, such as theology, philosophy, jurisprudence, and the sciences, Latin was no longer a universal literary language. The greatest age of English literature is often called the Elizabethan era because much of the English cultural flowering of the late sixteenth and early seventeenth centuries occurred during the reign of Queen Elizabeth I. Elizabethan literature exhibits the exuberance and pride associated with England's international exploits at the time. Of all the forms of Elizabethan literature, none expressed the energy and intellectual versatility of the era better than drama. And of all the dramatists, none is more famous than William Shakespeare (1564–1616).

William Shakespeare Shakespeare was the son of a prosperous glovemaker from Stratford-upon-Avon. When he appeared in London in 1592, Elizabethans were already addicted to the stage. In Greater London, as many as six theaters were open six afternoons a week. London theaters ranged from the Globe, which was a circular unroofed structure holding three thousand spectators, to the Blackfriars, which was roofed and held only five hundred. In the former, an admission charge of a penny or two enabled even the lower classes to attend; the higher prices in the latter ensured an audience of the well-to-do. Elizabethan audiences varied greatly, putting pressure on playwrights to write works that pleased nobles, lawyers, merchants, and even vagabonds.

William Shakespeare was a "complete man of the theater." Although best known for writing plays, he was also an actor and shareholder in the chief company of the time, the Lord Chamberlain's Company, which played in theaters as diverse as the Globe and the Blackfriars. Shakespeare has long been recognized as a universal genius. A master of the English language, he was instrumental in codifying a language that was still in transition. His technical proficiency, however, was matched by an incredible insight into human psychology. In tragedies as well as comedies, Shakespeare exhibited a remarkable understanding of the human condition (see Historical Voices, "William Shakespeare: In Praise of England," p. 482).

William Shakespeare: In Praise of England

 Why is William Shakespeare aptly described as not merely a playwright, but a "complete man of the theater"? Which countries might Shakespeare have meant by the phrase "the envy of less happier lands"?

WILLIAM SHAKESPEARE is one of the most famous playwrights of the Western world. He was a universal genius, outclassing all others in his psychological insights, depth of characterization, imaginative skills, and versatility. His historical plays reflected the patriotic enthusiasm of the English in the Elizabethan era, as this excerpt from *Richard II* illustrates.

William Shakespeare, *Richard II*

This royal throne of kings, this sceptered isle,
This earth of majesty, this seat of Mars,
This other Eden, demi-Paradise,
This fortress built by Nature for herself
Against infection and the hand of war,
This happy breed of men, this little world,
This precious stone set in the silver sea,
Which serves it in the office of a wall

Or as a moat defensive to a house
Against the envy of less happier lands—
This blessed plot, this earth, this realm, this England,
This nurse, this teeming womb of royal kings,
Feared by their breed and famous by their birth,
Renowned for their deeds as far from home,
For Christian service and true chivalry,
As is the sepulcher in stubborn Jewry [the Holy Sepulcher
    in Jerusalem]
Of the world's ransom, blessed Mary's Son—
This land of such dear souls, this dear dear land,
Dear for her reputation through the world,
Is now leased out, I die pronouncing it,
Like a tenement or pelting farm.
England, bound in with the triumphant sea,
Whose rocky shore beats back the envious siege
Of watery Neptune, is now bound in with shame,
With inky blots and rotten parchment bonds.
That England, what was wont to conquer others,
Hath made a shameful conquest of itself.
Ah, would the scandal vanish with my life,
How happy then were my ensuing death!

Source: G. B. Harrison, ed. *Shakespeare, The Complete Works* (New York: Harcourt Brace & World, 1952).

Spain's Golden Century The theater was also one of the most creative forms of expression during Spain's golden century. As in England, actors' companies ran the first professional theaters, which were established in Seville and Madrid in the 1570s. Soon a public playhouse could be found in every large town, including Mexico City in the New World. Touring companies brought the latest Spanish plays to all parts of the Spanish Empire.

Beginning in the 1580s, Lope de Vega (LOH-pay day VAY-guh) (1562–1635) set the agenda for playwrights. Like Shakespeare, he was from a middle-class background. He was an incredibly prolific writer; almost one-third of his fifteen hundred plays survive, which have been characterized as witty, charming, action packed, and realistic. Lope de Vega made no apologies for the fact that he wrote his plays to please his audiences. In a treatise on drama written in 1609, he stated that the foremost duty of the playwright was to satisfy public demand. Shakespeare undoubtedly believed the same thing, since his livelihood depended on public approval, but Lope de Vega was considerably more cynical about it: he remarked that if anyone thought he had written his plays for fame, "undeceive him and tell him that I wrote them for money."

French Drama As the great age of theater in England and Spain was drawing to a close around 1630, a new dramatic era began to dawn in France that lasted into the 1680s. Unlike Shakespeare in England and Lope de Vega in Spain, French playwrights wrote more for an elite audience and were forced to depend on royal patronage. Louis XIV used theater as he did art and architecture—to attract attention to his monarchy.

French dramatists cultivated a style that emphasized the clever, polished, and correct over the emotional and imaginative. Many of the French works of the period derived both their themes and their plots from classical Greek and Roman sources, especially evident in the works of Jean-Baptiste Racine (ZHAHNH-bah-TEEST ra-SEEN) (1639–1699). In *Phèdre*, which has been called his best play, Racine followed closely the plot of *Hippolytus* by the Greek tragedian Euripides. Like the ancient tragedians, Racine, who perfected the French neoclassical tragic style, focused on conflicts, such as between love and honor or inclination and duty, that characterized and revealed the tragic dimensions of life.

Jean-Baptiste Molière (ZHAHNH-bah-TEEST mohl-YAYR) (1622–1673) enjoyed the favor of the French court and benefited from the patronage of King Louis XIV. Molière wrote, produced, and acted in a series of comedies that often satirized the religious and social world of his time. In *Tartuffe*, he ridiculed religious hypocrisy. His satires, however, sometimes got him into trouble. The Paris clergy did not find *Tartuffe* funny and had it banned for five years. Only the protection of the king saved Molière from more severe harassment.

To many historians, the seventeenth century has assumed extraordinary proportions. The divisive effects of the Reformation had been assimilated and the concept of a united Christendom, held as an ideal since the Middle Ages, had been irrevocably destroyed by the religious wars, making possible the emergence of a system of nation-states in which power politics took on an increasing significance. The growth of political thought focusing on the secular origins of state power reflected the changes that were going on in seventeenth-century society.

Within those states, there slowly emerged some of the machinery that made possible a growing centralization of power. In those states called absolutist, strong monarchs with the assistance of their aristocracies took the lead in providing the leadership

for greater centralization. In this so-called age of absolutism, Louis XIV, the Sun King of France, was the model for other rulers. His palace of Versailles, where the nobles were entertained and controlled by ceremony and etiquette, symbolized his authority. Louis revoked his grandfather's Edict of Nantes, and he fought four costly wars, mainly to acquire lands on France's eastern borders. Strong monarchy also prevailed in central and eastern Europe, where three new powers made their appearance: Prussia, Austria, and Russia. Peter the Great attempted to westernize Russia, especially militarily, and built Saint Petersburg, a new capital city, as his window on the west.

But not all European states followed the pattern of absolute monarchy. Especially important were developments in England, where a series of struggles between king and Parliament took

place in the seventeenth century. The conflict between the Stuart kings, who were advocates of divine-right monarchy, and Parliament led to civil war and the creation of a republic and then a military dictatorship under Oliver Cromwell. After his death, the Stuart monarchy was restored, but a new conflict led to the overthrow of James II and the establishment of a new order. The landed aristocracy gained power at the expense of the monarchs, thus laying the foundations for a constitutional government in which Parliament provided the focus for the institutions of centralized power. In all the major European states, a growing concern for power and dynamic expansion led to larger armies and greater conflict. War remained an endemic feature of Western civilization.

But the search for order and harmony continued, evident in art and literature. At the same time, religious preoccupations and values were losing ground to secular considerations. The seventeenth century was a period of transition toward the more secular spirit that has characterized modern Western civilization to the present. No stronger foundation for this spirit could be found than in the new view of the universe that was ushered in by the Scientific Revolution of the seventeenth century, and it is to that story that we turn in the next chapter.

CHAPTER TIMELINE

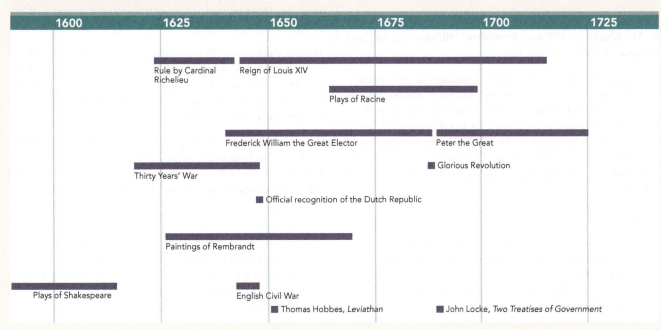

1600	1625	1650	1675	1700	1725

Rule by Cardinal Richelieu

Reign of Louis XIV

Plays of Racine

Frederick William the Great Elector

Peter the Great

Glorious Revolution

Thirty Years' War

Official recognition of the Dutch Republic

Paintings of Rembrandt

Plays of Shakespeare

English Civil War

Thomas Hobbes, *Leviathan*

John Locke, *Two Treatises of Government*

CHAPTER REVIEW

Upon Reflection

Q What theories of government were proposed by Jacques Bossuet, Thomas Hobbes, and John Locke, and how did their respective theories reflect concerns and problems of the seventeenth century?

Q What does the witchcraft craze tell us about European society in the sixteenth and seventeenth centuries?

Q What did Louis XIV hope to accomplish in his domestic and foreign policies? To what extent did he succeed?

Q What role did the nobility play in Poland and England?

Key Terms

absolutism (p. 453)
divine-right monarchy (p. 453)
intendants (p. 454)
parlements (p. 456)
boyars (p. 463)

procurator (p. 465)
Janissaries (p. 467)
gentry (p. 472)
Mannerism (p. 478)
Baroque (p. 478)

Full definitions also appear in the Glossary at the end of the book.

Suggestions for Further Reading

General Works For general works on the seventeenth century, see **T. Munck**, *Seventeenth-Century Europe, 1598–1700*, 2nd ed. (London, 2005); **Q. Deakin**, *Expansion, War, and Rebellion, 1598–1661* (Cambridge, 2000); and **J. Bergin**, *Seventeenth-Century Europe, 1598–1715* (Oxford, 2001).

Witchcraft Craze The story of the witchcraft frenzy can be examined in **R. Briggs**, *Witches and Neighbors: The Social and Cultural Context of European Witchcraft*, 2nd ed. (Oxford, 2002), **L. Roper**, *Witch Craze: Terror and Fantasy in Baroque Germany* (New Haven, Conn., 2006).

Thirty Years' War The fundamental study of the Thirty Years' War is **P. H. Wilson**, *The Thirty Years War: Europe's Tragedy* (Cambridge, Mass., 2009). For a brief study, see **R. Bonney**, *The Thirty Years' War, 1618–1648* (Oxford, 2002).

The Military Revolution On the military revolution, see **J. M. Black**, *A Military Revolution? Military Change and European Society* (London, 1996).

France and Spain For a succinct account of seventeenth-century French history, see **R. Briggs**, *Early Modern France, 1560–1715*, 2nd ed. (Oxford, 1998). A solid and very readable biography of Louis XIV is **A. Levi**, *Louis XIV* (New York, 2004). See also **J. Wilkinson**, *Louis XIV: The Power and the Glory* (New York, 2019). A good general work on seventeenth-century Spanish history is **H. Kamen**, *Spain, 1469–1714: A Society of Conflict* (London, 2014).

Central and Eastern Europe On the German states, see **P. H. Wilson**, *The Holy Roman Empire, 1495–1806*, 2nd ed. (New York, 2011). On the creation of Austria, see **P. S. Fichtner**, *The Habsburg Monarchy, 1490–1848* (New York, 2003). On Austria and Prussia, see **P. H. Wilson**, *Absolutism in Central Europe* (New York, 2000).

Russia On *Peter the Great*, see **P. Bushkovitz**, *Peter the Great* (Oxford, 2001), and **J. Cracraft**, *The Revolution of Peter the Great* (Cambridge, Mass., 2008).

English Revolutions Good general works on the period of the English Revolutions include **B. Worden**, *The English Civil Wars* (London, 2010), and **D. Purkiss**, *The English Civil War* (New York, 2006). On Oliver Cromwell, see **P. Little**, *Oliver Cromwell: New Perspectives* (New York, 2008), and the brief work by **D. Horspool**, *Cromwell: England's Protector* (New York, 2017).

United Provinces For a valuable but lengthy study on the United Provinces, see **J. Israel**, *The Dutch Republic: Its Rise, Greatness, and Fall* (New York, 1998). See also **M. Prak**, trans. **D. Webb**, *The Dutch Republic in the Seventeenth Century: The Golden Age* (Cambridge, 2005).

European Culture For a general survey of Baroque culture, see **F. C. Marchetti et al.**, *Baroque, 1600–1770* (New York, 2005). For a biography of Shakespeare, see **S. Greenblatt**, *Will in the World: How Shakespeare Became Shakespeare* (New York, 2005).

Notes

1. Quoted in Louis, duc de Saint-Simon, *Versailles, the Court and Louis XIV*, ed. L. Norton (New York, 1958), pp. 247–248.
2. Quoted in J. Klaits, *Servants of Satan: The Age of the Witch Hunts* (Bloomington, Ind., 1985), p. 68.
3. Quoted in P. H. Wilson, *The Thirty Years War: Europe's Tragedy* (Cambridge, Mass., 2009), p. 783.
4. Quoted in J. B. Wolf, *Louis XIV* (New York, 1968), p. 134.
5. Quoted in J. Wilkinson, *Louis XIV: The Power and the Glory* (New York, 2019), p. 139.

6. Quoted in J. B. Collins, *The State in Early Modern France* (Cambridge, 1995), p. 130.

7. Quoted in Wilkinson, *Louis XIV*, p. 237.

8. Quoted in Wolf, *Louis XIV*, p. 618.

9. Quoted in D. H. Pennington, *Europe in the Seventeenth Century*, 2nd ed. (New York, 1989), p. 494.

10. Quoted in J. H. Elliot, *Imperial Spain, 1469–1716* (New York, 1963), p. 306.

11. Quoted in B. H. Sumner, *Peter the Great and the Emergence of Russia* (New York, 1962), p. 122.

12. Quoted in the account of Peter by an eighteenth-century French writer in J. H. Robinson, *Readings in European History*, vol. 2 (Boston, 1906), p. 311.

13. Quote in P. Gaunt, *Oliver Cromwell* (London, 1996), p. 117.

14. Quoted in S. Schama, *A History of Britain*, vol. 2: *The Wars of the British, 1603–1776* (New York, 2001), pp. 182, 185.

15. T. Carlyle, *Oliver Cromwell's Letters and Speeches: with Elucidations*, vol. II, (London: Chapman & Hall, 1893), p. 250.

MindTap *Tips* Is writing a history paper part of your course grade? Check out the History Essay tutorial in the Skills Tutorial folder in MindTap, which will teach you effective ways to write a history paper.

CHAPTER 16

Toward a New Heaven and a New Earth: The Scientific Revolution and the Emergence of Modern Science

IMAGE 16.1 **A Nineteenth-Century Painting of Galileo Before the Holy Office in the Vatican in 1633**

Erich Lessing/Art Resource, NY

CHAPTER OUTLINE AND FOCUS QUESTIONS

16-1 Background to the Scientific Revolution

Q What developments during the Middle Ages and the Renaissance contributed to the Scientific Revolution of the seventeenth century? How did Hermeticism contribute to the Scientific Revolution?

16-2 Toward a New Heaven: A Revolution in Astronomy

Q How did Copernicus, Kepler, Galileo, and Newton each contribute to a new vision of the universe? How did their views differ from the Ptolemaic conception of the universe? Why was Galileo condemned by the Holy Office of the Catholic Church?

16-3 Advances in Medicine and Chemistry

Q What did Paracelsus, Vesalius, and Harvey contribute to a scientific view of medicine? How did their ideas about medicine differ from their predecessor, the Greek physician Galen?

16-4 Women in the Origins of Modern Science

Q What role did women play in the Scientific Revolution? How were women from France able to participate in the Scientific Revolution as compared to women from Germany? How did the Scientific Revolution impact the roles of women?

16-5 Toward a New Earth: Descartes, Rationalism, and a New View of Humankind

Q Why is Descartes considered the "founder of modern rationalism"?

16-6 The Scientific Method and the Spread of Scientific Knowledge

Q How and where were the ideas of the Scientific Revolution spread, and what impact did they have on society and religion?

CONNECTIONS TO TODAY

What scientific discoveries of the twentieth and twenty-first centuries have had as great an impact on society as those of the Scientific Revolution?

IN ADDITION TO THE POLITICAL, economic, social, and international crises of the seventeenth century, we need to add an intellectual one. The Scientific Revolution questioned and ultimately challenged conceptions and beliefs about the nature of the external world and reality that had crystallized into a rather strict orthodoxy by the Later Middle Ages. Derived from the works of ancient Greeks and Romans and grounded in Christian thought, the medieval worldview had become formidable. But the breakdown of Christian unity during the Reformation and the subsequent religious wars had created an environment in which Europeans became more comfortable with challenging both the ecclesiastical and the political realms. Should it surprise us that a challenge to intellectual authority soon followed?

The Scientific Revolution taught Europeans to view the universe and their place in it in a new way. The shift from an earth-centered to a sun-centered cosmos had an emotional as well as an intellectual effect on the people who understood it. Thus, the Scientific Revolution, popularized in the eighteenth-century Enlightenment, stands as the major force in the transition to the largely secular, rational, and materialistic perspective that has defined the modern Western mentality since its full acceptance in the nineteenth and twentieth centuries.

The transition to a new worldview, however, was far from easy. In the seventeenth century, the Italian scientist Galileo Galilei (gal-li-LAY-oh GAL-li-lay), an outspoken advocate of the new worldview, found that his ideas were strongly opposed by the authorities of the Catholic Church. Galileo's position was clear: "I hold the sun to be situated motionless in the center of the revolution of the celestial bodies, while the earth rotates on its axis and revolves about the sun." Moreover, "nothing physical that sense-experience sets before our eyes . . . ought to be called in question (much less condemned) upon the testimony of Biblical passages."[1] But the church had a different view, and in 1633, Galileo, now sixty-eight and in ill health, was called before the dreaded Inquisition in Rome. He was kept waiting for two months before he was tried and found guilty of heresy and disobedience. Completely shattered by the experience, he denounced his errors: "I curse and detest the said errors and heresies contrary to the Holy Church." Legend holds that when he left the trial room, Galileo muttered to himself: "And yet it does move!" Galileo had been silenced, but his writings remained, and they spread throughout Europe. The Inquisition had failed to stop the new ideas of the Scientific Revolution.

In one sense, the Scientific Revolution was not a revolution. It was not characterized by the explosive change and rapid overthrow of traditional authority that we normally associate with the word *revolution*. The Scientific Revolution did overturn centuries of authority, but only in a gradual and piecemeal fashion. Nevertheless, its results were truly revolutionary. The Scientific Revolution was a key factor in setting Western civilization along its modern secular and materialistic path.

16-1 Background to the Scientific Revolution

 FOCUS QUESTIONS: What developments during the Middle Ages and the Renaissance contributed to the Scientific Revolution of the seventeenth century? How did Hermeticism contribute to the Scientific Revolution?

To say that the **Scientific Revolution** brought about a dissolution of the medieval worldview is not to say that the Middle Ages was a period of scientific ignorance. Many educated Europeans took an intense interest in the world around them since it was, after all, "God's handiwork" and therefore an appropriate subject for study. Late medieval scholastic

philosophers had advanced mathematical and physical thinking in many ways, but the subjection of these thinkers to a strict theological framework and their unquestioning reliance on a few ancient authorities, especially Aristotle and Galen, limited where they could go. Many "natural philosophers," as medieval scientists were called, preferred refined logical analysis to systematic observations of the natural world. A number of changes and advances in the fifteenth and sixteenth centuries may have played a major role in helping "natural philosophers" abandon their old views and develop new ones.

16-1a Ancient Authors and Renaissance Artists

Whereas medieval scholars had made use of Aristotle, Galen, and Ptolemy in Latin translations to develop many of their positions in the fields of physics, medicine, and astronomy, the Renaissance humanists had mastered Greek and made available new works of Galen, Ptolemy, and Archimedes as well as Plato and the pre-Socratics. These writings made it apparent that other thinkers in antiquity had contradicted the unquestioned authorities of the Middle Ages, Aristotle and Galen. The desire to discover which school of thought was correct stimulated new scientific work that sometimes led to a complete rejection of the classical authorities.

Renaissance artists have also been credited with making an impact on scientific study. Their desire to imitate nature led them to a close observation of nature. Their accurate renderings of rocks, plants, animals, and human anatomy established new standards for the study of natural phenomena. At the same time, the "scientific" study of the problems of perspective and correct anatomical proportions led to new insights. "No painter," one Renaissance artist declared, "can paint well without a thorough knowledge of geometry."[2] Renaissance artists were frequently called on to be practicing mathematicians as well. Leonardo da Vinci devised "war machines," and Albrecht Dürer made designs for the fortifications of cities.

16-1b Technological Innovations and Mathematics

Technical problems such as accurately calculating the tonnage of ships also stimulated scientific activity because they required careful observation and precise measurements. The discovery of the New World and increased trading furthered the need for improved navigational and mathematical knowledge. The relationship between technology and the Scientific Revolution was not a simple one, however, for many technological experts did not believe in abstract or academic learning. Moreover, the early institutions that supported the academic study of technology, such as Spain's Casa de Contractación, or House of Trade, regarded their technological discoveries as state secrets and kept them hidden from the public. Indeed, many of the technical innovations of the Middle Ages and the Renaissance were accomplished outside the universities by people who emphasized practical rather than theoretical knowledge. In any case, the invention of new instruments and machines, such as the telescope and the microscope, often made new scientific discoveries possible. The printing press had an indirect but crucial role in spreading innovative ideas quickly and easily.

Mathematics, so fundamental to the scientific achievements of the sixteenth and seventeenth centuries, was promoted in the Renaissance by the rediscovery of the works of ancient mathematicians and the influence of Plato, who had emphasized the importance of mathematics in explaining the universe. Applauded as the key to navigation, military science, and geography, mathematics was also regarded as the key to understanding the nature of things. According to Leonardo da Vinci, since God eternally geometrizes, nature is inherently mathematical: "Proportion is not only found in numbers and measurements but also in sounds, weights, times, positions, and in whatsoever power there may be."[3] Moreover, mathematical reasoning was seen as promoting a degree of certainty that was otherwise impossible. In the words of Leonardo da Vinci: "There is no certainty where one can neither apply any of the mathematical sciences nor any of those which are based upon the mathematical sciences."[4] Copernicus, Kepler, Galileo, and Newton were all great mathematicians who believed that the secrets of nature were written in the language of mathematics.

16-1c Renaissance Magic

Another factor in the origins of the Scientific Revolution may have been magic. Renaissance magic was the preserve of an intellectual elite from all of Europe. By the end of the sixteenth century, Hermetic magic had become fused with alchemical thought into a single intellectual framework. This tradition believed that the world was a living embodiment of divinity. Humans, who it was believed also had that spark of divinity within, could use magic, especially mathematical magic, to understand and dominate the world of nature or employ the powers of nature for beneficial purposes. Hermetic magicians, who experimented with natural objects, were considered to be practitioners of idolatry because of their practice of distorting nature. However, it was their engagement with experimentation that perhaps contributed to the later practice of "experimental philosophy," or empirical science based upon observation. Was it Hermeticism, then, that inaugurated the shift in consciousness that made the Scientific Revolution possible, since the desire to control and dominate the natural world was a crucial motivating force in the Scientific Revolution? One scholar has argued:

> It is a movement of the will which really originates an intellectual movement. A new center of interest arises, surrounded by emotional excitement; the mind turns where the will has directed it and new attitudes, new discoveries follow. Behind the emergence of modern science there was a new direction of the will toward the world, its marvels, and mysterious workings, a new longing and determination to understand those workings and to operate with them.[5]

"This time," the author continues, "the return to the occult [Hermetic tradition] stimulates the genuine science."[6] Scholars debate the issue, but histories of the Scientific Revolution frequently overlook the fact that the great names we associate with the revolution in cosmology—Copernicus, Kepler, Galileo, and Newton—all had a serious interest in Hermetic ideas and the fields of astrology and alchemy. The mention of these names also reminds us of one final consideration in the origins of the Scientific Revolution: it largely resulted from the work of a handful of great intellectuals.

16-2 Toward a New Heaven: A Revolution in Astronomy

FOCUS QUESTIONS: How did Copernicus, Kepler, Galileo, and Newton each contribute to a new vision of the universe? How did their views differ from the Ptolemaic conception of the universe? Why was Galileo condemned by the Holy Office of the Catholic Church?

The greatest achievements in the Scientific Revolution of the sixteenth and seventeenth centuries came in the fields most dominated by the ideas of the Greeks—astronomy, mechanics, and medicine. The cosmological views of the Later Middle Ages had been built on a synthesis of the ideas of Aristotle, Ptolemy (the greatest astronomer of antiquity, who lived in the second century C.E.), and Christian theology. In the resulting Ptolemaic (tahl-uh-MAY-ik) or **geocentric conception**, the universe was seen as a series of concentric spheres with a fixed or motionless earth at its center (see Image 16.2). Composed of the material substances of earth, air, fire, and water, the earth was imperfect and constantly changing. The spheres that surrounded the earth were made of a crystalline, transparent substance and moved in circular orbits around the earth. Circular movement, according to Aristotle, was the most "perfect" kind of motion and hence appropriate for the "perfect" heavenly bodies thought to consist of a nonmaterial, incorruptible "quintessence." These heavenly bodies, pure orbs of light, were embedded in the moving, concentric spheres, which in 1500 were believed to number ten. Working outward from the earth, eight spheres contained the moon, Mercury, Venus, the sun, Mars, Jupiter, Saturn, and the fixed stars. The ninth sphere imparted to the eighth sphere of the fixed stars its motion, and the tenth sphere was frequently described as the prime mover that moved itself and imparted motion to the other spheres. Beyond the tenth sphere was the Empyrean Heaven—the location of God and all the saved souls. This Christianized Ptolemaic universe, then, was finite. It had a fixed outer boundary in harmony with Christian thought and expectations. God and the saved souls were at one end of the universe, and humans were at the center. They had been given power over the earth, but their real purpose was to achieve salvation.

This conception of the universe, however, did not satisfy professional astronomers, who wished to ascertain the precise paths of the heavenly bodies across the sky. Finding that their observations did not always correspond to the accepted scheme, astronomers tried to "save appearances" by developing an elaborate system of devices. They proposed, for example, that the planetary bodies traveled on epicycles, concentric spheres within spheres, that would enable the paths of the planets to correspond more precisely to observations while adhering to Aristotle's ideas of circular planetary movement.

Image Select/Art Resource, NY

IMAGE 16.2 Medieval Conception of the Universe. As this sixteenth-century illustration shows, the medieval cosmological view placed the earth at the center of the universe, surrounded by a series of concentric spheres. The earth was imperfect and constantly changing, whereas the heavenly bodies that surrounded it were perfect and incorruptible. Beyond the tenth and final sphere was heaven, where God and all the saved souls were located. (The circles read from the center outward as follows: 1. Moon, 2. Mercury, 3. Venus, 4. Sun, 5. Mars, 6. Jupiter, 7. Saturn, 8. Firmament (of the Stars), 9. Crystalline Sphere, 10. Prime Mover; and around the outside, Empyrean Heaven—Home of God and All the Elect, that is, saved souls.)

16-2a Copernicus

Nicolaus Copernicus (nee-koh-LAU-uss kuh-PURR-nuh-kuss) (1473–1543) had studied both mathematics and astronomy first at Krakow in his native Poland and later at the Italian universities of Bologna and Padua (see Image 16.3). Before he left Italy in 1506, he had become aware of ancient views that contradicted the Ptolemaic, earth-centered conception of the universe. Between 1506 and 1530, he completed the manuscript of his famous book, *On the Revolutions of the Heavenly Spheres*, but his own timidity and fear of ridicule from fellow astronomers kept him from publishing it until May 1543, shortly before his death.

Copernicus was not an accomplished observational astronomer and relied on his predecessors for his data. But he was a mathematician who felt that Ptolemy's geocentric system was too complicated and failed to accord with the observed motions of the heavenly bodies (see Historical Voices, "On the Revolutions of the Heavenly Spheres," p. 490). Copernicus hoped that his **heliocentric,** or sun-centered, **conception** would offer a simpler and more accurate explanation.

Copernicus argued that the universe consisted of eight spheres with the sun motionless at the center and the sphere of the fixed stars at rest in the eighth sphere (see Image 16.4). The planets revolved around the sun in the order of Mercury, Venus, the earth, Mars, Jupiter, and Saturn. The moon, however, revolved around the earth. Moreover, according to Copernicus, what appeared to be the movement of the sun and the fixed stars around the earth was really explained by the daily rotation of the earth on its axis and the journey of the earth around the sun each year.

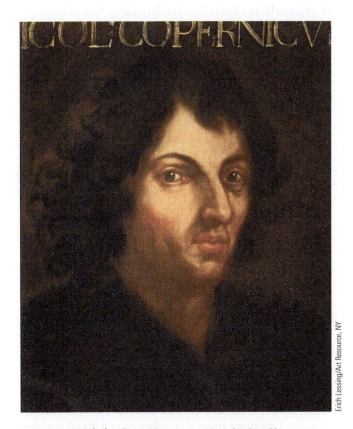

Erich Lessing/Art Resource, NY

IMAGE 16.3 Nicholas Copernicus. Copernicus developed his heliocentric (Sun-centered) conception of the universe, where the Sun, not the Earth, was at the center of the planetary system. The Copernican system challenged the earth-centered Ptolemaic concept of the universe.

On the Revolutions of the Heavenly Spheres

 What major new ideas did Copernicus discuss in this excerpt? What was the source of these ideas? Why might one say that European astronomers had finally destroyed the Middle Ages?

NICOLAUS COPERNICUS BEGAN A REVOLUTION in astronomy when he argued that the sun and not the earth was at the center of the universe. Expecting controversy and scorn, Copernicus hesitated to publish the work in which he put forth his heliocentric theory. He finally relented, however, and managed to see a copy of it just before he died.

Nicolaus Copernicus, *On the Revolutions of the Heavenly Spheres*

For a long time, then, I reflected on this confusion in the astronomical traditions concerning the derivation of the motions of the universe's spheres. I began to be annoyed that the movements of the world machine, created for our sake by the best and most systematic Artisan of all [God], were not understood with greater certainty by the philosophers, who otherwise examined so precisely the most insignificant trifles of this world. For this reason I undertook the task of rereading the works of all the philosophers which I could obtain to learn whether anyone had ever proposed other motions of the universe's spheres than those expounded by the teachers of astronomy in the schools. And in fact first I found in Cicero that Hicetas supposed the earth to move. Later I also discovered in Plutarch that certain others were of this opinion. I have decided to set his words down here, so that they may be available to everybody:

Some think that the earth remains at rest. But Philolaus the Pythagorean believes that, like the sun and moon, it revolves around the fire in an oblique circle. Heraclides of Pontus and Ecphantus the Pythagorean make the earth move, not in a progressive motion, but like a wheel in a rotation from the west to east about its own center.

Therefore, having obtained the opportunity from these sources, I too began to consider the mobility of the earth. And even though the idea seemed absurd, nevertheless I knew that others before me had been granted the freedom to imagine any circles whatever for the purpose of explaining the heavenly phenomena. Hence I thought that I too would be readily permitted to ascertain whether explanations sounder than those of my predecessors could be found for the revolution of the celestial spheres on the assumption of some motion of the earth.

Having thus assumed the motions which I ascribe to the earth later on in the volume, by long and intense study I finally found that if the motions of the other planets are correlated with the orbiting of the earth, and are computed for the revolution of each planet, not only do their phenomena follow therefrom but also the order and size of all the planets and spheres, and heaven itself is so linked together that in no portion of it can anything be shifted without disrupting the remaining parts and the universe as a whole . . .

Hence I feel no shame in asserting that this whole region engirdled by the moon, and the center of the earth, traverse this grand circle amid the rest of the planets in an annual revolution around the sun. Near the sun is the center of the universe. Moreover, since the sun remains stationary, whatever appears as a motion of the sun is really due rather to the motion of the earth.

Source: Copernicus, in E. Rosen, trans., *The Complete Works* (London: Palgrave Macmillan, 1978).

Copernicus, however, was basically conservative. He did not reject Aristotle's principle of the existence of heavenly spheres moving in circular orbits. As a result, when he put forth the calculations to prove his new theory, he retained about half of Ptolemy's epicycles and wound up with a system somewhat simpler than that of the Alexandrian astronomer but still extremely complicated.

Nevertheless, the shift from an earth-centered to a sun-centered system was significant and raised serious questions about Aristotle's astronomy and physics despite Copernicus's own adherence to Aristotle. It also seemed to create uncertainty about the human role in the universe as well as God's location. Protestant reformers, adhering to a literal interpretation of Scripture, were the first to attack the new ideas. Martin Luther thundered against "the new astrologer" who wants to turn the whole art of astronomy upside down. Luther's cohort at Wittenberg, Philip Melanchthon, condemned Copernicus as well:

The eyes are witness that the heavens revolve in the space of twenty-four hours. But certain men, either from the love of novelty, or to make a display of ingenuity, have concluded that the earth moves, and they maintain that neither the eighth sphere [of the fixed stars] nor the sun revolves. . . . Now it is a want of honesty and decency to assert such notions publicly, and the example is pernicious. It is the part of a good mind to accept the truth as revealed by God and to acquiesce in it.[7]

The Catholic Church remained silent for the time being; it did not denounce Copernicus until the work of Galileo appeared. The denunciation came at a time when an increasing number of astronomers were being attracted to Copernicus's ideas.

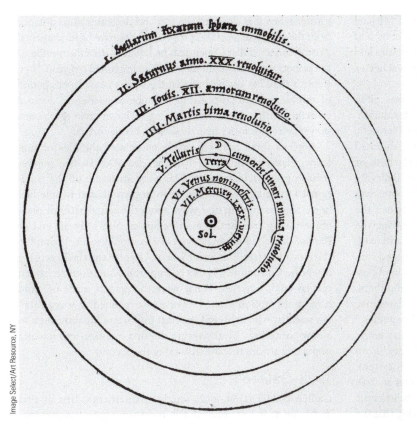

Image Select/Art Resource, NY

IMAGE 16.4 **The Copernican System.** The Copernican system was presented in *On the Revolutions of the Heavenly Spheres*, published shortly before Copernicus's death. As shown in this illustration from the first edition of the book, Copernicus maintained that the sun was the center of the universe and that the planets, including the earth, revolved around it. Moreover, the earth rotated daily on its axis. (The circles read from the inside out as follows: 1. Sun; 2. Mercury, orbit of 80 days; 3. Venus; 4. Earth, with the moon, orbit of one year; 5. Mars, orbit of 2 years; 6. Jupiter, orbit of 12 years; 7. Saturn, orbit of 30 years; 8. Immobile Sphere of the Fixed Stars.)

Q *What are the major differences between the medieval view of the universe (Image 16.2) and the heliocentric view put forth by Copernicus?*

16-2b Brahe

Copernicus did not have a great impact immediately, but doubts about the Ptolemaic system were growing. Johannes Kepler took the next step in destroying the geocentric conception and supporting the Copernican system. It has been argued, however, that Kepler's work would not have occurred without the material provided by Tycho Brahe (TY-koh BRAH) (see Image 16.5).

A Danish nobleman, Tycho Brahe (1546–1601) was granted possession of an island near Copenhagen by King Frederick II. On it, Brahe built the elaborate Uraniborg Castle, which he outfitted with a library, observatories, and instruments he had designed for more precise astronomical observations. For twenty years, Brahe patiently concentrated on compiling a detailed record of his observations of the positions and movements of the stars and planets, a series of observations described as the most accurate up to that time. In 1577, Brahe observed a comet, and again in 1585. Brahe's calculations of the comet's paths confirmed that celestial objects could cross one another and were not motionless. This body of data led him to reject the Aristotelian-Ptolemaic system, but at the same time he was unable to accept Copernicus's suggestion that the earth actually moved. Brahe's last years were spent in Prague as imperial mathematician to Emperor Rudolf II, who took a keen interest in astronomy, astrology, and the Hermetic tradition. While he was in Prague, Brahe took on an assistant by the name of Johannes Kepler.

16-2c Kepler

Johannes Kepler (yoh-HAHN-us KEP-lur) (1571–1630) had been destined by his parents for a career as a Lutheran minister. While studying theology at the university at Tübingen

Shutterstock.com

IMAGE 16.5 **Tycho Brahe.** His work at the Uraniborg observatory provided astronomers with the best data on the position of the celestial bodies. He published his results in *Of More Recent Phenomena of the Ethereal World* in 1588. He is depicted here in a sixteenth-century Dutch oil painting with a silver nose; his own nose was cut off during a duel.

(TOO-bing-un), however, he fell under the influence of Michael Mästlin (MEST-lin), Germany's best-known astronomer, and spent much time pursuing his real interests—mathematics and astronomy. He abandoned theology and became a teacher of mathematics and astronomy at Graz in Austria.

Kepler's work illustrates well the narrow line that often separated magic and science in the early Scientific Revolution. An avid astrologer, Kepler had a keen interest in Hermetic mathematical magic. In a book written in 1596, he elaborated on his theory that the universe was constructed on the basis of geometric figures, such as the pyramid and the cube. Believing that the harmony of the human soul (a divine attribute) was mirrored in the numerical relationships existing between the planets, he focused much of his attention on discovering the "music of the spheres." Kepler was also a brilliant mathematician and astronomer and, after Brahe's death, succeeded him as imperial mathematician to Rudolf II. There he gained possession of Brahe's detailed astronomical data and, using them, arrived at his three laws of planetary motion. These laws may have confirmed Kepler's interest in the "music of the spheres," but more important, they confirmed Copernicus's heliocentric theory while modifying it in some ways. Above all, they drove another nail into the coffin of the Aristotelian-Ptolemaic system.

Kepler published his first two laws of planetary motion in 1609. Although at Tübingen he had accepted Copernicus's heliocentric ideas, in his first law he rejected Copernicus by showing that the orbits of the planets around the sun were not circular but elliptical, with the sun at one focus of the ellipse rather than at the center. In his second law, he demonstrated that the speed of a planet is greater when it is closer to the sun and decreases as its distance from the sun increases. This proposition destroyed a fundamental Aristotelian tenet that Copernicus had shared—that the motion of the planets was steady and unchanging. Published ten years later, Kepler's third law established that the square of a planet's period of revolution is proportional to the cube of its average distance from the sun. In other words, planets with larger orbits revolve at a slower average velocity than those with smaller orbits.

Kepler's three laws effectively eliminated the idea of uniform circular motion as well as the idea of crystalline spheres revolving in circular orbits. The basic structure of the traditional Ptolemaic system had been disproved, and people had been freed to think in new ways about the actual paths of planets revolving around the sun in elliptical orbits. By the end of Kepler's life, the Ptolemaic system was rapidly losing ground to the new ideas (see Historical Voices, "Kepler and the Emerging Scientific Community," p. 493). Important questions remained unanswered, however: What were the planets made of? And how could motion in the universe be explained? It was an Italian scientist who achieved the next important breakthrough to a new cosmology by answering the first question and making important strides toward answering the second.

16-2d Galileo

Galileo Galilei (1564–1642) taught mathematics, first at Pisa and later at Padua, one of the most prestigious universities in Europe. Galileo was the first European to make systematic observations of the heavens by means of a telescope, thereby inaugurating a new age in astronomy (see Image 16.6). He had

IMAGE 16.6a

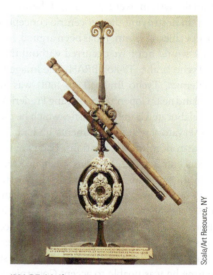

IMAGE 16.6b

IMAGE 16.6 **The Telescope.** The invention of the telescope enabled Europeans to inaugurate a new age in astronomy. Image 16.6a shows Johannes Hevelius (huh-VAY-lee-uss) (1611–1697), an eminent German-Polish astrologer, making an observation with his telescope. Hevelius's observations were highly regarded. He located his telescope on the roof of his own house, and by the 1660s, his celestial observatory was considered one of the best in Europe. Image 16.6b shows Galileo's original telescope, built in 1609.

Kepler and the Emerging Scientific Community

Q *What does the correspondence between Galileo and Kepler reveal about an emerging spirit of scientific inquiry? What other notable achievements must European society have reached even to make this exchange of letters possible? What aspects of European material culture made the work of these scientists easier?*

THE EXCHANGE OF LETTERS between intellectuals was an important avenue for scientific communication. After receiving a copy of Johannes Kepler's first major work, the Italian Galileo Galilei wrote to Kepler, inaugurating a correspondence between them. This selection contains samples of their letters to each other.

Galileo to Kepler, Padua, August 4, 1597

Your book . . . reached me not days ago but only a few hours ago, and as this Paulus just informed me of his return to Germany, I should think myself indeed ungrateful if I should not express to you my thanks by this letter. I thank you . . . for having deemed me worthy of such a proof of your friendship. . . . So far I have read only the introduction, but have learned from it . . . your intentions and congratulate myself on the good fortune of having found such a man as a companion in the exploration of truth. For it is deplorable that there are so few who seek the truth. . . . But this is not the place to mourn about the misery of our century but to rejoice with you about such beautiful ideas proving the truth. . . . I would certainly dare to approach the public with my ways of thinking if there were more people of your mind. As this is not the case, I shall refrain from doing so. . . . I shall always be at your service. Farewell, and do not neglect to give me further good news of yourself.

Yours in sincere friendship,
Galilaeus Galilaeus
Mathematician at the Academy of Padua

Kepler to Galileo, Graz, October 13, 1597

I received your letter of August 4 on September 1. It was a double pleasure to me. First because I became friends with you, the Italian, and second because of the agreement in which we find ourselves concerning Copernican cosmography. . . .

I would, however, have wished that you who have such a keen insight into everything would choose another way to reach your practical aims. By the strength of your personal example you advise us . . . to go out of the way of general ignorance and warn us against exposing ourselves to the furious attacks of the scholarly crowd. . . . But after the beginning of a tremendous enterprise has been made in our time, and furthered by so many learned mathematicians, and after the statement that the earth moves can no longer be regarded as something new, would it not be better to pull the rolling wagon to its destination with united effort? . . . For it is not only you Italians who do not believe that they move unless they feel it, but we in Germany, too, in no way make ourselves popular with this idea. Yet there are ways in which we protect ourselves against these difficulties. . . . Be of good cheer, Galileo, and appear in public. If I am not mistaken there are only a few among the distinguished mathematicians of Europe who would dissociate themselves from us. So great is the power of truth. If Italy seems less suitable for your publication and if you have to expect difficulties there, perhaps Germany will offer us more freedom. . . . Please let me know, at least privately if you do not want to do so publicly, what you have discovered in favor of Copernicus.

Source: C. Baumgardt, *Johannes Kepler, Life and Letters* (New York: Philosophical Library, 1951).

---

heard of a Flemish lens grinder who had created a "spyglass" that magnified objects seen at a distance and soon constructed his own after reading about it. Instead of peering at terrestrial objects, Galileo turned his telescope to the skies and made a remarkable series of discoveries: mountains and craters on the moon, four moons revolving around Jupiter, the phases of Venus, and sun-spots. Galileo's observations of Venus proved that it orbits the sun. Galileo's other observations demolished yet another aspect of the traditional cosmology in that the universe seemed to be composed of material substance similar to that of the earth rather than ethereal or perfect and unchanging substance.

Galileo's revelations, published in *The Starry Messenger* in 1610 (see Historical Voices, "The Starry Messenger," p. 494), stunned his contemporaries and probably did more to make Europeans aware of the new picture of the universe than the mathematical theories of Copernicus and Kepler did. The English ambassador in Venice wrote to the chief minister of King James I in 1610:

I send herewith unto His Majesty the strangest piece of news . . . that he has ever yet received from any part of the world; which is the annexed book of the Mathematical Professor at Padua [Galileo], who by the help of an optical

The Starry Messenger

Q *What was the significance of Galileo's invention? What impressions did he receive of the moon? Why were his visual discoveries so stunning, and how did he go about publicizing them?*

THE ITALIAN GALILEO GALILEI was the first European to use a telescope to make systematic observations of the heavens. His observations, as reported in *The Starry Messenger* in 1610, stunned European intellectuals by revealing that the celestial bodies were not perfect and immutable but composed of material substance similar to that of the earth. In this selection, Galileo describes how he devised a telescope and what he saw with it.

Galileo Galilei, *The Starry Messenger*

About ten months ago a report reached my ears that a Dutchman had constructed a telescope, by the aid of which visible objects, although at a great distance from the eye of the observer, were distinctly seen as if near; and some proofs of its most wonderful performances were reported, which some gave credence to, but others contradicted. A few days after, I received confirmation of the report in a letter written from Paris by a noble Frenchman, Jacques Badovere, which finally determined me to give myself up to inquire into the principle of the telescope, and then to consider the means by which I might compass the invention of a similar instrument, which a little while after I succeeded in doing, through deep study of the theory of Refraction; and I prepared a tube, at first of lead, in the ends of which I fitted two glass lenses, both plane on one side, but on the other side one spherically convex, and the other concave. Then bringing my eye to the concave lens I saw objects satisfactorily large and near, for they appeared one-third of the distance off and nine times larger than when they are seen with the natural eye alone. I shortly afterwards constructed another telescope with more nicety, which magnified objects more than sixty times. At length, by sparing neither labour nor expense, I succeeded in constructing for myself an instrument so superior that objects seen through it appear magnified nearly a thousand times, and more than thirty times nearer than if viewed by the natural powers of sight alone.

It would be altogether a waste of time to enumerate the number and importance of the benefits which this instrument may be expected to confer, when used by land or sea. But without paying attention to its use for terrestrial objects, I betook myself to observations of the heavenly bodies; and first of all, I viewed the Moon as near as if it was scarcely two semi-diameters of the Earth distant. After the Moon, I frequently observed other heavenly bodies, both fixed stars and planets, with incredible delight; and, when I saw their very great number, I began to consider about a method by which I might be able to measure their distances apart. . . .

Now let me review the observations made by me during the two months just past, again inviting the attention of all who are eager for true philosophy to the beginnings which led to the sight of the most important phenomena.

Let me speak first of the surface of the Moon, which is turned towards us. For the sake of being understood more easily, I distinguish two parts in it, which I call respectively the brighter and the darker. The brighter part seems to surround and to pervade the whole hemisphere; but the darker part discolors, like a sort of cloud, discolors the Moon's surface and makes it appear covered with spots. . . . These spots have never been observed by any one before me; and from my observations of them, often repeated, I have been led to the opinion which I have expressed, namely that I feel sure that the surface of the Moon is not perfectly smooth, free from inequalities, and exactly spherical, as a large school of philosophers considers with regard to the Moon and the other heavenly bodies, but that, on the contrary, it is full of inequalities, uneven, full of hollows and protuberances, just like the surface of the Earth itself, which is varied everywhere by lofty mountains and deep valleys.

Source: E. S. Carlo, *The Sidereal Messenger of Galileo Galilei: And a Part of the Preface to Kepler's Dioptrics Containing the Original Account of Galileo's Astronomical Discoveries* (London: Rivingtons, 1880), pp. 10–11, 14–15.

---

instrument . . . has discovered four new planets rolling about the sphere of Jupiter. . . . So upon the whole subject he has first overthrown all former astronomy. . . . By the next ship your Lordship shall receive from me one of the above instruments [a telescope], as it is bettered by this man.[8]

During a trip to Rome, scholars received Galileo as a conquering hero. Grand Duke Cosimo II of Florence offered him a new position as his court mathematician, which Galileo readily accepted. But even in the midst of his newfound acclaim, Galileo found himself increasingly suspect by the authorities of the Catholic Church.

Galileo and the Inquisition In *The Starry Messenger*, Galileo had revealed himself as a firm proponent of Copernicus's heliocentric system. The Roman Inquisition (or Holy Office) of the Catholic Church condemned Copernicanism and ordered Galileo to reject the Copernican thesis. As one cardinal commented, "The intention of the Holy Spirit is to teach us not how the heavens go, but how to go to heaven." The report of the Inquisition ran:

> That the doctrine that the sun was the center of the world and immovable was false and absurd, formally heretical and contrary to Scripture, whereas the doctrine that the earth was not the center of the world but moved, and has further a daily motion, was philosophically false and absurd and theologically at least erroneous.[9]

Galileo was told, however, that he could continue to discuss Copernicanism as long as he maintained that it was not a fact but a mathematical supposition. It is apparent from the Inquisition's response that the church attacked the Copernican system because it threatened not only Scripture but also an entire conception of the universe (see Opposing Viewpoints, "A New Heaven? Faith Versus Reason," p. 496). The heavens were no longer a spiritual world but a world of matter. Humans were no longer at the center, and God was no longer in a specific place. The new system raised such uncertainties that it seemed prudent simply to condemn it.

Galileo, however, never really accepted his condemnation. In 1632, he published his most famous work, *Dialogue on the Two Chief World Systems: Ptolemaic and Copernican*. Unlike most scholarly treatises, it was written in Italian rather than Latin, making it more widely available to the public, which no doubt alarmed the church authorities. The work took the form of a dialogue among Simplicio, a congenial but somewhat stupid supporter of Aristotle and Ptolemy; Sagredo, an open-minded layman; and Salviati, a proponent of Copernicus's ideas. There is no question who wins the argument, and the *Dialogue* was quickly perceived as a defense of the Copernican system. Pope Urban VIII had granted permission to Galileo to write the *Dialogue* under the condition that Galileo argue that all natural phenomena, such as planetary motion, have several possible causes, including God as a source of the earth's motion. Galileo did not fully comply with the Pope's wishes and was dragged once more before the Inquisition in 1633, found guilty of teaching the condemned Copernican system, and forced to recant his errors. Placed under house arrest on his estate near Florence, he spent the remaining eight years of his life studying mechanics, a field in which he made significant contributions.

Galileo and the Problem of Motion One of the problems that fell under the heading of mechanics was the principle of motion. The Aristotelian conception, which dominated the late medieval world, held that an object remained at rest unless a force was applied against it. If a force was constantly exerted, then the object moved at a constant rate, but if it was removed, then the object stopped. This conception encountered some difficulties, especially with a projectile thrown out of a cannon. Late medieval theorists had solved this problem by arguing that the rush of air behind the projectile kept it in motion. The Aristotelian principle of motion also raised problems in the new Copernican system. In the Ptolemaic

system, the concentric spheres surrounding the earth were weightless, but in the Copernican system, if a constant force had to be applied to objects to cause movement, then what power or force kept the heavy earth and other planets in motion?

Galileo made two contributions to the problem of motion. First, he demonstrated by experiments that if a uniform force was applied to an object, it would move at an accelerated speed rather than a constant speed. Moreover, Galileo discovered the principle of inertia when he argued that a body in motion continues in motion forever unless deflected by an external force. Thus, a state of uniform motion is just as natural as a state of rest. Before Galileo, natural philosophers had tried to explain motion; now their task was to explain changes in motion.

The condemnation of Galileo by the Inquisition, coming at a time of economic decline, seriously undermined further scientific work in Italy, which had been at the forefront of scientific innovation. Leadership in science now passed to the northern countries, especially England, France, and the Dutch Netherlands. By the 1630s and 1640s, no reasonable astronomer could overlook that Galileo's discoveries, combined with Kepler's mathematical laws, had made nonsense of the Aristotelian-Ptolemaic world system and clearly established the reasonableness of the Copernican model. Nevertheless, the problem of explaining motion in the universe and tying together the ideas of Copernicus, Galileo, and Kepler had not yet been solved. This would be the work of an Englishman who has long been considered the greatest genius of the Scientific Revolution.

16-2e Newton

Born in the English village of Woolsthorpe in 1642, Isaac Newton was an unremarkable young man until he attended Cambridge University (see Image 16.7). His first great burst of creative energy came in 1666, when fear of the plague closed Cambridge and forced him to return to Woolsthorpe for eighteen months. There Newton discovered his creative talents: "In those days I was in the prime of my life for invention and minded mathematics and philosophy more than at any time since."[10] During this period, he invented the calculus, a mathematical means of calculating rates of change; began his investigations into the composition of light; and inaugurated his work on the law of universal gravitation. Two years after his return to Cambridge, in 1669, he accepted a chair in mathematics at the university. During a second intense period of creativity from 1684 to 1686, he wrote his famous *Principia* (prin-SIP-ee-uh) (see Historical Voices, "Newton's Rules of Reasoning," p. 498). After a nervous breakdown in 1693, he sought and received an administrative post as warden of the royal mint and was advanced to master of the mint by 1699, a post he held until his death in 1727. Made president of the Royal Society (see "The Scientific Societies," in Section 16-6b) in 1703 and knighted in 1705 for his great achievements, Sir Isaac Newton is to this day the only English scientist to be buried in Westminster Abbey.

A New Heaven? Faith Versus Reason

 What does Galileo think is the difference between knowledge about the natural world and knowledge about the spiritual world? What does Galileo suggest that his opponents should do before dismissing his ideas? In what ways does Cardinal Bellarmine attempt to refute Galileo's ideas? Why did Galileo's ideas represent a threat to the Catholic Church?

IN 1614, GALILEO WROTE A LETTER to the Grand Duchess Christina of Tuscany in which he explained why his theory that the earth rotated around the sun was not necessarily contrary to Scripture. To Galileo, it made little sense for the church to determine the nature of physical reality on the basis of biblical texts that were subject to different interpretations. One year later, Cardinal Robert Bellarmine, a Jesuit and now a member of the church's Inquisition, wrote a letter to one of Galileo's followers that laid out the Catholic Church's approach to the issue of Galileo's theory.

Galileo, Letter to the Grand Duchess Christina, 1614

Some years ago, as Your Serene Highness well knows, I discovered in the heavens many things that had not been seen before our own age. The novelty of these things, as well as some consequences which followed from them in contradiction to the physical notions commonly held among academic philosophers, stirred up against me no small number of professors—as if I had placed these things in the sky with my own hands in order to upset nature and overturn the sciences. . . .

Contrary to the sense of the Bible and the intention of the holy Fathers, if I am not mistaken, they would extend such authorities until even in purely physical matters—where faith is not involved—they would have us altogether abandon reason and the evidence of our senses in favor of some biblical passage, though under the surface meaning of its words this passage may contain a different sense. . . .

The reason produced for condemning the opinion that the earth moves and the sun stands still is that in many places in the Bible one may read that the sun moves and the earth stands still. Since the Bible cannot err, it follows as a necessary consequence that anyone takes an erroneous and heretical position who maintains that the sun is inherently motionless and the earth movable.

With regard to this argument, I think in the first place that it is very pious to say and prudent to affirm that the holy Bible can never speak untruth—whenever its true meaning is understood. But I believe nobody will deny that it is often very abstruse, and may say things which are quite different from what its bare words signify. Hence, in expounding the Bible if one were always to confine oneself to the unadorned grammatical meaning, one might fall into error. Not only contradictions and propositions far from true might thus be made to appear in the Bible, but even grave heresies and follies. Thus, it would be necessary to assign to God feet, hands, and eyes, as well as corporeal and human affections, such as anger, repentance, hatred, and sometimes even the forgetting of things past and ignorance of those to come. These propositions uttered by the Holy Ghost were set down in that manner by the sacred scribes in order to accommodate them to the capacities of the common people, who are rude and unlearned. For the sake of those who deserve to be separated from the herd, it is necessary that wise expositors should produce the true senses of such passages, together with the special reasons for which they were set down in these words. . . .

This being granted, I think that in discussions of physical problems we ought to begin not from the authority of scriptural passages, but from sense-experiences and necessary demonstrations; for the holy Bible and the phenomena of nature proceed alike from the divine Word. . . . For that reason it appears that nothing physical which sense-experience sets before our eyes, or which necessary demonstrations prove to us, ought to be called in question (much less condemned) upon the testimony of biblical passages which may have some different meaning beneath their words.

Robert Bellarmine, Letter to Paolo Foscarini, 1615

First. I say that it seems to me that Your Reverence and Galileo did prudently to content yourself with speaking hypothetically, and not absolutely, as I have always believed that Copernicus spoke. For to say that, assuming the earth moves and the sun stands still, all the appearances are saved better than with eccentrics and epicycles, is to speak well; there is no danger in this, and it is sufficient for mathematicians. But to want to affirm that the sun really is fixed in the center of the heavens and only revolves around itself (i.e., turns upon its axis) without traveling from east to west, and that the earth is situated in the third sphere and revolves with great speed around the sun, is a very dangerous thing, not only by irritating all the philosophers and scholastic theologians, but also by injuring our holy faith and rendering the Holy Scriptures false. For Your Reverence has demonstrated many ways of explaining Holy Scripture, but you have not applied them in particular, and without a doubt you would have found it most difficult if you had attempted to explain all the passages which you yourself have cited.

Second. I say that, as you know, the Council [of Trent] prohibits expounding the Scriptures contrary to the common agreement of the holy Fathers. And if Your Reverence would read not only the Fathers but also the commentaries of modern writers on Genesis, Psalms, Ecclesiastes and Josue, you would find that all agree in explaining literally (*ad litteram*) that the sun is in the heavens and moves swiftly around the earth, and that the earth is far from the heavens and stands immobile in the center of the universe. Now consider whether in all prudence the Church could encourage giving to Scripture a sense contrary to the holy Fathers and all the Latin and Greek commentators. Nor may it be answered that this is not a matter of faith, for if it is not a matter of faith from the point of view of the subject matter, it is on the part of the ones who have spoken. . . .

Third. I say that if there were a true demonstration that the sun was in the center of the universe and the earth in the third sphere, and that the sun did not travel around the earth but the earth circled the sun, then it would be necessary to proceed with great caution in explaining the passages of Scripture which seemed contrary, and we would rather have to say that we did not understand them than to say that something was false which has been demonstrated. But I do not believe that there is any such demonstration; none has been shown to me. It is not the same thing to show that the appearances are saved by assuming that the sun really is in the center and the earth in the heavens. I believe that the first demonstration might exist, but I have grave doubts about the second, and in a case of doubt, one may not depart from the Scriptures as explained by the holy Fathers.

Source: "Letter to the Grand Duchess Christina (1614)" from *Discoveries and Opinions of Galileo* by Galileo, translated by Stillman Drake, translation copyright © 1957 by Stillman Drake. Used by permission of Doubleday, an imprint of the Knopf Doubleday Publishing Group, a division of Penguin Random House LLC. All rights reserved; Robert Bellarmine, Letter to Paolo Foscarini, 1615, in J. J. Langford, *Galileo, Science, and the Church* (New York: Desclee, 1966).

National Portrait Gallery, London/The Bridgeman Art Library

IMAGE 16.7 Newton. With a single law, that of universal gravitation, Isaac Newton was able to explain all motion in the universe. His great synthesis of the work of his predecessors created a new picture of the cosmos, one in which the universe was viewed as a great machine operating according to natural laws. Enoch Seeman painted this portrait of Newton one year before Newton's death.

Newton and the Occult Although Newton occupies a very special place in the history of modern science, we need to remember that he, too, remained extremely interested in aspects of the occult world. Newton believed in the concept of "original wisdom," a divinely revealed knowledge from centuries before that had been corrupted over time. In his early writings, Newton sought to reveal the "original wisdom" by studying theology, Greek myths, biblical passages, Hermeticism, and alchemy. He left behind hundreds of manuscript pages of his studies of alchemy, and in fact, his alchemical experiments were a major feature of his life until he moved to London in 1696 to become warden of the royal mint. The British economist John Maynard Keynes said of Newton after examining his manuscripts in 1936:

> Newton was not the first of the age of reason. He was the last of the magicians. . . . He looked on the whole universe and all that is in it as a riddle, as a secret which could be read by applying pure thought to certain evidence, certain mystic clues which God had laid about the world to allow a sort of philosopher's treasure hunt to the esoteric brotherhood. He believed that these clues were to be found partly in the evidence of the heavens and in the constitution of elements . . . but also partly in certain papers and traditions handed down by the brethren in an unknown chain back to the original cryptic revelation in Babylonia.[11]

Although Newton may have considered himself a representative of the Hermetic tradition, as was common for students of natural philosophy at the time, scholars placed greater emphasis on Newton's scientific works.

Universal Law of Gravitation Newton's major work, the "hinge point of modern scientific thought," was his *Mathematical Principles of Natural Philosophy*, known simply as the *Principia*, the first word of its Latin title. In this work, the last highly influential book in Europe to be written in Latin, Newton spelled out the mathematical proofs demonstrating his universal law of gravitation. Newton's work was the culmination of the theories of Copernicus, Kepler, and Galileo. Though each had undermined some part of the Aristotelian-Ptolemaic cosmology, until Newton

Newton's Rules of Reasoning

 What are Newton's rules of reasoning? How important were they to the development of the Scientific Revolution? How would following these rules change a person's view of the world, of European religious traditions, and of ancient "science"?

IN 1687, ISAAC NEWTON PUBLISHED HIS MASTERPIECE, the *Mathematical Principles of Natural Philosophy*, or *Principia*. In this work, Newton demonstrated the mathematical proofs for his universal law of gravitation and completed the new cosmology begun by Copernicus, Kepler, and Galileo. He also described the rules of reasoning by which he arrived at his universal law.

Isaac Newton, *Rules of Reasoning in Philosophy*
Rule 1

We are to admit no more causes of natural things than such as are both true and sufficient to explain their appearances.

To this purpose the philosophers say that Nature does nothing in vain, and more is in vain when less will serve; for Nature is pleased with simplicity, and affects not the pomp of superfluous causes.

Rule 2

Therefore to the same natural effects we must, as far as possible, assign the same causes.

As to respiration in a man and in a beast; the descent of stones in Europe and in America; the light of our culinary fire and of the sun; the reflection of light in the earth and in the planets.

Rule 3

The qualities of bodies, which admit neither intensification nor remission of degrees, and which are found to belong to all bodies within the reach of our experiments, are to be esteemed the universal qualities of all bodies whatsoever.

For since qualities of bodies are only known to us by experiments, we are to hold for universal all such as universally agree with experiments; and such as are not liable to diminution can never be quite taken away.

Rule 4

In experimental philosophy we are to look upon propositions inferred by general induction from phenomena as accurately or very nearly true, notwithstanding any contrary hypotheses that may be imagined, till such time as other phenomena occur, by which they may either be made more accurate, or liable to exceptions.

This rule we must follow, that the argument of induction may not be evaded by hypotheses.

Source: Newton, *The Mathematical Principles of Natural Philosophy* (London, 1803), pp. 160–162.

---

no one had pieced together a coherent synthesis for a new cosmology.

In the first book of the *Principia*, Newton defined the basic concepts of mechanics by elaborating the three laws of motion: every object continues in a state of rest or uniform motion in a straight line unless deflected by a force, the rate of change of motion of an object is proportional to the force acting on it, and to every action there is always an equal and opposite reaction. In book 3, Newton applied his theories of mechanics to the problems of astronomy by demonstrating that these three laws of motion govern the planetary bodies as well as terrestrial objects. Integral to his whole argument was the universal law of gravitation, which explained why the planetary bodies did not go off in straight lines but continued in elliptical orbits about the sun. In mathematical terms, Newton explained that every object in the universe was attracted to every other object with a force (gravity) that is directly proportional to the product of their masses and inversely proportional to the square of the distances between them.

The implications of Newton's universal law of gravitation were enormous, even though another century would pass

before they were widely recognized. Newton had demonstrated that one universal law, mathematically proved, could explain all motion in the universe, from the movements of the planets in the celestial world to an apple falling from a tree in the terrestrial world. The secrets of the natural world could be known by human investigations. At the same time, the Newtonian synthesis created a new cosmology in which the world was seen largely in mechanistic terms. The universe was one huge, regulated, and uniform machine that operated according to natural laws in absolute time, space, and motion. Although Newton believed that God was "everywhere present" and acted as the force that moved all bodies on the basis of the laws he had discovered, later generations dropped his spiritual assumptions. Newton's **world-machine**, conceived as operating absolutely in time, space, and motion, dominated the Western worldview until the twentieth century, when the Einsteinian revolution, based on the concept of relativity, superseded the Newtonian mechanistic concept.

Newton's ideas were soon accepted in England, possibly out of national pride and conviction and, as has been argued recently, for political reasons (see "Science and Society," in

CHRONOLOGY	Important Works of the Scientific Revolution	
Copernicus, *On the Revolutions of the Heavenly Spheres*	1543
Vesalius, *On the Fabric of the Human Body*	1543
Galileo, *The Starry Messenger*	1610
Harvey, *On the Motion of the Heart and Blood*	1628
Galileo, *Dialogue on the Two Chief World Systems*	1632
Cavendish, *Grounds of Natural Philosophy*	1668
Newton, *Principia*	1687

Section 16-6b). Natural philosophers on the continent resisted Newton's ideas, and it took much of the eighteenth century before they were generally accepted everywhere in Europe. They were also reinforced by developments in other fields, especially medicine.

16-3 Advances in Medicine and Chemistry

 FOCUS QUESTIONS: What did Paracelsus, Vesalius, and Harvey each contribute to a scientific view of medicine? How did their ideas about medicine differ from their predecessor, the Greek physician Galen?

Although the Scientific Revolution of the sixteenth and seventeenth centuries is associated primarily with the dramatic changes in astronomy and mechanics that precipitated a new perception of the universe, a third field that had been dominated by Greek thought in the Later Middle Ages, that of medicine, also experienced a transformation. Late medieval medicine was dominated not by the teachings of Aristotle but by those of the Greek physician Galen (GAY-len), who had lived in the second century C.E.

Galen's influence on the medieval medical world was pervasive in anatomy, physiology, and disease. Galen had relied on animal, rather than human, dissection to arrive at a picture of human anatomy that was quite inaccurate in many instances. Even when Europeans began to practice human dissection in the Later Middle Ages, instruction in anatomy still relied on Galen. While a professor read a text of Galen, an assistant dissected a cadaver for illustrative purposes. Physiology, or the functioning of the body, was also dominated by Galenic hypotheses, including the belief that there were two separate blood systems. One controlled muscular activities and contained bright red blood moving upward and downward through the arteries; the other governed the digestive functions and contained dark red blood that ebbed and flowed in the veins.

Treatment of disease was highly influenced by Galen's doctrine of four bodily humors: blood, considered warm and moist; yellow bile, warm and dry; phlegm, cold and moist; and

black bile, cold and dry. Since disease was supposedly the result of an imbalance of humors that could be discerned from the quantity and color of urine, the examination of a patient's urine became the chief diagnostic tool. Galenic medicine worked by administering "contrary cures": if a patient has a "cold," resulting from excess phlegm (the cold and wet *humor*), then hot and dry foods and remedies were prescribed. Although purging and bleeding to remedy the imbalance were often administered and harmful to patients, treatment with traditional herbal medicines sometimes proved beneficial.

16-3a Paracelsus

Three figures are associated with the changes in medicine in the sixteenth and seventeenth centuries: Paracelsus (par-uh-SELL-suss), Andreas Vesalius (ahn-DRAY-uss vuh-SAY-lee-uss), and William Harvey. Philippus Aureolus von Hohenheim (1493–1541), who renamed himself Paracelsus ("greater than Celsus," an ancient physician), traveled widely and may have been awarded a medical degree from the University of Ferrara in Italy. He achieved a moment of glory when he was appointed city physician and professor of medicine at Basel in 1527. But this, like so many other appointments, proved short-lived due to his vanity and quick temper. He could never disguise his contempt for universities and physicians who did not agree with his new ideas:

> I am *monarcha medicorum*, monarch of physicians, and I can prove to you what you cannot prove. . . . It was not the constellations that made me a physician: God made me. . . . I need not don a coat of mail or a buckler against you, for you are not learned or experienced enough to refute even one word of mine. . . . Let me tell you this: every little hair on my neck knows more than you and all your scribes, and my shoebuckles are more learned than your Galen and Avicenna, and my beard has more experience than all your high colleges.[12]

Paracelsus was not easy to get along with, and he was forced to wander from one town to another until his death in 1541.

Paracelsus rejected the work of both Aristotle and Galen and attacked the universities as centers of their moribund philosophy. He and his followers hoped to replace the traditional system with a new chemical philosophy that was based on a new understanding of nature derived from fresh observation and experiment. This chemical philosophy was in turn closely connected to a view of the universe based on the macrocosm-microcosm analogy. According to this view, a human being was a small replica (microcosm) of the larger world (macrocosm). All parts of the universe were represented within each person. As Paracelsus said, "For the sun and the moon and all planets, as well as the stars and the whole chaos, are in man. . . . For what is outside is also inside; and what is not outside man is not inside. The outer and the inner are one thing."[13] In accordance with the macrocosmic/microcosmic principle, Paracelsus believed that the chemical reactions of the universe as a whole were reproduced in human beings on a smaller scale. Disease, then, was not caused by an imbalance of the four humors, as Galen had argued, but was due to chemical imbalances that were localized in specific organs and could be treated by chemical remedies.

Although others had used chemical remedies, Paracelsus and his followers differed from them in giving careful attention to the proper dosage of their chemically prepared metals and minerals. Paracelsus had turned against the Galenic principle that "contraries cure" in favor of the ancient Germanic folk principle that "like cures like." The poison that caused a disease would be its cure if used in proper form and quantity. Despite the apparent effectiveness of this use of toxic substances as treatment (Paracelsus did have a strong reputation for actually curing his patients), his opponents viewed it as the practice of a "homicide physician." Later generations came to regard Paracelsus more favorably, and historians who have stressed Paracelsus's concept of disease and recognition of "new drugs" for medicine have viewed him as a father of modern medicine. Others have argued that his macrocosmic-microcosmic philosophy and use of "like cures like" drugs make him the forerunner of both homeopathy and the holistic medicine of the postmodern era.

16-3b Vesalius

The new anatomy of the sixteenth century was the work of Andreas Vesalius (1514–1564) (see Image 16.8). His study of medicine at Paris involved him in the works of Galen.

IMAGE 16.8 **Andreas Vesalius.** In this seventeenth-century French portrait of Andreas Vesalius, Vesalius is portrayed with one of his cadavers. His work established new understanding of the human body while the developments in artistic representation during the Renaissance allowed for more accurate representations of his findings, as seen here.

Especially important to him was a recently discovered text of Galen, *On Anatomical Procedures*, that led Vesalius to emphasize practical research as the principal avenue for understanding human anatomy. After receiving a doctorate in medicine at the University of Padua in 1536, he accepted a position there as professor of surgery. In 1543, he published his masterpiece, *On the Fabric of the Human Body*.

This book was based on his personal dissection of a body to illustrate what he was discussing. Vesalius's anatomical treatise presented a careful examination of the individual organs and general structure of the human body. Vesalius's text explained each illustration and anatomical feature in great detail. The book would not have been feasible without both the artistic advances of the Renaissance and technical developments in the art of printing. Together, they made possible the creation of illustrations superior to any done before.

Vesalius's hands-on approach to teaching anatomy enabled him to rectify some of Galen's most glaring errors. He did not hesitate, for example, to correct Galen's assertion that the great blood vessels originated from the liver since his own observations made it apparent that they came from the heart. Nevertheless, Vesalius still clung to a number of Galen's erroneous assertions, including the Greek physician's ideas on the ebb and flow of two kinds of blood in the veins and arteries. It was not until William Harvey's work on the circulation of the blood nearly a century later that this Galenic misperception was corrected.

16-3c William Harvey

William Harvey (1578–1657) attended Cambridge University and later Padua, where he received a doctorate in medicine in 1602. His reputation rests on his book *On the Motion of the Heart and Blood*, published in 1628. Although questions had been raised in the sixteenth century about Galen's physiological principles, no major break from his system had occurred. Harvey's work, which was based on meticulous observations and experiments, led him to demolish the ancient Greek's erroneous contentions. Harvey demonstrated that the heart and not the liver was the beginning point of the circulation of blood in the body, that the same blood flows in both veins and arteries, and most important, that the blood makes a complete circuit as it passes through the body. His efforts did not come without an ethical cost, however. Harvey chose as his experimental subjects people who had been convicted of murder or treason and operated on them while they were alive in order to assess certain organ function, such as the process of digestion. Although Harvey's work dealt a severe blow to Galen's theories, his ideas did not begin to achieve general recognition until the 1660s, when capillaries, which explained how the blood passed from the arteries to the veins, were discovered. Harvey's theory of the circulation of the blood laid the foundation for modern physiology.

16-3d Chemistry

Although Paracelsus had proposed a new chemical philosophy in the sixteenth century, it was not until the seventeenth and eighteenth centuries that a science of chemistry arose. Robert Boyle (1627–1691) was one of the first scientists to conduct controlled experiments. One of his most impressive experiments

Musee des Beaux-Arts, Orleans, France/Bridgeman Images

built upon the work of his predecessor, Otto von Guericke (1602–1686). Guericke's "Magdeburg sphere" had proven that air had weight and air could exist in a vacuum, challenging the Aristotelian notion that the world was completely full of matter. The sphere consisted of two halves built from copper, with a valve that controlled the air inside. When the air was released the two halves could not be separated because of the air's weight holding them together. Upon opening the valve, the two halves were easily pulled apart. In 1658, Boyle and Robert Hook built an improved version made of glass, allowing various objects to be sealed inside and observed as air was pumped out. His pioneering work on the properties of gases led to Boyle's law, which states that the volume of a gas varies with the pressure exerted on it. Boyle also rejected the medieval belief that all matter consisted of the same components in favor of the view that matter is composed of atoms, which he called "little particles of all shapes and sizes" and which would later be known as the chemical elements.

In the eighteenth century, Antoine Lavoisier (AHN-twahn lah-vwah-ZYAY) (1743–1794) invented a system of naming the chemical elements, much of which is still used today. In helping to show that water is a compound of oxygen and hydrogen, he demonstrated the fundamental rules of chemical combination. Many regard him as the founder of modern chemistry. Lavoisier's wife, Marie-Anne, was her husband's scientific collaborator. She learned English in order to translate the work of British chemists for her husband and made engravings to illustrate his scientific experiments. Marie-Anne Lavoisier is a reminder that women too played a role in the Scientific Revolution.

16-4 Women in the Origins of Modern Science

FOCUS QUESTIONS: What role did women play in the Scientific Revolution? How were women from France able to participate in the Scientific Revolution as compared to women from Germany? How did the Scientific Revolution impact the roles of women?

During the Middle Ages, except for members of religious orders, women who sought a life of learning were severely hampered by the traditional attitude that a woman's proper role was as a daughter, wife, and mother. But in the late fourteenth and early fifteenth centuries, new opportunities for elite women emerged as enthusiasm for the new secular learning called humanism led Europe's privileged and learned men to encourage women to read and study classical and Christian texts. The ideal of a humanist education for some of the daughters of Europe's elite persisted into the seventeenth century, but only for some privileged women.

16-4a Margaret Cavendish

Much as they were drawn to humanism, women were also attracted to the Scientific Revolution. Unlike females educated formally in humanist schools, women interested in

science had to obtain a largely informal education. European nobles had the leisure and resources that gave them easy access to the world of learning. This door was also open to noblewomen who could participate in the informal scientific networks of their fathers and brothers. One of the most prominent female scientists of the seventeenth century, Margaret Cavendish (KAV-un-dish) (1623–1673), came from an aristocratic background (see Image 16.9). Cavendish was not a popularizer of science for women but a participant in the crucial scientific debates of her time. Despite her achievements, however, she was excluded from membership in the Royal Society (see "The Scientific Societies," in Section 16-6b), although she was once allowed to attend a meeting. She wrote a number of works on scientific matters, including *Observations upon Experimental Philosophy* and *Grounds of Natural Philosophy*, published in 1668. In these works, she did not hesitate to attack what she considered the defects of the rationalist and empiricist approaches to scientific knowledge and was especially critical of the growing belief that through science, humans would be masters of nature: "We have no power at all over natural causes and effects . . . for man is but a small part. . . . His powers are but particular actions of Nature, and he cannot have a supreme and absolute power."[14]

IMAGE 16.9 **Margaret Cavendish.** Shown in this portrait is Margaret Cavendish, the duchess of Newcastle. She was a prolific writer, responsible for plays, biographies, poetry, and prose romances, as well as works in philosophy and science. Unlike most female authors of the time, who wrote anonymously, she used her own name on her works.

 Why was Cavendish critical of the new rationalist and empiricist approaches to science?

Margaret Cavendish: The Education of Women

 What arguments does Cavendish make to defend her right and ability to be an author?

MARGARET CAVENDISH'S HUSBAND, who was thirty years her senior, encouraged her to pursue her literary interests. In addition to scientific works, she wrote plays, an autobiography, and a biography of her husband titled *The Life of the Thrice Noble, High and Puissant Prince William Cavendish, Duke, Marquess and Earl of Newcastle.* The autobiography and biography led one male literary critic to call her "a mad, conceited and ridiculous woman." In an essay titled "The Philosophical and Physical Opinions," she discussed the constraints placed upon women, including education.

Margaret Cavendish, "The Philosophical and Physical Opinions"

But to answer those objections that are made against me, as first how should I come by so much experience as I have expressed in my several books to have? I answer: I have had by relation the long and much experience of my lord, who hath lived to see and be in many changes of fortune and to converse with many men of sundry nations, ages, qualities, tempers, capacities, abilities, wits, humours, fashions and customs.

And as many others, especially wives, go from church to church, from ball to ball . . . gossiping from house to house, so when my lord admits me to his company I listen with attention to his edifying discourse and I govern myself by his doctrine: I dance a measure with the muses, feast with sciences, or sit and discourse with the arts.

The second is that, since I am no scholar, I cannot know the names and terms of art and the divers and several opinions of several authors. I answer: that I must have been a natural fool if I had not known and learnt them, for they are customarily taught all children from the nurse's breast, being ordinarily discoursed of in every family that is of quality, and the family from whence I sprung are neither natural idiots or ignorant fools, but the contrary, for they were rational, learned, understanding and witty. . . .

But as I have said my head was so full of my own natural fantasies, as it had not room for strangers to board therein, and certainly natural reason is a better tutor than education. For though education doth help natural reason to a more sudden maturity, yet natural reason was the first educator: for natural reason did first compose commonwealths, invented arts and science, and if natural reason hath composed, invented and discovered, I know no reason but natural reason may find out what natural reason hath composed, invented and discovered with the help of education. . . .

Source: K. Aughterson, *Renaissance Woman: A Sourcebook* (London: Routledge, 1995); pp. 286–288.

As an aristocrat (she was the duchess of Newcastle), Cavendish was a good example of the women in France and England who worked in science (see Historical Voices, "Margaret Cavendish: The Education of Women," above). In Germany, women interested in science came from a different background. There the tradition of female participation in craft production enabled some women to become involved in observational science, especially entomology and astronomy. Between 1650 and 1710, one of every seven German astronomers was a woman.

16-4b Maria Merian

A good example of female involvement in the Scientific Revolution stemming from the craft tradition was Maria Sibylla Merian (MAY-ree-un) (1647–1717), who had established a reputation as an important entomologist by the beginning of the eighteenth century. Merian's training came from working in her father's workshop, where she learned the art of illustration, a training of great importance since her exact observation of insects and plants was demonstrated through the superb illustrations she made. In 1699, she undertook an expedition into the wilds of the Dutch colony of Surinam in South America to collect and draw samples of plants and insect life. This led to her major scientific work, the *Metamorphosis of the Insects of Surinam,* in which she used sixty illustrations to show the reproductive and developmental cycles of Surinam's insect life.

16-4c Maria Winkelmann

The craft organization of astronomy also gave women opportunities to become involved in science. Those who did worked in family observatories; hence, daughters and wives received training as apprentices to fathers or husbands. The most famous of the female astronomers in Germany was Maria Winkelmann (VINK-ul-mahn) (1670–1720). She was educated by her father and uncle and received advanced training in astronomy from a nearby self-taught astronomer. When she married Gottfried Kirch, Germany's foremost astronomer, she became his assistant at the astronomical observatory operated in Berlin by the Academy of Science. She made several original contributions, including a hitherto undiscovered comet, as her husband related:

Early in the morning (about 2:00 A.M.) the sky was clear and starry. Some nights before, I had observed a variable star, and my wife (as I slept) wanted to find and see it for herself. In so doing, she found a comet in the sky. At which time she woke me, and I found that it was indeed a comet. . . . I was surprised that I had not seen it the night before.[15]

Moreover, Winkelmann corresponded with the famous scientist Gottfried Leibniz (who invented the calculus independently of Newton), who praised her effusively as "a most learned woman who could pass as a rarity." When her husband died in 1710, she applied for a position as assistant astronomer for which she was highly qualified. As a woman—with no university degree—she was denied the post by the Berlin Academy, which feared that it would establish a precedent by hiring a woman ("mouths would gape"). Winkelmann continued to do much of the work at the Berlin Academy once her son Christophe was appointed astronomer.

Winkelmann's difficulties with the Berlin Academy reflect the obstacles women faced in being accepted in scientific work, which was considered a male preserve. Although no formal statutes excluded women from membership in the new scientific societies, no woman was invited to join either the Royal Society of England or the French Academy of Sciences until the twentieth century. All of these women scientists were exceptional, since a life devoted to any kind of scholarship was still viewed as being at odds with the domestic duties women were expected to perform.

16-4d Debates on the Nature of Women

The nature and value of women had been the subject of an on-going, centuries-long debate known as the **querelles des femmes** (keh-REL day FAHM)—arguments about women. Male opinions in the debate were largely a carryover from medieval times and were not favorable. Women were portrayed as inherently base, prone to vice, easily swayed, and "sexually insatiable." Hence, men needed to control them. Learned women were viewed as having overcome female liabilities to become like men. One man in praise of a woman scholar remarked that her writings were so good that you "would hardly believe they were done by a woman at all."

In the early modern era, women joined this debate by arguing against these male images of women. They argued that women also had rational minds and could grow from education. Further, since most women were pious, chaste, and temperate, there was no need for male authority over them. These female defenders of women emphasized education as the key to women's ability to move into the world. How, then, did the changes brought by the Scientific Revolution affect this debate over the nature of women? In an era of intellectual revolution in which traditional authorities were being overthrown, we might expect significant change in men's views of women. But by and large, instead of becoming an instrument for liberation, science was used to find new support for the old, stereotypical views about a woman's place in the scheme of things.

An important project in the new anatomy of the sixteenth and seventeenth centuries was the attempt to illustrate the human body and skeleton. For Vesalius, the portrayal of physical differences between males and females was limited to external bodily form (the outlines of the body) and the sexual organs. Vesalius saw no difference in skeletons and portrayed them as the same for men and women. It was not until the eighteenth century, in fact, that a new anatomy finally prevailed. Drawings of female skeletons between 1730 and 1790 varied, but females tended to have a larger pelvic area, and, in some instances, female skulls were portrayed as smaller than those of males. Eighteenth-century studies on the anatomy and physiology of sexual differences provided "scientific evidence" to reaffirm the traditional inferiority of women. The larger pelvic area "proved" that women were meant to be childbearers, and the larger skull "demonstrated" the superiority of the male mind. Male-dominated science had been used to "prove" male social dominance.

At the same time, during the seventeenth and eighteenth centuries, women even lost the traditional spheres of influence they had possessed, especially in the science-related art of midwifery. Women serving as midwives had traditionally been responsible for birthing. Similar to barber-surgeons or apothecaries (see Chapter 17), midwives had acquired their skills through apprenticeship. But the impact of the Scientific Revolution caused traditional crafts to be upgraded and then even professionalized as males took over. When medical men entered this arena, they also began to use devices and techniques derived from the study of anatomy. These were increasingly used to justify the male takeover of the traditional role of midwives. By the end of the eighteenth century, midwives were simply accessories to the art they had once controlled, except among the poor. Since little money was to be made in serving the lower classes, midwives were allowed to continue to practice their traditional art among them.

Overall, the Scientific Revolution reaffirmed traditional ideas about women. Male scientists used the new science to spread the view that women were inferior by nature, subordinate to men, and suited by nature to play a domestic role as nurturing mothers. The widespread distribution of books ensured the continuation of these ideas. Jean de La Bruyère (ZHAHNH duh lah broo-YARE), the seventeenth-century French moralist, was typical when he remarked that an educated woman was like a gun that was a collector's item, "which one shows to the curious, but which has no use at all, any more than a carousel horse."[16]

16-5 Toward a New Earth: Descartes, Rationalism, and a New View of Humankind

 FOCUS QUESTION: Why is Descartes considered the founder of modern rationalism?

The fundamentally new conception of the universe contained in the cosmological revolution of the sixteenth and seventeenth centuries inevitably had an impact on the Western

IMAGE 16.10 **Descartes.** Renè Descartes was one of the primary figures in the Scientific Revolution. Claiming to use reason as his sole guide to truth, Descartes posited a sharp distinction between mind and matter. He is shown here in a portrait done around 1649 by Frans Hals, one of the painters of the Dutch golden age who was famous for his portraits, especially that of Descartes.

view of humankind. Nowhere is this more evident than in the work of Renè Descartes (ruh-NAY day-KART) (1596–1650), an extremely important figure in Western history. Descartes began by reflecting the doubt and uncertainty that seemed pervasive in the confusion of the seventeenth century and ended with a philosophy that dominated Western thought until the twentieth century (see Image 16.10).

Descartes was born into a family of the French lower nobility. After a Jesuit education, he studied law at Poitiers but traveled to Paris to study by himself. In 1618, at the beginning of the Thirty Years' War, Descartes volunteered for service in the army of Maurice of Nassau, but he seems to have been interested less in military action than in traveling and finding leisure time to think. On the night of November 10, 1619, Descartes underwent what one historian has called an experience comparable to the "ecstatic illumination of the mystic." Having perceived in one night the outlines of a new rational-mathematical system, with a sense of divine approval he made a new commitment to mind, mathematics, and a mechanical universe. For the rest of his life, Descartes worked out the details of his vision.

The starting point for Descartes's new system was doubt, as he explained at the beginning of his most famous work, the *Discourse on Method*, written in 1637:

> From my childhood, I have been familiar with letters; and as I was given to believe that by their help a clear and certain knowledge of all that is useful in life might be acquired, I was ardently desirous of instruction. But as soon as I had finished the entire course of study, at the close of which it is customary to be admitted into the order of the learned, I completely changed my opinion. For I found myself involved in so many doubts and errors, that I was convinced I had advanced no farther in all my attempts at learning, than the discovery of my own ignorance.[17]

Descartes decided to set aside all that he had learned and begin again. One fact seemed beyond doubt—his own existence:

> But immediately upon this I observed that [while] I thus wished to think that all was false, it was absolutely necessary that I who thus thought, should be [something]; and as I observed that this truth, *I think, [therefore] I am*, was so certain and of such evidence, that no ground of doubt, however extravagant, could be alleged by the Sceptics capable of shaking it, I concluded that I might without scruple accept it as the first principle of the Philosophy of which I was in search.[18]

With this emphasis on the mind, Descartes asserted that he would accept only those things that his reason said were true.

From his first postulate, Descartes deduced an additional principle, the separation of mind and matter. Descartes argued that since "the mind cannot be doubted but the body and material world can, the two must be radically different." From this came an absolute duality between mind and body that has been called **Cartesian dualism**. Using mind or human reason, the path to certain knowledge, and its best instrument, mathematics, humans can understand the material world because it is pure mechanism, a machine that is governed by its own physical laws because it was created by God, the great geometrician.

Descartes's conclusions about the nature of the universe and human beings had important implications. His separation of mind and matter allowed scientists to view matter as dead or inert, as something that was totally separate from themselves and could be investigated independently by reason. The split between mind and body led Westerners to equate their identity with mind and reason rather than with the whole organism. Descartes has rightly been called the father of modern **rationalism** (see Historical Voices "The Father of Modern Rationalism," p. 505). His books were placed on the papal Index of Forbidden Books and condemned by many Protestant theologians. The radical Cartesian split between mind and matter, and between mind and body, had devastating implications not only for traditional religious views of the universe but also for how Westerners viewed themselves.

The Father of Modern Rationalism

 Describe Descartes's principles of inquiry and compare them with Newton's rules of reasoning. What are the main similarities between these systems of thinking?

RENÉ DESCARTES HAS LONG BEEN VIEWED as the founder of modern rationalism and modern philosophy because he believed that human beings could understand the world—itself a mechanical system—by the same rational principles inherent in mathematical thinking. In his *Discourse on Method*, he elaborated on his approach to discovering truth.

René Descartes, *Discourse on Method*

In place of the numerous precepts which have gone to constitute logic, I came to believe that the four following rules would be found sufficient, always provided I took the firm and unswerving resolve never in a single instance to fail in observing them.

The first was to accept nothing as true which I did not evidently know to be such, that is to say, scrupulously to avoid precipitance and prejudice, and in the judgments I passed to include nothing additional to what had presented itself to my mind so clearly and so distinctly that I could have no occasion for doubting it.

The second, to divide each of the difficulties I examined into as many parts as may be required for its adequate solution.

The third, to arrange my thoughts in order, beginning with things the simplest and easiest to know, so that I may then ascend little by little, as it were step by step, to the knowledge of the more complex, and in doing so, to assign an order of thought even to those objects which are not of themselves in any such order of precedence.

And the last, in all cases to make enumerations so complete, and reviews so general, that I should be assured of omitting nothing.

Those long chains of reasonings, each step simple and easy, which geometers are wont to employ in arriving even at the most difficult of their demonstrations, have led me to surmise that all the things we human beings are competent to know are interconnected in the same manner, and that none are so remote as to be beyond our reach or so hidden that we cannot discover them—that is, provided we abstain from accepting as true what is not thus related, i.e., keep always to the order required for their deduction one from another. And I had no great difficulty in determining what the objects are with which I should begin, for that I already knew, namely, that it was with the simplest and easiest. Bearing in mind, too, that of all those who in time past have sought for truth in the sciences, the mathematicians alone have been able to find any demonstrations, that is to say, any reasons which are certain and evident, I had no doubt that it must have been by a procedure of this kind that they had obtained them.

Source: N. K. Smith, trans., *Descartes' Philosophical Writings* (London: Palgrave Macmillan, 1958).

16-6 The Scientific Method and the Spread of Scientific Knowledge

 FOCUS QUESTION: How and where were the ideas of the Scientific Revolution spread, and what impact did they have on society and religion?

During the seventeenth century, scientific learning and investigation began to increase dramatically. Major universities in Europe established new chairs of science, especially in medicine. Royal and princely patronage of individual scientists became an international phenomenon.

16-6a The Scientific Method

Of great importance to the work of science was establishing the proper means to examine and understand the physical realm. This development of a **scientific method** was crucial to the evolution of science in the modern world.

Francis Bacon Curiously enough, it was an Englishman with few scientific credentials who attempted to put forth a new method of acquiring knowledge that made an impact on English scientists in the seventeenth century and other European scientists in the eighteenth century. Francis Bacon (1561–1626), a lawyer and lord chancellor, rejected Copernicus and Kepler and misunderstood Galileo. And yet in his unfinished work, *The Great Instauration*, he called for his contemporaries "to commence a total reconstruction of sciences, arts, and all human knowledge, raised upon the proper foundations." Bacon did not doubt humans' ability to know the natural world, but he believed that they had proceeded incorrectly: "The entire fabric of human reason which we employ in the inquisition of nature is badly put together and built up, and like some magnificent structure without foundation."

Bacon's new foundation—a correct scientific method—was to be built on inductive principles. Rather than beginning with assumed first principles from which logical conclusions could be deduced, he urged scientists to proceed from the particular to the general. From carefully organized experiments and thorough, systematic observations, correct generalizations could be developed.

Bacon was clear about what he believed his method could accomplish. His concern was for practical results rather than for pure science. He stated that "the true and lawful goal of the sciences is none other than this: that human life be endowed with new discoveries and power." He wanted science to contribute to the "mechanical arts" by creating devices that would benefit industry, agriculture, and trade. Bacon was prophetic when he said that he was "laboring to lay the foundation, not of any sect or doctrine, but of human utility and power." And how would this "human power" be used? To "conquer nature in action."[19] The control and domination of nature became a central proposition of modern science and the technology that accompanied it. Only in the twentieth century did some scientists begin to ask whether this assumption might not be at the heart of the earth's ecological crisis.

Descartes Descartes proposed a different approach to scientific methodology by emphasizing deduction and mathematical logic. As Descartes explained in the *Discourse on Method*, each step in an argument should be as sharp and well founded as a mathematical proof:

> Those long chains of reasonings, each step simple and easy, which geometers are wont to employ in arriving even at the most difficult of their demonstrations, have led me to surmise that all the things we human beings are competent to know are interconnected in the same manner, and that none are so remote as to be beyond our reach or so hidden that we cannot discover them—that is, provided we abstain from accepting as true what is not thus related, i.e., keep always to the order required for their deduction one from another.[20]

Descartes believed, then, that one could start with self-evident truths, comparable to geometric axioms, and deduce more complex conclusions. His emphasis on deduction and mathematical order complemented Bacon's stress on experiment and induction. It was Sir Isaac Newton who synthesized them into a single scientific methodology by uniting Bacon's **empiricism** with Descartes's rationalism. This scientific method began with systematic observations and experiments, which were used to arrive at general concepts. New deductions derived from these general concepts could then be tested and verified by precise experiments.

The scientific method, of course, was valuable in answering the question of *how* something works, and its success in doing this gave others much confidence in the method. It did not attempt to deal with the question of *why* something happens or the purpose and meaning behind the world of nature. This allowed religion to retain its central importance in the seventeenth century (see "16-6d Science and Religion," later in this chapter).

16-6b The Spread of Scientific Knowledge

Also important to the work of science was the emergence of new learned societies and journals that enabled the new scientists to communicate their ideas to each other and to disseminate them to a wider, literate public.

The Scientific Societies The first of these scientific societies appeared in Italy, but those of England and France were ultimately of greater significance. The English Royal Society evolved out of informal gatherings of scientists at London and Oxford in the 1640s, although it did not receive a formal charter from King Charles II until 1662 as the Royal Society of London for the Improvement of Natural Knowledge. The Royal Society grew quickly in esteem, with over 200 Fellows elected by the end of the seventeenth century. Every notable British natural philosopher of the period and since was a Fellow. The French Royal Academy of Sciences also arose out of informal scientific meetings in Paris during the 1650s. In 1666, Louis XIV formally recognized the group. The French Academy received abundant state support and remained under government control; the state appointed its members and paid their salaries. In contrast, the Royal Society of England received little government encouragement, and its fellows simply co-opted new members.

Early on, both the English and the French scientific societies formally emphasized the practical value of scientific research. The Royal Society created a committee to investigate technological improvements for industry; the French Academy collected tools and machines (see Images of Everyday Life, "The Science of Collecting," p. 507). This concern with the practical benefits of science proved short-lived, however, as both societies came to focus their primary interest on theoretical work in mechanics and astronomy. The construction of observatories at Paris in 1667 and at Greenwich, England, in 1675 greatly facilitated research in astronomy by both groups. Although both the English and the French societies made useful contributions to scientific knowledge in the second half of the seventeenth century, their true significance was that they demonstrated the benefits of science proceeding as a cooperative venture.

Scientific journals furthered this concept of cooperation. The French *Journal des Savants* (zhoor-NAHL day sah-VAHNH), published weekly beginning in 1665, printed results of experiments as well as general scientific knowledge. Its format appealed to both scientists and the educated public interested in the new science. In contrast, the *Philosophical Transactions* of the Royal Society, also initiated in 1665, published papers of its members and learned correspondence and was aimed at practicing scientists. It became a prototype for the scholarly journals of later learned and academic societies and a crucial instrument for circulating news of scientific and academic activities.

Science and Society The importance of science in the history of modern Western civilization is usually taken for granted. No doubt the Industrial Revolution of the nineteenth century provided tangible proof of the effectiveness of science and ensured its victory over Western minds. But how did science become such an integral part of Western culture in the seventeenth and eighteenth centuries? Recent research has stressed that one cannot simply assert that people perceived that science was a rationally superior system. Several factors, however, might explain the relatively rapid acceptance of the new science.

It has been argued that the literate mercantile and propertied elites of Europe were attracted to the new science because

The Science of Collecting

Q *How was the art of collecting significant in the development of science? Would collectors be considered scientists? Why or why not?*

THE ART OF COLLECTING was an important part of scientific culture. Early scientists maintained their relevance to the scientific community by their collections of drawings and specimens. Wealthy patrons were able to amass thousands of species of plants and insects as well as gems and scientific instruments for academic study and conservation. Sir Hans Sloane (1660–1753), portrayed with his drawings of plants (Image 16.11a), was an English physician who had spent fifteen months in Jamaica as a personal physician to the West Indies fleet in 1687. He collected around 800 species to bring back to England. His marriage to a wealthy heiress provided the capital to continue amassing his collection when he returned to London. By his death in 1753, he had gathered a collection of over 71,000 objects. He bequeathed his collection to the British nation, which used Sloan's collection as the foundation to the Natural History Museum. During his lifetime, Sloan's collection garnered considerable prestige and ensured his position as president of the Royal College of Physicians as well as the Royal Society. Various collections were kept in drawers, seen in this photo of specimens of beetles in the Jans Sloane collection (see Image 16.11b). However, botany collections were not only private endeavors, with royal patronage of botanical collections flourishing in the

seventeenth century. In France, the Royal Botanical Garden, founded in 1640, served as the leading center of botany in Europe; its gardens were divided into quarters representing Europe, Asia, Africa, and the Americas, as seen in a French drawing (see Image 16.11c).

IMAGE 16.11a

National Portrait Gallery, London, UK/Bridgeman Images

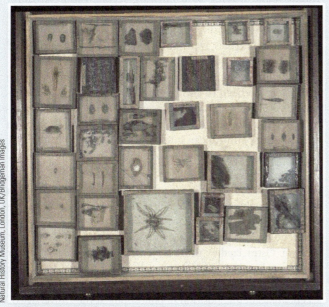

Natural History Museum, London, UK/Bridgeman Images

IMAGE 16.11b

Scala/White Images/Art Resource, NY

IMAGE 16.11c

it offered new ways to exploit resources for profit. Some of the early scientists made it easier for these groups to accept the new ideas by showing how they could be applied directly to specific industrial and technological needs. Galileo, for example, consciously sought an alliance between science and the material interests of the educated elite when he assured his listeners that the science of mechanics would be quite useful "when it becomes necessary to build bridges or other structures over water." At the same time, Galileo stressed that science was fit for the "minds of the wise" and not for "the shallow minds of the common people." This made science part of the high culture of Europe's wealthy elites at a time when that culture was being increasingly separated from the popular culture of the lower classes (see Chapter 17).

It has also been argued that political interests used the new scientific conception of the natural world to bolster social stability. One scholar has argued that "no single event in the history of early modern Europe more profoundly shaped the integration of the new science into Western culture than did the English Revolution (1640–1660)."[21] Fed by their millenarian expectations that the end of the world would come and usher in a thousand-year reign of the saints, Puritan reformers felt it was important to reform and renew their society. They seized on the new science as a socially useful instrument to accomplish this goal. The Puritan Revolution's role in the acceptance of science, however, stemmed even more from the reaction to the radicalism spawned by the revolutionary ferment. The upheavals of the Puritan Revolution gave rise to groups, such as the Levellers, Diggers, and Ranters, who advocated not only radical political ideas but also a new radical science based on Paracelsus and the natural magic associated with the Hermetic tradition. The propertied and educated elites responded vigorously to these challenges to the established order by supporting the new mechanistic science and appealing to the material benefits of science. Hence, the founders of the Royal Society were men who wanted to pursue an experimental science that would remain detached from radical reforms of church and state. Although willing to make changes, they now viewed those changes in terms of an increase in food production and commerce.

At the same time, princes and kings who were providing patronage for scientists were doing so not only for prestige but also for practical reasons, especially the military applications of the mathematical sciences. The use of gunpowder, for example, gave new importance to ballistics and metallurgy. Rulers, especially absolute ones, were also concerned about matters of belief in their realms and recognized the need to control and manage the scientific body of knowledge, as we have seen in the French Academy. In appointing its members and paying their salaries, Louis XIV was also ensuring that the members and their work would be under his control.

16-6c Science and Religion

In Galileo's struggle with the inquisitorial Holy Office of the Catholic Church, we see the beginning of the conflict between science and religion that has marked the history of modern Western civilization. Since time immemorial, theology had

seemed to be the queen of the sciences. It was natural that the churches would continue to believe that religion was the final measure of all things. The emerging scientists, however, tried to draw lines between the knowledge of religion and the knowledge of "natural philosophy" or nature. Galileo had clearly felt that it was unnecessary to pit science against religion when he wrote:

> In discussions of physical problems we ought to begin not from the authority of scriptural passages, but from sense-experiences and necessary demonstrations; for the holy Bible and the phenomena of nature proceed alike from the divine word, the former as the dictate of the Holy Ghost and the latter as the observant executrix of God's commands. It is necessary for the Bible, in order to be accommodated to the understanding of every man, to speak many things which appear to differ from the absolute truth so far as the bare meaning of the words is concerned. But Nature, on the other hand, is inexorable and immutable; she never transgresses the laws imposed upon her, or cares a whit whether her abstruse reasons and methods of operation are understandable to men.[22]

To Galileo, it made little sense for the church to determine the nature of physical reality on the basis of biblical texts that were subject to radically divergent interpretations. The church, however, decided otherwise in Galileo's case and lent its great authority to one scientific theory, the Aristotelian-Ptolemaic cosmology, no doubt because it fit so well with its own philosophical views of reality. But the church's decision had tremendous consequences, just as the rejection of Darwin's ideas did in the nineteenth century. For educated individuals, it established a dichotomy between scientific investigations and religious beliefs. As the scientific beliefs triumphed, it became almost inevitable that religious beliefs would suffer, leading to a growing secularization in European intellectual life—precisely what the church had hoped to combat by opposing Copernicanism. Many seventeenth-century intellectuals were both religious and scientific and believed that the implications of this split would be tragic. Some believed that the split was largely unnecessary, while others felt the need to combine God, humans, and a mechanistic universe into a new philosophical synthesis. Two individuals—Spinoza and Pascal—illustrate the wide diversity in the response of European intellectuals to the implications of the cosmological revolution of the seventeenth century.

Spinoza Benedict de Spinoza (spi-NOH-zuh) (1632–1677) was a philosopher who grew up in the relatively tolerant atmosphere of Amsterdam. He was excommunicated from the Amsterdam synagogue at the age of twenty-four for rejecting the tenets of Judaism. Ostracized by the local Jewish community and major Christian churches alike, Spinoza lived a quiet, independent life, earning a living by grinding optical lenses and refusing to accept an academic position in philosophy at the University of Heidelberg for fear of compromising his freedom of thought. Spinoza read a great deal of the new scientific literature and was influenced by Descartes.

Spinoza was unwilling to accept the implications of Descartes's ideas, especially the separation of mind and matter and the apparent separation of an infinite God from the finite world of matter. God was not simply the creator of the universe; he was the universe. All that is, is in God, and nothing can be apart from God. This philosophy of pantheism (or monism) was set out in Spinoza's book *Ethics Demonstrated in the Geometrical Manner*, which was not published until after his death.

To Spinoza, human beings are not "situated in nature as a kingdom within a kingdom" but are as much a part of God or nature or the universal order as other natural objects. The failure to understand God had led to many misconceptions—for one, that nature exists only for one's use:

> As they find in themselves and outside themselves many means which assist them not a little in their search for what is useful, for instance, eyes for seeing, teeth for chewing, herbs and animals for yielding food, the sun for giving light, the sea for breeding fish, they come to look on the whole of nature as a means for obtaining such conveniences.[23]

Furthermore, unable to find any other cause for the existence of these things, they attributed them to a creator-God who must be worshiped to gain their ends: "Hence also it follows, that everyone thought out for himself, according to his abilities, a different way of worshiping God, so that God might love him more than his fellows, and direct the whole course of nature for the satisfaction of his blind cupidity and insatiable avarice." Then, when nature appeared unfriendly in the form of storms, earthquakes, and diseases, "they declared that such things happen, because the gods are angry at some wrong done them by men, or at some fault committed in their worship," rather than realizing "that good and evil fortunes fall to the lot of pious and impious alike."[24] Likewise, human beings made moral condemnations of others because they failed to understand that human emotions, "passions of hatred, anger, envy and so, considered in themselves, follow from the same necessity and efficacy of nature" and "nothing comes to pass in nature in contravention to her universal laws." To explain human emotions, like everything else, we need to analyze them as we would the movements of planets: "I shall, therefore, treat of the nature and strength of my emotions according to the same method as I employed heretofore in my investigations concerning God and the mind. I shall consider human actions and desires in exactly the same manner as though I were concerned with lines, planes, and solids."[25] Everything has a rational explanation, and humans are capable of finding it. In using reason, people can find true happiness. Their real freedom comes when they understand the order and necessity of nature and achieve detachment from passing interests.

Pascal Blaise Pascal (BLEZ pass-KAHL) (1623–1662) was a French scientist who sought to keep science and religion united (see Image 16.12). An accomplished scientist and a brilliant mathematician, he excelled at both the practical, by inventing a calculating machine, and the abstract, by devising a theory of chance or probability and doing work on conic sections. After a profound mystical vision on the night of November 23,

Blaise Pascal (1623-62) (oil on canvas), Champaigne, Philippe de (1602-74)/Private Collection/Bridgeman Images

IMAGE 16.12 **Blaise Pascal.** Blaise Pascal was a brilliant scientist and mathematician who hoped to keep science and Christianity united. In his *Pensées*, he made a passionate argument on behalf of the Christian religion. He is pictured here in a portrait by Philippe de Champaigne, a well-known French portrait painter of the Baroque period.

1654, which assured him that God cared for the human soul, he devoted the rest of his life to religious matters. He planned to write an "apology for the Christian religion" but died before he could do so. He did leave a set of notes for the larger work, however, which in published form became known as the *Pensées* (pahn-SAY) (*Thoughts*).

In the *Pensées* (see Historical Voices, "Pascal," p. 510), Pascal tried to convert rationalists to Christianity by appealing to both their reason and their emotions. Humans were, he argued, frail creatures, often deceived by their senses, misled by reason, and battered by their emotions. And yet they were beings whose very nature involved thinking: "Man is but a reed, the weakest in nature; but he is a thinking reed."[26]

CHRONOLOGY	Consequences of the Scientific Revolution: Important Works	
Bacon, *The Great Instauration*		1620
Descartes, *Discourse on Method*		1637
Pascal, *Pensées*		1669
Spinoza, *Ethics Demonstrated in the Geometrical Manner*		1677

Pascal: "What Is a Man in the Infinite?"

 Why did Pascal question whether human beings could achieve scientific certainty? What is the significance of Pascal's thoughts for modern science?

PERHAPS NO INTELLECTUAL IN THE SEVENTEENTH CENTURY gave greater expression to the uncertainties generated by the cosmological revolution than Blaise Pascal, himself a scientist. Pascal's work, the *Pensées*, consisted of notes for a large unfinished work justifying the Christian religion. In this selection, Pascal presents his musings on the human place in an infinite world.

Blaise Pascal, *Pensées*

Let man then contemplate the whole of nature in her full and grand majesty, and turn his vision from the low objects which surround him. Let him gaze on that brilliant light, set like an eternal lamp to illumine the universe; let the earth appear to him a point in comparison with the vast circle described by the sun; and let him wonder at the fact that this vast circle is itself but a very fine point in comparison with that described by the stars in their revolution round the firmament. But if our view be arrested there, let our imagination pass beyond; it will sooner exhaust the power of conception than nature that of supplying material for conception. The whole visible world is only an imperceptible atom in the ample bosom of nature.

No idea approaches it. We may enlarge our conceptions beyond all imaginable space; we only produce atoms in comparison with the reality of things. It is an infinite sphere, the centre of which is everywhere, the circumference nowhere. In short it is the greatest sensible mark of the almighty power of God, that imagination loses itself in that thought.

Returning to himself, let man consider what he is in comparison with all existence; let him regard himself as lost in this remote corner of nature; and from the little cell in which he finds himself lodged, I mean the universe, let him estimate at their true value the earth, kingdoms, cities, and himself. What is a man in the Infinite? . . .

For in fact what is man in nature? A Nothing in comparison with the Infinite, an All in comparison with the Nothing, a mean between nothing and everything. Since he is infinitely removed from comprehending the extremes, the end of things and their beginning are hopelessly hidden from him in an impenetrable secret, he is equally incapable of seeing the nothing from which he was made, and the Infinite in which he is swallowed up. What will he do then, but perceive the appearance of the middle of things, in an eternal despair of knowing either their beginning or their end. All things proceed from the Nothing, and are borne towards the Infinite. Who will follow these marvellous processes? The Author of these wonders understands them. None other can do so.

Source: The Project Gutenberg EBook of Pascal's *Pensées*. Accessed from http://www.gutenberg.org/files/18269/18269-h/18269-h.htm.

Pascal was determined to show that the Christian religion was not contrary to reason: "If we violate the principles of reason, our religion will be absurd, and it will be laughed at." Christianity, he felt, was the only religion that recognized people's true state of being as both vulnerable and great. To a Christian, a human being was both fallen and at the same time God's special creation. But it was not necessary to emphasize one at the expense of the other—to view humans as only rational or only hopeless. Pascal even had an answer for skeptics in his famous wager. God is a reasonable bet; it is worthwhile to assume that God exists. If he does, then we win all; if he does not, we lose nothing.

Despite his own background as a scientist and mathematician, Pascal refused to rely on the scientist's world of order and rationality to attract people to God: "If we submit everything to reason, there will be no mystery and no supernatural element in our religion." In the new cosmology of the seventeenth century, "finite man," Pascal believed, was lost in the new infinite world, a realization that frightened him: "The eternal silence of those infinite spaces strikes me with terror." The world of nature, then,

could never reveal God: "Because they have failed to contemplate these infinites, men have rashly plunged into the examination of nature, as though they bore some proportion to her. . . . Their assumption is as infinite as their object." A Christian could only rely on a God who through Jesus cared for human beings. In the final analysis, after providing reasonable arguments for Christianity, Pascal came to rest on faith. Reason, he believed, could take people only so far: "The heart has its reasons of which the reason knows nothing." As a Christian, faith was the final step: "The heart feels God, not the reason. This is what constitutes faith: God experienced by the heart, not by the reason."[27]

In retrospect, it is obvious that Pascal failed to achieve his goal of uniting Christianity and science. The gap between science and traditional religion grew ever wider as Europe continued along its path of secularization. Of course, traditional religions were not eliminated, nor is there any evidence that churches had yet lost their followers. That would happen later. Nevertheless, more and more of the intellectual, social, and political elites began to act on the basis of secular rather than religious assumptions.

CHAPTER SUMMARY

The Scientific Revolution represents a major turning point in modern Western civilization. In the Scientific Revolution, the Western world overthrew the medieval, Aristotelian-Ptolemaic worldview and geocentric universe and arrived at a new conception of the universe: the sun at the center, the planets as material bodies revolving around the sun in elliptical orbits, and an infinite rather than finite world. This new conception of the heavens was the work of a number of brilliant individuals: Nicolaus Copernicus, who theorized a heliocentric, or sun-centered, universe; Johannes Kepler, who discovered that planetary orbits were elliptical; Galileo Galilei, who, by using a telescope and observing the moon and sunspots, discovered that the universe seemed to be composed of material substance; and Isaac Newton, who tied together all of these ideas with his universal law of gravitation. The contributions of each individual built on the work of the others, thus establishing one of the basic principles of the new science—cooperation in the pursuit of new knowledge.

With the changes in the conception of "heaven" came changes in the conception of "earth." The work of Bacon and Descartes left Europeans with the separation of mind and matter and the belief that by using only reason they could in fact understand and dominate the world of nature. The development of a scientific methodology furthered the work of the scientists, and the creation of scientific societies and learned journals spread its results. The Scientific Revolution was more than merely intellectual theories. It also appealed to nonscientific elites because of its practical implications for economic progress and for maintaining the social order, including the waging of war.

Although traditional churches stubbornly resisted the new ideas and a few intellectuals pointed to some inherent flaws, nothing was able to halt the supplanting of the traditional ways of thinking by new ways of thinking that created a more fundamental break with the past than that represented by the breakup of Christian unity in the Reformation.

The Scientific Revolution forced Europeans to change their conception of themselves. At first, some were appalled and even frightened by its implications. Formerly, humans on earth had viewed themselves as being at the center of the universe. Now the earth was only a tiny planet revolving around a sun that was itself only a speck in a boundless universe. Most people remained optimistic despite the apparent blow to human dignity. After all, had Newton not demonstrated that the universe was a great machine governed by natural laws? Newton had found one—the universal law of gravitation. Could others not find other laws? Were there not natural laws governing every aspect of human endeavor that could be found by the new scientific method? Thus, as we shall see in the next chapter, the Scientific Revolution leads us logically to the Enlightenment in the eighteenth century.

CHAPTER TIMELINE

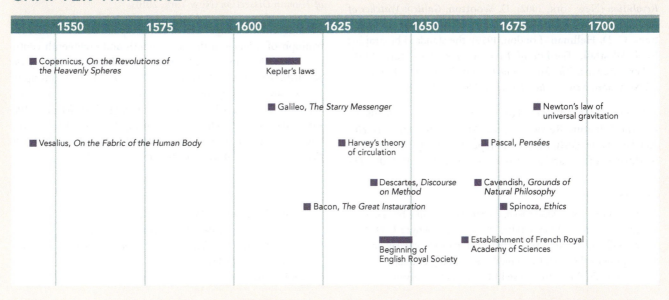

1550	1575	1600	1625	1650	1675	1700

- Copernicus, *On the Revolutions of the Heavenly Spheres*
- Kepler's laws
- Galileo, *The Starry Messenger*
- Newton's law of universal gravitation
- Vesalius, *On the Fabric of the Human Body*
- Harvey's theory of circulation
- Pascal, *Pensées*
- Descartes, *Discourse on Method*
- Cavendish, *Grounds of Natural Philosophy*
- Bacon, *The Great Instauration*
- Spinoza, *Ethics*
- Beginning of English Royal Society
- Establishment of French Royal Academy of Sciences

CHAPTER REVIEW

Upon Reflection

Q In what ways were the intellectual, political, social, and religious developments of the seventeenth century related?

Q How do you explain the emergence of the Scientific Revolution?

Q What do we mean by the "Newtonian world-machine," and what is its significance?

Q Compare the methods used by Bacon and Descartes. Would Pascal agree with their methods and interests? Why or why not?

Key Terms

Scientific Revolution (p. 487)
geocentric conception (p. 488)
heliocentric conception (p. 489)
world-machine (p. 498)
querelles des femmes (p. 503)

Cartesian dualism (p. 504)
rationalism (p. 504)
scientific method (p. 505)
empiricism (p. 506)

Full definitions also appear in the Glossary at the end of the book.

Suggestions for Further Reading

General Works   General surveys of the entire Scientific Revolution include J. Henry, *The Scientific Revolution and the Origins of Modern Science*, 2nd ed. (London, 2002), and D. Wootton, *The Invention of Science: A New History of the Scientific Revolution* (New York, 2015). See also P. Dear, *Revolutionizing the Sciences: European Knowledge and Its Ambitions, 1500–1700* (Princeton, N.J., 2001). On the Scientific Revolution in global perspective, see W. E. Burns, *The Scientific Revolution in Global Perspective* (New York, 2015). On the relationship of magic to the beginnings of the Scientific Revolution, see the pioneering work by F. Yates, *The Rosicrucian Enlightenment* (London, 1975). On the relationship between Renaissance artists and the Scientific Revolution, see P. H. Smith, *Body of the Artisan: Art and Experience in the Scientific Revolution* (Chicago, 2006).

A Revolution in Astronomy   On the important figures of the revolution in astronomy, see H. Margolis, *It Started with Copernicus: How Turning the World Inside Out Led to the Scientific Revolution* (New York, 2002); D. Wootton, *Galileo: Watcher of the Stars* (New Haven, Conn., 2013); M. Casper, *Johannes Kepler*, trans. C. D. Hellman (London, 1959), the standard biography; R. S. Westfall, *The Life of Isaac Newton* (New York, 1993); P. Fara, *Newton: The Making of Genius* (New York, 2004); and W. Newman, *Newton the Alchemist* (New York, 2018).

Advances in Medicine   For a general survey of medicine and the Scientific Revolution, see M. Lindemann, *Medicine and Society in Early Modern Europe* (Cambridge, 2010). The worldview of Paracelsus can be examined in P. Ball, *The Devil's Doctor: Paracelsus and the World of Renaissance Magic and Science* (New York, 2006). The standard biography of Vesalius is C. D. O'Malley, *Andreas Vesalius of Brussels, 1514–1564* (Berkeley, Calif., 1964). The work of Harvey is discussed in G. Whitteridge, *William Harvey and the Circulation of the Blood* (London, 1971).

Impact of Science   The importance of Francis Bacon in the early development of science is underscored in P. Zagorin, *Francis Bacon* (Princeton, N.J., 1998). A good introduction to the work of Descartes can be found in G. Radis-Lewis, *Descartes: A Biography* (Ithaca, N.Y., 1998).

Women and Science   On the subject of women and early modern science, see the comprehensive and highly informative work by L. Schiebinger, *The Mind Has No Sex? Women in the Origins of Modern Science* (Cambridge, Mass., 1989) and K. Park, *Secrets of Women: Gender, Generation, and the Origins of Human Dissection* (New York, 2010).

Science and Society   The social and political context for the triumph of science in the seventeenth and eighteenth centuries is examined in M. C. Jacobs, *The Cultural Meaning of the Scientific Revolution* (New York, 1988). On the relationship of science and industry, see S. Gaukroger, *The Emergence of a Scientific Culture: Science and the Shaping of Modernity, 1210–1685* (Oxford, 2006). On the relationship between the state and science, see J. Gascoigne, *Science and the State: From the Scientific Revolution to World War II* (New York 2019).

Notes

1. Excerpt(s) from *Discoveries and Opinions of Galileo* by Galileo, translated by Stillman Drake, translation copyright © 1957 by Stillman Drake. Used by permission of Doubleday, an imprint of the Knopf Doubleday Publishing Group, a division of Penguin Random House LLC. All rights reserved.

2. Quoted in A. G. R. Smith, *Science and Society in the Sixteenth and Seventeenth Centuries* (London, 1972), p. 59.
3. E. MacCurdy, *The Notebooks of Leonardo da Vinci* (London, 1948), vol. 1, p. 634.
4. Ibid., p. 636.

5. F. Yates, *Giordano Bruno and the Hermetic Tradition* (New York, 1964), p. 448.

6. Ibid., p. 450.

7. Quoted in Smith, *Science and Society*, p. 97.

8. L. P. Smith, *Life and Letters of Sir Henry Wotton* (Oxford, 1907), vol. 1, pp. 486–487.

9. Quoted in J. H. Randall, *The Making of the Modern Mind* (Boston, 1926), p. 234.

10. Quoted in Smith, *Science and Society*, p. 124.

11. Quoted in B. J. Dobbs, *The Foundations of Newton's Alchemy* (Cambridge, 1975), pp. 13–14.

12. Jolande Jacobi, ed., *Paracelsus: Selected Writings* (New York, 1965), pp. 5–6.

13. Ibid., p. 21.

14. Quoted in L. Schiebinger, *The Mind Has No Sex? Women in the Origins of Modern Science* (Cambridge, Mass., 1989), pp. 52–53.

15. Ibid., p. 85.

16. Quoted in P. Stock, *Better than Rubies: A History of Women's Education* (New York, 1978), p. 16.

17. *The Method, Meditations, and Selections from the Principles of Descartes*, Sixth Edition, trans. John Veitch (Edinburgh and London: William Blackwood and Sons, 1879), pp. 5–6.

18. Ibid., p. 33.

19. Francis Bacon, *The Great Instauration*, trans. Jerry Weinberger (Arlington Heights, Ill., 1989), pp. 2, 8, 16, 21.

20. Descartes, *Discourse on Method*, in *Philosophical Writings*, p. 75.

21. M. C. Jacob, *The Cultural Meaning of the Scientific Revolution* (New York, 1988), p. 73.

22. Excerpt(s) from *Discoveries and Opinions of Galileo* by Galileo, translated by Stillman Drake, translation copyright © 1957 by Stillman Drake. Used by permission of Doubleday, an imprint of the Knopf Doubleday Publishing Group, a division of Penguin Random House LLC. All rights reserved.

23. Benedict de Spinoza, *Ethics, trans.* R. H. M. Elwes (New York, 1955), pp. 75–76.

24. Ibid., p. 76.

25. Spinoza, *Letters*, quoted in Randall, *The Making of the Modern Mind*, p. 247.

26. Blaise Pascal, *Pensées*, trans. J. M. Cohen (Harmondsworth, U.K., 1961), p. 100.

27. Ibid., pp. 31, 52–53, 164, 165.

MindTap *Tips* What's a primary source? What's visual literacy? Get acquainted with all-important course concepts with the History Skills Tutorials in MindTap. These tutorials and associated online activities will help you succeed in the course!

GLOSSARY

A

abbess the head of a convent or monastery for women.

abbot the head of a monastery.

absolutism form of government in which the sovereign power or ultimate authority rested in the hands of a monarch who claimed to rule by divine right and was therefore responsible only to God.

Abstract Expressionism a post–World War II artistic movement that broke with all conventions of form and structure in favor of total abstraction.

abstract painting an artistic movement that developed early in the twentieth century in which artists focused on color to avoid any references to visual reality.

aediles Roman officials who supervised the public games and the grain supply of the city of Rome.

agricultural revolution the application of new agricultural techniques that allowed for a large increase in productivity in the eighteenth century.

Agricultural (Neolithic) Revolution *see* **Neolithic Revolution**.

anarchism a political theory that emerged in the late nineteenth century and holds that all governments and existing social institutions are unnecessary and advocates a society based on voluntary cooperation.

anticlericalism opposition to the power of the clergy, especially in political affairs.

anti-Semitism hostility toward or discrimination against Jews.

apartheid the system of racial segregation practiced in the Republic of South Africa until the 1990s, which involved political, legal, and economic discrimination against nonwhites.

appeasement the policy, followed by the European nations in the 1930s, of accepting Hitler's annexation of Austria and Czechoslovakia in the belief that meeting his demands would ensure peace and stability.

Arianism a Christian heresy that taught that Jesus was inferior to God. Though condemned by the Council of Nicaea in 325, Arianism was adopted by many of the Germanic peoples who entered the Roman Empire over the next centuries.

aristocracy a class of hereditary nobility in medieval Europe; a warrior class who shared a distinctive lifestyle based on the institution of knighthood, although there were social divisions within the group based on extremes of wealth.

audiencias advisory groups to viceroys in Spanish America.

Ausgleich the "Compromise" of 1867 that created the Dual Monarchy of Austria-Hungary. Austria and Hungary each had its own capital, constitution, and legislative assembly but were united under one monarch.

authoritarian state a state that has a dictatorial government and some other trappings of a totalitarian state but does not demand that the masses be actively involved in the regime's goals as totalitarian states do.

auxiliaries troops enlisted from the subject peoples of the Roman Empire to supplement the regular legions composed of Roman citizens.

B

balance of power a distribution of power among several states such that no single nation can dominate or interfere with the interests of another.

Baroque an artistic movement of the seventeenth century in Europe that used dramatic effects to arouse the emotions and reflected the search for power that was a large part of the seventeenth-century ethos.

bicameral legislature a legislature with two houses.

Black Death the outbreak of plague (mostly bubonic) in the mid-fourteenth century that killed from 25 to 50 percent of Europe's population.

blitzkrieg "lightning war." A war conducted with great speed and force, as in Germany's advance at the beginning of World War II.

Bolsheviks a small faction of the Russian Social Democratic Party who were led by Lenin and dedicated to violent revolution. They seized power in Russia in 1917 and were subsequently renamed the Communists.

bourgeoisie inhabitants (merchants and artisans) of boroughs and burghs (towns).

boyars the Russian nobility.

Brezhnev Doctrine the doctrine, enunciated by Leonid Brezhnev, that the Soviet Union had a right to intervene if socialism was threatened in another socialist state; used to justify moving Soviet troops into Czechoslovakia in 1968.

Burschenschaften student societies in the German states dedicated to fostering the goal of a free, united Germany.

C

caliph the secular leader of the Islamic community.

capital material wealth used or available for use in the production of more wealth.

capitalism beginning in the Middle Ages, an economic system in which people invested in trade and goods to make profits.

cartels combinations of independent commercial enterprises that work together to control prices and limit competition.

Cartesian dualism Descartes's principle of the separation of mind and matter (and mind and body) that enabled scientists to view matter as something separate from themselves that could be investigated by reason.

Catholic Reformation the movement for the reform of the Catholic Church in the sixteenth century. It included a revived papacy; the regeneration of old religious orders and the founding of new ones, most notably the Jesuits; and the reaffirmation of traditional Catholic doctrine at the Council of Trent.

celibacy complete abstinence from sexual activity. Many early Christians viewed celibacy as the surest way to holiness.

centuriate assembly the chief popular assembly of the Roman Republic. It passed laws and elected the chief magistrates.

chansons de geste a form of vernacular literature in the High Middle Ages that consisted of heroic epics focusing on the deeds of warriors.

chivalry the ideal of civilized behavior that emerged among the nobility in the eleventh and twelfth centuries under the influence of the church; a code of ethics that knights were expected to uphold.

cholera a serious and often deadly disease commonly spread by contaminated water; a major problem in nineteenth-century European cities before sewerage systems were installed.

Christian (northern Renaissance) humanism an intellectual movement in northern Europe in the late fifteenth and early sixteenth centuries that combined the interest in the classics of the Italian Renaissance with an interest in the sources of early Christianity, including the New Testament and the writings of the church fathers.

civic humanism an intellectual movement of the Italian Renaissance that saw Cicero, who was both an intellectual and a statesman, as the ideal and held that humanists should be involved in government and use their rhetorical training in the service of the state.

civil disobedience   a policy of peaceful protest against laws or government policies in order to achieve political change.

civilization   a complex culture in which large numbers of humans share a variety of common elements, including cities; religious, political, military, and social structures; writing; and significant artistic and intellectual activity.

civil rights   the basic rights of citizens, including equality before the law, freedom of speech and press, and freedom from arbitrary arrest.

Cold War   the ideological conflict between the Soviet Union and the United States after World War II.

collective farms   large farms created in the Soviet Union by Stalin by combining many small holdings into large farms worked by the peasants under government supervision.

coloni   free tenant farmers who worked as sharecroppers on the large estates of the Roman Empire (singular: *colonus*).

Columbian Exchange   the reciprocal importation and exportation of plants and animals between Europe and the Americas.

common law   law common to the entire kingdom of England; imposed by the king's courts beginning in the twelfth century to replace the customary law used in county and feudal courts that varied from place to place.

commune   in medieval Europe, an association of townspeople bound together by a sworn oath for the purpose of obtaining basic liberties from the lord of the territory in which the town was located; also, the self-governing town after receiving its liberties.

conciliarism   a movement in fourteenth- and fifteenth-century Europe that held that final authority in spiritual matters resided with a general church council, not the pope. It emerged in response to the Avignon papacy and the Great Schism and was used to justify the summoning of the Council of Constance (1414–1418).

condottieri   leaders of bands of mercenary soldiers in Renaissance Italy who sold their services to the highest bidder.

confession   one of the seven sacraments of the Catholic Church. It provided for the forgiveness of one's sins.

conquistadors   "conquerors." Leaders in the Spanish conquests in the Americas, especially Mexico and Peru, in the sixteenth century.

conscription   a military draft.

conservatism   an ideology based on tradition and social stability that favored the maintenance of established institutions, organized religion, and obedience to authority and resisted change, especially abrupt change.

consuls   the chief executive officers of the Roman Republic. Two were chosen annually to administer the government and lead the army in battle.

consumer society   a term applied to Western society after World War II as the working classes adopted the consumption patterns of the middle class and payment plans, credit cards, and easy credit made consumer goods such as appliances and automobiles affordable.

containment   a policy adopted by the United States in the Cold War. Its goal was to use any means, short of all-out war, to limit Soviet expansion.

Continental System   Napoleon's effort to bar British goods from the continent in the hope of weakening Britain's economy and destroying its capacity to wage war.

cosmopolitan   the quality of being sophisticated and having wide international experience.

cottage industry   a system of textile manufacturing in which spinners and weavers worked at home in their cottages using raw materials supplied to them by capitalist entrepreneurs.

council of the plebs   a council only for plebeians. After 287 B.C.E., however, its resolutions were binding on all Romans.

Crusade   in the Middle Ages, a military campaign in defense of Christendom.

Cubism   an artistic style developed at the beginning of the twentieth century, especially by Pablo Picasso, that used geometric designs to re-create reality in the viewer's mind.

cultural relativism   the belief that no culture is superior to another because culture is a matter of custom, not reason, and derives its meaning from the group holding it.

cuneiform   "wedge-shaped." A system of writing developed by the Sumerians that consisted of wedge-shaped impressions made by a reed stylus on clay tablets.

curiales   city councillors in Roman cities who played an important role in governing the vast Roman Empire.

D

Dadaism   an artistic movement in the 1920s and 1930s begun by artists who were revolted by the senseless slaughter of World War I and used their "anti-art" to express contempt for the Western tradition.

de-Christianization   a policy, adopted in the radical phase of the French Revolution, aimed at creating a secular society by eliminating Christian forms and institutions from French society.

decolonization   the process of becoming free of colonial status and achieving statehood. It occurred in most of the world's colonies between 1947 and 1962.

deconstruction   *see* poststructuralism.

deism   belief in God as the creator of the universe who, after setting it in motion, ceased to have any direct involvement in it and allowed it to run according to its own natural laws.

demesne   the part of a manor retained under the direct control of the lord and worked by the serfs as part of their labor services.

denazification   after World War II, the Allied policy of rooting out any traces of Nazism in German society by bringing prominent Nazis to trial for war crimes and purging any known Nazis from political office.

depression   a very severe, protracted economic downturn with high levels of unemployment.

de-Stalinization   the policy of denouncing and undoing the most repressive aspects of Stalin's regime; begun by Nikita Khrushchev in 1956.

détente   the relaxation of tension between the Soviet Union and the United States that occurred in the 1970s.

developed nations   a term used to refer to rich nations, primarily in the Northern Hemisphere, that have well-organized industrial and agricultural systems, advanced technologies, and effective educational systems.

developing nations   a term used to refer to poor nations, mainly in the Southern Hemisphere, that are primarily farming nations with little technology and serious population problems.

dialectic   logic, one of the seven liberal arts that made up the medieval curriculum. In Marxist thought, the process by which all change occurs through the clash of antagonistic elements.

Diaspora   the scattering of Jews throughout the ancient world after the Babylonian captivity in the sixth century B.C.E.

dictator   in the Roman Republic, an official granted unlimited power to run the state for a short period of time, usually six months, during an emergency.

diocese   the area under the jurisdiction of a Christian bishop; based originally on Roman administrative districts.

divination   the practice of seeking to foretell future events by interpreting divine signs, which could appear in various forms, such as in entrails of animals, in patterns in smoke, or in dreams.

divine-right monarchy   a monarchy based on the belief that monarchs receive their power directly from God and are responsible to no one except God.

domino theory   the belief that if the Communists succeeded in Vietnam, other countries in Southeast and East Asia would also fall (like dominoes) to communism; cited as a justification for the U.S. intervention in Vietnam.

dualism   the belief that the universe is dominated by two opposing forces, one good and the other evil.

dynastic state   a state in which the maintenance and expansion of the interests of the ruling family is the primary consideration.

E

economic imperialism   the process in which banks and corporations from developed nations invest in underdeveloped regions and establish a major presence there in the hope of making high profits; not necessarily the same as colonial expansion in that businesses invest where they can make a profit, which may not be in their own nation's colonies.

economic liberalism   the idea that government should not interfere in the workings of the economy.

Einsatzgruppen   in Nazi Germany, special strike forces in the SS that played an important role in rounding up and killing Jews.

empiricism   the practice of relying on observation and experiment.

enclosure acts   laws enacted in eighteenth-century Britain that allowed large landowners to enclose the old open fields, thereby combining many small holdings into larger units and forcing many small farmers to become tenant farmers or wage laborers on the large estates.

encomienda   in Spanish America, a form of economic and social organization in which a Spaniard was given a royal grant that enabled the holder of the grant to collect tribute from the Indians and use them as laborers.

enlightened absolutism   an absolute monarchy in which the ruler followed the principles of the Enlightenment by introducing reforms for the improvement of society, allowing freedom of speech and the press, permitting religious toleration, expanding education, and ruling in accordance with the laws.

Enlightenment   an eighteenth-century intellectual movement, led by the philosophes, that stressed the application of reason and the scientific method to all aspects of life.

entrepreneur   one who organizes, operates, and assumes the risk in a business venture in the expectation of making a profit.

Epicureanism   a philosophy founded by Epicurus in the fourth century B.C.E. that taught that happiness (freedom from emotional turmoil) could be achieved through the pursuit of pleasure (intellectual rather than sensual pleasure).

equestrians   a group of extremely wealthy men in the late Roman Republic who were effectively barred from high office but sought political power commensurate with their wealth; called equestrians because many had gotten their start as cavalry officers (*equites*).

estates   the traditional tripartite division of European society based on heredity and quality rather than wealth or economic standing, first established in the Middle Ages and continuing into the eighteenth century; traditionally consisted of those who pray (the clergy), those who fight (the nobility), and those who work (all the rest).

ethnic cleansing   the policy of killing or forcibly removing people of another ethnic group; used by the Serbs against Bosnian Muslims in the 1990s.

Eucharist   a Christian sacrament in which consecrated bread and wine are consumed in celebration of Jesus's Last Supper; also called the Lord's Supper or communion.

Eurocommunism   a form of communism that dropped its Marxist ideology. It was especially favored in Italy.

evolutionary socialism   a socialist doctrine espoused by Eduard Bernstein who argued that socialists should stress cooperation and evolution to attain power by democratic means rather than by conflict and revolution.

exchequer   the permanent royal treasury of England. It emerged during the reign of King Henry II in the twelfth century.

excommunication   in the Catholic Church, a censure depriving a person of the right to receive the sacraments of the church.

existentialism   a philosophical movement that arose after World War II that emphasized the meaninglessness of life, born of the desperation caused by two world wars.

F

family allowances   one aspect of the welfare state whereby the state provides a minimum level of material assistance for children.

fascism   an ideology or movement that exalts the nation above the individual and calls for a centralized government with a dictatorial leader, economic and social regimentation, and forcible suppression of opposition; in particular, the ideology of Mussolini's Fascist regime in Italy.

federates   German troops enlisted in groups to fight as allies for the Romans.

feminism   the belief in the social, political, and economic equality of the sexes; also, organized activity to advance women's rights.

fief   a landed estate granted to a vassal in exchange for military services.

Final Solution   the attempted physical extermination of the Jewish people by the Nazis during World War II.

Five Pillars of Islam   the major tenets of the Muslim faith: belief in Allah and Muhammad as his Prophet; standard prayer five times a day and public prayer on Friday; observance of the holy month of Ramadan by fasting from dawn to sunset; making a pilgrimage (the *hajj*) to Mecca in one's lifetime if possible; and giving alms to the poor.

folk culture   the traditional arts and crafts, literature, music, and other customs of the people; something that people make, as opposed to modern popular culture, which is something people buy.

free trade   the unrestricted international exchange of goods with low or no tariffs.

Führerprinzip   in Nazi Germany, a leadership principle based on the belief in a single-minded party (the Nazis) under one leader (Hitler).

functionalism   the idea that the function of an object should determine its design and materials.

G

general strike   a strike by all or most workers in an economy; espoused by Georges Sorel as the heroic action that could be used to inspire the workers to destroy capitalist society.

genocide   the deliberate extermination of a people.

gentry   well-to-do English landowners below the level of the nobility. They played an important role in the English Civil War of the seventeenth century.

geocentric conception   the belief that the earth was at the center of the universe and that the sun and other celestial objects revolved around the earth.

Girondins   a faction in the National Convention during the French Revolution that favored keeping the king alive; so called because their leaders came from the Gironde in southwestern France.

glasnost   "openness." Mikhail Gorbachev's policy of encouraging Soviet citizens to openly discuss the strengths and weaknesses of the Soviet Union.

global economy   an interdependent economy in which the production, distribution, and sale of goods are accomplished on a worldwide scale.

globalization   a term referring to the trend by which peoples and nations have become more interdependent; often used to refer to the development of a global economy and culture.

global warming   the increase in the temperature of the earth's atmosphere caused by the greenhouse effect.

good emperors   the five emperors who ruled from 96 to 180 (Nerva, Trajan, Hadrian, Antoninus Pius, and Marcus Aurelius), a period of peace and prosperity for the Roman Empire.

Gothic   a term used to describe the art and especially architecture of Europe in the twelfth, thirteenth, and fourteenth centuries.

Gothic literature   a form of literature used by Romantics to emphasize the bizarre and unusual, especially evident in horror stories.

Great Schism   the crisis in the late medieval church when there were first two and then three popes; ended by the Council of Constance (1414–1418).

greenhouse effect   the warming of the earth caused by the buildup of carbon dioxide in the atmosphere as a result of human activity.

guest workers   foreign workers working temporarily in European countries.

guilds   associations of people with common interests and concerns, especially people working in the same craft. In medieval Europe, guilds came to control much of the production process and to restrict entry into various trades.

gymnasium   in classical Greece, a place for athletics; in the Hellenistic Age, a secondary school with a curriculum centered on music, physical exercise, and literature.

H

heliocentric conception   the belief that the sun, not the earth, is at the center of the universe.

Hellenistic   literally, "imitating the Greeks"; the era after the death of Alexander the Great when Greek culture spread into the Near East and blended with the culture of that region.

helots   serfs in ancient Sparta who were permanently bound to the land that they worked for their Spartan masters.

heresy   the holding of religious doctrines different from the official teachings of the church.

Hermeticism   an intellectual movement beginning in the fifteenth century that taught that divinity is embodied in all aspects of nature; included works on alchemy and magic as well as theology and philosophy. The tradition continued into the seventeenth century and influenced some of the leading figures of the Scientific Revolution.

hetairai   highly sophisticated courtesans in ancient Athens who offered intellectual and musical entertainment as well as sex.

hieroglyphics   a pictorial system of writing used in ancient Egypt.

high culture   the literary and artistic culture of the educated and wealthy ruling classes.

Holocaust   the mass slaughter of European Jews by the Nazis during World War II.

home rule   in the United Kingdom, self-government by having a separate parliament but not complete independence.

hominids   the earliest humanlike creatures. They flourished in East and South Africa as long as 3 to 4 million years ago.

hoplites   heavily armed infantry soldiers in ancient Greece who entered battle in a phalanx formation.

Huguenots   French Calvinists.

humanism   an intellectual movement in Renaissance Italy based on the study of the Greek and Roman classics.

I

iconoclasm   a movement against the use of icons (pictures of sacred figures) in the eighth-century Byzantine Empire.

iconoclasts   members of an eighth-century Byzantine movement against the use of icons, which was condemned as idolatry.

ideology   a political philosophy such as conservatism or liberalism.

imperium   in the Roman Republic, the right to command troops that belonged to the chief executive officers (consuls and praetors); a military commander was known as an *imperator*. In the Roman Empire, the title *imperator* (emperor) came to be used for the ruler.

Impressionism   an artistic movement that originated in France in the 1870s. Impressionists sought to capture their impressions of the changing effects of light on objects in nature.

individualism   emphasis on and interest in the unique traits of each person.

indulgences   in Christian theology, the remission of part or all of the temporal punishment in purgatory due to sin; granted for charitable contributions and other good deeds. Indulgences became a regular practice of the Christian church in the High Middle Ages, and their abuse was instrumental in sparking Luther's reform movement in the sixteenth century.

infanticide   the practice of killing infants.

inflation   a sustained rise in the price level.

intendants   royal officials in seventeenth-century France who were sent into the provinces to execute the orders of the central government.

interdict   in the Catholic Church, a censure by which a region or country is deprived of receiving the sacraments.

isolationism   a foreign policy in which a nation refrains from making alliances or engaging actively in international affairs.

J

Janissaries   an elite core of eight thousand troops personally loyal to the sultan of the Ottoman Empire.

jihad   "striving in the way of the Lord." In Islam, the attempt to achieve personal betterment, although it can also mean fair, defensive fighting to preserve one's life and one's faith.

joint-stock company   a company or association that raises capital by selling shares to individuals who receive dividends on their investment while a board of directors runs the company.

joint-stock investment bank   a bank created by selling shares of stock to investors. Such banks potentially have access to much more capital than private banks owned by one or a few individuals.

justification   the primary doctrine of the Protestant Reformation, teaching that humans are saved not through good works but by the grace of God, bestowed freely through the sacrifice of Jesus.

K

Kulturkampf   "culture conflict." The name given to Bismarck's attack on the Catholic Church in Germany; has come to refer to conflict between church and state anywhere.

L

laissez-faire   "let (them) do (as they please)." An economic doctrine that holds that an economy is best served when the government does not interfere but allows the economy to self-regulate according to the forces of supply and demand.

latifundia   large landed estates in the Roman Empire (singular: *latifundium*).

lay investiture   the practice in which someone other than a member of the clergy chose a bishop and invested him with the symbols of both his temporal office and his spiritual office; led to the Investiture Controversy, which was ended by compromise in the Concordat of Worms in 1122.

Lebensraum   "living space." The doctrine, adopted by Hitler, that a nation's power depends on the amount of land it occupies. Thus, a nation must expand to be strong.

Leninism   Lenin's revision of Marxism that held that Russia need not experience a bourgeois revolution before it could move toward socialism.

liberal arts   the seven areas of study that formed the basis of education in medieval and early modern Europe. Following Boethius and other late Roman authors, they consisted of grammar, rhetoric, and dialectic or logic (the *trivium*) and arithmetic, geometry, astronomy, and music (the *quadrivium*).

liberalism   an ideology based on the belief that people should be as free from restraint as possible. Economic liberalism is the idea that the government should not interfere in the workings of the economy. Political liberalism is the idea that there should be restraints on the exercise of power so that people can enjoy basic civil rights in a constitutional state with a representative assembly.

limited monarchy (constitutional monarchy)   a system of government in which the monarch is limited by a representative assembly and by the duty to rule in accordance with the laws of the land.

M

major domus   the chief officer of the king's household in the Frankish kingdom.

mandates   a system established after World War I whereby a nation officially administered a territory (mandate) on behalf of the League of Nations. Thus, France administered Lebanon and Syria as mandates, and Britain administered Iraq and Palestine.

Mannerism a sixteenth-century artistic movement in Europe that deliberately broke down the High Renaissance principles of balance, harmony, and moderation.

manor an agricultural estate operated by a lord and worked by peasants who performed labor services and paid various rents and fees to the lord in exchange for protection and sustenance.

Marshall Plan the European Recovery Program, under which the United States provided financial aid to European countries to help them rebuild after World War II.

Marxism the political, economic, and social theories of Karl Marx, which included the idea that history is the story of class struggle and that ultimately the proletariat will overthrow the bourgeoisie and establish a dictatorship en route to a classless society.

mass education a state-run educational system, usually free and compulsory, that aims to ensure that all children in society have at least a basic education.

mass leisure forms of leisure that appeal to large numbers of people in a society, including the working classes; emerged at the end of the nineteenth century to provide workers with amusements after work and on weekends; used during the twentieth century by totalitarian states to control their populations.

mass politics a political order characterized by mass political parties and universal male and (eventually) female suffrage.

mass society a society in which the concerns of the majority—the lower classes—play a prominent role; characterized by extension of voting rights, an improved standard of living for the lower classes, and mass education.

materialism the belief that everything mental, spiritual, or ideal is an outgrowth of physical forces and that truth is found in concrete material existence, not through feeling or intuition.

mercantilism an economic theory that held that a nation's prosperity depended on its supply of gold and silver and that the total volume of trade is unchangeable. Its adherents therefore advocated that the government play an active role in the economy by encouraging exports and discouraging imports, especially through the use of tariffs.

Mesopotamia the valley between the Tigris and Euphrates Rivers.

metics resident foreigners in ancient Athens who were not permitted full rights of citizenship but did receive the protection of the laws.

Middle Passage the journey of slaves from Africa to the Americas as the middle leg of the triangular trade.

militarism a policy of aggressive military preparedness; in particular, the large armies based on mass conscription and complex, inflexible plans for mobilization that most European nations had before World War I.

millenarianism the belief that the end of the world is at hand and the kingdom of God is about to be established on earth.

ministerial responsibility a tenet of nineteenth-century liberalism that held that ministers of the monarch should be responsible to the legislative assembly rather than to the monarch.

mir a peasant village commune in Russia.

mobilization the organization of troops and supplies for service in time of war.

Modern Devotion a movement founded by Gerard Groote in the fourteenth century, aimed at a practical mysticism based on leading lives serving the needs of fellow human beings.

Modernism the artistic and literary styles that emerged in the decades before 1914 as artists rebelled against traditional efforts to portray reality as accurately as possible (leading to Impressionism and Cubism) and writers explored new forms.

monasticism a movement that began in early Christianity whose purpose was to create communities of men and women who practiced a communal life dedicated to God as a moral example to the world around them.

monk a man who chooses to live a communal life divorced from the world in order to dedicate himself totally to the will of God.

monogamy the practice of being married to one person at a time.

monotheism the doctrine or belief that there is only one God.

Mountain a faction in the National Convention during the French Revolution that represented the interests of the city of Paris and favored the execution of the king.

multiculturalism a term referring to the connection of several cultural or ethnic groups within a society.

multinational corporation a company with divisions in two or more countries.

mutual deterrence the belief that nuclear war could best be prevented if both the United States and the Soviet Union had sufficient nuclear weapons so that even if one nation launched a preemptive first strike, the other could respond and devastate the attacker.

mystery religions religions that involve initiation into secret rites that promise intense emotional involvement with spiritual forces and a greater chance of individual immortality.

mysticism the immediate experience of oneness with God.

N

nationalism a sense of national consciousness based on awareness of being part of a community—a "nation"—that has common institutions, traditions, language, and customs and that becomes the focus of the individual's primary political loyalty.

nationalities problem the dilemma faced by the Austro-Hungarian Empire in trying to unite a wide variety of ethnic groups (Austrians, Hungarians, Poles, Croats, Czechs, Serbs, Slovaks, and Slovenes, among others) in an era when nationalism and calls for self-determination were coming to the fore.

nationalization the process of converting a business or industry from private ownership to government control and ownership.

nation in arms the people's army raised by universal mobilization to repel the foreign enemies of the French Revolution.

nation-state a form of political organization in which a relatively homogeneous people inhabits a sovereign state, as opposed to a state containing people of several nationalities.

NATO the North Atlantic Treaty Organization, a military alliance formed in 1949 in which the signatories (Belgium, Canada, Denmark, France, Great Britain, Iceland, Italy, Luxembourg, the Netherlands, Norway, Portugal, and the United States) agreed to provide mutual assistance if any one of them was attacked; later expanded to include other nations.

natural laws a body of laws or specific principles held to be derived from nature and binding on all human societies even in the absence of written laws governing such matters.

natural rights certain inalienable rights to which all people are entitled, including the right to life, liberty, and property; freedom of speech and religion; and equality before the law.

natural selection Darwin's idea that organisms that are most adaptable to their environment survive and pass on the variations that enabled them to survive, while less adaptable organisms become extinct; "survival of the fittest."

Nazi New Order the Nazis' plan for their conquered territories. It included the extermination of Jews and others considered inferior, ruthless exploitation of resources, German colonization in the east, and the use of Poles, Russians, and Ukrainians as slave labor.

neoclassicism a late-eighteenth-century artistic movement that emerged in France. It sought to recapture the dignity and simplicity of the classical style of ancient Greece and Rome.

Neolithic Revolution the shift from hunting animals and gathering plants for sustenance to producing food by systematic agriculture that occurred gradually between 10,000 and 4000 B.C.E. (the Neolithic or "New Stone" Age).

Neoplatonism a revival of Platonic philosophy in the third century C.E., associated with Plotinus; a similar revival in the Italian Renaissance, associated with Marsilio Ficino, who attempted to synthesize Christianity and Platonism.

nepotism the appointment of family members to important political positions; derived from the regular appointment of nephews (Latin, *nepos*) by Renaissance popes.

New Economic Policy   a modified version of the old capitalist system introduced in the Soviet Union by Lenin in 1921 to revive the economy after the ravages of the civil war and war communism.

new imperialism   the revival of imperialism after 1880 in which European nations established colonies throughout much of Asia and Africa.

new monarchies   the governments of France, England, and Spain at the end of the fifteenth century, whose rulers succeeded in reestablishing or extending centralized royal authority, suppressing the nobility, controlling the church, and insisting on the loyalty of all peoples living in their territories.

nobiles   "nobles." The small group of families from both patrician and plebeian origins who produced most of the men who were elected to office in the late Roman Republica.

nominalists   members of a school of thought in medieval Europe that, following Aristotle, held that only individual objects are real and that universals are only names created by humans.

nuclear family   a family group consisting only of a father, a mother, and one or more children.

nuns   women who withdrew from the world and joined a religious community; the female equivalent of monks.

O

old order   the political and social system of France in the eighteenth century before the Revolution.

oligarchy   rule by a few.

optimates   "best men." Aristocratic leaders in the late Roman Republic who generally came from senatorial families and wished to retain their oligarchical privileges.

orders   *see* **estates**.

organic evolution   Darwin's principle that all plants and animals have evolved over a long period of time from earlier and simpler forms of life.

P

Paleolithic Age   the period of human history when humans used simple stone tools (ca. 2,500,000–10,000 B.C.E.).

pantheism   a doctrine that equates God with the universe and all that is in it.

panzer division   in the German army under Hitler, a strike force of about three hundred tanks and accompanying forces and supplies.

papal curia   the administrative staff of the Catholic Church, composed of cardinals and other officials who assist the pope in running the church.

parlements   provincial law courts in France.

pasteurization   a process developed by Louis Pasteur for heating a product to destroy the microorganisms that might cause spoilage.

paterfamilias   the dominant male in a Roman family whose powers over his wife and children were theoretically unlimited, though they were sometimes circumvented in practice.

patriarchal family   a family in which the husband dominates his wife and children.

patriarchy   a society in which the father is supreme in the clan or family; more generally, a society dominated by men.

patricians   great landowners who became the ruling class in the Roman Republica.

patronage   the practice of awarding titles and making appointments to government and other positions to gain political support.

Pax Romana   "Roman peace." A term used to refer to the stability and prosperity that Roman rule brought to the Mediterranean world and much of western Europe during the first and second centuries C.E.

Pentateuch   the first five books of the Hebrew Bible (Genesis, Exodus, Leviticus, Numbers, and Deuteronomy).

perestroika   "restructuring." A term applied to Mikhail Gorbachev's economic, political, and social reforms in the Soviet Union.

perioikoi   in ancient Sparta, free inhabitants but not citizens who were required to pay taxes and perform military service.

permissive society   a term applied to Western society after World War II to reflect the new sexual freedom and the emergence of a drug culture.

Petrine supremacy   the doctrine that the bishop of Rome (the pope), as the successor of Saint Peter (traditionally considered the first bishop of Rome), should hold a preeminent position in the church.

phalanstery   a self-sustaining cooperative community, as advocated by Charles Fourier in the early nineteenth century.

phalanx   a rectangular formation of tightly massed infantry soldiers.

philosophes   intellectuals of the eighteenth-century Enlightenment who believed in applying a spirit of rational criticism to all things, including religion and politics, and who focused on improving and enjoying this world, rather than on the afterlife.

Pietism   a movement that arose in Germany in the seventeenth century whose goal was to foster a personal experience of God as the focus of true religious experience.

pig iron   a type of iron produced by smelting iron ore with coke; of lower quality than wrought iron.

plebeians   the class of Roman citizens that included nonpatrician landowners, craftspeople, merchants, and small farmers in the Roman Republica. Their struggle for equal rights with the patricians dominated much of the Republic's history.

plebiscita   laws passed by the council of the plebs in the Roman Republica.

pluralism   the practice of holding several church offices simultaneously; a problem of the late medieval church.

plutocrats   members of the wealthy elite.

pogroms   organized massacres of Jews.

polis   an ancient Greek city-state encompassing both an urban area and its surrounding countryside; a small but autonomous political unit where all major political and social activities were carried out centrally.

political democracy   a form of government characterized by universal suffrage and mass political parties.

politiques   a group who emerged during the French Wars of Religion in the sixteenth century, placed politics above religion, and believed that no religious truth was worth the ravages of civil war.

polytheistic   believing in or worshiping more than one god.

Pop Art   an artistic movement of the 1950s and 1960s in which artists took images of popular culture and transformed them into works of fine art. Andy Warhol's painting of Campbell's soup cans is a good example.

popular culture   as opposed to high culture, the unofficial written and unwritten culture of the masses, much of which was traditionally passed down orally and centered on public and group activities such as festivals. In the modern age, the term refers to the entertainment, recreation, and pleasures that people purchase as part of the mass consumer society.

populares   "favoring the people." Aristocratic leaders in the late Roman Republic who tended to use the people's assemblies in an effort to break the stranglehold of the *nobiles* on political offices.

popular sovereignty   the doctrine that government is created by and subject to the will of the people, who are the source of all political power.

populism   a political philosophy or movement that supports the rights and power of ordinary people in their struggle against the privileged elite.

portolani   charts of landmasses and coastlines made by navigators and mathematicians in the thirteenth and fourteenth centuries.

Post-Impressionism   an artistic movement that began in France in the 1880s. Post-Impressionists sought to use color and line to express inner feelings and produce a personal statement of reality.

Postmodernism   a term used to cover a variety of artistic and intellectual styles and ways of thinking prominent since the 1970s.

poststructuralism   a system of thought, formulated by Jacques Derrida, that holds that culture is created in a variety of ways, according to the manner in which people create their own meaning. Hence, there is no fixed truth or universal meaning.

praetor a Roman executive official responsible for the administration of the law.

praetorian guard the military unit that served as the personal bodyguard of the Roman emperors.

predestination the belief, associated with Calvinism, that God, as a consequence of his foreknowledge of all events, has predetermined those who will be saved (the elect) and those who will be damned.

prefects officials appointed by the central government to oversee all aspects of a local government during the reign of Napoleon.

price revolution the dramatic rise in prices (inflation) that occurred throughout Europe in the sixteenth and early seventeenth centuries.

primogeniture an inheritance practice in which the eldest son receives all or the largest share of the parents' estate.

principate the form of government established by Augustus for the Roman Empire. It continued the constitutional forms of the Republic and consisted of the *princeps* ("first citizen") and the senate, although the *princeps* was clearly the dominant partner.

principle of intervention the idea, after the Congress of Vienna, that the great powers of Europe had the right to send armies into countries experiencing revolution to restore legitimate monarchs to their thrones.

principle of legitimacy the idea that after the Napoleonic wars, peace could best be reestablished in Europe by restoring legitimate monarchs who would preserve traditional institutions; guided Metternich at the Congress of Vienna.

procurator the head of the Holy Synod, the chief decision-making body for the Russian Orthodox Church.

proletariat the industrial working class; in Marxism, the class that will ultimately overthrow the bourgeoisie.

propaganda a program of distorted information put out by an organization or government to spread its policy, cause, or doctrine.

psychoanalysis a method developed by Sigmund Freud to resolve a patient's psychic conflict.

purgatory defined by the Catholic Church as the place where souls went after death to be purged of punishment for sins committed in life.

Puritans English Protestants inspired by Calvinist theology who wished to remove all traces of Catholicism from the Church of England.

Q

quadrivium arithmetic, geometry, astronomy, and music; four of the seven liberal arts (the others made up the *trivium*) that formed the basis of medieval and early modern education.

quaestors Roman officials responsible for the administration of financial affairs.

querelles des femmes "arguments about women." A centuries-old debate about the nature of women that continued during the Scientific Revolution as those who argued for the inferiority of women found additional support in the new anatomy and medicine.

R

rapprochement the rebuilding of harmonious relations between nations.

rationalism a system of thought based on the belief that human reason and experience are the chief sources of knowledge.

Realism a nineteenth-century school of painting that emphasized the everyday life of ordinary people, depicted with photographic accuracy.

realists subscribers to the medieval European school of thought that held, following Plato, that the individual objects we perceive are not real but merely manifestations of universal ideas existing in the mind of God.

Realpolitik "politics of reality." Politics based on practical concerns rather than theory or ethics.

reason of state the principle that a nation should act on the basis of its long-term interests and not merely to further the dynastic interests of its ruling family.

Reconquista in Spain, the reconquest of Muslim lands by Christian rulers and their armies.

relativity theory Einstein's theory that, among other things, (1) space and time are not absolute but are relative to the observer and interwoven into a four-dimensional space-time continuum and (2) matter is a form of energy ($E = mc^2$).

relics the bones of Christian saints or objects intimately associated with saints that were considered worthy of veneration.

Renaissance "the rebirth" of classical culture that occurred in Italy between ca. 1350 and ca. 1550; also, the earlier revivals of classical culture that occurred under Charlemagne and in the twelfth century.

rentier a person who lives on income from property and is not personally involved in its operation.

reparations payments made by a defeated nation after a war to compensate another nation for damage sustained as a result of the war; required from Germany after World War I.

revisionism a socialist doctrine that rejected Marx's emphasis on class struggle and revolution and argued instead that workers should work through political parties to bring about gradual change.

revolution a fundamental change in the political and social organization of a state.

revolutionary socialism a socialist doctrine that violent action was the only way to achieve the goals of socialism.

rhetoric the art of persuasive speaking; in the Middle Ages, one of the seven liberal arts.

risorgimento a movement in Italy in the nineteenth century aimed at the creation of a united Italian republica.

Rococo an eighteenth-century artistic movement that emphasized grace, gentility, lightness, and charm.

Romanesque a term used to describe the art and especially architecture of Europe in the eleventh and twelfth centuries.

Romanization the process by which Roman culture and institutions were spread to the provinces; often accomplished through the Roman army as colonies of veterans were established wherever the legions were stationed throughout the empire.

Romanticism a nineteenth-century intellectual and artistic movement that rejected the emphasis on reason of the Enlightenment. Instead, Romantics stressed the importance of intuition, feeling, emotion, and imagination as sources of knowing.

S

sacraments rites considered imperative for a Christian's salvation. By the thirteenth century, these consisted of the Eucharist or Lord's Supper, baptism, marriage, penance, extreme unction, holy orders, and confirmation of children. Protestant reformers of the sixteenth century generally recognized only two—baptism and communion (the Lord's Supper).

salons gatherings of philosophes and other notables to discuss the ideas of the Enlightenment; so called from the elegant drawing rooms (salons) where they met.

sans-culottes "without breeches." The common people, who did not wear the fine clothes of the upper classes and played an important role in the radical phase of the French Revolution.

satrap a governor with both civil and military duties in the ancient Persian Empire, which was divided into satrapies, or provinces, each administered by a satrap.

scholasticism the philosophical and theological system of the medieval schools, which emphasized rigorous analysis of contradictory authorities; often used to try to reconcile faith and reason.

scientific method a method of seeking knowledge through inductive principles, using experiments and observations to develop generalizations.

Scientific Revolution the transition from the medieval worldview to a largely secular, rational, and materialistic perspective that began in the seventeenth century and was popularized in the eighteenth.

scriptoria writing rooms for the copying of manuscripts in medieval monasteries.

scutage in the fourteenth century, a money payment for military service that replaced the obligation of military service in the lord-vassal relationship.

secularism the process of becoming more concerned with material, worldly, temporal things and less with spiritual and religious things; a characteristic of the Italian Renaissance.

self-determination the doctrine that the people of a given territory or a particular nationality should have the right to determine their own government and political future.

senate the leading council of the Roman Republic; composed of about three hundred men (senators) who served for life and dominated much of the political life of the Republica.

separation of powers a doctrine enunciated by Montesquieu in the eighteenth century that separate executive, legislative, and judicial powers serve to limit and control each other.

serf a peasant who is bound to the land and obliged to provide labor services and pay various rents and fees to the lord; considered unfree but not a slave because serfs could not be bought and sold.

Shi'ites members of the second largest tradition of Islam, which split from the majority Sunni tradition in the seventh century as a result of a disagreement over the succession; especially significant in Iran and Iraq.

skepticism a doubtful or questioning attitude, especially about religion.

social Darwinism the application of Darwin's principle of organic evolution to the social order; led to the belief that progress comes from the struggle for survival as the fittest advance and the weak decline.

socialism an ideology that calls for collective or government ownership of the means of production and the distribution of goods.

socialized medicine health services for all citizens provided by government assistance.

social security government programs that provide social welfare measures such as old-age pensions and sickness, accident, and disability insurance.

Socratic method a form of teaching that uses a question-and-answer format to enable students to reach conclusions by using their own reasoning.

Sophists wandering scholars and professional teachers in ancient Greece who stressed the importance of rhetoric and tended toward skepticism and relativism.

soviets councils of workers' and soldiers' deputies formed throughout Russia in 1917 that played an important role in the Bolshevik Revolution.

sphere of influence a territory or region over which an outside nation exercises political or economic influence.

squadristi in Italy in the 1920s, bands of armed Fascists used to create disorder by attacking Socialist offices and newspapers.

stagflation a combination of high inflation and high unemployment that was prevalent in the United States and elsewhere from 1973 to the mid-1980s.

Stalinization the adoption by Eastern European Communist countries of features of the economic, political, and military policies implemented by Stalin in the Soviet Union.

Stoicism a philosophy founded by Zeno in the fourth century B.C.E. that taught that happiness could be obtained by accepting one's lot and living in harmony with the will of God, thereby achieving inner peace.

subinfeudation the practice whereby a lord's greatest vassals subdivided their fiefs and had vassals of their own, who in turn subdivided their fiefs, and so on down to simple knights, whose fiefs were too small to subdivide.

suffrage the right to vote.

suffragists advocates of extending the right to vote to women.

sultan "holder of power." A title taken by Turkish leaders who took command of the Abbasid Empire in 1055.

Sunnites members of the largest tradition in Islam, from which the Shi'ites split in the seventh century as a result of a dispute over the succession.

surplus value in Marxism, the difference between a product's real value and the wages of the worker who produced the product.

Surrealism an artistic movement that arose between World War I and World War II. Surrealists portrayed recognizable objects in unrecognizable relationships in order to reveal the world of the unconscious.

syncretism the combining of different forms of belief or practice, as, for example, when two gods are regarded as different forms of the same underlying divine force and are fused together.

T

tariffs duties (taxes) imposed on imported goods, usually to raise revenue and to discourage imports and protect domestic industries.

tetrarchy rule by four; the system of government established by Diocletian (284–305 C.E.) in which the Roman Empire was divided into two parts, each ruled by an "Augustus" assisted by a "Caesar."

theocracy a government ruled by a divine authority.

Third Estate one of the traditional tripartite divisions (orders) of European society based on heredity and quality rather than wealth or economic standing, first established in the Middle Ages and continuing into the eighteenth century; consisted of all who were not members of the clergy or nobility (the first two estates).

three-field system in medieval agriculture, the practice of dividing the arable land into three fields so that one could lie fallow while the others were planted in winter grains and spring crops.

tithe a portion of one's harvest or income, paid by medieval peasants to the village church.

Torah the body of law in Hebrew Scripture, contained in the Pentateuch (the first five books of the Hebrew Bible).

totalitarian state a state characterized by government control over all aspects of economic, social, political, cultural, and intellectual life; the subordination of the individual to the state; and insistence that the masses be actively involved in the regime's goals.

total war warfare in which all of a nation's resources, including civilians at home as well as soldiers in the field, are mobilized for the war effort.

trade unions associations of workers in the same trade formed to help members secure better wages, benefits, and working conditions.

transformism the theory that societies evolve gradually.

transnational corporation *see* **multinational corporation**.

transubstantiation a doctrine of the Roman Catholic Church that during the Eucharist, the substance of the bread and wine is miraculously transformed into the body and blood of Jesus.

trench warfare warfare in which the opposing forces attack and counterattack from a relatively permanent system of trenches protected by barbed wire; a characteristic of World War I.

triangular trade a pattern of trade in early modern Europe that connected Europe, Africa, and the Americas in an Atlantic economy.

tribunes of the plebs beginning in 494 B.C.E., Roman officials who were given the power to protect plebeians against arrest by patrician magistrates.

trivium grammar, rhetoric, and dialectic or logic; three of the seven liberal arts (the others made up the *quadrivium*) that were the basis of medieval and early modern education.

Truman Doctrine the doctrine, enunciated by Harry Truman in 1947, that the United States would provide economic aid to countries that said they were threatened by Communist expansion.

tyrant in an ancient Greek *polis* (or an Italian city-state during the Renaissance), a ruler who came to power in an unconstitutional way and ruled without being subject to the law.

U

ultraroyalists   in nineteenth-century France, a group of aristocrats who sought to return to a monarchical system dominated by a landed aristocracy and the Catholic Church.

uncertainty principle   a principle in quantum mechanics, posited by Heisenberg, that holds that one cannot determine the path of an electron because the very act of observing the electron would affect its location.

unconditional surrender   complete, unqualified surrender of a belligerent nation.

utopian socialists   intellectuals and theorists in the early nineteenth century who favored equality in social and economic conditions and wished to replace private property and competition with collective ownership and cooperation.

V

vassalage   the granting of a fief, or landed estate, in exchange for providing military services to the lord and fulfilling certain other obligations such as appearing at the lord's court when summoned and making a payment on the knighting of the lord's eldest son.

vernacular   the everyday language of a region, as distinguished from a language used for special purposes. For example, in medieval Paris, French was the vernacular, but Latin was used for academic writing and for classes at the University of Paris.

viceroy   the administrative head of the provinces of New Spain and Peru in the Americas.

volkish thought   the belief that German culture is superior and that the German people have a universal mission to save Western civilization from "inferior" races.

W

war communism   Lenin's policy of nationalizing industrial and other facilities and requisitioning the peasants' produce during the civil war in Russia.

War Guilt Clause   the clause in the Treaty of Versailles that declared that Germany (with Austria) was responsible for starting World War I and ordered Germany to pay reparations for the damage the Allies had suffered as a result of the war.

Warsaw Pact   a military alliance, formed in 1955, in which Albania, Bulgaria, Czechoslovakia, East Germany, Hungary, Poland, Romania, and the Soviet Union agreed to provide mutual assistance.

welfare state   a sociopolitical system in which the government assumes primary responsibility for the social welfare of its citizens by providing such things as social security, unemployment benefits, and health care.

wergeld   "money for a man." In early Germanic law, a person's value in monetary terms, paid by a wrongdoer to the family of the person who had been injured or killed.

world-machine   Newton's conception of the universe as one huge, regulated, and uniform machine that operated according to natural laws in absolute time, space, and motion.

wrought iron   a high-quality iron first produced during the eighteenth century in Britain; manufactured by puddling, a process developed by Henry Cort that involved using coke to burn away the impurities in pig iron.

Z

zemstvos   local assemblies established in Russia in 1864 by Tsar Alexander II.

ziggurat   a massive stepped tower on which a temple dedicated to the chief god or goddess of a Sumerian city was built.

Zionism   an international movement that called for the establishment of a Jewish state or a refuge for Jews in Palestine.

Zollverein   the customs union of all the German states except Austria, formed by Prussia in 1834.

Zoroastrianism   a religion founded by the Persian Zoroaster in the seventh century B.C.E., characterized by worship of a supreme god, Ahuramazda, who represents the good against the evil spirit, identified as Ahriman.

INDEX